INSURANCE

PRINCIPLES AND PRACTICE

FOR GRADUATION AND PROFESSIONAL COURSES

M.N. MISHRA
Professor of Corporate Studies
Faculty of Commerce
Banaras Hindu University, Varanasi

Dr. S.B. MISHRA

S. CHAND
PUBLISHING

S Chand And Company Limited
(ISO 9001 Certified Company)

S Chand And Company Limited
(ISO 9001 Certified Company)
Head Office: D-92, Sector–2, Noida – 201301, U.P. (India), Ph. 91-120-4682700
Registered Office: A-27, 2nd Floor, Mohan Co-operative Industrial Estate,
New Delhi – 110 044, Phone: 011-49731800
www.**schandpublishing.com**; e-mail: **info@schandpublishing.com**

S. CHAND
PUBLISHING

Marketing Offices:

Chennai	:	Ph: 23632120; chennai@schandpublishing.com
Guwahati	:	Ph: 2738811, 2735640; guwahati@schandpublishing.com
Hyderabad	:	Ph: 40186018; hyderabad@schandpublishing.com
Jalandhar	:	Ph: 4645630; jalandhar@schandpublishing.com
Kolkata	:	Ph: 23357458, 23353914; kolkata@schandpublishing.com
Lucknow	:	Ph: 4003633; lucknow@schandpublishing.com
Mumbai	:	Ph: 25000297; mumbai@schandpublishing.com
Patna	:	Ph: 4011400; patna@schandpublishing.com

First Edition 1979
Subsequent Editions and Reprints 1982, 84, 86, 89, 93, 95, 97, 98, 99, 2001, 2002, 2003, 2004, 2005, 2006, 2007 (Twice), 2008, 2009, 2011, 2012, 2013, 2014
Twenty-Second Revised Edition 2016
Reprints 2017 (Twice), 2018 (Twice), 2020, 2021 (Twice), 2022 (Twice), 2023

Reprint 2025 (Twice)

ISBN: 978-93-856-7607-9 **Product Code:** H6INS48BAIN10ENAV16O

PRINTED IN INDIA

By Vikas Publishing House Private Limited, Plot 20/4, Site-IV, Industrial Area Sahibabad, Ghaziabad – 201 010 and Published by S Chand And Company Limited, A-27, 2nd Floor, Mohan Co-operative Industrial Estate, New Delhi – 110 044.

To

My Respected Parents

Who were Loving Me Lot

PREFACE TO THE TWENTY-SECOND EDITION

Insurance in India is at a galloping stage. It has shown maximum growth rate of 13.0 per cent in 2007 in the world after liberalisation although it has slightly declined in 2013 by one per cent. It is expected to grow by 4.2 per cent in 2016. De-tariffing since January 1, 2007 has facilitated the insurers to serve the society with quality and lowest cost in the competitive environment. Now, insurance is not limited only to life and property risks; it has expanded its scope to insure all the uninsurable risks. It has innovated awareness to manage all the risks attached to business, industry, individuals, institutions, agriculture, transport, banking and credit, householders, interests, Neon sign, pet animal, sports, shops, LPG and export, health, catastrophe, liability, guarantee and surety, bank assurance and Corporate Governance. Recently, many health insurers have tried to find out awareness to insure even HIV/AIDS and other occupational risks. New sections have been added for Transport Insurance, Commercial Insurance, Micro Insurance, Total Insurance and Social Security Schemes in this edition. Burglary and Personal Accident Insurance have been discussed under Urban Traditional Insurance. Reinsurance has been given more emphasis by bringing out from fire insurance to total insurance. It is expected that in future, political parties would go for insurance of the risks involved in election. However, the present state of insurance has tried to insure all the risks related to family, society, business, industry and other economic activities.

This edition has included all sorts of innovative insurance products. Long Term Care needs for ageing population have become a growing problems of the society. So, Long Term Care (LTC) insurance has been thoroughly discussed in the chapter of insurance innovation. New Pension Schemes, life insurance to weaker sections, social benefits schemes and micro life insurance are discussed under insurance for underpriviledged. Every chapter is thoroughly revised and new developments have been added in the respective chapters. International insurance scene is updated giving all the current information and data. Marine Insurance is known for its clauses and words which are added in the appendix. LIC has originated new life products which are given at a proper place.

This book is divided into seven parts. After discussing insurance concepts, life insurance, marine insurance and fire insurance in Parts One to Four; Part Five has discussed miscellaneous insurance which includes, transport insurance and motor insurance, miscellaneous forms of insurance such as employers' liability insurance, householder's insurance policy, Employees State Insurance Act, fidelity guarantee insurance, pedal cyde insurance, plate glass insurance, glow sign insurance, aviation insurance, livestock insurance, cattle insurance, crop insurance, credit guarantee insurance, engineering insurance, construction insurance, social security, sports insurance, shopkeepers insurance, export risk insurance; rural insurance including agriculture insurance; urban traditional and non-traditional insurance; progress of miscellaneous general insurance; progress of total general insurance and Appendix. Part Six of this book discusses prospects of insurance; privatisation of insurance industry, insurance innovation, and Long-Term Care (LTC) insurance risk management/and, commercial insurance; health insurance; catastrophe insurance; liability insurance; microinsurance, total and credit insurance; reinsurance; corporate governance and corporate social responsibility, bancassurance; international insurance scene and Appendix. Part seven of this book discusses insurance legislation in India.

For preparation of this present edition, we have taken the help of Sigma, IRDA and LIC. The Head of Economic Research and Consulting of Sigma has supplied all the information and data which we required for completing this edition. We are highly thankful to him and his team of researchers. We are indebted to IRDA officials, editors and friends who helped us a lot for updating the book. LIC has always been kind enough to us for writing this book since the beginning. Their officials have been excellent supporters throughout the period beginning from 1976 to 2015 for helping, guiding and discussing insurance problems. No word is enough to thank them. The book is comprehensively rewritten to educate the students of the latest development of insurance in India and abroad. Though the book is written primarily undergraduate and postgraduate students, it is becoming popular amongst the insurance personnel who are required to have general knowledge of insurance as well as develop their specialities in a particular field of insurance.

We are thankful to our family members who have been giving us sufficient time for rewriting the book. We hope that book will be a guiding star for all the insurance minded people. We shall feel obliged if comments and suggestions are given for the improvement of the book.

Varanasi **M. N. MISHRA**
2015 **Dr. S. B. MISHRA**

PREFACE TO THE FIRST EDITION

Insurance is as old as the civilization. It was present in the form of mutual help. Joint Stock Companies and Corporations are the recent forms of the insurance. The 'Yogakshena' has been the oldest term of insurance used in the Rigveda for some kind of insurance. Manu had emphasised that a special charge be made on goods carried from one town to another to ensure their safe carriage. Manusmriti says—

क्रयाविक्रयमध्वानं भक्तं च सपरिव्यम्।
योगक्षेमं च संप्रेक्ष्य वणिजों दापयेत्करान्।।

(Chap.7)

"The Trader should be made to pay taxes or duty taking into account the price of purchase, the price of sale, the length of the journey, incidental expenses and yogakshena *i.e.*, Risk and Safety". Ancient India was a prominent maritime power. Today, the nationalisation of life insurance business and general insurance business is expected to contribute maximum for the well-being and safety of the people by providing insurance services in every walk of life. The principles and practices of insurance have been changing from time to time according to needs.

The present book 'Insurance—Principles and Practices' has been written taking into consideration of the prevailing principles and practices in the different fields of insurance in India. The book has been written according to the Syllabi prescribed for the B.Com. and Honours examinations of Indian universities and of Federation of Insurance Institutes. Various authoritative works have been consulted so that all the required subject-matter could be given in a concised and comprehensive form. The book has been divided into Five Parts. Introduction, Life, Marine, Fire and Miscellaneous. Each part includes all the required chapters on the subject in a brief and illustrative form. It is expected that the book will be interesting for the general readers as well.

I am highly obliged to the officials of the LIC and the GIC who supplied all the information and statistics required by me.

I shall be grateful to receive comments and criticism of this book for the further improvement of the book.

M.N. MISHRA

CONTENTS

PART ONE
INTRODUCTION

PART TWO
LIFE INSURANCE

PART THREE
MARINE INSURANCE

PART FOUR
FIRE – INSURANCE

PART FIVE
MISCELLANEOUS INSURANCE

PART SIX

PROSPECTS OF INSURANCE COMPANIES

PART SEVEN

INSURANCE LEGISLATION

PART ONE
INTRODUCTION

1

DEFINITION AND NATURE OF INSURANCE

Insurance is defined as a co-operative device to spread the loss caused by a particular risk over a number of persons who are exposed to it and who agree to ensure themselves against that risk. Risk is uncertainty of a financial loss. It should not be confused with the chance of loss which is the probable number of losses out of a given number of exposures. It should not be confused with peril which is defined as the cause of loss or with hazard which is a condition that may increase the chance of loss. Finally, risk must not be confused with loss itself which is the unintentional decline in or disappearance of value arising from a contingency. Wherever there is uncertainty with respect to a probable loss there is risk.

Every risk involves the loss of one or other kind. The function of insurance is to spread the loss over a large number of persons who are agreed to co-operate each other at the time of loss. The risk cannot be averted but loss occurring due to a certain risk can be distributed amongst the agreed persons. They are agreed to share the loss because the chances of loss, *i.e.,* the time, amount, to a person are not known. Anybody of them may suffer loss to a given risk, so, the rest of the persons who are agreed will share the loss. The larger the number of such persons, the easier the process of distribution of loss. In fact; the loss is shared by them by payment of premium which is calculated on the probability of loss. In olden time, the contribution by the persons was made at the time of loss. The insurance is also defined as a social device to accumulate funds to meet the uncertain losses arising through a certain risk to a person insured against the risk.

FUNCTIONS OF INSURANCE

The functions of insurance can be studied into two parts (*i*) Primary Functions, and (*ii*) Secondary Functions.

Primary Functions

(*i*) *Insurance provides certainty.* Insurance provides certainty of payment at the uncertainty of loss. The uncertainty of loss can be reduced by better planning and administration. But, the insurance relieves the person from such difficult task. Moreover, if the subject matters are not adequate, the self-provision may prove costlier. There are different types of uncertainty in a risk. The risk will occur or not, when will occur, how much loss will be there? In other words, there are uncertainty of happening of time and amount of loss. Insurance removes all these uncertainty and the assured is given certainty of payment of loss. The insurer charges premium for providing the said certainty.

(*ii*) *Insurance provides protection.* The main function of the insurance is to provide protection against the probable chances of loss. The time and amount of loss are uncertain and at the happening of risk, the person will suffer loss in absence of insurance. The insurance guarantees the payment of loss and thus protects the assured from sufferings. The insurance cannot check the happening of risk but can provide for losses at the happening of the risk.

(*iii*) *Risk-Sharing.* The risk is uncertain, and therefore, the loss arising from the risk is also uncertain. When risk takes place, the loss is shared by all the persons who are exposed to the risk.

The risk-sharing in ancient time was done only at time of damage or death; but today, on the basis of probability of risk, the share is obtained from each and every insured in the shape of premium without which protection is not guaranteed by the insurer.

SECONDARY FUNCTIONS

Besides the above primary functions, the insurance works for the following functions:

(*i*) *Prevention of Loss.* The insurance joins hands with those institutions which are engaged in preventing the losses of the society because the reduction in loss causes lesser payment to the assured and so more saving is possible which will assist in reducing the premium. Lesser premium invites more business and more business causes lesser share to the assured. So again premium is reduced to, which will stimulate more business and more protection to the masses. Therefore, the insurance assist financially to the health organisation, fire brigade, educational institutions and other organisations which are engaged in preventing the losses of the masses from death or damage.

(*ii*) *It Provides Capital.* The insurance provides capital to the society. The accumulated funds are invested in productive channel. The dearth of capital of the society is minimised to a greater extent with the help of investment of insurance. The industry, the business and the individual are benefited by the investment and loans of the insurers.

(*iii*) It *Improves Efficiency.* The insurance eliminates worries and miseries of losses at death and destruction of property. The carefree person can devote his body and soul together for better achievement. It improves not only his efficiency, but the efficiencies of the masses are also advanced.

(*iv*) *It helps Economic Progress.* The insurance by protecting the society from huge losses of damage, destruction and death, provides an initiative to work hard for the betterment of the masses. The next factor of economic progress, the capital, is also immensely provided by the masses. The property, the valuable assets, the man, the machine and the society cannot lose much at the disaster.

DEFINITION OF INSURANCE

The definition of insurance can be made from two points: (*i*) Functional Definition and, (*ii*) Contractual Definition.

Functional Definition

Insurance is a co-operative device to spread the loss caused by a particular risk over a number of persons, who are exposed to it and who agree to insure themselves against the risk. Thus, the insurance is (*a*) a co-operative device to spread the risk; (*b*) the system to spread the risk over a number of persons who are insured against the risk; (*c*) the principle to share the loss of each member of the society on the basis of probability of loss to their risk; and (*d*) the method to provide security against losses to the insured.

Similarly another definition can be given. Insurance is a co-operative device of distributing losses, falling on an individual or his family over a large number of persons, each bearing a nominal expenditure and feeling secure against heavy loss.

Contractual Definition

Insurance has been defined to be that in which a sum of money as a premium is paid in consideration of the insurer's incurring the risk of paying a large sum upon a given contingency. The insurance, thus, is a contract whereby (*a*) certain sum, called premium, is charged in consideration, (*b*) against the said consideration, a large sum is guaranteed to be paid by the insurer who received the premium, (*c*) the payment will be made in a certain definite sum, *i.e.*, the loss or the policy amount whichever may be, and (*d*) the payment is made only upon a contingency. More specific definition can be given as follows—Insurance may be defined as a consisting one party (the insurer) agrees to pay to the other party (the insurer) or his beneficiary, a certain sum upon a given contingency (the risk) against which insurance is sought.

NATURE OF INSURANCE

The insurance has the following characteristics which are, generally, observed in case of life, marine, fire and general insurances.

1. Sharing of Risk

Insurance is a device to share the financial losses which might befall on an individual or his family on the happening of a specified event. The event may be death of a bread-winner to the family in the case of life insurance, marine-perils in marine insurance, fire in fire insurance and other certain events in general insurance, *e.g.*, theft in burglary insurance, accident in motor insurance, etc. The loss arising from these events if insured are shared by all the insured in the form of premium.

2. Co-operative Device

The most important feature of every insurance plan is the co-operation of large number of persons who, in effect, agree to share the financial loss arising due to a particular risk which is insured. Such a group of persons may be brought together voluntarily or through publicity or through solicitation of the agents. An insurer would be unable to compensate all the losses from his own capital. So, by insuring or underwriting a large number of persons, he is able to pay the amount of loss. Like all co-operative devices, there is no compulsion here on anybody to purchase the insurance policy.

3. Value of Risk

The risk is evaluated before insuring to charge the amount of share of an insured, herein called, consideration or premium. There are several methods of evaluation of risks. If there is expectation of more loss, higher premium may be charged. So, the probability of loss is calculated at the time of insurance.

4. Payment at Contingency

The payment is made at a certain contingency insured. If the contingency occurs, payment is made. Since the life insurance contract is a contract of certainty, because the contingency, the death or the expiry of term, will certainly occur, the payment is certain. In other insurance contracts, the contingencyis the fire or the marine perils etc., may or may not occur. So, if the contingency occurs, payment is made, otherwise no amount is given to the policy-holder. Similarly, in certain types of life policies, payment is not certain due to uncertainty of a particular contingency within a particular period. For example, in term-insurance the, payment is made only when death of the assured occurs within the specified term, may be one or two years. Similarly, in Pure Endowment payment is made only at the survival of the insured at the expiry of the period.

5. Amount of Payment

The amount of payment depends upon the value of loss occurred due to the particular insured risk provided insurance is there up to that amount. In life insurance, the purpose is not to make good the financial loss suffered. The insurer promises to pay a fixed sum on the happening of an event. If the event or the contingency takes place, the payment does fall due if the policy is valid and in force at the time of the event, like property insurance, the dependents will not be required to prove the occurring of loss and the amount of loss. It is immaterial in life insurance what was the amount of loss at the time of contingency. But in the property and general insurances, the amount of loss, as well as the happening of loss, are required to be proved.

6. Large Number of Insured Persons

To spread the loss immediately, smoothly and cheaply, large number of persons should be insured. The co-operation of a small number of persons may also be insurance but it will be limited to smaller area. The cost of insurance to each member may be higher. So, it may be unmarketable. Therefore, to make the insurance cheaper, it is essential to insure large number of persons or property because the lesser would be cost of insurance and so, the lower would be premium. In past years, tariff associations or mutual fire insurance associations were found to share the loss at cheaper rate. In order to function successfully, the insurance should be joined by a large number of persons.

7. Insurance is not a gambling

The insurance serves indirectly to increase the productivity of the community by eliminating worry and increasing initiative. The uncertainty is changed into certainty by insuring property and life because the insurer promises to pay a definite sum at damage or death. From a family and business point of view all lives possess an economic value which may at any time be snuffed out by death, and it is as reasonable to ensure against the loss of this value as it is to protect oneself against the loss of property. In the absence of insurance, the property owners could at best practice only some form of self-insurance, which may not give him absolute certainty. Similarly, in absence of life insurance, saving requires time; but death may occur at any time and the property, and family may remain unprotected. Thus, the family is protected against losses on death and damage with the help of insurance. From the company's point of view, the life insurance is essentially non-speculative, in fact, no other business operates with greater certainties. From the insured point of view, too, insurance is also the antithesis of gambling. Nothing is more uncertain than life and life insurance offers the only sure method of changing that uncertainty into certainty. Failure of insurance amounts gambling because the uncertainty of loss is always looming. In fact, the insurance is just the opposite of gambling. In gambling, by bidding the person exposes himself to risk of losing, in the insurance, the insured is always opposed to risk, and will suffer loss if he is not insured. By getting insured his life and property, he protects himself against the risk of loss. In fact, if he does not get his property or life insured he is gambling with his life on property.

8. Insurance is not Charity

Charity is given without consideration but insurance is not possible without premium. It provides security and safety to an individual and to the society although it is a kind of business because in consideration of premium it guarantees the payment of loss. It is a profession because it provides adequate sources at the time of disasters only by charging a nominal premium for the service.

PRINCIPLES OF INSURANCE

The insurance is based upon (*i*) Principles of Co-operation and, (*ii*) Principles of Probability.

(*i*) *Principles of Co-operation.* Insurance is a co-operation device. If one person is providing for his own losses, it cannot be strictly an insurance because in insurance, the loss is shared by a group of persons who are willing to co-operate. In ancient period, the persons of a group were willingly sharing the loss to a member of the group. They used to share the loss to a member of the group. They used to share the loss at the time of damage. They collected enough funds from the society and paid to the dependents of the deceased or the persons suffering property losses. The mutual co-operation was prevailing from the very beginning up to the era of Christ in most of the countries. Lately, the co-operation took another form where it was agreed between the individual or the society to pay a certain sum in advance to be a member of the society. The society by accumulating the funds, guarantees payment of certain amount at the time of loss to any member of the society. The accumulation of funds and charging of the share from the member in advance became the job of one institution called insurer. Now it became the duty and responsibility of the insurer to obtain adequate funds from the members of the society to pay them at the happening of the insured risk. Thus, the shares of loss took the form of premium. Today, all the insured give a premium to join the scheme of insurance. Thus, the insured are co-operating to share the loss of an individual by payment of a premium in advance.

(*ii*) *Principles and Theory of Probability.* The loss in the shape of premium can be distributed only on the basis of theory of probability. The chances of loss are estimated in advance to affix the amount of premium. Since the degree of loss depends upon various factors, the affecting factors are analysed before determining the amount of loss. With the help of this principle, the uncertainty of loss is converted into certainty. The insurer will have not to suffer loss as well have to gain windfall. Therefore, the insurer has to charge only so much of amount which is adequate to meet the losses. The probability tells what are the chances of losses and what will be the amount of losses.

The inertia of large number is applied while calculating the probability. The larger the number of exposed persons,, the better and the more practical would be the findings of the probability. Therefore, the law of large number is applied in the principle of probability. In each and every field of insurance the law of large number is essential. These principles keep in account that the past events will incur in the same inertia. The insurance, on the basis of past experience, present conditions and future prospects, fixes the amount of premium. Without premium, no co-operation is possible and the premium cannot be calculated without the help of theory of probability, and .consequently no insurance is possible. So these two principles are the two main legs of insurance.

QUESTIONS

1. What are the various functions of insurance?
2. State briefly a suitable definition of insurance.
3. Insurance is not to prevent risk, but to indemnify the losses arising from a certain risk'.—Comment.
4. What are the various principles of insurance?

2

EVOLUTION OF INSURANCE

The origin of insurance is lost in antiquity. The earliest traces of insurance in the ancient world are found in the form of marine trade loans or carriers' contracts which: included an element of insurance. Evidence is on record that arrangements embodying the idea of insurance were made in Babylonia and India at quite an early period. In Rigveda, the most sacred book of India, references were made to the concept 'Yogakshema' more or less akin to the well-being and security of the people. The codes of Hummurabi and of Manu had recognised the advisability of provision for sharing the future losses. However, there is no evidence that insurance in its present form was practised prior to the twelfth century.

1. Marine Insurance

The marine insurance is the oldest form of insurance. Under Bottomry bond, the system of credit and the law of interest were well-developed and were based on a clear appreciation of the hazard involved and the means of safeguarding against it. If the ship was lost, the loan and interest were forfeited. The contract of insurance was made a part of the contract of carriage, and Manu shows that Indians had even anticipated the doctrine of average and contribution. Freight was fixed according to season and was expected to be reasonable in the case of marine transport which was then very much at the mercy of winds and elements. Travellers by sea and land were very much exposed to the risk of loosing their vessels and merchandise because the piracy on the open seas and highway robbery of caravans were very common. Besides there were several risks. Many times, it might have been captured by the king's enemies or robbed by pirates or got sunk in the deep waters. The risk to owners of such ships were enormous and, therefore, to safeguard them the marine traders devised a method of spreading over them the financial loss which could not be conveniently borne by the unfortunate individual victims. The co-operative device was quite voluntary in the beginning, but now in modern it has been converted into modified shape of premium.

The marine policies of the present forms were sold in the beginning of fourteenth century by the Brugians. On the demand of the inhabitants of Burges, the Court of Flanders permitted in the year 1310, the establishment in this Town of a charter of Assurance, by means of which the merchants could insure their goods, exposed to the risks of the sea. The insurance development was not confined to the Lombards and to the Hansa merchants, it spread throughout Spain, Portugal, France, Holland and England. The marine form land lending prominence of Lombards merchants got a prominent section of the London City. They built homes there and took the name of Lombard Street. Later on, this street became famous in insurance history. The Lloyd's coffee-house gave an impetus to develop the marine insurance.

2. Fire Insurance

After marine insurance, fire insurance developed in present form. It had been observed in Anglo-Section Guild form for the first time where the victims of fire hazards were given personal assistance by providing necessaries of life. It had been originated in Germany in the beginning of sixteenth century. The fire insurance got momentum in England after the great fire in 1666 when the fire losses were tremendous. About 85 per cent of the houses were burnt to ashes and property worth of sterling ten crores were completely burnt off. Fire Insurance Office was established in 1681 in England. With colonial development of England, the fire insurance spread all over the world in present form 'Sun Fire Office' was successful fire insurance institution.

In India, the general insurer started working since 1850 with the establishment of the Triton Insurance, Calcutta. Again in 1861, the North British and Mercantile catered the requirements of insurance business. The general insurance in India could not progress much. The slow growth of joint-stock enterprise and mechanised production was another reason for the low level of general insurance business.

3. Life Insurance

Life insurance made its first appearance in England in sixteenth century, the first recorded evidence in England being the policy on life of William Gybbons on June 18, 1653. Even before this date annuities had become quite common in England, and marine insurance had, in fact, made its appearance three thousand years ago. The life insurance developed at 'Exchange Alley'. The first registered life office in England was the Hand-in-Hand Society established in 1696. The famous 'Amicable Society for a Perpetual Assurance Office started its operation since 1706. Life insurance did not prosper in the United States during the 18th century, because of serious fluctuations in death-rate, but soon after 1800 some active interest began to be shown in this enterprise because of the application of level premium plan which had by then been in operation in U.K. for more than a generation. In India, some Europeans started the first life insurance company in Bengal Presidency, viz., the Orient Life Assurance Company in 1818. The year 1870 was a year of a landmark in the history of Indian Insurance separating the early period of pioneering attempts at life insurance from the subsequent period of steady development at the establishment of Indian Life Office, viz., Bombay Mutual Life Assurance Society in 1871. The next important life office was Oriental Government Security Life Assurance Co., Ltd., which started its operation since 1874. Since then several offices developed in India.

4. Miscellaneous Insurance

The miscellaneous insurance took the present shape at the later part of nineteenth century with the industrial revolution in England. Accident insurance, fidelity insurance, liability insurance and theft insurance were the important form of insurance at that time. Lloyds's Association was the main functioning institution. Now, insurances such as cattle insurance, crop insurance, profit insurance, etc., are taking place. The scope of general insurance is increasing with the advancement of the society.

KINDS OF INSURANCE

The insurance can be divided from two angles: first, from the business point of view and the second, from the risk point of view.

Business Point of View

The insurance can be classified into three categories from business point of view: (*i*) Life Insurance, (*ii*) General Insurance, and (*iii*) Social Insurance.

(*i*) Life Insurance

Life Insurance is different from other insurance in the sense that, here, the subject matter of insurance is life of human being. The insurer will pay the fixed amount of insurance at the time of death or at the expiry of certain period. At present, life insurance enjoys maximum scope because the life is the most important property of the society or an individual. Each and every person requires the insurance. This insurance provides protection to the family at the premature death or gives adequate amount at the old age when earning capacities are reduced. Under personal insurance a payment is made at the accident. The insurance is not only a protection but is a sort of investment because a certain sum is returnable to the insured at the death or at the expiry of a period. The business of life insurance is wholly done by the Life Insurance Corporation of India.

(*ii*) General Insurance

The general insurance includes property insurance, liability insurance and other forms of insurance. Fire and marine insurances are strictly called property insurance. Motor, theft, fidelity and machine insurances include the extent of liability insurance to a certain extent. The strictest form of liability insurance is fidelity insurance, whereby the insurer compensates the loss to the insured when he is under the liability of payment to the third party.

(*iii*) Social Insurance

The social insurance is to provide protection to the weaker section of the society who are unable to pay the premium for adequate insurance. Pension plans, disability benefits, unemployment benefits, sickness insurance and industrial insurance are the various forms of social insurance. With the increase of the socialistic ideas, the social insurance is an obligatory duty of the nation. The Government of a country must provide social insurance to its masses.

Risk Point of View

Insurance is divided into property liability and other form from high point of view.

A. Property Insurance

Under the property insurance property of a person/persons are insured against a certain specified risk. The risk may be fire or marine perils, theft of property or goods, damage to property at accident.

(*a*) *Marine Insurance.* Marine insurance provides protection against loss of marine perils. The marine perils are collision with rock, or ship attacks by enemies, fire and capture by pirates, etc. These perils cause damage, destruction or disappearance of the ship and cargo and non-payment of freight. So, marine insurance insures ship (Hull), cargo and freight. Previously only certain nominal risks were insured but now the scope of marine insurance had been divided into two parts: (*i*) Ocean Marine Insurance and (*ii*) Inland Marine Insurance. The former insures only the marine perils while the latter covers inland peril which may arise with the delivery of cargo (goods) from the godown of the insured and may extend up to the receipt of the cargo by the buyer (importer) at his godown.

(*b*) *Fire Insurance.* Fire insurance covers risks of fire. In the absence of fire insurance, the fire waste will increase not only to the individual but to the society as well. With the help of fire insurance, the losses, arising due to fire are compensated and the society is not losing much. The individual is protected from such losses and his property or business or industry will remain approximately in the same position in which it was before the loss. The fire insurance does not protect only losses but it provides certain consequential losses also. War risk, turmoil, riots, etc., can be insured under this insurance, too.

(*c*) *Miscellaneous Insurance.* The Property, goods, machine, furniture, automobile, valuable articles, etc., can be insured against the damage or destruction due to accident or disappearance due to theft. There are different forms of insurances for each type of the said property whereby not only property insurance exists but liability insurance and personal injuries are also insured.

B. Liability Insurance

The general insurance also includes liability insurance whereby the insured is liable to pay the damage of property or to compensate the less of personal injury or death. This insurance is seen in the form of fidelity insurance, automobile insurance and machine insurance, etc.

C. Other Forms

Besides the property and liability insurances, there are certain other insurances which are included under general insurance. The examples of such insurances are export-credit insurances, State employees insurance, etc., whereby the insurer guarantees to pay certain amount at the certain events. This insurance is extending rapidly these days.

KINDS OF INSURANCE FROM RISK POINT OF VIEW

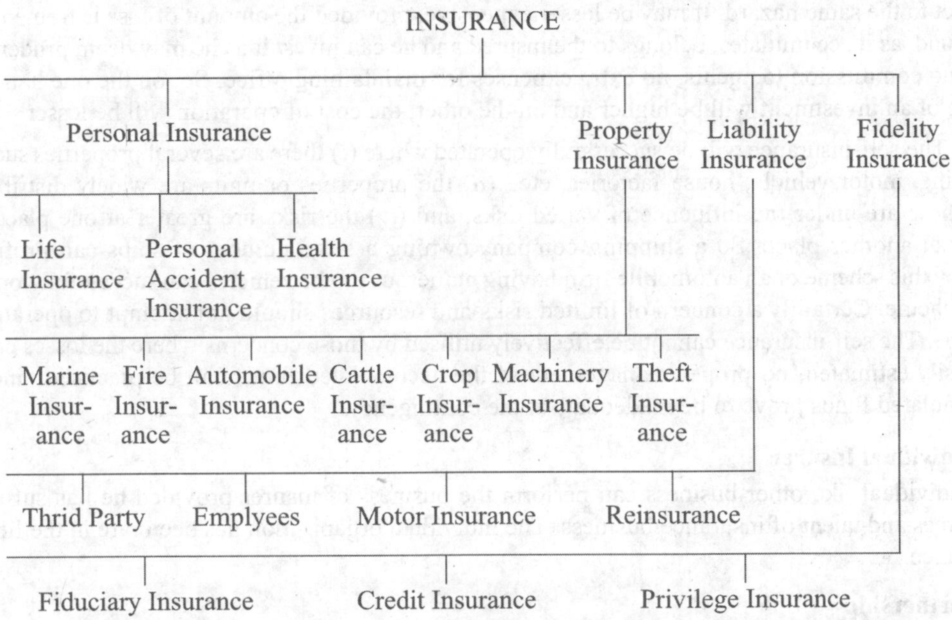

1. Personal Insurance

The personal insurance includes insurance of human life which may suffer loss due to death, accident and disease. Therefore, the personal insurance is further sub-classified into life insurance, personal accident insurance and health insurance.

2. Property Insurance

The property of an individual and of the society is insured against the loss of fire and marine perils, the crop is insured against unexpected decline in production, unexpected death of the animals engaged in business, break-down of machines and theft of the property and goods.

3. Liability Insurance

The liability insurance covers the risks of third party, compensation to employees, liability of the automobile owners and reinsurances.

4. Guarantee Insurance

The guarantee insurance covers the loss arising due to dishonesty, disappearance and disloyalty of the employers or second. The party must be a party of the contract. His failure causes loss to the first party. For example, in export insurance, the insurer will compensate the loss at the failure of the importers to pay the amount of debt.

TYPES OF INSURANCE ORGANISATIONS

The insurance organisation developed in different forms with the advancement of insurance practices. Some of the forms are discussed below.

1. Self-Insurance

The plan by which an individual or concern sets up a private fund out of which to pay losses is termed "Self-insurance". The person lays aside periodicallv certain sum to meet the losses of any contemplated risk. While it may be called "self-insurance", it is not, as a matter of fact, insurance at all because there is no hedge, no shifting or distributing of the burden of risk among larger persons. It is merely a provision for meeting the contingency. Here the insured becomes his own insurer for the particular risk. But, it can be successfully worked only when there is wide distribution of risks subject to the same hazard. It may be lesser expensive, provided the amount of loss is tremendous. The fund, as it accumulates, belongs to the insured and he can invest it as he may deem prudent. He pays no commission to agents, no extra expenses for maintaining office. So, on the one hand, the return of an investment will be higher and on the other, the cost of operation will be lesser.

The self-insurance will be successfully operated where (*i*) there are several properties such as, machine, motor vehicle, house factories, etc., (*ii*) the properties or units are widely distributed, (*iii*) these are under the influence of varied risks, and (*iv*) the risks are greater at one place and lesser at another place. So a shipping company owning a large number of ships can profitably employ this scheme or an automobile firm having numerous motor vehicles can successfully operate this scheme. Certainly a concern of limited risks and resources should not attempt to operate this scheme. The self-insurance cannot be effectively utilised by those concerns where the losses cannot be easily estimated, no proper management of the accumulated funds can be practised, and the accumulated funds prove to be inadequate at the contingency.

2. Individual Insurer

An individual like other business can perform the business of insurer provided he has sufficient resources and talent of insurance business. The individual organisation has been rare in the field of insurance.

3. Partnership

A partnership firm can also carry on the insurance business for the sake of profit. Since it is not an entity distinct from the persons composing it, the personal liability of partners in respect of the partnership debts is unlimited. In case of huge loss the partners have to pay from their own personal funds and it will not be profitable to them to start insurance business.

In the early period before the advent of joint stock companies many insurance undertakings were partnership or unicorporated companies. They were constituted by deed of partnerships which regulated the business. Before formation of joint stock companies, the crown had empowered to grant an application letters patent to such unincorporated companies to operate the business with limited liabilities. Sometimes, the policy-holders were permitted to share the management of the concern.

These forms of insurance had been completely disappeared with the advent of joint stock companies.

4. Joint Stock Companies

The joint stock companies are those which are organised by the share-holders who subscribe the necessary capital to start the business, are formed for earning profits for the stock-holders who are the real owners of the companies. The management of a company is entrusted to a Board of Directors who are elected by the share-holders from among themselves. The company can operate insurance business and the policy-holders have nothing to do with the management of the concern. But, in life insurance, it is the practice to share certain portion of profit among the certain policy-holders. The participating policy-holders are getting the bonus. Before nationalisation, according to Insurance Act, 1938, the policy-holders had a right to elect their representatives to the Board of Directors to the extent of one-fourth of the total number of directors of the company. The provision enabled the policy-holders to have an effective voice in the management of the company. Most of the insurance businesses were done on joint stock basis before nationalisation. They were operating within the memorandum of association and articles of association framed by them. They used to distribute only 5 per cent of divisible profit to the share-holders and more than 95 per cent of the divisible profit was distributed amongst the policy-holders.

5. Mutual Companies

The mutual companies were co-operative associations formed for the purpose of effecting insurance on the property of its members. The policy-holders were themselves the share-holders of the companies, Each member was insurer as well as insured. They had power to participate in, management and in profit to the full extent. When ever the income was more than the expenses and claims, it was accumulated in the form of saving and was entitled in reducing the rate of premium. Since the insured were insurers also, they always tried to reduce the management expenses and to keep the business at sound level.

The theoretical base of the mutual companies, is issuing of participating policies, *i.e.*, the policy-holders had full power in management and profit, whereas the joint-stock companies, strictly were to issue non-participating policies. But, in practice, the joint-stock companies were also issuing participating policies. It made them mixed companies *i.e.*, where the features of joint stock companies and of mutual companies were present.

6. Co-operative Insurance Organisation

Co-operative insurance organisations are those concerns which are incorporated and registered under Indian Co-operative Societies Act. The concerns are also called 'Co-operative Insurance Societies'. These societies like mutual companies are non-profit organisation. The aim is to provide insurance protection to its members at the lowest reasonable, net cost. The Indian Insurance Act, 1938, has provided special provisions for the co-operative insurance societies, but after nationalisation the societies have been ceased. IRDA has also permitted cooperative insurance organisation in 2005.

7. Lloyd's Association

Lloyd's Association is one of the greatest insurance institutions in the world. Taking its name from the Coffee House of Edward Lloyd, where underwriters assembled to transact business and pick-up news, the organisation traces its origin to the latter part of the seventeenth century. So, it is an oldest insurance organisation in existing form in the world. In 1871, Loyd's Act was passed incorporating the members of the association into a single corporate body with perpetual succession and a corporate seal. The powers of Lloyd's Corporation was extended from the business of marine insurance to other insurances and guarantee business. The Lloyd's association is an association of individual insurers known as 'underwriters'. They are also termed as 'Syndicates' or 'Names'. Any insurer who wants to become a member of such association has to deposit a certain fee as security for the regular payment of his liabilities. The association before enrolling the insurer as a member of the association will inquire about the financial position of the concern, business reputation and experience. On satisfactory proof the association admits him in the association. The business is effected by the insurers called underwriters, syndicates, or names. The association is merely a controlling and guiding body. Anybody desirous of taking insurance will approach to the 'underwriters' and not to the association. Each underwriter will be responsible for his business underwritten of a policy. Thus, a policy will be underwritten by several underwriters but their share or portion of business are fixed individually. When the policy becomes a claim, the insured realises money from all the underwriters who had underwritten the policy according to their respective shares. If an underwriter fails to pay his share of claim, the association will pay from his security which he had taken at time of enrolment of the underwriter. Never is one member or underwriter liable for the losses of other members either on a policy or in a syndicate. Underwriter assumes liability 'each for himself and not for another'.

Lloyd's as a corporation is never liable on a policy. It does supervise the conditions under which its members may issue policies; it undertakes to provide collective protection for the commercial and maritime interest of its members.

The Lloyd's has done commendable work not only in the field of marine insurance but in other insurances also. War risk election risk, export risk, aeroplane risk, etc., have been insured by the Lloyd's Association. The association also publishes, 'Lloyd's List' and 'Register of Shipping' for the information of insuring public and the insurers.

8. State Insurance

The Government of a nation sometimes owns the insurance and runs the business for the benefit of the public. The state insurance is defined as that insurance which is under public sector put; more specifically it can be stated that when governments have taken over the insurance business particularly life insurance. France had nationalised larger insurance companies in 1946. In Brazil, Japan and Mexico, the insurances are largely nationalised. Previously, the state undertook only those insurances which were regarded to be very vital for the public interest or where private companies were not able or willing to enter the field of insurance. Social security, unemployment, crop insurance, war risk insurance, export credit insurance, aeroplane insurance were generally under state insurance.

In India, the life insurance business was nationalised in 1956 and the general insurances were nationalised in 1971. Thus, the insurance business in India, today, is under the control and ownership of the Central Government although they are in different forms of insurances.

INSURANCE ORGANISATION IN INDIA

(*i*) *Departmental Organisation.* Departmental insurances are prevalent in different departments of the Central and State governments. The postal department of the country has its own system of insurances under which the employees of post-offices are insured, Similarly, the postal department as a carrier of goods has also provided insurance for the goods to be despatched. These insurances are not compulsory in India. The State Governments of different states have provided life insurance to their respective employees. Apart from this, the State Governments have also provided sickness maternity, disability, medical and pension insurances to respective employees.

(*ii*) *Corporations.* In India two corporations are established under separate Acts to deal with the insurance business.

(*A*) The Life Insurance Corporation of India Act, 1956, had provided for life insurance legislation for life insurance business conducted by the Life Insurance Corporation of India established under the said Act. It started its functions since Sept. 1, 1956. It owns all the life insurance business (including annuities) in India.

(*B*) The general Insurance Corporation of India established under the General Insurance Corporation of India Act, 1972 into four distinct companies which are (*i*) National Insurance Companies Ltd. (*ii*) New India Insurance Companies Ltd. (*iii*) Oriental Fire and General Insurance Companies Ltd. and (*iv*) United India Fire and General Insurance Companies Ltd. These companies would work separately maintaining their distinct features but they are controlled and guided by the General Insurance Corporation of India. This is a neo-techno scheme of nationalisation where the companies are also to work freely in the market. They will suffer and gain their own losses and profits. The monopoly on the concern, may be corporation, has gone in this new technique. These companies will be subsidiary to the G.I.C. (The General Insurance Corporation).

(C) Employees State Insurance Corporation

This corporation was established in 1948. This corporation provides social insurance to labourers of factories who are getting less than four hundred rupees per month., They are provided a definite assistance in sickness, maternity, disability, medical expenses and assistance to dependents.

(D) Deposit Insurance Corporation

This corporation was established in 1962. It provides protection to the depositors of a bank. In case the bank fails, the depositors can get returned their deposits up to rupees ten thousand.

(*iii*) *Government Companies.* Companies were established by the government according to the provision of Indian Companies Act. In 1957, export risks insurance corporation was established to insure the export risks. The name of this company was converted to Export Credit and Guarantee Corporation in 1964. Now all the general insurance businesses are conducted by the said four government companies.

QUESTIONS

1. Describe the main kinds of insurance and examine briefly the nature of risks protected by each kind of insurance.
2. Detail the different kinds of insurance oganisations and illustrate the merits demerits and of each organisation.
3. The latest and the oldest form of insurance is 'Lloyd's one'. Illustrate briefly.
4. Discuss the organisations of insurance business in India.

3

ROLE AND IMPORTANCE OF INSURANCE

The process of insurance has been evolved to safeguard the interests of people from uncertainty by providing certainty of payment at a given contingency. The insurance principle comes to be more and more used and useful in modern affairs. Not only does it serve the ends of individuals, or of special groups of individuals, it tends to pervade and to transform our modern social order, too. The role and importance of insurance, here, has been discussed in three phases: (*i*) uses to individual, (*ii*) uses to a special group of individuals, viz., to business or industry, and (*iii*) uses to the society.

USES TO AN INDIVIDUAL

1. Insurance provides Security and Safety

The insurance provides safety and security against the loss on a particular event. In case of life insurance payment is made when death occurs or the term of insurance is expired. The loss to the family at a premature death and payment in old age are adequately provided by insurance. In other words, security against premature death and old age sufferings are provided by life insurance. Similarly, the property of insured is secured against loss on a fire in fire insurance. In other insurance, too, this security is provided against the loss at a given contingency. The insurance provides safety and security against the loss of earning at death or in olden age, against the loss at fire, against the loss at damage, destruction or disappearance of property, goods, furniture and machines, etc.

2. Insurance affords Peace of Mind

The security wish is the prime motivating factor. This is the wish which tends to stimulate to more work, if this wish is unsatisfied, it will create a tension which manifests itself to the individual in the form of an unpleasant reaction causing reduction in work. The security banishes fear and uncertainty, fire, windstorm, auto-mobile accident, damage and death are almost beyond the control human agency and in occurrence of any of these events may frustrate or weaken the human mind. By means of insurance, however, much of the uncertainty that centres about the wish for security and its attainment may be eliminated.

3. Insurance protects Mortgaged Property

At the death of the owner of the mortgaged property, the property is taken over by the lender of money and the family will be deprived of the uses of the property. On the other hand, the mortgagee wishes to get the property insured because at the damage or destruction of the property he will lose his right to get the loan repayed. The insurance will provide adequate amount to the dependents at the early death of the property-owner to pay off the unpaid loans. Similarly, the mortgagee gets adequate amount at the destruction of the property.

4. Insurance eliminates dependency

At the death of the husband or father, the destruction of family need no elaboration. Similarly, at destruction of, property and goods, the family would suffer a lot. It brings reduced standards of living and the suffering may go to any extent of begging from the relatives, neighbours or friends. The economic independence of the family is reduced or, sometimes, lost totally. What can be more pitiable condition than this that the wife and children are looking others more benevolent than the husband and father, in absence of protection against such dependency. The insurance is here to assist them and provides adequate amount at the time of sufferings.

5. Life Insurance encourages saving

The elements of protection and investment are present only in case of life insurance. In property insurance, only protection element exists. In most of the life policies elements of saving predominates. These policies combine the programs of insurance and savings. The saving with insurance has certain extra advantages—(*i*) Systematic saving is possible because regular premiums are required to be compulsorily paid. The saving with a bank is voluntary and one can easily omit a month or two and then abandon the program entirely. (*ii*) In insurance the deposited premium cannot be withdrawn easily before the expiry of the term of the policy. As contrast to this, the saving which can be withdrawn at any moment will finish within no time. (*iii*) The insurance will pay the policy money irrespective of the premium deposited while in case of bank-deposit, only the deposited amount along with the interest is paid. The insurance, thus, provides the wished amount of insurance and the bank provides only the deposited amount. (*iv*) The compulsion or force to premium in insurance is so high that if the policy-holder fails to pay premiums within the days of grace, he subjects his policy to lapsation and may get back only a very nominal portion of the total premiums paid on the policy. For the preservation of the policy, he has to try his level best to pay the premium. After a certain period, it would be a part of necessary expenditure of the insured. In absence of such forceful compulsion elsewhere life insurance is the best media of saving.

6. Life Insurance provides profitable Investment

Individuals unwilling or unable to handle their own funds have been pleased to find an outlet for their investment in life insurance policies. Endowment policies, multipurpose policies, deferred annuities are certain better form of investment. The elements of investment *i.e.*, regular saving, capital formation, and return of the capital alongwith certain additional return are perfectly observed, in life insurance. In India the insurance policies carry a special exemption from income-tax, wealth tax, gift tax and estate duty. An individual from his own capacity cannot invest regularly with enough of security and profitability. The life insurance fulfils all these requirements with a lower cost. The beneficiary of the policy-holder can get a regular income from the life-insurer; if the insured amount is left with him.

7. Life Insurance fulfils the needs of a person

The needs of a person are divided into (*A*) Family needs, (*B*) Old-age needs, (*C*) Re-adjustment needs, (*D*) Special needs, (*E*) The clean-up needs.

(A) Family Needs

Death is certain, but the time is uncertain. So, there is uncertainty of the time when the sufferings and financial stringencies may be fall on the family. Moreover, every person is responsible to provide for the family. It would be a more pathetic sight in the world to see the wife and children of a man looking for some one more considerate arid benevolent than the husband or the father, who left them unprovided. Therefore, the provision for children up to their reaching earning period and for widow up to long life should he made. Any other provision except life insurance will not adequately meet this financial requirement of the family. Whole life policies are the better means of meeting such requirements.

(B) Old-age heeds

The provision for old-age is required where the person is surviving more than his earning period. The reduction of income in old-age is serious to the person and his family. If no other family member starts earning, they will be left with nothing and if there is no property, it would be more piteous state. The life insurance provides old age funds alongwith the protection of the family by issuing various policies.

(C) Re-adjustment Needs

At the time of reduction in income whether by loss of unemployment, disability, or death, adjustment in the standard of living of family is required. The family members will have to be satisfied with meagre income and they have to settle down to lower income and social obligations. Before coming down to the lower standard and to be satisfied with that, they require certain adjustment income so that the primary obstacles may be reduced to minimum. The life insurance helps to accumulate adequate funds. Endowment policy, anticipated endowment policy and guaranteed triple benefit policies are deemed to be a good substitute for old age needs.

(D) Special Needs

There are certain special requirement of the family which is fulfilled by the earning member of the family. If the member becomes disable to earn the income due to old age or death, those needs may remain unfulfilled and the family will suffer.

(i) Need for Education. There are certain insurance policies, and annuities which are useful for education of the children irrespective of the death or survival of the father or guardian.

(ii) Marriage. The daughter may remain unmarried in case of father's death or in case of inadequate provision for meeting the expenses of marriage. The insurance can provide funds for the marriage if policy is taken for the purpose.

(iii) Insurance needs for settlement of children. After education, settlement of children takes time and in absence of adequate funds, the children cannot be well placed and all the education go to waste.

(E) Clean-up funds

After death, ritual ceremonies, payment of wealth taxes and income taxes are certain requirements which decrease the amount of funds of the family member. Insurance comes to help for meeting these requirements. Multipurpose policy, education and marriage policies, capital redemption policies are the better policies for the special needs.

USES TO BUSINESS

The insurance has been useful to the business society also. Some of the uses are discussed below:

1. Uncertainty of business losses is reduced

In world of business, commerce and industry a huge number of properties are employed. With a slight slackness or negligence, the property may be turned into ashes. The accident may be fatal not only to the individual or property but to the third party also. New construction and new establishment are possible only with the help of insurance. In absence of it, uncertainty will be to the maximum level and nobody would like to invest a huge amount in the business or industry. A person may not be sure of his life and health and cannot continue the business up to longer period to support his dependents. By purchasing policy, he can be sure of his earning because the insurer will pay a fed amount at the time of death. Again, the owner of a business might foresee contingencies that would bring great loss. To meet such situations they might decide to set aside annually a reserve, but it could not be accumulated due to death. However, by making an annual payment, to secure immediately, insure policy can be taken.

2. Business-efficiency is increased with insurance

When the owner of a business is free from the botheration of losses, he will certainly devote much time to the business. The care free owner can work better for the maximisation of the profit. The new as well as old businessmen are guaranteed payment of certain amount with the insurance policies at the death of the person; at the damage, destruction or disappearance of the property or goods. The uncertainty of loss may affect the mind of the businessmen adversely. The insurance, removing the uncertainty, stimulates the businessmen to work hard.

3. Key Man Indemnification

Key man is that particular man whose capital, expertise, experience, energy, ability to control, goodwill and dutifulness make him the most valuable asset in the business and whose absence will reduce the income of the employer tremendously and up to that time when such employee is not substituted. The death or disability of such valuable lives will, in many instances, prove a more serious loss than that by fire or any hazard. The potential loss to be suffered and the compensation to the dependents of such employee require an adequate provision which is met by purchasing an adequate life-policies. The amount of loss may be up to the amount of reduced profit, expenses involved in appointing and training, of such persons and payment to the dependents of the key man. The Term Insurance Policy or Convertible Term Insurance Policy is more suitable in this case.

4. Enhancement of Credit

The business can obtain loan by pledging the policy as collateral for the loan. The insured persons are getting more loan due to certainty of payment at their deaths. The amount of loan that can be obtained with such pledging of policy, with interest thereon will not exceed the cash value of the policy. In case of death, this value can be utilised for setting of the loan alongwith the interest. If the borrower is unwilling to repay the loan and interest, the lender can surrender the policy and get the amount of loan and interest thereon repaid. The redeemable debentures can be issued on the collateral of capital redemption policies. The' insurance properties are the best collateral and adequate loans are granted by the lenders.

5. Business Continuation

In any business particularly partnership business may discontinue at the death of any partner although the surviving partners can restart the business, but in both the cases the business and the partners will suffer economically. The insurance policies provide adequate funds at the time of death. Each partner may be insured for the amount of his interest in the partnership and his dependents may get that amount at the death of the partner.

With the help of property insurance, the property of the business is protected against disasters and the chance of disclosure of the business due to the tremendous waste or loss.

6. Welfare of Employees

The welfare of employees is the responsibility of the employer. The former are working for the latter. Therefore, the latter has to look after the welfare of the former which can be provision for early death, provision for disability and provision for old age. These requirements are easily met by the life insurance, accident and sickness benefit, and pensions which are generally provided by group insurance. The premium for group insurance is generally paid by the employer. This plan is the cheapest form of insurance for employers to fulfill their responsibilities. The employees will devote their maximum capacities to complete their jobs when they are assured of the above benefits. The struggle and strife between employees and employer can be minimised easily with the help of such schemes.

USES OF SOCIETY

Some of the uses of insurance to society are discussed in the following sections.

1. Wealth of the society is protected

The loss of a particular wealth can be protected with the insurance. Life insurance provides loss of human wealth. The human material, if it is strong, educated and care-free, will generate more income. Similarly, the loss of damage of property at fire, accident, etc., can be well indemnified by the property insurance; cattle, crop, profit and machines are also protected against their accidental and economic losses. With the advancement of the society, the wealth or the property of the society attracts more hazardous and, so new types of insurance are also invented to protect them against the possible losses. Each and every member will have financial security against old age, death, damage, destruction and disappearance of his wealth including the life wealth. Through prevention of economic losses, instance protects the society against degradation. Through stabilization and expansion of business and industry, the economic security is maximised. The present, future and potential human and property resources are well-protected. The children are getting expertised education, working classes are free from botherations and older people are guiding at ease. The happiness and prosperity are observed everywhere with the help of insurance.

2. Economic Growth of the Country

For the economic growth of the country, insurance provides strong hand and mind, protection against loss of property and adequate capital to produce more wealth. The agriculture will experience protection against losses of cattle, machines, tools and crop. This sort of protection stimulates more production in agriculture, in industry, the factory premises, machines, boilers and profit insurances provide more confidence to start and operate the industry welfare of employees create a conducive atmosphere to work: Adequate capital from insurers accelerate the production cycle. Similarly in business, too, the property and human material are protected against certain losses, capital and credit are expanded with the help of insurance. Thus, the insurance meets all the requirements of the economic growth of a country.

3. Reduction in Inflation

The insurance reduces the inflationary resource in two ways. First, by extracting money in supply to the amount of premium collected and secondly, by providing sufficient funds for production narrow down the inflationary gap. With reference to Indian context it has been observed that about 5.0 per cent of the money in supply was collected in form of premium. The share of premium contributed to the total investment of the country was about 10.0 per cent. The two main causes of inflation, namely, increased money in supply and decreased production are properly controlled by insurance business. Insurance Need and Selling.

QUESTIONS

1. Describe in detail the importance of insurance. What are its uses to the business community and society as a whole?
2. 'Insurance is able to curtail inflation, so it should be made compulsory'. Comment.

4

INSURANCE CONTRACT

Insurance may be defined as a contract between two parties of whereby one party called insurer undertakes, in exchange for a fixed sum called premiums, to pay the other party called insured a fixed amount of money on the happening of a certain event. Since insurance is a contract, certain sections of Indian Contract Act are applicable. Section 10 of this Act says, "All agreements are contract if they are made by free consent of the parties, competent to contract, for a lawful consideration and with a lawful object and which are not hereby declared to be void". The insurance contract involves—(A) the elements of general contract, and (B) the element of special contract relating to insurance.

The special contract of insurance involves principles :(1) Insurable Interest, (2) Utmost Good Faith, (3) Indemnity, (4) Subrogation, (5) Warranties, (6) Proximate Cause, (7) Assignment and Nomination, (8) Return of Premium. So, in total, there are eight elements of insurance contract which are discussed below:

1. GENERAL CONTRACT

The valid contract, according to Section 10 of Indian Contract Act 1872, must have the following essentialities.

I. Agreement (offer and acceptance).

II. Legal consideration.

III. Competent to make contract.

IV. Free consent.

V. Legal object.

I. Offer and Acceptance

The offer for entering into contract may generally come from the insured. The insurer may also propose to make the contract. Whether the offer is from the side of insurer or from the side of insured, the main fact is acceptance. Any act that precedes it is offer or a counter-offer. All that precede the offer or counter-offer is an invitation to offer. In insurance, the publication of prospectus, the canvassing of the agents are invitations to offer. When the prospect (the potential policy-holder) proposes to enter the contract it is an offer and if there is any alteration in the offer that would be a counter-offer. If this alteration or change (counter–offer) ill accepted by the proposer, it would be an acceptance. In absence of counter-offer, the acceptance of offer will be an acceptance by the insurer. At the moment, the notice of acceptance is given to other party, it would be a valid acceptance.

II. Legal Consideration

The promiser to pay a fixed sum at a given contingency is the insurer who must have some return or his promise. It need not be money only but it must be valuable. It may be sums, right, interest, profit, or benefit. Premium being the valuable consideration must be given for starting the insurance contract. The amount of premium is not important to begin the contract. The fact is that without payment of premium, the insurance contract cannot start.

III. Competent to make contract

Every person is competent to contract (*a*) who is of the age of majority according to the law, (*b*) who is of sound mind, and (*c*) who is not disqualified from contracting by any law to which he is subject. A minor is not competent to contract. A contract by a minor is void excepting contracts for necessaries. A minor cannot sign a contract. A person is said to be of sound mind for the purpose of making a contract if at the time when he makes it, he is capable of understanding it and of forming a rational judgment as to its effect upon his interests. A person who is usually of unsound mind, but, occasionally of sound mind may make a contract when he is of sound mind. An alien enemy, an undischarged insolvent and criminals cannot enter into contract. Contract made by incompetent party/parties will be void.

IV. Free Consent

Parties entering into the contract should enter into it by their free consent. The consent will be free when it is not caused by—(1) coercion, (2) undue influence, (3) fraud, or (4) misrepresentation, or (5) mistake. When there is no free consent except fraud the contract becomes voidable at the option of the party whose consent was so caused. In case of fraud the contract would be void. The proposal for free consent must sign a declaration to this effect, the person explaining the subject matter of the proposal to the proposer must also accordingly make a written declaration on the proposal.

V. Legal Object

In order to make a valid contract, the object of the agreement should be lawful. An object that is (*i*) not forbidden by law, or (*ii*) is not immoral, or (*iii*) opposed to public policy, or (*v*) which does not defeat the provisions of any law, is lawful. In proposal from the object of insurance is asked which should ,be legal and the object should not be concealed. If the object of an insurance, like the consideration, is found to be unlawful, the policy is void.

2. INSURABLE INTEREST

For an insurance contract to be valid, the insured must possess an insurable interest in the subject matter of insurance. The insurable interest is the pecuniary interest whereby the policy-holder is benefitd by the existense of the subject-matter and is prejudiced death or damage of the subject-matter. The essentials of a valid insurable interest are the folowing:

(*i*) There must be a subject-matter to be insured.

(*ii*) The policy-holder should have monetary relationship with the subject-matter.

(*iii*) The relationship between the policy-holders and the subject-matter should be recognised by law. In other words, there should not be any illegal relationship between the policy-holder and the subject-matter to be insured.

(*iv*) The financial relationship between the policy-holder and subject-matter should be such that the policy-holder is economically benefited by the survival or existence of the subject-matter and or will suffer economic loss at the death or existence of the subject-matter.

The subject-matter is life in the life insurance, property and goods in property insurance, liability and adventure in general insurance. Insurable interest is essentially a pecuniary interest, *i.e.*, the loss caused by the happening of the insured risk must be capable of financial valuation. No emotional or sentimental loss, as an expectation or an anxiety, would be the ground of the insurable interest. The event insured should be one that if it happens the party suffers financially and if it does not happen, the party is benefited by the existence. But a mere hope or expectation, which may be frustrated by the happening of some extent, is not an insurable interest.

3. UTMOST GOOD FAITH

The doctrine of disclosing all material facts is embodied in the important principle 'utmost good faith' which applies to all forms of insurance. Both parties of the insuranre contract must be of the same mind (ad idem) at the time of contract. There should not be any mispepresentation, non-disclosure or fraud concerning the material. In case of insurance contract the legal maxim 'Caveat Emptor' (let the buyer beware) does not prevail, where it is regard of the buyer to satisfy himself of the genuineness of the subject-matter and the seller is under no obligation to supply information about it. But in insurance contract, the seller, *i.e.*, the insurer will also have to disclose all the material facts. An insurance contract is a contract of *uberrimae fidei*, *i.e.*, of absolute good faith both parties of the contract must disclose all the material facts and fully.

Material Facts

A material fact is one which affect the judgment or decision of both parties in entering to the contract. Facts which count materially are those which knowledge influence a party in deciding whether or not to offer or to accept such risk and if the risk, is acceptable, on what terms and conditions the risk should be accepted. These facts have a direct bearning on the degree of risk in relation to the subject of insurance. In case of life insurance, the material facts or factors affecting the risk will be age, residence, occupation, health, income, etc., and in case of property insurance, it would be use, design, owner and situation of the property.

Full and True Disclosure

The utmost Good Faith says that all the material facts should be disclosed in true and full form. It means that the facts should be disclosed in that form in which they really exist. There should be no concealment, misrepresentation, mistake or fraud about the material facts. There should be no false statement and no half truth nor nay silence on the material facts.

Duty of Both the Parties

The duty to disclose the material facts lies on both the parties the insured as well as the insurer, but in practice the assured has to be more particular, about the observance of this principle because he is usually in full knowledge of facts relating to the subject-matter which, despite all effective inspections of the insurer, wouid not be disclosed.

Facts need not be disclosed by the insured

The following facts, however, are not required to be disclosed by the insured:

(*i*) Facts which tend to lessen the risk.

(*ii*) Facts of public knowledge.

(*iii*) Facts which could be inferred from the information disclosed.

(*iv*) Facts waived by the insurer.

(*v*) Facts governed by the conditions of the policy.

4. PRINCIPLE OF INDEMNITY

As a rule all insurance contracts except personal insurance are contracts of indemnity. According to this principle, the insurer undertakes to put the insured, in the event of loss, in the same position that he occupied immediately before the happening of the event insured against. In certain form of insurance, the principle of indemnity is modified to apply. For example, in marine or fire insurance, sometimes, certain profit margin which would have earned in absence of the event, is also included in the loss. In true sense of the indemnity, the insured is not entitled to make a profit of his loss.

Uses

(*i*) To discourse over insurance the principle of indemnity it an essential feature of an insurance contract, in absence whereof this industry would have the hue of gambling and the insured would tend to effect over-insurance and then intentionally cause a loss to occur so that a financial gain could be achieved. So, to avoid this international loss, only the actual loss becomes payable and not the assured sum (which is higher in over-insurance). If the property is under-insured, *i.e.*, the insured amount is less than the actual value of the property insured, the insured is generally regarded his own insurer for the amount if under insurance and in case of loss one shall share the loss himself.

(*ii*) To avoid an Anti-social Act

If the assured is allowed to gain more than the actual loss, which is against the principle of indemnity, he will be tempted to gain by destruction of his own property after getting it insured against a risk. He will be under constant temptation to destroy the property. Thus, the whole society will be doing only anti-social act, *i.e.*, the persons would be interested in gaining after destruction of the property. So, the principle of indemnity has been applied where only the cash-value of his loss and nothing more than this, though he might have insured for a greater amount, will be compensated.

(*iii*) To maintain the Premium at Low-level

If the principle of indemnity is not applied, larger amount will be paid for a smaller loss and this will increase the cost of insurance and the premium of insurance will have to be raised. If premium is raised two things may happen—first, persons may not be inclined to insure and second, unscrupulous persons would get insurance to destroy the property to gain from such act. Both things would defeat thc purpose of insurance. So, principle of indemnity is here to help them because such temptation is eliminated when only actual loss and not more than the actual financial loss is compensated provided there is insurance up to that amount.

Conditions for Indemnity Principle

The following conditions should be fulfilled in full application of principle of indemnity.

(*i*) The insured has to prove that he will suffer loss on the insured matter at the time of happening the event and the loss is actual monetary loss.

(*ii*) The amount of compensation will be the amount of insurance. Indemnification cannot be more than the amount insured.

(*iii*) If the insured gets more amount than the actual loss, the insurer has right to get the extra-amount back.

(*iv*) If the insured gets some amount from third party after being fully indemnified by insurer, the insurer will have right to receive all the amount paid by the third party.

(*v*) The principle of indemnity does not apply to personal insurance because the amount of loss is not easily calculable there.

5. DOCTRINE OF SUBROGATION

The doctrine of subrogation refers to the right of the insurer to stand in the place of the insured, after settlement of a claim, in so far as the insured's right of recovery from an alternative source is involved. If the insured is in a position to recover the loss in full or in part from a third party due to whose negligence the loss may have been precipitated, his right of recovery is subrogated to the insurer on settlement of the claim. The insurers, thereafter, recover the claim from the thrid party. The right of subrogation may be exercised by the insurer before payment of loss.

Essentials of Doctrine of Subrogation

(*i*) *Corollary to the Principle of Indemnity.* The doctrine of subrogation is the supplementary principle of indemnity. The latter doctrine says that only the actual value of the loss of the property is compensated, so the formen follows that if the damaged property has any value left, or any right against a third party the insurer can subrogate the left property or right of the property because if the insurered is allowed to retain, he shall have realised more than the actual loss, which is contrary to principle of indemnity.

(*ii*) *Subrogation is the Substitution.* The insurer, according to this principle, becomes entitled to all the rights of insured subject matter after payment because he has paid the actual loss of the property. He is substituted in place of other persons who act on the right and claim of the property insured.

(*iii*) *Subrogation only up to the amount of payment.* The insurer is subrogated all the rights, claims, remedies and securities of the damaged insured property after indemnification, but he is entitled to get these benefits only to the extent of his payment. The insurer is, thus, subrogated to the alternative rights and remedies of the insured, only up to the amount of his payment to the insured. In the same way if the insured is compensated for his loss from another party after he has been indemnified by his insurer he is liable to part with the compensation up to the extent that the insurer is entitled to. In one U.S. case it was made clear "If the insurer, having paid the claim to the insured, recovers from the defaulting third party in excess of the amount paid under the policy, he has to pay this excess to the insured though he may charge the insured his share of reasonable expenses incurred in collecting.

(*iv*) *The Subrogation may be applied before Payment.* If the assured got certain compensation from third party before being fully indemnified by the insurer, the insurer can pay only the balance of the loss.

(*v*) *Personal Insurance.* The doctrine of subrogation does not apply to personal insurance because the doctrine of indemnity is not applicable to such insurance. The insurers have no right of action against the third party in respect of the damage. For example, if an insured dies due to the negligence of a third party his dependent has right to recover the amount of the loss from the third party along with the policy amount. No amount of the policy would be subrogated by the insurer.

6. WARRANTIES

There are certain conditions and promises in the insurance contract which are called warranties. According to Marine Insurance Act, "A warranty is that by which the assured undertakes that some particular thing shall or shall not be done, or that some conditions shall be fulfilled, or whereby he affirms or negatives the existence of a particular state of facts." Warranties which are mentioned in the policy are called express warranties. There are certain waranties which are not mentioned in the policy. These warranties are called implied warranties. Warranties which are answers to the question are called affirmative warranties. The warranties fulfilling certain conditions or promises are called promissory warranties.

Warranty is the very important condition in the insurance contract which is to be fulfilled by the insured. On breach of warranty the insurer becomes free from his liability. Therefore insured must have to fulfill the conditions and promises during the insurance contract whether it is important or not in connection with the risk. The contract can continue only when warranties are fulfilled. If warranties are not followed, the contract may be cancelled by the other party whether risk has occurred or not or the loss has occurred due to other reason than the waiving of warranties. However, when the warranty is declared illegal and there is no reverse effect on the contract, the warranty can be waived.

7. PROXIMATE CAUSE

The rule is that immediate and not the remote cause is to be regarded. The maxim is *sed causa proxima non-remota spectature*, *i.e.*; see the proximate cause and not the distant cause. The real cause must be seen while payment of the loss. If the real cause of loss is insured, the insurer is liable to compensate the loss; otherwise the insurer may not be responsible for loss. But, proximate cause is not a device to avoid the trouble of discovering the real cause or the common sense cause. Proximate cause means the active efficient cause that sets in motion a train of events which brings about a result, without intervention of any force started and working actively from a new and independent source.

The determination of real cause depends upon the working and practice of insurance and circumstances to losses. A loss may not be occasioned merely by one event. There may be concurrent causes or chain of causes. They may occur in a sequence or in broken chain. Sometimes, certain causes are excepted by the insurance contract and the insurer is not liable for the accepted peril.

The efficient cause of a loss is called the proximate cause of the loss. For the policy to cover the loss must have an insured peril as the proximate cause of the loss or also the insured peril must occur in the chain of causation that links the proximate cause with the loss. The proximate cause is not necessarily, the cause that was nearest to the damage either in time or in place, but is rather the cause that was actually responsible for loss.

Determination of Proximate Cause

(*i*) If there is a single cause of the loss, the cause will be the proximate cause and further if the peril (cause of loss) was insured,insurer will have to indemnify the loss.

(*ii*) If there are concurrent causes, the insured perils and excepted perils have to be segregated. The coneurrent causes may be first, separable and second, inseparable. Separable causes are those which can be separated from each other. The loss occurred due to a particular cause maybe distinguishly known. In such a case if any cause, is excepted peril, insurer will have to pay up to the extent of loss which occurred due to insured perils. If the circumstances are such that the perils are inseparable, then the insurers are not liable at all when there exists any excepted peril.

(*iii*) If the causes occurred in form of chain, they have to be observed seriously.

(A) If there is unbroken chain the excepted and insured perilfi have to be separated. If an excepted peril precedes the operation of the insured peril so that the loss caused by the latter is the direct and natural consequences of the excepted peril, there is no liability. If the insured peril is followed by an excepted peril there is valid liability.

(B) If there is a broken chain of events with no excepted peril involved, it is possible to separate the losses. The insurer is liabie only for that loss which caused by an insured peril; where there is an excepted peril, the subsequent loss caused by an insured peril will be a new and indirect cause because of the interruption in the chain of events. The insurer will be liable for the loss caused of insured peril which can be easily segregated. Similarly, if the loss occurs by an insured peril and there is, susbsequently loss by an excepted peril, the insurer will be liable for loss occurred due to the insured peril.

In brief, if the happening of an excepted peril is followed by the occurrence of an insured peril, as a new and independent cause there is a valid claim. If an insured peril is followed by the happening of an excepted peril, as a new and independent cause, there is a claim excluding loss or damage, caused by the excepted peril.

8. ASSIGNMENT OR TRANSFER OF INTEREST

It is necessary to distinguish between assignment of (*a*) the subject-matter of insurance, (*b*) the policy, and (*c*) the policy money when payable.

Marine and life policies can be freely assigned but assignment under fire and accident policies, are not valid,without the prior consent of the insurers—except changes of interest by will or operation of law. Moreover, assignments under fire and accident policies must be made before the insured parts with his, interest. Once he has lost the interest the policy is void and cannot be assigned.

The life policies can, be assigned whether the assignee has an insurable interest or not. Life policies are frequently charged, assigned or otherwise dealt with, for they are valuable securities. A marine policy is freely assignable unless it contains terms expressly prohibiting assignment. It assigned either before or after loss. A marine policy may be assigned by endorsement thereon or in other customary manner. In practice, a marine cargo policy is frequently endorsed in blank and becomes in effect a quasi-negotiable instrument. Thus, it will be appreciated, adds considerably to the convenience of mercantile transactions as the policy can be negotiated through a bank along with other documents of title.

Assignment in fire insurance cannot be recognised without prior consent of the insurer, change of interest in fire policies (unless by will or operation of law) are not valid unless and until the consent of the insurer has been given. The fire policies are not in the nature of assignment nor intended to be assigned from one person to another without the consent of the insurer. Assignment in fire insurance constitutes a new contract.

9. RETURN OF PREMIUM

Ordinarily the premium once paid cannot be refunded. However, in the following cases the refund is allowed.

(*i*) By Agreement in the Policy

The assured may pay full premium while effecting the insurance but it may be agreed to return it wholly or partly in the happening of certain events. For example, special packing may reduce the risk.

(*ii*) For Reasons of Equity

(*i*) *Non-attachment of risk.* Where the subject-matter insured or part thereof, has never been imperilled for example, term insurance with returnable premium where premium is returned to the policy-holder if death does not occur during period of insurance.

(*ii*) *Undeclared balace of on open policy.* The policy may be cancelled and premium may be returned for short interest allowed provided there was no further interest in the policy.

(*iii*) *Payment of Premium is apportionable.* The apportioned part of the consideration is refundable when a part of policy interest is not involved. For example, insurance may be taken for a voyage in stages, each stage being rated separately. In such a case if some stages are not completed the premium relating to incomplete stage is returnable.

(*iv*) Where the assured has no insurable interest throughout the currency of the risk, the premium is returnable provided the policy was not attached by way of wagering.

(*v*) Unreasonable delay in commencing the voyage may also entitle the insurer to cancel the insurance by returning the premium.

(*vi*) Where the assured has over-insured under an unvalued policy a proportionate part of the premium is returnable.

3. Over-insurance by Double Insurance

If there is over-insurance by double insurance, a proportionate part of the several premium is returnable provided that if the policies are taken at different times and any earlier policy has at any time born the entire risk or if a claim has been paid. On the policy in respect of the full insured thereby, no premium is returnable in respect of that policy and when double insurance is effected knowingly by the assured no premium is returnable.

DIFFERENCE BETWEEN DIFFERENT TYPES OF INSURANCE CONTRACT

1. Forms

The insurance contract may be divided into two forms—first life insurance contract and second contract of indemnity.

2. Occurring of Event

The event, the death, in life insurance is certain, but the only uncertainty is the time when the death will occur. In indemnity insurance (in fire and marine insurances) the even may not take place at all or may take place in part. Therefore, in life insurance, ordinarily every place will become a claim sooner or later but it is not certain in indemnity insurance.

3. Subject-Matter

The subject-matter in life insurance is life. The chances of death would increase along with the advance in age whatever precautionary measures may be taken for improvement of health whereas the property in other insurance can be repaired and replaced and may remain usually in good condition.

4. Variance in Premium

In life insurance premium is not much variable whereas in other insurance premium is variable in numerous forms.

5. Classification of Risk

The classification of risks is generally more simple in life insurance than in other types of insurance contract. In life contract it would be standard, sub-standard and uninsurable but in other insurance it may be several.

6. Period of Insurance

Generally the life insurance is taken for longer period. Whereas the other forms of insurance are taken for not more than one two years.

7. Protection and Investment

The life insurance contract provides protection against loss early death and investment to meet the old age requirements. Other forms of insurance do not provide investment because the premium paid is not returnable if the contingencies (hazards) do not occur within the period. Other forms of insurance provide only protection against loss on damage of the property against the insured perils.

8. Premium Payment

The mode of premium payment in life insurance is generally level premium whereas in other forms of insurances, it is single premium.

9. Insurable Interest

Insurable interest must be at the time of proposal in insurance but in property insurance it must be present at the time of loss.

DIFFERENCE BETWEEN FIRE INSURANCE AND LIFE INSURANCE

1. Type of Contract

The fire insurance is a contract of indemnity, where payment of loss will be made only when fire occurred, but the life insurance contract is a contract of certainty, wherein payment is certainly made.

2. Occurring of Event

The fire may or not occur in fire insurance but in life insurance the death will certainly occur.

3. Classification of risk

There are numerous types of risk in fire insurance whereas the risks in life insurance are divided into three classes—the standard risk sub-standard risk and uninsurable risk.

4. Period of Insurance

The term of insurance in fire insurance does not exceed generally more than one year but in life insurance it lasts for a very long period.

5. Protection and Investment

Fire insurance includes only the element of protection whereas the life insurance includes the element of protection and investment because the premium paid or sum assured is returnable in the latter case whereas no premium or amount is returnable in fire insurance.

6. Insurable Interest

In fire insurance, the insurable interest must exist from the date of the proposal to the date of completion of the contract whether by death or by expiry of term. In life insurances insurable interest must exist at the time of proposal. This is the reason that the insured property, insurance policy, or policy amount-cannot be assigned to others in fire insurance whereas it is freely assignable in life insurance.

7. Moral Hazard

The degree of moral hazard in fire insurance is maximum whereas it is very nominal in case of life insurance.

DIFFERENCE BETWEEN FIRE INSURANCE AND MARINE INSURANCE

Fire and marine insurance contracts are similar in most of the cases because both these contracts are indemnity contracts. But, the following differences are observed in both the contracts.

(*i*) Moral Hazard

In marine insurances, the chances of moral hazard do not exist so much as are in the fire insurance.

(*ii*) Insurable Interest

The insurable interest must exist both the time, at the inception and at the completion of the contract. This is the reason fire insurance policies cannot be freely assignable. The insurable interest in marine insurance must exist at the time of loss. So, the marine policies are freely assignable.

(*iii*) Profit

Marine policies generally allow certain margin of profit to be charged at the time of indemnification of loss, but the fire policies do not allow it ordinarily.

(*iv*) Valued Policies

Marine insurance policies are generally valued policies and the market fluctuation is avoided; but the fire polices strictly adher to the doctrine of indemnity and only the market value of the property at the time of loss (valuable amount) is compensated.

INSURANCE AND GAMBLING

Insurance and gambling was considered alike because there are uncertainty of events and payment is made when the event occurs. Like gambles the insured is unaware of the time and amount of loss. If the event occurs, the insured like the gambler gains, otherwise they are experiencing the loss. But there are certain differences between the insurance contract and gambling.

(*i*) Nature of risk

In insurance, risks are existing, they may occur at any time. For example, death, old age, fire, marine perils, accident, etc., may occur any time. If there is no insurance, the person will suffer at the occurrence of these perils, but if insurance is taken against these risks, the insurer will provide a fixed amount or indemnify the amount of loss occurred due to the insured perils. Thus, insurance is protection against these risks.

In case of gambling, the risk does not exist, it is being created for game or amusement while one will suffer and another will gain. In absence of such game, nobody will suffer. In absence of insurance the property owner will suffer while due to insurance, no party will suffer.

(*ii*) Insurable Interest

In insurance contract, insurable interest is essential. Without insurable interest, it would be wagering contract. Thus, this principle clearly distinguishes the insurance contract from the gambling.

QUESTIONS

1. What are the various essentials of insurance contract?
2. Explain fully insurable interest, utmost good faith, principle of indemnity doctrine of subrogation and warranties in insurance contracts.
3. Differentiate the types of insurance contract.
4. 'Proximate cause is not very essential in case of life insurance contract'. Explain in detail.

PART TWO

LIFE INSURANCE

5

NATURE OF LIFE INSURANCE CONTRACT

Life insurance contract may be defined as the contract, whereby the insurer in consideration of a premium undertakes to pay a certain sum of money either on the death of the insured or on the expiry of a fixed period. The definition of the life insurance contract is enlarged by Section 2 (*ii*) of the Insurance Act 1938 by including annuity business. Since, the life insurance contract is not an indemnity contract, the undertaking on the part of the insurer is an absolute one to pay a definite sum on maturity of policy at the death or an amount in instalment for a fixed period or during the life.

Features of Life Insurance Contract

(*i*) Nature of General Contract.

(*ii*) Insurable Interest.

(*iii*) Utmost Good Faith.

(*iv*) Warranties.

(*v*) Proximate Cause.

(*vi*) Assignment and Nomination.

(*vii*) Return of Premium.

(*viii*) Other Features.

In life insurance contract the first three features are very important while the rest of them are of complementary nature.

1. NATURE OF GENERAL CONTRACT

Since the life insurance contract is a sort of contract it is approved by the Indian Contract Act. According to Section 2 (H) and Section 10 of Indian Contract Act, the valid contracts must have the following essentialities:

(*i*) Agreement (offer and acceptance).

(*ii*) Competency of the parties.

(*iii*) Free consent of the parties, *i.e.*, the parties must be *ad. idem*.

(*iv*) Legal consideration.

(*v*) Legal objective.

1. Offer and Acceptance

An offer or proposal is an intimation to another of one's intention to do or to abstain from doing anything with a view to obtaining the assent of that other person to such an act or abstinence. When the person to whom the proposal or offer is made signifies his assent to it, the offer is said to be accepted. The offer and acceptance in life insurance is of typical nature. The proposal form is completed by the proposer and along with the proposal form first premium is paid. The same may be accepted at normal rates and terms. The Agents' canvassing or publication of prospects and of uses of insurance constitute invitation to offer because the public in general and individual in particular are invited to make proposal for insurance. Submission of proposal along with the premium is an offer and the despatch of acceptance-letter is the acceptance. The risk will commence as soon as the acceptance letter is despatched by the insurer. When proposal is not accompanied with the first premium, it would be an invitation to offer by the prospect and the letter of insurer (generally acceptance letter with modification is sent) asking the proposer to pay the first premium without any alteration is an offer and the payment of first premium by the prospect is acceptance. As soon as premium is despatched, acceptance is made provided there was no alteration in the terms and conditions.

Another case may be when the insurer desires to accept the proposal only on certain modifications. The letter (generally the acceptance letter) sent to the prospect about the desire of change in terms and conditions is an offer if the first premium was not sent along with the proposal. But if the first premium was sent along with the proposal, it would be a counter-offer. If the prospect accepts the terms and conditions and sends the first premium if the premium was not already sent, it would be an acceptance. Thus, the acceptance letter sent by the insurer is not always acceptance. It would be acceptance only when the first premium was accompanied with the proposal and the proposal is acceptable on normal rates and terms. In other cases it would be an offer or counter-offer.

2. Competency of the Parties

The essential element of a valid contract is that the parties to, it must be legally competent to contract. Every person is competent to contract who is of the age of majority according to the law, (2) who is of sound mind, and (3) who is not disqualified from contracting by any law.

The insurer will be competent to contract if he has got the licence to carry on insurance business. The insurer is working within the Article of Association and Memorandum of Association or the Deeds of Partnership. In India, the Life Insurance Corporation is solely authorised to carry on life insurance business.

Majority

Majority is attained when a person completes the age of 18 years. A minor is not competent to contract. A contract by a minor is void excepting contracts for necessaries. The minor can repudiate the contract at any time during his minority. If the life insurance policy is issued to a minor, the insurer cannot repudiate it but the minor can repudiate it during his minority. At the attainment of majority, he has to exercise the option, within a reasonable time, whether he would continue to carry on the policy or not. Generally, insurer accepts the proposal forms completed by the guardians of the minors. So, the incompetency of contract does not arise.

Person of Sound Mind

Persons of sound mind can enter into a contract. A person is said to be of sound mind for the purpose of making a contract if at the time when he makes it, he is capable of understanding it and of forming a rational judgment as to its effect upon his interests. A person who is usually of unsound mind, but occasionally of sound mind may make a contract when he is of sound mind. A person usually of sound mind, but occasionally of unsound mind, may not make a contract when he is of unsound mind. So, an intoxicated person cannot enter into a contract. The contract may be voidable at his option, but in order to be avoided, it must be repudiated by the insured within a reasonable time of his becoming sober. Similarly, when an originally valid contract has been entered into, it will not be affected by one of the parties becoming lunatic afterwards.

Other Disqualification

A contract with an alien enemy is void. An alien enemy is disqualified from, and is incapable of, entering into contract or enforcing it. When an alien with whom an insurance contract has been entered into becomes an enemy afterwards, the contract is either suspended or terminated as from the declaration of war.

3. Free Consent of the Parties

Both parties must be of the same mind at the time of contract. If the two parties do not meet in this respect, there is no perfect agreement between them. It is necessary to call it free consent of parties that the contract is not made (consent is not obtained) through coercion, undue influence, fraud, misrepresentation or mistake. In life insurance, both parties must know the exact nature of the risk to be underwritten. If the consent is not free, the contract is generally voidable at the option of the party whose consent was not freely given. According to Section 13 two persons are said to consent freely when they agree upon the same thing in the same sense.

4. Legal Consideration

The presence of a lawful consideration is essential for a legal contract. The insurer must have some consideration in return of his promise to pay a fixed sum at maturity or death whichever may be the case. The consideration need not be money only. It should be anything valuable or to which value may be assigned. It may be interest, right, dividend, etc. In Raj Narain vs. Hindustan Co-operative Insurance the insurance was accepted and the premium was paid but the policy was not issued by the insurers. The insured died and could get the policy amount in allegiance of policy because at the payment of premiums contract was complete. The first premium is consideration and subsequent premiums are merely conditions to contract.

5. Legal Objective

The contract would be legal only when the object is legal. The object of a legal life insurance contract is to protect oneself or one's family against financial losses at the death of the insured. The contract is, sometimes, to provide for financial emergencies that may occur in old age. In brief the contract will be lawful only when the objective is legal. The objective will be legal only when there is insurable interest. Without having this interest, the object of the contract would not be legal. It would be wager contract and against public policy.

2. INSURABLE INTEREST

Insurable interest is the pecuniary interest. The insured must have an insurable interest in the life to be insured for a valid contract. Insurable interest arises out of the pecuniary relationship that exists between the policy-holder and the life assured so that the former stands to loose by the death of the latter and/or continues to gain by his survival. If such relationship exists, then the former has insurable interest in the life of the latter. The loss should be monetary or financial. Mere emotion and expectation do not constitute insurable interest in the life of his friend or father merely because he gets valuable advices from them.

Insurable interest in life insurance may be divided into *two* categories: (1) insurable interest in own life, and (2) insurable interest in other's life. The latter can be sub-divided into *two* classes: (*a*) where proof is not required, and (*b*) where proof is required. Again this insurable interest, (*b*) can be divided into two classes: (*i*) insurable interest arising due to business relationship, and (*ii*) insurable interest in family relation.

Insurable Interest in Own's Life

An individual always has an insurable interest in his own life. Its presence is not required to be proved. Bunyon says, "Every man is presumed to possess an insurable interest in his estate for the loss of his future gains or savings which might be the result of his premature death." According to the definition of insurable interest it is also evident that the person will continue to gain financially while he is surviving and will suffer loss if he is dead because he will be unable to earn or protect the property.

The insurable interest in own life is unlimited because the loss to the insured or his dependents cannot be measured in terms of money and, therefore, no limit can be placed to the amount of insurance that one may take on one's own life. Thus, theoretically, a person can take a policy to any unlimited amount on his own's life; but in practice no insurer will issue a policy for an amount larger than amount seems suitable to the circumstances and means of the applicant. Generally, it is mentioned that one cannot purchase policy usually more than ten times of his one year's income. The premium can be paid by third party provided there was no intention to speculation. If there is possibility of wager contract it would be void.

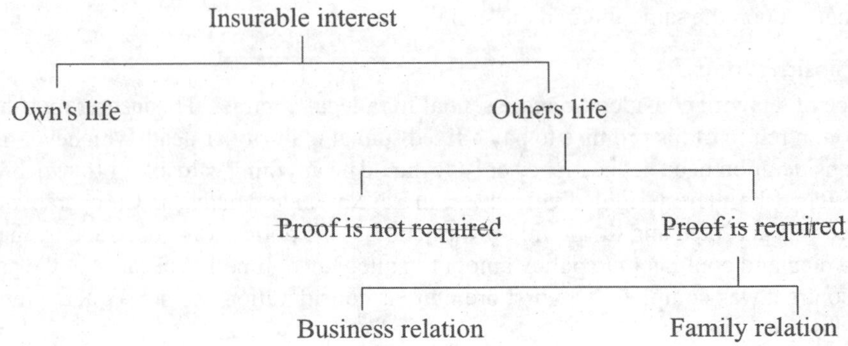

Insurable Interest in Other's Life

Life insurance can be effected on the lives of third parties provided the proposer has insurable interest in the third party. There are two types of insurable interest in other's life. First where proof is not required and second, where proof is required.

A. Proof not required

There are only two such cases where the presence of insurable interest is legally presumed and therefore need not be proved.

1. Wife has insurable interest in the life of her husband

It is presumed and decided by *Reed* vs. *Royal Exchange* (1795) that wife is presumed to have insurable interest in the life of her husband because husband is legally bound to support his wife. The wife will suffer financially if the husband is dead and will continue to gain if the husband is surviving. Since, the extent of loss or gain cannot be measured in this case, the wife has insurable interest in the husband's life up to an unlimited extent.

2. Husband has insurable interest in the life of his wife

The insurable interest is presumed to exist here and no proof is required. It was decided in *Griffith* vs. *Fleming* (1909) that the husband has insurable interest in his wife's life because of domestic services performed by the wife. If the wife is dead husband has to employ other person to render the domestic services and certain other financial expenditures will involve at her death which are not calculable. The husband is benefited at the survival of his wife, so it is self-proved that husband has insurable interest in his wife's life. Since the monetary loss at her death or monetary gain at his survival cannot be measured, there is unlimited insurable interest in the life of wife.

B. Proof is required

Insurable interest has to be proved in the following cases:

1. *Business Relationship.* The policy-holder may have insurable interest in the life of assured due to business or contractual relationship. In this case, the amount of insurable corresponds with the amount of risk involved. Some of such examples are narrated below:

(*a*) *A creditor has in the life or. his debtor.* The creditor may lose money if the debtor dies before the loan is repaid. The continuance of debtor's life is financially meaningful to the creditor because the latter will get all his money repaid at the former's survival. The maximum amount of loss to a creditor may be the amount of outstanding loan plus interest thereon and the amount of premium paid. So, the maximum amount of insurable interest is limited to the outstanding loan, plus interest and amount of premium expected to be paid. The interest is calculated on the estimation of duration of debt to be paid. The maximum amount of interest does not say about the payment of policy amount, it, merely, determines the chances of speculation. The full amount of policy is payable irrespective of the payment of loan and interest. Since it is life insurance, the full policy amount is paid.

(*b*) *A trustee has insurable interest in respect of the interest of which he is trustee* because at the survival of the other person the trustee is benefited and at his death he will suffer.

(*c*) *A surety has insurable interest in the life of his principal.* If the principal (the debtor) is dead, the surety is responsible for payment of outstanding loan, or obligated amount. At the survival of principal, he will not suffer this loss. The insurable interest is limited up to the amount of outstanding loan, interest and premium paid.

(*d*) *A partner has insurable interest in life of each partner.* At the death of a partner, the partnership will be dissolved and the surviving partner will lose financially. Even if the firm continues at the death of the partner, the firm has to pay deceased partner's share to his dependents. This will involve a huge financial loss to the partnership. Therefore, the firm collectively can purchase insurance policies in the life of each partner of the firm. Since the firm part of money up to the extent of deceased partner goodwill, capital, share of profit and reserve, the firm has insurable interest up to the extent in each partner. Similarly all the partners have insurable interest in life of each partner because they will financially suffer at a death.

(*e*) *An employer has in the life of a key-man.* A key-man is the person whose presence, capital, capacity cause profit to the business. If the key-man is dead, the business will reduce profit up to a certain extent. The business suffers reduced profit, expenses involved in appointing and training new persons and the amount to be given to the dependents of key-man at his death. So the business has insurance interest up to such extent in the key-man's life.

(*f*) *An insurer has in the life assured.* The insurer suffers at the death of life assured and, therefore, he can get reinsurance of the assured persons by him. The insurable interest is limited up to the policy amount.

2. Family Relationship

The insurable interest may arise due to family relationship if pecuniary interest exists between the policy-holders and life assured because mere relationship or ties of blood and of affection does not constitute insurable interest, the proposer must have a reasonable expectation of financial benefit from the continuance of the life of the person to be insured or of financial loss from his death. The interest must be based on value and not on mere sentiments. Similarly, mere moral obligation is not sufficient to warrant existence of insurable interest although legal obligation to get support will form insurable interest of the person who is supported in life of the person who is supporting. Thus, a son can insure his father's life only when he is dependent on him and the father can take insurance policy on his son's life only when he is dependent on his son.

GENERAL RULE OF INSURABLE INTEREST IN LIFE INSURANCE

1. Time of Insurable Interest

The insurable interest must exist at the time of proposal. Policy, without insurable interest, will be wager. It is not essential that the insurable interest must be present at the time of claim.

2. Services

Except the services of wife, services of other relatives will not essentially form insurable interest. There must be financial relationship between the proposer and the life assured. In other words, the services performed by the son without dependence of his father, will not constitute insurable interest of the father in the life of his soil. Vice-versa is not essential for forming insurable interest.

3. Insurable Interest must be valuable

In business relationship the value or extent of the insurable must be determined to avoid wager contract of the additional insurance. Insurance is limited only up to the amount of insurable interest.

4. Insurable interest should be valid

Insurable interest should not be against public policy and it should be recognised by law. Therefore, the consent of life assured is very essential before the policy can be issued.

5. The legal responsibility may be basis of insurable interest

Since the person will suffer financially up to the extent of responsibility, the proposal has insurable interest to that extent. For instance, a person will be under legal responsibility to expense at the funeral of his wife and children, he can purchase insurance in their lives up to that extent.

6. Insurable Interest must be definite

The insurable interest must be present definitely at the time of proposal. Mere expectation of gain or support will not constitute insurable interest.

7. Legal Consequence

The insurable interest must be there to form legal and valid insurance contract. Without insurable interest, it would be null and void.

3. UTMOST GOOD FAITH

The life insurance requires that the principle of utmost good faith should be preserved by both the parties. The utmost good faith says that both the parties, proposer (insured) and insurer, must be of the same mind at the time of contract because only then the risk may be correctly ascertained. They must make full and true disclosure of the facts material to the risk.

Material Facts

In life insurance material facts are age, income, occupation, health, habits, residence, family history and plan of insurance. Material facts are determined not on the basis of opinion, therefore, the proposer should disclose not only those matters which the proposer may feel are material but all facts which are material.

Duty of both parties

It is not only the proposer but the insurer also who is responsible to disclose all the material facts which are going to influence the decision of the proposer, whether apply or not to apply for insurance. Since the decision is taken mostly on the basis of subject-matter, the life to be insured in life insurance, and the material facts relating to the subject-matter are known or is expected to be known by the proposer; it is much more responsibility of the proposer to disclose the material facts.

Full and True Disclosure

Utmost good faith says that there should be full and true disclosure of all the material facts. Full and true means that there should be no concealment, misrepresentation, half disclosure and fraud of the subject matter to be insured.

Extent of the Duty

The duty of disclosure finishes at the moment when the proposal form has been fully and correctly fulfilled provided there is no such facts which he considers or expected to be considered material and have not been disclosed. The proposer cannot defened on the ground that he had omitted to disclose it by carelessness or by mistake or that he did not regard it material to the contract.

Legal Consequence

In the absence of utmost good faith the contract will be voidable at the option of the person who suffered loss due to non-disclosure. The intentional non-disclosure counts fraud and is void *ab initio* and the unintentional non-disclosure is voidable at the option of the party not at fault.

Once the voidable contract has been validated by the party not at fault, the contract cannot be avoided by him later on. For instance, if the insurer has continued to accept the premium when certain non-disclosure, say mis-statement of age, has been disclosed the insurer cannot invalid the contract and cannot refute to pay the amount of claim. If the party not at fault does not exercise its option, the contract will remain valid.

Indusputability of Policy

The doctrine of utmost good faith works as a great hardship for a long period on the plea of mis-statement at the time of proposal. In such cases, it would be very difficult to prove or disprove whether a particular statement made at the time of policy was true. Therefore, to remove this hardship, certain sections in the concerned Act are provided. In India, Section 45 of the Insurance Act 1938 deals with such dispute. It is called *indisputable clause*, "... No policy of life insurance, after expiry of two years from the date on which it was effected, be called into question by an insurer on the ground that a statement made in the proposal for insurance or in any report of a medical officer or referee or friend of the insured or in any other document leading to the issue of the policy was inaccurate or false, unless the insurer shows that such statement was on a material matter or suppressed facts which it was material to disclose and that it was fraudulently made by the policy-holder and that the policy-holder knew at the time of making it that the statement was false or that it suppressed facts which it was material to disclose. Provided that nothing in this section shall prevent the insurer from calling for proof of age at any time if he is entitled to do so.

FACTS NOT REQUIRED TO BE DISCLOSED

The following facts are not required to be disclosed:

(*i*) Circumstances which are diminishing the risk.

(*ii*) Facts which are known or reasonably should be known to the insurer in his ordinary course of business.

(*iii*) Facts which the insurer should infer from the information given.

(*iv*) Facts which are waived by the insurer.

(*v*) Facts which are superfluous to disclose by reason of a condition or warranty.

(*vi*) Facts of public knowledge.

4. WARRANTIES

Representation

For understanding warranties 'Representations' are to be thoroughly understood because in life insurance those representations which are embodied in the policy and expressly or impliedly forming part of the basis of the contract, are called *warranties*. Every information given by a proposer for insurance to the insurer during the negotiations is a representation. The representations may be material or non-material. The material representations are the basis of insurance contract as has been clear in the utmost good faith under material facts. If the proposer's representation is false or untrue, the contract may be voidable at the option of the insurer. The representations made during the negotiations do not form an integral part of the contract.

Warranties

Warranties are an integral part of the contract, *i.e.*, these are the bases of the contract between the proposer and insurer and if any statement, whether material or non-material, is untrue the contract shall be null and void and the premium paid by him may be forfeited by the insurer. The policy issued will contain that the proposal and personal statement shall form part of the policy and be the basis of the contract. So that representation will be warranty. As has been disclosed already that the warranties may be (*i*) informative, and (*ii*) promissory.

(*i*) *Informative Warranties.* In life insurance the informative warranties are more important. The proposer is expected to disclose all the material facts to the best of his knowledge and belief.

(*ii*) *Promissory Warranties.* Warranties relating to the future may only be statements about his expectation or intention, for instance, the proposer promises that he will not take up any hazardous occupation and will inform the insurer if he will take the hazardous occupation.

Breach of Warranty

If there is breach of warranty, the insurer is not bound to perform his part of the contract unless he chooses to ignore the breach. The effect of a breach of warranty is to render the contract voidable at the option of the other party provided there is no element of fraud. In case of fraudulent representation or promise, the contract will be void *ab initio*.

5. PROXIMATE CAUSE

The efficient or effective cause which causes the loss is called *proximate cause*. It is the real and actual cause of loss. If the cause of loss (peril) is insured, the insurer will pay; otherwise the insurer will not compensate. In life insurance the doctrine of *Causa Proxima* (Proximate Cause) is not applied because the insurer is bound to pay the amount of insurance whatever may be the reason of death. It may be natural or unnatural. So, this principle is not of much practical importance in connection with life assurance, but in the following cases the proximate causes are observed in the life insurance, too.

(*i*) *War-risk.* Where policy is issued on exclusion of war and aviation risks, the proximate cause of death is important because the insurer waives its liability if death occurred, in this case, while the insured was in field or is engaged in operation of war and aviation. Only premium paid or surrender value whichever is higher is payable and the total policy amount is not payable.

(*ii*) *Suicide.* If suicide occurs within one year of the policy, or there was intention to commit suicide and the payment of policy would be restricted, only up to the interest of the third party in the policy provided the interest was expressed at least one month before the suicide.

(*iii*) *Accident Benefit.* A problem arises when an insured under an accident policy is killed or suffers an injury which has an immediate cause and also a remote cause. In accident benefit policy, double of the policy amount is paid. So, the cause of death in this policy is of paramount importance.

6. ASSIGNMENT AND NOMINATION

The policy in life insurance can be assigned freely for a legal consideration or love and affection. The assignment shall be complete and effectual only on the execution of such endorsement either on the policy itself or by a separate deed. Notice for this purpose must be given to the insurer who will acknowledge the assignment. Once the assignment is completed, it cannot be revoked by the assignor because he ceases to be the owner of the policy unless reassignment is made by the assignee in favour of the assignor. An assignee may be the owner of the policy both on survival of the life assured, or on his death according to the terms of transfer. The life policies are the only policies which can be assigned whether the assignee has an insurable interest or not. Life policies are frequently charged, assigned or otherwise dealt with for they are valuable securities because a fixed sum is certainly paid, in life policies excepting a few, say, pure endowment and temporary polices.

Nomination

The holder of a policy of life insurance on his own life may either at the time of affecting policy or at any subsequent time before the policy matures, nominate the person or persons to whom the money secured by the policy shall be paid in the event of his death. A nomination can be cancelled before maturity, but unless notice is given of any such cancellation to the insurer, the insurer will not be liable for any bona fide payment to a nominee registered in the records. When the policy matures, or if the nominee dies, the sum shall be paid to the policy-holder or his legal representatives.

7. RETURN OF PREMIUM

Ordinarily, the premium once paid cannot be refunded. However in the following cases the premiums paid are returnable.

1. For reason of Equity

Equity implies a condition that the insurer shall not receive the price of running a risk he runs. Thus, there the contract does not come into effect or it is held to be void *ab initio*. For example, on account of misrepresentation or breach of warranty, the insured, in the absence of any express condition to the contrary, can claim the return of any premiums paid. But if the policy runs for a time and becomes void later on, the insured is not entitled to the return of any part of the premium.

Where the insured is guilty of fraud in obtaining a policy, he will fail in his claim to the sum assured. He cannot also ask for a return of the premiums because he will have to allege his own fraud to succeed in his claim and no court will assist such person.

8. OTHER FEATURES

Life insurance policies have the following additional features:

Life insurance contract is (*i*) an Aleatory contract, (*ii*) a unilateral contract, (*iii*) a conditional contract, (*iv*) a contract of Adhesion, and (*v*) not a contract of indemnity.

(*i*) *Aleatory Contract.* Aleatory contract means contract depends on chance. In ordinary contract approximately equal value is exchanged by both parties; but in life insurance contract, the full sum assured may be payable even if all premiums are not paid. Thus, on the chance of death, higher amount is payable. It should be clear, here, that, this does not make the contract of wager because of insurable interest.

(*ii*) *Unilateral Contract.* Life insurance contract is unilateral contract because, here, only the insurer makes an enforceable promise. The proposer had already performed his duty of payment of premiums. If the first premium is paid, the insurer is bound to accept subsequent premium and to pay the amount claim when it arises except on the ground of fraud.

(*iii*) *Conditional Contract.* Life insurance contract is conditional contract because the insurer shall pay the assured sum only when the contract is continuing by payment of premium. In addition, the insurer's promise to pay the sum assured is also conditional upon the furnishing of satisfactory proof of death and other conditions mentioned in the policy.

(*iv*) *Contract of Adhesion.* Contract of adhesion means that the terms of the contract are not arrived by mutual negotiations between the parties as in the case of ordinary contracts. The proposer is not in a position to bargain about the terms of contract because these terms are already determined. The only course open to the proposer is whether to accept or not a particular policy.

(*v*) *Indemnity contract is not applied.* In life insurance the indemnity contract is not applicable because the value of loss at death cannot be ascertained. It is not possible to ascertain the time up to which the insured would have survived and it is also difficult to ascertain the amount of money to be earned by him during life-time. So, the doctrine of subrogation is also not applicable. In life insurance a fixed sum is paid which may be the sum assured and bonus if the policy is participating one.

QUESTIONS

1. Describe the essential features of life insurance contract.
2. Explain in detail how insurable interest, utmost good faith, warranties and proximate cause are applicable in life insurance.
3. 'The policies are freely assignable in case of life insurance.' Discuss.

6

CLASSIFICATION OF POLICIES

The life insurance contract provides elements of protection and investment. After getting insurance, the policy-holder feels a sense of protection because he shall be paid a definite sum at the death or maturity. Since a definite sum must be paid, the element of investment is also present. In other words, life insurance provides against pre-mature death and a fixed sum at the maturity of policy. The two elements of protection and investment exist in various degrees in different types of policies. Not only this, but these elements will vary according to the different times in the same policy. The older the policy, the lesser the element of protection and higher the element of investment and vice-versa is also true.

Having different elements in different policies, the policy-holders are free to choose the best policies according to their requirements. It would be known that no one policy is the best policy for all the policy-holders due to variance in cost, elements of investments and protection, requirements of the policy-holders and availability of the policy.

The life insurance policies can be divided on the basis of (*a*) Duration of policy, (*b*) Method of Premium payments, (*c*) Participation in profit, (*d*) Number of lives covered, (*e*) Method of payment of claim amounts and (*f*) Non-conventional Policies.

A. POLICIES ACCORDING TO DURATION OF POLICIES

The life insurance policies according to the duration may be (*i*) whole-life, (*ii*) term insurance, (*iii*) endowment insurance and (*iv*) survivorship policy.

(*i*) *Whole-life policies.* Whole-life policies are issued for life. It means that the policy amount will be paid at the death of the life assured. The life assured, thus, cannot get the policy amount during his life time; only his dependents will get the advantages of this policy. The whole life policies can be effected either by payment of (*i*) single premium, (*ii*) continuous premium, payment or (*iii*) limited premium. The single premium payment is not very common whereas the limited premium payment is the most popular form of whole-life policies because, it is convenient to the policy-holder to arrange the payment of premium during his income-earning period. In continuous premium payment, this benefit is not available because premium is payable up to the life of the policy-holder. This is losing its importance because only the dependents of life assured are getting the benefit. Also, in extreme cases, he pays, more by way of premium than the benefits relievable under the policy and that too when earning capacity of the assured is reduced. This plan is cheaper and suits to an young man with limited resources and whose requirements for protection is maximum. It is, also beneficial to pay estate duty. If payment of premiums, ceases after at least, 3 years' premiums have been paid, a free paid up policy for such reduced sum, as can be allowed according to the rules, will be automatically secured provided the reduced sum assured is not less than ₹ 250.

(*ii*) *Limited Payment Whole-Lite Policies.* The payment of premium is limited to certain period, although the amount secured under this plan is payable on the death of the policy-holder. Premium under this plan is higher than the premium payable under a whole life plan. The amount of premium depends upon the number of annual premiums stipulated since premiums are payable for a selected period of years or until death if it occurs within this period, the life assured is satisfied to know the amount of maximum premium payable. If the life assured survives the premium paying period, the policy continues in full force, provided all premiums have been paid, but no further premiums are required to be paid. With profits limited payment policies do not cease to participate in profits after completion of the premium-paying period but continue to share in the periodical bonús distribution.

This plan is suitable for persons in whose case the need for money would arise only on the happening of the death, but who either on account of personal and family history are not eligible for a whole life plan or do not want to extend the premium-paying period beyond their earning years. The minimum amount for which a policy will be issued under this plan is ₹ 1,000.

(*iii*) *Convertible Whole-Life Policy.* This is a whole-life policy which gives its holder an option to get it converted at the end of five years, into an endowment policy. If this option is exercised, the policy no longer remains a whole-life policy, if it is not exercised the policy continues to be, a whole-life policy. The policy is designed to meet the needs of the young man who is on the threshold of his career and has prospect for increase in income after a short period. The object is to provide maximum insurance protection at a minimum cost and at the same time to offer a flexible contract which can be allowed to an endowment policy, at the end of five years of the policy. If the option is not exercised, the policy continues as a whole life assurance with premiums ceasing at age 70. If the policy is converted into endowment, the premium is suitably increased. However, no difference in premiums for the previous five years, and interest thereon, will be charged and he is not required to go under fresh medical examination. The vested bonus additions would be altered to an amount which the policy would have earned had it been effected from the commencement as an endowment policy and further, the policy would thereafter be entitled to bonus at the rate applicable to endowment assurance. The minimum sum assured for which a policy will be issued under this plan is ₹ 5,000 and the maximum age at entry shall be 45 years.

TERM INSURANCE POLICIES

Term insurance is far a short period of years ranging from 3 months to seven years. Sum assured is payable only in the event of death of the life assured occurring during the period; but the assurance comes to an end, should the life assured survive. The selected term premiums are usually payable throughout the term of the policy or till the prior death of the life assured. Term insurance policies are the cheapest policies. Without profit term insurance issued at age 35 requires a single premium of ₹ 13.62 for a ₹ 1,000/- whereas the single premium rate far whole life without profit policies issued at corresponding age is ₹ 519.69. Term insurance policies are always 'without profits'.

The term insurance policies are useful to those (*i*) who need extra-protection far a short duration or (*ii*) who need protection for long duration but are unable to purchase for the time-being due to ill-health or lesser income, (*iii*) a young businessman can take the policy to save the business-disaster during initial stage of the business, (*iv*) key-men's insurances are generally on term insurance basis, (*v*) a mortgagor of the property may be benefited by this scheme, (*vi*) a father can take this policy during the period of education of his child, and (*vii*) any such persons who are willing to provide insurance far a shorter period.

Term insurances are of the following types in India.

(*i*) *Straight-Term (Temporary) Insurance.* The corporation issues term-insurance for two years, which is also called as two-years temporary assurance policy. The sum assured will be payable only in the event of the life assured's death occurring within two years from the commencement of the policy. A single premium is required to be paid at the outset. The policies are issued only under, the without profits plan. The proposes is required to pay the medical examination fee. The policy is not entitled to any surrender value and no loan can be granted on the security thereof because, it is not of accumulative nature and payment is not always certain. This plan cannot be converted into other plans.

This policy is beneficial to the dependents who are required to pay Estate Duty and to those persons who are given charity or donation of fixed property.

(*ii*) *Renewable Term Policies.* These policies are renewable at the expiry of term for an additional period without medical examination; but the premium rate will be altered according to the age attained at the time of renewal. This policy is beneficial to those whose health are deteriorating and will be uninsurable at an advanced age. With the help of this policy, they continue to enjoy the insurance benefit without going under fresh medical examination. However, the premium rate will be increasing according to the attained age. The policy-holder can renew it many times provided the attained age has not crossed 55 years.

(*iii*) *Convertible Term Policy.* Under this policy, option to convert it into whole life or endowment policy is available. In corporation, the life assured under this plan has an option to convert the policy, provided it is in full force, into either a limited payment life policy or an endowment assurance policy, without having to undergo fresh medical examination, at any time during the specified term except the last two years. If the option of conversion is exercised, a new policy under the limited payment life-plan or endowment assurance plan will be issued as the case may be subject to the rates of premium and terms and conditions prevailing on the date of conversion. In other words, the premium rates ,will be increased according to the age attained.

This policy is issued only to first class lives. Persons aged over 40 years nearer birthday at entry and those following hazardous occupation including persons in the Armed Forces will not be eligible for assurance under this plan. Proposals on the lives of ladies are also not considered under this plan. Proposals for policies under this scheme will be entertained only from persons in government or quasi-government service, or in the service of reputed commercial firms. The cost of medical, examination will have to be borne by the proposer. The minimum sum assured is ₹ 5,000 and the term is 5, 6, or 7 years. Admission of age before issuing of policy is essential. Premium may be single, yearly or half-yearly instalments only. No surrender values loan, paid-up values, no rebate in premium whether for large sum or for mode of payment of premium are allowed under this policy.

This plan is of much use to those who are initially unable to pay the larger premium required for a whole life or endowment policy. This is useful to those who desire to leave the final decision of permanent insurance at later date. The premium rate is considerably lower in this case. It is specially suitable to a young man with large family just entering in life who, due to his low, income, is unable to afford high premium required to give him adequate protection under a permanent policy.

ENDOWMENT POLICIES

The endowment policies can be several, of which important endowment policies are discussed below:

1. Pure Endowment Policy

The sum assured is payable on the life assured's surviving the endowment term. In the event of his death within the term (endowment), premiums may be returnable or not. In corporation, all premiums paid, without any deduction, will be refunded to. Thus the pure endowment policy is opposite of the term policy, because the insured is paid if he survives in pure endowment and if dies with, in the term in term policy. Actually, these two policies, *i.e.*, pure endowment and term policies, are the bases of all other policies. Pure endowment is for the benefit of the policy-holder and term policy is for the benefit of others. So, the pure endowment policy has the element of investment and the term policy has the element of protection. Pure endowment grants protection against 'living long' while the term policy grants protection against living too short. The former is old-age protection while the latter is family protection.

This policy can be issued in the life of adult as well as in the life of child. In the case of a policy effected on the life of a child payment of premiums does not case on the death of the proposer but must be continued during the whole currency of the policy. Paid-up and surrender values are allowed on this policy. The mode of payment of premium under this plan is only yearly or half-yearly.

This policy is useful to the person who does not care to present himself for medical examination. This is also beneficial to those who, for reasons of health, would be unacceptable for life insurance on standard premium. It is a sort of compulsory saving for old age.

2. Ordinary Endowment Policy

This is the policy which actually represents the life insurance in true sense. It provides an ideal combination of both the family protection and the investment. It is taken out for a specified term of years, the sum assured being payable either on the life assured's death during the period or on his survival to the end of the period. Premiums are payable throughout the term of the policy or to a limited period or till the prior death of the life assured. Ordinary endowment policy is the combination of term insurance and of pure endowment. So, the net premium rate for an ordinary endowment policy is equal to the net premiums of term and pure endowment policies issued at the same age, for the same period of time.

This provides solutions to various problems of life whether living too long or too short. In other words, the old age provision and the family protection is possible by purchasing only this single policy. Moreover, compulsory saving is possible due to this policy which is not present in other types of savings. It is a means of hedging against the possibility of saving period being cut short by death. The next advantage of this policy is to meet the marriage; education or other requirements of the family.

3. Joint Life Endowment Policy

This policy covers more than one life under a single policy. Under this plan, the sum assured is payable on the expiry of the term or on the death of one of the assured lives during the endowment period. Premiums are payable throughout the endowment period or till the prior-death of anyone of the lives assured. The premium is calculated with certain modification according to the age of all insured partners. Paid-up and surrender values are payable on the policy.

This policy is suitable to partners of a firm because firm will not discontinue on the tremendous outflow of the funds at the death of a partner. This policy is also beneficial to a couple. The practice of granting insurance to husband and wife under this plan was withdrawn in 1960; but it has again been reinstated. The ceiling on the sum to be assured will be determined by the earned income on the wife or the husband whichever is less and also taking into account the previous insurance held on that life.

4. Double Endowment Policy

Under this policy, if the life assured dies during the endowment period, the basic sum assured is payable and if he survives to the end of the term, double of the sum assured is paid. Premiums are payable throughout the endowment term or till the prior death of the life insured. The premiums, are generally quoted according to the endowment period, irrespective of the age at entry subject to the provision that maturity age is not beyond 65. The term of policy is ranging from 10 years to 40 years but no policy is insured to mature at an age exceeding 65 years. This policy is combination of an endowment insurance and a pure endowment (without return of premiums) for the same period and for the same amount.

This plan is beneficial to the person who by reason of some physical disability is not eligible for acceptance at the tabular rates under any of the other classes of insurance. This is also to benefit to those who are confident of living long but would like to have some cover in the event of his early death. The investment element is higher than the protection element in this plan.

5. Fixed Term (Marriage) Endowment Policy

Under this plan, the sum assured is payable only at the end of a stipulated period, but the premium ceases if death of the policy-holder occurs earlier. In such an event the policy will remain fully paid until the maturity date but the beneficiary may discount the policy before maturity. This plan is issued on without profit basis, paid-up values are paid under this policy. This policy is designed to meet the needs of a family man who wants to make available a certain sum for marriage of a female dependents.

6. Educational Annuity Policy

Like marriage endowment policy, this policy is also taken out on the life of the father or guardian who undergoes medical examination, The child for whose benefit (education) policy is taken is called beneficiary. The difference is that the sum assured is not payable in, a lump sum but is payable, in equal instalments over a period of five years. It is payable in half-yearly instalments for five years.

7. Triple Benefit Policy

This policy is a combination of a whole life limited payment and a pure endowment (without return of premium) with a guaranteed annual bonus payable on death during the endowment term. This policy is granted for a fixed terms of 15, 20 or 25 years. Premiums are payable throughout the term or till prior death of the life assured.

The special feature of the plan is that there is a guaranteed and steadily increasing family provision during the selected period along with the old age benefit. The provision for the family does not terminate when the old age benefit is paid at the end of the period and no further premiums are payable thereafter; but a sum equal to the original sum assured still remains to be paid on the death of the life assured thereafter.

The following benefits are guaranteed provided the policy remains in force for the original sum assured.

A. If death occurs within the stipulated period

The benefits payable to the dependents, in this case, are:

(*i*) The basic sum assured, and

(*ii*) A guaranteed bonus per annum equal to ₹ 25/- per - 1,000/- sum assured for each full year's premium paid excluding the first year's premium.

This is a non-participating scheme where under the sum assured increases by fixed amounts during the term. The amount of guaranteed bonus is fixed and does not defend on the profits of the insurer.

B. On survival to the Selected Term

The following amounts are paid at the survival of the life assured at the selected term:

(*i*) The basic sum assured in cash, and

(*ii*) Actually paid-up whole life assurance for a like amount payable at death thereafter.

However, the life assured is given the following options in lieu of these two benefits:

An increased cash payment

OR

fully 'paid-up whole life policy for an increased sum assumed.

The alternative benefit of an increased paid-up assurance will be allowed without medical examination subject to the exercise of this option not less than three years before expiry of the selected term. Paid-up values are also given in this case. The benefits available under the policy on maturity will also be reduced in the same proportion. The policy so reduced will thereafter be free from all liability for payment of premiums but shall loose all rights to the guaranteed additions assured in the event of death subsequent to the date of the conversion into a reduced paid-up value. Guaranteed surrender value is applicable to this policy.

The plan is useful to a person who, in addition to providing cover for his family, wants to make some provision for his old age. It overcomes the main drawback of the whole life policy, *i.e.*, the assured is permitted to get the policy amount. The other advantage is that the insurance element is greater than in an ordinary endowment assurance policy.

8. Anticipated Endowment Policy

This policy is similar to endowment assurance except that a part of the sum assured is paid at certain interval before death within maturity of the policy and the balance of the sum assured is payable at maturity. In the event of death at any time during the term of the policy, *i.e.*, before the maturity date, full sum assured is payable without any deduction of installments paid earlier. The policy may be issued both under with and without profit plan. The term may be 15, 20 or 25 years.

The payment of policy amount by the corporation is as below:

1. 1/5 of the sum assured becomes payable on the life assured's surviving 5, 10 or 15 years according as the selected term of insurance is 15, 20 or 25 Years;
2. Another 1/5 of the sum assured on his surviving 10, 15 or 20 years according as the selected form of assurance is 15, 20 or 25 years; and
3. The balance 3/5th of the sum assured on his surviving the selected term of years.

But in the event of death at any time within the selected term the full sum assured is payable without any deduction or adjustment for amount that may have been paid earlier by way of survivance benefit. The LIC has discontinued this policy.

The money back policy is useful for those who, besides desiring to provide for their own old age and family, feel the need for lump sum benefits at periodical intervals. Under this scheme, the following benefits are payable:

(*i*) For a policy with a term of 12 years, 1/5th of the sum assured becomes payable on the life assured's surviving 4 years, a further 1/5th of the sum assured becomes payable on his surviving 5 years and the balance 3/5th of the sum assured on his surviving to the end of the term of 12 years.

(*ii*) For a policy with a term of 15 years, 1/4th of the sum assured becomes payable on the life assured's surviving 5 years, a further 1/4th of the sum assured becomes payable on his surviving 10 years and the balance 1/2 of the sum assured becomes payable on his surviving to the end of the term of 15 years.

(*iii*) For a policy with a term of 20 years, 1/5th of the sum assured becomes payable on the life assured's surviving 5 years, a further 1/5th of the sum assured becomes payable on his surviving 10 years, a further 1/5th of the sum assured becomes payable on his surviving 10 years, a further 1/5th of the sum assured becomes payable on his surviving 15 years and the balance 2/5th of the sum assured becomes payable on his surviving to the end of the term of 20 years.

(*iv*) For a policy with a term of 25 years, 1/5th of the sum assured becomes payable on the life assured's surviving 10 years, a further 1/5th of the sum assured becomes payable on his surviving 15 years, a further 1/5th of the sum assured becomes payable on his surviving 20 years and the balance 2/5th of the sum assured becomes payable on his surviving to the end of the term of 25 years.

However in the event of death at any time within the selected term the full sum assured is payable without any deduction or adjustment for the amount that may have been paid earlier by way of survivance benefit. The bonus additions to the policy will be reckoned of the full sum assured and are payable at the end of the selected term of years or at the life assured's death, if previous.

In the event of cessation of payment of the premiums under this policy, a paid up assurance, payable at the end of the selected term of years or at the life assured's death if previous, is automatically secured provided premiums have been paid under the policy for not less than three years and a minium paid up assurance of ₹ 250 exclusive of any attached bonus is secured. All bonuses declared and attaching to the policy at the date of cessation of payment of premiums remain attached to the reduced paid up policy but the policy is not entitled to participate in the profits declared thereafter. No loan will be granted under this policy. The minimum amount for which a policy will be issued under this plan is ₹ 5,000. Further, policies will be issued for terms of 12, 15, 20 and 25 years only.

10. Progressive Protection Policy with Profits

This policy is very useful for those who want to provide additional insurance benefits for additional responsibilities. Only first class lives will be accepted under this plan. For' the purpose of Non-Medical (Special) Scheme, this policy will be deemed to be for double the sum assured. The sum assured increases automatically by half the initial sum assured at the end of five years and again by half the initial sum assured at the end of ten years, irrespective of the state of health of the policy-holder at that time. In other words, medical evidence of health will not be required on the occasion of subsequent increase in the sum assured under the policy. After ten years the benefits under the policy will be double the initial sum assured, payable on survival at the end of the selected term or on death within the term.

For the first five years, premiums will be for the initial sum assured. At the end of five years, and again at the end of ten years, the premiums will increase with the increase in the sum assured. Bonus will be paid at the end of the selected term or at the death of the life assured, whichever is earlier, and will be calculated on the initial sum assured for the first five years. After the increase in the sum assured, bonus will be calculated on the increased sum assured from the date of increase. Loans will be available within the surrender value of the policy. If, after at least three full years premiums have been paid in respect of this policy, any subsequent premium be not duly paid, this policy shall not be wholly void, but the sum assured by it shall be reduced to such a sum as can be allowed according to the rules of the Corporation. The policy so reduced shall not be entitled to participate in future profits. The existing vested bonus additions, if, any, will remain attached to the reduced paid up policy. The maximum age at entry is 45 years and maximum maturity age is 65 years. The policy is offered for 20, 25, 30 and 35 years. The minimum sum assured for which it policy will be issued under this plan is Re. 5,000/- and the maximum will be ₹ 1,00,000. All policies taken under, this plan will be taken into account while arriving at the maximum sum assured.

11. Anticipated Whole Life Policy With Profits

This policy provides two distinct types of benefits in one policy—the benefit of Whole Life Limited Payment Policy and anticipated payments at five yearly intervals. It provides complete long-range insurance protection or the family and in addition helps meet various short-term needs through periodical payments. The following benefits are available under this policy:

(*i*) For a policy with a term of 20 years, 1/8th of the sum assured becomes payable on the life assured's surviving 5 years, a further 1/8th of the sum assured becomes payable on his surviving 15 years and a final 1/8th of the sum assured becomes payable on his surviving to the end of the term of 20 years.

(*ii*) For a policy with term of 25 years, 1/10th of the sum assured becomes payable on the life assured's surviving 5 years, a further 1/10th of the sum assured becomes payable on his surviving 10 years, a further 1/10th of the sum assured becomes payable on his surviving 20 years and a final 1/10th of the sum assured becomes payable on his surviving to the end of the term of 25 years.

However, in the event of death at any time, the full sum assured is payable without any deduction or adjustment for the amount that may have been paid earlier by way of survivance benefit. Premiums are payable for 20 or 25 years depending upon the premium paying term selected or till death if it occurs within the period. The bonus will be reckoned on the full sum assured and will be payable at the life assured death. The policy will not cease to participate in profits after completion of premium paying period but will continue to share in the periodical bonus distribution for full sum assured until the death of the life assured.

No loan is payable under the policy during the premium paying period, but after the policy becomes fully paid up, loan will be available within the surrender value of the policy for such amounts and on such terms and conditions as may be prescribed from time to time. The minimum amount for which a policy will be issued under this plan is ₹ 5,000. The maximum age at entry is 50 years for a policy with premium paying term of 20 years and 45 years for a policy with premium paying term of 25 years.

12. New Jana Raksha Policy

This policy has been designed taking into account the problem of non-payment of premiums in time. A special facility whereby the policy continues to provide full cover for three years on payment of an initial extra single premium has been incorporated under this policy. The benefits under this policy are, the same as those applicable for all Endowment Assurance Policy with Profits.

The policy will be issued to male lives only. Policies will issued with, maximum age at entry of 40 years. The minimum age at entry will be 18 years completed. Policies will be issued for terms 12, 15 and 40 year only. The minimum sum assured for which policy will be under this plan is ₹ 5,000 and tile maximum sum assured will ₹ 16,000. The sum assured will be issued in the denomination or ₹ 5000, ₹ 10,000 and ₹ 15,000.

In the event of non-payment of premiums within the days of grace, after the payment of premium for the first two years, the policy will be kept in force for the full sum assured for a period of three years on payment of a single extra premium along with the first premium at a rate of ₹ 10.50 per thousand, for ages at entry 29 years and below and at a rate of ₹ 15.00 per thousand for ages at, entry 30 years and above. No commission is payable on this additional premium. If any portion of this extra premium is not utilised for the risk cover, this unutilised portion will be refunded without interest at the time of claim arising by maturity or by death or at the time of surrender. After atleast two years' premiums have been paid, if default occurs in the payment of premium, full death cover is continued for a period of three years from the first unpaid premium due date. At any time during the first 36 months from the date of first unpaid premium, the policy-holder can pay the arrears of premium in full with interest or arrears of first two unpaid premiums with interest or arrears of first unpaid premium with interest. No evidence of health will be required. In ease the arrears of premiums are paid in full, the facility of temporary assurance cover for further three years can be availed of at a future date, during the term of the policy. If the arrears of the premium are paid in part only, the amount will be utilised towards the adjustment of premium starting from the first unpaid premium due date onwards; but no gaps in the adjustment of premium will be allowed.

The policy can be revived by payment of full arrears of premiums with interest, if the period elapsed from the first unpaid premium due date is more than 36 months but not more than 60 months. For revival after three years' default in payment of premiums, a Declaration of Good Health is necessary. After revival, the facility of temporary assurance cover for a further period of three years will be available.

13. Mortgage Redemption Assurance Policy

This policy meets the requirements of institutions and individual borrowers to ensure that the outstanding loan is automatically extinguished in the event of the borrower's death. The benefits under the plan at any time during the currency of the policy would be the amount of outstanding loan at the beginning of the year as envisaged at the beginning of the transaction, and would become payable in the event of death of the borrower. A schedule showing the amounts of outstanding loan at the beginning of each year would be drawn up at the outset on the basis of predetermined rate of interest. The benefits payable would be fixed as shown in the schedule and only these amounts will be paid under the policy irrespective of the actual loan payments. The policies would normally be issued only to male lives aged upto 50 years at entry subject to the condition that the insurance cover would in no case extend beyond 65 years. It means the loans should be liquidated by the time the borrower attained age of 65. The policy may be taken either by single premium or annual premiums. Policies on which premiums are payable annually or monthly will not carry any surrender value. The minimum sum assured, under the above plan shall be ₹ 10,000 except ill the case of large institutional lenders *e.g.* a Co-operative House Mortgage Society and the minimum sum assured for individual will be ₹5,000.

14. Children's Deferred Endowment Assurance

Sometimes a parent or guardian or near relative of a child wishes to take an insurance policy on the lift of the child under which the premium is paid by the proposer during the first few years and by the life assured (*i.e.* by the child) thereafter. This can be done by taking the children's deferred endowment assurance. The low premium rate under this plan is a great attraction. A parent can help to his children to take a policy at a rate which is considerably lower than that what they would be called upon to pay at the attaining of majority. The second advantage of this policy is that the habit of thrift is developed among the child and from the very beginning tries to save some money. The third advantage is that the cash value if the policy is discontinued before or at majority, can be available for meeting specific expenses of education and marriage. The policy is taken on the life of child and not on the life of parent. The parent is merely a proposer and is contracting on behalf of the child. The policy can be issued on whole life basis, too; but the corporation issues it on endowment basis.

Commencement of Risk

The risk does not commence immediately at the issue of policy but only on the policy anniversary, following completion of 18 or 21 years. The policy envisages two stages, one covering the period from the date of commencement of policy to the deferred date, *i.e.*, the date of commencement of risk on the child's life, called deferment period, and the other covering the period from the deferred date to the date on which the policy emerges as a claim by the death of the child or its survival to a stipulated date. A combined policy is issued to cover both the aforesaid periods. Policies under this scheme are issued on the lives of children, both male and female who have completed one year of age but have not completed 18 year. No medicinal examination is required where the deferment period is 10 years or more. Policies under this scheme will not be issued for deferment period less than 4 years. The risk may commence on the life of child since 18 or 21 years of his age, as desired by the proposer.

The provisions of this policy make it obligatory on the life assured to adopt the policy in writing at any time after attaining majority but before the deferred date. This provision is necessary to ensure that the life assured will be a major on the deferred date, *i.e.*, will be of age 18 years. On such adoption by the life assured, the policy will be deemed to be a contract between the corporation and the life assured as the absolute owner of the policy and the proposer or his estate shall not thereafter have any right or interest in the policy. The person entitled to the policy money will have the option of taking a cash payment in entire cancellation of the policy contract before the deferred date.

In the event of the life assured, death (the child's death) before the deferred date, *i.e.*, the date of commencement of risk, the policy shall stand cancelled and all premimums paid.

15. Children Anticipated Policy with Profits

This policy can be taken by parent or legal guardian or any near relative on the life of a child on whose life risk will commence at the age of 18 completed, or 21 years as required by the proponent. The policy will automatically vest in the child at the end of the deferment period and half of the premiums paid during this period will be paid to him in lump sum. Risk will commence at the Deferred Date and full sum assured will be payable on survival of the life assured to the date of maturity or on his death, if earlier. The policy will attach bonus from the Deferred Date at the Endowment Assurance Rate. This policy is issued on the lives of children both males and females upto the age of 14 years. Like Children's Endowment Policy, medical examination is not required where the deferment period is 10 years or more. Where it is less than 10 years, medical examination of the child is required. Policies are issued for maturity ages 35, 40, 45, 50, 55 and 60 years. Policies under this plan will not be issued for deferment periods less than four years. The proposals on the lives of minor girls will be entertained only when the father and other insurable members of the family are of adequately insured and the social, cultural, and educational back-round of the family is good. An extra-premium on account of sex will be payable from the Deferred Date. If the premiums due prior to the Deferred Date have been paid, an amount equal to 90 per cent of the total amount of premiums paid excluding the premiums for the first year is payable as a cash option.

The policy will be cancelled in case the life assured dies before the Deferred Date. A sum of money equal to the premiums paid will become payable to the person entitled to the policy moneys in such event provided the policy is in full force. The payment of premiums does not cease on death of the proposer during the deferment period.

No loan will be granted on this policy during the deferment period. Disability benefit unless specifically excluded will be available on this policy with effect from such date.

PLANS WITHDRAWN BY LIC

1. Anticipated Endowment Assurance
2. Convertible Whole Life with Profits
3. Centenary Policy
4. Grihalakshmi Policy
5. Cash and Cover Policy

Premium rates have been reduced in certain policies and some of the policies have been modified. Jana Raksha Policy has been introduced in June 1981.

16. 'Jeevan Saathi'

'Jeevan Saathi' is the new Joint Life Plan with a difference. The Plan is designed to gift a total protection to families; particularly for the working couple.

Row 'Jeevan Saathi' is different from the existing Joint Life Plan!

Under the existing Joint Life Plan two persons' lives can be jointly covered and the Sum Assured becomes payable either on the first death or on the expiry of the selected term.

Under the Jeevan Saathi Plan, only the lives of husband and wife are jointly covered. The basic S.A., together with vested bonuses are payable in event of survival to maturity of either or both of the partners. In the event of the first death of anyone of the lives assured, the survivor gets the basic Sum Assured. Again basic Sum Assured with bonuses is payable to the nominee, in the event of the premature death of the second partner.

Another important feature of this plan is that the premium under the policy ceases on the first death and the surviving partner need not have to pay any more premiums. But inspite of non-payment of premium after the first death, the policy will continue to participate the bonuses will accrue till the final settlement.

From the benefits available it could be seen that a family that is used to certain economic comforts, gets a lump sum immediately, if one of the partners dies, to maintain a certain level of economic stability. Once again the basic Sum Assumed is paid to the surviving partner on, maturity or in the event of other early death, to the nominee. Thus this plan gives a total and complete insurance protection to the whole family.

What are the eligibility condition for purchasing life insurance, under this plan?

Policies under this plan will be issued on the lives of husband and wife, provided the latter belongs to Category-I.

The plan is available for specified Terms of 15, 20 and 25 years only· The age of the older life at maturity should not be more than 65 years.

The minimum basic Sum Assured, under this plan, is ₹ 5,000/- and the maximum is ₹ 1,00,000/- under one or more Policies.

The premium should be minimum ₹ 3 per thousand. S.A. over the premium under Endowment Assurance on older life for the same term. The minimum difference between the Double Joint Life Endowment Assurance premium and Endowment Assurance premium, as calculated in the aforesaid manner, is ₹ 3 per thousand S. A. only against ₹ 5 per thousand S. A. applicable to existing Joint Life Endowment Assurance plan.

17. Married Women's Property Act Policy

A married man can effect a policy on his own life, wife and/or children and shall be deemed to be a trust for their benefits and shall not, so long as any object of the trust remains, be subject to the control of the husband or his creditors, or form part of his estate. The policy effected under Sect. 6 of the Married Women's Property Act 1874 for the above purpose, shall not be aggregated with his other property provided the trust is absolute. The term 'children' means sons and daughters only and excludes an adopted son by Hindus. Grih Lakshmi Policy issued in December, 1975, is an important instance of Married Women's Property Act Policy.

18. Survivorship, Reversionary or Centingent Assurance

There are two persons in this policy, first a named insured and another named person. The sum assured is payable if the life assured dies before another specified person (named person) or counter life. If the counter life dies first, nothing is payable and the contract ceases. These assurances usually arise in connection with reversionary transactions. Suppose in terms of a trust or will A will be entitled to certain property at the death of B provided A is then living, Here A possesses a contingent interest in that property and his interest has a market value. But the purchaser of the interest will receive nothing if A precedes B and, therefore, he effects a contingent assurance for the amount of capital. The purchaser is thus fully protected because (*a*) the purchaser is thus fully protected, as he receives the capital from trust or will if A is living at B's death, (*b*) he receives the policy money if A dies before B.

The rate of premium depends upon the age of the insured, of named person. When the life assured is young and the counter life is old the risk and premium, therefore, would be possible equal to that of a short period temporary insurance. If the ages are equal to or the counter life is younger the premium is roughly that of a whole life assurance. This policy is not widely written.

B. POLICIES ACCORDING TO PREMIUM PAYMENT

The policies according to the premium payment may be of the following types:

1. Single Premium Policy

In this policy, the whole premium is paid at the beginning of the policy. As compared to the annual premium payable, it is costlier; but as compared to aggregate of all annual premiums payable, it is much smaller because all the premiums are received in advance and the insurer can earn additional amount on the premiums received.

This type of policy can be afforded by those who got a windfall income and are expected not to continue such return in subsequent years. The single premium policy is not useful to other persons because of chances of death whereafter the subsequent premiums are not required to be paid.

2. Level Premium Policy

Under this policy regular and equal premiums are paid at a definite interval. This premium is lesser than the single premium and is convenient to make premium at a regular period. This may take the shape of an expense and can be constantly paid. The equal installments may be paid monthly, tri-monthly (quarterly), half yearly and yearly. So, it suits the requirements of different types of the policy-holders. Since, originally the premium is calculated and charged on annual basis, the unpaid premiums for the year are required to be paid at the time of payment of claims due to death. The amount of each monthly, quarterly and half-yearly is not just the one twelfth. One-fourth and one-half of the annual premium because the insurer is involved in more expenses while collecting more frequent premiums and is at loss of the interest for the balance of the annual premium. For monthly installments an additional charge of 5 per cent on the annual premium is made to cover loss of interest and additional cost of collection. The additional charge of 5 per cent of the premium shall be waived if the premiums are paid through a co-operative society or by trustees of a staff provident or super-annuation fund or are collected by deduction from salary and remitted by or under the supervision of the Corporation. If premiums are payable yearly or half-yearly reduction of Re. 0.75 and Re. 0.50 per thousand of sum assured is ordinarily deductible from the annual premium. There is no deduction or reduction in quarterly premium. The level premium policy may be either a continuous level premium or a limited level premium policy.

C. POLICIES ACCORDING TO PARTICIPATION IN PROFITS

Policies according to participation in profits may be (*i*) without profit policies, and (*ii*) with profit policies.

(*i*) *Without Profit Policies or Non-participating Policies.* The holders of without profit policies are not entitled to share the profits of the insurer. These policy-holders get only the sum assured and no bonus is given to them.

(*ii*) *With Profit Policies or Participating Policies.* The holders of the with profit policies are entitled to share the profit of the insurer. Since the policy-holders can share the profit and not the loss, they can not be treated as co-owner of the insurance business. If there is loss, the policy-holders cannot get bonus, *i.e.*, the share in profit. They are entitled to get the share of profit, *i.e.*, the bonus only when there is profit. The amount of bonus depends on the profit after deducting provision for taxes, contingency, etc. In participating policy there is no guarantee that the insured will get something by way of profit every year. The only law is that the corporation has to distribute 95 per cent of its profits among the policy-holders. Thus, if there is no profit in a year, no amount can be distributed to the participating policy-holders. However, the Corporation has decided that at least bonus rate of previous years should not decrease while declaring bonus in the present year.

The Corporation issues both types of policies, *i.e.*, participating and non-participating. Since the participating policies share profit the premium rate is higher in this case. The difference between the premiums of participating policies and of non-participating polices is called 'bonus loading' because the additional premium in participating policies is charged for allowing bonus. The amount of insurance to be paid is certain in non-participating policies but it is not certain in participating policies due to accrual of bonus, the rate of which is not constant.

D. POLICIES ACCORDING TO THE NUMBER OF PERSONS INSURED

On the basis of number of persons insured in a policy, the policy may be (*i*) single life policies, and (*ii*) multiple life policy.

(*i*) *Single Life Policies.* Under single life policies, only one individual is insured. It is not necessary that the policy should be issued in one's own life, it may be in other's life; but the fact is that this policy insures only one life. The policy amount is payable only when the assured event occurs.

(*ii*) *Multiple Life Policies.* In this policy more than one life is insured. It may be (*a*) Joint Life policy, and (*b*) Last Survivor Policy.

(*a*) *Joint Life Policy.* This policy covers two or more lives and the policy amount is payable on the first death. This is beneficial to the partners of a firm and to a couple.

(*b*) *Last Survivorship Policy.* The policy amount is payable at the last death. So long as any one of the insured is alive, no payment is made.

E. POLICIES ACCORDING TO THE METHOD OF PAYMENT OF POLICY AMOUNT

The policy amount may be paid in (*i*) Lump sum policies or (*ii*) installments.

(*i*) *Lump Sum Policies.* Where the sum assured is paid in lump sum at the events insured against.

(*ii*) *Installment or Annuity Policies.* Under this policy, the policy amount is payable in installments. It is beneficial to those whose earning capacities are reduced to minimum in old age. At that time, this policy may be more helpful. He may continue to get up to a fixed period or up to death or both.

Non-Conventional Policies

The Life Insurance Corporation of India has introduced several non-conventional policies to meet the requirements of the population. The conventional policies have the main attributes of protection at early death or living too long; but majority of the population, is interested mainly in investment. The LIC has designed several new policies from time to time to meet these requirements. Some of the important new policies are described here.

1. Policies under LIC Mutual Fund
2. Jeevan Akshay
3. Jeevan Dhara.
4. Jeevan Kishor
5. Jeevan Chhaya

The LIC is conducting market research to find suitable policies to meet the requirements of the people. Every year, some policies are issued to benefit the population.

1. POLICIES UNDER LIC MUTUAL FUND

LIC launched its Mutual Fund with a promise to the investors to provide high returns alongwith safety and security of investment. LIC Mutual Fund entered the Indian capital market on 19th June 1989. During the first year of operation LIC Mutual Fund came up with 5 schemes which provide distinct benefits to various cross sections of investors. Out of the 6 schemes, 3 are close ended schemes viz., Dhanashree 1989, Dhan 80 CC (I) and Dhanvarsha while the other two schemes viz.,. Dhanaraksha 1989 and Dhanavridhi 1989 are open ended schemes. Dhan 80 CC B (I) has been introduced since Feb. 11, 1991. The salient features of Dhanasahayog and Dhan 80 CC B (1) are given to illustrate the LIC Mutual Fund Policies.

I. Dhanasahayog

Introduction. LIC Mutual Fund was set up as a separate Trust by Life Insurance Corporation of India. The basic objectives of LIC Mutual Fund are mopping up the savings of people, especially from rural and semi-urban areas and providing good returns, liquidity and security to the investors through investment in the capital market for productive purposes.

LIC Mutual Fund mobilised nearly ₹ 375 crores in the very first year of operations from $1\frac{1}{2}$ lakh investors. Other schemes launched by the Mutual Fund are also having very good response from investors.

LIC Mutual Fund has declared a handsome income distribution (dividend) for 1989-90 which is higher than that promised under various schemes. For example, a rate of 12% was promised under Dhanashree 1989 but the dividend declared is 13.50% p.a. under this scheme.

LIC Mutual Fund has already launched seven schemes which are primarily income and growth oriented. However, several requests have come from investing public to launch an income and growth oriented scheme which is to be available on tap. The investors can invest in this scheme depending upon their liquid position and convenience.

The details of Dhanasahayog are as follows:

1. Who can apply for Dhanasahayog units?

(*a*) Resident citizens of India who are (*i*) Adult individual or individuals not exceeding three in number jointly or on either/anyone or survivor(s) basis, (*ii*) Minors through their parents/step-parents/guardians (No joint ownership is permitted with minors), (*iii*) Hindu Undivided Family (by the Karta acting on behalf of H.U.F.).

(*b*) Companies registered in India, Bodies Corporate, Trusts, Societies, Co-operative Societies, Schools, Colleges, Universities, Clubs created under the applicable laws and authorised to invest in the units of the Mutual Fund.

(*c*) Non-Residents of Indian Nationality/Origin on non-repatriation basis.

Exploration: A person shall be deemed to be of Indian origin if (*i*) he/she, at any time, held an Indian passport, or (*ii*) he/she, or either of his/her parents or any of his/her grandparents was an Indian and a permanent resident of undivided India at any time.

However, Pakistani and Bangladeshi nationals, even though they satisfy the definition of Indian Origin shall not be eligible to apply for the units.

The wife of a citizen of India or a person of Indian Origin shall also be deemed to be of Indian Origin even though she may be of non-Indian parentage.

Note: Partnership firms and others not mentioned, above are not eligible to apply.

2. How much one can Invest?

There is no upper limit, on investment. The face value of the units will be ₹ 10/- each. Minimum investment for individual investor is 100 units and in multiples of 50 units thereafter. In case of Trusts, Societies, Companies. etc., the minimum investment will be 1000 units and thereafter in multiples of 100 units. The amount payable will be calculated on the basis of the prevailing selling price per unit of Dhanasahayog scheme.

3. Where can you submit your application with subscription?

(*a*) At any designated branch of Central Bank of India (CBI). The branches of CBI authorised to collect subscriptions under the earlier schemes of LIC Mutual Fund are the designated branches for this purpose. The application alongwith the bank draft for the amount of investment less the bank draft commission may be sent to any designated branch of CBI. The facility of deduction of bank charges is available only in places where there is no designated branch of CBI .

(*b*) Non-Residents of Indian Nationality/Origin should remit their application money to authorised dealers of CBI branches as mentioned in the instructions on the back of the application form.

4. Selling and Repurchase price of the units

The scheme is open for subscription from 1st January 1991 and the units will be sold at ₹ 10/- to the investors in this scheme upto September 1991. Thereafter the selling price of the units will be fixed every month. On and after 1st January 1992, units can be sold back to LIC Mutual Fund at the rate fixed by LIC Mutual Fund.

5. Incentive for early subscription

Incentive for the period upto 31st March 1991 will be payable as follows:

Period of Collection	Incentive amount
01.1.1991 to 15.1.1991	3.0%
16.1.1991 to 31.1.1991	2.5%
01.2.1991 to 15.2.1991	2.0%
16.2.1991 to 28.2.1991	1.5%
01.3.1991 to 15.3.1981	1.0%
16.3.1981 to 31.3.1991	0.5%

6. Plans of Investment

The investor has a choice between the following two plans:

Plan A: Under this plan, dividend declared after the close of each accounting year will be remitted to the investor.

Plan B: Under this plan dividend declared after the close of each accounting year will be reinvested under the scheme the prevailing selling price.

The investor will indicate his/her choice between the above plans in the application form. In case where the applicant does not tick the relevant plan column, it will be considered that he/she has opted for Plan B. The investor is free to switch from Plan A to Plan B or vice versa after payment or accrual of two annual dividends from the date of earlier option. Any dividend declared will be treated as per the option exercised and recorded last.

7. Benefits

Safety: The investment will be safe as the risk is distributed among a huge number of investors and the funds are invested in varied securities and spread over a wide range of sector wise industries.

Regular Income: The investment will be so managed as to ensure a flow of regular income consistent with safety.

Growth: Growth in income and capital will be achieved through investment planning and constant monitoring to resort to profitable switching operations.

8. Tax benefits

The following tax benefits will be available to the sole/first individual applicant only.

(*i*) **Benefits under Section SOL of Income. Tax Act, 1961:** Permissible maximum deduction of ₹ 10,000/- from the taxable income under Sec. 80L of Income Tax Act, 1961 as follows:

(*a*) Income on Dhanasahayog together with other income from specified securities/deposits etc., shall be eligibly for deduction from total income upto a maximum of ₹ 7,000/- [Sec. 80L (1) (Va)].

(*b*) A further deduction from total income upto a maximum of ₹ 3,000/- is also available on income from Dhanasahayog along with income from certain other specified categories [proviso to sec. SOL (I)].

The dividend certificates will be issued under Plan B for claiming tax relief under the Section.

(*ii*) **Wealth Tax Exemption:** Investment in Dhanasahayog would be treated at par with investments entitled to exemption within the overall limit of ₹ 5,00,000/- referred to in Sec. 5 (1) (XXIVa) of Wealth Tax Act, 1957.

(*iii*) **Long Term Capital Gains:** If the investor holds Dhanasahayog Units for a minimum period of three years, he/She is eligible to the following Capital Gains Relief, along with gains from other assets, under Sec. 48 (2) of Income Tax Act, 1961. (*a*) Total exemption of capital gains upto ₹ 10,000/,- (*b*) A deduction of 60% of the capital gains in excess of ₹ 10,000/-. If the investor is a company, the deduction rate is 30%.

(*iv*) **No deduction of tax at source:** There shall be no deduction of tax at source.

9. Liquidity

Loan facility: Dhanasahayog certificate holders can avail of loan facility from Central Bank of India as per their terms and the instructions/guidelines issued to them by Reserve Bank of India.

II. Dhan 80 CCB (1)

Introduction: LIC Mutual Fund was set up as a separate Trust by Life Insurance Corporation of India. The basic objectives, of LIC Mutual Fund are mopping up the savings of people especially from rural and semi-urban areas and providing good returns, liquidity and security to the investors through investment in the capital market for productive purposes.

LIC Mutual Fund mobilised nearly ₹ 375 crores in the very first year of operations from about $1\frac{1}{2}$ lakh investors. Various schemes launched by LIC Mutual Fund are receiving very good response from investors.

All the close of first Accounting year LIC Mutual Fund has declared a handsome income distribution (dividend) for 1989-90 which is higher than that promised under various schemes. For example, a rate of 12% was promised under Dhanashree-1989 but the dividend declared is 13,5% p.a. under this scheme.

LIC Mutual Fund has already successfully launched eight schemes of various types. Out of these, there have been as many as three open ended schemes. One tax savings scheme viz. Dhan 80CC (I) was also introduced by the Mutual Fund in the year 1990. LIC Mutual Fund has been in forefront in catering to the diverse needs of investors. Keeping this in view, LIC Mutual Fund has seen to it that Dhan 80CCB (I) scheme is launched at the earliest to enable its investors to take advantage of the tax concessions. The scheme is formulated under the Equity Linked Savings Scheme, 1991.

1. Who can apply for Dhan 80CCB (1) Units

(*a*) **Resident Citizens of India who are:** (*i*) Adult individual or individuals not exceeding three in number jointly or on either/anyone or survivor basis (*ii*) Minors through, their Parents/Step-parents (No joint ownership is permitted with minors) (*iii*) Hindu Undivided Family (by the Karta acting on behalf of H.U.F.).

(*b*) **An association of persons** or body of individuals consisting, in either case, only of husband and wife governed by the system of community of property in force in the State of Goa and the Union Territories of Dadra and Nagar Haveli and Daman and Diu.

2. Minimum Investment

Units of face value of ₹ 10/- each will be issued at par. Investment can be made in a **minimum of 50 units and in multiples of 50 units thereafter**. These units will be called 'Capital Units'. There is, no upper limit on Investment. Investment can be made maximum four times in a financial year. Each investment will be subject to the minimum specified above.

3. Where can you submit your application with subscription?

At any designated branch of central Bank of India. The branches of Central Bank of India authorised to collect subscriptions under the earlier schemes of LIC Mutual Fund are the designated branches for this purpose.

4. Scheme Period and Issue Period

The scheme would be terminated at the close of the 10th financial year from the financial year of subscription. The scheme will be open for subscription from 11th February, 1991 to 30th March, 1991 only. However, LIC Mutual Fund reserves its right to close the issue earlier after giving due public notice, but in any case not before 15th March, 1991.

5. Selling and Repurchase Price of the Units

The Selling and Repurchase prices Mutual Fund periodically after one year from the date of allotment of the Units.

6. Incentive for early subscription

Incentive on subscription amount will be payable as follows while issuing the unit certificates. The unit certificates will be issued before 31st July, 1991.

Period oj Collection	Incentive amount
11.02.1991 to 15.02.1991	2.0%
16.02.1991 to 28.02.1991	1.5%
01.03.1991 to 15.03.1991	1.0%
16.03.1981 to 30.03.1991	0.5%

7. Plan of Investment

The investor has a choice out of the following plans:

Plan A—Annual Income

Under this plan, dividend declared after the close of each accounting year will be remitted to the investor.

Plan B—Accumulation with 8OL Benefits

Under this plan, dividend declared after the close of each accounting year will be reinvested under the scheme at the prevaling selling price. The certificate, as to the quantum of dividend declared and reinvested, will be issued to the investor to enable him to claim tax benefits under Sec. 80L of Income Tax Act, 1961. The units issued against the dividend declared will be called 'Dividend Units'.

Plan C—Growth with Capital Gains Benefits

Under this plan, units equivalent to dividend in value will be allocated to the investor at the prevailing selling price, but no certificate for claim under Sec. 80L of Income Tax Act,. 1961 will be issued. Units thus allocated will be called 'Dividend Units'. On encashment of such units, the investor will be liable to pay Capital Gains Tax.

The investor will indicate his/her choice out of the above plans. In case where the appıicant does not tick the relevant plan box, it will be considered that he/she has opted for Plan A. The investor is free to switch from Plan A to B or vice versa after payment or accrual of 2 annual dividends from the date of earlier option. Any dividends declared will be treated as per the option exercised and recorded last. The Plan option C, once exercised cannot be interchanged with Plan option Aor B.

Benefits

Safety: The investment will be safe as the risk is distributed among a large number of investors and the funds are spread over a wide range of sector-wise industries.

Regular Income: The investment will be so managed as to ensure a flow of regular income consistent with safety and capital appreciation.

Growth: Growth in income and capital will be achieved through investment planning and constant monitoring to resort to profitable switching operations.

9. Tax Benefits

The following tax benefits will be available to the sole/first individual applicant only.

(i) **Benefits under Section 80 CCB of Income Tax Act, 1961:** A deduction in computation of income under Sec. 80 CCB of the Income Tax Act, 1961, of so much of the amount, invested as does not exceed the amount of ₹ 10,000/- will be allowed. Provided however, any amount invested by the assessee in the capital units in respect of which a deduction has been allowed is returned in whole or in part either by way of repurchase of such units or on the termination of the Scheme by the Mutual Fund, as the case may be, it shall be deemed to be the income of the assessee and charged to tax.

Provided further, where a partition has taken place among the members of a Hindu Undivided Family (H.U.F.) or where an association of persons has been dissolved after a deduction has been allowed, the person in receipt of income referred in the provided herein before shall have to pay tax.

(ii) **Benefits under Section SOL of Income Tax Act. 1961:** Permissible maximum deduction of ₹ 10.000/- from the taxable income under Section 80L of Income Tax Act, 1961 as follows will be available under Plans A and B.

(*a*) Income on Dhan 80 CCB (1) together with other income from specified securities/deposits etc. shall be eligible for deduction from total income upto a maximum of ₹ 7.000/- [Sec, 80L (1) (Va)],

(*b*) A further deduction from total income upto a maximum of ₹ 3,000/- is also available on income from Dhan 80 CCB (1) along with income from certain other specified categories [proviso to Sec. 80L (1)].

(iii) **Wealth Tax Exemption:** Investment in Dhan 80CCB (1) would be treated at par with investments entitled to exemption within the overall limit of ₹ 5,00,000/- referred to in Section 5 (1) (XXIVa) of Wealth Tax Act, 1957.

(iv) **Long Term Capital Gains:** Under Plan C the investor will be eligible to the following Capital Gains Relief, along with gains from other assets, under Section 48 (2) of Income Tax Act, 1961.

1. Total exemption of Capital Gains upto ₹ 10,000/-.
2. A deduction of 80% of the Capital Gains in excess of ₹ 10,000/-.

(iv) **Tax Deduction:** There shall be no deduction of tax at source on the Dividend declared under Plans A and B. However, when the units are encashed in whole or in part other by way of repurchase of these units or on termination of the scheme by the trustees as the case may be, the amount invested by the assessee in 'Capital Units' shall be deemed to be the income of the assessee as per the provisions of Section 80 CCB of Income Tax Act, 1961 and tax at the standard rate of 20% as per Section 194F of Income Tax Act, 1961 will be deducted. The Mutual Fund shall issue certificate of tax so deducted at source.

10. Termination of the Scheme

The scheme will be terminated at the end of the Scheme Period. The Scheme may also be terminated after 90% of the investors withdraw from the scheme, If so decided by the Trustees. The Scheme's assets will be realised and distributed among the Unit holders on books at that time in proportion to their total investment in Capital and Dividend Units. Thus there would be 100% participation in Capital Growth.

11. Liquidity

The Units issued under the Scheme can, be encashed at any time after the initial locks in period of three years is over from the date of allotment at the applicable repurchase price. No partial encashment of the Unit Certificate would however be allowed.

In the event of the death of sole/first applicant, the units can be encashed at any time after the completion of one year from the date of allotment of the units.

The Units Issued under the Scheme, save as provided in Sub-section (3), of Section 89 CCB of Income Tax Act, 1961, **cannot be transferred assigned or pledged.**

2. JEEVAN AKSHAY

In return for purchase price paid by the purchaser a monthly pension will be paid during the lifetime or the purchaser of the pension.

The last payment would be falling due prior to the date of death of the pensioner. No medical examination is necessary to get the policy.

Post-dated monthly cheques are sent in advance for the whole year. No existence certificate is required for receipt of the pension.

Pension cheques are payable at par on all branches of the Central Bank of India and such other nationalised bank which LIC may notify.

On the death of the pensioner, the original amount invested by the employee along with an additional bonus will be returned to the nominee or his legal heirs.

The minimum amount to be invested (premium) is ₹ 10,000 and in multiples of ₹ 100 thereafter. There is no maximum limit.

For every ₹ 10,000 purchase price, pension payable would be ₹ 100 per month.

Minimum age at entry is 50 years. There is no restriction as regards maximum age at entry. Only persons aged 50 or more can avail of pension benefits on their own lives.

Since the pension is payable monthly, the gross annual return works out to nearly 12.7 per cent—an excellent return by any standard on a safe, long-term investment. The plan guarantees the return for the lifetime of the pensioner which can be as long as 50 years or more. No other investment guarantees such a high rate of return for such a long period. The rate of return is guaranteed even when the rate of interest falls in the future.

The Jeevan Akshay policies also enjoy various tax benefits:

3. JEEVAN DHARA

The payment of annuities in respect of policies under Jeevan Dhara has to start one month after the completion of the deferment period. In order to enable the annuitant to get the payment on the due date, the annuity cheque has to be posted at least two weeks earlier. Since Jeevan Akshay/Jeevan Dhara payments are centralised at Zonal Offices, it means that the input forms for building master records for payment of annuities have to reach the Zonal Machine Department well in advance to enable them to process it and despatch the cheques to the annuitant about two weeks before the date of vesting.

However, in the case of policies under SSS, the payment of final installment premium will be received only after the date of vesting, making it impossible to build the master record in time. The delay in building of master record will be much more when there are gaps, in premium payment. This is one of the reasons behind discontinuing issue of Jeevan Dhara policies under Salary Savings

Scheme.

The problems involved in building the master record in time are being faced, to a lesser extent, in the case of policies under are half-yearly mode of payment also.

In order to obviate these difficulties, wherever the mode is other than single premium, it has been decided to limit the premium paying term under Jeevan Dhara Plan to one year less than the deferment period. That is, if the deferment period under a policy is 20 years, the premium paying term will be limited to 19 years. (The amount of annual premium shown against term 20 in the Premium Table will be payable for 19 years). If the deferment period is 15 years, the premium paying term will be limited to 14 years. Policies with deferment period of 2 years will be issued only as single premium policies.

Revival of Jeevan Dhara Policy which has been in a lapsed condition will not be permissible in the last year of the policy term because of the problems involved in preparation of cheques in time.

The revised rates of annual premium for Jeevan Dhara Policies is enclosed herewith (Annexure I).

Mode of payment of premium: The premium can be paid yearly or half-yearly or Salary Savings Scheme only.

Jeevan Dhara Policies under SSS: Effective from 1st December, 1990, Jeevan Dhara policies can be issued under Salary Savings Scheme.

Rebate for mode of payment of premium: A rebate of 1.5% of the Tabular Premium is allowed if the mode of payment of premium is yearly. No rebate is allowed for other modes of payment.

Rebate for large premium: The allowed in case of large premiums:

Mode	**Rebate**	**Eligible Amount**
Yearly	1.5%	Portion of the instalment premium in excess of ₹ 5,000/-.
Half-yearly	1.5%	Portion of the instalment premium in excess of ₹ 2,500/-.
Monthly (SSS only)	1.5%	Portion of the instalment premium in excess of ₹ 417/-.

4. JEEVAN KISHOR

The salient features of the plan are as follows:

Who are eligible?

Children, both male and female, between the ages of 1 (last birthday) and 12 (last birthday) are eligible to be proposed for , insurance under this Plan.

Who can propose?

(*a*) If both parents are alive, generally the father should propose. However, if the mother has an income of her own, she can be, the proposer.

(*b*) If father is not alive, mother can propose.

(*c*) If both parents are not alive, then the legal guardian can propose.

Commencement of risk

The risk will commence either-two years after the date of commencement of the policy or from the policy anniversary falling immediately after the completion of 7 years of age, whichever is later. However, the date of commencement of risk will not, in any case, go beyond the policy anniversary falling immediately after the completion of 12 years of age.

The following table will further clarify the point:

	Age (last birthday at entry)	Risk to commence from
(*i*)	1 to 4	Policy anniversary falling immediately after completion of 7 years of age.
(*ii*)	5 to 10	Second policy anniversary from the date of commencement of policy.
(*iii*)	11	First policy anniversary from the date of commencement of policy.
(*iv*)	12	From the date of commencement.

Waiting Period

The period starting from the date of commencement of the policy to the date of commencement of risk will be known as the 'Waiting Period'.

Bonus

The policy is eligible for bonus even during the waiting period. However, the bonus for the waiting period will vest only on the policy anniversary from which the risk is covered or at the end of five years from the commencement of the policy, whichever is later, provided the policy is then in force for full sum assured.

Vesting of the Policy

The policy shall automatically vest in the Life Assured on the policy anniversary falling on or immediately following his/her attaining majority.

Benefits

The Sum Assured alongwith vested bonus and final additional bonus, if any, will be payable on maturity or on death if earlier, provided the death occurs on or after the date of commencement of risk.

In case of death of the child before the date of commencement of risk, the premiums paid (excluding the premiums for premium waiver benefit) will be refunded.

Substitution of child will not be permitted.

Premium Waiver Benefit

There is also the provision for waiving of premium under the policy till the child attains majority, in the event of death of the proposer. This premium waiver benefit is available subject to payment of a small, additional premium and medical examination of the proposer.

Medical Examination of the child

No medical examination will be necessary if the age of the child as on the date of proposal is less than 10 years (last birthday). Otherwise, medical examination will be necessary. Only Standard Lives will be eligible for Insurance under this plan.

Other Conditions

(*a*)	Minimum Term	:	15 years
(*b*)	Maximum Term	:	35 years
(*c*)	Maximum Sum Assured	:	₹ 5,00,000/-, if the age (last birthday) as on the date of proposal is less than 10. In all other cases, it will be ₹ 10,00,000/-
(*d*)	Minimum Sum Assured	:	₹ 10,000/-
(*e*)	Mode of Payment of Premium	:	Only Yearly

5. JEEVAN CHHAYA

"Jeevan Chhaya" introduced in March 1991, can be considered to be a combination of '*Jeevan Mitra*' and '*Money Back*' plans.

Couples having a child (not an adopted one), of age less than one year can avail of this plan, in order to ensure that an adequate financial provision is made for the higher education of the child. The child should not have completed one year of the date of registration of the proposal. Either father age or mother or each one of them individually can take policies or under this plan.

Premium payment

The premiums under this plan payable during the life time of the life assured and shall cease on the death of the life assured or on the expiry of the term of the policy, whichever is earlier.

Benefits

The benefits under the '*Jeevan Chhaya*' plan are:

Fixed Benefits

The following benefits (on all inforce policies) are payable whether or not the life assured survives the term of the policy:

(*i*) One fourth of the sum assured each at the end of $(n-3)$, $(n-2)$, $(n-1)$ and nth year (where n is the term of the policy).

(*ii*) Bonus for the full term on the full sum assured on the date of maturity.

For example, if the term of the policy is 20 years, one-fourth the sum assured will be payable at the end of the 17th, 18th, 19th and 20th year. The bonus on full sum assured for the full term of the policy along with final additional bonus, if any, will be payable at the end of 20 years.

Death Benefit

In addition to the above fixed benefits, one additional sum assured will be payable on the death of the policy-holder at any time during the term of the policy. (Future premiums, falling due from the policy anniversary following the date of death will stand waived.)

For example, if the term of the policy is 21 years, one-fourth the sum assured is payable at the end of 18th, 19th, 20th and 21st year. If death occurs during the 19th year, full sum assured (without bonus) will be payable immediately. One instalment of one fourth the sum assured would have already been paid at the end of the 18th year. The balance three instalments of one fourth sum assured, each due at the end of the 19th, 20th and 21st year, and the bonus on full sum assured (for the full term) due at the end of the 21st year shall be paid to the person eligible to receive the policy moneys.

Restrictions

(*i*) The term can be 20, 21, 22, 23, 24 or 25.

(*ii*)	Minimum sum assured	₹ 10,000
	Maximum sum assured	₹ 1,00,000
(*iii*)	Minimnm age at entry	20 (nearer birthday)
	Maximum age at entry	40 (nearer birthday).

The maximum age at entry can be raised to 45 if the original or attested *xerox copy* of birth certificate or school certificate is submitted as age proof.

(*iv*)	Maximum maturity age	65 (nearer birthday)

Underwriting

Proposals under this plan can be entertained under non-medical (general) scheme, both in respect of male and female lives upto Rupees one lakh sum assured. However, if anything adverse is indicated at the time of underwriting and the case cannot be accepted under non-medical, then the regular underwriting procedures like calling for full medical report, special reports (if need be) are to be followed.

In the case of female lives, the following three restrictions will apply:

(*i*) Only category-I and category-II female lives will be eligible for insurance under this plan.

(*ii*) No proposal will be entertained within 3 months of the date of delivery.

(*iii*) In case the female life had undergone a caesarian operation, a single extra premium of ₹ 5 per thousand sum assured is to be charged.

The father and, mother should, jointly sign a declaration regarding the date of birth of the child.

Similarly Jeevan Suraksha has ,been introduced on Aug. 15, 1996 to meet the requirements of all categories of people.

6. JEEVAN KISHORE

Jeevan Kishore— With Profit Plan further curtails the age from which the risk on child's life is covered. As previsions of this policy, risk commences either two years from third the date of commencement or from the policy anniversary following immediately after the completion of 7 years of age, whichever is later. Contrary to participation in bonus from the deferred date, or the risk date or vesting date, this policy allows participation in bonuses from the very date of commencement of policy. However, vesting of the bonus was allowed either from the risk date 5 years from the commencement of the policy, whichever is later.

7. JEEVAN SUKANYA

Jeevan Sukanya—With Profit is designed exclusively for female children. The premiums under this plan are payable for a limited period only. The premium ceases from the policy anniversary following on or immediately after completion of 20 years of age by the life assured. The policy matures on the policy anniversary following or immediately after completion of 50 years by the child. The policy provides following benefits:

Death Benefits

(*a*) Before the commencement of risk, the premiums paid, excluding premiums for premium waiver benefit are refunded.

(*b*) Fun sum assured alongwith vested bonuses after commencement of risk but before maturity of the policy.

(*c*) After marriage of the life assured and commencement of the risk cover on the life of the husband but before the date of maturity full sum assured without bonus in case husband predeceases the wife.

Survival Benefits

(*a*) Full sum assured on the life assured's surviving till the end of the end of the premium-paying term.

(*b*) The vested bonuses are paid on the life assured's surviving up to the age of maturity (bonuses continue to vest upto the end of the policy term).

8. CHILDREN'S MONEY BACK PLAN

Children's Money Back Plan—Yet another innovative plan has been introduced by LIC with effect from 16th January 1995. The plan envisages full and complete growth of the child. The plan provides for educational as well as start in life expenses—a series of financial benefits at the time when the child needs them most. Under a policy of ₹ 5 lakhs sum assured, ₹ 1 lakh is paid as survival benefit on the policy anniversary immediately after the child completes 18 years of age. A similar amount is paid on the policy anniversary two years hence. The amount is increased to ₹ 1.5 lakhs as survival benefit payable on the policy anniversary immediately after completion of 22 years of age. A similar amount is paid on the policy anniversary two years hence. The guaranteed additions at the rate of ₹ 80/- per thousand sum assured are payable on the maturity date *i.e.*, the policy anniversary immediately after commencement. The sum of the guaranteed and loyalty additions would be as under:

	Age at entry at last birthday		
	0	***5***	***10***
Total Guaranteed Additions	10,40,000	8,40,000	6,40,000
Loyalty Addition, if Policy is			
Annual Premium Policy	3,00,000	1,75,000	1,25,000
Net, Annual premium payable	26,525	39,815	67,995

All the premiums are paid by the parents. They can claim tax concession under Section 88 of Income Tax Act 1961. The single premium policy under the above plan can be gifted to the child for his advancement by close relations. The policy can be taken even for a new born child upto 10 years of age last birthday—the age on the commencement of the policy.

"*any sum received under a life insurance policy,*
including the sum allocated by way of bonus on such
policy".

The benefits payable under the policy are exempt in terms of section 10(10D) of Income Tax Act 1961. The provisions are reproduced for ready reference:

The maturity proceeds in the form of guaranteed and loyality additions will stand in good stead when the child takes up his career.

Another attractive feature of the plan is an option available to the proposer to obtain insurance in the form of term rider on his life to the extent of 20% of the sum assured under the policy not exceeding ₹ 50,000/-. The cover being in the form of term rider, the cost is nominal as granting of it does not involve administrative expenses.

This is the first time that the Corporation is granting a covery in the form of term rider. The insurance protection to the family will provide additional assistance in the event of unfortunate death of the bread-winner.

1994 happened to be the Year of the Family, the intention of the plan is to cover up two of the family members together.

The payment of survival benefits does not in any way reduce the insurance protection. In case of death of the life assured after commencement of the risk, the full sum assured together with guaranteed additions is payable without any deduction for the amount that may have been paid earlier by way of survival instalment. Loyalty addition is another novel feature which will depend upon Corporation's experience with regard to three factors viz. Mortality Expenses and Interest. In case the Corporation's experience is maintained at the current level without any further improvement, a good percentage of sum assured will accrue as Loyalty Addition.

LIC has taken interest for introducing different new policy schemes to cater the needs of customers of different segments—Asha Deep, Bima Kiran, Jeevan Shree, Jeevan Adhar, Bima Sandesh, Bhavishya Jeevan, Jeevan Surabhi, Jeevan Mitra, Jeevan Sathi, Jeevan Sarita, Jeevan Balya and Jeevan Griha have been introduced by LIC.

9. JEEVAN SURAKSHA

Jeevan Suraksha plan was introduced on 15th August, 1996. It enables individuals to provide for retirement income from a chosen date. The Policy is with life cover but can be taken without life cover under certain conditions. The Policy holder taking policy with life cover provides minimum of 50% of the target pension to spouse on death during the deferment period. Spouse's pension is not provided under without life cover plan. On vesting, the policy holder, has the option to receive 25% of the notional cash option in lumpsum and balance in annuity.

10. JEEWAN SNEHA

Jeevan Sneha introduced on 16th June 1997 is specially designed for women. The plan is without profits money back type plan with the added feature of guaranteed additions.

Loyalty addition, encashment of survival benefit, as and when required, flexibility to pay premium in advance, in-built accident cover. Free insurance cover for a period of 3 years from the date of first unpaid premium provided at least 2 full years' premiums have been paid and option to receive pension in lieu of maturity benefits.

Comments on New Policy

Remember when Jeevan Shree Plan (112) was launched in 1994/95 almost everyone felt that it will not sell as it was minimum 5 lakhs policy. During those days the high sum assured cases were very rare and the average size of LIC policy was ₹ 25,000/- only. A rebate of Re. 1 for sum assured more than ₹ 25,000/- and ₹ 2/- for sum assured more than ₹ 50,000/- was offered. That meant even a policy of ₹ 25,000/- was high sum assured then.

One more interesting fact; most of our policies will be sold in the size of ₹ 25,000/-, ₹ 50,000/- and ₹ 1,00,000/-. Because when the primary salesperson *i.e.*, agent discusses a policy he may begin with ₹ 1 lakh sum assured if he is little courages but on further negotiation and discussions, he will directly come down to ₹ 50,000/ - in 99% of the cases as the "Ready Reckoner" with him gives the premium rates for ₹ 50,000/- instantly. The agent normally will not talk of sum assured of ₹ 75,000/ - or ₹ 90;000/- even though the customer could have gone for that sum. This may be called Ready Reckoner yndrome.

Now imagine the scenario today. Agents all across the country are selling high sum assured policies. The Jeevan Shree was withdrawn last year in January 2002 but has made a big contribution that our average agents also started talking and selling ₹ 5 lakhs policy. Had Jeevan Shree not been there perhaps even today selling ₹ 5 lakhs or more policy would have been difficult for most of us.

After Jeevan Shree (112), New Jeevan Shree (151) has arrived on the scene. The sales have been very moderate so far. Let us examine what are the myths and mindsets that are coming in our way in selling some of our newly launched plans.

(A) New Jeevan Shree: Misconception about the Plan is minimum sum assured and premium is high

Fact: (i) Jeevan Shree (112) with minimum sum assured of ₹ 5 lakhs was sold in large numbers (26387 in Mumbai D.O. III) last year based on high yield. It means people will buy even high sum assured policies if product is attractive yield-wise or benefitwise.

(*ii*) The guaranteed additions @ ₹ 70/- per thousand sum assured per year with accident benefit and term assurance of ₹ 15 lakhs each makes this plan attractive. Even with the higher premium the yield is upto 7%. We should always see the benefits and not the cost. Cost is only relative to benefit.

Selling Points

- Ideal for executives, professionals, businessmen, artists having limited span of active earning life/career and wish to provide for later part of life.
- Suitable for Key Man Insurance. Short term is suitable as Keyman may keep changing his job.
- Transferability between employers under Key Man Insurance.
- Limited premium paying term and single premium option.
- Loan is permissible after 2 years.
- Ideal for gift under single premium.

(B) Jeevan Rekha-Misconception about the plan is money back is after every 5 years which is long survival gap compared to plan life Mahalife of Tata AIG.

Fact: (*i*) It is true that money is returned after every 5 years on survival. However what need to be analysed is that money back is quicker *i.e.*, after just 5 years from DOC and at higher rate *i.e.*, 10% of sum assured-thereby offering good liquidity whereas Mahalife has long initial waiting period of 12 years. For example a 13 years person will get his full sum assured back under survival benefits by 63 years of age. Further the life cover with bonuses continue till death. Longer the life, higher the benefit under Jeevan Rekha. As there is choice of premium payment terms an even single premium, life long unlimited Survival Benefited security and savings can be

Selling Points:

- Regular–life long money back @ 10% sum assured every five years.
- Life long cover for full S.A. irrespective of S.B. paid.
- Bonus and sum assured payable to dependants, as a parting gift.
- As a birthday or anniversary gift every 5th year.
- Single and Limited premium payment terms as per one's convenience 5, 10, 15,20,25 and for life.
- As a provision of foreign tour or holiday every 5th year.
- Most suitable for short career profession as like sports persons/singer artists who can take 5 Single Premium or 5 years' term policies for, successive 5 years and get regular tax free income every year until life. This is all the while necessary in view of increased average longevity.

(C) New Jeevan Dhara-I, New Jeevan Akshay-l, New Jeevan Suraksha-l: Misconception about the plan is:

***(i)* No guaranteed pension or annuity**

Fact: (*i*) The pension schemes available in the Insurance market are almost on LIC's pattern, No company can afford to guarantee a pension that too after 20-25 years at the current interest rates. The interest rates are very volatile and are changing fast. There is lot of risk interest rates and increased longevity. Therefore almost all insurance companies or pension funds are going for "defined contribution" from "defined benefit" type of annuities.

***(ii)* The annuities are low**

It has been specified that annuity rates for New Jeevan Surakhsa-l/ New Jeevan Dhara-I will be same as that of New Jeevan Akshay-I current at the time of vesting. Today, New Jeevan Akshay-I, an immediate annuity plan offers life long guaranteed pension @ 6.66% p.a. to 8.11 % p.a. with return of purchase price depending on age of annuitant being 40 or 79 years.

By all counts in today's scenario this yield which is guaranteed and safe should be considered excellent. We need to market "New Jeevan Akshay-l" not only as immediate annuity plan but also as scheme which can give you a regular income with safety of your capital.

(*iii*) No bonus indicated in New Jeevan Surakhsa-I/New Jeevan Dhara-I

Fact: By now all of us know that bonus depends on surplus fund generated by LIC. However we offer more bonus to long term and high premium policies as they give higher reserve for surplus. Traditionally we have been selling policies like endowment and money back by presuming a bonus rate however, same is not being done in New Jeevan Suraksha-I. While computing in the latest valuation should be added to NCO while computing annuity rates.

Selling Points:

New Jeevan Suraksha-I

- o Single Premium payment availability.
- o The most flexible deferment period 2–35 years in New Jeevan Suraksha- I.
- o Income tax exemption upto ₹ 10,000/- p.a. u/s. 80 CC (I)
- o Tax free commutation of 25% of NCO + Bonuses.
- o 5 different options to receive annuity.
- o Tax rebate available for persons with more than ₹ 5 lakhs of income also.

New Jeevan Akshay-I

- o Available from 40 years to 79 years of age. Suitable for middle aged and short careerists also.
- o Minimum of purchase price ₹ 25,000/- only.
- o 5 convenient pension options.

LIC has got very powerful products – each one of them having its own distinctive and specific features which we need to highlight. Our need based ideal product range include some of the plans where sales are low as we have not understood fully the entire spectrum of benefit of the plan in totality. I will recommend Plan 5, 89,91, 103, 109, 121, 150, 151, 143, 149, 152, 159 in particular apart from our usual 'bread and butter' plans 14 & 75.

Given below are the highlights of some of the other favourite plans:

Plan 89: Jeevan Sathi

- o A superb plan.
- o Two lives are covered at little over half the cost of separate Endowment Plans.
- o P.W.B. offered free after 1st death + Free risk cover for another life till maturity.
- o Both lives get accident benefit if death of both lives take place in the same policy year by accident.

Plan 91: New Jana Raksha:

- o Ideal Endowment policy for persons with irregular or uncertain income and even salaried class working in companies/factories facing job security syndrome.
- o After the premiums are paid for 2 years, free risk cover in case of non-payment of premiums upto 3 years from F.D.P.
- o Easy revival terms.

Plan 103: Jeevan Chhaya

- o Ideal for annual educational expenses of children.
- o Free term assurance on proposer's death during term.
- o Free P.W.B. after death of life assured.
- o **Guaranteed Policy benefits:** Education provision guaranteed during life time or even in the contingency of premature death of Life Insured.

Plan 121: Asha Deep

- A policy combining benefits of health and life Insurance.
- Four critical illnesses covered.
- Free P.W.B.
- Immediate contingent benefit equal to 50% of sum assured in case of policy holder suffers from critical illness.
- Balance 50% Sum Assured repaid in 10 equal instalments.
- Full risk cover in case of death.

Plan 153: Bima Nivesh Triple Cover

- Ideal for younger people — VRS at middle age or retirees from Army.
- Guaranteed returns and thrice sum assured risk cover.
- Convenient single premium.

Every product has distinct segment, only and eagle's eye will pave the way to enlarge the compass of clientile.

JEEVAN PRAMUKH

BENEFITS

Guaranteed Additions

Guaranteed Additions @ ₹ 50/- per thousand Sum Assured for each completed year, for the first five years.

Participation in profits: The policy shall participate in profits of the Corporation from the 6th year onwards and shall be entitled to receive bonuses declared as per the experience of the Corporation.

Maturity benefit: Sum Assured together with accrued Guaranteed Additions and accrued Simple Reversionary Bonuses and Final Additional Bonus, if any, will be paid to the Policy-holder on surviving the term of the policy provided the policy is in full force for full sum assured.

Death benefit: On death of the Life Assured during the term of the policy an amount equal to the Sum Assured along with accrued Guaranteed Additions and accrued Simple Reversionary Bonuses and Final Additional Bonus, if any, will be paid provided the policy is in full force for full Sum Assured.

Grace period: A grace period of 30 days will be available for payment of yearly, half-yearly or quarterly premiums and 15 days for monthly premiums.

15-day cooling-off period: If you are not satisfied with the 'Terms and Conditions' of the policy you may return the policy to us within 15 days.

Paid-up value: The policy will acquire paid-up value after more than one year's premiums have been paid subject to Terms-and Conditions.

Guaranteed surrender value: The policy can be surrendered for cash after more than one year's premiums have been paid. The Guaranteed Surrender Value allowable under the policy will be equal to 30% of the total amount of premiums paid excluding the premiums for the first year and the extra premiums, if any.

The cash value of any existing vested Guaranteed Additions and vested simple reversionary bonuses, if any, will also be payable after completion of 3 years.

Revival: The policy-holder can revive his lapsed policy by paying arrears of premium together with interest within a period of five years from the date of first unpaid premium subject to satisfactory evidence of health and continued insurability of the Life Assured. The rate of interest will be as determined by the Corporation from time to time. Currently, the rate of interest is 9% p.a.

Loan: Subject to Terms and Conditions loan is permissible after the policy has acquired paid-up value. The rate of interest charged on such loan amount would be determined from time to time. The present rate is 10.5% p.a. payable half-yearly.

Payment of premium: Premium under this policy are payable over a period of 3, 4 or 5 years. The following modes of payment of premium are allowed – Yearly. Half-yearly. Quarterly or Monthly.

Policy Term: 5, 10, 15, 20 or 25 years.

Eligibility conditions and other restrictions:

(*a*) Minimum Age at entry - 18 years completed
(*b*) Maximum Age at entry - 65 years (age nearer birthday)
(*c*) Maximum Maturity age - 75 years (age nearer birthday)
(*d*) Policy Term - 5, 10, 12, 20 or 25 years
(*e*) Sum Assured - Minimum Rs. 10 lakhs. Thereafter in multiples of ₹ 1,00,000

Rebate for mode of premium payment:

yearly - 2% of tabular premium
Half-yearly - 1 % of tabular premium
Quarterly - Nil
Monthly - 5% extra of tabular premium

Sum assured rebate:

Up to and including ₹ 50 lakhs : Nil
Above ₹ 50 lakhs : ₹ 0.50 per thousand Sum Assured

Exclusions: This policy will be void if the Life Assured commits suicide within one year from the date of commencement of risk under the policy.

SPECIMEN PREMIUM RATES
Premium Paying Term 3 years

Age	*Policy Term*				
	5	***10***	***15***	***20***	***25***
20	362.70	306.00	256.40	213.85	177.85
25	362.75	306.05	256.55	214.10	178.40
30	362.75	306.10	256.75	214.65	179.55
35	362.85	306.35	257.35	215.95	181.85
40	363.10	306.90	258.60	218.30	185.80
45	363.50	307.85	260.65	222.05	191.95
50	364.30	309.55	264.00	228.00	201.55
55	365.55	312.05	269.00	236.95	000.00
60	367.25	315.75	276.75	000.00	000.00
65	370.35	322.30	000.00	000.00	000.00

Premium Paying Term 4 years

Age	*Policy Term*				
	5	***10***	***15***	***20***	***25***
20	277.60	234.20	196.25	163.65	136.15
25	277.65	234.25	196.35	163.90	136.55
30	277.65	234.30	196.50	164.30	137.45
35	277.75	234.50	197.00	165.30	139.25
40	278.05	235.00	198.00	167.15	142.25
45	278.50	235.85	199.70	170.15	147.10
50	279.40	237.40	202.50	174.90	154.60
55	280.80	239.70	20.65	182.05	000.00
60	282.75	243.05	213.05	000.00	000.00
65	286.20	249.05	000.00	000.00	000.00

Premium Paying Term 4 years

Age	*Policy Term*				
	5	***10***	***15***	***20***	***25***
20	239.95	202.45	169.65	141.50	117.70
25	240.00	202.50	169.75	141.70	118.70
30	240.00	202.55	169.90	142.05	118.85
35	240.15	202.75	170.35	142.95	120.40
40	240.50	203.30	171.30	144.60	123.10
45	241.05	204.15	172.85	147.25	127.30
50	242.10	205.70	175.45	151.55	134.00
55	243.75	208.05	179.35	158.00	000.00
60	246.05	211.55	185.45	000.00	000.00
65	250.20	217.70	000.00	000.00	000.00

Benefit Illustration

Statutory Warning

Some benefits are guaranteed and some benefits are variable with returns based on the future performance of your Insurer carrying on life insurance business. If your policy offers guaranteed returns then these will be clearly marked 'guaranteed' in this illustration table on this page. If your policy offer variable returns then the illustrations on this page will show two different rates of assumed future investment returns, These assumed rates of return are not guaranteed and they are not the upper or lower limits of what you might get back, as the value of your policy is dependent on a number of factors including future investment performance".

Age at Entry	*35 years*	*Yearly Premium (₹)*	*178213*
Term	*25 years*	*Sum Assured*	*1000000*
ppt	*3 years*		

End of Yrs.	*Total Premium paid (₹)*	*Death Benefit/Maturity Benefit (₹) payable at end of year*				
		Guaranteed	*Variable*		*Toral*	
			Scenario 1	*Scenario 2*	*Scenario 1*	*Scenario 2*
1	178213	1000000	0	0	1000000	1000000
2	356426	1050000	0	0	1050000	1050000
3	534639	1100000	0	0	1100000	1100000
4	534639	1150000	0	0	1150000	1150000
5	534639	1200000	0	0	1200000	1200000
6	534639	1250000	22000	104000	1272000	1354000
7	534639	1250000	44000	208000	1294000	1458000
8	534639	1250000	66000	312000	1316000	1562000
9	534639	1250000	88000	416000	1338000	1666000
10	534639	1250000	110000	520000	1360000	1770000
15	534639	1250000	220000	1040000	1470000	2290000
20	534639	1250000	440000	2080000	1690000	3330000
25	534639	1250000	586000	2773000	1836000	4023000

(i) *This illustration is applicable to a non-smoker male/female standard (from medical, life style and occupation point of view) life.*

(ii) *The non-guaranteed benefits (1) and (2) in above illustration are calculated so that they are consistent with the protected Investment Rate of Return assumption of 6% p.a. (Scenario 1) and 10% p.o. (Scenario 2) respectively. In other words, in preparing this benefits illustration, it is assumed that the Projected Investment Rate of Return that LICI will be able to earn* ***throughout the term of the policy will be*** *6% p.a. or 10% p.a., as the case may be. The Projected Investment Rate of Return is* ***not guaranteed.***

(iii) *The main objective of the illustration is that the client is able to appreciate the features of the product and the flow of benefits in different circumstance with some level on quantification.*

(iv) *Future bonus will depend on future profits and as such is not guaranteed. However, ones bonus is declared in any year and added to the policy, the bonus so added is guaranteed.*

(v) *The Maturity Benefit is the amount shown at the end of the policy term.*

Section 41 of Insurance Act 193د

(1) No person shall allow or offer to allow, either directly or indirectly as an inducement to any person take out or renew of continue an insurance in respect of any kind of risk relating to lives or property in India, any rebate of the whole or part of the commission payable or any rebate of the premium shown on the policy, nor shall any person taking out or renewing or continuing a policy accept any rebate except such rebates as may be allowed in accordance with the published prospectuses or tables of the insurers provided that acceptance by an insurance agent of commission in connection with a policy of life insurance taking out by himself on his own life shall not be deemed to be acceptance of the rebate of premium within the meaning of this sub-section if at the time of such acceptance the

insurance agent satisfies the prescribed conditions establishing that he is a bona fide insurance agent employed by the insurer.

(2) Any person making default in complying with the provisions of this Section shall be punishable with a fine, which extend to 500 rupees.

LIC'S JEEVAN NIDHI

SALIENT FEATURES

(*a*) **Guaranteed Additions:** Guaranteed Additions @₹50/- per thousand Sum assured for each completed year, for the first five years.

(*b*) **Participation in profits:** The policy shall participate in profits of the Corporation from the 6th year onwards and shall be entitled to receive bonuses declared as per the experience of the Corporation.

(*c*) **Benefits on Vesting:**

1. *Option to commute* up to 1/3rd of the amount available on vesting, which shall include the Sum Assured under the Basic Plan together with accrued Guaranteed Additions, simple Reversionary Bonuses and Terminal Bonus, if any.
2. *Annuity as per the option selected:* Annuity on the balance amount if commutation is exercised, otherwise annuity of the fun amount.

(*d*) **Death Benefit on death before annuity vests:** One the death of the Life Assured during the deferment period of the policy, *i.e.,* before the annuity vests, an amount equal to the Sum Assured under the Basic plan along with the occurred: Guaranteed Additions, simple Reversionary Bonuses and Terminal Bonus, if any, will be paid in a lump sum to the appointed nominee, provided the policy is in force for full Sum Assured. Nominee will also have the option to purchase an annuity with this amount.

(*e*) **Annuity Options:** On vesting, the annuity instalment, mode of annuity payment and type of annuity which shall be made available to the Life Assured (Annuitant/Nominee will depend upon the then prevailing Immediate Annuity plan of the Life Insurance Corporation of India and its terms and conditions.

Currently the following options are available under LICs Immediate Annuities:

1. **Annuity for life:** The annuity is paid to the life assured as long as he/she is alive.
2. **Annuity Guaranteed for certain periods:** The annuity is paid to the life assured for periods of 5 or 10 or 15 or 20 years as chosen by him/her, whether or not he/she survives that period. After the chosen period, the annuity is paid to the life assured as long as he/she is alive.
3. **Annuity with return of purchase price on death:** The annuity is paid to the life assured as long as he/she is alive. On the death of the life assured, the purchase price of the annuity is paid as death benefit. The purchase price includes the Sum Assured under the Basic Plan, the accrued Guaranteed Additions and any accrued bonuses, excluding the commuted value, if any.
4. **Increasing annuity:** The annuity is paid of the life assured as long as he/she in alive. The amount of annuity increases every year at a simple rate of 3% per annum.
5. **Guaranteed Surrender Value:** Before the annuity vests, the policy can be surrendered at any time after the completion of 3 policy years. For a regular premium policy, the Guaranteed Surrender value is available provided 3 years premiums are paid, and it is 30% of the premiums paid excluding premiums paid in the first year. For a Single Premium policy, the Guaranteed Surrender Value available after completion of 3 policy years is 90% of the Single Premium: Any extra premiums and premiums for Term Assurance Rider Option, Critical Illness Rider option and Accident Benefits, if any will be excluded.

The cash value of any existing vested Guaranteed Additions and vested Simple Reversionary Bonuses. If any, will be allowed in the surrender value.

(*g*) **Grace Period:** A grace period of 30 days will be available for payment of yearly, half-yearly or quarterly premiums and 15 days for monthly premiums.

(*h*) **15 – day Cooling-off period:** If policy-holder is not satisfied with the 'Terms and Conditions" of the policy, he/she may return the policy to us within 15 days.

(*i*) **Paid-up Value:** The policy will acquired paid-up value after at least 3 full year's premiums have been paid.

(*j*) **Revival:** The policy-holder can revive his lapsed policy by paying arrears or premium together with interest within a period of five years from the date of first unpaid premium subject to satisfactory evidence of health. The rate of interest for this purpose will be decided by the Corporation from time to time. The present rate of interest in 9% p.a.

(*k*) **Options:** 1. *Accidental Death and Disability Benefits:* In case of death accident (within 180 days) an additional amount equal to the Accident Benefit Sum assured will be payable. In case of Total and Permanent disability arising due to accident an amount equal to accident benefit sum assured will be able over a period of 10 years in monthly instalments. However, the payment of accident benefits will be subject to an overall limit of ₹ 25 lakh under all policies of the Life Assured with the Corporation taken together.

The disability due to accident should be total and such that the Life Assured is unable to carry out any work to earn a living. Following disabilities due to accident are also covered.

(*a*) irrevocable loss of the entire sight of both eyes or
(*b*) amputation of both hands at or above the wrists of
(*c*) amputation of both feet at or above ankles, or
(*d*) amputation of the hand at or above the wrist and one foot at or above the ankle.

Not benefit will be paid in case of accidental death or disability due to accident in case of:

(*a*) international self-injury, attempted suicide, insanity or immorality or the Life Assured is under the influence of intoxicating liquor, drug of narcotic,
(*b*) engagement is aviation or aeronautics other than that a passenger in any air craft
(*c*) injuries resulting from riots, civil commotion, rebellion, war, invasion, hunting, mountaineering, steeple chasing or racing of any kind
(*d*) accident resulted from committing any breach of law
(*e*) accident arising from employment in armed forces or military services of police organisation.

2. **Term Assurance Rider Option:** Term Assurance as optional rider will be available under this plan. Premiums for this option are payable during the premium paying term and an amount equal to Term Assurance Sum Assured will be payable on death during the policy term. The maximum cover for this rider will be ₹ 25 lakh under all policies of the Life Assured with the Corporation taken together.

3. **Critical Illness Rider Option:** An amount equal to the Critical Illness Rider Sum Assured as optional rider will be payable in case of diagnosis of defined categories of Critical Illness subject to certain terms and conditions. The maximum cover for this rider will be ₹ 5 lakh under all policies of the Life Assured with the Corporation taken together.

ELIGIBILITY CONDITIONS AND OTHER RESTRICTIONS UNDER THIS PLAN

For Basic Benefit

(*a*) Minimum age at entry:	18 years (completed)
(*b*) Maximum age at entry:	65 years
(*c*) Minimum age at vesting:	40 years
(*d*) Maximum age at vesting:	75 years
(*e*) Policy terms:	6 to 35 years under Single Premium policies and 5 to 35 years under Regular Premium policies
(*f*) Modes of premium payment:	Yearly, Half-yearly, Quarterly, SSS & Single Premium
(*g*) Sums Assured allowed:	₹ 50,000/- and in multiples of Rs. 5,000/- thereafter, with no upper limit
(*h*) Minimum Annual Premium:	₹3,000/-
(*i*) Minimum Single Premium:	₹ 10,000/-

For Term Assurance Rider Option:

(*a*) Minimum age at entry:	18 years (completed)
(*b*) Maximum age at entry:	50 years
(*c*) Maximum age at vesting:	60 years
(*d*) Policy terms:	6 to 36 years under Single Premium mode and 10 to 35 years under regular
(*e*) Minimum Sum Assured:	₹ 1,00,000/-
(*f*) Maximum Sum Assured:	An amount equal to the Sum Assured under the Basic plan subject to a limit to ₹ 25,00,000/- taking all Term Assurance Rider Sum Assured under all policies of a life assured
(*g*) Multiples of Sum Assured:	₹ 25,000/-

For Term Assurance Rider Option:

(*a*) Minimum age at entry:	20 years (completed)
(*b*) Maximum age at entry:	50 years

A BLEND OF HAPPINESS AND SECURITY
JEEVAN ANAND

Table No. 149

A two-in-one policy that gives the advantage of both whole life & Endowment schemes.

- **Survival Benefit:** Sum Assured + Bonus at the end of the selected term and risk cover continues.
- **Death Benefit:** Sum Assured + Bonus if death takes place during the selected term and policy comes to an end. However, if death takes place after the selected term, then the Sum Assured alone is payable to the nominee/legal heirs.
- **Accident and Disability Benefit:** Exclusive in-built accident and disability benefit up to ₹5,00,000.

- **Minimum Sum Assured:** ₹ 1,00,000.
- **Loan facility:** Available

The LIC has introduced five new policies during 2005-2006. These are LIC's Golden Jubilee Policy—Bima Gold, LIC's Jeevan Plus, LIC's Bima Bachat, LIC's Amulya Jeevan and LIC's Jeevan Tarang. Similarly, LIC's Jeevan Akshay III was repriced and replaced as LIC's Jeevan Akshay IV. New Bima Gold (Table 179) having regular premium money back plan with return of total premium in instalments at prescribed intervals with loyalty additions, if any, at maturity and extended free risk cover was introduced in 2008.

SOCIAL SECURITY SCHEMES

Janashree Bima Yojana : The object of this scheme is to provide insurance protection to the rural and urban poor below the poverty line or marginally above it. 50% of the premium is subsidised from the Social Security Fund maintained by LIC and the remaining 50% is contributed by members / Nodal Agency / State Government. Persons aged between 18 and 59 years are covered for an amount of ₹ 30,000/- each under this scheme. In case of death or total disability (including loss of 2 eyes / 2 limits of use) due to accident, a sum of ₹ 75,000 and in case of partial permanent disability (loss of 1 eye /1 limit of 1 use) due to accident, a sum of ₹ 37,500/- is payable to the nominee / beneficiary.

HIGHLIGHTS OF LIC'S JEEVAN AROG
(Plan No. 903)

- A unique non linked benefit type plan offering both life and health cover up to age 80 yrs.
- Single policy for self (Principal insured-PI) and entire family including parents and parents-in-law.
- Health Benefit for Listed as well as unlisted surgeries.
- Benefits type of policy without any link to actual expenses incurred.
- No exclusion of first 24 hours, if hospitalization exceeds 6 days 4 hours.
- Attractive rebates on higher HCB Slabs.
- Premium paid will be eligible for IT exemption under section 80D up to ₹ 15,000/- (₹ 30,000/- if parents are covered)

Plan Features

- Eligible Age—PI and Spouse–18 to 65: Parents and Parents-in-law-18 to 75;
- Children–3 months to 17 yrs.
- Modes of premium payment–Yly, Hly, Qly and (ECS (Mly)–Mode rebate for Yly & Hly.
- Premiums are guranteed for 3 years with automatic renewal facility.

Unique Benefits

1. Hospital Cash Benefit (HCB)
2. ICU Benefit
3. Major Surgical Benefit (MSB)
4. Day Care procedure Benefit (DCPB)
5. Other Surgical Benefit (OSB)
6. Quick Cash facility
7. Ambulance charges Benefit
8. Premium Waiver Benefit
9. Term Assurance rider (Death Benefit)
10. Accident Benefit rider (AB)
11. No Claim Benefit

- **Hospital Cash Benefit** from ₹ **1000/- to** ₹ **4000/-** per day (to be opted by the policy holder in multiples of ₹ 1000/-).
  - Double the Benefit for **ICU**.
  - Maximum **720** days for each member including **360** days ICU benefit, throughout the policy term up to 80 years of age; for children up to 25 years of age.
  - Automatic increase in HCB of **5%** of initial HCB every year up to **50%** of the initial HCB
- Major surgical benefit for 140 Listed Surgical Procedures.
  - MSB is equal to 100 times of HCB.
  - Automatic increase in MSB by **5%** of initial MSB every year up to **50%** of the initial MSB.
  - Maximum 3 times of MSB throughout policy term (1 MSB per annum)
  - Upto 80 years of age for other than children – for children **up to 25 yers of age.**
- **Day Care Procedure Benefit** for 140 day care procedures. **5 times** of Applicable Daily Cash Benefit (ADB). **3 times** in a year and **24 times** in the policy full term.
- **Other Surgical Benefit**–for any surgery **not covered under** MSB. **2 times** of applicable Daily Cash benefit–**45 days** in a year **360 days** in the policy full term (15 days-First Year)
- **Quick Cash Facility**–This is the facility available for all insured, where instant cash can be paid as an advance up to **50%** of eligible **57** MSB surgeries of category 1 & 2.
- **Ambulance Charges**–for **57** surgeries eligible of **MSB** listed under **category 1 and 2.**
  – Benefit @ ₹ **1000** per insured per policy year.
- **Premium Waiver Benefit**–For **57** surgeries eligible for **MSB** listed under **category 1 and 2** one year premium will be waived.
- **Term Assurance Rider :** Death Benefit MSB is covered under this policy by payment for additional premium.
- **Accident Benefit Rider**–Accidental Death Benefit up to initial MSB is available by payment of additional premium.

No Claim Benefit–If there is no claim from any insured between two automatic renewal date (ARD) **5% of IDB** will be added to the ADB from net ARD for all insured.

Sample Premium chart (Yearly)

	A : Immediate family = PI + spouse + children					
	PI	**Spouse**	**Son**	**Daughter**	**Total**	**Medical/Non-Medical**
HCB/Age->	35	31	10	7		
1,000	2,426	1,737	796	783	5,742	NMG
2,000	4,353	3,224	1,342	1,317	10,236	NM for cat, I and II ladies
3,000	6,279	4,711	1,888	1,850	14,728	NM for cat, I and II ladies
4,000	8,205	6,198	2,434	2,383	19,220	NM for cat, I and II ladies

Sample Premium Chart (Yearly)

B : Immediate family + parents of PI

	PI	Spouse	Son	Daughter	Father	Mother	Total
HCB/Age->	35	31	10	7	60	56	
1,000	2,426	1,737	796	783	4,651	3,170	13,563
2,000	4,353	3,224	1,342	1,317	9,052	6,091	25,379
3,000	6,279	4,711	1,888	1,850	13,453	9,011	37,192
4,000	8,205	6,198	2,434	2,383	17,854	11,932	49,006

Sample Premium Chart (Yearly)

Extended family = Immediate family + parents of PI + parents of spouse

	PI	Spouse	Son	Daughter	Father	Mother	Father-in-Law	Mother-in-Law	Total
HCB/Age->	35	31	10	7	60	56	55	51	
1,000	2,426	1,737	796	783	4,651	3,170	4,020	2,859	20,442
2,000	4,353	3,224	1,342	1,317	9,052	6,091	7,790	5,468	98,637
3,000	6,279	4,711	1,888	1,850	13,453	9,011	11,559	8,077	56,828
4,000	8,205	6,198	2,434	2,383	17,854	11,932	15,329	10,686	75,021

JEEVAN ANKUR (T. NO. 807)

The Jeevan Ankur plan is the latest offering from the bouquet of LIC in New Year 2012. This with profit plan was launched on 23rd Jan, 2012.

This plan is specially designed for the benefit of the children. A child is totally dependent on his parents during his growing up period. This plan can meet the various financial needs that arise during that period.

Under Jeevan Ankur Plan, Parent is the Life Assured and Child is the Beneficiary. It is available to parents aged between 18 yrs to 50 yrs having child upto 17 yrs (completed) including newborns.

Since the policy is on the life of parent, the premium can be paid by the grandparent of the child. Thus it can become a grand gift from a grandparent to his/her grandchild.

Particulars	*Minimum*	*Maximum*
Entry Age-Life Assured	18 yrs (completed)	50 yrs (NBD)
Entry Age-Child	0 yr	17 yrs (completed)
Term	18 minus age of Child (subject to minimum 8 yrs)	25 minus age of child
Sum Assured	₹ 1 lac	No limit

Besides Single Premium, other available modes of payement of premium include Yearly. Half-yearly, Quartely and Monthly (ECS and SSS).

Salient Features

The features of the plan are aimed at providing financial security to the child by paying lumpsum amount in case of untimely death of Life Assured (father/mother) during the term of the policy. This payment would help the family to meet financial needs which arise on demise of the Life Assured. In addition, it then starts taking care of upbringing / educational / other needs of the child by paying 10% of the Sum Assured till maturity date.

At Maturity Date, again the Sum Assured is payable along with Loyality Additions (if any).

In effect, this plan guarantees the payment of Sum Assured to the child at a time (i.e. Maturity date) which is planned in advance today and irrespective of the fact whether parent is alive that time or not.

OPTIONAL BENEFITS

Jeevan Ankur plan has provision for three riders to customize the policy, viz:

1. Accident Benefit Rider
2. Critical Illness Rider
3. Premium Waiver Benefit under Critical Illness Rider

Jeevan Ankur as a gift to the child

Sample illustration:

Age of Life Assured: 35 yrs

Age of child: 0 yr (new born)

Term: 25 yrs

Mode of payment: Single Premium

Particulars	*Various Gift Options*		
Gift amount	10 lacs	5 lacs	2 lacs
Exact premium*	10,02,605	4,99,256	2,04,613
Basic Sum Assured	24,50,000	12,20,000	5,00,00
Risk Cover:			
1. Basic SA	24,50,000	12,20,000	5,00,000
2. Income Benefit	2,45,000 per year	1,22,000 per year	50,000 per year
3. Maturity Benefit	24,50,000 + LA**	12,20,000 + LA**	5,00,000 + LA**
Maturity Benefit:	24,50,000 + LA**	12, 20, 000 + LA**	5,00,000 + LA**

* includes Service tax (at current rate)

** LA ® Loyality Additions; Based on Corporation's Experience.

Death Benefit

1. Basic Sum Assured amount immediately after death.

2. Income Benefit equal to 10% of Basic Sum Assured payable on every policy anniversary coinciding with or next following the date of death of Life Assured till the end of policy term.

3. Another amount equal to Basic Sum Assured payable on Maturity date along with loyalty Additions, if any.

LIC'S NEW ENDOWMENT PLAN (UIN: 512N277V01)

LIC's New Endowment Plan is a participating non-linked plan which offers an attractive combination of protection and saving features. This combination provides financial support for the family of the deceased policyholder any time before maturity and good lump sum amount at the time of maturity for the surviving policyholders. This plan also takes care of liquidity needs through its loan facility.

1. BENEFITS:

Death benefit:

In case of death during the policy term provided all due premiums have been paid Death benefit, defined as sum of **"Sum Assured on Death"** and vested Simple Reversionary Bonuses and Final Additional bonus, if any, shall be payable. Where, **"Sum Assured on Death"** is defined as higher of Basic Sum Assured or 10 times of annualised premium. This death benefit shall not be less than 105% of all the premiums paid as on date of death.

Where premiums exclude service tax, extra premium and rider premiums, if any.

Maturity Benefit: Basic Sum Assured, along with vested simple reversionary bonuses and Final Additional bonus, if any, shall be payable in lump sum on Survival to the end of the policy term provided all due premiums have been paid.

Participation in Profits: The policy shall participate in profits of the Corporation and shall be entitled to receive Simple Reversionary Bonuses declared as per the experience of the Corporation, provided the policy is in full force.

Final (Additional) Bonus may also be declared under the policy in the year when the policy results into a claim either by death or maturity, provided the policy has run for certain minimum term.

2. ELIGIBILITY CONDITIONS AND OTHER RESTRICTIONS:

For Basic plan

1. Minimum Basic Sum Assured : ₹ 100,000
2. Maximum Basic Sum Assured : No Limit

(The Basic Sum Assured shall be in multiples of ₹ 5000/-)

1. Minimum Age at entry : 8 years (completed)
2. Maximum Age at entry : 55 years (nearest birthday)
3. Maximum Maturity Age : 75 years (nearest birthday)
4. Minimum Term : 12 years
5. Maximum Term : 35 years

3. PAYMENT OF PREMIUMS

Premiums can be paid regularly at yearly, half-yearly, quarterly or monthly mode (through ECS only) or through salary deductions over the term of policy.

However, a grace period of one month but not less than 30 days will be allowed for payment of yearly or half-yearly or quarterly premiums and 15 days for monthly premiums.

4. SAMPLE PREMIUM RATES:

Following are some of the sample tabular premium rates (exclusive of service tax) per ₹ 1000/- Basic Sum Assured:

AGE/TERM	15	25	35
20	71.20	40.10	28.10
30	71.50	40.75	29.40
40	72.85	43.25	33.15
50	77.10	49.40	

5. MODE AND HIGH S.A. REBATES:

Mode Rebate:

Yearly mode – 2% of Tabular Premium

Half-yearly mode – 1% of Tabular premium

Quarterly & Salary deduction – NIL

High Sum Assured Rebate:

Basic Sum Assured (B.S.A)		Rebate (₹)
1, 00,000 to 1, 95,000	-	Nil
2, 00,000 to 4, 95,000	-	2.00 % o B.S.A.
5, 00,000 and above	-	3.00% o B.S.A.

LIC'S NEW MONEY BACK PLAN – 25 YEARS (UIN: 512N278V01)

LIC's New Money Back Plan-25 years is a participating non-linked plan which offers an attractive combination of protection against death throughout the term of the plan along with the periodic payment on survival at specified durations during the term. This unique combination provides financial support for the family of the deceased policyholder any time before maturity and lump sum amount at the time of maturity for the surviving policyholders. This plan also takes care of liquidity needs through its loan facility.

1. BENEFITS:

Death benefit:

On death during the policy term provided the policy is in full force, death benefit, defined as sum of **"Sum Assured on Death"** and vested Simple Reversionary Bonuses and Final Additional Bonus, if any, shall be payable. Where, **"Sum Assured on Death"** is defined as higher of 125% of the Basic Sum Assured or 10 times of annualized premium. This death benefit shall not be less than 105% of the total premiums paid as on date of death.

The premiums mentioned above exclude tax, extra premium and rider premium, if any.

Survival Benefits: In case of Life Assured surviving to the end of the specified durations 15% of the Basic Sum Assured at the end of each of 5th, 10th, 15th, % 20th policy year.

Maturity Benefit: In case of Life Assured surviving the stipulated date of maturity, 40% of the Basic Sum Assured along with vested Simple Revers'ɔnary Bonuses and Final Additional Bonus, if any, shall be payable.

Participation in Profits: The policy shall participate in profits of the Corporation and shall be entitled to receive Simple Reversionary Bonuses declared as per the experience of the Corporation, provided the policy is in full force.

Final Additional Bonus may also be declared under the policy in the year when the policy results into a claim either by death or maturity, provided the policy has run for certain minimum term.

2. ELIGIBILITY CONDITIONS AND OTHER RESTRICTIONS:

For Basic plan

1. Minimum Basic Sum Assured : ₹ 100,000

2. Maximum Basic Sum Assured : No Limit

(The Basic Sum Assured shall be in multiples of ₹ 5000/-)

1. Minimum Age at entry for Life Assured : 13 years (completed)

2. Maximum Age at entry for Life Assured : 45 years (nearest birthday)

3. Maximum Maturity Age for Life Assured : 70 years (nearest birthday)

4. Term : 25 years

5. Premium paying term : 20 years

3. PAYMENT OF PREMIUMS:

Premiums can be paid regularly at yearly, half-yearly, quarterly or monthly mode (through ECS only) or through salary deductions over the term of policy.

However, a grace period of one month but not less than 30 days will be allowed for yearly, half-yearly, quarterly modes and 15 days for monthly mode of premium payment.

4. SAMPLE PREMIUM RATES:

Following are some of the sample tabular annual premium rates (exclusive of service tax) per ₹ 1000/- Basic Sum Assured:

Age(in years)	Premium (₹)
20	60.00
30	61.45
40	65.95
45	70.15

5. MODE AND HIGH S.A. REBATES:

Mode Rebate:

Yearly mode - 2% of Tabular Premium

Half-yearly mode - 1% of Tabular premium

Quarterly & Salary deduction - NIL

High Sum Assured Rebate:

Basic Sum Assured (B.S.A)		**Rebate (₹)**
1, 00,000 to 1, 95,000	-	Nil
2, 00,000 to 4, 95,000	-	2.00 %o B.S.A.
5, 00,000 and above	-	3.00%o B.S.A.

LIC'S NEW JEEVAN ANAND (UIN: 512N279V01)

LIC's New Jeevan Anand Plan is a participating non-linked plan which offers an attractive combination of protection and savings. This combination provides financial protection against death throughout the lifetime of the policyholder with the provision of payment of lumpsum at the end of the selected policy term in case of his/her survival. This plan also takes care of liquidity needs through its loan facility.

1. BENEFITS:

Death benefit:

Provided all due premiums have been paid, the following death benefit shall be paid:

On Death during the policy term: Death benefit, defined as sum of **"Sum Assured on Death"** and vested Simple Reversionary Bonuses and Final Additional bonus, if any, shall be payable. Where, **"Sum Assured on Death"** is defined as higher of 125% of Basic Sum Assured or 10 times of annualised premium. This death benefit shall not be less than 105% of all the premiums paid as on date of death.

The premiums mentioned above exclude service tax, extra premium and rider premiums, if any.

On death of policyholder at any time after policy term: Basic Sum Assured.

Benefits payable at the end of Policy Term: Basic Sum Assured, along with vested Simple Reversionary Bonuses and Final Additional Bonus, if any, shall be payable in lump sum on survival to the end of the policy term provided all due premiums have been paid.

Participation in Profits: The policy shall participate in profits of the Corporation and shall be entitled to receive Simple Reversionary Bonuses declared as per the experience of the Corporation during policy term provided the policy is in full force.

Final (Additional) Bonus may also be declared under the plan in the year when the policy results into death claim during the policy term or due for the survival benefit payment provided the policy is in full force and has run for certain minimum term.

2. ELIGIBILITY CONDITIONS AND OTHER RESTRICTION :

For Basic plan

(a) Minimum Basic Sum Assured : ₹ 100,000

(b) Maximum Basic Sum Assured : No Limit

(The Basic Sum Assured shall be in multiples of ₹ 5000/-)

(c) Minimum Age at entry : 18 years (completed)

(d) Maximum Age at entry : 50 years (nearest birthday)

(e) Maximum Maturity Age : 75 years (nearest birthday)

(f) Minimum Policy Term : 15 years

(g) Maximum Policy Term : 35 years

2. PAYMENT OF PREMIUMS:

Premiums can be paid regularly at yearly, half-yearly, quarterly or monthly intervals (through ECS only or through salary deductions) over the Policy Term.

However, a grace period of one calendar month but not less than 30 days will be allowed for payment of yearly or half-yearly or quarterly premiums and 15 days for monthly premiums.

3. SAMPLE PREMIUM RATES:

Following are some of the sample tabular premium rates (exclusive of service tax) per ₹ 1000/- Basic Sum Assured:

Policy Term (in years)

Age (in years)	**15**	**25**	**35**
20	79.05	44.30	29.95
30	82.45	46.75	32.30
40	88.20	51.40	37.10
50	97.70	59.65	

4. MODE AND HIGH S.A. REBATES:

Mode Rebate:

Yearly mode - 2% of Tabular Premium

Half-yearly mode - 1% of Tabular premium

Quarterly & Monthly mode - NIL

High Sum Assured Rebate:

Basic Sum Assured (B.S.A)		**Rebate (₹)**
1, 00,000 to 1, 95,000	-	Nil
2, 00,000 to 4, 95,000	-	1.50%o B.S.A.
5, 00,000 and 9, 95,000	-	2.50%o B.S.A.
10, 00,000 and above	-	3.00%o B.S.A.

LIC'S NEW MONEY BACK PLAN - 20 YEARS (UIN: 512N280V01)

LIC's New Money Back Plan-20 years is a participating non-linked plan which offers an attractive combination of protection against death throughout the term of the plan along with the periodic payment on survival at specified durations during the term. This unique combination provides financial support for the family of the deceased policyholder any time before maturity and lump sum amount at the time of maturity for the surviving policyholders. This plan also takes care of liquidity needs through its loan facility.

1. BENEFITS:

Death benefit:

On death during the policy term provided the policy is in full force, death benefit, defined as sum of **"Sum Assured on Death"** and vested Simple Reversionary Bonuses and Final Additional Bonus, if any, shall be payable. Where, **"Sum Assured on Death"** is defined as higher of 125% of the Basic Sum Assured or 10 times of annualized premium. This death benefit shall not be less than 105% of the total premiums paid as on date of death.

The premiums mentioned above exclude tax, extra premium and rider premium, if any.

Survival Benefits: In case of Life Assured surviving to the end of the specified durations 20% of the Basic Sum Assured at the end of each of 5th, 10th & 15th policy year.

Maturity Benefit: In case of Life Assured surviving the stipulated date of maturity, 40% of the Basic Sum Assured along with vested Simple Reversionary Bonuses and Final Additional Bonus, if any, shall be payable.

Participation in Profits: The policy shall participate in profits of the Corporation and shall be entitled to receive Simple Reversionary Bonuses declared as per the experience of the Corporation, provided the policy is in full force.

Final Additional Bonus may also be declared under the policy in the year when the policy results into a claim either by death or maturity, provided the policy has run for certain minimum term.

2. ELIGIBILITY CONDITIONS AND OTHER RESTRICTIONS:

For Basic plan

1. Minimum Basic Sum Assured : ₹ 100,000
2. Maximum Basic Sum Assured : No Limit

(The Basic Sum Assured shall be in multiples of ₹ 5000/-)

1. Minimum Age at entry for Life Assured : 13 years (completed)
2. Maximum Age at entry for Life Assured : 50 years (nearest birthday)
3. Maximum Maturity Age for Life Assured : 70 years (nearest birthday)
4. Term : 20 years
5. Premium paying term (PPT) : 15 years

3. PAYMENT OF PREMIUMS:

Premiums can be paid regularly at yearly, half-yearly, quarterly or monthly mode (through ECS only) or through salary deductions over the term of policy.

However, a grace period of one month but not less than 30 days will be allowed for yearly, half-yearly, quarterly modes and 15 days for monthly mode of premium payment.

4. SAMPLE PREMIUM RATES:

Following are some of the sample tabular premium rates (exclusive of service tax) per ₹ 1000/- Basic Sum Assured:

Age (in years)	Premium (₹)
20	78.00
30	79.10
40	82.95
50	92.05

5. MODE AND HIGH S.A. REBATES:

Mode Rebate:

Yearly mode – 2% of Tabular Premium

Half-yearly mode – 1% of Tabular premium

Quarterly & Salary deduction – NIL

High Sum Assured Rebate:

Basic Sum Assured (B.S.A)		**Rebate (₹)**
1, 00,000 to 1, 95,000	–	Nil
2, 00,000 to 4, 95,000	–	2.00 % o B.S.A.
5, 00,000 and above	–	3.00% o B.S.A.

LIC'S SINGLE PREMIUM ENDOWMENT PLAN (UIN: 512N283V01)

LIC's Single Premium Endowment Plan is a participating non-linked savings cum protection plan, where premium is paid in lump sum at the outset of the policy. This combination provides financial protection against death during the policy term with the provision of payment of lump sum at the end of the selected policy term in case of his/her survival. This plan also takes care of liquidity needs through its loan facility.

1. BENEFITS

Death Benefit:

(a) On death during the policy term before the date of commencement of risk: Return of single premium excluding service tax and extra premium, if any, without interest.

(b) On death during the policy term after the date of commencement of risk: Sum Assured along with vested Simple Reversionary Bonuses and Final Additional Bonus, if any.

Maturity Benefit: Sum Assured, along with vested Simple Reversionary Bonuses and Final Additional Bonus, if any, shall be payable.

Participation in profits: The policy shall participate in profits of the Corporation and shall be entitled to receive Simple Reversionary Bonuses declared as per the experience of the Corporation.

Final (Additional) Bonus may also be declared under the policy in the year when the policy results into a claim either by death or maturity on such terms and conditions as may be declared by the corporation from time to time.

2. ELIGIBILITY CONDITIONS AND OTHER RESTRICTIONS:

1. Minimum entry age : 90 days (completed)
2. Maximum entry age : 65 years (nearest birthday)
3. Maximum maturity age : 75 years (nearest birthday)
4. Minimum policy term : 10 years
5. Minimum age at maturity : 18 years (completed)
6. Maximum policy term : 25 years
7. Minimum Sum Assured : ₹ 50,000
8. Maximum Sum assured : No limit

Sum Assured will be in multiples of ₹ 5000 /- only.

1. Premium Payment Mode: – Single Premium Only.

Date of Commencement of risk: In case the age of Life Assured at entry is less than 8 years, risk under the plan will commence either 2 years from the date of commencement or form the policy anniversary coinciding with or immediately following the attainment of 8 years of age, whichever is earlier. For those aged 8 years or more, risk will commence immediately.

3. SAMPLE PREMIUM RATES:

The sample premium rates (exclusive of taxes) are as under:

Single Premium per 1000 Sum Assured			
Age (Nearest Birthday)	**Term**		
	10	**15**	**25**
10	756.90	640.30	463.10
20	757.60	641.55	465.85
30	757.95	642.60	470.90
40	759.75	647.65	488.35
50	766.05	662.25	527.35
60	777.50	688.60	-

4. REBATE FOR HIGH SUM ASSURED:

High Sum Assured Rebates:

Sum Assured (S.A)		**Rebate (₹)**
50,000 to 95,000	–	Nil
1,00,000 to 1,95,000	–	18% o S.A.
2,00,000 to 2,95,000	–	25% C.S.A.
3,00,000 and above	–	30% o S.A.

LIC'S NEW BIMA BACHAT (UIN: 512N284V01)

LIC's New Bima Bachat is a participating non-linked savings cum protection plan, where premium is paid in lump sum at the outset of the policy. It is a money-back plan which provides financial protection against death during the policy term with the provision of payment of survival benefits at specified durations during the policy term. In addition, on maturity, the single premium shall be returned along with Loyalty Addition, if any. This plan also takes care of liquidity needs through its loan facility.

1. BENEFITS:

Death benefit:

On death during the first five policy years: Sum Assured.

On death after completion of five policy years: Sum Assured along with Loyalty Addition, if any.

Survival Benefits:

Payable as given below in case of Life Assured surviving to the end of the specified durations:

For policy term 9 years: 15% of the Sum Assured at the end of each of 3rd & 6th policy year

For policy term 12 years: 15% of the Sum Assured at the end of each of 3rd, 6th & 9th policy year

For policy term 15 years: 15% of the Sum Assured at the end of each of 3rd, 6th, 9th & 12th policy year

Maturity Benefit:

Payment of Single Premium (excluding taxes and extra premium, if any) along with Loyalty Addition, if any, in case of Life Assured surviving to the end of the policy term.

Loyalty Addition

Depending upon the Corporation's experience the policies shall be participate in the profits and shall be eligible for Loyalty Addition. The Loyalty Addition, if any, is payable on death after completion of five policy years and on policyholder surviving to maturity, at such rate and on such terms as may be declared by the Corporation.

2. ELIGIBILITY CONDITIONS AND OTHER RESTRICTIONS :

(a) Minimum entry age : 15 years (completed)

(b) Maximum entry age : 66 years (nearest birthday) for term 9 years
63 years (nearest birthday) for term 12 years
60 years (nearest birthday) for term 15 years

(c) Maximum maturity age: : 75 years (nearest birthday)

(d) Policy Term : 9, 12 or 15 years.

(e) Minimum Sum Assured : ₹ 35,000 for term 9 years
₹ 50,000 for term 12 years
₹ 70,000 for term 15 years

(f) Maximum Sum assured : No limit
Sum Assured will be in multiples of ₹ 5,000 /- only.

(g) Premium payment mode : Single Premium only

3. SAMPLE PREMIUM RATES:

The sample premium rates (exclusive of taxes) are as under: -

Single Premium per 1000 Sum Assured (₹)			
Age (Nearest Birthday)	**Term**		
	9	**12**	**15**
15	767.95	771.00	771.55
25	768.95	772.00	772.70
35	771.70	775.35	776.80
45	782.65	787.15	789.25
55	803.80	808.10	810.70
65	836.85	-	-

4. REBATE FOR HIGH SUM ASSURED :

High Sum Assured Rebates (As percentage of Tabular Premium) :

Term – 9 years

Less than ₹ 75,000 : NIL

₹ 75,000 and Less than ₹150,000 : 6 %

₹ 150,000 and above : 8 %

Term – 12 years

Less than ₹ 100,000 : NIL

₹ 100,000 and Less than ₹ 200,000. : 4 %

₹ 200,000 and above : 6 %

Term – 15 years

Less than ₹ 150,000 : NIL

₹ 150,000 and Less than ₹ 300,000 : 3 %

₹ 300,000 and above : 5 %

LIC'S JEEVAN RAKSHAK (UIN: 512N289V01)

LIC's Jeevan Rakshak Plan is a participating non-linked plan which offers a combination of protection and savings. This plan provides financial support for the family in case of unfortunate death of the policyholder any time before maturity and a lump sum amount at the time of maturity for the surviving policyholder. This plan also takes care of liquidity needs through its loan facility.

1. BENEFITS:

Death benefit:

In case of death of the policyholder during the policy term provided all due premiums have been paid, **"Sum Assured on Death"** shall be payable, which is the highest of

- Basic Sum Assured or
- 10 times of annualized premium or
- 105% of all the premiums paid as on date of death.

The premiums defined above exclude service tax, extra premium and Accident Benefit rider premium, if any.

In addition to the above, Loyalty Addition, if any shall also be payable if death occurs after completion of 5th policy year.

Maturity Benefit:

Basic Sum Assured, along with Loyalty Addition, if any, shall be payable in lump sum on Survival to the end of the policy term provided all due premiums have been paid.

Participation in Profits:

Provided the policy is in full force, then depending upon the Corporation's experience the policies under this plan will be eligible for Loyalty Addition. The Loyalty Addition, if any, is payable at such rate and on such terms as may be declared by the Corporation, on death after completion of 5th policy year or on Policyholder surviving to the maturity.

2. OPTIONAL BENEFIT:

LIC's Accident Benefit Rider:

Accident Benefit Rider is available as an optional rider by payment of additional premium. In case of accidental death, the Accident Benefit Sum Assured will be payable as lumpsum along with the death benefit under the basic plan.

3. ELIGIBILITY CONDITIONS AND OTHER RESTRICTIONS:

For Basic plan

(This plan is only available for standard healthy lives without undergoing any medical examination)

(a) Minimum Basic Sum Assured per life* : ₹ 75,000

(b) Maximum Basic Sum Assured per life* : ₹ 200,000

(The Basic Sum Assured shall be in multiples of ₹ 5000/-)

(c) Minimum Age at entry : 8 years (completed)

(d) Maximum Age at entry : 55 years (nearest birthday)

(e) Minimum Policy Term : 10 years

(f) Maximum Policy Term : 20 years

(g) Maximum Age at Maturity : 70 years (nearest birthday)

* The total Basic Sum Assured under all policies issued to an individual under this plan shall not exceed ₹ 2 lakh.

For LIC's Accident Benefit Rider

(a) Minimum Accident Benefit Sum Assured : ₹ 75,000

(b) Maximum Accident Benefit Sum Assured : An amount equal to the Basic Sum Assured under the Basic Plan subject to the maximum of ₹ 50 lakh overall limit taking all existing policies of the Life Assured under individual as well as group schemes including policies with inbuilt accident benefit taken with Life Insurance Corporation of India and the Accident Benefit Sum Assured under the new proposal into consideration.

The Accident Benefit Sum Assured shall be in multiples of ₹ 5,000.

(c) Minimum Entry Age : 18 years (completed)

(d) Maximum Entry Age : The cover can be opted for at any policy anniversary during the policy term

(e) Maximum Cover Ceasing Age : Same as under the Basic Plan.

4. PAYMENT OF PREMIUMS:

Premiums can be paid regularly at yearly, half-yearly, quarterly or monthly mode (through ECS only) or through salary deductions over the term of policy.

However, a grace period of one month but not less than 30 days will be allowed for payment of yearly or half-yearly or quarterly premiums and 15 days for monthly premiums.

5. SAMPLE PREMIUM RATES:

Following are some of the sample tabular annual premium rates (exclusive of service tax) per ₹ 1000/- Basic Sum Assured:

AGE/TERM	10	15	20
10	85.90	51.70	35.20
20	86.25	52.05	35.55
30	86.45	52.35	35.95
40	87.35	53.70	37.80
50	90.65	57.80	42.70

6. MODE AND HIGH BASIC SUM ASSURED REBATES:

Mode Rebate:

Yearly mode - 2% of Tabular Premium

Half-yearly mode - 1% of Tabular premium

Quarterly, Monthly (ECS) & Salary deduction - NIL

High Basic Sum Assured Rebate:

Basic Sum Assured		Rebate (₹)
75,000 to 1,45,000	-	Nil
1,50,000 and above	-	1.50% o SA

VARISHTHA PENSION BIMA YOJANA (UIN: 512G291V01)

1. INTRODUCTION:

Government of India in the Union Budget 2014-2015, announced the revival of Varishtha Pension Bima Yojana. Excerpts from budget speech by Honourable Finance Minister are, "NDA Government during its last term in office had introduced the Varishtha Pension Bima Yojana (VPBY) as a pension scheme for senior citizens. Under the scheme a total number of 3.16 lakh annuitants are being benefited and corpus amounts to ₹ 6,095 Crore. I propose to revive the scheme for a limited period from 15th August 2014 to 14th August 2015 for the benefit of citizens aged 60 years and above."

LIC of India has been given the sole privilege to operate this scheme.

2. BENEFITS :

(a) Pension Payment :

During the lifetime of Pensioner, a pension in the form of immediate annuity as per mode chosen by the Pensioner shall be payable.

(b) Death Benefit:

On death of the Pensioner the Purchase Price shall be refunded.

3. ELIGIBILITY CONDITIONS AND OTHER RESTRICTIONS:

(a) Minimum Entry Age : 60 years (completed)

(b) Maximum Entry Age : No limit

(c) Minimum Pension : ₹ 500 per month
₹ 1,500 per quarter
₹ 3,000 per half year
₹ 6,000 per year

(d) Maximum Pension : ₹ 5000/- per month
₹ 15,000/- per quarter
₹ 30,000/- per half-year
₹ 60,000/- per year

Ceiling of maximum pension is for a family as a whole i.e. total amount of pension under all the policies issued to a family under this plan shall not exceed the maximum pension limit. The family for this purpose will comprise of pensioner, his/her spouse and dependants.

4. PAYMENT OF PURCHASE PRICE:

The plan can be purchased by payment of a lump sum Purchase Price. The pensioner has an option to choose either the amount of pension or the Purchase Price.

The minimum and maximum Purchase Price under different modes of pension will be as under:

Mode of Pension	Minimum Purchase Price	Maximum Purchase Price
Yearly	₹ 63,960/-	₹ 6,39,610/-
Half-yearly	₹ 65,430/-	₹ 6,54,275/-
Quarterly	₹ 66,170/-	₹ 6,61,690/-
Monthly	₹ 66,665/-	₹ 6,66,665/-

The Purchase Price to be charged shall be rounded to nearest multiple of ₹5/-.

5. MODE OF PENSION PAYMENT:

The modes of pension payment are monthly, quarterly, half-yearly & yearly. The pension payment shall be through ECS/NEFT only.

The first instalment of pension shall be paid after 1 year, 6 months, 3 months or 1 month from the date of purchase of the same depending on the mode of pension payment i.e. yearly, half-yearly, quarterly or monthly respectively.

6. SAMPLE PENSION RATES PER ₹ 1000/- PURCHASE PRICE

The pension rates for ₹1000/- Purchase Price for different modes of pension payments are as below:

Yearly	:	₹ 93.8069 p.a.
Half-yearly	:	₹ 91.7045 p.a.
Quarterly	:	₹ 90.6767 p.a.
Monthly	:	₹ 90.0000 p.a.

The pension instalment shall be rounded off to the nearest rupee.

These rates are not age specific.

LIC'S JEEVAN SHAGUN (UIN: 512N290V01)

LIC's Jeevan Shagun is a participating, non-linked, savings cum protection single premium plan wherein the risk cover is a multiple of single premium.

The proposer will have an option to choose the Maturity Sum Assured. The single premium payable (exclusive of service tax) shall depend on the chosen amount of Maturity Sum Assured and age of the life assured.

A percentage of Maturity Sum Assured shall be payable on surviving to the end of the specified durations and on maturity. This plan also takes care of liquidity need through its loan facility. The plan will be open for sale for a maximum period of 90 days from the date of launch.

1. BENEFITS:

(a) Death Benefit:

On death during first five policy years:

Basic Sum assured i.e. 10 times the tabular single premium shall be payable.

On death after completion of five policy years:

Basic Sum assured i.e. 10 times the tabular single premium along with Loyalty Addition, if any, shall be payable.

(b) Survival Benefit:

On Life Assured surviving to the end of the specified durations, the following Survival benefit shall be payable.

- At the end of 10th policy year: 15% of the Maturity Sum Assured.
- At the end of 11th policy year: 20% of the Maturity Sum Assured.

(c) Maturity Benefit:

On maturity, 65% of the Maturity Sum Assured along with Loyalty Addition, if any, shall be payable.

(d) Loyalty Addition:

Depending upon the Corporation's experience, a policy shall participate in the profits in the form of Loyalty Addition. The Loyalty Addition, if any, shall be payable on death or surrender, provided the policy has run for atleast five policy years, or on policyholder surviving to the maturity, at such rate and on such terms as may be declared by the Corporation.

2. ELIGIBILITY CONDITIONS AND OTHER RESTRICTIONS:

(a) Minimum Entry Age : 8 years (completed)
(b) Maximum Entry Age : 45 years (nearest birthday)
(c) Minimum/Maximum Basic Sum Assured : 10 times of tabular single premium paid
(d) Minimum Maturity Sum Assured : ₹ 60,000/-
(e) Maximum Maturity Sum Assured : No Limit
Maturity Sum Assured shall be available in multiples of ₹ 5,000/-.
(f) Policy Term : 12 years
(g) Premium payment mode : Single premium only

3. SAMPLE PREMIUM RATES:

Specimen tabular Single Premium rates for some of the ages per ₹1000/- Maturity Sum Assured are as under:

Age at entry (Nearest Birthday)	Tabular Single Premium Rates (₹)
10	494.95
20	508.20
30	521.25
40	595.40

Note: Tabular premiums do not include any extra premium or taxes and is before applying high Maturity Sum Assured rebate.

4. REBATE FOR HIGH MATURITY SUM ASSURED:

Maturity Sum Assured	Reduction in Tabular premium per 1000/- Maturity Sum Assured
Below ₹ 150,000	Nil
₹ 150,000 to ₹ 395,000	₹ 15
₹ 4,00,000 and above	₹ 20

QUESTIONS

1. What are the various kinds of life insurance policies?
2. 'Multipurpose policy is fulfilling almost all types of human needs'. Comment.
3. "These days Children's Deferred Endowment Policies are gaining ground." Discuss in detail.
4. Describe the different types of endowment and term policies.
5. "Life insurance is insurance against dying too soon and endowment insurance is insurance against living too long." Explain.
6. Explain the distinctive features of (*a*) Anticipated Policies. (*b*) Double endowment policies and, (*c*) Simple benefit policies.
7. Explain the salient features of Jeevan Chhaya.
8. Describe the terms and conditions of "Jeevan Pramukh" what is LIC's Jeevan Nidhi? Explain with advantages.

7

ANNUITIES

An annuity is a periodical level payment made in exchange at the purchase money for the remainder of the life time of a person or for a specified period. The recipient is usually as an annuitant. In annuity contract, the insurer undertakes to pay certain level sums periodically up to death or expiry of the term. Since at the early death, the insurer does not suffer loss, no medical examination is necessary. However, evidence of age is essential at the time of proposal.

The annuity is beneficial to those who do not want to leave amount for others but want to use their money during their life-time. During the life-time, they may make maximum use of the money by purchasing annuity which is not possible otherwise. In bank, he may leave certain amount at early, death or may suffer loss in living long due to stoppage of the money after a certain period. The payment of annuity generally continues up to the life. So the premium rate is determined according to longevity. The amount premium is higher at younger age and lower at advanced age.

Difference between Annuity Contracts and Life Insurance Policies

Annuity contract is just opposite of the insurance contract.

(*i*) The annuity contract liquidates gradually the accumulated funds whereas the life insurance contract provides gradual accumulation of funds.

(*ii*) The annuity contract is taken for one's own benefit but the life assurance is generally for benefits of the dependents.

(*iii*) In annuity contract generally the payment stops at death whereas in life insurance the payment is usually given at death.

(*iv*) The premium in annuity contract is calculated on the basis of longevity of the annuitant but the premium in life insurance is based on the mortality of the policy-holder.

(*v*) Annuity is protection against living too long whereas the life insurance contract is protection against living too short.

Both of these contracts complete the economic programme of an individual from beginning to an end. When life insurance stops to serve the annuity contract starts to help the individual up to his survival.

Classification of Annudeties

The annuities can be defined according to (*i*) commencement of income, (*ii*) number of lives covered, (*iii*) mode of payment of premium, (*iv*) disposition of proceeds, and (*v*) special combination of annuities.

Annuities According to Commencement of Income

1. Immediate Annuity

The immediate annuity commences immediately after the end of the first income period. For instance, if the annuity is to be paid annually, then the first instalment will be paid at the expiry of one year. Similarly, in half-yearly annuity, the payment will begin at the end of six months. The annuity can be paid either yearly, half-yearly, quarterly or monthly. The purchase money (or consideration) is in single amount. Evidence of age is always asked for at the time of entry. The advantage of this is that with this help, it is possible to obtain a larger income than can be secured from the yield of investments. The form of contract is of special interest to persons without dependents and it provides maximum possible consistent income.

2. Annuity Due

Under this annuity, the payment of instalment starts from the time of contract. The first payment is made as soon as the contract is finalised. The premium is generally paid in single amount; but can be paid in instalments as is discussed in deferred annuity.

The difference between the annuity due and immediate annuity is that the payment for each period is paid in its beginning under the annuity due contract while at the end of the period in immediate annuity contract. The annuity due contract is beneficial for acturial valuation.

3. Deferred Annuity

In this annuity contract, the payment of annuity starts after a deferment period or at the attainment by the annuitant of a specified age. The premium may be paid as a single premium or in instalments. Generally the deferred annuity is sold on level premium. The payment of premium continues until the stated date for commencement of the instalments or until prior death of the annuitant. At the death, the premium may be returned without interest. The deferred annuity can be surrendered for a cash amount (or cash option) at the end of or before the deferment period. The surrender value is normally 950 per cent of the premiums paid excluding first premium before deferment period. No surrender value is payable after the deferment period.

The deferred annuity can be issued to male or female lives. The female lives are generally able to avail lesser amount due to their higher longevity as compared to male lives after certain age. The corporation does not require any medical examination but only proof of age is required. The corporation also issues this annuity provided the amount of annuity is not less than ₹ 100 per annum or the instalment of annuity is not less than ₹ 25 per month or the cash option is not less than ₹ 1,000.

This annuity is useful to those who desire to provide a regular income for themselves and their dependents after the expiry of specified period.

CLASSIFICATION OF ANNUITY ACCORDING TO THE NUMBER OF LIVES

1. Single Life Annuity

Under this annuity one single person following is contractor. This annuity is most beneficial to those who have no dependent and want to use all this saving during his life-time.

2. Multiple Life Annuity

In this annuity more than one life is contracted. The annuity is also of *two* types: (*a*) Joint Life Annuity where payment of annuity stops at the first death, and (*b*) Last survivor annuity where payment continues up to the death of the last person of the group.

Classification of Annuities according to Mode of Premium

The annuities according to payment of premium can be level single premium annuities.

1. Level Premium Annuities

For availing the annuity, the annuitant can deposit some amounts periodically so that, at the end, he can get sufficient amount of annuity in equal instalments. During the accomolation period, *i.e.*, before commencement of the payment of annuity, he is given option to get the surrender value in cash or to get the paid up values reduced in proportion to the premium paid to the premium payable. At the death of the depositor, the beneficiary can get the surrender values or premiums paid whichever is higher.

2. Single Premium Annuities

The annuity in this case is purchased by payment of a single premium. Generally, the life insurance amount is utilised for purchasing this annuity.

Classification according to the disposition of Proceeds

The annuities according to this classification may be (*i*) Life Annuity; (*ii*) Guaranteed Minimum Annuities; and (*iii*) Temporary Annuities.

1. Life Annuity

This annuity offers a regular income to the annuitant throughout his life-time. No payment is made after his death. This is beneficial not in every case. When the annuity dies before receiving all the amounts of the purchase price he is at loss. But, if he survives for a longer period than expected, he is benefited by this annuity. When we talk of annuity we mean such types of annuity. In other words, annuity means annual payment up to life. But this annuity will be treated as fair-weather friend and the dependents may be at loss because the father who had accumulated a large amount could not use the funds at early death.

2. Guaranteed Minimum Annuity

Annuity payment up to a period is guaranteed by the insurer. If the annuitant dies before the specified period, annuity will continue up to the unexpired period. This annuity may be of two types, (*i*) Immediate Annuity with guaranteed payment, and (*ii*) Deferred annuity with guaranteed payment.

(*i*) *Immediate Annuity with Guaranteed Payment.* To safe-guard the loss in case of early death of the annurant, this annuity is issued where payment for a fixed number of years will continue, irrespective of death. Sometimes, instead of continuing the annuity payments after the death of the policy-holder, the difference of the purchase money and annuity instalments already paid is returned as a lump sum to the legal representative of the annuitant. This annuity may be of *two* types: first, where payment is continued up to the fixed period and second, where payment continues up to the fixed period and up to life thereafter. The corporation issues the second type of annuity where payments are guaranteed for 5, 10, 15 or 20 years and thereafter up to life. It means that payment certainly be made up to this period whether the annuitant is alive or dead within this period and if the annuitant survives after period, he is paid the annuity up to this survival.

(*ii*) *Deferred Annuity with Guaranteed Payment.* During the deferment period, there is no difference between this annuity and ordinary deferred annuity. After deferment period, the payment under this policy will continue for a fixed period, say 5, 10, 15 or 20 years and up to life, thereafter. This policy also guarantees refund of cash value of the balance of annuity where the insurer promises to pay a lump sum to the beneficiary or to the annuitant's estate, the difference, if any, between the total of annuities received before the annuitant's death and the purchase price.

3. Temporary Life Annuity

Under this plan, annuity payments cease at the end of a specified period or at the death whichever is earlier. The corporation does not issue such annuity.

4. Retirement Annuity Policy

This annuity is useful employees at the time of retirement. This annuity is issued under the following conditions: (*i*) The main object of the annuity contract must be the provision of life annuity to the individual in old age; (*ii*) During the life of the individual no sum other than the annuity to the individual shall be payable under the contract; (*iii*) All annuities must be payable in India only; (*iv*) The annuity must commence between the ages of 58 and 68; (*v*) The annuity payable shall not be capable of surrender, commutation or assignment; (*vi*) The annuity will ordinarily be payable for the life of the annuitant but if so desired provision can be made for annuity to continue for a specified period notwithstanding the death of the annuitant within the term on condition that such period of guarantee for payment of the annuity does not exceed ten years. This Annuity Policy will not be issued for an annuity of less than ₹ 600 per annum or where the annuity instalments are payable for a monthly instalment of less than ₹ 50.

8

SELECTION OF RISK

The selection of a risk is a process whereby inferior lives are "weeded out". The function of the selection process is to determine whether the degree of risk presented by applicant for insurance is commensurate with the premium established for persons in his category or some additional premium should be charged or the applicant should be rejected the insurance.

Purpose of Selections

(*i*) The first and the foremost purpose of the selection of risk is to determine whether the proposal should be accepted or not.

(*ii*) The second objective of the selection is to determine the rate of premium to be charged from the assured. The premium depends upon the amount of risk. Higher is the risk the more will be amount of premium. Each and every proposal should be evaluated to determine the amount of risk for calculation of premium. The evaluation of risk is also known as the *selection of risk*.

(*iii*) Since there are various degrees of risk to a person and so theoretically at least, all the persons should be charged different premiums, but it is not practicable to charge so many premiums as many applicants are. Therefore for practical purpose the risks are classified and premiums are determined accordingly. This is discussed in the next section of this chapter.

Insurance risk may be classified into standard or sub-standard on the basis of selection. It is possible to determine what risks are to be accepted at normal rate of premium and what at extra premium what not to be accepted at all.

(*iv*) The fourth aim of selection is to avoid any discrimination on the part of the lives assured. Since the degree of risk is not the same to all the persons, different premiums should be charged from different groups. If one premium is charged from all the proposers, it would be unjustified. For instance, it would be wrong to charge the same premium from the persons who are engaged in the hazardous occupation and from the persons who are enjoying robust health and conducive occupation.

(*v*) The selection of risk is also essential to avoid adverse-selection: Selection of risk is very essential to check the anti-selection or adverse-selection which means selection of the persons for insurance who are not insurable and charging of lesser premium for those who are to be charged higher premium. The persons in adversity of insurance, *i.e.*, the person who are imminent to death may try to purchase insurance at any cost to gain. If it is permitted not only the insurer will be losing, but the honest insured would be required to pay more premium to meet the total loss of the insurer. If they accept the higher premium they are purchasing insurance at higher cost, and if they are not going to purchase the policy, the insurer will be losing sounding business and would be again at loss. Therefore, it is very essential to select standard risk at standard cost and sub-standard risk at extra premium to avoid inequality of cost and unfavourable selection of risk.

FACTORS AFFECTING RISK

In life insurance, the factors which may affect the risk are usually those factors which are affecting the mortality; they are also called *factors affecting longevity of a person*. The mortality is not the only risk but the capacity and willingness of a person also influence the insurance decision. These factors are discussed in following paragraphs:

1. Age

The age of the life to be assured is the most important factor to affect mortality. Except for a few years of the childhood, the premium is determined at every year of the completion of age. The corporation asks for the age nearer to birthdays. The person below six months and the person above six months older of the age will be treated of the same age. For instance, a person of 22 years 7 months and another person of 23 years 5 months will be treated the age of 23 years.

The age proof is very essential for calculating premium rate. So, unless age is proved payment of claim is not made if the age was not admitted at the time of proposal. Now it has been the common practice that the age should be admitted at the time of proposal to avoid dispute. On the basis of age, in future, if a misstatement is discovered after the policy has become a claim, the amount of the claim is adjusted in accordance with the rectification of age. Age proof is essential at the proposal if the policy is term insurance, non-medical policies and immediate annuity or the insurance is taken at advance age or for a child because they are maximum and minimum limits of age.

Minimum and Maximum limit of age

The maximum age limit is fixed to avoid adverse selection. At advance age, the need for insurance is a doubtful proposition, *i.e.*, the chances of moral hazard is higher. The third reason for fixing maximum limit is the medical examination will disapprove most of the proposal at that stage. Mortality is certainly increased at that age. The minimum age limit is meant to avoid risk of infant mortality.

2. Build

Build refers to physique of the proposed life and includes height, weight, the distribution of weight and chest expansion. There are standards of weight according to maximum weight reveal the indication of certain hidden diseases. Therefore this sign is not favourable. The relationship between height, weight, girth and expansion of chest are the basic determinants of mortality expectations.

Overweight is dangerous in advanced age and underweight is similarly not desirable at younger age, say, below 35 years. The corporation, for example, has fixed the minimum weight, and maximum weight at a specified height. If the assured life is not within the standard the proposal may not be accepted at the time of proposal and it may be postponed or may be accepted at extra-premium or may be rejected at all.

3. Physical Condition

The physical condition of the age life proposed has a direct bearing on the mortality of the life. Insurers are, therefore, very particular about the conditions of an applicants' sight, hearing, heart, arteries, lungs, tonsils, teeth, kidneys, nervous system, etc. The experts in the field can assess the longevity or mortality of a person due to impairment of certain organs. The questions are also designed to elicit information on the physical status of the applicant in the proposal form. The information is confirmed and supplemented by a medical examination. The primary purpose of the medical examination is to detect any malfunctioning of the vital organs of the body.

4. Personal History

The personal history of the life proposed would reveal the possibility of death to him. The history may be connected with the (*i*) health record, (*ii*) past habit, (*iii*) previous occupation, (*iv*) insurance history.

(*i*) *Health Record.* The past health record is the most important factor under personal history because it affects the longevity or mortality of a person to a greater extent. It includes any operations of the life proposed. The medical examination may reveal these facts. These information is also given by the applicant. Particular emphasis is placed on the recent injuries and illness. It is customary to consult attending physicians. It has been the practice not to accept the proposal form of the applicants who are suffering from illness. If the applicant has suffered from certain serious disease or operation during the past 5 years, he may be under the possibility of getting it again.

(*ii*) *Past Habits.* The insurers want to know the past habit the life proposed, for drugs or alcohol because the cure may be only temporary. The past history is usually expected to be repeated. Therefore, past history is very cautiously examined.

(*iii*) *History of Occupation.* If the proponent was employed in hazardous or unhealthy occupation, there is a possibility that he may still retain ill-effects therefrom or may revert to such occupation. An intimate association within a person suffering from a contagious disease may influence the health of the life proposed. The past hazardous occupations generally affects, health slowly occupational diseases are contacted. Inorganic dust may create silicosis.

(*iv*) *Insurance History.* The previous amount of insurance may disclose the degree of risk of the applicant. If he was refused insurance, it might be a suspicious factor of his insurability. If it was found that the applicant was already insured for adequate amount this request for more insurance is regarded with suspicions.

5. Family History

Like the personal history, family history also requires information of habit, health, occupation and insurance of other family members, particularly of the parents, brother and sisters. The children's history of health is also required. The certain diseases, like tuberculosis and insanity, etc., and longevity of the parents will be relevant factors for determining the degree of risk of the proponents. The favourable family history, however, is not considered for offsetting the adverse effect of the personal history. The family history is considered significant to know the transmission of certain, characteristics by heredity. Heart, lungs, build, etc., follow family.

6. Occupation

Occupation is an important factor to affect the risk. It affects the occupation in various ways. Firstly, the nature of work may be hazardous because he may suffer an accident at any time while at work. Secondly, the morale of the workers may go down. They may be tempted to indulge in intoxicating or liquor or other forms of immoral living. Thirdly, the chemical effect may be poisonous. For instance, the workers may contact poison while engaged in match or chemical factories. Fourthly, the dusty or unventilated house, unhealthy or insanitary environments may deteriorate the health of the workers. Fifthly, in certain occupation, the occupational diseases are common. Sixthly, excessive mental and nervous strain may cause financial worries, and lastly, the lesser income may affect the health of the worker.

7. Residence

The residence also affects the risk. The risk will be lesser in a good climate area and more in a bad climate although the difference is narrowed down because of better medical and sanitary facilities. Information about the previous residence is equally important. The geographical location, atmosphere, political stability, climate, construction of house, travel, etc., are important factor which may affect the risk.

8. Present Habits

The general mode of living of the proposer affects the risk. Drunkards and non-temperate persons cause increase in mortality. Similarly, temperate habits tend to increase longevity of a person. Excessive and careless smoking tends to shorten the life due to development of nicotine poisoning. The past habits are also considered important. The intoxication affects the health of a person and consequently his mortality. The general mode of living is also considered in habits.

9. Morals

It has been observed that the departure from the commonly accepted standards of ethical and moral conduct involve extra mortality. Infidelity and departure from the code of sex behaviour are seriously regarded because these may affect the health. Unethical conduct is considered to be another form of moral hazard. Insurance is not generally given to bankrupt and reputed dishonest persons.

Consideration, of morals is essential to determine the moral hazard. There are two types of hazards—(l) Moral and Physical hazards—we have discussed factors affecting physical hazards in the other sections. Moral hazard will be discussed only under this heading.

The moral hazard occurs due to intention of the insured whereas the physical hazard is beyond his approach. The former is present where the policy is taken not with a view to protect one-self against losses but to obtain gain through crooked means. The moral hazard is judged by the reputation and fairness in dealings. The moral hazard is expected to present where insurance is taken at advanced age, where person is suffering from serious disease, proposal is on other's life and the proponent is engaged in hazardous occupation.

10. Race and Nationality

The mortality rate differs from race to race and nation to nation. In India, persons of high, race or caste are expected to live longer than the scheduled castes or tribes. Similarly, countries near to equator have more mortality. The climate and way of life of a country affect the health conditions of the people.

11. Sex

Mortality among female sex is, generally, higher than that of male sex because the physical hazard of maternity is present in the former case. Moreover, the ladies are physically more handicapped. The lesser education, conservatism and non-employment of the ladies also affect the mortality. The absence of proper examination of the ladies also count more hazard. The chances of moral hazard are also present in the female insurance. So, unless woman has good financial reasons for insurance, her proposal is not generally conceded.

12. Economic Status

It is essential to examine that the family and business circumstances of the proponents are such as to justify the amount of insurance applied for. This investigation also reveals whether the income of the applicants bears a reasonable relationship to the amount of insurance which he proposes to carry. The higher economic status generally provides a better field for insurance due to various reasons. Educational, financial and professional consciousness make the proponent insurance minded. The chances of death is also lower in higher strata of the society.

13. Defence Services

Though there has been much improvement in defence technology, yet flying or gliding, etc., is still considered hazardous one. Sometimes, certain restrictive clauses are imposed for insuring persons engaged in such services. In some other works, extra premiums are required. In commercial flying, no occupational extra is required. The war clause is added to avoid the occupation risk in defence, say, navy, air force and military.

14. Plan of Insurance

Certain plans involve more responsibility to the insurer at death and so these plans are restricted to only first class lives, Similarly, some plans have lesser risk and, therefore, can be issued without any extra investigations. For example, the multi-purpose policy is issued only to first class lives and the pure endowment policy can be issued to any one irrespective of health.

SOURCES OF RISK INFORMATION

Information on the factors affecting risk is collected before it can be evaluated to determine the degree of risk. It is collected from various sources because it is not possible to get all information from one source. Moreover, information from various sources on a particular item will provide an effective check.

1. The Proposal Form

The first and the important source of risk information is application form. The proposer is required to disclose all the material facts truly and fully. If any information is not asked by the insurer, the proponent should reveal the information if he thinks it to be material. Usually, the agent asks all the questions which are written in the proposal form.

The proposal form is divided into *two* parts:

1. Application form; and
2. Personal Statement.

The application includes questions pertaining to home, address, term of insurance, sum to be assured, mode of premium payment, date of birth, object of insurance, name of the nominee, previous insurance history, acceptance or rejection of the proposal, engagement in navy, air force and military services or the intention to be engaged in these services. Double accident benefit is sought or not. There are some additional questions to be answered by formal proposers, which are about education, their income, income occupation and insurance of husband. There is declaration in the end of the form which form the basis of contracts between the insured and the insurer.

Part II of the proposal form is called *personal statement* which is filled by (*i*) either the life to be assured, or (*ii*) the agent or the development officer, writing at the dictation of the life to be assured. This statement mentions name of the life to be assured, family history of father, mother, brothers and sisters in connection with their health and illness and cause of death. Questions about the bodily impairments, serious disease, habits, operation, accident or injury. There are special questions for such as observing of predate, conceptions, miscarriages and abortion for female proposers. Declaration of the proposer is also essential.

In non-medical proposals some detail information is also required. Name and address of family physicians, absent on ground of ill-health, height, weight, name and address of present and previous employers and declaration.

The proposal form gives all the required information of risk. Different types of proposal forms are used for different policies.

2. Medical Examiner's Report

The medical examiner has to identify the applicant to avoid the case of impersonation. The knowledge of medical examiner to the assured is also required. General appearance is an important question where proposal's apparent age, general health, habit, vaccination, deformity are asked. Measurement of height, weight, conditions of teeth, gums, ears, chest, heart, digestive tract, gentito-urinary system, nervous system operations and other details, etc. are inquired by physical test of the life to be assured. There are special questions for female proposers. Opinions of the medical examiner for the longevity, suspected health, first class lives, etc., are required. He has to declare that the findings are true and correct.

The information given by medical examiner is deemed to be correct and it is expected that the medical examiners would give true and fair picture; but certain cases in India have revealed that the reports of medical examiner are not hundred per cent reliable. Therefore, the underwriting officers at divisional or zonal office are required to go into details of suspected cases because once proposal has been accepted it cannot be repudiated on the ground of wrong medical reports.

3. Agent's Report

Although agents has to pursue or canvass a lot for getting proposal, yet he is required to state whether the life to be assured, is insurable or not. He has to furnish information of sum assured, name, acquaintances with the proposer, time and place of first introduction, identity of the life, medical examiners, name and address, monthly income and occupation of the proposer, general state of health, relationship with the agent, etc. The agent has also to disclose the financial and social position of the proposer. The agent is required to disclose all the unfavourable information of the life proposed. The agent's report can be of great value to the underwriting department because he has personal acquaintances with the life proposed and can give a full and correct information of all the factors affecting the risk.

Insurers do not place too much reliance on the agent's certificate because, he, in his zeal to increase his commission, might tend to colour his judgement. The comparision of agent's reports with information of other sources may reveal the fair or unfair reports of the agent. In case of wrong information of material facts, his licence may be cancelled.

4. The Inspection Report

The insurers generally verify the information obtained by an independent agency. Sometimes this investigation is conducted without the knowledge of the applicant. Today, the insurers have their own inspection staff who are generally known as inspectors or field officers or development officers. When the amount of insurance is not large, the inspectors make a general inquiry but when the amount is substantial, a deep and thorough inquiry of habits, character, social condition, occupation and health is required. In this case, the inspector interviews the applicant's neighbours, employers, bankers, business associates and other who have had special information pertaining to business, personal ethics, temperate habit, social behaviour and health.

The main advantage of this source is that the inspectors provide fair and frank information because they have no interest in the outcome of the case.

5. Private Friends Reports

The information from private friends is not generally required. But for some checking purposes, confidential reports of the friends of the proposer are considered. They are requested to reply those questions which are generally asked in agents report. Since friends are fully aware of the personal and private life of the proposer, they can give better information than the agents. But naturally the real friend does not want to harm his friend. So friends report may not always be correct.

6. Attending Physicians

The attending or family physicians can give better records of health, history of the proposed life and his family. It has been revealed that the family physicians have given true and fair reports of the required information by the insurers. The family physicians give the information only after charging a certain amount of fees.

7. Medical Information Bureau

The organisation commonly known as 'MIB' is an effective bureau for furnishing confidential medical reports. This bureau is common in U.S.A, but in India such bureau has not started. The insurers are members of this bureau and pay a certain fees annually. Sometimes they are required to pay commission for furnishing information. The MIB has recorded sufficient information of reputed and distinguished persons so the bureau is competent enough to report adequate and fair information.

8. Neighbours and Business Associates

Confidential reports about the applicant can be easily obtained from the neighbours and business associates although it may be prejudice to the extent of friendship or enemity with the proposer. The obtained information can be tallied with other information.

9. Commercial Credit Investigation Bureau

The bureau assembles financial and social information of businessmen. The credit worthiness is decided by the Bureau. The information given by the Bureau is treated confidential. These reports are expected to be correct and fair to a greater extent.

INSURANCE OF LADIES AND MINORS

Proposals on the lives of minor boys and girls who have not completed 15 years of age will be considered only under Children's Deferred Endowment Assurance and Children's Anticipated Plans. The proposals on the lives of minor boys and girls who have completed 15 years of age will be entertained only under Limited Payment Life Endowment Assurance, Double Endowment, Guaranteed Triple Benefit, Anticipated Whole Life, Convertible Whole Life Assurance, Children's Deferred Endowment. Assurance and Children's Anticipated Plans. Proposals under Progressive Protection Plan will be considered on the lives of minor boys and not girls provided they have completed 16 years of age. All such proposals will be entertained subject to medical examination except under Children's Deferred Endowment Assurance and Children's Anticipated Plans where the deferment term is 10 years or more.

The minor girls can get the benefits of insurance coverage subject to the condition that she should be studying in the school/college, the maximum limit of ₹ 1 lakh on total sum assured, usual extra-premium for sex if applicable, the amount of insurance would depend, *inter alia* on the financial status of the family and amount of insurance on the lives of parents, brothers and sisters.

The proposal form must be signed by the father/mother. In absence of both the parents, it will have to be signed by the legal guardian of the minor. A policy issued on the life of a minor under a plan of insurance, except the Plan Endowment, Children's Deferred Assurance or Children's Anticipated Plan will automatically vest in the life assured on his attaining the age of majority, provided no application for surrendering the policy is received before the date on which the life assured attains majority. A policy under Children's Deferred Assurance or Children's Anticipated Plan will vest in the life assured on the Deferred Date as per Special Provisions applicable to the policy and it is in no event assignable by the proposer before the Deferred Date. Such policy is not assignable by the proposer to any person other than the life assured. If the policy issued on the life of minor has vested in the life assured, the life assured may appoint a nominee/s or create an assignment thereof.

Precautions and Conditions. The treatment of proposals on the lives of ladies and minors should be made at extra precautions because physical and moral hazards are very high in such cases. The proposed lives should have a genuine need for life insurance, adequate income and employment, educational standard, marital status, social background etc. If the merit of proposal is unwarranted for acceptance on above grounds, the proposals may be rejected. The terms and conditions laid down for treatment of such proposals should be maintained.

The following rating is done for female lives under Endowment Assurance and Whole Life Plans.

Category of lives	*Rating*	*Amount of Maximum Insurance*
1. Woman with earned income	Same as in the case of men	Same as in the case of men.
2. Women with unearned income attracting income	— do —	Equal to 5 times her own average assessed income for the last 3 years but not exceeding the insurance

Category of lives	*Rating*	*Amount of Maximum Insurance*
tax or with sizeable personal properties likely to attract Estate Duty.		cover on husband's life or ₹ 5,00,000 whichever is lower. For Estate Duty purposes, upto the amount of estimated Estate Duty.
3. Women not covered by 1 and 2	Extra 3%	(*a*) *Single Woman*—On consideration of insurance needs, subject to maximum of ₹ 1,00,000; the actual amount would depend on the financial status etc., of the family and the father and other insurable members of the family being sufficiently insured.
		(*b*) *Married Women*—Not exceeding 3/4th of husband's insurance in force for full sum assured with a maximum of ₹ 2.50 lakhs.
		(*c*) *Widows*—On consideration of insurance needs.

No policy is issued under Convertible Term Assurance Plan to ladies.

Restrictions and Conditions. (1) Proposals for assurance on the lives of ladies who have not undergone a normal full time confinement are accepted with the first pregnancy clause. This clause may be removed on payment of a single-extra-premium of ₹ 5 per thousand. This clause may be waived in the case of ladies who may be expected to go to qualified doctors for delivery.

2. Proposals for assurance on the lives of ladies after a child birth are considered only six months after delivery. Where menstruation has not been re-established even after six months from the date of delivery the acceptance of proposals in such cases are subject to the one year pregnancy clause.
3. Proposals on the lives of ladies who are pregnant at the time of proposals are not enter-tained.
4. Proposals are not entertained on the lives of ladies who observe *purdah* whether full or partial.
5. Proposals are not entertained on the lives of ladies who have had many miscarriages.
6. Proposals are not entertained on the lives of those married ladies who, though not divorced, live separately from husbands as a matter of precaution against contracting an infectious disease from which the husband is suffering or for any other reason which raises reasonable doubts as to moral hazard.

JEEVAN BHARATI (TABLE NO. 160)

On International Women's Day, Life Insurance Corporation of India as a tribute to Indian women has launched an exclusive policy Jeevan Bharati. LIC has chosen the best way to honour women on this very special day by devising this very plan for them because LIC cares and understands the Indian Women.

Women excel everywhere—as anchor at home, achiever at work. They give life and LIC protects theirs. The woman takes care of so many lives that she is hardly ever left with time for her own. LIC's Jeevan Bharati Policy protects and nurtures her life.

All female lives including physically handicapped with certain conditions are covered. This policy is most suited for entrepreneurs and professionals like software engineers, doctors, managers, officials, self-employed, artists, salaried class, home-makers, students in the age group of about 18 to 50 years.

What is so exclusive about this plan?

1. Female Critical Illness (FCI) Cover

For the first time ever, FCI cover's for the women will be available under the umbrella of this plan. No other Indian Insurer has a product having such a unique inbuilt feature. It is indeed a brave step taken by LIC in corning out with Jeevan Bharati with additional benefits. In today's world, the most prevalent cancer among women is Breast and Ovarian Cancer, which are covered under this plan. FCI benefit offers 100% of Sum Assured (maximum ₹ 2 lakh) on diagnosis of such critical illness.

2. Congenital Disability Benefit (CDB) Cover

Some unfortunate women have to endure the pain of bringing up children born with congenital disabilities. To alleviate their hardships and to reimburse to a certain extent the expenses of treatment for rectifying the disability and the cost of bringing up such disabled child, CDB Cover offers 50% of Sum Assured (maximum ₹ 1 lack—upto 2 children).

The payment of FCI benefit or CDB does not restrict the original benefit *i.e.*, basic risk cover throughout the term and maturity benefit as well.

The plan provides for payment of 20% of Sum Assured at the end of 5 years and 10 years in case of 15 years' policy and at the end of 5, 10 and 15 years in respect of 20 years' policy. Balance Sum assured along with guaranteed addition at the rate of ₹ 50 per thousands Sum Assured for the first five years and thereafter, reversionary bonuses is payable on maturity of the policy. The policy provides an option to the female policyholder to retain survival benefit with LIC and withdraw it after its due date subsequently depending upon her need. This provision will take care of unforeseen contingencies like covering of medical expenses of family members, celebrating certain occasions like wedding, engagement, etc. of their beloved ones. The policyholders also exercise this option to plan for payment of fees of her child's education.

3. Another feature of this plan is option to receive maturity Proceeds in the form of an Annuity. People at advanced stage find it difficult to manage investment of lumpsum amount and at times there is an apprehension that the lumpsum amount may be spent on luxury items etc. Instead they prefer safety of investment with regular income. This option takes care of such women who may desire to have regular income for routine family maintenance without spending the capital amount.
4. Free risk cover for basic Sum Assured for three years in case of default of premiums after payment of the premiums for at least two years is another unique feature of this plan. The provision especially takes care of housewives and women with irregular income who may find it difficult to pay premium in unavoidable circumstances.
5. As the mode of payment of premium is yearly only, for the of convenience who may not be able to pay the premium in lumpsum, a provision to deposit premium in advance in maximum three instalments is also available under the plan.
6. In case of death of the policyholders during the term of the policy, basic Sum Assured along with guaranteed additions and reversionary bonuses, if any, is payable irrespective of survival benefits paid earlier.

The plan also provides for accident benefit and disability benefit upto an overall limit of ₹ 25 lakh Sum Assured.

Other Details

- Diseases covered under Critical Illness are Breast Cancer, Ovarian/Fallopian Tube Cancer, Cervical Cancer/Uterine Cancer/Vaginal/Vulval cancer.
- The Congenital Disabilities on the life of new born child include Downs Syndrome, Spina Bifida, Tetralogy of fallot, Oesophageal Atresia & Tracheoesophageal Fistula, Anal Atresia, Imperforate anus, Cleft Palate with or without Cleft Lip.
- Minimum and Maximum Sum Assured is ₹ 50,000 and ₹ 25 lakh (in multiples of ₹ 5,000) respectively.

- The plan is granted under Medical Scheme only.
- Being a money back plan, policy loan is not available.

(An attempt is made to give as much details as possible. For waiting period and exclusions, original circular/plan brochure please be referred).

Specimen Premium Calculation Under Jeevan Bharati (Table No. 160)

(I) Policy Particular

(*i*) Age of the Life Assured	:	30 years (last birthday)
(*ii*) Term	:	20 years
(*iii*) Sum Assured	:	₹2,00,000
(*iv*) Mode	:	Yearly

Premium Calculation:				(₹)
Tabular Premium for Basic Plan (Table 1)	:	71.45 × 200	=	14,290
Tabular Premium for Special Benefits of FCI Table (2)	:	1.35 × 200	=	270
Tabular Premium for Special Benefits of CDB (Table 3)	:	2.75 × 200	=	550
Total Tabular Premium	:			15,110
Less: Sum Assured Rebate for full Sum Assured	:			−400
Total Instalment Premium	:			14,710

(II) Policy Particulars:

(*i*) Age of the Life Assured	:	30 years (last birthday)
(*ii*) Term	:	20 years
(*iii*) Sum Assured	:	₹5,00,000
(*iv*) Mode:		Yearly

Premium Calculation:				
Tabular Premium for Basic Plan (Table 1)	:	71.45 × 500	=	35,725
Tabular Premium for Special Benefits of FCI (Table 2)	:	1.35 × 200*	=	270
Tabular Premium for Special Benefits of CDB (Table 3)	:	2.75 × 200*	=	550
Total Tabular Premium	:			36,555
Less: Sum Assured Rebate for full Sum Assured	:			−1,000
Total Instalment Premium				35,545

(*The maximum benefit available under FCI and CDB is ₹2,00,000/-).

Note:

1. The total instalment premium is to be rounded off to the nearest rupee.
2. CDB premium is payable upto age 40 years and hence the total instalment premium reduces by CDB premium from age 41 (e.g. in case (II) premium of ₹35,545 reduces by ₹550 from age 41).
3. Method in Case (II) is applicable for Sum Assured above ₹2 lacs.

NON-MEDICAL BUSINESS

Some lives are insured without undergoing medical examinations. It has been observed that medical examination may be clearly dispensed within insuring certain standard lives. There are *two* types of non-medical business: (1) Non-medical General Scheme, and (2) Non-Medical Special Scheme.

1. *Non-medical General Scheme.* Under Non-medical General Scheme, a special report is completed. The special report replaces the medical report and is prepared by those officers and agents who are related to the proponents.

Classes of lives acceptable. Male lives not more than 40 years nearer birthday are accepted for non-medical general schemes; but minors are not issued policies under this scheme. Illiterate male lives must have earned income for getting the benefits of this scheme and must be below 40 years.

Maximum Sum Assured. The maximum sum assured under this scheme is ₹ 7,500.

Types of Policies. Only Endowment, Double Endowment, Marriage Endowment, Educational Annuity, Limited Payment Endowment and Money Back Policies are issued under this scheme. The illiterate lives are insured with minimum lien of 50% during first 6 months and 25% during next six months. If lien is not desired Medical Examination will be necessary.

Maximum Age. The maximum age at maturity is 60 nearer birthday. The Maximum Policy Term is 25 years.

2. *Non-medical (Special) Scheme*. The Non-medical (Special) Scheme is available to males who are literate, not more than 45 years nearer birthday and are employed in special types of employment such as Government offices, Quasi-Government offices e.g., Municipalities, Distt. Boards, Local Boards: etc.; Schools, Hospitals etc. run by Government offices and Quasi-Government offices; State Corporations, Government Industrial Undertakings; Reputed Commercial Firms who keep accurate leave records and non-Government Industrial Undertakings on merit.

   Types of Policies. The Non-medical (Special) Scheme covers only Limited Payment Life, Endowment, Double Endowment, Marriage Endowment, Educational Annuity, Guaranteed Triple Benefits Convertible whole Life, Money Back, Progressive Protection and Anticipated Whole Life Policies.

   Maximum Sum. The maximum sum assured under this scheme is ₹ 20,000. The special condition for this scheme is that the employee should not be less than one year.

   Non-Medical (Special) Scheme to Commissioned Officers in Armed Forces. This scheme is available to Commissioned Officers in Armed Forces who are not more than 45 years.

   The types of policies as mentioned above are also available in this scheme. The maximum sum assured is ₹ 40,000. The Officer should not be put in lower category during the two years prior to the date of the proposal.

   The existing non-medical limits are based on the total sum assured under all plans taken together and once the limits are exhausted there is no further scope for taking policies under non-medical. The current basis as also the limits were reviewed and it has been decided to make the following revisions:

Basis for non-medical limits

The maximum limits are now based on sum under consideration *i.e.*, rated up sum assured during current and last calendar year (on the basis of date of commencement). Any insurance taken under non-medical business prior to the latest two calender years is not to be considered while deciding the eligibility under non-medical business.

Limits

The upper limits under non-medical business are revised upwards as shown below:

Non-medical (Special) Business

1. To Personal employed with length of service not less than one year in
   (*i*) Government and Quasi-Government Offices.
   (*ii*) Schools, Hospitals etc. run by Government/Quasi Government.
   (*iii*) State Corporations, Industrial Undertakings, Private schools, Colleges, etc.

Classes of Lives	*Maximum Sum Assured (based on SUC only)*
(*i*) Literate major males and SSC passed major females not aged over 45 years	₹ 8 lakhs Maximum aggregate basic sum assured under table nos. 88, 89, 103, 106, 107, 108, 121, and 150—₹ 2 lakhs.
(*ii*) Literate males and SSC passed females aged between 46 and 50 years	₹ 2 lakhs Maximum aggregate basic sum assured under table nos. 88, 89, 103, 106, 107, 108, 121 and 15—₹ 1 lakh. Maximum sum assured under Table-91—₹ 1 lakhs

2. Commissioned Officers in Armed Forces

(*i*) Length of service not less than one year.

(*ii*) Not below medical category A-1.

(*iii*) Not been placed in a lower category during the 2 years period prior to the date of proposal.

Classes of Lives	*Maximum Sum Assured (based on SUC only)*
(*i*) Commissioned Officer in armed forces not aged over 45 years	₹ 10 lakhs Maximum aggregate basic sum assured under table nos. 88, 89, 103, 106, 107, 108, 121, and 150—₹ 2 lakhs. Maximum sum assured under Table 91—₹ 2 lakhs
(*ii*) Commissioned Officer in armed forces aged between 46 and 50 years	₹ 4 lakhs Maximum aggregate basic sum assured under table nos. 88, 89, 103, 106, 107, 108, 121, and 150—₹ 1 lakhs. Maximum sum assured under Table 91—₹ 1 lakhs

Non-medical (General) business

1. Self-employed professionals

Chartered Accountants, Cost Accountants, Engineers, Architects, Management/Computer consultants, Doctors, Lawyers, Teachers, LIC Agents, etc.

Classes of Lives	*Maximum Sum Assured (based on SUC only)*
(*i*) Professionals not aged over 45 years	₹ 6 lakhs Table allowed are 5, 8, 14, 27, 48, 75, 90, 91, 93, 95, 152, 154, 155, 156, 157 Maximum sum assured under Table 91—₹ 1 lakhs
(*ii*) Professionals aged between 46-50 years	₹ 3 lakhs Tables allowed are 5, 8, 14, 27, 48, 75, 90, 91, 93, 95, 152, 154, 155, 156, 157 Maximum sum assured under T 91—₹ 50,000/-

2. Others

(*i*) Major males and literate females with own income (earned or (unearned) not\aged over 40 years	₹ 2 lakhs Tables allowed are 14, 48, 75, 90, 91, 93, 95, 154, 155, 156, 157 Maximum SA under T91—₹ 50,000/- Maximum maturity age for non-standard age proof: —65 years for endowment type —60 years for money back type Maximum term—25 years

(*ii*) Males and literate females with own income (earned or unearned) not aged between 40 and 45 years with standard age proof	₹ 1 lakhs Tables allowed are 14, 48, 75, 90, 91, 93, 95, 154, 155, 156, 157 Maximum SA under T91—₹ 50,000/- (Provisions of Circular Ref: Act 1/1775/4 dated 2nd January 2002 regarding self-declaration will remain unaltered)
(*iii*) Males and literate females with own income (earned or unearned) not aged between 46 and 50 years with standard age proof	₹ 40,000/- Tables allowed are 14, 48, 75, 90, 91, 93, 95, 154, 155, 156, 157

Non-medical (Express) business

Maximum sum under consideration—₹ 10 lakhs

Special Reports

Only sum under consideration (not modified SUC) will be the basis for calling for special reports. Where SUC is such that it falls within the limits of non-medical business, no special reports are to be called for.

Plans not allowed under non-medical business

Table Nos. 2, 43, 52, 58, 131, 133, 143, 153, 160.

All other existing rules in respect of non-medical schemes remain unaltered.

P.S.: All ages mentioned above are Nearer Birth Day.

CLASSES OF RISK

The various life risks cannot be treated individually, so they are put under a few broad categories based on the degree of each risk. There are *two* main classes of risk:

(*i*) Uninsurable Risks; and

(*ii*) Insurable Risks.

(*i*) *Uninsurable Risks*. If the insurance can be purchased at higher premium, there should not be any uninsurable risk. Theoretically, after investigating all the factors affecting a risk, the life insurance company should be able to give each due consideration and determining the premium charge for the insurance. Practically, however, there are a number of reasons why some persons are not insurable. The premium would be much high for these persons which will be against the insurance principle because higher premium will stimulate only to those who are at death bed. If they are allowed it would be a case of speculation because after payment of a few premiums he will be gaining. It would be unfair to other healthy policyholders. The second reason is that unknown risk cannot be insured to avoid the existing policyholders. So, in order to protect existing policy-holders, the insurance company must accept those risks against which it can assess adequate and fair premiums to provide for claims.

(*ii*) *Insurable Risks*. The insurable risks are those which after the selection process can be carried out by an insurer although there can be different terms and conditions for different policy-holders. There is a standard of risk, if the risk is not too great (*i.e.*, uninsurable) it can be insured as sub-standard risks even if he does not meet the requirement of a standard risk. The risk of death among sub-standard lives varies, but in all cases it is higher than that of standard lives. Insurable risks are divided into *three* broad classes—standard, sub-standard and super-standard. Every insurer, however, does not use all these classifications. Generally distinction between standard and super-standard is not made.

(a) *Standard Risk.* The standard risk is related with the normal life where there is no much or no less risk. There is certain criteria on which the risks are judged as normal life. It does not refer to ideal or first class life but it is rather a mix of good and bad lives. This group does not contain only those persons who are free from all impairments nor those persons who are under serious illness. It is the group where majority of the persons can be included and who may be either more or less than the average.

(b) *Sub-Standard Risk.* Sub-standard risks are those risks which are higher though insurable than the standard risk. Thus, the sub-standard risks are above the standard risk and below the uninsurable risk. If the life proposed crosses the maximum limit of sub-standard risk, that will be treated as uninsurable. The sub-standard risk is insured after payment of additional premium. This has been discussed in detail in chapter on Treatment of sub-standard risk.

(*iii*) *Super-Standard Risk.* The super-standard risk is present where there is lesser risk than the standard risk. This is also called a *preferred risk*. An insurer does not prefer to issue preferred risk policies because it increases the premium on other standard risk which may cause reduction in loss of business.

METHODS OF RISK CLASSIFICATION

There are two methods of classification of risk. First, the judgment method and second, the numerical rating system.

1. The Judgment Method

Under this method the individual decisions of experienced persons, in the medical, actuarial, underwriting and other departments are combined. These persons are qualified and permitted to take decision. Unlike the other method, no rigid rules and scales are prescribed and followed. Personal judgment, therefore, plays vital part in the whole system of underwriting. Under this system the routine cases are processed with a minimum of consideration by assistants trained in the review of applications and doubtful or significant cases or border line cases are resolved by experts who take the decision on their experience and general impressions. This method is still used in India by the Life Insurance Corporation.

The judgment method is generally used where a single factor is to be considered or where the decision for acceptance or rejection is to be taken. The second use of this method is that where numerical rating fails to decide, this method comes to much assistance because the merit of each and every factor is personally considered. The personal decision of the officers and experts may be quick and significant. The various difference in the reports, thorough inquiries is made and personal judgment is substituted by the other method.

The disadvantage of this method is that the personal direction may be biased by the whims and negligence of the officers. Inexperienced decision may harm the insurance business. The second criticism is that it is not very much scientific. There is no basis except the personal experience, for taking correct decision.

To avoid the weaknesses of the judgment method, a method known as the numerical rating system was devised and is commonly used by the insurers.

2. Numerical Rating System

This system is based upon the principle that a large number of factors enter into the composition of a risk and that the impact of each of these factors on the longevity of the risk can be determined by a statistical study of lives possessing that factor. It assumes that a standard risk has a rating of 100. Each factor has 100 if they are standard and no marks will be assigned. Information for each factor one by one is considered. Favourable factors are assigned negative values called *credits* while unfavourable factors are assigned positive values called *debits*. The particular percentages to be added or deducted for each factor will depend upon the degree of its variation from the situation assumed for the normal risk and the experience of each insurer. The algebraic summation of the debits and credits added to the per value of 100 represents the numerical value of risk. In practice, value are generally assigned to the important factors such as build, physical condition, personal history, family history, occupation, residence, habits, moral and plan. The value assigned to the various factors are on the basis of mortality. For example, if the mortality experience of a group of insured lives with a particular medical history reflected a certain degree of overweight has been found to be 135 per cent of that among all standard risk, a debit (+) of 35 marks will be assigned to such medical history. Similarly, the degree of risk on the basis of each factor is evaluated in terms of percentage. If it is more than 100, *i.e.*, if the risk is more than the standard the extra percentage will be debited (+) and if the degree of risk expressed in percentage is less than the 100, the lesser percentage will be credited (–) up to the difference.

One example of numerical rating system will make it clear. A married man having two children of the age 3.2 has good physical condition. He is over-weight by 60 per cent. His expanded chest measurement is one inch less than the girth of his abdomen. He has no indication of adverse effect on longevity. His family was from tuberculosis, insanity etc. He was working as blacksmith. His habits and morals are good. He lives in a posh house in good surrounding. The plan of insurance is twenty-year endowment. According to following table, he is given 60 marks in debit (+) side for overweight. The unfavourable build (girth greater than chest expanded) is a basis of an additional debit of 10 marks. The family history is favourable which has been given him 15 marks in credit side. The plan of insurance 20-year's endowment would call for an additional credit of 10 marks. The residence, habits, good behaviour, occupation and physical conditions have no credit marks, only debit marks are assigned to these.

Table 8.1

Factory	*Debit* (+)	*Credit* (–)
1. Build (Overweight)	60	—
2. Physical condition (Favourable)	—	—
3. Build unfavourable (Chest in lesser the girth)	10	—
4. Family History (Superior)	—	15
5. Occupation: favourable	—	—
6. Residence: normal	—	—
7. Habits and morals: favourable	—	—
8. Plan of insurance 20 year's endowment	—	10
	70	25

Net rating = 70 – 25 = 45

So, Total Rating 100 + 45 = 145

Extra Premium	₹ per thousand of sum assured.
1. For unfavourable occupation	2/-
2. For Higher Rating	2/-

145 – 125 = 20

Age and occupation are separately valued, so they are excluded from the rating table.

The rating, thus, makes it easier to classify the risk.

Super-standard/	Standard/sub-Standard/	Uninsurable
75	125	500

If the rating is below 75, it is generally treated as super-standard and if the rating is between 75 and 125, it is standard risk, if the rating is more than 125 and below 500, it is sub-standard and the rating of more than 500 is uninsurable. The degree of rating for classification may vary from insurer to insurer.

The numerical rating system follows the same procedures as that is followed by those who judge a risk with only difference of allotting marks. The same factors are considered and the final decision is based upon the relationship of the various favourable and unfavourable features of the risk. The numerous method is objective standards which assist in the final valuation of risk and makes for greater consistence of decision. The method expedites the handling of cases and holding done the expense of the selection process. It enables to make decision on the medico-acturial investigation and reduces the operation of the subjective factor in the under-writing of risks to a minimum. The basic ratings are continuously reviewed in the height of up-to-date trends in insurance.

Various criticisms have been levied on the system. The system is thought to be too arbitrarian. There are many impairments concerning which knowledge is too limited to permit the assignment of numerical values. The interrelated factors are non-additive. Too many minor debits and credits are taken into account in evaluating risk. Ratings have often to be modified by taking into account the interaction of various aspect of the risk and in particular, the probable influence on the risk of occupation, habits, mode of living, socio-economic status, moral hazard, etc.

Supporters of the system recognise its flaws but fell that it is still superior to any other method. The numerical ratings arrived at can only be regarded as a guide, and the selection of risk depends to a considerable extent on the individual judgment and skill of the medical examiner, actuaries and underwriting officers of the life insurance business.

QUESTIONS

1. What is risk and how risk is determined in life insurance?
2. Critically examine the various factors affecting risk. From where these information of risk is obtained ?
3. Examine the 'Judgments Method' and Numerical rating system of evaluating risk.
4. What are the various classes of life insurance risk?
5. Explain in detail (*a*) Proposal form, (*b*) Medical Examination, (*c*) Proof of age, and (*d*) Insurance of female lives.

9

MEASUREMENT OF RISK AND MORTALITY TABLE

The risks are measured or evaluated for fixation of premium be charged by the insurer. There are *two* methods of calculation of Premium: (*i*) Value of Service, (*ii*) Cost of Service.

(*i*) *Value of Service.* The value of service determines the rate of premium according to the utility of insurance to each proponent. Since, the value or utility to each person differs, the premium rate will also vary. The *value of service* principle cannot be used in insurance because its utility to each individual cannot be determined. Moreover, the value is higher to the proper section of society and to the head of large family; but they cannot be charged higher premium than the premium charged by richer class of the society. Moreover, the higher premium will not attract business from them. The value of service cannot be used due to its impracticability.

(*ii*) *Cost of Service.* In fact, the premium should be charged according to cost to the insurer. In insurance demand side does not play important role. Therefore, it is called that the insurer is no bought, but it is sold. So, the insurer must fix the cost or premium to be charged on a particular risk or policy. Insurance business may carry on only when the cost of insurance is met. The cost includes all expenses of the business plus small profit margin. Above the profit margin, insurer is not expected to gain. This is the reason that insurance business is expected to run on 'no loss, no gain', basis. The most important cost to insurer is cost of claim. Therefore, the insurer must charge at least so much of premium that can be used to pay the full amount of claim. Technically, the premium charged to meet the amount of claim, is called *net premium*. Another cost to insurer is cost of administration. It includes all expenses of management and other amount for provisions of contingency. The cost of administration may be of *two* types, (*i*) fixed cost, and (*ii*) recurring cost. The fixed cost is spread over the policy-life but the recurring expenses do not involve much problem of allocation. The method of distribution of the expenses is called loading which, is discussed in detail in a separate chapter. With the help of loading net premium is enhanced to charge a fixed amount regularly from the policy-holders, which is called gross premium or office premium. So, the first problem before the insurer is to calculate the cost of claims.

Cost of Claims

The claims may arise at the death of the life assured or at the of the policy. In annuity contract the payment shall continue to death therefore, the expectation of survival will be the basis of the cost. In life insurance, in most cases, payment of claims depends upon the death. The death is certain but when it will take place is not certain.

Therefore, the main problem before the insurer is to decide when the death will take place. The forecasting of death is very important factor to decide the period and amount of claim. If the period and amount of claims have been decided, the premium can be easily calculated. The forecasting of death can be done on (*i*) experience of medical science, and (*ii*) On the experience of past records. If the medical science of insurance has been sufficiently advanced and its knowledge could be perfectly used, the same, then, might have projected the time of death of each applicant. The medical science can be useful to modify the past experience according to the present mortality prospects. The insurer bases the calculating of time of death on the basis of experience of past death with certain modification in special cases. The insurer has to rely upon the past experience which is treated as a basis for germinating future mortality. It has been assumed that there is law of mortality on the basis of which deaths have been taking place in future. Evidently, the death of one life cannot be forecasted; but the expectation of a number of deaths from a group of persons of the same age can be forecasted on the basis of (*i*) Theory of probability and (*ii*) The law of large numbers.

Theory of Probability

The theory of probability reveals the possibility of occurring a certain event or not occurring a certain event out of the given events. Thus, in insurance, the theory of probability reveals the chances of death of a person out of a group of persons. The theory of probability can be of three types: (*i*) certainty, (*ii*) simple probability and (*iii*) compound probability.

1. Certainty

The probability of certainty is expressed as one. It means the chance of happening a certain event, say death, is 100 per cent. It sure that the death will occur in this expression. Naturally factor, *i.e.*, certainty is taken as the, basis of comparison. In other words, the chance of death is related with the unity or one or certainty.

2. Simple Probability

When the events are mutually exclusive or when only event is present, the probability will be known as simple probability. For example; if at the age of 40, 2 persons die out of 10,000 the probability of death of a person, who is of 40 years, can be expressed as:

$$\frac{2}{10,000} = .02 \text{ per cent or} = 0.0002 \text{ of units.}$$

Generally, the probability is expressed in term of unity or one, *i.e.*, the probability is related with one which can be expressed in the decimals. Similarly, if there are more than one person and the death rate of each person is to be calculated separately, the simple probability is applied. For example, if there are two persons of ages 40 and 42 years the causes of death of one person only can be expressed as probability of death of first person plus probability of death of second person.

3. Compound Probability

Multiplication is a applied when the probability of the combined happening of two or more independent events, if the probabilities their separate happening are known when two or more events occur together, their joints occurrence is called compound event. For example; if the probability of death of A at the age of 40 is 0.002 and the probability of death of B at the age of 42 is 0.0003, the compound probability shall be calculated when we are required to know the probability of death of any of the persons. Thus, the probability of death of any of the, persons, will be $0.0002 \times 0.0003 = 0000006$. In insurance, the simple probability is generally used to calculate death rate of one person.

Estimation of Probability

The probability can be estimated whether (*i*) Priori basis and or (*ii*) Posteriori basis.

(*i*) *Priori Basis.* In this case, the probability is estimated merely on the basis of knowledge. It is not derived after experiment or practice. It is also called deductive reasoning where estimation is based on from general to particular. Although it is not exirically tested, but it is useful to correct the defects of experimental probability where the probability not expected to give hundred per cent correct results. It is well known fact that the death rate after 50 years, will not decline but it will go on increasing year after year. If in any year there is fluctuation in mortality which has been calculated on the basis of experiment that is corrected with the help of interpolation or graphical method. Thus, the apriori, probability is of much use in such circumstances.

(*ii*) *Posteriori Probability.* The probability in this case is calculated on the basis of experiment. It is also called as Inductive method because in this case, estimation is based from particular to general. The posterioi probability can give correct result only when the experiment involves a large number of units and the data are correct. In mortability estimation we cannot depend merely on the posteriori probability because cent per cent accuracy and universal experiment are not possible.

Hundred per cent correct results. It is well known fact that the death after 30 years will not decline but it will go on increasing year after year. If in any year there is fluctuation in mortality which has been calculated on the basis of experiment that is correct.

Law of Large Numbers

The accuracy of probability depends on two factors:

(*i*) Accuracy of data;

(*ii*) The large number of units.

The important fact to be considered is that the probable experience should be nearest to the actual experience. If there is difference between the actual and probable experience, the probability will be of no use. To avoid this deviation or difference, the data of estimation should be accurate enough and the experiment should base on a large number. It has been observed that the larger the number, the lesser the deviation between actual and probable estimation. So far calculating death rate or mortality rate a large number of persons should be selected and their age should be correctly recorded.

MORTALITY TABLE

Definition

Mortality table is such data which records the past mortality and is put in such form as can be used in estimating the course of future data. Thus the mortality table is to predict future mortality. It is also described as the picture of a generation of individuals passing through time. A large number of persons are selected and served for death and survival rated till all of them is dead.

Features

(*i*) Observation of Generation

In preparation of mortality table persons of a generation (*i.e.*, persons of a single age) are selected and they are observed up to death. No new entries or withdrawals are assumed at any stage of the study.

(*ii*) Start from a point

The mortality table starts from a point, which depends on the requirement of the insurer, and will continue up to the point all of them has been dead.

(*iii*) Yearly Estimation

The mortality table records the yearly death or survival rate. Each and every year is considered for calculating the rates.

(*iv*) Mortality and Survival Rates

The mortality and survival rates of the generation who are selected at a particular age are considered each and every year. Any table giving mortality rates only is not mortality, table unless mortality rate of a generation is calculated every year. Each year's number, living is the previous year's number of living minus previous year's number dying and, therefore, as persons go on dying year after year the number of living goes on shrinking till it is reduced to zero and modality table ends there.

CONSTRUCTION OF MORTALITY TABLE

The best method of construction of mortality table will be to select a large number of persons at attained age. Attained age means age nearer to birth date. For example, persons of 19 years 6 months to 20 years 5 months and 29 days will be treated as the age of 20 years. The attained age will be selected at which policy is to begin. The selected persons of the attained age will be observed and the number of deaths will be recorded during a year till the persons selected are dead. Theoretically speaking this type mortality table will be the actual mortality table. The number of death in a year is deducted from the number of living at the beginning of year to get the number of living in the begining of the ne year.

Criticism

(*i*) Preparation of such table is difficult because a large number of persons or an attained age is impracticable to get.

(*ii*) Constant, watch on them is not possible.

(*iii*) It will require a long-period to construct the table and for which a permanent officer, say for about 100 years, is required.

(*iv*) A lot of money and time will be wasted to record number of deaths every time.

(*v*) However, if such impossibilities are dared to do the mortality table will be quite obsolete because it had been constructed at least within 100 years during, which a lot of changes might have occurred.

Age	*Number of Living*	*Number of Death*	*Death Rate*	*Survivers Rate*
20	10,00,000	2,000	0.002	0.998
21	9,98,000	3,000	0.003	0.997
22	9,95,000	4,000	0.004	0.996

CONSTRUCTION OF DEATH RATE ON YEARLY BASIS

To avoid the above difficulties, death rate is calculated on yearly basis. The death rate is calculated for every age. Separate sample is taken for each age. The number of living in each age is observed and number of death during the age is recorded. By dividing number of death by number of living in each age, the death rate for the age is calculated. A year is selected because a year constitute various types of weather and, therefore, low, high and normal mortalities are averaged in the year. Secondly, rates of premium in insurance are quoted on an yearly basis and so the cost depending on mortality showed also be based on yearly basis.

SOURCES OF MORTALITY INFORMATION

For construction of mortality table, number of living of the beginning of each age and the number of deaths during the age are required. The mortality table should be constructed to represent the past experience as accurately as possible. So the figures of mortality construction should be as accurate as possible and based on a large number of persons. The sources of mortality construction can be obtained either from (*i*) population statistics, and (*ii*) records of life insurers.

Population Statistics

The insurer gets number of living at each age from the census records and the number of deaths from municipal and other death records. The population statistics will reveal how many persons have died at what age. So, with the radix of total number of persons at the beginning, it can be calculated how many died in a particularly age. The calculation of mortality table on this basis is not very easy and correct.

Criticism

The population statistics is not very much useful to insurers. It was applied only when there was no insurance experience in this field.

(*i*) The accuracy of population statistics is doubtful in absence of age-proof. There has been over-estimation or under-estimation in several cases. Sometimes, members of a certain section of society are unaware of ages.

(*ii*) It has been also noticed that some deaths are unrecorded. It is difficult to know exactly how many deaths are unrecorded and similarly. It is also difficult to know exactly how many deaths occurred a particular age.

(*iii*) Census figures are available only after 10 years and therefore, it would not be very recent figure. A particular census figure may be biased with the abnormality of the year.

(*iv*) Interpolation and extrapolation are involved and correct figures are generally not known.

(*v*) The population statistics will give statistics of all types persons without any separation while the insurer requires mortality of only insurable lives. Mortality for standard and substandard lives are required separately.

2. Records of Insurers

The records of insurer give a correct figure because the death rates can be correctly recorded. No death will go unrecorded, correct number of persons living and dead for each age can be known. Collection of figures is done from the records of as many insurers as possible in large numbers but is not more than 10 years covering, favourable and favourable years. Generally 10-year period may be quite sufficient. The abnormal years are excluded from the sample. Separate mortality tables may be prepared for standard lives, sub-standard lives, female and male lives. Sub-classification according to sex, marital status, occupation, geographical area, class may be made and tables are constructed separately.

The counting of persons is done very cautiously, withdraw and lapsation are excluded. Persons included for calculation caused exposed to risk. If the calculation starts at the withdrawal from this number is excluded.

Yearwise aggregation of number of deaths and number of loving persons is done from the information of all insurers. Mortality rate at every age will be counted by dividing the number of expired lives by number of exposed lives.

CONSTRUCTION OF MORTALITY TABLE

An example is taken for construction of mortality table. For example 10,000 persons are taken at age 20,2,000 persons at age 21,5,000 persons at age 22 and so on. The number of deaths observed at these ages are 20, 80 and 15 respectively. Therefore the death rate will be 0.002, 0.004 and 0.003 respectively at this stage and the death rate is calculated by the formula.

$$\text{Death rate} = \frac{\text{Number of deaths during the year}}{\text{Number of living at the begining of the year}}$$

Table 9.1 Yearly Death

Age	*Number of Living*	*Number of Death*	*Death Rate*	*Survivers Rate*
20	10,000	20	0.002	0.002
21	20,000	80	0.004	0.003
22	5,000	15	0.003	0.004
23	10,000	60	0.006	0.005
24	20,000	100	0.005	0.006

Crude and Graduated Mortality Rates

It has been observed on the basis of the theoretical analysis that the death rate normally decreases gradually from 1 to 10 years age. It increases thereafter and fastly increases after the age of 50. The yearly death rate may not be given the same phenomena because (*i*) the generation of an age is not observed. Different persons at different ages are observed, (*ii*) there may not be a large numbers for observation, and (*iii*) the date may be cent per cent correct. Therefore, there may be fluctuation in the death rate. Therefore, the death rates calculated on yearly basis having fluctuations are called Crude Death Rate. This death rate is not used for calculation of premium due to absence of a certain trend.

The graduated Mortality Rates are those which are obtained by smoothing the fluctuations of crudes rate. The smoothing or graduation is done with the help of interpolation or graphical methods. The above crude death rate is graduated by the graphical methods as below:

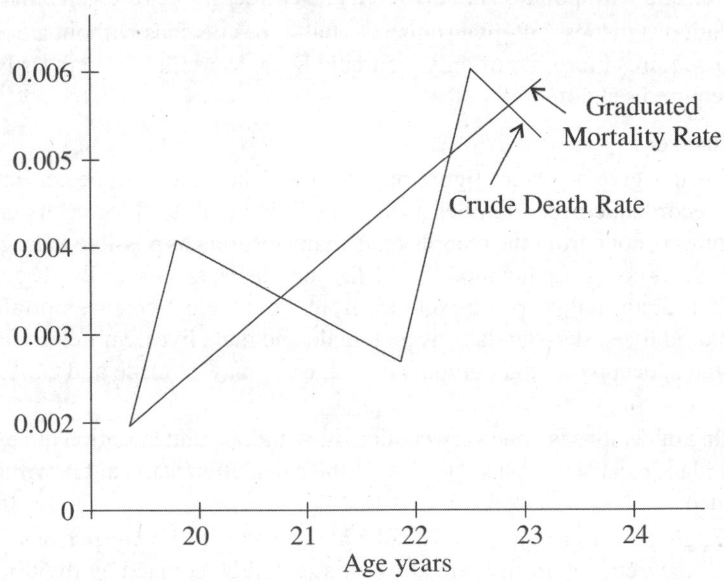

The graduated mortality rate is used for construction of mortality table. Assumption of a large number of persons at the radix is made.

Table 9.2 Mortality Table

Age	*Number of Living*	*Number of Death*	*Mortality Rate*	*Survival Rate*
x	l_x	dx	qx	$px = 1 - qx$
20	10,00,000	2,000	0.002	0.998
21	9,98,000	2,994	0.003	0.997
22	9,95,006	3,980	0.004	0.996
23	9,91,026	4,955	0.005	0.995
24	9,86,065	5,716	0.006	0.994

The number of death at a particular age is calculated by multiplying number of living at the age with the, mortality rate. Thus, $dx = 1x \times qx$. Here at age 20 the $d_{20} = 1_{20} \times q_{20} = 10,00,000 \times 0.002 = 2,000$. Similarly the number of living persons to the net age is calculated by deducting number of death s from the number of living persons during the age.

$$1_{21} = 1_{20} - d_{20} = 10,00,000 - 2,000 = 9,98,000$$

The graduated mortality rate is not sufficient to calculate or the death rate or survival rate after a certain period, so the number of living and number of deaths at every age are calculated. This makes possible to calculate the death or survival rate, after a certain period. For example, the death rate of a person aged 20 after 3 years cart be calculated as—

$$q_{x+3} = \frac{1x - 1x + 3}{1x}$$

$$q_{20+3} = \frac{1_{20} - 1_{20+3}}{1_{20}}$$

$$q_{20+3} = \frac{10,00,000 - 9,19,026}{10,00,000}$$

$$= 0.008974$$

The Annuity Tables are also constructed besides the life table as discussed above. The only difference is that the Annuity Table will last 5 or 10 years longer to the Life Mortality Table which is commonly known as *Mortality Table.*

A Complete Mortality Table

Apart from the ordinary mortality table, the insurer uses complete mortality table. All the components of complete mortality table are discussed in the following mortality table.

H^m Maikaham Graduation Mortality Table

Age	*No. of Living at x*	*No. of Deaths between x and x + 1*	*Death Rate*	*Survival Rate*	*Force of Mortality at age x*	*No. of Survival at min age lx and lx + 1*	*Total Survival No.*	*Complete Expectation of life at age x*	*Age*
Age	*No. of*	*No. of*	*Death*	*Survival*	*Force of*	*No. of*	*Total*	*Complete*	*Age*
x	l_x	dx	$q_x = \frac{dx}{l_x}$	$p_x = 1 - q_x$	U_x	$Lx = ½ (l_x + l_{x+1})$	$T_x = \Sigma L_x$	$^{o}e_x = \frac{T_x}{L_x}$	x
20	96061	548	0.00572	0.99428	0.00550	95787	4044238	42.101	20
21	95513	582	0.00608	0.99392	0.00592	95222	3948451	41.339	21
22	94931	609	0.00643	0.99357	0.00629	94626	3853229	40.590	22
23	94322	631	0.00668	0.99332	0.00659	94007	3758603	39.849	23
24	93691	647	0.00691	0.99309	0.00682	96367	3664596	39.114	24

1. ***Column* (x).** Column x denotes the age of the prospect. The mortality table can start from any age and continue to 100 to 120 years, as required by the insurer.
2. ***Column* (l_x).** This column indicates the number of living persons at the beginning of each year. If the table starts from age 0, the number in the l_x column against this age that is to say l_0 is any convenient number like 9,000,000 or even an arbitrary number and represents the number of persons of age 0 *i.e.,* the number of persons just born. Having fixed the starting number l_0, any other number l_x in the column appearing against age x gives the number of persons living, out of the l_o persons born, who reach age x. All mortality tables may not start with age 0. If the table starts with, say age 30, any number can be assumed, for the starting value of the l_x column *i.e.,* for l_{30}. The figures in the l_x column have a meaning in relation to the starting value like l_0, l_{30} etc. and it is wrong to describe l_x as the number of persons living who are of age x in a given population.

3. **Column (dx).** Number of persons dying between x and $x + 1$ are given under this column. The difference $l_x - l_x + 1$ is the number of persons who die between ages x and $x + 1$. Thus, $dx = l_x - l_x + 1$.

   So, we get $l_x + 1 = l_x - dx$. The next value of the l_x column *i.e.*, $l_x + 1$ can be obtained by subtracting dx, from l_x. This process continues until all the living number are dead or the mortality table is completed. Thus, the sum of all the deaths on and after age x to the extreme age w is equal to the number living at that age.

4. **Column (q_x).** This column indicates the probability of death. It gives for successive values of x the probability that a person aged x dies within one year *i.e.*, before reaching age $x + 1$. Thus, the death rate or mortality at age x is equal to number of deaths at age x divided by the number of living at age x or $q_x = \frac{dx}{l_x} = \frac{l_x - l_{x+1}}{l_x}$. So, $dx = l_x + q_x$; the values of dx can be found from the corresponding l_x by multiplying l_x by the rate of mortality q_x. Except at the very young rates, the rate of mortality (q_x) increases as age (x) advances. At the extreme age (w) the mortality will be equal to 1 as $q_{w-1} = \frac{l_{w-1} - l_w}{l_{w-1}} = 1$ as $l_w = 0$.

5. **Column (p_x).** The column (p_x) indicates the rate of survival. It gives for successive ages the probability that a life aged x survives to age $x + 1$. Thus, the probability of survival (p_x) is equal to number of survivors to age $x + 1$ divided by total number living at age x. Hence, $p_x = \frac{l_{x+1}}{l_x}$.

   Except at very young ages, the value of p_x decreases as x increases *i.e.*, probability of survival decreases as age advances.

   So,
$$q_x = \frac{dx}{l_x} = \frac{l_x - l_{x+1}}{l_x}$$
$$= 1 - \frac{l_{x+1}}{l_x} = 1 - p_x$$

   It is also known as $p_x = 1 - q_x$

   The mortality table can be used for calculating the various probabilities of survival and death.

   (*a*) np_x. The probability that a person aged x survivers n years is denoted by np_x. So, this probability is equal to the number of persons living at age $x + n$ divided by number of persons living at age x. *i.e.*, $np_x = \frac{l_{x+n}}{l_x}$.

   (*b*) m/q_x. The probability that a person aged x dies within the next m years is denoted by mq_x. This probability is equal to number of death within m years out of persons now aged x divided by number of persons living at age x *i.e.*, $\frac{l_x - l_{x+m}}{l_x} = 1 - \frac{l_{x+m}}{l_x} = 1 - mp_x$.

   (*c*) m/q_x. It is the probability that a person aged x dies in the year of age $x + m$ to $x + m + 1$.

   This is equal to $m/q_x = \frac{dx + m}{l_x}$.

   It is different from $\frac{d_{x+m}}{l_{x+m}}$ *i.e.*, q_{x+m}

It can be expressed as:

$$m/q_x = \frac{d_{x+m}}{l_x} = \frac{l_{x+m}}{l_x} \cdot \frac{d_{x+m}}{l_{x+m}}$$

$$= mp_x \cdot q_{x+m}$$

6. Force of Mortality (U_x). The force of mortality at age x is denoted by U_x. The force of mortality at age x can thus be defined as the limiting value of the nominal yearly rate of mortality at age x, over a small interval of time d_t as the length of interval d_t, tends to zero. In practice the smallest interval we can consider is one day *i.e.*, $d_t = 1/365$ days of a year. The deaths between age x and $x + \frac{1}{365}$ are $(l_x - l_{x+1/365})$ and the rate of mortality at age x per day is $\frac{l_x - l_{(x+1/365)}}{l_x}$ and the corresponding yearly rate is

$$\frac{l_x - l_{(x+1/365)}}{\frac{1}{365} l_x} = \frac{365\,(l_x - l_{x+1/365})}{l_x}$$

7. No. of survival at mid age x and $x + 1$ (L_x). The number of persons in the population between ages x to $x + 1$ is denoted by L_x. Thus,

$$L_x = \tfrac{1}{2}\,(l_x + l_{x+1}) = l_{x+1/2}$$

Also, $l_{x+1} = l_x - d_x$ and hence, $L_x = \tfrac{1}{2}\,(l_x + l_x - d_x) = l_x - \tfrac{1}{2}\,d_x$

8. Total Number of Survival (T_x). The total number of survival at any age is equal to summation of number of persons living between mid age x to the end of the table. Thus,

$$T_x = L_x + L_{x+1} + L_{x+2} \cdots L_{w-1}$$

In particular, T_0 represents the whole population at all ages and is given by:

$$T_0 = L_0 + L_1 + L_2 \ldots\ldots$$

$$= \frac{1}{2}[(l_0 + l_1) + (l_1 + l_2) + \ldots\ldots]$$

$$= \frac{1}{2} l_0 + (l_1 + l_2 + l_3 + \ldots\ldots)$$

$$= \frac{1}{2} l_0 + N'_0$$

where $N'_0 = \quad = l_2 + l_2 + l_2 \ldots\ldots\ldots\ldots l_w$

9. Complete Expectation of Life at age x ($°e_x$). This column is known as the complete expectation of life denoted by the symbol $°e_x$. The expectation of life (e_x) is the average number of complete years of life lived by each person aged x, after reaching age x. It is an average obtained by dividing by l_x, the total number of future years of life lived by the l_x persons. The total number of completed years lived by l_x persons after reaching age x is given by $(l_{x+1} + l_{z+2} \ldots\ldots)$ which is denoted by N'_x. The expectation of life will be obtained by dividing this quantity N'_x by l_x. Thus

$$e_x = N'_x / l_x$$

This expectation of life is called the curtate expectation of life as it takes into account only complete years of life lived and ignores fraction of the year lived in the year of death. If fractions are taken into account we get the complete expectation of life denoted by $°e_x$. The additional number of years of life to be included in respect of the fractional years lived is equal to $\frac{1}{2}(d_x + d_{x+1}........) = \frac{1}{2}l_x$. Therefore, the total number of years lived by the l_x persons, taking fractions of a year into account is:

$$N'_x + \frac{1}{2}l_x$$

The complete expectation of life at age x *i.e.*, $°e_x$ is obtained dividing this quantity by l_x. Thus,

$$°e_x = \frac{N'_m + \frac{1}{2}l_x}{l_x} = \frac{T_x}{l_x}$$

Types of Mortality Tables

There are three types of mortality tables: (*i*) Aggregate Table. (*ii*) Select Table, and (*iii*) Ultimate Table.

(*i*) *Aggregate Table.* A table constructed without distinguishing the select, and ultimate lives is called an Aggregate Mortality Table. The lives from which the mortality rates of the aggregate lives are derived being a mixture of the 'Select' lives and Utimate lives, the aggregate rates lie between the select and ultimate rates for the same age attained, that is to say, they are lighter than ultimate rates but heavier than the select rates. This is also called Mix or General Mortality Tables. In this table persons of same age irrespective of the consideration whether they were insured at age 30 or some years before the age 30. The above table is the example of aggregate table.

This table is used where no selection is required, or non-medical policies are issued. This table is also used in Group Insurance.

2. *The Select Table.* Mortality table giving rate depending on both age and duration elapsed since entry are called, select mortaility tables. Thus, persons taking policies at different ages ,are separate from each other for the purpose of the calculation, even though they all may be of the same age now. This is done because mortality rate among them will not be the same despite the same attained age. It will vary according to the duration of insurance because at the initial stage, all the policy-holders are selected after a thorough inquiry of health. The method to select, only insurable live is called 'Selection'. It has been observed that the effect of this selection wears out quickly and that two groups of persons so seleeted at different times will not experience the same mortality though they are of the same age. The group which has been selected first now is found to experience lighter mortality than another of the age at present but selected some time ago. The effect of selection may be eliminated altogether after a certain pariod *i.e.*, 5 years.

Table 9.3 Mortality Rate per 1000 (d_x)*

Age	*Years of insurance*					*6 years*	*Age*
	1	*2*	*3*	*4*	*5*	*& over*	*attained*
20	2.73	3.59	3.80	3.96	4.13	4.31	25
21	2.78	3.66	3.86	4.01	4.18	4.35	26
22	2.83	3.72	3.91	4.07	4.21	4.38	27
23	2.86	3.76	3.06	4.08	4.24	4.41	28

* Life Insurance by O.S. Gupta Page, 139

The above table shows that the mortality, rate is 2.86 per, thousand at age 23 during 1 year after selection, 3.72 per thousand at 22 during 2 years after selection, 3.86 per thousand at age 21 during 3 years after selection and 3.96 per thousand at age 20 during 4 years after selection. Thus, it reveals that as the selection period passes the mortality rate increases although they are of the same age at present. The effect of selection is removed after 5 years and the mortality rate will be approximately equal if there are not approximately the same, there will be a case of spurious selection, *i.e.*, where effect of selection is not required.

Form a Select Table

It should be noted that in the select table the values of number of living at each are not related. Thus, $l_{(x)}, l_{(x+1)}, l_{(x+2)}$...... will not be interlinked as bas been observed earlier, but $l_{(x)+1}, l_{(x)+2}$ will be linked together.

Table 9.4 Select Mortality Table

Age	*Number of living*	*Number of Death*	*Death Rate per thousand*
X	l_z	l_x	*l*
35	1,00,000	316	3.16
35 + 1	99,684	428	4.29
35 + 2	99,256	454	4.57
35 + 3	99,802	474	4.80
36	1,00,000	323	3.23
36 + 1	99,677	411	4.42

Select table is useful where lowest and accurate death rates required. It has been used for calculating short-term and participating policies.

3. *Ultimate Morlality table.* A mortality table in which the rates in the select period are omitted and only the ultimate rates are tabulated is called an ultimate mortality tables. In other words, figures for policies that still have the effects of selection are not included. In the above example, the mortality rates for the years will not be included for preparing an ultimate mortality table.

Table 9.5 Ultimate Mortality Table

Age at entry	*6 and over*	*Age attained*
20	4.31	25
21	4.35	26
22	4.38	27
23	4.41	28

But, generally both the 'Select' and 'Ultimate' Mortality tables are shown together. In the Table No. 9.3 the select table was up the 5 years of the selection (6) and over with attained age was ultimate table.

The ultimate table is used for valuation purposes. Where insurer wants to have a reasonable safety margin and where policies are participating ones, the ultimate table is used. It gives maximum possible rate of death.

INTEREST FACTOR

The second factor after death rate is interest factor for calculating net premium because the premium is obtained in advance and claim is paid subsequently. So, during this period the insurer can earn certain rate of interest. Since the insurer can earn additional amount on the premium collected, its benefit should be given to the policy-holders. The insurer, therefore, is required to assume a rate of return that may be earned taking into consideration various factors that would affect such earnings. Insurers are generally conservative in assuming such rate of return. Since the premium is determined in advance the present value or pre sent net worth should be calculated so that this value at an assumed compound rate of interest must be adequate to pay the amount of claim. The present value is calculated by the following formula:

$$P = \frac{S}{(l+i)}$$

where P stands for present value of the given sum.

S stands far the given sum of which present value is to be calculated.

i stands far assumed rate of interest.

n stands for the number of years before which present value is to be calculated.

There is the third factor called loading which is discussed in detail in the next Chapter.

QUESTIONS

1. 'The risk can be measured by the mortality rate in life insurance'— Explain.
2. 'The martolity rate can be ascertained by the mortality table'—comment.
3. Explain how mortailty table is constructed.
4. The information of insurers' is one of the several sources of constructing the mortality table'— critically examine the various sources of information of construction of mortality tabes.
5. What are the different types of mortality table? State the fundamental principles on which mortality tables are constructed.
6. Fill up the banks in the following portion of a life table:

Age	*Living Numbers*	*No. of Deaths*	*Probability of Death*	*Probability of Survival*
x	l_x	d_x	q_x	p_x
20	10,00,000	—	0.0050	—
21	—	—	0.0045	—
22	—	—	—	0.9960
23	—	—	—	0.9965
24	—	—	—	0.9970
25	—	—	0.0025	—

7. From the following information find the number living at age 43 and l_{x+4}.

Age	*Living Numbers*	*No. Dying*	*Probability of Death*	*Probability of Survival*
x	l_x	d_x	q_x	p_x
40	—	400	0.006	—
41	—	—	0.007	—
42	—	—	0.008	—
43	—	300	—	—

8. From the table given below, evaluate $3p_{(21)+1}$ and $1/2q_{20}$.

Select Table

Age at Entry x	$l_{(x)}$	$l_{(x)+1}$	$l_{(x)+2}$	Attained Age
20	4,95,393	4,94,534	4,93,633	22
21	4,94,480	4,93,620	4,92,716	23
22	4,93,566	4,92,702	4,91,795	24
23	4,92,647	4,91,781	4,90,868	25

9. From the select mortality table (period of selection 2 years given below; find out $2p_{(30)+1}$; / $2q_{(31)+1}$; $I/q_{(32)}$.

Age at entry	$l_{(x)}$	$l_{(x)+1}$	$l_{(x)+2}$	Attained Age x + 2
30	4,86,024	4,85,094	4,84,096	32
31	4,85,028	4,85,080	4,83,305	22
32	4,84,012	4,83,042	4,81,994	34
33	4,83,000	4,82,000	4,81,000	35

10. Fill up the blanks in the following portion of a life table.

Age x	Living Numbers l_x	No. of Deaths d_x	Probability of Death q_x	Probability of Survival p_x
20	10,00,000	—	0.00409	—
21	—	—	0.00370	—
22	—	—	—	0.99653
23	—	—	—	0.99658
24	—	—	0.00342	—
25	—	—	0.00335	—

10

CALCULATION OF PREMIUM

The premium is of two types: (1) Net Premium and (2) Gross Premium. The two premiums are further sub-divided into two parts: (*i*) single premium, and (*ii*) level premium. The net premium: is based on the mortality and interest rates whereas the gross premium depends upon the mortality rate, the assumed interest rate, the expenses and the bonus loading. Single premium is paid in one lump sum while the level premium is paid periodically in instalments. The level premium may be yearly, half-yearly, quarterly and monthly. Firstly, net single premium is calculated and other premiums are based on this calculation.

Net Single Premium

Net single premium is that premium which is received by the insurer in a lump sum and is exactly adequate, along with the return earned thereon, to pay the amount of claim wherever it arises whether at death or at maturity or even at surrender. It does not provide for expenses of management and for contingencies.

Steps for Calculation

1. Determine what constitutes a claim (*a*) death, (*b*) survival or (*c*) both.
2. Determine when claims are paid (*a*) at the beginning, (*b*) at the end, or (*c*) during the year.
3. Determine the number of insured.
4. Determine the duration of the policy.
5. Determine the probable number of claims per year.
6. Determine the value of claims per year.
7. Determine the number of years of interest involved and find the present value of a rupee.
8. Determine the present value of the claim for each year.
9. Determine the present value of all future claims.
10. Determine the net single premium, (*i.e.*, present value of future claims) divided by number assumed for buying policy.

The step of premium calculation vary according to the nature of the policy which will be clear later on. When premium is calculated several questions emerged simultaneously.

Assumptions underlying Rate Computations

There are certain variables which are to be assumed at a level for calculation and alterations in premium calculation are made at later stage according to the change in the variable. The following factors are assumed while calculating the net single premium.

(*i*) As many policies of the given type are being issued as are the number of persons.

(*ii*) Premiums are collected in advance or in the beginning of the period.

(*iii*) All collections are immediately invested and will remain invested until money is needed for the payment of claims.

(*iv*) The insurer will receive an assumed rate of interest. The assumed rate should be conservative to avoid future decline in interest rate.

(*v*) The interest or dividend or any return of the invested funds is immediately invested for re-earning.

(*vi*) Mortality rate will be the same as given in the mortality table and will he uniformly distributed throughout the year.

(*vii*) All policies are of the same amount, say, ₹ 1,000.

(*viii*) Claims will be paid only at the end of the period.

These assumptions may not be totally practicable, but they are taken as for making calculation easy. The changes in assumption can be adjusted accordingly.

Calculation of Net Single Premium

The calculation of net single premium is discussed in different types of policies.

Term Insurance

This is the simplest type of contract whereby, payment is made only when the life assured dies within the term specified. Nothing will be paid if death does not occur during the designated term. This is also called temporary insurance. The premium is received in advance and it will not be returned if life assured survives. The premium is paid only once in a single sum at the inception of the policy. Death claims will be paid at the end of the year in which they occur and not at the end of the term. Thus the probability of death in each year along with the present value, of the claim for each year will be calculated because the death may occur at any moment and the insurer may be required to pay. The term may be one, two, five or seven years. Here we assume that the period of term insurance is 5 years. Before we start we assume that the (1) rate of return on investment is 3 per cent and the mortality experience will be like the one shown in the oriental 1953-54 Experience Life Table. The person is proposing at the age of 40 for the period of 5 years.

Table 10.1 Oriental 1953-54 Experience Life Table, Ultimate Table

Age	*Number of Persons living*	*Number of deaths*	*Mortality Rate per 1,000*
40	96,463	273	2.83
41	96,190	302	3.14
42	95,888	336	3.50
43	95,552	375	3.92
44	95,177	418	4.39
45	94,759	467	4.03

The number of details can be known from the above table we assume that each person dead will be paid ₹ 1,000. The next factor of calculation is that the insurer will earn a fixed return on the investment, therefore, only the present value of the claim should be taken as a premium. Thus, the net single premium for each year will be calculated:

Number of deaths × Amount of claims × Present value of ₹ 1 = Present value of claims.

Table 10.2 Net Single Premium for 5 years Term Policy

Year of Insurance	*Age attained*	*Number of living*	*Number of death*	*Amount of claims per death*	*Present value of Re. 1.0*	*Present value of 4 × 5 × 6*
1	2	3	4	5	6	7
1	40	96,463	273	1000	0.971	2,65,083
2	41	96,190	302	1000	0.943	2,84,786
3	42	95,888	336	1000	0.915	3,07,440
4	43	95,552	375	1000	0.888	3,33,000
5	44	95,177	418	1000	0.863	3,60,734

Present value of all claims = ₹ 15,51,043

Total premium to be charged on all 96,463 policies = ₹ 15,51,043.

Therefore, premium per policy = ₹ 15,51,043/96,463 = ₹ 16.18.

The present value of the first year will be calculated for one year in the first year of insurance because of death occurs during the first year, the insurer can earn interest at least for one year. Similarly, in the second year of insurance, the present value of ₹ 1 is calculated for two years at 3.0 per cent· per annum. The formula for calculating present value is $P = \frac{S}{(1+i)^n}$. In this case:

$$P = \frac{1}{(1 + 0.03)^2} = P = \frac{1}{(1.03 \times 1.03)} = 0.943$$

where P stands for the present value, S for the amount of which present value is to be calculated and i for the rate of interest and n for number of years for which present value is to be calculated.

Thus, the present value of claim for the first year will be 273 × 100 × 0..971 = 265083 because the number of deaths are 273 and the total amount of claim, so, would be 2,73,000. If multiplied by factor of present value it gives present value of claim. The formula can be used for the calculation

$$NSP = \frac{Vd_x + V^2 d_{x+1} + \ldots..V^2 d_{x+n}}{l_x}$$

where V represent present value of Re. 1.0.

d_x represent deaths

l_x = numbers of living in the beginning.

Another Method of Calculation of Premium on a Single Policy

The probability of death is taken into account while the premium for one policy is to be calculated:

Table 10.3

Year of Insurance	*Age*	*Probability of Deaths expression in units*	*Amount of policy of*	*Present value of Re. 1.0*	*Net single Premium*
1	40	0.00283	1000	0.971	2.74793
2	41	0.00314	1000	9.943	2.96102
3	42	0.00350	1000	0.915	3.20250

Year of Insurance	*Age*	*Probability of Deaths expression in units*	*Amount of policy of*	*Present value of Re. 1.0*	*= Net single Premium*
4	43	0.00392	1000	0.888	3.48096
5	44	0.00439	1000	0.863	3.78857
					₹ = 16.8098
					₹ 16.18

Thus the net single premium will be the same whether it has to be calculated on the basis of group policy or on the basis of single policy; The probability method is generally used for calculation of premium.

Net Single Premium in Whole Life Policies

A whole life policy continues for the whole of life and promises to pay the sum assured upon the death of the insured to his beneficiary. This policy is like the term insurance policy with only difference that instead of being limited to a definite number of years, it continues for the largest possible length of life and will certainly be paid at some time. It has been assumed in most of the mortality table that the life will continue up to 100 years. Therefore, the calculation of premium will start from the date of commencement of risk to the 100th year. If a person has taken policy at age 45, the calculation will continue until 100th year.

The chances of death in each separate year will be multiplied by the face value of the policy and this amount is discounted by the present value for the period.

Table 10.4 Calculation or Net Single Premium on the basis or CSO Mortality Table

Age	*Probability of Death*	×	*Policy amount*	×	*Present value of Re. 1.0 @ 2.5%*	=	*Present value of the claim*
45	$\frac{7340}{852554}$	×	1000	×	0.975610	=	8.399441
46	$\frac{7801}{852554}$	×	1000	×	0.951814	=	9.039243
99	$\frac{125}{852554}$	×	1000	×	0.257151	=	10.037703
			Net Single Premium				= ₹ 551.372587

The amount ₹ 551.37 is the present value of all the death claims payable from age 45 until the mortality table ends, which will be the single premium amount which can purchase policy of ₹ 1,000. The sum assured is payable upon the insured's death when ever it may take place. Therefore, the chance of death in each year is taken into account. The present value in the 99 years was the lowest because the chance of survival at this stage is very nominal. Second, the sum deposited at the inception of the contract to hedge this possibility would earn interest for 55 years. Therefore, very nominal amount 0.25751 is charged for making it ₹ 1.0 at the end of 99th year.

Actuarially the net single premium in a whole life policy will be-:

$$NSP = \frac{V_{dx} + V^2{}_{dx+2} + V^3{}_{dx+3} \text{.... for the end of the mortality table}}{I_x}$$

The expression of the symbols has been made in the previous section of the chapter.

Net Single Premium in Pure Endowment Policy

In this policy, insurer promises to pay the insured value in case the holder survives a certain fixed period. Thus the holder of 5 years pure endowment will be paid only when he survives at the end of 5 years. The insured ,cannot get possession of the money invested in a pure endowment before the expiration of the endowment period. If the insured dies during this period, all the premium paid is fourfeited.

Table 10.5 Single Premium Pure Endowment

Actually form of calculation is	*Probability of Survival*	×	*Policy Amount*	×	*Present value of Re. 1.0 for the endowment period*	=	*Net single premium*
$NSP = \frac{V^n l_{x+n}}{l_x}$							
$= \frac{94689}{93463}$	= 0.981	×	1000	×	0.863	=	846.603

Thus, the net single premium of ₹ 1000/ for 5 years pure endowment will be ₹ 846.60.3

Net Single Premium in Ordinary Endowment Policy

Under this policy payment of claim amount is made at the survival of the term or at the death of the life assured whichever is earlier. Payment in this case is certain. Since payment is based on the death and survival, the net premium is calculated on death and survival rate. The net single premium on the basis of death has been discussed in case of term insurance and on the basis of survival in case of pure endowment assurance. For example, we have to complete net single premium of ordinary endowment policy of 5 years, we can easily base our calculation on death and survival rates.

1. Net single premium on the basis of death for 5 years =₹ 16.18
2. Net single premium survival at the end of 5 year =₹ 846.60

₹ 862.78

Net single premium on the basis of death and survival rate = ₹ 862.78

Thus,

The net single premium in ordinary endowment policy of ₹ 1,000 for 5 years is ₹ 862.78.

Actually the formula for calculating net single premium in ordinary endowment is:

$$NSP = \frac{Vd_x + V^2 d_{x+1} ... V^n{}_{dx+n-1}}{l_x} + \frac{V^n l_{x+n}}{l_x}.$$

Net Single Premium in Double Endowment

Under this policy, double of the amount is paid if the life assured survives at the end of the term of policy and only single amount will be paid if the death occurs within the term. Thus, it is first like ordinary endowment policy with only difference that double of the policy amount is paid if life assured survives up to the term. Since the double of the policy amount is paid at the survival, one more premium on the basis of pure endowment is added to the premium of ordinary endowment policy. For example, double endowment policy is to be calculated of ₹ 1,000 for 5 years.

The Net Single Premium of Ordinary Endowment + Net single premium of Pure Endowment Policies for 5 years issued at same age.

= policy for 5 years issued at the same age.

= ₹ 862.78 + 846.60 = 1709.38.

Thus, the net single premium of double endowment policy of ₹ 1,000 for 5 years will be ₹ 1.709.38. If death occurs within the term, he is paid merely ₹ 1,000 and ₹ 709.38 will be a loss to him; but if he survives up to the period, he is paid ₹ 2,006 only on payment of ₹ 1,709.38.

Actuarial expression of net single premium in this case will bc:

$$NSP = \frac{(Vd_x + V^2 d_{x+1} + V^2 d_{x+2} ... V^n d_{x+n-1} + 2V^2 l_{x+n}}{l_x}$$

Net Single Premium for a Joint Life Policy

Under this policy payment of claim will bc made at the first death of the assured lives who may be two or more. Here, the process of calculation will be the same as has been discussed in term insurance with only difference that the probability of death is compound one. The compound probability of death is calculated by addition of the probability of deaths of one other and all of the envy aged.

For example:

Compound Probability of any one of the two lives assured will be

(*a*) Probability of death of the younger person

+

(*b*) Probability of death of the older person

+

(*c*) Probability of death of both the persons.

It is calculated by multiplying the probability of death of each person. The compound probability may also be calculated by the following method.

$$= 1 - \left(\frac{\text{Probability of Survival of}}{\text{younger life}} \times \frac{\text{Probability of Survival}}{\text{of older life}} \right).$$

Net Single Premium for Last Survival Policy

The policy amount is payable, under this policy, only when all lives covered by the policy expire. The compound probability of all policy-holders is calculated. The calculation will continue up to the youngest life's reaching to the highest age of the mortality table, it will not stop at the first death. Thus, the compound probability will be

= Probability of death of one person × Probability of death of other person.

When the youngest son is supposed to be dead, calculation stops.

NET SINGLE PREMIUM IN ANNUITIES

An annuity may be defined as a contract whereby for a cash consideration, (called premium) one party (the insurer) agrees to pay the other (the annuitant) a stipulated sum (the annuity), throughout life, or during the life within a fixed term, either annually, semiannually quarterly or monthly. The purpose of the annuity, is to protect a hazard–the outliving of one's income. It is just opposite of insurance contract. The annuity protects against the absence of income in old age. A periodical amount is given by the insurance to the insured up to his life or up to a fixed period life thereafter.

Under this annuity the payment of annuity starts from the date of first annuity period. For example, if annuity is to be paid six monthly and contract of annuity, *i.e.*, payment of purchase price is made on 1st Jan., 1976, the first annuity will be paid on 1st June, 1976. Therefore, up to this period, the insurer can enjoy the premium paid six months ago. If he survives to next period of instalment, the insurer has to pay the second instalment of annuity. The immediate annuity may be (1) Life Annuity, and (2) Term Annuity.

(1) *Net Single Premium in Life Annuity.* In this case, the payment of annuity shall continue up to the life of the annuitant. No annuities are paid after his death nor is any part of the consideration refunded to his beneficiaries. The cost of annuity depends upon his survival, therefore, the calculation is based upon the probability of survival.

Suppose, net single premium for an immediate annuity of ₹ 1,000 to be paid annually issued at the age 105 is to be calculated. Assuming a rate of 3 per cent of interest and 1937 Standard Annuity Mortality Table, the calculation will be as below:

Age	*Probability of Survival*	×	*Amount of Annuity*	×	*Present value of Re. 1,00*	=	*Present value of Annuity*
106	97/249	×	1000	×	0.971	=	94187/249
107	30/249	×	1000	×	0.943	=	28290/249
108	6/249	×	1000	×	0.915	=	5490/249
109	1/249	×	1000	×	0.888	=	888/249
110	0/249	×	1000	×	0.863	=	0/249

= ₹ 128855/249

Present value of total amount = ₹ 517.

(2) *Net Single Premium for Temporary (Term) Annuity.* The process of calculation is the same as discussed above with only difference that the calculation continues only up to a fixed period. It does not, like annuity, continue up to the completion of Annuity Mortality Table. For example, an annuity of ₹ 1,000 to be paid annually is taken at the age of 70 and continues up to 5 years. The net single premium will be as below if rate of interest is $2\frac{1}{2}$ p.a.

Age	*Probability of Survival*	×	*Amount of Annuity*	×	*Present value of Re. 1.0*	=	*Present value of Annuity*
71	$\frac{553332}{577445}$	×	1000	×	0.975610	=	934.87
72	$\frac{5238443}{577445}$	×	1000	×	0.951814	=	871.04
73	$\frac{502843}{577445}$	×	1000	×	0.928599	=	808.63
74	$\frac{476611}{577445}$	×	1000	×	0.905951	=	747.75
75	$\frac{449841}{577445}$	×	1000	×	0.883854	=	688.54

Present value of total amount ₹ 4,050.79.

Actuarial Expression of Immediate Annuity:

(i) Life Annuity:

$$NSP = \frac{Vl_{x+1} + V^2 l_{x+2} + V^2 l_{x+3} \text{....life}}{l_x}$$

(*ii*) Temporary Annuity:

$$NSP = \frac{Vl_{x+1} + V^2 l_{x+2} + V^2 l_{x+2} \text{(if it is for 3 years)}}{l_x}$$

DEFERRED ANNUITIES

In this case payment of annuity starts after a fixed period called deferred period or deferment period. Since the premium has been received at the time of contract and payment shall start only at the end of the deferment period, the present value will defer with the deferment period. The survival rate will also be calculated after the deferment period.

For Example:

Age	*Probability of Survival of 100,000 persons*	×	*Amount of Annuity*	×	*Present value of Re. 1.0*	=	*Present value of Annuity*
40	Year of Contract		—		After 30 years		—
70	deferred date $\frac{2000}{100000}$	×	1000	×	0.477	=	9.540
71	$\frac{1000}{10000}$	×	1000	×	0.465	=	4.650
72	$\frac{500}{100000}$	×	1000	×	0.454	=	2.270
							₹ 16.46

$$NSP = \frac{V^{i+1} l_{x+i+1} + V^{i+2} l_{x+i+2} + \ldots\ldots}{x}$$

Net Single Premium for Minimum Payment Annuity

(*i*) Under this contract a minimum specified number of annuity payments have to be made on each contract irrespective of the death of the annuitant.

(*ii*) Thereafter annuity is paid so long as annuitant lives.

(*iii*) The probability of survival up to the fixed period will be treated as one because payment of annuity is certain up to this period and thereafter the actual probability of survival at that age will be taken into consideration.

(*iv*) It is a combination of Annuity certain and life Annuity. Therefore, for payments guaranteed for a certain period, the amount of annuity is certainly paid irrespective of death and survival rate is not required.

Net Single Premium for Annuity Due

Under this, annuity payment begins from the start of the period and not at the end of the period. For example, if annuity is taken, on annual basis on 1st July, 1975, the first payment will be made at that time and second payment will be made on 1st July 1976, while in other annuity contract, it is the first payment. Since first payment is certain it is not based on survival rate. In other words, for the first payment the survival rate is treated to one.

Actuarial expression is:

$$NSP = \frac{l_x + Vl_{x+1} \quad V^2 l_{x+2} .....life}{l_x}$$

Calculating of Net Level Premium

The net level premium is collected periodically while, the net single premium is charged only once in the beginning of the contract. The net level premium cannot be calculated first by dividing net single premium by the number of premiums payable in instalments because in net single premium whole of the premium is received in advance and will remain invested until is paid as a claim whereas the net level premium will be invested. The second reason is that the net single premium will be paid by all the policy-holders whereas the level premiums could be paid only by the surviving policy-holders.

The net single premium is the present value of all claims and the present value of all net level premiums is also equal to the total of present values of all claims. It means the present value of all net level premiums is equal to the net single premium. So, if the present value of a unit level premium is known, the net single premium can be converted into level premium.

CALCULATION OF LEVEL PREMIUMS

The single premium of a given policy can be easily converted into level premium by establishing ratio between net level premium and net single premium. The ratio will differ according to the age at the beginning, nature and duration of the policy. This calculation of the ratio is illustrated in the following table. The single premium in 5 years Term policy is to be converted into level premium on annual basis for 5 years. Assuming that the net level premium for the policy is ₹ 1.0 per thousand of sum assured, the calculation of the present value of all the level premium is given as below.

Using Oriental 1953-54 Experience Life Table–

Ultimate and 3 per cent rate of interest.

Year of Insurance	*Age*	*Number of persons living*	*No. of premium received*	*Amount of premium received*	*Present value of Re.1*	*Present value of Premium received*
1	40	96,463	96,463	96,463	1,000	96,463
2	41	96,190	96,190	96,190	0.971	93,400
3	42	95,880	95,880	95,880	0.943	90.415
4	43	95,552	95,552	95,552	0.915	87,430
5	44	95,177	95,177	95,177	0.888	84,517

Total Present value = ₹ 4,52,225.

The present, value of all level premiums to be received during the five years is ₹ 4,52,225 on all policies which comes to ₹ 4,52,225/96,463 per policy. Since, the present value per policy of all the net level premiums is equal to the net single premium of all the policy, the ratio between level premium and net single premium is 1:4 [illegible]25/96463. Thus, the ratio for converting net single premium of term policy for 5 years is, establishe[illegible] as

I. : 452225/96463

On this ratio the net single premium of ₹ 16.18 $= \frac{15551043}{96463}$ can be converted into several premium policy.

Since, For N.S.P. of ₹ $\frac{452225}{96463}$ the NLP is = Re. 1.0

$\therefore$ For N.S.P. of ₹ 1 the NLP $\dfrac{1 \times 96463}{452225}$

$\therefore$ For N.S.P. of ₹ $\dfrac{1551043}{96463}$ the NLP $\dfrac{96463 \times 1551043}{452225 \times 96463}$

= ₹ 3.43 p.a.

This ratio was easily calculated in this policy of 5 years, but it is very difficult in the case of whole life and endowment policies because, the calculation is made for a very large number of years.

Annuity Due Principle

The second method of calculating the net level premium is on the basis of annuity due principle because the annuity due for the same period and issued at the same age is just like level premium. In the life insurance for the same period and issued at the same age is just like level premium. In both the cases, the payments are made in the beginning of the period and so long as the assured is alive. It may be limited to a particular period also like term and endowment policies. For purchasing life insurance single premium is given and for purchasing annuity due purchase price of the annuity due is given. In exchange if the purchase price of the annuity due, periodical annuity is paid constantly up to the life or up to the fixed period as the case may be similarly in exchange of the single premium, the issued is not required to pay the level premium. Since net purchase price of annuity due issued at the particular age for a particular period or up to life is equal to the net single premium of the life insurance issued at the same age for the same period. Therefore, if the payment of periodical annuity due is known, the level premium for the same period can be easily known.

Thus, the expression can be made as :

Net level premium (Px) : Net single premium (Ax) :Annuity· due amount: Purchase price to the annuity due contract (ax)

or,

$$\text{Net level Premium (Px)} = \frac{\text{Net Single Premium } (Ax) \times \text{ Annuity Due}}{\text{Purchase price of Annuity Due } (ax)}$$

Here we assume that Annuity due io Re 1.0 per annum.

$$P_x = \frac{(Ax)(1)}{ax}$$

If the purchase price of Annuity due of Re. 1.0 and net single premium are known, the net level premium can be easily converted into net level premium.

CALCULATION OF GROSS PREMIUM

The gross premium is that premium which is charged by the insured to meet the amount of claims and expenses. Thus, the gross premium includes the net premium and loading.. Loading is the process to add the expenses to net premium. The loading may add a certain amount to meet the bonus charges on participating policies. The policy-holders are required to pay this gross premium and they even do not know the net premium. Therefore the gross premium is also know as 'Office Premium'. The policy-holder are, thus, required to pay amount to meet the cost or claim, expenses of business, and loading for bonus if the policy is participating one.

Allocation of Expenses

.As has been made it clear that the expenses of business are allocated amongst the net premiums. So, in allocation, the insurer faces two problems (*i*) Allocation of expenses over various policies and (*ii*) Allocation of expenses over duration of the policy.

(*i*) *Allocation of Expenses over Various Policies.* The allocation of expenses over various policies should be equitable. It means that every policy should be allotted the due share of its expenses, some policies involve higher expenses than others and should, therefore, bear higher loading. The policies involving lesser expenses should be lesser share of the total expenses. The total expenses are, therefore, classified so that equitable distribution can be easily done.

CLASSIFICATION OF EXPENSES ON THE BASIS OF VARIATION

There are three classifications on the basis:

1. Those expenses that vary with the size of the premium, for example, first year or renewal commissions.
2. Those expenses that vary with the amount of policy, for example, stamp fee, and medical examiner's fee.
3. Those expenses that are independent of both, being either the same per policy or the expenses are incurred for the business as a whole for example, salaries, and establishment charges.

These expenses would be equitably distributed only the relationship between the premium, policies or fixed is determined. For example,

Loading = A fixed percentage of net premium
+ A fixed amount per 1,000 of sum assured
+ A fixed amount per policy.

The insurer will have to establish what expenses are varying at what degree with premium, policy or policy amount. Therefore, he has to analyses the expenses and to determine the percentage.

(*i*) Analysis of Expenses

All the expenses incurred during a particular period are classified into (*i*) those expenses which are related to the premium, (*ii*) those expenses which are related with the policy, and (*iii*) those expenses which are independent of these two.

(*ii*) Determination of Percentage

After classifying the expenses it is essential to determine the percentage according to the premium or policy or with other factor. The percentage is determined on the basis of past, experience. If it has been known that ₹ 10,000 will be expended in connection with premium of ₹ 10,00,000, it can be established that the expenses varying with the premium will be 1 per cent of the premium collected. Similar percentage in relation to policy amount and to policy number can be easily established. Thus the net premium can be easily loaded with these percentage or fixed amount per policy.

The expenses should be allocated according to policies amount, premium amount and per policy although various methods have been derived for allocation of expenses.

Methods of Loading

The expenses can be allocated by any of the following methods:

1. Constant Addition Loading

Under this method a fixed amount per thousand of sum assured is loaded to the net premium. This method is not scientific because it assumes that all expenses vary according to the amount of the policy which is not correct. Some expenses vary according to variation in the rate of premium.

2. Percentage Addition Loading

According to this method a fixed percentage of net premium is added to the net premium. It assumes that all expenses vary according to the premium amount. But there are certain expenses which vary according to the policy amount or per policy.

3. Modified Percentage Method

Under the method, the loading is divided into two parts: (*i*) expenses varying according to net level premium of the given, policies and (*ii*) expenses varying according to net level premium, of the whole life policy issued at the given age. This method is modification of the above two methods; but it does not relate the expenses according to their variations.

4. Constant and Percentage Addition Method

Under this method, the loading is done under two parts (*a*) a constant amount per thousand of the sum assured and (*b*) a fixed percentage related to the net premium of the policy. The percentages are determined on the basis of past experience. This method assumes that the expenses vary either with the net premium or the sum assured, but the expenses also vary with the amount per policy which is not taken into account. However, this method is more scientific than the methods discussed above.

B. DISTRIBUTION OF EXPENSES OVER THE PERIOD OF POLICY

There are certain expenses which are incurred in the inception of the policy, certain expenses incur every year of the policy and certain expenses incur only in the end of the policy. The allocation of expenses requires that equal amount should be distributed every year. Therefore, firstly, the nature of expense according to occurrence and secondly, equal distribution of the expenses every year are to be done for equitable distribution of loading.

1. Classification of expenses

The expenses for the above purpose are distributed into four categories :

(*a*) *The Initial Expenses.* The initial expenses are those expenses which incurred at first before or at the time of issuing the policy. The expenses, for example, may be medical examiner's fees, inspection of risk of agents' commission, expenses involved for preparation of the policy and correspondence expenses and so on.

(*b*) *The Recurring Expenses.* The recurring expenses are those expenses which are incurred every year for the policy. Some of them may be limited only up to the period of premium collection The expenses may be expenses for issue of premium notices, premium receipts, keeping accounts and payment of renewal commissions to agents.

(*c*) *The Final Expenses.* The final expenses are incurred at the time of payment of claims or of surrender values. They are expenses for approving the claims, cost of paying surrender values and cost of correspondence, etc.

(*d*) *The General Expenses.* These expenses are fixed and incurred for the business as a whole. The important general expenses are accounting expenses actuarial and legal expenses, maintenance and establishment charges. They are not related to a particular policy or point of time.

The recurring and final expenses, normally, vary with the policy amounts, premium amount or per policy. But the general expenses may not vary in the above manner.

Equal Distribution of the Expenses

All the above expenses should be equally distributed over the policy year. The main problem of distributions of initial expenses is that a heavy expense is involved in the beginning of the policy but it has to be distributed over the life of the policy, *i.e.*, over the period of premium payment.

Dr. Sprague's Formula for Loading

Dr. Sprague's formula can be discussed as below:

(*a*) A single percentage of sum discussed to cover the initial expenses.

(*b*) A percentage of net premium to cover recurring renewal expenses.

(*c*) A fixed amount to cover general office expenses.

The inital expenses are equally spread over the period of premium payment by dividing it by the present value of Annuity due, of Re. 1.0 over the given period.

Thus,

Office Premium = Per cent of sum Assured + Per cent of

$$\text{Net level Premium} + \frac{\text{Initial Expenses}}{\text{Present value of Annuities Due of Re. 1.0 for the period}}.$$

Actually, the gross premium is calculated as below:

$$P = P + I / a + \frac{r}{100} P + c$$

where P is gross premium, P is net premium, I is the initial expenses, is the present value of annuity due of Re. 1.0, r is the renewal expenses as a percentage of Office Premium and c constant addition, for fixed renewal expenses. The above formula can be refined as below:

$$P = P + I / a + c \div \left(1 - \frac{r}{100}\right)$$

QUESTIONS

1. What are the various assumptions underlying the calculation or premium.
2. What are the various factors affecting the calculation of premium.
3. Net Single Premium and loading compute gross premium—explain in detail.
4. Illustrate the methods of computing premiums in different types of policies and annuities.
5. What are the various methods of Loading?
6. Loading of expenses and Bonus are done in two parts—(*a*) Distribution according to time and (*b*) distribution according to policies.
7. From the following mortality table, calculate net level premiums in Term Insurance for five years, Endowment Insurance for five years, Pure Endowment for five years and Double Endowment for five years, assuming 5 per cent rate of interest and ₹ 1,000 policy amount in each policy.

x	25	26	27	28	29	30
lx	100000	99500	98900	98200	97400	96500
dx	500	600	700	800	900	1000

8. Calculate the value of an anticipated endowment assurance for a person aged 25 with the following benefits.
   (*i*) a sum of ₹ 100 at the end of 2nd year.
   (*ii*) a sum of ₹ 200 at the end of 3rd year.
   (*iii*) a sum of ₹ 300 at the end of 5th year if the life assured is alive at the end of respective years.
   (*iv*) a sum of ₹ 600 whenever the dies during the 5 years period.

   Use the data given above with 5 per cent rate of interest.
9. Calculate on the basis of mortality table given below, net annual premium at 5% rate of interest for a 5 year Term Insurance for ₹ 1,000 effective at the age of 60 years.

Age	*Number Living*	*Number Dying*
60	1000	20
61	980	22
62	958	25
63	933	33
64	900	40
65	860	45

10. Calculate the net annual level premium for a Double Endowment Assurance of ₹ 100 for a person aged 60 years, the assured benefit being ₹ 100 in the case of his death before attaining age 63 and ₹ 200 if he survives to age 63. Use the above mortality table and rate of interest.
11. Using the above mortality table and rates of interest, calculate level premium for the Anticipated Endowment Policy of ₹ 1000 where ₹ 200 is paid in the case of death in the second year, ₹ 200 is paid in the case of death in the third year, ₹ 600 in case of death in the fourth year and ₹ 1000 in case of survival upto five years.
12. If the annual premium for an endowment assurance of ₹ 1000 for a person aged 40 years for a term of 20 years is ₹ 30.00, calculate the office premium, making the following provisions:
    (*a*) Initial Expenses at ₹ 40 per 1000 S.A.
    (*b*) Renewal Expenses at 10% of office premium.
    (*c*) A constant expenditure of ₹ 2.50 per thousand sum assured.
    Given $a_w : 19 =$ ₹ 16.00
13. The net premium for an endowment assurance of ₹ 1000 for a person aged 30 for a term of 25 years is ₹ 30.97. Calculate the office premium, making the following provisions:
    (*a*) Initial Expenses at Rs. 40 per 1000 B.A.
    (*b*) Renewal Expenses at 8% of office premium.
    (*c*) A constant expenditure of Rs. 2.50 per thousand sum assured.
    Given $a_w : 29 =$ ₹ 15.640
14. The following particulars are given:

x	25	26	27	28	29	30
l_x	97380	97088	96794	96496	96124	95887
dx	292	294	298	302	307	313

    Calculate, using a rate of interest of 3% p.a.
    (*a*) The value of a Temporary Assurance of ₹ 1000 for 2 years for a person aged 25.
    (*b*) The value of Endowment Assurance benefit of ₹ 1000 for 4 years to a person aged 25.
    (*c*) The value of a pure Endowment of ₹ 600 for a person aged 27, receivable on attaining age 30.
15. Find the value of a Pure Endowment Benefit of ₹ 600 for a person aged 40, payable on his surviving to age 60 at 4% p.a. compound interest; given:
    $a_{40} : 20 = 13.060$ and
    $a_{40} : 19 = 12.691$ at 3% p.a. compound interest.
16. Calculate the net annual premium for an Endowment Assurance of ₹ 2500 for a period of 5 years for a person aged 25 using mortality table in question no. 7 at 3% rate of interest.
17. Find the office annual premium at 3% rate of interest for a whole life assurance on the life of a person, aged, 36 years. Make provision for expenses at 80% of office premium for first year and 7% for all premiums, including that for, the first year.
    Given $a_{35} = 18.182$.

11

TREATMENT OF SUB-STANDARD RISKS

We have discussed how some of the accepted risks are considered as 'standard' and others a 'sub-standard'. The standard risks are accepted at standard or normal premium rates. In this chapter, we shall discuss what treatment may be given to sub-standard risks so that equity is maintained as between standard risks and sub-standard risks. Equity can be maintained only when the extra-risk in sub-standard risk is given special treatment or additional premium is charged.

Types of Sub-standard Risks

The sub-standard risks are divided into three categories according to the incidence and intensity of extra-risk.

(*a*) Increasing Extra-Risk

In this category, the extra mortality increases as the life assured grows older. For example, patients of diabetes, occupational diseases, overweight, etc. The effect of extra-risk in these cases tend to rise with the passage of time and on the lives assured becoming order.

(*b*) Decreasing Extra-Risk

In this category, the extra hazard decreases with increase in age. The extra mortality, consequently, would be experienced more in the early years and would be going down as time passes. In some cases, the extra-mortality tends to decrease until the extra risk might, have disappeared. For example, persons of defective past history.

(*c*) Constant Extra-Risks

Here, the extra hazard remains at the same level throughout the life-time of the assured. There cannot be any risk which are strictly constant. They may decrease or increase to some extent. However, there are certain cases when risks are approximately constant. For example, blindness, or loss of limb, deafness, etc.

Such a classification permits the company to assess premiums according to the incidence of the extra deaths, that is, assuming the company expects the same number of extra-deaths to occur in two groups more will have to be collected for the extra-risk in a group where the deaths occur early (decreasing risk) than where the deaths occur later (increasing risk), because the effect of reserves have to be estimated. In level premium plan the reserve increases year after year and so, the amount at risk decreases along with the increase in reserve. The rate at which reserves are accumulated is also very important. For meeting decreasing risk, higher reserve should be made in the beginning and for increasing risk, the rate of reserve should constantly increase as the time passes. The rate of reserve in constant risk may remain at par.

METHODS OF TREATING SUB-STANDARD RISKS

The Sub-standard risks may be treated in five ways:

1. Increase in premium,
2. decrease in death, benefits,

3. change in class and period of assurance,
4. any combination of the above-mentioned methods, and
5. postponement of risk.

1. Increase in Premium

The premium can be increased in any of the following manners:

(*a*) Rating up of Age

Under this method, the life assured is assumed to be a number of years older than his real age. The premium rate is calculated according to the assumed higher age. So, the cash value, loan, paid up and surrender values are also increased according to the increased premium. The extra number of years to be added is determined according to the extra risk involved with the life assured. The policies issued under this plan will be similar to those issued at standard premium. The only difference is that the premium is increased according to the assumed higher rate. Once the premium determined, cannot be decreased. So, this method is not suitable in decreasing risk. The rated up plan is best adopted to the increasing type of extra-risk although it does not deal equitably with all risks of this type.

The plan has certain advantages. It is easy for the insured to understand; it appeals him because of the increased surrender values and loans. It is simple for insurer to handle. There are certain disadvantages, too. The insured may take advantage of higher surrender values and can get back a substantial part of the premium paid by surrendering the policy.

(*b*) Flat Extra Premium

Under this method a flat annual extra premium of so many rupees per thousand sum assured per year is charged. Thus, a Constant additional premium is added to standard premium; but unlike the rated up age, the extra premium is not taken into accounting for surrender and paid up values. The extra-premium is constantly charged up to the life of policy or up to the existence of the extra risk. In practice, however, it is usual to charge a level extra premium when the extra risk is constant or decreasing one (as in the case of hazardous occupations or even in the case of decreasing extra risk such as a young under-weight). Extra premium is also charged for certain defects and deformity like imputed arms and legs, partial or total blindness, deafness, etc., or in the case of standard imprepairments. Under numerical rating system, the extra-hazard risk is treated by charging that extra according to the degree of extra-hazards.

The extra premium should not be flat or constant when there is heavy and immediate risk in the inception. Otherwise as soon as the period of heavy extra passed, there will be a tendency to drop the policy. In such cases, therefore, if extra is to be charged, a heavier extra should be charged for initial period of so many years when the risk is considered to be very heavy and the extra is removed there-after.

The Life Insurance Corporation of India charges flat extra premium for a Scheduled Occupation. This extra rating mostly vary from ₹ 2/- to ₹ 6/- per thousand of sum assured per annum. Heavy extra flat is also charged from commissioned officers in submarines.

(*c*) Extra Percentage Plan

There are certain classes of sub-standard risks which are determined by numerical rating system. For each class of extra risk, a certain percentage of the standard premium is charged. This extra percentage is added to the standard premium and is charged along with the standard premium. The classes of sub-standard risks are divided on the basis of incidence of extra risk on the mortality. Once the extra premium is determined on the standard premium, it would not vary later on and will be charged according to that extra premium. The difference has in the fact that the amount of extra percentage premium will vary according to the standard premium. Thus, it will be higher when standard premiums are higher. But, in case of flat extra, the same extra premium is charged irrespective of the age or standard premium. Thus, the rate of extra premium as compared to standard premium is higher in the early age and lower in the advanced age. The extra percentage may be used in increasing risks also while the flat extra premium will not be suitable to increasing risks.

2. Decrease in Death Benefits

The death benefits may be reduced in two ways:-

(*a*) Lien Method; and

(*b*) Restrictive Clause.

(*a*) Lien Method

The amount payable under this method would be the sum assured less the outstanding lien at the particular time of the policy. The lien is for a fixed number of years. If the life assured dies within this period, the amount of lien is deducted from the policy amount and rest is paid to the beneficiary but if the life assured survives the period of lien, the whole of the policy amount is paid at the claim.

The amount of lien goes on decreasing in most of the cases, as time passes until whole of the lien is finished. Thus, the amount of claim will go on increasing as time expires because lesser amount of lien is to be deducted at later age. The premium charged is the standard one but only policy amount is reduced. Thus, the effective premium per thousand of the sum payable will be higher in the beginning and lower at the later stage and consequently, in the end, when the lien is terminated, it will be equal to the standard premium.

For example, a reducing lien of ₹ 500 per ₹ 1,000 sum assured for 10 years would mean that the sum payable would be reduced by ₹ 500 if death occurs in the first year, by ₹ 450 if in the second year, and ₹ 400 if in the third year and so on, so that the full sum assured will he paid if death occurs only after the expiry of 10 years. The lien may be constant, and decreasing for the first few years. The type, amount and term of lien would always depend on the nature and extent of extra-risk.

This method is most appropriate when the extra-risk is of decreasing type. As the risk decreases, the amount of lien decreases. For example, an underweight young man with family history of tuberculosis is subject to an extra risk of death during the early years but as age advances, the effect of this extra risk reduces. In this case the lien would be most suitable because other treatments may not provide sufficient fund at the early death. The insured may also be willing to purchase the policy at standard premium only. Thus, the insurer is not at loss if death occurs during the first few years of the policy because he can deduct a certain sum before payment. The insured is also assured of getting the policy amount after the lien period without payment of extra-premium. The plan is simple in operation and is readily understood.

The method is not useful for increasing extra-risk. A small degree of extra mortality may ripe out a substantial amount of claim at the early death. The method appears to be arbitrary in its working as the extra-risk operates fully on one day and then suddenly on the next day, the assured becomes a first class life. The next disadvantage is that a lien reduces the protection substantially during the early years when the need for it is the greatest.

The corporation, therefore, uses this method in special cases. For example, lien is allowed when the life assured is underweight and the life is aged below 33 and there is specific request from the proposer. The lien is used to factory workers, low income people, persons from mofussil centres with inadequate or no income, no arrangements for medical examination, personal or family history of tuberculosis or plurisy and suspicion of moral hazard.

(*b*) Restrictive Clause

Under this clause, the extra hazard is accepted with a restrictive clause which limits death benefit under certain circumstances. Such a clause usually states that the amount payable under this policy will be on a reduced basis which any be surrender value or return of premiums paid, in case death occurs due to the specified extra hazard, For example, the first pregnancy clause which excludes the risk of death arising from causes connected with first pregnancy is often applied to lives of ladies who have not undergone a normal full-time confinement and who do not wish to pay extra premium to cover the extra-hazard. Similarly, in aviation clause, the amount of claim is restricted to surrender value or premiums paid if death occurred while the life assured was engaged in flight.

This method can be used satisfactorily where the cause of death can be distinctly known. In India this method is used in certain life assured "with certain types of policies".

3. Change in the Class and Period of Assurance

The life assured is not given all types of insurance and for a longer period. There is neither a lien on the policy nor any extra premium by way of flat nor rating up to ages. The policy is given at standard premium but all types of policies are not issued. The types of policies to which the choice is restricted are those which carry a higher rate of premium such as ordinary endowment policy. Whole life, multipurpose or triple benefit policies are not given because in these cases the degree of risk is higher as compared to accumulation of reserves. This plan is useful where the extra-risk is expected to occure later in life, such as the case of an over-weight, unfavourable family history. Special dividend plans may be issued to those who are expected to give share of dividend or bonus with higher mortality. By declaring lower bonus rates the insurer is in a position to charge an extra amount for the extra risk assumed. This plan can be used only for the participating policies.

The period of assurance in all types of insurance is limited. The age at the inception or maximum maturity ages for policies are fixed in various types of policies.

4. Any Combination of the above-mentioned Methods

For certain proponents, any of the above methods can he used, which depends on the practical experience of the insurer. For example, a proposal for a multipurpose plan may be accepted under an endowment Assurance Plan with a lien, if the proponent is young and underweight.

5. Postponement

Consideration of proposal is postponed for a period, when the initial risk is so heavy that there is little hope of offering insurance immediately and the proposal is postponed. In future when health will improve, the proposal can be accepted. Postponement in different type of risk are different. It has been observed that the postponement vary from 3 months to 3 years.

The extra premium or line etc. may be removed later on when the extra-risk is improved and the extra-mortality was nominal discreet and no chance of recurrence. In practice the extra are removed in special cases when there are agreement for this.

QUESTIONS

1. What do you understand by sub-standard risks! How far it is distinguished from standard risks?
2. What are the various methods of treating sub-standard risks?
3. "Classification of increasing, decreasing and constant sub-standard risks are very crucial while treating them." Comment.
4. 'Is the sub-standard risk the same as is uninsurable risk?' Distinguish them.

12

THE RESERVE

Nature

The reserve in life insurance is different from the reserve in other business. It is not an accumulation of profit. In Insurance, it is a liability which is to be met by the insurer at and when it arises. It represents a liability which must be adequately met.

Definitior

The reserve is that fund, which, together with future premiums and interest, will be sufficient to pay the future claims. This is called prospective definition because here the future amounts are considered. Another definition of the reserve is the retrospective definition under which the reserve is considered as the accumlation at interest of the difference between the net premiums received in the past and the claims paid out.

The reserve has nothing to do with an insurer's actual past experience. It is always calculated on the assumption that experience has been in accordance with the mortality table selected and interest rate assumed. However, the assumptions as to future interest and mortality are made on a safe basis. It is, thus, clear that on each policy a certain sum must be accumulated every year to be increased at an interest to form fund to meet the future liability of the policy. This accumulated is called the Reserve on the Policy.

Origin of Reserve

The reserve in any group of policies originates in the excess of premium receipts over payment of claims. The premium receipts are more than the payments in the beginning and less after a point. The excess receipts are accumulated at the assumed rate of interest and build up the 'Reserve' up to a point of time, the 'reserve' grows, particularly, because of such receipts. It is to be noted again here that the reserve is accumulated on the assumed mortality and interest. The reserve based on this assumptions is compared to the funds based on the actual experience. The difference may create 'surplus', or deficit. As has been noted that the reserve accumulates at a point and starts declining thereafter because of heavy mortality and receipts of premium at the advanced age.

Sources of Reserve

1. The first and the foremost source of reserve is premium. It should be noted that reserve is accumulated in level premium plan because the premium is more the actual cost of insurance in the beginning. In other two methods of premium, reserve cannot be accumulated. This is discussed as below:

(*a*) Assessment Premium Plan

The members of a group would, under this plan, contribute to a fund which could be utilised in rendering assistance at the time of death to the deceased's dependents. The payment is made by contribution only at the time of death. Therefore, there is no need to accumulate amount for payment of the claim.

(b) Natural Premium Plan

Under this plan, the rate of premium will increase as the insured grows older. It is based on the risk. Since risk increases as time passes, the premium charged from the policyholder also increases. The premium increases year after year with the increase in mortality rate and, so it is also called yearly renewable premium plan. The reserve is not accumulated in this case, because premium increases as cost of insurance increases.

(c) Level Premium Plan

Here, the premiums to be paid are levelled so that usually the same premiums are paid every year. The premiums in the early years are greater than the actual cost (determined by the mortality rate) with the result that the excess payments of premium in the earlier years are accumulated as reserve which makes up any deficiency out of lower premium in later years.

2. The second source of reserve is interest because the accumulated fund is not remaining idle, it is invested. While calculating premium it was assumed that the insurer will earn a certain rate of interest, so to earn at least that much of amount, the accumulated funds have to be invested. The assumed rate of interest is the source of reserve.

3. Nature of Policy

The reserve can be calculated only in those policies where payment is not certain, reserve is generally not requiring. Thus the amount of reserve depends upon the duration of the policy and nature of the policy.

Need for Reserves

The reserves in life insurance is required for the following reasons:

I. To Meet the Amount of Claims

The reserve is required to meet the amount of claim whenever the given event takes place. The incurring of this liability does not bother the insurer at all if in any given period it receives by way of consideration from the policyholders concerned an amount which is equal to the amount it has to pay during this period. The insurer must have sufficient amount to meet the claims. Therefore, the reserve is essential to meet these claims.

II. To Build up Funds

Besides being essential for meeting future cost of claims, the 'reserve' is also useful to build up funds that can be invested for long period to earn at least assumed rate of return. The invested funds help not only to the insurer to obtain a required amount of return but are also helpful for the economic development of the country. The insurers are in a position to accumulate a huge fund and, therefore, can contribute a significant amount for country's advancement.

III. Policyholders are Benefited

The accumulated fund or the reserve belongs to policyholders. This fund is safely and profitably invested by the insurer who are in a position to do that.

The main purpose of creating reserve is to meet the obligation of payment of claims whenever it arises. How should the reserve be created is the main problem of the insurer. The assumed rates of mortality and interest are mainly taken into consideration while calculating reserve for a particular policy, assumed mortality rate, assumed rate of interest, nature of policy, period of premium payments and duration of policy.

METHODS OF CALCULATING RESERVE

The reserve can be calculated by applying retrospective method or by prospective method. The reserve calculated by either of these methods will give the same result provided the mortality rates and interest rates remain the same in both the methods. Reserve can be calculated either on all the policies or on a single policy. This can be expressed by the following illustration–

I. Present value of all premiums	=	Present value of all benefits
II. Accumulated value of past premium + discounted value of future premiums	=	Accumulated value of past benefits + discounted value of future benefits
III. Accumulated value of past premiums–Accumulated Value of past benefits	=	Discounted value of future benefits + Discontinuity value of future premium.
IV. Retrospective Reserve	=	Prospective Reserve

RESERVE

- Retrospective Method
  - Group policies
  - Single policy
- Prospective Method
  - Group policies
  - Single policy

RETROSPECTIVE METHOD

Under this method, the reserve is derived entirely by reference to past experience. The reserve represents the net premiums collected by the insurer for a particular class of policies plus interest at an assumed rate, less the death claims paid out. We calculate for each year how much would have been received by way of premiums on the basis of assumed mortality figures, how much interest would have been earned on the basis of assumed interest rate and how much would have been paid by way of claims on the basis of assumed mortality figures.

Group Approach

The calculation begins with the first year when the total net premium has been received for the first time. We, then, determine the amount of interest that this total of net premium receipts will earn for one full year at the assumed rate of interest. For the total of these two claims paid for the first year are deducted to get the reserve. Again in the second year, we carry forward the reserve.

The net premium received from the surviving policyholders is added to the reserve of past year which is taken together and is called initial reserve of the second year. This process continues until all the policyholders are dead or policy period expires. Per policy reserve can be calculated by dividing the total reserve by the number of policies. It can be illustrated with the following formula.

For example, there are 10 policyholders insured for ₹ 10,000 each for the period of 10 years. They are required to pay net premium of ₹ 1,000 each. The rate of interest is 10 per cent per annum.

First Year

Net premiums of 10 policyholders @₹ 1000/–each	10000
Add interest @ 10%	1000
Total amount	11000
Less	
Claims paid out (no claims)	—
Terminal reserve	₹ 1100

Second Year

Net premium of 10 policyholders	
@₹ 1000/–each	1000
Add Terminal reserve of last year	11000
Initial Reserve	21000
Add Interest @₹ 10 per cent	2100
	23100
Less claims paid out	10000
(one death)	
Terminal Reserve ₹	13100

The process of calculating reserve continues till the 10th year. In the third year, the net premium will be paid by only 9 policy-holders because one person is dead during second year.

Reserve in a Particular Year

The reserve at a particular time can be calculated by the following formula–

Reserve = Reserve at the close of the previous year (if any)
+ Premium of the Year.
+ Interest thereon at the assumed rate for one year
– Claims for the year

With this help reserve can be calculated at any moment provided the initial reserve is known.

Another Method on Accumulation Basis

The accumulated value of premiums over the accumulated value of claims will be the retrospective reserve.

Reserve = Accumulated value of Past Premiums
– Accumulated value of Past Claims

The accumulated value is calculated on the basis of assumed death rate per year and assumed rate of interest. The accumulation factors can be known from the interest table. Thus, the calculation is simple in this method.

Individual Approach

The retrospective reserve may also be calculated on every policy. The method of calculation is the same as discussed above with only difference that the reserve will be calculated on the basis of cost of insurance instead of claims paid on. The 'cost of insurance' reveals how much amounts will have to be shared by the policyholders in payment of claims of other policy-holders. Technically, the po-rate share of death claims in any particular year is called the 'cost of insurance'. It is the amount which must be paid for the protection. The cost of insurance is arrived by multiplying amount at the risk with the probability of death to him. The amount at risk is the amount which is obtained by deducting the initial reserve of the policy-holders from the policy amount.

In brief-

Cost of Insurance =Amount at risk × Probability of Death.
= (Policy Amount-Initial Reserve) × Probability of death.

The individual reserve can be explained by an illustration. For example, a policyholder takes policy of ₹ 10,000 (for ten years) and pays ₹ 1,000 an annual premium, the rate of interest being 10 per cent. The probability of death in the first year is 0.002 and in the second year 0.003. We have to calculate reserve for two years.

First Year

	₹
Net Premium	1,000
Add interest @ 10%	100
	1,100
	₹
Less: 'Cost of Insurance'	
= Amount of risk × probability of death	
= Policy amount – Reserve × Prob. of Death.	
= 10,000 – 0 × 0.002	20
	1,080

Second Year

Net Premium	1,000
Add Reserve of Previous Years	1,080
Initial Reserve	₹ 2,080
Add Interest @ 10%	208
Total:	2,288
Less: Cost of Insurance (10,000 – 1,080) × 0.003 = 8920 × 0.003	26 approx.
Terminal Reserve	₹ 2,262

At a Particular Year

Thus, Individual Reserve can also be calculated at a particular year =

Reserve = Initial Reserve + Interest at assured rate – Cost of Insurance.

The accumulation method can also be used for the calculation of Reserve = Accumulated Value of Premiums paid – Accumulated Value of Cost of Insurance.

Difference between Group Reserve and Individual Reserve

1. The group reserve increases up to a point of time and decreases thereafter until it is finished completely. The individual reserve increases each year and in the end it becomes equal to the policy amount.
2. The group reserve will be zero when payments of claims of all the policy-holders are made whereas the individual reserve must be equal to the face value of the policy at the maturity.

PROSPECTIVE METHOD

The second method of calculating reserve is prospective method. Under this method we determine how much is required to be paid in future and how much premium will be received in future. So, how much the insurer should arrange for payment. The present values of future claims and of future premiums are calculated. In other words, the reserve is the difference between the present value of future benefits and the present value of premiums. At the beginning of the contract the present value of future claims or benefits (PVFB) is exactly equal to the present value of the future premiums. Thus, PVFB =PVFP at the inception of the policy. But as soon as one premium is paid, the present value of future benefit exceeds the present value of future premiums. This is because less premiums remain to be paid and the present value of future benefits increases as the policy is nearer to the claim.

The difference will go on increasing up to the point when the present value of future benefit equals the policy amount and the present value of future claims goes on decreasing until it becomes zero. The difference between these two must be held by the insurer. This difference is reserve because so much of amount must be with the insurer to pay the amount of claim.

Reserve = PVFB – PVFP

Since, the net single premium of a policy is equal to the present value of future benefits, the PVFB can be replaced by NSP (net single premium).

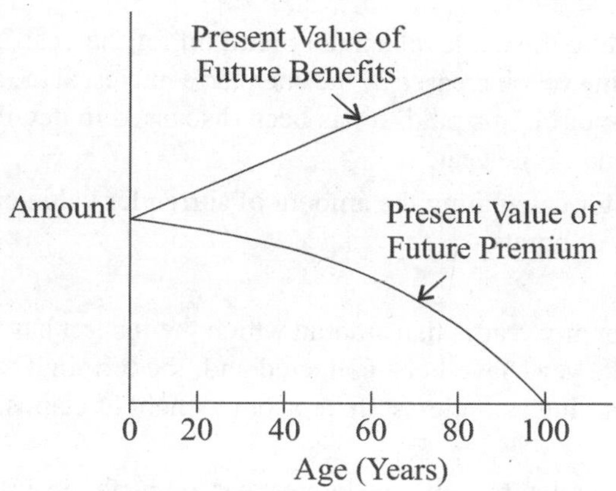

Fig. 12.1

Present Value

The present value, which invested to a given rate over a number of years, will amount to Re. 1.0. The Re. 1.0 is called the accumulated value. The calculation is reverse of accumulation value. To find the accumulated value (A) of Re. 1.0 it was multiplied by one plus the rate of interest (i) raised to the power equal to the number of time units (n) in the period of calculation. Thus,

$$\text{Accumulated } (A) = ix\ (1 + i)^n$$

To find the present value of 1.0 it is to be divided by one plus the rate of interest raised to the power equal to the number of time units in the period, or

$$\text{(Present value) PV} = \frac{1}{(1+i)^n}$$

Thus the present value of any amount can be calculated by multiplying it by $= \dfrac{1}{(1+i)^n}$

Now,

Prospective Reserve = NSP – PVFP

The present value of future premium must necessarily be equal to the net level premium (NLP) for the contract under consideration multiplied by the present value of a life annuity due (PV AD) of Re. 1.0 for the remaining premium paying period. Now the equation will be—

Reserve = NSP – (NLP × PVAD of Re. 1.0).

The reserve can be calculated at any time during the policy period. The NSP will vary according to the time. The PVAD will be calculated for the remaining period of premium payment. NLP is the same as was at issue of policy. Thus,

Reserve (age of valuation)	= NSP (age of valuation)	– NLP (age of issue)	× PVAD of Re 1.0 (remaining premium paying period).

The method of calculation of NSP, NLP and PVAD have been discussed in the previous chapter. They are easily calculated on the basis of tables.

Terminal, Initial and Mean Reserves

1. Terminal Reserve

It is obtained by adding the net level annual premium for the year in question to the terminal reserve of the preceding year increased by the one year's interest at the assumed rate and deducted the cost of insurance or claims paid. It has been discussed in detail in previous section. It is obtained out at the end of the year.

The reserve is used for calculating the amount of surrender value or paid up values. It is also used for distribution of bonus.

2. Initial Reserve

The initial reserve for any year is that amount which the insurer has with him in the beginning after premium for the year have been collected and, the terminal reserve of the last year has been added before earning any interest thereon or payment of claims. It has also been discussed already.

This reserve is used for determining the interest earned by the insurer.

3. Mean Reserve

The mean reserve is the arithematic average of initial reserve and terminal reserve during a year. This is used in connection with the Annual statements. Mean reserve is used for valuation purposes.

QUESTIONS

1. How is reserve created and for what is it created?
2. Discuss the two methods of calculating reserves.
3. What are the uses of Terminal Initial and Mean Reserves?
4. 'Reserve is to determine solvency' discuss in the light of insurance fund.
5. Calculate the retrospective policy value at 2% interest at the end of 3 years for a Temporary Assurance of ₹ 1000 for a period of 6 years on the life of a person aged 40. Use the following mortality table on the basis of which a net annual premium of ₹ 3.89 per thousand has been charged.

Age (x)	40	41	42	43	44
l_x	475	474	472	470	465

6. A person aged 28 is insured for Rs. 1000 for a term of 6 years with the following benefits.
   (*a*) ₹ 200 on survival to age 30
   (*b*) ₹ 300 on survival to age 32
   (*c*) ₹ 500 on survival to age 34
   (*d*) ₹ 1000 at the end of year of death before 34.

   If the net annual premium is ₹ 150.61, find the retrospective policy value at 3% interest at the end of 3 years. Given the following mortality table.

Age (x)	28	29	30	31	32	33	34
l_x	966	962	958	953	950	946	940

7. Find the prospective policy value in the following cases :

$a_{31}:\overline{31} = 2.801; a_{31}:\overline{21} = 1.90; a_{31}:\overline{11} = 0.966$

8. Find the prospective policy value using the data given in Q. 6.
9. 8969 persons aged 30 insure under 1 year temporary assurance for sum assured of ₹ 1000 each at a single premium of ₹ 29.20. Sum assured is payable at the end of the year of death. Premium is based on 3% interest, ignoring expenses. Number of survivors year after year are.

$l_{30} = 9987$	$l_{36} = 8533$
$l_{31} = 8899$	$l_{37} = 8458$
$l_{32} = 8829$	$l_{38} = 8367$
$l_{33} = 8759$	$l_{39} = 8272$
$l_{34} = 8688$	$l_{40} = 8125$
$l_{35} = 8613$	

Calculate the balance of accumulated funds at the end of 4th year after meeting all the claims.

10. A man now aged 40 effected 5 years ago a Whole Life Assurance for ₹ 1000, the number of annual premiums being limited to a maximum of 20. He now desires to alter it to an Endowment Assurance maturing at age 55. Find the amount of the Whole Life Assurance at present.
11. On the basis of above information of survivals and the 3% rate of interest, calculate the value of an Endowment Assurance Policy for ₹ 5000 granted 5 years ago to a person now aged 40 at an annual premium of ₹ 250.
12. An insurer is having the following Children Differed Assurances on its books as on 31-12-85.

Years of issue	*No. of Policies*	*Total Sum Assured*	*Total office Annual Premium*
1974	6	30,000	900
1978	4	25,000	1000
1982	10	40,000	1080

Assume that policies were issued on 31st Dec. in the year of issue, that the premium due on 31-12-85 has been paid and that all the policies are running in the deferment period. If policy conditions provide return of 90% office-premium with 2% interest in case of death of child during deferment period, find the minimum amount the insurer has to keep in reserve to meet his obligations as above.

13

INVESTMENT OF FUNDS

While calculating premium, it has been assumed that the accumulated premiums are invested. The funds are invested to earn at least assumed rate of interest. The needs of investment of funds are given here in brief.

NEEDS OF INVESTMENT

1. Payment of Claims

The first and most important obligation of the insurer is to pay the amount of claims whenever they arise. For this, insurer is getting a substantial amount in form of premiums and has to preserve them for payment later on. To keep such amounts idle will be a failure on the part of the insurer who is expected to invest them on behalf of the policy-holders.

2. To Avoid Financial Deficit

If funds are not invested, the total income of the insurer will fall short of its requirements for meeting its commitments because a particular rate of interest on its investments has been assumed while calculating the rate of premium. Again, if funds are not invested and interest not earned, it would be an under-estimation of its future liability which may prove disastrous at the time of higher mortality.

3. National Interest

A huge fund of the society is taken by the insurers in form of premiums. Therefore, it is essential for the insurers to invest the funds for the economic development of the nation.

SOURCES OF FUNDS

The funds with the insurers are accumulated from the various sources, some of which are given below:

(*i*) Premiums

The main source of funds is the premiums collected by the insurer. The premiums may be single premium, level premiums or annuity considerations. The excess of these premiums over the needed premiums for meeting claims and expenses is the source of funds.

(*ii*) Interest

The second source of funds is the excess interest earned over the assumed rate of interest. The assumed rates are lesser than the actual rate in most of the cases. In reverse, the funds will decline.

(*iii*) Capital Gain

Funds obtained from the sale of share capital and debentures are included under capital gains.

(*iv*) Savings in Expenses

Savings in expense loadings, bonus loadings or mortality savings are also contributing to the funds of the insurers.

(v) Non-Payment of Claims

In pure endowment or term insurance, the claims may not arise, therefore, the premiums paid for such benefits are saved. Sometimes, in certain cases, the claimants do not come for payment at all. Thus, the saved money also form a part of the funds of insurers.

PROBLEMS OF INVESTMENT

While investing the funds, the insurer will have to face various problems, some of which are given in the following sections:

1. The main problem of investment is to preserve the interest of the policy-holders. The insurer keeps the money of the policy-holders as a trust money. To maintain the trusteeship it is essential that the fund must be invested in such securities which are safe and secured.
2. The payment of the claim amount is the second problem of the life insurer. The insurer must have sufficient funds to pay the claims. So, the interest earned from the investment must be adequate enough.
3. The assets of the insurer should be protected from any elements of fluctuations. Therefore, the insurer must earn sufficient amount to pay its expenses. Moreover, the earning should be constant and the market price of the securities must not fall considerably.
4. There should be complete good faith of the public in the insurer's management of funds. In case of doubtful investment the purpose of public may be defeated. The insurer, therefore, may be loosing its business in future.
5. A great care has to be taken while selecting suitable channels of investment. The principles of investment should be followed to a considerable extent. Investment should be such that profit thereon should be maximum without hampering safety and marketability.

THE PRINCIPLES OF INVESTMENT

The canons of investment are safety, profitability, liquidity, diversification and increasing of life business.

1. Safety

The securities in which the funds of insurer is to be invested should never at any time fall in their face values, otherwise the liability will be more than its corresponding assets. The primary purpose of investment is not to earn maximum profit but to maintain a complete security. Therefore, speculative investments involving possibilities of large profits of large losses are not suitable for life insurance funds. On account of trusteeship status, the insurer should invest the funds only in sound channels. Security of principal amount is more important consideration. Therefore, in India, the investment regulations are made whereby the life insurer is required to invest at least 50 per cent of his controlled funds in Government Securities.

Safety includes safety of principal amount and interest, thereon. It means that the principal and interest must not fall, below the expected level at any time. This principle is the keystone of investment.

2. Profitability

The insurer must earn at least the assumed rate of interest otherwise he will suffer loss. The investment, so, should be made in such securities which yield the highest return consistent with the principle of safety. The insurer can reduce his future premiums by earning higher interest and thus will be able to increase his business. It has been realized that the safety and the profitability principles are opposite to each other. The most safe securities earn little profit and vice-versa is also true. Therefore, the investment department has to establish a proper balance between safety and profitably. However, there are certain securities where the safety and the profitability principles are fully observed. Gilt-Edge-Securities, National-Defence Securities are some of the examples of such securities.

A very large portion of funds may be invested in safe-securities which might yield at least assumed rate of interest while the other small portion may be invested in profitable securities guaranteeing at least safety of principal amounts. In addition, an investment fluctuation funds may also be created to meet any possible losses on account of fluctuations in return. In profitability reasonable rate of return with regularity and stability of income is essential. The second factor to be considered is no fluctuation in capital and lesser expenses of investments. The third factor *i.e.,* taxation is also important because unfavorable taxation may reduce the net income of the insurer.

3. Liquidity

It represents convertibility of investments into cash without undue loss of capital. The principle is essential because of immediate requirement of money for payment of claims. However, there is no higher chance of maximum outflow at any time because the maturity, unlike the bank withdrawal, may not fall within a short period. The claims are, generally, following a set-trend on the maturity and death experience. A rough estimation can be made of the payments of claims, surrender values, policy loans and regular expenses 'Funds' should be invested according to the requirements of the insurers, *i.e.,* investments are so made that the maturities will occur at intervals adjusted to meet the needs of maturity obligations.

For meeting the daily outflow of funds, it is not essential to keep maximum amount in cash or in readily convertible securities because a vast inflow of cash is observed in form of premium return on investment and sale of securities. For the established and financially stronger insurers, the liquidity is not much essential. Moreover, the insurer can insert a clause of delay in payment for a specific period.

The principle of liquidity is against the principle of profitability because the idle cash will earn nothing and invested cash will have no liquidity.

4. Diversification

Diversification of investment may mean spreading investment over different channels. The spreading may take place in the following manners.

(*a*) Diversification on the basis of geographical distribution.

(*b*) Distribution of the protfolio over the different economic enterprises of the country, political changes and time.

(*c*) Diversification may be according to number of investment in a security, maturity of security and duration of security.

(*d*) The distribution of funds according to industries, firms and sectors.

The diversification provides maximum security with high yield and better liquidity provided the diversification was done taking into account of all these factors. Do not invest all the funds at one place in an industry, in a security and for a period of maturity. Investments should spread over the widest possible range to minimise unfavourable consideration and to gain favourable advantages. Under diversification, the law of average reduces the losses to minimum.

5. Increasing of Life Business

Investments should also be made in those sectors which are going to benefit the business in the return. Naturally, the social objective principle helps in increasing the business. For example, the life funds, if utilised to finance the schemes of housing, sanitation, medical and education, it will go a greater way to lower the mortality and to increase the standard of people. Decreased mortality and increased income cause more business to insurer because the lower mortality tends to reduce the rate of premium which increases the business. Higher income induces person to get more policies.

Principles of Investment as laid down by Mr. A. H. Bailey

Mr. A. H. Bailey was actuary of the London Assurance Corporation. He contributed a paper in 1862, which was published in Journal of Institute of Actuaries, Vol. X. The principles are commonly known as 'Bailey's Canons' which remain as much applicable to insurance business today as they were in 1862. However, their mode of application can be changed with the changing conditions. His principles of investment are summarised as below:

(*i*) That the first consideration should invariably be the security of the capital.

(*ii*) That the highest practicable rote of interest be obtained, but that this principle should always be subordinate to the previous one, *i.e.*, the security of capital.

(*iii*) That a small proportion of the total funds (the amount varying according to the individual circumstances of each case) should be held in readily convertible securities for the payment of current claims.

(*iv*) That the remaining and much larger proportion may be safely invested in securities that are not readily convertible.

(*v*) That as far as possible the capital should be employed to aid the life insurance business.

COMMENTS ON THE PRINCIPLES

1. The presentation of the principles shows that Mr. Bailey was fully aware of the safety, profitability and liquidity principles but he presented in an exemplary way which did not reveal all scheme of a picture. He would have presented it in a simple way.
2. He was extra cautious with the negative relationship between the safety and profitability. But there are certain securities where the safety and profitability principles are fully applicable simultaneously. In gift-edge securities and postal certificates or national defence bonds may achieve both security of capital and maximum return. Moreover, Investment Fluctuation Fund may be created for meeting losses on investments.
3. He put undue stress on liquidity. Liquidity, at least for established concerns, are not very essential because a vast fund inflows daily to the business in form of premium, return on investment and other sales proceeds.
4. He discussed the principle of diversification in his second, third and fourth principles which can be given only under one principle of diversification because the diversification may also be according to profitability and liquidating besides according to class, character and geographical locations.

USEFULNESS OF MR. BAILEY'S PRINCIPLES

Mr. Bailey's principles are as much useful today as were in his time.

1. Security of Capital

As he thought, security of capital is very useful today also, because of fiduciary relationship of the insurer and insured. Therefore, he pointed out first principle of security in his canons.

2. Profitability

He suggested the second principle only after the first one because he was aware of the negative correlationship between high security and high profitability. It is correct in most of the cases even today. He tried to establish happy balance between the first and second principles. Therefore, he suggested that a fund should be invested in safe security first and in profitable securities, later on. At least the assumed rate of interest must be earned to avoid losses.

3. Liquidity

The negative correlationship between liquidity and profitability was fully known to him. Therefore, he suggested that a larger portion of funds should be invested in non-liquid securities and a smaller part in the liquid securities, *i.e.,* which can be easily converted into cash.

4. Social Objective

His fifth rule to increase life insurance business is now gaining more importance because of awareness of the government towards Social objectives. He suggested that life insurer should make investment in social institutions such as municipal boards, hospitals, housing societies, health centres and schools because these will help in reducing mortality which will tend to reduce premium rates. The life business will increase, consequently.

SUITABILITY OF VARIOUS TYPES OF INVESTMENTS

There are various types of investments having their own advantages and disadvantages. Skill and sound judgment may influence the result. The suitability of some of the investments is discussed here.

1. Government Securities

Government Securities are deemed to be the safest securities in the senses theat there are no substantial fluctuations in their values. Securities of Central Government are safer than that of State Governments. The return on these securities may not be higher. The foreign government securities are not much favourable due to fluctuation and political conditions. The social objective principle is also fulfilled by these securities because the stronger government can look after better its masses.

2. Industrial Securities

The shares and debentures of business and industrial units are included in this category. The rate of return on these securities is comparatively higher than the return on government securities but the safety principle is not so much applicable as in latter case. They are also desirable investments for fulfilling socio-economic purposes. Maximum diversification of investments industry-wise, nature-wise and sector-wise etc. is very much possible.

Relative Importance of Shares and Debentures

Debentures and bonds offer a greater amount of security. The preference shares are more secure than the equity shares. The returns on debentures and preference share being fixed are not more profitable than the return on equity shares. But, the return is more stable in the former case. However, the rate of return depends largely on the normal rate of the concerns, size and nature of business and management of the unit. For example return on shares of a well managed and sound concern will be better than that of financially unsound concerns. Moreover, the equity shares will be more secured in the former case than the debentures of the lattern concern. The investment department of the insurer must have constant vigilance over the prices of such securities, and securities of only those concerns should be selected which promise constant and regular income and lesser or no fluctuations in their price. From return point of view the equity shares of sound concerns are better investment. Some experts are of the opinion that the equity shares do not form proper investment because it tempts to secure full control of the business units, which is beyond the purview of insurance business. The government has also laid down various regulations of investment in shares. The investment of a very large proportion of the funds of a life insurance is undoubtedly objectionable, but it is not necessary to prohibit such investments altogether.

Preference shares give lower yield but the return is more assured while ordinary stocks involve more speculation about the return. Debentures rank high in order of security and are placed next to government securities. Debenture-holders are creditors and as such have prior right to both interest as well as capital over shareholders of a particular unit.

3. Mortgages

Loans are, generally, granted on the mortgage of buildings and land. Usually loans are given to a lower amount than the value of property to provide sufficient margin for safety. Adequate rate of return is observed on such loans and there are sufficient scopes of diversification. Moreover, these loans are relatively expensive to initiate and to service. The marketability of such loans is also doubtful. But a mortgage loan carrying a provision of amortization whereby the loan is entirely paid off in a particular period, are perfectly satisfactory. Mortgages are a specified form of investment and, as such, need skill and experience in their managements.

4. Real Estate

The purchase of land and buildings is included under investment in real estate. This is not a proper investment for insurer because there are a huge fluctuations in the prices of real estate. Moreover, he real estate does not guarantee a constant and higher income apart from the lesser marketability. Therefore, the insurer has only as much real estate as is needed for his own requirements, *i.e.,* for opening offices. Investment in real estate requires specialised knowledge. Hence, the insurer has a special department for its management.

5. Policy Loans

Policy loans are given to the policy-holders against the security of the surrender value of the policy. The amount of loan and interest thereon will not be more than the surrender value of the policy. The loan, if not paid, can be taken over from the amount of surrender. The liquidity factor is not bright because the unpaid loans cannot be treated as unpaid until the duration of the policy. The rate of expenses in handling such loans are very high. However, this is an important investment as it improves business and customer relationship and provides facilities to the policy-holders.

6. Other Assets

The funds of the life insurer may be invested in the business it self in the shape of cash, machine, furniture and properties etc. These investments are as essential as other forms of investment because they assist in smooth running of the business.

Bases for Formulation of Investment Policy by a Life Insurer

1. Basic Principles

The safety, profitability, liquidity diversification and aid to business are guiding principle for formulating the investment policies. These principles vary according to the nature and size of business. However basically, these principles have to be, applied for proper investment policy.

2. The Outlook of Management

Apart from the basic principles, the investment portfolio is affected with the attitude of the management of the concern. If the management wishes to earn maximum profit, investment will be made in high-yielding securities rather than in safe securities. The sound and effective management will always try to invest in safe and constant earning securities.

3. The Present Composition of Investment Portfolio

Where the present composition of investment portfolio shows heavy concentration on government securities, fresh investment may be made in industrial securities. An effective investment policy will have to establish a proper balance between all types of investment channels.

4. Present Position of the Insurer

Investment of the insurer is affected mostly with the size, age, capital and progress rate of the business. For example, new insurer must see safety to the maximum level while the established concern may invest in high-yielding security.

5. Availability of Suitable Securities

When the most suitable securities are not available, investment will have to be confined to the next suitable investment. The requirement of time may also bound the investment portfolio, e.g., during war period, government securities are considerably used.

6. Adequacy of Funds

If there is adequate fund with the insurer investment may be made in high-yielding securities and if funds are insufficient, safety principle is the most considerable factor.

7. Socio-Economic Needs

Bailey had also suggested that investment must be made according to the social and economic requirement of the society. It has been discussed earlier that for meeting social objectives, investment, sometimes, is made even in low yielding securities.

Environment of the Country

Political and economical environment of the country also affect the investment portfolio. International and national relationship are also taken into account while investing the funds.

9. Limitation of Investment

Investment of funds is subject to two limitation:—

(*a*) Legal; and

(*b*) Self-imposed.

(*a*) Legal Limitations

It can be of two types:—

(*i*) Quantitative; and

(*ii*) Qualitative

(*i*) Quantitative Limitation

The quantitative aspects of investment regulations stem from the specification of eligible types of investment and the minimum quality criteria for individual investments within the eligible categories.

(*ii*) Quantitative

Limitations may be imposed on the amounts that can by placed in eligible investments. For example, in India at least 50 per cent of the controlled funds should be invested in government securities.

(*b*) Self-Imposed Limitations

Life insurers also place limitation on their investments which is determined by the tradition and outlook of management. These limitations may be change from time to time.

INVESTMENT REGULATIONS FOR LIFE INSURERS

The Insurance Regulatory and Development Authority (IRDA) Formulated Investment Regulations in August, 2000 and subsequently amended them in May 2001. The latest regulations which are applicable are as per Regulation (3).

S.No.	*Type of Investment*	*Percentage*
(*i*)	Government Securities	25%
(*ii*)	Government Securities or other approved Securities (including (*i*) above)	Not less then 50%

Contd...

(*iii*)	Approved Investments as Specified in Schedule	
(*a*)	Infrastructure and Social Sector Explanation: For the purpose of this requirement, Infrastructure and Social Sector Shall have the meaning as given in relation 2(h) of Insurance Regulatory and Development Authority (Registration of Indian Insurance Companies) Regulations, 2000 and as defined in the Insurance Regulatory and Development Authority (Obligations of Insurers to Rural and Social Sector) Regulations, 2000 respectively.	Not less than 15%
(*b*)	Other to be governed by Exposure norms as specified in regulations 5. Investments in "other than approved Investment in "other than approved Investments" can in no case exceed 15% of the fund.	Not exceeding 35%

Regulation 3. "1. Life Business: In terms of explanation is Section 27A of the Act, the Authority has determined that assets relating to Pension business, Annuity business and Linked Life Insurance business shall not form part of the Controlled Fund for the purpose of that section.

Without prejudice to Section 27 or Section 27A of the Act, Every insurer carrying on the business of life-insurance shall *invest and at all times keep invested* his controlled fund (other than funds relating to pension and general annuity business and unit linked life insurance business) in the following manner.

2. **'Pension and General Annuity Business':** Every insurer *shall invest and at all times keep invested* funds belonging to his Pension Business, General Annuity Business in the following manner:

Sr. No.	*Type of Investment*	*Percentage*
(*i*)	Government Securities, being not less than	20%
(*ii*)	Government Securities of other approved Securities (inclusive (I) above, being not less than)	40%
(*iii*)	Balance to be invested in Approved Investments as specified in Schedule 1 and to be governed by Exposure/Prudential Norms specified in Regulation 5	Not exceeding 60%

Note: for the purposes of this sub-regulation no unapproved investments shall be made.

3. 'Unit Linked Life Insurance Business': Every insurer shall invest and at all times keep invested his segregated fund of unit linked life insurance business as per investment offered to and approved by the policy-holders. Uni Linked policies may only be offered here the units are linked to categorie of assets which are both marketable and easily realizable. However, the total investment in other than approved category of investments shall at no time exceed 25% of the fund.

An attempt has been made to discuss the issues arising out of the investment regulations pertaining to life business.

- The inclusion of infrastructure appears to aim for channeling insurance funds into infrastructure projects which need long term funds in significant amounts. Further in the changed economic scenario, the funds could be invested in Corporate Sector for implementing he infrastructure projects.
- Earlier also the mandated investments were directed towards social sector. However the definition of social sector under IRDA regulations is more rigorous and basically these investments are meant for the development of economically backward segments in both urban and rural sectors.
- Even though the objectives are laudable, given the slow pace of progress in the implementation of infrastructue projects thereby slowing the off take of funds coupled with the rigorous definition

of social sector the insurers, more so the existing players may find it difficult to deploy the funds in the social Sector on accretion basis, as per the Regulations.

- The regulator may consider under the definition infrastructure Oil and Gas Pipelines, CNG, LNG Terminals, which also need huge sums of money. Further, it may also consider investments in funds exclusively devoted for infrastructure sectors as investments under infrastructure.
- Many Infrastructure projects have foreign collaborations. The companies, for implementing these projects, are being incorporated as Private Limited Companies. On doing so, apparently, the foreign partners in these Companies enjoy certain tax benefits. But the insurance Act, 1938 as amended, explicitly states that an insurer shall not out of his controlled fund invest or keep invested any sum in the shares or debentures of a private limited company. The act therefore effectively bars any investment in a private limited company. This provision may act as an impediment for flow of funds into private limited companies implementing infrastructure projects. This issue therefore needs to be re-examined.
- In addition, the definition of rural and social sector is quite rigorous. It is indeed quite challenging for the insurance companies to evolve norms for granting loans in the social sector, wherein mostly the loanees are individuals with little or no security.
- The insurance companies, as they are not equipped to identify the beneficiaries/genuine credit needs, may have to involve village level panchayats, NGOs, Co-operative Societies and other government agencies to lend for the social sector. Even by lending through these organisations, the issue of monitoring will still be left unanswered, in view of the lack of administrative mechanisms available with insurers. The regulator may have to look into these practical aspects and review this regulation. Alternatively, the insurance companies may be directed to lend to government rural organisations/nodal agencies either directly or by way of refinancing and such investments may be treated as investments under social sector.
- The regulation does not specify any definite percentage of investments separately for infrastructure and social sectors. However, in a recent amendment proposed, it explicitly mentions that every insurer shall endeavor to maintain a proper balance between the investments made in infrastructure and social sectors thus inhibiting insurers from investing in one sector completely and complying with the regulation.
- The compliance with this regulation may not be easy for existing life insurer *i.e.,* LIC, as it has a huge controlled fund approximating to ₹ 200,000 Cr. 15% of this will amount to ₹ 30,000 Cr. If one has to strike balance in the investments between infrastructure and social sector, the investment figures are mind boggling and to deploy that kind of money in the social sector may not be very easy. Even on accretion basis, wherein the yearly accretions are in the range of ₹ 28,000 to 30,000 Crs. compliance with this regulation will be difficult as the numbers involved are about ₹ 4200-₹ 4500 Cr. If a balance has to be struck between the investments in infrastructure and social sector, at least an amount of ₹ 1000-1500 Cr. may have to be invested in the social sector. Therefore to comply with the regulation on year to year accretion basis, let along on total control fund, would be very difficult.
- These investments, notwithstanding the issues mentioned above, have to comply with the norms as specified in Schedule-1. The recent amendments to Schedule-1 say that bonds issued for development of infrastructure and social sectors, duly guaranteed by government or otherwise rated AA by an independent rating agency, issued by others would qualify as approved investment.
- Most of the infrastructure projects are implemented under new companies without any track record. General view among the rating agencies is that project bonds/debentures will not get a rating of more than A+ on their own accord. As these projects involve substantial investments, the guarantees from parent companies may not be forthcoming. Therefore in practice bonds

may not qualify as approved investment. It is assumed that "others" means other than Government.

- The IRDA, under Section 27A, amended the following clause:

"All secured loans, secured debentures, secured bonds, other secured debt instruments, shares and preference shares and debt instruments issued by all India Financial Institutions recognised as such by RBI-investments to be made in terms of investment policy guidelines, benchmarks and exposure norms/limits approved by the Board of Directors of the Insurer".

The Notes 2 to 4 under regulations 3 & 4 mention that all investment in assets/instruments which are capable of being rated as per market practice be rated and should carry a minimum rating of AA. If sufficient investments of this grade are not available, Investment Committee may approve investments in instruments rated A+.

Going by the workings of the clause, one may infer that all the project loans/debentures etc., which are generally secured by a first charge on the assets of the company and are not rated as per market practice may qualify as approved investments.

Another significant issue is point 7 in the notes which states "investments in equity shares listed on a recognised stock exchange should be made in actively traded and liquid instruments viz., its trading volume does not fall below 10,000 in any trading session during the last 12 months or trading value of which exceeds ₹ 10 lacs in any trading session during last 12 months".

It is presumed that it pertains to only secondary market operations. By virtue of this note, it is assumed that the insurer is not prohibited from investing in IPOs, project equities and other privately placed equities in companies which may not be listed immediately. In fact many infrastructure project companies seek equity investments as part of project finance and these companies generally propose to get listed only after the project is commissioned and start earning profits. Further, many infrastructure related funds are being floated for initial project development and these funds need equity Investments.

- The regulations mention that other approved investments shall be governed by Exposure Norms. Hence it may be inferred that Exposure Norms may not apply for Infrastructure and Social Sector Investments.
- The regulator has included Commercial Paper with "very strong" or more rating, inter alia, in the approved investments. In view of the developing market for Securitisation, the regulator may also consider including "Pass Through Certificates" issued with "very strong rating" as approved investments. In recent times, PTCs have slowly started coming into the market and will provide a good investment opportunity for insurers as these are generally backed by cash flows and also asset cover in the case of mortgage backed securities and suitable credit enhancement facilities. In recent times, all PTC issued were rated as "AAA (so)". It may be noted that in the domestic market, none of the securitised deals has experienced default as of today.

SEBI in its latest move has banned the carry forward trading and introduced options on individual equities w.e.f. 2nd July. The Index futures have already started trading. Options and futures, world over, are used by insurance companies as portfolio hedging instruments. As per the reporting formats prescribed by the IRDA, it appears there is no bar on insurance companies to deal in derivative instruments. However, detailed guidelines may be necessary in view of the varied risk profile of derivatives depending upon the purpose for which they are traded in/held. For example if an insurance company holds derivative instruments purely for hedging its portfolio, which will enable it to reduce the investment risk on the portfolio, it may be considered as an approved investment.

- As already mentioned above, many infrastructure projects are being implemented as Private Ltd. companies. Besides, many of these projects are coming up with structured products such as Take Out Finance etc. These instruments may be considered as part of the financing instruments for the projects along with the traditional instruments.

EXPOSURE NORMS

The IRDA Regulations also provide norms regarding investment exposure to individual companies.

The Exposure Norms briefly are as follows:

- The Capital Employed is defined as total of ordinary and preference shares, debentures, long/medium/short term loans (excluding public deposits), free reserves but excluding revaluation reserves of the investee company as shown in the last audited balance sheet.
- The regulator would have done well by giving a definition of each of the terms used in the regulations as there is wide scope for different interpretations of definitions such as capital employed, free reserves etc.
- The investments in equity (ordinary, preference and convertible portion of debentures) should not exceed 50% of the above mentioned exposure norms. In effect in the case of individual Investee Company, insurance companies and existing insurers should not exceed 5% and 10% of the capital employed respectively. Further, the regulator restricts investment in the promoters' groups of the life insurance Company to 5% of the controlled fund.
- The norms are uniform for all insurers in principle, limiting exposure to individual company, group and industry sector and to promoters' groups reduces the risk of concentration and excessive self-investments.

Type of Investment (1)	*Limit for Investee Company* (2)	*Limit for the entire group to which the Investee company belongs* (3)	*Limit for the industry sector to which the Company belongs* (4)
Equity/Preference Shares/Convertible portion of Debenture at face value Debenture—(face) value) including Private place	As on any date Not exceeding 20% of the total Capital Employed	As on any date Not exceeding 15% of the total Capital Employed of group companies	As on any date Not exceeding 15% of the total Capital Employed in all such companies.
NCDs and Non-Convertible portion of Convertible Debentures Short/Medium/ Long Term Loans and "any other financial assistance	During the year not exceeding 5% of estimated annual accretion of funds	During the year not exceeding 10% of estimated annual accretion of funds	

PRUDENTIAL NORMS

- The regulator has earlier specified various prudential norms for investments in NCDs and Terms Loans. However, in the latest amendment, the Regulator has left prudential norms to the discretion of the board thus removing a major impediment. This provides leeway as the board, keeping in view the availability of skills for appropriate risk assessment of an investment with the company, may evolve the norms such that the policyholders funds enjoy highest amount of safety.

- The discussion in the foregoing paragraphs clearly indicate that the regulations are prescriptive in nature, with an objective to protect the funds of the policyholders and as in the case of any prescription impose constraints on the flexibility and innovative ability of the insurer in investing the funds. By no means these restrictions are undesirable, given the nascent development of Indian financial markets, inability of various regulators to prevent market manipulations, inadequate and lack of prompt punitive system and slow and complicated legal systems.

Some Concluding Remarks

- If we compare the Indian regulations with those prevailing in U.K., the developed insurance market, there are no restrictions on the investment pattern in U.K. The value of assets has to be maintained at more than the value of liabilities. However, for valuation, which is based on market value of assets, the admissible of asses and caps on investments in particular assets have been specified. However, these rules do not preclude insurers from holding assets, which are not admissible, as long as they demonstrate solvency. The insurer has to disclose all his investments completely so that policyholders are aware of the investment pattern and its performance.
- On the other hand, the regulations in US are again prescriptive with quantitative qualitative restrictions on the investments of insurers even though the markets are well developed and efficient. India over a period of time, as its gains experience may gradually progress towards the US pattern and from there to UK pattern, if our markets and legal systems are fully developed and equipped to deal with any eventuality efficiently.

(*The views in the article are those of the author. The article is an obridged version of a presentation made by the author at National Insurance Academy, Pune*)

INVESTMENT PATTERN OF LIC AND OVERVIEW OF INVESTMENTS AS ON 31ST MARCH, 2002

The investment of LIC are governed by Section 27A of the Insurance Act, 1938 and the (Investment) Regulations as prescribed by the Insurance Regulatory and Development Authority (IRDA). LIC follows a very prudent and sound systems of investment. The decision for investments are taken by a high level committee comprising Chairman of LIC, Managing Director and some members of the Board of the corporation, and an investment is made only if the decision to do so is taken with unanimity. In all its investments LIC follows the exposure and prudential norms prescribed by the Investment Committee and the IRDA. In our investment decisions the emphasis is on obtaining the highest yield commensurate with the total security of our funds. The pattern of Investments as prescribed for LIC is as under:

Investment Norms for LIC: Life Business

Sr.No	*Type of Investment*	*IRDA Norm*
1.	Govt. Securities	Not less than 25%
2.	Govt. Securities of other Approved Securities. (including item no. 1)	Not less than 50%
3.	Approved investments	
	(*a*) Infrastructure and Social Sector	Not less than 15%
	(*b*) Others	Not exceeding 35%

Investment Norms for LIC: Pensions and Group Schemes Business Not less than 15%

Sr.No	*Type of Investment*	*IRDA Norm*
1.	Govt. Securities	Not less than 20%
2.	Govt. Securities of other Approved Securities including 1 above	Not less than 40%
3.	Balance in Approved Investment	Not exceeding 60%

The Break-up of investment are as under:

LIC's Investments (₹ Cr.) As on 31st March

Sr.No	*Type of Investment*	*2001-02*	*2003-2004*	*2006-2007*
1.	Govt. Securities and Govt. Guaranted Bonds	126752	99256	272498
2.	Other approved securities	2982	2630	64285
3.	Investments in Infrastructure and Social Sector	4492	11747	73746
	(*i*) Others to be governed by exposure norms Specified in Regulation 5.			
	(*ii*) Out of the above 35% percentage of investment in Other than Approved Investments not to exceed 15%	60874	15198	
	Total Investments	195100	128831	410529

INVESTMENTS IN THE INFRASTRUCTURE AND SOCIAL SECTOR

LIC has been investing in Infrastructure and Social sector in a major way. As per IRDA norms, LIC is required to invest 15% of the accretion to the controlled fund in Infrastructure and Social Sector. The major investments in social sector are as under:

Total Investments And Outstanding Position In The Social Sector As on 31st March

Sector	*Total investment* *2002*	*(₹ in Crore)* *2007*
Housing	4817.28	22451
Power	135.16.44	37881
Road Railways, Port & Bridges	892.84	1516
Irrigation / Water Supply & Severage	3950.28	7500
Others	3404.70	4398
Total	26581.54	73746

LIC'S INVESTMENTS ARE WELL DIVERSIFIED AND SECURE

LIC has a very strong and robust base of investment and is one the largest financial institutions in the country. The Asset bases of LIC stands at ₹ 2,45,387 Crore as on 31st March 2002 which includes investments of ₹ 2,15,392 Crore. LIC's investment activities are well distributed in all categories of

Sectoral Investment by Life Insurers as at March 31, 2006

Insurer	Life Fund (Rs. Crores)												Pension and General annuity			
	Central Govt Securities		State Govt Securities and other approved Securities Including central Govt Securities		Infrastructure / Social Sector		Investment Subject to Exposure Norms (INCL. OTAI)		Other than Approved Investments (OTAI)		Total (Life fund)		Central Govt Securities		State Govt Securities and other approved securities including central Govt Securities	
Public Sector	31/3/05	31/3/06	31/3/05	31/3/06	31/3/05	31/3/06	31/3/05	31/3/06	31/3/05	31/3/06	31/3/05	31/3/06	31/3/05	31/3/06	31/3/05	31/3/06
LIC	1,67,718.86	1,97,419.39	206,906.87	2,41,103.52	44,660.40	48,182.22	1,09,861.60	1,00,161.78	26.111.98	26,286.06	3,61,428.87	3,89,447.52	5,650.77	18,987.86	9,083.36	28,881.26
Total (A)	1,67,718.86	1,97,419.39	2,06,906.87	2,41,103.52	44,66.40	48,182.22	1,09,861.60	1,00,161.78	26,111.98	26,286.06	3,61,428.87	3,89,447.52	5,650.77	18,987.86	9,083.36	28,881.26
Private Sector																
HDFC STD	286.29	463.82	286.29	463.82	85.80	213.28	108.67	233.43	19.58	14.82	480.77	910.53	117.37	215.39	117.37	215.39
MAX NYI	109.02	505..97	315.67	505.6	89.08	130.90	11.62	57.06	15.06	29.80	436.37	693.90	281	14.79	12.90	14.79
ICICI PRU	552.82	683.64	552.82	683.64	159.04	226.11	258.77	404.34	75.82	67.37	970.63	1314.09	121.87	184.53	121.87	184.53
Birla Sun	84.73	141.95	110.75	141.95	3174	41.97	27.58	68.72	9.56	7.25	170.06	252.64	0.06	0.15	0.06	0.15
Tata-Aig life	311.91	511.43	311.91	511.43	64.66	121.50	16.19	91.37	1.33	4.69	392.76	724.30	58.25	72.93	58.75	72.93
Om Kotak	103.11	128.97	113.10	180.53	66.92	59.99	40.64	##	0.73	1.98	200.52	338.54	8.23	##		
SBI life	587.78	758.38	792.78	780.18	155.26	264.96	212.86	500.76	88.48	167.70	960.89	1545.91	55.36	90.85		
Allianz Bajaj	235.67	403.04	235.67	403.04	74.02	141.91	72.79	178.15	20.89	30.94	382.28	723.10	7.13	18.12	7.13	18.12
Metlife	101.51	127.20	101.51	127.20	30.05	43.87	25.63	37.40	13.34	17.69	157.18	208.67	0.21	0.36	0.21	0.36
Reliance life	63.54	95.80	65.30	95.80	22.94	34.34	-22.47	33.81	6.58	6.00	110.71	163.98	27.87	50.38	27.87	50.38
ING Vysya	132.91	196.16	132.91	196.16	46.63	75.93	61.69	99.4	14.30	49.01	241.22	371.73	0.00	37.85	0.00	37.85
Vysya Life	79.70	128.91	79.70	128.91	30.21	38.15	35.04	51.24	0.00	4.94	144.95	218.29	0.00	0.00	0.00	0.00
Ahara Life	60.47	48.42	102.90	90.52	24.27	28.37	15.32	26.00	0.01	2.71	142.48	145.69	0.06	0.32	0.06	0.32
Hriram life		65.25		65.25		34,95		29.55		7.59		129.75		0.00		0.00
Total (B)	2,714.53	4,258.93	3,001.31	4,374.41	860.61	1,456.23	929.07	1,910.49	265.75	412.50	4,790.98	7,741.13	399.22	694.79	414.32	723.18
Total (A+B)	1,70,433.39	2,01,678.32	2,09,908.18	2,45,477.93	45,521.01	49,638.45	1,10,790.66	1,02,072.27	26,377.73	26,698.56	3,66,219.85	3,97,188.65	6,049.99	19,682.65	9,492.68	29,604.44

Note: The figures are based on provisional Returns filed with IRDA

Fund (Rs. Crores)				Group excluding froup Pension and Annuity Fund (Rs. Crores)								Unit Linke fund (Rs. Crores)									
Estatement Subject to Posure norms		Total (Pension Fund)		Central Govt Securities		State Govt Securities and other approved Securities Including central Govt Securities		Investment Subject to Exposure Norms		Total (Group Fund)		'Other Approved Investments		Other than Approved Investments		Total (Unit Linked fund)		Total (All Funds) (₹ Crores)	
31/3/05	31/3/06	31/03/05	31/3/06	31/3/05	31/3/06	31/3/05	31/3/06	31/3/05	31/3/06	31/3/05	31/3/06	31/3/05	31/3/06	31/3/05	31/3/06	31/3/05	31/3/06	31/3/05	31/3/06
2,378.66	7,276.38	11,462.03	36,157.64	25,039.54	16,665.46	33,297.31	21,231.45	9,342.11	5,506.08	42,639.42	26,737.53	2,547.87	10,269.86	210.80	1,158.59	2,758.67	11,428.45	4,18,288.99	4,63,771.14
2,378.66	7,276.38	11,462.03	36,157.64	25,039.54	16,665.46	33,297.31	21,231.45	9,342.11	5,506.08	42,639.42	26,737.53	2,547.87	10,269.86	210.80	1,158.59	2,758.67	11,428.45	4,18,288.99	4,63,771.14
34.56	57.24	151.91	262.63	0.00	0.00	0.00	0.00	0.00	0.00	0.00	0.00	280.17	1,396.26	10.49	21.86	290.67	1,418.13	921.39	286.79
1.13	1.06	14.03	15.83	1.45	3.76	6.81	3.76	0.44	0.16	7.25	4.92	20.11	142.33	0.33	28.85	20.44	121.18	478.09	885.85
44.77	60.02	166.64	244.55	0.00	0.00	0.00	0.00	0.00	0.00	0.00	0.00	1,896.27	5,270.23	440.89	656.63	2337.16	5,926.86	3,474.43	485.50
0.00	0.00	0.06	0.16	0.00	0.00	0.00	0.00	0.00	0.00	0.00	0.00	1,047.34	1,862.92	78.38	235.13	1,125.72	2,098.05	1,295.85	2,350.85
18.53	23.69	76.78	96.62	14.70	40.69	14.70	40.69	0.00	0.00	14.70	40.69	76.00	325.79	4.81	34.95	80.81	360.74	565.05	1,222.35
5.13	9.56	13.36	20.68	205	3.52	2.05	3.52	0.00	0.49	2.05	4.00	304.75	750.35	3.57	10.26	308.33	760.61	524.40	1,123.82
18.60	160.49	78.97	277.75	420	0.00	4.20	0.00	6.57	0.00	10.77	0.00	3.46	193.27	0.08	18.06	3.54	211.33	1,054.17	2,034.98
2.15	0.00	9.28	18.12	127	8.00	1.27	8.00	0.00	5.82	1.27	13.82	336.14	2,325.67	33.10	243.65	369.24	2,569.32	762.07	3,324.36
0.00	0.08	0.21	0.44	252	5.76	2.52	5.76	0.00	0.53	2.52	6.29	1.62	50.52	0.12	0.00	1.74	50.52	161.66	265.92
22.58	39.21	50.45	89.58	0.00	0.00	0.00	0.00	0.00	0.00	0.00	0.00	21.40	93.25	0.00	6.09	21.40	99.34	182.56	352.90
0.00	37.11	0.00	74.96	0.00	0.00	0.00	0.00	0.00	0.00	0.00	0.00	73.70	214.12	4.91	31.56	78.61	245.68	319.83	692.36
0.00	0.00	0.00	0.00	0.76	0.76	2.06	1.54	0.80	0.77	2.85	2.32	122.95	490.87	8.18	41.27	131.13	532.15	278.93	725.76
0.00	0.00	0.06	0.32	0.02	0.06	0.02	0.06	0.00	0.00	0.02	0.06	0.00	15.57	0.00	0.21	0.00	15.79	142.56	161.86
	0.00		0.00		0.00		0.00		0.00		0.00		0.00		0.00		0.00		129.75
147.43	383.46	561.75	1,106.65	26.97	62.55	33.63	63.33	7.81	8.77	41.43	72.09	4,183.91	13,131.15	584.86	1,328.53	4,768.77	14,459.68	10,162.94	23,379.55
2,526.09	7,659.84	12,023.78	37,264.29	25,066.52	16,728.01	33,330.93	21,294.78	9,349.92	5,514.85	42,680.85	26,809.62	6,731.78	23,401.01	795.66	2,487.12	7,527.45	25,888.13	4,28,451.93	4,87,150.69

investments such as Treasury Bills, Government Securities, State Government Securities, Equity, Projects Financing, Infrastructure, Social Sector etc. LIC is one of the largest investors in Government Securities and social sector and infrastructure investment thereby contributing in a significant way to the economic growth of the nation.

Sectoral Investment by Life Insurers as at March 31, 2006

QUESTIONS

1. What is fund and why the fund is invested?
2. Give the various solutions of the problems of investment.
3. Critically examine the connons of investment.
4. How far is Bailey's principle of investment suitable to modern life insurance? Comment in the light of socialistic goal of a country.

14

SURRENDER VALUE

Nature and Meaning

It has been revealed in previous chapter that the premiums received by the insurer are accumulated with a certain rate of interest, which form the shape of reserve. When the insured wishes to surrender his policy or fails to pay his premium, reserve is no longer accumulated and the insured, generally, is given a surrender value. The surrender value will not be equal to the accumulated reserve because certain expenses or losses are involved in payment of surrender values. Now, the definition of surrender value can be as that amount of premiums paid which is returned to the policy-holder at the time of surrendering the policy. Normally no surrender value is paid if the policy lapses within two or three years of its issue because huge expenditures are involved during the inception of the policy. It has been realised that the insurer may return the excess of receipts over expenditure only after two years of the policy. In India, the policy can be surrendered for cash after the premiums have been paid for at least two years or to the extent of one-tenth of the total number, stipulated for in the policy, provided such one-tenth exceeds one full year's premium.

BASES OF CALCULATING SURRENDER VALUES

There are two bases of calculating surrender values:–

I. Accumulation Approach and

II. Saving Approach.

I. The Accumulation Approach

Under this approach, surrender value is the accumulation of overcharges in the net premium, which upon the surrender of the policy is no longer required to pay the amount of claims, therefore, theoretically he should pay all the accumulated reserve but if it is allowed, the insurer will be left a vary small amount for meeting other obligations because a huge expenses are involved at the time of surrender.

The accumulation approach is very scientific because it allows surrender values to all types of policies, whereas, in practice surrender values on the term policies and pure endowment policies are not allowed because there the question of payment may or may not arise. Had the surrender values allowed on these policies, the insurer may be losing when claims would not arise on the policies.

The accumulation approach regards reserve for policy as the basis of distribution of surrender values. The reserve is calculated in this case on gross premium. So the expenses are also deducted from the premium received. Thus, the reserve would be equal to all the premiums paid and interest earned thereon minus shares of death claims and of over all expenses of the insurer. The surrender value can be the largest amount which the insurer can pay without going into loss. The full amount of reserve to a particular policies cannot be given as a surrender value because there are certain expenses and loss because of surrendering the policies. Thus,

Surrender Value = Full Reserve–Surrender Charges

Surrender Charges

The surrender charges are those expenses and losses which occurred on account of a surrender or lapsation of policy. The surrender charges are discussed below:

***(i)* Initial Expenses**

In the beginning of the contract, certain expenses are involved for processing the proposals, payment of commission to agents and medial officer, correspondence and issuing of policy. The initial expenses are so high that the first year's premium is unable to meet all the expenses. These expenses, actually, are recouped after several years' continuation of the policy. Moreover, the initial expenses involved are equally distributed throughout the premium paying period. If policy is lapsed or surrendered before maturity, a part of the initial expenses are left unpaid. So, it is a justified matter to charge the unpaid initial expenses from the reserve of the policy which is surrendered. If it is not done, it would be a great injustice to remaining policy-holders who are willing to continue the policy. The surrender values are lesser in the beginning and higher at later stage because initial expenses to be recouped in the beginning are more than at later age.

***(ii)* Adverse Financial Selection**

During the period of business depression, the surrendering of policies weaken the financial standing of the insurer because at that time most of the policy-holders will rush for surrender values and the insurer's funds will be reduced to minimum. In such cases the policyholders should not be allowed to receive surrender values more than the realized values of the invested funds. The insurer has to liquidate some assets at depressed prices. The demand of surrender values necessitates some liquid assets with the insurer, which means the insurer is unable to earn sufficient amount on the liquid assets.

***(iii)* Adverse Mortality Selection**

It is well-known fact that the persons in extremely poor health are not likely to surrender their policies. They will beg, borrow or steal to maintain the protection. Those who do surrender are expecting longer lives than those who do not surrender. Consequently at every surrender, the average or actual mortality tends to increase more than the assumed mortality. Thus, the increased mortality should be adjusted while surrender value is permitted.

***(iv)* Contribution to Contingency Reserve**

While calculating gross premium a small amount for contribution to contingency reserve is charged from the policyholders to meet the sudden and accidental rise in claims due to wars and epidemics. If the policy is surrendered in the beginning, the contribution is left unrealised.

***(v)* Contribution to Profits**

The policy is expected to contribute a fund towards the profit. If the policy surrendered, the expectation is lost. So this contribution should also be treated as surrender charges while permitting surrender of policy.

***(vi)* Cost of Surrender**

The insurer will incur a certain amount of expenses in processing the surrender of policies. Sometimes, the cost of surrender is like other expenses, spread over the premium paying period. In early surrender, the cost is left unrealised and a deduction from the reserve is permitted.

These expenses and losses are estimated by the actuary. He tries to allow maximum surrender values keeping all the above factors.

II. Saving Approach

An insurer is responsible for payment of claims whenever it may arise; but if a policy is surrendered, the insurer is relieved of its obligation for payment of the assured sum. He is in a position to save something due to non-payment of claims. Thus, where the insurers is relieved of the responsibility of payment of claims, he is in a position to return some amounts to the insured. But where he may not be required to pay the claims, he is not relieved of the responsibility and no surrender value can be given to the policyholders. For example, in Term Insurance and Pure Endowment policies, the insurer may or may not be required to pay the claims. So the insurer is not bound to pay the amount of surrender. The insurer may certainly agree to pay a cash surrender value to the policy-holder in lieu of paying the sum assured at maturity or death.

The saving approach is more scientific because it reveals the reason of payment of surrender value. Thus, it forbids payment of surrender values on term and pure endowment policies and agrees to pay the surrender amount on whole life and endowment policies.

Under this method, the surrender value is paid in lieu of the claim amount. Here it is to be understood that the amount of saving in non-payment of claim can be calculated only after considering various transactions from the inception of the policy up to its surrender and from the date of surrender up to the maturity or deaths. Had, instead of surrendering the policy, the insurance continued, the insurer would have received the level premiums on the policy and have earned interest on invested amounts and would have occupied certain expenses. Thus, at the surrender of the policy, the insurer does not get certain income and has not to occur future expenses in relation to the policy. The incomes or expenses will continue up to the policy life. Therefore, the life expectancy is to be known while determining the saving in expenses or loss of income. So, at the time of surrender of the policy, it is expected that the policy would have continued up to the maturity or till the end of mortality table. The surrender value on a policy can be calculated as below:

Surrender Value = (Sum assured + Accumulated value of future expenses + Future reversionally bonus, if participating policy) – (Accumulated value of all future premiums + expenses incurred in processing the surrender value).

On the basis of above formula, at the time of maturity or death, the surrender, value is calculated; but it does not mean that the surrender value is paid only at that time. A provisional sum, called minimum surrender allowance, is paid at the time of surrender and then, at the time of maturity or death the surrender value is adjusted. The adjusted amount will be the full surrender value minus the accumulated value of the minimum surrender allowance.

FORMS OF PAYMENT OF SURRENDER VALUES

The policyholder can get the surrender values in any of the following forms:

1. Cash Surrender Value

The policyholder can get the value of surrender in cash. When the policyholder gets the cash, the contract comes to an end and the insurer has no further obligation to pay on that particular policy. Since all the amounts surrendered is given at the time of surrender, the cash benefit is generally less than the other benefits. However, the cash surrender value gives immediate relief to the policyholders; so it is generally preferred by them.

2. Reduced Paid up Insurance

In this case, the surrender value is not paid immediately, but the original amount of policy is reduced in certain proportion and the reduced amount is paid according to the term of Policy . Thus, if, after at least two full years' premiums have been paid in respect of the policy, any subsequent premium be not duly paid, the policy shall not be wholly void, but the sum assured by it shall be reduced to such a sum as shall bear the same ratio to the full sum assured as the number of premiums actually paid shall bear to the total number premiums payable as originally stipulated for in the policy provided such reduced sum together any attached bonus in the case of a policy for a sum assured of ₹ 1,000 or over be not less than ₹ 100 and in the case of a policy for or a sum assured of less than ₹ 1,000 be not less than ₹ 50.

Since, January 1, 1976 the provision for non-forfeiture clause has been altered as below.

1. If the premium under the policies have been paid for a period of five years or 1/4 of the original premium paying period of the policy whichever is less but subject to the condition that minimum 3 years' premiums are paid.
2. The paid up value under the policy is not less than ₹ 250 excluding of attached bonuses for policies where under original sum assured is ₹ 1,000 or more and Rs. 100 exclusive of attached bonus where the original sum assured is less than ₹ 1,000.

The above non-forfeiture condition would apply to proposals completed on and after 1-1-1976.

3. Extended Term Insurance

The net cash value arisen at the time of surrender of a policy can be used for payment of as single premium for purchase of term insurance, where the sum assured will be paid only when death of the life assured occurs within the term of the policy. The main disadvantage of this scheme is that if the life assured does not die within the specified time, the premium paid is forfeited by the insurer. Thus, the surrender value would be lost with no use to the insured. However, in case of death during the term, the policy-holder would be benefited for a higher amount with only a small sum of surrender value. Moreover, the term insurance under this scheme is given without medical examination.

4. Automatic Premium Loan

Under this scheme, the surrender value is used for payment of future premium. Thus, the policy will continue up to the period the surrender value is adequate enough to meet the amount of further premiums. Each premium is paid automatically as it comes due by creation of a loan which with interest becomes a lien upon the face of the policy amount until paid. The premiums continue to be paid until the surrender value is completely exhausted. After this period the policy stands cancelled and no amount is paid to the policy-holder because all the surrender value has been used for payment of premiums.

The advantage of this scheme is that if the policyholder dies after surrender but before expiry of the surrender value, full policy amount minus the loan and interest thereon is paid. The policy does not lapse but remains in full force subject to the lien. The insured is permitted to regain his original status without furnishing an evidence of insurability by simply repaying the amount which he owes to the insurer.

The rate of interest on loan is now 9 per cent p.a. with effect from Feb. 1974. The loan can be granted only up to 90 per cent of surrender value if policy was in force.

5. Purchase of Annuity

The policyholder, with the surrender value, can purchase an annuity. Thus instead of taking surrender value in cash, the annuity is purchased from the available surrender value. The amount of annuity depends upon the amount of net cash value, the attained age of the policyholders and the type of annuity required. The option of an annuity is better alternative to those who require to use all their savings during their life-times.

QUESTIONS

1. Discuss the method of calculating Surrender Value.
2. What are the various forms of payment of Surrender Values?

15

VALUATION AND SURPLUS

Valuation is a process to value the net liabilities of a life insurer as on a particular date. It determines the total amount of reserve that an insurer must have to meet his obligations. It means that the valuation, firstly, determines the total net liabilities of the insurer and secondly, compares his liabilities with the available funds. Ultimately, it can be revealed whether the insurer has sufficient funds to meet his obligations or not.

Purpose of Valuation

There are two main objectives of the valuation (*i*) to determine the solvency of the insurer and (*ii*) to determine the distributable surplus amongst the participating policyholders.

(*i*) ***To determine the Solvency.*** The life insurer must find out whether he has sufficient funds to meet the current obligations or not. In case of insolvency, he has to curtail his expenses and increase the income. He has to raise the premium rates and has to stop bonus distribution. Extra-precaution has to be applied in restraining the outflow of funds.

(*ii*) ***To determine the divisible Surplus.*** The excess of receipts over expenditures of a period cannot be regarded as profit of the year because unless all the claims are paid out, insurer cannot know the actual amount of profit. Since the insurer transacts a continuing business, he cannot know the exact amount of profit at a point. The valuation comes to help the insurer at this stage. The net profit or net loss is estimated through the comparison of net liability at a particular point of time with the available funds at that time. If the funds are more than the net liability, a part of the excess can be distributed as a bonus or as a dividend to shareholders. How much will be distributed depends upon the amount of surplus at that time.

THE CALCULATION PROCESS

The valuation involves calculation of net liabilities apart from this main process, the valuation also includes comparison of insurance funds with the net liabilities during a particular period. The comparison will reveal the surplus or deficiency which is treated accordingly. If the fund is more than the net liabilities (reserves), it would be a case of surplus. Similarly, deficiency will occur where the insurance fund is less than the net liabilities.

1. Calculation of Net Liabilities

The Net liabilities may be calculated with prospective method or retrospective method. Whatsoever method may be applied, the result will be the same provided the past assumptions are also applicable to future estimations. In other words, if deaths occurred as anticipated, interest earned is also as expected and expenses are also incurred according to assumptions, there will be no difference between the value accumulated (retrospective reserve) and the present value required (prospective reserve) to meet the obligations. This brings out the fact that policy value would be the same whether obtained retrospectively from past experience or prospectively on future anticipation. But in practice, the assumed rate of mortality has been observed more than the anticipated mortality. Similarly, the assumed rate of interest has been lesser than the future rate of interest. Thus, the retrospective value has been more than the prospective values.

It has been made clear while explaining the relative merits of these methods that the valuation is made on the gross premium. In the chapter of reserve we have dealt with the calculation of reserve on the basis of net premium. But, so far determination of solvency is concerned, reserve or value is calculated on gross premium where we take into account not only mortality and interest but expenses also.

(*a*) **Prospective Value**

The excess of present value of future claims over the present value of the future premiums is called net liability. There will always be excess because the net liability is calculated after some time of the commencement of the policies. The calculation has been explained in detail in the chapter of reserve. There is only difference of gross and net premium. Here the value is calculated on the basis of gross premium. The method reveals the net liabilities up to which the Insurer must have sufficient funds.

VALUATION BALANCE SHEET AS ON 31ST MARCH 1983

Liabilities			*Assets*
	₹		₹
Net Liabilities	90,17,20,00,000	Life Insurance Fund	98,00,38,00,000
	783,18,00,000		
	9800,38,00,000		9800,38,00,000

The above balance sheet reveals that the Life Insurance Fund is ₹ 783.18 crores more than the net liabilities.

(*b*) **Retrospective Method**

Under this method, the premium is accumulated every year with certain rate of interest after meeting the claims. The accumulated excess is called life values (reserves). The actual accumulated funds should always be more than the assumed reserves. But if the insurer has experienced heavier mortality than what he expected, earned less interest, or incurred greater expenses, the excess of his income over outgo would be less than what it ought to be. If it were so, the insurer's position is not solvent because if this state of affairs were left to continue, he would not be able to meet his future obligations. Similarly, if his experience had been favourable, he would have accumulated more than what he ought to have accumulated and this difference is therefore the 'Surplus'.

1. Bases of Valuation of Net Liabilities

While calculating rates of premium, the insurer bases his calculation on mortality rates, interest, expenses and bonus loading on past experience. But, at the time of valuation of net liabilities, assumptions would have been changed completely and the estimation of 'net liabilities' would be erroneous. Therefore, it is very essential to calculate the 'net liabilities' only on the future estimation which are expected to occur because the net liabilities do not represent past; it reveals the future responsibilities. These bases of calculation of net liabilities are discussed in the following sections.

(*i*) **The Mortality Rate**

The morality rate is assumed that which is likely to be experienced in future during the policy. The past mortality which is revealed recently is modified in the light of present conditions and future prospects of the mortality rates.

(*ii*) **Rate of Interest**

Like mortality rates we are not depending upon the past assumed rate; but we should base our valuation on such rates which may reasonably be anticipated. The expectation of future earnings is well regarded although some conservative rates are used for valuation.

(*iii*) Rate of Expenses

The appropriate expenses should be assumed. Past expenditure ratios may not be the correct figure of valuation. The future expense may be unduly heavy, if businesses are expanding or viceversa is also true. All the classes of expenses are well anticipated for purpose of valuation.

(*iv*) Bonus Rate

Premiums on the participating policies are loaded with bonus extras. In exchange of the bonus loading, the participating policyholders are getting bonus. At last, past years' bonus should be distributed. So the bonus loading must assume at least previous loading.

2. Calculation of Life Insurance Fund

The Life Fund is obtained from the revenue account of the insurer. The previous fund is shown in the credit side of the revenue account in respect of life insurance. During the period, all incomes including premiums, interest, rents, etc., are credited to the revenue account and all payments, like policy claims, annuities, management expenses etc., are debited to the account. The difference of the two sides will disclose the Life Insurance Funds available to insurer at the end of the period. The excess of the incomes over the expenditures during the year will disclose the life insurance fund of the year. Thus, the Life Insurance Fund at a particular date is the accumulation of previous excesses of actual total income to total expenditures in respect of life insurance business. Here, it should be noticed that the Life Insurance Fund is different from Life Insurance Reserve. The Fund reveals the actual amount with the insurer whereas the Reserve discloses the net liabilities of the insurer. Reserve ensures what amount should be with the insurer to pay the claims and Fund replies what amount is with the insurer.

3. Comparison of Net Labilities with Life Insurance Fund

The valuation in India is done in every alternate year because the process of valuation of 'net liabilities' is very different and it cannot be estimated every year. The insurance Act has provided that the valuation should be done once in a period of 3 years. However, the Life Insurance Corporation of India has taken a liberal attitude and makes the valuation once within 2 years. The last valuation was done on 31st March, 1977 and the next valuation will be on 31st March, 1979:

The comparison of net liabilities with Life Insurance Fund will disclose surplus or deficiency. If the former is less than the latter one, surplus is created and when the former is more than the latter one, deficiency is arrived.

Treatment of Deficiency

When deficiency arises, the insurer has to apply some drastic actions such as the expenses are curtailed, profitable investments are sought and bonus is not declared. The premium rates are increased. But increase in premium rates causes reduction in business.

Treatment of Surplus

The surplus arrived on can be distributed among the policyholders and shareholders only after certain provisions. The provisions may be General Contingency Fund, Dividend Equalisation Fund, Bonus Equalisation Fund, and Taxation Fund. As is clear from their names, these funds are provided for meeting certain objectives, *e.g.*, constant rate of bonus to the policyholders or dividend to shareholders.

SOURCES OF SURPLUS

1. Excess Interest

While calculating the net liabilities, a certain rate of interest is assumed; but if the insurer gets more than this rate, the surplus is originated. In other words, the excess of actual interest over the assumed one gives rise to surplus. Sale of securities at more than the book value also contributes the surplus.

2. Savings from Mortality

If the actual rate of mortality is lesser than the assumed rate of mortality, surplus is created by the excess amount. It has been observed that the mortality rate assumed in calculation of policy value has always been lesser than the actual death-rate. Had the former been higher than the latter one, there would be a deficiency, but the insurer, to avoid the deficiency, assumes a very conservative rate of interest.

The savings from mortality act in three ways to induce surplus. Firstly, lesser death causes higher amount of premium which shall be received from the persons more than the expected one. Secondly, lesser payment of claims on account of lesser death causes Surplus to a great extent. Thirdly, the extra-premium will not be required due to death less than the expected one.

3. Savings from Loading

A certain amount is added to the net premium to obtain the office premium for meeting the expenses of the insurance-business. If this assumed loading is more than the actual expenses, surplus will arise.

4. Lapses and Surrenders

Early termination of policy during policy-life may give rise to surplus, if the surrender value given is less than the reserve accumulated or amount of surrender to be given. Actually, this is not surplus because the excess amount will be required to meet the losses on account of surrender.

5. Bonus Loading

On participating policies, bonus loading is added to declare at least a certain minimum rate of bonus. The unutilised portion of it along with interest thereon is added to surplus.

Miscellaneous Sources

Saving in various types of annuity contract may give rise to surplus. Similarly in pure-endowment or Term insurance, some amount may remain unpaid, which will be taken as a surplus.

DIFFERENCE BETWEEN SURPLUS AND PROFIT

As the surplus is a cash sum, being the excess of the funds over the net liabilities brought out by the valuation, the surplus is not the same thing as profits. After having sent some of the surplus to these various funds, what the insurer is left with may be called 'profit'. Thus, to estimate profit, surplus is calculated. The difference between the two arises on account of provisions for various funds.

Divisible Profit

After setting aside certain portion of surplus to various funds, the profit is to be distributed. The supreme consideration for this distribution is legal requirements. For example, Section 28 of the LIC Act, 1956 requires that not less than 95 per cent of the surplus of the Corporation shall be allocated to or reserved for the policy-holders of the Corporation.

BASES OF ALLOTMENT OF PROFIT

The losses of allotment of profit are simplicity, equity, suitability, popularity and flexibility.

1. Simplicity

It is desirable from the expense point of view and from understanding point of view.

2. Equity

The most important principle is 'Equity'. Due weightage should be given to each policyholder according to his contribution to surplus. But in practice, this cannot be rigidly adhered to. So, a broad equity or rough justice in distribution of divisible surplus is taken into account.

3. Suitability

A system of distribution of surplus should be suitable according to the nature, size and age of the insurance business.

4. Popularity

The system should not be confirmed merely to the acturial undersanding but it should be popularly known to the policyholders.

5. Flexibility

The better system of divisible profit will be that which can be changed or altered according to the requirement.

In practice hundered per cent equity is not possible. So the flexibility, simplicity and popularity are generally practised.

METHODS OF DISTRIBUTION OF SURPLUS

The divisible profit is to be distributed amongst the policyholders and shareholders. The main problem is distribution of profit to policyholders. Two methods (*i*) Uniform Bonus Plan and (*ii*) Contributory Plan are assured while distributing the profit to policyholders.

1. Uniform Bonus Plan

Under this method, a uniform bonus rate is given to all policyholders of a particular type. The bonus rate is based on the policy amount. For example, ₹ 25 per thousand on whole life policies have been declared as bonus. Thus, the only equity with this plan is the amount of policy. Higher the policy amount, higher will be the bonus amount to a policy. The bonus rate is determined simply by calculating the total amount of divisible profit and multiplying it with the amount of insurance of ₹ 1,000 and again dividing the whole sum by the amount of insurance under participating policies, at the time of valuation. Thus the bonus per thousand can easily be calculated for a particular period. Thus, this system is popular, simple and flexible, but it is not very much equitous or it makes no distinction between policies on the basis of their contribution to the surplus. However, some persons argued that taking the long term duration, it would be equitous because in the early period of the policy when his contribution is smaller, he is getting higher amount and at the later stage when his contribution will be higher he will be getting lesser amount of bonus. Thus taking the total duration of policy, he is getting equal share of his contribution.

2. Contribution Method

The essential principle of this method is that the divisible surplus should be allotted to the various policies in proportion to the individual contribution of each policy to the surplus. The higher the contribution of a policy, the higher should be the amount of bonus declared on it. Since there are several sources of surplus, contribution of each source should be analysed. For this purpose two things have to be taken into account.

1. The contribution of a particular type of policy to the total surplus.
2. Contribution of each source of surplus of a particular policy to the total surplus is to be determined. Then, on the basis of the contribution of each policy, the surplus is allocated. The calculation has been made simple by taking only three sources of surplus viz. Mortality, Interest arid Expenses savings. This is called 'Three Factor Contribution Plan' . Sometimes, mortality saving is ignored and only two factors viz. excess interest and loading saving are taken into consideration for determining the amount of contribution of each policy.

This method observes mostly the equity principle. But in practice, the calculation is very hard and complicated. Therefore, it is not popular.

CLASSIFICATION OF BONUS

The bonus can be classified on the bases of calculation, resting of bonus and results of calculation.

1. Bonus on the Basis of Calculation

There are two methods of calculation of bonus. Therefore, the bonus may be either uniform bonus or contributory bonus. Where the rate of bonus varies according to the policy amount, that is known uniform bonus and where the contribution method is applied the bonus is known as contributory bonus.

2. Bonus on the Basis of Vesting

The bonus may vest as soon it is declared or after a period when the declared bonus is payable soon as it is declared, it is known as the immediate bonus and when the bonus does not become a liability of the insurer as soon as it is declared, it is called as deferred bonus. In the latter case bonus is payable only when particular conditions are fulfilled. The bonus having already been declared is only in the nature of one of contingent liabilities. The bonus remains with the insurer and ultimately is shared by those policy-holders who satisfy the given condition.

3. Bonus on the Basis of Results

Under this category, bonus is determined on the basis of actual results or fixed on an adhoc basis. When the actual valuation has taken place, the bonus declared is known Final Bonus, and the bonus declared before the acturial valuation is known as Interim Bonus. It is a rough estimation of bonus that will take place in future. It is required where the policy matures before the valuation takes place on the basis of guess the bonus for the interim period is declared.

BONUS OPTIONS

1. Cash Bonus

Under this plan, the bonus when declared is paid to the assured in cash and the original sum assured alone is payable at claim. However, the cash bonus can be converted into other options of bonus.

2. Reversionary Bonus

The bonus is allotted as a uniform percentage addition to the sum assured or sum assured plus existing bonus addition and is payable along with the sum assured according to the terms of the policy. The former case is known as 'Simple Reversionary Bonus' and the latter is known as 'Compound Reversionary Bonus'. The former is simple popular and flexible as every time a bonus is distributed some addition is made to the policy amount. The compound reversionary becomes more equitable but is hard to calculate. So, the simple reversionary bonus is practically used today.

3. Reduction in Premium Bonus

When the bonus is not added to the assured sum but is utilised for permanent reduction in the future premium payable, it is called 'Reduction in Premium Bonus'. As soon as the yearly bonus will be equal to the yearly premiums payable, the policy becomes paid up and no future premiums are required. After this point, the additional increase in bonus may be added to the policy amount.

4. Accumulation at Interest Bonus

The bonus on the policy is kept in deposit with the insurer. The insurer gives a fixed rate of interest on the deposited amount and the insured at any time can withdraw the accumulated bonus or can use it for payment of future premiums.

5. Endowment Option

Under this option, the bonus is accumulated with a certain rate of interest and when the accumulated value of the policy becomes equal to the policy amount, the policy amount is paid in full before maturity. The accumulated value of the policy will increase with the amount of bonus reserves and interest thereon. Thus, before maturity at any time the accumulated value of the policy will be equal to the policy amount.

In India, the Corporation declares simple reversionary bonus at the interval of one year. The bonus can also be used for payment of future premiums.

QUESTIONS

1. What are the factors of valuation? How is valuation done?
2. What do you-mean by profit in L.I.C. and how it is estimated and distributed?
3. What are the various option of Bonus?

16

POLICY CONDITION

The policy conditions are studied in five forms:

1. Conditions relating to commencement of risk,
2. Conditions of Premium,
3. Conditions relating to continuation of policies,
4. Lapse-conditions, and
5. Claims conditions.

CONDITIONS RELATING TO COMMENCEMENT OF RISK

1. Commencement of Risk

The letter of acceptance is not a cover note, it only intimates that the risk will commence when the first premium is offered to and accepted by the insurer. If premium was paid along with the proposal form, the date of letter of acceptance will be the date of commencement of risk. After acceptance of risk, policy is issued. The policy contains terms and conditions of the insurance and is a document which can be used as a proof of insurance.

2. Proof of Age

The proof of age must be produced at the time of proposal or immediately after the proposal because the rate of premium depends upon the age of the life assured. The insurer does not withhold the issue of the policy for want of proof of age, but does not admit any claim unless the age is proved to the satisfaction of the insurer. However, if it is subsequently found that the age at entry was mentioned lower than the correct age, the assured sum is reduced to such amount as would have been purchased at the true age.

If the actual age comes out to be lower than the stated age, the difference is either refunded or adjusted towards future premium or policy amount. The proof of age is very essential at the time of proposal in the term policies. Multi-purpose policy, children's Defered Endowment Assurance, Immediate Annuity and defered annuity, where the life assured has not completed 20 years or where the life to be assured has completed 50 years of age or the proposal is under the Salary Saving Scheme.

CONDITIONS OF PREMIUMS

1. Payment of Premiums

The premium rate is calculated annually, but for the convenience of the assured, it can be paid half-yearly, quarterly or even monthly. It should be remembered that these premiums are not just the portion of yearly premium because the insurer losses interest on the unpaid premium of a year and expenses are involved for frequent calculation of premium. When premiums are not annual but fractional and if death takes place before all the premiums have fallen due for the current policy year, the corporation deducts the unpaid instalments from policy year, the corporation deducts the unpaid instilments from the assured sum at the time of settling the claim.

2. Days of Grace

Premium is paid at or before the due date. But for convenience of the policyholders, certain additional period called days of grace, is allowed to pay, the premium. The insured can pay the premium within the days of grace and the policy would not lapse up to the days of grace. However, the policy will lapse if the due premium is not paid even within the days of grace.

One calendar month but not less than 30 days of grace is allowed for payment of yearly, half-yearly and quarterly premiums, and fifteen days for payment of monthly premiums. The days of grace are to be counted excluding the due date of the premium. When the days of grace expire on a Sunday or a holiday observed by the office of the insurer where premiums are payable, the premium must be paid on the following working day to keep the policy in force. The insurer is not responsible for any delay in remittance caused through the post office or otherwise.

3. Premium Notice

In order that the policyholder may not forfeit the benefit of his policy, notice of premiums falling due will be regularly sent to him except in the case of policies under which the mode of payment of premium is monthly where no such notice is required, the insurer is not bound to give any such notice and the want of it cannot be admitted as an excuse for not paying the due premium in time.

CONDITIONS RELATING TO THE CONTINUE POLICIES

1. Indisputable Clause

In order to protect the interests of the assured, indisputable clause is added which provides that the policies shall be indisputable after a state period, viz., two years from the date of issue except for non-payment of premiums or for fraud. Section 45 of the insurance Act has provided that the policy will not be disputed on ground of unintentional misstatement, misrepresentation or non-disclosure of a material fact after two years of the issue of the policy. However, on ground of fraud it can be disputed at any time during the currency of the policy.

2. Alterations in Policies

The insurer permits certain alterations in terms and conditions of the policies at the request of the policyholders. The insurer reserves the right to decline such requests without assigning any reason. Alteration may be change: in class or term, reduction in sum assured, increase in sum assured, change in mode of premium payment, splitting up of a policy into two or more policies and so on. The insurer, generally, does not permit alterations which increase the amount of risk to the insurer.

3. Exclusion

Ordinarily, the insurer does not assure the hazardous occupation. If any insured person has taken up or intends to take up hazardous occupation, he has to pay extra-premium. The hazardous occupations have been listed, by the Corporation in India. The policies issued at standard rates are free from all restrictions to change in occupation. However, the policies issued to students are on the term of hazardous occupation because a student's occupation is not determined till he completes his education and hence the degree of risk is not known. Standard premium rates are not sufficient to cover the risk of war mortality, therefore, war clause is included in such policies where it is mentioned that if the death will occur due to war the liability of the insurer is limited to the premium paid or surrender value whichever is higher. The total sum assured will not be paid in this case.

4. Lost Policy

The insured must inform to the insurer whenever the policy is lost or destroyed. On the satisfactory evidence of loss or destruction, the insurer will issue a duplicate copy after advertising the fact and will charge the assured the fee for issuing the duplicate copy.

5. Loans

The insurer may grant loan on the security of the surrender value of the policies. In India, loans are granted on unencumbered policies up to 90 per cent of the surrender value in case of policies which are in force for full sum assured and 85 per cent of the surrender value in the case of policies which are paid up being in force for reduced sum assured. In case, policies are due to mature within three years a larger percentage may be granted. The minimum amount for which a loan can be granted is ₹ 150 and the rate of interest is 7½ per cent per annum payable half-yearly. Loans are not granted on certain type of policies where surrender values are not accumulated.

6. Nomination

According to Section 39 of the Insurance Act, 1938, the holder of a policy of life insurance on his own life may, when effecting the policy or at any time before the policy matures for payment, nominate a person or persons to whom the policy money secured by the policy shall be paid in the event of his death. Nominee is the person named by the policyholder to whom the policy amount may be paid if the policy amount is payable on death and the nominee is alive when the life assured expires. In absence of any of these, the nominee does not acquire a right in the policy. If policy matures by expiry of time, the policy amount is payable to the insured himself and not to the nominee.

Notice of Nomination

When such nomination is made for the first time, the corporation will register it even if no notice is served, provided the nomination is in order. But for all cancellation, changes and for all nominations subsequent to the first, the Corporation insists on a notice of nomination in the light of Sec. 39 of the Ins. Act, 1938, otherwise it will not be liable for any payment.

7. Assignment

A transfer or assignment of a policy of life insurance, whether with or without consideration, may be made only by an endorcement upon the policy itself or by a separate instrument, signed in either case by the transferor or by the assignor or has duly authorised agent and attested at least by one witness, specifically setting forth the fact of transfer or assignment. The transfer or assignment shall be complete and effectual upon the execution of such endorsement or instrument only attested until a notice in writing of the transfer or assignment and either the said endorsement or instrument itself or a copy thereof have been delivered to the insurer. The priority of claims will go by the date on which the notice of assignment is served on the Corporation. The insurer has to record the fact of the transfer or assignment and has to give a written acknowledgment of receipt of such notice. As a result of the assignment, all the rights and liabilities under the policy will be transferred to the assignee subject to any condition contained in the assignment.

The assignment can be of two kinds

l. Absolute and 2. Condition. An absolute assignment is an assignment where all rights, title and interest of assignor in the policy pass to assignee without reversion to the former or his estate in any event. Under such an assignment, the policy rests absolutely in the assignee and forms part of his estate on his death. A conditional assignment provides that on the happening of a specified event which does not depend on the will of the owner, the assignment shall be either wholly or partially inoperative. An example of the conditional assignment is one which reverts to the assured in the event of his surviving the date of maturity or in the event of his being alive on the death of the assignee.

8. Suicide

In the event of suicide committed by the assured within one year from the date of commencement, whether insured or not, at the time, the liability of the Corporation shall be limited to the extent of the beneficial interest which any person shall prove to the satisfaction of the. Corporation to have been acquired in the policy bona fide and for valuable consideration, of which notice in writing shall, at least one calendar months previous to death, have been given to the, within mentioned, divisional office of the Corporation and save and except to that extent, this policy shall be void and all claims to any benefit, advantage or interest in the funds of the Corporation by virtue of this policy shall cease.

9. Double Accident Benefit

This provides for payment of double of the sum assured on death by accident. If the life assured sustain any bodily injury resulting solely and directly from accident caused by outward violent and visible means and if such injury within 90 days of its occurrence, solely directly and independently of all other intervening causes results in the death of the life assured, double of the sum assured will become payable. The benefit is available only to limited proposals. The aggregate limit of assurance under this policy is ₹ 1,00,000.

10. Disability Benefit

This benefit will be granted to all lives assured under all plans except pure endowment, term assurances, children's Differed Endowment, Deferred and Retirement Annuities. Life assured disabled by accident from earning his livelihood, will be exempted from paying premiums on his policy, falling due after the date of disablement. This benefit is granted on the first ₹ 20,000 of assurance. The example of permanent disablement are loss of sight of both eyes or amputation of both hands at or above the wrists or amputation of both feet and hands.

11. Extented Disability Benefit

It provides for waiver of premiums and also for payment of an amount equal to the sum assured on permanent total disability as a result of an accident. The example of permanent total disability is given above. This benefit is available by paying extra premium of ₹ 2/- per thousand of sum assured.

LAPSE CONDITIONS

1. Lapse of Policies

The insurer shall remain liable for the payment of the claim so far the assured continues to pay the premiums when they fall due. If the policyholder fails to pay any of the due premiums within the days of grace, the insurance liability ordinarily ceases under the policy and the contract comes to an end. Thus the policy is lapsed and all the benefits related to the policy are terminated. The insurer, however, provides certain alternatives to help the insured at the time of lapsation.

2. Revival of Lapsed Policies

If a policy lapses by non-payment of premium within the days of grace, it may be revived to the full policy amount at any time during the life time of the life assured, but within a period of five years from the due date of the first unpaid premium and before the date of maturity. The revival is possible within six months from the due date of the first unpaid premium without evidence of health on payment of the premiums in arrears with interest at the rate of 7 ½ per cent per annum compounded half yearly. The revival after the first six months from the due date of the first unpaid premium but before five years from the due date of the first unpaid premium will be effective only on satisfactory production of evidence of health and habits of the life assured and no adverse change in personal or Family History or occupation.

3. Special Revival Scheme

Many policyholders find it difficult to pay the arrears of premiums with interest to revive their policies. For them the special revival scheme is beneficial to gain the cover of insurance. Under this scheme, the date of commencement of policy will be fixed by dating back the policy. The period for which the policy will be dated back depends upon the amount of premium paid. The plan and period of insurance will be the same as those under the original policy. The revival will be effected ordinarily by issue of a fresh policy.

The special revival is possible only when all of the following conditions are fulfilled.

1. The policy must not have acquired surrender value.
2. Period from the date of lapse must not be less than 6 months and not over two years.
3. Such a revival is not allowed more than once under the same policy.

4. Surrender Value

When the assured is unable to revive his policy, he can surrender his policy and can get cash surrender value. With this payment, the contract comes to an end and the assured will get the cash value without any liability to pay further premiums. In India, the Corporation has guaranteed surrender value if the premiums have been paid for at least two years or to the extent of one-tenth of the total number of premiums stipulated for in the policy provided such one-tenth exceeds one full year's premium. The minimum surrender value allowable under this policy is equal to 30 per cent of the total amount of the, within mentioned, premium paid excluding the premiums for the first year and all extra premium. The percentage increases along with the increase in duration of premium payment because the amount of the surrender on any policy depends on its reserve value. Thus, on such policies which do not have any reserve, no surrender value is allowed.

Since January 1st, 1976, the provision for non-forfeiture clause has been amended.

1. If the premiums under the policy have been paid for a period of five years or 1/4 of the original premium paying period of the policy, whichever is less but subject to the condition that minimum 3 years' premiums are paid.
2. The paid up value under the policy is not less than ₹ 250 (excluding of attached bonuses) for policies whereunder original sum assured is ₹ 1,000 or more and ₹ 100 exclusive of attached bonus where the original sum assured is less than ₹ 1,000.

The above non-forfeiture conditions would apply to proposals completed on and after 1-1-1976.

Since April, 1980, the above conditions have been changed. Surrender value is secured only when the policy was continued for three years.

5. Extended Term Insurance

If a premium remains unpaid at the end of the days of grace and the policy has been in force for at least three years, the insurance will continue as paid up for the full sum assured up to a period called term.

The term depends upon the amount of premium paid. During this period, if the life assured dies payment will made up to the full amount. But, if the assured survives the period, no payment is made. Actually, the amount of premium paid before the lapsation is utilised as a single premium or purchasing term insurance and the duration of the term insurance upon the amount of premium paid for meeting as single premium.

6. Automatic Premium Loan

The assured may use the option of automatic premium loan before the maturity of the policy. In this case, if the assured is unable to pay the premiums the insurer will not allow the policy to lapse but will automatically pay the premiums out of the net surrender value. The assured can repay the unpaid premiums with interest at any time while the policy is so kept in force without furnishing evidence of insurability. If the whole of surrender value is exhausted by advances on account of payment of premium, the policy will lapse and can be revived only after payment of all the premiums unpaid and interest thereon at the rate of 7½ per cent per annum compounded half yearly. This option can be exercised only when premiums of consecutive three years have been paid.

In this case one benefit is also available that if after at least three years, premiums have been paid, the assured dies without payment of the premium within six months from the due date of the first unpaid premium, the policy amount will be paid subject to deduction of unpaid premiums with interest thereon up to the date of death.

7. Reduced Paid-up Insurance

When the policyholder is unable to pay further premiums and does not want cash immediately he can paid up the policy. The sum assured under the policy is reduced in the same proportion as the amount of premiums paid bears to the total premiums payable. The reduced sum assured is payable according to the original term of the policy. Where uniform premiums are payable, as in the case of endowment or whole life limited payment assurances, this proportion is easily ascertained. The paid up value of whole life policy is calculated as per the formula $1-\frac{dx}{d(x+n)}$ sum assured, where *dx* is the premium for the age when the policy was affected, and *d* (*x* + *n*) is the premium for the present age of the life assured when policy is surrendered.

CLAIMS CONDITIONS

1. Settlement of Claims

The policy amount becomes payable either on the assured's death during the term of insurance or on his surviving till the end of the term, *i.e.,* on maturity. In case of death claims proof of death, proof of title and age proof are essential. In case of maturity proof of title and age proof are required. The age proof is required only when the age was not admitted before to the claims. In maturity claim, the policyholder is generally advised well before the actual date of maturity in order that the necessary papers may be completed. The proof of death may be certificate from the doctor who attended the deceased in his last illness, or certificate of Registration of the Death by the Official Registrar of Deaths, or Certificate from employer identifying the deceased or if the deceased was not in service a certificate of identity from a responsible person acquainted with the deceased. In case of assignment and nomination, or assured having the policy right, no proof of title is required. In other cases, proof of title is essential, the probate of Will or succession certificate or Administration General's Certificate may be used as a proof of title.

2. Settlement Options

The claim amount may be paid in cash or in instalment. The instalment payment may be of different types payment of interest annually for a particular period or up to survived and the sum assured at a time may be paid. Annuity may be purchased for life or for a particular period and life thereafter.

PERFORMANCE OF COMPETITIVE LIFE INSURANCE INDUSTRY IN DEATH CLAIMS SETTLEMENT IN 2009-2010

It is now a decade since the insurance industry has been opened up to private players. True to expectations, the life insurance market has expanded and and there has been substantial growth in life insurance business as reflected by life insurance penetration of 4.6% (percentage of life insurance premium to the Gross Domestic Product) of our country in 2009 as against 2.15% in 2001. (Source: Swiss Re, Sigma No. 3/2010). Against this background it is also worthwhile to assess the extent to which the industry has fulfilled its obligations towards the policyholers, especially in the matter of settlement of death claims, which area constitutes the true test of the ability of the life insurers to live up to the promises made by them under their life insurance contracts with speed, sensitivity and empathy.

While LIC since nationalization has developed its own effective systems of claim settlements with evolution of appropriate benchmarks of performance and constantly improved upon its performance reaching an enviable prime position in the industry, an attempt has been made by this author to study the comparitive performance in Death Claims area under individual policies in the year 2009-10 between LIC and the Private life insurers as a whole on the one hand and among the private life insurers per se on the other.

The major parameters on which the life insurers were compared were;

(*a*) the ratio of outstanding claims to total death claims payable, both in terms of number and benefit amount,

(*b*) the ratio of repudiated claims to total death claims payable both in terms of number and benefit amount.

TABLE 1 and TABLE 3 below give the statistics of idividual death claims in the year 2009-10 in terms of number and benefit amount respectively. TABLE 2 and TABLE 4 give the critical ratios in death claims in respect of number of policy claims and benefit amount of claims resepctively, based on the figures in the former two tables.

LIC ON TOP

A persual of the tables will reveal the convincing superiority of LIC in the death claims performance with the lowest outstanding ratios of 1.41% and 2.35% respectively in terms of number of claims and benefit amount of claims against 7.48% and 11.25% respectively of the private life insurers. (See Table 1 & Table 2) This is understandable considering the well steamlined claim settlement mechanism devised by LIC over a period of over 54 years with a claimant-friendly approach and a well decentralized network of Branches spread over the entire country for rendering service to customers. Another aspect in which LIC has distinguished itself commendably is in the ara of ratios of repudiated claims payable which were 1.21% and 1.59% respectively in terms of number and benefit amount much lower than 7.6% and 11.02% of the private life insurers respectively. The low ratios of repudiation have been achieved progressively over time with a more claimant sensitive decision making process reinforced by the decisions of the Claims Review Committees including outside judicial members from time to time both at the zonal level and the Central Office levels minimizing the scope for repudiation at decision points.

The following table clearly illustrates the superior death claims performance of LIC in relation to the market share in the policies in force as well as the total premium income in 2009-10. While the percentage share of repudiation of LIC is higher than that of the private life insurers in number of death claims, that in terms of benefit amount of claims repudiated is much lower bringing in sharp focus the higher sum assured policies being repudiated by the private insurers.

	Market Share in total policies in force (%) as on 31st March, 2010	*% of number of Death - claims paid of 2009-10*	*Market share in total premium income (%) in 2009-10*	*% of benefit amount of Death claims paid in 2009-10.*	*% of repudiated number of Death claims in 2009-10*	*% of repudiated benefit amount of Death Claims in 2009-10*	*% of pending no of claims as at 31st March, 2010*	*% of pending Benefit amount of claims as at 31st March 2010*
Private	12.5	9.9	29.9	19.4	44.0	67.2	0.016	1.46
LIC	87.5	90.1	70.1	80.6	56.0	32.8	0.003	2.58
Industry	100	100	100	100	100	100	0.01	2.24

One significant feature that comes out of the yearly data is while LIC has paid higher amount of death claim benefits, the quantum of benefit amounts repudiated and those pending at the end of the year 2009-10 is far higher in case of the private insurers as a whle than in case of LIC. This is a clear demonstration of more claimant-friendly performance in death claims settlement by LIC than is exhibitted by the private sector.

COMPARTIVE PERFORMANCE OF PRIVATE LIFE

The performance of LIC is not strictly comparable with specific private players for the reason that the composition of claims payable of the former is distinctly different from the latter who, having been in life insurance business for barely 10 years or less would definetely have a higher proportion of early death claims entailing more dealy in obtaining requirements and conducting claims entailing more delay in obtaining requirements and conducting claim investigations as may be needed before decisions can be taken either to admit or reject the claims. Nevertheless, the performance of private players can be assessed releatively on the metrics of claim performance. With that end in view, the private life insurers were classified into "low", "high", and "medium" category performers in terms of outstanding ratio of death claims to total death claims payable both in terms of number and benefit amount, with similar categorization in respect of repudiation of claims. These have been indicated in the MATRIX I and MATRIX II given below. The "high" category was determined by taking the life insureres falling under the top 25% of the group above the aggregate average of the private life insurance sector. Similarly, the bottom 25% of the group below the aggregate average of the private life insurance sector, were considered to fall under the "low" ratio category. The remaining companies falling under the middle 50% segment on either side of the private sector average were categorized under "medium" category.

OUTSTANDING DEATH CLAIM RATIO

The degree to which an insurer is able to dispose of maximum number and benefit amounts of death claims out of those payable during the year determines its claim settlement efficiency as measured by the outstanding claims ratio at the end of the year. Judged from this standard, the best performance has come from this standard, the best performance has come from Bharti Axa Life, Birla Sunlife, SBI Life Aviva and Reliance registering the relatively lowest ratios on both the number of death claims and benefit amount. (see MATRIX I). ICICI Prudential has recorded a low ratio on benefit amount while falling in the medium category in terms of outstanding number of claims, implying a lower average benefit amount per claim outstanding. On the contrary, IndiaFirst, Shriram and Canara - HSBC- OBC have shown the highest oustanding ratios on both counts. Shriram Life, having been relatively in the sector for a longer period than the other two, having a high ratio of pending claims may indicate a relatively negative performance. IDBI Federal and Future Generali had a high ratio of pending benefit amount, while star Union Dai-ichi and DLF Pramerica had a high ratio of outstanding pending claims. Aegon Religare is the only relatively new entrant which finds a place in the medium category on both counts. Even among the companies in the medium category, Sahara and Max Newyork (on both number and amount) and MetLife (on amount) are relatively high on ratios among the categorized companies. The pattern that emerges may lead us to conclude that the more established a life insurer is, the better is the performance in terms of outstanding claims ratio.

RATIO OF REPUDIATED CLAIMS

The sensivity and prudence with which a life insurer decides to objectively and with a sense of fairness and justice to reject a claim on valid and justifiable grounds of nondisclosure of material facts in the proposal is reflected by the ratio of repudiated death claims to claims payable. Judged from this angle, Star Union Dai-ichi, ICICI Prudential, ING Vysya and Kotak Mahindra are the four companies who were having the least incidence of repudation on both number of claims and benefit amount (See Matrix II). DLF Pramerica and Sahara had medium repudiation in number but low repudiation in benefit amount. This may perhaps indicate that average benefit amount repudiated by these companies may be relatively lower. At the other extreme, Aegon Religar, Future Generali, Bharti Axa Life and Shriram Life had the highest incidence of repudiation. It is interesting to note that Aegon Religare figures in the medium category in outstanding claims ratio, while Bharti Axa Life figures in the star league of low outstanding ratio insureres. The benefits amounts repudiated by Aegon Religare adn Future Generali exceeded the benefit amounts paid for the year. HDFC Standard Life had low incidence of repudiation in number, but medium incidence by benefit amout. IDBI Federal had a high incidence in terms of amount. MetLife insurance company had a high incidence of repudation by amount while having medium incidence of number. Out of the remaining, Birla Sunlife (by amount) and Canara HSBC OBC (by number) were having higher incidence than the other insurers in the medium category.

Shriram Life insurance company is the single non recent insurer to have a high outstanding ratio as well as a high incidence of repudiation.

AVERAGE SIZE OF DEATH CLAIMS

An incidental study was also made of the average size of death cliams payable, death claims repudiated and death claims outstanding. While the average claim amount per policy was quite proximate in respect of Claims pending at the start of the year and the total claims payable, the average amount per policy claim repudiated as well as per claim pending at the end of the year was significantly higher as follows:

	Repudiated claim per policy claim as multiple of average claim amount payable	*Average Claim per policy claim pending as at 31st March 2010 as multiple of average claim amount payable*
Private Life Insurers	1.58	1.64
LIC	1.33	1.69
Industry	2.03	2.20

Please also see TABLE 5 and FIGURE 5 and FIGURE 3. This pattern leads us to conclude that repudation of deaths trend to be concentrated on high sum assured policies and most of the death claims pending for higher sums assured are potential repudiable claims kept pending for gathering evidence to strengthen repudiation. The size of the repudiated policy of private insurers is much higher than that of LIC. Another significant fact that emerges in thsi comparison is that the average sizes of the claim playable, paid are repudaited of private life insurers are more than double those of LIC which may be the logical outcome of sale of higher sum assured policies by the former compared to those of the latter as is revealed by the divergence in the average sum assured in force per policy between private players and LIC as at 31st March, 2010 as will be apparent from FIGURE 3.

SUMMING UP

In the area of death claims, LIC has maintained its supremacy in effective and efficient settlement of death claims with minimal denials presumably on justifiable grounds. At the same time, LIC cannot afford to be complacent, but needs to maintain its current status of excellence in the years ahead as well. Five or ten years down the line, the Corporation is likely to be challenged with a much more improved claims performance by private life insurers like ICICI Prudential, HDFC Standard Life, Bajaj Alianz, Reliance and Life, SBI Life. Once the companies cross the breakeven point in terms of business profitability they are likely to focus more on customer service, especially claims settlement to differentiate them. Incidentially, the comparitive claims settlement data throw up interesting marketing insights. Ever since the industry has been opened up, private insurers have been selling higher ticket policies than LIC. In spite of death claims settlement performance relatively inferior to LIC, the private sector continues to maintain its trend in selling higher premium/ higher sum assured policies than LIC. With the kind of excellent track record achieved in claims performance, it is apparent that LIC has tremendous potential to set its marketing sights higher and sell a higher proportion of high volume policies by targeting HNI's (High Net worth Individuals) by using its superior claims performance as a competive advantage. Such a strategy will facilitate a happy blend of business growth and sustained customer delight. The marketing intermediaries of LIC have a great opportunity before them.

(Note: The hard data furnished in the various tables have been taken from the Annual Report for 2009-10 of IRDA and the ratios havbe been worked out and charts have been prepared by this author wherever not given in the Annual report.)

INDIVIDUAL DEATH CLAIMS STATISTICS-2009-10(Number of Death Claims)

Life insurer	*No of claims pending at start of year*	*No. of claims intimated/ booked*	*Total No of Claims*	*No of Claims paid*	*No of Claims repudiated*	*No of Claims written back*	*No of Claims pending at the end of the year*
Aegon Religare	2	48	50	24	22	0	4
Aviva 59		128	1749	1877	1635	183	0
Bajaj Alianz	524	22516	23040	20316	1197	0	1527
Bharti AXA	4	487	491	382	109	0	0
Birla Sunlife	14	5907	5921	5275	629	3	14
Canara HSBC	8	85	93	36	15	0	42
DLF Pramerica	0	10	10	4	1	0	5
Future Generali	4	449	453	176	133	0	144
HDFC Std	210	3627	3837	3497	197	0	161
ICICI Prudential	886	15171	16057	14479	525	0	1053
IDBI Federal	25	185	210	104	50	0	56
IndiaFirst	0	13	13	7	1	0	5
ING Vysya	216	1710	1926	1720	82	12	112
Kotak Mahindra	178	2102	2280	1983	100	0	197
Max New York	87	5932	6019	3943	741	0	1335
MetLife	139	1207	1346	1111	80	3	152
Reliance Life	287	8467	8754	7797	617	6	334
Sahara	187	544	731	461	50	0	220
SBI Life	355	6877	7232	6022	1067	1	142
Shriram	287	879	1166	461	230	0	475
Star Union Dai-ichi	0	60	60	35	3	0	22
Tata AIG	298	3197	3495	2732	452	5	306
Private Total	3839	81222	85061	72200	6466	30	6365
LIC	13076	664298	677374	653909	8227	5711	9527
Industry Total	16915	745520	762435	726109	14693	5741	15892

Source: IRDA Annual Report, 2009-2010

MATRIX I

OUTSTANDING DEATH CLAIMS RATIO MATRIX OF PRIVATE LIFE INSURERS IN 2009-10

O/S ratio of more than 34% (by benefit amount) (HIGH)		IDBI Federal (26,67,50.35) Future Generali(31.79, 34.7)	IndiaFirst(38.46.52.94) Shriram(40.74, 45.06) Canara HSBC OBC (45. 1665.68)
O/S ratio of more than 8% and less than or equal to 34% (by benefit amount) (MEDIUM)		HDFC Std(4.20,9.13) ING Vysya(5,82, 9.74) Bajaj Allanz(6.63, 9.18) Aegon Religare(8.0, 14.34) Kotak Mahindra OM(8.64, 12.43) Tata AIG(8.76, 15.26) MetLife(11.29, 22.90) Mex Newyork(22, 18, 23.96) Shara(30.10, 29.86) **Private Average = (7.48, 11.25)**	Star Union Dai-ichi (36, 67, 32.97) DLF Pramerica (50.0, 30.0)
O/S ratio of 8% or less (by benefit amount) (LOW)	Bharti Axa Life(0, 0) Birla Sunlife(0.24, 0.5) SBI Life(1.96, 4.82) Aviva(3.14, 5.58) Reliance (3.82, 7.75) **IC (1.41, 2.35)** **Industry(2.08, 4.38)**	ICICI Prudential(6.56, 7.85)	
	O/S ratio of 4% or less (by number) (LOW)	O/S ratio of more than 4% and less than or equal to 35%(by number) (MEDIUM)	O/S ratio of more than 35% (by nuber) (HIGH)

Note: The first figure in the brackets is outstanding ratio by number and the second figure is outstanding ratio by benefit amount.
Source of Data: IRDA Annual Report, 2009-2010

MATRIX II

REPUDIATION RATIO MATRIX OF PRIVATE LIFE INSURERS IN 2009-10

Ratio of Repudiated Claims of more than 22% (by benefit amount) (HIGH)		MetLife (5.94, 24.12)	Shriram(19.73, 23.54) Bharti Axa Life(22.20,31.56) Future Generalli (29.36, 34.53) Aegon Religare (44.0, 43.80)
Ratio of Repudiated Claims of more than 5.5% and less than or equal to 22% (by benefit amount) (MEDIUM)	HDFC Std(4.67, 7.39)	Bajaj Allianz(5.20, 7.30) Reliance(7.05, 15.27) india-First(7.69,5.88) Aviva(9.75, 14.41) Birla Sunlife(10.63, 20.32) Tata AIG(12.93, 15.92) SBI Life(14.75, 5.74) Canara HSBC OBC (16,13, 10.11) Private Insurers' Average = (7.60, 11.02)	IDBI Federal (23.81, 18.55) Max Newyork(12.31, 14.35)

Ratio of Repudiated/ Claims of 5.5% or less (by benefit amount) (Low)	ICICI Prudential (3.27, 4.42) ING Vysya(4.26, 5.32) KotakMahindra OM (4.39, 5.31) Star Union Dai-ichi (5.0, 0.0) **LIC (1.21, 1.59)** **Industry (1.93, 3.74)**	Sahara(6.84, 3.52) Dlf Pramerica(10.0, 1.43)	
	Ratio of Repudiated Claims of 5% or less (by number) (LOW)	Ratio of Repudiated Claims of 5% Or more and less than or equal to 18% (by number)	Ratio of Repudiated Claims of more than 18% (by number) (HIGH) (MEDIUM)

Note : The first figure in the brackets is repudation ratio by number and the second figure is repudiation ratio by benefit amount Source of Data: IRDA Annual Report, 2009-2010

QUESTIONS

1. What are the various conditions relating to commencement of risk, payment of premium and continuation of policies?
2. Discuss in detail the conditions of lapsation and claims.

17

LIFE INSURANCE FOR THE UNDER—PRIVILEGED

Under-privileged persons are those persons whose incomes are too low to purchase life insurance policies, who have no adequate provision for old age and family security and who become incapable to earn adequate income due to accident injury or disease. For them, four alternatives are generally provided in life insurance, which are (*i*) Industrial Life Insurance, (*ii*) Group Life Insurance Policies, (*iii*) Disability Benefit Policies, (*iv*) Pension Plans and (*v*) Micro Insurance.

INDUSTRIAL LIFE INSURANCE

Industrial Life Insurance is a form of life insurance specially designed to meet the requirements of wage earning population of industry. It may also apply to low income classes of business or even of the population. It may be issued without medical examination. The premiums may be collected by agents on weekly or monthly basis. Industrial insurance should not be confused with social insurance, which means workmen's compensation, employers, liability, etc.

Purpose

The main purpose of industrial life insurance is to provide at least clean up funds to meet lest expenses of the assured. Since, the amount of industrial life insurance is not much, family protection is not always possible. The second aim is to educate the habit of saving amongst the low income group to meet their contingencies. Weekly premium can be easily saved and it may provide funds to create property.

COMPARISON OF INDUSTRIAL AND OTHER FORMS OF LIFE INSURANCE

Industrial insurance is a form of life insurance, therefore, most of the characteristics of life insurance are present in this insurance apart from the following dissimilarities:

(*i*) The premiums in industrial insurance are payable weekly and monthly whereas in ordinarily life insurance, they are payable annually, semi-annually, quarterly and monthly.

(*ii*) The premiums, instead of being payable at the office of the insurer are collected in most of the cases at the houses of the assured persons by insurance agents.

(*iii*) The amount of a policy in industrial insurance is generally not more than ₹ 1,000 whereas in other forms of insurance it is usually more than ₹ 1,000.

(*iv*) In Industrial insurance, medical examination is not essential, but in other forms of life insurance, medical examination is required in most of the cases.

(*v*) Industrial insurance is extended to every member of the family. Thus, it covers more areas than the other forms of insurance.

Types of Contracts. The policies issued under this form of the insurance are generally limited payment life or endowment plans because saving element in these plans are maximum.

Cash Values

The Industrial Policy should be in force for a longer period for getting cash or paid up values. It may be from 3 years to 5 years. Extended term assurance is available after payment of premiums for at least six weeks.

Loan Values

Since the servicing cost of the loan is higher and the protection element is elapsed in granting loan, the policy does not bear the provision for loan.

Assignment

Assignment of the Industrial Policy is prohibited because the amount secured may not be useful to the assured in case of assignment.

Indisputable Clause

The industrial policy becomes indisputable after one year of the issue whereas the ordinary life insurance policies become indisputable after two years on any ground except that of fraud and age admission.

Suicide

The suicide waiver clause does not apply to this policy.

Reinstatement

Industrial policies that have been in force more than 5 years and are not more than six months in arrears may usually be reinstated without medical examination.

Conversion of Plan

The industrial policy can be converted into ordinary endowment policy or whole life policy.

Beneficiaries

The beneficiaries of the policy may be usually those persons who got the insurable interest in the life of assured.

Premium Rates

The premium rates in industrial life policies are generally higher than that of ordinary life insurance policies because of higher mortality cost, higher cost of administration and higher lapse rates.

In India, the form of Industrial Insurance Policy is Janata policy which is issued generally to comparatively poorer sections of the society. The maximum amount under this policy is ₹ 1,000, the minimum sum assured is ₹ 250 and the maximum sum assured to a policyholder is ₹ 3,000. The maximum age at entry is limited to 45 years. No medical examination is required up to 35 years. A lapsed policy can be revived during a period of 3 years from the due date without medical examinations. No loans or other benefits are granted on this policy.

Janata Personal Accident Policy

This scheme would benefit industrial workers, domestic servants, road transport operators and the like who are engaged in hazardous jobs.

The scheme is truly a Janata Scheme for anybody between the ages of 16 to 60 can join it. The annual premium is ₹ 12 or one rupee per month. Risk cover is for ₹ 10,000. The scheme is designed to give insurance protection of ₹ 10,000 to the family of any person in case the subscriber is fatally injured and ₹ 200 as cash help for hospital expenses. According to Chairman, G. V. Kapadia of GIC, it is meant for the worker, the office goer, truck operator, rickshaw-puller, students or just anybody. Such a scheme would be a great help to the people, it covers apart from death and hospitalisation, loss of limbs and eyes and disablement.

2. Group Life Insurance

Under this plan a large number of persons are insured by a single policy without medical examination at a low cost. The group consists employees of a common employer, debtors of the same creditor or members of the same trade union. The policy is issued to the employer, creditor or the trade union although the number and information of all the assured lives are mentioned, in the policy.

Minimum Number of Persons Insured

The minimum number to be insured is fixed according to the nature of business, number of employees and methods of contribution. The contributory plan is that where employees are also liable to pay a portion of the premium. In non-contributory plan, only employer pays the whole amount of premium. In non-contributory plan, all the employees should be included under this plan whereas in the contributory plan all employees may not be insisted for contribution. However, 75 per cent of the employees must be covered by this scheme.

Eligibility

Only regular and permanent employees are included under this scheme. Seasonal and part time employees are excluded from this scheme.

Termination of Employment

The employee who is terminated may elect within thirty-one days and without medical examination to take an ordinary policy in his own name.

Group Term Insurance Scheme by Corporation

This scheme is a form of renewable term insurance. In the event of death of life assured while in service, the sum assured is paid to the dependents of the deceased persons. A policy is issued to the employer and each member included in this scheme is given a certificate thereto. The sum assured cannot be assigned or mortgaged.

The scheme is applicable to all the permanent employees of an employer. The amount of insurance to each employee is determined by mutual understanding of the employer and the Corporation. In case of non-contributory scheme all existing permanent employees must join the scheme. The amount of insurance is generally fixed for all employees of a given class. There may be different amounts for a different classes of employees.

Group Insurance for U.P. Government Employees

The U.P. Government has enforced the scheme of group insurance for their gazetted and non-gazetted government servants since March 1, 1976. The scheme will, however, not apply to those State Police Personnel who had already been provided with group insurance cover separately. The members of the teaching community and legal profession in the State had also been brought within the ambit of group insurance scheme earlier.

Under the scheme, each Government servant would be required to subscribe ₹ 10 per month in lieu of which the Life Insurance Corporation of India will pay ₹ 12,000 to the family of the Government servants who die in harness. Otherwise, the employee concerned will, on retirement, be paid his share of money deposited. The employee concern will, on retirement, be paid his share of money deposited by him along with compound interest at the rate of six per cent per annum.

3. Disability Benefit

This benefit is granted to all the lives assured excepting a few policies such as Pure Endowment, the Temporary Assurance, Mortgage Redemption Assurance, Convertible Term Assurance, the deferred Annuity, Retirement Annuity and Restrictive Policies. The benefit is offered free of cost and no premium is charged for the purpose.

The Nature and Extent

If a life assured is disabled by accident from earning, he will be exempted from paying premiums on his policy falling due after the date of disablement. This benefit will be granted only on the first ₹ 20,000 of assurance on a life.

The policy must be in force for the full sum assured at the time the disability occurs. The disability must be result of an accident and must be total and permanent and such that there is no scope to do any work, occupation, or profession. Satisfactory proof of the disability must be furnished to the Corporation within 90 days.

Extended Disability Benefit

The extended disability benefit provides for waiver of premiums and also for payment of an amount equal to the sum assured on permanent total disability as a result of an accident. The accident must occur before the age 60 during the continuation of the policy.

Benefits

1. Payment in monthly instalments spread over 10 years an additional sum equal to the sum assured by the policy, the first instalment becoming payable one month after the date of disablement. However, if the policy becomes a claim before the expiry of the said period, the disability benefit instalments which have not become due will be paid along with the claim.
2. Waiver of payment of future premiums up to an assurance of ₹ 1,00,000.

   The annual premium for this benefit is ₹ 2 per thousand.

Conditions

The disability of the Life Assured shall not

1. be caused by intentional self-injury, attempted suicide, insanity or immorality or while the Life Assured is under the influence of intoxicating liquor, drug or narcotic; or
2. taken place as a result of accident while the Life Assured is engaged in aviation or aeronautics in any capacity other than that of fare-paying, part or non-paying passenger; or
3. be caused by injuries resulting from riots, civil commotion, rebellion, war, invasion, hunting, mountaineering, steeple chasing or racing of every kind; or
4. be result from the Life Assured committing any breach of law; or
5. arise from employment of the Life Assured in the armed forces or military service of any country at war.

The disability must be disability which is the result of an accident and must be total and permanent and such that there is neither than nor at any time thereafter any work, occupation or profession that the Life Assured can never sufficiently do or follow to earn or obtain any wages, compensation or profit. Recently Bajaj alliance has insured Seva Sakti Suroba Bima.

SOCIAL SECURITY SCHEMES

India is known for its huge geographical spread and magnitude of its populations. It has a huge working population of 460 million. Almost 92% of this workforce is in the unorganized sector. There are numerous occupational groups pursuing economic activities from generation to generation without formal schooling and scattered all over the country with diffused employer-employee relationship.

The occupationwise distribution of employment indicates that 62% of the workers are engaged in agriculture, 11% in industry and 27% in the services sector. A characteristic feature of the employment situation in the country is that the percentage of workers employed on regular salaried employment is small. The Organized Sector already has a structure through which social security benefits are extended to workers covered under the legislations. And hence they do not need Social Security Support. The bulk of the workforce is either self-employed or employed in casual wage employment in the unorganized sector characterized by the lack of labour law coverage, seasonal and temporary nature of occupations, high labour mobility, lack of organizational support etc. Their families have nothing which they can fall back upon in times of contigencies such as death, disability, accident and old age of the earning member of their family and are forced into vicious circle of debt and deprivation. Thus, they need social security support.

Role of LIC in Social Security Schemes

To extend the system of Social Security to the weaker sections of the society, a Social Security Fund was set up in the year 1988. Funds were deposited by the Central Government and LIC in 1988 and 1989 to provide subsidy in the premia under the various Group Insurance Schemes covering persons of weaker sections. LIC was entrusted with the task of implementing various social security schemes that were devised by the Central Government.

Social Security Schemes administered by LIC

At present major schemes for the benefit of weaker sections is the 'Janashree Bima Yojana' and 'Aam Admi Bima Yojana' which have an addon benefit of Shiksha Sahayog Yojana free of cost.

JANASHREE BIMA YOJANA

Under 'Janashree Bima Yojana', LIC covers rural and urban people living below the poverty line or marginally above it. This scheme offers life insurance cover to persons aged between 18 to 59 years, preferably heads of families engaged in any of the specified 46 vocations/occupations.

The scheme is mobilized thro' Nodal Agency, which shall mean the Panchayats, NGO's Self Help Groups and any other institutionalized arrangements. The Nodal Agency acts for and on behalf of the insured members in all matters relating to the scheme and is a Master Policy holder.

Persons between age 18 to 59 years are eligible for entering into the scheme.

The groups to be insured are identified in consultation with State Government/Nodal Agency. Minimum group size is 25 and the member should normally be the head of the family.

The scheme provides for an insurance cover of ₹ 30,000/– on natural death. On death/total permanent disability due to accident, the benefit is ₹ 75,000/–. On partial permanent disability due to accident, the benefit is ₹ 37,500/–. The premium for the scheme is ₹ 200/– per member per annum, 50 percent of which is met out of Social Security Fund. The balance premium is borne by the member and/or Nodal Agency.

Scholarship as a Free Add-on benefit is provided to a maximum of two children of the beneficiary studying between 9th to 12th standard @ ₹ 100/ per month for each child payable half yearly i.e. on 1st July and on 1st January, each year. Students studying in 9th to 12th standards. (including ITI courses) and whose parents are covered under Janashree Bima Yojana are eligible for this benefit. If a student fails and is detained in the same standard, he will not be eligible for scholarship for the next year in the same standard. Scholarship of ₹ 600/– per half year per child is paid for a maximum period of four years. The benefit is restricted to two children per member (family) only.

AAM ADMI BIMA YO JNA

AAM ADMI BIMA YOJANA is Government of India's Insurance Scheme – for the Rural landless households (weaker sections of the society), that is administered by Life Insurance Corporation of India Total Lics covered are **2.02 crores** as at 31.03.2012.

The State Government/Union Territory which opts for the scheme acts as Nodal Agency. The Nodal Agency shall identify the members to be covered under AAM ADMI BIMA YOJANA in consultation with the Panchayati Raj Institutions where feasible and shall intimate the total number of lives to be covered under the scheme to the designated P & GS Unit along with the share of 50% of the premium. The Nodal Agency shall be the Master Policyholder under the scheme.

Persons between ages 18 to 59 years are eligible for entering into the scheme and the member should normally be the head of the family or one earning member in the family of a rural landless household.

The scheme provides for an insurance cover of ₹ 30,000/ on natural death. On death/total permanent disability due to accident, the benefit is ₹ 75,000/. On partial permanent disability due to accident, the benefit is ₹ 37,500/-. The premium for the scheme is ₹ 200/- per member per annum, 50 percent of which is met out of Aam Admi Bima Yojana Fund. The balance premium is borne by the State Government.

Scholarship as a Free Add-on benefit is provided to a maximum of two children of the beneficiary studying between 9th to 12th Standard @ ₹ 100/ per month for each child payable half yearly-on 1st July and on 1st January, each year. Students studying in 9th to 12th standards (including ITI courses) and whose parents are covered under Aam Admi Bima Yojana are eligible for this benefit. If a student fails and is detained in the same standard, he will not be eligible for scholarship for the next year in the same standard. Scholarship of ₹ 600/ per half year per child is paid for a maximum period of four years. The benefit is restricted to two children per member (family) only.

Benefits paid under 'Janashree Bima Yojana' & 'Aam Aadmi Bima Yojana' during last Financial Year:

Under Janashree Bima Yojana

1. LIC has paid more than ₹ 205.97 crore by way of claims to families below poverty line during last financial year.

2. Further, 20.90 lakh number of scholarships amounting to ₹ 180.25 crore were also disbursed to the children of the insured members.

Under Aam Aadmi Bima Yojana

1. LIC has paid more than ₹ 197.85 crore by way of claims to families below poverty line during last financial year.

2. Further 4.45 lakh number of scholarships amounting to ₹ 47.25 crore were disbursed to the children of insured members.

Towards a Universal Social Security System

The effectiveness of social security programmes for all workers in the economy is predicated on the success of extending social security cover to unorganized workers. The contribution of the unorganized sector alone to the national income is around 60 per cent of the total. In order to sustain high economic growth, it is essential to provide social security cover to the families of the deprived sections of the society as a part of the financial inclusion programme of Government of India so that they can become a part of the economic growth model. We have to make sustained efforts to cover all the eligible persons under our Social Security Schemes. So far due to the initiative & efforts of our officials all over the country coupled with the support from the various State and Central Government Departments, we have been successful in covering more than 4.79 crore lives as at 31.03.2012. However, LIC's endeavour is to provide insurance cover to all the families who are living below poverty line or are marginally above poverty line. This will also help us in achieving our vision 2020 of having "A POLICY IN EVERY POCKET".

4. Pension Plans

Today several schemes, providing regular pensions to the employees after their retirement, which may continue even after his death, may be for a specified time or during the life time of his wife as was chosen.

Deferred Annuity Plan is the effective method to provide for the pension. The pension plan can be purchased through the employer or it can be purchased individually. In case of non-contributory plan, participation by all the eligible employees in specified categories is compulsory. The existing employees in other categories may be given the option of joining the scheme.

Benefit on Death During Service

If the member dies while in service, all contributions with interest thereon at a rate ascertained by the Corporation are returned to him.

National Pension System – A Brief Overview

Pension is an assured monthly income receivable by an individual after retirement which enables him to maintain his standard of living even after his salary income has ceased. With changing times, the support system available to earlier generation by way of joint family system has diminished. Increase in life expectancy and nuclear families have made financial independence after retirement a necessity. It is observed that secured income leads to improved mental health of senior citizens.

Hitherto, Central and State Governments were the largest employers in the past. However, with computerisation, substantial increase in population and globalisation, private enterprises are emerging as most preferred employers of majority of young aspirant working class. There is considerable increase in employment in the private and unorganized sector. Generally, there is lack of commitment from the employers in this sector to provide for a pension to its employees. Due to more number of opportunities available, the rate of attrition has also been very high and the responsibility to provide for pension has slowly shifted from the employer to the individual employee. Awareness and increase in income levels has opened up an opportunity for garnering and chanelising long-term savings from the untapped pension business to provide a secure pension to senior citizens.

World over, pension funds are the largest fund managers covering majority of the working population. Funds Managed by top Government Pension Funds in the US are close to US $617 billion. Australian pension market is also developed and manages funds to the extent of USD 1,250 billion. Japanese Pension Funds are around USD 3,500 billion. Pension fund assets are 60% and above of GDP in these countries.

As compared to this, the pension penetration is very low in India. Total funds managed by Indian Pension Fund managers under National Pension System are around ₹22,000 crore. Total pension fund assets (including NPS) amount to USD 103 billion which is around 8% of GDP. This is due to the huge population dependent on agriculture, having uncertain income, lack of laws making it mandatory for the private sector employers, to provide for pension benefit to the employees as also lack of awareness in the weaker sections to invest in pension products.

PFRDA was established by Government of India on 23rd August, 2003. The government has, through an executive order dated 10th October 2003, mandated PFRDA to act as a regulator for the pension sector. The mandate of PFRDA is to develop and regulate pension sector in India.

As a first step towards pension reforms, the pension scheme applicable to central government employees was changed from defined benefit pension to defined contribution based pension for its new recruits joining services from 1st January, 2004. Since 1st April, 2008, pension funds of central government employees are covered under National Pension System (NPS).

Sibsequently, many State Governments have also joined the scheme. So far, 26 state governments have adopted NPS for their employees.

Under the NPS, contributions from employees and the central/state government are handed over to select Pension Fund Managers (PFM) having sponsors with strong financial background for investing as per pattern stipulated by PFRDA and generating reasonable returns for subscribers. Pattern of Investment applicable to Central/State Government and NPS Lite Scheme is as under:

Sr.No.	*Investment Pattern*	*Percentage amount to be invested*
1.	Government Securities	Upto 55%
2.	NCD/NCB	Upto 40%
3.	Money market Instruments including units of money market mutual funds	Upto 5%
4.	Equity (Share of Corporates on which derivatives are available in BSE/NSE or Equity linked schemes of Mutual Funds regulated by SEBI	Upto 15%

NPS Trust constituted under the Indian Trust Act, 1882 monitors the performance of the PFM's and ensures compliance to the market practices and Investment Management Agreement signed with them. PFM's declare NAV (Net Asset Value) on a daily basis and all entry and exits are NAV based.

From 1st May 2009, the scheme was made open to all citizens of India and they were given the choice to choose the pattern of investment consisting of equity allocation of maximum 50% and balance in fixed income securities. The subscribers can also choose their Pension Fund Manager and switch over from one PFM to another once in a year.

Exit from the scheme by the subscribers is normally after reaching superannuation age. The subscriber can withdraw maximum 60% of the accumulated pension wealth and balance 40% is utilized to buy an annuity which ensures steady cash flow throughout the life time of the subscriber. In case a subscriber chooses to exit before retirement age, it is mandatory to annuitize 80% of the accumulated wealth and balance 20% can withdrawn in one lumpsum. In case of death of the subscriber, the pension wealth is paid to the nominee or an option to continue in the scheme is permitted.

The scheme offers reasonable returns at low cost with transparency and flexibility to the subscribers.

LIC'S NEW JEEVAN NIDHI

LIC's New Jeevan Nidhi can form an integral part any individual's financial plan. It is open to persons aged 20 to 60 years of age, the vesting age can be anywhere between 55 to 65 years and deferment period between 5 to 35 years. The plan has both Regular and Single Premium options. Under Regular Premium, the plan can also be taken for yearly, half-yearly, quarterly and monthly (ECS or SSS) modes. The minimum Sum Assured is ₹150000 and ₹100000 for Single and Regular premium plans respectively, there is no upper limit for Sum Assured. The plan can be customized by opting for Accident Benefit Rider under regular premium policies. LIC's New Jeevan Nidhi acquires a paid-up value after payment of at least 3 years premium. In case of surrender, it is compulsory to purchase an immediate Annuity or a new single premium deferred pension plan through the surrender proceeds.

LIC's New Jeevan Nidhi is a brilliant pension plan. The word "Retirement" has made news headlines and is no longer an abstract concept as it was during our joint family and extended family days. Retirement planning cannot rest on speculative financial decisions, it has to be a carefully reasoned out process right from the start of one's career. Every drop that we save today adds to the ocean from which we can draw in our later years. LIC's New Jeevan Nidhi has been designed carefully to create a golden cocoon for the golden years so that it can be the most fulfilling time of life.

Illustration of Age 40 – Single Premium

Age at entry	40 years
Sum Assured	500000
Mode	Single Premium
Age at Vesting	60 years
Premium	307500/
Guaranteed Additions	125000/
Simple reversionary Bonus assuming Bonus @₹ 35%	262500/
Policy Proceeds at Vesting	500000 + 12500 + 262500 + Final Additional Bonus

PROGRESS OF SOCIAL SECURITY SCHEME

LIC has designed following life products for social benefits of people:

1. Landless Agricultural Labourers Group Insurance Scheme w.e.f. 15.8.1987. (Closed on 14.8.2000)
2. Group Insurance Scheme for the beneficiaries of Integrated Rural Development Programme w.e.f. 1.4.1988. (now for the beneficiaries of Swarna Jayanti Gram Swarojgar Yojana)
3. Social Security Group Insurance Scheme (SSGS) for certain sections of society, pursuing certain occupations (24 approved occupations) w.e.f. 1.4.1988. (Selling of new schemes closed w.e.f. 10.8.2000)
4. Rural Group Life Insurance Schemes w.e.f. 15.8.1995. (closed w.e.f. 1.4.2000)
5. Janashree Bima Yojana w.e.f. 10.8.2000. (Merged with Aam Aadmi Bima Yojana from 1.1.2013)
6. Aam Admi Bima Yojna for rural landless households w.e.f. 02.10.2007 (merged with new Aam Aadmi Bima Yojana w.e.f. 1.1.2013)
7. Aam Admi Bima Yojana covering 48 occupations w.e.f. 1.1.2013 by adding another 24 occupations since the SSGS Scheme.

The P&GS Deptt. Which has been assigned the job of spreading such life insurance cover all along has taken the job in the right earnest since inception. Upto 31st March, 2013, we have not only settled 6,90,401 claims with an outgo of ₹ 2138.15 crs. but also paid 1,28,53,247 scholarships of ₹ 1027.09 crore to the eligible children of the people covered.

Moreover, to provide bigger thrust to the on-going efforts of providing cover to wider sections of the society and for reviewing coverage of Social Security Schemes to the market.

We have, thus covered 4.81 crores of lives upto 31.03.2013 and the figure as on 30.09.2013 is 5.44 crores as per the state-wise given below:

STATE WISE IN FORCE SOCIAL security LIVES AS AT 30.09.2013

Sr. No.	*State*	*Total Lives in Force as at September 2013*
1.	Andhra Pradesh	12928760
2.	Madhya Pradesh	9308106
3.	Maharashtra	6260698
4.	U.P.	5594038
5.	Chhattisgarh	4462545

(*Contd.*)

6.	Rajasthan	3524136
7.	Karnataka	2197335
8.	Tamil Nadu	1866497
9.	Gujarat	1656210
10.	Orissa	1554237
11.	Kerala	1288461
12.	West Bengal	1227915
13.	Uttrakhand	728804
14.	Bihar	493605
15.	Assam	353555
16.	Jharkhand	310649
17.	J & K	119001
18.	Punjab	88158
19.	Himachal Pradesh	86675
20.	Haryana	84342
21.	Pondicherry	82029
22.	Delhi	54070
23.	Tripura	46938
24.	Goa	46788
25.	Manipur	29025
26.	Meghalaya	21180
27.	Nagaland	18587
28.	Arunachal Pradesh	12572
29.	Mizoram	4324
30.	Sikkim	2582
31.	A & N Island	1379
32.	Chandigarh	1073
33.	Dadra & N Haveli	
34.	Daman & Diu	214
35.	Lakshadweep	203
	Total	**54455157**

Recognition of selfless service

We have been doing this service to vulnerable sections of society with utmost dedication and our efforts have been lauded at all levels. With the Govt. aming at Financial inclusion by offering pension and health benefits, Swavalamban Scheme of PFRDA has also been given to LICHFL & LIC P&GS Deptt as aggregators.

SALEINT FEATURES OF AAM ADMI BIMA YOJANA

Ministry of Finance, Government of India has approved the merger of Social Security Schemes, viz., Aam Admi Bima Yojana (AABY) and Janashree Bima Yojana (JBY). The merged scheme is renamed **"Aam Admi Bima Yojna"** and has come into effect from 01.01.2013.

Object:

The object of this scheme is to provide life insurance protection to the rural and urban poor persons living below poverty line and marginally above poverty line.

Eligibility:

1. Persons between age 18 years and 59 years.
2. The groups will be identified and notified by LIC in consultation with State Government/ Nodal Agency.
3. Minimum Membership should be 25.
4. The member should normally be the head of the family.

Benefits

On Natural Death	₹ 30,000
On Death or Total Permanent Disability due to accident	₹ 75,000
On Partial Permanent Disability	₹ 37,500

Premium : per member per annum

Member/Nodal Agency/State Govt. ₹ 100

Social Security Fund ₹ 100

Nodal Agency

Nodal Agency shall mean the Panchayats, NGO's, Self Help Groups and any other institutionalized arrangements. The Nodal Agency will act for and on behalf of the insured members in all matters relating to the Scheme.

Claim Procedure

The beneficiary of the deceased member will be required to furnish the original death certificate to the Nodal Agency who will arrange to forward the same along with the claim papers to LIC i.e. the Branch wich has originally finalized the scheme. LIC will settle the claims by drawing 'A/C Payee' Cheque to the beneficiary. In case of accidental claim police inquiry report will also be required to be submitted.

New vocational/occupational groups if suggested by State/Central Government/NGOs can be approved by LIC if members are eligible as per eligibility criterion.

SCHOLARSHIP

It is a free add-on benefit under the Aam Admi Bima Yojana & NO premium is charged for the scholarship.

ELIGIBILITY

Scholarship is paid to the students studying in 9th to 12th standards (including ITI courses), **whose parents are covered under Aam Admi Bima Yojana**. If a student fails and detained in the same standard, he/she will not be eligible for scholarship for the next year in the same standard.

BENEFITS

Scholarship of ₹ 600/- per half year per child will be paid for a maximum period of four years. The benefit is restricted to two children per member (family) only.

Insurance of Weaker Section of Society

The Government of India has provided insurance to the weaker section of the society to the tune of ₹ 5,000 at the death. Other people may get benefit of this insurance provided they pay ₹ 75 per annum premium to the LIC. Half of the premium will be met by the State Government and Central Government as provided in the budget 1995-96. The amount of insurance has increased to ₹ 10,000 w.e.f. 15-8-96. It has been extended to all types of people who were unable to purchase policies on their lives.

Customised products for the weaker sections

The need of the hour is products which give simple coverages at an affordable price – apart from pure term life insurance covers, pure term with some guaranteed savings element – in the nature of simple universal life products with low ticket size is also required. This would help in effectively supporting the micro finance with a sustainable micro insurance model.

Another area is affordable health insurance to weaker sections. Tamil Nadu government has taken the initiative of signing up for health insurance for the people of the state with a health insurer. Such government sponsored insurance schemes must be promoted so that insurance coverage reaches the masses.

Micro insurance Budget

The Microinsurance channel has achieved the distinction of achieving its budget for the first time since inception. As against the budget of 25 lakh policies, they have secured 29.51 lakh policies (118%-achievement to budget). We know that Micro Insurance is a medium of financial inclusion by reaching out to the poorest of the poor to satisfy their need of insurance.

5. Micro Life Insurance

Micro in surance typically refers to insurance products designed for low-income individuals. The wordd 'micro' represents the relatively small transaction size of lower premiums, a concept similar to microfinance with small ticket loans. Microinsurance differs from traditional insurance in many ways. Such as the size of premiums, coverage limits, product features, distribution, policy administration and target customers. The objectives of microinsurance also vary amongst different stakeholders. For governments and policymakers, for instance, microinsurance is a way to ensure inclusive growth and support the livelihoods of the vulnerable segment of the society. For social and developmental organizations, microinsurance can be an effective tool to help alleviate poverty. For insurers and other market participants. It is an opportunity to tap into new market segments and support economic and insurance growth of emerging markets.

Rural India is the big opportunity. Indian rural market constitutes approximately 72% of total Indian population even as of date. This is spread across approx through 638.635 villages across the states and union territories of India. More than half of the Indian population residing in these areas has seasonal income while the other part of the population draws irregular income. Majority of rural population is involved in farming sector either directly or indirectly (farming, marginal farming, and marginal land labourers, etc.) and the balance of the large population comprises of skilled labourers; artisans which includes carpenters, masons, etc; and small scale shop owners, etc.

Non-agrisector like infrastructure (construction, electricity, gas and water supply), rural health services, education, tourism, transport, communication etc. are all exhibiting high growth rates. Financial services providers like banks, mutual funds, Life and Non-Life insurers, card distributors, chit funds etc.

Benefits the society and the insurance sector

Strong need for financial and risk protection at the bottom of the pyramid

Based on World Bank statistics, around 4 billion people are living under $ 4/day (in 2005 international dollars based on purchasing power parity). This figure includes 2.6 billion people living under $2/day. This vast section of the population is usually under-served and has very limited access to the basic necessities of life. Their livelihoods are dependent largely on informal sectors with no regular income flows adn limited or negligible financial resources. In addition, they face numerous risks and usually do not have access to formal risk coping solutions, including conventional insurance products. As a result, it becomes extremely difficult for such households to manage unforeseenexpenditures or loss of income, rendering them highly vulnerable to life, health and financial shocks. Health risk in particular is often the biggest concern for low-income families (see Figure), but other risks are also important considerations.

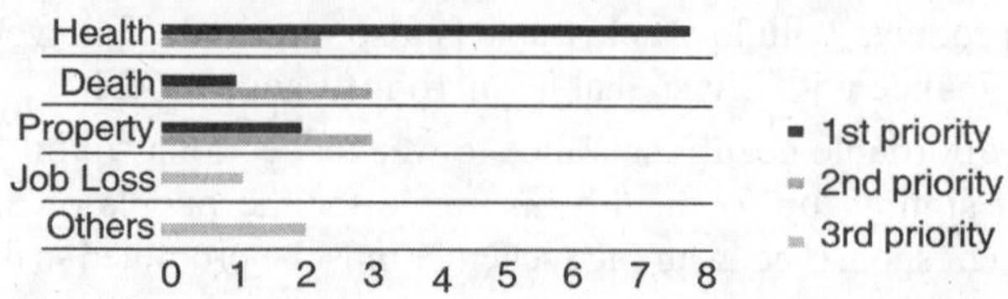

Low-income individuals usually have limited access to formal risk solutions (see Figure 4). Ex-ante measures such as precautionary savings help in mitigating the impact; however, savings – if any - are seldom sufficient to compensate for the loss of property or life. As such, they usually resort to support from family and their community, sell off their assets or take emergency loans. At the same time, the availability of formal mechanisms, including social protections schemes and mutual/cooperative programmes, is often limited to low-income families. In effect, the weakest segment of the society is usually the least protected and could suffer the most due to the limited range of available risk management tools. They have significant unmet demand for financial protection against risks related to health, life events, crop harvest failure and loss of assets.

Challenges in Distribution of Micro Insurance Products

As is the case with any other insurance product, even in Microinsurance there are huge challenges that are seen in the development and distribution of such products.

(*a*) *Infrastructure:* Due to the very nature of low premium products, it may not be physically viable for insurance companies to have their own offices to cater to this population in rural India. as such alternative distribution mechanism, which has long-term perspective and well set requlated. Systems and procedures in place to manage premium collection and servicing is required.

(*b*) *Medical Network:* Establishing medical network in this area is another challenge which then restricts the development of certain types of products, which could be offered to rural population, which might necessitate medical examination, either pre or post issuance.

(*c*) *Manpower:* The quality of manpower available in rural India is low on knowledge and capability for distribution of these products. Secondly, rural markets are not a preferred location for employment of today's youth.

(*d*) *Technology:* This is another limiting factor and the challenge in servicing. The technology factor is a huge hindrance in remote underwriting and printing of policy document.

(*e*) *Actuarial Limitation:* Lack of correctness of mortality data available and veracity of lapsation data is another huge challenge in this segment.

(*f*) *Awareness:* Low awareness of life insurance itself and specially its products (the term, and term with return of premium) is a huge challenge in the segment Low literacy rate, misguiding products or channels of distribution (multi level marketing where people have lost money) have created negative feeling lowends such products.

- No hidden charges of small lettering which could confuse the rural population.
- Plain, simple and easy to understand communication.

Integrated process:

The process of pre-sale, sale and post sale have to be simple and efficient.

It system in the bank should support prscessing with seamless instegration with inurer's IT system.

Affordable:

- The premium charges on these products have to be affordable to the targeted population.

- They should be structured in the manner which should take care of seasonality/irregular incomes.

Reaching end customer

- Most important and cricical aspects of sale.
- Need to adequately educate the sales force.
- Equip them with necessary sales tolls to help reach the customer.

Untapped target for Microinsurance

There is a huge population who are categorised as belonging to Below Poverty Line (BPL). The population, which is today covered under the MNEREGA scheme. Most of their payments happen through the banking system and is a perfect example of how this population which needs the protection the most is totally neglected. Apart from this we also have large Self Help Groups (SHG) operating in rural market, large unorganized sector, daily wagers and small organized group like weavers, fishermen, toddy tapper, farm laborer artisans etc., that can be tapped through the sale of Micro insurance products through the large Bancassurance channel.

Role of PSU Banks

Traditionally, the banks (especially the PSU banks) have been providing all the financial security and stability to the rural. India. The loyalty factor of the rural population in this segment is very high. When we think of distributing of financial products like Microinsurance, which have a long tenure (5 to 20 years) with low premiums and which require continuous and regular follow up in terms of collections and servicing, the bank is an excellent channel that can give financial stability, viability, consistency; and proviedservices by leveraging its trust and brand equity with its customers. The inherent strength of the bank can do wonder in this channel as.:

(*a*) *Reach:* especially the PSU banks, have the reach (approximately 37% of total bank branch operates in rural area and are classified as rural branches by Reserve Bank of India (RBI). Another 23.66% of the branches operate in this Semi Urban demarcated areas in India by RBI.)

(*b*) Brand Equity and Stability: Almost 95% of these branches operating in Rural and Semi Urban India are pertaining to PSU banks. They have **Customer loyality :** Due to its very nature of being PSU bank branches which have entered rural India with a social obligation of meeting the financial inclusion objective, the customer loyality is very high. They also disburse a lot of Govt. sponsored programmes to this population which requires this population to physically visit the bank branches.

Knowledge of customers financial and protection need: As these bank branches operated in limited geography and environment where usually population does not exceed 10,000 the bank branch officials are fully aware of the customer's needs, both financial and protection needs, as such this helps tremendously in understanding the customer "needs" and meet the same.

Micro-Insurance: Very nature of microinsurance offer of protection to low/irregular income household against specific pertils. This protection is in exchange of affordable premium, which is based on the likelihood and the cost of the risk involved.

Purpose of Microinsurance: The cover so provided should reduce the exposure and multiple risks; soften the impact of natural calamities and disasters; and provide an overall economic and psychological security to be population.

QUESTIONS

1. Discuss the main proviso of Industrial Life Insurance.
2. 'Group Life Insurance is becoming more popular', discuss its appealing feature.
3. 'Disability and Pension Plans are useful to under-privileged,'—comment it.

18

PROGRESS OF LIFE BUSINESS OF LIC

The life insurance was carried on by the private insurances before 1956; but since January 19, 1956, the Life business came under the control and ownership of government. In June 1956, a Bill was passed for establishing Life Insurance Corporation of India, which started functioning since September 1, 1956. The Corporation is a body corporate having perpetual succession and a common seal with powers to acquire, hold and dispose of property and may be its name sue and be sued. There will be not more than 15 members including a Chairman thereof. The Corporation is charged with the main duty to carry on life insurance business. It has one Central Office, 7 Zonal Offices and several Divisional and Branch offices.

Table 18.1 A New Business (1957-1994)

1. New Business **(inclusive of Group Insurance Business)**

(Amount in crores of ₹)

Business in India			*Business Outside India*	*Total Business*
December 31,	1957	277.67	5.40	283.07
31st March	1963	734.72	11.24	745.96
31st March	1970	1,025.80	10.28	1,036.08
31st March	1974	2,575.01	11.32	3,112.43
31st March	1975	3,100.70	11.73	3,112.43
31st March	1976	5,373.02	12.32	5,385.34
31st March	1980	7,998.16	11.22	8,009.38
31st March	1981	8,787.26	14.41	9,801.67
31st March	1984	11,917.20	18.30	11,945.50
31st March	1985	13,033.38	22.64	13,056.02
31st March	1989	33,473.96	45.74	33,519.70
31st March	1990	43,490.34	100.00	43,590.34
31st March	1994	80,560.88	19.07	80,759.95
31st March	2001	2,03,049.39	179.01	2,03,228.40
31st March	2002	2,88,503.80	212.69	2,88,716.49

Note: *The statutes are now given as per IRDA rules as is attached in the end of this chapter.*

The new business of individual insurance (excluding annuities) has increased from 86.54 lakhs policies in 1990-91 to ₹ 108.88 lakhs policies in 1994-95 and 140-07 policies in 1995-96; amounting to ₹ 2,824 crores, ₹ 55,46,882 crores and ₹ 68,039.16 crores in the respective years. It indicates that the LIC is trying hard to increase its new business at a very rapid speed that is, more than 2 times during the period of five years. The business out of India, increased to ₹ 240.32 crores in 1994-95 under 13 thousand policies. The total individual business touched the minimum of ₹ 1,24,950.63 crores in 2001 and ₹ 1,92,784.96 in 2002.

Table 18.1B New Business Individual Insurance (Excluding Annuities)
(No. of policies in lakhs; sum assured in crores of ₹)

	In India		*Out of India*		*Total*	
Year	*No. of*	*Sum*	*No. of*	*Sum*	*No. of*	*Sum*
1990-91	86.45	28139.07	0.09	100.03	86.54	28239.10
1991-92	92.38	32064.44	0.10	131.86	92.48	32196.30
1992-93	99.58	35956.82	0.10	158.98	99.68	36115.80
1993-94	107.26	41813.83	0.12	199.07	107.38	42012.90
1994-95	108.75	55228.50	0.13	240.32	108.88	55468.82
1995-96	110.21	51815.54	0.13	255.99	110.34	52071.53
1996-97	122.68	56740.50	0.12	253.44	122.81	56993.94
1997-98	133.11	63617.69	0.14	310.14	133.25	63927.83
1998-99	148.44	75316.28	0.13	289.98	148.57	75606.26
1999-2000	169.77	91214.25	0.13	276.69	169.89	91490.94
2000-2001	196.57	124771.62	0.08	179.01	196.65	124950.63
2001-2002	224.91	192572.27	0.08	212.69	225.00	192784.96
2002-2003	242.68	179.51	0.10	298.95	242.79	179.81

Table 18.1C
New Business Progress under Group Insurance (Including Group Gratuity and GSLI) Scheme

	New Schemes			*New Business under existing Schemes*		*Existing Members*		*Total*	
Year	*No. of schemes*	*No. of Member (in lakhs)*	*Sum Assured ₹ in crores*	*No. (in lakhs)*	*Sum Assured ₹ in crores*	*No. in lakhs*	*Increases in Sum Assured ₹ in crores*	*Renewable of Term Insurance ₹ in crores*	*Total Sum Assured ₹ in crores*
1990-91	11548	17.08	3392.05	11.61	1,257.56	112.89	1,844.90	19,417.57	25,912.08
1991-92	12293	34.83	3837.23	4.97	1,221.66	116.71	2,443.32	21,439.57	28,941.78
1992-93	6465	26.49	2923.43	11.63	1,841.13	139.63	3,682.25	31,459.84	39,906.65
1993-94	6529	9.94	2382.77	9.58	835.58	188.60	1,123.11	34,687.42	38,723.88
1994-95	6772	10.49	2773.06	4.85	468.30	195.47	1,346.29	46,064.20	50,651.85
1995-96	9078	11.77	2657.22	8.18	923.32	207.29	2,769.95	56,368.01	62,718.50
1996-97	8381	18.89	3237.59	12.08	718.03	192.81	2,154.11	56,582.15	62,691.88
1997-98	8640	15.80	3692.24	9.43	867.18	201.95	2,601.54	67,987.26	75,148.22
1998-99	8832	15.84	3793.93	5.31	541.21	195.56	1,895.53	63,327.47	69,558.14
1999-2000	9266	17.59	3571.12	4.95	632.78	212.39	1,927.38	60,488.15	66,619.43
2000-2001	8492	14.91	4563.20	3.95	739.15	195.94	2,217.45	70,614.86	78,134.66
2001-2002	5957	21.57	6703.08	3.73	752.62	221.88	3,296.55	77,749.49	88,501.74

The, renewable term insurance, under group insurance, has, gone up from ₹ 19,417.57 crores in 1990-91 to ₹ 46,064.20 crores in 1994-95, whereas the sum assured has increased from ₹ 25,912.08 crores in 1990-91 to ₹ 50,651.85 crores in 1994-95. During 1994-95 many new schemes of group insurance have been added to the extent of 6772 amounting to ₹ 2773-06 crores, covering 10-49 lakhs people. The total business under the schemes increased to the maximum of ₹ 78,134.66 crores in 2001 and ₹ 88,501.74 crores in 2002.

Table 18.1D New Business Progress under Group Superannuation Schemes

Year	New Schemes		New Members		Existing Members		Total	
	No. of Schemes	*No. of Members*	*Annuities per annum*	*Number*	*Annuity per annum*	*Number*	*Increase in amounts*	*Annuities per annum*
1990-91	275	12165	5.49	5036	2.28	176317	2.54	10.31
1991-92	306	15028	6.78	7559	3.42	215263	2.10	12.30
1992-93	249	28411	9.10	6298	3.01	234662	2.31	14.42
1993-94	273	31695	11.65	10487	3.85	271480	2.67	18.17
1994-95	328	31299	14.85	9407	4.46	313662	4.93	24.24
1995-96	353	75692	49.34	12384	4.52	330906	5.47	59.33
1996-97	373	125272	78.42	9676	5.53	419156	8.92	92.87
1997-98	393	33143	122.45	9401	8.63	530000	13.92	145.00
1998-99	369	51592	80.92	10902	17.10	691101	34.40	132.42
1999-2000	323	64004	82.62	11762	20.24	733123	36.06	138.92
2000-2001	408	93695	84.35	4908	23.96	785168	37.80	146.11
2001-2002	427	59814	92.14	2135	26.69	918341	44.21	163.35

The number of existing members under group super-annuation schemes has increased from 176317 in 1990-91 to 313662 in 1994-95 *i.e.*, by more than 15 times, but the amount of total annuity increased only by more than 2 times from ₹ 10.31 crores in 1990-91 to ₹ 24.24 crores in 1994-95. It shows that the Corporation is trying to increase the number of assured people under this scheme. It has increased to ₹ 146.11 crores in 2001 and ₹ 163.35 crores in 2002.

Business in India

The new business in India has tremendously increased during the period of 25 years. It has gone up from ₹ 277.67 crores in 1957, to ₹ 734.72 crore in 1963 and to ₹ 1,025.80 crores in 1970 and again to ₹ 8,787.26 crores in 1980-81 and ₹ 43,490.34 crores in 1989-90 and ₹ 80,560.88 crores in 1993-94. Thus, it had shown a satisfactory progress so far new business was concerned upto 31 March 1990 from ₹ 13,033.38 crores in 1985. It has gone to ₹ 2,88,503.80 crore in 2002.

Business outside India

The new business outside did not rise satisfactorily. It has gone up from ₹ 5.40 crores in 1957. ₹ 11.73 crores in 1975 and to ₹ 14.41 crores in 1981, and ₹ 28.30 crores in 1984. The cause of the lesser rate of increase was that the Corporation has to compete with other concerns outside India whereas in India it is a monopolistic concern. However, it improved in 1989-90 when it rose to ₹ 100.00 crores and ₹ 199.07 crores in 1993-94 and ₹ 212.69 crore in 2002.

Total Business

The total new business had also gone up significantly from ₹ 283.07 crores in 1957 to ₹ 745.96 crores in 1963 to ₹ 2,586.33 crores in 1974 and further to ₹ 3,112.43 crores in 1975 and to ₹ 5,385.34 crores in 1976; but it declined to ₹ 5,119.23 crores in 1977 and increased to ₹ 8,009.38 crores in 1980, ₹ 9,801.67 crores in 1981 and ₹ 13,056.02 crores in 1985. It touched the highest of ₹ 43,590.34 crores in 1989-90 and ₹ 80,759.95 crores in 1993-94 and ₹ 2,03,228.40 crores in 2001 and ₹ 2,88,716.49 crore in 2002.

2. Average amount per policy

The average amount per policy has also been rising constantly in India and outside India. The average policies has increased from ₹ 3,425 in 1957 to ₹ 7,345 in 1970 and further to ₹ 9,807 in 1975, ₹ 13,041 in 1980, ₹ 14,789 in 1981. ₹ 1,99,134 in 1985, ₹ 39,125 in 1994 and ₹ 50,945 in 1995. Thus, the average sum assured has risen by about 12.3 times during the period of last 30 years. The growth in average sum per policy was not as fast as the sum assured had risen. The rise in the average sum outside India was higher than the rise in India. The total average sum assured has also risen more than 12.4 times during this period. The sum assured per policy went upto ₹ 63,539 in 2001 and ₹ 85,682 in 2002.

Table 18.2 Average sum Assured per Policy (New Business) Individual

	India	*Outside*	*Total*
1963	4179	11834	4220
1970	7345	22055	7394
1974	9344	24518	9378
1975	9807	27985	9848
1976	10502	30750	10581
1980	13041	40129	13077
1981	14789	39020	14835
1984	18541	57439	18622
1985	19913	43256	19959
1989	28804	59457	28843
1990	31411	117523	31510
1994	38986	160851	39125
1995	50786	180637	50945
1996	47015	196915	47192
1997	46250	211200	46408
1998	47793	221528	47975
1999	50738	223061	50889
2000	53728	212838	53853
2001	63474	223762	63539
2002	85622	265862	85682

3. New Business in Rural Areas

One of the main purposes of nationalisation was to spread the life insurance business to rural areas where population was less than one lakh. The amount of rural business in absolute term is rising whereas the percentage share of rural business to total business is going down. The definition of Rural/Social Sector has been redefined by the Insurance Regulatory and Development Authority (IRDA) Insurance legislation in India under Section V.

Table 18.3 Rural Business as compared to Individual Business of LIC

	Policies		*Business*	
	Lakhs of Policies	*% to total Policies*	*₹ in crores*	*% to Total Business*
1969–1970	4.61	33.0	251.76	24.5
1973–1974	6.43	31.3	498.17	19.2
1974–1975	5.72	35.7	464.27	14.9
1975–1976	6.50	32.5	563.53	26.8
1979–1980	5.91	28.16	603.77	22.0
1983–1984	8.30	35.00	1260.24	28.54
1984–1985	9.52	35.20	1569.62	29.07
1969–1970	4.61	33.0	251.76	24.5
1988–1989	24.12	40.29	5818.22	33.69
1989–1990	30.48	41.19	8086.35	34.68
1992–1994	48.56	45.3	16680.41	39.9
1994–1995	49.02	45.1	21571.00	39.1
1995–1996	52.57	47.7	21263.59	41.0

Contd....

	Policies		Business	
	Lakhs of Policies	*% to total Policies*	*₹ in crores*	*% to Total Business*
1996–1997	60.33	49.2	24278.73	42.8
1997–1998	68.40	51.4	27550.69	43.3
1998–1999	81.23	54.7	35372.94	47.0
1999–2000	97.04	57.5	44168.19	48.7
2000–2001	35.34	18.2	17955.88	14.6
2001–2002	37.01	13.7	25461.94	16.9
2002–2003	45.23	18.9	23547.69	13.37
2003–2004	62.19	17.85	35651.99	17.85
2004–2005	55.03	22.97	46037.01	25.18
2005–2006	74.66	23.65	60971.85	21.21
2006–2007	88.50	23.16	68497.21	22.60

Note: This decline is as per the definition of rural/social sector as stated by the Insurance Regulatory and Development Authority.

The share or rural business to total business has been continuously declining from 31.8 per cent in 1961 to 24.5 per cent in 1970 and further to 14.9 percent in 1975. It improved from 22.0 per cent in 1980 to 34.68 per cent in 1975. It improved from 22.0 per cent in 1980 to 34.68 per cent in 1990. Not only this but the percentage of policies issued in rural areas to total policies has also been decreasing from 38.5 percent in 1962-63 to 31.3 per cent in 1974 although it has a slight improvement in 1975. This, evidently, reveals that the percentage of rural business to total new business, instead of going up, is going down which is very discouraging sign. The figure of 1981 has revealed that the percentage Share of rural business in total number of policies and in total amount of business has been improved slightly in 1985. It has improved in 1990 and touched the highest figure in 1994. It decline to 13.7 per cent to total policies and 16.9 per cent of total sum assured.

The most discouraging sign is that the number of policies and amount of insurance in rural areas had been fluctuating. Thus the Corporation could not achieve its main objective of expansion of rural insurance.

4. Annuities

The amount of annuities has been declining with fluctuations. The deferred annuities in India has gone down from ₹ 14.05 crores in 1966 to ₹ 12.68 crores in 1970 and further to ₹ 9.67 crores in 1975. However, there has been a slight improvement so far immediate annuities are concerned. It has gone up from ₹ 1.90 crores in 1966 to ₹ 2.07 crores in 1975. Thus, the immediate annuities was gaining popularity. Moreover, the Group Super Annuation Scheme has given a significant rise, it has gone up from ₹ 106.20 lakhs per annum. During 1979-80, 681 Immediate Life Annuity amounted to ₹ 30.78 lakhs per annum and 141 Deferred Life Annuity amounted to ₹ 6.98 lakhs per annum. It declined in 1985 to the level of 28 Immediate Life Annuity Policies of ₹ 1.27 lakhs and 88 Deferred Life Annuity Policies of ₹ 4.10 lakhs per annum. The number of annuities has been ₹ 1.85 lakhs to the extent of ₹ 1261.19 crores in 1989-90. Immediate annuities of ₹ 2.50 crores and Deferred Life Annuities of ₹ 7.11 crores were sold during 1994-95 which were ₹ 6.54 crores and ₹ 6.48 crores respectively in 1998-99.

Non-Medical Schemes

The increase in non-medical insurance is a sign of rapid progress of the insurance business. The amount of non-medical business has increased from ₹ 155.67 crores in 1963 to ₹ 223.65 crores in 1970, to ₹ 447.26 crores in 1974 and further to ₹ 375.0 crores in 1975 and ₹ 422.86 crores in 1977, although the percentage share to total business has declined from 21.2 per cent in 1963, to 21.8 per cent in 1970, 17.3 per cent in 1974 and further to 12.0 per cent in 1975 and increased to 20.0% in 1977. The number of policies issued under this scheme has also gone up from 7.12 Lakhs in 1963 crores ₹ 8.42 lakhs in 1975 although it touched the highest number of 6 lakhs in 1977. New Business under the Non-Medical Scheme amounted to ₹ 519.3 lakhs under 8.35 lakhs policies in 1980 and ₹ 1,508.94 crore under 13.63 lakhs policies in 1985. New business under the Non-Medical schemes increased to ₹ 10,234.94 crores under 40.37 lakhs in 1989-90.

New Schemes

The Group Insurance Scheme has been extended to groups other than those of employees working for a single employer. Deposit Linked Insurance and Cooperative Housing Financial Societies schemes have been formulated in 1970. Centenary Policy Unit Link Insurance Plan, Group Insurance Schemes for handloom weavers, for Government employees, for teachers of Primary and Junior High Schools has also been extended to the employees of Military, Navy and Air Force departments in 1975. The Corporation is, thus making every effort to popularise the insurance benefits among the masses. Money Back, Cash and Cover Plan and Progressive Protection Policies had been introduced during 1976-77. With effect from 1st April 1980, Grihalakshmi Policies, Anticipated Endowment Assurance, Cash and Cover, Centenary Policy and Convertible Whole Life Policies have been withdrawn. Jeevan Sathi and modified New Jana Raksha Policies were introduced in 1985. Jeevan Chhaya has been introduced in March 1991 and Jeevan Shree in 1995. Bima Kiran Plan and Jeevan Shree Plan were introduced in 1996. The sum assured under Bima Nivesh was ₹ 3,594.85 crore under 357665 policies in 2002-2003. Jan Shree was ₹ 3,285 crore under 636116 policies in 2002-2003.

BUSINESS IN FORCE

A. Individual Business

The life insurance business in Force in India has been continuously from ₹ 1,473 crores in 1957 to ₹ 3,168 crores in 1963; to ₹ 6,425 crores in 1970; and further to ₹ 11,852 crores in 1975 and ₹ 19,114 crores in 1980; and ₹ 94408 crores in 1990. Thus the business, in force, has been increased by more than 4 times during the period of last 10 years. The total business in force has increased to ₹ 19,243 crores in 1980 and ₹ 30,426 crores in 1984, ₹ 94,823 crores in 1990, ₹ 2,08,619 crores in 1994 and ₹ 2,54,572 crores in 1995 and ₹ 645042 crores in 2001 and ₹ 8,11,017 crore in 2002.

Table 18.4 Total Business in Force Individual Insurance

	Indian	*Non-Indian*	*Total Business*
Dec. 31st			
1951	793	80	873
1955	1128	92	1220
1960	2176	109	2285
March 31st			
1966	4282	112	3878
1969	5606	119	5725
1974	10725	124	10849
1975	11725	124	11852
1976	13248	124	13372
1980	19114	129	19243
1981	20923	134	21067
1984	30266	160	30426
1985	3785	166	33951
1989	74129	300	74429
1990	94408	415	94823
1994	207601	1018	208619
1995	253333	1239	254572
1996	294336	1422	295758
1997	343018	1601	344619
1998	398959	1789	400748
1999	457435	1766	459201
2000	534589	1862	536451

Contd....

	Indian	Non-Indian	Total Business
2001	643241	1801	645042
2002	809170	1847	811017

The business in-force of Group Insurance Schemes has rapidly been increasing from ₹ 39.0 crores in 1967 to ₹ 6137.46 crores in 1980 and ₹ 1021856 crores in 1985, ₹ 23049.64 crores in 1990, ₹ 46,742.75 crores in 1994 and ₹ 51,034.71 crores in 1995. The business-in-force of Group Superannuation Schemes has increased from ₹ 1.79 crores of annuities in 1967 to ₹ 61.02 crores of annuities in 1980 and ₹ 146.51 crores in 1985 and further to ₹ 245.11 crores in 1990 and ₹ 403.51 crores in 1994 and ₹ 422.66 crores in 1995. This reveals that the Group Insurance has been constantly and rapidly rising in India. It is a very good indicator of the popular form of life insurance which can be adopted to benefit the masses, individually as well as a group. The group insurance scheme amounted ₹ 89,326.19 crores under 84,203 schemes and group Superannuation Scheme 5753 giving ₹ 1,137.72 crores in 2001, and ₹ 1,271.94 crore in 2002.

Table 18.4a Business in Force

(₹ in Crores)
(Sum Assound and Bonus)

Individual Insurance:				
	2002-2003	*2003-2004*	*2004-2005*	*2005-2006*
Assurance	956675.20	11114198.37	1288468.80	1535439.60
Annuities	1449.53	1406.02	1189.80	1296.16
Jeevan Suraksha	8899.81	8611.92	3136.27	3208.08
			(No. of Policies in Lakh)	
Assurance	1388.77	1541.88	1649.35	1835.77
Annuities	9.84	9.98	9.31	9.79
Jeevan Suraksha	13.02	15.95	19.38	19.44
			(Sum Assured in Crore ₹)	
Group Schemes:				
Group insurance	124312.26	1541.88	1649.35	1835.77
Annuities for annum	1488.98	1705.50	1916.64	2189.28
			(No. of schemes)	
Group insurance	95325	10005.50	106912	109995
Group Superannuation	6461	7232	7321	6135
			(No. of Lives in lakhs)	
Group insurance	240.99	253.46	306.50	302.71
Group Superannuation	10.86	12.34	12.73	12.52

Table 18.5 Group Insurance and Superannuation Schemes Business-in-Force

(Business in crores)

As on March 31	***Group Insurance Schemes***		***Group Superannuation Schemes***	
	Number of Scheme	*Sum assured (in Crores of Rupees)*	*Number of Schemes*	*Amount of Annuities (in Crores of Rupees)*
1967	259	39.00	Included in Group Insurance Schemes	1.79
1970	385	77.00		3.12

As on Group InsuranceGroup Superannuation

Contd....

March 31	Schemes Number of Scheme	Schemes Sum assured (in Crores of Rupees)	Schemes Number of Schemes	Amount of Annuities (in Crores of Rupees)
1975	2062	1457.07	366	6.59
1980	7442	6137.46	639	61.02
1981	8537	6960.32	783	69.90
1984	10624	9251.33	1287	118.67
1985	14521	10218.56	1391	146.51
1989	30028	20052.48	2095	213.95
1990	37089	23049.64	2405	245.11
1994	64426	46742.95	3314	403.51
1995	71726	51034.71	3642	427.66
1996	72592	64651.54	3977	483.05
1997	78372	64606.60	4349	545.59
1998	78600	4798.75	4719	682.84
1999	80785	77918.65	4963	815.96
2000	83254	76384.53	5246	971.15
2001	84203	89326.19	5753	1137.72
2002	93836	100597.64	6109	1271.94

The lapsation of policy is harmful for the insurers as well as insured because the goodwill and reputation of the former decline whereas the benefits of insurance are not available to the latter one. Therefore, attempts should be made to reduce the lapse-per-centage. It is a very encouraging sign that the percentage of net lapses to mean life insurance-business-in-force has declined from the highest of 8.1 per cent in 1963 to 3.8 percent in 1980 and 5.6 percent in 1990. Even this percentage is vcry high and Corporation should try to minimisc thc lapsc-ratio. But it could not improvc thc problems of lapses as the lapse-ratio. But it could not improve the problems of lapses as the lapse-ratio increased to 4.5 per cent in 1984 but declined to 4.2 per cent in 1985 and again increased to 5.8 per cent in 1990 and 6.3 per cent in 1994 and 6.1 per cent in 1995 and 5.0 per cent in 2003.

Table 18.6 Percentages of Net Lapses to Mean Life Insurance Business-in-force

Year	Percentage
Dec.31, 1957	6.4
Dec.31, 1960	6.6
March 31, 1963	8.1
" " 1970	5.9
" " 1975	5.4
" " 1976	5.4
" " 1980	3.8
" " 1981	3.8
" " 1984	4.5
" " 1985	4.2
" " 1989	5.0
" " 1990	5.6
" " 1994	6.3
" " 1995	6.1
" " 1996	6.4
" " 1997	5.1
" " 1998	5.0
" " 1999	4.9

Year	Percentage
" " 2000	5.1
" " 2001	4.9
" " 2002	5.5
" " 2003	5.0

Working Results

The working results of LIC can be evaluated by various indicators such as Life Insurance Fund, Premium-Income, Total Income, Expenses, Interest Rates, Investment, Claims-settlements, Number of offices, Productivity of Agents and so on.

(*i*) *Life Insurance Fund.* An increasing trend of life insurance found is a clear indication of progressive business. If the rate of increase of life insurance fund is progressive, it is undoubtedly a significant increase in life insurance business.

The, life insurance fund has been increasing at a faster rate bring the period of 33 years. It is a very encouraging sign that the life insurance fund has increased from ₹ 410.47 crores on Dec. 31, 1957 to ₹ 5,818.09 crores on March 31, 1980 by more than 13 times. It increased to ₹ 9,800.38 crores in 1984 by more than 24 times and again to ₹ 11,191.09 crores in 1985. It has gone up to ₹ 9,568.79 crores in 1989, ₹ 23,471.84 crores in 1990. ₹ 8,667.53 1994 and ₹ 10,313.08 crores in 1995.

Table 18.7 Total Income, Outgo and Funds

(In crores of ₹)

An on	Total Income	Total Outgo	Total Funds
Dec. 31, 1957	101.98	58.91	410.41
Dec. 31, 1960	117.90	62.28	560.38
Mar. 31, 1963	186.25	96.03	120.10
" " 1970	346.35	169.11	1611.04
" " 1915	690.02	360.65	3033.19
" " 1916	190.84	383.66	3440.91
" " 1980	1291.18	596.01	5818.09
" " 1981	1461.25	631.94	6641.44
" " 1984	2113.22	1004.56	9800.88
" " 1985	2519.99	1194.56	11191.09
" " 1989	5310.41	2426.22	19568.79
" " 1990	6835.04	2931.99	23471.84
" " 1994	15212.31	6544.18	8661.53
" " 1995	18102.32	1189.24	10313.08
" " 1996	22046.16	9245.60	12801.16
" " 1991	25933.09	10841.58	14919.90
" " 1998	30132.60	12659.61	18012.93
" " 1999	36352.59	14196.42	21556.11
" " 2000	44129.61	18101.93	26621.61
" " 2001	53968.46	21981.45	31981.02
" " 2002	12169.91	28283.50	44486.41
" " 2003	80981.82	40886.08	40101.14
" " 2004	93088.91	44106.11	48382.14
" " 2005	112346.24	48460.10	63885.54
" " 2006	139146.88	52251.57	
" " 2007	173527.08	77938.52	

(*ii*) *Total Income.* Total income has also increased from ₹ 107.98 crores in 1957 to ₹ 2,519.99 crores in 1985 by more than 23 times during the period. It has increased to ₹ 6,835.04 crores in 1990. ₹ 15,212.31 crores in 1994, ₹ 18102.32 crores in 1995 and ₹ 53,968.46 crores in 2001 and ₹ 72,769.91 crore in 2002.

(*iii*) *Total Outgo.* Total outgo includes payment to policy-holders, expenses of management, commission to agents, salaries and other benefits to employees. Other outgo such as other expenses, taxes, reserves etc. It has increased from ₹ 58.97 crores in 1957 to ₹ 1,194.56 crores in 1985 by more than 19 times. Thus, the income has increased at a faster late than the increase in III outgo. The outgo has gone upto ₹ 2,931.99 crores in 1990 and ₹ 6,544.78 crores in 1994 and ₹ 7,789.24 crores in 1995 and ₹ 21,987.45 crores in 2001 and ₹ 28,283.50 crore in 2002.

(*iv*) *Premium Income.* Increase in premium income has been considerably high as it has increased in absolute as well as in relative term. The percentage increase per annum has been rising year after year. The percentage change over previous year was the highest 15.06 per cent in 1976 and the lowest 7.90 per cent in 1963.

The Premium income has increased from ₹ 88.6,5 crores in 1957 to ₹ 875.37 crores in 1980 by about 10 times and to ₹ 1,355.10 crores in 1984 by more than 15 times and again to ₹ 1,559.33 crores in 1985. It has touched the highest level of ₹ 4,489.39 crores in 1990 and ₹ 9,735.34 crores in 1994, ₹ 11,527.80 crores in 1995 and ₹ 34,207,78 crores in 2001 and ₹ 48,963.60 crores in 2002.

Table 18.8 Premium Income

	Premium income crores of ₹	*Percentage increase over previous year*
Dec. 31, 1957	88.65	
Dec. 31, 1960	97.55	12.68
March 31,1963	151.05	7.90
" " 1970	260.41	10.92
" " 1975	511.24	12.39
" " 1976	588.25	15.06
" " 1980	875.37	12.95
" " 1981	964.88	10.22
" " 1984	1355.10	11.86
" " 1985	1559.33	15.07
" " 1989	3432.72	28.48
" " 1990	4489.39	30.78
" " 1994	9735.32	21.88
" " 1995	11527.80	18.41
" " 1996	14181.77	23.02
" " 1997	16351.39	15.30
" " 1998	19252.07	18.55
" " 1999	22805.80	18.46
" " 2000	27461.71	20.42
" " 2001	34207.78	24.56
" " 2002	48963.60	13.14
" " 2003	54602.37	9.63
" " 2004	62130.26	15.63
" " 2005	75083.37	18.25
" " 2006	90759.20	20.88
" " 2007	127782.26	

(*v*) *Expenses.* The expenses as a percentage to total premium should not increase. The overall expense-ratio and renewal. Expense Ratio are the important expense ratio. The overall expense ratio had touched the highest figure of 30.48 per cent in 1975 and declined to 24.52 percent in 1980 and further to 22.37 per cent in 1984. It increased to 23.84 per cent in 1990 and declined to

21.39 per cent in 1995. The Renewal Expense ratio has also gone down from 18.97 per cent in 1975 to 13.01 per cent in 1980 and again to 13.92 per cent in 1985. It was merely 3.04 per cent in 1990. ₹ 4.95 percent in 1995,6.32 per cent in 1995 and 2.43 per cent in 2001 and 4.20 per cent in 2002.

Table 18.9 Expenses as a Percentage to Total Premium

Year ending on	*Overall Expense Ratio*	*Renewal Expenses Ratio*
Dec. 31, 1957	27.20	15.89
Dec. 31, 1960	28.45	12.90
Mar. 31, 1963	29.31	14.13
Mar. 31, 1970	27.69	16.15
" " 1975	30.48	18.97
" " 1976	29.66	18.14
" " 1980	24.52	13.01
" " 1981	24.24	12.62
" " 1984	22.37	11.16
" " 1985	24.68	13.92
" " 1989	25.52	6.89
" " 1990	23.84	3.04
" " 1994	21.83	4.95
" " 1995	21.39	6.32
" " 1996	20.79	7.00
" " 1997	21.43	7.09
" " 1998	20.53	6.09
" " 1919	20.48	5.38
" " 2000	21.16	5.63
" " 2001	19.89	2.43
" " 2002	17.72	–4.20%
" " 2003	17.62	2.40
" " 2004	17.30	2.73
" " 2005	16.57	2.30
" " 2006	14.47	2.69
" " 2007	12.72	2.35

(*vi*) *Interest Rate.* The interest rate reveals the profitability of the concern. The rising rate of interest is a promising sign. In LIC, the gross interest rate has increased from 4.58 per cent in 1957 to 7.89 per cent in 1980 and the net interest rate has increased from 3.74 per cent in 1957 to 7.44 percent in 1980 and 9.76 per cent in 1985. It has increased to 11.13 per cent in 1990, 12.21 per cent in 1995 and 11.60 per cent in 2001. Thus, it is clear that the profitability position of LIC has been improving gradually.

Table 18.10 Interest-Rate earned on Mean Life Insurance Fund

Year ending on	*Gross Interest Rate*
Dec. 31, 1957	4.68
" 1960	4.58

Contd....

Mar. 31, 1963	4.76
" 1970	6.06
" 1975	6.93
" 1976	7.13
" 1980	7.89
" 1981	8.21
" 1984	9.19
" 1985	9.46
" 1986	10.95
" 1990	11.13
" 1994	12.43
" 1995	12.21
" 1996	12.29
" 1997	12.39
" 1998	12.37
" 1999	11.96
" 2000	12.08
" 2001	11.60
" 2002	11.59
" 2003	10.40
" 2004	9.57
" 2005	9.93
" 2006	8.72
" 2007	8.21

Table 18.11a Amount of Investment

As on	*Investment in crores of ₹*
Dec. 31, 1957	329.75
" 1960	457.43
Mar. 31, 1963	678.81
" 1970	1528.66
" 1975	2803.20
" 1976	3134.64
" 1980	5747.51
" 1981	6534.32
" 1984	9613.74
" 1985	10804.03
" 1986	17342.70
" 1990	20503.74
" 1994	46560.63
" 1995	56182.44
" 1996	68275.60
" 1997	82665.17
" 1998	98947.77
" 1999	120445.40

" 2000	139032.15
" 2001	175491.18
" 2002	221697.50
" 2005	413800.95
" 2006	613266.58

(*vii*) *Investment.* The amount of investment has been constantly increasing from ₹ 329.75 crores in 1957 to ₹ 5747.51 crores in 1980 by more than 18 times and ₹ 10804.03 crores in 1985 by 30 times. It had gone upto ₹ 20503.74 crores in 1990, ₹ 46560.63 crores in 1994 and ₹ 56182.44 crores in 1995 and ₹ 221697.50 crore in 2002. The investment has contributed significantly in the development of the nation.

The percentage distribution of LIC investment reveals that LIC has favoured public sector as more than 79 per cent of total investment was made in public sector. The investment in cooperative sector has also been rising but in 1980 it declined to 9.7 per cent and increased to 10.2 per cent in 1984 and came down to 6.5 per cent in 1990. Investment in private sector had gone down from 22.7 per cent in 1957 to 11.6 per cent in 1977 but it improved to 12.5 per cent in 1980, 13.7 per cent in 1990, 13.8 per cent in 1995 and 86.5 per cent 2002. LIC investment has been directed towards socially oriented securities. It is a great achievement that LIC has tried to develop electricity, health, drinking facilities, water and sewerage schemes, small-scale industries, fertilisers, housing and other infrastructures.

Table 18.11b Percentage Distribution of LIC Investment in Different

As on	*Public Sector*	*Cooperative Sector*	*Private Sector*
Dec. 31, 1957	77.3	—	22.7
" 1960	78.7	—	21.3
Mar. 31, 1963	76.8	3.3	19.4
" 1970	73.6	9.5	16.5
" 1975	75.4	12.0	12.6
" 1976	76.3	11.8	11.9
" 1980	63.4	9.7	12.5
" 1984	79.3	10.2	10.5
" 1985	79.6	8.4	10.6
" 1989	80.9	7.2	11.9
" 1990	79.8	6.5	13.7
" 1994	82.1	3.9	14.0
" 1995	82.9	3.3	13.8
Mar. 31, 1996	84.63	2.90	12.47
" 1997	84.58	2.49	12.93
" 1998	84.66	2.17	13.17
" 1999	84.49	1.84	13.67
" 2000	84.2	1.5	14.3
" 2001	84.6	1.3	14.1
" 2002	86.5	1.0	12.5

Note — Joint Sector is included under private sector.

(*viii*) *Claims-Settlement.* The claims settlement is an indicator of the efficiency of the LIC in meeting claims-obligation. The percentage of outstanding claims to claims intimated should decline. It has been observed that percentage of outstanding claims to total claims intimated has decreased from 60.52 per cent in 1957 to 14.14 per cent in 1977. It was a tremendous achievement in the field of claim-settlements; but it has again deteriorated and percentage of claims outstanding to total claims intimated has increased to 17.08 per cent in 1980. It decreased to 11.23 per cent in 1995 and 5.96 per cent in 1990 and 4.86 per cent in 1994 and increased to 5.26 per cent in 1995 and 3.70 per cent in 2001 and declined to 1.85 per cent in 2002.

Table 18.12 Claims—Settlement

(In crores of ₹)

As on	*Claims intimated*	*Claims outstanding*	*Percentage of claims outstanding to claims intimated*
Dec. 31, 1957	28.70	13.03	60.53
" 1960	30.60	13.47	43.89
Mar. 3 1. 1963	43.95	13.55	38.45
" 1970	81.44	24.29	29.83
" 1975	148.32	31.72	21.39
" 1976	162.73	28.60	17.58
" 1980	283.00	48.35	17.08
" 1981	314.20	67.05	21.34
" 1984	517.28	73.62	14.23
" 1985	638.29	73.23	11.53
" 1989	1211.08	84.71	6.61
" 1990	1425.14	90.56	5.96
" 1994	3845.45	171.50	4.86
" 1995	4130.80	226.23	5.26
" 1996	4594.69	288.70	6.28
" 1997	6722.38	319.59	5.58
" 1998	6673.07	315.62	4.73
" 1999	7615.78	348.22	4.57
" 2000	9266.25	403.17	4.35
" 2001	11666.82	432.01	3.70
" 2002	14358.55	273.34	1.85
" 2003	—	213.98	0.23
" 2004	—	—	1.11
" 2006	—	—	0.82
" 2007	—	—	0.68

Number of Offices. The number of offices has not increased satisfactorily. As compared to the bank-branches, the expansion in LIC offices has been almost negligible. The total offices of LIC have increased from 735 in 1963 to 888 in 1980 and 1160 in 1985 and 1603 in 1990. The number of branch offices has been growing from 340 in 1963 to 738 in 1980 and 1023 in 1984 and 1528 in 1990. The number of sub-offices increased to 179 in 1963 and declined to only 4 sub-offices in

1980. The number of development centres has also been decreasing from 175 in 1963 to 100 in 1980 and further to only 5 in 1985. The total number of LIC offices in 1995 was 2128, out of which 2021 were branch offices.

The total number of LIC offices increased to 2155 in 2001 but of which 2048 were branch offices.

Table 18.13 Number of Offices

As on	*Zonal offices*	*Divisional offices*	*Branch offices*	*Sub offices*	*Development centres*	*Total offices*
Dec. 31, 1957	5	33	105	45	—	278
Mar. 31, 1963	5	36	340	179	175	735
" 1970	5	36	424	115	123	703
" 1975	5	41	651	29	105	831
" 1976	5	41	659	23	110	838
" 1980	5	41	738	4	100	888
" 1981	5	42	826	—	63	936
" 1984	5	43	1023	—	12	1083
" 1985	5	43	1107	—	5	1160
" 1989	5	64	1427	—	—	1496
" 1990	6	69	1528	—	—	1603
" 1994	7	100	2008	—	—	2115
" 1995	7	100	2021	—	—	2128
Mar 31, 1996	7	100	2021	—	—	2128
" 1997	7	100	2023	—	—	2130
" 1998	7	100	2046	—	—	2153
" 1999	7	100	2048	—	—	2155
" 2000	7	100	2048	—	—	2155
" 2001	7	100	2048	—	—	2155
" 2002	7	100	2048	—	—	2155
" 2003	7	100	2048	—	—	2156
" 2004	7	101	2048	—	—	2156
" 2005	7	101	2048	—	—	2156

(x) *Productivity of Agents*. The productivity or Active Agents has been constantly increasing from ₹ 31,000 in 1957 to ₹ 2,47.641 in 1980 by about 8 times and ₹ 3,63,772 in 1985 by 11 times. The productivity of agent has been ₹ 6,66,605 in 1990, ₹ 7,97,324 in 1994, 1063101 in 1995 and ₹ 12,59,013 in 1999 and ₹ 7,44,003 in 2002.

Table 18.14 Productivity of Agents

As on	*Number of Active Agents*	*Business Per Active Agents in ₹*
Dec. 31, 1957	8900	31,000
1960	1,01,600	47,900

Contd....

As on	*Number of Active Agents*	*Business Per Active Agents in Rs.*
Mar. 31, 19631,41,000	52,070	
" 1970	1,32,790	77,241
" 1975	1,46,103	1,20,518
" 1976	1,44,385	1,45,722
" 1980	1,10,366	2,47,641
" 1984	1,32,947	3,29,980
" 1985	1,47,783	3.63.722
" 1989	2,96,713	5,80,455
" 1990	3,48,325	6,66,605
" 1994	5,24,427	7,97,324
" 1995	5,19,504	10,63,101
Mar. 31, 1996	5,13,897	10,08,286
" 1997	5,33,133	10,64,284
" 1998	5,58,517	11,39,047
" 1999	5,98,217	12,59,013
" 2000	6,83,190	13,28,292
" 2001	7,43,064	16,56,370
" 2002	7,44,083	23,55,697
" 2003	9,02,199	19,51,767
" 2004	10,03,241	21,97,675
" 2005	10,41,737	—

Valuation

The valuation of life assets and liabilities is very important process to assess the solvency of the concern. Prior to nationalisation the insurers were required to make an acturial valuation at least once in three years. In terms of the Life Insurance Corporation Act 1956, the Corporation has to conduct valuation of its assets and liabilities at least once in two years. The rate of reversionary bonus has increased very slowly from ₹ 16.00 per thousand in 1957 to ₹ 31.00 per thousand in 1981 in case of Whole Life Policy and form.

Table 18.15 Valuation of Life Assets

As on	*Policyholders share, excluding interim bonus (in crores of ₹)*	*Government's share (in crores of ₹)*	*Rewrsionary* *Endowment*	*Bonus Declared per thousand ₹* *Whole-life*
Dec. 31, 195727.56	1.45	12.80	16.00	
" 1959	24.48	1.28	12.80	16.00
" 1961	32.73	1.27	12.80	16.00
Mar. 31, 196325.03	1.32	14.00	17.50	
" 1965	58.93	3.10	16.00	20.00

Contd....

As on		Policyholders share, excluding interim bonus (in crores of Rs)	Government's share (in crores of Rs)	Rewrsionary Endowment	Bonus Declared per thousand Rs. Whole-life
"	1967	68.67	3.61	16.00	20.00
"	1969	90.30	4.75	17.60	22.00
"	1971	110.18	5.80	17.60	22.00
"	1973	144.34	7.60	17.60	22.00
"	1975	172.43	9.07	17.60	22.00
"	1977	241.04	12.69	20.00	25.00
"	1979	354.30	18.65	24.80	31.00
"	1981	495.83	26.10	28.00	35.00
"	1983	743.98	39.16	34.00	42.50
"	1985	997.17	52.48	44.00	55.00
"	1989	905.02	47.63	62.00	77.50
"	1990	1128.58	58.40	64.00	80.00
"	1993	2368.10	118.43	75.00	96.00
"	1995	2803.00	140.15	75.00	96.00
"	1996	3362.31	171.69	78.00	95.00
"	1997	2768.65	198.35	80.00	97.00
"	1998	4439.36	233.64	85.00	102.00
"	1999	5635.00	265.0	87.00	104.00
"	2000	5035.48	265.02	89.00	106.00
"	2001	6016.26	316.65	89.00	106.00
"	2002	7232.60	380.66	89.00	106.00
"	2003	9767.00	488.13	89.00	106.00
"	2004	10087.60	548.13	89.00	106.00
"	2005	13951.69	696.60	—	—
"	2006	12463.0	621.71		
"	2007	15156.0	757.81		

₹ 12.80 per thousand to ₹ 24.80 per thousand in case of endowment policy. The bonus per thousand has been 64.0 in case of endowment and 80.00 in whole life in 1990 which increased to 75.00 and 96.00 respectively in 1993. The Reversionary bonus in 1995 per thousand for was ₹ 75 whole life which increased to 106 per thousand and 89 per thousand in 2002.

Organisation Scheme of the LIC

As per the suggestions of Era-Sezhiyan Committee, the LIC has adopted reorganisation schemes of its divisional and branch offices. At present the reorganisation work has been completed in all the divisions and branches.

Reorganised Divisions: The reorganised divisions have nine departments. The marketing department, planning and review department and divisional management committee are important departments of the divisions. There are discussed in the following sections:

1. Marketing Department

It is responsible for branch performance and is the single point of contact for supervising them. The department is responsible for judging the quality of work done in branches through its sections sales, policy-holders' service section, sales training section and branch support section.

(*a*) *Sales Section.* It is responsible for carrying out supervisory functions relating to sales and the field-force and customer-satisfaction.

The major task of the sales managers in charge of the sales section is the supervision of the sales functions at the branches and the performances of the field-personnel. This section is also responsible for spreading awareness among the general public about the benefits of life insurance and the nature of cover that LIC's policies provide and how section assesses the quality of business of the various branches and effectiveness of their plans in penetrating the respective territories and markets assigned.

(*b*) *Policyholders' Service Section.* It is responsible for supervising the policyholder servicing function including claims and the operational function of early settlement of claims. It handles matters referred to divisional office by branches in respect to all policyholder's service functions. It may undertake the training of branch staff and carry out timeliners and the quality of the service rendered by the branches to the policyholders. This section has also to deal with the individual cases referred to by branches. All old claims have to be got investigated and settled by this section.

(*c*) *Sales Training Section.* This section is entrusted with responsibility for training in product, in selling and sales planning in the field personnel. It arranges and conducts training of field-personnel, such as ABM(D), development officers and agents.

(*d*) *Branch Support Section.* It is responsible for providing secretarial support to the various sections in marketing department. It provides administrative support to the sections under the Marketing Manager. This section is responsible for analysis of budget proposals and monthly review of data. They analyses the performance data, raise special issues concerning the performance of branches and generally help the various sections in the marketing department to process work and perform liaison work with other departments and take up routine functions as assigned to them. They have to undertake general follow up of routine matters with the branches and with other departments of the Divisional Office.

The marketing department controls the entire sales and service functions in the Divisional area and also services as a single point contract between the branches and the departments of the divisional office.

2. New Business and Acturial Department

New Business and Acturial Department is responsible as specialists to decide on the proposal referred to the divisional office in respect to all individual, SSS and GSD proposals, cheque, Delined Life Index Cards and undertake supervisory, inspection tasks, vis-a-vis branches. They also have the responsibility to train new business incumbents in branches according to their judgment of their capabilities and of their needs. This department is responsible for supervision of branch functions from under-writing to issue of policy, appointment and control of medical examiners etc. It underwrites proposals of higher sum assured, which are beyond the powers of the branches and conducts acturial valuation and undertakes acturial research.

3. Accounts Department

The Accounts Departments is responsible for supervision of accounts in the branches, collection of branch accounts and all the accounting functions in the division, also training of staff and test-checking how well the work in branches is being done. Accounts department has two sections: (*a*) Branch Accounts Section has responsibility for supervision of branch accounts, expenses and training of staff. They analyses the trial-balances from branches and recommend suitable action to divisional management, (*b*) General Accounts Section which has three units: (*i*) Cash and Banking Section; (*ii*) Salary and Provident Fund Section; and (*iii*) Final Accounts Section.

4. Legal and Mortgage Department

The legal and mortgage department has the responsibility for all legal and mortgage loan work in the division, They advise branches when required for mortgage loans and legal matters.

5. Office Management Department

The office management department consists of two divisions; (*a*) Purchase Section which has responsibility for purchases, inventory and materials utilisation and (*b*) Service Section that consists of security despatch, duplicating and office services, transportation etc.

6. Machine Department

It is responsible for data processing and offers service to user-departments in the Divisional office and to branches that do not have machine support. It has two sections (*a*) System Section which is responsible to oversee the systems and programmes of data processing machines in branches and division; (*b*) Operations Section that is responsible for providing machine support to branches that do not have an in-house system, as also to the divisional office.

7. Personnel Department

It consists of three sections:

(*a*) *Management Development Section.* This section is responsible for management forecast, management development and career planning of staff. It has responsibility to ensure that branches implement the policies laid down in letter and spirit. They carry out periodic personnel audit to ensure that the corporate plans and policies are implemented satisfactorily.

(*b*) *Industrial Relations Section.* It is responsible to develop relations with trade unions and to carry out negotiations in matters that relate to the division as a whole.

(*c*) *Training Section.* It is responsible for organising programme for supervisors and middle management personnel within the division. This section is also responsible to organise functional programmes according to the needs of various departments in the divisional office.

8. Planning and Review Department

The planning and review department has responsibilities in two main areas. One is the operation section with responsibility for locality data suitable for planning, education and developing among concerned people, the understanding of the concepts and their applications, review of performance budget proposals and review of monthly, quarterly or six monthly performance reports. The other is the Special Studies Section with responsibility for undertaking studies that the performance data may indicate or the divisional management may consider necessary.

REORGANISED BRANCH OFFICE

The reorganised branch offices of the LIC have the following sections:

1. Sales Section

This section is responsible for supervision of development officers agents and for building up the agency force in its jurisdiction. It has to plan and review business performance and take remedial action where necessary. It registers new proposals, settles commission and make all payments to agents and development officers.

2. New Business Section

This section is responsible for underwriting all new business and issue of new policies. It sends recommendations and obtains approval for business beyond its permmissible limits, from higher authority.

3. Policy holders' Servicing Section, Including Claims

This section is responsible for total servicing of policies, including loans and claims and to obtain approval from higher authority for matters beyond their sanctioned powers. A separate section for claims and salary saving scheme is created, if the volume of work justifies.

It is responsible for providing the required support to all departments. An in-house machine will be provided only where size justifies it. In other cases, such support will come from the divisional office.

5. Office Service Section

It is responsible for establishment and personnel matters in the Branch.

6. Accounts Section

This section is responsible for Cash and Banking, preparation of trial balance of the branch, reconciliation of various accounts and issue and control of premium, receipts.

7. Branch Management Committee

This committee consists of the Branch Manager and all the heads of sections and has higher financial powers. The members of the Branch Management Committee are Section Heads, Higher Grade Assistants, Superintendents, Assistant Administrative officers or Administrative officers. The Committee has also been vested with a financial authority beyond the power of the officer in charge of the branch in matters relating to underwriting and policy-services. The decisions of the Management Committee on all matters have to be unanimous and in case of differences in the committee the matters have to be referred to the Divisional office.

The basic function of the Committee is to review the performance of the branch, discuss its work-status and evolve methods to overcome problems facing the branch. The review of the performance of the branch has to be made in relation to some standards. The performance budget for the branch, agreed between the Division and the Branch provides the yardstick for this comparison.

This review would be meaningful if the planning and budgeting itself is done after a thorough discussion at the Management Committee, so that all members of the Committee have a sense of commitment and identity with the plan. The review of the performance at the Branch Management Committee provide feedback for future planning and enables suitable measures to be taken speedily wherever necessary to bring performance in line with plans, by a careful analysis of the reasons for its deviation.

The performance plan and budget evolved, after discussions in the Management Committee provides common goals for the branch to reach and the involvement of individual departmental heads in evolving these goals. It brings in them a sense of commitment so that when reviews are made individual departmental heads become prepared to sacrifice narrow departmental interests, Whenever required, in the interest of the branch attaining the common objectives. The review of performance and analysis of the problems faced which the Committee does enable emergence of a problem-solving culture. It leads to a realisation that operational problems can be solved primarily by putting heads together, identifying the causes and tackling the issues that provide the cause and not by referring to higher officers and awaiting their advice or directions. Only those matters are referred to higher authority, which are beyond the powers and levels of expertise available at the branch.

CUSTOMERS RELATIONS MANAGEMENT

In order to provide individual attention to the policyholders and to monitor continuously the quality of service delivery, the LIC has introduced the CRM initiatives during 2001-2002. As a part of the initiatives Managers (CRM) at the Divisional Office are positioned. Customer Relations Executives

(CRE) and Customer Relations Group (CRG) have been constituted at branch level Helplines Letters etc. Standing committees on customer Relations have been Constituted.

INSURANCE OMBUDSMAN

The office of Insurance ombudsman was created in the year 1998 for arbitration between the customers and the insurance companies. These are 12 insurance ombudsmen in the country. There is no cost involved in taking the grievance to the ombudsman and generally the decisions are more expeditions. The ombudsmen are empowered to receive and consider disputes arising of repudiation of claims by an insurer premiums paid or payable in terms of the policy, legal construction of the policies relating to claims, delay in settlement of claims, non-issue of any insurance document to customers after receipt of premium.

UPGRADING OF INFORMATION TECHNOLOGY

The LIC is one of the largest users of Information Technology in terms of hardware and in house developed application software. The "Green Channel" is for on the spot policy completion and the "Single Window" provides all policy servicing at one single point. The "CRM" module shows all the relevant details of a customer displaying his individual interest in particular plans and giving marketing leads to meet his future needs.

The LIC has Wide and Metro Area Network Connect 90 centres covering 101 division and 2037 branches.

Through the LIC's website www.licindia.com, people get information about the Corporation's products services, subsidies, and addresses of branches and about the premium payment through the internet. The LIC has installed **Information**. Kiosles at prominent places in India.

LIC (INTERNATION) LTD.

The branches at Fiji and Mauritius have shown very good business growth. Similarly LIC (Int.) Behrain, LIC (Nepal) Ltd., LIC (Lanka) Ltd. The branch at UK in progress-process. Botswana, Tanzania, Maldives and New Zealand are getting LIC services.

INFORMATION RELATING TO PRIVATE INSURANCE (LIFE)

Bank of Punjab (BoP), announced its tie up with the state-owned life insurance major LICI for distributing the latter's insurance products.

The Indian Cricket Board will launch a unique insurance policy offered by LICI for its players wherein their returns would rise by 43 per cent annually compared to an existing benevolent fund.

All the life insurance companies in India have decided to jointly work out a standardised individual pension product. The N.K. Shinkar Committee which was appointed by the IRDA has submitted its report on the same.

Vijaya Bank, Punjab National Bank (PNB), the Principal Financial Group of the US and a leading tyre company have signed a memorandum of understanding (MoU) and have applied to IRDA for a license for a life insurance venture.

Private insurance players are targeting Non-resident Indians (NRIs) as the premiums coming from this segment of society are huge. Birla Sun Life Insurance Company and SBI Life Insurance are coming up with special insurance-cum-investment products targeted at NRIs.

LIC is toying with the idea of launching a credit-cum-debit card in a tie up with one of the largest financial companies-Capital One Financial of the US, a Fortune 500 company with a customer base of 46.4 million.

The Supreme Court has ruled that an insurance company which has issued a Third Party (TP) liability policy has to pay compensation to the victims of a road accident even if the driver of the vehicle which meets with an accident had a fake driving licence.

LIC is looking at extending insurance cover to HIV–infected women under the Jeevan Bharati plan. The life insurance company will need national level data on AIDS/HIV infection and relevant statistical information to take any decision on extending insurance cover to women affected by this disease.

IRDA has granted in-principle permission to the Sahara Group to enter the life insurance business, subject to the latter fulfilling some regulatory requirements.

In the context of declining interest rates, Senior citizens ate awaiting for the launch of LIC's pension scheme, guaranteeing an annual return of 9%, in the form of monthly pension scheme.

Reliance General Insurance has been slapped with a penalty of ₹ Two lakh by IRDA for failing to meet the insurance regulator's rural business target for the fiscal 2001-02 .

RECENT PROGRESS OF LIC

1. LIC Plans Micro-risk Products for Rural Poor

The Life Insurance Corporation of India (LIC) is planning to forge an alliance with the four state-owned general insurance companies to jointly develop micro-insurance products affordable for the rural poor. The new Insurance Reguatory and Development Authority (Irda) regulations permit life insurance companies for offer non-life micro-insurance products, provided the life insurer has a tie-up with a non-life insurance company. Similarly, nonlife insurance companies can also offer life products if they have a tie-up with a life insurer.

"LIC would perfer to have an arrangement, preferable with all the government owened general insurance companies, but a final decision would depend on Irda's views." T.S. Vijayan, managing director of LIC, told reporters on the sidelines of a seminar on corporate governance organised by the Indian Merchant's Chamber.

LIC would be able to distribute micro-insurance policies through its existing agent network and will also appoint agents only to hawk micro-insurance products. Besides servicing policies, the micro-insurance agents would also collect premium.

Vijayan said LIC would have to rework its organisational network to make the business of micro-insurance cost-effective and also make it serve the target customer segment.

The minimum and maximum cover for accident, health and endowment policies would range between ₹ 5,000 to ₹ 50,000 per policy.

The remuneration or commission to agents would be a maximum of 10 per cent for single premium life product and 20 per cent for other products. For non-life products, the commission to micro-insurance agents would be upto 15 per cent of the premium.

2. LIC to Add Corporate Agencies

The 10 lakh plus army of individual agents has been one of the core strengths of the Life Insurance Corporation but now the life insurer is looking at corporate agencies to complement this channel, "We are looking at tying up with as many banks as possible to reach out to more customers. As of now the banking channel accounts for a small per cent of our business but in the next five-l0 years this will go to about 20-25%", S. Viswanathan, executive director (marketing-bancassurance and alternate channels) said.

The bancassurance channel currently brings in premium of ₹ 200 crore out of a total ₹ 12,000 crore for LIC. LIC has tied up 38 bancassurance deals with the latest being the MoU with Bank of maharashtra which was signed in pune on Wednesday. Ashok Kumar Dugade, ED, Bank of Maharashtra said bancassurance would be introduced in 200 select branches and gradually rolled out across its network of 1 ,300 branches. In the first year the bank is looking at an income of ₹ 10 crore through selling of life insurance. Mr. Viswanathan said LIC had, tied up with nine PSU banks and 21 cooperatives banks and it had and it had a good equation with PSU banks. "Two PSU banks come to us after they severed ties with private insurance companies and some more will come in the near future. He said "Apart from the alternate channels, LIC is currently working on its foray into micro-insurance products for the rural markets and low-income groups through NGOs, SHGs and banks," he said.

3. LIC to Hire Consultant for Credit Card biz

The country's largest life insure. Life Insurance Corporation Ltd. (LIC) will appoint a consultant soon for weighing the credit card business options. Many banks are approaching LIC for tying up offe₹ LIC has decided to appoint a consultant before diversifying into such ventures. Speaking to FE, TS Vijayan, managing director, LIC said, "Lot of banks are approaching us for entering into the business. We, are in the process of appointing a consultant in January for this purpose. The report would be expected in another six months.

The consultant would provide views on two issues: one, what are the value addition LIC's customer would get from such a product and second, what are the stand-alone profitability and break even points from the business, "We would like to see that by a venturing into this new business what are the value addition we would be able to provide for our customer for example, if the customer could pay the premium through the card and other aspects.

In addition, the consultant will also measure the stand alone profitability of the new entity and the break even point," Mr. Vijayan added. If LIC, finally, launches such card, it would be the first insurance firm in India to enter the plastic money business. The industry expects that the insurance gant can change the rules of the game by offering lower interest as compared to the existing card issuers.

4. LIC Plans to Foray Into New Zealand

Plans composite company in Riyadh

The Life Insurance Corporation of India plans to start a composite company in Riyadh, the capital of Saudi Arabia soon and also make a foray into the insurance sector in New Zealand.

Talking to reporters here recently, its Managing Director, K, Sridhar, said the LIC was working out a strategy to establish itself in New Zealand. The decision on whether to establish a subsidiary or a branch or take up joint venture would hinge upon the result of the ongoing survey, he said. The LIC owned subsidiaries in Bahrain, Sri Lanka and Nepal and had overseas branches in Fiji, Mauritius and London. The Zonal Manager, G Prabhakara, said till November-end, the Southern Zone achieved 41.43 per cent of annual target in selling policies and 51.06 per cent in premium income mobilisation and stood number two in the country in performance.

5. BOM, LIC Tie up for Bancassurance

The giant insurer, Life Insurance Corporation of India has signed Memorandum of Understanding **(MOU)** with Bank of Maharashtra (BoM). Putting its plan into action, the insurance products will be initially made available at selected 200 branches, which will move to 500 branches later on. The expansion levels are aimed to be achieved within a span of two years.

This is the 35th tie up of bancassurance for LIC, It had earlier tied up with a couple of public and private sector banks. It has also apped in 22 cooperative banks for its bancassurance venture. Other options like NGOs are also being considered. For non insurance products, BoM will approach United India Insurance Company.

NEW BUSINESS (INDIVIDUAL)

	In India			*Out of India*			*Total*		
Year	*No. of Policies*	*Sum Assured/ NCO/APA ₹ in crores*	*Annual Premium Receivable (₹ in crores)*	*No. of policies*	*Sum Assured/ NCO/APA ₹ in crores*	*Annual Premium Receivable (₹ in crores)*	*No. of Policies*	*Sum Assured/ NCO/APA ₹ in crores*	*Annual Premium Receivable (₹ in crores)*
Individual Assurance									
2001-02	22490852	192569.11	16009.13	8695	212.68	12.57	22499547	192781.79	16021.70
2002-03	24267282	179504.34	12504.19	10359	298.95	18.85	24277641	179803.29	12523.04
2003-04	2646320	198707.12	12540.82	11562	341.40	23.27	26467882	199048.52	12564.09
2004-05	21817967	179481.39	11224.19	13807	409.27	26.50	21831774	179886.66	11.250.69
2005-06	129284800	283763.74	15157.76	13370	416.10	25.24	29298170	284179.84	15183.00
2006-07	20910041	201620.74	11672.72	12059	403.71	24.94	20922100	202042.45	11697.66
General Annuity									
2001-02	515948	740.38	125.08	14	0.15	0.03	515962	740.53	125.11
2002-03	6394	17.36	8.34	0	0	0	6394	17.36	8.34
2003-04	6777	31.93	10.78	0	0	0	6777	31.93	10.78
2004-05	4577	15.43	1.26	0	0	0	4577	15.43	1.26
2005-06	4678	26.73	0.75	—	—	—	4678	26.73	0.75
2006-07	5903	132.16	0.65	—	—	—	5903	132.16	0.65
Pension									
2001-02	259515	6596.37	255.99	0	0	0	259515	6596.37	255.99
2002-03	234390	2165.03	243.39	9	0.05	0.01	234399	2156.08	243.40
2003-04	318761	2826.63	342.87	23	0.16	0.04	318784	2826.79	342.91
2004-05	413441	3590.40	320.15	11	0.06	00	413452	2590.46	320.15
2005-06	40842	270.07	35.78	—	—	—	40842	270.07	35.78
2006-07	16288	207.63	18.86	—	—	—	16288	207.63	18.86
Unit Linked									
2001-02	452	3.15	0.32	0	0	0	452	3.15	0.32
2002-03	1134	7.89	1.19	0	0	0	11341	7.89	1.19
2003-04	170061	990.90	19.12	0	0	0	70061	990.90	19.12
2004-05	7190.85	3378.88	122.51	0	0	0	719085	3378.88	122.51
2005-06	35692	153.53	8.07	—	—	—	35692	153.53	8.07
2006-07	—	—	—	—	—	—	—	—	—
Future Plus started in 2004-05									
2004-05	1004633	260.961	166.52	0	0	0	1004633	260.96	166.52
2005-06	1902505	279.41	133.62	—	—	—	1902505	279.41	133.62
2006-07	1273443	71.44	86.23	—	—	—	1273443	71.44	86.23
Jeevan Plus started in 2005-06									
2005-06	304030	3612.97	273.37	—	—	—	304030	3612.97	273.37
2006-07	228570	2846.11	314.78	—	—	—	228570	2846.11	314.78
Market Plus Started in 2006-07									
2006-07	4993655	699.14	1419.55	—	—	—	4993655	699.14	1419.55
Market Plus									
2006-07	4975762	681.75	1409.23	—	—	—	4975762	681.75	1404.23

NEW BUSINESS (GROUP)

Year	*No. of Schemes*	*No. of Members (in lakh)*	*Sum Assured/Annuity annum (₹ in crore)*
Group Insurance (incl. Social Security)			
2001-2002	15957	22.33	88501.74
2002-2003	15329	25.20	110763.34
2003-2004	15797	44.48	128047.85
2004-2005	18189	81.00	117662.56
2005-2006	18160	114.68	177317.32
2006-2007	20434	140.38	152864.52
Group Superannuation			
2001-2002	427	0.62	163.35
2002-2003	305	1.08	186.87
2003-2004	344	1.72	214.90
2004-2005	231	0.43	82.50
2005-2006	127	0.71	91.10
2006-2007	263	1.12	212.09
Linked Business G-plus			
2006-2007	20	0.14	97.68

NEW BUSINESS (INDIVIDUAL)

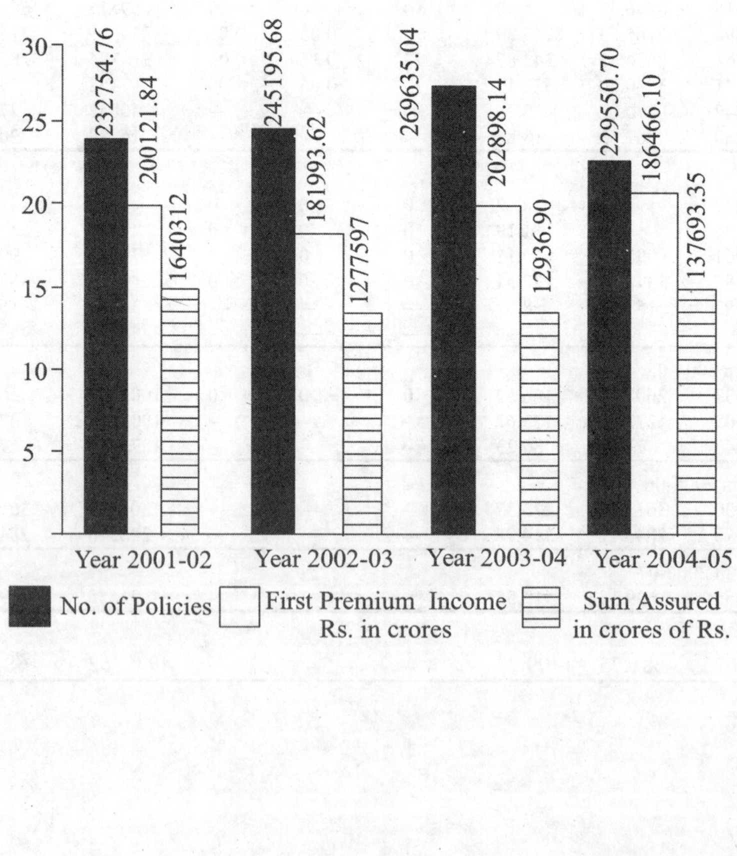

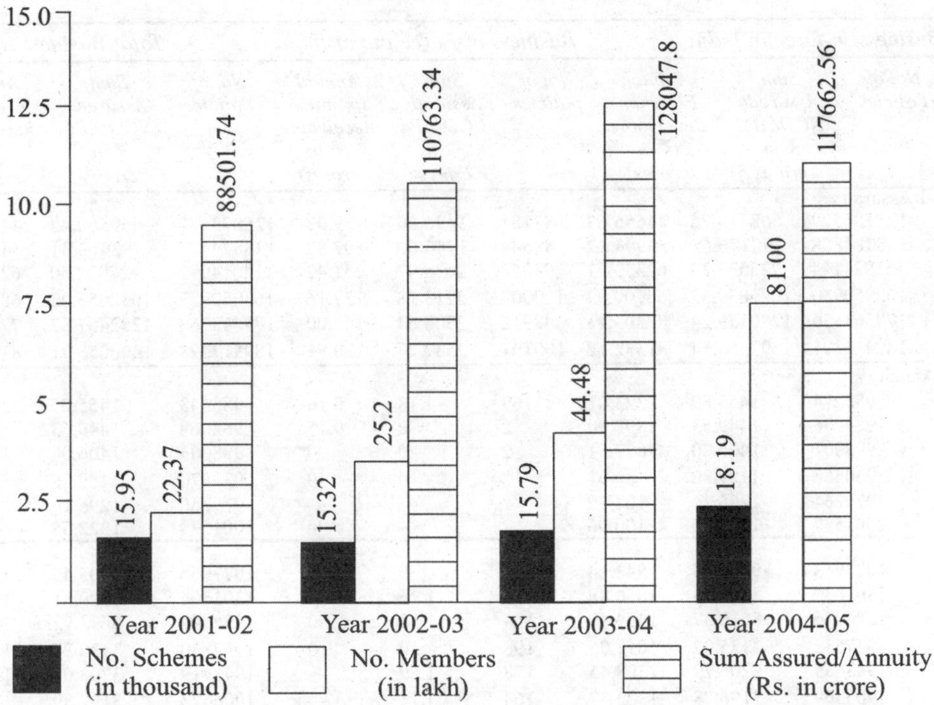

NEW BUSINESS (GROUP INSURANCE)

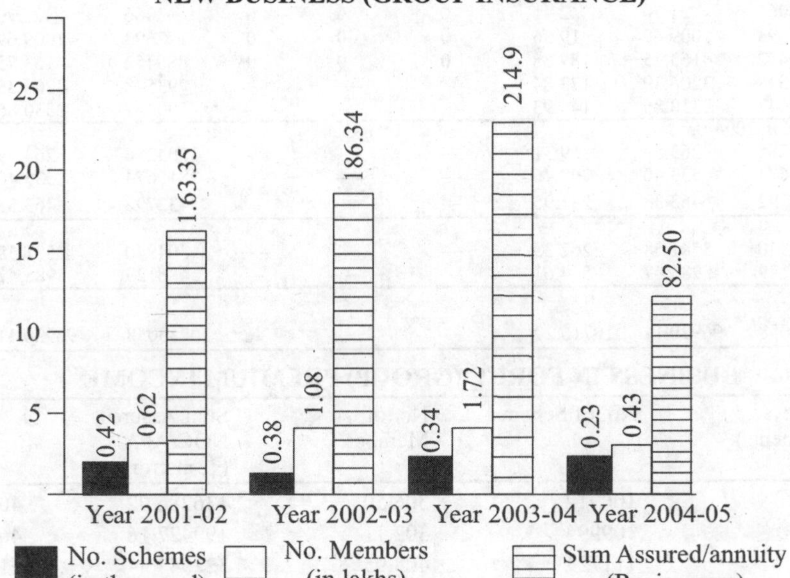

BUSINESS IN FORCE

	Business in-force in India			*Business in-Force out of India*			*Total Business in force*		
Year	*No. of Policies*	*Sum Assured/ NCO/APA ₹ in crores*	*Annual Premium Receivable (₹ in crores)*	*No. of policies*	*Sum Assured/ NCO/APA ₹ in crores*	*Annual Premium Receivable (₹ in crores)*	*No. of Policies*	*Sum Assured/ NCO/APA ₹ in crores*	*Annual Premium Receivable (₹ in crores)*
Individual Assurance									
2001-02	125786529	668113.76	44656.63	87181	1476.66	79.01	125873680	669590.42	44735.64
2002-03	138784878	790176.65	53994.12	89544	1746.66	107.82	138874422	792463.31	54101.94
2003-04	153921144	925033.33	62333.71	93853	2038.97	131.42	154014997	927072.30	62465.13
2004-05	162950920	1029839.55	68700.99	100007	2213.18	137.16	163050927	1032053.03	68838.15
2005-06	179563850	1280159.24	77303.43	98912	2308.64	145.00	179662768	1282467.87	77448.43
2006-07	189417301	1397468.14	81382.12	100197	2587.77	139.81	189517498	1400055.91	81521.93
General Annuity									
2001-02	985274	1453.89	2323.01	169	1.18	0.16	985443	1455.07	2323.17
2002-03	984066	1449.53	1892.90	2	0	0.15	984068	1449.53	1893.05
2003-04	998001	1406.20	1877.51	2	0	0	998003	1406.02	1877.51
2004-05	930568	1189.80	89.01	2	0	0	930570	1189.80	89.01
2005-06	979264	1296.16	107.32	2	—	—	979266	1296.16	107.32
2006-07	1001537	1322.55	100.96	2	—	—	1001539	1322.55	100.96
Pension									
2001-02	1077963	9005.45	842.24	0	0	0	1077963	9005.45	842.24
2002-03	1301630	8898.55	1056.88	174	1.26	0	1301804	8899.81	1056.88
2003-04	1594946	8610.57	1454.48	194	1.35	0	1595140	8611.92	1454.48
2004-05	1937632	3135.07	1617.05	198	1.20	0	1937830	3130.27	1617.05
2005-06	1943639	3206.79	1398.45	178	1.29	—	1943819	3208.08	1398.45
2006-07	1906309	3196.78	1322.37	164	1.11	—	1906473	3197.89	1322.37
Unit Linked									
2001-02	2308	17.47	0.30	0	0	0	2308	17.47	0.30
2002-03	3066	21.70	2.41	0	0	0	3066	21.70	1.41
2003-04	172693	1009.69	19.56	0	0	0	172693	1009.69	19.56
2004-05	880452	4163.75	187.88	0	0	0	880452	4163.75	187.88
2005-06	793548	3206.39	173.84	—	—	—	793548	3206.39	173.84
2006-07	590447	2330.86	148.93	—	—	—	590447	2330.86	148.93
Future Plus started in 2004-05									
2004-05	1004285	263.59	69.31	—	—	—	1004286	263.59	69.31
2005-06	2815674	533.40	209.40	—	—	—	2815674	533.40	209.40
2006-07	3432792	463.33	231.95	—	—	—	3432792	463.33	231.95
Jeewan Plus									
2005-06	304940	3581.58	262.33	—	—	—	304940	3581.58	262.33
2006-07	486129	5985.47	564.61	—	—	—	486129	5985.47	564.61
Money Plus									
2006-07	10755058	96920.11	10716.29	—	—	—	10755058	96920.11	10916.29

BUSINESS IN FORCE (GROUP) PREMIUM INCOME

Group Insurance (inc. social segments)	No. of Schems	No. of Member	Sum Assured NOC/APA (₹, in crore)	
2004-2005	106912	306.50	136286.92	4019.57
2005-2006	109995	302.71	199427.16	4669.76
2006-2007	111729	405.95	322042	11462.91
Group Superanuation				
2004-2005	7321	12.73	1916.64	3723.75
2005-2006	6135	12.52	2189.28	2946.11
2006-2007	6180	12.93	2575.98	4051.36
Linked Business G=Plus				
2006-2007	20	0.14	97.68	1737

As per IRDA, life Insurers are required to publish their new business and business in force under Individual Insurance General Annuity, Pension and Unit Linked. The LIC is experiencing increasing trends in all respects.

MARKET INTELIGENCE

LIC to Introduce Rima Nivesh 2005

LIC's Bima Nivesh 2005, a single-premium product, will offer a return of 5.5% for a 10-year policy and 5.3% for a 5-year cover. Bima Nivesh 2004 offers 5% on a 10-year policy and 4.8% on a 5-year cover. Since 2000, when the original single premium policy, Bima Nivesh, came into being, the assured rate or return on this plan has been slipping from a height of 10.5% for a 10-year cover. This is the first time the return will go up.

Bima Nivesh 2005 is awaiting approval from the insurance Regulatory and Development Authority, IRDA, and is expected to be launched before the close of the financial year. With market interest rates rising, the 50 basis point increase is in line with the growth in returns. LIC is also awaiting approval for its unit-linked pension plan filed earlier this years. Despite the removal of tax exemption on this plan, on account of its being a single-premium product, LIC has seen a growth rate of 474% in sales of this product this years.

Between April 2004 and January 2005, LIC mopped up ₹ 2,071 crore (₹ 20.71 billion) from the sale of single-premium products, a large portion accounted for by Bima Nivesh 2004. LIC sold single-premium plans worth ₹ 360 crore (₹ 3.6 billion) in the corresponding 10-months period last year. With Bima Nivesh 2005, that is expected to be introduced before the end of 2004-2005, LIC hopes to push this growth rate further. Despite the removal of the tax exemption under Section 88 for single-premium plans, policyholders of Bima Nivesh enjoy tax-free returns at end of the policy period under Section 10 (10D). Thus, many individuals who are not in the tax bracket tend to put large sums of this plan.

LIC to Have Separate Investment Units

LIC has decided to carve out the investment activity of group business into a separate division. From April the investment activities of group and pension business will be conducted separately. Until now the corporation had a common investment department for both individual as well as group business.

The group business, which currently accounts for an investment portfolio of around ₹ 30,000 crore (₹ 300 billion) has a different investment outlook compared to long-term life insurance policies.

Last year, the corporation had decided to create separate strategic business units for pension and group business, international operation and real estate. The SBUs have also been given a separate actuary.

LIC to Recruit Lakh Agents

The Life Insurance Corporation of India plans to recruit around one lakh agents mainly from areas that have not contributed much towards premium income.

The corporation, apart from increasing the number of agents also plans to work out ways to increase the productivity of the existing agent work force. It plans to cross ₹ 3.11 crore new policies by March 2005 an increase of about 15%.

Life Insurers Ready to Share Network With MFs

The life insurance industry has indicated a desire to work in collaboration with the mutual funds, offering them its distribution strength. The move comes ill the wake of mutual funds complaining to the Securities and Exchanges Board of India (SEBI) of life insurers encroaching into mutual funds territory with unit-linked plans. Life insurance companies feel that by working together, both the insurers and the asset management companies can increase their share of the savings pie, which they feel is under threat from increased spending of FMCG, White goods and automobiles. They feel that with over 40% of domestic savings in banks, insurance companies (14.5% share) and mutual funds (1.1%) can grow without hurting each other's prospects.

Unlike traditional products where investment details and various charges are kept under wraps, ULIPs project all this information up-front. But at the same time the investor also takes upon himself the investment risk.

PNB Plans Life Insurance Foray

Punjab, National Bank (PNB), the country's second largest public sector banks, is now planning to diversity into life insurance business. PNB has already applied to the Reserve Bank of India (RBI) in this regard. The company will set up the life insurance business in a joint venture with the Principal Finance Group of the US, Vijay Bank and Berger Paints with equity participation of 24%, 12% and 34% respectively. The PNB will have 30% stake. The joint venture will be the country's first agent-less life insurance office. The proposed joint venture, which will start operations in the next six months has a model distinct from the other 14 life insurance ventures in the country and is being planned to be the country's first agent-less life insurance office.

Principal Group has plans only to sell group and corporate life insurance policies and would not venture into retail insurance products. It would prefer to sell through bancassurance tie-ups.

IRDA May Allow NGOs to Sell All Insurance Products

The Insurance Regulatory and Development Authority may allow Non-Governmental Organisation (NGOs) and self-help groups (SHGs) to act as agencies for life and non-life insurance companies under the new micro-insurance scheme. Until now NGOs and SHGs were allowed to sell health insurance products only. However, they are now likely to be allowed to distribute other life and non-life products as well.

Non-governmental organisation and self-help groups are not required to have the mandatory capital base of ₹ 100 crore, as applicable to insurance companies. The scheme will be unveiled soon. It is expected to help in better distribution of products in rural areas. The comprehensive scheme will cater to the poorer section of society. The IRDA has decided to relax its norms in a bid to offer insurance products for a minimum assured sum of ₹ 10,000.

IRDA Irked with Inconsistent Pricing

Unhappy with the present pricing, the IRDA has asked insurance companies to be consistent in pricing critical illness products by sticking to one standard data. With no reliable data available at present to base the rates on life insurance companies are modifying the critical illness rates provided by reinsurer based on the experience abroad.

The insurance regulator has asked the Actuarial Society of India (ASI) to suggest reference tables that can be the basis till a morbidity table in drawn up. Once that happens, insurance companies will have to follow the said data for pricing products.

Life Insurers Want to Keep Tabs on Mortality Trends

Life insurers are coming together to unravel the mystery of mortality. With some serious number crunching on mortality trends and sickness incidence, life insurers aim to get a clear view to design their products and work out premium. At present, all life insurance payers depend on the data on mortality of the Life Insurance Corporation of India. The move, proposed by the Life Insurance Council; is to set up a Mortality and Morbidity Investigation Bureau in collaboration with the Actuarial Society of India. The exercise will be funded by the life insurance industry and technical support will be provided by ASI. It will be a joint venture entity.

The whole exercise would be based on decoding statistical data on death rate in every age group. The mortality rates are improving in the country with access to better healthcare facilities. On the other hand, there is a rise in sickness level and there is no data available correlating age, nature and extent of sickness.

TECHNILOGICAL UPGRADING OF LIC

LIC's Alternate Channel of Premium Payment is just a way of bringing Premium Payment near the doorstep for the policyholders.

Life Insurance Corporation of India, the pioneer Insurance Company has an in-house information Technology and a team, which any industry can be proud of. Several marketing and service tools including different avenues for premium payment have been developed through the IT initiatives which have kept LIC always ahead of its competitors in all aspects. There are more than half a dozen options to pay premium and every year new options are getting added. These technology driven initiatives as alternate Channels of Premium Payment not only provide convenience to the policyholders but also equip LIC with economical and advantageous modes of payment. Cashless transactions are a boon to national economy as well as it keeps away the risk of fake currency and money laundering.

Collections of premium through alternate channels is accounted by an Unit **"Premium Collection Management Cell (PCMC)"** under Central Office, CRM Dept. In addition to PCMC there are 10 more ECS centers across the country for ECS administration. MASH (METRO Area Services Hub) centers at the Zonal headquarters and 3 additional Mash centers at Pune, Ahmedabad and Bangalore are accounting ECS payments.

Alternate channels for premium collection in LIC can be classified as Offline and Online channels. **Offline channels** like ECS, Direct Debit, EBPP are the payment modes where policyholders are required to register either at LIC branch or at their Bank. A database is created by LIC and whenever due, invoice is sent and payment received is accounted as bulk adjustment. Receipts are printed and dispatched by LIC.

Online mode of payment is accounting of transactions through the Online Data Store (ODS) adn updation happens in real time. Here the policyholder gets receipt immediately either online or through the collection centers. Online portal payment, collection by Banks, franchisees and Merchant collection are online channels.

Under offline modes, **ECS or Electronic Clearance System** is the most sought after and important payment mode, Under ECS mode policyholder authorizes LIC to raise ECS debit to his bank for collecting LIC premium, simultaneously he authorizes his bank to debit his bank account. Policyholder has to submit a copy of ECS mandate form attested by his banker to LIC as well as an authorization to his bank for availing ECS facility. Banks may dishonour the ECS debit mandate if they do not receive debit authorization by the account holder.

ECS facility can be opted at proposal stage as also anytime after completion of policy. ECS can be opted for all modes and all plans including Ulip and Health insurance plans. Plans where Mly mode is not allowed and ECS Mly mode also is not specified separately are not eligible for ECS Mly mode.

ECS facility can be availed only at the location where RBI or RBI authorized Clearing House for ECS are available. At present, there are 89 locations where ECS facility can be made available. LIC has enabled ECS at all these locations. In addition to these location ECS is available in few states through RECS.

R-ECS or Regional ECS is progeny of the ECS system which has been introduced at a few Regional offices of Reserve Bank of India. In all locations of State where R-ECS is enabled can opt for ECS facility. At present R-ECS (Debit) has been made operational by LIC at RBI Bangalore for **Karnataka**, RBI Chennai for **Tamil Nadu**, RBI Hyderabad for **Andhra Pradesh**, RBI Jaipur for **Rajasthan**, RBI Chandigarh for **Punjab, Haryana, Himachal Pradesh, and Chandigarh -Union Territory**.

With introduction of ECS mode (ECS MLY with waiver of 5% extra premium) ECS has become a popular mode of premium payment. ECS is now a marketing tool also for canvassing business.Direct Debit is a facility through which non-ECS centers can also provide convenience of premium collection by debiting customer's account through standing instructions.

In LIC Direct Debit facility will be made available shortly through ICICI & SBI Bank

EBPP or Electronic Bill Presentment and Processing or Bill Pay is a mode of payment where policyholder registers for premium payment with authorized Banks or service providers for LIC premium payment. This registration data is sent to LIC by these banks/service providers for Bill Pay master creation. Invoice is sent by LIC to the respective vendor and payment received from them is accounted by PCMC. Under EBPP system Monthly mode and ULIP plans is not accepted. Under EBPP, policyholder can pay premium by giving standing instructions to this bank to debit his account, through Net banking, Mobile banking or any other mode as enabled by his bank for payment. Authorized vendors for EBPP are:

Banks – ICICI Bank, HDFC Bank, CITI Bank, Axis Bank, Corporation Bank and Federal Bank.

Service Providers – Bill Desk and Tech Process and LIC Credit Cards.

Through the service providers all the major banks are covered.

Premium collection through **ATMs** is also similar to EBPP where premium is paid through ATM. Axis Bank, Corporation Bank and ICICI Bank allow their customers to pay LIC premium through ATM.

Online Premium Payment through **LIC's Portal Payment Gateway** is another important payment mode. Premium can be paid through LIC's website using Net banking facility or through VISA or Master Credit and Debit Cards issued in India. For premium payment through cards a small amount as interchange or convenience fee is charged. This is a discounted flat fee which the card issuing bank charges for any card payment. The levied charges are as below:

Card Type	*Convenience or interchange Fee* ₹
Debit Cards	12
Credit Cards upto ₹ 5000	18
Credit Cards above ₹ 5000	35

Service taxes are to be paid extra. Premium can be paid online by the portal registered users as well as un-registered customers. For online payment digitally signed receipt is instantly generated and same is sent to the policyholder on his mail-id also.

Premium can be paid at any Branch cash counters of the *authorized Banks* i.e. Axis Bank and Corporation Bank in cash or cheque drawn on these Banks.

APOnline in Andhra Pradesh, **MPOnline** in Madhya Pradesh, M/S **Suvidhaa Invorserve** and **Easy Bill Ltd.** pan India are authorized to collect LIC premium. Customers can walk into any of the collection centers of these franchisees and pay premium in cash. Premium for ULIP and Health Insurance plans cannot be paid at Bank and the service providers counters.

Premium collection by **Authorized Agents, SBAs, ASBAs** and retired LIC employees which is referred as **Merchant Collection** is the major alternate channel. They are authorized to collect premium in cash as well as cheque. For Merchant Collection, funds collected by them in cash or cheque can be remitted in any LIC Branch Office. Cash collections can be remitted in any Axis Bank Branch or Online through LIC

Portal using Net Banking facility.

Different customers can have different choices of payment. LIC's Alternate channels of premium payments has an option for each type of payment preference.

At present one third of the total renewal premium collection of LIC is through Alternate Channels. This year the target is to take ratio of premium collection at Cash Counter to Alternate Channels should be 50:50; which will be a step towards preparation of 20:20.

To achieve this target involvement by one and all at all levels is required. Various offices are trying to give wide-spread publicity to the alternate channels for premium payment in their own creative ways.

Analysis of Market Share of Life Insurance

Sl. No.	Interval	Percentage share in Total Premium (%) 2001–02	2004–05	2005–06	2006–07	2007–08	2008–09	Rank in 2004–05	Rank in 2008–09	Share in Policies (%) 2001–02	2004–05	2005–06	2006–07	2007–08	2008–09	Rank in 2004–05	Rank in 2008–09
1.	ICIC-Prudential	2.96	6.51	7.20	6.97	8.93	7.82	II	II	0.96	2.63	2.78	4.24	5.73	5.60	II	II
2.	SBI-Life	0.59	2.35	1.85	3.31	4.38	6.18	V	III	0.07	0.48	0.75	0.98	1.82	1.84	VII	VIII
3.	Bajaj-Alliance	0.44	2.70	7.29	5.66	698	5.16	IV	V	0.46	1.11	2.17	4.51	7.36	5.08	III	III
4.	Riliance-Life			5.90	1.22	2.96	4.03	–	V	–	–	0.23	0.53	2.11	4.36	–	IV
5.	Birla-Sunlife	1.21	2.85	1.80	1.17	2.10	3.24	III	VI	0.26	0.84	0.84	0.92	1.35	2.72	VI	V
6.	HDFC-Standard	1.08	1.91	2.97	2.15	2.88	3.03	VI	VII	0.49	0.91	1.23	1.13	3.98	2.11	V	VII
7.	Max Newyork	0.62	0.26	1.38	1.22	1.71	2.12	XI	VIII	0.29	0.19	1.57	1.20	1.72	2.37	XI	VI
8.	Kotak Mahindra	0.25	0.79	0.76	0.82	1.91	1.54	IX	IX	0.13	0.26	0.30	0.36	0.62	0.97	X	X
9.	Tata-AIG	0.48	1.51	1.60	0.85	1.04	1.32	VII	X	0.36	1.11	1.12	0.89	0.97	1.37	IV	VIV
10.	Met-Life	0.05	–	0.43	0.46	0.89	1.31	–	XI	0.04	–	0.35	1.46	0.46	0.64	–	XIII
11	Aviva	0.10	0.87	1.112	0.96	1.14	0.83	VIII	XII	0.07	0.38	0.52	0.64	0.77	0.72		XI
12.	ING-Vyasya	0.14	0.55	0.75	0.62	0.76	0.79	X	XIII	0.11	0.48	0.40	0.50	0.71	0.70	VIII	XII
13.	Shriram Life	–	–	–	0.24	0.33	0.35		XIV				0.21	0.21	0.25		XVI
14.	IDBI Fortis Life	–	–	–	0.20	0.01	0.34		XV					.006	0.16		XVIII
15.	Canara HSBC	–	–	–	–	–	0.34		XVII					.000	0.04		XIX
16.	Bharti Axa Life	–	–	–	0.01	0.12	0.33		XVIII				0.01	0.15	0.38		XV
17.	Star-Union–Dai-ichi	–	–	–	–	0.19							00	0.20	0.20	XVII	XVII
18.	Future Gaurd Life	–	–	–	–	0.001	0.17		XIX					00	0.02		XXI
19.	Sahara life	–	–	–	0.06	0.13	0.15		XX			0.08	1.46	0.46	0.64		XIV
20.	Argon-Riligare	–	–	–	–	–	0.003		XXI					00	0.03		XX
21.	DCF	–	–	–	–	–	0.003		XXII					00	00		XXII
22.	LIC	92.03	78.10	72.30	60.65	63.64	59.76	I	I	96.70	90.41	87.67	82.83	64.10	70.52	I	I
	Total (Rs Crors)					9298871	8710762							5,08,74,157	5,09,23,377		

Eligibility of UCB's lowered to ₹ 50 crore

Urban co-operative banks toying with the idea of taking a plunge into insurance as a corporate agent can now be a happier lot. For, the Reserve Bank of India (RBI) has brought down the minimum eligibility to ₹ 50 crore from ₹ 1000 crore. Urban cooperative banks UCBs will now be able to undertake risk business on a referral basis without RBI approval.

The apex bank had earlier laid down stringent rules to ensure that only those UCBs that are financially strong participated in the insurance business. But, with the relaxation allowed. It has said that no restrictive practice should be adopted by UCBs and that customers should be allowed to exercise their own choice. Also it has said that the UCB's agreement with an insurance company should be for a period not exceeding three years.

Insurance Costs to Increase Post April 1, 2007

Insurance policies will become dearer from April 1. This means that a policyholder will have to sell out 1.2-1.2% addition premium in the coming financial years, depending on the type of product chosen, and the composition of savings and risk elements within the cover. The less the savings element, the higher the additional premium a policyholder will have to bear as the service tax is being loaded on the risk portion of the cover. Following the government's decision to load a 10% service tax on the risk portion of insurance premium plus the 2% education cess, policyholders will have to bear the tax, which has till now been absorbed by the insurance companies.

In a meeting of the life insurance council, which has representation of all the 14 life payers, it was decided that insurance companies would pass on the tax liability to policyholders with respect to unit-linked plans, pure term insurance covers and group plans. In case of a pure term insurance plan, the tax will be levied at the rate of 10.2% . On traditional plans, it was decided that individual companies would decide whether they would bear the burden and absorb the costs, or pass it on to the policyholders

There is a divergence among private players when it comes to passing on the tax to customers in the case of traditional policies. LIC is bearing the entire cost of the service tax. As it is not possible to segregate the risk and savings portion on existing policies, the corporation will absorb the tax liability. It has yet to take a final view on the road ahead when the percentage of service tax rises.

S. No	*Life Insurance Company*	*Market Share in% Premium Share*				*No. of Policies Sold in%*			
		2001-02	2004-05	2005-06	2006-07	2001-02	2004-05	2005-06	2006-07
1	LIC	92.03	78.10	72.30	60.65	96.70	90.41	87.67	82.83
2	ICICI Prudential	2.96	6.51	7.20	6.97	0.96	2.63	2.78	4.24
3	Birla Sunlife	1.21	2.85	1.80	1.17	0.26	0.84	0.84	0.92
4	HDFC Standard	1.08	1.91	2.97	2.15	0.49	0.91	1.23	1.13
5	MAX New York	0.62	0.26	1.38	1.22	0.29	0.19	1.57	1.20
6	SBI Life	0.59	2.35	1.85	3.31	0.07	0.48	0.75	0.98
7	TATA-AIG	0.48	1.51	1.60	0.85	0.36	1.11	1.12	0.89
8	Bajaj Allianz	0.44	2.70	7.29	5.66	0.46	1.11	2.17	4.51
9	Om Kotak	0.25	0.79	0.76	0.82	0.13	0.26	0.30	0.36
10	Ing Vysya	0.14	0.55	0.75	0.62	0.11	0.48	0.40	0.50
11	Aviva	0.10	0.87	1.12	0.96	0.07	0.38	0.52	0.64
12	Met Life	0.05	—	0.43	0.46	0.04		0.35	1.46
13	Amp Sanmar	0.04	—	—	—	0.06		—	—
14	Reliance Life	—	—	05.9	1.22			0.23	0.53
15	Sahara Life	—	—	0.06	0.06			0.08	1.46
16	Bharti Axa Life	—	—	—	0.01				0.01
17	Shriram Life	—	—	—	0.24				0.21

Life Insurance Corporation of India Report on relief measures by LIC or India to Tsunami affected (As on 17th February, 2005) No. of Claims Settled)

INDIVIDUAL

Division	*No.*	*Amount*	*Division*	*No.*	*Amount*
Tamil Nadu (South Zone)					
Vellore	35	3129160	Vellore	16	800000
Tirunelveli	39	3337779	Tirunelveli	18	900000
Thanjavur	159	10374061			
Chennai I	12	1148084	Chennai-I	1	105034
Madurai	28	3717670	Madurai	2	139995
Chennai II	17	3272496			
Coimbatore	2	342233			
Salem	2	278577			
Kerala (South Zone)					
Trivandrum	5	338000			
Kottayam	5	269986			
Emakulam	8	1148707			
Andhra Pradesh (SC Zone)					
Machilipatnam	3	869350			
Nellore	3	699230			
Visakhapatham	2	187900			
Andaman (Eastern Zone)					
Andaman	6	1045298			
Total	326	30158531	**Total**	37	1945029

NO. OF CLAIMS REPORTED

Individual	341	(Settled: 326, Pending: 15)
Group	44	(Settled: 37, Pending: 7)

Insurance Indications Premium Volume USD (Millions)

	Total			*Life*			*Non-Life*			*Population (millions)*		*GDP (USD billion)*	
	2004	*2005*	*2006*	*2004*	*2005*	*2006*	*2004*	*2005*	*2006*	*2005*	*2006*	*2005*	*2006*
1. South Korea	68623	85097	101179	48680	60683	72298	19944	24414	28881	48.1	48.8	685	911
2. China	52171	60144	70805	35407	39604	45092	16765	20540	25713	1299.0	1323.6	1599	2613
3. Taiwan	43236	48984	51562	33851	38788	41245	9385	10169	10318	22.7	22.9	309	355
4. South Africa	30682	34773	40731	24381	27596	33106	6301	7177	7624	43.9	47.6	213	255
5. India	21249	27410	43032	16919	22587	37220	4330	4823	5812	1077.0	1119.5	595	901
6. Brazil	18042	23947	30930	8199	10553	13699	9843	13394	16691	178.5	188.9	600	1067
7. Russia	16352	17336	21904	3544	894	571	12809	16442	20932	142.9	142.5	566	929

Source: Sigma R 5/2005 and 4/2007

Global Market Share of Insurances

Ranks		*Home Market*	*Premium in USD in 2004*	*Global Market Share 2004/1998*	
1.	AIG	USA	66837	3.6%	1.8%
2.	Metropolitan Life	USA	58732	3.2%	2.4%
3.	AXA	France	58422	3.2%	3.3%
4.	Allianz	Germany	56178	3.0%	1.8%
5.	ING	Netherlands	45978	2.5%	1.5%
9.	Aviva	U.K.	37612	2.0%	0.9%
13.	Prudential (US)	U.S.A.	27751	1.5%	1.3%
23.	Standard Life	U.K.	18719	1.0%	0.6%
28.	Sun Life	Canada	15406	0.8%	0.6%
30.	LIC	India	13746	0.7%	0.4%

Source: signs 1 /2006

Progress of Life Insurance

Sl. No.	Insurer	Premium u/w (Rs. in Crores)		No. of Policies/Schemes		No. of lives covered under group Schemes	
		Upto March, 10	Upto March, 09	Upto March, 10	Upto March, 09	Upto March, 10	Upto March, 09
1	**Bajaj Allianz**						
	Individual Single Premium	802.87	470.91	117949	107390		
	Individual Non-Single Premium	3082.43	3729.72	2111540	2482553		
	Group Single Premium	76.39	8.60	16	9	82230	264579
	Group Non-Single Premium	489.40	282.41	1181	813	18210216	7201816
2.	**ING Vysya**						
	Individual Single Premium	6.92	22.48	996	2772		
	Individual Non-Single Premium	626.52	634.84	289759	355436		
	Group Single Premium	8.86	13.34	0	1	2181	5625
	Group Non-Single Premium	0.24	17.51	0	100	4942	105633
3.	**Reliance Life**						
	Individual Single Premium	264.83	405.83	47864	91043		
	Individual Non-Single Premium	3123.43	2936.18	2277767	2128230		
	Group Single Premium	24.80	136.88	213	22	701119	49019
	Group Non-Single Premium	507.46	35.17	310	383	245348	812353
4.	**SBI Life**						
	Individual Single Premium	560.99	519.26	79206	92965		
	Individual Non-Single Premium	3934.18	2839.69	1274025	844528		
	Group Single Premium	197.94	302.49	6	14	85479	246653
	Group Non-Single Premium	2347.55	1725.02	186	155	1527769	7459886
5.	**Tata AIG**						
	Individual Single Premium	21.05	40.24	3969	8662		
	Individual Non-Single Premium	1113.82	953.71	685227	689156		
	Group Single Premium	27.34	32.21	11	7	45066	82944
	Group Non-Single Premium	159.32	116.29	74	83	119877	308531
6.	**HDFC Standard**						
	Individual Single Premium	267.50	159.47	281332	154311		
	Individual Non-Single Premium	2488.51	2293.87	668928	919704		
	Group Single Premium	7.30	151.53	200	174	187251	385946
	Group Non-Single Premium	497.84	39.16	62	16	206311	16719

7.	**ICICI Prudential**						
	Individual Single Premium	121.41	244.79	10213	36236		
	Individual Non-Single Premium	5092.14	5121.31	1751014	2601439		
	Group Single PRemium	161.50	221.86	302	214	1407255	697290
	Group-Single Premium	959.25	1224.56	341	349	657389	650773
8.	**Birla Sunlife**						
	Individual Single Premium	42.39	42.36	135203	160689		
	Individual Non-Single PRemium	2244.32	2438.40	1635518	1222780		
	Group Single Premium	0.34	16.38	3	2	924	41768
	Group Non-Single Premium	671.39	326.77	285	206	583595	261322
9.	**Aviva**						
	Individual Single PRemium	55.33	46.24	6270	6672		
	Individual Non-Single PRemium	686.45	651.28	233273	360688		
	Group Single Premium	0.05	0.05	3	0	51	66
	Group Non-Single PRemium	56.83	26.09	118	80	2018985	1079352
10.	**Kotak Mahindra Old Mutual**						
	Individual Single PRemium	187.81	18.81	10107	2410		
	Individual Non-Single Premium	924.83	1175.93	310066	492466		
	Group Single Premium	62.41	36.82	18	12	197358	135532
	Group Non-Single Premium	158.93	111.47	544	428	803834	587331
11.	**Max New York**						
	Individual Single Premium	193.94	241.48	6265	16103		
	Individual Non-Single PRemium	1564.53	1571.31	945575	1190613		
	Group Single Premium	7.67	7.71	30	11	1027066	206762
	Group Non-Single PRemium	81.93	23.21	607	335	7730169	259110
12.	**Met Life**						
	Individual Single Premium	31.36	8.02	4451	2238		
	Individual Non-Single Premium	911.24	1067.64	287286	325896		
	Group Single Premium	......	....	....	....	....	
	Individual Single Premium	42.29	59.05	59.05	....	....	....
	Individual Non-Single Premium	64.89	78.95	72036	95930		
	Group Non-Single Premium	19.83	3.80	6	16	2212630	325067

14.	**Shriram Life**						
	Individual Single Premium	113.79	135.29	17174	21929		
	Individual Non-Single Premium	269.19	177.23	122462	104697		
	Group Single Premium	36.97	0.00	4	0	147686	0
	Group Non-Single Premium	0.47	0.64	11	4	61663	44783
15.	**Bharti Axa Life**						
	Individual Single Premium	6.21	5.57	15576	18071		
	Individual Non-Single Premium	405.33	275.34	163174	193504		
	Group Single Premium	26.13	11.67	8	4	31016	44550
	Group Non-Single Premium	0.00	0.00	0	0	0	0
16.	**Future General Life**						
	Individual Single Premium	9.03	5.24	1297	1079		
	Individual Non-Single Premium	445.02	132.71	334396	102851		
	Group Single Premium	0.11	0.13	1	1	1917	671
	Group Non-Single Premium	31.66	14.36	111	82	2916319	265867
17.	**IDBI Fortis Life**						
	Individual Single Premium	115.02	132.57	15841	21008		
	Individual Non-Single Premium	285.42	184.19	80923	62993		
	Group Single Premium	0.00	0.00	0	0	0	0
	Group Non-Single Premium	0.11	0.03	5	2	41442	22602
18.	**Canara HSBC OBC Life**						
	Individual Single Premium	11.98	7.59	581	499		
	Individual Non-Single Premium	621.70	291.12	99275	35230		
	Group Single PRemium	6.52	0.00	4	0	3863	0
	Group Non-Single Premium	0.07	0.02	1	1	8073	2500
19.	**Aegon Religare**						
	Individual Single Premium	3.90	2.30	4913	1193		
	Individual Non-Single Premium	146.42	28.91	44947	22392		
	Group Single Premium	0.05	0.00	3	2	7632	2745
	Group Non-Single Premium	0.00	0.00	0	0	0	0

20.	**DLF Pramerica**						
	Individual Single Premium	1.38	0.00	192	0		
	Individual Non-Single Premium	35.97	3.38	19292	2795		
	Group Single Premium	0.00	0.00	0	0	0	0
	Group Non-Single Premium	0.01	0.01	1	1	7500	2602
21.	**Star Union Dal-ichi@**						
	Individual Single Premium	239.07	14.70	23227	2206		
	Individual Non-Single Premium	250.98	32.26	84995	11039		
	Group Single Premium	25.79	4.25	7	2	22754	4101
	Group Non-Single Premium	3.65	0.55	33	2	48300	5587
22.	**IndiaFirst #**						
	Individual Single Premium	38.85		3456		0	
	Individual Non-Single Premium	162.74		67300		0	
	Group Single Premium	0.00		0		0	
	Group Non-Single Premium	0.00		0		0	
	Private Total						
	Individual Single Premium	3137.92	2574.76	798099	762093		
	Individual Non-Single Premium	28480.09	26617.98	13558778	14244920		
	Group Single Premium	712.96	1013.90	829	641	3969006	2479839
	Group Non-Single Premium	6068.36	3947.07	4067	3056	37990790	19411920
23	**LIC**						
	Individual Single Premium	26539.59	22159.02	5951076	5188193		
	Individual Non-Single Premium	23575.90	18070.18	32887823	30703139		
	Group Single Premium	20775.56	12724.72	23763	21335	38733489	31770561
	Group Non-Single Premium	0.00	0.00	0	0	0	0
	Grand Total						
	Individual Single Premium	29677.51	24733.78	6749175	5950286		
	Individual Non-Single Premium	52055.90	44688.16	46446601	44948059		
	Group Single Premium	21488.51	13738.61	24592	21976	42702495	34250400
	Group Non-Single Premium	6068.36	3947.07	4067	3056	37990790	19411920

Source = IRDA-Journal May 2010

Report Card:Life

First Year Premium of Life Insurers for the Period ended March, 2011

Sl. no.	Insurer	Premium U/W (₹ in crores)			No of Policies/Schemes			No. of lives covered under Group Schemes		
		March, 11	Upto March	Upto March, 10	March, 11	Upto March, 11	Upto March, 10	March, 11	Upto March, 11	Upto March, 10
1.	**Bajaj Allianz**									
	Individual Single Premium	117.67	779.83	802.87	14621	102659	117949			
	Individual Non-Single Premium	241.72	1808.68	3082.43	184769	1439346	2111540			
	Group Single Premium	111.27	373.76	76.39	14	84	16	30019	172074	82230
	Group Non-Single Premium	100.87	500.14	489.40	119	1414	1181	1322185	19935010	18210216
2.	**ING Vysya**									
	Individual Single Premium	4.76	19.26	6.92	566	2745	996			
	Individual Non-Single Premium	118.94	633.25	626.52	43770	271656	289759			
	Group Single Premium	0.35	7.10	8.86	0	0	0	64	1371	2181
	Group Non-Single Premium	0.00	0.25	0.24	0	0	0	0	138	4942
3.	**Reliance Life**									
	Individual Single Premium	233.23	719.73	264.83	26380	91377	47864			
	Individual Non-Single Premium	180.08	1938.88	3123.43	177236	1811308	2277767			
	Group Single Premium	1.39	30.59	24.80	15	202	213	30801	610337	701119
	Group Non-Single Premium	247.14	345.75	507.46	59	180	310	70718	227521	245348
4.	**SBI Life**									
	Individual Single Premium	520.08	1936.28	560.99	44092	171390	79206			
	Individual Non-Single Premium	405.70	2851.42	3934.18	115272	768588	1274025			
	Group Single Premium	690.88	2261.92	197.94	53	158	6	114034	445277	85479
	Group Non-Single Premium	108.75	521.10	2347.55	34	86	186	336796	1060051	1527769
5.	**Tata AIG**									
	Individual Single Premium	22.60	182.03	21.05	1803	20829	3969			
	Individual Non-Single Premium	137.09	933.63	1113.82	54142	532374	685227			
	Group Single Premium	7.20	42.48	27.34	0	11	11	18295	110375	45066
	Group Non-Single Premium	71.66	172.57	159.32	16	75	74	219261	571673	119877
6.	**HDFC Standard**									
	Individual Single Premium	167.64	588.85	267.50	655	202908	281332			
	Individual Non-Single Premium	416.44	2905.68	2488.51	90694	627624	668928			
	Group Single Premium	123.41	131.42	7.30	40	226	200	158559	421448	187251
	Group Non-Single Premium	110.27	439.45	497.84	19	64	62	45605	297905	206311

7.	**ICICI Prudential**									
	Individual Single Premium	394.08	1929.44	121.41	25346	123599	10213			
	Individual Non-Single Premium	268.86	3492.00	5092.14	110344	1226895	1751014			
	Group Single Premium	25.97	240.22	161.50	17	154	302	432341	2519428	1407255
	Group Non-Single Premium	1461.53	2199.33	959.25	41	76	341	113601	617019	657389
8.	**Birla Sunlife**									
	Individual Single Premium	16.73	45.39	42.39	511	28167	135203			
	Individual Non-Single Premium	242.30	1595.46	2244.32	83662	975926	1635518			
	Group Single Premium	0.49	5.65	0.34	1	3	3	115	1255	924
	Group Non-Single Premium	136.44	430.63	671.39	49	243	285	110257	744397	583595
9.	**Aviva**									
	Individual Single Premium	19.59	88.74	55.33	469	4565	6270			
	Individual Non-Single Premium	111.55	577.23	686.45	28728	186438	233273			
	Group Single Premium	0.18	0.76	0.05	0	3	3	885	4364	51
	Group Non-Single Premium	35.40	78.33	56.83	24	149	118	– 27335	1419364	2018985
10.	**Kotak Mahindra Old Mutual**									
	Individual Single Premium	166.58	280.37	187.81	13250	23148	10107			
	Individual Non-Single Premium	69.33	684.96	924.83	23661	235635	310066			
	Group Single Premium	17.53	115.80	62.41	1	6	18	64238	487655	197358
	Group Non-Single Premium	42.49	172.02	158.93	63	655	544	150844	1470913	803834
11.	**Max New York**									
	Individual Single Premium	38.11	233.34	193.94	3	1275	6265			
	Individual Non-Single Premium	214.87	1700.75	1564.53	87948	814984	945575			
	Group Single Premium	13.25	53.06	7.67	3	32	30	– 166319	1317775	1027066
	Group Non-Single Premium	3.95	72.48	81.93	37	680	607	–903377	7271051	7730169
12.	**Met Life**									
	Individual Single Premium	10.79	141.08	31.36	1154	19100	4451			
	Individual Non-Single Premium	86.66	492.70	911.24	35829	180111	287286			
	Group Single Premium	1.17	11.48	42.78	3	9	0	3582	12772	18158
	Group Non-Single Premium	22.96	58.69	82.42	43	298	191	35935	2519370	586428
13.	**Sahara Life**									
	Individual Single Premium	9.68	43.52	42.29	2168	9799	12017			
	Individual Non-Single Premium	8.50	47.50	64.89	13176	59733	72036			
	Group Single Premium	0.00	0.00	0.00	0	0	0	0	0	0
	Group Non-Single Premium	0.01	0.02	19.83	5	8	6	396	1108	2212630

14. Shriram Life									
Individual Single Premium	47.83	325.26	113.79	5319	37308	17174			
Individual Non-Single Premium	16.84	157.68	269.19	12667	84022	122462			
Group Single Premium	12.15	88.27	36.97	0	1	4	44742	352022	147686
Group Non-Single Premium	0.29	3.97	0.47	4	11	11	28143	417477	61663
15. Bharti Axa Life									
Individual Single Premium	13.05	17.81	6.21	25483	28478	15576			
Individual Non-Single Premium	33.87	320.81	405.33	20406	153730	163174			
Group Single Premium	6.51	23.78	26.13	0	6	8	8423	17668	31016
Group Non-Single Premium	0.00	0.00	0.00	0	0	0	0	0	0
16. Future Generali Life									
Individual Single Premium	40.03	81.65	9.03	5243	10834	1297			
Individual Non-Single Premium	42.53	329.17	445.02	33938	303120	334396			
Group Single Premium	0.00	0.10	0.11	0	1	1	0	2241	1917
Group Non-Single Premium	10.94	37.92	31.66	16	109	111	10558	2162534	2916319
17. IDBI Federal									
Individual Single Premium	35.56	181.37	115.02	2644	18704	15841			
Individual Non-Single Premium	39.46	251.86	285.42	14153	89686	80923			
Group Single Premium	0.00	0.0	0.00	0	0	0	0	0	0
Group Non-Single Premium	3.49	11.72	.11	0	11	5	89312	696305	41442
18. Canara HSBC OBC Life									
Individual Single Premium	0.00	5.31	11.98	0	254	581			
Individual Non-Single Premium	88.89	692.60	621.70	15990	111044	99275			
Group Single Premium	1.31	15.27	6.52	0	3	4	451	8366	3863
Group Non-Single Premium	53.51	109.57	0.07	2	6	1	44758	95785	8073
19. Aegon Religare									
Individual Single Premium	11.73	23.11	3.90	8445	9855	4913			
Individual Non-Single Premium	49.20	236.67	146.42	15847	83328	44947			
Group Single Premium	0.08	0.61	0.05	1	1	3	10152	11484	7632
Group Non-Single Premium	14.47	14.47	0.00	10	10	0	11195	11195	0
20. DLF Pramerica									
Individual Single Premium	2.83	5.00	1.38	318	604	192			
Individual Non-Single Premium	9.22	69.02	35.97	6588	36287	19292			
Group Single Premium	0.00	0.00	0.00	0	0	0	0	0	0
Group Non-Single Premium	0.00	0.00	0.01	0	0	1	0	0	7500

21.	**Star Union Dal-Ichl**									
	Individual Single Premium	104.41	364.31	239.07	6472	23682	23227			
	Individual Non-Single Premium	45.40	225.72	250.98	14125	74048	84995			
	Group Single Premium	7.00	50.45	25.79	1	5	7	4349	41.36	22754
	Group Non-Single Premium	100.27	118.07	3.65	16	67	33	121736	312958	48300
22.	**India First #**									
	Individual Single Premium	93.00	261.68	38.85	6266	18968	3456			
	Individual Non-Single Premium	24.33	251.93	162.74	9078	92882	67300			
	Group Single Premium	4.23	14.87	0.00	1	8	0	3017	120036	0
	Group Non-Single Premium	154.30	176.28	0.00	14	30	0	561781	1284878	0
	Private Total									
	Individual Single Premium	2070.00	8253.37	3137.92	191208.00	950248.00	798099			
	Individual Non-Single Premium	2851.78	22197.59	28480.09	1192023	10158765	13558778			
	Group Single Premium	1024.36	3467.58	712.96	150	913	829	757748	6548984	3969006
	Group Non-Single Premium	2678.74	5462.76	6068.36	571	4172	4067	2665769	41116652	37990790
23.	**LIC**									
	Individual Single Premium	3117.74	27620.15	26539.59	572097	4643865	5951076			
	Individual Non-Single Premium	5317.79	24583.49	23575.90	7007531	32368412	32887823			
	Group Single Premium	4398.40	22889.13	20775.56	4205	19292	23763	3027579	21567555	38733489
	Group Non-Single Premium	489.20	11351.95	0.00	1230	6217	0	1030450	14092644	0
	Grand Total									
	Individual Single Premium	5187.74	35873.52	29677.51	763305	5594113	6749175			
	Individual Non-Single Premium	8169.56	46781.08	52055.99	8199554	42527177	46446601			
	Group Single Premium	5422.76	26356.71	21488.51	4355	20205	24592	3785327	28116539	42702495
	Group Non-Single Premium	3167.94	16814.72	6068.36	1801	10389	4067	3696219	55209296	37990790

Note: 1. Cumulative premium/No. of policies upto the month is net of cencellations which may occur during the free look period.
2. Compiled on the basis of data submitted by the insurance companies.

Comparative Study of Performances of LIC and Other Life Insurances (First Year Premium) (2000–01 to 2009-10)

(₹ Crore)

Insurer	2009-10	2008-09	2007-08	2006-07	2005-06	2004-05	2003-04	2002-03	2001-02	2000-01
I. LIC	71521.90	53179.08	59996.57	56223.56	28515.87	20653.06	17347.62	15976.76	19588.77	9700.98
	(34.49)	(-11.36)	(6.71)	(97.17)	(38.07)	(19.05)	(8.58)	(-18.44)	(101.93)	-
II Private Insurers										
Aegon Religare	150.37	31.21	-	-	-	-	-	-	-	-
Aviva	798.37	724.56	1053.98	721.35	407.12	192.29	46.96	13.47	-	-
Bajaj Allianz	4451.10	4491.43	6674.48	4302.74	1716.77	857.45	179.55	63.39	7.14	-
Bharti AXA	437.43	292.93	113.24	7.78	-	-	-	-	-	-
Birla Sun Life	2960.01	2820.85	1965.01	882.72	678.12	621.31	449.86	129.57	28.11	0.32
Canara HSBC	622.62	296.41	-	-	-	-	-	-	-	-
DLF Pramerica	37.38	3.37	-	-	-	-	-	-	-	-
Future Generali	486.08	149.97	2.49	-	-	-	-	-	-	-
HDFC Standard	3257.51	2651.11	2685.37	1648.85	1042.65	486.15	209.33	129.31	32.78	0.002
ICICI Prudential	6334.03	6811.83	8034.75	5162.13	2602.50	1584.34	750.84	364.11	113.33	5.97
IDBI Federal	400.56	316.78	11.90	-	-	-	-	-	-	-
India First	201.59	-	-	-	-	-	-	-	-	-
ING Vysya	642.43	688.95	704.44	467.66	283.98	282.98	71.10	17.66	4.19	-
Kotak Mahindra	1333.98	1343.03	1106.62	614.94	396.06	373.99	125.51	35.21	7.58	-
Max New York	1849.08	1842.91	1597.83	912.11	471.36	233.63	137.28	67.31	38.80	0.16
Met Life	1061.85	1144.70	825.35	340.44	148.53	57.52	23.41	7.70	0.48	-
Reliance	3920.78	3513.98	2751.05	329.11	193.56	91.33	27.21	6.32	0.28	-
Sahara	124.83	134.01	122.12	43.00	26.34	1.74	-	-	-	-
SBI Life	7040.74	5386.64	4792.82	2563.84	827.82	484.85	207.05	71.88	14.69	-
Shriram	419.50	314.47	309.99	181.17	10.33	-	-	-	-	-
Star Union Dai-ichi	519.87	50.19	-	-	-	-	-	-	-	-
TATA AIG	1322.01	1142.67	964.51	644.82	464.53	297.55	181.59	59.77	21.14	-
III Private Total	38372.12	34152.00	33715.95	19425.65	10269.67	5564.57	2440.71	965.69	268.51	6.45
	(12.36)	(1.29)	(73.56)	(88.84)	(84.55)	(127.99)	(152.74)	(259.65)	(4061.70)	
IV Industry Total	109894.02	87331.08	93712.52	75649.21	38785.54	26217.64	19788.32	16942.45	19857.28	9707.43
	(25.84)	(-6.81)	(23.88)	(94.96)	(47.94)	(32.49)	(16.80)	(-14.68)	(104.56)	

Note : Figure in bracket indicates the growth over the previous year in per cent. "–" indicates the company has not started its operation.

(₹ Crore)

Insurer	2010-11	2009-10	% Variation
ICICI Pru	7860.98	6334.31	+24.10%
SBI Life	7570.72	7040.66	+7.52%
HDFC Life	4065.41	3261.14	+24.66
Bajaj Allianz	3462.41	4451.09	-22.21
Reliance Life	3034.96	3920.52	-22.58
Birla Sun Life	2077.13	2958.45	-29.78
Max New York	2059.62	1848.07	+11.44
Tata AIG	1330.70	1321.54	+0.69
Kotak Mahindra	1253.14	1333.98	-6.06
Canara HSBC	822.76	640.27	+28.50
Star Union Daichi	758.56	519.49	+46.02
Aviva	745.05	798.66	-6.71
India First	704.77	201.59	+249.60
MetLife	703.95	1067.81	-34.07
ING Vysya	659.85	642.55	+2.69
Shriram life	575.18	420.42	+36.81
Future Generali	448.85	485.82	-7.60
IDBI Federal	444.95	400.56	+11.08
Bharti Axa Life	362.39	437.67	-17.20
Aegon Reigaire	274.87	150.37	+82.79
Sahara Life	91.05	127.01	-28.31
DLF Pramerica	74.01	37.36	+98.09
Total (Private) Insurers	39381.33	38399.32	+2.55
LIC	86444.72	70891.05	21.94%
Total for Industry	125826.03	109290.37	15.13

Look at it from a different perspective. After a decade of supposedly intense competition from twenty two odd private insurance companies, LIC is still able to hold on to 68.70% of the market share (2010-11) and leaving just 31.30% to the private players. (The market share in number of policies is even higher at 76.91%). While this undoubtedly speaks well of the manner in which LIC has stood up to competition there is a perception that the private insurance companies could and should have performed better. After having been in business for a period of ten years a total of 22 companies have managed to garner barely 31.3% of the market share. Let us have a look at the performance of the private insurance companies, especially those eleven which were amongst the first to set up shop in 2001-2002! It is revealing that nine (9) out of these eleven (11) companies are also the nine (9) out of the 22 currently in business that had crossed 1000 crores in first year premium in their tenth/eleventh year of competition. Needless to add the remaining 11 (including the two that started work in 2001-02) have yet to breach the one thousand crore landmark premium income.

LIC Sold 3,70,12,277 Policies.

Four companies sold over Ten Lakh policies.

(Reliance Life – 19,02,685, Bajaj Allianz – 15,42,005, ICICI Pru – 13,50,494, Birla Sunlife – 10,04,093.)

Four companies sold between 5 lakh – 10 lakh pols.

(SBI Life – 9,39,978, HDFC Life – 8,30,532, Max New York – 8,16,259, Tata AIG – 5,53,203.)

Ten companies sold between one Lakh – 5 lakh pols.

(Future Generali – 3,13,954, ING Vysya – 2,74,401, Kotak Mahindra Om – 2,58,783, Met Life – 1,99,211, Aviva – 1,91,003, Bharti Axa – 1,82,208, Shri Ram Life – 1,21,330, IndiaFirst – 1,11,850, Canara HSBC – 1,11,298, IDBI Federal – 1,08,390.)

Four companies sold less than 1 Lakh policies.

(Star Union Daichi – 97,730, Aegon Religaire – 93,183, Sahara Life – 69,532, DLF Pramerica – 36,891.)

			% Over 09-10	Mar. Share
Total For Private Player	11109013	-	22.6%	23.09%
Total For LIC	37012277	-	4.70%	76.91%
Total For Industry	48121290	-	9.53%	100.00%

Although the performance of life insurance companies world wide is assessed on the basis of premium income (new and renewal) in India with its large population and low penetration the number of policies sold which is an indication of lives insured and insurable population covered is an equally important measure to asses the performance of life insurance companies. During the year 2001-02, LIC sold 2.32 crore new policies (a small number was contributed by the private insurers) which increased to 3.70 crore policies for LIC and 4.81 crores for the industry in 2010-11 an increases of 59.30% for LIC and more than double (107.10%) for the industry, after ten years. Interestingly the number of policies sold by all insurers, as also for the LIC, was the highest ever not last year (2010-11) but in the previous year (2009-10) when 5.32 crore policies were sold with LIC contributing 3.88 crore policies (the number came down to 3.70 crores in 2010-11). the market share of LIC for policies sold was 76.9% while that of the remining insurers was 23.1%; the fact that LIC's market share in policies (76.9%) is higher than its market share in new business premium income (68.7%) is indicative of the greater sales activity of the LIC agent vis-a-vis his counterpart in the private sector and may lead one to infer that the focus of the private players is more on premium income and perhaps less on the number of sales or policies sold. The overwhelming supermacy of LIC over its competitons in both these important spheres of activity is unamatched and unrivalued. LIC has thus been able to seli not only higher premium but higher number of policies also. As against 3.70 crores policies sold by LIC 2010-11 there were just four companies that sold over 10 lakh policies (Reliance life, Bajaj Allianz, ICICI Prudential, Birla Sun Life.) and three that came very close to the 10 lakh (SBI life, HDFC life and Max New York life) Eleven companies i.e., half the number of all, sold between one and six lakhs, while the remaining five ended the year with less than one lakh policies it needs to be mentioned here that most companies including LIC sold a vastly higher number of policies in 2009-10 than in 2010-11.

	First Year Premium		No. of Policies Income	
Year	**LIC**	**Private Insurance**	**LIC**	**Private Players**
2001-02	98.64%	1.36%	NA	NA
2002-03	94.30%	5.70%	96.75%	3.25%
2003-04	87.66%	12.34%	94.20%	5.80%
2004-05	78.77%	21.23%	91.48%	8.52%
2005-06	73.52%	26.48%	89.08%	10.92%
2006-07	74.32%	25.68%	82.83%	17.17%
2007-08	64.02%	35.98%	73.93%	26.07%
2008-09	60.89%	39.11%	70.52%	29.48%
2009-10	65.08%	34.92%	73.01%	26.99%
2010-11	68.70%	31.30%	76.91%	23.09%

As the life insurance industry has completed ten years of competition it is interesting to see that LIC occupies a major share of the market in respect of both first year and number of policies. As a matter of fact its market share in 2010-11 rose to 68.70 in premium income and 76.91 in no. of policies.

It is also worth nothing that in no year in the last decade the market share of LIC has gone beow 60.89% in premium income and 70.52% in policies. This is a fantastic performance which is unrivalled any where else. Heartiest congratulation to LIC, its marketing team (including agents) and administrative staff.

A closer look at the performance of the industry in the last ten years shows that progress has not been very even; there were years of phenomenal growth (2001-02, 04-05, 05-06, 06-07 and 09-10) and periods when growth was modest (2003-04 and 2007-08) or even years when growth was negative (2002-03 and 08-09). Overall the progress has been steady with industry failing to register positive growth in only two of the last ten years.

As LIC has been in existence for 55 years now and private companies have been operating for a decade or even less a comparison between the two on the basis of percentage growth-the base of the private players being much smaller-would not reflect a correct or fair picture nonetheless it is interesting to see that right from 2001-02 to 05-06 i.e. for five years straigt and in 07-08 the growth of the private sector companies far outstripped that of LIC; it is in the years 2006-07, 09-10 and 10-11 that the insurance behemoth seems to be re-asserting its strength and registering growth rates higher than that of the industry and even that of the private companies. Will this trend-observed in the last two years-continue and are the private companies, after the initial burst, losing their steam in the long run?

After a decade of competition-most would agree intense competition-LIC continues to stand head and shoulders above all other companies-individually and collectively its market share in first year premium in 2010-11 was 68.70% while in respect of number of policies sold in that year it was higher at 76.91 at no point in the history of competition in these ten years has the market share of LIC slipped to below 60% in premium income-the lowest was 60.89% in 08-09 and below 70% in no. of policies (it was 70.52% in 08-09). It will thus be observed that while the year 08-09 represents that year in last decade when LIC's market share was the lowest the year 06-07 saw its market share peaking at 74.32% (premium income) and 81.83 (policies) respectively. The issue of market share in the first five years of competition is not very relevant as the private companies were then in the nascent stage of their operations with the size of their operations-not very big even now-was verysmall five years back.

Insurer	Pols (Ind)	Lives (group)	Total
Private Insurers	1,11,09,013	4,76,65,636	5,87,74,649
LIC	3,70,12,277	3,56,60,199	7,26,72,476
Industry	4,81,21,290	8,33,25,835	13,14,47,125

Note :

Normally one should bot be combining no. of lives with policies because one of life or person can have 9and do have0 more than one policy on their lives. The purpose behind the above statement is to give a more holistic (through not entirely accurate) idea of the coverage provided through individual policies and group schemes. As would be seen the combined figure comes to 13,14 crores but a more realistic number would be around 11-12 crores which is very impressive. For the first time the private sector has overtaken LIC is no. of lives covered through group schemes largely because of good work done by Bajaj Allianz.

It will be observed from the enclosed charts that the tsunami of recession and financial crisis that affected the world economy also left its impact on the performance of the life insurance industry in India. This was reflected in the performance of the industry in 2008-09 when the performance of all companies witnessed a decline vis-a-vis the performance of the previous year; however the performance in the immediate next year (09-10) witnessed a strong bounce back by the industry with an even more robust performance by the LIC. This was as true of LIC's performance in the area of premium income as it was in policies where its growth rates outstripped those of the private sector companies; the performance of the life insurance industry mirrored the state of the Indian economy.

The picture in the year 2010-2011 is some what different - LIC performed very well by clocking an impressive growth of 21.94% as dis some of the bigger private companies especially. ICICI Pru (24.10%), HDFC Life (24.66%) and Max New York Life (11.44%) together with good performances by medium sized companies and relatively recent entrants (incidentally all but one promoted by big banks) to the life insurance scene like CANARA, HSBC, OBC Life (28.50%) Star Union Daichi (46.02%), India First (249.68%) and Shri Ram Life (36.81%). However a less encouaging aspect of the performance of 2010-11 was that as many as nine companies performed at level that were lower than in the previous year amongst the major companies that have been in the market for over ten years, have strong and recognized brands, and were perceived to be doing well there were quite a few e.g. Bajaj Allianz, Reliance Life, Birla Sun Life, Kotak Mahindra OM, Aviva and Metlife whose premium income in 10-11 was less than in the previous year. The poor performance of these companies contributed to an overall negative growth by the private sector insurers notwithstanding the good performances by some of the other companies. (Annexure II)

There is no doubt that competition has had a salutary impact on the life insurance industry. As we have shown earlier the first year premium expanded (for the industry) from 19857 crores (01-02) to 1,25,826.23 crores (in 10-11) a growth of 533.65% in a period of ten years; in terms of policies sold the growth from 2,32,49,651 in 2001-02 to 4,81,51,884 has also been very impressive at more than double or 107.10% over the performance of 2001-02. Annexure–VI. It is quite evident that in this first decade of competition LIC has acted as the major trigger in driving the growth in the life insurance indistry. LIC sold 3.70 crores policies in 10-11 (the number was 3.88 crores in 09-10) which represents an increase fo nearly 60% over its performance in 2001-02 the growth in first year premium income in this period of ten years has been much higher and quite phenomenal from 19588.77 crores (01-02) to 86444.72 crores (2010-11) an increase of 341.29%. That competition has been good for the industry and even of LIC is amply proved by performance figure in the decade before competition (92-93 to 01-02). The premium income of LIC increased from 995.25 crores in 92-93 to 19588.77 crores in 2001-02 but accelerated from 19588.77 crores to 86,444.72 crores.

Percentage of Single Premium to Total First Year Premium

	2010-11		**% of Single Premium**
	Single Premium	**Non Single**	**To total First Year Premium**
Private Insurers	8253.37	22197.59	27.10%
LIC	27620.15	24583.49	52.90%
Industry	35873.52	46781.08	43.40%

	2009-10		**% of Single Premium**
	Single Premium	**Non Single**	**To total First Year Premium**
Private Insurers	3137.92	28480.09	9.92%
LIC	26539.59	23575.90	52.95%
Industry	29677.51	52055.99	36.31%

Death Claims statistics in percentage terms (To total no of death claims payable) for 2009-2010

Life Insurer	*No of Claims paid*	*No of Claims repudiated*	*No of Claims written back*	*No of Claims pending at end of the year*
Aegon Religare	48.00	44.00	0.00	8.00
Aviva	87.11	9.75	0.00	3.14
Bajaj Allianz	88.88	5.20	0.00	6.63
Bharti AXA	77.80	22.20	0.00	0.00
Birla Sunlife	89.09	10.62	0.05	0.24
Canara HSBC	38.71	16.13	0.00	45.16
DLF Pramerica	40.00	10.00	0.00	50.00
Future Generali	38.85	29.36	0.00	31.79
HDFC Std	91.14	4.67	0.00	4.20
ICICI Prudential	90.17	3.27	0.00	6.56
IDBI Federal	49.52	23.81	0.00	26.67
India First	53.85	7.69	0.00	38.46

ING Vysya	89.30	4.26	0.62	5.82
Kotak Mahindra	86.97	4.39	0.00	8.64
Max New York	65.51	12.31	0.00	22.18
MetLife	82.54	5.94	0.22	11.29
Reliance Life	89.07	7.05	0.07	3.82
Sahara	63.06	6.84	0.00	30.10
SBI Life	83.27	14.75	0.01	1.96
Shriram	39.54	19.73	0.00	40.74
Star Union Di-ichi	58.33	5.00	0.00	36.67
Tata AIG	78.17	12.93	0.14	8.76
Private Total	84.88	7.60	0.04	7.48
LIC	96.54	1.21	0.84	1.41
Industry Total	95.24	1.93	0.75	2.08

Statistics on Benefit Amount of Death Claims for 2009-2010 (Amount in ₹ Cr.)

Source : IRDA Annual Report, 2009-2010

Life Insurer	*Benefit amount pending at start of year*	*Benefit amount claims intimated/ booked*	*Total Benefit amount of Claims amount*	*Benefit amount of Claims paid*	*Benefit amount of Claims repudiated*	*Benefit amount of Claims written back*	*Benefit amount of claims pending at the end of the year*
Aegon Religare	0.1	2.48	2.58	1.08	1.13	0	0.37
Aviva	2.36	29.35	31.71	25.37	4.57	0	1.77
Bajaj Allianz	14.21	338.9	353.11	294.92	25.79	0	32.4
Bharti AXA	0.17	10.9	11.06	7.57	3.49	0	0
Birla Sunlife	0.77	129.44	130.21	102.76	26.46	0.32	0.67
Canara HSBC	0.46	4.29	4.75	1.15	0.48	0	3.12
DLF Pramerica	0	0.7	0.7	0.48	0.01	0	0.21
Future Generali	0.06	11.67	11.73	3.61	4.05	0	4.07
HDFC Std	8.16	71.59	79.75	66.58	5.89	0	7.28
ICICI Prudential	16.9	231.62	248.52	218.04	10.98	0	19.5
IDBI Federal	0.55	8.13	8.68	2.7	1.61	0	4.37
India First	0	0.17	0.17	0.07	0.01	0	0.09
ING Vysya	4.75	24.93	29.68	24.91	1.58	0.3	2.89
Kotak Mahindra	5.25	62.72	67.97	55.91	3.61	0	8.45
Max New York	1.82	124.73	126.55	78.07	18.16	0	30.32
MetLife	7.4	69.23	76.63	40.5	18.48	0.1	17.55
Reliance Life	7.14	96.33	103.47	79.61	15.8	0.04	8.02
Sahara	1.82	5.28	7.1	4.73	0.25	0	2.12
SBI Life	8.08	95.27	103.35	92.44	5.93	0	4.98
Shriram	3.61	13.81	17.42	5.47	4.1	0	7.85
SBI Life	8.08	95.27	103.35	92.44	5.93	0	4.98
Shriram	3.61	13.81	17.42	5.47	4.1	0	7.85
Star Union Dai-ichi	0	0.91	0.91	0.61	0.00	0	0.3
Tata AIG	10.71	64.85	75.56	52	12.03	0	11.53
Private Total	94.31	1397	1491.61	1158.58	164.41	0.76	167.86
LIC	148.53	4900.90	5049.43	4799.55	80.36	51.07	118.45
Industry Total	242.84	6298.20	6541.04	5958.13	244.77	51.83	286.31

Source: IRDA Annual Report, 2009-2010

Claims Statistics in Percentage Terms (To Total Benefit Amount of Death Claims) for 2009-10

Life Insurer	*Benefit amount of Claims paid*	*Benefit amount of Claims repudiated*	*Benefit amount of Claims written back*	*Benefit amount of Claims pending at the end of the year*
Aegon Religare	41.86	43.80	0.00	14.34
Aviva	80.01	14.41	0.00	5.58
Bajaj Allianz	83.32	7.30	0.00	9.18
Bharti AXA	68.44	31.56	0.00	0.00
Birla Sunlife	78.92	20.32	0.25	0.51
Canara HSBC	24.21	10.11	0.00	65.68
DLF Pramerica	68.57	1.43	0.00	30.00
Future Generali	30.78	34.53	0.00	34.70
HDFC Std	83.49	7.39	0.00	9.13
ICICI Prudential	87.74	4.42	0.00	7.85
IDBI Federal	31.11	18.55	0.00	50.35
India First	41.18	5.88	0.00	52.94
ING Vysya	83.26	5.31	0.00	9.74
Kotak Mahindra	82.26	5.31	0.00	12.43
Max New York	61.69	14.35	0.00	23.96
MetLife	52.85	24.12	0.13	22.90
Reliance Life	76.94	15.27	0.04	7.75
Sahara	66.62	3.52	0.00	29.86
SBI Life	89.44	5.74	0.00	4.82
Shriram	31.40	23.54	0.00	45.06
Star Unon Dai-ichi	67.03	0.00	0.00	32.97
Tata AIG	68.82	15.92	0.00	15.26
Private Total	77.67	11.02	0.05	11.25
LIC	95.05	1.59	1.01	2.35
Industry Total	91.09	3.74	0.79	4.38

Source: IRDA Annual Report, 2009-2010

Average Size of Death Claims

Average size of Death Claims for the year 2009-10 (in ₹)

Life Insurer	*Average amount per policy on Total Claims payable*	*Average amount per policy on Total clims paid*	*Average Bennefit amout per policy on Claims repudicated*	*Average Benefit amount per policy Claim at pending at the end of the year*	*Average Sum assured per policy in force as at 31/3/2010*
Private Insurers	175358	160468	254268	263723	242634
LIC	74544	73398	97678	124331	82912
Industry Total	85791	82056	166590	180160	102912

F.No. 300 (Rev. '74)

Office use only
Date of Receipt ....
....
Inward No. Initials
Is licience in force? .... Initials ....

LIFE INSURANCE CORPORATION OF INDIA

(Established by the Life Insurance Corporation Act, 1956)

PROPOSAL FOR INSURANCE ON OWN LIFE

(*Not to be used for Insurance on the Lives of Minors*)

Divisional Office: .... **Branch Office:** .... **Proposal No.** ....

Agent's Name .... **Licence No.** .... **Date of Expy.** .... **Agent's D.O's. Code Nos.** ....

(*All answers to be filled in legibly. Answers must be given in words. Strckes of the pen or date of dashes will not be accepted as replies*)

1. (*a*) Name in full ....
(IN BLOCK LETTERS) ....
(*b*) Short Name ....
(*c*) Nationality ....
(*d*) Address which will be incorporated in the Policy and at which notices will be sent ....
....
(*e*) Permanent Residential Address ....
....
(*f*) Father's Name in full ....
....
(*g*) Present Occupation ....
(*h*) Nature of Duties ....
(*i*) Name of present employer ....
(*j*) Length of service with him ....
(*k*) Name of previous employer ....

2. Table and Term of Assurance Sum to be Assured Rs. State if premiums are payable Yearly Half-Yearly, Quarterly or Monthly. Amount of the deposit If policy is to be dated back, state date.

3. Date of Birth	Age Nearer Birthday	Nature of Age Proof	Place of Birth	If Age proof is service record, what proof was submitted to employer?	

4. Do you desire to secure Double Accident Benefit and Extended Permanent. Disability Benefit? ....
N.B.: *The maximum Double Accident Benefit or Combined Double Accident Benefit and Extended Permanent Disability Benfit allowed on any one life under one or more policies of the Corporation or of the insurers whose business has been taken over by the Corporation, shall be limited to ₹ 1,00,000.*

Contd....

5. What is the object of this assurance? ....

N.B. —If the policy is to be effected (a) under the Married Women's Property Act, 1987, or (b) for the purpose of paying Estate Duty, or (c) for the Marriage of a dependent female relation, please state so. If the object is as per (d) please complete the relevant addendum.

6. A. If you wish to nominate under Section 39 of the Insurance Act, 1983, a person to whom the moneys secured by the policy applied for are to be paid in the event of your death, please state:

Full Name of Nominee .... Relationship to Yourself .... Age ....
(IN BLOCK LETTERS)

Full Address ....

B. If the nominee is a minor, please state the name of the person whom you wish to appoint to receive the policy money in the event of the claim arising during the minority of the nominee. The appointee must sign below to show his/her consent to the appointment.

Full Name of the Appointee ....
(IN BLOCK LETTERS)

Full Address ....

Signature of the Appointee .... Age ....

7. N.B. — For non-medical ....

8. If you are already ... Armed

(a) The wing to which you belong	(b) Your ra	Medical Examination	Your medical category after Medical Examination	(e) Were you below A-I category? If so, when?

9 Have you any prospect or intention of engaging in Aviation or of enterior Naval or Millitary Service or taking up any other hazardous occupation or pursuit? If so give details. ....

10. Is your life now being proposed for another assurance to, or is any other perposal, or an application for revival of a policy, on your life, under consideration of this or any other Office of the Corporation? If so, which is the Office and give details. ....

Contd....

11. State below details of all your previous Policies under. *(*A*) Medical basis, +(*B*) Non-Medical Basis:

Name of the Divl. Office of the Corp. or of the Insurer	Policy Number	Sum Assured	lan of Absence	Year of issue of Policy	Whether accepted as proposed at ordinary rates	With or Without Accident Benefit	Whether in force, for the full sum Assured?	*If not, give due date of last premium paid and mode of payment
**A*								
+*B*								

*N.B.: Corporation does not entertain any fresh proposal for Insurance where previous policy has lapsed or converted into paid up policy within last three years.

12. Has a proposal on your life on an application for revival of a policy on your life made to this or any other Office of the Corporation or any Insurer ever been.

(*a*) withdrawn or dropped? .... (*c*) accepted with an extra premium or lies? ....

(*b*) deferred or declined? .... (*d*) accepted or terms otherwise than those proposed? ....

If so, give details ....

Additional questions to be Answered by Female Proposers (Qns. 13 and 14)

13. (*a*) Your educational qualification, if any .... (*b*) Your average monthly income, if any ....

(*c*) State Sources of income .... (*d*) Whether you pay Income-tax ....

14. If you are married, please state:

(*a*) Husband's full name ....

(*b*) His occupation .... (*c*) His average monthly Income Rs. ....

(*d*) The following details of his life insurance:

Contd....

Office of the Corporation	Policy Number	Sum Assured	Table and Term	Present condition

15. Family History

		LIVING		DEAD		
	Age	State of Health (if not good, give full details)	Year of Death	Age of Death	Duration of last illness	Cause of death
Father						
Mother						
Brothers ... No. Total Living ... Total Dead ...						
Sisters ... No. Total Living ... Total Dead ...						
Wife/Husband ... No.						
Children ... Total Living ... Total Dead ...						

16. Has any of your relations, living or dead, suffered from any hereditary or infectious disease like diabetes, insanity, epliepsy, gout, asthma, tuberculosis, cancer, leprosy, etc.? ... .

....

Contd....

17. (*a*) What has been your usual state of health? .... (*a*) ....

(*b*) Have you any bodily defect or deformity? If so, give details. .... (*b*) ....

(*c*) Have you had (*i*) Small Pox or (*ii*) Successful vaccination .... (*c*) (*i*) .... (*ii*) ....

(*d*) (*i*) Are you suffering from Pyorrhea? .... (*d*) (*i*) ....

(*ii*) State number of missing teeth, if any .... (*ii*) ....

(*iii*) For how many missing teech a denture is worn? .... (*iii*) ....

18. Have you ever suffered from or are you suffering from:	Answers "Yes" or	If 'yes' describe fully each ailment giving its nature the number of attacks, dates, duration, seycrity, treatment taken, result and names and address of doctors consulted, giving reference to Question No. for questions 18 to 22.
(*a*) Presistent cough, asthma, bronchitis, pneumonic pleurisy, spitting of blood, tuberculosis or any other disease of lungs?	(*a*)	Details of Q. No. ....
(*b*) High or low blood pressures, rhenumatic fever, pain chest, breathlessness, palpitation, infraction, or any disease of the heart of arteries?	(*b*)	
(*c*) Peptic ulcer, colitis, jaundice, anaemia, piles, dysentery or any disease of the stomach, liver, spreen, gall bladdeer or, pancreas?	(*c*)	
(*d*) Any disease of kidney, prostate, or urinary system?	(*d*)	
(*e*) Paralysis, insanity, epilepsy, fits of any kind or nervous breakdown or any other disease of the brain or the nervovs system?	(*e*)	
(*f*) Hernis, hydrocele, varicocele, fistula, varicose venis, skin eruption, filariasis, goitre, gonorrhea, syphilis or any other venereal disease?	(*f*)	
(*g*) Cancer, leprosy, rheumatism, gout, enlarged glands or tumours?	(*g*)	
(*h*) Any disease of the ear, nose, throat or eyes, including defective sight or hearing and discharge from the ears?	(*h*)	

Contd....

19.	Have you been suspected of diabetes or are you suffering from diabetes or have ever passes sugar, albumen, pus or blood in urine?	....	
20.	Have you consulted a raodical practitioner, within the last five years for any ailments requiring treatment for more than a week?	....	
21.	Have your remained absent from place of your work on ground of health during the last 5 years?	....	
22.	(*a*) Did you ever have any operation, accident or injury? (*b*) Have you ever had, an electrocardiogram, X-ray or screening, blood, urine or stood examination? (*c*) Have you ever been in any hospital, asylum, or panatorium for check-up, observation, treatment or any operation?	(*a*) .... (*b*) .... (*c*)	
23.	Do you use or have you ever used alcoholic drinks, narcotics or any other drugs? If so, what? Also state quantity consumed per day.	....	

For Females only

24.	(*a*) Do you observe purdah?	(*a*)	(*f*) Have you had any abortions or miscarriages?	(*f*) ....
	(*b*) Have the menstrual periods always been regular and painless?	(*b*)	(*g*) Did you have any complications related to pregnancy?	(*g*) ....
	(*c*) State the date of last menstruation.	(*c*)	(*h*) Have you any weakness or injury resulting from child bearing or miscarriage?	(*h*) ....
	(*d*) Are you pregnant now?	(*d*)	(*i*) Have you suffered or are you suffering from any disease of breast, ovaries or uterus?	(*i*) ....
	(*e*) State the date of the last delivery.	(*e*)		

Contd....

DECLARATION BY THE PROPOSER

I ....the person whose life is hereinbefore proposed to be assured, do hereby declare that the foregoing statements and answers have been given by me after fully understanding the questions and the same are true, and complete in every particular and that I have not withheld any information and I do hereby agree and declare that these statements and this declaration shall be the contract of assurance between me and the Life Insurance Corporation of India and that if any untrue averment be contained therein the said contract shall be absolutely null and void and all moneys which shall have been paid in respect thereof shall stand forfeited to the Corporation.

SPECIMEN SIGNATURE ....

Notwithstanding the provisions of any law, usage, custom or convention for the time being in force prohibiting any doctor, hospital, and/or employer from divulging any knowledge or information about me concening my health or employment, on the grounds os secrecy, I, my heirs, executors, administrators and assigns or any person or persons, having interest of any kind whatsoever in the policy contract issued to me hereby agree, that such autbority having such knowledge or information, shall be at liberty to divulge any such knowledge or information to the Corperation.

And I further agree that if after the date of submission of the Proposal but before the issue of First premium Receipt (*i*) any change in my ccupation or any adverse circuumstance connected with my financial position or the general health of myself or that of any member of my family, occurs or (*ii*) if a Proposal for assurance or an application for evival of a policy on my life made to any Office of the Corporation hasbeen withdrawn on dropped, deferred or declined, or accepted at an increased premium or subject to a lien or on terms other than as proposed I shallforthwith intimate the same to the Corportion in writing to reconsider the terms of acceptance of assurance. Any omission on my part to do so shall render this Assurance invalid and all moneys which shall have been paid in respect thereof forfeited to the Corporation.

Dated at..............................on the .... day of 197

Signature of Witness ....

Occupation & Address ....

....

.... Signature or thumb impression of the Proposer.

Contd....

If in this form the answers to the questions and/or signature of the Proposer is/are in vernaoular then he should declare in his own handwriting above his signature that all questions were explained to him and that his replies were given after fully and properly understanding the same.

1. This declaration should be made by the person filling in the form

(I) I hereby declare that I have fully explained the above questions to the Proposer and I have truthfully recorded the answers given by the Proposer.

Address of the declarant ....

....

Signature

2. The thumb impression of the proposer should be attested by a person of standing whose identity can easily be established, but unconnected with the Corporation and this declargtion should be to the questions has affixed his thumb impression to the proposal

(I) I hereby declare that I have explained the contents of the proposal form to the proposer in .... (language) and that I have read out to the Proposer the answers made by from after fully understanding the contects thereof.

Address of the declarant ....

....

Signature

Extracts from Section 41 of the Insurance Act, 1938:

1. No person shall allow or offer to allow, either directly or indirectly, as an inducement to any person to take out or renew or continue an insurance in respect of any kind of risk relating to lives or property in India, any rebate of the whole or part of the commission payable or any rebate of the premium shown on the Policy, nor shall any person taking out or renewsing or continuing a Policy accept any rebate, except such rebate as may be allowed in accordance with the published prospectuses or tables of the Insurer.
2. Any person making defaut in complying with the provisions of this section shall be prunishable with fine which may extend to five hundred rupees.

THE CORPORATION ALLOWS THE FOLLOWING REDUCING IN THE ANNUAL PREMIUM

Reduced Premiums for Policies of Large Amounts:

In respect of Policies for ₹ 5,000/- and upwards, there will be allowed a reduction in the Annual Premium per thousand Sum Addured of (*i*) Re. 0.50 for each policy for ₹ 5,000/- and upwards, but less than ₹ 10,000/- (*ii*) Re. 0.75 for each policy for ₹ 10,000/- and upwards but less than ₹ 20,000/- and (*iii*) Rupee one for each policy for ₹ 20,000/- and upwards. These reductions are not applicable to Single Premium Policies or to policies effected under the (*i*) Pure Endowment,

Contd....

(*ii*) Multi-purpose, (*iii*) Children's Deferred Assurance, (*iv*) Convertible Term Assurance, (*v*) Immediate Annunity and (*vi*) Deferred Annuity Plans. However, under the Multi-purpose Plan, a reduction of Re. 0.50 per thousand basic sum assured would be allowed in the Annual Premium in respect of Policies for ₹ 5,000/- and upwards. In the case of the Educational Annuity Policy, the above reduction will be calculated on the nominal sum assured.

Reducted Premium where the Mode of Payment is Yearly or Half-Yearly:

If the premiums are payable yearly or half-yearly, a reduction of Re. 0.75 and Re. 0.50 respectively will be allowed in the Annual Premium per thousand sum assured under all classes of assurance except under the Pure Endowment, Children's Deferred Assurance and Deferred Annuity Policies where the reductive will be the rate of ₹ 0.37 and Re. 0.25 respectively. These reductions are not applicable to (*i*) the Immediate Annuity Policy, (*ii*) the Convertible Term Assurance Policy, (*iii*) the additional premium payable to secure the Premium Waiver Benefits under the Children's Deference Assurance Policy, (*iv*) the additional premium payable to secure the Supplementary Benefis under the Multi-purpose Policy and (*v*) the Janata Policy. In the case of the Deferred Annuity Policy the above reduction will be calculated on the cash option, while under the Educational Annuity Policy the said reduction will be calculated on the nominal sum assured.

Croup and Superannuation Scheme:

Special rates will apply to policies issued under these Schemes.

FOR MEDICAL CASE ONLY

"I certify that the Proposer has signed/put his/her thumb impression in my presence after admitting that all the answer to Question Nos. 15 & onwards of this from have been correctly recorded.

....

Signature or thumb impression of the Life Proposal

N.B.: Signature or thumb impression should be affixed in presence of Medical Examiner.

....

(Signature of the Medical Examiner)

To be completed by the Agent

Branch No. ....

Agent's Name ....

Dev. Off. Name ....

Proposal No ....

Policy No. ....

LIFE INSURANCE CORPORATION OF INDIA

(Established by the Life Insurance Corporation Act, 1956)

MEDICAL EXAMINER'S CONFIDENTIAL REPORT

(*i*) Please satisfy yourself about the identify of the Life Proposed to guard against impersonation.

(*ii*) Give full detials of ailment or impairment detected. Ascertain & give details such as dates & duration etc.

(*iii*) If this is a new proposal, obtain proposal form completed as per instractions therein & attach it with this.

(*iv*) The Life Proposed and the person introducing him/her to you should sign in your presence. Do not use the form signed in advance.

Full Name of the Life to be examined .... **Age** .... **Years**

Father's Name .... **Occupation of the Life Proposal** ....

Introduced by .... **His designation** .... **His signature** ....

1. Identification	
(*a*) Is the examinee known to you (*i*) personally or (*ii*) professionally?	(*a*) (*i*) .... (*ii*) ....
(*b*) Give identification marks	(*b*) ....
	....
2. Appearance	
(*a*) (*i*) What is his/her apparent age?	(*a*) (*i*) ....
(*ii*) Does he/she look older than the stated age?	(*ii*) ....

Contd....

Question	Answer	OFFICE REMARKS
(*b*) Is the general appearance healthy?	(*b*)	
(c) Does the person appear to be of sober and temperate habits?	(*c*)	
(*a*) Are there marks of (*i*) small pox or (*ii*) successful vaccination?	(*d*) (*i*) .... (*ii*)	
(*e*) Is those any defect or deformity, swellings of joints, enlarge ment of thyroid or lymphatic glands or any cicatrices?	(*e*)	
(*f*) Is there any evidence of filariasis, varicose veins or skin disease?	(*f*)	
(*g*) Is there any evidence of pesent or past malignancy?	(g)	
3. Measurements and Weight		
(*a*) Chest (over nipples) on (*i*) complete expiration ..	(*a*) (*i*) .... cms.	....
(*ii*) full inspiration	(*ii*) .... cms.	....
(*b*) Abdomen (over naval)	(*b*) .... cms.	....
(*c*) Height (without shoes)	(*c*) .... cms.	....
(*d*) Height (with thin clothes)	(*d*) .... cms.	....
4. Mouth, Eyes, Ears and Throat		
(*a*) Are the gums, teeth and tongue healthy	(*a*)	
(*b*) Is there any pyorshea? If so, is it moderate or marked?	(*b*)	
(*c*) (*i*) Are there any missing teeth? If so, how many? ..	(*c*) (*i*)	
(*ii*) For how many missing teeth a denture is worn? ..	(*ii*)	

Contd....

(*d*) Is there any evidence of past or present disease of the eyes, ears nose or throat? (If the visioner hearing is affected, degree should be stated. Ascertain and mention the power of glasses.)	(*d*) ....
5. Respiratory System	
(*a*) Is the chest symmetrical and well formed?	(*a*) ....
(*b*) Are there any symptoms or signs suggesting abnormality of disease of the repiratory system?	(*b*) ....
6. Cardiovascular System	
(*a*) Is the heart normal in size, position and impulse? Are the heart sounds normal?	(*a*) ....
(*b*) (*i*) State pluse rate (*ii*) Describe abnormalities, if any.	(*b*) (*i*)..................(*ii*)..................
(*c*) Is the condition of blodd vessels healthy?	(*c*) ....
(*d*) Blood Pressure : (in supine position with a mercury manometer)	(*d*) Ist reading systolic ....mm.Hg.......... „ Diastolic..........mm.Hg.......... 2nd reading Systolic..........mm.Hg.......... „ Diastolic..........mm.Hg..........
N.B. If the Systolic reading is 140 or over, or Diastolic reading is 90 or ocer, a second reading should be 90 or over, a second reading should be taken in supine position after 10 minutes rest.	
7. Abdomen	
(*a*) Is there any evidence of disease or of enlargement of liver or spleen? If so, its degree.	(*a*) ....
(*b*) Is there any evidence of gastric or duodenal ulcer? ..	(*b*) ....

Contd....

(*c*) Is there any lump or tenderness or free fluid in the abdomen?	(*c*) ....
(*d*) Is there any evidence of piles or fistula?	(*d*) ....
8. Genito-Urinary System	
(*a*) Urine: (The sample of urine must be passed under such circums-	(*a*) (*i*) Sugar..................(*ii*) Sp. Gravity..................
	(*iii*) Albumen..................(*iv*) Other Abnormalities..................
(*b*) Is there any evidence of past or present venereal disease?	(*b*) ....
(*c*) Is hernia present? If so, state side, type, size reducible or not whether a properly fitting truss is worn & history of strang lation	(*c*) ....
(*d*) Are the testis normal in location, size and consistency? ..	(*d*) ....
(*e*) Is hydrocele present? Is so, give the maximum horizontal circumference of the whole scrotum.	(*e*) ....
9. Nervous System	
(*a*) Is there any evidence or nervous disease, such as, paralysis, epilepsy, wasting, tremors, involuntary movements, etc.?	(*a*) ....
(*b*) Are the kenee-jerks and pupil reflexes normal?	(*b*) ....
10. Operation and other details	
(*a*) Is there any evidence of any operation, accident or injury? State the degree of impairment if any. Give the location, size and condition of scar.	(*a*) ....

Contd....

(*b*) Has the person ever undergone any ECG, X-Ray, Screening, Blood, urine or stool examinatiens? If so, ascertain nature of test, date, reason and result.	(*b*) ....
11. For Female Applicants only	
(*a*) Is there any disease of teh breasts?	(*a*) ....
(*b*) Is there any evidence of pregnancy?	(*b*) ....
(*c*) Do you suspect any disease of uterus, cervix or overies? ..	(*c*) ....
(*d*) Is there any weakness or injury resulting from childbearing or miscarriage?	(*d*) ....
12. (*a*) Have you carried out ECG or any other special examination give such as heart report etc. alongwith this examination? If so, details.	(*a*) ....
(*b*) Are there any other circumstances or findings which might affect the longevity?	(b) ....
(*c*) Do you suspect any adverse feature of past history or habits or existence of any other disease or any other complaint not noted above.	(*c*) ....
(*d*) Do you consider the life to be first class? If not, state the reason.	(*d*) ....

Space for Additional Remarks:

Dated at .... on the .... day on .... 97, at .... a.m. / p.m

Contd....

I hereby certify that I have this day examined the above Life to be assured personally, in private and have recorded in my own hand the true and correct findings. I declare I am not related to the party.

Signature of the Life Prospo sed Signed in my presence
Signature of the Medical Examiner

Signature of the Medical Examiner

Qualification .... Code No. ....

Name & Address ....

....

F.No. 300 (Rev. '75)

Office use only
Name of Agent..
Agency No..
Prosposal No..

LIFE INSURANCE CORPORATION OF INDIA

(Established by the Life Insurance Corporation Act, 1956)

AGENT'S CONFIDENTIAL REPORT

N.B—Agent should complete this report only after medical examination is arranged.

Full name of the Proposer...Age.......................years.

Full Name of the Life to be Assured...Age.......................years.

Residence .... **ccupation**...

.... **Sum Proposed**...

1. (*a*) How long you have known the life to be assured?	(*a*) ....
(*b*) Are you related to him? If so, how?	(*b*) ....
2. (*a*) Give (*i*) name of medical examiner and (*ii*) date of medical examination.	(*a*) (*i*)....................(*ii*)....................
(*b*) State if any special reports were done and if so, give date, doctors' name and nature of reports.	(*b*) ....
3. (*a*) Does he look older than the stated age? If so, by how many years?	(*a*) ....
(*b*) What is the educational qualification of the Life to be Assured?	(*b*) ....
4. What is his monthly income and state the sources:	....
(*i*) Employment (*ii*) Business or Profession	(*i*) ....(*ii*)....................
(*iii*) Other sources (to be specified) (*iv*) H. U.F., if any	(*iii*) ....(*iv*)....................
N.B.—*State also income of life to be assured, if he is different from proposer*	....
5. (*a*) What is general state of health of the Life to be assured? ..	(*a*) ....
(*b*) Is there anything unhealthy about his appearance, such as being very thin and emaciated, anaemic etc.? ..	(*b*) ....

Contd....

(*c*) Has he any deformity, impaired sight or hearing, amputation? ..	(*c*) ....
(*d*) Is he (*i*) tall or short (*ii*) underweight or overweight? ..	(*d*) (*i*) ....(*ii*)..................
(*e*) Have you any knowledge of his having suffered from any	(*e*) ....

6. Have you verified the particulars relating to the previous policies? If so, give following particulars.

(*a*) Policy No.	Date of last Premium Receipt	Policy No.	Date of last Premium Receipt

(*b*) State whether the policy document shows that the age is admitted? ....

(*c*) Verify/ascertain what proff of age was submitted under previous policy ....

7. (*a*) Give mark of identification. ..	(*a*) ....
(*b*) Does he bear marks of (*i*) successful vaccination (*iii*) small pox? ..	(*b*) (*i*)..................(*ii*)..................
(*c*) Give below weight and physical measurements; (Please see not below)	(*c*)
(*i*) Exact Height (*ii*) Exact Weight ..	(*i*) ....cms.(*ii*)..................kgs.
(*iii*) Girth of abdomen at level of navel ..	(*iii*) ....cms.
Girth or chest at nipple (*iv*) on expiration (*v*) on inspiration ..	(*iv*) ....cms. (*v*)..................cms.

N.B.— Height and girths of chest and abdomen should be found by measurement. Places where weighing machines are available actual weight should be given. Places where a weighing machines is not available, weight should be estimated and the word 'Estimated' should be added after the estimated figure of weight.

8. Are you aware of anything in the occuptaios, financial or social position of the life to be assured, his personal habits or any other circumstances which might be likely to add to the risk?	

Contd....

9. Do you recommend the acceptance of the proposal?

I hereby declare that the foregoing statements are true and correct to the best of my knowledge and belief.

Dated at ....on the ....day of..19.

Signature of the Agent.

The agent should type here or write in block letters his name and address so that the acceptance advice may be sent to him without any delay. ....

From No. 460-A(Revised)

LIFE INSURANCE CORPORATION OF INDIA

(Established by the Life Insurance Corporation Act, 1956)

PERSONAL STATEMENT REGARDING HEALTH

Divisional Office..Branch Office..Proposal/Policy No..years.

Agent's Name...Agent's Code No..

(All answers to be filled in legibly. Answers must be given in words. Srokes of the pen or dots or dashes will not be accepted as replies).

Instruction:— Please fill this form

(*i*) When specifically requested, if you apply for the issue of a new policy

(*ii*) When more than 6 months have passed since the date of lapse; if you apply for the revival of a lapsed policy. (when this form is used in respect of assurances under Non-medical Schemes, detect room the first line of Question 3 hereunder the words "Your last medical examination for ")

1. Name in full (in BLOCK LETTERS)..

   Full address ....

2. Is this application for: (*a*) Issue of a new Policy?	If the answer is 'Yes' please give the Proposal Number or the Policy Number.
(*b*) Rvival of a lapsed Policy?	(*a*) .... Proposal No....................... (*b*) .... Policy No..........................
3. Since the date of your last Medical Examination for the above mentioned proposal or Policy: (*a*) Have you suffered from any physical or mental illness, injury or disability? If so, give details. (*b*) Have you been required to take medical treatment? If so, give details (Such as date and duration of illness, effect of treatment etc. as also name and address of the doctor who treated you).	(*a*) .... (*b*) ....

Contd....

(*c*) What deaths or illness have there been in your family (parents, wife/husband, brothers, sisters or children)? Give age at death, date of death and duration of illness.	(*c*) ....
(*d*) Has there been any change in your mode of life habits and occupation? If so, give details	(*d*) ....
(*e*) Has a proposal on your life or an application for revival of a policy on your life made to this or any other office of the Corporation or any. Insurer ever been withdrawn or dropped, deferred or declined, accepted with an extra premium or lien or on terms otherwise than those proposed? If So, give details.	(*e*) ....
4. Are you at present in sound health?	
5. Have you paid any deposit or arrears of premiums? If so, give details.	(*i*) Amounts: Rs.................... (*ii*) Dates:.................... (*iii*) How paid:....................
6. Since the date of your last Medical Examination for the abovementioned Proposal or Policy: (*a*) Have you been menstruating regularly? .. .. (*b*) Have you had any miscarriages?	 (*a*) .... (*b*) ....
7. Please give the date of : (*a*) Last menstruation. .. .. .. (*b*) Last delivery	 (*a*) .... (*b*) ....
8. Are you pregnant now?	

Contd....

I,.. do hereby declare that the foregoing statements and answers are true in every particular and agree and declare that these statements and this declaration along with my Proposal for Insurance shall be the basis of the contract of *assurance/ revival of the lapsed policy, between me and the Life Insurance Corporation of India and that if any untrue averment be contained therein the said contract shall be absolutely null and void and all moneys which shall have been paid in respect thereof shall stand forfeited to the Corporation.

(* Delete words not applicable)

**And I further declare that if the Corporation revives the policy on the original terms or otherwise and (*i*) if any change in my occupation or any adverse circumstance connected with my financial position or the general health of myself of that of my family, however unimportant I may consider the same, occurs or (*ii*) if a Proposal for assurance or any application for revival of a policy on my life made to any office of the Corporation is pending or has been withdrawn or dropped, deferred or declined or accepted at an increased premium or subject to a lien or on terms other than as proposed or (*iii*) if I have been selected for service in any of the branches of Military, Naval or Air Force Services between the date of this declaration and the date of revival of the policy, the Revival shall be absolutely null and void and all moneys which shall have been paid in respect thereof forfeited, unless intimation of such event be made in writing to the Corporation and the revival be reapproved by the Corporation.

(** Delete this paragraph in case of application for the issue of a new policy.)

Dated at..............................on the..............................day of..............................197

Signature of Witness..............................

Occupation..............................

Address..............................

Signature of Thumb Impression of the Proposer/Life Assured.

If the answers to the question in this form are given in vern acular or if the answers to the questions are given in English but the Proposer/Life Assured signs in vernacular then the Proposer/Life Assured should declare in his own handwriting above his own signature that all questions were explained to him and that his replies were given after fully and properly understanding the same.

In case the Proposer/Life Assured is illiterate:

1. This declaration should be made by the person filling in the form.

   Address of Declarant..............................

   ....

I hereby declare that I have fully explained the above questions to the Proposer/ Life Assured and I have truthfully recorded the answers given by the Proposer/Life Assured.

.... (*Signature*)

2. The thumb impression of the Proposer/Life Assured Should be attested by a person of standing whose identity can easily be established, but unconnected with the Corporation, and this declaration should be made by him.

Address of Declarant..............................

....

I hereby declare that I have explained the contents of the statement to the Proposer/ Life Assured in (language) .... and that I have read out to the Proposer/Life Assured the answers to the questions dictated by the proposer/ Life Assured and that the Proposer/Life Assured has a fixed his thumb impression to the statement after fully understanding the contents thereof.

..............................(*Signature*)

If the life assured/to be assured is different from the proposer, the questions are to be answered in respect of the life assured/to be assured.

Contd....

LIFE INSURANCE CORPORATION OF INDIA

SHORT MEDICAL REPORT

Instructions: (*i*) Please have this report completed by an authorised medical examiner of the Corporation.

(*ii*) The fee of ` 8/- for this report is to be paid to the medical examiner by the policyholder/proposer.

On the life of Shri/smt./Ku...

who was introduced by Shri/smt./Ku...

1. (*a*) Is the person to be examined known to you (*i*) personally or (*ii*) professionally? .. .. (*a*) ....
   (*b*) Are you satisfied about his identity? .. .. (*b*) ....
   (*c*) Describe personal marks or peculiarities by which we may be identified. .. .. (*c*) ....
   (*d*) Is the general appearance of the applicant healthy? .. (*d*) ....
   (*e*) Are there any physical defects or deformities? .. (*e*) ....

2. Are the breath sounds normal over whole of the chest?

3. (*a*) State the character of heart's action. .. .. (*a*) ....
   (*b*) Are its sounds and rhythm regular and normal? .. (*b*) ....
   (*c*) Are there any indications of disease of heart or blood Vessels? .. .. (*c*) ....

4. Do you find any evidence of the past or present disease of the following:
   (Give details where necessary)
   (*a*) Brain or the nervous system? .. .. .. (*a*) ....
   (*b*) Respiratory System? .. .. .. (*b*) ....
   (*c*) Digestive organs, missing teeth or Pyorrhea? .. (*c*) ....
   (*d*) Genito-urinary tract, syphilis, gonorrhea or stricture? (*d*) ....

Contd....

(*e*) Hernia or Hydrocele? .. .. .. (*e*)......................................

(*f*) Eye, ear or throat? .. .. (*f*)......................................

---

5. Height..............................cms. 6. Wt..................................Kgs.

7. Chest (over nipples) stripped 8. Abdomen..........................cms.

On complete expiration........................cms.

On full inspiration..............................cms.

N.B: If the systolic reading is. 140 mm. Hg. or over, or the 5th phase diastolic reading is 90 mm. Hg. or over, a second reading should be taken in a supine position after 10 minutes.

---

11. For Female Applicants.

(*a*) Is there any evidence of pregnancy? .. .. (*a*)......................................

(*b*) Does your examination show any disease of the breast or of the uterus? .. .. (*b*)......................................

---

12. Do you consider the life to be first Class? If not state reasons for your opinion .. ..

I hereby certify that I have this day examined the above life to be Assured personally, in private and have recorded in my own hand the true and correct findings. I declare I am no related to the party.

Dated..on the..day of...197

....

Signature of the Life Assured/Life to be Assured. *Signature of the Life Assured/Life to be Assured.*

(*N.B.* –The Medical Examiner should see that the applicant signs in his presence).

PARTICULARS OF THE MEDICAL EXAMINER

Appointed by the Corporation or not.. Medical Degree and name of the University..

....

Medical Examiner's Code No.................................. Year in which degree obtained..

(allotted by the Corporation)

Name and Address (IN BLOCK LETTERS)..

....

....

PART THREE
MARINE INSURANCE

19

NATURE OF MARINE INSURANCE CONTRACT

Definition

Marine insurance has been defined as a contract between insurer and insured whereby the insurer undertakes to indemnify the insured in a manner and to the interest thereby agreed, against marine losses incident to marine adventure.

Section 2(13)A of the Insurance Act 1938 defines marine insurance as follows:

"Marine insurance business" means the business of effecting contracts of insurance upon vessels of any description, including cargoes, freights and other interests which may be legally insured in or in relation to such vessels, cargoes and freights, goods, wares, merchandise and property of whatever description insured for any transit by land or water or both, and whether or not including warehouse risks or similar risks in addition or as incidental to such transit and includes any other risks customarily included among the risks insured against in marine insurance policies.

SUBJECT MATTER OF MARINE INSURANCE

Hull insurance , Cargo Insurance, Freights Insurance and liability Insurance are the subject matter of Marine Insurance :

A. HULL INSURANCE

Insurance of vessel and its equipments are included under hull insurance. There are a number of classification of vessels such as ocean steamers, sailing vessels, builders, risks fleet policies and so on. It is concerned with the insurance of hull and machinery of ocean-going and other vessels like barges, tankers, fishing and sailing vessels.

Insurance of construction risks or builder's risks deal with hull insurance for vessels when they are under construction. A recent development in hull insurance has been the growth of insurance of offshore oil/gas exploration and production units as well as connected construction risks.

It is covered with specialised class of business particularly for Fishing Vessels, Trawler's, Dredgers, Inland and Sailing Vessels are available.

The subject matter of hull insurance is the vessel or ship. There are many types of designs of ships. Most of them are constructed of steel and welded and are capable of sailing on the sea in ballast or with cargo.

The ship is to be measured with GRT (Gross Register Tonnage) and NRT (Net Register Tonnage). GRT is calculated by dividing the volume in cubic feet of the ship's hull below the tonnage dock, plus all spaces above the deck with permanent means of closing. NRT is the gross tonnage less certain spaces for machinery, crew accomondation ballast spaces and is intended to encompass only those spaces used for carriage of cargo. DWT (Dead Weight Tonnage) means the capacity in tons of the cargo required to load a ship to her loadline level.

Subdivision of Hull Insurance

The Hull Insurance is further Subdivision into –

(*a*) General Cargo vessels

(*b*) Dry Bulk Carriers

(*c*) Liquid Bulk Carriers

(*d*) Passenger Vessels

(*e*) Other Vessels.

These can be further divided into ocean going and coastal tonnage. Ocean going general cargo vessels is usually in the 5000 to 15000 GRT range, coasters are smaller in size and one engaged in the carriage of bulk cargoes. Coastal tonnage does not withstand the same strains as ocean going vessels.

General Cargo Vessel

The general cargo vessels may be container ships, large carriers (LASH – Lighter Abroad Ship)

Ro-Ro (Roll on Roll off) vessels, Refers (Refrigerated Vessels General Cargo) Many general cargo vessels are built for specific purpose Vessels may be subdivided into Liners and Tramps.

Liners loads at an advertised berth and runs to an advertised schedule calling can route at a varying number of ports according to the particular service. It tries to maintain Time schedule although there are heavy risk of seas. It requires huge capital investment. Liners are always fit and well maintained at all times. Liners have high standard of officers and crew.

Tramp carries cargo whenever and wherever it is available. Mostly bulk cargo very often are seasonal in character for which she is usually chartered. Vessels are built to comply with the particular needs of the owner's trade.

Dry Bulk Carriers

Dry Bulk Carriers are specially constructed vessels in the size range of thousands GRT for coasters and 70,000 GRT for ocean going tonnage. The main bulk cargoes carried are iron ore, coal, grain bauxite and phosphate .The main features of these vessels are the single weather deck and large holds with wide hatches to facilitate loading and discharge by mechanical means. Most bulk carriers have sloping upper wing tanks to assist in trimning the cargo and thus produce a safer slow.

Nature of cargo, routs conversation into bulk cargoes and stability are the main considerations for underwriting.

Liquid Bulk Carriers

Tankers are strongly constructed to carry bulk liquid. The tankers have using tanks which do not extend across the breadth of the tanker. Due to the live nature of the liquids cargo, tankers sustain heavier damage than other cargo ships. Tanker has shorter life due to corrosive effect. There is considerable danger of fire and explosion. Before a tanker is allowed to enter a dry dock for repairs, a gas free certificate is required. The risk of pollution following a casualty makes salvage operation more difficult and expensive.

The tankers may be VLCC (Very Large Crude Carrier) and ULCC (Ultra Large Crude Carrier)

LASH and Sea Bee vessels are mother ships which carry floating containers in the form of barges up to 1000 tonnes displacement. A RO- RO (Roll on Roll off) vessel is one having facility for shipping lorries, trailers, etc. without need for cranes.

Passenger Vessels

There are cruise vessels or passenger liners which sail on voyages to distant areas of scenically beautiful but rocky or shallow coasts or near the icy waters of the Arctic and Antarctic. They possess modern navigational systems.

Other Vessels

There are other types of vessels such as fishing vessels, offshore oil vessels and others.

Fishing Vessels

Fishing vessels bulk of steel and fiberglass (GRP) are much more prevalent. Geographical/physical features of the area of operations vary from comparatively sheltered waters of inshore fishing to the full rigurs of the open seas with exposure to gales, heavy seas fog ice and snow. The vessels may be classed or unclassed. Classed vessels are reacognised by Classification Society, and may possess class granted by it. Unclassed vessels are surveyed out of water and all machinaries are thoroughly examined. There are special tariff for fishing vessel in India. The nature, type, age, geographical limits, etc. are examined for insurance cover and rating.

Offshore Oil Vessels

The offshore oil vessels are used for explanation or for commercial production of oil from the ocean beds. The comprehensive cover given covers not only the operations at site but also the transporter of plant and equipment to the drilling sales which may be hundred of kilometers away in mid sea. These vessels are veritable artificial islands where the risks are present in one form or another.

The jack up units are self-elevating platform which can float freely with legs retracted by a jacking system for movements in tow. Casualties may occur during tows or whilst jacking up or down. The sem-submersible or culumn established drilling platform can be bottom supported and or free floating. They can operate is deeper water and usually have multi anchoring system employing up to 10 separate lines. Another ship shape unit is basically a modified conventional ships, with a slot for drilling through, located in the centre. It is capable of much deeper water drilling. Again another fixed structure is usually a platform construction on four or more piled legs. The platforms are stationary.

Hull and Machinery Insurance

The policy covers the hull, machinery and equipment and stores, etc. on board but does not cover cargo. The insurance cover, the requirements of the individual ship owner and protects him against partialy loss, total loss, ship's proportion of general average and salvage charges, sue and labour expenses and ship owner's liability towards other vessels arising from collisions.

Hull Underwriting

Hull underwriting requires the following information to assure the risk

Type, construction, builders, age, tonnage, demension, equipment, propulsion machines, engine, fire extinguisher; classification society, merchant shipping act, warranties, navigation physical and moral hazerd.

B. CARGO INSURANCE

Cargo insurance is covered under risk policy or floating policies. The cargo may be of any description, for example wares, merchandise, property, goods and so on. Transit clause of ICC (A), (B),and (C) describes the duration of the risk as attaching from the time the goods leave the warehouse or other place of storage at the placement in the policy for commencement of transit. The risk then continues during the ordinary course of transit to terminate on delivery.

Cargo insurance has coverage of loss or damage caused by war, civil war, revolution, rebellion, insurrection or civil strife or any hostile act, capture, seizure, arrest, restraint detainment, general average and salvage charges, strikes, riots, etc.

Trade coverage covers the insurance needs of various type of cargoes of general nature. A number of commodities and foodstuff provide for particular hazards. Institute of London Underwriters (ILU) have adopted uniform trade practices. Which are followed by other insurers for insurance of cocoa, coffee, cotton, fats oil knots, hids, skins, leather, metal, oil seeds, sugar, tea ans so on are assured under standred policy. There are separate insurance of coal. Jute, Rubber, tanker, bulk oil , frozen products.

Risks Covered :

All risks clause covers inland Transit risks also for the cargo insurance. Loss or damage are covered if the risks occurred due to:

fire
lightning
explosion
Riot, strikes, malicious damage
impact by any rail /road vehicle
storm, cyclone flood, inundation
earth-quake, burglary
accidental physical loss or damage.

A special declaration policy (SDP) is a form of floating policy issued to insured who have a large turnover with many and frequent despatches of goods anywhere within the country by rail or road or in water warp.

C. FREIGHT INSURANCE

Freight is to be payable for the carriage of cargoes or if the vessel, is chartered, the money to be paid for the use of the vessel. The carriage is unable to earn freight if the goods or properties (cargoes) are not safely transported.

Pre-paid freight payable in advance is at the risks of the cargo owner who includes it in the value of the goods insured under a cargo policy. But freight payable only on delivery of the goods at the destination is at the risk of the shipowner who has insurable interest in it and therefore can insure it. The disbursement warranty of the ITC (Hulls) allows the ship owner to effect in conjugation with 12 months insurance on the ship's hulls and machinery etc. Time insurance on freight and/or charters freight and/or anticipated freight. When the ship is lost, it also results in loss of her profit earring capacity and the termination of freight contracts already entred into. A certains amount of freight is insured by a ship owner for a period of 12 months under the Institute Time Clauses (freight). Additional policies are insured on a voyage basis. The freight at risk on any voyage exceeds the amount of insured for time. The Institute Voyage Clauses (freight) are then used.

Time charter hire is payable to the ship owner for the use of his ship for carriage of goods for a specific period of time. If any events occur, such as breakdown of machinery damage to the vessel etc. which prevents the operation of the vessel for more than 24 consecutive hours, of the payment hire shall cease until the ship become operational. This freight is at the risk of the shipowner.

Freight Standard Clauses

The standard clauses in use are Institute Time Clauses-Freight (1.10.83) and Institute Voyage Clause-Freight (1.10.83). Freight is insurable on a time basis. Shipowners usually insure a certain amount on freight for a power of 12 months. Additional policies on voyage basis are issued if the freight at risk on any one voyage exceeds the amount insured for time.

A loss of freight to the carrier who may be a shipowner or a character—can only arise when the freight is payable at destination and the carrier runs the risks of not receiving it by reason of loss of ship and/or loss or damage to cargo.

No such loss can arise to the shipowner where freight in advanced of prepaid and is not repayable if the ship and/or cargo is lost because in such cases the freight is usually merged with the value of the cargo and any claim would be made under the policy covering cargo. The freight may be prepaid freight ; freight payable on ship or cargo lost or not lost, freight payable on delivery, lump sum freight, time charter hire. Prepaid freight is not refundable in case of non-delivery of the goods and hence it is not at risk of shipowner.

D. LIABILITY INSURANCE

The Marine Insurance policy may include liability hazards such as collision or running down. Insurance can also be taken for the expenses involved in non-compliance of rules and regulations without any intention to deceive. It should be clear here that the marine perils insurance covers not only the "ocean but also the inland perils", The parils to be included in the policy are clearly defined and the insurer will be liable only for the insured perils.

Third Party Liability covers third party liability which insurer undertakes to indemnify the insured in respect of

(*i*) legal liability for accidental loss or damage to property of other persons, and

(*ii*) legal liability for fatal or non-fatal injury to the third party directly consequent upon or solely due to erection operations

There will be liability for damage where negligence is shown or where liability has been assumed under contact. To succeed in an action in tort, the claimant plaintiff has the onus of showing one that the loss resulted from the defendent's negligence. Negligence has been defined as doing something which ought either to be done in a different way or not at all or omitting to do something which ought to be done.

The liability must arise as the result of tort committed by the insured vessel. The clause does not extend to indemnify the assured against payments which arose out of contractual relationship and not in consequence of actionable fault committed by the insured vessel.

Form of Liability

There are two type of liabilities : Cross Liabilities and Single Liabilities

Cross Liability : where both vessels are to blame, then unless the liability of one or both vessels become limited by law, the indemnity shall be calculated on the principle of cross liability.

When the respective owners had been compelled to pay each other such proposition of each other's damages as has been properly allowed.

Exclusions : There is no liability under the clause is respect of :

(*i*) removal or disposal of obstructions wrecks, cargoes.

(*ii*) any real or personal property

(*iii*) cargo or other property

(*iv*) loss of life, personal injury or illness

(*v*) pollution or contamination of any real or personal property.

Single Liability :

Single liability is only a liability on the parts of the vessel under the lesser damages to that with the greater. When both vessels are to blame in a collisions, the court decides the legal liability by

– assessing the degree of fault

– apportioning the liability according to the degree of fault, and

– deciding settlement on a single liability basis which is determined by the difference between the two liabilities

Limitation Of Liability

The right to limit liability is based on the international convention relating to the limitation of liability of owners of Sea-going ship, 1957. India has incompleted it in part X A of the Merchant shipping act 1958. Under the 3/4 the collision liability of clause the principle of "Cross Liability" will not apply were either ship or both ships limit liability. In such instances, the indemnity under clause No.8 will be " Single Liability" principle upon which the case is adjustised at law between the respected owners.

DOCUMENT OF MARINE INSURANCE

Marine Insurance underwriting requires a knowledge of how trade (domestic and international) is conducted. These trades are generally conducted through agents,brokers and intermediaris. They are commission agents, warehouse keepers, shipping agents, freight forwarding agents and Stevedores,. Commission agents sell goods on behalf of the principal for which they receive a commission. Brokers are agents, who for a commission negotiate sale or purchase of goods on behalf of other parties. They do not acquire title to the goods and do not assume possession of goods. Warehouse keepers receive the goods for the purpose of storage in their warehouses. Shipping agents have special arrangements with the ship companies. They formulate the various shipping documents arrange for the insurance of goods and pass the custom entry. Freight forwarding agents make special arrangements with the transport authorities. They collect numerous packages from different traders and make up large consignment for which they obtain special rates. Stevedores are contractors appointed by shipping companies for leading and discharging cargoes. They plan, arrange equipment receive cargo from vessels bringing import cargo. Some specific documents such as open covers and Marine Policy should be properly understood for Marine Insurance.

Open Cover

Open cover is an agreement, binding in honour where by, the insures undertake to insure all shipments declared by the insured and the assured to declare each and every shipment which comes within the scope of the open cover. Premium is payable on each declaration against which specific stamped certificate/policy in issued.

Advantages

The advantage of the open cover is automatic and continuous insurance. Once arranged the insured is granted protection on the agreed basis for all shipment subject to declaration of full shipping, details. The client is relieved of the necessity to negotiate the insurance of every shipment individually. The premium rates are agreed at inception and this assist the insured to identity his cost of insurance right at the outset.

However, for legal purpose open cover is treated like a cover note. It is not a policy and therefore, is not stamped. The basis of valuation is the prime cost of the goods plus expenses to shipping, freight for which the assured is liable and cost of insurance plus ten per cent. The assured is bound to declare each and every shipment as they go forward and obtain a certificate of insurance from the insurer as required either for individual shipment or for group of shipment. Section 23 of the Act states " A contract of marine insurance is deemed to be concluded when the proposal of the insured is accepted by the insurer whether the policy is issued or not reference may be made to the ship, covering note or other memorandum.

Marine Policy

Section 24 of the Marine Insurance Act 1963 States "A contact of marine insurance shall not be admitted in evidence unless it is embodied in a Marine Policy in accordance with this Act. The policy may be executed and issued either at the time when the contract is concluded or afterwards. Section 25 of the Act states that the policy must specific the name of the assurred, or of some person who effect the insurance on his behalf; the subject-matter insured and the risk insured against the voyage or period of time or both as the case may be, covered by the insurance; the sum or sums insured the name or names of the insurer or insurers.

Policy Schedule

The standard form of the Marine Policy has a schedule showing following details:

(*i*) Policy number, place and date of issue

(*ii*) Name of assured with address where the transaction is financed by a Bank, the name of the Bank.

(*iii*) Name of the vessel carrying the insured cargo.
(*iv*) Description of the voyage/transit.
(*v*) The subject-matter insured and the classification packing.
(*vi*) Risks covered, risk excluded, duration other term and conditions.

Surveyor's Note

The Surveyor's note contains the

(*i*) Name and address of the surveyor who may be contacted at destination point to conduct a survey on damaged goods insured under the policy and issue a surveyor report.

(*ii*) Name and Address of the claims Setting Office at destination which may be contacted so that the claim could be serviced processed on ultimately settled on behalf of the insurer concerned.

PROCEDURE TO EFFECT MARINE INSURANCE

The proposer may approach to the insurer directly or through an agent or broker. Generally, the proposal is made through brokers because they are well known of the insurance practices. The broker prepares a slip where material information are recorded. This slip is presented to the insurer who will signify his acceptance by initialling the slip and indicating the sum they are prepared to· accept. The risk may commence from the date of acceptance or from at any other date which is mutually agreed.

Sometimes, the insurer asks additional information from the broker. When the additional information called closing slip has been accepted by the insurer he may issue policy. Before issuing the policy, open cover is issued to the insured, which becomes inoperative as soon as policy is issued. The document containing the term of the contract is called policy. The assured cannot lagally make any claim over the underwriter if the loss occurs before a final policy is issued. The 'open cover' or 'slip' is not legally binding on the insurers. In practice, however, the insurer pays the amount of claims even before the issue of policies. Insurers in marine insurance generally called 'underwriters'

ELEMENTS OF MARINE INSURANCE CONTRACT

The marine insurance has the following essential features which are also called fundamental principles of marine insurance, (1) Features of General Contract, (2) Insurable Interest, (3) Utmost Good Faith, (4) Doctrine of Indemnity, (5) Subrogation, (6) Warranties, (7) Proximate cause, (8) Assignment and nomination of the policy. (9) Return of premium.

1. FEATURES OF GENERAL CONTRACT

(*a*) Proposal

The broker will prepare a slip upon receipt of instructions to insure from shipowner, merchant or other proposers. Proposal forms, so common in other branches of insurances, are unknown in the marine insurance and only the 'slip' so called 'the original slip' is used for the proposal. The original slip is accompanied with other material information which the broker deems necessary for the purpose. The brokers are expert and well versed in marine insurance law and practice. The various kinds of marine proposals are altogether too diverse, so elaborate rating schedules are not possible and the proposals are considered on individual merits.

(*b*) Acceptance

The original slip is presented to the Lloyd's Underwriters or other insurers or to the Lead of the insures, who initial the slip and the proposal is formally accepted. But the contract cannot be legally enforced until a policy is issued. The slip is an evidence that the underwriter has accepted an insurance and that he has agreed subsequently to sign a policy on the terms and conditions indicated on the slip. If the underwriter should refuse to issue or sign a policy, he could not legally be forced to do so.

(*c*) Consideration

The premium is determined on assessment of the proposal and is paid at the time of the contract. The premium is called consideration to the contract.

(*d*) Issue of Policy

Having effected the insurance, the broker will now send his client a cover note advising the terms and conditions, on which the· insurance has been placed. The broker's cover note is merely an insurance memorandum and naturally has no value in enforcing the contract with the underwrites. The policy is prepared, stamped and signed without delay and it will be the legal evidence of the contract. However, after issue of the policy the court has power to order the rectification of the policy to express the intention of the parties to the contract as evidenced by the terms of the slip.

2. INSURABLE INTEREST

Section 7, 8 and 9 to 16 provide for insurable interest. An insured person will have insurable interest in the subject-matter where he stands in any legal or equitable relation to the subject-matter in such a way that he may benefit by the safety or due arrival of insurable property or may be prejudiced by its loss, or by damage thereto or by the detention thereof or may incur liability in respect thereof. Since marine insurance is frequently effected before the commercial transactions to which they apply are formally completed it is not essential for the assured to have an insurable interest at the time of effecting insurance, though he should have an expectation of acquiring such an interest. If he fails to acquire insurable interest in due course, he does not become entitled to indemnification. Since the ownership and other interest of the subject matter often change from hands to hands, the requirement of the insurable interest to be present only at the time of loss makes a marine insurance policy freely assignable.

Exceptions

There are two exceptions of the rule in marine insurance.

1. Lost or Not Lost

A person can also purchase policy in the subject-matter in which it was known whether the matters were lost not lost. In such cues the assured and the underwriter are ignorant about the safety or otherwise of the goods and complete reliance was placed on the principle of Good Faith. The policy terminated if anyone of the two parties was aware of the fact of loss. In this case, therefore, the insurable interest may not be present at the time of contract because the subject-matter would have been lost.

2. P.P.I. Policies

The subject-matter can be insured in the usual manner by P.P.I. (Policy Proof of Interest), *i.e.*, interest proof policies. It means that in the event of claim underwriters may dispense with all proof of insurable interest. In this case if the underwriter does not pay the claims, it cannot be enforced in any court of law because P.P.I. policies are equally void and unenforceable. But the underwriters are generally adhering on the terms and pay the amount of claim.

The insurable interest in marine insurance can be of the following forms:

I. According to Ownership

The owner has insurable interest up to the full value of the subject-matter. The owners are of different types according to the subject-matter.

(*a*) In Case of Ships

The ship-owner or any person who has purchased it on charter-basis can insure the ship up to its full price.

(*b*) In Case of Cargo

The cargo-owner can purchase policy up to the full price of the cargo. If he has paid the freight in advance, he can take the policy for the full price of the goods plus amount of freight plus the expense of insurance.

(*c*) In Case of Freight

The receiver of the freight can insure up to the amount of freight to be received by him.

II. Insurable Interest in Re-insurance

The underwriter under a contract of marine insurance has an insurable interest in his risk, and may re-insure in respect of it.

III. Insurable Interest in other Cases

In this case all those underwriters are included who have insurable interest in the salary and own liabilities. For example, the master or any member of the crew of a ship has insurable interest in respect of his wages. The lender of money on bottomry or respondentia has insurable interest in respect of the loan.

3. UTMOST GOOD FAITH

Section 19, 20, 21 and 22 of the Marine Insurance Act 1963 explained doctrine of utmost good faith. The doctrine of caveat emptor (let the buyer beware) applies to commercial contracts, but insurance contracts are based upon the legal principle of uberrimae fides (utmost good faith). If this is not observed by either of the parties, the contract can be avoided by the other party.

The duty of the utmost good faith applies also to the insurer. He may not urge the proposer to effect an insurance which he knows is not legal or has run off safely. But the duty of disclosure of material facts rests highly on the insured because he is aware of the material common in other branches of insurance are not used in the marine insurance. Ships and cargoes proposed for insurance may be thousands of miles away, and surveys on underwriters' behalf are usually impracticable. The assured, therefore, must disclose all the material information which may influence the decision of the contract. Any non-disclosure of a material fact enables the underwriter to avoid the contract, irrespective of whether the non-disclosure was intentional or inadvertent. The assured is expected to know every circumstance which in the ordinary course of business ought to be known by him. He cannot rely on his own inefficiency or neglect.

The duty of the disclosure of all material facts falls even more heavily on the broker. He must disclose every material fact which the assured ought to disclose and also every material fact which he knows. The broker is expected to know or inquire from the assured all the material facts. Failure in this respect entitles the underwriter to avoid the policy and if negligence can be held against the broker, he may be liable for damages to his client for breach of contract. The contract shall be *ab initio* if the element of fraud exists.

Exception

In the following circumstances, the doctrine of good faith may not be adhered to:

(*i*) Facts of common knowledge.

(*ii*) Facts which are known should be known to the insurer.

(*iii*) Facts which are not required by the insurers.

(*iv*) Facts which the insurer ought reasonably to have in ferred from the details given to him.

(*v*) Facts of public knowledge.

4. DOCTRINE OF INDEMNITY

Under Section 3 of the Act at is provided 'A contact of marine insurance is an agreement whereby the insurer undertakes to indemmify the assured in the manner and the extentagreed upon. The contract of marine insurance is of indemnity. Under no circumstances an insured is allowed to make a profit out of a claim. In the absence of the principle of indemnity it was possible to make a profit. The insurer agrees to indemnify the assured only in the manner and only to the extent agreed upon. Marine insurance fails to provide complete indemnity due to large and varied nature of the marine voyage. The basis of indemnity is always a cash basis as underwriter cannot replace the lost ship and cargoes and the basis of indemnification is the value of the subject-matter. This value may be either the insured or insurable value. If the value of the subject matter is determined at the time of taking the policy, it is called 'Insured Value'. When loss arises the indemnity will be measured in the proportion that the assured sum bears to the insured value. In fixing the insured value, the cost of transportation and anticipated profits are added to original value so that in case of loss the insured can recover not only the cost of goods or properties but a certain percentage of profit also. The insured value is called agreed value because it has been agreed between the insurer and the insured at the time of contract and is regarded as sacrosanct and binding on both parties to the contract. In marine insurance, it has been customary for the insurer and the assured to agree on the value of the insured subject-matter at the time of proposal. Having, agreed of the value or basis of valuation, neither party to the contract can raise objection after loss on the ground that the value is too high or too low unless it appears that a fraudulent evaluation has been imposed on either party. Insured value is not justified in fire insurance due to moral hazard as the property remains within the approach of the assured, while the subject-matter is movable from one place to another in case of marine insurance and the assured value is fully justified there. Moreover, in marine insurance, the assured value removes all complications of valuation at the time of loss.

Technically speaking the doctrine of indemnity applies where the value of subject-matter is determined at the time of loss. In other words, where the market price of the loss is paid, this doctrine has been precisely applied. Where the value for the goods has not been fixed in the beginning but is left to be determined ai the time of loss, the measurement is based on the insurable value of the goods. However, in marine insurance insurable value is not common because no profit is allowed in estimating the insurable value. Again if the insurable value happens to be more than the assured sum, the assured would be proportionately uninsured. On the other hand, if it is lower than the assured sum, the underwriter would be liable for a return of premium of the difference.

Exceptions

There are two exceptions of the doctrine of indemnity in marine insurance.

1. Profits Allowed

Actually the doctrine says that the market price of the loss should be indemnified and no profit should be permitted, but in marine insurance a certain profit margin is also permitted.

2. Insured Value

The doctrine of indemnity is based on the insurable value, whereas the marine insurance is mostly based on insured value. The purpose of the valuation is to predetermine the worth of insured.

5. DOCTRINE OF SUBROGATION

Section 79 of the Act explains doctrine of subrogation. The aim of doctrine of subrogation is that the insured should not get more than the actual loss or damage. After payment of the loss, the insurer gets the light to receive compensation or any sum from the third party from whom the assured is legally liable to get the amount of compensation. The main characteristics of subrogation are as follows:

1. The insurer subrogates all the remedies rights and liabilities of the insured alter payment of the compensation.
2. The insurer has right to pay the amount of loss after reducing the sum received by the insured from the third party. But in marine insurance the right of subrogation arises only after payment has been made, and it is not customary as in fire and accident insurance, to alter this by means of a condition to provide for the exercise of subrogation rights before payment of a claim. At the same time the right of subrogation must be distinguished from abandonment. If property is abandoned to a marine insurer, he is entitled to whatever remains to the property irrespective of value of subrogation.
3. After indemnification, the insurer gets all the rights of the insured on the third parties, but insurer cannot file suit in his own name. Therefore, the insured must assist the insurer for receiving money from the third party. If the insured is revoking from filing suit against the third party, the insurer can receive the amount of compensation from the insured. Section 80 of the Act deals with the right of contribution between two or more insurers where there is over insurances by double insurance . It is corollary of principle indermity

6. WARRANTIES

A warranty is that by which the assured undertakes that some particular thing shall or shall not be done, or that some conditions shall be fulfilled or whereby he affirms or negatives the existence of a particular state of facts. Warranties are the statement according to which insured person promises to do or not to do a particular thing or to fulfil or not to fulfil a certain condition. It is not merely a condition but statement of fact. Warranties are more vigorously insisted upon than the conditions because the contract comes to an end if a warranty is broken whether the warranty was material or not. In case of condition or representation the contract comes to end only when these were material or important. Warranties are of two types:

(1) Express Warranties, and (2) Implied Warranties.

1. Express Warranties

Express warranties are those warranties which are expressly included or incorporated in the policy by reference.

2. Implied Warranties

These are not mentioned in the policy at all but are tacitly understood by the parties to the contract and are as fully binding as express warranties.

Warranties can also be classified as (1) Affirmative, and (2) Promissory. Affirmative warranty is the promise which insured gives to exist or not to exist certain facts. Promissory warranty is the promise in which insured promises that he will do or not do a certain thing up to the period of policy.

In marine insurance, implied warranties are very important. These are:

1. Seaworthiness of Ship.
2. Legality of venture.
3. Non-deviation.

All these warranties must be literally, complied with as otherwise the underwriter may avoid all liabilities as from the date of the breach. However, there are two exceptions to this rule when a breach of warranty does not affect the underwriter's liability: (1) Where owing to a change of circumstances the warranty is no longer applicable. (2) Where compliance would be unlawful owing to the enactment of subsequent law.

1. Seaworthiness of ship

The warranty implies that the ship should be seaworthy at the commencement of the voyage, or if the voyage is carried out in stages at the commencement of each stage. This warranty implies only to voyage policies, though such policies may be of ship, cargo, freight or any other interest. There is no implied warranty of seaworthiness in time policies. A ship is seaworthy when the ship is suitably constructed, properly equipped, officered and manned, sufficiently fuelled and provisioned, documented and capable of withstanding the ordinary strain and stress of the voyage.

The seaworthiness will be more clear from the following points:

1. The standard to judge the seaworthiness is not fixed. It is a relative term and may vary with any particular vessel at different periods of the same voyage. A ship may be perfectly seaworthy for Trans-ocean voyage. A ship may be suitable for summer but may not be suitable for winter. There may be different standard for different ocean, for different cargo, for different destination and so on.
2. Seaworthiness does not depend merely on the condition of the ship, but it includes the suitability and adequacy of her equipment, adequacy and experience of the officers and crew.
3. At the commencement of journey, the ship must be capable of withstanding the ordinary strain and stress of the sea.
4. Seaworthiness also includes "Cargo-Worthiness". It means the ship must be reasonably fit and suitable to carry the kind of cargo insured. It should be noted that the warranty of seaworthiness does not apply to cargo. It applies to the vessel only. There is no warranty that the cargo should be seaworthy. It cannot be expected from the cargo-owner to be well-versed in the matter of shipping and overseas trade. So, it is admitted in seaworthiness clause that the cargo would be seaworthy of the vessel and would not be raised as defence to any claim for loss by insured perils.

It should be noted that the ship should be seaworthy at the port of commencement of voyage or at the different stages if voyage is to be completed in stages.

2. Legality of Venture

This warranty implies that the adventure insured shall be lawful and that so far as the assured can control the matter it shall be carried out in a lawful manner of the country. Violation of foreign laws does not necessarily involve breach of the warranty. There is no implied warranty as to the nationality of a ship. The implied warranty of legality applies total policies, voyage or time. Marine policies cannot be applied to protect illegal voyages or adventure. The assured can have no right to claim a loss if the venture was illegal. The example of illegal venture may be trading with an enemy, violating national laws, smuggling, breach of blockade and similar ventures prohibited by law.

Illegality must not be confused with the illegal conduct of the third party *e.g.*, barratry, theft, pirates, rovers. The waiver of this warranty is not permitted as it is against public policy.

3. Other Implied Warranties

There are other warranties which must be complied in marine insurance.

(*a*) No Change in Voyage

When the destination of voyage is changed intentionally after the beginning of the risk, this is called change in voyage. In absence of any warranty contrary to this one, the insurer quits his responsibility at the time of change in voyage. The time of change of voyage is determined when there is determination or intention to change the voyage.

(*b*) No Delay in Voyage

This warranty applies only to voyage policies. There should not be delay in starting of voyage and laziness or delay during the course of journey. This is implied condition that venture must start within the reasonable time. Moreover, the insured venture must be despatched within the reasonable time. If this warranty is not complied, the insurer may avoid the contract in absence of any legal reason.

(*c*) Non deviation

The liability of the insurer ends in deviation of journey. Deviation means removal from the common route or given path. When the ship deviates from the fixed passage without any legal reason, the insurer quits his responsibility. This would be immaterial that the ship returned to her original route before loss. The insurer can quit his responsibility only when there is actual deviation and not mere intention to deviation.

Exceptions

There are following exceptions of delay and deviation warranties:

1. Deviation or delay is authorised according to a particular warranty of the policy.
2. When the delay or deviation was beyond the reasonable approach of the master or crew.
3. The deviation or delay is exempted for the safety of ship or insured matter or human lives.
4. Deviation or delay was due to barratry.

7. PROXIMATE CAUSE

According to Section 55 (i) Marine Insurance Act, 'Subject to the provisions of the Act and unless the policy otherwise provides the insurer is liable for any loss proximately caused by a peril insured against, but subject to as aforesaid he is not liable for any loss which is not proximately caused by a peril insured against.' Section 55 (2) enumerats the losses which are not payable are (*i*) misconduct of the assured (ii) delay although the delay be caused by a peril insured against (iii) ordinary wear and tear, ordinary leakage and breakage inherent vice or nature of the subject matter insured, or any loss proximately caused by rates or vermin or any injury to machinery not proximately caused by maritime perils

1. The insurer is not liable for any loss attributable to the wilful misconduct of the assured, but, unless the policy otherwise provides, he is liable for any loss proximately caused by a peril insured against.
2. The insurer will not be liable for any loss caused by delay unless otherwise provided.
3. The insurer is not liable for ordinary wear and tear, ordinary leakage and breakage, inherent vice or nature of subject-matter insured, or for any loss proximately caused by rats or vermin, or for any injury to machinery not proximately caused by maritime perils.

Dover says .... "The causa proxima of a loss is the cause of the loss, proximate to the loss, not necessarily in time, but in efficiency. While remote causes may be disregarded in determining the cause of a loss, the doctrine must be interpreted with good sense." So as to uphold and not defeat the intention of the parties to the contract. Thus the proximate cause is the actual cause of the loss. There must be direct and non-intervening cause. The insurer will be liable for any loss proximately caused by peril insured against.

8. ASSIGNMENT

A marine policy is assignable unless it contains terms expressly prohibiting assignment. It may be assigned either before or after loss. A marine policy may be assigned by indorsement thereon or on other customary manner. A marine policy is freely assignable unless assignment is express prohibited. A marine policy is not an incident of sale. So, if there is intention to assign a plicy when intrest passes, there must be an agreement to this effect. Sections 53 of the Marine Insurance Act, 1963 states, Where the assured has parted with or lost his interest in the subject-matter insured and has not, before or at time of so doing, expressly or implidly agreed to assign the policy, any subsequent assignment of the policy is inoperative. 'Section 17 of the Act states, "where the asserted assigns or otherwise parts with his interest in the subject-matter insured, he does not thereby transfer to the assignee his rights under the contracts of insurance.

The feature of return of premium has been already discussed in the portion of life insurance.

HISTORICAL PREVIEW OF MARINE INSURANCE

Marine insurance is the oldest form of insurance. Is Rigveda marine insurance was provided in the form of Risk and Safety insurance Historian traced into the period 900 B.C. when the Rhodian merchant trading in the Mediterranean sea introduced certain maritime customs and practices.

There were problems of maritime financing. This led to "Bottomry" and "Respondentia" loans. Bottomry was a loan raised by the captain of a vessel when money was urgently needed. It was given on the security of vessel. Respondentia was loan on the security of the Cargo. There was an lement of insurance in these transactions.

When goods were thrown into the sea, the loss of goods so scarified was made good by the owner of ship and goods saved. Thus sharing of losses of few by many has given the birth of insurance. This practice spread and is now known as General Average which is part of maritime law.

Marine insurance as practiced today had its crude beginning is the 12th century in Italy from where it spread to England. In the 17th century maritime insurance began to be transacted in the coffee house of the Edward Leoyd and so was Lloyd's of London was born.

The Marine Insurance Act 1906 was passed in the U.K. for first time.

The United Kingdom, the U.S.A., Japan and the Continent of Europe are major international markets. The years following the end of World War II have seen a period of economic nationalism, particularly stimulated by the political independence attained by many countries previously within the colonial empires,. for example, India, Indonesia, the Philippines, East and West Africa, the Arabian Gulf countries. The Middle East countries and others. In such countries indigenous insurance markets have developed, which in several instances, cater almost exclusively to their domestic market and usually depend on the reinsurance facilities. U.K.,USA, Germany and Japan have developed tremendous capacity of reinsurance. Domestic companies are obliged to cede amount in excess of their prescribed retentions to their national reinsurance company, which in turn, arranges reinsurance in the international market.

The marine insurance market in U.K. its major centre in London Lloyd's's Association and other Institute are developing marine insurance internationally.

THE ORGANIZATION OF LLOYD'S

The Corporation of Lloyd's is a corporate entity, financed primarily by subscriptions from underwriting members. The subscription help to provide the premises, administrative staff and services which enable the underwriting members to transact insurance business. The Corporation does not itself accept insurance or assume liability for business transacted by its underwriting members. This premier world marine insurance market had its origin in a small coffee house of Edward Lloyd in Tower Street, London in 1680s. As the coffee house was meeting place for those interested in shipping, it is reasonable to deduce that Lloyd's as a marine insurance market had its beginnings there. Lloyd's Act of 1871 gave Lloyd's a legal status. The Act incorporated the members of Lloyd's and at the same time, it provided for a committee of members to manage the Society's affairs.

For detail study see marketing management of Insurance by proof M.N. Mishra publishing by RSBA, Jaipur.

Lloyd's Act of 1982 established a Council of Llyod's to manage and regulate the Society's affairs. The Council has 28 members of whom 16 are elected from and by the working members of Lloyd's and 8 from and by the external members of Lloyd's. The remaining 4 member (who must not be member of Lloyd's) are appointed by the Governor of the Bank of England. Each year the council elects from amongst its working members a Chairman and two Deputy Chairman of Lloyd's. The council is responsible broadly for the management and superintendence of the affairs of Lloyd's. The underwriting members through their underwriting agents, form groups called "Syndicates". The members are called "Names". Each Syndicate will have an appointed underwriter to accept business on behalf of the members. The members, in most cases, do not take active part in the day to day running of the Syndicate. Although in a Syndicate, the underwriting members transact business on his own behalf and is legally liable in respect of his engagements under Lloyd's policies to the full extent of his means. Much of the non-underwriting work, such as signing of policies and settlement of claims, has been delegated to special departments. Lloyd's Policy Signing Office (L.P.S.O.) checks and executes all Lloyd's policies on behalf of the subscribing underwriters. The policies are prepared by the brokers placing the risk and they lodge the policies, along with relevant "slips" and accounting documents, with L.S.P.O. Also L.S.P.O. initiates the procedure for premium accounting and adjustment to policies. Lloyd's Underwriters Claims and Recoveries office (L.U.C.R.O.) handles the settlement of claims, effecting reconversion from third parties and dealing with settlements in respect of general average and salvage. Lloyd's has also standardised various forms which are used internationally, for example, Lloyd's Standard Form of Salvage Agreement (also called "Lloyd's Open Form") and Lloyd's Average Bond.

Lloyd's Brokers

Insurance brokers may be elected to membership and be authorised to designate themselves as Lloyd's brokers". Insurance brokers, to qualify for election, must satisfy the Committee of Lloyds as regards their intergrity and financial standing. During their continuance as members, they must annually satisfy the Committee as to their solvency. They are also required to satisfy the Committee that they are in a position to bring to Lloyd's reasonable portfolio of business and in their conduct they are expected to conform to the high traditions of Lloyd's.

Underwriting members are to be found at Lloyd's in the underwriting room (usually called "The Room"). The general public are denied access to the Room and Lloyd's underwriters will only transanct business through a recongnised Lloyd's broker. A Lloyd's broker, therefore, is a very responsible person as it is his duty to move amongst the underwriters in the Room, obtaining the best terms possible for his client.

On being requested to place an insurance at Lloyd's, the broker will prepare a "Slip" containing brief details of the risk to be placed. He will then approach underwriters who specialise in that class of business with a view to obtaining one or them as a "Leader" of "Leading Underwriter". Such an underwriter gives a lead by quoting an appropriate rate of premium and accepting a certain percentage or proportion of the risk. The broker will then approach other underwriters until 100% of the insurance is placed.

The broker is subject to the ordinary law of agency and also the law of professional negligence and failure on his part to exercise reasonable care and skill in effecting insurance in accordance with his client's instructions may expose him to an action for damages, if the client is prejudiced by his lapses. The broker has a duty to make full disclosure of all material facts to the insurer and observe the principle of "uberrima fides" in all respects.

Underwriting are directly liable to the assured for claims and returns of premium. They cannot set off premiums not paid to them by the broker. A broker has lien on the policy and may retain it until the assured pays the premium. These particular sections which deal with policies effected through brokers is omitted from our Indian Marine Insurance Act, 1963 because business comes direct to the Companies in India or through ordinary agents.

Lloyd's Agents

By Act of Parliament in 1871 in the U.K. Lloyd's was incorporated and given the power to appoint Agent in other parts of the world, where permitted by the country concerned. Lloyd's Agents are found in most major ports and in many cities of the world. The primary duty of the agents is to keep

Lloyd's information of shipping movements, casualties and other matters of interest to the maritime community. Lloyd's Agents survey damage to ship or cargo and issue Survey Reports for use in claiming against insurers. Moreover, if the policy certificate makes provision of settlement of claims abroad, the Lloyd's Agent adjusts and settles such claims. Their income consists of surveys fees charged on a time and trouble basis for surveys and settling commission for adjustments of claims. Lloyd's Agents are not underwriting agents. Their services are used by all underwriters, companies, world wide as well as by Lloyd's. Usually the Lloyd's Agent is connected with a leading shipping establishment at that place. Lloyd's Agency department is responsible for the appointment and control of Lloyd's Agents and includes a team of Inspectors who regularly visit and closely analyses the Agents and their work.

Lloyd's Underwriters Association

Established in 1909 it is a body comparable to the Institute of London Underwriters. All marine underwriters at Lloyd's are members of the Association. Its purpose is to deal with matters generally affecting the business of marine underwriting at Lloyd's. The Association administers market agreement and maintains liason with ILU and Lloyd's. Insurance Broker's Committee. The Association is managed by a committee the of 15 members elected annually with Chairman and Dy Chairman of Lloyd's as ex-officio members.

MARINE PUBLICATIONS

Objective Of Lloyd's

One of the objects of Lloyd's, as defined in the Lloyd's Act of 1911 is: "collection, publication and diffusion of intelligence and information". Underwriters are assisted by a number of publications which give latest information on matters of vital importance to their business. Details of some of the more important publications are set out below:

Lloyd's Maritime Atlas

The Atlas covers the world with special emphasis on ports and world weather conditions and seasons. Large scale maps of areas of particular interest and a list of ports on a country by country basis are also given.

Lloyd's Register of Shipping

It is an organisation independent of the Corporation of Lloyd's and publishes "Register of Ships"together with other ancillary publications. The "Register of Ships", published annually, contains particulars of all known ocean-going merchant ships of 100 tons gross and upwards. The Register is kept up-to-date by means of cumulative monthly supplements containing changes of name, ownership, flag, tonnage, etc., for all ships together with a cumulative list of new ships not recorded in the Register itself.

Lloyd's Confidential Index

This Index is published twice a year in March and September and gives an alphabetical list of world shipowner and details of vessels owned/managed by them. Listed are names of vessels with former names, year of acquisition by present owner/manager, type, where built, year of build, gross, net and deadweight tonnages, classification society, flag and brief details of trading area. Importantly, also shown is the record of each owner/manager with regard to total losses dating back up to ten years with prior periods is summary form.

Lloyd's Shipping Index

A daily publication, the Index records the movements and latest reports at Lloyd's of almost all merchant vessel with the exception of vessels engaged in coastal trade. Following details of vital importance to marine underwriters are listed :

(*i*) Name of vessel, arranged in alphabetical order with previous name(s), if any.

(*ii*) Type of vessels (merchant vessel carrying general cargo, bulk carriers, tanker, Ro-Ro,etc.)

(*iii*) Owner or manager of vessel (this detail enables the underwriter to check the bonafides and past records of concerned owners/managers as regards their reputation and financial stability).

(*iv*) Flag (this detail throws light on whether the vessel is Registered in a "flag of convenience" country).

(*v*) Registration (Class). This detail will inform the underwriter on whether the vessel is entered in one of the recognised Classification Societies and whether she is holding the Class of that Society.

(*vi*) Gross, net and deadweight tonnages (this will throw light on whether or not the vessel is under-tonnage).

(*vii*) Year of build (this detail will inform whether the vessel is over-age).

(*viii*) Smiling and destinations ports (this detail will identify the voyage of the vessel at the material time).

(*ix*) Brief details of any recent casualty involving the vessel.

Casualty Report Service

Subscribers to this service are advised daily of casualties or occurrences likely to affect underwriters. These advises are reproduced later in the "Lloyd's List" and in the "Weekly Casualty Reports". Such information enables underwriters to estimate claims on major casualties which are yet to materialise on each year's account and provide for them as outstanding claims. The Institute of London Underwriters compiles detailed casualty stastistic of vessels 500 GRT and over and these are published each month.

Lloyd's List

This is a daily publication listing shipping and aviation reports and news, details of marine and non-marine causalities review of freight markets, details of port developments, law reports, conditions of various markets, details of port developments, law reports, conditions of various markets,i.e., money and stock exchange, also currency and exchange rates, technical review of marine and other equipment and other information of a similar nature.

Lloyd's Survey Handbook

First published in 1952, and revised several times since, this is a very useful publication containing a wealth of information for underwriters, loss adjusters, surveyors, shipowners, consignees and others engaged in the survey and treatment of damaged goods.

The book is in five sections alongwith an appendix :

(*i*) Surveys on damaged goods

(*ii*) Origins of damage

(*iii*) Containers

(*iv*) Hazardous cargo

(*v*) Commodities – Their nature and subceptibility to loss or damage, with guideline on possible treatment and reconditioning of damaged cargo.

Appendix::- Weights, Measures, Test Tables, etc.

Lloyd's Law Reports

This is fortnightly publication giving full reports and usually verbatime judgments of High Court shipping and insurance cases and includes leading maritime decisions in other courts.

Other Institutes

The other institute working and marine insurance are

1. The Institute of London Underwriter's
2. The Salvage Association
3. The International Union of Marine insurance
4. The International Maritime Bureau
5. Marine insurance market in India

The Institute of London Underwriter

When the Institute of London underwriter (ILU) was incorporated in 1884 in London there was membership of 20 companies. The Institute now has over 100 insurance companies as members. The Institute holds dominant place among marine underwriting association. It fosters market agreements and in general provides a form for discussions of marine insurance problems on natural or international level. The Institute Cargo, Hull and other clauses which are more or less used internationally are creation of ILU. The objects of the Institute are the advancement of marine insurance and the protection of the interests of companies writing marine business by consultation, and united action. The Institute is responsible for standardisation of marine insurance clauses a matter which is delegated to the Technical and Clauses committee which works also in association with Lloyd's Underwriter's Association and other interested bodies.

The Salvage Association

Incorporated by Royal Charter in U.K. in 1856, it is governed by a committee drawn from Lloyd's and Company underwriters. Its main activities consists of :

(*i*) providing expert advice and supervision of salvage operations with commercial salvors undertaking the work needed on a "no cure no pay" basis, usually under Lloyd's Open Form;

(*ii*) undertaking damage and condition surveys of hull and cargo;

(*iii*) supervision of repairs, towage and voyage approvals;

(*iv*) site and lay-up surveys;

(*v*) oil industry damage surveys; and

(*vi*) preparing the case for insurers when important litigation is in prospect.

The services of the Salvage Association are available to underwriters, shipowners and others on request from the interested parties. It has offices in many important ports and has a world-wide network of correspondents.

The International Union of Marine Insurance

The Union was constituted in Germany in 1874 with founder members who were Swedish, German, Austrian and Russian marine underwriters. In those early days, absence of unity among marine underwriters had been the principle cause of unjustifiable rating concessions to the insuring public, thus putting the business of insurance on unsound lines. The prime objective of the Union are to safeguard and develop marine insurance interests by providing a forum for advancement of constructive propositions for improvement of business and also providing opportunities for making contacts between markets and exchange of information. Britain joined the Union in 1925 and after the difficult years experienced during the World War II, the Union has survived and is now one of the important marine insurance associations in Britain with delegates representing associations from several countries of the world. Tariff Advisory Committee and GIC of India are members of this Union.

International Maritime Bureau

It was realised that the only possible answer to the problem of international maritime frauds lies in a non-governmental body to get to grips with the problem. This was the idea behind the International Chamber of Commerce's International Maritime Bureau, which will give the industry an opportunity to show that it can deal with its own particular problems. I.M.B. started operations in London in 1981 with the overall object to collect and collect information concerning illegal practices and trends and thus seek to do two things:

- by dissemination of information of the intelligence gained to thwart future crimes; and
- by formulation of proposals for improved commercial practices to enable marine cargo transportation to become self protecting.

Four services are offered which have a prevetive function.

(*i*) An education service. Members will be able to seek advice on how to supplement their present training programmes with material on the prevention of maritime fraud.

(*ii*) The provision of general information. This is made available through the publication of a bulletin to allow members to keep abreast of latest developments in various parts of the world.

(*iii*) Advice on whether potential trading partners are known to have previously been involved in fraudulent or suspect practices. Prior knowledge of this could save much anguish and financial loss on numerous occasions.

(*iv*) The final preventive service involves authenticating trading documents for banks and others that may need such assistance.

As well as preventive services, the I.M.B. also offers following remedial ones :

(*a*) To advise and suggest avenuses of procedures to those who suspect they have been defrauded.

(*b*) A " deviation search". A variation of cargo theft occurs when a vessel fails to arrive at its intended port of destination because the cargo has illegally been sold and off-loaded else where. The name of the vessel is frequently changed, at least once during this operation. The purpose of the "deviation search" is to locate the vessel regardless of name change-very often not an easy task. Once located, appropriate action can be taken.

(*c*) In-depth surveys into particular losses. Such surveys enable the I.M.B. To discover the particulars of frauds with a view to arrive at an accurate picture of the over all extent of the problem. If the system currently used in international maritime trade is at fault and requires amendments, surveys for this type will provide the International Chamber of Commerce, through the I.M.B., with the necessary insight.

Amongst a number of good publications, may be mentioned the following :

(*i*) "Indian Shipping & Transport News". This is a daily publication on shipping, ports, Railways, Roadways and Aviation. Apart from shipping news, it publishes also

(*a*) schedule of movement of ships due in Bombay and Nhava Sheva for export loading;

(*b*) movement of ships due for import discharge;

(*c*) ships at berth at docks in Bombay and at Jawaharlal Nehru Port (Nhava Sheva); and

(*d*) container schedules.

(*ii*) "Indian Shipping". Published monthly, this is a journal of the India National Shipowners' Association, Bombay. It contains articles of interest to shipowner and essential statistics relating to ships and shipping.

(*iii*) "The Marine Times". This is a Journal published every alternate Saturday containing articles of interest devoted to maritime trade, ports shipping and allied matters.

Marine Insurance Market in India

Marine insurance business was transacted by the four subsidiaries viz; New India, Oriental, National and United India of the G.I.C. Of India. Marine cargo and hull insurance accounts for roughly 20% of the total gross premium income of the Indian Market. Insurance operations, including marine insurance, are subject to the Insurance Act, 1938, (as amended) and the General Insurance Business (Nationalisation) Act, 1972. Now some private insurers have entered in this field.

The other laws, which directly or indirectly concern marine insurance are :

(*a*) Marine Insurance Act, 1963, which is, more or less, a copy of the Marine Insurance Act, 1906 of the U.K.

(*b*) Carriage of Goods by Sea Act, 1924 (COGSA) which defines the rights responsibilities, etc. of sea carriers, cargo owners and other parties. The Act gives effect to the protocol signed by maritime nations at Brussels in 1924, called the "Haugue Rules". These Rules were improved upon in 1968 by the "Haugue Visby Rules".

(*c*) Carriers Act, 1865 defines a 'Common Carrier' and its responsibilities in respect of cargo carried in trucks etc.

(*d*) Railways Act, 1989 is a comprehensive legislation relating to railway operations, but also includes provisions on rights, responsibilities, etc. of railways in respect of goods carried.

(*e*) Carriage by Air Act.

(*f*) Multi Modal Transport of Goods Act, 1993 provides for rights and liabilities of relative carriers in respect of carriage of goods by more then one mode of transport i.e., land, inland, waterways, sea, etc.

(*g*) Merchant Shipping Act, 1958. This is the base legislation governing all the shipping operations such as ragistration of ships, maintenance of ships, etc.

There are also other laws such as Bill of Lading Act, Foreign Exchange Regulation Act, etc. The Tariff Advisory Committee (TAC), formed under the provisions of the Insurance Act, 1938 is empowered to lay down rules, regulations, rates, terms and conditions for transaction of marine business in India, both Cargo and Hull. There are tariffs for cargo insurance e.g. Tea, coffee, etc, and for hull insurance e.g.fishing sailing, inland vessels, etc. The All India Marine Cargo Tariff has been discontinued from 1.4.1994 but the provisions of the Tariff are applied as guidelines by the companies. A special feature of the Indian market is the screening and approval of vessels carrying cargo. This is an underwriting safeguard. Active measures are taken in the sphere of loss prevention by the Loss Prevention Association of India (LPA) sponsored by GIC and its four subsidiaries. Loss Prevention Association was established in January, 1978. Its main objectives amongst others are :

– to provide advice and expertise on techniques of loss prevention and risk improvement;

– to organise supervision and monitoring facilities at marine terminals for cargo loss minimisation;

Cargo Loss Minimisation Cells established at various major ports in India, undertake cargo supervision and tracing work, largely at the request of the concerned insurers. Facilities are extended for supervision of loading and unloading of sensitive and valuable cargo at India ports and for tracing missing or misplaced packeges.

QUESTIONS

1. What are the subject-matters which are insured by Marine Insurance?
2. Discuss how are the Insurable Interest, Utmost Good Faith and Indemnity applicable to Marine Insurance?
3. What do you mean by warranties? What are the important warranties in Marine Insurance?
4. Discuss Lloyd's Powers and Functions.

20

MARINE INSURANCE POLICIES

The marine insurance policy is issued only when the contract has been finalised and it would be legal documents of evidence of the contract. The form of marine insurance policies has been taken from pretty old times. There has been a slight change in the wordings of the policies. For example, 'Be it known that' is substituted for the words 'In the name of God, Amen'. The old form of policy has been practised today due to its practicabilities which took after a numerous legal decisions during the past centuries. It has also been practised that only form of policy is standarised and different clauses are added for applying to various types of policies. The standard policy generally contains the following information:

(*i*) Name of insured or his agent.

(*ii*) Subject matter insured. It may be ship (hull) cargo and freight.

(*iii*) Risks insured against.

(*iv*) Name of vessel and officers.

(*v*) Description of voyage or period of insurance.

(*vi*) Amount and term of insurance.

(*vii*) Premium.

There are various clauses which are suitably inserted according to the nature and type of policies. Hull, cargo and freight policies have different standard clauses. In case of hull insurance, the clauses provide that if the insured vessel at the expiration of the policy is at sea, or at a port of refuge. Generally the ship may be covered until arrival at port of destination. In case of cargo policies—with Average, Free of particular Average, or All Risks are generally used. There are standard clauses which are invariably used in marine insurance. Firstly, policies are constructed in plain, ordinary and popular sense, and, later on, specific clauses are added to them according to terms and conditions of the contract. Clauses attached to the policy would override the printed wording in the policy.

CLASSES OF POLICIES

Different classes of policies are used in marine insurance.

1. Voyage Policies

The policy is issued to cover a particular voyage from one port to another and from one place to another. The policy mentions the port of departure and the port of destination, between which the risks are generally underwritten. This policy is not suitable for hull insurance as a ship usually does not operate over a particular route only. However, this policy may include time factor also as from Bombay to London for one year. In this case the risk may be covered from one place to another covering a period of one year.

The policy is used mostly in case of cargo insurance. The goods remain covered even when the ship halts at intermediate ports. The risks at the port of departure and at the port of destination may be covered by incorporating suitable, clauses in the policy. The liability of the insurer continues during landing and re-shipping of the goods.

2. Time Policies

Under this policy, the subject-matter is insured for a definite period of time, *e.g.*, from 6 a.m. of 1st January, 1976 to 6 a.m. of 1st January, 1977. The policy is generally taken for one year although it may be for less than one year. This policy is commonly more used for hull insurance than for the cargo insurance. The policy may cover, while navigating the vessel or while under construction. Risks covered under construction are for more than 12 months. There are standard clauses in relation to freight, premium, interests, etc., which are added to this policy. The time policy may be taken in case of goods and other movable vessels.

3. Voyage and Time Policy or mixed Policies

In this policy, the elements of voyage policy and of time policy are combined in under this policy. The reference is made certain period after completion of voyage. For example, 24 hours after arrival. It may be beneficial to hull as well as to cargo insurance.

4. Valued Policies

Under this policy the value of loss to be compensated is fixed and remains constant throughout the risk except where there is fraud and excessive over-valuation. The value of the subject-matter is agreed between the insurer and the assured at the time of taking the insurance. It is also called insured value or agreed value. It forms the measure of indemnity at the time of loss. The insured value is not necessarily the actual value. It may be total of invoice, *e.g.*, cost of goods, freight; shipping charges, insurance and a certain percentage of margin (generally 10 per cent) to cover anticipated profits.

5. Unvalued Policies

When the value of policy is not determined at the time of commencement of risk but is left to be valued when the loss takes place. The value thus left to be decided later on is called the insurable value or unvalued or valuable policy. In deciding the value, the invoice cost, freight, shipping and insurance charges are included and no margin for anticipated profit is added. Usually unvalued policies are not common in marine insurance because evaluation of loss at the time of damage poses a difficult problem. It is extremely difficult when consignment goes nearer the port of destination.

In hull insurance, the insurable value is determined taking into account the value of the ship at the commencement of risk including provision and, stores for officers and crew plus the charges of insurance. In insurance on freight whether paid in advance or otherwise, the insurable value is the gross amount of freight plus the charges of insurance. Similarly, in cargo insurance it would be the cost of goods plus expenses and insurance charges.

A limitation of insurable value is desirable not only to fix the measure of indemnity under an unvalued policy, but also to provide an approximate basis for the calculation of value in a valued policy.

6. Floating Policies

This policy describes the general terms and leaves the amount of each shipment and other particulars to be declared later on. The declaration is made in order of despatch of shipment. The policy is taken for a round large sum which is specified at each declaration and is attached to each shipment. With each declaration the amount will be reduced till it is exhausted when the insured sum is said to be 'closed' and the policy is 'fully declared' or, 'run off'.

The most popular form of contract is 'Open Cover'. It is an agreement between the insured and the insurer by which the assured on his part agrees to declare, and the insurer on his part agrees to accept all the shipments falling within the scope of the 'open cover' which is merely an original ship'. It is not a legal contract of marine insurance and suffers from the same legal disability as the 'original 'ship'. However the insured and the insurers are honour bound. To give 'Open Cover' a legal form, a policy is issued for the purpose. Separate policies are not issued in case of each shipment but only one policy is issued at the time of entering into contract. All declarations are written on the back of the policy. A classification clause is usually inserted in 'open cover' to provide the agreed rates of premium. Similarly, valuation clauses are also inserted to provide the basis for valuation in the event of loss taking place.

This policy is suitable for a cargo-owner who makes regular shipments of cargoes. All his shipments are automatically covered as soon as the declarations are made. The floating policies are mostly used in the age of gigantic trade.

7. Blanket Policies

The policy is taken to cover losses within the particular time and place. The policy is taken for a certain amount and premium is paid on the whole of it in the beginning of the policy and is re-adjusted at the end of the policy according to the actual amount at risk. If the actual coverage of risk is less than the total amount of insurance, the premium related to the excess amount is returned to the insured. On the other hand, if the amount of shipments are greater than the insured sum, additional premium is charged over the excess protection.

8. Named Policies

Under this policy, the name of the ship and the amount of insured cargo are mentioned. These policies are specific policies.

9. Single Vessel and Fleet Policies

A ship or a fleet of ships is insured in a single policy. When one policy is assured, it is called single vessel policy and when a fleet of ship is insured in single policy, it is called fleet insurance policy. The advantages of the fleet policies are that even old and weak ships are also insured. This insurance facilitates easy and smooth functioning of insurance benefits.

10. Block Policies

This policy insures incidental inland risks, too, along with the marine perils. For example, cotton is insured from the time of processing to the time when it was delivered at the point of destination.

11. Currency Policies

Policies issued in foreign currency is called currency policy, where the sum assured is stated in foreign currency, This policy avoids the fluctuation in foreign currencies because the claim amount is determined in the foreign currency and the fluctuations in the exchange rates of the inland and foreign currencies up to the period of the policy are meaningless.

12. P.P.I. Policies

The policy is issued to avoid the complication of the principle of insurable interest. This is called 'Policy Proof of Interest' and are honoured by the insurer even in absence of insurable interest. This policy is based on mutual understanding, so, it is called honoured policies. This is also called wagering policies because insurable interest is not required; consequently, it cannot be legally enforceable.

13. Special Declaration Policy

A special declaration policy (SDP) is a form of floating policy issued to clients who have a large turnover with many and frequent dispatches of goods. The minimum annual estimates despatches shall be ₹ 3 Crore for the individual company concerned. Issue one of SDP to transport operators/ agents or forwarders is prohibited. The policy shall not be issued in joint names. However, financial intests of a bulk or the financial institution may be recorded in the policy. Special declaration policy is not assignable or transferable. The sum insured shall be on the basis of the previous year's turnover. Mid-term increase in the sum insured may be allowed once only during the currency of the policy. Insurance may be renewed subsequently for an amount not less than the total amount of the expiring year turnover. Annual turnover means total insured value of goods in transit. It many include all incoming and outgoing consignments comprising capital goods, raw materials, stores, finished and semi finished products. Total value of the goods shall be declared at periodical intervals but at least once on completion of each quarter in the form of certified statement.

14. Annual Policy

The Annual Policy is insured for a period of 12 months to cover goods belonging to the assured or held in trust by the assured. The policy in not assignable or transferable. The policy is not allowed to be issued to transport operators/contractors, clearing, fowarding and commission agents or to freight forwarders. Nor can this policy be issued in Joint Names. The sum insured is the aggregate maximum estimated value on rail/road at any one time of all the insured goods in respect of a specified transit.

The policy shall be subject to condition of average stipulating that if at the time of any loss damage, the total value of goods in transit is more than the sum assured in respect of that specified transit, the assured shall be considered as being his own insurer for the difference and shall bear a rateable proportion of the loss accordingly.

Sum assured under the Annual Policy shall stand, reinstated as from the time of the happening of an event giving rise to a valid claim and the assured shall remain responsible for a pro-rata additional premium for the remaining period of the policy on the amount reinstated continuing from the date of the loss.

15. Inland Transit Cargo Policy

Inland Transit Policy covers all risk for inland transit for rail on road. It may cover only a few risks such a fire or theft or strikes, riots, civil commotion.

The cover may be extended up to 7 days after arrival at distination. It may be extended per week additional premium for a subject to not exeeding 8 weeks. This extension apply to goods only which is lying in railway or road carrier's premises or in clearing and forwarding agents' warehouse in bonded warehouse at the destination.

16. Inland Vessel Policy

Inland vessel policy covers all cargoes carried on rivers, canals or other smooth waters including F.O.B shipment. General average sacrifice and jettison are not included in the risk coverd. The rate of premium is based on age, propelled angine, steel, wooden boats, etc.

17. Indian Coast Ports Policy

This policy covers cargo on coastal voyage, covered by self propelled vessels of iron or steel construction which are not over 15 years of age and not under 450 tons GRT/Rates depend upon Voyage between different category of ports. For timber stored on deck, insurance shall be limited to Free of all Average (FAA) and Institute Cargo Clauses (ICC) covers both including jettison and washing over board.

18. Free on Board Policy

The policy is arranged by the buyer overseas for his own account and benefit. Risks under the buyer's policy commence on loading of the cargo on the overseas vessel, becuase it is at that juncture of transit that the risk passes from the seller to the buyer. The covers start from the time the cargo leave the warehouse till such goods are loaded on the ship. The policy also cover loss/damage reasonally attributable to craft, raft or lighter being stranded, grounded, sunk or capesized.

19. Sailing Vessels Policy

Sailing vessels include country craft total and/or constructive total loss of the subject-matter insured attributable to fire or shinking or stranding. Loss/Damage are also covered of subject-matter insured caused by jettison due to stress of weather stranding sinking or buruning or collision at sea.

20. Package Policy

This policy has bear devised under the tariff to cater to the special requirments of certain categories of business such as tea estates coffee estate and Export Promotion under Duty Exemtion Scheme.

QUESTIONS

1. What are the various kinds of Marine Insurance Policies?
2. Discuss the feature of marine insurance policies.
3. Explain SDP and Annual Policies.

21

POLICY CONDITIONS

The old form of policy is even used today. In order to make the standard policy suitable for the different types of contracts, suitable conditions are added to the policy. The conditions are inserted in the policy in the form of clauses. The clauses took the standard form with special meanings. They may be pertaining to Hull, Cargo and Freight.

1. Hull Clauses

These clauses are mainly framed with the insurances on vessels and are incorporated in hull policies. The clauses may be pertaining to losses resulting from collision, standing, general average, etc. 'All risks policy' may be issued or certain risks may be excluded from the policy by inserting suitable clauses. 'Inland or Port Risk Clauses' may be incorporated in the policy to determine the extent of loss. These clauses are known as 'Institute Time Clauses'.

2. Cargo Clauses

These clauses are used in the insurance of goods and are incorporated in cargo policies. The clauses describe the nature, extent; and scope of the insurance and define comprehensive conditions and restrictions. The additional marine perils against which cover may be sought or which are excluded from the policies are inserted through special clauses. Terms and conditions of Cargo insurance are specially incorporated in the policies. 'With Average (W.A.) or With Particular Average, (W.P.A.),' 'Exposed during transit', etc., are the important clauses of cargo insurance. The underwriting of cargo-risks depends upon the nature of goods, the susceptibility of the goods, intentions of the insurer and insured and willingness of the assured to pay extra premium. This clause is known as 'Institute Cargo Clause'.

3. Freight Clauses

The clauses are framed in connection with the loss of freight due to maritime perils which may be insured for a period or for a voyage. A person which paid the freight in advance and the person who will receive the freight on completion of voyage are interested in covering the risk. The General Average (G.A.), Particular Average (P.A.) etc. are used in the freight clauses. The clauses are known as 'Institute Freight Clauses'.

The clauses to be incorporated in the policy are generally taken from Lloyd's Association.

LLOYD'S FORM OF POLICY

BE IT KNOWN THAT ..... as well in....... own name as for and in the name and names of all and every other person or persons to whom the same doth, may or shall appertain, in part or in all doth make assurance and cause, and them, and every of them, to be insured lost or not lost, at and from.

Upon any kind of goods and merchandise, and also upon the body, tackle, appeared, ordinances munition, artillery, boat, and other furniture, of and in the good ship or vessel called the.

Whereof is master under God, for this present voyage or whosoever else shall go for master in the said ship, or by whatsoever other name or names the said ship, or the master thereof, is or shall be named or called, beginning the adventure upon the said goods and merchandises from the loading thereof abroad the said ship.

Upon the said ship and so, shall continue and endure, during her abroad there.

Upon the said ship, & c. And further, until the said ship, with all her ordinance, tackle, apparel, and goods and merchandises whatsoever shall be arrived at.

Upon the said ship, & c, until she hath moored at anchor twenty-four hours in good safety; and upon the goods and merchandises, until the same be there discharged and safely landed. And it shall be lawful for the said ship, & c, in this voyage, to proceed and said to and touch and stay at any ports or places whatsoever without prejudice to this insurance. The said ship, & c., goods and merchandises, & c., for so much as concerns, the assured by agreement between, the assured and assurers in this policy, are and shall be valued at.

Touching the adventures and perils which we the assurers are contented to bear and do take upon us in this voyage. They are of the seas, men of war ...

... And it is agreed by us the insurers, that this writing or a policy of assurance shall be of as much force and effect as the surest writing or policies of assurance heretofore made is Lombard Street, or in the Royal Exchange, or elsewhere in London.

DESCRIPTION OF THE CLAUSES

The usual clauses which are or may be incorporated in a marine policy are:

(*i*) Assignment clause,
(*ii*) Lost or not lost,
(*iii*) At and from clause,
(*iv*) Warehouse to warehouse clause,
(*v*) Deviation, touch and stay clause,
(*vi*) Inchmaree clause,
(*vii*) Running down clause,
(*viii*) Sue and Labour clause,
(*ix*) Reinsurance clause,
(*x*) Memorandum clause,
(*xi*) Continuation clause.

1. Assignment Clause

The clause of assignment is as below .... as well as in his/their own name as for and in the name and names of all and every other person or persons to whom the same doth may or shall appertain, in part or in all doth make assurance ... and cause ... and them and every of them, to be insured ....

This clause makes it clear that the marine policy is freely assignable unless this is expressly prohibited. The policy can be assigned to anyone who may acquire an insurable interest in the subject-matter as soon as the assured parts with his interest. Cargo policy is freely assignable and no notice, thereof is essential to be given to the underwriter. But, in case of hull insurance the policy cannot be assigned freely and the consent of underwriter is essential because the degree of risk of the subject-matter is materially changed when the management and ownership of the vessel is changed. Since the owner of cargo has no control over the cargo in transit, blank endorsement may be permitted. But in hull insurance, specific endorsement of an assignment is essential.

It is interesting to note that marine policy can be assigned even after it takes place, but the assignee does not get a better title than the assignor. However, where the assured has parted with his interest in the subject, matter insured and has not, before or at time of so doing, expressly or impliedly agreed to assign the policy and subsequent assignment of the policy is inoperative.

2. Lost or Not Lost Clause

The clause is as ..... to be insured, lost or not lost. The policy was taken in good faith. The meaning of the clause is that the insurer insures the subject-matter irrespective of the fact that it has already been lost or not lost before the issue of the policy. It is taken in such a case where a merchant receives information of the shipment of his cargo very late after the sailing of the steamer and, therefore, when he submits the risk to the underwriter and effects insurance it was not known whether the subject-matter to be insured was lost or was not lost. So, to provide full protection to shipment, the words, 'Lost or not Lost' are inserted. It means that the insurer undertakes to indemnify the insured whether the subject matter before the date of issue of the policy was already lost or not. In this case, it is assumed that the assured and the underwriters are ignorant about the safety or otherwise of the subject-matter. The policy terminates if it is proved later on that one of the two parties was aware of the subject-matter at the time of loss. The introduction of this clause has a retrospective effect to provide for any loss which have occurred during the period from the date of shipment to the date of issue of policy. This clause was mostly prevalent in olden times when the media of communication were not developed so much. Now, the clause has lost much of its importance.

3. At and From Clause

This clause is applicable in voyage policies insuring hull, and freight. It determines the time when the actual risk commences. As soon as the ship will arrive at the port, the risk will commence. It means that the policy covers the subject-matters while it is lying at the port of departure and from the time the ship sails when the policy contains From only instead of 'At and Form.' From means the risk commences from the time of departure of the ship and not previous to that.

In case of cargo policy this clause is amended as the risk may commence boom the 'time the cargo is loaded on the vessel. In voyage policy, if the ship is not at that place when the contract is concluded, the risk commences as soon as the ship arrives there in good safety. If the place of departure is specified by the policy, and the ship sails from other place than the specified one, the risk does not attach.

Termination of Risk

The wordings of policy in this case are as follows:

"And upon the goods and merchandises until the same be there discharged and safely landed."

When the ship arrives the port of destination, the goods must be landed within a reasonable time and if they are not landed the risk ceases. The risk of landing within the reasonable time is permitted in most of the cases. But, where it is allowed with standard policy, clauses such as craft, lighters, etc., are inserted to the policy.

4. Warehouse to Warehouse Clause

Generally, underwriters are responsible for the risk commencing from the time of loading to the time of unloading the cargo. But, in certain cases the risks are beyond these two limits, *i.e.*, departing and destination. So, in order to cover the inland risks from the original place of departure to the port of sailing and from the port of discharge to the place of final destination are insured under 'Warehouse to warehouse clause'. Under this policy, the risk commences from the specified place and continues to the specified place of destination named in the policy. Thus, the risk of land, craft transport and transhipment are also covered under a single marine insurance policy. Sometimes, time-limit is also inserted in the policy and extra cost is required from the insured to cover the remaining voyage. But, where goods are wilfully detained, the underwriter shall cease his liability.

The clause as appeared in the Institute Cargo clause is as follows:

"The risks covered by this policy attach from the time the goods leave the Warehouse and/or Store at the place named in the policy for the commencement of the transit and continue during the ordinary course of transit, including customary transhipment, if any, until the goods are discharged overside from the overseas vessel at the final port. Thereafter the risks covered are continued whilst the goods are in transit and/or awaiting transit until delivered to final warehouse at the destination named in the policy or until the expiry of 15 days (30 days if the destination to which the goods are insured is outside the limits of the port) whichever shall first occur. The time limit referred to above to be from midnight of the day on which the discharge overside of the goods hereby insured from the overseas vessel is completed. Transhipment, if any other than as above, and/or delay in excess of the above time limits arising from circumstances beyond the control of the assured, held covered at a premium to be arranged.

5. Deviation Touch and Clauses

The ship should not deviate from the course of the voyage described in the policy or where the course is not a specifically designated one, from the customary course. Any departure from the specified course or a customary course amounts to deviation. A deviation is different from change of voyage. In the latter case, the destination agreed upon is changed, while in the former case the destination is the same as agreed, but the course thereto is deviated from. In the change of voyage the underwriter's liability comes to an end from the time the intention or decision to change the voyage is taken, but in deviation mere intention to deviation is not material; there should be an actual deviation to avoid the policy. Once deviation has taken, place the risk ceases to attach for the rest of the voyage even though loss has occurred after the vessel had reverted to the proper course.

Where the ship deviates without lawful excuse the underwriters are relieved of the liability as from the time of deviation. The fact that deviation did not increase the risk or that the ship regained her route before any loss occurred, would not amount to non-deviation. This clause applies only to voyage policies. In time policies, this clause does not apply.

Deviation is excused under certain circumstances but it should be noted that the ship must resume her course and prosecute the voyage with reasonable despatch. Deviation or delay is excused in the following cases:

1. Where authorised by any special term in the policy. The special term must be incorporated in the policy. Underwriters are usually willing to extend the protection of the policies after charging additional premium.
2. Where deviation is caused by circumstances beyond the control of the master and his employer.
3. Where deviation or delay is necessary to comply with an express or implied warranty.
4. The deviation or delay is necessary for the safety of the ship or subject-matter insured.
5. For the purpose of saving human life or aiding a ship in distress where human life may be in danger. For, and for obtaining medical or surgical aid, deviation or delay is required.
6. Where deviation is caused by the barratrous conduct of the master or crew, if the barretry be one of the perils insured against.

Touch And Stay

It accords liberty to the vessel to touch and stay at any port, or place whatsoever. In absence of the clause, the liberty to touch and stay at any port or place whatsoever does not authorise the ship to depart from the course of her voyage from the port of departure to the port of destination. Where several ports are specified, the ship may touch or stay at all or any of them. In the absence of any usage or sufficient cause to the contrary the ship must proceed to the designated ports. Following wordings are incorporated in the standard policy.

"And it shall be lawful for the said ship, etc., in the voyage to proceed and sail to and touch and stay at any ports or places whatsoever without prejudice to this insurance."

It means that the vessel in course of the voyage must touch and stay at such ports and in such order as are mentioned in the policy or if no course is mentioned in the policy, the ports must be in the ordinary course of the voyage.

6. Inchmaree Clause

The clause protects the shipowners against losses to be included in claims by the assured. This clause is taken from an illustration of a steamer called 'Inchmaree'. The donkey pump of the steamer was damaged due to salt. Claim was covered under the "and all other perils, losses, and misfortunes clause". The court decided that due to negligent such losses were outside the scope of the insurance and should not be covered by it. So, now to provide indemnity for the insured for damage to the hull or machinery resulting from the negligence of the master or crew, at well as from explosion or latent defects, a clause was introduced into hull policies which is commonly known as 'Inchmaree clause'. This clause is also incorporated in cargo policies.

Hague Rules

A Maritime Law Committee of the International Law Association sat at The Hague in 1921 and framed a set of rules regarding the rights and liabilities of cargo-owners and shipowners in connection with Bills of Lading so that no complication may arise in settlement of claims.

7. Running Down Clauses (R.D.C.)

This clause is also called collision clause and is included in hull policies. It provides that the underwriter agrees to take upon the liability of the owner of the ship for damage done by his vessel to another vessel on collision to the extent of three-fourths of such liability. The underwriter will be responsible only when this clause is added in the policy. The assured himself has to bear one-fourth of the loss so that he may exercise greater care in the navigation of the vessel. The full protection can be given by deleting the words 'Three-fourths' from the clause. In case the ship sinks in a collision and is held liable for the damage done to the other vessel, the underwriter may have to pay a total loss and a heavy claim under the R.D.C. The amount of damage extends to include damage done to other ship, her cargo and compensation for loss of employment in consequence of the collision.

8. Sue and Labour Clause

This clause reads as follows: "And in case of loss of misfortune it shall be lawful to the assured, their factors, servants and assigns to sue, labour and travel for in and about the defence, safeguards, and recovery of the said goods and merchandises, and ship, ete., or part thereof, without prejudice to this insurance, to the charges whereof we, the assurers, will contribute each one according to the rate and quantity of his sum herein assured".

Thus, it is the duty of the assured and his agents to act in such a way that they are uninsured and to take such measures as may be reasonable for the purpose of averting or minimising loss or damage. This clause requires underwriters to pay any expenses properly incurred by the assured or his agents in preventing or minimising loss or damage to the subject-matter. The reasonable expenditure is payable even though it may be, in addition, to total loss.

The essential features of Sue and Labour Charges are:

(*i*) The expenses must be incurred for the benefit of the subject-matter insured. If occurred for the common benefit they may become a part of general average which is not recoverable under this clause.

(*ii*) They must be reasonable.

(*iii*) They may be incurred by 'the assured, his factors, his servants or assigns'. The clause excludes salvage charges.

(*iv*) The expenses are incurred to avert or minimise a loss from a peril covered by the policy. Expenses incurred for purpose of averting or diminishing any loss not covered by the policy are not recoverable under this clause.

9. Reinsurance Clause

The reinsurance clause .... "being a reinsurance and subject to the same clauses and conditions as the original policy, and to pay as may be paid thereon." .... is generally added to the original policies. The reinsurer is liable only for claims for which the original underwriter is liable. If the reassured has paid a claim for which he is not legally liable under his policy, the reinsurer is under no obligation to reimburse him. The cost incurred by the original insurer in contesting liability under the original policy, need not be paid by the reinsurer. The reinsurance policy is closely linked with the original insurance and any alteration in the original policy must be agreed with the reinsurer.

10. Memorandum Clause

The memorandum clause reads as under:

"Corn, fish, salt, fruit, flour and seed are warranted free from average, unless general, or the ship be stranded—sugar, tobacco,... are warranted free from average, ... and all other goods, also the ship and freight, are warranted free from average, ..."

This clause is meant to provide a minimum limit to be underwriter's liability regarding claims for particular average by exempting him from such claims.

11. Continuation Clause

This clause refers that the vessel shall continue to be covered even after completion of voyage under the policy at a *pro rato* premium to her port of destination provided previous notice was not given.

12. Institute Cargo Clauses

These clauses are used to cover various types of general merchandise involving transit by sea. The risks clauses, general average clause and collison clause are included in these clauses. These clauses are ICC (A) (B) and (C).

RISKS COVERED BY ICC (A)

This clauses includes all risks of loss or damage to the subject-matter insured except by risks specifically excluded, General average and Salvage charges incurred to avoid loss from any cause or causes except those excluded by the policy liability under Both to Blame collision clause of the contract of affreightment. Under this clause, the assured has only to show that the insured cargo was lost or damaged during the currency of the insurance. General average is there where any extraordinary sacrifice or expenditure is voluntarily and reasonably made or insurred at a time of peril for the purpose of preserving the property imperilled in the commen adventure. There is a direct liability on the insurer for general average sacrifice which is treated in the same manner as particular average or partial loss claim. The Jettison is also included under this clause which relates to cargo or other property thrown overboard at time of peril to save the adventure from total loss. When ship and cargo belong to different owners, such jettison would constitute a general average sacrifice but where only one interest (ownership) is involved, there would be no claim for general average sacrifice. This clause also covers loss overboard of any sort. When goods are lost or damaged in an accident to the overland conveyance, this clause deamed to be covered. The institute malicious clause is also covered.

Institute Cargo Clauses (B) and (C)

These clauses are identical with only different of risks clause. The risks covered by these clauses are fire or explosion, vessel or craft being standared, granted sunk or capsized, overturning or derailment of land conveyance , collision on or contract of vessel craft, or conveyance with any external object other than water discharge of cargo at a port of distress, general average sacrifice and jettison. Additional risks covered under ICC (B) are earthquake volcanic eruption or lightning, washing overloard lake or river water into the vessel, craft, gold, conveyance, container, liftkan or place of storage. Similarily ship loss is also included which relates to total loss of any package lost overboard or dropped during loading or unloading operations of the vessel or craft. These clauses are on the basis of "Named perils with exclusions" while ICC (A) is based on "All risks with exclusion" under the clauses of the "Named risks with exclusions" an additional burden on the assured is there because he has not only to show that the loss/damage occurred during the policy period but also that it was due to the operation of one of the named perils. The assured is entitled to indemnity under the policy unless the insurers are able to establish that the loss/damage arose because of the operations of an excluded peril.

13. Institute War Clauses

The risks covered under these clauses are war, civil war, revolution, rebellion, insurrection or civil strife arising there from, or any hostile act by or against a belligerant power. It also includes capture, seizure, arrest, restraint or detainment arising from risks covered under (a) above and the consequences there of any attempt threat, torpedoes, bombs or other derelect weapon of war.

These clauses also cover general average and salvage charges adjusted or determined according to the contract of affreightment and/or the governing law and practice, incurred to avoid, or in connection with the avoidance of loss from a risk covered.

There is exclusion of frustration which mean that the insurance does not generate the completion of the voyage and the arrival of the goods at destination.

14. Incresed Value Insurance Clause

Insurance may be arranged to cover increased value of the cargo i.e. the market value of goods at destination port in the date of landing is higher than CIF and duty value of the cargo. The assured is the holder or assignee of the import license or is the actual user who has purchased goods from a recognised Export House. This policy is not assignable. No claim shall be paid for increased value until the claim under the CIF value insurance policy is payable and proof of liability for loss under that policy shall be furnished to the company. This polilcy is not valid if effected after arrival of the vessel at destination. Insurance in not on agreed value basis. The claim payable together with CIF value, duty policy and increased value policies shall not exceed the specified proportion of the market value of the goods at destination.

QUESTIONS

1. What are the various clauses of marine insurance policies?
2. Discuss in detail Touch and Stay, Running Down Clause, At and From, Sue and Labour Clause.
3. Explain ICC with referance to India.

22

PREMIUM CALCULATION

Premium can be ascertained either by numerical rating system or by judgment method. The numerical rating system evaluates each and every item and marks are assigned to them according to their merits and degrees of influencing risk. Since the marine perils are varied, the only numerical rating system cannot be successfully utilised. However, tabulation of statistical experience on many risks can serve the purpose as a basis of supplementary factors for underwriter's judgment. Marine insurance grants protection against a large number of perils which are viewed in relation to (*i*) the inherent character of a large variety of subject-matter of insurance (*ii*) the effects of season, adverse physical forces and trade customs, (*iii*) the policy conditions.

Individual insurance account is used for personal valuation by a leading underwriter who enter into the making of marine insurance rates very materially. The judgment and personal evaluation is very vital in rate making. There are various factors to influence the risk. The management and ownership are very important factors while risks are evaluated for the purpose of rate making. Residents in India are not permitted to take marine insurance cover with insurance companies in foreign countries without prior permission of RBI.

RATE MAKING IN MARINE INSURANCE

Hull Insurance

1. Management

One management may be efficient in the upkeep of the vessel and the appointment of officers and crew. Other management, through negligence, indifference and undue economy, may show a bad record. To treat these managements alike would be an injustice to the better managed concerns. It would penalize efficiency and carefulness and put a premium on inefficiency and carelessness.

2. Natural Forces and Topography

The underwriters consider the character of the route, the construction, type and the nationality of the vessel and conditions of the contract. Some natural hazards are permanent while others are of seasonal dangers. References are made to storms, submerged shoals, shifting sand bars, shallow water, narrow channels, ice, currents, tides and seaquakes while calculating the premiums to a particular route. Dangers from an underwriting point of view are associated with the ports of departure, call or destination. Some ports are known for insufficient depth, absence of good anchorage ground, lack of protection against tides or tidal waves.

3. Construction, Type and Nationality of the Vessel

The quality and fitness of the vessel to serve as a carrier on the particular route is naturally of the utmost importance. The underwriter wants to know the vessel with respect to its builder and owner, structural plan, material used in construction, type of propulsion, structural strength to resist stresses and strains, adaptability to carry various kinds of cargo and its age and physical condition. In foreign countries, certain societies are formulated to promulgate rules for the construction of vessels, supervising such construction and assigning a class to each vessel. The Lloyd's Register contains information to numerous vessels of other countries, name and nationality of the vessel, materials of construction, details of the decks, the engine and boiler equipment of the vessel. Periodical changes are noted down there. Nationality of the vessel is important to insurer because it discloses the dependence of the nations upon the ocean trade. The nationality reveals the acumanship or skilfulness of the masters and crew. The rates may vary greatly as to the standard or commercial honour in trade, high standard and commercial ethics. Premium rates are based on age of the vessel, propelling method body-structure, risks covered, distance for transit and nature of the vessel, tonnage capacities, port-classification and season of sailing.

4. Policy Conditions

Innumerable clauses are used to limit or increase the underwriter's liability. Some policies may cover against total loss. Some may cover partial losses. Others may relate only to general average or particular average.

Cargo Rates

The premium on cargo depends upon the following factors:

1. Ownership

It may happen that two separate ownerships of the same kind of cargo, carried on the same ship and to the same place will command different rates. Proper packing, profitable accounts and previous refusal of insurance may determine the rate.

2. Character of the Cargo

The difference in hazard between various kinds of commodities, different forms of the same commodity, different shipments, different types of packing and durability of the commodity may influence the premium rates.

3. Hazards and Customs

The natural forces and topography considered in the case of ship are also considered in the case of cargo. The effect of seasons has important bearing upon commodities that are seriously affected by cold or heat. The season or climate at the port of destination may influence the risk. In certain season the port is busy with a particular cargo. Varying trade customs associated with the different commercial routes will influence cargo rates materially. The moral hazard is greater on certain routes.

4. Quality and Suitability of the Vessel used as Carrier

The underwriters take into account the fitness of the vessel to carry the particular cargo. The premiums are higher in the case of ship of slower speed due to longer exposure of the cargo. In case of highly perishable goods, moving in large quantities, special types of vessels have been designed to carry such commodities.

5. Duration of Voyage and Policy Conditions

Insurers take into account the length of time. Sometimes, loading of the goods aboard the vessels and protection of the goods while on the dock are considered in calculation of premium.

6. Miscellaneous Factors

The operating efficiency or proved experience of ship may affect the risk on cargo. The methods of handling and stowing cargo, the regularity of the service, etc., are the various factors to influence the premium rate.

RETURN OF PREMIUM

Circumstances may happen when the proposed shipment of goods may not take place or only a reduced quantities may be shipped. In the following circumstances the premium is returnable.

1. By Agreement in the Policy

The assured may pay full premium while effecting the insurance. The insurer may agree to return it wholly or partly at the happening of a certain event. The premium is returnable by agreement in the following circumstances:

(*i*) Improvement in the character of insurance. For example, change of ship to safer routes, use of first class liner, good packing, etc.

(*ii*) The insurer may encourage to return a part of the premium if claims do not arise.

(*iii*) Cancellation of policy due to change in the ownership of hull.

(*iv*) Mutual cancellation of the policy.

2. For Reasons of Equity

The premium is returnable for reasons of equity.

(*i*) *Non-attachment of risk:* Where the subject-matter has never been under the risk, or the risk has not been started. For example, the voyage might not have been made or the goods might be short shipped.

(*ii*) Undeclared balance of an open policy is entitled for return of premium. The premium shall be returned only when there has no further interest to declare within the scope of the policy.

(*iii*) Where there is a total failure of an apportionable part of the consideration, the apportionate part of the premium is returnable to the assured provided where is no fraud or illegality on the part of the assured or his agents. Where voyage was to be completed in stages and each stage is being rated separately. If some stages are not completed, the premiums relating to uncompleted stages are returnable.

(*iv*) When the assured has no insurable interest throughout the life of the policy the premium is returnable provided the policy does not amount to fraud.

(*v*) The insurer can cancel the voyage when there is unreasonable delay in commencing the voyage.

(*vi*) In case of over-insurance, a proportionate part of the premium is returnable. Where two or more policies are effected by or on behalf of the assured on the same adventure and interest or any part thereof, and the sums insured exceed the indemnity allowed, the assured is said to be over-insurance by double insurance. In this case, a proportionate part of the several premiums is returnable, provided that if the policies are taken at different times, and any earlier policy has at anytime borne the entire risk, or if a claim has been paid on the policy in respect of the full sum insured, no premium is returnable in respect of that policy.

Special Premium Rates for different purposes and cargoes

Vessel or LASH barges : A flat extra premium is charged for extension of cover upto on board the overseas vessel in addition to the appropriate premium chargeable for inland transit. Additional rate is charged for extension of storage risks at port/docks.

Additional rates for shut-out cargo is charged from the goods which arrives too late for a vessel at a loading port or else the goods are not loaded became the vessel has a full cargo load. Its rate depends on coastal and overseas ex-craft, raft or lighter in midstream will depend upon category of port and type of inland transit cover. In the event of the goods are returned to the shipper's warehouse involving rail/road transit, appropirate full premium as per Inland. Transit (Rail/Road) risks; schedule shall apply for the return journey in addition to the above.

Sailing Vessels

The premium for sailing vessels depend upon voyage between ports and type of cover. Premium rates apply for non-mechanised sailing vessels. A discount of $33\frac{1}{3}$% on the premium rates are allowed for shipments by mechanised sailing vessels. Where the vessel involves the West Coast of India, there is increased hazard of shipping during monsoon month. Suitable loading of rates take place between certain dates. Extra primium is charged for that. Thus reduction for machanised vessels and tonnage of vessels is applicable. Extra premium is charged based on commodity and period.

Bullion and Species

Two rates apply for sending them through insured post : one for sending within India and the other for sending from India to any foreign country and *vice versa.* The policy covers all risks from the time the peril is delivered. Securities shall be insured for their face value or market value whichever is less and 40% of the schedule premium rate is charged. When valuable are carried in the Bullion Room of a liner, 75% of the schedule rate is charged.

Major Commodities

When commodities are transit by sea, the rates are indicated for cargoes carried by steamers, classed in accordance with the Institute Classification Clause. Where the cargo is carried in vessel not so classed, extra premium for over age, undertonnage and non-classification shall apply. Insurance of petroleum product, cement, edible oil, bagged rice, coffee, tea, etc. are charged different. The premium for cargo is decided on the vessel, voyage, nature of cargo, type of packing and insurance cover bases.

Vessel: cargo carried on vessels not complying with or not coming within the classification clause will be subject to additional premium and possibly a restriction in cover. Additional premium is payable for the vessel not on regular trading pattern and is over 15 years old, vessel in under 1000 GRT and over 15 year old, when the vessel is on a regular trading pattern but is over 25 years old, when the vessel is not a mechanically propelled steel vessel, where vessel is not classed.

Voyage : "warehouse to warehouse" clause includes risks of land transit by rail or load from the time the goods leave the warehouse to the port of shipment. There is no cover during any permit before transit actually commences; transit to a container terminal for stuffing into a container, a period in the warehouse awaiting customs formalities inspection and shipment.

Nature of cargo : There are goods which are specially valnerable to damage in transit. The nature of the product or commodity insured from the point of view of susceptibility to tonnage through various causes is a vital consideration for an underwriter to take into account. The tendency is to require protection which is as comprehensive as possible. Inherent vice is not covered unless the policy specially so provides. Some commodities lose weight by evaporation of their moisture content. The insurance does not cover also ordinary leakage, ordinary loss in weight or volume or ordinary wear and tear.

Packing : The purpose of packing goods for transit overseas or inland is to ensure as far as possible that the goods reach destination the same perfect condition. It should be made certain that the goods are packed in a manner which will enable them to withstand normal handling during transit. Normally insurance covers content of the package not the packing material except when this specifically included. Insurers may not pay for the loss aggravated by inadequate packing. Packing involves strength of the packing material weight of the packing unit, handling mobility inherent qualities of the commodities and hazards involved in the transit.

Insurance cover: Rating should take into consideration each material element of the risks involved whether it is the characteristic of a given vessel or voyage or the nature of cargo and packing. These are common area of risk in all sets of Institute Cargo Clauses (ICC-A,B,C) There are some risks which are covered only in (B) of ICC i.e. earthquake volcanic eruption or lighting, washing overcovered entry of sea, lake or river water into vessel loading. However, ICC (A) covers "all risks" whereas ICC(B) and ICC(C) are named risks."

QUESTIONS

1. What are the factors to effect premium calculation?
2. When is premium of marine insurance returnable?
3. Discuss special premium rates for different purposes and cargos

23

MARINE LOSSES

Losses in marine insurance business are result of the various perils. Marine insurance policy does not necessarily cover all the risks. All insurer is liable to indemnify an insured in respect of only losses which result from perils insured against. When the loss occurred is beyond the insured peril, the insured himself shall have to bear. The onus of proof under a policy of marine insurance is upon the insured to establish that the loss was proximately, caused by an insured peril. When goods are insured against 'All Risks', the onus of proof of loss is transfered to the insurer.

Marine Perils

The perils insured against are mentioned in the policy and the underwriter shall be liable for damages caused by the insured perils.

"Marine Perils means the perils consequent on", or incidental to the navigation of the sea, that is to say, perils of the seas, fire, war perils (enemies), pirates, rovers, thieves, captures, seizures, restraints and detainment of princes and peoples, jettisons, barratry and other perils, either of the like kind or which may be designated by the policy."

1. Perils of Sea

Under perils of sea, ordinary action of the winds and waves, ordinary wear and tear to the vessel, inherent risk of the cargo are not included. The underwriter may be liable for losses caused by Perils of the sea, he is not necessarily liable for perils on sea. Pertils of the sea refers to fortuitous accidents or casualties of the sea. If the loss arising out of any of the perils of the sea insured is attributable to the fraud or wilful misconduct of the assured, the underwriter is acquitted from the liability under the policy.

2. Fire

In olden times fire was the biggest maritime perils, but recently it has been under control to a greater extent. Damage resulting from fire and smoke is included under fire-peril. The water used for extinguishing fire may cause damage to the insured goods. So, this peril is also insurable. The damage due to spontaneous combustion may be maritime peril and be insured against. Damage done due to lightning, explosion and fire originating from negligence of the crew is recoverable from underwriters. The losses which are not included in the standard policy can be covered by having special clauses and paying extra-premium.

3. Man-of-War

This is the vessel which is authorised by nations for the purpose of defence or attack in the event of hostilities. Any damage to the goods or ships arising out of collision against a man-of-war is insurable.

4. Enemies

The ships belonging to the foe (enemy) may cause loss to the insured and is re-underwritten by the marine policy. This policy extends to all the persons of the enemy country and to their hostile acts provided such acts form part of the enemy actions.

5. Pirates, Rovers, Thieves

The perils on account of pirates, rovers and thieves were common in olden times, but it has been reduced considerably these days. These acts are generally committed for the pursuit of individual gain by the persons beyond the jurisdiction of a state. The term 'thieves' does not mean clandestine theft or a theft committed by anyone of the crew or officers or passengers.

Jettison

Jettison means voluntary throwing away of the cargo or part of a vessel's equipment for the lightening or relieving the ship for common safety. The aim of the intentional throwing away of the goods or property is to relieve the vessel from some imminent peril. Accidental falling of things does not constitute jettison. The own inherent-vice of cargo is also not included in the jettison.

Barratry

Barratry includes every wrongful act wilfully committed by the master or crew the prejudice of the owner. The act of barratry must be committed without the knowledge of the owner. The theft, the setting fire to ship, fraudulent selling of vessel and cargo without the connivance of the ship-owner are the various examples of the barratry. The insurer, if barratry insured, is liable for losses arising out of barratry.

Restraints and Detainments

The prevention to free use of a port by the government of the country is called restraints. It may cause interruption and possible loss of voyages involving such ports and sacrifice of cargo. The term 'detainments' covers losses resulting from the detention of a vessel and its cargo by blockage or possibly quarantine regulation or other interference by the police power of a nation while a vessel is in port. It does not cover losses which are the result merely of delay or interruption of the voyage, or loss of market or some other remote result.

The Free of Capture and Seizure Clause (F.C. & S. Clause)

The policy generally covers war perils. But, to include perils of sudden declaration of war, the war clause or free of capture and seizure clause is added to relieve war perils. By deletion of this clause, the policy is automatically restored to its original condition and adequate premiums are charged for the purpose.

Explosion

The risk of explosion has greatly increased. The explosion on board of a vessel damaging hull or cargo or both could be constructed as a peril on the sea. An explosion on shore might damage a ship or its cargo. Marine cargo policies were amended to include the risk of explosions not clearly caused by war perils. The explosion, in case of hull policies, 'on shipboard or elsewhere' is covered in the amended "Inchmaree or Negligence clause".

Strikes, Riots and Civil Commotion Clause

The marine insurance on cargo is extended to cover from warehouse to warehouse or otherwise insures the goods on shore prior to shipment and after discharge, the danger of underwriters being held liable for losses, resulting from the unlawful acts of strikers from riots or civil commotions is materially enhanced. The insurers are unwilling to assume liability for losses due to unlawful acts.

All Other Perils

Loss occurred by salt water of the sea, action of worms on timber, cattle dying due to want of fodder as a result of lengthy voyage constitute sea perils. There may be other damages due to oil, sweat, heat, which are insured under other perils.

MARINE LOSSES

If the loss takes place on account of any of the perils insured against with the insurer, the insurer will be liable for it and shall have to make good the losses to the assured. If the peril is insured, the insurer will indemnify the assured, otherwise not. The doctrine of causa proxima is to be applied while calculating the amount of loss. It means for payment of losses, the real or proximate cause is to be taken into account. If the proximate cause is insured, the insurer will pay, otherwise not. It has been discussed in a previous chapter.

TOTAL LOSS

According to S. 57(1) of the Marine Insurance Act, there is an actual total loss where the subject matter insured is destroyed or so demaged as to cease to be a thing of the kind insured or where the assured is irretrievably deprived thereof. Losses are deemed to be total or complete when the subject-matter is fully destroyed or lost or ceases to be a thing of its kind. It should be distinguished from partial loss where only part of the property insured is lost or destroyed. In case of total loss, the insured stands to lose to the extent of the value of the property provided the policy amount was to that limit.

1. Actual Total Loss

Actual total loss is a material and physical loss of the subject-matter insured. Where the subject-matter insured is destroyed or so damaged as to cease to be a thing of the kind insured, or where the insured is irretrievably deprived thereof, there is an actual total loss. When a vessel is foundered or when merchandise is so damaged as to be valueless or when ship is missing it will be an actual total loss.

The actual total loss occurs in the following cases:

1. The subject-matter is destroyed, *e.g.*, a ship is entirely destroyed by fire.
2. The subject-matter is so damaged as to cease to be a thing of the kind insured. Here, the subject-matter is not totally destroyed but damaged to such an extent as the result of the mishap, it is no longer of the same specie as originally insured. The examples of such losses are—foodstuff badly damaged by sea water became unfit for human consumption, hides became valueless as hides due to admission of water. These damaged foodstuffs or hides may be used as manure. Since the characters of the subject-matters are changed and have lost their shapes, they are all actual total loss.
3. The insured is irretrievably deprived of the ownership of goods even they are in physical existence as in the case of capture by enemy, stealth by thief or fraudulent disposal by the captain or crew.
4. The subject-matter is lost. For example, where a ship is missing for a very longtime and no news of her is received after the lapse of a reasonable time. An actual total loss is presumed unless there is some other proof to show against it.

In case of actual total loss, notice of abandonment of property need not be given. In such total losses, the insurer is entitled to all rights and remedies in respect of damaged properties. In no case, amount over the insured value or insurable value is recoverable in a total loss form the insurers. If the property is under-insured, the insured can recover only up to the amount of insurance. If it is over-insured he is not over-benefited but only the actual loss will be indemnified.

Where the subject-matter had ceased to be of the kind insured, the assured will be given the full amount of total loss provided there was insurance up to that amount, and the insurer will subrogate all rights and remedies in respect of property. Any amount realised by the sale of the material will go to the insurer.

2. Constructive Total Loss

Section 60 of the Act defines constructive Total Loss. Where the subject-matter is not actually lost in the above manner, but is reasonably abandoned when its actual total loss is unavoidable or when it cannot be preserved from total loss without involving expenditure which would exceed the value of the subject-matter. For example, the cost of repair and replacement was estimated to be ₹ 50,000, whereas the ship was estimated to be ₹ 40,000. The ship may be abandoned and will be taken as constructive total loss. But if the value of ship was more than ₹ 50,000 it would not be constructive total loss. Here it is assumed that retention of the subject-matter would involve financial loss to the insured.

The constructive total loss will be where—

(*a*) the subject-matter insured is reasonably abandoned on account of its actual total loss appearing to be unavoidable;

(*b*) the subject-matter could not be preserved from actual total loss without an expenditure which would exceed its repaired and recovered value.

The insured is not compelled to abandon his interest, where the goods are abandoned, the insurer will have to pay the full insured value. Where there is constructive total loss, the assured may either treat the loss as a partial loss or abandon the subject-matter insured to the insurer and treat the loss as if it was an actual total loss.

Notice of Abandonment

The notice of abandonment is essentially given to the insurer to claim the loss as constructive total loss. If he fails to do so, the loss can only be treated as a partial loss. The notice can be given orally or in writing. The notice should be unconditional and absolute. The insurer may either elect to accept or decline the proposal. But, when the insurer elects to object the notice, the insured should at once commence legal action against the insurer to claim 'the loss' under constructive total loss. In brief, the notice of abandonment involves the following:

1. Subject to the contrary provision, where the insurer elects to abandon the subject-matter insured to the insurer, he must give notice of abandonment. If the insured fails to furnish the notice, the loss can be treated as a partial loss.
2. The notice can be given in writing or orally. It may be given in any terms which indicate the intention of the assured to abandon his insured interest in the subject-matter insured unconditionally to the insurer.
3. Notice of abandonment must be given with reasonable diligence after the receipt of reliable information of loss, but where the information is of a doubtful character, the insured is liable to furnish the required information.
4. If notice of abandonment is properly given, the rights of the assured are not prejudiced by the fact that the insurer refuses to accept the abandonment.
5. The acceptance of an abandonment may be either express or implied from the conduct of the insurer. The mere silence of the insurer is not an acceptance.
6. Where notice of abandonment is accepted the abandonment is irrevocable.
7. Notice of abandonment is unnecessary where there is no possibility of benefit to the insurer if notice was given to him.
8. Notice of abandonment may be waived by the insurer.

Effect of Abandonment

1. In case of valid abandonment the insurer is entitled to take over the interest of the assured in, whatever may remain of the subject-matter insured.
2. At the time of abandonment of ship, the insurer is entitled of any freight in course of being earned.

In case of constructive total loss, the insurer have a right, after the settlement of the claim in full, to take over the property or whatever may remain of it. Where the insurers elect to take over the remainders of the wreck, the cost of removing the wreck is borne by the insurers. But, in case insurers elect not to take over the destroyed party, it becomes the liability of the ship-owners to remove the wreck and incur necessary expenditure for the same. The constructive total loss in the case of vessels is distinguished from the constructive total loss in cargo or freight. In case of cargo, the constructive total loss will be there where the assured is deprived of the goods by insured perils. In case of damage to the goods there is a constructive total loss where the cost of reconditioning the goods and forwarding the goods to the destination would exceed their value an arrival. Hull policy covers total and partial losses and partial losses are paid in full irrespective of the insured amount, the insured amount merely serves as the maximum limit.

Difference between Actual and Constructive Total Loss

Actual total loss is related with the physical impossibility and the constructive total loss is related with the commercial impossibility. For example, if the hides are so damaged that it is impossible to prevent the hides from the destruction and it may become a mass of putrefied matter, the case is of an actual total lass. But if it was possible to restore the hides to their original condition, though the cost of so doing would exceed their value at destination, the damaged hides can be claimed as constructive total loss because the completion of the adventure has became commercially impossible.

Salvage Loss

Where actual total loss occurred, and the subject-matter is so damaged as to cease to be a thing of the kind insured or when they have been sold before reaching the destination, there is a constructive total loss. The usual form of settlement is that the net sale proceeds will be paid to the assured. The net sale proceeds is calculated by deducting expenses of the sale from the amount realised by the sale. The insured will recover from the insurer the total loss less the net amount of sale. This amount received from the insurer is called a 'Salvage Loss'.

PARTIAL LOSS

Section 56 of the Act provides that any loss other than a total loss is a partial loss. Partial loss is there where only part of the property insured is lost or destroyed or damaged. Partial losses, in contradiction from total losses, include *(a)* Particular Average Losses, *i.e.*, damage, or total loss of a part, *(b)* General Average Losses (General Average) *i.e.*, the sacrifice expenditure, etc., done for common safety of subject-matter insured, *(c)* Particular or special charges, *i.e.*, expenses incurred in special circumstances, and *(d)* salvage charges.

PARTICULAR AVERAGE LOSS

Section 64 of the Act defines Particular Average loss as 'a partial loss' of the subject-matter insured caused by a peril insured and is not a general average loss. The general average loss or expense is voluntarily done for the common safety of all the parties insured. But, the particular average loss is fortuitous or accidental. It cannot be partially shifted to others but will be borne by the persons directly affected. The particular average loss must fulfil the following conditions:

1. Particular Average Loss is a partial loss or damage to any particular interest caused to that interest only by a peril insured against.
2. The loss should be accidental and not intentional.
3. The loss should be of the particular subject-matter only.
4. It should be the loss of a part of the subject-matter or damage thereto or both. The distinguishing feature in this matter is that where the properties insured are all of the same description, kind and quality and they are valued as a whole in the policy, the total loss of a part of this whole is a particular loss, but where the properties insured are not all of the same description, kind and quality and they are separately valued in the policy, the loss of an apportionable part of the interest is a total loss.

In case of total loss of a part of recoverable either as a total loss or as a particular average loss, the basis of settlement will be on the total loss of the whole lot and the insurer will be liable to pay in proportion according to the insured or insurable value of the whole interest.

Particular Average on Cargo

The particular average loss may be either the damage and depreciation of a particular interest or a total loss of its part. If the property is insured under one value for the whole and is all the same kind, quality or description, a total loss of part will be recovered as a particular average loss. In case where goods are delivered in a damaged condition or where the value is depreciated, the resulting particular average loss will be adjusted upon the basis of comparison between the gross sound value and damaged value. The process of valuation is as follows:

1. The gross sound value of the goods damaged is found out. This is the value for which the goods would have been sold if the goods had reached the port of destination in sound condition.
2. After calculating the above value, the gross damaged value of the goods damaged or depreciated is found out on the basis of market price at that time.
3. Deduct the gross damaged value from the gross sound value. The difference is the measure of the actual damage or depreciation.
4. The ratio of the damage or depreciation is calculated by dividing the amount of damage or depreciation by the gross sound value.
5. Apply the above ratio to the value (insured or insurable value as the case may be) of the damaged or depreciated goods which will give the amount of particular average loss.
6. Of the amount thus arrived at, the insurer is liable for that proportion which his sum insured bears to the value (insured or insurable).

ILLUSTRATION

For example, the cargo was of ₹ 20,000. Half of the goods are damaged which realised ₹ 4,000 at destination. If the damaged goods would have realised (*a*) ₹ 8,000, (*b*) ₹ 16,000 had they reached undamaged.

(*a*)	Gross sound value on arrival	₹ 8,000
	Gross realised value on arrival	₹ 4,000
	Damage	₹ 4,000

Damage is ₹ 4,000 which is 1/2 of gross sound value. Therefore, the claim on policy is 1/2 of ₹ 10,000 (20,0002)-₹ 5,000.

(*b*)	Gross sound value on arrival	₹ 16,000
	Gross realised value on arrival	₹ 4,000
	Damage	₹ 12,000

Damage is ₹ 12,000 which is 3/4 of gross sound value. Therefore, the claim on policy is 3/4 of ₹ 10,000 = ₹ 7,500. The main reason for the above computation was to keep the underwriter free from the liability or otherwise of the rise or fall in the price of the damaged goods.

Valuation by Services

The valuation by services removes the defects of memorandum clause which is used to free certain commodities from particular average and in the case of other commodities the damage has to amount to at least 5 per cent to become recoverable. Specifically, the provisions are:

1. Corn, fish, salt, fruit, flour and seed, etc., are warranted free from particular average unless the ship be stranded.
2. Sugar, tobacco, hemp, flax, hides and skins, etc., are warranted free from particular average unless the ship be stranded or unless amounting to 5%.

3. All the other goods are warranted free from particular average unless the ship be stranded or unless amounting to 3%.

The stranding of the ship vitiates the Memorandum and renders insurers liable for any particular average which has occurred on the voyage irrespective of the franchises mentioned. Percentage has to be taken into consideration in ascertaining whether the franchise is reached, but when attained the damage is paid in full. If the particular average reaches the stated percentage, the insurer becomes liable in respect of the whole loss and not merely for the excess over the franchise or exemption limit.

As has been mentioned above, the particular average loss can be claimed only when it exceeds 'certain fixed percentage' of the total value of the goods. But this limit or percentage may account a huge amount when a very large amount has been insured. In such a case, it will work as a great hardship to the assured as he will have to suffer this partial loss himself. In order to lessen the rigours of memorandum clause, the subject-matter is divided in sections known as 'series' and the franchise *i.e.,* the exemption limit will be considered for each series separately for the purpose of calculating particular average loss. The subject-matter may vary according to the type of interest, packing, original localities. The last series which does not fulfil the required limit or amount is called tail series. A tail series is dealt as a complete series. The assured is free to recover particular average in respect of each series separately.

Particular Average on Ship

In case of partial loss of ship the following factors are considered:

1. Where the ship has been repaired, the assured is entitled to the reasonable cost of the repairs less the customary deductions. The amount of repair shall not be more than the sum insured.
2. Where the ship has been only partially repaired; the assured is entitled to the reasonable cost of such repairs, reasonable depreciation.
3. If the ship has not been repaired and has not been sold in her damaged state during the risk, the assured is entitled to be indemnified for the reasonable, depreciation arising form ,the unrepaired damage.

The measure of indemnity for particular average is the reasonable cost of repairing the damage less the customary deductions 'new for old'. If the damaged parts of the ship are old then the insurers is obliged to indemnify the insured only to the extent of the value of the old parts. But when new parts are added, the difference between the value of the new parts and the value of the old parts are made. Insurers are liable for the cost of repairing particular average damage to the ship irrespective of the insured or actual value of the ship where temporary repairs are necessary the insurers are liable for such repairs in addition to the permanent repairs. Where a ship cannot be repaired at the port of refuge, cost of removal to another port is regarded as part of the cost of repairs. Extra expenses involved in 'over-time' working are not allowed.

Particular Average in Case of Freight

Where there is a partial loss of freight, the measure of indemnity is such proportion of the sum fixed by the policy in the case of a valued policy, or of the insurable value in the case of an unvalued policy as the proportion of freight lost by the assured bears to the whole freight at the risk of assured under the policy.

GENERAL AVERAGE

Section 66 of the Act defines General Average as a loss caused by or directly consequential on a general average act which includes a general average expenditure as well as a general average sacrifies. The general average loss will be there where the loss is caused by an extraordinary sacrifice or expenditure voluntarily and reasonably made or incurred in time of peril for the purpose of preserving the property imperilled in common adventure. The following elements are involved in general average.

1. The loss must be extra ordinary in nature. The sacrifice or expenditure must not be related to the performance of routine work. A state of affairs may compel the master to do something beyond his ordinary duty for the preservation of the subject-matter.
2. The whole adventure must be imperilled. The peril should be something more than the ordinary perils of the sea. It should be imminent and real.
3. The general average act must be voluntary and intentional accidental loss or damage is excluded.
4. The loss, expenses or sacrifice must be incurred or made reasonably and prudently. The master of the ship is proper person to decide the reasonableness of a particular circumstance.
5. The sacrifice, loss or expenditure should be made for the preservation of the whole adventure. It should be made for the common safety.
6. If the sacrifice proved abortive, it will be allowed as the total loss. Therefore, to call it general average, it must be successful at least in part.
7. In absence of contrary provision, the insurer is not liable for any general average loss or contribution where the loss was not incurred for the purpose of avoiding, or in connection with the avoidance of a peril insured against.
8. The loss must be direct result of a general average act. Indirect losses such as demurrage and market losses are not allowed as general average.
9. General average must not be due to some default on the part of the person whose interest has been sacrificed.

Difference between General Average Loss and Particular Average Loss

1. General average is incurred for the benefit of all interests but the particular average is in connection with any of the interests.
2. General average is always voluntary and intentional but the particular average is an accidental or fortuitous.
3. General average is shared by all those who is benefited by the general average act. Particular average is paid by the insurer.
4. General average may include expenditure and sacrifice along with loss, whereas the particular average results from a loss or damage.

TYPES OF GENERAL AVERAGE LOSS

The general average losses are divided into two classes.

1. General Average Sacrifices

The general average sacrifices are made for common safety. For example 'jettison' which means throwing away of the cargo in order to lighten the ship. Similarly, the use of cargo as fuel, cutting away of a spare and sails.

2. General Average Expenditure

The general average act involves expenditure. In this case extra expenditures are involved for common safety. Here, additional charges are incurred at the port ship is repaired, expenses may be involved for lightening and re-loading of the cargo.

GENERAL AVERAGE CONTRIBUTION

The general average loss is rateable contributed by the parties interested. In contribution of general average loss the contributory interest, amount to be made good and contributory values are considered.

1. Contributing Interests

The interests saved by the general average act are liable to contribute rateably to make good the sacrifices or expenses. There are certain articles which are not required to contribute towards general average loss. For example, postal articles, parcel, crews, effects and the personal effects of passengers not shipped under a bill of lading. There are three main contributing interests—ship, freight and cargo. When a general average loss occurred among different interests, it is of vital importance that the interest which has been sacrificed must also rateably contribute to the loss, otherwise it would be in a better position than the interests saved by general average act.

2. Amounts to be Made Good

The amount to be made good in general average differs from adventure to adventure.

(*a*) *Ship.* The amount to be made good in general average in respect of a ship is measured by reasonable cost of repairs less the actual deduction (if any) new for old. The costs of repairs are taken into account as they have been actually effected either at a port of refuge or at destination.

(*b*) *Cargo.* The amount of general average in case of goods is their net value. The net value is calculated taking into account the value of goods sacrificed at their safe arrival and from this the expenses (*i.e.,* freight unpaid, duty and landing charges) which would have been incurred had the goods arrived safely, are deducted. Thus, the net value of goods is obtained. The remaining cargo arrives damaged from causes which would have actually affected the sacrificed goods. The amount to be made good for general average purposes is their net value based on what the goods sacrificed would have realised, had they reached the destination damaged to some extent as the other cargo. For goods arriving damaged owing to general average sacrifice, the allowance is the difference between their net value in sound condition and net value in damaged state.

(*c*) *Freight.* Where the freight is to be paid at destination in respect of a cargo which is used for general average act, the shipowner will lose it and it would be made good in general average. The shipowner is entitled for the gross freight which he would have earned, had the goods not been sacrificed less the charges which he would have incurred to earn such freight during the remainder of the voyage, but which he has not incurred as a result of the sacrifice.

(*d*) *Expenses.* All the extra ordinary expenses properly incurred by the shipowner in time of peril for the common safety of all the interests are also made under the general average contribution.

3. Contributory Values

The third process is to determine what are the bases to contribute to general average. The interest contributes on their net value at the place where the voyage ends, *i.e.*, at destination or at intermediate port if the voyage be abandoned there. The values are contributory values. It may be of three types.

(*i*) *Ship.* The shipowner will contribute on the ship's value as saved by the sacrifice. The value is the amount for which the shipowner as a reasonable man would be willing to sell her on arrival at her destination. Any amount that may have been contributed in respect of general average damages is added to this value to arrive at contributory value.

(*ii*) *Cargo.* The cargo owner will contribute on the market value of goods saved at the place where the voyage ends. To arrive at the value the expenses incidental to the safe arrival of the cargo is deducted from the selling price of the cargo.

(*iii*) *Freight.* If the freight has been paid in advance, it would have been included in the value of separate interest. The goods arrived safely at destination will have to contribute on the basis of the net value of freight saved if the freight was not paid in advance. The contribution of freight will arrive at by ascertaining the actual sum of freight received at port of destination less the expenses of earning it from the date of general average act.

Applicaation of General Average to Insurance

In absence of contrary to the contract, the general average losses and contributions are recoverable from the respective marine insurers insuring ship, freight and cargo if the general average has been incurred for the purpose of avoiding a peril insured against. The extent of insurers, liability for general average contribution is the full amount of the contribution provided the contributory value does not exceed the insured value.

The York-Antwerp Rules 1950

The York-Antwerp rule was formulated in 1877. The rule was again revised and extended at a meeting of the International Law Association held at Stockholm in Sept. 1924. The rule was again amended in 1950 and 1974. Now, the rule is called the York-Antwerp Rules 1974. It has been formulated in two forms (1) Lettered Rules and (2) Numbered Rules.

Lettered Rules

There shall be a general average act when and only when any extra-ordinary sacrifice or expenditure is intentionally and reasonably made or incurred for the common safety for the purpose of preserving from peril. The general average sacrifices and expenses shall be borne .by the different contributing interests. Only such losses, damages, or expenses which are the direct consequence of the general average act shall be allowed as general average. The lettered rules are described from A to G.

Numbered Rules

The numbered rules I to XIX specify the various losses and expenses that are considered to be general average sacrifices. The last three rules XX, XXI and XXII govern the banking arrangements in connection with the adjustment. It is provided that cash deposits paid to the adjusters as security for the final general assessment shall be treated as a fiduciary funds and placed in a special bank account.

Jettison of Cargo, Fire

No Jettison of cargo shall be made good as general average unless such cargo is carried in accordance with the Rule I and II.

Rule III

Extinguishing fire on shipboard done to a ship and cargo or either of them by water or otherwise will be included in general average.

Rule IV and V

Cutting Away wreck, stranding: Where a vessel has been partially wrecked by a sea peril and portion of the spares remain, the cutting away of these remnants is not allowed for in general average. The place of stranding should be voluntarily selected by the master. Loss or damage incurred in refloating such stranded ship shall be allowed as general average.

Rule VI and VII

Damage or loss caused to soils and spares and machinery shall be allowed in general average if it was due to general average act.

Rule VIII to XII

Expenses involved from lightening a ship to the reloading or discharge of cargo are involved in general average ships' materials and stores build for fuel are also taken as general average. Wages ana maintenance of crew and other expenses at a port of refuge are taken into general average if these are involved for general average act.

Rule XIII

In adjusting claims for general average repairs to be allowed in general average shall be subject to deductions in respect of "new for old" according to the rules. Temporary repairs made for the common safety shall be admitted as general average (Rule XIV).

Rule XVII

This rule mentioned that the contribution to a general average shall be made upon the actual net value of the property at the termination of the adventure to which values shall be added the amount made good as general average for property sacrificed.

Rule XV, XVI, XVII, XVIII

These deal with the loss of freight, amount to be made good for large and damage to ship.

Rule XIX

This rule deals with the undeclared value of goods without the knowledge of the shipowner or his agent or to goods wilfully misdescribed of the shipowner or his agent or to goods wilfully misdescribed at the time of shipment shall not be allowed to general average but such goods shall remain liable to contribute.

Rules XX, XXI and XXII deal with the banking provision of the general average.

EXPENSES

The expenses are (*i*) Particular charges and (*ii*) Salvage charges.

1. Particular Charges

Where the policy contains a "Sue and Labour" clause, the engagement thereby entered into is deemed to be supplementary to the contract of insurance and the assured may recover from the insurer any expenses properly incurred pursuant to the clause. The clause requires the insurers to pay any expenses properly incurred by the assured or his agents in preventing or minimising loss or damage to the subject-matter by an insured peril. The essential features of the clause are as below :

1. The expenses must be incurred for the benefit of the subject matter insured. The expenses incurred for the common benefit will be a part of general average.
2. The expenses must be reasonable and be incurred by "the assured, his factors, his servants or assigns" and this provision effectively excludes salvage charges.
3. They are recoverable only when incurred to avert or minimise a loss from a peril covered by the policy.

Sue and Labour

Sue and labour charges are a type of particular charges. They are incurred short of destination *i.e.* reconditioning costs and follow upon loss or damage, whereas particular charges may be incurred when loss in threatened imminant but is avoided by expenses for that purpose. In real and actual sense sue and labour is a sort of particular charges.

Extra charges

Extra charges are the expenses of proving a claim *e.g.* survey fees. These are payable only if the loss is payable under the policy. Where extra charges are payable by insured, insurance cover is given. For example sale, charges and auction fees incurred in disposing of damaged cargo.

2. Salvage Charges

Section 65 of the Act defines salvage charges as those recoverable under maritime law by a salvor independents of contract. It is the remuneration or reward payable according to maritime law to salvors who voluntarily and independently of contract render services to rescue or save property at sea *i.e.* hull, cargo and freight. No reward for services or payments for loss or expenses can be claimed by salvors where the services were unsuccessful and the property was totally lost.

Average Adjusters :

The adjustment of general average losses is entrusted to an average adjuster. The specialised knowledge and the reputation for strict impartiality ensure that their findings are acceptable to all coverenced. The adjuster's fees are allowed in general average. This is also allowed in particular average loss.

QUESTIONS

1. What are the procedures of adjusting marine insurance losses?
2. What do you mean by the following terms:

   Particular Average Loss, General Average Loss, Constructive and Total Losses.

24

PAYMENT OF CLAIMS

When the policy has been issued the risk for the peril insured against is covered. The contingency against which protection is given or not materialised when the loss insured against actually occurs, the insured has got to make a claim on the insurer for in-demnification of loss. If loss does not occur, no payment would be made to the insured.

Evidence

Before admitting a claim, relevant evidence in connection with the policy is required. In marine insurance the policy is generally issued on mutual understanding and Good Faith of both the parties. But, at the time of claim, the insurer should satisfy himself on the information furnished by the insured. Value of subject-matter, nature of the subject matter; warranties, insurable interest, etc. are some of the matters to be considered at the time when the claim arises. For these purposes, the production of certain documents becomes necessary.

Notice of Claim

A prompt notice of claim by the insured is required. The receipt of notice or approval of the course of action taken by the insured does not mean that the liability of any loss is acknowledged. The damage notice must be given prior to survey by insurer's representative and the survey report signed by him.

The compliance with the rules of notice is necessary to enforce the right of recovery of the loss by the insured. After the notice, the insured must take delivery of the damaged goods at once or otherwise deal with the damage because the insurer is not responsible for further and continued depreciation of the interest damaged. In case of any theft or pilferage, the insured must give notice to the insurer within 10 days from the date on which the risk expired. If ship owner is also liable for any loss or damage, he or his agent is also entitled to a written notice. The notice is generally given at the time of taking delivery of goods. But if loss could not be determined or detected before such delivery, the notice is to reach the ship-owner or his representative within 3 days of the delivery. The notice is an important factor in the matter of claim.

DOCUMENTS REQUIRED FOR CLAIM

The following documents are required at the time of claim.

(*i*) Policy or certificate of insurance.

(*ii*) **Bill of lading.** It determines the scope of the contract of carriage.

(*iii*) **Invoice or bill** stating terms and conditions of sale.

(*iv*) **Copy of protest.** In the event of stranding of or accident to the vessel, the master of the ship notes 'protest' before a counsel or notary public. The protest states that everything was done to bring to safety the ship and cargo and loss or damage was not due to lack of diligence on the part of the master or crew.

(*v*) **Certificate of Survey.** This is necessary to find out whether the necessary franchise is reached or not in case of particular average.

(*vi*) **Account sales or Bill of sale.** Similar documents where goods have been sold. The difference between gross sound value and proceeds as per account sales might be accepted as amount of loss.

(*vii*) **Letter of subrogation.** It gives the underwriters to sue and recover compensation from third parties where the same is due.

DOCUMENTS IN DIFFERENT TYPES OF CLAIMS

Total Loss

(*i*) **Insurance policy.** It furnishes an evidence of the terms and contract of insurance.

(*ii*) **Bill of lading.** It is the correspondence of the insurance contract with the voyage and vessel.

(*iii*) **Copy of the invoice.** A copy of the Invoice relating to the goods insured should be sent. It will help in estimating the correct value of the goods.

(*iv*) ***Protest.*** A copy of protest is required when the total loss is due to the loss of the vessel or other accident.

(*v*) **Letter of subrogation.** A letter of subrogation is sent if anything remains of the subject-matter insured after the total loss or if there are rights or remedies regarding the interest or against third parties.

(*vi*) **Notice of Abandonment.** If there is a constructive total loss, the notice of abandonment is given in the manner described in previous chapter.

Partial Loss

In case of partial average loss:

(*i*) the policy or the certificate,

(*ii*) the invoice for the whole shipment,

(*iii*) the bill of lading should be sent to the underwriters and

(*iv*) the copy of the Master's protest or an extract from logbook of the ship is to be presented with the policy if the particular average is recoverable in certain circumstances according to the terms of the policy, *e.g.*, standing of the vessel, accident, heavy weather, etc.

(*v*) **A Surveyor's Report.** A surveyor's report prepared by some recognised surveyor should be appended to the above documents when evidence is necessary to show that the settled franchise has reached.

(*vi*) **Bill of Sale.** When there is a sale of the damaged goods the bill of sale is required by the measures.

(*vii*) **Letter of Subrogation.** The letter of subrogation should be duly furnished by the insured if required by the insurers.

(*viii*) **Cost of Protection.** On the proof, the cost of protection is paid by the underwriters apart from the particular average if there was a successful claim. In unsuccessful claims, insurers are not liable to pay these charges.

Particular Charge

When claim is made under those heads, shipping and insurance documents with evidence for the amount of the particular charges are required. When the case is taken up by an Average Adjuster, his report or the appropriate extract will have to be furnished to the underwriters.

General Average

While making a claim for general average loss, all the documents required for claims in total losses or in particular average losses if partial sacrifices are required to be represented to the underwriter. The Average Adjuster's Statement or the appropriate extract from it will have to be presented when claims for General Average Contribution are made. When the Average is claimed for General Average Deposits. the insurers will require the deposit receipt to enable them to recover any refund that may be due to them.

Salvage Charges

The documents in support of a salvage claim and the procedure to be followed are almost identical to those for a General Average Claim.

EXTENT OF LIABILITY

The insured can recover from the underwriter a loss to the extent of the insurable value of the property insured if it was an unvalued policy. In case of a valued policy, the assured can recover the loss to the full extent of the value fixed by the policy. Subject to the average-clause, where there are two or more underwriters, they shall bear the loss in the proportion of their subscription.

Successive Losses

The underwriters are generally not liable for more than the insured value; but they may be liable for successive losses which may in the aggregate exceed the insured value, by payment of extra premium and stamp duty. This provision is made by 'reinstatement clause'. Where there is partial loss which has not been repaired or otherwise made good is followed by a total loss, the assured can recover only the total loss. For example, where a damaged ship in an unrepaired state is lost, the insurers are liable only for total loss and not for unrepaired damage.

Other Charges

The amount of claim cannot include survey fees, cost of certificates and professional average adjuster's fees. Once the claim is proved to be recoverable, these charges can be recovered in full from the underwriters. The 'Sue and Labour' clause defines the procedure of payment of the expenses. Expenses incurred by or on behalf of the assured for the safety or preservation of the subject-matter insured, other than general average and salvage charges, are called particular charges. The underwriter is liable for particular charges and other expenses properly incurred pur sant to the provision of the suing and labouring clause in order to avert a loss insured against.

Effect of Over-Insurance and Under-Insurance

If two or more policies are effected by or on behalf of the assured on the same adventure and interest or in respect of any part thereof, and the sums insured exceed the minimum amount allowable as indemnity, the assured is said to be over-insured. Where the assured is insured for an amount less than the insurable value, he is said to be under -insured. In this case, he is deemed to be his own insurer in respect of the uninsured balance. Where the assured is over-insured, each insurer is bound as between himself and the other insurers to contribute rateably to the loss in proportion to the amount for which he is liable under his contract.

Subrogation

Where the insurer pays for a total loss, either of the whole, or in the case of goods, of any apportionable part, of the subject-matter insured, he thereupon becomes entitled to take over the interest of the assured in, whatever may remain of the subject-matter so paid for, and he is thereby subrogated to all the rights and remedies of the assured in and in respect of that subject matter. Subject to the foregoing provisions where the insurer pays for a partial loss, he acquires no title to the subject matter insured, or such part of it as may remain, but he is thereupon subrogated to all rights and remedies of the assured in and in respect of the subject-matter insured as from the time of the casualty causing the loss, in so far as the assured has been indemnified. The right of subrogation ensures that the assured should not make a profit out of the contract.

Salvage

The salvage is the remuneration or reward payable according to maritime laws to salvors who voluntarily and independently of contract render services to maritime property at sea. Salvage charges insured in preventing a loss by perils insured against may be recovered as a loss by those perils. The salvage awarded to salvors is apportioned over the values saved. This charge is not recoverable from marine underwriters.

Claims and 'Causa Proxima'

In determining the amount of the loss, the rule of Causa Proxima Non Remota Spectature is applied. It means that when there are more than one cause for the loss or damage the proximate cause and not the remote cause is regarded. The underwriter will pay the amount of loss only when the real or the proximate cause is insured. The peril insured against must be the proximate cause of the loss and it must not be due to the fault or misconduct of the insured.

The insurer is not liable for any loss attributable to the wilful misconduct of the assured, but unless the policy otherwise provides, he is liable for any loss proximately caused by a peril insured against, even though the loss would not have happened but for the misconduct or negligence of the master or crew. Unless the policy otherwise provides, the insurer on ship of goods is not liable for any loss proximately caused by delay although the delay be caused by a peril insured against. Unless the policy otherwise provides, the insurer is no liable for ordinary wear and tear, or dinary leakage and breakage, inherent vice or nature of the subject-matter insured or for any loss proximately caused by rate or vermin or for any injury to machinery not proximately caused by maritime perils.

SOME PRACTICAL PROBLEMS

Example 1

25 personal computers were insured for ₹ 35,00,000 with following invoice value:

Model A-20 Pc @ ₹ 1,00,000 each 20,00,000
Model B-5 Pc @ ₹ 2,00,000 each 10,00,000
Total value CIF = 30,00,000

when consignment arrived at the destinaction, it was found that one of Model A and one Pc of Model B were missing

Invoice value of missing PC
Invoice value of one Pc Model A ₹ 1,00,000
Invoice value of one Pc Model B ₹ 2,00,000
₹ 3,00,000

Total invoice value of Rs. 30,00,000 insured for 35,00,000

So, claim amount

$$\frac{3,00,000 \times 35,00,000}{30,00,000} = ₹3,50,000$$

Example 2

A consignment of goods insured for ₹ 22,00,000. The Gross Arrived Damaged Value (GADV) at destination is ₹ 8,00,000. And the Gross Arrived Sound Value (GASV) is ₹ 20,00,000. The depreciation is

	GASV	20,00,000
less	GADV	8,00,000
Difference		₹ 12,00,000

$$\text{The loss is} = \frac{\text{Differnce} \times 100}{\text{GASV}} = \%$$

$$\text{in this case} = \frac{12,00,000 \times 100}{20,00,000} = 60\%$$

So,

60% of the insured value of ₹22,00,000 = ₹13,20,000 will be paid as claim.

It should be noted here that gross value includes wholesale price, (or the estimated value) with freight, landing charges and duty paid.

Example 3

A consignment of goods under ICC (A) was insured for ₹24,00,000. On arrival broken consignment loss was Rs. 1,06,800 the invoice value was ₹21,50,000. ₹3000 was paid for sorting charges. The claim worked out

$$\frac{1,06,800 \times 24,00,000}{21,50,000} = ₹119220+3000 = ₹1,22,220$$

Example 4:

A consignment of apple in 400 cases was booked from Mumbai to New York and was insured for ₹40,00,000. At the destination, it was noticed that

(i) 120 cases were damaged by fire - depreciation 30%
(ii) 40 cases damaged by sea water - depreciation 50%
(iii) 50 cases were found to be missing due to pilferage
(iv) 10 cases were lost overboard during discharge
(v) 218 cases arrival sound, The survey fee was ₹10,000

Find claim amount if insurance is under ICC(A), ICC(B), and ICC(C)

	Particulars	*Insures value*	*Depreciation*	*Claim*
(i)	120 cases fire damaged	12,00,00	30%	3,60,000
(ii)	40 cases seawater damaged	4,00,000	50%	2,00,000
(iii)	50 cases missing (pilferage)	5,00,000	—	5,00,000
(iv)	10 cases lost overboard	1,00,000	—	1,00,000
				9,60,000

A- **Claim Under** – ICC(A)-All Risks

	Rs.
All claims	9,60,0000
+ Survey fees	10,000
	9,70,000

B. Claim Under – ICC(B) named risks in this clause pilferage is not insured. So total claim - loss by pilferage

= ₹9,60,000 – 5,00,000 = ₹4,60,000 + survey fees ₹10,000

₹4,70,000

C. Claim under ICC(C) – named risks. Other losses are not covered under ICC(C). Only fire damaged in insured.

Thus :	3,60,000
plus survey fee	10,000
	3,70,000

Example 5

There were consignment for ₹ 3,00,000 under Institute Cargo Clauses (B) of 500 bales. There was 21 bales unidentified and 22 bales were lost. Insurance claim of 500 bales insured for ₹ 3,00,000

The claim	Rs.
1. 50% of 21 bales unidentified.	6300
$₹ = \frac{21 \times 600 \times 50}{100}$	
2. 22 bales were lost @ 600	13200
	₹ 19,500

Example 6

At the time of the general average act, the vessel had unrepaired damage from a previous accident amounts to Rs. 2,00,000.

		₹
The Sound Value on arrival at destination was		1,00,00,000
The damage sustained on the current voyage was		5,00,000
The contributory value would be sound value		1,00,00,000
Less cost of repairs	₹ 2,00,000	
outstanding at destination	₹ 5,00,000	7,00,000
contributory value		₹ 93,00,000

Any amount made good, will be added

Example 7 :

	₹
1. Cargo Jettisoned on which freight payable at destination	40,00,00
cost of discharging cargo	90,000
Amount to be made good for loss of freight	
	₹ 3,10,000

Example 8.

1. Sound value of the ship	50,00,000
2. Deduct estimated cost of repairing particular average damage	10,00,000
3. Value of Vessel immediately preceding the general average sacrifice	40,00,000
4. Amount realised by the sale of the vessel	4,00,000
5. Amount to be made good in general average in respect of the sacrifices	36,00,000
	₹ 36,00,000

Example 9

Adjust the general average given the following facts :

Sound market value of slip at destination	8,00,00,000
Damage caused by collision	2,00,0,000
Damage in existence from previous content	1,00,0,000
C&I value of 1000 containers	3,00,00,000
Freight due on all containers	8,00,0,000

use of discharge @ ₹ 200 per container 20% of the containers were jettison for common safety and the vessel was then able to proceed to destination

General Average Allowed

		₹
1. 20% container Jettisoned *i.e.* 200 containers		60,00,000
2. Freight 20% of Rs. 8,00,000	1,60,000	
Less Expenses saved i.e. 200 × ₹ 200	40,000	
		12,00,000
		72,00,000
Ship :		
sound market value ship		8 ,00,00,000
deduct damage		30,00,000
		7,70,00,000
Cargo :		
C & I value		3,00,00,000
deducts 200 containers lost		60,00,000
		2,40,00,000
Freight add made good		60,00,000
		3,00,00,000
Freight :		
Gross freight		64,00,000
add made good		12,00,000
		76,00,000

Thus ₹ 7,70,00,000 + ₹ 3,00,00,000 + ₹ 76,00,000 = 11,46,00,000

QUESTIONS

1. Discuss the procedures of settlement of claims.
2. How is the extent of liability determined by the insurer?

25

PROGRESS OF MARINE INSURANCE BUSINESS IN INDIA

The marine insurance business was nationalised, along with other general insurance by the General Insurance (Emergency Provisions) Ordinance 1971, which was subsequently replaced by the General Insurance (Emergency Provisions) Act, 1971. The management of the insurers carrying on General Insurance Business in India was taken over by the Central Government with effect from 13th May, 1971. The General Insurance Corporation of India was formed on 22nd Nov. 1972, under the General Insurance Business (Nationalisation) Act 1972 and by virtue of the same Act, 55 Indian General insurance companies became subsidiaries of the General Insurance Corporation of India and the undertakings of the other erstwhile insurers were merged in one or the other of four selected ultimate companies which were to operate in the nationalised set-up, viz., National Insurance Company Ltd., New India Assurance Company Limited, Oriental Fire & General Insurance Company Ltd. and United India Fire & General Insurance Company Limited. On 1st January, 1974, the 55 Indian insurance companies were also merged into the four ultimate companies by schemes merger. The setting up of a new organisational set-up for the four ultimate companies is still in the process of being completed. Thus the period from 13th May, 1971 to 31st Dec. 1974 has been a period of transition. The progress of marine insurance has been analysed under progress before nationalisation and progress after nationalisation.

Business of Indian Insurers Progress Before Nationalisation

The Gross Premium of Indian Insurers has increased from ₹ 21.06 crores in 1969, *i.e.*, 76.6 per cent of the gross premium received by the marine insurers, to ₹ 31.61 crores, *i.e.*, 79.4 per cent of the gross premium in 1972. Thus, the gross premium has increased not only in absolute term but it has increased in relation of total gross premium. The business of non-Indian insurers has decreased from 23.4 per cent of total gross premium in 1969 to 20.6 per cent or gross premium in 1972. The non-Indias insurers were unable to increase their share in total business. The total gross premium income of nationalised insurers have increased from ₹ 70.83 crores in 1975 to ₹ 98.32 crores in 1978.

Not only the share of gross premium to Indian Insurers, but, the share of net premium to Indian Insurers has also increased from 75.2 per cent of net premium to 78.2 per cent of net premium in 1972. The share of non-Indian insurers has decreased from 24.8 per cent of total net premium to 21.8 per cent of total net premium in 1972. The total net premium has been constantly rising from ₹ 17.96 crores in 1969 to ₹ 27.79 crores in 1972.

As compared to general total general insurance business, the Indian insurers have booked less business in the form in marine insurance business as the share of Indian insurers to total general insurance business in 1969 was 80.2 per cent of total net received by all general insurers which increased to 81.7 per cent in 1971 and 82.8 per cent in 1972 while the corresponding percentage in case of marine insurance was 25.2, 76.9 and 78.2 per cent respectively. Thus, the share of marine insurance of Indian insurers was not so high as was total business in case of general insurances.

Table 25.1 Marine Insurance Business in India, (1969-1981)

(All Insurers) **₹ in Crores**

Year	Gross Premium					(Net Premium)					Total General Insurances (Net Premium)				
	Indian Insurers		Non-Indian Insurers		Total	Indian Insurers		Non-Indian Insurers		Total	Indian Insurers		Non-Indian Insurers		Total
	₹	% to total	₹	% to total	₹	₹	% to total	₹	%to total	₹	₹	% to total	₹	to% total	₹
1969	21.06	76.6	6.44	23.4	27.5	13.50	75.2	4.46	24.8	17.96	73.22	80.2	18.12	19.8	91.35
1970	24.31	77.8	6.95	22.2	31.26	14.45	74.5	4.94	25.5	19.38	84.41	81.5	19.13	18.5	103.57
1971	30.22	79.4	7.85	20.6	38.07	18.48	76.9	5.56	23.1	24.04	93.76	81.7	20.94	18.3	114.70
1972	31.61	79.4	8.22	20.6	39.84	21.73	78.2	6.06	21.8	27.79	119.11	82.8	23.46	17.2	136.57
*1975					70.83					39.32					247.07
1977					95					85					326
*1978					102					92					370
1979					115					103					398
*1980					137					117					481
1981					168					146					599

*Figure relate subsidiary companies of GIC.

The net premium in marine has also increased from ₹ 17.96 crores in 1969 to ₹ 24.04 crores in 1971 and ₹ 27.79 crores in 1972 and ₹ 48.71 crores in 1977. The net premium of all insurances has also increased from ₹ 91.35 crores in 1969 to ₹ 114.70 crores in 1971 and further to 136.57 crores in 1972.

Table 25.2 Analysis of Ratio to Net Premium (%) (1970-1981)

Year	Indian Insurers						Non-Indian Insurers					
	Net claim Payable	Net Commssion	Expenses of Mang.	Incerease in Reserve	Misc. Income	Balance of Income	Net claim Payable	Net Commission	Expenses of Mang.	Increase in Reserve	Misc. Income	Balance of Income
1970	65.7	2.4	19.5	2.7	0.6	4.8	62.8	–1.5	32.4	4.8	0.1	1.4
1971	59.7	1.2	17.1	10.5	5.5	16.6	68.0	–0.4	32.9	5.6	0.7	–6.2
1972	61.3	2.2	17.3	5.1	6.7	20.6	68.4	–0.3	35.2	4.1	2.8	–5.1
1975	49.9	18.9	0.6	16.5		14.1						
1977	41.1	18.0	0.9	2.8	—	37.2						
1978	54.3	17.2	1.0	10.6	—	16.9						
1980	68.5	17.9	0.8	20.9	—	8.1						
1981	61.3	18.2	0.8	18.9	—	0.8						

Note: Figure of 1975, 1977 and 1978 are related with the nationalised business.

—(Not Applicable)

Indian Insurers

The percentage of net claim to net premium has declined from 65.7 in 1970 to 59.7 percent in 1971 and increased to 61.3 per cent in 1972 while non-Indian insurers have experienced correspondingly a higher percentage viz. 62.8, 68.00 and 68.9 per cent. It reveals that the Indian insurers were rational in payment of claims and were gaining on ground of payment claims. But so far payment of commission was concerned Indian insurers were not saving as compared to that of non-Indian insurer. Indian insurers paid net commission as high as 24 per cent of net premium in 1970. But the Indian insurers were controlling their management expenses more effectively than that of non-Indian insurers who experienced 32.4 per cent of net premium at the minimum while the Indian-insurers experienced the expenses of 19.5 per cent of the net premium at the rnaximum. More-over, the expenses ratio was declining. This shows that the Indian-insurers were more efficiently managing their business and were gaining much more than the non-Indian insurers. The non-Indian insurers suffered loss to the tune of 6.2 per cent of net premium whereas the Indian insurers got the balance of income as low as 14.8 per cent of net premium which has increased to 16.6 per cent in 1971 and 30.6 per cent in 1972 and 16.9 per cent in 1978. Thus the Indian Insurers were more benefited at every level so far as ratios to net premiums were concerned.

Table 25.3 Analysis of Ratio to Gross Premium (%) (1958-1972)

Year	*Indian Insurers*						*Non-Indian Insurers*					
	Gross claim pay-able	*Direct Commi-ssion*	*Expen-ses of Mang.*	*Incre-ase in Reserve*	*Misc. Income*	*Balance of Income*	*Gross claim pay-able*	*Direct Commi-ssion*	*Expen-ses of Mang.*	*Increase in Reserve*	*Misc. Income*	*Balance of Income*
1958	56.7	7.4	19.2	—	—	16.4	49.5	8.6	27.0	—	—	14.9
1970	49.8	2.6	14.2	6.6	2.6	29.4	63.2	4.4	23.0	3.6	0.1	5.8
1971	41.7	2.4	13.5	9.8	2.7	35.1	57.6	4.5	23.3	5.1	0.5	8.9
1972	50.7	2.7	14.8	0.9	3.1	33.9	64.2	4.4	25.9	2.2	2.1	5.0

Indian Iusurers

The percentage of gross claims payable to gross premium has been constantly declining from 56.7 per cent in 1958 to 46.8 per cent in 1970 to 41.7 per cent in 1971 and further to 50.7 per cent in 1972. As compared to that of non-Indian insurers, it has been about two-thirds of their ratios. Thus the Indian insurers were saving much in shape of payment claim. Similarly, the Indian-insurers were also curtailing their expenses in the form of payment of direct commission which has been as low as 2.4 per cent of the gross premium in 1971 whereas it was 4.5 per cent in the case of non-Indian-insurers. The expenses of management were also curtailed more effectively by the Indian insurers as were done by the non-Indian insurers. The Indian insurers had expended only 19.2 per cent of the:r gross premium at the maximum in 1958 whereas it was 23.3 in 1971 of Non-Indian insurer. The Indian insurers were experiencing declining ratios of management expenses to gross premium. The increase in reserve to the Indian insurers were more than the increase in reserve of the non-Indian insurers. The balance of income to Indian insurers was rising rapidly from 16.4 per cent of gross premium in 1958 to 35:1 per cent in 1971 whereas the non-Indian insurers were grossing the share of balance of income to gross premium. Conclusively, it can be stated that the Indian insurers were improving their business and were doing business more effectively than that of non-Indian insurers.

Table 25.4 Indian Insurers, Ratio to Gross Direct Premium Income Outside India (%) (1970-1972)

	1970	*1971*	*1972*
1. Gross claims Payable	64.3	91.9	64.0
2. Direct Commission	10.8	11.8	12.6
3. Expenses of Managing	16.6	14.2	15.0
4. Increase in Reserve	–8.2	1.8	2.8
5. Misc. Income	5.1	5.4	8.3
6. Balance of Income	17.2	–18.6	17.9

The Indian insurers were losing their business outside India as the balance of income has decreased from 17.2 per cent of gross premium in 1970 to — 18.8 per cent of gross premium. Similarly, the percentage of gross claims payable to Gross Direct Premium has increased from 64.3 per cent in 1970 to 91.9 per cent in 1971 and declined to 64.0 per cent in 1972. The direct commission has also increased from 10.8 per cent in 1970 to 11.8 per cent in 1971. However the management expenses has declined from 16.6 per cent in 1970 to 14.2 per cent in 1971 and increased to 15.0 per cent in 1972.

Table 25.5 Net Premium Income Marine Insurance (1975-1981)

(In crores of ₹)

	1975	*1977*
In India	39.32	48.91
Outside India	14.28	17.75
Total	53.60	66.66

Total Insurance

	1975	*1977*	*1978*	*1979*	*1980*	*1981*
In India	166.12	254	287	323	385	486
Outside India	63.75	72	83	75	96	113
Total	229.87	326	370	398	481	599

The net premium income of marine insurance out of India has increased from ₹ 14.28 crores in 1975 to ₹ 17.75 crores in 1977. The net premium income in case of total General Insurance out of India has also increased from ₹ 63.75 crores in 1975 to ₹ 71.46 crores in 1977.

1. Gross Direct Premium Income

The gross direct premium has been analysed under the GIC and the four subsidiary companies. They are National Insurance Company Ltd., New India Assurance Company Ltd., Oriental Insurance Company Ltd. and United India Insurance Company Ltd.

Table 25.6 Gross Direct Premium Income in Marine in Insurance (*In Crores of* ₹)

	GIC	*National*	*New India*	*Oriental India*	*United*	*Total*
1975	—					70.83
1980	—	28.02	32.49	37.34	34.76	132.61
1981	—	35.26	49.58	48.77	51.13	185.04
1982	—	40.18	60.70	53.65	55.09	209.62
1984	—	49.15	67.70	58.97	71.58	247.40
1985	—	57.31	79.85	64.12	73.91	275.19
1986	—	62.40	86.52	69.96	85.02	303.90
1987	—	68.27	93.56	78.59	97.19	337.61
1988-89*	—	92.78	129.01	108.08	135.03	464.90
1989-90*	—	88.30	129.01	97.01	125.44	439.77
1994-95	—	165.30	230.16	170.56	260.83	826.85
1997-98	—	209.76	312.64	217.14	286.13	1025.67

*Note: 1988-89 has 15 months period.

The gross direct premium income has increased from ₹ 70.83 crores in 1975 to ₹ 132.61 crores in 1980, ₹ 275.19 crores in 1985, ₹ 464.90 crores in 1988-89 and ₹ 826.85 crores in 1994-95. The rate of increase has been higher in the later period. It shows that the general insurance industry has been very particular to extend its benefits to a larger population of the country. United India has increased its premium income from ₹ 34.76 crores in 1980 to ₹ 135.03 crores in 1988-89 and ₹ 260.83 crores in 1994-95. New India has also tried to increase its business from ₹ 32.49 crores in 1980 to ₹ 129.01 crores in 1988-89 and ₹ 230.16 crores in 1994-95. They have regular and constant progress. On the other hand, Oriental has increased its business very slowly from ₹ 37.34 crores in 1980 to ₹ 108.08 crores in 1988-89 and ₹ 170.56 crores in 1994-95. National has the least amount of business. It increased its business from ₹ 28.02 crores in 1980 to ₹ 92.78 crores in 1988-89 and ₹ 165.30 crores in 1994-95.

2. Net Premium Income

Net premium income has been observed in the GIC because it does accept reinsurance functions although it does not work directly for marine and fire insurance. The amount of net premium of the GIC has increased from ₹ 38.11 crores in 1982 to ₹ 102.81 crores in 1988-89 and ₹ 187.43 crores in 1994-95. It has maximum business than those of subsidiaries. The total net premium income in marine insurance has increased from ₹ 48.00 crores in 1973 to ₹ 156.38 crores in 1982 by more than three times. This premium could not increase at faster rate at later part of the period. It increased to ₹ 260.36 crores in 1985, ₹ 433.01 crores in 1988-89 and ₹ 734.33 crores in 1994-95. United India has shown satisfactory progress from ₹ 34.88 crores in 1982 to ₹ 93.27 crores in 1988-89 and ₹ 133.85 crores in 1994-95. New India has shown rapid progress from ₹ 31.05 crores in 1982 to ₹ 96.56 crores in 1988-89 and ₹ 179.84 crores in 1994-95. Oriental has been at the last place for promoting its business from ₹ 30.10 crores in 1982 to ₹ 70.66 crores in 1988-89 and ₹ 113.07 crores in 1994-95. National insurance has improved its position from the lowest to the second lowest position.

Table 25.7 Net Premium Income in Marine Insurance

(In crores of ₹)

	GIC	*National*	*New India*	*Oriental India*	*United*	*Total*
1973						48.00
1975						68.00
1980						117.00
1982	38.11	22.24	31.05	30.10	34.88	156.38
1983	44.35	27.53	40.66	34.37	42.70	189.61
1984	61.75	33.29	45.10	38.25	82.48	227.21
1985	72.59	37.95	53.35	40.78	55.69	260.36
1986	71.93	44.79	61.87	45.64	62.79	287.02
1987	77.69	51.53	68.34	50.23	74.41	322.20
1988-89	102.81	69.77	96.56	70.66	93.27	433.01
1989-90	95.47	64.37	95.90	65.48	85.33	311.08
1994-95	187.43	120.14	179.84	113.07	133.85	734.33
1997-98	221.90	136.36	188.74	124.07	151.41	822.48

*Note : The GIC transacts mainly reinsurance business.

3. Underwriting Experiences in Marine Insurance

The underwriting profit/loss experience of marine insurance has decreased from ₹ 6.86 crores in 1982 to ₹ 5.88 crores in 1985 but increased to ₹ 37.81 crores in 1988-89 and ₹ 56.61 crores in 1994-95. It shows that the underwriting profit has increased rapidly at later part of the analysis. But as percentage to net premium, it has increased from 4.3 percent in 1982 to 12.70 per cent in 1988-89 and declined to 7.0 per cent in 1994-95. National and New India have shown losses in 1994-95. National, Oriental and United India have experienced losses in some years, whereas United India has the highest underwriting profit. National and New India have shown higher rate of claims. Oriental have the lowest claim-ratio. United India and Oriental have higher expense-ratio than those of New India.

Table 25.8 Underwriting Experience in Marine Insurance

		% to Net Premium						
	Net Premium ₹ crores	*Net Claims payable %*	*Net commission %*	*Expenses to Management %*	*Miscellaneous Outgo %*	*Unexpired Risks Reserve %*	*Underwriting Profit/Loss (–) %*	*Underwriting Profit/Loss (–) ₹ Crores*
1985								
GIC	72.59	61.5	17.4	–0.9	—	14.9	5.3	3.88
National	37.95	70.6	–7.6	25.3	0.3	12.3	–0.3	–0.13
New India	53.35	64.0	–6.9	21.3	–0.6	16.5	6.7	3.55
Oriental	40.78	82.7	–9.8	26.1	–0.4	6.2	–4.8	–1.96
United India	55.69	69.4	–3.5	20.8	—	12.3	1.0	0.54
Total	260.36	68.4	—	16.8	–0.2	12.7	2.3	5.88
1989-90								
GIC	95.47	47.5	18.9	1.26	–0.02	13.8	18.5	17.64
National	64.37	64.5		19.6		13.3	22.6	1.67
New India	95.90	51.6		18.9		19.4	10.1	9.67
Oriental	65.48	57.7		21.5		13.7	7.1	4.65
United India	85.33	63.0		19.5		12.6	4.9	4.18
Total	311.08	56.9		18.4		14.6	12.6	37.81
1994-95								
GIC	187.43	53.5	17.6	1.0	–0.6	7.5	21.0	39.50
National	120.14	97.7	–5.0	23.50	0.30	–5.80	–9.70	–11.60
New India	179.85	86.0	–2.1	17.9	—	–1.2	–0.6	–1.13
Oriental	113.07	70.0	–7.6	23.90	—	1.0	12.7	14.39
United India	133.85	80.5	–11.5	25.00	—	–5.6	11.6	15.53
Total	734.34	77.34	–1.72	18.26	—	–0.82	7.0	56.61
1997-98								
GIC	221.90	45.5	18.1	0.9	0.00	3.6	31.9*	70.82
National	136.36	75.63	–9.46	24.33 (*b*)	0.08	6.51	3.07	4.19
New India	188.74	54.39	–9.37	25.49	–@	–9.03	38.52	72.70
Oriental	124.07	74.3	—	28.3	–11.1	–0.1	8.6	10.67

Contd...

	Net Premium ₹ crores	Net Claims payable %	Net commission %	Expenses to Management %	Miscellaneous Outgo %	Unexpired Risks Reserve %	Underwriting Profit/Loss (–) %	Underwriting Profit/Loss (–) ₹ Crores
	% to Net Premium							
United India	151.41	70.3	–13.5	30.9	16.3	7.9	5.4	8.15
Total	822.48	320.12	–14.23	109.92	5.28	7.97	87.49	166.53

*Note: @ includes commission also (*b*) includes miscellaneous outgo

Progress of Marine Insurance after Privatisation

(In crores of ₹)

Year	*National*	*New India*	*Oriental India*	*United*	*Total*
1998-1999	199.2	297.7	208.9	291.9	997.7
1999-2000	198.0	310.4	209.8	276.8	995.0
2000-2001	203.8	313.8	187.9	279.6	985.1
2001-2002	207.1	339.3	205.6	255.2	1003.7

Gross Direct Premium Outside India

Year	*National*	*New India*	*Oriental India*	*United*	*Total*
1998-1999	3.5	16.8	6.8	0	27.1
1999-2000	3.4	18.2	7.7	0	29.3
2000-2001	3.7	19.2	7.2	0	30.1
2001-2002	4.0	23.4	8.9	0	—

Total Gross Direct Premium

Year	*National*	*New India*	*Oriental India*	*United*	*Total*
1998-1999	202.7	314.5	215.7	291.9	1024.8
1999-2000	201.4	328.6	217.5	276.8	1024.3
2000-2001	207.5	333.6	195.1	279.6	1015.2
2001-2002	211.2	362.7	214.6	255.2	

Financial Highlights of Marine Insurance

(*₹ in crores*)

Year	*Net Premium*		*Net Incurred Claim*		*Commission*		*Expenses of Managment*		*Other income (–) outgo (+)*		*Increase in Reserve for Unexpired Risks*		*Investment Income*		*Under Working Profit Less +*	
	₹	% to GP	₹	% to NP	₹	%	₹	%	₹	%	₹	%	₹	%	₹	%
General Insurance Corporation																
1998-1999	221		108.2	47	40.8	18		–	–	–	7.4	3	–	–	72.9	32
1999-2000	233.3		130.0	55.7	39.8	17.1	2.08	0.9	0.25	0.10	3.98	1.7	–	–	57.21	24.5
2000-2001	296.8		89.0	39.6	36.0	15.9	2.03	0.9	52.6	0.2	–6.53	–2.9	64.2	27.5	105.01	46.3
2001-2002	207.6		131.0	57.8	43.0	19.0	1.7	0.3	00.3	–0.1			56.5	24.9	51.2	22.6
National Insurance Co. Ltd.																
1998-1999	14.3	71	126.8	88	27.3	19					6.9	5			–17.7	–12
1999-2000	139.3		110.13	79	–6.8	–4.9	37.24	26.74	–0.62	–0.01	–3.9	–2.9	344.4		2.65	1.90
2000-2001	149.1		56.9	38	–9.11	–6.1	35.05	23.50	0.13	0.08	9.8	6.6	381.8		56.26	37.7
2001-2002	132.8		78.0	58.8	–6.51	–4.9	38.3	283	–0.07	–0.05	–16.31	–12.3	30.4	22.9	69.7	52.5
The New India Assurance Co. Ltd.																
1998-1999	190.3	61	96.8	51	14.5	8					1.6	1			77.4	40
1999-2000	192.1		122.4	63.7	–17.64	9.18	50.88	26.48			1.78	0.93			34.69	18.06
2000-2001	188.12		141.8	75.4	–17.22	–9.2	54.19	28.80			–4.00	–2.13	50.71	24.14	13.40	7.12
2001-2002	220.69		131.33	62.51	10.34		51.64	24.5	80.09		21.97	10.46	35.22	37.41	15.49	7.33

(₹ *in crores*)

Year	*Net Premium*		*Net Incurred Claim*		*Commission*		*Expenses of Managment*		*Other income (–) Management Risks*		*Increase in Reserve for outgo (+)*		*Investment Income Unexpired*		*Under Writing Profit Less +*	
	₹	%	₹	%	₹	%	₹	%	₹	%	₹	%	₹	%	₹	%
							The Oriental Insurance Company Ltd.									
1998-1999	132.1	61	85.9	65	22.4	17									15.7	12
1999-2000	132.08	60.7	97.01	73.4	40.41	30.6	–9.40	–7.1			0.04	0.01	367.53		4.11	3.1
2000-2001	121.71	62.4	91.35	75.1	33.48	27.5	–6.95	–5.7			–10.37	8.5	396.23		14.20	11.7
2001-2002	139.11	64.0	74.27	53.3	41.18	29.6	–4.66	–3.3			–40.10	28.8	–24.21	–17.4	94.30	67.8
							United India Insurance Company Ltd.									
1998-1999	145.8	50	92.6	64	26.3	18					–5.6	–4			32.5	2.2
1999-2000	149.51		99.80	66.8	–25.34	–16.95	41.10	27.49			3.74	2.50			30.21	20.21
2000-2001	142.77		118.85	83.2	–18.99	–13.3	44.45	31.37			–6.73	4.71			4.85	3.40
2001-2002	126.60		81.64		–15.24		41.36		–6.56		–16.18		39.33		67.84	
							Indian Market Total									
1998-1999	840.8	82	510.3	61	131.3	16					18.4	2			180.5	21
1999-2000	846.3	83	559.3	66	152.6	18					5.5	1			128.9	15
2000-2001	828.4	82	498.7	60	153.0	18					–17.8	2			194.5	24
2001-2002																

MARINE INSURANCE APPENDIX

FRENCH MARINE HULL INSURANCE POLICY FOR ALL VESSELS

excluding fishing vessels, pleasure craft, sailing ships, and vessels with auxilary engines

(Policy form of 1st January 1998* as amended 1st January 2002)

GENERAL CONDITIONS

SUMMARY

PREAMBLE – Applicable law

CHAPTER I–EXTENT OF THE INSURANCE

Article 1 – Risks covered
Article 2 – Insurers' total liability
Article 3 – Exclusions

CHAPTER II–TIME AND PLACE OFTHE INSURANCE

Article 4 – Navigation and mooring
Article 5 – Trading limits
Article 6 – Continuation of the insurance

CHAPTER III–AGREED VALUE

Article 7

CHAPTER IV–RIGHTS AND DUTIES

Article 8 – Disclosure
Article 9 – Classification
Article 10 – Premium
Article 11 – Preventive measures
Article 12 – Sue and labour
Article 13 – Application for survey and repair of damage
Article 14 – Penalties
Article 15 – Premium payment provisions
Article 16 – Lay up in port
Article 17 – Avoidance or cancellation of the insurance

CHAPTER V–SURVEY OF LOSS OR DAMAGE

Article 18

CHAPTER VI–CALCULATION OF THE INDEMNITY

Article 19
Article 20 – Partial loss
Article 21 – Abandonment
Article 22 – General average
Article 23 – Salling in ballast
Article 24 – Third party claims
Article 25 – Salvage
Article 26 – Collision or salvage services between vessels belonging to the same assured

CHAPTER VII–PAYMENT OF IDEMNITY

Article 27 – Payment of loss or damage

CHAPTER VIII–PROCEDURAL MATTERS

Article 28

CHAPTER IX–INSURANCE OF SEVERAL VESSELS UNDER ONE POLICY

Article 29

* Original policy form of 1st December 1983 as amended 13th December 1984 and 30th January 1992

PREAMBLE–APPLICABLE LAW

This contract is governed by French law and in particular by those provisions of Title VII. Book 1, of the Code des Assurances which affect the marine insurance contract whether or not reference is made to them in the policy.

CHAPTER 1–EXTENT OF THE INSURANCE

ARTICLE 1–Risks covered

This policy covers loss, damage, third party liability or expenses caused by perils of the seas (fortunes de mer) and other accidents to the insured vessel.

It therefore covers:

1. subject to a limit of the agreed value, **loss or damage incurred by the vessel**, even if caused by the decision of a govermmental authority to avoid or minimize a risk of pollution arising from a peril insured against;
2. subject to a limit of the agreed value, **third party liablity incurred by the vessel in consequence of her collision** with an overseas vessel or inland craft, a floating object or structure, **or in consequence of the insured vessel's contact** with any other property or installation, as well as (and subject to the same limit) third party liability incurred in respect of damage caused by the insured vessel's hawsers, anchors, chains or tenders while attached to the vessel or being handled or used in the operation of the vessel;
3. subject to a limit of the agreed value, the vessel's contribution to general average, salvage and salvage charges, and legal costs incurred with insurer's agreement in respect to insured third party liability, as well as expenses reasonably incurred to save the vessel from an insured peril or to minimze such a peril.

ARTICLE 2–Insurers' total liability

Insurers' liability for all cover under article 1 **is limited to a total of twice the agreed value**.

ARTICLE 3–Exclusions

This insurance excludes:

1. loss, damage, liability or expenses caused by:
   - blockade running, smuggling, forbidden or chandestine trade, findes, confiscation, sequestration and requisition;
   - any seizure, bond or other financial guarantee;
   - wilful misconduct or gross negligence of the assured or his senior officers, viz, directors and officers, agency managers, superintendents or heads of technical departments;
   - inherient vice, wear and tear;
   - removal, destruction or marking of the wreck of the insured vessel;
   - immobilisation of or delay to the vessel, quarantine, health measures or disinfection;
   - impediments to commercial operation of the vessel;
   - death or injury to persons;
   - war or civil war, hostilities, reprisals, torpedoes, mines and all other weapons of war and, generally, all accidents and misfortunes of war, as well as acts of sabotage or terrorism of a political nature or related to war;
   - capture, takings at sea, arrest, seizure, restraint, molestation or detention by any government or other authority;
   - riots, civil commotions, strikes, lockouts and other similar events;
   - piracy of a political nature or related to war;
   - any direct or indirect effects of an explosion, release of heat, irradiation or any other nuclear power supply due to the transmutation of atoms or radioactivity as well as any effects of raditaion caused by the artificial acceleration of particles, whether through civil or military use or exploitation.

2. Loss or damage incurred by the vessel as a result of cargo being shipped in a manner not in accordance with current regulations and recognized trade practice where the assured is privy to such shipment.

   Expenses resulting from repair or replacement of parts affected by latent defect.
3. Liability incurred by the insured vessel for damage or other financial detriment:
   – in respect of cargo on board the insured vessel;
   – in respect of any liability resulting from the engagements assumed by the assured solely under a contract;
   – to the environment or as a consequence of pollution or contamination of any property or installation other than vessels or craft (or cargoes thereon) resulting from a collision with the insured vessel, when arising from escape or release of pollutant substances from that vessel.

Consequently, shall not be convered under this insurance, the "special compensation" payable to a salvor under Art. 14 of the International Convention on Salvage, 1989, to the extent specified in paragraph 4 of that article or under any other rovision similar in substance.

4. Expenses incurred for refloating, salvage or recovery of the vessel in case of stranding resulting from normal tidal movements, unless the vessel is in a place normally used for commercial operations.

CHAPTER II – TIME AND PLACE OF THE INSURANCE

ARTICLE 4 – Navigation and mooring

The vessel is covered verywhere within the geographical limits of the policy, whether in use, moored, laid up or under repair, and whether floating or in dry dock.

It remains covered when engaged in salvage operations. Insurers are liable for damage incurred in such operations only to the extent taht the assured is ubale to revover elsewhere.

It also remains covered when effecting towage or transhipment outside its normal commercial operations subject to prior notice to insurers who may require any precautionary measures apporpriate to the situation.

ARTICLE 5 – Trading limits

In the absence of prior notice there is no cover:

A. – During sailing and mooring within the zones defined below unless the vessel is obliged to enter by force majeure or to render salvage services.

1. Waters north of Lat. 70°N and Greeland waters other than voyages direct to or from any port or place in Norway or Kola Bay.
2. Beharing Sea, Eastern Asia north of Lat. 46° N; any port or place in Siberia except Nakhodka and/or Valdivostok.
3. To or from any port or place on the Atlantic coast of North America, tis rivers or adjacent islands as follows:
   a. at any time of year, north of Lat 52° 10¢N and west of Long. 50°W;
   b. between 21st December and 30th April (both dates inclusive) south of Lat. 52°10′N within the area bounded by lines drawn between:
      – Battel Harbour and Pistolet BAy
      – Cape Ray and Cape North (Nova Scotia)
      – Port Hawkesbury and Port Mulgrave
      – Bale Comeau and Matane
   c. between 1st December and 30th April (both dates inclusive) within the area between Montreal to the west and a line drawn between Baie Comeau and Matane to the east.

4. Any port or place on the Great Lakes or the St. Lawrence Seaway west of Montreal.
5. To or from any port or place on the Pacific coast of North America, its rivers or adjacent islands north of Lat 54°30N and west of Long 130°50′W.
6. To or from Kerguelen or Crozet or south of Lat 50°S, except ports of places in Patagonia, Chile or the Falkland Islands, but the vessel may enter waters south of Lat. 50°S for the sole purpose of reaching or returning from ports or places not excluded by this article.
7. Baltic Sea and adjacent waters east of Long 15°E as follows:
   a. north of a line between Mo (Lat 63°24′N) and Vasa (Lat. 63° 06′N) between 10th Decmeber and 25th may, (both dates inclusive);
   b. east of a line between Viipuri (Vyborg) (Long. 28° 47′E) and Narva (Loing. 28° 12′E) between 15th December and 15th May, (both dates inclusive);
   c. north of a line between Stockholm (Lat. 59°20′N) and Tallinn (Lat. 59°24′N) between 8th January and 5th May, (both dates inclusive);
   d. east of Long. 22°E and south of Lat. 59°N between 28th December and 5th May, (both dates inclusive)

B. – When the vessel is in tow other than in port, in the roads, in rivers or in canals, other than in the course of salvage operations.

ARTICLE 6 – Continuation of the insurance

If at expiry of the policy the vessel is under repair for damage covered by the policy or is on a voyage and suffereing fro such damage, cover under this policy is extended at a pro rata daily additional primum until either the repair or the voyage is completed (whichever shall first occur).

In case of total loss or abandonment during such extension premium for a further six moths is payable to insurers in addition.

CHAPTER III–AGREED VALUE

ARTICLE 7

The vessel's agreed value shall be conclusive, each party to this insurance undertaking not to use any other estimate unless in case of fraud, and subject to the provisions at articles 22 and 25.

The agreed value includes jointly the hull and machinery of the vessel as well as appurtenances and fittings owned by the assured and including ship's stores in particular.

if insurance is taken out without agreement of the vessel's insurers on an increased value basis or other supplementary interests, then the sum insured is reduced by the same amount in case of total loss or abandonment.

CHAPTER IV–RIGHT AND DUTIES

ARTICLE 8–Disclosure

1. The assured must disclose, on concluding the contract of insurance, all circumstances of which he is aware that would influence the insurers in assessing the risks to bge covered, in particular the flag, the classification society and the class of the vessel.
2. The assured must disclose to the insurers, as soon as he is himself aware of them, circumstances affecting the risk which occur during the time of the insurance.
3. The assured must immediately disclose any change in the vessel's flag or classification society and any alteration, cancellation or withdrawal of her class.
4. The assured must disclose to the insurers any marine mortgage on the insured interest at the time the contract is concluded or during the currency of the policy. In such cases the premium must be paid immediately unless the mortagees guarantee its payment on expiry of the insurance.

ARTICLE 9–Classification

1. The assured undertakes to comply, by the dates required by the vessel's classification society, with any recommendations, requirements or restrictions imposed by that society, which relate to the vessel's seaworthiness.
2. Subject to the authorisation of the assured or of his duly authorised representative and after setting out his reasons, the leading insurer witll be entitled to request from the vessel's classification society to consult the vessel's classification file.

ARTICLE 10–Premium

The assured must pay the premium at the agreed places and times.

ARTICLE 11–Preventive measures

The assured must take all reasonable care to ensure the safety of the vessel. He must take all reasonable measures to safeguard the vessel from an insured peril or to minimize the consequences of such a peril. In case of failure to comply with these duties, the insurers may intervene in his place to take such measures deemed necessary without thereby admitting liability for their consequences.

ARTICLE 12–Sue and labur

1. If an insured peril occurs :
   - the assured must and insurers may take or require all measures necessary to preserve or safeguard the insured property;
   - the assured must take all measures necessary to preserve his rights against third parites who may be liable.
2. The assured must preserve insurers' right against repair yards.

   Nothwithstanding this obligation, the insurers shall not take advantage of possible assured's partial or total waivers to claim against repair yards, when such waivers arise from the general conditions of the said yards.
3. The assured undertakes to notify the insurer as soon as he is aware of any waivers that might give rise to the payment of a specific additional primum.

ARCTICLE 13–Application for survey and repair of damage

The assured must declare the occurance of any insured peril as soon as he is aware of it and take steps to survey and repair loss and damage according to the conditions laid down in articles 18 and 20.

ARTICLE 14 – Penalties

Non-compliance with the duties listed above may lead, according to the particular circumstances, to :

- the policy being declared void (articles 8–1° and 8–4°),
- cancellation of the policy at three days' notice or proportionate reduction of the indemnity (articles 8-2°, 8°3° and 9–1°),
- cancellation of the policy (article 9-2°),
- suspension or cancellation of the policy under the conditions imposed in Article 15 (article 10),
- forfeiture of the right to indemnity (article 13),
- proportionate reduction of the indemnity (articles 11 and 12).

ARTICLE 15 – Premium payment provisions

Premium is payable 30 days after attachment of the policy.

If the insurance is for twelve months the assured may – if agreed before attachement of the policy – pay the premium in four quarters, that is :

the first quater 30 days after attachment;

the second quarter 3 months after attachment;

the third quarter 6 months after attachment;

the fourth quarter 9 months after attachment.

The assured's failure to pay a premium gives insurers the right either to suspend the insurance or to require its cancellation. Such suspension or cancellation will only take effect eight days after a demand for payment sent by registered letter to the assured's latest address known to the insurers. Suspension will automatically occur on expiry of such eight days and until 0000 hours on the day after payment of the delayed premium.

Insurers have no liability for any even occurring during the period when cover is suspended, but retain full rights against the assured as to performance of the contract, and in particular their right to receive full payment of the premium.

Premium for the whole period of cover is due in case of total loss or abandonment recoverable under the policy. If total loss or abandonment is not so recoverable, the premium is due proportionately to the time on risk until total loss or notice of abandonment, but subject to a minimum payment of three months' premium.

Premium is refunded in case of total loss, sale or bareboat charter of the vessel before attachment; if the contract is broken before such attachment by the assured for any other reason, insurers are entitled to payment of half the agreed premium up to a maximum of 0,50% of the sum insured.

The cost of the policy and any taxes, fees and duties thereon is payable by the assured. Such amounts are payable in full in all cases, and without any deduction, when due.

ARTICLE 16–Lay up in port

1. If at the inception of the period of insurance the vessel remains in port for at least fifteen consecutive days a return of 1/24 (one twenty-fourth) of the annual navigating premium will be made after deduction of the premium stated in the policy for port risks. If the period in port is longer than fifteen days, return of premium will be calculated as indicated above and for each consecutive fifteen days after the first fifteen days.
2. If during the period of insurance the veseel remains at least thirty days in port, a return of 1/12 (one twelth) of the annual navigating premium will be granted subject to deduction of the premium stated in the policy for port risks. if the period in port is longer than thirty days, returns for port risks will be calculated for each period of fifteen consecutive days after the first thirty days.

   Nevertheless if repairs for insurers' account are carried out during the time spent in port the number of days required for such repairs will be deducted from the total of days spent in port when the return preimum is assessed.

   The total of such days must in any case attain the minimum period specified above before a return of premium is assessed.

   The total of such days must in any case attain the minimum period specified above before a return of premium is payable.

   If repairs are carried out simultaneously for account of both the assured and insurers, the exact length of each set of repairs will be determined by surveyors appointed with the insurers' agreement.
3. Days of arrival and departure and days when repairs are started or completed do not count towards any entitlement to a return of premium.
4. The returns under paragraphs 1 and 2 of this article are not payable to the assured if there has been a settlement for total loss or abandonment. They are only assessed after of each six month period of insurance.

ARTICLE 17–Avoidance or cancellation of the insurance

In addition to the cases listed in article 14, the policy may be avoided or cancelled in the following circumstances:

Any insurance–whether or not concluded 'lost or not lost'–taken out after an accident involving the vessels is void if it is proved that news of the accdient had in any way reached the domicile of the assured or insurers, even if reaching third parties unknown to either, unless the assured can prove his good faith.

In case of bankruptcy or insolvency of the assured, whether an individual or a company, either the receiver, the assured when authorized by the judge or the official liquidator as the case may be, or the insurer, may cancel the policy by sending a registered letter to the other party within three months as from the proceedings are started. Cancellation will occur automatically eight days after such sending and the insurer will waive any rights to premium in respect of the cancelled period of insurance.

If the policy is not cancelled as provided for in paragraph above, the receiver or the assured duly authorized to manage the business shall have to pay in cash the premiums payable in respect of the continued contract.

In case of bankruptcy and insolvency of an insurer, the assured may exercise the same rights in respect of such insurer as provided above.

where any insurer's authorization to trade is revoked by the authorities the policy becomes invcalid as far as privided under articles L 326-12 and R*326-1 of the Code des Assurances in respect of the cover granted by such insurer.

If the vessel is subjected to public sale or bareboat charter, the policy terminates automatically with effect from the date of sale or charter.

If the vessel or at least half the interest insured is sold the policy is terminated from the date of sale unless there is prior agreement to the countrary.

If the vessel is chartered other than on a bareboat basis this policy continues unless otherwise agreed and subject to an additional premium if required.

The policy may be cancelled by mutual agreement before expiry of the period of insurance, iwth a proportionate return being made for each complete period of fifteen days not yet commenced; nevertheless net premium payable in such circumstances may not be less than half the premium charged for the full period of insurance.

The policy may be cancelled by the insurers at three days' notice if any change attributable to the assured is made either to the property insured or to any course of action agreed at the time the contract was concluded, if as a result the risk shows a marked deterioration.

The policy may be cancelled by the insurers at the month's notice at any time after the first three months if the cost of repairs in France has risen by more than 20% compared with such costs at attachment of the policy; in such cases a proportionate return of premium will be made. In case of dispute the coefficient of price increase used will be subject to artbitration by the French Shipreparriers' Association (Chambre Syndicale des Reparateurs de Naveires).

CHAPTER V–SURVEY OF LOSS OR DAMAGE

ARTICLE 18

In the absence of prior agreement by the insurers the assured must proceed with a joint survey of damage with insurers' representatives within sixty days of the accident at the latest; if damage occurs at a port this period is reduced to fifteen days.

Surveyors appointed by mutual agreement or, if not, by the courts, are to investigate the cause of loss, ascertain its nature and extent, and draw up the specification of repairs acknowledged by them as necessary to restore the vessel's seaworthiness.

The assured must arrange for these repais to be carried out without delay. If for any reason, including force majeure repairs are not carried out within six months of the date of accident, the sum for insurers; account may not exceed that which would have been payable if reparis as estimated by surveyors had been carried out within this period.

CHAPTER VI–CALCULATION OF THE INDEMNITY

ARTICLE 19

A separate settlement is made for each casualty.

Settlement is made without deductible in case of total loss or abandonment. All other indemnities due in respect of a single event are settled after deuction of the amount indicated in the schedule attahced to this policy

Surveryors' and average agents fees and expenses, as provided in article 18, are fully recoverable from the insurers.

ARTICLE 20–Parial loss

1. In adjustment of partial loss insurers are liable only for the cost as proved by receipted invoices for replacement and repair recognized by surveryors as necessary to restore the vessel's seaworthiness. The assured may claim no other indemnity whether for depreciation, loss of hire or any other reason whatever.
2. Crew wages and maintenance, and any bunkers used are not for insurers' account except as specified below.
3. Before taking any action relating to carrying out repairs the assured must inform the insurers, who have the right to demand that replacement or repair is carried out after tenders. If the assured fails to observe this condition 25% of the total replacement or repair cost will be deducted from the settlement without taking into account any other franchise or deduction provided by the policy.
4. During the time between the drawing up of repair's specifications and acceptance of the tender, crew wages and maintenance and bunkers are for insurers' account.
5. When the vessel stays at a port of refuge waiting for spare parts essential to enable the voyage to continue, crew wages and maintenance and bunkers are for insurers account while such spare parts are in transit. Additional expenses incurred to reduce the time spent in transit are also for insurers account.
6. When repairs cannot be carried out or are too expensive at the port where the vessel is situated, then the insurers will also pay the cost of temporary reparis essential to permit the vessel to reach a port where repairs can be carried out at a lower price, the cost of any incidental fowage which may be incurred, and crew wages and maintenance and bunkers used during the voyage.
7. Bank charges, interest and all other expenses associated with the repair such as dry-docking expenses and port dues are adjusted and paid by the insurers in proportion to the various repairs carried out at the same time.
8. For special expenses in respect of the ship's bottom, shall only by payable by insurers, as proved by receipted invoices the expenses incurred for supplying and applying anticorrosion layer, first coats of primer, top anti-fouling paints and self-polishing coats to the underwater surfaces of the vessel, when such repairs are allowed as partial average.

   When as a consequence of a prticular average, the vessel must stay in drydock for so long a period that the above-mentioned layers lose their efficiency, half of those special expenses incured in respect of the vessels's bottom should be allowable in particular average for half of their amount.

ARTICLE 21–Abandonment

Abandonment of the vessel may take place in the following cases;

- total loss;
- where the total cost or repair for insurers' account amounts to the agreed value, provided that the total sum is calculated in accordance with the provision governing settlement of partial loss and including if necessary the costs of refloating the vessel;
- where no news of the vessel has been received for more than three months; loss is then deemed to have occurred at the date when the last news of the vessel was received;
- when the vessel cannot be repaired, Nevertheless, **loss of the vessel merely from insufficient funds to pay repair or other costs does not entitle the assured to abandon her to the insurers.**

Abandonment must be notified to the insurers within three months of the event giving rise to it or within three months of the period permitting such abandonment.

In notifying abandonment the assured must disclose all insurances which he has taken out or of which he is aware.

In all cases giving rise to abandonment, the insurers to whom the insured property has been abandoned are entitled to accept abandonment or to settle the claim as a total loss without transfer of ownership.

Nevertheless, they are bound to inform the assured of their decision within thirty days of the date by which the assured has submitted all relevant evidence of his right to abandonment.

Cover under this policy shall terminate as from the time the insurers give written notice either of :

- their acceptance of abandonment or,
- their admitting the claims as total loss without any change of ownership

ARTICLE 22–General average

The vessel's contribution to general average is recoverable under this insurance. However, the insurers will only pay such proportion of general average as the agreed value bears to the full contributory value, their payment being subject to reduction for any partial loss recoverable under this insurance.

With regard to settlement between the insurers and the assured no derogation from this insurance is permitted, any general average adjustment being readjusted if necessary in accordance with the provisions of the policy.

The master and the assured have authority not to declare general average in respect of loss of expenses involving the vessel or cargo where the amount in question is not expected to exceed 1% of the agreed value for hull and machinery provided that such loss or expenses do not exceed EUR 60 000.

ARTICLE 23 – Sailing in ballast

When the vessel sails in ballast and there is no other contributory interest the provisions of article 22 apply to expenses and sacrifice which would have had the nature of general average if the vessel had been carrying cargo.

ARTICLE 24 – Third party claims

If the assured does not invoke any limitation of liability to which he may be entitled under applicable law, the total indemnity payable by the insurers shall not exceed that payable if such limitation had been invoked.

ARTICLE 25 – Salvage

In case of salvage of the insured vessel the proportion of salvage and salvage charges incurred by her is for insurers' account, the insurers will only pay such proportion of salvage and salvage charges as the agreed value bears to the full contributory value.

ARTICLE 26–Collision or salvage services between vessels belonging to the same assured

If the insured vessel collides with a vessel owned by the assured or receives salvage services from such vessel, the indemnity payable by the insurers shall be adjusted as if the vessels belonged to different shipowners.

The same applies if the vessel comes into contact with property or installations belonging to the assured.

In the absence of an agreed settlement between the insurers and the assured, liability for collision or payment for salvage services shall be determined by a sole arbitrator in accordance with the provisions of the Nouveau Code de Procedure Civile (Livre IV) or, in the case of failure to agree on a sole arbitrator, by the Chambre Arbitrale Maritime de Paris.

CHAPTER VII–PATYMENT OF INDEMNITY

Article 27–Payment of loss or damage

All loss or damage for insurers' account are apayable thirty days after presentation of all relevant evidence to the bearer of such evidence and of this policy, without power of attorney being required.

When loss or damage is indemnified all premium payable by the assured up to the time of settlement, is set off against the indemnity in case of bankruptcy or insolvency and any bond containing a promise to pay insurers is redeemable immediately.

If neither bankruptcy nor insolvency is declared the insurers are only entitled to set off premium due for expired and unexpired periods under this insurance.

After the occurrence of any causlty leading to recovery under this insurance the sum insured is reinstaled automatically subject to an addtional premium to be agreed.

CHAPTER VIII–PROCEDURAL MATTERS

ARTICLE 28

If this policy is underwritten by more than one insurer then each shall be liable only for his own respective proportion of the sum insured and has **no joint liablity with any other insurer**.

The leading insurer is empowered to receive on behalf of all interested insurers all evidence and documentation relating to the operation of the policy **but he does not thereby have any authority to represent his coinsurers at law**.

The insurers are vested with the rights of the assured to the extent of the indmnity they have paid and only on completion of such payment. The assured undertakes, when required by the insurers, to restate this transfer of right in the adjustment in any reciept for settlement or other document.

Any actions under this insurance policy shall be barred at the end of two years.

The insurers may only be sued before the Tribunal de Commerce of the place where the leading insurer's insurance market is situated.

CHAPTER IX–INSURANCE OF SEVERAL VESSELS UNDER ONE POLICY

ARTICLE 29

The proportion underwritten by each insurer and expressed in relation to the total sum insured remains constant over the respective sums insured.

The insurance shall be deemed to be a separate policy on each vessel.

FRENCH MARINE CARGO INSURANCE POLICY
"ALL RISKS" COVER

(POLICY FORM DATED JUNE 30, 10983 AS MODIFIED FEBRUARY 16, 1990-OCTOBER 22, 1998 AND JULY 1ST, 2002)

APPLICABLE LAW: This contract is governed by French law and in particular by those provisions of Title VII, Book I, of the << Code des Assurances >> which affect the marine insurance contract, whether or not reference is made to them in the policy.

CHAPTER I-APPLICATION OF THE INSURANCE

ARTICLE 1.–

This insurance applis, within the limits of the insured voyage, to the cargo designated hereafter when transported or received for shipment by shipping or forwarding companies in accordance with recognized trade practice.

ARTICLE 2.–

This insurance applies to cargo in new condition packed or prepared for transit, loaded on overseas vessels less than 16 years old, over 500 GT and with the highest classification issued by a classification Society full member of the International Association of Classification Socieiteies (I.A.C.S.).

When, unknown to the Assured, the above requirements for the vessel are not met, the insurance remains in forced subject to the Assured disclosing the circumstances to the insurer as soon as he is aware and subject to payment of an additional premium if required.

ARTICLE 3.–

1. The insurance does not apply to :
   (a) liability for any reason which the Assured or any other beneficiaries of this insurance, whether on their own account or on account of the insured cargo, could incur, in respect of third parties or joint contracting parties :
   (b) the consequences of trade barriers, or hindrance to the commercial transactions of the Assured or any other beneficiaries of the insurance;
   (c) the illegal or clandestine trading of cargo.
2. The insurance applies only where :
   (a) the "safety management certificate" is held by the carrying vessel,
   (b) and the "document of compliance" is held by her company, as required under the SOLAS Convention 1974 as amended, establishing the international Safety Management (ISM) Code.

Nevertheless, when the carrying vessel and her company do not hold the above-mentioned documents. Such non-compliance with the requirements of the ISM code shall not be opposable either to the assured or to the holder of the insurance certificate, when he proves that in the ordinary course of business, he was not aware of that situation.

"Company" means the owner of the ship or any organization or person such as the manager or the bareboat charterer, who has assumed the responsibility for operation of the ship from the owner of the ship and who on assuming such responsibility has agreed to take over all the duties and responsibilities imposed by the International Safety Management Code.

ARTICLE 4.–

The insurance is invalid if it is proved that before the contract had been concluded, news of an even involving the insured cargo had reached the place where the policy was signed or the place where the Assured was without there being any need to prove that the Assured was personally aware of it.

CHAPTER II-EXTENT OF THE INSURANCE

1 — COVER

ARTICLE 5.–

This insurance covers physical loss or damage and loss in weight or quantity of the insured carge.

Nevertheless.

1. shortage of all or part of the contents of a package will only be indemnified by the insurer if a forcible opening or breaking has been confirmed in the manner indicated in article 17. The **disappearance** of one or more entire packages is only covered on presentation of a certificate or other docutment confirming non delivery;
2. **cargo loaded on deck or on the superstructure of vessels or craft not designed for this purpose** is only covered if the physical loss or damage, or loss in weight or quantity has been caused by one of the following events : sinking, capsizing, stranding or grounding of the vessel or craft; fire or explosion; tidal wave; lightning; collision or contact of the vessel or craft with a fixed movable or floating object including ice; falling aircraft; entry of water causing the vessel or craft to enter a port of refuge and there discharge all or part of its cargo; the insured package falling or being dropped overboard during loading aboard, transhipment or unloading from vessel or craft. Such cargo is also covered on payment of an additional premium against loss or damage from jettison, or from washing or falling or being dropped overboard on condition that the Assured discloses to the insurer such loading of cargo on deck or on the superstructure as soon as he is himself aware of it.

ARTICLE 6.–

This insurance also covers in full, proportionately to the insured value, any expenses in the following list unless excluded by one of the provisions in article 7:

1. expenses reasonably incurred for the purpose of protecting the insured cargo from insured physical loss or damage or of minimizing such loss or damage;
2. expenses reasonably incurred through interruption or termination of the voyage for unloading, warehousing, transhipment or forwarding of the insured cargo to the destination named in the policy, on condition that such expenses have not been incurred as a result of financial default of the owners manager or charterers of the carrying vessel;
3. general average and salvage charges on the insured cargo, the insurer furthermore agreeing to pay any general average deposit or providing a guarantee of payment of general average or salvage charges.

2—EXCLUSIONS

ARTICLE 7.–

This insurance excludes physical loss or damage, loss in weight or quantity of the insured cargo resulting from:

1. confiscation, sequestration, requisition, blockade running, smuggling any kind of arrest or seizure, the insurer furthermore not being liable for any security payable for release of the insured cargo in such circumstances:
2. wilful misconduct or gross negligence of the Assured or any other beneficiaries of the ipnsurance or their servants, representatives or other authorized persons;
3. inherent vice of the insured cargo; worm and vermin unless caused by contamination during the insured voyage, effect of atmospheric temeprature, ordinary leakage or ordinary loss in weight or volume;
4. absence, inadequacy or unsuitability of:
   - preparation, packing or packaging of cargo.
   - securing or stowing of cargo in a shipping unit, when carried out by the Assured, his representatives or any benificiary of the insurance, or when carried out prior to attachment of the insurance.
5. delay in forwarding or arrival of the insured cargo unless resulting from sinking, capsizing or stranding or grounding of the vessel or craft, fire or explosion, collision or contact of the vessel or craft with a fixed

movable or floating object including ice; falling aircraft; entry of water causing the vessel or craft to enter a port of refuge and there discharge all or part of its cargo;

6. any direct or indirect effects of an explosion, release of heat, irradiation or any other nuclear power supply due to the transmutation of atoms or radioactivity as well as any effects of radiation caused by the artificial acceleratio of particles, whether through civil or military use or exploitation.

7. (a) war or civil war, hostilities, reprisals, torpedoes, mines and all other weapons of war, and generally all accidents and misfortunes of war, as well as acts of sabotage or terrorism of a political nature or related to war;
   (b) capture, taking at sea, arrest, seizure, restraint, molestation or detention by any government or authority;
   (c) riots, civil commotions, strikes, lockout and other similar events;
   (d) piracy of a political nature or related to war.

CHAPTER III - TIME AND PALACE OF THE INSURANCE

ARTICLE 8.–

Unless otherwise agreed, this insurance attaches when the insured cargo as defined in article 2 leaves the warehouse at the place named herein for the commencement of the insured transit and terminates on delivery to the warehouse of the consignee, his representatives or other authorized persons at the place of destination. Warehouse of the consignee, his representatives or other authorized persons, is deemed to include any place - whether belonging to them or not - where such parties stored cargo on arrival.

ARTICLE 9.–

Without prejudice to the provisions of article 11, this insurance remains in force, subject to the payment of an additional premium if required, during any change of the insured voyage or extension of its normal duration provided such change of extension of voyage is beyond the control of the Assured or other beneficiearies of the insurance.

ARTICLE 10.–

This insurance terminates on any delivery of the insured cargo to the Assured or to any other beneficiearies of the insurance or to their servants, representatives or other authorized persons before normal termination of cover in accordance with the provisions of this chapter.

ARITLCE 11.–

This insurance terminates no later than 60 days after the completion of discharge overside of the insured cargo from the last overseas vessel

CHAPTER IV-INSURED VALUE

ARTICLE 12.–

The insured value, which must be proved in case of loss or damage, shall not exceed the highest of the amounts caluculated as follows :

1. the cost of the insured cargo at the place of destination, plus the expected profit;
2. the value at the place of destination on the date of arrival as determined by customary published commodity prices;
3. the provisions in the contract of sale;
4. replacement cost in the case of manufactured cargo provided that the corresponding invoices are produced as evidence of such replacement.

CHAPTER V - DUTIES OF THE PARTIES TO THE INSURANCE

1.– DUTIES OF THE ASSURED AND OTHER BENEFICIARIES OF THE INSURANCE.

ARTICLE 13.–

The whole premium is payable to the insurer as soon as cover attaches. It is payable in full to the insurer at the place of underwriting and at the time of issue of this policy. In case of loss or damage, the insurer may deduct the amount of the due premium from the indemnity paid to the beneficiaries of the insurance.

ARTICLE 14.–

1. The Assured shall disclose, on concluding the contract of the inssurance, all circumstances of which he is aware that would infulence the insurer in assessing the risks to be covered.
2. In the same way, he must disclose to the insurer, as soon as he is himself aware of it, any circumstance affecting the risk which occurs during the time of the insurance.

ARTICLE 15.–

The Assured, his representatives and all beneficiaries of the insurance must take all reasonable care to ensure the safety of cargo. They shall also take all resonable measures to safeguard cargo or avert or minimize loss of or damage to it. In case of failure to comply with these duties, the insurer may intervene in their place to take such measures deemed necessary without prejudice to his liability.

ARTICLE 16.–

The Assured, his representative and all beneficiaries of the insurance shall also take all measures to preserve the possiblity of recovery and other rights against carriers and any other third parties who may be liable and, should the occasion arise, to allow the insurer to institute any proceedings which he may deem necessary.

ARTICLE 17.–

They must on arrival of cargo at the place of destination of the insured voyage and where required by the apparent condition of such cargo, apply to the claims agent (commissaire d'avaries) of the "Comité d' Etudes et de Services des Assureurs Maritimes et Transports de France (CESAM)" or, in the absence of such, to any organisation nominated under the item "claims agent" of the special conditions of this policy, to obtain a contradictory survey ("expertise contradictoire"). Application for survey shall be made within three days of termination of cover, not including non-working days, as determined in chapter III. Any counter-survey ("contre-expertise") must be conducted in the presence of the insurer and of the Assured (or representatives of either party) within fifteen days of the initial survey.

ARTICLE 18.–

Non-compliance with the duties listed above will lead either to avoidance of the policy in the event of non-disclosure or misrepresentation by the Assured (article 14-1°), cancellation of the policy in the event of non-disclosure by the Assured of material circumstances affecting the risk (article 14-2°), reduction of measure of idemnity (articles 15 and 16) or forefeiture of the right to indemnity (article 17). Where, in the cases enumerated in article 14-1° and 2° the utmost good faith of the Assured is proved, only reduction of the measure of indemnity shall apply.

2. DUTIES OF THE INSURER : CLAIMS ADJUSTMENT AND PAYMENT OF THE INSURANCE INDEMNITY.

ARTICLE 19.–

Claims adjustment and payment of indemnity are made separately on each package except for cargo transported in bulk where it is made per hold, per tank, by individual account or on the total shipment.

ARTICLE 20.–

The amount of loss, ascertained as above, is determined by comparison of the value of the insured cargo in its damaged condition with that which it would have had in sound condition at the same time and place, the percentage of depreciation so calculated to be applied to the insured value. The measure of indemnity shall include surveyor's and claims agents expenses and fees due as provided in article 17.

ARTICLE 21.–

In the case of sale short of destination which has been agreed as a result of insured physical loss and damage, the indemnity is calculated as the difference between the insured value and the net proceeds.

ARTICLE 22.–

If through insured physical loss or damage, the insurer decides to send all or part of the insured cargo back to the place of manufacture for repair, the resulting expenses and risk are for his account even if he must thereby pay an amount higher than the total insured value.

ARTICLE 23.–

When total profict cannot be proved. It is limited to a maximum of 20% of the price of the cargo at the place of destination as mentioned in article 12-1°.

ARTICLE 24.–

In respect of adjustment of loss or damage, increased value insurances are subject to the same provisions as double insurance.

ARTICLE 25.–

Where a franchise is agreed, it does not include ordinary leakage or loss in weight or volume.

ARTICLE 26.–

The insured cargo may only be abandoned in the following cases :

1° In the case of loss without news of the carrying vessel : after 4 months counting from the date of the last news received.

2° when the carrying vessel is admitted to be clearly unfit to continue the voyage: after 4 months counting from the date of the declaration of unseaworthiness of the vessel made by the carrier if during that time it has not been possible to reforward cargo to the place of destination;

3° when the total of physical loss or damage to be indemnified by the insurer amounts to at least three quaters of the insured value.

ARTICLE 27.–

The idemnity due by the insurer is payable in full at the latest 30 days after production of all necessary documents to the bearer of those documents and on surrender of the original policy document.

No one may recover under this insurance without proof of having suffered loss of damage.

ARTICLE 28.–

After any event leading to idemnity by the insurer the full insured value is automatically reinstated on payment of an additional premium.

ARTICLE 29.–

If this policy is underwritten by several insurers, each shall be liable only for his own respective proportion of the sum insured.

ARTICLE 30.–

The leader is empowered to receive on behalf of all interested insurers all documentation and evidence relating to the operation of this policy, **but he does not thereby have any power to represent at law the co-insurers.**

CHAPTER VI - PROCEDURAL MATTERS

ARTICLE 31. –

The insurer is vested with the rights of the assured to the amount of the indemnity he has paid and only on completion of such payment. The Assured undertakes if asked by the insurer - to restate this transfer of rights in the adjustment, in any receipt of settlement or any other document.

ARTICLE 32.–

Any action under this insurance policy shall be barred at the end of two years.

ARTICLE 33.–

The insurer may only be used before the Tribunal de Commerce of the place of underwritting of the policy.

TERMS USED IN MARINE INSURANCE

Act of God

A natural event such as flood, storm, lightning, or earthquake not caused by nor preventable by any human agency, and for which no transporter can be held accountable.

Adventure

The commercial enterprise involving uncertainties, risks and hazards. In which a vessel and cargo are subjected to the peril of a loss, delay or damage at sea. Merchandise is shipped by the seller on speculation to arrive safely at a foreign port to be sold for a profit. The vessel carries the merchandise in order to earn freight. The vessel and cargo together make up the "common venture." In clipper ship days, the captain participated in the profits of the venture to give him the incentive to make profitable voyages for the owners. fishing vessel owners still give their crew "shares" of the venture's profits.

All Risks

The broadest form of insurance coverage available providing protection against all perils of physical loss or damage from an external cause. Loss must be fortuitous. i.e. accidental, to be covered. All risks does not cover inevitable loss, wear and tear, dealy, inherent vice, preshipment condition, inadequate packaging, or loss of market.

Approved Merchandise

Under any Open Cargo Policy, goods that are approved by the insurance company for coverage under the specified insuring conditions and rates fo the policy. Other goods can be "held covered," but subject to terms and conditions to be determined.

Approved Packing

Packing that meets the packaging industry standards of sufficient design and construction to protect the cargo from the normal hazards expected to be encountered during the intended voyage, including normal domestic handling and storage from point of origin to final destination.

Approved Vessel

In the American market, a cargo-carrying vessel over 1,000 net registered tons and under 20 years of age that insurance companies accept to carry the insured cargo without additional premium. Shipments aboard other vessels are accepted and may be subject to additional premiums, called "penalties," which results in these vessels being called "penalty vessels." The London market uses a different standard.

Blocking and Bracing

Materials (usually wood-timber) used to secure, immoblize and protect cargo by preventing its free movement or shifting during transit.

Bumbershoot

A marine insurance policy covering multiple liability coverage's in excess of one or more different underlying policies (comparable to the Commercial Liability Umbrella covering liabilities on land). "Bumbershoot" is the English word for "Umbrella," i.e. "all encompassing."

Carnet

An international customs document, acting as a passport for merchandise that allows goods to temporarily enter certain foreign countries and return to the United States without paying duty or posting customs bonds in either country; e.g. goods for trade shows, display, or demonstration

Certificate of insurance

In Marine Insurance, a document issued on behalf of an insurance company covering a specific shipment. It states the terms are conditions of the cargo insurance and is subject to the terms and conditions of the underlying open cargo policy. It is not a "stand-alone" policy. It is used when evidence of insurance is required, especially by a bank issuing a letter of credit.

Declaration

An insurance form filled out by the Assured for reporting/declaring individual shipments under an Open Cargo Policy. It is usually used for declaring import shipments where evidence of insurance is not required. A multi-entry declaration is called a bordereau.

General Average (GA)

An ancient principle of equity, recognized by maritime nations, predating the concept of insurance and still valid today, in which all parties involved in a sea adventure (vessel, cargo, and freight) proportionately share losses resulting from a voluntary and successful effort to save the entire venture from an imminent peril. There are two types of General Average Acts:

1. Voluntary Sacrifice of a part of the vessel or a part of the cargo, e.g. jettison of property to stabilize the vessel during heavy weather.
2. Extraordinary Expense necessarily incurred for the joint benefit of vessel and cargo, e.g. towing charges incurred to assist a disabled vessel to a port of refuge.

General Average Agreement

A guarantee by the owner of the cargo (usually the consignee) to pay that proportion of the general average contribution, salvage, or special charges owed by the shipment, and to give information about its value so an Average Adjustment can be prepared. The vessel owner will not release cargo for delivery to the consignee until the cargo owner signs this average agreement or bond, which is prepared by the general average adjuster.

Inherent Vice

A loss caused by the nature of the thing insured and not the result of a fortuitous external cause; e.g. spontaneous combustion of bulk grain.

Institute Clauses

Clauses agreed in the London insurance market and offered by the institute of London Underwriters. (Clauses offered by the American market are titled "American Institute of Marine Underwriters Clauses.")

Insurable Interest

A real stake in a specific property to the extent that loss of or damage to the property could cause a financial loss.

Letter of Credit (LC) (LOC)

A document issued by a bank and used to pay for cargo. The buyer arranges a letter of credit from its local bank, creating a fund in a foreign bank near the seller in a specified amount in the seller's favour. The buyer authorizes the seller to draw drafts against the fund for goods purchased by the buyer. A sum of money is paid to the seller under specific terms and conditions, including the receipt by the bank of certain documents within a given time.

Negligence

Doing something that a reasonable and prudent person would not do, or not doing something that a reasonable and prudent person would do in a particular situation. The failure to exercise normal care or act reasonably under the circumstances.

Non-Delivery

A loss in which an entire shipping package and its contents are missing at destination. Non-delivery does not include pilferage of cargo from a package where the package itself is delivered.

Open Policy

A cargo policy with no expiration date that provides automatic coverage of cargo shipments to or from an Assured in a specified trade at agreed rates, terms, and conditions. The marine and war policies are usually two separate open policies.

Partial Loss

Any loss to cargo or a vessel that is less than a total loss. If the partial loss is directly caused by a peril insured against, it is a particular average loss.

Particular Average (PA)

A partial loss of the property insured (vessel or cargo, including total loss of part of a cargo shipment) caused by a peril insured against, and which is not a General Average loss.

Recovery

Amount received from a third party responsible for a loss on which a claim has been paid.

Risk

A fortuitous peril or hazard; i.e. something that may happen, not something that is inevitable.

Sacrfice

The deliberate destruction or jettisoning of property to prevent greater loss.

Settiling Agent

An insurance company's representative in a foreign country who is authorized to settle claims and make payment on behalf of the insurance company.

Special Drawing Rights (SDR)

An international monetary unit used to measure and compare the changing market values of currencies of member countries of the International Monetary Fund. It is equal to the market value of currencies of the 5 member countries: United States, France, Germany, Japan and England.

Valuation Clause

The clause in the Marine Policy that contains a consistent basis of valuation agreed upon by the Assured and the insurance company and which establishes the insured values of the cargo or vessel when the insurance attaches.

Warehouse to Warehouse Clause

A clause in a cargo policy defining when coverage attaches and terminates. Coverage attaches when the cargo leaves the warehouse at the place named in the policy, and continues during the ordinary course of transit after discharge at the final port. Coverage ends when one of the following first occurs.

When the cargo is delivered at the final warehouse at the destination named in the policy, or 15 days after discharge if the final destination is within the port, or 30 days after discharge if the final destination is outside the port.

Warranty

An undertaking in which the Assured promises to comply with certain conditions. Non-compliance constitutes a breach of warranty and the insurance company is discharged from liability from the date of the breach.

Expressed Warranty

An agreement written in the policy that the Assured must srictly and literally comply with. A violation thereof voids the insurance; e.g. trading warranties.

Implied Warranty – Fundamental conditions implied in a contract of marine insurance:

1. Seaworthiness of the vessel;
2. Legality of the adventure

War Risks

Those risks related to two (or more) belligerents engaging in hostilities, whether or not there has been a formal declaration of war. Such risks are excluded by the F.C. & S. (Free of Capture and Seizure) Warranty, but may be covered by a separate War Risk Policy, at an additional premium.

Wear and Tear

The ordinary wearing away of the various parts of a vessel, machinery and equipment through use. Such damage is not accidental in nature, but is inevitable.

CFR(Cost and Freight)

The seller pays for the carriage of goods to the named destination and clears the goods for export. CFR is only used for sea and inland waterway transportation. The buyer undertakes the risk of loss of damage once the goods are delivered to a carrier.

CPT(Carriage paid to)

The seller pays for the carriage of goods to the named destination and clears the goods for export. CPT is used for any mode of transportation. The buyer undertakes the risk of loss or damage once the goods are delivered to the first (or only) carrier.

D/A (Documents Against Acceptance)

It is one of common payment methods for international trade. Exporters, via the remitting bank, instruct the banks (collecting bank via remitting bank) to release the title right and other shipping documents to the importers subject to acceptance of the drafts by the importers. Exporters will face the higher risk. Non-payment risk at maturity of the draft.

D/C (Documentary Credit)

It is one of common payment methods for international trade. D/C is an instrument issued by buyer's bank who undertakes to settle payment to the seller when the seller acts and fulfills all terms and conditions of the credit.

ETA (Estimated Time of Arrival)

The projected date and time a shipment scheduled to arrive at its destination.

ETD (Estimated Time of Departure)

The projected date and time a shipment scheduled to depart.

EU (Europian Union)

An economic trade region in Europe comprising 27 members, namely Austria, Belgium, Bulgaria, Cyprus, Czech Republic. Denmark, Estonia, Finland, France, Germany, Greece, Hungary, Ireland, Italy, Latvia, Lithuania, Luxembourg, Malta, Netherlands, Poland, Portugal, Romania, Slovakia, Slovenia, Spain, Sweden and United Kingdom.

EXW (Ex Works)

The seller makes the goods available to the buyer at the seller's own premises. The buyer bears all costs and risks involved in taking the goods from the seller's premises to the desired destination.

FCL (Full Container Load)

A full container load means a container with goods from one consignor to one consignee.

FOB (Free On Board)

The seller fulfills his obligation to deliver when the goods have passed over the ship's rail and cleared for exports at the named port of shipment. Buyer bears all costs and risks of goods from that moment.

TEU (Twenty-foot Equivalent Unit)

A unit for calculating the carrying capacity of container vessels. The unit is based on the twenty foot container.

UCP (Uniform Customs and Practice of Documentary Credits)

Rules of the international Chamber of Commerce (ICC) governing a letter of credit issued in respect of goods shipped.

VARIOUS ABBREVIATIONS USED IN MARINE INSURANCE

A.H.F American Hull Form
A.H.I.S American Hull Insurance Syndicate
A.I.T.H American Institute Time Clauses (Hulls)
A.O.A. Anyone accident
A.O.B. Anyone bottom
A.O.L. Anyone loss or Any one location
A.O.V. Anyone vessel
A.P. Additional Premium
A.P.L. As per list (Lloyd's Shipping Index)
A.R. All Risks
A.T.C. Automatic Termination Clause (War Risks)

B.L or B/L Bill of Lading
B.O.V. Basis of Valuation
B.D.I. Both days inclusive
BDLS Bundles
B.N.A. British North America
B.O.C. Breach of Contract, Bulk off Cluses

C. & F. Cost and Freight
C.D. or C/D Country damage
CGO Cargo
CF Cost and Freight
C.I.F. Cost, Insurance and Freight
C.N. Cover Note
C.P. Charter Party
C.T.L. Constructive Total Loss

D.A. Deductible Average
D.B.B. Deals, Battens and Boards

D.D. Damage done, Dry Dock
D.P.R. Daily pro rata
D.T.B.A. Date to be advised
E. & E.A. Each and every accident
E. & E.L. Each and every loss
E. & E.O. Each and every occurrence
E.C. East Coast, English Conditions, Extended Coverage
E.P.I. Earned Premium Income
E.S.D. Echo Sounding Device
E.V. Equal Values, Each Vessel
F.A.A. Free of all average
F. & D. Freight and Demurrage
F.A.S. Free alongside
F.I.A. Full interest admitted
F.I.O Free in and out
F.O.B. Free on board
F.O.C. Flags of Convenience, Free of Cost, Free of Claims
F.O.D. Free of Damage
F.P.I.L. Full Premium if Lost
F.R.O. Fire Risk Only
FRT Freight
F.W.D. Freshwater Damage

G.A. General Average
G.M.T Greenwhich Mean Time UTC
G.N.P.I Gross Nett Premium Income
G.P.I. Gross Premium Income
G.O.R. Gross original Rate
G.R.T. Gross Registered Tonnage

H.C. or H/C Held Covered
H and O Hook and Oil Damage
HSSC Heating, sweating, spontaneous combustion
HWD heavy weather damage

I. and/or O. In and/or Over Under and/or on Deck
I.C.C. Institute Cargo Clauses
I.L.U. Institute of London Underwriters
INS VAL Insured value
I.O.P. Irrespective of Percentage
I.T.C. Institute Time Clauses
I.V. Increased Value, Inherent Vice

J. & W.O. Jettison and Washing Overboard
J.C.C. Joint Cargo Committee
J.H.C. Joint Hull Committee

LCL Less container load
L.O.A. Length Overall
L.O.H. Loss of Hire
Ltr Lighter
Ltrg Lighterage
L.U.A. Lloyd's Underwriters Association
L.U.R. Lay-Up Return

M.D. or MALD Malicious Damage
M.I.A. Marine Insurance Act
Mindep. Minimum and Deposit Premium
M.S. Motor Ship
MV or M/V Motor Vessel

N.C.A.D. Notice of Cancellation at Anniversary Date
N.C.R. No Claim return
N.D. Non-Delivery, No Discount
N.R.A.D. or N.R.A.L. No Risk after Discharge/Landing
N.R.T.O R. No Risk after Discharge/Landing
N.R.T.O.R. No risk attached until on Rail
N.R.L. Nett Retained Line
N.U.R. Not Under Repair

O.C. Open Contract, Open Cover, Off Cover, Original Condition
O.C.A. Outstanding Claims Advance
O.D. On Deck
O.GP. Original Gross Premium
O.GR. Original Gross Rate
O.N.P Original Nett Premium
O.N.R. Original Nett Rate

P.A. Particular Average, Per Annum
P.C. Profit Commission
P.D. Property Damage
P.E. Personal Effects
P. & I. Protection and Indemnity Risks
P.I. Personal Injury, Premium Income
P.L. Public Liability, Partial Loss
P.P. Professionally Packed
P.P.I. Policy Proof of Interest
P.R. Pro rata
Q.S. Quota Share

R & C.C. Riots and Civil Commotions
R.D.C. Running Down Clause (Collision Clause)
R.I. Reinsurance
R.R.I. Respective Rights and Interests
R.O.D. Rust, Oxidization and Discolouration
RoRo Roll on Roll off - Drive on service loading vessel
R.P. Return Premium
R.T.B.A. Rate to be agreed
R.F.W. Rain and Freshwater

S.A. Subject Approval, South Africa, South America
Salvage Association (London)
S.G. Ship and Goods
S.L. Sue and Labour charges
S.O.L. Shipowners' Liability
S.R. & C.C. Strikes, Riots and Civil Commotions
S.R.L.L. Ship Repairers' Legal Liability
S. of S. Service of Suit Clause
S.V. Sailing Vessel

T. or C.T.L Total or Constructive Total Loss
T.C.A. Comp Total or Constructive or Arranged or compromised
T.L.V.O. Total Loss of Vessel Only
T.P.L. Third Party Liability
T.P. & N.D. Theft, Pilferage and Non-Delivery
T.O.R. Time on Risk
T.S. Transhipment
T.T.F.C. Timber Trade Federation Clauses

U.D. Under Deck
U.E.P. Unearned Premium
U.K.C. (B/H) United Kingdom and/or continent of Europe Bordeau-Hamburg range.
U.N.L. Ultimate Nett Loss
U.R. Under Repair

V.C. Valuation Clause
V.O.P Valued as in Original Policy

W.A. With Average
W.B.S. Without Benefit of Salvage
W.C. West Coast
W.C.S.A. West Coast of South America
W.D.F. Wireless Direction Finder
W.P. Without Prejudice
W.P.A. With Particular Average
W.R.O. War Risks Only
W.W. Worldwide

INSURANCE PROPOSAL FORM

Fill in details and click the submit button.

We welcome enquiris for marine cargo insurance including large values, even commodities. However, we do need full information such as, names and addresses of: enquirer, owner of the goods, supplier and consignee. Plus method of transport and name (s) of vessel (s) expected to be used or being negotiated.

Actual transit or voyage e.g. ex works or warehouse, F.O.B., C.&F. with discharge port and final destination.

The goods to be insured, in bulk or how packed, if F.C.L. or L.C.L.

The sum to be insured and if this is C.I.F. plus Duty or G.S.T. plus 10%. In other words, all the information tha you need to supply in order to comply with your Duty of Disclosure.

Name and Address of Proposer

Name and Address of Remover

Name and Address of Professional Packer Please state if owner packed

VOYAGE
Address from which Goods are to be moved

Date (s) of packing/uplift

Address to which Goods are to be sent

If Exact Address is Not Known State Destination

Goods will be Sent by

○ Sea ○ Air ○ Rail ○ Road

If Sea State name of Vessel (See note 1)

STORAGE
Have Goods been in Store? Yes; Since When?

○ Yes ; Since when?

Will Goods be stored Prior to Shipment?	No
	Yes ; How long?
Will Goods be stored at Destination?	No
	Yes ; How long (See Note 2)?
Value of goods at destination	No
What Currency are you using	

Cover will continue during the normal course of transit (including up to one month at packer's premises) from the time the goods are take up at the above address until set down at the final address (including up to one month after discharge from Ship awaiting delivery).

When name of vessel is unknown a quotation will be given on the basis that the vessel is approved by underwriters. In such cases it is possible

Note 1. that when the Underwriters are eventually informed of the name of the vessel an additional premium may be required, especially should the vessel be over 15 years old.

In the event of any storage taking place before arrival at final address, cover will cease on arrival at such place of storage unless prior notice is

Note 2 given to New Zealand Shipping stating full details of the location, storage facilities and period, and an additional premium paid.

FCRA NO. AC/36

Accident Department

The New India Assurance Comapny ltd.

Regd. & Head Office: 87, Mahatama Gandh Road, Fort, Mumbai - 400001, Website : http:/www

Settlement Intisation Voucher

Address of D.O. Br. ....
....
....

Claim No. ....
Srl. No. : 1
Vehicle No. ....

Receved this .... day of ....
from THE NEW INDIA ASSURANCE COMPANY LTD.
....
....
which I/we agree to acept in full/partial satisfaction and dicharge of the claim under
Policy No. .... in respect to ....
which occured on or about ....
.... Name ....
Occupation ....
Address ....

Please affix revenue stapd of Re.1/- if the amount exceed Rs. 5000/- (Sign. Across the Revenue Stamp)

....
....
....

I/We hereby authorise the Insurance company that about stated above say be paid to the hirer On Account Payment Disbursed : ₹ ....
Date ....

TATA AIG GENERAL INSURANCE COMPANY LIMITED

Marine Insurance Application Form

WITH YOU ALWAYS

1. Name and Address of the applicant/Bank, if any*
2. Phone & Fax nos. & e-mail address
3. Merchandise/Goods to be insured*
4. Nature of Packing*
5. Marks & Nos.
6. Conveyance* Sea Air Closed Rail Wagons/Covered Trucks Courier Post Others
7. Name of the Vessel
8. B/L, AWB, RR/CN no. and date
9. Voyage/Transit* From To
10. Transshipment &/or storage if any (specify place and period)
11. Basis of Valuation*
12. Value declared for insurance* in foreign currency in Indian Rupees
13. Terms of cover required* All Risks Basic
14. Specify LC wordings, if any, to be incorporated.
15. Any other details about the risk:
16. Producer Name & Code, if applicable:*

Corporate office : Ahura Centre, 4th Floor, 82 Mahakali Caves Road, Andheri (E), Mumbai - 4000093.

(Regd. Office : Bombay House, 24 Homi Mody Street, Mumbai-400001)

Fore more information, call the Tata AIG Toll-free-24 hours Helpline at - 1,600-119966 1 of 2

Declaration by Applicant

I/We hereby declare that the statements made by me/us herein and in attachments hereto are true to the best of my/our knowledge and belief and I/We hereby agree that this Proposal shall form the basis of the insurance contract between me/us and Tata AIG General Insurance Company Ltd.

SURVEYOR'S REPORTS

Seaside Marine Surveyors LLC
Gary Friend, MMS, SA
P.O.Box 25, Port Jefferson Station, N.Y. 11776
Phone 631-838-7450
USSA, SAMS
www.SeasideMarineSurveyors.com

Marine Survey Work Order

Client Name ________________________________ Date: ____________

Address: ____

City: ____________________ State: ____________ Zip: ____________

Survey Location: ____

Year/MFG/Model: ____________________________ VesselNo. ________

Survey Type: Pre-Purchase __________ Insurance/Finance ________ Sea Trial _____ Other _____

Guidelines: The Survey guidelines used for the inspection conform to the common practice by members of the Society of Accredited Marine Surveyors, and the U.S. Surveyors Association, The mandatory standards are promulgated by the U.S. Coast Guard under the authority of the Code of Federal Regulations, Parts 33 and 46 as published for pleasure craft, and the U.S. Coast Guard Navigation Rules. The voluntary standards and recommended practices are developed by the NFPA 302 pleasure and commercial motor craft standards, and the ABYC Standards for small craft. The guidelines for determining fair market value are the N.A.D.A Appraisal Guide, BUC Value Guide, a national search of the Internet for comparable vessels, and local market conditions. The surveyor is committed to providing accurate surveys which meet or exceed these standards. It is not possible to determine the full extent of compliance with some standards due to the nature of a vessels construction but I will report all findings and observations as they relate to the above standards to the best of my ability.

Scope and Limitations: The survey report represents a statement of visually observable conditions on all normally accessible parts of the vessel, and constitutes a statement of opinion only as observed on the date of inspection. The survey is neither a guarantee nor a warranty of the condition of the vessel, its hull, machinery, unforeseen or undetectable damages or other conditions that may exist, and accordingly, shall suffer no liability for errors or omissions or for not being able to properly evaluate parts of perform the requested services as stated within this work order. The sole remedy for a dissatisfaction of services will not exceed the total fee paid to the surveyor for the survey services with the sole remedy expiring in six months from the date of inspection. The surveyor reserves the right to amend the final survey report if additional information is presented. This survey should not be construed as an engineering or engine analysis and is not considered a complete mechanical inspection. The survey is limited in its nature. It is not possible to verify or determine the types of fiberglass, resins, cores, or laminating schedule the manufacturer has used in the construction of the vessel. There will be no withdrawal of any shafts. There will be no opening of joiner work, paneling, tankage or bulkheads. There will be no removal of stores or equipment. There will be no removals of decking or destructive testing undertaken. There will be no disassembly of the hull structure, engines, machinery, electrical system, plumbing or other equipment. An inspection of the internal parts of the engine is not possible. Seaside Marine Surveyors recommends that the client consider contracting the services of a certified engine surveyor for a complete gas or diesel engine and generator analysis. The spars and rigging for sailboats are inspected at deck level only, unless un-stepped. It is not practical or cost effective to list every cosmetic deficiency, it is not possible to discover hidden flaws if no outward signs or evidence of such exist. Assessment there is limited to what is externally visible, reasonably accessible, and/or ascertainable from operation. The client fully understands the potential for errors and inaccuracies resulting from the inability to evaluate portions of the vessel due to these limitations as well as any other limitations that may be encountered during the inspection.

Fees: The quote for your survey is $ _____ and is due at the time of inspection. Should unexpected, significant delays be incurred such as unexpected travel, additional consultation time, engine repairs or yard delays, an additional charge of $80.00 per hour may be incurred. Haul out fees are paid for by the client. The contracting of additional services such as an engine surveyor, rigging inspector or other technicians is the responsibility of the client.

On Site Survey Termination: If the survey is terminated during the on site inspection due to unsatisfactory findings or any other reason within the control of the client, the charge will be a minimum of 75% of the quoted fee. A written report will not be provided. **The written survey report** will detail all systems on the vessel that were accessible and inspected including their apparent condition and recommendations or repairs if required. The fair market value and current condition along with replacement value will be given.

The report is completed and mailed or e-mailed in approximately 3-5 business days. If the survey is rejected by an insurance company or bank due to the quality or limitations of the survey, the company should send a letter to the surveyor stating the reasons for rejection, and following the receipt of this letter; a full refund for the survey will be issued to the survey purchaser within 30 days. By signing below, the client contracting the services of the marine surveyor accepts the scope, terms and limitations, outlined above.

Signed: ______________________________ Dated: ______________

(Client)

Seaside Marine Surveyors LLC

Gary Friend, MMS, SA

P.O. Box 25, Port Jefferson Station, N.Y. 11776

Phone. 631-838-7450

USSA, SAMS

www.SeasideMarineSurveyor.com

Survey Customer Data Sheet

Customer.____ Date:

Town/State/ Zip:____

Phone:____/Work/Cell:__________________

Vessel Year/Make/Model:____

LOA:______________________________Beam:_____________Hull Type: Deep Vee/Mod. Vee/Displacement

Engine/Make/Year:____Single / Twin Screw / IB / OB / SD

Engine Refitted/Year:____

Generator / Make / Mode / Year.____

Intended Use: Pleasure / Commercial, Hull Modified or Customized:______________

Seller / Broker:____

Vessel Location :____

Trailer Make and Model:____

Comments:____

Mileage:____

Type of Survey : Pre-Purchase. C & V, Appraisal, Damage, Sea Trial, Corrosion, Compression Test, Lower Unit Test, Oil Analysis, Osmosis Test, Electronics Inst.

SeasideMarineSurveyors.com

Seaside Marine Surveyors LLC

Gary Friend, MMS, SA

P.O. Box 25, Port Jefferson Station, N.Y.11776

Phone. 631-838-7450

USSA, SAMS

www.SeasideMarineSurveyors.com

Survey Preparation List

1. If vessel is to be hauled, it must be properly blocked and secured and the hauler should be contacted to insure the time and schedule.
2. Insure the vessel is prepared and operational for the sea trail. If repairs are needed, this should be performed before the day of the sea trial.
3. Remove all anchors, chains, and ropes it they cannot be properly viewed in their lockers.
4. Have contents of lockers prepared for easy viewing and inventory.
5. Have all safety equipment together for inspection. (PFD"s, throw cushions, rings, flares, sound device, fire extinguishers, life rafts etc.)
6. Have all bridge areas dry for viewing of pumps, thru-hull fittings, and glass work.
7. Have all necessary paper work available. (previous surveys, maintenance records, Registration, documentation, etc.)
8. The owner or purchaser of this survey may be present during this inspection and is encouraged to do so.
9. If a sea trial is to be conducted, the owner or broker needs to be present to operate the vessel.
10. If a trailer is to be inspected, be sure to have all necessary paper work available. (registration,

maintenance records, etc.)

Seaside Marine Surveyors

Seasidemarinesurveyors.com

What is Marine Survey?

Before you purchase the vessel of your dreams, have a thorough inspection performed by a competent marine surveyor. The inspection can uncover items that may lead to costly repairs or issues that can compromise the safety of the vessel and its passengers. There are several types of surveys available. The two most popular are, pre-purchase surveys and condition and valuation surveys. Both surveys are concerned first and foremost with the safety of the vessel and its passengers. Pre-purchase surveys are for the person buying a new or used boat and wants to find out as much about as possible the condition, value and maintenance history of the vessel. This survey consists of an overview of all visible areas of the hull structure and its many different systems for proper working conditions. Another popular survey is the condition and valuation survey or the insurance survey. This type of survey does not approach the scope of a Pre-Purchase Survey, but will address the overall condition of the vessel along with safety and compliance issues of the vessel.

Some of the items typically covered during a survey are :

* Electrical system
* Plumbing system
* Fuel system
* Sanitation system
* Underwater gear
* Engine components
* Generator operation
* Hull, stringer and bulkheads
* Safety Gear
* Assess the vessel for compliance with USCG CFR, ABYC, and NFPA recommendations
* Conduct a sea trial to evaluate performance
* Give a fair market value or appraisal

Your survey will be concluded with a written report, detailing the vessel and a list of recommendations. repairs or upgrades that the vessel may need, These

Why hire a surveyor? A professional surveyor will provide objective opinions through experienced eyes. Buying a boat is emotional. People tend to fall in love with the prospect of a new car, or house and a boat is no different. Love may be blind, but a surveyor is working for you eyes wide open. Most banks and insurance underwriters require a survey on vessels over two years old. They will want to know her condition and fair market value in order to insure or finance her. The most important reason to survey your vessel however is for the safety of her passengers and crew.

CHOOSING A MARINE SURVEYOR:

Anyone can start a business and title him or herself a Marine Surveyor. Certain organizations, such as the U.S. Surveyors Association, or SAMS, require members to meet strict professional, technical ethical standards. Surveyors should provide you with a professionally prepared report that can be accepted by your bank and / or insurance company. Talk with prospective surveyors and ask questions! How long will the survey take? What does the survey include, and what type of reporting format is used ? Do they use ABYC, NFPA and USCG standards in their surveys? How much will the inspection cost? A through inspection will not be rushed and will depend on the type of survey required based on size, equipment and on board systems. There may be additional services required such as haul out, engine surveys, oil analysis, galvanic and stray current corrosion testing, moisture testing, ultrasonic testing, as well as other non-destructive tests. There may be additional charges for these and other services. Remember that a well conducted survey can provide important information about the condition of the vessel, but they are not guarantees. The surveyor reports the condition in accessible areas as it existed at the time of the inspection.

The New India Assurance Company Limited

Head Office: 87, MG Road, Fort, Mumbai-400001

SUNDRY HULL CLAIM FORM

ISSUANCE OF THIS FORM IS NOT BE TAKEN AS ADMISSION OF LIABILITY

I. Name of the insured and Address:

II. Name of the Assignee, if any:

III. Particular of the Insured Vessel :

a. Name — b. GRT

c. Registration No. — d. Place of Registration

e. Classified as — f. Construction

g. Year Built — h. Engine No.

IV. Particulars of the Tindal & Crew Members

Tindal — Name & Address

Tindal's Father — Name & Address

Crew Members — Name & Address

1. — 2.

3. — 4.

5. — 6.

V. Policy Particulars

No. — Issuing Office

Period of Cover — Terms

Sum Insured ₹

VI. Detailed particulars of the casualty giving to this claim indulging place (Anchor-bearing) Time, Date and the cause of the casualty:

VII. Action taken to save the vessel from imperilment:

VIII. Actual loss / damage suffered :

IX. Human lives lost/saved – How and by whom ?

X. Has the casualty been reported to the authorities–Port Officer / Police / Notary Public ? If so, give particulars :

XI. Was the vessel seaworthy in all respects before commencement of the ill fated voyage or immediately before the casualty?

XII. (a) When was the vessel last repaired ?

(b) What was the repair work carried out ?

XIII. Particulars of loss minimization efforts and expenses incurred, if any:

XIV. Estimated Loss :

The above particulars are true to the best of my knowledge. I/We further declare that no other person has any interest in the said properly, as Owner Mortgagee. Trustee of otherwise, and as that it is not otherwise insured against with this or any other Office, except as above stated.

Place :

Date :

Signature of Insured.

NATIONAL INSURANCE COMPANY LIMITED

(*Regd. Office* : 3, *Middleton Street, Calcutta* - 700 071)
Regional Office : 6, *Shahnajaf Road, Lucknow* – 226 001

ISSUING OFFICE

The issue of this form is not to be construed as an admission of liability on the part of the Company and should be completed and returned to the Branch of the Company whom it was issued within seven days.

"ALL RISKS" CLAIM FORM

Note : A list of lost and damaged property must be furnished in the space provided overleaf

Name of Insured.. Policy No.................................

Address.. ....

....Telephone No.....................

1. When and where was the missing property last seen ?

2. On what day and at what hour was the loss or damage discovered ?

3. State the circumstances of the loss or damage. Full particulars must be given.

4. Have the Police Authorities been informed of the loss ? It so. on what date and at which Police Station and the Diary No.

5. (a) Has a thorough search been made for the articles?

   (b) What steps have been taken to recover the property?

6. Is the Claimant the sole owner of the property lost or damaged ?

7. Are there any other insurances upon the same property ? It so, give full particulars.

8. Has the claimant sustained other losses of the same nature ? If so, given full particulars.

9. If claim in respect of jewellery, when was the property last overhauled by a Jeweller ? Name and address of the Jeweller should be stated.

I...of...

....do herbey affirm and declare that the above statements and the statements contained in the list lost or damaged articles overleaf are in all respect true and complete and are made without reservation of any kind, and accordance with the particulars given in the said list I claim the sum of₹..

I do further affirm and declare that to my knowledge no other person than myself has any interest in the said property by bill of sale or as owner, mortgagee, trustee or otherwise, and that thereare no other insurances effected on the said property by me, or so far as I am aware, by any other person.

Dated this...day of 19

Signature of Claimant ....

Please turn overleaf

An "All Risks" Police being a contract of INDEMNITY, all claims must be based upon the actual value of the atricles at the time of the Theft, Loss or Damage, but not exceeding the sums for which they are respectively insured, due allowance being made for depreciation and wear and tear.

No. of Item of Schedule of Policy	Full description of article lost or damaged	From whom purchased or by whom presented (Receipt or vouchers should be attached for perusal and return)	Date purchased or received	Cost		Deduction for wear and tear		Amount claimed	
				₹	P.	₹	P.	₹	P.

PP – 100 Pads /10 - 85

NATIONAL INSURANCE COMPANY LIMITED

(Regd. Office : 3, Middleton Street, Calcutta - 700 071)
Regional Office : 6, shahnajaf Road, Lucknow - 226 001

Claim
Reference :

MARINE CLAIM FORM

1. Name of Applicants.

2. Policy No. / Declaration No.

3. GOODS as per SCHEDULE despatched form..on..........................
under Rly. inv/ R.R/ PWB/ Motor Lerry. R. No..Date..........................
and transhipment at ....on................and arrived at..........................
on ....and was cleared on ....

   (a) Remarks on Rly. Inv. /R.R/ PWB / Motor Lorry. R. No.

   (b) How the delivery was taken:

   (c) Date of taking delivery :

   (d) Reason for delay, if any :

   (e) Has claim been made against the carriers.

   (f) If so, what is the result?

   (g) If not, what are the reasons?

5. External condition of Packages at the time of delivery :

6. Nature of Packing.

7. Nature of Damage.

8. Attributed cause of Damage.

9. Gross sound arrived market value of goods.

10. (a) Invoice Value.

    (b) Insured Value.

11. Date of opening the Cases
Reasons for delay, if any

12.

Mark & Nos.	Total No. of Packages	No. of Packages Damaged	Contents Sound	Contents Short	Contents Damaged

13. Number of Packages to be examined.

14. Damaged Packages lying at.

15. Details of Damage if goods are examined prior to application of survey).

16. (a) Salvage Value.
(b) Further Remarks:

Date...........................

....
Signature of Consignee/Applicants

N. B : We enclose herewith the following papers in support of the above claim, receipt of which please acknowledge,

1.

2.

3.

5.

6.

A.P.P-17000/9/86.

Tata AIG General Insurance Company Limited
Marine Insurance Application Form

1. Name and Address of the applicant/Bank, if any*
2. Phone & Fax nos. & e-mail address
3. Merchandise / Goods to be insured *
4. Nature of Packing *
5. Marks & Nos.
6. Conveyance * ☐ Sea ☐ Air ☐ Closed Rail wagons/ Covered Trucks
7. Name of the Vessel ☐ Courier ☐ Post ☐ Others
8. B/L, AWB, RR/CN no. and date
9. Voyage / Transit * From To
10. Transshipment &/ or storage if any (specify place and period).
11. Basis of Valuation *
12. Value declared for insurance* In foreign currency In Indian Rupees
13. Terms of cover required* ☐ All Risks ☐ Basic
14. Specify LC wordings, if any, to be incorporated:
15. Any other details about the risk:
16. Producer Name & Code, if applicable: *

Corporate Office : Ahura Centre, 4th Floor, 82 Mahakali Caves Road Andheri (E) Mumbia-4000093.
(Regd. Office: Bombay House, 24 Homi Mody Street, Mumbia -400001)
For more information call the Tata AIG Toll-free-24 hours Helpline at - 1-600-119966

Declaration by Applicant

I/We hereby declare that the statements made by me/us herein and in attachments hereto are true to the best of my/our knowledge and belief and I/We hereby agree that this Proposal shall form the basis of the insurance contract between me/us and Tata AIG General Insurance Company Ltd. (referred to as the Company). I/We further confirm that if any additions or alterations are carried out in the risk proposed for insurance herein after the submission of this Proposal then particulars of such shallbe forthwith conveyed to the Company. I/We further agree that the submission of this Proposal to the Company and its receipt thereof shall not constitute an acceptance of the risk. by the Company.

Place		Signature of Applicant	
Date		Name & Designation	
Time		Cheque no. and Date	
Amount of Cheque			

ATTACHMENTS

Invoice/Packing List/ LC wordings BL or contract of affreightment/ if other, specify.

(IMPORTANT) Prohibition of Rebates (Section) 41 of the Insurance Act 1938

1. No person shall allow or offer to allow either directly or indirectly as inducement to any Person to take out renew or continue an Insurance in respect of any kind of risk relating to lives or property in India any rebate of the whole or part of the commission payable or any rebate of the premium shown on the Policy, nor shall any person taking our or renewing or continuing a Policy accept such rebate except such rebate as maybe allowed in accordance with the published prospectuses or tables to the Insure.
2. Any person making default in complying with the provision of this section shall be punishable with fine which may extend to five hundred rupees only

NOTE:

1 Premium cheque to be drawn in favour of Tata AIG General Insurance Company Limited.
2 Policies proposed and taken after commencement of transit shall be deemed to be nuil and void.
3 Non-disclosure or misrepresentation in application form will render the contract null and void.
4 For Sea shipments - Institute Classification Clause (extended for Vessels upto 20 years.) Vessels <20 years> 25 years additional premium @ 0.125%.
VESSELS NOT TO EXCEED 25 YEARS.
5 Insurance policy taken should run concurrent to your sale terms and not exceeding the same.
6 This application shall form part of the policy and in case of a dispute referred to as base document.
7 Fields marked in* are Mandatory fields.
8 Please ask for copy of the Clauses in case you require it alongwith the Policy document
9 Shipment details to be furnished within 7 days of sailing

FOR OFFICE USE

Corporate Office: Ahura Centre, 4the Floor, Mahakali Caves Road, Andheri (E) Mumbai - 4000093.
(Regd. Office : Bombay House, 24 Homi Mody Street, Mumbai - 400001)
For more information, call the Tata AIG Toll-free-24 hours Helpline at - 1-600-119966

2 of 2

Effective from 31-1-1989

Application form for issue of

MARINE CARGO SPECIAL DECLARATION POLICY

The ________________________________ Insurance Company Limited.

Branch : ____________ Division : ____________ Region : ____________

PART - A

To be filled in by the Insured only

1. Name and Address of the Proposer :
2. Commencement date of the Special Declaration Policy, i.e, the data on which it was issued for the first time:
3. Date from which Special Discount has to be sanctioned by the Committee on the basis of the application:
4. Description of goods to be covered and their packing and estimated Annual Turnover:

Goods	**Packing**	**Estimated Annual Turnover** ₹
(i)		
(ii)		
(iii)		
(iv)		Total :

5. Mode of Conveyance :
6. Journey : From/To
7. Risks to be covered under the proposed policy :
8. Whether extension of period of cover beyond 7 days period provided in the Transit Clause is required after the goods reach destination point but remaining in the custody of carrier waiting clearance ?

   If yes indicate the number of weeks for which extension is required.

   Yes, for ____________ weeks.
9. Whether cover against Strike, Riot and Civil Commotion risks required :

   Yes/No

10. Details of previous Insurance for Marine Transit Cover, it any, for the last three years :

(i) Whether the goods in Transit which are proposed for insurance were in the past insured and, it so, the type of policy taken :

(a) Annual Transit Policy :

(b) Special Declaration Policy :

(c) Open Policy subject to declaration of each transit :

(ii) If Special Declaration Policy or Open Policy subject to Declaration of each Transit, please state :

(a) Annual Turnover :

(b) Nature of Cover :

(C) Details of Rates, Charged :

Basic Cover :

Wider Cover :

SRCC Cover :

Extension of Cover e.g. Period of Storage, Distance etc :

(iii) Name of the previous Insurer and Division :

(iv) Whether Special Declaration Policy discount was allowed in the past, and if so, the percent there of :

11. Whether a separate Special Storage Risks Insurance (Annual cover) as provided under the Special Storage Risks Insurance Tariff is required in conjunction with the Special Declaration Policy ?

12. Whether cover against Terrorist Risk is also required?

Note : It may be noted that the cover for Terrorist Risk can be granted only if the preceding Special Declaration Policy

I/We declare that the answers given by me/us are true and correct and that I/We have not withheld any information which might influence acceptance of this proposal. I/We agree that this declaration and the answers given by me/us shall be the basis of the Insurance contract between me/us and the Company and shall be deemed to be incorporated in the Policy. I/We further agree to accept the policy subject to the terms, conditions and exceptions prescribed by the Company.

Signature of the Proposer

Date : __________ Name : __________ Designation : __________

PART - B

To be filled in by the Insurer only

13. Loss Experience for the fover granted under any type of policy other than Special Storage Risks Insurance Policy during the last three years.

1	2	3	4	5	6	7
U E A R	Sum Insured	Type of policy	Rate (Basic + loading for wider coverage and SRCC etc., to be shown separately)	Premium paid	Losses paid and losses outstanding (to be shown separately)	Loss Ratio %

Total of the above :

Average Loss Ratio for the last three years (%) :

14. Details of Rates charged by insures :
    (a) Basic Cover with Statistical Code of the Tariff :
    (b) Wider Cover :
    (c) SRCC Cover :
    (d) Extension of Cover - e.g. Period of Storage, Distance etc :

15. Insurer's request with reasons :
    (i) Whether continuation of Old Tariff rates, terms/conditions desired : Yes/No
    (ii) Whether continuation of New Tariff rates, terms/conditions desired : Yes/No
    (iii) Percent of special Discount requested:________________
    (iv) The date from which sanction of Special Discount is requested :________________

16. We confirm that we have checked Part 'A' filled in by the Insured and the answers given in Part 'A' & 'B' are true.

________________ ________________

Incharge of Divisional Office | Officer of the Regional Office

Date : ________________

HDFC ERGO General Insurance Company Ltd.

PROPOSAL FOR MARINE CARGO INSURANCE (OPEN POLICY/ OPEN COVER)

Name of the Agent/ Broker		Code	

(a) Client Data:

1.	*Name of the Proposer*				
2.	*Address*				
3.	*Phone Nos./ Fax*	*Fax*		*Ph:*	
4.	*e-mail*				
5.	*Key Person (Insurance)*				
	Thone Nos./Fax	*Fax*		*Ph:*	
6.	*Description of the Trade/Business*				
7.	*Years in Trade*				
8.	*Annual Turncver(Last 3 Years) Rs.*	*Yr*	*Yr*	*Yr*	
	(as shown in the annual report)	*Amt.*	*Amt*	*Amt.*	

(a)	**Policy Date:**
	(Please answer all questions)

1.	Type of Policy required	One Voyage/transit	Open Policy (Annual)	Others (specify)
2.	Is the policy being taken for the first time ?		If"NO"please give details as below	
	(a) Present Insure		Date of commencement of policy	

(b) Premium Paid and Claims Received & Outstanding for the last 3 years :

Year	Premium (₹).	Claims Paid (r)	Outstanding Claims(r).	Claims Ratio

3. It the claim experience of any year is adverse due to a me or/ unusual loss, please give brief details of the claim including claim amount received :

HDFC ERGO General Insurance Company Limitec

The intention of this Form is to meet your entire Marine Insurance requirement under one Policy document. Kindly therefore, complete the Form carefully

(c)	**Cargo Data :**					
1	Merchandise/Goods to be Insured *Input : Raw Materials, CKD, SKD,etc* *Output : Finished Products, etc*	Input (Imports)				
		Output (Exports)				
		Domestic Input				
		Domestic Output				
2	Packing of Cargo E.g. Gases, crated, manufacture's export cartons, bulk, bagged, and then palletised and wrapped	Input (Imports)				
		Output (Exports)				
		Domestic Input				
		Domestic Output				
3a	Will the cargo be containerised ?			If "YES", is it		
3b	If FCL, will cargo be destuffed at final destination warehouse			If "No", where will destuffing take place ?		
4	Estimated Annual volume to be insured (**₹ In Lacs**)	**(4a)** Exports (₹)		**(4b)** Imports (Rs.)	Input Domestic (₹)	Output Domestic (₹)

4a	**Principal** countries to which	Country	**US/Canada**	**U.K.& Continental Europe (EC)**	**Middle/ South east**	**Far East/ Australia/ Newzealand**	**Others**	**Total**
	goods are **exported**	CIF % of Total						0
	(Mention only **PERCENTAGE**)	Value Rs. Lacs	0	0	0	0	0	0
		FOB/C&F % of totals						0
		Value Rs. Lacs		0	0	0	0	0
4b	Final **Destination Towns** in India for **Imports**	Location						Total
		% of Total						0
	(Mention only **PERCENTAGE**)	Value Rs. Lacs	0.00	0.00	0.00	0.00	0.00	0.00

5	**Conveyance:**		**Air**	**Sea**	**Postal**	**Courier**	**Other Conveyance (Please specify)**		
	Please tick	**Export**							
		Import	**Air**	**Road**	**Rail**	**Inland Water**	**Coastal Water**	**Postal**	**Courier**
		Domestic							
5a	What percentage of total shipments will be by **AIR TRANSIT**					Exports	%	Imports	%
5b	Will the Courier shipments exceed **10%** of the Total Shipments ?								
5c	Do the Couriers have any insurance police covering their liability as carriers?								
6	Will there be any transshipment ? If **"Yes"** please give details.					Transhipment at :			
7	**Geographical Limits for Policy**			From		To			
		Import	Exports						
		Export	Imports						
		Domestic Input							
		Domestic Output							
8	Basis of Valuation for Policy		**Imports**	**FOB+ %**	**C & P %**		**Domestic Input**	**Purchase Invoice + %**	
	(The Percentage to be shown should not include % age towards Increased **Value or Customs Duty)**		**Export**	**FOB+ %**	**C&F+ %**	**CIF+ %**	**Domestic Output**	**Sale Invoice+ %**	
9	Limits of Insurance required for the Policy (₹)		By any one vessel on Deck under			By Registered or P.O Insured Parcel			
			By any one vessel on Deck			By Unregistered or Ordinary Parcel Post			
			By any one aircraft			By Courier			
			By any one Truck/Rake			By any other mode			
			By any one Barge (Inland vessel)			By any other mode			
10	Limit for any one Location **(Accumulation)**	₹							

11	**Terms** of Cover required		
	"Basic"(Named Perils), "All risk", "SRCC", "War" etc.		
12	Do you require cover for Custom Duty ?		
	(Please note that this is not an **"agreed value"** cover)	If "YES" please state	(₹)
		(a) Maximum amount per shipment	
		(b) Annual Amount	
13	Do you require "Increased value "for imports ?		
	(Please note that this is not an **"agreed value"** cover	If "YES" please state	(₹)
		(a) Maximum amount per shipment	
		(b) Annual Amount	
14	Do you require storage cover at intermediate inland locations, originating ports (exports), arrival ports (import etc?		
		If "YES" please state	For more than one locations, attach separate sheet
		(a) Location (City /Town/Port)	
		(b) Number of days /weeks	
		(c) Amount per Location	₹
15	Reasons for storage ? e.g consolidation, processing, packing, blending etc.	(d) Are the godowns owned/hired by you ?	
		If the Godowns are not owned/ hired by you, they belong to whom?	
16	Have you entered into a special contract with any Carrier restricting their liability ?		
	If "YES" Please give details.		
17	Would you like to opt for a **"Voluntary Excess" ?**		
	If **" yes"** , please mention the amount.		₹
18	Any other information you would like to provide		

Decleration Prohibition of Rebates

HDFC ERGO General Insurance Company Limitec

I/We the undersigned hereby declare that the above statements and particulars are true and complete and I/We declare and agree that this declaration and the answers given above shall be held to be promissory and shall be the basis of the contract between me/us and the Company.

Proposer's Signature

Place————

Date ————

Place							Signature of the Applicant		

SECTION 41
PROHIBITION OF REBATES

1. No person shall allow or offer to allow, either directly or indirectly as an Inducement to any person to take out or renew or continue an Insurance in respect of any kind of risk relating to lives or property in India any rebate of the whole of the commission payable or any rebate of the premium shown in the policy nor shall any person taking out or renewing or continuing a policy accept any rebate except such rebate as may be allowed in accordance with the published prospectuses or tables ofthe insurer.

2. Any person making default in complying with the provislons of this section shall be punishable with fine which may extend to Rs. 500/- (Rupees Five Hundred)

NEW INDIA ASSURANCE

(Incorporated in India)

Registered Office : New India Assurance Building, 87 Mahatma Gandhi Road, Fort, Bombay-400 023, India

MARINE POLICY (CARGO)

WHEREAS the ASURED named in the schedule hereto, have represented to THE NEW INDIA ASSURANCE COMPANY LTD (hereinafter called the "COMPANY)" that they are intersteded or duly authorised to make the insurance mentioned and described and have to pay the premium hereinafter stated.

THE COMPANY HEREBY PROMISES AND AGREES with the Assured, their Executors, Administrators, and Assigns that the Company will insure against loss damage liability or expense t to the clauses, endorsements conditions and warranties contained in the Schedule.

SCHEDULE

ASSURED			POLICY NO.
Vessels & / or Conveyance			In lieu of Cover Note NO.
Local vessel or conveyance	From (local port or place or holding)	Currency	Issued at Date or Issue Sailing on or about
Ocean vessel etc.	Seaport of loadlng		
Sea port of discharge	Final Destination/ transshipment		
Subject matter Insured			From : To:
Amount Insured hereunder $ In figures $In words			

Special conditions & Warranties:

Subject to Important Notice attached hereto

THE ATTACHED CLAUSES AND ENDORSMENTS FORM PART OF THIS POLICY

SURVEY AND	In the event of loss or damage which may result in a claim under this insurance, immediate notice be given to Who are the company's agents at port of discharge, in order that may examine the goods and issue a survey report where the s company has no agent, the notice must be given to Lloyd's Agent
CLAIMS SETTLEMENT	Payable at BY

Code Number and full address of issuing office

IN WITNESS WHEREOF SIGNED FOR AND ON BEHALF OF THE COMPANY

OP/8260/96

Duly Constituted Attorney (s)

IMPORTANT

PROCEDURE IN THE EVENT OF LOSS OR DAMAGE FOR WHICH

UNDERWRITERS MAY BE LIABLE

LIABILITY OF CRRIERS BAILEES OR OTHER THIRD PERTIES

It is the duty of the Assured and their agents, in all cases, to take such mearues as may be reasonable for the purpose of averting or minimizing a loss and to ensure that all right against Carriers, bailees or other third parties are properly take steps and failure too comply with these requirements may prejudice any claim under this polciy/certificate.

1. To claim immediately on Carriers, Port Authorities or other bailees for any missing packages.
2. To apply immediately for survey by carriers' or other Bailees' Representatives if any loss or damage be apparaent and claim on the Carriers or other Bailees for any actual loss or damage found at such survey.
3. In no circumstances, except under written protes, to give clean receipts where goods are in doubtful condition.
4. To give notice in writing to the Carriers or other Bailees within 3 days of delivery if the loss was not apparent at the time of taking delivery.

NOTE: – The Consignees or their Agents are recommended to make themselves familiar withthe Regulations ofthe Port Authoriteis at the port of discharge.

SURVEY AND CLAIM SETTLEMENTS

In the event of loss or damage which may involve a claim under this insurance immediate notic of such loss or damage should be given to an a Survey Report obtained from Lloyd's Agents or othe agents nominated for the purpose in this Policy and who are authorised to adjust and settle claims on behalf of the Company named within.

DOCUMENTATION OF CLAIMS

To enable claims to be dealt with promptly, Assured or their Agents are advised to submit all available supporting documents with out delay, including when applicable :–

1. Original policy or certificate of insurance.
2. Original or copy of shiipping invocies, together with shipping specification and/or weight notes.
3. Original bill of Lading and/or other contract of carriage.
4. Survey report or other documentary evidence to show the extent of the loss or damage.
5. Landing account and weight notes at final destination.
6. Correspondence exchanged with the carrier and other Parties regarding their liability for the loss or damage

Form of Marine Insurance Policy

(SECTION 24 OF THE MARINE INSURANCE ACT. 1963)

BE IT KNOWN THAT … as well in … own name as for and in the name and names of all and every other person or persons to whom the same doth, may or shall operate appertain, in past or in all doth make assurance and cause them and every of them, to be insured lost or not lost, at and from upon and kind of gods and merchandise, and also upon the body, tackle, apparel, ordnance, ammunition, artillery, boat and other furniture, of and in the good ship or vessel called the _____ whereof___ is master for this present voyage or whosoever else shall go for master in the said or by whatsoever other name or names the said ship, or the master thereof, is or shall be named or called beginning the adventure upon the said goods and merchandise from the loading thereof aboard the said ship, upon the said ship etc... And further until the said ship with all her ordnance, tackle, apparel etc. And good and merchandise whatsoever shall be arrived at ____ upon the said ship etc. until she hath moored at anchor twenty four hours in goods safety; and upon the goods and merchandise, until the same be there discharged and safely landed. And it shall be lawful for the said ship etc. in this voyage to proceed and sail to and touch and stay at any ports or places whatsoever without prejudice to this insurance. The said ship etc. good and merchandise etc. for so much as concerned the assured by agreement between the assured and assurers in this policy, are and shall be valued at _____

Touching the adventures and perils which we the assurers are contended to bear and to do take upon us in this voyage; they are of the seas, men of war, fire, enemies, pirates, rovers, thieves, jettisons, letters of mart and countermart, surprisals, takings at sea, arrests, restraints, and detainments of all kings, princes, and people, of what nation condition or quality whatsoever, barratry of the master and mariners, and of all nation, condition and all other perils losses and misfortunes that have or shall come to hurt, detriment, or damage of the said goods and merchandise, and ship etc. or any part thereof.

And in case of any loss or misfortune it shall be lawful to the assured, their factors, servants, and assigns, to sue, labour and travel for, in and about the defence, safeguards and recovery of the said goods and merchandises and ship etc. or any part thereof, without prejudice to this insurance; to the charges whereof we, the assurers; will contribute each one according to the rate and quantity of his sum herein assured.

And it is especially declared and agreed that no acts of the insurer or insured in recovering, saving, or preserving the property insured shall be considered as a waiver, or acceptance or abandonment. And so we, the assurers are contended, and do hereby promise and bind ourselves, each one for his own part, our heirs, executors and goods to premises, confessing ourselves paid the consideration due unto us for this assurance by the assured, at and after the rate of …

IN WITNESS WHEREOF we, the assurers, have subscribed our names and sums assured in.

MEMORANDUM N.B. Com, fish, salt, fruit, flour and seed are warranted free from average, unless general or the ship be stranded-sugar tobacco, hemp, flax, hides and skins are warranted free from average, under five per cent, and all other goods, also the ship and freight, are warranted free from average, under three per cent, unless general, or the ship be stranded.

RULES FOR CONSTRUCTION OF POLICY.

The following are the rules referred to by the Marine Insurance Act 1963 for the construction of the policy in the above or other like form, where the context does not otherwise require.

1. Lost or not lost. Where the subject matter is insured "lost or not lost" and the loss has occurred before the contract is concluded, the risk attaches unless, at such time the assured was aware of the loss, and the insurer was not.
2. From: Where the subject matter is insured "from" a particular place the risk does not attach until the ship starts on the voyage insured.
3. At and from -- (a) Where a ship is insured "at and from" a particular place, and she is at that place in good safety when the contract is concluded, the risk attaches immediately.
   1. (b) If she be not at that place when the contract is concluded, the risk attaches as soon as she arrives there is good safety, and unless the policy otherwise provides, it is immaterial that she is covered by another policy for a specified time after arrival.
   2. (c) Where chartered fright is insured "at and from" a particular place and the ship is at that place in good safety when the contract is concluded the risk attaches immediately. If she be not there when the contract is concluded, the risk attaches as soon as she arrives there in good safety.
   3. (d) Where freight, other than chartered freight is payable without special conditions and is insured "at and from" a particular place, the risk attaches pro rata as the goods or merchandise are shipped; provided that, if there be cargo in readiness which belongs to the ship-owner, or which some other person has contracted with him to ship, the risk attaches as soon as the ship is ready to receive such cargo.
4. From the loading thereof- where goods or other movables are insured "from the loading thereof" the risk does not attach until such goods or movables are actually on board, and the insurer is not liable for them while in transit from the shore to the ship.
5. Safely landed; where the risk on goods or other movables continues until they are "safely landed", they must be landed in the customary manner and within a reasonable time after arrival at the port of discharge and if they are not so landed the risk ceases.
6. Touch and stay: in the absence of any further license or usage, the liberty to touch and stay "at any port or place whatsoever" does not authorize the ship to depart from the course of her voyage from the port of departure to the port of destination.
7. Perils of the Seas: The term "Perils of the Seas" refers only to fortuitous accidents or casualties of the seas. It does not include the ordinary action of the winds and waves.
8. Pirates: The term "Pirates" includes passengers who mutiny and rioters who attack the ship from the shore.
9. Thieves: The term "Thieves" does not cover clandestine theft or a theft committed by any one of the ship's company, whether crew or passengers.
10. Restraint of Princes: The term "arrests, etc. of kings, princes and people" refers to political or executive acts, and does not include a loss caused by not or by ordinary judicial process.
11. Barratry: The term "Barratry" includes every wrongful act willfully committed by the master or crew to the prejudice of the owner, or as the case may be, the charterer.
12. All other perils: The term "all other perils" includes only perils similar in kind to the perils specifically mentioned in the policy.
13. Average unless General: The term "average unless general" means a partial loss of the subject matter insured other than a general average loss, and does not include "Particular charges".

14. Stranded: Where the ship has stranded, the insurer is liable for the excepted losses although the loss is not attributable to the stranding, provided than when the stranding takes place the risk has attached and, if the policy be on goods, that the damages goods are not on board.
15. Ship: The term "ship" includes the hull, material and outfit, stores and provisions for the officers and crew, and, in the case of vessels engaged in a special trade, the ordinary fittings requisite for the trade, and also, in the case of a steamship the machinery, boilers, and coals and engine stores, if owned by the assured and also in the case of a ship driven by power other than steam, the machinery fuels and engine stores, if owned by the assured.
16. Freight: The term freight includes property derivable by a ship-owner from the employment of his ship to carry his own goods or movables, as freight payable by a third party , but does not include passage money.
17. Goods: The term "Goods" means goods in the nature of merchandise, and does not include personal effects or provisions and stores for use on board.

In the absence of any usage to the contrary deck cargo and living animals must be insured specifically and not under the general denomination of goods.

.... Claim No:

DISCHARGE VOUCHER

I/WE have this day taken delivery of .... marine .... Registered No .... and here by certify the the whole of the replacement for which I/We have claimed have been carried out to my/our entire satisfaction by ....

I/WE hereby authorize and direct NEW INDIA ASSURANCE COMPANY LIMITED to pay the accounts for such and such adn such payments will LIMITED from all liability in connection with my/our claim for damage to such marine and alieds arising out of accident which occured on : .... (date) .... (month) .... (year)

Signature of Insured:

....

Witness: ....

Date: ....

N.B. No account recognized unless accompanied by this discharge voucher.

PART FOUR

FIRE-INSURANCE

26

NATURE AND USE OF FIRE INSURANCE

Fire insurance has not a long history. The real establishment of fire insurance came only after the Great Fire of London in 1066. This fire lasted for four days and nights burning over 436 acres of ground and destroying over 13,000 buildings was the most disastrous fire in history and forcibly awakened the people to the necessity for a form of protection against such calamities. The main cause of its late development was slow progress of trade and commerce. After a certain period when the business and commerce ran high, fire insurance received a real fillip. Previously there was no basis on which the premimium could be based. There were a few concerns which made a remarkable progress. Gradually as they gained experience the data went on accumulating and the premium rates became more equitable and scientific. The decisions of law court also brought the principles of fire insurance to a standard form. With increasing competition and experience, the fire insurance is evolved in its present scientific form. However, the progress in fire insurance was not so tremendous and categorical as was in the case of life insurance.

Definition and Nature

Section 2 of the Insurance Act 1938 defines fire insurance as "the business of effecting, otherwise than incidentally to some other class of insurancc businccs, contract of insurance against loss by or incidental to fire or other occurrence customarily included among the risks insured against in fire insurance policies." The occurrence of a fire will result not only in loss of or damage to material property but also other consequential losses such as loss of production causing loss of profit. The function of fire insurance is to make good the financial loss suffered as a result of fire. It is not the function of fire insurance to replace the economic loss termed the 'fire waste'. Such damage apart form causing financial loss to the owners, dislocates the economic activity of the community. Inspite of sustained efforts made by human ingenuity to achieve complete mastery of fire, material property continue to be liable in varying degree to destruction or damage by the escape of fire from its contract. Some of the insurable properties are buildings, electrical installation, contents of building such as machines plant and equipment accessories, etc. goods such as raw materials, goods in process, finished goods, goods in the open or in the premises, contents in dwellings, shops, hotels furniture, fixture and fitting and other movable and immovable properties.

Fire insurance is a device to compensate for the loss consequent upon destruction by fire. Thus the fire insurer shifts the burden of fire losses from their actual victims over to all the members of the society. It is a cooperative device to share the loss. It relieves the insured from the horror of the fire losses to which he is exposed.

Functions

It is a wellknown fact that the fire causes huge losses every year. The individual owner by taking fire insurance can prevent the fire waste to some extent. The insurer acts as a middle man between all the members of the society who are exposed to the fire risk on the one hand and the members who will be the actual victims of the fire losses on the other. The insurer charges the premium from all the insured members and makes good the losses when they occur to any of them.

The system of fire insurance cannot save the society from the economic loss to the community to the extent of the property lost by fire, but it compensates someone and this saves him from a ruinous loss, at the cost of group of some others.

Causes of Fire

Fire waste is the result of two types of hazard, *viz.*, 'physical' and 'moral'.

1. **Physical Hazard:** It refers to the inherent risk of fire in the property which may occur due to inflammable nature, construction, artificial lighting and heating, lack of extinguishing apparatus use of the property, etc. It may also cover other risks such as explosion, riot, strike, etc.
2. **Moral Hazard:** The moral hazard depends upon the man as physical hazard depends on the property. The property may be set on fire by the owner or by any person with his willingness, carelessness and lack of sense of duty may also increase the fire waste. Sometimes, when market price is going down the owner can willingly set fire on the property and gain from the payment of insurance money. Thus, where the property was destroyed with the willingness of the property owner, moral hazard exists.

Prevention of Less

Insurance is meant for indemnification of loss and not for prevention of loss although every reasonable step can be taken to eliminate it or minimise it through the agencies engaged in prevention of loss. Thus, insurance may help in two ways 1. Indemnification and 2. Preventive efforts.

1. **Indemnification or curative efforts:** According to doctrine of indemnification, the financial loss suffered by the perils insured against will be compensated in full, not more than this and not less than this. The insurance provides protection by indemnifying the financial loss suffered by insured person which occurred beyond the control of insured and insurer.
2. **Preventive efforts:** The loss cannot be prevented by insurance. But, the insures help those who are engaged in the preventive efforts by granting financial and other assistance. This will benefit insurers as well because if the loss of society is reduced, they can charge lesser premium which will stimulate the public for purchasing more insurance policies because of cheaper rate of insurance. Fire insurers stimulate the installation of protective devices and better types of construction through granting credit. They help in installation of fire-fighting apparatus, water supply and engineering services.

   Preventive efforts are divided into two parts (*i*) private activities and (*ii*) public activities.

(*i*) Private Activities

Private activities are those which include those activities which the property owner may engage in for the purpose of preventing fire loss. Insurers given sincere advice of financial help to property owner on the following factors.

(*a*) **Construction:** In construction of building, fire resistive materials, fire proof construction, greatest care in exercising selection of the type and planning of the construction, availability of fire extinguisher, water supply, proper passage in emergency are various activities which reduce the chance of fire. For these activities, the insurers provide advice and assistance.

(*b*) **Fire Services:** The important thing is to extinguish fire before it reaches large proportions. The owner should consider equipping his building with an automatic sprinkler system. Similar fire fighting equipment may be established. Such services can be provided by insurers with the help of fire fighting associations.

(*c*) **Occupation:** There are considerable hazard in certain occupation *e.g.* in oil or coke or chemical industry. Insurance in these concerns is available at higher rate. Insurers help by stimulation and charging lesser premium in fire fencing occupation.

(*d*) **Management:** Good management of property may reduce the chances of fire. Carelessness and indifference cannot be over-emphasized because these increase the chance of fire.

(*e*) **Exposure:** Fire insurance rates are determined on the basis of possibility of exposure. Fire-proof services may reduce the chances of exposure to a greater extent.

(*ii*) Public Fire Prevention Activities

Fire insurers have performed numerous important services to reduce the fire waste with the help of public institutions which are engaged in fire fighting activities.

(*a*) **Community Surveys:** Engineering survey of the cities and localities is made. As a result of its investigation many have improved their fire departments, water supplies and other facilities involved in the protection against fire.

(*b*) **Standard schedule for grading cities:** Under this schedule a number of cities, town, or mohallas are divided, according to fire preventive devices. The deficiencies in each part is sorted out and attempts are made to remove them.

(*c*) **Underwriters' laboratories:** The laboratories are to find out the possible causes of fire losses. Every time research or investigation is made to find out the possible attempts to prevent fire losses.

(*d*) **Equipment:** Fire can be properly checked only through the possession and maintenance of adequate equipment, personnel fire alarm system and water supply. Fire fighting apparatus and equipment for any city or town can be determined by the Fire Protection Association.

(*e*) **Salvage Corps and salvage works by fire deparments:** The chief aim of the corps is to protect property from unnecessary smoke and water damage. The protective benefits are extended to all those who suffer fire damages. The protective benefits are extended to all those who suffer fire damages regardless of whether they are insured or not. Training school and colleges are, sometimes, engaged in giving general education to all and particular education to few students to train them in fire fighting methods and fire preventive methods.

(*f*) **Legislation and Regulation:** National Board of fire underwriters' fire brigade and other such associations are engaged in fire preventive and protective efforts under a certain law. The property owner and the fire protection engineer must keep in mind the numerous legal requirements relating to the various phases of fire prevention.

(*iii*) General Devices

Apart from the above contribution to prevention protection, the following devices are utilised for preventing the losses.

(*i*) The insurer compensates loss at a reasonable cost.

(*ii*) Serious hazards are to be cooperatively reinsured.

(*iii*) Loans are provided for better construction and building.

(*iv*) Fire insurers stimulate the installation of protective devices to reduce losses.

(*v*) Fire fighting methods are organised with public utility concerns.

(*vi*) Insurers investigate the causes of loss and attempts are made to reduce the causes.

(*vii*) Insurers study various devices for fire proof, protection and problems of special processes.

(*viii*) Periodical examination of insured property is made and instructions are issued for the purpose of investigation.

QUESTIONS

1. What do you understand by the fire insurance?
2. What are the uses of the Fire Insurance?

27

FIRE INSURANCE CONTRACT

Fire insurance contract may be defined as "an agreement, whereby one party in return for a consideration undertakes to indemnify the other party against financial loss which the latter may sustain by reason of certain defined subject-matter being damaged or destroyed by fire or other defined perils up to an agreed amount." The party responsible to indemnify the loss is called the insurer, the party who is to be indemnified is called the insured, the consideration for the contract is termed 'the premium', the defined subject-matter is termed 'the property insured" the sum set forth in the contract is called the assured sum, and the document containing the terms and conditions of the contract is known as 'the policy.'

The contract of insurance involves all the elements of an ordinary contract and insurance contracts. The elements of contract are discussed in following paragraphs.

Before discussing the elements of the fire insurance contract, the special meaning of the 'Fire' must be understood.

Fire

Fire, in order to make the insurer liable under the contract, must satisfy two conditions. First, there should be actual fire or ignition, and second, the fire must be fortuitions in its nature.

Ignition

The expression in the policy we have to construct is loss or damage occasioned by fire. This means that loss or damage must be either by ignition of the article or property or premises or part thereof. In other words, the damage should be occasioned by fire. Loss or damage caused by excessive fire heat cannot be included in 'loss or damage by fire'. If should be proved here, that the loss should be caused by fire. The cause of fire is not important. The fire even if caused by the negligence of the servant or himself may come under the definition of fire. There should be no fraud or wilful misconduct by the assured. There should be actual ignition but a process resembling fire may not be fire. For example, the damage done due to smoke due to faulting chimney, or overheated iron are not the example of fire. Similarly chemical actions, explosion, lighting, etc. are not occasioned or example of fire.

Fire should be accidental and not intentional

Any loss caused by fire lighted purposively is not a loss by fire if it was intentional. However, the property burned accidentally in an ordinary fire, such as domestic fire, the loss is covered even if the fire remains under control. When a fire was purposively lighted but became out of control at a later stage is taken under the definition of fire. The object of fire insurance is to indemnify the insured against accidental loss by fire.

ELEMENTS OF FIRE INSURANCE CONTRACT

1. Features of General Contract. All the features of general contract are also applicable to the fire insurance contract. Such as proposal and acceptance, consideration, agreement between the parties, legal competence of the parties and legal venture.

(*a*) **Proposal:** The proposal for fire insurance can be made either verbally or in writing. The proposer gives the necessary description of the property to be insured. In practice the printed proposal form is used for the purpose. Introduction, type of properties, value of properties, construction, occupation, etc., are the various information which are required by the insurer. The answers to these questions must be completely correct. The assured must disclose all the material facts and should observe utmost good faith. The description of the subject-matter of insurance is the basis of contract for assessing the risk and fixing the premium.

(*b*) **Acceptance:** On receipt of the proposal form, the insurer will assess the risk. Sometimes, when the contents and subject-matters are not of very high amount, the insurer may accept on the basis of proposal forms only. When the subject-matters is of larger magnitude and where the hazard involved is of a variable or unknown nature, the insurer may send his surveyor to survey the property. The surveyors being expert in the field of insurance evaluation will consider the proposal in the light of this report. The unknown proposers are required to submit an evidence of respectability. The insured is required to submit a certificate from some known and respectable person about honesty and integrity. As soon as the proposal is accepted, the assured is informed about the decision.

(*c*) **Commencement of risk:** The risk commences as soon as the contract is completed provided there is no specific time for the purpose. As soon as the proposal is accepted, risk will commence irrespective of the fact that no policy was issued and no premium was paid. Where risks are unknown and tremendous, the payment of premium will be the basis of the completion of the contract. The risk will commence only when the premium has been paid and not before that when the policy has been issued, payment of premium will not be the basis of commencement of risk.

(*i*) **Cover note:** The insurer issues a 'Cover Note' or 'Interim Protection Note' when the risk was accepted provisionally or subject to the condition of payment of premium. This note will cover the property so far the final policy has not been issued. If loss occurs before issue of policy the cover note will be sufficient to prove insurance. The cover note, however is not taken at par to the policy.

Policy

The insurer issues a duly stamped policy which will bear all the terms and conditions of the contract. Any contract of fire insurance, comes within the meaning of the word 'policy'. It is a statutory and formal document of insurance contract. There are different forms of policies for different types of policies. However, a standard form is also used. The policy contains the name and address of the insured, the subject-matter of insurance, the sum insured, the term and the premium. There are various clauses governing the conditions of insurance contract. The terms and conditions of the policy can be changed.

Period of Fire Insurance Policies

Usually fire policies are issued for one year and are called 'Annual Insurance.' Policies issued for a period shorter than one year are known as 'Short-term Policies' and those issued for a period more than one year are called 'Long-term Polices'. But in practice only annual policies are common. 'Short-term' and 'Long-term' policies are rarely used. Long-term policies are generally issued in case of building. Alteration in the policy will be made according to the change in building and terms of insurance. The premium rate is determined according to the nature, location, construction of the property.

Moreover, the period of insurance is also taken into account for computing premiums.

More than one fire during a Period

When there is more than one fire in respect of the same subject-matter insured, the insurer is not bound to pay more than the sum assured. During the policy-life, payment of each loss, automatically, reduces the amount of the policy by the amount so paid. When, after payment of certain losses, the property insured is totally destroyed, the insurer will pay loss not more than the balance of insured amount remaining after compensation of the previous losses.

However, if the insured is willing to get payment of full loss, he can reinstate the assured sum to the original amount by paying a fresh premium on a pro-rata basis to the date of expiry.

More than one Policy

If the same subject-matter is insured with more than one insurer, he cannot realize more than the actual loss from all the insurers. Each insurer will pay his ratable proportion of loss to the property insured against fire. If there is average clause, then the insurers will pay accordingly.

2. Insurable Interest. Insurable interest is the general principle of insurance without which an insurance cannot lawfully be enforced for an insurance unsupported by an insurable interest would be a gambling transaction. Insurable interest will be there where the subject-matter should be in such a position that the insured may suffer loss at the time of damage and may gain by its protection. The insurable interest in fire insurance must be present at the time of contract continue throughtout its currency and at the time of loss. Insurance contract will be invalid if the property is sold to another party. Similarly if there is no insurable interest at the time of insurance, the contract will be invalid. The following conditions must be fulfilled to constitute an insurable interest.

(*i*) There should be a physical object capable of being damaged or destroyed by fire.

(*ii*) The object must be the subject matter of insurance.

(*iii*) The insured must stand in such relationship as recognized by law where the insured is benefited by the safety of the subject-matter or be prejudiced by its loss.

The insurable interest is the 'pecuniary interest'. The fire insurance is a personal contract between the insured and the insurer. So, the transfer of interest would invalidate the contract.

The following persons have insurable interest in the subject-matter concerned.

1. The owner of the property or asset whether fixed or current has as insurable interest whether he is the legal owner or the equitable owner. The owner may be a single or joint, holder.' Partial owner can take policy for full value as trustee of all the property. A Life tenant entitled to the use of the property during his life time only has an insurable interest.
2. An agent has insurable interest in the property of his principal.
3. A partner has an equitable interest in the firm's property.
4. A creditor has an insurable interest in property on which he has a lien for the debt.
5. An insurer has it in respect of risks underwritten by him for the purpose of reinsurance.
6. Where the subject-matter is mortgaged, the mortgagor has an insurable interest in the full value thereof and the mortgagee has an insurable interest in respect of any sum due to become due under the mortgage.
7. A bailee can insure any article or property bailed. He may be a gratuitous bailee or bailee for reward.
8. A trustee has insurable interest in the property put on trusteeship.

3. Principle of Good Faith. The contract of fire insurance is one in which the observance of the utmost good faith-uberrima fides-by both the parties are of vital significant. The utmost good faith in fire insurance has two aspects-first, disclosure of material facts and second, preservation of the property insured.

The insurer and the insured must furnish detailed information regarding the subject-matter to be insured. The insured, since he has more, information about the subject-matter, must disclose all the information asked truly and fully. The, assured is also required to disclose all the material information which are known to him although it was not asked by the insurer; material fact is one which influences the decisions of the insurance. The decision may be pertaining to the acceptance or declination or determination of the premium. In case of fire insurance the examples of material facts are construction of buildings. If the assured has not observed good faith, the contract can be avoided by other party. It was immaterial to plead that the insured was unaware of the fact and could not disclose. In a given circumstance, it is expected from the insured to-know all the material facts. The insurer has also to disclose such material facts as are within his knowledge.

The second phase of good faith is preservation of property. Thus, the observance of good faith is necessary not only during the negotiations of the contract but throughout the term of the policy and in making claims. Any change after commencement of risk must be communicated to the insurer. The insured or his agents as well as the insurer must take all such steps as may be reasonable for averting or minimising loss. Since the insured is near to the property, he must act to prevent the fire and if fire occurred, he must do his utmost to extinguish it. In such cases he must act as if he was not insured.

Exceptions

In the following circumstances, the insured is not required to disclose information.

1. All those circumstances which diminish the risk.
2. All those facts which are known or reasonably presumed to be known to the insurer.
3. Information which are of common knowledge.
4. Those facts which the insurer in the ordinary course of his business ought to know or which the insurer ought reasonably to have inferred from the details given.
5. Those facts which are superfluous to disclose by reason of a condition or warranty.

4. Principle of indemnity. The doctrine of indemnity aims to compensate the insured for a loss sustained, and the compensation should be such as to place him as nearly as possible in the same pecuniary position after the loss as he occupied immediately before the occurrence. The insured cannot claim anything in excess of the amount required to recoup the actual loss sustained. The insurers undertake to make good the insured's loss by monetary payment or by reinstatement or replacement so that the insured shall be fully indemnified, but this is subject to the sum insured. The law does not sanction any insurance which would enable the insured to profit by the destruction of the thing destroyed. It will check the temptation to destroy the property insured thereby to secure the money.

The assured amount is not the measure of indemnity but it sets an upper limit up to which the loss can be indemnified. The actual amount of indemnity will be the market value of the subject-matter destroyed or damaged by fire at the time and place of the occurrence of fire. It will never exceed the assured amount. When the actual loss is more than the assured amount then only the insured sum will be paid and nothing more is paid. But, this principle does not hold good when the policy is valued policy. Here, the basis of indemnity will not be the actual cash value of the property at the time of loss but the insured value which is named in the policy when it was taken. In a valued policy, no consideration is given to the actual loss. Thus, the amount of claim may be greater or less than the actual loss at the time of fire in case of valued policies.

Interpretation of Indemnity

The insured is entitled to perfect indemnity subject to the sum assured being sufficient. But, in practice such perfection may be difficult to attain. Previously, the meaning of the word 'indemnity' was understood in the sense of material indemnity only, *i.e.,* tangible and material property only. The intangible loss, *i.e.,* loss of profit, rent, etc. was not compensated. It worked as a great hardship to the honest insured persons. Now, the insurance is extended to cover not only the material loss of property insured but also to cover the 'consequential loss'. When a business property is burnt, not only the material loss on account of the destruction of building, plant and stock are covered but the consequential loss of profits on account of cessation of sales, salaries, taxes, rent, rates, etc., are also indemnified. Now a days tangible and intangible losses are insured and the consequential loss is also within the meaning of indemnity.

REINSTATEMENT VALUE (RIV)

Reinstatement value is the value at which the damaged property can be reinstented or replaced by new property. Insured whilst taking insurance should decide the cost of reinstatement of his property in future.

The reinstatement value may be market value or book value. Market value is the value of property of the same age and conditions at which it can be bought and sold. It is determination for insurance purposes with references to the present cost of construction of the property. The market value of plant and machinery is arrived at by deducting suitable depreciation for age, usage, wear and tear, etc. from the current replacement cost. Depreciation refers to actual intrinsic physical depreciation and most depreciation rates used for accounting purposes. Book value is very nominal and cannot be adequate for insurance purposes as it is arrived at by applying depreciation on the original cost of the property. Book value is ignored while fixing the sum assured. Thus, only market value is adequate for insurance purpose. The purpose is to have reinstatement value of insured property.

The sum assured of buildings, plant, machinery and accession, fixture, furniture and fittings, electrical installation households properties, etc. is decided by market value or reinstatement value. The sum assured for raw material is based on marked value *i.e.* the cost at which the insured can purchase it in the market to replace the damaged raw material. Similarly for semi-finished goods and finished goods, the sum assured is based on the cost of raw material plus all the overhead expenses incurred.

Contribution

The principle of contribution which is also a corollary of the principle of indemnity provides that if the same property is insured under more than one policy, insured cannot recover more than his loss, he can recover only a rateable properties of the loss under each policy.

Consequences of Indemnity

The consequences of the doctrine of indemnity are as below:

1. The insured may claim only the amount of the loss sustained.
2. In case of partial damage, the insured may claim compensation only for the amount of damage done.
3. The insured must transfer to the insurer any rights which he may possess against a third party in respect of the loss.
4. If the insured have effected more than one policy, he is precluded from obtaining more than one complete indemnity.

Measure of indemnity varies with the type of property. For damaged buildings, the measure of indemnity is the cost of repairing or reinstating the buildings to their pre-loss condition. Similarly, for machinery, the measure of indemnity is the market value which is arrived at after taking into account wear and tear and depreciation. For stock in trade, the measure is the net cost to the insured. The indemnification may be in the form of cash, repair, replacement and reinstatement.

5. Doctrine of Subrogation. Subrogation means the right of one person to stand in the place of another and to avail himself of the latter's rights and remedies. The principle of subrogation is just a corollary to the principle of indemnity. The insured can realise only the actual value of the loss or damage to the property according to the principle of indemnity and it follows that if the damaged property has any value left or the assured can recover the lost property or has any right against a third party regarding that property. These must pass on to the insurer. If the assured is allowed to retain them, he shall have realised more than the actual loss which is contrary to the indemnity principle. The assured can proceed against the third party, if he so, desires, and if he recovers damages the insurer is relieved of liability. If the insured has received the full amount of his loss any sums obtained from the third party belong to the insurer up to the amount of their disbursement.

The right of subrogation is exercisable at common law after the insurer has paid the claim made against him.

6. Warranties. The contents of proposal form are expressly incorporated in the policy, which form warranty. Warranty is that by which the assured undertakes that some particular thing shall or shall not be done, or that some conditions shall be fulfilled or whereby he affirms or negatives the existence of a particular state of facts. Warranties which are mentioned in the policy are called express warranties and those warranties which are not mentioned in the policy are called implied warranties.

Implied warranties

The first implied warranty is that the property structure is not inferior *e.g.* kachhahouse should not be made of wooden-roof of thatched leaves grass, hay or bamboo cloths, etc. There is second warranty that Fire Extinguishing Appliances should be fixed with the property. Annual maintenance is essential. There should not be possibility of silent risks i.e. new construction addition. The special articles and property exposed to fire must be provided with the safety services against fire. The subject-matter of insurance must exist when the contract is effected and should be identified in the event of loss. The identification is based on the, locality, municipal number, surrounding and full description of the place. A breach of warranty enable the insurer to avoid the claim.

Warranties must be complied with literally and the effect of a breach of warranty is to render void the relevant item of the policy, even if no increase in risk is involved. Every warranty to which the property insured or any item thereof is, or may be, made subject, shall from the time the warranty attaches apply and continue to be in force during the whole currency of the policies, and non-compliance with any such warranty, whether it increases the risk or not, shall be a bar to any claim in respect of such property or item. The condition states that every warranty is attached during the whole currency of the policy and if during this period a warranty has not been complied with, the insured will not entertain any claim in respect of the property or item affected. However, if the policy is renewed and there was breach of a warranty before the renewal date and not after it and a loss occurs after the renewal is effected, in such a case the claim can be made. Non-compliance with a warranty prior to the current renewal period of a policy is not a bar to a claim. The non-compliance with a warranty avoids a cover only during the period of insurance in which the breach occurred.

7. Proximate Cause. The rule is that the immediate and not the remote cause is to be regarded–causa proxima non-remota spectature. Proximate cause is very important in fire insurance. The principle of proximate cause has already been discussed in detail. The insurer always takes the proximate cause while paying the claim. If the property insured is burned but the fire was preceded and brought into operation by an excepted peril, the legal position depends upon whether the excepted peril was the proximate. The remote cause is when an incendiary bomb damaged the property, the proximate cause is enemy action. Proximate cause is the active efficient cause that sets in motion a train of events which brings about a result without the intervention of any force stated and working actively from a new and independent source. It is dominant, effective and proximate cause to the exclusion of all other causes which are too remote. If the loss is attributed to the insured periles, the direct and unavoidably result that direct causal relationship is established, the insurer is liable for loss.

QUESTIONS

1. Discuss the features of Fire Insurance Contract.
2. 'Assignment is set possible in fire insurance' Comment.

28

KINDS OF POLICIES

The policies can be of various types which are discussed in the following paragraphs.

1. Valued Policy. The value of the property to be insured is determined at the inception of the policy. In this case, the insurer pays the total admitted value irrespective of the then market value of the properties. The measure of indemnity is, in consequence, not value at the time of fire, but a value agreed at the inception of the policy. The insurer pays the insured a fixed sum following the destruction of the insured property. The amount fixed may be greater or less than the actual market value of the property destroyed by fire at the time of loss. In this policy, the measure of indemnity is based on the value of properties rather than on the market values of the property destroyed. This policy is used for insuring specially pictures, sculptures, works of art, jewellery, rare things, articles of everyday use. Since the value of damage of these articles cannot be easily determined at the time of loss, the valued policies are commonly used. Strictly speaking the valued policies are betrayal from the principle of indemnity because the market price is not paid in this case.

The valued policy is beneficial to the insured because he is relieved of proving the value of property at the time of loss by searching of invoices and receipts. The disadvantages is that the new purchases and replacement cannot be added to the valued policy. The valuation, therefore, is revised at frequent intervals. The insurer will have to pay more than the actual loss if the market price of the property has gone down. It may increase the moral hazard. There may be difficulty in settling the partial losses. The valued policies can be disputed on grounds of fraud.

2. Valuable Policy. Valuable policy is that policy where claim amount is to be determined at the market price of the damaged property. The amount of loss is not determined at the time of commencement of risk but is determined at the time and place of loss. This policy is truly representing the doctrine of indemnity.

3. Specific Policy. Where a specific sum is insured upon a specified property in case of a specified period, the whole of the actual loss is payable provided it does not exceed the insured amount. Here the value of property insured has no relevance in arriving at the measure of indemnity in a specified policy and the insured sum sets a limit up to which the loss can be made good.

4. Floating Policy. The floating policy is the policy taken to cover one or more kinds of goods at one time under one sum assured for one premium and in relation to the same owner. This policy is useful to cover fluctuating stocks in different localities. Since the properties are spread over various localities and in different forms, the physical and moral hazards are also varying and, therefore, it makes difficult to determine premium rates. In India, the premium rate is approximately the same in such case except the case of most hazardous risk. Such policies are specially taken by big manufacturers or traders whose merchandise might be lying in parts at warehouse, godown, port, or railway station. In such cases, it is very difficult for the owner of such goods to take specified policy for each good because the quantities of the goods deposited in each will fluctuate from day to day, place to place, according to sales or consumption or consequent removal and replacement. The average rate of premium is ascertained by taking into account the total premium payable had the property been insured by specific policies. The floating policy contains the 'average' and 'marine' clauses. The policy is taken only on stocks. The policy cannot be issued in respect of immovable property. The address of each godown has to be declared by the insured. Unspecified locations cannot be covered. The entire complex is under the control of insured. There is extra premium for the addition risks.

5. Average Policy. Policy containing 'average clause' is called an Average Policy. The amount of indemnity is determined with reference to the value of the property insured. If the policy holder has taken policy for lesser amount than the actual value of the property, the insured will be deemed to be his own insurer for the amount of under-insurance. The insurer will pay only such proportion of the actual loss as his insurance amount bears to the actual value of the property at the time of loss. For example, the property worth ₹ 30,000 is insured for ₹ 20,000 is damaged up to ₹ 12,000, the insurer will pay only ₹ 8,000 as is evident from the following:

Claim = Insured amount / value of property × actual loss

= 20,000 / 30,000 × 12,000 = ₹ 8,000

The insured, thus, will suffer himself up to ₹ 4,000 and the insurer will pay only ₹ 8,000 out of ₹ 12,000. In this case, if the insurance was taken up to the full value of the property, the assured would have been paid all the financial loss, *i.e.*, ₹ 12,000. Since the insurance was taken for lesser than the actual value of property, the assured is compensated the loss in that proportion.

The average clause is operative only in case of an under-insurance. This clause is ineffective when the property is insured for the full value as in that case the insured is protected to the extent of his total loss. The under-insurance penalises the assured by inserting 'average clause' to the policy because he is supposed to insure himself for the amount by which he under-insures his property and, therefore, is supposed to contribute in that ratio to the loss sustained. The average clause is accompanied, sometimes, with the co-insurance clause which is discussed in the next chapter.

6. Excess Policy. Sometimes, the stock of a businessman may fluctuate from time to time and he may be unable to take one policy or specific policy. If he takes policy for a higher amount, he has to pay a higher premium. On the other hand, if he takes insurance for lower amount, he will have to bear the proportionate amount of loss. The insured in this case can purchase two policies, one 'First Loss Policy" and second, 'excess policy.' The 'First Loss Policy' will cover that stock below which the stock never goes. The minimum level of stock can be found out from the past experience and for the other portion of stock which exceeds the minimum limit, he can purchase another policy called 'excess policy'. The actual value of the excess stock is declared every month. The amount of premium is calculated on the average monthly excess amount. Since the chances of payment on the excess amount are very remote, the rate of premium is also very nominal. Thus, the insured will pay very nominal premium as compared to the premium payable on the total amount had the policy been specific one. The average .clause also applies to this policy.

7. Declaration Policy. The excess policy contributes to only a rateable proportion of the loss because if the amount of excess stock exceeds the sum set in the excess policy the businessman will not have a full cover owing to average condition. Moreover, if the First Loss Policy was also subject to average condition the assured will be at a loss. The declaration policy will give a better protection in such cases where the stock fluctuates from time to time. Under the declaration policy, the insured takes out an insurance for the maximum amount that he considers would be at risk during the period of the policy. On a fixed date of every month or a specific period, the insured furnishes a declaration of the amount. The premium is provisionally paid to 75% of the annual premium amount. Practically, the annual premium is determined on the average of these declarations. If the premium is higher than the provisional premium already paid, the insured has to pay the difference to the insurer. On the other hand if the premium so calculated is lesser than the premium already paid, the excess is returned to the policyholder. The declaration must be made on a specified day or within the next 14 days, otherwise the sum insured will be deemed to be the declaration value. The policy is applicable only to stocks and the sole property of the insured.

The great advantage of this policy is that the premium is limited to the actual amount at risk irrespective of the sum insured. Unlike the excess policy, the premium is not unnecessarily paid. Moreover, the insurer may pay up to the full sum insured throughout the period of the policy because the premium amount can be adjusted accordingly. The value of risks is average of the each day of the month or the highest value at risk during the month. Declaration policy is not available for a short period stock in process, stock at Railway siding. Premium is adjusted at the expiry of policy. The policy is very advantageous to those business men whose stocks fluctuate from time to time. The amount of the declaration offers scope for fraud because the insured may pay lesser premium by undervaluing the stock. Therefore, this policy is issued only to reputed concerns.

8. Adjustable Policy. The above disadvantage is removed by adjustable policy. This policy is nothing but an ordinary policy on the stock of the businessman with liberty to the insured to vary at his opinion, the premium is adjustable pro-rata according to the variation of the stock. In case of declaration policy, since the excess premium is refundable at the end of the year, the insured may put fire to the property. This danger is avoidable in an 'Adjustable Policy'. This is issued for a definite term on the existing stock. The premium is calculated in the ordinary manner and is paid in full at the inception of the policy. Whenever, there is variation in the stock, the insured informs the insurer. As soon as the information of variation is received, the policy is suitably endorsed and ,the premium is adjusted on a pro-rata basis. The policy amount will, thus, be changeable from time to time. The premium is also settled accordingly.

Difference between Declaration and Adjustable Policies

In case of declaration policy, the insurer's liability is the insured amount but in the case of adjustable policy, the insurer's liability is the value of the last declaration made. The periodical declarations have no direct bearing on the measurement of indemnity in case of declaration policy but these have been the basis of measurement of indemnity. The advantage of the declaration policy over the adjustable policy is that in the former a margin of safety is present because the maximum amount insured is always at the risk, but in the latter case the cover is always for the declared value. The declaration in the case of declaration policy is meant only for the purpose of ascertaining the average of the actual cover given throughout the year to arrive at the figure to which the actual premium will be calculated, but in case of adjustable policy the declaration is the basis of policy amount adjusted by endorsement. The drawback of this policy is that the insured will have to deposit 75 per cent of the premium fixed for the maximum cover in the beginning although a portion of it if found in excess of the actual premium required for the full coverage will be returned at the end of the year. In case of adjustable policy, the premium is adjusted from time to time according to the variation of the risk and the liability of the insurer.

9. Maximum Value with Discount Policy. Under this policy no declaration or adjustment of policy is required, but the policy is taken for a maximum amount and full premium is paid thereon. At the end of the year, in case of no loss, one-third of the premium paid is returned to the policy holder. This policy is similar to the declaration policy where the botheration of checking and recording declarations is avoided. It serves as a rough and ready method of coverage for maximum amount. This policy is not issued on all types of commodities and is confined only to selected commodities.

10. Reinstatement Policy. This policy is issued to avoid the confict of indemnity. In other types of policies only the market value of the damage or loss is indemnified but, this policy under takes to reinstate the insured property lost by fire to new condition irrespective of its value at the time of loss.

In other types of policies, in case of building or machinery, the actual loss is arrived at by deducting the regular depreciation from the original cost of it. The amount of indemnity will be lesser than the amount to be spent in reinstating the property destroyed or damaged. In order to provide full coverage 'reinstatement or replacement' policies are issued. Under this policy, the basis of settlement in the event of destruction is the cost of rebuilding the premises or in case of plant and machinery, the placement is done by similar machinery. The reinstatement of the damaged property indicates the meaning of repair of the damages. The restoration of the damaged portion of the property to a condition substantially the same is but not better or more extensive than its condition, at the time of its renovation. The cost of the property when partially destroyed will not be more than the cost which would have been insured if such a property has been totally destroyed. The payment of the actual expenditure on replacement will not be made until the expenditure has actually been incurred. This policy is also called 'New for Old' policy because the old property is replaced by new properties. However, such policies are issued only on building, plant and machinery. This policy is not issued on stock, merchandise or materials. Each item of the insured property is subject to average. The policy provides the definite amount in case of purchase of new property in place of the old property destroyed. The reinstatement Policy stipulates that reinstatement must be carried out by the insured in order to obtains the special basis of settlement agreed. The reinstatement must be commenced and carried out with reasonable despatch and in any case must be complete within 12 months after the destruction or damage or until reinstatement carried out and expenditure incurred, the liability under the policy remain on the normal indemnity basis. The insurance by this policy intends to include such additional cost of reinstatement as may be incurred solely by reason of the necessity to comply with the building, etc. by any Act of Parliament, Municipal or Local Authority. No additional premium is charged for the purpose. This policy does not cover any destruction or damage occurring prior to the granting of this extension.

11. Comprehensive Policy. This policy undertakes full protection not only against the risk of fire but combining within the risk against burglary, riot, civil commotion, theft, damage from pest, lightning. The policy is also termed as 'All in policies'. Here the 'Comprehensive' does not mean that every type of risk is covered. There may be many exclusions and limitations. This policy is beneficial to the insured and the insurer. The insurer can get higher premium and the assured is protected against losses due to several specified perils.

12. Consequential Loss Policy. The fire insurance is originally purchased to indemnify the material loss only. The intangible interest was not indemnified. This provided a check on the insured to exercise a greater care with respect to the property. However, the settlement of a loss covering material damage only was not sufficient. The consequential loss was also to be provided. Thus, the consequential loss policy includes the loss of tangible and intangible properties.

Thus, this policy provides an indemnity to the insured for loss of net profits, payment of standing charges and expenditure in respect of increased cost of working. As a consequence of fire, there is a reduction in the volume of business which in its turn leads to a reduction in the net profit which the lost business would have ordinarily contributed and to an increase in the proportion of the standing charges such as rents, rates, salaries and others to the total business done. Thus, the policy is to indemnify the insured against financial loss which he may sustain due to the interruption of his business following a fire. Previously the measure of indemnity was a specified percentage of the amount payable under an ordinary fire policy in respect of a material loss. The insurer, thus, used to pay the amount of loss and a specified percentage of the loss. However, now, the measure of indemnity is changed because the specified percentage cannot be the true estimation of the intangible loss. So, the resultant loss is calculated by estimating figures of loss of profits based on a reduction in turnover or output and secondly, increased cost of working in maintaining the business on its pre-fire level.

13. Sprinkler Leakage Policies. This policy insures destruction of or damage to by water accidentally discharged or leaking from automatic sprinkler installation in the insured premises. However, the discharge or leakage of water due to heat caused by fire, repair or alteration of building or sprinkler installation, earthquake, war, explosion are not covered by this policy.

14. Add on Covers Policy : An insured may like to cover his property against to delete some of the exclusions. The cover in respect of these perils is provided by insurer by charging additional premium. This additional cover is effected by either deletion of some of the excluded perils or addition of other specified perils. The perils which are covered by an endorsement of the basic fire policy are collectively called, Add on Covers. For example, earthquake damage are added to the fire policy.

There are certain principles to add on covers. It is extension of the basic standard fire policy. The liability shall in no case under the extension of the policy exceed the sum insured of the policy. All the conditions of the basic fire policy shall apply to the insurance granted by extension. Add on cover is mid-term inclusion but the annual premium has to be charged and not short period premium. If the insured requests for the add on cover to be cancelled mid-term then no refund of premiums for the cancellation will be allowed unless the entire policy is cancelled.

15. Escalation Policy

This insurance allows automatic regular increase in the sum insured throughout the period of the policy in return for an additional premium to be paid in advance. There are certain conditions for escalation insurance. The escalation of policy amount shall not be more than 25 per cent of sum assumed. The additional premium payable in advance, will be at 50% of the full rate. This policy applies to policies covering building, machinery and accessories only and will not apply to policies covering stock. The clause cannot be opted for during the currency of the policy but only at inception or renewal. The effect of this policy/clause is to provide for a daily increase in the sum assumed based on the percentage selected spread over the period of the policy: It also allows automatic regular increase up to 25% of the sum insured of throughout period of the policy in return of an additional premium to be paid in advance.

16. Specialised Policies

Special policies for different risk exposed products are also issued specifically with their respective premium term and warranties. The important specialised policies are petrochemical policy, industrial all risks policy, machinery breakdown policy, material damage policy, business interruption policy, engineering good policy, electrical installation policy, housekeeping policy, mega risk policy and consequential loss policy.'

QUESTIONS

1. What do you mean by the following policies—Valued Policies, Reinstatement Policies and Adjustable Policies?
2. Discuss the essential features of fire insurance policies.
3. Discuss Add on cover policy.

29

POLICY CONDITIONS

The fire insurance may be defined as a contract by which the insurer agrees to make good any loss suffered by the insured through damage or destruction of properties by fire up to the sum assured in consideration of payment called premium. The contract of fire insurance is expressed in a document described as a policy. It provides for the payment of a sum of money as representing the pecuniary loss incurred by the insured through the damage or destruction by fire of the property described in the policy or alternatively the restoration or replacement of what has been damaged or destroyed. Only Standard Fire and Special Perils Policy with the permitted "Add on" covers can be issued.

Standard Form of Policy

The conditions in fire insurance may be of varied nature, but the standard form of policy includes several conditions which are common to most of the fire policies. The fire insurance contract, principle and practice are governed by the conditions contained in the policy. The standard form of policy at present is the outcome of several vicissitudes in the past. In the beginning, the conditions were very few but with the advancement of the fire insurance several conditions were introduced. Now the conditions became very complex and varied. Now, therefore, several conditions are deleted from the policy and sometimes, the policy is called 'conditionless policy' although no policy can be conditionless at a time.

Needs have arisen about the common conditions of the policy. The leading insurers agreed on a code of essential conditions which are embodied in the standard form of policy. The standard form of policy is now commonly used by the fire insurers. According to standard form the condition of fire-policies are divided into two parts: (*i*) informative and (*ii*) proper conditions. The informative conditions are also divided into two parts: (*i*) Preamble and (*ii*) Perils insured.

1. Specimen of Fire Policy

"In consideration of the insured named in the schedule hereto having paid to the .... insurance company limited(hereinafter called the company) the full premium mentioned in the said schedule, the company agrees (subject to the conditions and exclusions contained herein or endorsed or otherwise expressed here on) that if after payment of the premium, the property insured described in the said schedule or any part of such property be destroyed or damaged by any of the perils specified hereunder during the period of insurance named in the said schedule or of any subsequent period in respect of which the insured shall have paid and the company shall have accepted the premium required for the renewal of the policy, the Company shall pay to the insured the value of the property at the time of the happening of its destruction or the amount of such damage or at its option reinstate or replace such property or any part there of"

British Law

British Law is the guideline for fire insurance

1. There must be an actual fire or ignition, hence a more heating or fermentation will not be sufficient to render the insurers liable for loss occasioned thereby.

2. There must be something on fire which ought not to have been on fire.
3. There must be something in the nature of casualty or accident but a fire occasioned by the wilful act of a third person, without the privity or consent of the assured is to be regarded as accidental for purpose of this rule. Any loss attributable to the fire, whether by actual burning or by scorching or cracking or by smoke or otherwise is within the contract.

The important ingredients in the definition are

(*a*) Ignition

(*b*) Accidental

Ignition

The fire should be actual. Ignition means the presence of flames. Mere damage by smoke heating, scorching or charring without actual burning is not considered a fire. Damage caused by acid is not fire damage. Chemical buring is not burning by fire.

Accident

The ignition has to be fortuitious or accidental. This applies to the insured. If a third party deliberately sets fire to insured property, it is also accidental so far as the insured is concerned provided the third party is not acting with connivance of the insured. A fire caused by the negligence of the insured or of his employees will be payable so long as there is no element of fraud.

A fire lighted for a definite purpose and confined to its own property limits *e.g.* cooking, heating or manufacturing purpose is not a fire within the meaning of the Policy. Destruction of lighted lamp by its own fire does not come within the fire policy. However, fire caught by the side of the lamp is within the fire policy. There is improper or accidental ignition.

Once there is a fire within the meaning of fire policy, the damage caused by smoke and heat, scorching, falling walls, collapse of roofs, floors, etc. is also covered within the fire insurance. Damage caused deliberable or accidently by fire brigades in discharged of duties are also covered. For example damage caused by water or extinguishing agents or blowing up the property to prevent spread of fire.

Contents of policy

1. Name and address of the insured
2. Policy number the agent's code no.
3. Name and address to the policy issuing office
4. Property covered / sum assined
5. Property owner, location, independent or peril of some buildings
6. The occupation of the premises
7. The occupation of the premises by other
8. The construction of building
9. General and special warranties
10. Rate of tariff
11. Endorsements

Preamble of the Policy

The preamble of the policy sets forth the agreement between the insurers and the insured subject to the conditions of the policy. Payment of premium is an essential consideration of the contract. The insurer, therefore, undertakes to pay to the insured the value of loss to the property at the time of its destruction or the amount of the damage done or to reinstate or replace the property or any part thereof. The agreement clause sets forth that the insurer's liability shall not exceed the sum set opposite each item.

The second clause of the preamble provides for the conditions and terms of the renewal of the policy which limits the liability of the insurer to any term in respect of which the insured shall have paid and the insurer shall have accepted the premium in renewal of the policy.

The third part contains the schedule where the name of the insured, the property insured, sum assured, the total sum assured, period of insurance and premium amount are mentioned.

Perils Insured

The next important part of the policy is description of the perils insured. The perils insured under the standard form of policy are described below.

1. Fire

Fire (whether resulting from explosion or otherwise) is not occasioned by or happening through:

(*a*) its own spontaneous fermentation or heating or its undergoing any process involving the application of heat,

(*b*) earthquakes, subterranean fire, riot, civil commotion, war, invasion, act of foreign enemy, hostilities (whether war be declared or not), civil war, rebellion, revolution, insurrection or military or insured power.

To constitute fire within the meaning of contract of fire insurance two essentials must be present, *viz.*, (1) there must be ignition and (2) the fire, so far as the insured is concerned, must be fortuitous in origin. The 'fire' must be understood in its popular sense, it does not include chemical actions which result in no ignition. The term 'fire' does not include a fire lighted for a specific purpose while confined to its limits. Fire used for cooking, warming or manufacturing is not a fire within the meaning of the contract because there is nothing fortuitous about it. Any loss occasioned by such a fire, whether by burning of any property in the fire itself, or by the scorching or cracking of any property adjacent to it owing to its intense heat, if unaccompanied by origin, is not covered by the contract since the cause of the loss cannot be regarded as a peril insured against. However, if the fire causes ignition by throwing out sparks or otherwise, outside its proper limits it will be fire in the sense of fire insurance. The fire thus occurred, being fortuitous in its origin, is a fire within the meaning of the contract and any loss occasioned thereby, whether by direct building, or by scorching or cracking, or by smoke is within the meaning of fire insurance. The assured must show that he has sustained a loss by fire within the meaning of the fire insurance. The fire caused deliberately by insured or at his convenience will not be included in the meaning of 'fire'. However, the fire caused by incendiarism without the knowledge or connivance of the insured will be included under fire insurance.

The following forms of loss or also indemnified provided they are proximately caused by fire since.

(*i*) damage caused during or immediately following fire by smoke, scorching and falling walls or part of the building in which fire takes place,

(*ii*) damage caused by firemen and others in the discharge of their duties by using water or other extinguishing agent, demolition of buildings to prevent spreading of fire, and damaging property so as to gain access to fire,

(*iii*) damage to property immediately after removal from burning building caused by exposure to weather, provided the removal was justified.

2. Lightning

The lightning may be a form of fire, but loss occasioned by lightning without ignition is not a loss by fire; where the lightning results in ignition, a loss occasioned by such ignition is a loss by fire. However, in practice any damage caused by lightning whether ignition results or not is covered under fire insurance.

3. Explosion/Implosion

Explosion is when the atmospheric pressure in lower than the pressure in the vessel and therefore the vessel brusts open under the pressure generated within it. Implosion is when the atmosphere pressure is greater than the pressure in the vessel and, therefore the vessel is pressed in and damaged by outside pressure. The explosion of gas used for illuminating and domestic purposes in a building in which gas is not generated and which does not form part of gas works will be insured under fire insurance.

POLICY CONDITIONS

The policy conditions may be precedent to the contract conditions subsequent to the contract and conditions precedent to liability. The conditions must be fully complied with to make the insurer liable under the contract. The conditions may be implied or express. Conditions which are set out in the policy are known as express conditions which may be either of general nature and, therefore, printed on the policy or conditions specially designed with reference to a particular contract and are incorporated in the policy. The implied conditions are not mentioned on the policies but are deemed to be present with reference to the policy.

A. Implied Conditions

The following conditions are implied conditions in fire insurance.

(*a*) **Existence of property:** The subject-matter of insurance should exist when the policy is effected.

(*b*) **Insured property:** When the fire occurs the property damaged should be the property insured for obtaining claim on the property.

(*c*) **Insurable interest:** The insured must have insurable interest from the time of the commencement of risk up to the completion of the contract.

(*d*) **Good Faith:** The insured must observe good faith towards the insurer. He must disclose all the material facts truly and fully, and should try to prevent the fire and extinguish the fire, if it occurred, with a reasonable care.

(*e*) **Identity:** The subject-matter of insurance should be described in the policy as to identify it clearly and so define the risk which insurers have undertaken.

B. Express Conditions

The express conditions in fire insurance are discussed in the following paragraphs.

1. Misdescription

The policy shall be voidable in the event of misdescription, misrepresentation or non-disclosure of any material facts. If there is any material misdescription of any of the property insured, the insurer shall not be liable upon this policy so far as it relates to property affected by any such misdescription, misrepresentation or omission. This condition is a reiteration of the implied condition of utmost good faith. Therefore, if the assured fails to disclose all material facts or be guilty of misrepresentation or misdescription in any way, the policy shall be voidable at the insurer's option. Under Common Law, a breach of utmost good faith goes to the root of the whole contract. By virtue of this condition, insurer will limit the avoidance of the contract to that part only of the property affected if risk is divisible into distinct parts. If the misrepresentation, under good faith, relates to a part of the policy only, it will render the whole contract voidable, for a breach of good faith cuts at the root of the whole contract. According to the condition of misdescription, any misrepresentation, misdescription or omission must be material. Usually all the questions asked in the proposal forms are material. Therefore, they should he answered correctly and fully. The insurer should be protected in the manner described in this condition should it be subsequently discovered that the insurance has been obtained through an inaccurate statement on the part of the insured.

2. Alteration

The insurance contract may be avoided if there is any alteration after the commencement of this insurance. The alteration may be of the following types.

(*a*) **Removal:** The removal of the insured property without the consent of the insurer makes the contract voidable. If without the consent of the insurer, the property is removed from one place to another, the insurer will no longer be responsible for any loss arising in relation to the property removed. For example, if the furniture insured has been removed from dewelling house to factory, the risk has increased. In this case, the insured is responsible to inform the insurer who may accept or refuse to cover the furniture in the new place because risk has increased. Nevertheless the insured is always responsible for informing the insurer whether the risk has increased or not by removal.

(*b*) **Increase in risk:** The alteration may take place where the risk of the insured property has increased. The insurer can avoid the policy in respect of the item altered. However, if the insurer is agreed to continue the contract the charging extra-premium on the increased risk, after getting information of alteration, he can do so. If the assured has not informed the insurer, the insurer can waive the contract. The insurer usually accommodates the insured either by waiving his right or by charging extra-premium depending on the circumstances.

(*c*) **Change of interest:** Without the consent of the insurer the interest on the insured property cannot be changed. If the interest has been changed, the insurer will cease his responsibility. The assignment, or transfer of property, interest thereon and policy will be valid only when it has been made after the express consent of the insurer. Except the case of change to hazardous or more risky assignment, the insurer generally accepts the proposal of assignment. Without the consent of the insurer, the assignment or transfer will be invalid.

The insurer can accept the assignment or transfer and the interest of the vendor and of the purchaser may remain intact. Now a days, by inserting 'optional memorandum', the property can be transferred under good faith and the interests of both the parties are protected.

Exception

The change in interest is ceaseable in the case where the property changes on account of will or operation of law. The insurer in this case will be liable though the consent has not been obtained.

3. Exclusions

The risks which are excluded from the fire policies are called exceptions or exclusions. The exclusions are explained below:

(*i*) Destruction or damage by explosion (whether the explosion be occasioned by fire or otherwise) except as stated on the face of the policy.

(*ii*) Goods held in trust or on commission, money, securities, stamps, documents, manuscripts, business books, patterns, models, moulds, plans, designs, explosives unless specially insured by the policy.

(*iii*) Destruction of or damage to property which at the time of the happening of such destruction or damage is insured by any Marine Policy.

The above exceptions can be covered or modified by payment of extra-premium. The meaning of certain words should be clarified. Damage by explosion is not covered but damage by fire consequent on explosion is covered. Goods held in trust can be insured by the trustee provided he has an insurable interest in them. The trustee must have some legal liability or reputation at stake for the loss of the goods to create an insurable interest for which he can insure. Money, securities, documents and business books are practically uninsurable under an ordinary policy for the very nature of them, except that money can be covered up to a certain small amount under a comprehensive policy. Documents and business books can be insured for the cost of their reinstatement. Some classes of goods when in stock are liable to spontaneous fermentation or heat on account of the internal temperature engendered by compression. There are many heating processes regularly used in trade and in many business. Such cases are underwritten only on payment of additional premium. Stamps, manuscripts, plants, designs are highly perishable articles, and it is very difficult to assess their values. However, they can be covered by payment of a special rate. Earthquake, riot, civil commotion, foreign enemy, etc., can be covered by payment of a special rate of premium and under special conditions. The burden of proof that the fire occurred due to excepted perils lies on the insurer. Destruction or damage caused by forest fire are excluded. But bush fire is accidental and is insured. Forest fire can be insured on extra premium.

General Exclusions

There are nine exclusion under the fire policy

1. 5% of each and every claim resulting from the operation of lighing /STFT subsidence and landslide including Rock slide
2. Loss or damage caused by war, civil war and kindered perils
3. Loss or damage caused by nuclear risks
4. Loss or damage caused by pollution or contamination.
5. Loss or damage to bullion or unset precious stones
6. Destruction or damage to the stock in cold storage premises caused by change of temperature
7. Loss, destruction or damage to electrical appliances
8. Expenses incurred on Architects, Survey or and Consulting Engineers Fees.
9. Loss of earning, loss by delay, loss of market, or other consequential or indirect loss or damage or anykind

Some of the above exclusions are covered by payment of extra-premium

4. Fraud

Fraud always invalidates a contract and the following provision is made in the standard policy.

"If the claim be in any respect fraudulent or if any fraudulent means of devices be used by the insured or anyone acting on his behalf to obtain any benefit under this policy or if any destruction or damage be occasioned by the wilful act or with the connivance of the insured of benefit under this policy shall be forfeited."

The clause clarifies that the fraud would forfeit all the benefits under the policy. It contemplates three eventualities—presentation of a fraudulent claim, use of fraudulent means and acts of wilful destruction like arson, etc. Fraudulent does not necessarily include improper or excessive claims. Fraud cannot necessarily be in case of price. However, it may be in respect of quantities. Excepted property if included under insured properties would amount fraud. False valuation of insured properties comes under fraud. Incendiarism or arson committed by the insured or by anyone else with his connivance will be fraud and will avoid the policy.

5. Claim

The claim clause runs as below—

"On the happening of any destruction or damage the insured shall forthwith give notice thereof in writing to the insurer and shall within fifteen days after such destruction or damage, or such further time as the insurer may in writing allow, containing as particular on account as may be reasonably practicable of the several articles or portions of property destroyed or damaged and of the amount of destruction or damage thereto respectively having regard to their value at the time of the destruction or damage together with details of any other insurances on any property hereby insured. The insured shall also give to the insurer all proofs and information with respect to the claim as may reasonably be required together with (if demanded) or statutory declaration of the truth of the claim and of any matters connected therewith. No claim under this policy shall be payable unless the terms of this conditions have been complied with."

From the Above clause, it appears that the notice of loss is to be given forthwith after its occurrence though details can be given thereafter. The expenses of claim will be borne by the insured. The insured has to disclose other inferances in respect of the property for the purpose of determining the contribution that may be payable by other insurer. The insured must give immediate written notice of any destruction or damage and should be followed with a written notice within 15 days of the claim. The time may be extended by the insurer where there is a reasonable case for it. The insured must furnish all reasonable proofs and information required together with a statutory declarations as to the truth of the claim or any matters connected there with.

6. Reinstatement Clause

The insurer has the option to discharge his liability by reinstating or replacing the damaged property. The cash payment of actual loss is not made under this clause. It needs as below:

If the company elects to reinstate or replace any property, the insured shall, at his own expense, furnish the company with such plans, specifications, measurements, quantities and such other particulars as the company may require and no acts done or caused to be done by the company with a view to reinstatement or replacement shall be deemed an election by the company to reinstate or replace.

The insurer shall not be bound to reinstate exactly or completely, but only as circumstances permit and in reasonably sufficient manner, and in no case shall the insurer be bound to expend more in reinstatement than it would have cost to reinstate such property, as it was at the time of the occurrence of such loss or damage, nor more than the sum insured by the insurer thereon. If in any case the insurer is unable to reinstate or repair the property thereby insured, because of certain regulations, the insurer may be liable to pay such sum as would be requisite to reinstate or repair such property if the same could lawfully be reinstated to its former condition.

The clause removes the dispute between insured and insurer because the insurer can replace the goods by similar ones without submitting to the stated value given to them by the insured. The reinstatement is optional with the insurer and not with the insured, but once the former has elected to reinstate or replace he has no right to reverse his decision.

7. Insurer's Rights after a Fire

On the happening of any loss or damage to any of the property insured by this policy, the company may:

(*a*) enter and take and keep possession of the building or premises where the loss or damage has happened;

(*b*) take possession of or require to the delivered to it any property of the insured in the building or on the premises at the time of the loss or damage;

(*c*) keep possession of any such property and examine, sort, arrange, remove or otherwise deal with the same; and

(*d*) sell any such property or dispose of the same for account of whom it may concern.

The powers conferred by this condition shall be exercisable by the company at any time until notice in writing is given by the insured that he makes no claim under the policy or, if any claim is made until such claim is finally determined or withdrawn, and the company shall not by any act done in the exercise or purported exercise of its powers hereunder, incur any liability to the insured or diminish their right to rely upon any of the conditions of this policy in answer to any claim. If the insured or any person on his behalf shall not comply with the requirements of the company or shall hinder or obstruct the company in the exercise of its powers hereunder, all benefit under this policy shall be forfeited.

8. Subrogation

The clause subrogation reads as below:

Any claimant under this policy shall at the request and at the expenses of the company do and concur in doing and permitting to be done all such acts and things as may be necessary or reasonably required by the company for the purpose of enforcing any rights and remedies, or of obtaining relief or indemnity from other parties to which the company shall be or would become entitled or subrogated upon its paying for or making good any destruction or damage under this policy, whether such acts and things shall be or become necessary or required before or after his indemnification by the company.

The clause is corollary to the doctrine of indemnity. It makes clear that the insured is precluded from obtaining more than the actual loss. When the insurer has indemnified the insured against a loss the insured must transfer all the rights regarding the property damaged. The insured cannot recover from the third party as well as from the insurer more than the actual loss. However, both the parties can indemenify only up to the amount of loss. The insured is entitled to receive payment from the third party, by reason of negligence of law or agreement. The insurer cannot recover from third party more than the sum paid by him. The excess amount can be retained by the insurer only as the trustee of the insured.

The insurer is entitled to the advantage of every right of the insured whether such right consists in contract, fulfilled or unfulfilled or in remedy for tort capable of being insisted on or already insisted on or in any other right whether by way of condition or otherwise. The insured is bound to give all necessary facilities to the insurer which the latter may require in enforcing his rights against third parties. The steps taken in such field are in the name of the insured. The cost will be borne by the insurer. Amounts recovered by the insurer become his property subject to the right of the insured to be fully indemnified.

9. Warranties

The warranties clause is as follows:

Every warranty to which the property insured or any item thereof is or may be made subject shall from the time the warranty attaches apply and continue to be in force during the whole currency of this policy, and non-compliance with any such warranty, whether it increases the risk or not, shall be a bar, to any claim in respect of such property or item, provided that if this policy is renewed a claim in respect of loss or damage occurring during the renewal period shall not be barred by reason of warranty not having been complied with at any time before the commencement of such period.

The compliance of warranties is very essential Non-compliance with any of the warranty or even substantial compliance is fatal to the contract whether the risk thereby has increased or not. According to the clause the warranties of the previous policies or policy may not essentially be applied to renewed policies.

10. Arbitration

The arbitration clause in the policy is mentioned as below:

"If any difference arises as to the amount of any loss or damage such difference shall independently of all other questions be referred to the decision of an Arbitrator, to be appointed in writing by the parties in difference, or if they cannot agree upon a single Arbitrator, to the decision of two disinterested persons as arbitrators, of whom one shall be appointed in writing by each of the parties within two calendar months after having been required so to do in writing by the other party. In case either party shall refuse or fail to appoint an arbitrator within two calendar months after receipt of notice in writing requiring an appointment, the other party shall be at liberty to appoint a sole arbitrator, and in case of disagreement between the arbitrators, the difference shall be referred to the decision of an umpire who shall have been appointed by them in writing before entering on the reference and who shall sit with the arbitrators and preside at their meetings."

The above clause is meant to avoid undue litigation and settle the dispute by arbitration. It is a very simple, cheap and expeditious method of settling disputes.

11. Purchaser's Interest Clause

Sometimes a further memorandum in the following terms is also added to the policies:

If at the time of destruction or damage to any building hereby insured, shall have contracted to sell his interest in such building and the purchase shall not have been but shall be thereafter completed, the purchaser on the completion of the purchase, if and so far as the property is not otherwise insured by or on behalf of the purchaser against such destruction or damages, shall be entitled to the benefit of this policy so far as it relates to such destruction or damage without prejudice to the rights and liabilities of the insured or the company under this policy up to the date of completion.

The above clause is useful to the vendor and purchaser up to the date of completion of the sale for their respective interests. If the purchaser elects to continue the insurance in his own name, in that case the purchase price will include the value of the unexpired insurance.

12. Loss Procedure

It is the responsibility of the insured to inform about the loss as soon as the loss occurs. The insurer will send a claim form to the insured. In this form a detailed information about the loss, the place and the circumstances under which it occurred and the description of the property insured are given. The insurer will examine the claim form and if find it reasonable, claim is paid at once. If the loss is serious and disputable the insurer may appoint an assessor called adjuster. The assessor or the adjuster will examinc the cause of fire, the amount of loss and the amount of salvage. The details of the examination are sent to the insured and the insurer. The completed claim form and the consent of the insured are also sent to the insurer. The insurer will see whether warranties are complied with or not. If the insurer is satisfied and the insurer is agreed, the amount of claim is paid. In case of dispute, the arbitrators and umpire may settle the dispute as has been described above.

In case the property was insured for more than one insurer, the leading office may pay the amount of the claim.

Ex Gratia Payment

When the insurer pays certain portion of the claim before final settlement, it is called ex gratia payment. It is an act of grace. It is paid to avoid the hardship to the insured and also to keep the reputation of the insurer.

13. Contribution and Average

The contribution and average clauses are as below:

If at the time of any loss or damage happening to any property hereby insured there be any other subsisting insurance or insurances, whether effected by the insured or by any other person or persons, covering the same property, this company shall not be liable to pay or contribute more than its rateable proportion of such loss or damage.

If the property hereby insured shall, at the breaking out of any fire, be collectively of greater value than the sum insured thereon, then the insured shall be considered as being his own insurer for the difference and shall bear rateable proportion of the loss accordingly. Every item, if more than one, of the Policy shall be separately subject to this condition.

The contribution clause clarifies that if there is more than one insurance, all the insurers will indemnify according to their proportion to the total insurance. So, the liabilities of the insurers are limited to their rateable proportions of the loss. One alternative is also available that the insured can recover the whole of the loss from any one insurer leaving him to collect the proper contributions from the other insurers. The contribution clause simplifies the claim settlement. The rateable proportion of each insurer is arrived at by dividing the sum insured under his policy by the total insured sum of all policies on the risk.

The following conditions must be fulfilled for this clause:

(*i*) The subject-matter of insurance must be common to all the policies.
(*ii*) The peril which is insured again must be common to all of them.
(*iii*) The same insured must be interested in all the policies.
(*iv*) All the policies must be in force at the time of the loss.

The average clause in fire insurance penalises as under-insurance by a corresponding under-payment of loss. The clause reveals that the loss will be paid in proportion to the insured amount and total amount of property. For example

$$\text{Loss} \times \frac{\text{Amount of Insurance}}{\text{Amount of the Property}}$$

The pro rata condition of average is applicable to all policies issued by tariff offices in India.

QUESTIONS

1. What do you mean by policies conditions?
2. What are the important conditions of policies?
3. Discuss Contribution and Average Clause.

30

RATE FIXATION IN FIRE INSURANCE

The rate fixation in fire insurance is not so scientific as in life insurance. The physical hazard can be estimated satisfactorily but the moral hazard, being varied and unknown, cannot be ascertained so correctly. While calculating the premium, various relevant factors of both the hazards are properly estimated and evaluated. The premium must be adequate enough to provide for full payment of claims including catastrophic losses, expenses of management and a margin of profit. The tariff offices follow the collective system of tariff rating. After nationalisation of general insurance businesses, the tariff rating is applied. The basic principles of premium rating are physical hazard, classification of risk, past loss experience, discrimination differentiates, industrial and non industrial risks.

SYSTEM OF RATE FIXATION

The actual process of rating consists of three steps: 1. Classification, 2. Discrimination and 3. Fixing rates or schedule rating.

1. Classification

Properties to be insured are of various nature and risk. Since the premium is fixed in relation to the class of risk, the properties are classified accordingly. Properties are generally divided into three main classes, *viz.*, (*i*) common or ordinary, (*ii*) hazardous and (*iii*) doubly hazardous. Different premium rates are fixed for each class. These classifications do not hold good for a long time because of varied nature of risk. Now the risks are classified into various classes according to factors affecting fire risk.

(*i*) **Construction or Structure:** The construction of the building has always been of great importance in rating. Building made of brick will be more sound than the building made of wood. Today, the construction of building is divided into two types of structure. First fire-proof building and second, building without fireproof. The height of the building, the area, the number of unprotected floor openings, construction of walls, floors, roof, etc., are considered in calculating the fire hazard.

(*ii*) **Occupancy:** The risk considerably varies according to the nature of occupancy, *i.e.,* the use to which the building is devoted. One building may be used as a dry goods store or hardware store, or furniture-store or for residential purposes. The building may have different risks because of the different substances and processes which they contain and the different uses to which they are put. There is inherent connection between the building and its contents. It is essential for companies to change their rates to meet changing business conditions. Rate making in fire insurance does not present constant factors. Justice demands that the insurer should recognise the important changes. A building occupied as a residence or an office is a better risk than a retail shop. A storeroom used for the storage of highly combustible goods is more hazardous from a fire insurance viewpoint than a grocery shop. The process of manufacture, the nature of raw materials used, the type of machinery are important factors to influence the physical hazard.

(*iii*) **Nature of Flooring:** The nature of flooring influences the risk to a greater extent. Existence of wooden floors in the building introduces an additional physical hazard. Wooden floor becomes a fuel in the event of fire. It may collapse easily causing damage to property. The risks inspection in based upon general features, lighting, heating and power ; process of manufacture, exposures appliances, management and supervision and so on. A risk inspection report must satisfy three essential requirements of clarity, conciseness and completeness. The report must be free from ambiguities.

(*iv*) **Height:** The height adds difficulty in fighting a fire on the upper floors. There may be risk of water damage to property on the lower floors when water is used to extinguish a fire on the upper floors. The floors involve heavy risk of collapse of the upper floors.

(*v*) **Floor and wall opening:** Openings in the floor for lifts and belts constitute higher physical hazard. It may cause greater chances of ignition of fire and difficulty of extinguishing the fire.

(*vi*) **Exposure:** The chances of risk may differ from property to property according to the degree of exposure. A building or property may be situated in a congested conflagration locality involving greater danger to the property. Exposure stands second as a cause of fire and is more than the occupancy hazard.

(*vii*) **Lighting, Heating and Power:** The fire may occur due to short-circuit. Combustion can also arise from faulty installation and dampness. The lighting system *e.g.* by gas or oil, leakage of fuel and naked flames cause more hazard to property.

(*viii*) **Place or Situation:** The location of the property, nature of adjoining premises, the distance from a fire brigade station or the source of water supply, the degree of congestion in the area are some of the important factors to influence the degree of risk.

(*ix*) **Protection:** The availability of protection against fire influences the degree of risk. The protection facilities may be public or private. When protection facilities are available the fire may be extinguished in its incipiency. The fire extinguishing apparatus, water supply, police system, etc. can reduce the degree of risk. Smaller premium is charged where modern devices for preventing and extinguishing fires are present. It would be injustice to charge the same rate for all types of risk.

(*x*) **Time:** The time of loss must be kept into consideration. The annual loss ratio is by no means uniform every year. So, the rate fixation must account for good or bad years to determine approximately the real loss. Therefore, a long period of time is taken into consideration while calculating the premium.

2. Discrimination

The differentiation of the rates for individual risks in a particular class is known as discrimination. Each additional feature of risk is charged extra premium. The better types of risks are encouraged and attracted by the insurer. Lesser premium is charged where fire extinguishing appliances or fire-resisting construction are present. The tariff system is based on the law of average and graded schedule is formulated where different rates are ascertained for the different types of risks. Thus, the different risks are put in a specified class, and are differentiated from each other according to the merits and demerits of the individual risk. It aims at a more equitable basis of rating. For example, dwelling house is a class and, therefore, all the dwelling houses are put in the same class. Since the dwelling houses are of different type, the class may be sub divided into several classes according to the degree of hazard. An appropriate discount could be given for those houses which have fire extinguishing appliances, nearness to fire brigade station and absence of exposure in the vicinity. There are Non-manufacturing risks. Industrial/Manufacturing risks, Utilities located outside the industrial, manufacturing risks, storage risks and Tank farms risks.

3. Schedule Rating

It is a plan by which hazards with respect to any particular risk are measured. It is defined as, "..........

an empirical standard for the measurement of relative quantity of fire hazard. Schedule rating takes into consideration the various items influencing the peril of fire. It is based on the theory that the aggregate fire hazard of any risk is capable of ultimate analysis into its component factors to each of which could be assigned an appropriate charge. A standard or average premium is determined as a base for calculating the premium. The average premium rate for a class of risk is determined taking into account the total loss and the sums assured during a period of year. The period should be such that the experience of good as well as bad years may be taken into account. A large number of items, as far as possible, are taken so that the law of average may apply. Larger the number, the more representative will be the rate of premium.

Thus the average fire rate is calculated as follows:

$$L/V \times 100$$

Where L represents the losses, and V represents the values of insured amount.

The rate arrived at will be net premium which is just sufficient to meet all the losses in that particular risk. This basic or net premium is loaded with expenses of management, commission, rents and a margin for profit to arrive at the gross premium or office premium.

The rate so calculated is called 'normal rate' or average rate for the particular group. In each group, risks may differ from one another and in order to maintain equity between different types of risk and between the insurer and the insured, it is necessary to apply the principle of discrimination, *i.e.,* differentiation, of individual risks in a group taking into account their particular features. Extra rates are provided for bad features, *i.e.,* for inferior construction, timber flooring, height, situation in a congested area and discounts are granted for good features, *i.e.,* for fire extinguishing appliances, automatic sprinklers ets. The rebate will be allowed taking into account the efficacy of the means adopted. The schedule contains name and address of the proposer, brief description of the property insured, sum insured, period of insurance, perils covered, rates of premium and the serial number of the cover note.

PRINCIPLES OF RATE FIXATION

The fire insurance rates are determined by three ways: 1. Personal judgement, 2. Tabulated experience and 3 by schedule.

1. Personal Judgement Rating

This method was the first to be generally used. Under this method, the rates so made indicate the opinion or judgement of the rate makers. The judgement is the result of the experience and observation of many years. The rate made were equitable. No attempt was made to take account of minor differences. All the good features and all the defective features were put together and the rate was calculated by differentiating from the average premium.

Since the personal judgements differ greatly, different rates may be determined to the same risk. With the increasing complexities of modern properties, the shortcomings of this system became more and more apparent. This method may create dissatisfaction amongst the policyholders because of different premiums to the same type of properties. Now less reliance is placed upon personal judgement in making rates.

2. Experience Rating

The method is not essentially based upon judgement. The combined judgement of a large number of individuals is taken into account. It is based on the experience of several years and of several persons. Therefore, it reflects a reasonably accurate treatment of the various elements to measure the fire hazard. Under this method, the risks are classified according to their loss experiences.

This system may not be practical as so many classes of risks would be necessary. The experience collected in the past will be of no great value in the future. However, rates made on this basis may more correctly be utilised as compared to that of other systems.

3. Schedule Rating

Under this method, fire hazard is separated into various elements and each element is assigned a particular value. The schedule describes a property as 'Standard'. For each standard risk, a standard premium is assigned. To this basic rate or standard premium, a certain stipulated charges are made for defects in construction and arrangement of property and certain deductions are made for unusually good features as compared with the standard.

The advantages of the schedule rating system are that it provides more equitable treatment of all insured. Due to the systematic treatment of the risk, the premium rates come approximately the same. The second advantage is that it reduces friction between the company and the insured because the insured is able to understand how his rate is made in every case. The third advantage is that it tends to reduce the Fire Waste because it encourages proper construction of buildings by intelligently charging for deficiencies from standards and recognizing exceptionally good construction by deductions. The fourth advantage is that it secures more thorough inspection and rating.

TARIFF RATES

Fire insurance business is governed by the tariffs formulated by the Tariff Advisory Committee which is a statutory body established under the provisions of the Insurance (Amendment) Act 1968 "to control and regulate the rates, advantages, terms and conditions that may be offered by insurers in respect of general insurance business. The Tariffs provide rates of premium for almost all classes of risks as also rules and regulations governing the business and standard form of wordings for the contract and its extensions. The Tariff Advisory Committee has constituted four Regional Committees at Delhi, Calcutta, Madras and Bombay.

Delhi: The States of Jammu and Kashmir, Punjab, Haryana, Rajasthan, Uttar Pradesh, Himachal Pradesh and the Union Territories of Delhi.

Calcutta: The States of Assam, Bihar, Orissa, West Bengal and the Union Territories of Andaman and Nicobar Islands, Manipur and Tripura.

Madras: The States of Andhra Pradesh, Kerala, Tamil Nadu and Karnataka and the Union Territories of Laccadiv, Minicoy and Amindive Islands.

Bombay: The States of Gujarat, Maharashtra and Madhya Pradesh.

Each region has its own Tariff providing for rates, warranties and other regulations applicable to risks situated in its territorial jurisdiction. The Tariffs applicable to each of the regions are similar in broad outline but differ in matters of detail such as actual rates which reflect local hazards and past experience of the area. These Tariffs are formulated by applying the principles of fire insurance rating discussed earlier. Risks are classified into principal groups and rates are provided for each group on the basis of loss experience of each such group. After classification, discrimination is another feature of the tariff system of rating. In the same group of risks, there will be differences in the circumstances of individual risks. The differences are dealt with by charging extra premium for unfavourable feature and granting discount for favourable features.

The following three broad principles are adopted by the Tariff :

Occupancy: Risks are classified according to the occupation of premises. Goods stored are classified into hazardous or non-hazardous. Under this factor manufacturing process heating, lighting and power, the nature of goods, combustion and damage by smoke and water, etc.

Construction: Buildings are classified into 3 or 4 categories according to materials used in the construction of external walls and roof. Fire resisting materials, fire extinguishers, etc., are considered.

Situation: Risks are estimated according to the situation of the property, big cities, smaller towns, narrow streets, fire brigade facilities, water supplies, survey facilities, etc.

The tariff provides:

1. Definition of the class of risks.
2. A minimum basic rate for a normal risk in a class.
3. Extra rates for specified, common and special hazards of a particular risk, *e.g.*, situation in the mofussil, conflagration area, height, night work, etc.
4. Discount in the premium for improvements in the risk, *e.g.*, sprinkler installation, fire extinguishing appliances.
5. General rules and regulations governing the business.
6. Standard wording for the policy forms, clauses and warranties.

THE TARIFF SYSTEM IN PRACTICE

The Tariffs have prescribed the order in which the various additional rates and discounts are to be applied to the final rate.

1. Tariff rates as mentioned against the relevant item in the tariff.
2. Extra rate mentioned in the item itself.
3. Extra for inferior reconstruction.
4. Conflagration extra.
5. Artificial light extra.
6. Extra for the use of mobile goods handling appliances.
7. Mofussil or classified towns extra.
8. Extra for electrical installation not in accordance with the Tariff regulations.
9. Night work extra.

QUESTIONS

1. Discuss the methods of Rate Fixation in Fire Insurance Policies.
2. What are the principles of rate fixation in fire insurance?

31

PAYMENT OF CLAIM

The insurer should be informed about the loss as soon as the loss occurs. On receiving the notice, the Insurer appoints an assessor to examine the facts of the case and to determine the amount of liability. The assessor is an expert person having the ability and experience in handling claims. The assessor is empowered to act and make necessary arrangement on behalf of the insurer. He goes to the site of fire and, personally, examines the damaged property and collects all available information. The assessor gets the idea of 'the nature' and extent of the damage, the origin and cause of fire. Usually, the assessor asks from the insured about the loss to avoid future dispute between the insured and the insurer. The insured is suggested to separate the salvage or undamaged part from the damaged part to reduce the possibilities of further damage and to evaluate the amount of loss correctly.

Steps are taken to check that

(*i*) the policy is in force on the date of occurrence of the loss or damage;

(*ii*) the loss or damage is by a peril insured by the policy;

(*iii*) the property affected by the loss is the same as insured under the policy.

(*vi*) notice of loss is received without undue delay.

After the initial check up, a number is allotted to the claim and entered in the claims register. A separate docket is opened for filling the claim papers and a copy of policy. The face of the docket provides for printed columns for incorporating claim number, policy number, date of loss, estimated amount of loss, date of survey, name of the surveyor, etc.

A claim form is issued to the policyholder. The claim form requires the following information:

(*i*) Full description of circumstances of the loss such as date of loss time, the place of fire.

(*ii*) Cause of fire.

(*iii*) Particulars of the property affected by the loss such as description, value at the time of fire, value of salvage and the claim amount.

(*iv*) Statement of other insurances on the property, name of the insurer, the policy number and the sum insured.

(*v*) Sound value of all the property.

The claim is recorded in the docket of claim, where facultative reinsurance is involved, an advice of the loss is sent to the insurers.

The survey report of the assessor contains the following information.

(*i*) **Cause of loss:** It is necessary to know whether the fire was caused by an excepted peril or was caused by the negligence of a third party or there was any evidence of fraud. So, the cause of fire is clearly obtained. Often the exact cause and origin of fire cannot be accurately established. In such cases the available evidence will have to be carefully examined to support a plausible cause.

(*ii*) The amount recommended for payment which is determined on the basis of current market value and under-insurance.

(*iii*) Detail and value of salvage. The method to dispose it of.

(*iv*) Details of expenses involved in extinguishing fire and salvage corps charges.

(*v*) The position in respect of compliance with the warranties.

(*vi*) Apportionment of the loss and expenses among the insurers where there are more than one insurer.

(*vii*) The assessor can judge whether the fire has been started at more than one place and whether it is a case of arson. He will inquire whether there is a breach of warranty or negligence on the part of the insured.

(*viii*) The exact amount of loss payable by the insurer. The presence of the average clause in the policy will determine the amount of loss payable.

On receipt of the claim form duly completed and the survey report, the claim is processed and, if it is in order, a discharge voucher is to be signed by the insured. The amount of loss payable by the insurer is usually settled by agreement between the insurer and the insured otherwise the matter has to be referred to arbitration. Market value of the damaged property is usually taken into account while calculating the amount of loss. Sometimes, the cost of replacement is considered for the puropse. But, it is prevalent only in advanced countries because the insurers have well-equipped staff of replacement.

Before the cheque in settlement of the claim is released, the payment is recorded in the claims register and the claim docket. It is essential that the salvage recoveries should be correctly recorded in the claims register. The payment is recorded in the relative policy file and the sum insured is reduced by the amount of the claim. The sum assured can be reinstated on payment of proportionate premium from the date of reinstatement of the sum insured to the date of expiry of the policy. When the amount of loss is estimated to be small and the cost of investigation is disproportionately high, the survey is dispensed with and the claim is processed and settled on the basis of the complete claim form. When the insurance is on co-insurance basis, the surveyor is appointed by the leading office. Each co-insurer is sent a preliminary advice of the claim followed by a copy of the final survey report which indicates the apportionment of the loss among the co-insurers. Generally the leading office settles the entire loss and recovers the proportionate shares of the loss and expenses from the co-insurers.

Salvage Corps

Fire Salvage Association was incorporated in 1925 as a company registered by guarantee and the insurance companies are members of the Association. The main objects of the Association are to provide a fully trained corps to salvage materials from the buildings on fire, to protect them from water damage, to restore them to serviceable conditions after fire fighting operations are completed. The corps also renders following services to the fire sub-committee, Bombay, of the Tariff Advisory Committee.

1. Checking the fire hydrants in the Cotton Green Storage area.
2. Inspection of sprinklers in the godowns in the Cotton Green area.
3. Training of the fire fighting squads in the textile mills.
4. Provision of facilities to the Fire Sub-committee to test fire sprinkler heads and other fire extinguishing appliances.
5. Reporting on unusual features observed on the premises at the time of fire extinguishment.

Application of Average Clause in Payment of Claim

When insurance is subject to the ordinary, or Pro Rata condition of Average, *i.e.,* under-insurance, the liability of the insurers is restricted to that proportion of the loss that the sum insured bears to the value of the property at the time of the destruction or damage. The insurer's liability in the event of a claim under a policy subject to average, the loss is assessed in the ordinary manner, but the amount payable is determined after a comparison of the sum insured and the value of the property. Where under-insurance exists, the liability of the insurers is limited.

The Pro Rata Condition of Average

"Whenever, a sum insured is declared to be subject to average, if the property covered thereby shall at the breaking out of any fire or at the commencement of any destruction of or damage to such property by any other peril hereby insured against the collectively of greater value than such sum insured, then the insured shall be considered as being his own insurer for the difference and shall bear a rateable share of the loss accordingly."

The operation of the condition can be shown as below

	₹
Sum assured	1,500
Loss	300
Value of the property at the time of fire	1,800

The insurer's liability is $\frac{\text{sum asured}}{\text{value of property}} \times \text{loss}$

$$= \frac{1500 \times 300}{1800} = ₹250$$

Thus the insured will bear ₹ 50 and the insurer will pay ₹ 250.

The insurers cannot be called upon to pay the full sum insured. If the property is totally destroyed, there will be a total loss under the policy.

CONTRIBUTION

Contribution is a corollary of the principle of indemnity. It prevents the insured from receiving more than the total amount of the loss. It applies where two or more insurance cover the same interest, the same subject matter against the same peril. There is no right of contribution where the policies cover different interest e.g., lessor and lessee mortgage, bailor and bailee. Both policies must cover the item is respect of which a claim is made. One insurance may cover more perils than the other but contribution will arise if both policies include the perils which has caused the loss.

Pro rata contribution

The insurer shall not be liable to pay or contribute more than its rateable proportion of loss. The insured is obliged to claim from each insurer, a rateable proportion of his loss. Rateable proportion of the policy is defined as the proportion of the loss as the sum insured under the policy bears to the total sum insured under all the policies.

For example 1

If two policies A and B have been taken for ₹ 30,000 of a building respectively at ₹ 10,000 from A and ₹ 20,000 from B and loss is ₹ 6,000. The policy A will pay

$$= \frac{10,000}{30,000} \times 6,000 = ₹2,000$$

Policy B will Pay $= \frac{20,000}{30,000} \times 6,000 =$ ₹4,000

Total ₹6,000 paid

Example 2:

If the value is ₹ 60,000 in the above example, the payment will be

Policy A $= \frac{10,000}{60,000} \times 6,000 =$ ₹ 1,000

Policy B $= \frac{20,000}{60,000} \times 6,000 =$ ₹2,000

Total ₹ 3,000

In this case insured is not paid full amount of loss because of under insurance

Example 3

In the example 1 if the insured value of the building is Rs. 20,000, the payment is made by

Policy A $= \frac{10,000}{20,000} \times 6,000 =$ ₹ 3,000

Policy B $= \frac{20,000}{20,000} \times 6,000 =$ ₹ 6,000

Total = ₹ 9,000

Here more than loss (Rs. 6000) *i.e.* ₹ 9000 is payable to the insured who will receive the payment only to the extent of loss *i.e.* ₹ 6,000

So Policy A $= \frac{3000}{9000} \times 6,000 =$ ₹ 2,000

Policy B $= \frac{6000}{9000} \times 6,000 =$ ₹ 4,000

Actual claim = ₹6,000

Coinsurance

When a large risk is shared between two or more insures, it is done on a co-insurance basis *i.e.* each insurer accepts only a specified percentage of risks below:

Apportionment

Insurance company	*Sum assured*	*Share of loss*	*Share of expenses*
A	%	₹	₹
B	%	₹	₹
Total	100%		

Example:

The sum assured Rs. 20,000 by A Co. and Rs. 40,000 by B Co. The amount is Rs. 12,000 and expenditure to extinguish fire is Rs. 6,000. The insurance companies will share the loss and expenses as below in proportion to their respective sum assured.

Apportionment of Coinsurance

Insurance company	*Sum assured* ₹	*Share of loss* ₹	*Share of expenses* ₹
A	20,000	40,00	2,000
B	40,000	8,000	4,000
Total	60,000	12,000	6,000

Loss *Expenses*

$$A=\frac{20,000}{60,000}\times 12,000=₹4,000 \qquad A=\frac{20,000}{60,000}\times 6000=₹2,000$$

$$B=\frac{40,000}{60,000}\times 12,000=₹8,000 \qquad B=\frac{40,000}{60,000}\times 6000=₹4,000$$

Thus A Co. and B Co. will share the loss and expenses.

Special Condition of Average

"Whenever a sum insured is declared to be subject to the special condition of Average, then, if such sum shall at the breaking out of any fire or at the commencement of any destruction of or damage to the property by any other peril hereby insured against, be less than three-fourths of the value of the property insured in that amount the insured shall be considered as being his own insurer for the difference between the sum insured and the full value of the property insured at the time of such fire or at the commencement of such destruction or damage and shall bear a rateable share of the loss accordingly."

This condition shall operate only if the sum assured is less than the three-fourths of the value of the property. If the sum assured exceeds this proportion of the value at risk, the insured recovers, the full amount of his loss up to the sum insured.

The assessor in the fire insurance deals with some typical tasks which are described in the following paragraphs. The assessor is also called 'Adjuster'.

Task of Adjuster

The adjuster has to examine and collect the following information:

(*i*) What policies and agreement covered the property at the time of loss.

(*ii*) Whether the property described in the policy is really located and placed at the described place. Whether property had been removed at the safer place at the time of loss.

(*iii*) The nature and extent of the insurer's interest in the property.

(*iv*) Loss occurred after the commencement and before the expiration of the contract.

(*v*) Whether loss was the direct result of fire or other insured perils.

(*vi*) Whether any part of the loss was caused directly or indirectly by enemy attack, military offence, etc.

(*vii*) Whether the loss occurred while the hazard was increased by any means within the control or knowledge of the insured.

(*viii*) Whether before or after the loss the insured wilfully concealed or misrepresented any material facts.

The adjuster must do the following:

(*i*) Fix by agreement with the insured or by appraisal, the actual cash value of the property at the time of loss and the amount of loss thereto.

(*ii*) Exclude from the claim, uninsurable property or excepted property.

(*iii*) Determine the extent of the application of the insurance and the contribution to be made by the insurer to the loss.

(*iv*) If there are two or more policies covering the property, apportion the loss among these policies.

(*v*) See that the requirements in case of loss that are necessary to produce informative essentals to establish the status of liabilities under the policy or the value or loss of the property are complied with.

(*vi*) Consider the interest of any mortgagee named as payee in the policy and the action that should be taken by the insurers.

(*vii*) Investigate any disputed cancellation of the policy.

(*viii*) Exercise the option to take all or any part of the property at the agreed or appraised value.

(*ix*) Preserve any right of recovery from third parties to the loss.

PAYMENT AND DISCHARGE BY ADJUSTER

The adjuster should:

(*i*) Meet the insured or the person who will act for him in the adjustment, discuss the loss with him and make any necessary examination of records.

(*ii*) Examine his policy if it cannot easily be produced, the record of insurer's agents or broker's record should be searched.

(*iii*) Inspect the scheme of the loss and examine any of the property still in evidence.

(*iv*) Examine available records or reports covering the occurrence of the loss, those of fire department, peril or salvage corps, police, etc.

(*v*) Examine records or documents deeds or mortgages, contracts of sale, leases, etc.

(*vi*) Consider whether any insurance held by others should bear the loss or any part of it.

(*vii*) Withdraw if the insurance is not liable for the loss from contract with the insured and report to the insurer or have nonwaiver agreement.

(*viii*) Estimate the situation and the probable results of adjustments.

(*ix*) Choose the method of adjustment used.

(*x*) Make any necessary preparation for conducting the adjustment according to the method chosen.

(*xi*) Negotiate an agreement with the insured as to value and loss, submit the disagreement.

(*xii*) Check any claim for possible errors and omissions also for improper inclusion, of property.

(*xiii*) Apply contract conditions and determine the sum for which any policy or contract is liable.

(*xiv*) Forward to insurer with final report and supporting papers.

(*xv*) Account the salvage and its proceeds with the final report.

WAIVER AND ESTOPPEL

Waiver

Waiver is defined as the voluntary relinquishment of a known right. The waiver may be (*i*) expressed or (*ii*) implied. An insurer is informed that a policy under which claim is made is void because the person insured had no insurance interest in the property; but still, the insurer is going to pay it as a waiver. The example of implied or waiver by conduct is where after having learned of a misstatement on a proposal neverthless, in full knowledge accepts the insurer.

Estoppel

Estoppel is the legal bar raised by a person's own action against asserting a right that he once possessed or making a choice that once was open to him. An insurer may be estopped from exercising its option to take all or any part of the property at the agreed or appraised value if it delays its notice to the insured that it intends to do so. When the insurer has sought to fix the amount of loss through arbitration, it is estoppel from exercising its option to reinstate or replace.

QUESTIONS

1. Discuss the procedure of settlement of fire insurance claims.
2. Explain—Estoppel, Adjuster, Waiver and Estoppel.

32

PROGRESS OF FIRE INSURANCE

The fire insurance has not a long history. The real establishment of fire insurance came only after the Great Fire which took place in London in 1666. This fire lasted for four days and destroyed over 13,000 buildings, which awakened the people to the necessity for a form of protection against such calamities. The insurance received a real fillip only after the growth of commerce. There were a few companies which tried to be more scientific even in some cases, their rates remain standard even now. The decisions of law courts brought the principles of fire insurance to a standard form.

In India, the fire insurance business is not so developed as in foreign countries. With nationalisation of General Insurance Business, it is expected to have a new turn in annals of fire insurance. Before nationalisation the fire insurance had got the following position.

The Gross Premium to Fire Insurers had increased from ₹42.83 crore in 1969 to ₹51.52 crores in 1971 and further to ₹55.29 crore in 1972 and ₹117.64 crore in 1978. The share of Indian insurers to the gross premium has increased from 72.72 per cent in 1969 to 74.0 per cent in 1970 which declined to 73.6 per cent in 1971 and increased to 78.0 per cent in 1972. Thus, the Indian insurers were not experiencing established business and were not well off as compared to non-Indian insurers. The percentage of net premium received by Indian fire insurers to the total net premium had increased from 76.2 per cent in 1969 to 78.8 per cent in 1970 which declined slightly to 78.1 per cent in 1971 and increased to 78.9 per cent in 1972. The non-Indian insurers were losing their business up to 1970 and got a slight improvement in 1971. The net premium has increased from ₹ 33.59 crores in 1969 to ₹42.12 crore in 1971 and further to ₹50.98 crore in 1972 and ₹98.61 crore in 1977. The Indian insurers were far away in the field of fire insurance as compared to total general insurance. The share of Indian insurers to the net premium of total general insurance has increased from 80.2 per cent in 1969 to 81.7 per cent in 1971 and further to 82.8 per cent in 1972. The total net premium has increased from ₹91.34 crores in 1969 to ₹ 114.70 crores in 1971 and further to ₹ 136.57 crore in 1972 and ₹268.43 crores in 1977. It reveals that the Indian fire insurers were not doing more effective business than that of non-Indian insurers.

Indian Insurers

The percentage of net claims payable to net premium has declined to 36.3 per cent in 1970 to 33.5 per cent in 1971 and increased to 35.6 per cent in 1972 giving an increase in balance of income which has gone up from 29.1 per cent of net premium in 1970 to 36.0 per cent in 1971 and increased to 30.4 per cent in 1972. However, the net commission has increased from 8.8 per cent of net premium in 1970 to 9.0 per cent in 1971 and further to 13.0 per cent in 1972. It was a satisfactory state of affairs that the expenses of management had gone down from 21.6 per cent of net premium in 1970 to 20.1 per cent in 1971 and further to 19.5 per cent in 1972. But the percentage of reserve has declined from 5.5 per cent in 1970 to 3.8 per cent in 1971 and increased to 4.7 per cent in 1972. The Indian insurers were experiencing higher proportion of the net claims as compared to that of non-Indian insurers which declined from 29.7 per cent of net premium in 1970 to 22.6 per cent of net premium in 1971. The expenses of commission were missing in case of non-Indian insurers, whereas the Indian insurers

Table 32.1 Premium: Fire Insurance Business (1969-81)

Year	Gross Pemium					Net Premium					All Types of General Insurance (Net Premium)				
	Indian Insurers		Non-Indian Insurers		Total	Indian Insurers		Non-Indian Insurers		Total	Indian Insurers		Non-Indian Insurers		Total
	₹	%to total	₹	%to total	₹	₹	%to total	₹	%to total	₹	₹	%to total	₹	%to total	₹
1969	31.13	72.7	11.71	27.3	42.83	25.59	76.2	8.00	23.8	33.59	73.22	80.2	18.12	19.8	91.34
1970	35.17	74.0	12.35	26.0	47.52	30.72	78.8	8.25	21.2	38.97	84.44	81.5	19.13	18.5	103.57
1971	37.93	73.6	13.60	26.4	51.53	32.92	78.1	9.20	21.9	42.12	93.76	81.7	20.94	18.3	114.70
1972	43.11	78.0	12.18	22.0	55.29	40.21	78.9	10.76	21.1	50.98	113.11	82.8	23.45	17.2	136.57
1975					91.90					87.02					229.87
1977					110					117					326
1978					121					130					370
1979					124					130					398
1980					148					157					481
1981					180					189					599

Table 32.2 Ratio to Net Premium Income (1970-1981)

(In Percentage)

Year	*Indian Insurers*						*Non-Indian Insurers*					
	Net Claims Payable	*Net Commission*	*Expenses of Mangement*	*Increase in Reserves*	*Misc. Income*	*Balance of Income*	*Net claims Payable*	*Net Commission*	*Expenses of Management*	*Increase in Reserves*	*Misc Income*	*Balance of Income*
1970	36.5	8.8	21.6	5.5	2.1	29.1	29.7	9.2	42.1	1.2	0.2	36.3
1971	33.5	9.0	20.1	3.8	2.6	36.0	22.6	–12.1	42.2	4.2	0.6	43.4
1972	35.6	13.0	19.5	4.7	3.5	30.4	23.0	–4.2	37.0	5.8	—	38.3
1975	23.2	36.6	1.2	8.9	—	30.1						
1977	28.6	38.7	2.0	–0.7	—	31.4						
1978	26.8	38.5	2.1	6.0	—	26.6						
1980	30.5	36.1	1.9	7.4	—	24.1						
1981	32.8	35.7	1.6	10.0	—	19.9						

Table 32.3 Percentages of Gross Direct Premium (1970-1972)

Year	*Indian Insurers*						*Non-Indian Insurers*					
	Gross Claims Payable	*Direct Commis-sion*	*Expenses of Mange-ment*	*Increase in Reserves*	*Misc. Income*	*Balance of Income*	*Gross claims Payable*	*Direct Commis-sion*	*Expenses of Manage-ment*	*Increase in Reserves*	*Misc. Income*	*Balance of Income*
1970	25.1	4.2	24.1	4.5	1.6	43.5	24.8	4.4	28.9	2.1	0.2	40.7
1971	22.3	4.2	23.8	2.9	1.6	48.3	19.6	4.6	28.5	3.7	0.4	43.8
1972	23.6	4.3	24.1	2.9	2.0	47.0	19.8	5.1	32.6	4.6	—	47.0

were controlling their expenses of management. The non-Indian insurers were benefited by higher balance of income as compared to that of Indian Insurers.

The share of gross claims payable to gross direct premium has declined from 25.1 per cent in 1970 to 22.3 per cent in 1971 and increased to 23.6 per cent in 1972. The payment of direct commission remarked at the same level while the expenses of management have declined from 24.1 per cent of gross direct premium in 1970 to 23.8 per cent in 1971 but increased to 24.1 per cent in 1972. The proportion of miscellaneous income remained at the same level. Thus, the balance of income has increased from 43.5 per cent in 1970 to 48.3 per cent in 1971 and declined to 47.0 per cent in 1972.

The non-Indian insurers have saved more in the shape of gross claims payable. It has declined from 24.8 per cent in 1970 to 19.6 per cent of gross direct premium in 1971.

Direct commission in case of non-Indian insurers has increased. So, the balance of income has not increased so much in the case as had increased in the case of Indian insurers.

Table 32.4 Indian Insurers Business written outside India (1970-72)

	1970	*1971*	*1972*
1. Gross Claims Payable	42.6	26.9	69.0
2. Direct Commission	28.8	28.0	29.1
3. Expenses and Management	25.4	26.4	23.4
4. Increase in reserve	–1.5	–1.8	0.9
5. Miscellaneous Income	3.2	6.8	13.3
6. Balance of Income	0.8	25.3	10.4

The gross claims payable outside India has declined from 42.6 per cent of gross direct premium in 1970 to 26.9 per cent in 1971 and increased to 69.0 per cent in 1972. It reveals that the Indian Insurers were able to save in payment of claims outside India. However, the expenses of management has increased from 25.4 per cent of gross direct premium in 1970 to 26.4 per cent in 1971 and decreased to 23.4 per cent in 1972. Miscellanenous Income has also increased. The balance of income has increased tremendously from 0.8 per cent in 1970 to 25.3 per cent of gross premium in 1971 but became negative in 1972.

Table 32.5 Net Premium Income (1975-77)

	1975	1977
Fire Insurance		*(In crores ₹)*
In India	63.47	70.36
Outside India	23.55	28.25
Total	87.02	98.61
Total Insurance	1975	1977
In India	166.12	196.97
Outside India	63.75	71.46
Total	229.87	268.43

The net premium income in case of fire insurance outside India has revealed that the business out of India has been increasing. The total net premium income in case of fire insurance has gone upto ₹98.61 crores in 1977.

PROGRESS AFTER NATIONALISATION

The progress of fire insurance after nationalisation has been analysed under 1. gross direct premium 2. net premium and 3. underwriting experiences.

1. Gross Direct Premium in Fire Insurance

The gross direct premium in fire insurance has increased from ₹96.00 crores in 1975 to ₹142.28 crores in 1980, ₹318.94 crores in 1985, ₹581.91 crore in 1988-89 and ₹1248.18 crore in 1994-95. New India has been the first company to procure maximum fire insurance business. It has increased its business from ₹ 38.79 crore in 1980 to ₹ 179.67 crore in 1988-89 by 463.19 per cent. Its gross premium was ₹415.44 crore in 1994-95. The business of United India increased by 405.99 per cent from ₹38.72 crores in 1980 to ₹ 157.20 crores in 1988-89 and its business was ₹ 327.19 crores in 1994-95. These companies have shown a higher rate of increase, as well as a higher amount of business. Oriental has been at the third place and increased its business from ₹ 34.27 crore in 1980 to ₹ 128.41crore in 1988-89 by 374.70 per cent. Its gross premium was ₹262.21 crore in 1994-95. National has increased its business from ₹ 30.50 crore in 1980 to ₹116.63 crore in 1988-89 by 382.39 per cent and ₹243.34 crore in 1994-95. New India has been at the top for increasing its gross direct premium with the help of a larger number of offices. National has been at the lowest ladder in all types of general insurance. It has the smallest number of offices and the lowest figure of employees. New India has the maximum number of employees. It has higher productivity also. The fire insurance business in India increased fastly after nationalisation.

Table 32.6 Gross Direct Premium in Fire Insurance

	GIC	*National*	*New India*	*Oriental*	*United India*	*Total*
1975	—	—	—	—	—	96.00
1980	—	30.50	38.79	34.27	38.72	142.28
1981	—	40.52	62.12	48.08	56.43	207.15
1982	—	47.63	72.44	57.81	63.22	241.10
1984	—	56.40	85.41	64.00	71.24	277.05
1985	—	66.29	95.29	72.48	84.88	318.94
1986	—	76.24	115.18	86.13	100.29	377.84
1987	—	86.68	129.75	94.43	115.93	426.79
1988-89*	—	116.63	179.67	128.41	157.20	581.91
1989-90*	—	118.44	187.17	128.33	155.04	588.98
1994-95	—	243.34	415.44	262.21	327.19	1248.18
1997-98	—	390.58	624.17	401.13	500.22	1916.10

2. Net Premium

Net premium of fire insurance has increased from ₹ 85 crore in 1973 to ₹ 106 crore in 1975, ₹ 157 crore in 1980, ₹ 354.02 crore in 1985, ₹ 493.88 crore in 1988-89 and ₹ 1333.21crore in 1994-95. New India has increased its net premium from ₹ 53.01 crores in 1982 to ₹ 142.20 crore in 1988-89 by 268.20 per cent whereas the net premium of Oriental increased from ₹ 38.21 crores in 1982 to ₹ 102.20 crore in 1988-89 by 267.47 per cent. United India increased its business from ₹ 48.44 crore in 1982 to ₹ 129.24

crore in 1988-89 by 266.80 per cent. National increased its net premium from ₹ 35.93 crore in 1982 to ₹ 108.40 crore in 1988-89 by 301.70 per cent. Thus, the National Company having the lowest amount of net premium has shown the highest rate of growth. New India has shown the second highest growth with the maximum amount of net premium. This company has been more efficient in expanding its fire insurance business than those of other companies. GIC has increased its reinsurance business from ₹ 38.27 crore in 1982 to ₹ 118.40 crore in 1988-89 by 309.38 per cent which stood at ₹ 277.26 crore in 1994-1995. The nationalised companies have shown satisfactory progress. Before nationalisation, the fire insurance was not popular in India. These four companies have taken special initiatives to increase fire insurance coverage to a larger market and have shown a higher amount of net premium in 1994-95, *i.e.,* ₹ 349.33 crore by New India, ₹ 269.79 crore by United India, ₹ 216.08 crores by Oriental and ₹ 220.75 crores by National Insurance.

Table 32.7 Net Premium in Fire Insurance

	GIC	*National*	*New India*	*Oriental*	*United India*	*Total*
1973						85
1975						106
1980						157
1982	38.27	35.93	53.01	38.21	48.44	213.86
1983	50.27	43.55	68.73	48.48	61.67	272.70
1984	65.80	50.90	71.29	54.32	67.14	309.45
1985	77.52	58.96	82.84	56.21	78.49	354.02
1986	78.76	67.15	95.88	67.65	81.65	391.09
1987	88.54	78.38	108.31	76.40	95.66	447.29
1988-89	118.40	108.40	142.20	102.20	129.24	493.88
1989-90	105.34	102.76	156.25	102.83	123.87	380.36
1994-95	277.26	220.75	349.33	216.08	269.79	1333.21
1997-98	377.80	320.81	504.59	323.68	392.08	1919.02

3. Underwriting Experiences

The underwriting profit of all the companies have increased from ₹ 63.69 crores in 1982 to ₹ 95.40 crores in 1988-89 by 149.79 per cent which raised to ₹ 1217.49 crores in 1994-95. The maximum amount of underwriting profit was ₹ 79.13 crores in United India in 1994-95. It is quite a satisfactory profit amount, as its underwriting profit to net premium has also been the highest in that year. National had the lowest amount of profit in 1982, 1988-89 and in 1994-95. Claims-ratio has been 44.7 per cent in 1982, 51.8 per cent in 1985, 50.3 per cent in 1988-89 and 63.3 per cent in 1994-95 in case of New India. It shows that the maximum claims-ratio has taken away a larger position of net income. Oriental had the least claims-ratio and the highest expense-ratio in 1988-89. New India and National faced higher claims-ratio. New India and Oriental has higher expenses-ratio also. The higher claims-ratios have been associated with the gross direct premium. Highest rate of profit in United India is attributed to lower claim and expenses-ratios in 1994-95.

Table 33.8 Underwriting Experience in Fire Insurance

		% to Net Premium						
Premium ₹ Crores	*Net Payable*	*Net Claims Commis-sion*	*Net to Manag-ement*	*Expenses Outgo*	*Miscellaneous Risks Reserve*	*Unexpired ting Profi/ Loss(–)*	*Underwri- ting Profit/ Loss (–) ₹ Crores*	*Underwri-*
1985								
GIC	77.52	46.8	34.4	1.7	–	7.6	9.5	7.37
National	58.96	53.6	–3.0	29.9	0.4	6.8	13.1	7.71
New India	82.84	51.8	–1.2	28.4	–1.3	7.0	15.3	
Oriental	56.21	46.8	–6.7	35.5	–0.8	1.7	23.5	13.24
United India	78.49	57.5	–0.1	27.0	0.1	7.2	8.1	6.32
Total	354.02	51.5	5.7	23.6	–0.5	6.3	13.4	47.31
1989-90								
GIC	105.34	35.4	34.8	3.18	–	5.0	21.8	22.94
National	102.76	50.4	–	34.4	–	7.8	7.4	7.63
New India	156.25	36.0	–	28.3	–	13.6	21.2	33.12
Oriental	102.83	43.0	–	32.7	–	10.2	14.1	14.46
United India	132.83	40.2	–	26.7	–	8.3	24.8	30.80
Total	380.36	41.2	–	37.74	–	8.98	19.6	108.85
1994-95								
GIC	277.26	47.4	35.0	2.0	–0.4	6.0	10.0	28.02
National	220.75	61.49	–0.85	31.66	0.67	–1.45	5.59	12.34
New India	349.33	63.3	–14.8	31.9	–	4.5	15.1	52.74
Oriental	216.08	48.3	–7.2	33.9	–	4.0	21.0	45.26
United India	269.79	46.4	–8.3	29.0	–	3.6	29.3	79.13
Total	1333.21	58.38	+0.77	25.69	–	3.91	16.20	1217.49
1997-98								
GIC	377.86	37.1	34.6	1.8	–0.20	3.8	22.90	86.43
National	320.81	43.13	–5.0	32.2	–0.25	1.84	27.77	89.09
New India	504.59	41.04	–8.87	33.12	–8.5	–4.35	30.36	153.17
Oriental	323.68	38.7	–	34.2	27.9	4.1	31.4	101.63
United India	392.08	39.3	–8.0	35.7	+3.9	7.9	28.9	113.28

Progress of Fire Insurance After Privatisation Gross Premium Income of Fire Insurance

	National	*New India*	*Oriental India*	*United*	*Total*
		In India			
1998-1999	423.10	681.80	434.8	548.20	2087.9
1999-2000	460.87	760.29	485.03	606.03	2312.22
2000-2001	408.09	654.24	471.28	526.11	2059.72
2001-2002	491.83	859.88	521.67	635.89	2504.97
		Out of India			
1998-1999	2.9	84.7	6.30	1.00	94.9
1999-2000	3.07	87.04	6.66	1.02	97.8
2000-2001	4.21	125.15	8.94	1.11	139.1
2001-2002	4.32	246.81	9.36	1.09	261.58
		Total of India			
1998-1999	426.00	766.5	441.10	549.20	2182.8
1999-2000	463.94	847.33	491.69	607.05	2409.9
2000-2001	412.30	779.39	480.22	527.22	2199.1
2001-2002	496.16	1106.70	531.03	636.98	2766.55

Financial Highlights of Fire Insurance

Year	Net Premium		Net Claim		Commission		Expenses of Management		Other Outgo		Increased in unexpired Risks reserve		Investment Income		Under writing Profit	
	₹	%	₹	%	₹	%	₹	%	₹	%	₹	%	₹	%	₹	%
General Insurance Corporation																
1998-1999	402.0		157.10	39	143.4	36	–	–	–	–	12.1	3.0			89.4	22
1999-2000	451.09		169.61	37.6	156.10	34.6	8.90	2.0	0.32	0.1	24.54	5.4			91.62	20.3
2000-2001	379.16		230.76	60.9	129.32	34.1	7.24	1.9	0.34	0.1	–35.96	–9.5			47.46	12.5
2001-2002	634.99		356.23	70.25	212.05	41.8	7.66	1.51	–1.61	–0.32			65.88	13.0	–67.25	–13.26
National																
1998-1999	354.7	83	163.10	46.0	113.5	32					17.0	5.0			61.1	17
1999-2000	395.51	85	163.18	41.3	–20.11	–5.08	141.35	35.7	0.29	0.07	20.38	5.15			90.42	22.86
2000-2001	365.51	89	179.03	49.0	–11.99	–3.28	121.03	33.1	0.35	0.09	–15.00	4.10			92.08	25.19
2001-2002	367.6		192.36	52.3	–17.66	–4.80	126.47	34.0	0.37	0.10	1.04	0.3	44.55	12.11	109.57	29.80
New India																
1998-1999	526.7	69	210.9	40.0	139.0	26.0					11.1	3.0			165.7	31.0
1999-2000	655.72	77	297.30	45.3	–48.95	–7.47	208.56	31.81			64.52	9.84			134.29	20.48
2000-2001	599.64	77	392.69	65.5	–1.25	–0.21	200.11	33.37			–28.04	–4.68	73.40		36.13	6.03
2001-2002	758.84		371.77	49.0	8.50	1.12	211.47	27.87			79.60	10.5	73.50		87.5	11.53

Financial Highlights of Fire Insurance

Year	Net Premium		Net Claim		Commission		Expenses of Management		Other Income		Increased in unexpired Risksin reserve		Investment Income		Under writing Profit	
	Rs.	%	Rs.	%	Rs.	%	Rs.	%	Rs.	%	Rs.	%	Rs.	%	Rs.	%
Oriental																
1998-1999	335.3	76.0	148.9	45.0	92.2	27					5.8	2.0			88.4	26.0
1999-2000	412.72	83.94	173.17	42.0	–3.98	–1.0	152.67	37.0	82.3		38.72	9.4	367.53		52.13	12.6
2000-2001	393.43	81.93	266.28	67.7	–19.55	–5.0	133.49	33.9	45.5		–9.64	–2.5	396.23		22.86	5.8
2001-2002	392.22	73.86	192.75	49.1	–186.4	–4.7	145.41	37.1			–0.61	–0.2	–3.36	0.80	125.29	31.9
United India																
1998-1999	426.0	78	169.1	40	105.3	25					17.0	4			134.6	31.0
1999-2000	487.65	80	159.32	32.7	–38.93	–7.98	163.80	33.59	–17.42		30.81	6.32	444.46		172.65	35.40
2000-2001	487.33	78	288.19	69.9	–38.34	–9.30	136.63	33.14	–55.80		–37.66	–9.13	484.29		63.51	15.40
2001-2002	480.28		175.60	36.6	–37.45		148.74		–11.48		33.98		63.93		211.86	
Indian Market Total																
1998-1999	2044.7	94	849.1	42.0	593.4	29					63.0	3			539.2	26
1999-2000	2402.7	100	962.6	40.6	720.0	30					178.9	–			541.2	23
2000-2001	215.4	98	1357.1	63.6	657.3	31					–126.3	6			262.0	10
2001-2002	2998.94			46.6												

Agency.. **FIRE INSURANCE PROPOSAL-FORM** C/Note No. ....

Code No.. Policy No. ....

THE ORIENTAL FIRE AND GENERAL INSURANCE COMPANY LIMITED

1. Name of Proposer in full ....
(In case of mortgage or other interests the names of all parties should be given)

2. Address in full ....

3. Business or Profession ....

4. Period of Insurance: From .... 19 to 19

Please insure as follows:

5. **Sums Insured:**

(*a*) On the Building(s).................................... } ₹ ....

(*b*) On household goods, furniture, fixtures, fittings and personal effects .... ₹ ....

(*c*) On Merchandise and stock-in-trade consisting of (in shop or godown) .... ₹ ....

(*d*) On furniture, fixtures and fittings in trade .... ₹ ....

(*e*) On Machinery/Accessories .... ₹ ....

(*f*) On stock and stock-in-process .... ₹ ....

(*g*) On Electrical Installations .... ₹ ....

Contd....

(*h*) Any other items (to be specified) .... ₹ ....

Total ₹ ____________

Note:–(*i*) Unless otherwise stated in the Policy this Insurance does not cover Securities, Bond or Paper money or Claques, Obligations or Documents of any kind, Stamps or Stamp Collections, Coin Collections, Books of Accounts or Manuscripts or other business Books, Computer system records. Any . curiosity or work of Art for an amount exceeding ₹ 250/-

(*ii*) It is desirable that the property is insured for its full value as only a proportionate amount will be recoverable in the event of under insurance.

(*iii*) If more than one building is to be Insured se ate particulars and Sum Insured must be given.

The above property is situated at:

(*a*) Name of Building and other means of identification ....

(*b*) Street No. and Name/Municipal No. .... (*c*) Town ....(*d*) District......................

6. Construction:

The said building consists of ground floor and .... upper floors.

The wall are built of ....Cement / Set in lime mortar / mud. The roof of..laid over Rcc / steel frame / timber

The walls are built of ....on ground floor and of .... on upper floors.

How are the premises lighted and heated ....
(i.e. electric light, oil, lanterns, etc.)

The said building belongs to .... of ....

7. Adjacent Buildings:

Is the building detached? If so, the distance from the nearest building ..

Contd....

	CONSTRUCTION		How occupied
If any of the adjacent buildings are within 50 feet, state the construction	Of Walls	Of Roof	
(*a*) Building to the North?	(*a*)		
(*b*) Building to the south?	(*b*)		
(*c*) Building to the East?	(*c*)		
(*d*) Building to the West?	(*d*)		

8. Use of Building

(*a*) Are you the sole occupier of the building? ..	(*a*)
(*b*) Give full particulars of how each ..	(*b*)
(*c*) If any goods are stored, state nature of such goods (Distinguish between hazardous and non-hazardous goods as per list overleaf)	(*c*)
(*d*) If any trade or process of manufacture is carried on, give full particulars. ..	(*d*)
(*e*) If the proposed insurance applied to business premises state how long have you carried on business in the supremacies, and if in other premises, where and how long?	(*e*)
Also state:	
(*a*) How frequently stock is taken? ..	(*a*)
(*b*) Whether a proper set of Account Books is kept? ..	(*b*)
(*c*) Whether the Account Books are liked up in a fireproof Safe, or removed to another Building at all times when the Premises are not open for business purposes?	(*c*)
	Riot and Strike Yes/No

Contd....

9. Additional Perils:

Do you wish to insure against any additional perils given opposite? If so, please indicate Yes/No.

N.B.—An additional premium will be charged for covering these perils.

Malicious Damage	Yes/No
Earthquake, Fire and Shock	Yes/No
Flood & Inundation	Yes/No
Storm and Tempest	Yes/No
Aircraft Damage	Yes/No
Explosion	Yes/No.

10. Existing/Previous Insurance:

Has the property been previously insured or are there any existing insurances with this or any other Company of the same property? If so, state

Name of Company	Amount Insured	Premium	Period of Insurance From to

11. Previous Experience:

Has any Company—

(*a*) declined to insure this or any other property belonging to you? .. (*a*)

(*b*) Cancelled any of your Insurance Policy .. (*b*)

(*c*) refused to renew any Policy? If so, give details .. (*c*)

12. Have you over sustained loss by Fire, or any other Perils now proposed for insurance..? If so, state full particulars.

Name of the Co.	Sum Insured	Date of Fire	Amount of Loss

13. Do you wish the Insurances on buildings/machinery to be on the basis of Reinstatement Value?

Contd....

INDIAN INSURANCE ACT 1938

Section-3 " This proposal is only acceptable on the terms and conditions lodged with the Controller of Insurance."

DECLARATION

I/We hereby declare that the above statements are true and that I/We have withheld no information which might influence the acceptance of this Proposal. I/We further declare that the Sum proposed for Insurance represents and will be maintained at no less than full value of the property. I/We agree that this proposal shall be the basis of the Contract between me/us and the Company and deemed to be incorporated in the Policy.

Date.. *Signature of proposer:* ....

No Insurance in force until the Proposal has been accepted by the Company and the premium paid.

HAERRDOUS GOODS

The following is a list of goods deemed hazardous, but as other goods may be equally hazardous, this list is not necessarily a complete one. In case of doubt, reference may be made to the company.

Acetylene (liquid)
Acids of all kinds except Acetic (but not Glacial Acetic), Boric Citric and Tartaric
Aluminium Carbide, Bust, Powder and Resinate
Aniline
Areca Nuts (unshelled)
Asphalt
Bomboo Mats
Benzyl Acetate
Bichromate of potash
Biri Leaves

Blacks of all kinds [except as Provided in N.B 1(e)]
Calcium Carbide
Calcium Cyanamide, unless certi fied to contain not more than 0.3% of Carbide and packed in air-tight metal containers
Camphene
Camphor
Candles
Caustic Potash and Caustic Soda
"Celluloid" and "Xylonite" and other similar substances

Sopra, copra Cake and Copra neal
Cardass Sisal (loose and/or in hags)
Cotton (whether is fully pressed bales is otherwise)
Creosote
Diethyl Pthalare
Disinfectant Liquids and Liquid Insecticides with flash point Below 65.5°C (250°F)
Explosives of all kinds [including

Fish Guano and Fish Manure
Ganja
Ghee [other than Vegetable ghee in tins not exceeding 4.5 Kg. (10 1b.) in weight and/or in bottles]
Glycerine [except as provided in N. B. 1 (b)]
Grasses of all kinds and straw
Grass Mats (other than in fully-) Pressed bales)
Gunnies and/or Hessians (other

Contd....

Bi-Sulphide of Carbon
Bitumen (other than emulsified
  Bitumen containing not less
  than 45 per cent of water
  and packed in metal drums)
Inflammable Liquids
Inks, Printing
Jute (in fully-pressed bales or)
  otherwise)
Leaves, dried, of all kinds
  except tobacco)
Lime (Unslaked)
Liquefied petroleum Gas
  oil and other mineral products
Matches of all kinds
Matting, used
Metallic Potassium
Mungo
Nephthalene
Nitrates of all kinds

Charcoal
Chlorates of all kinds
Codilla
Coir Yarn, Coir matting and Coir
  rope
Nitro-cellulose plastics
Oils of all kinds [other than
  vegetable oils in tins not
  exceeding 4.5 kg. (10 lbs.)
  in weight and/or in bottles]
Oil Seed Cake (including Cotton
  Seed Cake)
Oil Seed meal
  ble base
Paper, Waxed, Asphalted and
  Oiled
Perchlorate or Potash and
  Perchlorate of Soda
Permanganate of Potash and
  Permanganate Soda
Peroxide of Potash and Peroxide
  of Soda
Phosphorus
Pitch

  Ammunition and Percussion
  caps) (except as provided
in N. B. 1 (d)]
Films, non-safety
Fireworks of all kinds
Poisons, if stored on the same
  floor as or on floors above
  foodstuffs
Rags
Rayon fibres and rayon waste
Resins, natural
Rubber (unmanufactured) if
  stored with other goods
Rubber, Foam
Rubber Goods, Foam
Rubber, Waste and Reclaimed
Sawdist
Shoddy
Spirits of all kinds except potable
  Spirit in bottles and/or jars
Staple (man-made Fibre)
Stearine

  than in fully pressed bales)
  (except as provided in N. B.)
  1 (C))
Herbs, dried, of all kinds
Hyool
Sulfides, metallic, generally
Sulphur
Sulphur dyes or colour [exclud-
  ing those packed in air tight
  metal vessels, labelled with a
  Certificate by the manufac-
  tuerers that the dyes (or
  colours) contain at least 10 per
  cent inert inorganic salts]
Tallow (manufactured or un-
  manufactured)
Tar and/or its liquid products
  (other than in bottles)
Tarred Cloth, Felth, Rope, String
  and Twine
Varnish
Vegetable fibres of all kinds
Waste of all kinds (excluding
  silk and tea waste)
Wax of all kinds

N.B.1 The Following articles may be treated as non-hazardous if stored in the manner indicated:

(*a*) "Ruberoid" and/or "Pioneer" roofing material and/or small quantities of "Carbo lastic" and "Sealtite" in air-tight kegs.

(*c*) Loose Gunnies for packing purposes provided the quantity will never be largely in excess of that required for imediate packing purposes.

Contd....

(*b*) Glycerine in tins, cases, steel drums or other large packages subject to the following warranty: glyceriene will not be stored with or within 6 metres (20 feet) of permanganate of soda or potash nitrates, metallic sulfides, strong acids, fibres or fibrous goods or blacks such as lamp black."

(*d*) Loaded cartridges not exceeding in all 5% of total value of stockes.

(*e*) Gas Carbon Block if stored in a separate buidling.

(*f*) Betel Nuts (Unshelled).

(*g*) Rubber goods other than foam rubber goods.

(*h*) Titanium dioxide (Powder).

THE ORIENTAL FIRE AND GENERAL INSURANCE COMPANY LIMITED

(Incorporated in India)

Subsidiary to General Insurance

Corporation of India

Refistered Office:

Jeevan Udyog, Asaf Ali Road, New Delhi

Issuing Officer:

PROHIBITION OF REBATING

Section 41 of the Insurance Act 1933 as amended provides as follows:-

1. No person shall allow or offer to allow, either directly or indirectly, as an induscement to any person to take out or renew or continue an insurance in respect of any kind of risk relating to lives or property in India, any rebate of the whole or part of the commission payable or any rebate of the premium shown on the Policy, nor shall any person taking out or renewing or continuing a Policy accept any rebate except such rebate as may be allowed in accordance with the published prospectuses or tables of the insurer.
2. Any person making default in complying with the provisions of this section shall be punishable with fine which may extend to five hundred rupess.

FIRE INSURANCE

The Oriental Fire and General Insurance Company Limited

THE ORIENTAL FIRE AND GENERAL INSURANCE COMPANY LIMITED

Classes of Business Transacted

FIRE* MARINE * AVIATION

LOSS OF PROFITS

MOTOR CAR

WORKMENS COMPENSATION

BURGLARY

PERSONAL ACCIDENT

FIDELITY GUARANTEE

MONEY IN TRANSIT

ETC., ETC.

TheCompany's policies are liberal contracts free from restrictive conditions and the premiums charged are strictly moderate consistent with absolute security.

Quotalions on Application to the company or its Agents

PART FIVE

MISCELLANEOUS INSURANCE

33

TRANSPORT INSURANCE AND MOTOR INSURANCE

This chapter discusses Transport Insurance as well as Motor Insurance.

TRANSPORT INSURANCE

Transport insurance provides protection against damage or injury to property, goods and people in transit.*

Some risks are covered by personal insurance but most transport insurance is purchased in wholesale markets.

Marine, aviation and other transit (MAT) insurance are often considered together, although there are important differences.

MAT insurance can include policies to cover both commercial and recreational activities. They are together known Transport Insurance as one insurer underwrites all the above risks under one policy i.e.Transport Insurance.

General aviation insurance is distinct from commercial airline cover and insurance for professional shipping is separate from insuring pleasure craft.

Nature of Cover

Marine, Aviation and other Transit (MAT) insurance is often considered together to refer to wholesale insurance for aircraft and ships themselves as well as the goods and persons on-board. But this grouping belies important differences in the forms of insurance along various dimensions including: the class of business, the type of cover, the type of policy, type of policyholder and the type of peril/ hazard.

Class of business

Typically, transport insurers distinguish between commercial insurance policies – those offering risk protection for businesses or professionals engaged in transporting people and cargoes – and recreational insurance which is geared towards insuring individuals or firms against losses incurred in the private use of vehicles.

Thus in aviation, commercial airline insurance is separate from general aviation insurance, which includes flights ranging from gliders and powered parachutes to corporate jets. Similarly, marine insurance for small boats/yachts and pleasure craft is distinct from cover for commercial shipping. In some countries for example in the US, ocean marine policies refer to insurance against incidents that might occur at sea. Other types of transit insurance covering transportation via inland waterways (lakes, rivers, canals) as well as roads are sometimes known as inland marine.

---

* Source: Swiss Re Economic Research Consulting Reports.

Type of policyholder

The nature of the insurance contract will also reflect the type of policyholder. For example, distinct insurance policies are available for ship-owners, aircraft owners, port facilities manufacturers and repairers as well as leasing and chartering companies. Aviation insurance typically distinguishes cover for airlines, aerospace (manufacturer, service providers), general aviation (industrial aid, commercial, private business and pleasure (PBP)), and space (risks associated with the transportation, storage, launch and operation of satellites). The physical damage and liability exposures of offshore energy exploration and extraction companies are typically covered under marine insurance.

Type of cover

There are three general types of transport cover: hull, cargo and liability.

Hull insurance: refers to the protection against damage to the structure and machinery of a vessel, both ships and aircraft, from perils such as collision or sinking of the ship, capsizing or stranding, fire, jettisoning (throwing overboard of property to save other property). This type of insurance is mainly purchased by the owner or charterer of the craft and generally covers physical damage incurred either in motion or while in port.

Cargo insurance: caters specifically to the transportation of goods or merchandise packed or in bulk and shipped either by sea, air or land.

Liability insurance: protects the policyholders against possible claims they may face in respect of unintentional damage suffered by third parties, including passangers. A key insurance product is cover for the liability exposures of ship-owners (so-called protection and indemnity, P&I) although other transport-related operations also purchase insurance to protect against legal liabalities.

Structure

Transport insurance is typically arranged through wholesale a subscription co-re/insurance markets

Under a subscription arrangement, the customer (usually acting through a broker) will negotiate terms and conditions, including the premium, with are/insurer who will agree to cover a certain part of the risk and is referred to as the 'lead' co-re/insurer. If the selected leader is not willing to underwrite 100% of the risk, or if the broker and his client are unwilling for one re/insurer to underwrite the entire risk, other re/insurers are invited to cover the remaining part of the risk as 'followers'.

Typically, the following re/insurers accept the same terms and conditions as the leader, (although sometimes the leader receives an additional fee or commission for having the principal responsibility for policy administration and claims handling). However, there are a situations where different terms and conditions can be negotiated with following re/insurers. Such 'verticalised' arrangements are not common, although they are prominent feature of airline fleet insurance programmes. It is possible for risks to be placed using a combination of subscription and vertical underwriting, with a group of underwriters accepting the business on a subscription basis but others requiring separate terms and conditions.

Evolution in the role of mutuals

In addition to wholesale subscription markets, transport insurers sometimes organise formal insurance pools to share risks. In fact, three of the largest aviation insurers, Global Aerospace, USAIG, and La Reunion Adrienne, are pools, each of which writes business on behalf of five or six different insurance companies from various countries. Similarly, pools such as France's GAREX specialise in underwriting marine war risks.

Owners of aircraft or ships also enter into co-insurance arrangements amongst themselves. In the maritime sector, for example, Protection and Indemnity (P & I) clubs have evolved to provide the vast majority of the world's shipping fleet with insurance cover against legal liabilities to third parties. Some P & I clubs co-operate to form a club of clubs, the most famous of which is the

International Group (IG). Under the IG's pooling agreement, all qualifying claims in excess of USD 9 million are shared between member Clubs. This claim-sharing agreement, is underpinned by an extensive reinsurance programme which the IG also arranges.

Such mutual insurance arrangement remain important. In large part this reflects the nature of the underlying risks which would otherwise be difficult to cover through other co-re/insurance market arrangements. In the case of the P&I Clubs too, the ancillary services offered such as claims handling and legal representation reinforce their value proposition to their members, Sharing risks across Clubs allows the underwriting of potentially very large claims that could exhaust the resources of an Club.

However, as commercial insurer's appetites for transport risks have evolved, underwriting capacity has been extended to include areas previously dominated by mutuals. This, together with tougher competition rules and regulations, has to a number of the aviation pools being dissolved – for example, the Swiss Poll for Aviation Insurance was placed into run-off in July 2007. At the same time, a number of commercial insurers have begun to write marine insurance for third-party liabilities on a fixed premium basis.

These fixed-premium P&I facilities, which tend to target charterers or owners of smaller vessels principally operating in coastal or inland waters, have grown considerably over recent years with many more new entrants than exits, especially in 2011. Nonetheless, the market remains relatively small, accounting for only around a tenth of total P&I premiums. In response, some P&I clubs have introduced "Owners P&I" fixed-premium policies for established shipping fleets. Similarly, some P&I Clubs have developed fixed-premium facilities for smaller inland craft and yachts, to compete with commercial insurers.

PROGRESS OF TRANSPORT INSURANCE

The sources of demand for transport insurance have typically been international. Policyholders want consistency and certainty of cover regardless of the location of the insurer. In the case of cargo policies, protection may typically be arranged by the buyer of the goods or the seller either of whom in priniple could choose to insure with a local or an overseas carrier. Likewise, the owners of ships and aircraft (or charterers/leasers of these craft) may take out hull and liability insurance in a jurisdiction unrelated to locations where the vessels or craft are employed.

International transport insurers have expanded throughout world specially in Asia

In response to increased competition, specialist insurers such as Lloyd's and other international insurers have set up insurance units in emerging economies. Many operate in multiple locations, either as branch officers or as independently capitalised entities. For example, in 2004 Lloyd's formed its Lloyd's Asia platform enabling local syndicates in Singapore, Hong Kong and Shanghai to write business across the region. The number of Lloyd's Asia syndicates had increased from three initially to eighteen by 2011 while corresponding MAT premiums have more than doubled over the past five years. Most of this regional premium growth has been cross-border.

International insurers have not only expanded into Asia, but also into other emerging regions. For instance, a number of international insurers operating out of the Dubai International Financial Centre provide the Middle East region with specialy risk solutions including marine and aviation insurance. Similarly, global insurers have sought to penetrate Latin American transport insurance markets.

Together with the emergence of domestic players, the entry of foreign insurers has encouraged the development of regional insurance centres. Singapore in particular has become an important hub for Asian Insurance, particularly for marine. This probably reflects Singapore's low tax status, liberal regulatory and political environment, openness to foreign capital, strong talent pool and its close ties with shipping and oil related businesses.

Consistent with the growing importance of regional hubs, according to the International Underwriting Association the proportion of business written overseas by London Market participants represented around one fifth of their total market premiums in 2011. Indeed, Catlin – a publicly-listed specialist London re/insurer – increased its share of non-UK business to around 50% in 2012, supported by significant growth in its regional operations in Asia-Pacific and the US (which covers specialty business for Latin America).

Influence of local regulations

The international nature of transport risks means that restrictions on the cross-border provision of marine and aviation insurance have typically been less onerous than other lines of insurance. But while it once would have been accepted that MAT insurance can only be bought in specialist markets, this view is increasingly being challenged as global insurance capacity expands and as national regulators seek greater protection for their own markets. As a result, transport companies may be obliged to purchase insurance cover for local risks from domestic insurers or from locally-licenced foreign insurers.

The barriers to entry for new insurers are more significant in some regions than others. For example, India can be a difficult market for foreign transport insurers to penetrate, although things are improving with reduced limits on domestic retentions. Asia and to some extent Latin America are relatively more liberal in terms of market access, although some countries such as Brazil prescribe that the import or export of cargo should be insured with companies registered locally.

CHALLENGES OF TRANSPORTH INSURANCE

Coping with persistent surplus insurance capacity

The recent long run of poor underwriting performance in some transport insurance lines such as marine hull raises the question of why risk capital has not left this segment in search of higher returns elsewhere. Indeed, fresh underwriting capacity reportedly continues to enter transport insurance markets, for example, in terms of new Lloyd's syndicates offering aviation and marine hull cover.

Part of the explanation could be that MAT risks typically form a relatively small part of an insurer's overall portfolio and offering the cover may bring other benefits. For many large continental European insurers for example, marine insurance is seen as an important service to clients which helps market other products. So the incentive to actively withdraw capacity may be less than for other risks such as property or motor where poor performance can have a large impact on an insurer's financial results.

By the same token, the fixed costs of maintaining specialist expertise in transport insurance may make it difficult for insurers to switch underwriting resources. This would also explain inertia in risk absorbing capacity in MAT lines.

Strategic considerations too may be important. The actions of one or more large insurers to exit the sector or reduce the percentage of the risk they are willing to underwrite could prompt a re-pricing of risk. Yet to the extent that this encourages others to increase capacity to take advantage of prospective higher premiums this might serve only to limit any rate hardening in the market. The result is a collective action problem – few if any insurers have an incentive to reduce their exposure even though all might potentially benefit if they all adopted strategies to reduce overall market capacity.

The potential diversification benefits from including transport insurance lines in insurers overall portfolios also helps to explain their attraction to insurers. MAT risks tend to be uncorrelated with other lines of business – the correlation of marine hull and world non-life loss ratios is estimated at less than 0.1, while the correlation of aviation hull and liability with world non-life loss ratios is less than 0.3. Moreover, such diversification benefits are being hard coded into the new European Solvency II capital requirements.

The positive impact of diversification is however, no substitute for persistently weak or even negative underwriting results. Ultimately insurers need to at least cover their expenses associated with an insurance class (including the cost of capital employed to support the business) even if the business helps to lower the overall riskiness of the insurance portfolio. This is especially true in the current environment with persistently low interest rates restraining investment returns.

Several of the factors sustaining capital allocation in MAT insurance lines and hindering price increases despite weak underwriting profits seem likely to persist. Indeed, the growth of regional insurance capabilities. Increased competitiveness of the major players, aggressive and ever larger clients and enhanced regulatory incentives for insurers to hold MAT exposure given their perceived low correlation with other risks could underpin a structural change in the premium rate cycle. Even if such a change was not permanent, given that other business lines are also facing many of the same pressures, insurers may simply prefer to remain in transport insurance markets in case its pricing turns before other business lines.

Against that backdrop, and without a large catastrophic event large enough to prompt a sudden and significant withdrawl of capacity in the market or a material reduction in risk appetite that led insurance prices to rise, insurers will need to rely more than ever on their underwriting expertise to improve profitability. This may include tighter terms and conditions, product innovation or constraining insurable values.

Opportunities for transort insurers

Despite these underwriting challenges, there are a number of ways that transport insurers can improve the effectiveness of MAT insurance. In particular, product, process and organisational innovations could open up various opportunities.

Responding to emerging risks

Most hull, cargo and liability insurance contracts routinely involve 'manuscript' policy wording changes to reflect individual needs, circumstances and preferences of the policyholder and insurer. Such on-going policy modifications, often labelled "deal-by-deal" innovation, can be vitally important not only in maintaining cover but in encouraging policyholders to adopt appropriate riskeduction measures.

There is also scope for insurance to cover new, emerging transport-related risks. For example, the increased threat of piracy has prompted a number of marine insurers to provide new protection products for piracy-related losses. In particular, dedicated kidnap and ransom cover has been introduced to protect ship-owners against ransom payments, as well as the other costs associated with seizure. Similarly, cover for loss of hire/earnings due to piracy has been offered.

More generally, in common with other insurance lines, marine and aviation cover has progressively sought to provide protection against risks associated with non-physical damage–for example, business interruption costs. A marine cargo policy may therefore sometimes include incidental project delay cover to insure against costs that could be incurred due to the cargo being delayed. Following the airline business interruption during the iceland volcano ash cloud of 2010, a number of major insurers initiated additional covers aimed at helping airlines deal with such challenges, although the take up has been very low.

The transport sector could be especially vulnerable to cyber risk – the potential failure, malfunction, or misuse of information technology infrastructure. Transport companies first line of defence against such risks is likely to be greater investment in security technology and more robust risk management. Cyber-attacks are commonly excluded from "All-risk" marine and aviation policies. But with corporate awareness of the threat increasing, demand for cyber risk extensions to existing policies, as well as dedicated cover against related business interruption losses and liability claims, has risen.

As with other risks such as terrorism, insurers must be careful not to overstep the boundaries of insurability. In some cases, public-private partnership may be necessary to support insurance solutions and new risk protection products. A debate is in progress over whether the US government terrorism insurance backstop should include cyber attacks.

Designing new product features

As well as responding to new or evolving risks, some insurers have sought to redesign features of existing insurance policies. One topic that is currently under review by marine insurers is General Average (GA), the principle that in the event of an emergency leading to cargo being jettisoned or expenses incurred, the loss is shared proportionately by all parties with a financial interest in the voyage. In the modern world of ultralarge container ships, GA has become increasingly problematic. The logistical challenges of tracing and securing collateral from vast numbers of cargo owners can be severe. Since the cargo and ships cannot typically be released until security is in place, this potentially causes significant disruption to supply chains adding to insurance losses.

In light of these problems, the Landmarks Consortium (a collection of insurance companies, led by Swiss Re) has proposed an insurance product which would set an agreed, nominal value for each container in the event of an incident, albeit with a cap on total exposure. In addition, a ship-owner would be the sole policyholder, which in turn should help speed up establishment of appropriate security and release of cargos as well as expedite the processing of claims.

A possible fertile area for product innovation relates to the adoption of renewable energy. Thus far transport insurers involvement has largely been passive, providing extensions to cover for machinery upgrades to the latest green standards, hybrid or alternative fuel discounts, builders' risks for environmentally sustainable construction, etc. But insurance can play a more proactive role in promoting renewable energy projects through the provision of innovative risk transfer and financing schemes. Examples in transport include solar powered aircraft and the use of gas turbine fuel cell hybrids in ships.

Upgrading underwriting practices

There are signs that the transport insurance sector is responding to shifts in the risk landscape and upgrading its underwriting practices. Accumulation management is becoming more sophisticated and risk based. Some re/insurers have developed formal models, to understand better the increasingly complex and interdependent risks. Such tools can improve the quantification and therefore the insurability of potential highly-accumulated losses. They complement more traditional methods to assess tail risk exposure such as Realistic Disaster Scenarios routinely employed within the Lloyd's market.

Regulatory initiatives are also encouraging insurers to take accumulation risks seriously. In particular within Europe, the proposed Solvency II regime requires insurers to hold a level of capital commensurate with the full potential costs of the insured peril.

New tracking technology, along with enhanced electronic data processing is also bringing down hull and cargo monitoring costs. The practical difficulties of processing potentially vast quantities of information should not be underestimated. But in partnership with technology companies, progress is being made in designing better and more secure data tracking systems (eg CargoNet). In turn, this raises the prospect of a return to policies written on the basis of detailed declarations of individual shipments, at least for some cargo business.

Given the significance of natural catastrophe exposure, reinsurers with sophisticated modelling capabilities play an important role in assessing and underwriting transport risks. A better understanding of natural catastrophe risks may ultimately help to locate transport infrastructure in less exposed locations, and improve building codes to mitigate earthquake, windstorm, and flood damages.

Exploiting expertise across insurance classes

Despite the trend towards intermodal transportation, the associated provision of insurance trends to be organised via business units which are normally split functionally along individual lines of business. Even where an insurer collects transport insurance classes together within a team, in practice there is often limited collaboration between the dedicated underwriters.

In part at least this reflects the history of how the separate markets have evolved. Effective underwritting of transport-related risks requires specialist knowledge which typically needs to be built up over time and informed by loss experience of past events. Good underwriters must combine technical expertise with subjective judgement about both the likelihood of events and insurers' sensitivity to those events. In practice, therefore, the synergies between MAT insurance lines may not be especially large.

Yet history suggests that large, unexpected losses are rarely due to a single underlying cause, but rather are the result of a combination of multiple, often unrelated, factors that combine to produce catastrophic impacts. Consequently, insurers that are organisationally equipped to appreciate better their exposure to interdependent risk drivers are likely to prosper.

With the application of modern risk management tools and techniques, arguably there is increased scope to cross-fertilise ideas and share insights from across transport insurance markets as well with other lines such as property and casualty. The key is for insurers to harness the skilled underwriter's knowledge with the increased use of sofware and data analytics. This could become especially important as less experienced underwriters join the industry ranks and as institutional memory fades about major loss events.

Looking ahead, the longer-term prospects for marine and airline insurance are tied to the outlook for international transport activity and the associated developments in risk exposures. To the extent that the world economy continues to recover and pre-crisis trends in trade and travel are broadly re-established, marine and aviation markets will likely expand robustly. This is the most probable outcome. But there are risks to that outlook, both on the upside and downside, relating to any lasting impact of the financial crisis on the trade and travel intensity of economic growth and the sensitivity of premiums to changes in transport activity. Transport insurers, therefore need to ensure that their business and underwriting models are sufficiently nimble and sophisticated enough to respond.

Distribution channels

Despite shifts in the international marketplace, brokers and agents remain the key distribution channel for MAT insurance. Some insurers have introduced direct marketing approaches. For example in 2012. Zurich Insurance Group launched a web-based portal to issue marine cargo insurance certificates. In general though, there are few signs of disintermediation. This reflects the complexity of risks and the need for non-standard insurance which often requires specialised knowledge that brokers and agents provide.

Underwriting management agents (UMAs) – entities that have the authority to enter into or sign insurance policies on behalf of insurers – also continue to play an important role in marine and aviation markets. Especially in countries where specialist underwriting expertise may be limited. UMAs can channel capacity from general insurers who might otherwise be relucant to cover MAT risks. In turn, this can help to tailor policies to meet local needs, enhance competitive pricing and provide more effective claims processing.

Accumulation risk in transport insurance

The changing transportation environment has increased the potential for much larger than expected losses arising from accumulation risk (where a single event can lead to multiple claims). In turn, this can be linked to different types of exposure concentration which can build up in insurance portfolios.

Value concentration. Larger, more expensive craft carrying bigger quantities of diverse and highly valued cargo or more passengers expose insurers to potentially very large losses in the event of an accident. Moreover, urbanisation has increased the potential losses from an aircraft crashing in a densely populated city.

Geographical concentrations. While normally mobile, aircraft and ships can often reside in one place for a length of time – for example, in ports/airports where there are many ships/aircraft, stored and loaded/unloaded cargo, and a high density of associated equipment and buildings. This means that insured risks can accumulate significantly at these storage or interchange locations. The development of regional trade and passenger hubs has increased this vulnerability.

Policyholder concentration. The widely used system to open policies for cargo insurance (with a rate based on turnover for a vessel or storage facility rather than declarations of the precise shipments) means an underwriter generally does not know how many policy holders have cargo on board the same vessel and to what extent. An insurer must estimate his exposure based for example on past average shipments which could mask considerable variation in cargo values. Not only might transit involve various stages and different modes of transport, but containerised cargoes may be falsely declared.

A feature of airline insurance is that a significant share of premiums comes from a relatively small number of customers. Individual insurers can therefore potentially have a large exposure across a small number of risks. This makes it difficult for airline insurers to diversify risks over policyholders.

A feature common to many mobile risks is that they come together for a certain period of time in transshipment and trading hubs such as ports and distribution warehouses. As a result, accidents, delays or disruptions – for example, strikes – at ports or other key transport hubs can contribute to a sudden increase in risk accumulations. Some major international ports and airports are especially vulnerable to concentrated risk exposures.

Shifts in natural catastrophe exposure

Natural catastrophe exposure is highly significant for transport systems, particularly because windstorm exposure is often highest near major ports. Earthquake and tsunami exposures are also important near some coastal areas, while aviation is especially susceptible to weather interruptions. Even when cargo and vessels are static, there is considerable natural catastrophe exposure. Recent natural disaster events, such as Hurricane Sandy in 2012 and the 2011 Thailand floods, led to major losses for the marine and aviation industries. For example, Hurricane Sandy caused over 5000 flight cancellations, affected 9% of worldwide capacity and led to the largest cumulative marine losses on record. Similarly, the ash cloud that formed following the eruption of icelandic volcano Eyjafjallajökull in 2010 led to over 100000 flight cancellations and affected around 10 million passengers.

To the extent that climate change leads to permanent shifts in weather patterns (e.g. increased frequency and intensity of extreme weather events) this could increase the likelihood of delays, disruptions, damage and failures across land-based, air and marine transport. It is important that as more evidence emerges about such effects insurers build these sorts of factors into their underwriting assessments.

Such loss severity issues could come increasingly to the fore with the widening of the Panama Canal, which could encourage a significant shift in intermodal transport. Larger ships will be able to use the canal to access ports on the east coast of the USA for freight bound for other parts of the country, affecting the risks to which ships and cargos are exposed. While western USA is vulnerable to rare earthquake events, the east coashas windstorms that occur much more regularly. Similarly, plans for the expansion of Arctic scailing routes will reduce voyage times but pose hazards for ships including extreme weather and temperature in a highly eco-sensitive environment. Proposals for a canal in Nicaragua are still very preliminary, but a canal there would concentrate in a narrow area even larger ships than the widened Panama Canal.

Motor insurance got recently a great momentum. In the older times, persons, who were injured or killed through the negligence of the motorists, could not get financial redress either to them or to their legal heirs because no scheme of insurance was present at that time. To mitigate the financial hardship caused to the persons, the Motor Vehicles Act, 1939, as amended from time to time, has made it compulsory for the motorists to insure against the risk of liability to third parties.

The rate of premium is standardised because the business is tariff. No insurer can charge lower rates than the tariff rates and no insurer can grant benefits exceeding than those prescribed by the tariff.

Vehicles for the purpose of insurance are classified as below:

(*i*) Private Cars (not used for carrying passengers for hire or reward).

(*ii*) Commercial vehicles such as goods carrying vehicles, passenger vehicles, tractors and others.

(*iii*) Motor cycles, scooters and autocycles.

KINDS OF POLICIES

The policies under motor insurance are as follows:

(*i*) Act Liability only.

(*ii*) Third Party only.

(*iii*) Comprehensive Policy.

1. Act Policies

This policy is designed to meet the requirements of Motor Vehicles Act, 1939, which provides for compulsory insurance in regard to liabilities arising out of use of motor vehicles in a public place. This kind of policy is limited to bodily injury or death of the third parties. Section 95(2) of the Motor Vehicles Act lays down that a policy of insurance shall cover any liability incurred in respect of anyone accident up to the following limits:

(*i*) *Goods Vehicle.* Rs. 50,000 in all including the liabilities if arising under the W.C. Act, 1923, in respect of death of or bodily injury to employees (other than the driver) not exceeding six in number being carried in the vehicle. This means that liabilities if any towards driver and employees (above six) being carried in the vehicle under W.C. Act in addition to Rs. 50,000.

(*ii*) *Passenger Vehicles.* Vehicles in which passengers are carried:

(*a*) For hire or reward.

(*b*) By reason of or in pursuance of contract of employment.

(1) in respect of persons other than passengers carried for hire or reward—₹ 50,000 in all.

(2) in respect of passengers.

₹ 50,000 in all where the vehicle is registered to carry not more than 30 passenger;

₹ 75,000 in all where the vehicle is registered to carry not less than 30 but not more than 60 passengers;

₹ 1,00,000 in all where the vehicles are registered to carry more than 60 passengers; and

Subject to the limit aforesaid, ₹ 10,000 for each individual passenger where the vehicle is a motor car (used to carry not more than 6 passengers excluding the driver) and ₹ 5,000 for each individual passenger in any other case.

(*iii*) *Other Vehicles.* The amount of liability incurred except as provided otherwise.

The Act Policy besides the cover as required under the Motor Vehicles Act provides for indemnification of the claimants costs and expenses which the insured shall become legally liable to pay as also costs and expenses incurred with the written consent of the insurer. The policy may extend to indemnify any driver who is driving the motor vehicles on the Insured's order or with his permission provided, he is not entitled to indemnify under any other policy.

2. Third Party Policy

This policy cover the liabilities of the third parties who suffered less in connection with the damage of property and personal injury or death. Thus, this policy indemnifies the insured against his legal liability in respect of damage to property of third parties over and above 2000. The limit of liability is as follows:

(*a*) Private Car—Unlimited.

(*b*) Commercial Vehicle.

(*i*) Goods or passenger-carrying vehicles—₹ 20,000.

(*ii*) Other miscellaneous or special type of vehicles—₹ 50,000, Motor cycle—Unlimited.

The policy may be extended to include:

(*a*) fire,

(*b*) theft risks,

(*c*) legal liabilities to persons employed in connection with the operation and/or maintenance and/or loading and/or unloading of motor vehicles.

The private car policy extends to indemnify the insured (individual only) against legal liabilities incurred by him subject to limitations of indemnity whilst personally driving a private motor car. Private car policy covers legal liability of the insured to passengers (not for hire or reward) in the car although under the passengers (not for hire or reward) in the car although under the Motor Vehicles Act, it is not required to be covered. Liabilities arising while the motor cat is being used in private places is covered. The policy covers bodily injury or death, property damage and medical expenses. Due to the amendment to the Motor Vehicles Act, 1994, liability on third party claims has gone up as 'No fault' liability compensation has been enhanced and Structured Compensation has been introduced.

3. Comprehensive Policy

The comprehensive policy covers the following risks

1. Damage to car parts or body.
2. Removal charges for repairs.
3. Third Party Liabilities.
4. Costs and Expenses incurred with risk.
5. Repair Charges.
6. Medical expenses.

At the payment of extra premiums, the following risks are also insured:

(*i*) Death or injury to family members who are above 16 years and below 65 years.

(*ii*) Riots, strikes, thefts, larceny, etc.

(*iii*) Loss of Rugs.

Jald Rahat Yojna (Pre-litigation Settlements) has been introduced to help claimants to get payment of compensations without approaching courts. Structured Compensation formula has been used for quick settlements of claims.

PROCEDURES OF INSURANCE

The proposal form is completed for making proposal for motor insurance. The form is divided into three parts:

(*i*) *identification of vehicles*—registered number, horse-power shape and size, model, etc.

(*ii*) *Risk-information*—past insurance, type of policy got previously, equipments, vehicles.

(*iii*) *Declaration*—The declaration of true and full statement of the questions is made at the end of the policy.

Rating the Motor Insurance

Since the motor insurance is subject to tariff, basic premium is determined by the tariff association. Additional premium is added to the basic premium on the basis of shape, size, horse power, use, value of the motor car, etc. The higher the risk, the more will be the amount of premium. Rebate in premium is allowed if the insured has more than one car, is a member of Automobile Association and there was no loss in the previous years. The car was under the personal use and care of the owner.

Issue of Policy

As soon as the proposal form is accepted, cover note is issued. The cover note is a certificate of insurance although it cannot be used as a proof of insurance in a court of law. As soon as the policy is issued the cover note is cancelled.

Term of Insurance

The motor insurance policy is issued generally for one year. However, the policy can be issued for less than one year but the premium rate will be higher, *e.g.*, the premium rate is three-fourths of annual premium of the policy issued for six months.

Additions of Benefits

During the currency of policy, after payment of extra-premium additional benefits can be added to the original policy. Thus additional risks can be included to the original policy.

Change of Vehicle

The insured vehicles can be disposed of along with the policy. The term of policy will remain the same. The policy will continue up to the unexpired period with the purchaser of the car. Similarly the insured can replace another car under the same policy.

Furlough Concessions

When risk is reduced, the proportionate share of premium is returned or the period of coverage is extended by the excess premium. This is called 'furlough concessions'.

Settlement of Claims

As soon as the damage occurs, notice of that is given to the insurer. The evidence or eye-witness should be placed to the insurer. When the insurer is satisfied with the notice and evidence, he can issue claim form which is returned to the insured after completing it in all respects. Personal injury is also made in connection with the personal injury, damage to property, defence and prosecution.

Negligence of the Parties

The insurer will pay the amount of liability only when the insured is at negligence. In other words, the insurer shall pay only when the insured not legally liable for indemnification to third party.

Knock for Knock Agreement

This clause says that the liability of the insurers will be limited only to the liability to the insured. In this case the third party liabilities do not arise.

Halving Agreement

Under this agreement the loss of both partners (insured) and third party and is equally divided amongst the insurer.

Private Car

Cover is granted against the loss of or damage to motor car and its accessories whilst thereon, anywhere in India, caused by any of the following perils:

1. Accidental, external means
2. Fire

3. External explosion
4. Self-ignition.
5. Lighting
6. Frost
7. Burglary, house breaking or theft, and
8. Malicious act.

The cover is also operative whilst the car is in transit by road, rail, in land, waterway, lift or elevator.

The following are excluded:

(*i*) Consequential loss;
(*ii*) Depreciation;
(*iii*) Wear and tear; and
(*iv*) Mechanical or electrical breakdowns, failures or breakages.

Damage to tyres is ordinarily not payable. If, however, the insured car is also damaged at the same time, the damage to tyres is payable but the amount payable in that event is limited to 50% of the cost of replacement of the tyres. The exclusion applies to damage to tyres and, therefore, losses of tyres due to theft is payable.

If the motor car is disabled as a result of damage covered by the Policy, the insurers bear a reasonable cost of protecting the car and removing it to the nearest repairs, as also of redelivery to the insured. The amount so borne by the insurers is limited to ₹ 150 in respect of any one accident.

Normally, repairs arising out of damage covered by the policy can be carried out only after they are authorised by the insurers. In terms of this section of comprehensive policy, the insured may authorise the repair to the car provided that:

(*a*) the estimated cost of such repair does not exceed ₹ 300;
(*b*) the insurers are furnished forthwith a detailed estimate of the cost; and
(*c*) the insured gives the insurers every assistance to ensure that such repair is necessary and that the charge is reasonable.

Section II

It provides for the cover in respect of liability to the third parties.

Section III

If any bodily injury is caused to the insured or to any occupant of the motor car by violent accidental, external and visible means, as the direct result of an accident to the motor car, and if the insured incur medical expenses for the treatment of such injury, the medical expenses reasonably incurred by the insured in this behalf are reimbursed to him, subject to a limit of ₹ 350 in respect of any accident. A notable feature of this provision is that insured car must meet an accident in order to attract the benefit.

General Exceptions

The insurer is not liable under the policy in respect of:

(*i*) any accident, loss, damage and liability caused, sustained or incurred outside the Geographical Area specified in the schedule of the policy, *i.e.*, India. On request it can be extended to Nepal, Sikkim and Bhutan.

(*ii*) Any claim arising out of any contractual liability. If, however, the liability arises independent of the contract, the claim is payable.

(*iii*) Any claim arising whilst the vehicle is being:

(*a*) used otherwise than in accordance with the limitations as to use specified in the schedule of the policy; or

(*b*) driven by any person other than a driver described in the schedule of the policy.

(*iv*) Any claim arising after any variation in or termination of the insured's interest in the vehicles.

(*v*) Any claim directly or indirectly arising from:

(*a*) Ionising, radiations or contamination by radio-activity from any nuclear waste from the combustion of nuclear fuel.

(*b*) Nuclear weapons material.

(*c*) Flood, typhoon, hurricane, volcanic eruption, earthquakes or other convulsions of nature.

(*d*) war, invasion, act of foreign enemies, hostilities or war-like operations, civil war, strike, riot, civil commotion, invasion, rebellion, military or usurped power.

(*e*) Driving of the car under the influence of intoxicating liquor or drugs.

(*vi*) This does not cover use for hire or reward or gaining, pace-making, reliability trial, speed testing, the carriage of goods (other than samples) in connection with any trade or business or use for any purpose in connection with motor trade.

Extra Benefits

The policy may be extended to cover the following extra-benefits. On payment of additional premium:

(*i*) Accidents to insured or any named person (not less than 16 not more than 65 years of age) other than a paid driver or cleaner. This provide for specified scale of benefits in the nature of personal accident cover.

(*ii*) Accidents to insured and wife. Benefits and limits are similar to (*i*) above. In the event of both the insured and his wife being in the same car at the time of an accident the benefits will apply to insured and his wife to the extent of 50% only.

(*iii*) Accidents to unnamed passenger other than insured and his paid driver or cleaner. The benefits and age limits are similar to (*i*) above.

(*iv*) The legal liabilities to employees of the insured who may be travelling in or driving the employer's car (other than paid drivers).

(*v*) Business use by fellow employers. The policy extends to include use by persons other than insured for the business of the insured's employer and to indemnify such person. The additional premium depends upon whether use of one named person or use by unnamed is desired.

(*vi*) Accident to soldiers/sailors/airmen employed as by officers in their private capacity.

(*vii*) Trailers. Trailers may not be insured separately and the cover on the trailers must correspond to the cover on the car.

(*viii*) Riot and strikes.

(*ix*) Earthquake (fire and damage).

(*x*) Flood, inundation, typhoon and hurricane.

(*xi*) Rugs, coats and luggage.

(*xii*) Legal liability of passengers for acts of negligence; and

(*xiii*) Reliability trials and rallies.

Commercial Vehicles

The following points of difference between this policy and private car policy comprehensive policy should be noted:

(*a*) Loss of or damage to the vehicle and its accessories whilst thereon is not covered.

(*i*) against the risk of frost.

(*ii*) if loss or damage is due to overloading or strain or by explosion of the boiler or the motor vehicle.

(*b*) Loss or damage to accessories whilst on the vehicle is covered against the risk of burglary, house-breaking or theft only if the vehicle is stolen at the same time.

(*c*) The insured can authorise repairs if estimated cost of repairs does not exceed ₹ 150 (against ₹ 300 in the case of Private Car).

(*d*) There is a compulsory excess for each and every claim in respect of goods carrying vehicles, taxis or private car type vehicles plying for public hire and public passenger service vehicles, buses and motorised rickshaws.

(*e*) Loss of or damage to tyre, lamps, bumpers, mudguards and Painting of vehicles is not covered except in case of total loss.

Application of Limit of Indemnity

It is provided that if out of an accident indemnity is available to more than one person the limit of-indemnity prescribed by the policy applied to the total of the amounts payable to all eligible persons and if the limit is less than the total of the amounts due, the insured will have priority, in indemnification. For example, if an indemnity of ₹ 40,000 is due to the insured and of ₹ 20,000 to some other person against a limit of ₹ 50,000 under the policy, the insured will be paid ₹ 40,000 first and only the balance of ₹ 10.000 will be paid to the other person.

Motorcycle

Under this policy following points should be noted:

(*i*) The cost of removal, etc., in one event of an accident is limited to ₹ 50;

(*ii*) The amount up to which the insured is authorised to repair is specified at ₹ 50; and

(*iii*) The polices covering motor scooters are made subject to an excess of ₹ 50 for each and every claim.

The liability in respect of death or bodily injury to any person being conveyed in or on the motor cycle is excluded. Such liability is, however, covered if the said person is being conveyed by reason of or in pursuance of a contract of employment in terms, and subject to, limitation of indemnity. Under this section the insured individual is indemnified whilst personally driving a motor cycle not belonging to him and not hired to him under a Hire Purchase System. The extension, however, is not available for policies issued in respect of auto-cycles or mechanically assisted pedal cycles.

Extra Benefits

The following extra benefits may be granted on payment of additional premium:

(*a*) increase in the limit of indemnity for liability to public risks can be effected;

(*b*) full liability under Workmen's Compensation Act, 1923, Indian Fatal Accidents Act or at Common Law for accidents to paid driver, cleaner or conductor can be covered on payment of extra annual premium per head of ₹ 5; and

(*c*) in the case of vehicles plying for hire—(*i*) legal liability for loss or damage to goods caused by accident whilst being conveyed on the insured vehicle can be covered; (*ii*) Fire risk whilst vehicle is garage can be covered.

Underwriting Considerations

Relating to the insured and driver. The insured himself persents a great hazard in Motor insurance; he is likely to be the principal driver, particularly in private cars. Besides he will have a good deal of influence in the selection of other drivers. If the insured is a firm, the underwriter may have to examine the policy of the proposed firm in the matter of selection of drivers.

The business or profession of the insured is another important consideration, because this would show how, where and to what extent the vehicle will be used.

The nationality of the proposer is an underwriting consideration because:

(*i*) Foreigners are not accustomed to the local road and traffic conditions;

(*ii*) It is not always possible to ascertain their (insurer) history and driving experience;

(*iii*) In the event of an accident, they may not be available when they are required as witnesses for their own defence; and

(*iv*) Language difficulties may make them unsatisfactory witnesses.

Age of the driver is also important as very young persons are prone to accident as well as very old persons. The physical condition of the driver should also be considered when underwriting the risk. All convictions for driving offences are also material facts and must be reported to the insurers. The underwriter may ignore a series of convictions for minor offences but may take serious note of a single conviction for a major and dangerous offence. Drunken drivers have always been posing a serious problems to the under writers.

After examining the proposal and assessing the risk, the underwriter will decide on anyone or more of the following lines:

(*i*) accept the risk at normal terms,

(*ii*) increase the premium,

(*iii*) impose a compulsory excess in respect of each and every loss, under one or more sections of the policy,

(*iv*) restrict the cover to third party, fire and theft risk only,

(*v*) restrict the cover to third party risk only,

(*vi*) restrict the cover to act liability only, and

(*vii*) decline the risk. The declinature is, however, resorted to in exceptional circumstances only.

Table 33.1 Progress of Motor Insurance

(In crores ₹)

	Motor				Miscellaneous			
	Premium Less Reinsure-ance	*Expenses of Manage-ment*	*Incurred Claims*	*Working Results Profit/ Loss(–)*	*Premium Less Reinsurs-ance*	*Expenses of Manage-ment*	*Incurred Claims*	*Working Results Profit/ Loss(–)*
1991-92								
GIC*					368.08	4.42	294.71	–41.71
National*					302.02	77.49	224.58	–25.84
New India	334.07	71.74	293.48	–57.00	193.85	51.09	123.85	13.48
Oriental	219.11	86.46	184.36	–17.84	117.25	–	68.46	–
United India	230.97	50.90	213.33	–55.05	146.27	31.25	104.23	–0.11
Total	784.15	209.10	691.17	–129.89	1127.47	164.25	815.83	41.82
1994-95								
GIC*					553.61	5.30	585.12	–198.94
National*					428.04	107.25	452.22	–155.56
New India	510.28	96.32	633.71	–268.64	293.99	77.87	815.65	39.60
Oriental	314.25	122.70	439.49	–190.44	178.50	–	106.92	–
United India	321.70	57.44	452.29	–209.87	211.52	43.79	157.75	4.29
Total	1146.23	276.46	1525.49	–668.95	1665.66	234.21	2117.66	–310.61

* Includes Motor Insurance and Miscellaneous Insurances.

Motor insurance business in India has suffered loss to the extent of ₹ 668.95 crores in 1994-95 whereas other insurance has experienced loss of ₹ 310.61 crores.

The Motor Third Party business of ₹ 2114 crore is 11 per cent of the total market. It grew by ₹ 34 crore only in 2004-05.

Table 33.2 Progress of Motor Insurance After IRDA

(₹ in crore)

	Company Performance All General Insurance		*Motor Business*		*Motor TP Business*		*Motor OD Business*	
	2003-04	*2004-05*	*2003-04*	*2004-05*	*2003-04*	*2004-05*	*2003-04*	*2004-05*
Earned Premium	1972	2122	916	1035	292	342	624	693
Net Incurred claims	1587 (80%)	1908 (90%)	981 (107%)	1238 (120%)	694 (238%)	832 (243%)	287 (46%)	406 (59%)
Net O/S claims	2552	2859	1984	2256	1825	2066	159	190

Source — IRDA Journal.

Table 33.3 Place of Motor Insurance in General Insurance

	Total Premium	*Motor Premium*	*Motor OD Premium*	*Motor TP Premium*
2003-04	16550	6460 (39%)	4377 (27%)	2080 (12%)
2004-05	18860	7500 (40%)	5384 (29%)	2114 (11%)

Motor insurance constitutes about 40% of total general insurance. Motor OD premium higher than motor TP premium whereas claims of TP insurance are very high *i.e.*, 243%.

MOTOR INSURANCE APPENDIX

मोटर वाहन बीमा कवर नोट-Motor Vehicle Insurance Cover Note

दि न्यू इन्डिया एश्योरन्स कम्नी लिमिटेड

The New India Assurance Co. Ltd.

पंजीकृत कार्यालय: न्यू इन्डिया एश्योरन्स बिल्डिंग, 87 महीत्मा गाँधी मार्ग, फोर्ट, मुंबई-400 001

Regd. & Head Office : New India Assurance Bldg., 87 M.G Road, Fort Mumbia - 400 001

कवर नोट सं0
Cover Not No.
KNP/ 42/B

ORIGINAL

नीचे दिए गये फार्म "52" में वर्णित बीमाकृत व्यक्ति द्वारा मोटर वाहन (वाहनों) के लिए बीमा करवाने को प्रस्ताव तथा........रू. बतौर प्रीमियम राशि का भुगतान करने पर कम्पनी के प्रचलित पॉलिसी फार्म की शर्तो (व नीचे दी गई विशेष शर्तो) के अन्तगर्त जोखिम का तब तक वहन किया गया समझ जायेगा जब तक कम्पनी लिखित सूचना द्वारा इस बीमे को समाप्त न कर दे। ऐसी स्थिति में उस/इन वाहन/वाहनों का बीमा समाप्त हो जाएगा और कम्पनी ने जितने समय तक इसके/इनके लिए जोखिम वहन किया है, उसके लिए प्रीमियम के आनुपातिक अंश को वसूल किया जाएगा जो अन्यथा देय होता।

The Insured described in form '52' referred to below having Proposed for Insurance in respect of the Motor Vehicle (s) described there in and having paid the sum of Rs...... ....as premium the risk is hereby held covered under the terms of the Company''s usual form of .... Policy applicable there to (subject to any Special conditions mentioned below) unless the cover be teminated by the company by notice in writing in which case the insurance will thereupon ceases and a proportionate part of the premium otherwise payable for such insurance shall be charged for the time the company had been on risk.

जारी करने वाला कार्यालय
Issuing Office

वाहन का मेक और रजिस्ट्रेशन Make & Registration No. of the Vehicle	निर्माण का वर्ष Year of Mfg.	धन क्षमता Cubic Capacity	वाहन का ग्रास वेट (भार वाहन) Gross Vehicle Weight (SVW) (Goods Carrying yehicle)	लाइसेन्स भार वाहन क्षमता (सवारी वाहन) Licensed Carrying Capacity (LCC) Passenger Carrying Vehicle	बीमाकृत घोषित मूल्य Insured's Declared Value (IDV) वाहन का मूल्य रू0 For Vehicle Rs	 ब्रिØी मूल्य बिना किसी वाहन सम्बन्धित उप साधनों का मूल्य For Accessories not included in Mfrs. listed selling price

1234566070708708,,

इंजन नं0 Engine No. ______________

चेसिस नं0 Chasis No ______________

फार्म 52 (भारत)/FORM 52 (INDIA)
मोटर वाहन नियम 1989 का नियम संख्या 142 (1) देखें
See Rule 412 (1) of Motor Vehicles Rules 1989

अतिरिक्त जोखिम यदि कोई हो / Additional Risks, If any..........
विशेष शर्तें / Special conditions

1. बीमित वाहन का रजिस्ट्रेशन फार्म और नं0 अथवा विवरण
   Registration mark and number or description of the vehicle insured

2. बीमाकृत व्यक्ति का नाम और पता Name and address of insured	
3. अधिनियम के प्रयोजन के लिए प्रभावी होने की तिथि Effective date and time of commencement of insurance for the purpose of this Act	समय / Time .... दिनांक / Date............ से / From..........
4. बीमा समाप्ति की तिथि Date of expiry of insurance	मध्य रात्रि / Mid Night on .... दिनांक / Date............ तक /To......................
5. वाहन चलाने के हकदार व्यक्ति या व्यक्तियों का वर्ग Persons of classes of persons entitled to drive	
6. उपयोग की सीमाएँ Any limitations as to use. of motor vehicle	
7. इस कदर नोट की विधिमान्यता की अवधि समाप्ति की दिनांक The period of validity of this cover note will expire on	

मैं/हम इसके द्वारा प्रमाणित करता हूँ करते है कि यह कवर नोट वाहन अधिनियम 1988 (XI) के प्रावधानों के अनुसार जारी किया गया है।
I/We here by certify that this Cover Note is issued in accordance with the provisions of Chapter XI of the Motor Vehicles Act 1988.

Office Code

In case of any Assistance
Please Contact:-
DEEP KACKER AM (D)
Mob. No. - 9415380197

कृते वि न्यू इन्डिया एश्योरन्स कम्पनी लिमिटेड
For The New India Assurance Co. Ltd.

प्राधिकृत बीमाकर्ता
Authorised Insures

मूल / Original

(किसी भी कारण से चैक अस्वीकृत होने पर जोखिम के लिए कम्पनी उत्तरदायी नही होगी)
(The Company will not be on risk in case of dishonored of cheque for any reason)

SHRIRAM
GENERAL INSURANCE
be insured... rest assured

Shriram General Insurance Co. Ltd.
(A joint venture with Sanlam, South Africa)
Corpt. Office :E-8, EPIP, RIICO Sitapura, Jaipur 302022 (Raj.)
Phone : +91-141-3220900/2/4, 3928400 ,Fax : +91-141-2770 692/3
Website : WWW.shriramgi.com, Toll free No. : 1800-180-7474, 1800-300-30000

Branch Name:__________
Branch Code:__________
IMD Code:__________
Sub IMD Code:__________

Cover Note No:__________

Motor Vehicle Cover Note

The insured described under form no."52" referred to below having proposed for insurance in respect of the Motor Vehicle(s) described therein and having paid the sam of Rs.__________as premium, the risk hereby held covered under the terms of the Company's usual form of ____________________policy applicable thereto (subject to any special condition mentioned below) unless the cover be terminated by the company by the notice in writing in which case the insurance will thereupon ceaseand a proportionate part of the premium otherwise payable for such Insurance shall be charged for the company had been at risk.

Registration Number	Registration Authority	Make	Model	Sub Model	Manuf. Year	Cubic Capacity

Licensed Carrying Capacity		Insured's' Declared Value	Electrical Accessories	Non-Electrical Accessories	CNG/LPG Kit	Total
Goods	Passenger					

Lease	Hire purchase	Hypothecation

Engine No:____________________

Chassis No:____________________Name of the Financier__________

Additional risk if any____________________

Special Conditios if any____________________

FORM 52
SEE RULE 142 (1) OF MOTOR VEHICLE RULES 1989

Policy is subject to exclusion of damages noted down by our authorised representative during their inspection

1. Name of the Insured:____________________
2. Address of Insured____________________
   City / Village__________Pin__________Tensil Taluk__________Distric__________State__________
3. Telephone No____________________Email:____________________
4. Period of Insurance (start time):__________A.M./P.M. of __________to__________
5. Person or classes of persons entilted to drive (see overleaf) dd mm yy dd mm yy
6. Date of Issue:____________________Time:____________________A.M/P.M.
7. Limitation as to use (see overleaf)
8. **The period of this Cover Note will expire on completion of 60 days from the date of issue.**
9. **THE COVER NOTE BECOMES VOID AB INTTION CASE OF DISHONOUR OF PREMIUM CHEQUE.**
10. **PREMIUM CALCULATION:**

Own Damage		B. Liability	
(i) Basic OD		(i) TP Premium	
(ii) Elec. Accessories		(ii) PA to Owner Driver	
(iii) Non-Elec. Accessories		(iii) L.L.to Paid driver Passenger Employee	
(iv)CNG/LPG Kit			
(v) Discount		(b) Total	
(vi) Loading		Net Premium__________ (a + b)	
(vii) NCB		S.T. __________	
(a) Total		Final Premium__________	

Payment Details:
CASH/ CHEQUE/ DD / Others (Strike out whichever is not applicable)
Cheque /DD No.__________
Cheque /DD Date.__________
Bank Name __________

Following Excess are over & above Compulsory Excess.

Additional Excess Rs.__________

Voluntary Excess: Rs__________

I/We hereby certify that this Cover Note is issued in accordance with the provisions of Chapter XI of the Motor Vehicles Act, 1988

I/We have been explained salient features of the policy and express conditions mentioned on the covernote in vernacular language. I agree to the terms and conditions of the same.

(Authorised Insurer Duly Constituted Attorney (s)

Signature of the Insured

PLEASE SEE OVERLEAF FOR CONDITIONS

PERSONS OR CLASSES OF PERSONS ENTITLED TO DRIVE

Any person including insured provided that a person driving holds an effective driving license at the time of accident and is not disqualified from holding or obtaining such a license.

Provided also that the person holding effective learner s license may also drive the vehicle and such a person satisfies requirements of Rule 3 of the Central Motor Vehicles Rules, 1989

LIMITATIONS AS TO USE

Passenger carrying vehicle

Used only for carriage of passengers in accordance with the permit (Contract Carriage or stage Carriage) issued within the meaning of the Motor Vehicles Act, 1988.

The policy does not cover.

1. Use for organized racing, pace making, reliability trials or speed testing.
2. Use whilst drawing a trailer except the towing (other than for reward) of any one disabled mechanically propelled vehicle.

For private car and motor cycle/scooter

Use only for social, domestic and pleasure purpose and insured's own business. The Policy does not cover use for hire or reward or for organized racing, pace making, reliability trials, speed testing, carriage of goods (other than samples) in connection with any trade or business or use for any purpose in connection with Motor trade.

For goods carrying Vehicles

Use only for carriage of goods within the meaning of the Motor Vehicles Act.

This Policy does not cover:

1. Use for organized racing, pace making, reliability trials or speed testing.
2. Use whilst drawing a trailer except the towing (other than for reward) of any one disabled mechanically propelled vehicle.
3. Use for carrying passengers in the vehicle except employees (other than the driver) not exceeding the number permitted in the registration document and coming under the purview of Workmen's Compensation Act 1923.

CLAIMS

1. In case of Claim, Please Call on Tool Free Nos. 1800-7474 or 1800-300-30000
2. Please ensure that information related to Policy Number, Estimated Loss/ Description, Date & Time of Accident, Place where Vehicle can be surveyed and your Contact Details are ready with you before you call on above mentioned Toll Free No.

PROHIBITION OF REBATES

The Insurance Act, 1938:

No person shall allow or offer to allow, either directly or indirectly, as an inducement to any person to take out or renew or continue an insurance in respect or any kind or risk relating to lives or property in India, any rebate of the whole or par... the commission payable or any rebate of the premium shown on the policy, nor shall any person taking out or renewing or continuing a policy accept any rebate, except such rebate as may be allowed in accordance with the published prospectuses or tables or the insurer.

ANY PERSON MAKING DEFAULT IN COMPLYING WITH THE PROVISIONS OF THIS SECTION SHALL BE PUNISHABLE WITHFINE WHICH MAY EXTEND TO RS. 500/- (RUPEES FIVE HUNDRED)

VERY IMPORTANT

अगर आपकी किसी समस्या का समाधान 15 दिनों के अन्दर न हो तो कृपया md@shriramgi.com पर मैनेजिंग डायरेक्टर को सूचित करें या अपना शिकायत पत्र प्रथम पृष्ठ पर दिये गये पते पर भेजें।

In case your complaint is not resolved within 15 days, you can inform Managing Director on md@shriramgi.com or sent your complaint letter to the address mentioned on 1st page

Regd. office : 5th Floor, "Greams Dugar', 149, Greams Road, Chennai-600006

THE NEW INDIA ASSURANCE CO. LTD.
DIVISIONAL OFFICE, VARANASI (420700)

ASSESSMENT AND CONSIST SHEET

DATE..........................

POLICY NO... FROM.......................TO......................

INSURED'S NAME..

VEHICLE NO.. MAKE..

CHASSIS NO... ENGINE NO.......................................

DATE OF LOSS.. DATE OF REGISTRATION.....................

PLACE OF ACCIDENT...TIME..........................

VEHICLE INSPECTED.......................................VEHICLE INSPECTED...

NAME OF DRIVER...

CAUSE & NATURE OF ACCIDENT...

....

....

AFTER INSPECTION THE DAMAGES OF THE VEHICLE AND COMPARING THE SAME WITH THE ESTIMATE. IT WAS DISCUSSED WITH THE INSURED/INSURED'S REPRESENTATIVE MR............... THE FINAL AMOUNT ASSESSED ON REPAIR BASIS FOR RS................................AS LABOUR PLUS PARTS AS MENTIONED BELOW —

1.
2.
3.
4.
5.
6.
7.
8.
9.
10.
11.
12.
13.
14.
15.
16.
17.
18.
19.
20.

LESS DEPRICIATION ....% ON PARTS AND LESS CLAUSE ....SALVAGE TO BE COLLECTED/ SALVAGE VALUE RS ....TO BE DEDUCTED.

THE ABOVE ASSESSMENT IS FULL AND FINAL WHICH IS ACCEPTABLE TO THE INSURED SUBJECT TO POLICY TERMS AND CONDITIONS. THERE WILL NOT BE ANY SUPPLEMENTARY CLAIM LODGED IN FUTURE FOR THIS ACCIDENT.

AUTHORITY LETTER OF THE INSURED IN FAVOUR OF THE AFORESAID PERSON AS INSURED'S REPRESENTATIVE IS ATTACHED HEREWITH.

SIGNATURE..

INSURED/INSURED'S REPRESENTATIVE ....

NAME..

....

ADDRESS

....

....

....

....

SIGNATURE.....................................

OFFICE...

NAME...

DESIGNATION...................................

DATE..

THE NEW INDIA ASSURANCE CO. LTD

DIVISONAL OFFICE, VARANASI (420700)

D. 58/12-A-1, SATYA SAMEER, SIGRA, VARANASI - 221010

SELF SURVEY BILL

1. NAME OF THE INSURED :

2. VEHICLE NO :

3. CLAIM NO :

4. COVERNOTE / POLICY NO :

5. PERIOD : FROM ....TO..............................

6. PLACE OF ACCIDENT :

7. DATE OF ACCIDENT :

8. DATE OF SURVEY :

9. CONVEYANCE CHARGED : ₹ ....

Signature :

Name :

S.R. No :

34

MISCELLANEOUS FORM OF INSURANCE

EMPLOYERS' LIABILITY INSURANCE

Introduction

The genesis of employers' liability insurance can be traced to the industrial development. It was, however, thought the employer had no more than ordinary duty of care to his employees. Hence an employee injured as a result of negligence on the part of his employer had just the same right of action against the employer for damage as any other citizen had. The employer's duty of care to his employees was to provide:

(*a*) a safe place of work;

(*b*) proper plant, tools, machinery and working implements and for their maintenance in good working order;

(*c*) a safe system of work with adequate warning to the employee of any danger of which he might not be aware; and

(*d*) competent and sober fellow employees.

It would appear that the duties of an employer were wide enough to encompass all situations in which an employee might be placed that would give him automatically a right of action against the employer and enable him to obtain damages.

The underwriting by insurers of employers' liability arising under the status or in common law is a comparatively later development. In India most employers' liability policies are issued in respect of their liability under the Fatal Accidents Act 1955, the Workmen's Compensation Act 1923 and common law. In India these are referred to as workmen's compensation policies.

The Fatal Accidents Act was nevertheless an inadequate measure, as it made no provision for the employees who were not killed but were maimed and totally or partially disabled. The Workmen's Compensation Act 1923 filled the gap and also made employers' liability more rigorous. Though the liability of employer under the Act for accidental injuries sustained by his workmen arising out of and in the course of employment is absolute, in certain circumstances employer is not liable. Section 3 of the Workmen's Compensation Act 1923 provides that the employer is not liable to pay compensation in respect of any injury not resulting in death caused by an accident which is directly attributable to—

1. the workmen having been at the time of injury under the influence of drink or drugs,
2. the wilful disobedience of the workmen to an order expressly given or a rule expressly framed, for the purpose of securing the safety of the workmen, or,
3. the wilful removal or disregard by the workman of any safetyguard or other device which he knew to have been provided for the purpose of securing the safety of the workman.

An employment injury which may be personal injury sustained or an occupational disease specified in the Workmen's Compensation Act contracted by a workman in the course of fulfilling his duties to his employer. An occupational disease peculiar to an employment which a person exposed to the rigours of that employment contracts.

Classification of Risk and Coverage

In India the business of Workmen's Compensation Insurance is governed and regulated as to underwriting coverage, proposal and policy forms and endorsements by the Workmen's Compensation Tariff. The tariff is administered by the Tariff Advisory Committee, which is a statutory body set up under Section 54 of the Insurance Act 1938. The tariff applies to all policies issued to employees to provide reimbursements of compensation to their employees in respect of accidents and occupational diseases. The tariff provides three forms of insurance, viz.—

Table 'A'

Table 'B'

Table 'C'

Whatever may be the form of cover issued, no policy is to be issued to cover liability in excess of that provided by the tariff forms of policies and endorsements unless specifically authorised and no policy is to be issued which does not include all employees (other than individuals employed on monthly wages exceeding ₹ 500) in the Insured's Service. The premium to be paid has to be calculated on the total wages of the employees, since the actual wages may not be available in advance, a provisional premium calculated on the estimate of the total wages is paid and at the expiry of the policy the actual premium is calculated on the actual total wages and the difference between the provisional and the actual premium is made good a further payment by the insured or a refund by the insurers as the case may be.

Policy Form

The Policy Form is prescribed by the tariff and all insurers have to use the form. The wording is the same for all the three **tables A, B and C except that when a table 'A' policy is to be issued**, the laws in respect of which the policy is issued are to be mentioned in the schedule in the space provided therefor viz. the Workmen's Compensation Act 1923 and subsequent amendments to the said Act prior to the date of the issue of the policy and the Fatal Accidents Act 1855.

Extensions to the Policy

The extensions granted are as follows:

(*i*) The tariff permits the inclusion of the risk of the insured in respect of the empolyees of contractors at a premium calculated at the tariff rate for the work contracted for;

(*ii*) Where the insured are themselves contractors to a certain principal, policy may be extended to include the vicarious liability of the principal.

(*iii*) Occasional domestic labour may be covered for common law (tortious) liability at an additional premium of 25% of the premium charged for the permanent servants. When no permanent servants, the charge for occasional domestic labour must be a minimum of ₹ 6.25 to cover legal liability only.

(*iv*) Table 'A' and 'C' policies may be extended on the following scale and provide for the payment of medical, surgical or hospital expenses (including cost of transport to hospitals) incurred by the insured.

Limit (Per case)	Additional Premium
₹ 50/	12½%
₹ 75/	15%
₹ 100/	17½%
₹ 250/	20%
₹ 500/	25%

The Proposal Form

An employer desirous of insuring himself against his liability arising under the Workmen's Compensation Act 1923, the Employer's Liability Act 1938, the Common Law and Fatal Accidents

Act, 1855, has to approach the insurer for this purpose. He has to fill in and submit a proposal form to the insurer. The particulars required in this form are the proposer's name, proposer's business, address, proposer's trade or occupation, particular hours of work, description of employees, estimated number of employees, estimated annual wages, salaries and other earnings, insurance cover required and other particulars regarding the nature of the work done in the employer's premises. The proposer has also to state whether any proposal or renewal of insurance of his liability was never declined (or withdrawn). Finally he has to sign the declaration to the effect that every information supplied in the proposal form is correct. Any concealment or misstatement of material facts will render the policy void.

Duration

The tariff makes it compulsory for all policies to be issued for 12 months. The exceptions are:

1. Policies which may be issued for a period in excess of 12 months where an additional odd period is required to make a policy renewable on a particular date to meet the convenience of the insured.
2. Policies which may be issued for a period less than 12 months in cases of specific contracts or work which will be completed in less than 12 months provided the policies are written for the full period involved.

HOUSEHOLDER'S INSURANCE POLICY

Brief Description

The Householder's Insurance Policy is a comprehensive shelter that protects your house and the various contents in it against a variety of risks. It is a single policy that takes care of a number of contingencies.

The policy is divided into 10 sections. Sec 1(B) and a minimum of any 2 other sections are compulsory. Section 1: Fire and Allied Perils. Section 2: Burglary. Section 3: All risks. Section 4: Plate Glass. Section 5: Breakdown of domestic appliances. Section 6: T.V. Set. Section 7: Pedal Cycles. Section 8 : Baggage Insurance. Section 9: Personal Accident. Section 10: Public Liability

Covered Risks

Buildings of class 'A' construction, Plate Glass, Breakdown of domestic appliances, TV Set, Pedal Cycles, Baggage Insurance, Personal Accident, Public Liability

History of Householder's Insurance Policy

The first homeowners policy *per se* in the United States was introduced in September 1950, but similar policies had existed in Great Britain and certain areas of the United States. In the late forties US insurance law was reformed and during this process multiple line statutes were written, allowing homeowners policies to become legal.

Prior to the 1950s, there were separate policies for the various perils that could affect a home. A homeowner would have had to purchase separate policies covering fire losses, theft, personal property, and the like. During the 1950s, policy forms were developed allowing the homeowner to purchase all the insurance they needed on one complete policy. However, these policies varied by insurance company, and were difficult to comprehend.

The need for standardization grew so great that a private company based in Jersey City, New Jersey, Insurance Services Office, also known as the ISO, was formed in 1971 to provide risk information and issued a simplified homeowners policy for resell to insurance companies. These policies have been amended over the years.

Types of Policies

Currently, the ISO has seven standardized homeowners insurance forms in general use:

HO1 – Basic Homeowner Policy

A basic policy form that provides coverage on a home against 11 listed perils; contents are generally included in this type of coverage, but must be explicitly enumerated. The perils include fire or lightning, windstorm or hail, vandalism or malicious mischief, theft, damage from vehicles and aircraft, explosion, riot or civil commotion, glass breakage, smoke, volcanic eruption, and personal liability. Exceptions include floods, earthquakes.

HO2 – Broad Homeowner Policy

A more advanced form that provided coverage on a home against 17 listed perils (including all 11 on the HO1). The coverage is usually a "named perils" policy, which lists the events that would be covered.

HO3 – All Risk Homeowner Policy

The typical, most comprehensive form used for single-family homes. The policy provides "all risk" coverage on the home with some perils excluded, such as earthquake and flood. Contents are covered on a named peril basis.

HO4 – Renter's Insurance

The "Tenants" form is for renters. It covers personal property against the same perils as the HO2.

HO5 – Premier Homeowner Policy

Covers the same as HO3 plus more

HO6 – Condominium Policy

The form for condominium owners.

HO8 – Older Houses

The "Modified Coverage" form is for the owner-occupied older home whose replacement cost far exceeds the property's market value.

Coverage Rates

According to a 1998 NAIC report, 83% of homes were covered by owner-occupied homeowners policies. Of these, 87% had the HO3 Special and 9% had the more expensive HO5 Comprehensive. Both of these policies are "all risks" or "open perils", meaning that they cover all perils except those specifically excluded. 3% were the HO2 Broad, which covers only specific named perils. Others include the HO1 Basic and the HO8 Modified, which is the most limited in its coverage. HO8, also known as older home insurance, is likely to pay only actual cash value for damages rather than replacement.

The remaining 13% of home insurance policies were covered by renter's or condominium insurance. Two-thirds of these had the HO4 Contents Broad form, also known as renter's insurance, which covers the contents of an apartment not specifically covered in the blanket policy written for the complex. This policy can also cover liabilities arising from accidents and intentional injuries for guests as well as passers-by up to 150' of the domicile. Common coverage areas are events such as lightning, riot, aircraft, explosion, vandalism, smoke, theft, windstorm or hail, falling objects, volcanic eruption, snow, sleet, and weight of ice. The remainder had the HO6 Unit-Owners policy, also known as a condominium insurance, which is designed for the owners of condos and includes coverage for that part of the building owned by the insured and for the property housed therein. Designed to span the gap between the coverage provided by the blanket policy written for the entire neighbourhood or building and the personal property inside the home. The liability coverage may cover incidents up to 150 feet from the insured property, all valuables within the home from theft, fire or water damage or other forms of loss. The Associations Bylaws determine the total amount of insurance necessary.

In addition, about 2.4% of homes were covered by a dwelling fire policy, which covers property damage to a structure and is typically sold to non-commerical owners of rented houses. It may also cover the owner's personal property (such as appliances and furnishings). The owner's liability is generally extended from their own primary home insurance, and does not comprise part of the Dwelling Fire policy.

Typically consumers can save money by purchasing their insurance directly from a company rather than through an agent, but there are not many companies which sell home insurance directly.

Householders Insurance Policy

Householders Insurance Policy is a comprehensive package policy that protects householders from a wide gamut of potential risks and perils. It covers almost all your personal belongings and household possessions, including furniture, domestic equipment, electrical appliances, furnishing, food and drink, some valuables and cash up to a certain limit, against loss or damage. Applicants can either choose a comprehensive cover where all the 10 sections will get covered or the specific sections in which they want coverage. Public sector companies require one to take the coverage of a minimum of three sections, of which the first two sections, namely fire coverage and burglary, are mandatory.

In the present times, the householder's insurance policy available in the market features 'new for old' cover. In such a case, the policyholder gets full cost of replacing an old item with a new one if it is damaged or stolen. However, some items, for example clothing and bedding, are not usually covered on a 'new for old' basis. There are some householder's insurance policies that provide lump sum money in case the applicant or his/her spouse dies as a result of a fire, theft, or an accident in the home. Household contents insurance policies do not usually cover personal possessions taken out of the home. However, by paying an extra sum, applicants might be able to get cover for such items as well.

Formalities

The householder's insurance policy, being a package policy, requires only one proposal form to be completed instead of separate proposal forms for individual policies, thus doing away with the tedious procedure associated with individual policies. Applicants are required to submit the completed proposal form giving full details of the property to be insured, full value of jewelry and individual values of each item to be given. In case the applicant opts for more number of sections, a discount in the premium is allowed for non-tariff covers. Know more about the contents of householder's insurance policy and how to make the right choice.

Content of Householder's Insurance Policy

The householder's package policy includes 10 sections. Apart from the below mentioned section, the policy also covers perils, such as floods, cyclone, lightning, explosion, riots, strikes, damage to electrical & electronic equipment due to breakdowns/short circuits and even accidental injury to your family members or even your driver/maid-servant.

- Fire Insurance of the building and household contents
- Burglary, housebreaking, larceny and theft
- All Risks Insurance for jewelry, ornaments and other valuables
- Domestic Appliances (electrical and mechanical failures)
- TV, VCR & VCP and music systems
- Plate Glass Insurance
- Personal baggage while on travel
- Pedal cycle Insurance
- Personal accident
- Third Party Liability

Choosing Household Contents Insurance

At the time of getting household insurance, you need to work out how much insurance you actually need/require. Calculate the cost of replacing the cost of all your possessions in a crisis-situation.

Instead of signing the deal with the first insurer, the best bet would be to get quotes from several and then evaluate the best deal.

- Know in detail what each policy covers and its exclusions, if any.
- What is the price of the policy? Is there any discount being offered? Is it worth that amount of premium you would have to pay in a specific period?
- The premium you pay would be dependent on your age, the place you live in, how much cover you want and the value of your possessions. The more valuable your possessions are, the more premium you would have to pay for your policy.
- Look out for additional clauses that mention restriction or additional conditions on your cover.
- Find out the no-claim bonus, for every year you make no claim against your policy. Also, calculate the amount by which the no-claims bonus would be reduced if you made a claim.

Employees State Insurance Act, 1948

The scheme envisaged under the Act applies compulsorily to all persons working in factories using power and employing twenty or more persons but seasonal factories are excluded; so also the dependents of workers in perennial factories. The scheme is applicable only to Industrial workers and excludes agricultural labourers. The scheme provides for five-fold benefits, namely, medical, sickness, maternity, disablement and dependents. Medical treatment is provided free of charges to the sick insured persons; and this medical cost is provided through the panel system of the doctors. Under this system, panel of approved doctors is drawn up and the insured person is given the choice to select his own doctor from among the list. The insured is qualified to receive benefit during the benefit period if he has paid at least a minimum number of twelve weekly payments in the course of sixteen weeks or two-thirds of the number of weeks in the 'Contribution period'. The amount of cash sickness benefit is about half the daily wage of the insured person. He can claim it for a maximum of fifty-six days in any period of 365 days.

For the administration of Employees State Insurance Scheme, a statutory corporation known as the Employees State Insurance Corporation has been established. The scheme is contributory, the contributions to be paid by both the employer and employees. The amounts of compensation are on a scale more liberal than those payable under the Workmen's Compensation Act. The Employees State Insurance Act comes into force at the very region where it is interested to extend by a notification by the Government of India.

In the case of risk coming under the purview of the Employees' State Insurance Act 1948 it is permissible under the tariff to issue separate table 'B' or 'C' 'Workmen's Compensation Policies covering those members of staff who are not 'employees' within the meaning of the Act provided all such employees (other than individuals employed on monthly wages exceeding ₹ 500) in the insured's service are included hereunder.

Fidelity Guarantee Insurance

Fidelity Guarantee is one of the main classes of insurance written in the accident department. As a handmaid of business and commerce, it is an essential insurance protection, for it seeks to indemnify the employer against direct pecuniary loss that he may sustain through acts of fraud or dishonesty by an employee in the course of his employment. The basis for a fidelity guarantee originates from an employer and employee or a fiduciary relationship where confidence or trust reposed plays a crucial part.

Broadly, fidelity guarantee business can be divided into the following sections:

(*i*) Commercial Fidelity Guarantees,

(*ii*) Court Bonds, and

(*iii*) Government Bonds.

Types of Policy

The following types of policy are in general demand:

(*a*) Individual Policy

This type of policy is used where only one individual is to be guaranteed.

(*b*) Collective Policy

Where the entire staff or a number of selected individuals are to be covered, a collective policy is issued.

(*c*) Floating Policy or Floater

This is an extension to the collective form of contract in which the names and duties of the individuals to be covered are inserted in schedule but instead of individuals amounts of guarantee a specified sum of guarantee is floated on the whole group.

(*d*) Positions Policy

This is similar to a collective policy with the difference that instead of using names, the position is guaranteed for a specified amount so that a change in the person holding the position does not affect the cover. It is noted to be that the liability of the insurers in respect of each position remains limited to the amount guaranteed for, irrespective of the number of persons acting in that position.

(*e*) Blanket Policy

This policy covers the entire staff without showing names or positions. No enquiries about the employees are made by the insurers. Such policies are only suitable for an employer with a large staff and the organisation to make adequate enquiries into the antecedents of employees.

(*f*) Excess Floating Policy

This is a combination of collective policy and a floating policy.

Proposal Form (Employer's Form)

Several different types of proposal form are in use for the various classes of fidelity guarantee. For commercial guarantees the employer has to complete an employer's statement. This statement may be likened to the proposal form as it forms the basis of the contract between employer and the insurers.

Commercial Fidelity Guarantee

Application Form

The applicant (the person to be guaranteed) has to fill in an application form which requires in addition to his name, age and address the name, address and business activities of the employer, the position to be covered by the guarantee, the salary or other remuneration to be received, details of past guarantees as also details of the applicant's status (single or married) and dependents, if any. The extent of debts, private income, whether or not the applicant has ever been bankrupt or insolvent, details of past employment, whether he is householder and owns furniture and details of his life assurance are also required.

Private Referee's Form

At one time great significance was attached to private referees' forms. This is a form which may be sent to persons whose names and addresses have been supplied by the applicant.

Previous Employers' Form

A reference for the applicant from all the employers for the previous five years is an important underwriting tool to the insurers. This form is only for the proof of applicant's integrity and honesty.

Collective Proposals

For collective floating and blanket policies, individual applicants' forms are dispensed with. The employer has to set out in a statement all such particulars relating to the employees to be covered as are required for individual policies.

Underwriting Considerations

The main considerations are employers' style of establishment, methods of selection of employees, working conditions generally emoluments and benefits in relation to responsibilities and other organisation and how far the system of check and control measures are effective and what supervision is exercised over the employees. To improve the risk, the insurers may make suggestions to the employer for tightening up the system of check. But where the system is fundamentally unsatisfactory no piecemeal improvement is of any avail. An entirely new system may have to be agreed upon.

Risks Covered

The perils covered are variously described under different insurers, but the risk of pecuniary loss to the employer by reason of breach of trust and misuse of office is uniform. The normal wording runs as follows:

If the employee in the course of the duties, specified commits any act or acts of forgery or of embezzlement, larceny and fraudulent conversion of moneys or goods of the insured the insurer will make good to the Insured any loss which the insured shall thereby directly sustain up to an amount not exceeding the amount insured.

Following points should be noted in connection with Risk:

(*i*) The cover granted is against a direct pecuniary loss and not a consequential one;

(*ii*) The pecuniary loss should be sustained by the insured in respect of the moneys or goods; and

(*iii*) The act should be committed in the course of the duties specified.

Period of Discovery

Unlike other classes of business, fidelity guarantee policies stipulate time limit for discovery of losses. This is also because the loss can occur over a long period without discovery. Investigation of such losses would be troublesome and recoveries may become legally and practically difficult. The customary time limit provided is that the act or acts insured against should be discovered not later than six months after the resignation, dismissal, retirement or death of the employees or not later than three months after the termination of the policy. Whichever be the earlier the time limit may be increased up to 12 months, if the insurers agree to it.

Some of the important conditions are considered here viz.—Application of control measures, notice of claim, prosecution condition, subrogation and contribution.

Hazardous Risks

Not all risks proposed for insurance are accepted at normal terms; certain risks are considered not good for insurance because of the very high degree of hazard associated therewith and the high incidence of claims. A representative list of such risks is given below:

(*i*) Collection agents whose financial limits are disproportionately high compared to their remuneration and the security deposit given by them;

(*ii*) Jewellery Travellers;

(*iii*) Cashiers in eating houses, cinema houses and other places of entertainment;

(*iv*) Estate Agents;

(*v*) Treasurers of friendly societies of Associations;

(*vi*) Employees of bullion merchants, antiques, furs and other valuables.

Service Security Policies

Another offshoot of the fidelity guarantee business is guaranteeing a minimum period of service an employee has agreed to render an employer in return for the training imparted to him by the employer in enabling the employee to acquire qualifications. In the event of failure by the employee to honour his commitment, the policy has to pay the amount guaranteed. Here again it is doubtful, whether this type of policy falls within the province of fidelity guarantee though some insurers are inclined to treat breach of minimum service conditions a default and write the business in the fidelity guarantee department.

Rating of Fidelity

Guarantee Business premium under individual and collective policies is charged as a rate per cent of the amount guaranteed subject to a minimum premium. The rate per cent varies from risk to risk depending upon the merits of each case. Generally speaking it ranges from 0.25% to 1.50%. The premium for a floating policy comprises a percentage charge and a per capita charge. The percentage charge is applied on the amount guaranteed and the per capita charge on the number of employees to be guaranteed. For example, if a floating policy has to be issued covering 200 employees for an amount of ₹ 2,00,000 and the percentage charge is, say, 1%, and per capita charge of ₹ 5, the premium payable would be ₹ 3,000 arrived at as shown below:

Percentage charge @ 1% of ₹ 2,00,000	₹ 2,000
Per capita charge @ ₹ 5 for 200 persons	
(200 × 5)	₹ 1,000
Total	₹ 3,000

A minimum premium is always insisted upon because the expenses accruing of proposal, issue of policy, stationery, cost etc., would be the same whether the cover is for ₹ 1,000 or ₹ 1,00,000.

Extensions under Fidelity Guarantee Policies

It is not unusual for employers to ask for extending the conventional Policy to cover negligence or lack of care on the part of the employee, government departments, the Posts and Telegraphs Directorate Railways and many. Public Sector institutions, as a rule, demand such extension. Since the terms of negligence and lack of care do not admit of precise definitions it is not a safe underwriting proposition to cover them. Nevertheless, some insurers do cover such risks.

Administration Bonds

The appointment of the administrator is made by the Court by the grant of letters of administration spelling out the duties and obligations of the administrator.

The amount of bond is stipulated by the court making the appointment and it depends upon the value of both the real and the personal estate of the deceased. The administrator may be an individual or a corporate body but whoever he is, he would be thoroughly screened by the court before making the appointment. All the same insured who have to be satisfied about the bona fides of the applicant for the bond have to make exhaustive enquiries before accepting the proposal.

Unlike a Commercial Fidelity Guarantee Policy, an administration bond is a special contract to be executed under seal and it attracts stamp duty higher than the ordinary policy. The stamp duty varies from state to state depending on the rules framed under the Stamp Act. An administration bond provides for payment up to the amount guaranteed as a Penalty on demand and hence considerations of utmost good faith, disclosure of material facts etc. would not arise. Only in the event of fraud, the insurers can raise a plea of no liability before the court, but the onus of proof that the bond was obtained fraudulently rests on the insurers.

Difference Between Commercial Guarantee & Court Bonds

1. Commercial guarantees are simple contracts, whereas court bonds are special contracts executed under seal.

2. The proposal made by the employer is the basis of a commercial guarantee and it is deemed to be incorporated in the policy and hence any misrepresentation or inaccuracy in the proposal will make the policy void or voidable. In the court bonds the proposer does not form part of the contract and hence the contract is not affected even if the proposal contains materially inaccurate particulars.
3. The commercial guarantee is subject to conditions the breach of which may render the policy void or voidable, but no such conditions are incorporated in court bond.
4. Commercial guarantees are normal annual contracts which the insurers may renew at their option. But court bonds are automatically renewable, unless the insurers give sufficient notice to the court of their intention not to renew the bond.
5. In a court bond the person guaranteed is a party to the contract, whereas in commercial guarantee he is not.
6. In order to obtain a payment under a commercial guarantee the insured has to prove to the satisfaction of the insurers that he has suffered a pecuniary loss arising out of the insured contigencies. In a court bond a demand from the appropriate authority of the amount guaranteed for a failure in the discharge of duties or obligations by the person guaranteed is sufficient.
7. Commercial guarantees are stamped with an ordinary insurance stamp, while court bonds have to be stamped in accordance with the stamp duty.
8. The cover under a commercial guarantee is restricted in scope as compared with that under a court bond.
9. Commercial guarantees prescribe time limits within which the insured has to intimate defaults to the insurers. Court bonds are not subject to this restriction of time limit.

Government Bonds

Government bonds are like court bonds. They can be classified in two parts viz. custom bonds and excise bonds.

Custom bonds are to be executed by importers in favour of the controller of imports and exports agreeing, inter alia, to perform the conditions stipulated in the import trade control regulations. Excise bonds are to be executed by manufacturer in the country in respect of finished products assembled or produced in the company which are dutiable. The excise is to be paid to the Excise Department in lieu of which a bond may be executed. Manufacturers of alcohol, sugar, textiles, automobiles etc. are the categories of persons required to execute the bond.

Liquidator's and Recovership Bond

Estates which are under dispute and referred to the court for adjudication are temporarily placed under the care of a receiver during the pendency of the case. The receiver has to administer the estate and render proper accounting of the estate when under his care to the court. A receiver may also be appointed to administer the estate of a minor who is placed under the court of wards till he attains majority or of a person who is pronounced mentally incapable.

Liquidators are appointed by the court to deal with the estates of persons who filed insolvency petitions before the court or are declared insolvent by the courts. Unlike the receivers, the liquidators have to meet the claims of the insolvent's creditors and realise amounts due to the insolvent's estate from his debtors. The liquidator has to produce a bond guaranteeing his honest and faithful accounting of the estate.

Other Classes of Accident Insurance

Accident department also deals with some other types of insurance:.

PEDAL CYCLES INSURANCE

The cover is generally granted in respect of:

(*a*) Loss of or damage to the Pedal Cycle described in the schedule of the Policy by fire, lightning, explosion, burglary, housebreaking, theft or accidental external means. The loss or damage to the Pedal Cycle by accidental external means is subject to an excess of ₹ 10 in respect of each claim.

(*b*) Insured's legal liability for bodily injury to the public and for damage to the property of the public limit of ₹ 15,000 in all limit may be increased.

The premium rates depend on the cover desired by the insurance (*i.e.*, whether comprehensive or third party liability only) and the limit of indemnity selected by the insured in respect of third party cover. Some insurers grant a discount of, say, 10% if more than two cycles are insured under a single policy.

PLATE GLASS INSURANCE

The policy provides cover against the breakage of the plate glasses fixed to display windows or showcases of commercial establishments by any reason whatever, except those that are specifically excluded by the policy. Breakage normally excluded from the policy are by reason of:

(*i*) Fire and explosion,

(*ii*) Typhoon, flood, hurricane, volcanic eruption, earthquake or other convulsions of nature; and

(*iii*) Fight, strikes, war and kindred risks (riot and strike risks may be covered on payment of additional premium).

Unless specifically stated in the Schedule of the Policy, glass means plain glass and does not include any embossing, silvering, lettering or ornamental work. Damage to frames and the cost of removal or replacement of any fittings or fixtures necessitated for replacing the broken glass are not paid for under the policy.

The rate of premium depends on the type of glass, situation, previous experience and neighbourhood. The rate ranges from 5% to 10% of the value of the glass.

Missing Documents Indemnity

Documents like share certificates, bank deposit receipts, life insurance policies, etc., sometimes get lost or misplaced and consequently the owners of these documents may have to apply for the issue of duplicate documents. Since there is no guarantee that the original documents have perished or they have not fallen into wrong hands who may misuse them, there is element of risk in the issue of duplicate documents. The authorities concerned, therefore, ask for an indemnity from an insurance company before they issue duplicate documents. The indemnity issued by insurers seeks to indemnify the authority issuing the duplicate documents or paying any sums under the missing documents against any loss that it might sustain as a result of its having issued a duplicate document or having made any payment under the missing document. Insurers, while granting such an indemnity, almost always obtain a counter-indemnity in order to safeguard their interests.

There are no standard premium rates for this indemnity, because the risk varies from case to case.

Neon Sign Insurance

Neon Sign Insurance covers loss or damage to the neon sign installation by accidental external means or fire, lightning, external explosion and theft. The loss or damage includes burning out of any bulbs/tubes, repair, clearing, removal or erection, overruning, overheating or strain atmospheric conditions, natural risks, war and kindred perils and consequential loss. Strikes, riot, curl common are covered on extra premium

Warranties. The neon sign must be examined and inspected at regular interval within six months by a qualified electrician and engineer. It should be properly and adequately fastened and attached to its framework. The foundation of the structure should be adequately strong and properly attached to the ground or floor and safety measures should be adopted for the prevention of loss or damage occurring as a result of the collapse of the sign. The physical characteristics of the property on which the sign is erected or attached and the features of the surroundings are important factors for consideration of insurance. Age, height, building built, territory prone to windstorms with high velocity winds blowing during certain seasons. Third party liability is also covered on extra premium.

Neon Sign/Glow Sign Insurance

The Neon Sign Insurance Policy General Insurance is especially suitable for those having business or slow rooms or shopping centres, hotels, theatres etc. where damage of neon sign or hoardings to insured party is covered for. The neon sign Insurance policy from General Insurance is a **yearly** and it is applicable to all types of accidental damage or breakage to neon or hoardings of the corporate establishment. The coverage includes the estimated cost of damage.

Neon Sign Insurance is being basically formulated to provide cover to the damage/losse that occurs due to neon sign installation.

As per the terms and conditions of the insurance policy the insured neon sign must be properly inspected and examined at regular interval of **6 months** by some professional electricals engineer or any electrician.

The Company General Insurance may just restore or repair the neon/glow sign instead of paying in cash. This policy is being basically formulated to provide cover to damage/loss that occurs due to neon sign installation.

Exclusions of Coverage

- Damage and destruction due to terrorism or nuclear threats.
- Damage due to repairing or changing.
- Damage if the sign is not properly or securely fixed or is in the process of fixing.
- Scraping or defacement or breakage of lettering on the glow/neon sign without damage of the entire glow/neon sign.
- Damage to property as a result of damage to neon/glow/hoarding.
- Repair, cleaning, wear and tear, erection or removal, depreciation or deterioration, overheating or strain, overrunning, fusing or burning from short circuit or mechanicaly breakdown natural risk or war and kindred risk, atmospheric conditions and any other consequential losses.

Risk Coverage

Neon Sign Insurance provides covers damage/losses such as lightning, fire, external explosion, theft and other means of external accidents that occur due to the neon sign installation.

There are **certain criteria** that the Insurer must fulfil —

- The insurer has to ensure that the property is safe against accidents.
- Upon occurrence of any (excluded items) event the insurer has to inform the company in writing with the copy of the policy certificate.

The insurer must observe the terms and conditions that are specified in the policy.

Neon sign advertisements are well known form of advertising and therefore it occupies a very important place. These signs are located in crowded public places so as to get the attention of the people. As a result of this the neon signs are very much vulnerable to loss. The neon signs are also an important fixed asset of the advertising agencies and the assets need to be covered with reliable insurance policy.

Scope of insurance has been classified in two sections—

- Cover the losses regarding the damage to a neon sign by means of any external accident, vicious act or damage caused by fire or explosion.
- Losses that are incurred due to legal liability.

Like other general insurance it has one year validity. This policy is helpful in advertising business.

AVIATION INSURANCE

This class of insurance has been mainly because of the steep increase in the values of aircraft and the consequent phenomenal increase in the limits of indemnity under third party and other legal liability covers. It may be interesting to note here that the Jumbo Jets which are being operated by Air India are covered for a sum of ₹ 18,75,00,000 each and the third party legal liability and passenger legal liability that may be incurred by Air India out of the operation of this aircraft are covered for a combined limit of ₹ 75,00,00,000. Gross direct premium collected by General Insurance Corporation of India amounted to ₹ 119.51 crores during 1994-95. The overall operations have given a profit of ₹ 8.99 crores in that year.

Flights operated on scheduled routes by recognised airlines as also chartered flights are covered. The rate of premium for chartered flights is higher because of the greater hazard involved.

Aircraft Comprehensive Policy

The policy is divided into three sections, viz.—

(*i*) loss of or damage to aircraft;
(*ii*) third party legal liability; and
(*iii*) legal liability to passengers.

(*i*) Loss of or Damage to Aircraft

The indemnity is provided for loss of or damage to the aircraft (also known as aircraft hull, *i.e.*, the body of the aircraft and its component parts) by any cause whatever except those that are specifically excluded by the policy. The cover is also granted in respect of standard component parts (of the aircraft) temporarily detached in connection with overhaul or repair while in the custody or control of the insured. The cover is operative whilst the aircraft is in flight or is taxiing or is on the ground or is moored.

Wear and tear and gradual deterioration are excluded. The losses or damage arising from mechanical, structural or electrical breakdown or failure are excluded, but if the loss or damage is caused by fire, explosion or impact of the aircraft with an external object, the said loss or damage is payable even though the fire, explosion or impact might have been caused by the breakdown or failure referred to above.

In addition to the actual cost of repairs, the following are also payable in the event of valid claim:

(*a*) The reasonable expenses incurred by the insured with the written consent of the insurers in respect of:
   (*i*) maintenance of watch on the damaged aircraft and safeguarding it from further loss or damage;
   (*ii*) transportation of the necessary materials, parts and/or technical personnel to the site of the accident;
   (*iii*) transportation of aircraft from the site of the accident to the repairers.

(*b*) Such proportion of the cost of obtaining a new certificate of Airworthiness as shall apply to the period from the date of accident to the date of expiry of the current certificate of Airworthiness.

The rate of the premium varies with the value of the aircraft, and has a bearing on the type of aircraft. The premium, in respect of low valued aircraft like 'Pushpak' which are valued around ₹ 20,000 is charged at a high rate as 15%. The rate of premium charged for Jumbo Jets of Air India which are insured for as high as ₹ 18,75,00,000 is about 2.5% only.

(*ii*) Third Party Legal Liability

Insurers indemnify the insured or any member of the operative crew of the aircraft acting in the course of their duties with the insured, against all sums which they may become legally liable to in respect of death, sickness or disease, and bodily injury sustained by any person and caused by an accident arising out of the ownership, maintenance or use of the aircraft. There are ordinarily two limits under third party liability: a limit per accident and a limit per policy year. Under this section of the aircraft comprehensive policy, however, limit per accident is the only limit that is specified. In other words, the liability of the insurers per policy year is unlimited. The limit of indemnity depends on the type of aircraft to be covered and the route over which it is to be flown.

The following are not treated as third parties for the purpose of this section of the policy:

(*i*) any member of the insured's household or family;

(*ii*) any sub-contractor whilst such person is engaged in his duties as such or any other person claiming by virtue of any contract the insured;

(*iii*) any passenger whilst entering into, being carried in or alighting from the aircraft; and

(*iv*) any member of the crew of the aircraft or any person working in or about the aircraft.

(*iii*) Passenger Legal Liability

Insurers indemnify the insured or any member of the operative crew of the aircraft acting in the course of his duties with insured in respect of all sums which insured or any such member of crew shall become legally liable to pay as compensation in respect of:

1. death, personal injury, sickness or diseases caused to any passenger by an occurrence arising out of the ownership, maintenance or use of such aircraft whilst such passenger is entering into, being carried in or alighting from the aircraft;
2. loss of or damage to passenger's baggage and personal effects whether registered or personally retained by the passengers whilst in the course of carriage by the insured.

The insurers are not liable in respect of death, personal injury, sickness or disease, damage or loss caused to or sustained by any member of the insured's household or family, any sub-contractor of the insured or any agent or servant of the insured or of any such sub-contractor whilst such person is engaged in his duties as such.

General Exceptions

The policy will not pay under both the sections, hull and liability, in respect of bodily injury, disease, loss, damage or liability under the following contingencies:

(*i*) Whilst the aircraft is being used for any illegal purpose or for the purpose other than that stated in the policy or whilst outside the geographical limit specified in the policy.

(*ii*) Whilst the aircraft is being piloted by a person other than the one specified in the policy.

(*iii*) Whilst the aircraft is being flown at night (*i.e.*, one hour after sunset and one hour before sunrise) unless due to force carriage.

(*iv*) Whilst the aircraft is being transported.

(*v*) Whilst the aircraft is using unlicensed landing areas unless due to force major use.

(*vi*) Due to or arising out of the use of the aircraft for racing, speed trials, acrobatics, etc.

(*vii*) Contractual liability other than that assumed by the insured under an approved contract of carriage.

(*viii*) War and allied risks including hijacking and riot, strikes and civil commotion.

(*ix*) Whilst the total number of passengers carried exceeds the seating capacity.

The exception relating to night flying is normally removed without charging extra-premium since most of the modern aircraft are filled night-flying equipment.

Freight Liability Policy

In addition to the passengers and the crew, an aircraft carries passengers' baggage, cargo and mail. The airline operating the aircraft is, therefore, liable if the baggage, cargo or mail is lost or damaged. The liability for the passengers' baggage is dealt with under the aircraft comprehensive policy. The freight liability policy deals with the cargo carried on the aircraft. In terms of the provisions of this policy, the insurers indemnify the insured against all sums which the insured may become legally liable to pay to the owners of cargo as a result of loss or damage to cargo or delay in delivery of the cargo or the mishandling of the cargo. The limits of indemnity that appears in the freight liability policy range from ₹ 1 lakh to ₹ 25 lakhs for any one accident.

Airmail Liability Policy

This is similar to freight liability policy, except that this policy provides cover per liability in respect of mail carried on the aircraft. The limits of the liability that appear in the airmail liability policy range from ₹ 1 lakh to ₹ 5 lakhs.

Personal Accident Policy for Crew Members

The crew members can be granted personal accident insurance cover under this policy. Pilots, flight navigators, radio officers, air-hostesses, etc., are covered. The benefits are more or less similar to those granted under the personal accident insurance policies.

LIVESTOCK INSURANCE

Livestock insurance refers mainly to the insurance of horses and cattle. Since cattle insurance is discussed later in this section, we shall confine our discussion here to the insurance of horses alone.

A proposal form together with a report from a qualified veterinary surgeon on the form drawn up by the insurers is always insisted upon to minimise the difficulty of identification; each horse must be adequately described giving colour, all natural markings and age. All horses of a particular type owned by the proposer must be insured, so as to eliminate the possibility of the proposer making a selection against the insurers. The policy provides indemnity against the loses of a horse by death resulting either from accident or a disease specified in the policy, including the destruction of the animal on human grounds arising from an accident or disease.

Exclusions

Death of the animal, arising out of the following, are excluded:

1. War and allied risks, strikes, riot and civil commotion;
2. Slaughter of the animal without prior consent of the insurers;
3. Fire, lightning, seagoing transit, surgical operations, breeding and loss occasioned by the animal becoming unfit or incapable of fulfilling the functions for which it is kept or employed.

CATTLE INSURANCE

This insurance provides cover against death of animals, like bulls, buffaloes, cows and heifers, arising as a result of accident, disease, parturition or pregnant condition, as the case may be. The insurance is arranged on a sort of the excess basis, and provides for payment of an amount in excess of a certain other amount which is known as first loss. The Policy excludes, inter alia, destruction in compliance with any statute or orders of any government or local authority, or because of unfitness or incapacity from fulfilling duties for which the animal is kept. Any death arising out of castration or other surgical operation is also excluded. The number of animals covered by cattle insurance in India has increased from 2.10 lakhs in 1976 to 43.72 lakhs in 1 980, 160.79 lakhs in 1985 and 256.22 lakhs in 1988-89.

Pet Insurance

Pet insurance is a cover for financial losses suffered by a policyholder due to unexpected emergencies in his/her pet's life. This insurance covers medical expenses that you may need to bear due to your pet's illness, allergy or accident. However, the insurance policy does not pay for routine or preventative treatment.

This policy also provides cover for kennel fees in case you are hospitalized. A dog insurance policy can help you cover losses to a third party in case your pet has destroyed their property.

Pet Insurance : Types of Coverage

One can select different types of pet insurance policies, based on individual needs, pets and budgets. The following are the various types of pet insurance policies.

(1) Lifetime Cover:

This policy covers expenses related to a pet contracting any long term or chronic illness. The illnesses covered in this policy include arthritis, eczema or any other sickness that requires your pet to be treated by a vet for a long period of time. Under this type of policy a policyholder is entitled to a specific sum of money every year. This maximum limit can be reset when the policy is renewed. This cover is especially available for pet insurance bought for dogs and cats.

(2) Time-Limited Cover:

Through this cover, pet owners receive financial protection for a specific period after a pet suffers an injury or contracts any disease that requires him/her to be treated by a vet. This cover is usually cheaper than the lifetime cover and is extremely popular among people who own crossbreed cats and are worried about incurring high treatment costs.

(3) Money-Limit Cover:

Through this cover, pet owners can receive monetary benefit for every condition that falls under the purview of pet insurance coverage. There is no time limit and a policyholder can claim for as long the money limit is not reached. This cover is generally costlier than the lifetime cover, but cheaper than the time-limited cover.

Pet insurance plans can cover such eventualities as your pet having an accident, sickness, compensation for having to cancel your holiday, money for advertising or to pay a reward if your pet is lost or stolen. The level of cover varies with each policy, but most provide cover for the following categories:

(*i*) Vet fees.
(*ii*) Death Benefit.
(*iii*) Holiday cancellation.
(*iv*) Boarding fees.
(*v*) Theft/Straying.
(*vi*) Advertising/Reward.
(*vii*) Third party Liability.
(*viii*) Accidental Damage.

Dog Insurance

This policy covers indigenous, cross-bred or exotic dogs which are pets, watch dogs, sheep dogs and hunting dogs and provides insurance against death due to accident and or diseases during the period of insurance to the dogs. Age: 8 weeks to 8 years. Insured dogs must be suitably identified by one of the following methods:

(*i*) Tattooing.

(*ii*) Nose point.

(*iii*) Coloured photograph.

(*iv*) In the case of pups.

One more coloured photo may be taken at 6 to 8 months age. Normal physical identification marks and breed, sex, age etc. should be clearly described in the veterinary certificate and proposal form. The policy may be extended as per the following sections and the proposer may be chosen to cover risk under any section by payment of extra premium:

Section: 1 –

Death by accident in transit by air, railroad and water and show risk.

Section: 2 –

Death by accidental poisoning.

Section: 3 –

Breeding risk – (*a*) Death by whelping, (*b*) loss of litter in case the whole litter dies within 14 days after birth.

Section: 4 –

Lost or stolen dogs (including burglary or housebreaking).

Section: 5 –

Loss of show entry fees (max. limit ₹ 250) when dog registered with the kennel dub is unable to attend the show because of accident or disease.

Section: 6 –

Loss of value resultant upon an accident.

Section: 7 –

Liability for personal injury and damage to property (including animals, poultries or third parties) up to ₹ 5,000/.

Section: 8

Worldwide transit clause.

Pet Health Insurance

Pet health insurance offers family pets coverage for veterinary care when injuries or illnesses occur with many animals being a part of their human families, companions. These policies offer coverage for office visits, routine care, illnesses and emergency care. Terminal illnesses arc usually not covered, though with medical costs for pets rising and the average vet visit costing $ 100 to $ 150 option for pet medical insurance is an option some may choose.

Dog Health Insurance

Dog health insurance provides coverage for veterinary costs. This type of health insurance can help the dog owner provide routine veterinary care such as vaccinations and necessary veterinary care to treat unexpected health problems and injuries from accident. The dog owner can choose from dog health insurance policies that cover all veterinary costs for a high monthly premium or one that overs only unexpected veterinary costs that may occur for a lower monthly premium.

Pet Dog Insurance

Life insurance policy is taken as a financial security after the death of Life Insured. For some of the people, their pets are very loving and they take care of their pets like their own children. So, it becomes evident that for them, how important their pet's health and death is? So, providing financial security or as the principle of insurance pet dog insurance exists.

Contents of Proposal From of Pet Dog Insurance

1st Section

1. Application form Number:
2. Policy commencement date:
3. Cover note no. ......

2nd Section

Your Personal Details

1. Name:
2. Address:
3. E-mail, Mobile no.
4. Data of Birth:

3rd Section

Your Pet's Details

1. Your Pet's name;
2. Date of Birth;
3. Sex – Male, Female, Desexed
4. Breed –
5. Colour
6. Tattoo – no –
7. Purchase price –
8. Has your pet had ANY Injury or illness that required vet Treatment – Yes/No.
9. Has your pet had an injury or illness BUT did not require vet Treatment – Yes/No.
10. If you have other pets give their details also.
11. Has a claim or complaint involving your pet has been lodged in last five years – Yes/No.
12. Is your pet used in any trade, profession/occupation or go to work with you – Yes/No.

Name of Vet Practice Your Pet Attends

1. Name:
2. Address:
3. Phone

Choose Your Dog Plan

1. **Vet's Fees and Alternative Treatment:** For illness and injury, including hospitalization, referal and medicine.
2. **Death from illness:** Losing a dog is a great sadness, this plan will refund the purchase price.
3. **Death from injury:** Nothing can replace a loved dog but this plan will refund the purchase price.
4. **Boarding kennel fees:** Or home care with a friend if you are hospitalized for more than 4 days.
5. **Advertising and Reward:** If your dog gets lost or stolen we will pay for local newspaper advertising and a reward.
6. **Theft or straying:** If your dog is lost or stolen, we will pay for local newspaper advertising and a reward.
7. **Third party liability:** If your dog causes damage or injury and you are legally payable.

All these plans have different charges and total of all these charges will be premium for Dog insurance plan.

Payment Details

Mode of Payment: Monthly/Annually

Method of Payment:

(*i*) By cheque
(*ii*) debit card
(*iii*) credit card
(*iv*) cash

If paid by credit card/debit card, give the card declaration:

– card number
– card holder's name
– signature

Declaration: At last, a declaration would be made by the proposer that proposer is fully satisfied with the procedure and plan and all information provided by proposer are right.

Signature of the Applicant	Date Place

Claim Form Pet Dog Insurance

1. Policyholder to complete following details in claim Form while making Claim:

(*a*) Policy No.
(*b*) Name of policyholder and Address
(*c*) Telephone No.

About Pet Insured:

– Pet's name
– Pet's date of birth
– Breed
– Is your pet insured with any other company – Yes/No.
– If yes, please state which company.

Details of your pet condition:

– Is the condition are you claiming for Illness, or Injury or Death.
– If illness or injury, then
– Date condition first noticed
– Date pet seen by vet
– Time pet seen by vet
– Did the illness or injury result in death of your pet – Yes/No
Date of Death.

Some information would be filled by vet:

– Name
– Address
– Telephone Number
– Make a house visit
– Fees for treatment
– Condition of the pet: details

- Treatment dates from ..... to .....
- Data of death
- Declaration by the veterinary doctor:

Signature

These are some fundamental information an insurer company asks while making claim. The insurance company may ask for other information as required by them.

Table 34.1 Progress of Cattle Insurance in India

	Number Covered (in Thousand)	*Premium (In ₹ lacs)*
1974	30	25.84
1975	63	48.45
1976	210	132.93
1977	589	247.18
1978	1410	472.02
1979	3230	948.16
1980	4372	1333.78
1981	5676	1908.98
1982	8235	2633.03
1983	10578	3389.58
1984	14267	4596.45
1985	16079	5135.90
1986	18969	5935.00
1987	18536	69.45
1988-89	25622	10188.00
1989-90	19921	8604.00

CROP INSURANCE

Crop insurance on a restricted scale is being underwritten in the Fire department where damage by fire to standing sugarcane crops is insured. Insurance of all crops against all risks of loss or damage has not found a beginning in our country so far. One of the chief reasons why crop insurance has not gained currency in the country is the inadequate data available on the position of loss. Since our country is dependent to a large extent on agriculture, such non-availability of data acts as a damper on undertaking the job. The climate conditions in the country vary from extreme hot to extreme cold and from swamping rains to severe drought. All the same, a beginning has been made and some crops have been insured on input basis, *i.e.*, the indemnity comprises the cost of all inputs like seeds, pesticides, weedicides, fertilizers, manure; labour; water; crop spraying, etc. The crops insured are crops like cotton where controlled conditions of cultivation can be applied. The experiment too is still rudimentary and may be extended to other crops like rubber, coffee and tea. GIC has taken up insurance of cotton grown by small and marginal farmers through adoption of Nursery Technology in Gujarat and Maharashtra.

Crop insurance scheme introduced by the Government of India commenced from kharif 1985-86. The corporation has been entrusted with the task of administering the scheme on behalf of the Government. The insurance charges and claims in respect of crops insured in any State is shared between the Central Crop Insurance Fund and Crop Insurance Fund set up by the State Government concerned in the ratio of 2: 1. The number of farmers covered has been 4226 thousand for Kharif 1989 and 661 thousand for Rabi 1989-90. The claims have been ₹ 28085 lakhs and ₹ 622 lakhs respectively. However the number of farmers covered and premium income declined in 1994-95 to the tune of 4072 thousand for kharif and 545 thousand for rabi while premium income declined to ₹ 21.90 crores and ₹ 3.35 crores respectively.

Contract guarantee also known as solvency guarantee comes under the classification of insurance of interest, when contracts for works or for supply of materials are awarded the awarders are required to guarantee that the contract awarded will be executed within the time stipulated or within such extension of time as may be allowed and in accordance with the terms of the contract and the specifications stipulated therein. The amount of guarantee varies with the nature of contract. Generally, it ranges from 1% to 10% of the contract. The purpose of a contract guarantee is two-fold. Firstly, by the deterrent of calling in the insurance guarantee for payment the contractor is discouraged from slowing down or the making down the quality of the work. Secondly, the requirement of a guarantee may dissuade all and sundry from rushing in to secure the award of the contract.

The risk under a contract guarantee is the skill, ability and intention of the person who is guaranteed. Hence, like fidelity guarantee it covers on intangible. The insurer who underwrites this class needs specialised knowledge and wide experience. Apart from the natures of contract, the important considerations are the financial status and reputation of the contractor, the experience he has in executing work similar to that contract, or the manpower, equipment and capital base he has and the skill and ability he has as may be judged from his completed contracts or as reflected in his existing contracts. A pitfall that has to be avoided as a tendency on the part of contractors to overtrade, that is, contractors trying to take more contracts on hand than he could successfully execute.

Contract guarantee takes on three distinct forms as stated below:

1. *Performance Bonds:* The bond undertakes to indemnify the principals against any failure on the part of the contractor to execute the contract works in accordance with the specifications and terms of the contract and within the time stipulated in the contract or in case of supply contracts if the materials, goods or products supplied by the contractor fall short of the standards set by the principals.
2. *Earnest Money (Bid) Bonds*: The bond is issued in lieu of the earnest money which every intending contractor has to pay to a principal while submitting his tender or bid. The bond provides for payment of the amount guaranteed if the contractor fails to enter into a contract with the principals after they have accepted his tender or bid.
3. *Security Depositor Retention Money Bond*: Before the commencement of this contract works, the contractor is required to provide as security deposit a certan percentage of the contract value for due performance of the contract. A security deposit bond issued in lieu of the security deposit undertakes to pay the amount guaranteed should there be any failure on the part of the contractor to perform the contract. Instead of a security deposit, the principals may deduct from each running bill of the contractor a fixed percentage as security for the due performance of the contract. This is known as retention money. A bond issued in lieu of the retention money is known as retention money bond.

Credit Guarantee

Credit guarantee is also an insurance of interest. It has for its risk the credit of any buyer or borrower to a supplier or financier. The term credit as used here means commercial credit and it connects the trust reposed and time allowed in making a payment or repayment. The trust is not only in relation to the integrity and honesty of the person who has to make the payment but also in the business ability of the person for his conducting the entire business and making a profit enough to repay one "debt". The subject-matter of insurance in credit guarantee is also called as finance guarantee. Like contract guarantee for credit guarantee also a very elaborate proposal is required to be submitted. In addition all the other particulars as called for in a contract guarantee are required to be provided.

As no contracts are involved here, the proposer need not furnish details about his past or present contracts. Also a cash flow statement detailing as to how funds would be generated for repayment of the debt is required to be given. Full details of the purpose for which the loan is obtained and any security given to the financier have to be furnished.

Credit guarantee takes on many forms. A few are explained briefly below:

1. Hire Purchase Guarantee

Bank and other financial institutions may advance money to transport operators or fleet owners to enable them purchase motor cars or truck chassis. The advances with interest are repayable within a certain period by instalments. This transaction is known as hire purchases. The banks or financiers who advance as the money invariably requires an insurance guarantee as security. The guarantee covers only up to 75% or 80% of the total purchase price of vehicle including sales taxes and other local taxes. The balance of 25% or 20% has to be paid in cash by the person buying the vehicle or has to be borne by the bank or financier, as the case may be. In respect of second hand vehicle, it may even be as low as 40% of the total purchase price. In the event of any failure on the part of the hire purchaser to pay any amount, the vehicle in question may be seized and disposed of.

2. Deferred Payment Guarantee

Various industrialists (Large Scale and Small Scale) need credit from banks for the purchase of machinery or capital goods both from foreign suppliers and indigenous suppliers. The credit may not be necessarily monetary credit. It may be in the form of guarantee and payment on behalf of the clients from the bank to the suppliers of machinery or capital goods. In the case of foreign suppliers the opening of a letter of credit is with the supplier's bank. The payment of the purchase price may be spread over a period of years and for payment of each instalment a date may be stipulated in the purchase agreement. The deferred payment guarantee provides for payment of any loss arising from any default committed by the purchaser in the payment of the instalments.

3. Cash Credit or Overdraft Guarantee

Businessmen frequently resort to overdraft or cash credit facilities with bank for obtaining working capital. The guarantee undertakes to indemnify the bank against any loss arising out of the failure of the borrower in repaying the amount advanced or the interest thereon .

4. Bills Discounting Guarantee

It is an established practice in business circles to discount bills of exchange banks. The banks which discount the bills proceed to collect the amount due thereon from the makers or acceptors thereof only on the dates of payment under those bills which may be dishonoured on their due dates. Banks, therefore, insist or insurance guarantee indemnifying them against such losses.

Period of Guarantee

The period of guarantee has to be concurrent with the period of the original agreements which they cover. In some cases they may even overstretch the period of the original agreements by a month or more. This is done to facilitate the principal parties to process their claims, if they have any under the insurance guarantees.

Counter-Guarantees and Tangible Security

A counter-guarantee is a document executed in favour of the insurers by the party who is guaranteed by the insurers. The counter-guarantee may be from the guaranteed party only or it may be joined co-guarantors. When insurers pay a loss under an insurance the guarantee insurers lose. Insurers as a rule make it obligatory for the guaranteed party to execute a counter-guarantee.

In addition to counter-guarantee, insurers may also obtain some tangible security where they feel it is warranted. The tangible security may be by way of an equitable mortgage of the immovable assets or it may be assignment of life insurance policies or even a negative lien over the assets of the guaranteed party or pledge of share scripts, banks lodgement receipts, etc. Guarantees and counter-guarantees are specially contracts. Hence they have to be executed under the seal.

ENGINEERING INSURANCE

Engineering insurance is growing in India due to rapid industrialisation. The machines are exposed to accidental breakdown or unforeseen damage. There are heary costs involved and third party liability. There are two main types of engineering insurance: Construction and operational policies. The origin of engineering insurance goes back to Industrial Revolution in U.K. Due to frequent explosions of boiler, heavy losses to property and life occurred. The Manchester Steam Users Association was formed in 1854 to prevent losses occurring due to explosions. Eventually, the Steam Boiler Assurance Company was formed in 1858. New India Assurance Company Ltd. started engineering insurance for the first time in India followed by other general insurance companies Engineering experts are appointed by the insurance companies for evaluating risk and rate fixing.

Underwriting :

Proposal form and questionnaire are fulfilled by the proposer, which is inspected by the inspector of the company. The proposal form includes name and address of the principal contractor and sub-contractor, full description of the contract construction nature, location, special risk involving earthquakes etc. sum assured, material used, limit of accident period of insurance third parties liabilities.

The hazard of special types are assessed with foundations materials of installation/erection, tall building possibilities of scaffolding fire, contact with aircraft. Underground risks are also assessed, pipelines, tunneling, hydroelectric, road construction, reservoirs, bridge construction and so on.

Types of Policies

There are two main engineering insurance policies: Construction policies and operational policies. The construction policies are issued for the period of the project i.e., one time policies and the operational policies are issued for one year with renewable facility.

Construction Policies:

1. Contractor's All Risks (CAR) Policy.
2. Erection All Risks (EAR) Policy.
3. Storage Cum Erection (SCE) Policy.
4. Marine Cum Erection (MCE) Policy.
5. Contract Works (CW) Policy.
6. Advance Loss of Profits (ALOP) Policy.
7. Delay in Start Up (DSU) Policy.

Operational Policies.

1. Machinery Insurance (M1) Policy.
2. Machinery Breakdown (MB) Policy.
3. Boiler and Pressure Plant (BPP) Policy.
4. Machinery Loss of Profits (MLOP) Policy.
5. Contractor's Plant and Machinery (CPM) Policy.
6. Civil Engineering Complete Risks (CECR) Policy.
7. Electronic Equipment (EE) Policy.
8. Deterioration of Stocks (DOS) Policy.

Principles of Contract

All the principles of general insurance contract are applicable to engineering insurance i.e.utmost good faith, insurable interest, indemnity and subrogation. etc.

A. CONSTRUCTION INSURANCE

Construction insurance of engineering is generally one-time policy. for the period of the project. It has several forms of insurance as defined above.

1. Contractor's All Risks (CAR) Policy:

This is issued to protect the interests of contractors and principals for civil engineering projects like construction of building bridges etc. It is All Risk cover unless the risks are specifically excluded.

The insured perils are - fire, lightning, explosion, flood, inundation, windstorm, theft, burglary, landslide, earthquake, accidental damage, collapse, acts of terrorism. Third party liability is also covered by paying extra premium.

The subject matter of insurance are civil engineering projects like building, warehouse, hospitals, schools, churches, theatres, cinemas, factories, bridges, dams, canals, tunnels, water supply systems, road, railways, airport and so on.

Claims :

The losses as described above are made good by repair or replacement the cost of clearance and removal of debris will also be reimbursed if insured for. Cost of alterations, additions and improvements shall not be recoverable. The payment of loss or damage caused by its own mechanical or electrical breakdown or derangement is not paid here in this policy as there is a separate policy for mechanical and electrical breakdown. The claim would be the cost of repairs necessary to restore the property to their conditions immediately before the occurrence of the damage less salvage or in case of total loss, the actual value of property before the occurrence of loss less salvage.

The cover of third party liability is at the option of the insured. The indemnity applies to legal liability of the insured to pay compensation for accidental loss of or damage to property of other persons and or fatal or non-fatal injury to any person.

2. Erection All Risks (EAR) Policy :

Erection All Risks policy is concerned with erection of electrical plant and machinery and equipment and structures. It is also known as Storage Cum Erection (SCE) Policy. The insurable plants are boilers, transformers, switchgear, compressors and plant for manufacturing purposes etc. The policy covers structural steel work, tanks, oil refinery, plant, blast furnaces etc.

The individual machine, turbine, generator etc., are also covered under this policy. Civil engineering works necessary for the project may be covered in his policy. If the actual erection period is shorter than the period indicated in the schedule, no refund of premium shall be allowed.

Underwriting : Special attentions are paid for transit insurance machinery and equipment are duly inspected by the insurer. no unusually prolonged storage period is involved. The risk is not exposed to extraordinary hazards of storm, flood, inundations, subsidence and cyclone. The project will be completed within the time schedule. Most of the reinsurers follow their own rating pattern, which varies from the nature of project, location, size, period of insurance. Tariff Advisory Committee have standardised the rates and excess for this class of business.

Claims : The loss producing events are the same as discussed in Contractor's All Risks (CAR) Policy.

The Marine-Cum-Erection (MCE), Contract Works (CW) insurance, Advanced Loss of Profits (ALOP) insurance or Delay in start up (DSU) insurance have all the terms and conditions as described above.

The Erection All Risks insurance policy covers plant and machinery under erection. The cover normally commences from the arrival at site of erection of the materials and it operates during storage of the material, erection and test run of the plant and terminates on the commissioning of the plant.

Civil engineering works, provided they are incidental to erection of plant of machinery, are also covered. Third party liability arising out of the insured's activities with the erection work is also covered. The erection policy is issued for the entire period of erection including trial run.

Excess: It is customary for excess to be applied under machinery breakdown and erection policies. Boiler explosion is, however, not subject to excess. The purpose of excess is two:fold, first, to eliminate small claims thereby reducing clerical work for the insurance and second, to make the insured more conscious of this responsibility to take adequate precautions and to observe all safety regulations and statutory rules.

B. OPERATIONAL INSURANCE

Operational insurance under engineering insurance is generally for one year which is removable. Machinery insurance and Boiler Insurance are important engineering insurance.

Machinery Insurance.

Accidents under machinery insurance policy occur more frequently than under any other insurance. The machinery insurance includes electrical equipment, oil firing equipment, fans and blowers; mechanical plant including engines, turbines, blowers, compressors, pumps, machine tools and presses, lifting equipment including cranes with fixed installation, conveyors and lifts.

The perils insured are short circuits, failure of insulations, malfunctioning of control and protection circuits, faulty materials, faulty design, faulty casting, vibration, loosening of parts, stress, centrifugal force, explosion due to internal/external pressure, failure of connected machinery, protection devices, etc and external factors causing breakdown and damage to insured machinery.

Exclusions:

1. Fire, lightning, theft, collapse of building, landslide, flood, volcano, earthquake etc.
2. Damage occasioned by war and civil war, riot, strike, nuclear risks
3. Damage resulting from experiments or overload.
4. Loss or damage caused by the wilful act or gross negligence.

The purpose of the exclusions is to exclude the actual wastage, wear or deterioration but not sudden and unforeseen damage to other parts resulting therefrom.

Claims :

The damage can be repaired. The basis of indemnification is the cost of restoration working order based on the customary daily rates of wages together with normal freight and erection costs. Where the insured item is totally destroyed or is a constructive total loss, the basis of indemnification is the market value of the item immediately before the accident plus the cost of removing the damaged machinery loss the value of the salvage

Policy Conditions :

The special conditions in this policy relate to proper maintenance of insured machinery and observance of manufacturers instructions. All mechanical and electrical parts shall be inspected notice of material change in the risk, alterations etc. to an insured item, deviation from prescribed operating conditions and change of insurable interest so that the policy may be suitably endorsed.

The machine will not be used except while being turned over periodically for maintenance purpose.

Rating:

The tariff is separately provided each for electrical machine, machinery in cold storage, major equipments, glass and graphite equipments and mechanical items.

Extension:

The machinery insurance can be extended to cover third party personal injury and property risks, expenses incurred for overtime, express freight, cost incurred in the clearance and removal of debris and loss or damage to the existing surrounding property on payment of extra premium.

The fire policy covers loss or damage to machinery only if the loss or damage is attributable to fire or any of the extraneous perils covered by the fire policy. But where loss or damage has originated from breakdown, fire policy is of no avail. This gap is made good by the machinery breakdown policy which provides indemnity against any unforeseen and sudden damage to the machinery by causes such as short circuit, action of centrifugal forces, shortage of water in boilers, faulty design, bad workmanship, erection faults, lack of skill, carelessness, malicious damage etc. and also extended to cover some allied risks by payment of extra premium as given in extension clause.

Boiler and Pressure Plant Insurance

The boiler and pressure plant insurance covers boilers and pressure vessels and seeks to indemnify the insured against damage, other than by fire to the boilers and other pressure plants and to surrounding property of the insured, legal liability of the insured on account of bodily injury, fatal and non-fatal to the person or damage to the property of third parties. "Boiler" means any fired closed vessel or a combined container piping system in which steam is generated under pressure. Pressure Plant means any unfixed closed container under steam gas or fluid pressure. "Explosion" means the sudden and violent rendering or tearing a part of the permanent structure of a boiler or pressure plant or any part thereof by force of internal steam, gas or fluid pressure causing bodily displacement of the said structure and accompained by the forcible ejectment of its contents. It is necessary that the boilers and pressure plants insured are inspected normally by inspectors appointed by the appropriate statutory authority and that they are operated by attendants holding a valid certificate of competencies.

"Collapse" means the sudden and dangerous distortion of any part of a boiler or pressure plant by bending or crushing caused by steam, gas or fluid pressure.

"Flue Gas Explosion" means and explosion of ignited gases in the furnaces or flues of the boilers economisers and superheaters.

"Chemical Explosion" means an explosions arising out of chemical reaction in any plant.

The boiler and pressure plant insurance covers the losses or damages arising out of explosion, collapse, flue gas explosion or chemical explosion.

Warranties

The boiler and pressure plants insured are inspected by inspectors appointed by the appropriate Government Authorities, they are operated by attendants holding a valid certificate of competency

Sum Assured

Sum Assured will be new replacement value of the plant which is inclusive of freight and customs duties and erection cost. Wherever super heaters or economisers do not form an integral part of the Boiler installation, they should be described separately and specifically while completing the policy schedule. The sum assured in respect of the insured's own surrounding property damage and Third Party Liability may be fixed separately on a first loss basis

The other forms of operational insurance e.g. Contractor's Plant and Machinery (CPM), Civil Engineering Completed Risk (CECR), Electronic Equipment Insurance (EEI) and Deterioration of Stocks (DOS) insurance are insured as described in Machinery Insurance and Boiler and Pressure Plant Insurance.

Loss of Profit Insurance:

As in the fire department, the interruption risk arising out of machinery breakdown can be covered under a loss of profits insurance policy taken in conjunction with a basic machinery breakdown policy. The cover is similar to what is granted in the fire department excepting that the period of indemnity is restricted to 9 months ordinarily and 12 months in special cases.

SOCIAL SECURITY COVERAGE IN INDIA

Most social security systems in developed countries are linked to wage employment. In India, situation is entirely different. The key differences are:

1. We do not have existing universal social security system.
2. We do not face the problem of exit rate from the workplace. Rather on the contrary, lack of employment opportunities is the key concern.
3. 92 % of the workforce is in the informal sector which is largely unrecorded and the system of pay roll deduction is difficult to apply.

New Initiatives In Social Security :

Janashree Bima Yojana: The objective of this scheme is to provide life insurance protection to the rural and urban persons living below poverty line and marginally above poverty line. The main features are:

Eligibility: Person between 18 years and 59 years is benefited under the scheme. The member should normally be the head of the family.

Benefits:

Natural Death ₹ 30,000/-

Accident Death/
Permanent Total Disability ₹ 75,000/-

Partial disability due to
accident ₹ 37,500/-

Aam Admi Bima Yojana: This scheme provides coverage to Rural Landless Households.

Eligibility: Person between 18 years and 59 years. The member should normally be the head of the family.

Benefits: As per Janashree Bima Yojana.

This scheme is fully subsidized by Central and State Government.

Janashree Bima Yojana for Women SHG's Credit Linked to Banks

Target for F.Y. 2008 - 09 covering 2.5 lacs SHG group

Other Social Security Schemes Implemented through LIC of India:

	Schemes	Commencement	Coverage (31/3/2008)
1.	Khadi Karigar Janashree Bima Yojana	15/8/2003	2,34,436
2.	Bima Yojana for Handicraft Artisan	July, 2003	97,636
3.	Mahatma Gandhi Bunkar Bima Yojana	02.10.2005	4,66,484
4.	Aanganwadi Karyakartri Janashree Bima Yojana	01.04.2004	15,26,970
5.	Kendriya Bhed Palak Bima Yojana	01.01.2008	3,435

Government of India has created Social Security Fund with LIC of India to provide subsidy to all the Social Security Schemes.

SPORTS INSURANCE

Claims Made and Notified Cover

The Professional Indemnity Section 3 is a 'claims made' cover. This means that the policy covers you for claims first made against you during the period of insurance and notified to the insurer during such period of insurance.

This extension does not provide cover in relation to:

- Events which occurred prior to the period of insurance or such earlier retroactive date as may be stipulated in the policy schedule;
- Claims made against you after the expiry of the period of insurance even though the event giving rise to the claim may have occurred during the period of insurance;
- Claims arising from or attributable to any facts, circumstances or occurrences noted on the proposal for the current period of insurance or on any previous proposal or of which notice had been given under any previous policy;

Claims arising from or attributable to any facts, circumstances or occurrences of which you were aware and knew (or ought reasonably to have realised) prior to the commencement of the period of insurance may give rise to a claim.

As explained above, the policy does not provide cover for claims made after the expiry of the period of insurance cover provided by the Policy.

Section 40(3) of the Insurance Contracts Act 1984 however provides that an insurer is not relieved from liability under a contract of insurance in respect of a claim by reason only that the claim was made after the expiry of the period of insurance cover provided by the contract where the insured has given notice in writing to the insurer:

- of the facts that might give rise to a claim against the insured;
- as soon as was reasonably practicable after the insured became aware of those facts; and
- before the expiry of the period of insurance.

It is therefore important that you advise the insurer of any circumstances that could rise to a claim during the period of insurance to protect your position in case the circumstances give rise to a claim after the expiry of the period of insurance.

Important Notices

Please read these notices before completing this form.

Sports Personal Accident Duty of Disclosure

This duty of disclosure applies to Sports Personal Accident cover.

What you must tells us

When answering our questions you must be honest and you have a duty under law to tell us anything known to you, and which a reasonable person in the circumstances would include in the answer to the question. We will use the answers in deciding whether to insure you and anyone else to be insured under the policy, and on what terms.

Who needs to tell us?

It is important that you understand you are answering our questions in this way for yourself and anyone else whom you want to be covered by the policy.

If you do not tell us

If you do not answer our questions in this way, we may reduce or refuse to pay a claim, or cancel the policy. If you answer our questions fraudulently, we may refuse to pay a claim and treat this policy as never having been in force.

You, Your or Yours Means –

- Each person who is shown in this form; — Each legal entity that is shown in this form.

Your Duty of Disclosure

This policy is subject to The Insurance Contracts Act 1984. Under that Act You have a Duty of Disclosure. This means;

- When You ask for cover, You must tell Your Insurer all that You know about the risk You want covered that may affect Their decision: — To offer You cover; and — The Terms and the cost of such cover.
- if You ask for the cover to be renewed, extended, altered or reinstated You must tell Your Insurer:
- if there have been any changes in what is covered, and — Of all things that may increase the chances of a claim.

If Things Change

After Your Insurer has agreed to cover You and while You are covered You must tell Them of all changes that may increase the chances of a claim. The sort of changes that may increase the chances of a claim are if:

- You vary the scope of activities You conduct: — You change the facilities You provide;
- You increase the size of Your operations.

Non-Disclosure

If You don't tell Your Insurer something that You know which may affect Their decision To offer You cover or the terms of that cover They may be allowed to:

- Reduce that amount that They have to pay for a claim. This may mean that They would pay You nothing.
- Cancel this policy. They may even be allowed to cancel this policy from the date that the cover started if:
- You lie to Them; — Deliberately keep information from Them, or — Mislead Them.

What You Don't Have to Tell Your Insurer

You do not have to tell Them of anything:

- That reduces the chances of a claim, but, if You Do, it may let Them offer You better terms or a lower price
- That is common knowledge; — That They should know as a normal part of Their business;
- If They waive Your Duty of disclosure.

If You Reduce Your Insurer's Rights

They will not pay that part of a claim where You have by agreement limited or excluded Your rights to recover Your loss from any person or entity.

Declaration

I represent that the following statements and facts are true and that no material facts have been suppressed or mis-stated.

I understand that completion of this form does not bind coverage. The company's acceptance of this proposal required before cover may be bound and the policy issued.

Furthermore, 1:

1. have either completed all the questions on this form personally or they have been completed by somebody else on my behalf and the answers have been checked for fullness and accuracy by me.
2. have read and understood the information concerning claims made cover, important notices and duty of disclosure.
3. agree to the Insurer obtaining from my previous insurer(s) any information it may need about prior claims or insurance history.
4. agree to the Insurer making enquiries from any third party to verify claims history and other information disclosed here in or statements made by myself in making this application.
5. agree to the Insurer disclosing to any insurance intermediary appointed by myself or to any former or future insurer of myself the claims history or any other information as may be determined.

Please Sign Below

NAME: ....

(Please Print)

SIGNATURE: ....

POSITION: ....

DATE: ..../ ..../ ....

NOTE: Please attach any additional information that you wish to tell Your Insurer as part of Your Duty of Disclosure on a separate page.

Shopkeeper's Insurance Policy

A number of insurance companies in India have come up with attractive insurance policies for people owning small or medium-sized shops. It covers all the risks and contingencies faced by small or medium-sized shopowners. The policy provides protection for the property and the interests of the shopowners (including their partners) in the business venture who has applied for the insurance cover.

SHOPKEEPER'S INSURANCE POLICY IN INDIA

The shopkeeper's insurance policy contains 11 sections, including the shop's building, its contents, money stored in transit/counter/safe, pedal cycle, plate glass, neon and glow signs, baggage, fidelity of the employers, the owner's public liability, workmen's compensation liability as well as interruption of business.

The estimated cost of rebuilding the shop is calculated, which in turn gives the value of the shop in question.

The value and time of purchase of the contents of the shop are assessed before providing an insurance cover to the shopkeepers. The valuables shall include electrical as well as mechanical appliances present in the shop.

Commercial outlets with a larger value at risk have to obtain separate coverage for different perils. Loss or damage to livestock, motor vehicles, security stamps, deeds, bullion, bonds, bills of exchange, stocks and share certificates, promissory notes, business documents, manuscripts, precious stones and valuables cannot be claimed under the Shopkeeper's Insurance Policy.

Other prominent exclusions include any misdemeanor involving any partner or employer of the insured or his/her family member as principal or accessory, in a housebreaking case. The insured cannot invoke the fidelity guarantee, regarding any infidelity by a person other than a salaried employee of the insured.

Exclusions

1. Loss or damage in the shop due to natural calamities such as earthquake, cyclone, flood etc is not covered by the insurance policy.
2. If a family member of business staff is directly/indirectly involved in the actual theft of the shop, then the damage caused by the situation shall not be included in the policy cover.
3. Some companies may charge extra money for the damage caused due to terrorist activity.
4. Damage due to war, invasion, foreign enemy, hostilities, civil war, mutiny, civil commotion, or nuclear activity is not covered by the insurance policy.
5. If the property insured has been removed to another place for the purpose of renovation, cleaning or repairing, then the policy doesn't guarantee its coverage.

Types of Coverage

Shop insurance provides cover for losses that might arise due to unexpected events, such as theft, fire or natural disasters. A single policy can cover all risks associated with a shop or showroom. Shopkeeper's insurance includes cover for the shop building and its contents, cash-in-transit or in the counter, public liability, employer's liability and business interruption.

- Stock Protection – Insurers generally allow shopkeepers or owners to choose the quantity of stock to cover for protection against theft, fire and unexpected circumstances.
- Business Interruption Insurance – This cover is a standard part of shop insurance, which provides coverage for loss of business income and additional costs after insured property is damaged.

- Public Liability Insurance – Public liability insurance covers the damage or legal costs of defending against any legal claim that arises from any person other than an employee.
- Employer's liability insurance – Employer's liability insurance is a legal liability for any business firm to compensate for damages sustained by employees on the premises.

Features

- Fire and allied perils – Provides protection for for the property and interests of the insured against fire, burglary, theft or any fortuitous event.
- Covers breakdown of office equipment.
- Covers liability towards workmen under the Workmen's Compensation Act.
- Covers business interruptions suffered due to fire and allied perils fidelity guarantee.
- Covers money carried to the bank, plate glass, neon sign and other electronic equipment in shop.
- Provides protection against fraudulent and dishonest employees.
- Covers for damage to data media, software and cost of recovery of lost data.
- Personal accident insurance provided for the shopkeeper and the permanent employees.

Advantages

- Single policy covering all risks in a shop.
- Complete coverage at lower premium.
- Simple documentation.
- Covers for unanticipated loss.
- Saving on costs.
- Smooth functioning of the business.
- One-stop shop/solution for the client's business related needs.

Who Can Take the Policy

This policy can be taken by the small shopkeepers whose shop building value and contents value does not exceed ₹ 10 lacs. In case it exceeds ₹ 10 lacs, this policy cannot be given. This policy is meant for shops only. Mere registration under Shops and Establishments Act does not entitle the premises to be insured under this policy.

How to Select the Sum Insured

The shop building should be insured on market value basis *i.e.,* depreciated value basis. The contents should be insured on cost price basis. The sum insured for contents under sections I and II should be identical. The sum insured under sections III, IV, V, VI, VII, VIII, IX, X, and XI is limited to specified percentage of the sum insured for contents.

How to Claim

In case of any incident giving rise to a claim under this policy, one should take the following steps:

1. Take necessary steps to minimize the loss/damage.
2. In case of fire, inform fire brigade immediately.
3. In case of theft, larceny or burglary inform the police immediately along with a list of items stolen and their approximate value.
4. Inform insurance company by phone or fax and in writing.
5. Extend full co-operation to the surveyor appointed by the Insurance Co. and provide necessary documents to substantiate the loss.
6. In case any rights of recovery exists against any other party responsible for the loss, the rights of recovery have to be subrogated to the insurance company on payment of claim.

EXPORT RISK INSURANCE

Exporters face a problem of not being paid by the overseas importer because of various reasons like outbreak of war or civil war, a coup or an insurrection, economic difficulties or balance of payment problems faced by importers country and commercial risks like insolvency or protracted default of buyer. All these reasons may block the amount or delay the amount. The loss of amount brings a disaster for any exporter, howsoever he is financially sound, intelligent and competent. Export credit insurance provided by ECGC helps in preventing the above risks. With insurance cover, exporters can do business confidently and in the process can increase or expand the business significantly without fear of loss. This paper examines export insurance system in the country and the role played by ECGC.

In order to provide export credit insurance support to Indian exporters, the Government of India set up the **Export Risks Insurance Corporation (ERIC)** in 1957. The name of the Corporation was changed in 1964 as **"Export Credit & Guarantee Corporation Limited" (ECGC)**. To bring the Indian identity into the name, the Corporation's name was changed as the present **Export Credit Guarantee Corporation of India Limited** in 1983. The Government of India owns ECGC. It works under the administrative control of the Ministry of Commerce and is managed by a Board of Directors representing Government, Banking, Insurance, Trade and Industry.

ECGC Covers

1. Standard policy issued to exporters to protect them against payment risks involved in exports on short-term credit and small exporter policy issued for the same purpose to exporters with small exports;
2. Specific Policies designed to protect Indian firms against payment risks involved in
   (*a*) Export on deferred terms of payment,
   (*b*) Services rendered to foreign parties, and
   (*c*) Construction works and turnkey projects undertaken abroad;
3. Financial guarantees issued to banks in India to protect them from risks of loss involved in their extending financial support to exporters at the pre-shipment well as post-shipment stages; and
4. Special schemes, viz., Transfer guarantee meant to protect banks which add confirmation to letters of credit opened by foreign banks, insurance cover for buyer's credit; Line of Credit, Overseas investment insurance and Exchange fluctuation risk insurance.

How does ECGC help Exporters?

1. Offers insurance protection to exporters against payment risks
2. Provides guidance in export-related activities
3. Makes available information on different countries with its own credit ratings
4. Makes it easy to obtain export finance from banks/financial institutions
5. Assists exporters in recovering bad debts
6. Provides information on creditworthiness of overseas buyers

Risks Involved

There are a number of risks facing exporters, while there is an element of risk in all commercial transactions, the complexity of the environments that exporters must operate in, multiplies these risks.

1. **Credit risk** (because of the large distances and alien environments involved)
2. **Poor quality risk** (if the goods to be exported are not inspected)
3. **Transportation and logistic risks** (movement of goods from one continent to another, the risk of theft, damage and possibly the goods not even arriving at all.)
4. **Legal risks** (international laws and regulations change frequently and/or may be applied differently from that of the exporter's own country.)
5. **Political risk** (the political stability of a foreign country into which a company is exporting)
6. **Unforeseen risks** (natural disaster, terrorist action, unexpected occurrences could completely destroy an export market)
7. **Exchange rate risks** (the currency will weaken and thus resulting in the benefit of a weaker exchange rate being passed onto the importer and not benefiting the exporter.)

8. **Culture and language risk** (the importer and exporter come from different cultures and express themselves with different languages.)

Managing Risks

The task of managing your export-related risks beings with knowing what the risks are. First step is therefore to identify the risks that you are likely to encounter and to give some 'weighting' to the seriousness of the risk. Three main types of risk cover include **credit risk cover, country risk cover and transit risk cover.**

Types of Export Risk Insurance

Insurance is a crucial consideration in the export process. The purpose of any insurance is to protect you from loss as a result of actions outside of your control (such as your customer not paying you, or the ship containing your cargo sinking). There are various types of export-related insurance that you may wish to take out. Perhaps the most common is **marine insurance.** The purpose of marine insurance is to insure your cargo from various transport-related risks while it is being shipped to the importer (note that it is called marine insurance even if you send the cargo by air).

Other types of insurance include

- **export credit insurance** (to protect you from the risk of non-payment on the part of the importer) and
- **political risk insurance** (to protect you should the importing country take some action that results in your non-payment).

Approaching to Export Risk Insurance

To obtain insurance, you would approach a specialist insurance firm; a marine insurance company in the case of cargo or marine insurance, or a credit insurance firm, such as **Credit Guarantee.** As far as marine insurance is concerned, your freight forwarder can help you in this regard and will either put you in touch with an insurance provider or obtain the insurance on your behalf.

Need for Export Risk Insurance

Payments for exports are open to risks even at the best of times. The risks have assumed large proportions today due to the far-reaching political and economic changes that are sweeping the world. An outbreak of war or civil war may block or delay payment for goods exported. Economic difficulties or balance of payment problems may lead a country to impose restrictions on either import of certain goods or on transfer of payments for goods imported. In addition, the exporters have to face commercial risks of insolvency or protracted default of buyers. The commercial risks of a foreign buyer going bankrupt or losing his capacity to pay are aggravated due to the political and economic uncertainties. Export credit insurance is designed to protect exporters from the consequences of the payment risks, both political and commercial, and to enable them to expand their overseas business without fear of loss.

Insurance Documentation

All insurance documentation is unique to the insurer in question and the documentation will differ from insurer to insurer. Normally they will provide you with an insurance application form which you need to complete. On this form you will provide all the relevant and pertinent information that *they* need to know in order to be able to judge your level of risk and to decide on an appropriate insurance premium to charge you. If they agree to insure you, the insurance provider will normally issue you with an insurance certificate. As these documents differ from firm to firm, we cannot provide you with generic copies. Nevertheless, an example of an insurance certificate is provided below for your information.

Conclusion

Export business is very risky and problem may fall from any side all of a sudden. Export Risk insurance enables exporters to avoid risks on payment of a very nominal fee. Export Credit Guarantee Corporation, the four subsidiaries of General Insurance Corporation, namely, National Insurance, Oriental Insurance, New India Assurance and United India are doing a predominant role. In order to increase foreign trade from country, the Government of India and the Private sector should work hand in hand. With Export risk insurance, exporters feel easy of doing business and feel pleasure of doing the business. Profits to exporters and risks to insurance companies. Looks nice for exporters always.

APPENDICES

A. Householders Insurance

B. Neon Signs

C. Pet Insurance

D. Sports Insurance

E. Shopkeepers Insurance

F. Liquified Petroleum Gas Insurance

G. Export Risk Insurance

A. Householder's Insurance

eTiQa

Insurance

Houseowners/Householders Insurance Proposal Form

Important Notice

1. Pursuant to Section 149(4) of the Insurance Act (Malaysia) 1996, you are to disclose in this Proposal Form, fully and faithfully all the facts, which you know or ought to know, otherwise, the policy issued may be void.
2. In line with our group's strategy to promote usage of technology and to help preserve the country's natural resources, we no longer print the full policy wordings. Do visit www.etiqa.com.my for the full policy wording. Printout may also be obtained from our offices nationwide or from our agents.

Individual Proposer		Company Proposer
Title		Company Name
Name		
MyKad No.		Company Registration No.
Army/Police/Passport No.		Date of Company Registration
Gender	Date of Birth	
Marital Status	☐ Single ☐ Married ☐ Divorced ☐ Widowed	Contact Person
Occupation		Nature of Business
Phone No. (Mobile/House/Office)	Fax No.	E-Mail
Correspondence Address		
Postcode	Town	State

To be filled by Individual proposer only				
Education Level	☐ Primary	☐ Secondary	☐ Diploma	☐ Bachelor Degree
	☐ Master	☐ Doctorate	☐ Professional	
No. of children in family (please indicate the number)		☐ 0 - 12 years	☐ 12 years to 18 years	☐ 18 years +
Monthly Household Income	☐ Up to RM1,500	☐ RM1,501 - RM2,500	☐ RM2, 501 - RM5,00	☐ RM5,001 - RM8,000
	☐ RM8,001 - RM15,000	☐ RM15,001 - RM20,000	☐ RM20,001 +	

Details Of Insurance Required

1. Period of Insurance from to

2. Location of building to be insured

   Postcode Town State

3. Of what materials is the dwelling constructed?

   (i) Walls .... (ii) Roof ....
   (Bricks/Concrete/Wood/Others) (Concrete/Tiles/Zinc Others)

4. Number of storey? ....

5. Are there outbuildings and, if yes, how are they constructed? ☐ Yes ☐ No

   (i) Walls .... (ii) Roofs ....
   (Bricks/Concrete/Wood/Others) (Concrete/Tiles/Zinc/Others)

6. Is there any profession, business or trade carried on in the dwelling or in any portion of the premises of which the dwelling forms a part? If yes, please give details. ☐ Yes ☐ No

7. (i) Please state the nature of your residence

   (a) Private Dwelling House - detached ☐

   (b) Private Dwelling House - non-detached ☐

   (c) Flat/Apartment/Condominium ☐

   (ii) Is the dwelling occupied solely by you and your family and servants? If no, state number of other tenants, lodgers or paying guests. ☐ Yes ☐ No

8. Will the dwelling regularly be left unoccupied? Kindly note that the cover against theft will be suspended if the building is unoccupied for more than 90 days unless specially agreed by the Company. ☐ Yes ☐ No

9. Is the building in a good state of repair and will it be maintained? ☐ Yes ☐ No

10. Have you ever sustained loss from any of the hereinmentioned perils other than those referred to in item (9) above? If yes, please give particulars. ☐ Yes ☐ No

11. Is insurance required against:

    (a) Full theft (under Contents only) ☐ Yes ☐ No

    (b) Riot, Strike and Malicious Damage (under Building and Contents) ☐ Yes ☐ No

    (c) Accidental damage to plate glass (under Building only) ☐ Yes ☐ No

    (d) Rent Insurance under Section 111(A) of the Policy in excess at the 10% at the Total Sum Insured on Buildings and/or contents. ☐ Yes ☐ No

12. Have the Building and/or contents suffered damage by flood, windstorm, typhoon, cyclone or hurricane during the past five (5) years? If yes, please give particulars. ☐ Yes ☐ No

13. (a) During your occupancy of the premises, has there been any entry or attempted entry by thieves? If so, state when and how access was obtained or attempted. ☐ Yes ☐ No

(b) Is any burglar alarm system fitted? If so, please give details. ☐ Yes ☐ No

(c) Is your building door and window fitted with iron grilles? ☐ Yes ☐ No

14. Have you any other policies in force covering any of the contingencies to be insured against? If yes, please give particulars. ☐ Yes ☐ No

15. If this proposal is in lieu of any insurance with this company, please give particulars. ☐ Yes ☐ No

16. Has any Insurer/Takaful Operator, in respect of any of the contingencies to which this proposal applies:

(a) Declined your proposal? ☐ Yes ☐ No

(b) Required special terms to insure/cover you? ☐ Yes ☐ No

(c) Cancelled or refused to renew your insurance? ☐ Yes ☐ No

(d) Increased your premium on renewal? If yes, please give particulars. ☐ Yes ☐ No

Note: for questions 11(a) to (d), rates will be quoted on application.

Property To Be Insured

The Sum to be insured must represent Full Value of the building and/or contents. The proposer is required to sign a declaration to the effect below. The insurance will be subject to average, which means that if at the time of loss or damage, the sum insured is less than the full value of the property, the amount payable is proportionately reduced.

Section 1 - The Building	Sum to be insured
The Proposers Private Dwelling House (or Flat) and all the Domestic Offices, Stables, Garages and Out-Building used solely in connection therewith and on the premises including Fixtures and Fittings there in and the Walls, Gates and Fences around and pertaining thereto situate.	RM................................
Section 2 - The Contents	**Sum to be insured**
On Household Good and Personal Effects of every description (except as after mentioned) the property of the contents belonging to the Proposer or any member of the Proposer's family and domestic staff normally residing with the proposer and Fixtures and Fittings the Proposer's own or for which the proposer is legally responsible in the Proposer's Private Dwelling and all the Domestic Offices. Stables, Garages and Outbuildings used solely in connection therewith and on the same building.	RM................................

No one article (furniture, pianos, household appliances, wireless and television set and organs excepted) will be deemed of greater value than five per cent (5%) of the total Sum Insured on the said Contents unless such article is specially declared as a separate item.

Specify here any such article of greater value than five percent (5%) of the Total Sum Insured on the said Contents.

No.	Item Description	Sum Insured
1.		RM...
2.		RM...
3.		RM...
4.		RM...
5.		RM...
	Total Sum Insured on Contents	RM...

Note

1. The value of Platinum, Gold and Silver Articles, Jewellery and Furs payable under the policy is limited to one-third (1/3) of the Total Sum Insured on Contents.

2. This policy is for Private Dwelling and/or Contents contained therein, occupied solely for residential purposes or residential and domestic office purposes. No manufacturing or deposit or storage of merchandise may be allowed in the Private Dwelling or in any portion of the premises of which the Private Dwelling forms a part.

3. This policy does not cover property more specifically insured or, unless specially mentioned: Deeds, Bonds, Bills of Exchange, Promissory Notes, Cheques, Securities of Money, Stamps, Documents of any kind, Cash, Currency Notes, Bank Notes, Manuscript, Medals and Coins, Motor Vehicles and Accessories.

Important Notice

1. If there is insufficient space to complete an answer, please attach a signed and dated addendum. Any documents attached shall form part of this proposal form.

2. Your attention is drawn to the 60 days Premium Warranty attached to the Policy. By this warranty, the insurance policy is automatically cancelled unless the full premium is paid to the insurer within 60 days from the commencement date of cover. Please note that if this insurance is transacted through your insurance broker, the broker is acting on your behalf for the purpose of formation of this contract of insurance. It is important that you ensure your insurance broker remits your premium to the insurer concerned in strict compliance with the provisions of the Premium Warranty.

Declaration

I/We hereby declare that the information given is true and complete to the best of my/our knowledge and believe that all material information affecting the assessment of this application have been disclosed.

I/We understand that this insurance will not be enforced until and unless this proposal has been accepted by Etiqa Insurance Berhad (hereinafter referred to as "Company").

I/We also declare that The Total Sums To Be Insured Represent Not Less Than The Full Value Of The Property, as above mentioned, and I/we agree that no insurance shall commence until the proposal has been accepted by the Company.

Signature of Proposer/Company Stamp

Verification Of Proposer's Identity

In Compliance With Section 16/2 Of The Anti-Money Laundering Act 2001

I/We hereby certify that the Proposer's original NRIC/Business Registration Certification was verified and authenticated by me/us at the Point of Sales.

Third Party Verification*

Name of Officer/Intermediary .... Signature

NRIC/Business Registration Certification .... Date ....

* "Third Party" means by Insurance Agents, Insurance Brokers or staff of Insurance Companies.

Note:
To retain a copy of NRIC for Applicant(s)/Proposer(s) for Individual Policy Insurance where the premium is exceeding RM50,000.00 per annum and a copy of Business Registration Certificate for Group Policy Insurance is exceeding RM100,000.00 per annum.

For Office Use

Source: HQ/Branch .... Sales Channel Code: ....

Channel: .... Sales Channel Name: ....

The New India Assurance Company Limited

Head Office: 87, M G Road, Fort, Mumbai-400001

PROPOSAL FORM FOR THE INSURANCE OF NEON SIGNS AND/OR HOARDINGS

Name of Proposer (in full)

Address:

Occupation or Business Paid Up Capital (if applicable):

1	Particulars of the Hoarding or Neon Signs (a) Full description along with measurements of its size (b) Year of manufacture (c) By whom manufactured (d) Price paid by proposer	
2	Particulars of the Foundation and/or supporting structure on which Sign and/or Hoarding is erected. The measurements of and materials from which such foundation and/or supporting structure is constructed should be given	
3	Has the structure of the sign been approved and passed by the Municipal or other Government Authority concerned? Does it require such approval?	
4	Will the Sign its foundation, supporting structure, fastening attachments etc. be regularly inspected by a duly qualified Electrician and Engineer if so, by whom and at what intervals?	
5	Will the repairs or defects found by these inspections be immediately carried out or set right?	
6	What are the measures adopted for the prevention of loss or damage occurring as a result of the falling down of the Sign?	
7	Particulars of the property on which the sign is erected and/or attached to (a) Is the sign affixed to the wall or erected on the roof of a building (b) State the address and the situation of the building (c) What is the approximate age of the building?	

	(d) Is the building in a sound condition? (e) Is the building abutting on to a main thoroughfare? (f) How far away is the nearest building or structure from the building on which the Sign is installed? (g) How far away is the building concerned situated from the Road or Street or Kerb on all sides? (h) Give brief information and particulars of the surrounding area of the building. (i) If the Sign/Hoarding is erected or placed on the roof of a building, please state whether the roof is flat or gabled and how far it is from the edge of the roof on all sides. (j) If the sign is erected on the ground give full particulars of its surroundings. How far away is it from any public or other pathways, thorough fares, streets, roads, etc.? (k) How high is the Sign/Hoarding from ground level? (I) How high is the Sign/Hoarding from roof level?	
8	Have any claims been made against you in the last five years in respect of accidents caused directly or indirectly by the Sign/Hoarding? If so, give full particulars.	
9	Has any Company: (a) declined your proposal? (b) refused to renew your policy? (c) demanded an increased rate on renewal? (d) cancelled any of your insurances?	
10	Have you received any notice from any person or authority regarding any defect in the Sign/Hoarding?	
11	Amount of Indemnity required: (a) In respect of loss of or damage to the Sign/Hoarding? (b) In respect of Third Party Liability: (a) Any one Accident: (i) Personal Injury (ii) Damage to Property (c) For all Accidents in any one period of Ins	

I/WE HEREBY DECLARE AND WARRANT that the above statements are true and complete. I/We desire to effect an Insurance with The Company, and I/We agree that this proposal and declaration shall be the basis of the contract between me/us and the Company and I/We agree to accept a Policy subject to the conditions prescribed by the Company.

Proposer's Signature ....

Date ....

Note
1. The liability of the company does not commence until the proposal has been accepted by the Company and full premium paid.
2. If space is found insufficient, please attach separate sheets for details.
3. Insurance is the subject matter of solicitation.

PROHIBITION OF REBATE -- Section 41 of the Insurance Act 1938

No person shall allow or offer to allow, either directly or indirectly, as an inducement to any person to take out or renew or continue an insurance in respect of any kind of risk relating to lives or property in India, any rebate of the whole part of the commission payable or any rebate of the premium shown on the policy nor shall any person taking out or renewing or continuing a policy accept any rebate, except such rebates as may be allowed in accordance with the published prospectuses or tables of the Insurer.

Any person making default in complying with the provisions of this section be punishable with fine which may extend to Five Hundred Rupees.

For Office Use -

MARKETING/DEVELOPMENT OFFICER'S REPORT

The Proposer is known to me/my agent/Broker for_____years and I recommend acceptance of this proposal.

Name and Code No. Signature of Dev. Officer / A/AO-D

ACCEPTED BY DATE & TIME RATE REMARKS

CODES - OFFICE/DEV. OFFICER/AGENT/BROKER-

COLLECTION/SCROLL NO POLICY NO.

The New India Assurance Company Limited

Head Office: 87, M G Road, Fort, Mumbai-400001

Claim Form For Neon Sign/Glow Sign

THE ISSUE OF THIS FORM IS NOT TO BE TAKEN AS AN ADMISSION OF LIABILITY

Policy No.....................................

Claim No......................................

1. Name of the Insured:
2. Address:
3. Address where the glass situated (Please state position of Neon Sign)
4. Size of Neon Sign
5. Cause of Breakage
6. Date of Breakage
7. Name and address of the person causing breakage
8. Was he in any way employed by the Insured?
9. The make and Origin of the Neon Sign
10. Cost of Neon Sign (Paid)
11. Additional observations, if any:

I/We hereby declare that the foregoing statements are made by myself/ourselves and are true in all respects and that I/We have not attempted to conceal from the Company anything which it ought to be made acquainted.

Signature of the Claimant

Date:

N.B. Please give a rough sketch of the breakage on the reverse

C. PET INSURANCE

Pacific Pet Plan – Proposal Form

About you...

Name : ______________________________

Address : ______________________________

Country ______________

Telephone : + ______________ Mobile + ______________

Email : ______________________________

About your Pet(s)

Name	Cat or Dog	Breed/Crossbreed	Date of Birth	Male or Female

Is your Pet(s) used for any breeding purposes? ***YES / *NO**

Does your Pet(s) have any pre-existing medical conditions? ***YES / *NO**

Any ongoing claims concerning your Pet(s)? ***YES / *NO**

If "YES" to any of the above, please give details: ______________________________

____

Dog Owners Only

If your Dog is a crossbreed, has it been bred with any of the following excluded breeds? Chinese Shar Pei; Pit Bull (American & Staffordshire); Rottweiler; Dog Argentions; any Breed of Wolf? ***YES / *NO**

Please tick the Plan you would like...

Diamond

Gold

Silver*

Important note: * Silver plan is not available in N. America, EU, Japan, Hong Kong, Singapore and Australasia

Declaration: I (we) have read and understood the terms and conditions and that Pacific Casualty and General Insurance Ltd is incorporated in the Republic of Vanuatu and I (we) hereby submit our application for the Pacific Pet Plan insurance as above and I (we) declare the information provided herein is accurate and complete to the best of my (our) knowledge and believe that all material facts affecting the assessment of this application have been disclosed. I understand that this application will not come into effect until this proposal has been accepted by Pacific Casualty and General Insurance Ltd and agree that this proposal shall be the basis of the contract.

____

Signature

Date: ______________________

Brokers Company Stamp

Pacific Casualty & General Insurance Co. Ltd is incorporated in the Republic of Vanuatu

VPI PET
insurance

VPI PET INSURANCE CLAIM FORM

No Cover Sheet Necessary. Fax to: 714-989-5600 No. of pages: ____

Take this form to your veterinarian to complete Section 2. Veterinarian's signature not required.

1 Policyholder Information

POLICY NO: ____________

PET NAME: ____________

BREED: ____________

AGE: ____________

NAME: ____________

ADDRESS: ____________

CITY: ____________

STATE: ________ ZIP: ________

PHONE (H): ____________

PHONE (B): ____________

EMAIL: ____________

2 **Fill in below. ONE CLAIM FORM PER PET.** You must submit itemized receipts. You must provide us with veterinary medical records when we request them. Claims that are NOT COMPLETE or MISSING itemized, legible receipts or invoices may be delayed.

Wellcare Treatments	Treatment Date	Hospital/ Clinic
❑ Annual Exam	/ /	
❑ Annual Lab Tests	/ /	
❑ Vaccinations	/ /	
❑ Dental	/ /	
❑ Spay/Neuter	/ /	
❑ Heartworm/Flea Medication	/ /	

DIAGNOSIS(ES) **Please provide a diagnosis, or a tentative diagnosis, not a description of services performed.**	TREATMENT DATE	HOSPITAL/CLINIC
	/ /	
	/ /	
	/ /	
	/ /	
	/ /	
	/ /	
	/ /	

3 **TOTAL AMOUNT SUBMITTED**

$ ____________

You must submit receipts for all veterinary service charges. All submitted fees may not be eligible for coverage. Fees that exceed benefit schedule limits are your responsibility.

By signing this Claim Form, I confirm that to the best of my knowledge the information I have provided is true and correct. I authorize the release of my pet's medical records to Veterinary Pet Insurance Company/DVM Insurance Agency.

4 **POLICYHOLDER SIGNATURE and DATE**

X ____________ / /

5 **FAX:** *(Preferred Method)* **714-989-5600**

OR

MAIL:
VPI Claims Department
PO Box 2344, Brea CA 92822
PLEASE DO NOT USE STAPLES, PAPER CLIPS OR TAPE to attach receipts or Invoices to your claim form.

To download claim forms: petinsurance.com/forms
QUESTIONS? Customer Care Dept: 800-540-2016

VPI DOCUMENT CENTER USE ONLY

CLAIMS NOTES (VPI use only)

Fax Only The Front of This Claim Form. No Cover Sheet Required.

CLAIM FORM CHECKLIST ✓

- ❑ I entered in my policy number, pet information and my contact information.
- ❑ This claim form includes only one pet.
- ❑ My veterinarian helped me complete Section 2 with the diagnosis(es), treatment date and the name of the hospital/clinic.
- ❑ I included all of my itemized and legible receipts/invoices.
- ❑ My pet's name and policy number are clearly identified on each receipt/invoice.
- ❑ I added up all my eligible receipts and entered the Total Amount Submitted.
- ❑ I signed and dated this claim form. (My veterinarian is not required to sign this form.)
- ❑ I submitted this claim form and all supporting receipts/invoices to the VPI Claims Department. I understand that claim forms that are incomplete or missing itemized and legible supporting receipts/invoices may be delayed.
- ❑ I kept a back-up copy of all documentation submitted for my records.
- ❑ If medical records are requested to process this claim, I understand that it is my responsibility to provide them to VPI.

Two ways to submit your claim:

Fax 714-989-5600

– OR –

VPI Claims Department, PO Box 2344, Brea, CA 92822

If FAXING your claim, DO NOT MAIL IT IN. Duplicate claims submission may delay processing.

Fraud Warning: Any person who knowingly and with intent to defraud any insurance company or other person files an application for insurance or statement of claim containing any materially false information or conceals for the purpose of misleading, information concerning any fact material thereto commits a fraudulent insurance act, which is a crime and subjects such person to criminal and civil penalties.

Not applicable in Nebraska, Oregon and Vermont.

PET DOG INFORMATION

How to work out your MONTHLY PREMIUM

1 Choose your Dog Plan		Budget Dog Plan	Standard Dog Plan	Supreme Dog Plan
Vet's Fees & Alternative Treatment	For Illness & injury, including hospitalisation, referral & medicines.	$9,000 each year	$14,000 each year	$18,000 each year
Death from illness	Losing a dog is a great sadness but We will refund the purchase price.	Nil	Nil	$2,000
Death from injury	Nothing can replace a loved Dog but We will refund the purchase price.	Nil	$1,000	$2,000
Boarding kennel fees	Or home care with a friend if You are hospitalised for more than 4 days.	$500 each year	$1,000 each year	$2,000 each year
Advertising & Reward	If Your Dog gets lost or stolen We will pay for local newspaper advertising & a reward.	$500	$1,000	$2,000
Theft or Straying	If Your Dog is lost or stolen and not found despite all efforts We will refund the purchase price.	Nil	$1,000	$2,000
Holiday Cancellation Cost	If Your Dog has urgent life saving surgery or goes missing up to 7 days before or while you are away.	Nil	$1,000	$2,000
Third party Liability	If Your Dog causes damage or injury and you are legally liable.	$1m	$3m	$5m
You may choose from 3 different Plans for Your dog. Please refer to your Petplan policy wording and Product Disctosure Statement for full details of the cover provided by each type of Plan A copy can be viewed on our website at http:/www.p.......... orby phoning 1300 738 225	(Price Includes GST) This is how much you pay monthly (Price Includes GST) Annual Premium	$36.90 $415.70	$41.00 $466.30	$46.70 $533.00

2 Choose your Dog Plan		Budget Cat Plan	Cat Plan	Supreme Cat Plan
Vet's Fees & Alternative Treatment	For Illness & injury, including hospitalisation, referral & medicines.	$8,000 each year	$9,000 each year	$12,000 each year
Death from illness or injury	Losing a cat is a great sadness but We will refund the purchase price.	Nil	Nil	$1,000
Boarding Cattery Fees	Or home care with a friend if You are hospitalised for more than 4 days.	$500 each year	$500 each year	$1,000 each year
Advertising & Reward	If Your Cat gets lost or stolen We will pay for local newspaper advertising & reward.	$500	$500	$2,000
Theft or Straying	If Your Cat is lost or stolen and is not found despite all efforts We will refund the purchase price.	Nil	$1,000	$2,000
Holiday Cancellation Cost	If Your Cat has urgent life saving surgery or goes missing up to 7 days before or while You are away.	Nil	$1,000	$2,000
You may choose from 3 different Plans for Your cat. Please refer to your Petplan policy wording and Product Disctosure Statement for full details of the cover providing by each type of Plan A copy can be viewed on our website at http:/www.p.......... orby phoning 1300 738 225	(Price Includes GST) This is how much you pay monthly (Price Includes GST) Annual Premium	$21.90 $223.65	$23.00 $237.45	$27.40 $294.95

Pet% Share - the cheaper option

This is the low cost option where you select one of the three plan options above and when you have .... pay the fixed excess, plus 23% of the cost of the treatment. In return you get around 25% discount off the annual premium, i.e. If you select Budget Dog Plan the annual premium is $41............ with Pet% Share option, the premium is $311.90 annually. Ring 1300 738 225 for monthly & annual premiums for Pet%Share. Excesses can be viewed in our Policy Wording & Product Disclosure .... on our website.

Important Information about Your Cover

- You can start your Pet's insurance from 8 weeks of age and before their 6th birthday (5th birthday for Select Breeds dog).
- Cover for Injury starts as soon as we accept Your application. Illness cover starts after the 21st day of cover, after we accept your application.
- We cannot provided cover for any **Injury** or **Illness** that happened or showed **Clinical Signs** before taking out **Your Policy,** or any **Illness** occuring or showing **Clinical Signs** in the first 21 days of **Your** Insurance.
- If after receiving Your Certificate of Insurance and Policy Terms and Conditions you are not happy you have 14 days during which you can cancel the policy and receive a full refund of any premium paid (providing you have not made a claim in the 14 day cooling off period).

Select Breeds

Bandog, Beauceron, Bernese Mountain Dog, Eulldog, American Bulldog, Bull Arab, Deerhound, Dogue de Bordeaux, Estrela Mountain Dog, Great Dane, Irish Wolfhound, Leonberger. All Mastiff Breeds, Newfoundland, Minlature Bulldog, Old English Sheepdog, Pyrenean Mountain Dog, Pottweiler, Shar Pei, St Benard or any crosses of these breeds.

Multi-pet Discount

If you are insuring three or more pets, we will give you a 10% discount, please advise if you quality for a multi-pet discount when sending in your application.

Dog & Cat **Application Form 0800 255 426**
Phone free for immediate cover or more information, or fill out and post ....
Policy Commencement Data / / To / /
Cover Note Number: ....

Your personal details		
Surname *(Mr/Mrs/Miss/Ms)*		
Christian Names(s)		
Address		
	Postcode	
Email		
Your Date of Birth / /	Daytime Ph No	

Your pet's details						
Your Pet's Name						
Date of Birth / /	Male		Female		Desexed	
Breed (if crossbred tell us what breeds make up the mix) Colour						
Microchip/Tattoo No					Purchase	$
You are required under your Duty of Disclosure to list ALL injures, illnesses & .... your Pet has had.						
Has your pet had ANY injury or illness that required Vet treatment?	Yes		No			
Has your pet had an injury of illness BUT did not require Vet treatment?	Yes		No			
If Yes Please give details of injury illness and date treated. If space insufficient details on a separate sheet.				Date		
Do you own any other Pets Besides this Pet? If YES provide details of your other pets.	Yes		No			
Are your Pets insured? If NO provide details as to why	Yes		No			

If you answer yes to any of the following questions please give details on a separate sheet.

Has a claim or complaint involving your pet been lodged in the last 5 yrs?	Yes		No	
Does your pet have vicious tendencies?	Yes		No	
Is your pet used in any trade/profession occupation go to work with you?	Yes		No	

Name of Vet Practice your Pet attends If your .... has attended other ....
Name
Address
Phone

Declaration and Signature

Declaration - 1/We declare that

- Received a copy of that policy word.... and product disclosure statement or have read it online;
- Read the information concerning the .... of disclosure and other important notices.
- Answered every question fully & frankly.
- Either completed this proposal form personally or, if it has bee completed by somebody else, have checked the question have been fully and accurately answered.
- The Pet that is being proposed for insurance is in a sound state of health and the sums stated represent their full value;
- I/We authorise any Vet to supply Petplan my Pet's complete medical history or to supply details of claims and other relevent information.
- I acknowledge that I have read and understood the Privacy Act 1993 information and consent to the collection, storage, use and disclosure of personal and sensitive information of all persons covered by **this proposal**, with their approval.

Applicants's
Signature .... Date / /

Policy No: **(Office Use Only)**

Your choice of cover						
Dog	Budget plan		Standard plan		Supreme plan	
Cat	Budget plan		Cat plan		Supreme plan	
Pet%Share						

How do you want to pay		
Choose your payment method		
Monthly by direct debit		Please complete Pitect Debit Request
Monthly by credit card		Fill in credit card details below
Annually by credit card		Fill in credit card details below
Annually by cheque		Attach to proposal form and remit

Amount you are paying	**Monthly**	**Annually**
Premium please refer to the enclosed leaflet and select the premium for the plan you have selected	$	$
Pensioner Discount Deduct monthly $1.00 per pet insured.	$	$
If you are insuring more than 3 pets, please phone us for a discount		
Total Monthly/Annual payment	$	$

Credit Card Details					
Please charge my					
Visa Card		Monthly		Annually	
Master card		Monthly		Annually	
And debit my credit card		Monthly		Annually	
Unless cancelled by me in writing					

Card number

Card Expiry Date

Card Holder's Name

Card Holder's Signature

Direct Debit Request

User Identification No.:

To: Petplan ABN 64 069 468 542

I/We	Insert your name $ address
Of	

Request you until further notice in writing, to debit my our account as described in the schedule below, any amounts due and payable to you under my/our insurance policy with you. I/We acknowledge and agree that:

1. This Direct Request ("DDR") is governed by the terms & conditions of the Direct Debit Client Agreement ("Agreement") provided to me/us;
2. By stoning this DDR, I/We acknowledge that I am/we are bound by all the terms & conditions of the Agreement; and
3. You may vary the amount and frequency of future debits under this DDR and the Agreement by prior arrangement and advice to me/us in accordance with the terms of the agreement.

....

....

(If total account, all signatures may be required)

The Schedule

....

Address of Plans or Financial ....

Name of account to be credited

BSB Number							Account Number									

Please note: Direct debiting is not available for all accounts. If in doubt please contact your bank or financial institution.

Administrator

Petplan Australasia Ply Ltd. ABN 64 069 468 542 AFSL No. 245663 is the sole Administrator of the policy.

Petplan Is a Registered Trade Mark, and Products sold under this Trade Mark. In Australia are sold excusively by Petplan Australasia Pty-Ltd under Licence to Petplan UK Limited.

Head Office

1-3 Smolic Crt, Tullamarine, Vic, 3043
Ph: 1300 738 225 Fax: (03) 9339 3377
info@petplan.com.au : http://www.petplan.com.au

"Introductory offer applies only for new policies Cannot be used in conjunction with any other Petplan offer

Petplan® the pet insurance people

For petplan use only

Claim Form for Veterinary Fees

New Condition ☐ Continuation Condition ☐ Previous claim no _______

Please make sure this claim form is completed CLEARLY and IN FULL to ensure the correct assessment of your claim.
If you are submitting a CONTINUATION CLAIM, please complete the YELLOW SHADED BOXES MARKED WITH A 'C'.
Please complete using BLACK PEN and BLOCK CAPITALS.

NoteN

- **Please use a separate claim form for each pet, each illness or injury and each treating Veterinary Practice.**
- **If you are claiming for a NEW CONDITION and the claim amount does not exceed the Excess stated on Your Certificate of Insurance, you are not eligible to make a claim.**

We're happy to help
If you have any questions call us on
1300 738 225

1. Policyholder to complete — POLICY NUMBER:

2. Policyholder to complete — ABOUT YOU

Policyholder's name C

Daytime telephone no.

Email address

Policyholder's address

Postcode

Please tick here if this is different to the address on your Certificate of Insurance ☐

3. Policyholder to complete — ABOUT YOUR PET

Pet's name C

Pedigree name (If applicable)

Is your pet a Dog ☐ Cat ☐

Pet's date of birth / / Male ☐ Female ☐

Breed

Is this pet insured with any other company? Yes ☐ No ☐

If Yes, Please state which company

Have you, or are you intending to lodge a claim for this illness/injury with them? Yes ☐ No ☐

4. Policyholder to complete — DETAILS OF YOUR PET'S ILLNESS

What condition(s) are you claiming forS?

Please tell us the date you noticed any signs that your pet was unwell before booking an appointment with your vet. Your claim may be delayed if you do not give us this information.

Date Condition first noticed / / am pm

Date Pet seen by Vet / / am pm

Do you own any other pets NOT insured with Petplan? Yes ☐ No ☐

Did the illness or injury result in the death of your pet? Yes ☐ No ☐

Date of Death / /

Please tell us the name A addresses of all vet surgeries where your pet has been treated before or the vet that referred you. (If there is more than one, please use a separate piece of paper)

Name

Address

Postcode

Telephone no.

Date: from / / to / /

If your pet was injured - How did the injury occur (detail on separate sheet if space is insufficient)

Is anyone else responsible for the injury, if so supply name A address of person (s)

5. Policyholder to complete — PAYEE DETAILS

Cheques will be automatically made payable to the policyholder(s) named on your certificate of Insurance, unless we are instructed otherwise.

Is any insured registered for GST A entitled to an ITC Yes ☐ No ☐

If yes, what is your ITC percentage ☐ T ABN

PLEASE COMPLETE ONE OF THE FOLLOWING

Please note we will not pay your vet unless it has been previously agreed with them to do so. Please check with your vet

☐ A. Pay Vet - please tick C

I/We have arranged with my/our vet and would like this claim paid directly to them, less my excess and any other non claimable items.

Name of the vet practice

Customer Id

Vet Practice sign here Date / /

☐ B. Pay Policyholders(s) - please tick C

I/We wish the claim to be paid to the policyholder(s) named on the certificate of Insurance.

☐ C. Issue Cheque with a different name to policyholder(s) - please tick C

I/We wish to have the Cheque issued with the following details.

Name

Account Name

INCOMPLETE CLAIM FORMS WILL BE RETURNED TO THE POLICYHOLDER

In order for your claim form to be processed in a timely manner please make sure that you have completed the claim form in full, have your vet complete their section, and it is signed by both You and Your Vet, and includes itemised invoices. If you fax/email your Claim, Petplan still require originals of all faxed/emailed items to be sent in the post.

Are all sections of the claim form completed	Yes ☐	No ☐	if not claim form will be returned
Has the Vet completed all their sections of the claim	Yes ☐	No ☐	if not claim form will be returned
Have You signed the claim form	Yes ☐	No ☐	if not claim form will be returned
Has Your Vet signed the Claim Form	Yes ☐	No ☐	if not claim form will be returned
Have included all itemised invoices with Claim	Yes ☐	No ☐	if not claim form will be returned

Privacy: The Privacy Act 1993 requires us to tell you that as an insurer we collect your personal and sensitive information in order to calculate your loss and entitlement, determine our liability, compile data and handle claims. When handling claims, we may disclose your personal and other information to third parties such as other insurers, loss adjusters, external claims data collectors, investigators and agents, to the Insurance Reference Service (IRS), etc, or other parties as required by law. You have the right to see access to your personal Information and to collect it at any time. Please contact us on 1300 738 225 EST 9am-5pm Mon-Fri and advise us of the changes.

IDR Statement: Disputes are not an everyday occurrence at Petplan. However we do provide an internal dispute resolution process should any dispute arise. Please feel free to ask for details. If you are not satisfied with the outcome of this process, we will advise you how to contact the insurance industry's external independent complaints scheme (subject to eligibility).

I/We certify the information given on this form is truthful, accurate and complete. No information likely to affect this claim has been withheld. I/We understand that this claim may be refused if information is untrue, inaccurate or concealed. I/We acknowledge that I/We have read and understood the Privacy Act 1993 and consent to the collection, storage, use and disclosure of personal and sensitive information to all persons affected by this claim. I/We acknowledge that if I/We do not agree to the collection of this personal and sensitive information then Petplan will be unable to process my/our claim.

I confirm that I have checked the information on this claim form and that it is all correct to the best of my knowledge and belief

Please sign here ✗ Date / /

*Not covered by your policy - Routine and preventative healthcare eg. Shampoo, nail clipping, teeth cleaning, worming, desexing and vaccination, any illness within your waiting period and pre-existing conditions

IMPORTANT NOTES • Please send completed claim forms including copies of all receipts to Petplan Australasia Pty Ltd, 1-3 Smolic Crt, Tullamarine, Vic 3043

Petplan Australaisa, ABN 64 069 468 542 AFSL No: 245663 administers the policy on behalf of Allianz Australia Insurance Limited ABN 15 000 122 AFSL 234708 which underwrites the policy.

ASK YOUR VET TO COMPLETE THESE THREE SECTIONS

1. Vet to Complete — GENERAL INFORMATION

When was this pet first registered at your practice / /

If this pet has been referred please give the name, address and telephone number of the practice which referred it

Name

Address

Telephone no

In connection with treatment claimed did you:

Make a house visit? Yes ☐ No ☐

Or provide out of hours treatment? Yes ☐ No ☐

If Yes, why was the house visit/out of hours treatment necessary?

Is any part of this claim for a condition the pet can be vaccinated against? Yes ☐ No ☐

If Yes, were the pet's vaccinations up to date at time of treatment?

Yes ☐ Please give date of last vaccination / / No ☐ Don't know ☐

Is any part of this claim for dental treatment? Yes ☐ No ☐

If Yes, please enclose a full clinical history over the last 2 years. If this is not attached this will delay the client's claim

Is any part of this claim for treatment of a urinary problem? Yes ☐ No ☐

If Yes, is the cost of diet food included in this claim? Yes ☐ No ☐

If Yes, please provide the name of the diet food being used and total cost being claimed

Name Amount $ -

Were crystals present? Yes ☐ No ☐

If Yes, are the crystals Oxalate ☐ Struvite ☐ Other ☐

If other, please specify

Please give date and results of last two urine tests

Date / / Result

Date / / Result

2. Vet to Complete — ABOUT THE ILLNESS OR INJURY

Condition

Name of the illness or injury (if no diagnosis has been made please give clinical signs)

Is this claim a continuation of a previous claim? Yes ☐ No ☐

When did this illness or injury begin or show clinical signs (as stated by the client and noted in your records)? / /

Treatment dates: from / / to / /

Did death or euthanasia result from this illness or injury? Yes ☐ No ☐

Date of death / /

If the pet was put to sleep, did you recommend this? Yes ☐ No ☐

To your knowledge has this pet been seen before for

This illness or injury Yes ☐ No ☐

Any similar or related illness or injury Yes ☐ No ☐

Any similar or related clinical signs Yes ☐ No ☐

If Yes, please provide the history with dates? Date / /

Date / /

Total amount being claimed (inc GST) $ -

PLEASE ENCLOSE FULL ITEMISED INVOICES AND RECIEPTS TO SUPPORT THIS CLAIM
ONE CONDITION PER CLAIM FORM

3. Vet to Complete — DECLARATION BY THE VETERINARY PRACTICE

This practice has authorised to have the claim(s) paid direct Yes ☐ No ☐

I have checked the information on this claim form and confirm that it is all correct to the best of my knowledge and belief

Name

Position in practice

Petplan Practice No:
If you do not know - leave blank

Ph:

Fax:

Email address:

Vet practice stamp here

Signature X Date / /
Vet/Practice Managers

D. Sports Insurance Proposal Form

ORGANISATION DETAILS

Full Name of Organisation:

___

Is the Organisation Incorporated? ☐ YES ☐ NO

ABN Number: ___ Input Tax Credit: ___%

Street Address: ___

___ State: ___ Postcode: ___

Postal Address: ___ State: ___ Postcode: ___

Contact Name: ___

Business Phone: ___ Business Fax: ___

Mobile: ___ Web: ___

Email: ___

Name of State or National Sporting Organisation you are affiliated with (if applicable):

___

SPORT DETAILS

What sport(s) does your organisation conduct? ___

Please describe all the activities of your organisation: ___

___

___

SPORTING CLUBS/ASSOCIATIONS

Number of Junior Members: ___

Number of Senior Members: ___

Number of Non-Playing Officials: ___

Number of Qualified Coaches/Referees/Instructors. ___

COACHING/TRAINING/INSTRUCTION ORGANISATIONS

Number of Registered Clients: ___

Number of Sessions run per week: ___

Average number of clients per session: ___

Number of qualified Coaches/Referees/Instructors: ___

Are your activities conducted continuously throughout the year or are they conducted in competition seasons? ☐ Continuously ☐ Seasons

If Seasons, how many competition seasons do you have in a year? ___

If Seasons, what is the duration (in weeks) of each competition season? ___

If Seasons, how many fixture matches does each of your teams play in each competition season?

Senior (open age) ___

Juniors - Up to & including Under 18 ___

Are all your Coaches, umpires/referees and other officials accredited? ☐ YES ☐ NO

General Details

What is the annual turnover of your organisation? $ ____________

Does your organisation own its premises or are they hired/leased? ☐ OWN ☐ LEASED

If owned, are these premises hired out to others? ☐ YES ☐ NO

If yes, please provide details: ____________

If yes, is the hirer required to have its own public liability insurance for a minimum of $10,000,000? ☐ YES ☐ NO

Does your organisation hire out any equipment? ☐ YES ☐ NO

If yes, please provide details: ____________

____

Are there any grandstands at your organisation's premises? ☐ YES ☐ NO

If yes, please advise seating capacity and type of construction (e.g. 10,000, brick, steel and concrete):

____

Does your organisation operate licensed premises? ☐ YES ☐ NO

If yes, please provide licence details (how often open, hours of licence).

____

Does your organisation have poker machines? ☐ YES ☐ NO

If yes, please advise number: ____________

Does your organisation sell goods to the public? ☐ YES ☐ NO

If yes, please provide details: ____________

Has your organisation entered into any contracts where it has assumed the liability of others or agreed to hold them harmless? ☐ YES ☐ NO

If yes, please provide details ____________

____

____

RISK MANAGEMENT DETAILS

Does your organisation have documented risk management policies and procedures in place? (copies of these documents may be requested) ☐ YES ☐ NO

Does your risk management program include policies/procedures regarding:

- Member: Protection (i.e. child protection, discrimination, harassment, codes of conduct, etc.) ☐ YES ☐ NO
- Facility and equipment maintenance and safety ☐ YES ☐ NO
- First Aid, including blood and infectious diseases ☐ YES ☐ NO
- Emergency/disaster plan e.g. very serious injury/ies ☐ YES ☐ NO

Was any consultant involved or specialised computer program used in preparing these risk management policies and procedures? ☐ YES ☐ NO

If yes, please provide details?

____

Does your organisation operate using an Indemnity/Waiver Form? ☐ YES ☐ NO

If yes, please provide a copy.

Insurance Cover Required:

Note: Whilst Sports Personal Accident, Public Liability and Professional Indemnity insurance is usually organised on a package basis, we can provide both Personal Accident and Public Liability in isolation, however Professional Indemnity can only be provided in conjunction with Public Liability.

Required period of insurance ____/ ____/ ____ to ____/ ____/ ____

1. Personal Accident (Sports Injury) ☐ YES ☐ No

If YES, please complete the following:

☐ **GOLD cover** ☐ **SILVER cover** ☐ **BRONZE cover**

Loss of Income cover required? ☐ YES ☐ NO

Three options of cover (Gold, Silver or Bronze) are available.

Outlined below are the differences in cover between the 3 options, plus details of cover common to all three options.

(a) GOLD cover

— Death and Permanent Disability as per scale (Capital Benefits) $ 75,000

— Non Medicare medical expenses – 85% to a maximum of $2,500 with a $50 excess if no private health insurance; nil excess if private health insurance

Gold Optional Loss of Income Extras

— Loss of Income - $500 per week up to 52 weeks with a 7 day excess, or

— Student Assistance Benefit - $500 per week up to 52 weeks with a 7 day excess or

— Home Help Benefit - $500 per week up to 52 weeks with a 7 day excess

(b) Silver cover

— Death and Permanent Disability as per scale (Capital Benefits) $50,000

— Non Medicare medical expenses - 85% to a maximum of $2,000 with a $50 excess if no private health insurance; nil excess if private health insurance

Bronze Optional Loss of Income Extras

— Loss of Income - $350 per week up to 52 weeks with a 7 day excess, or

— Student Assistance Benefit - $350 per week up to 52 weeks with a 7 day excess, or

— Home Help Benefit - $350 per week up to 52 weeks with a 7 day excess

(c) Bronze cover

— Death and Permanent Disability as per scale (Capital Benefits) $50,000

— Non Medicare medical expenses – 85% to a maximum of $1500 with a $50 excess if no private health insurance; nil excess if private health insurance

Bronze Optional Loss of Income Extras

— Loss of Income - $250 per week up to 52 weeks with a 7 day excess, or

— Student Assistance Benefit - $250 per week up to 52 weeks with a 7 day excess, or

— Home Help Benefit - $250 per week up to 52 weeks with a 7 day excess

The following covers are included under all of Gold, Silver and Bronze covers in addition to the benefit outlined above.

— Parents inconvenience allowance - $25 per day to a maximum of $1,500

— Funeral Expenses to a maximum of $5,000

— Ancillary non medical expenses to a maximum of $1,500

— Home/car modification benefits to a maximum of $10,000

— Vocational Tuition to a maximum of $3,000

— Rehabilitation expenses to a maximum of $500

— In Memoriam expenses to a maximum of $1,000

— Home Nursing Care benefit $300 per week up to 52 weeks with a 7 day excess

— Dependent Children's Allowance to maximum of $500

— Unexpired membership benefit to a maximum of $500

— HIV Positive benefit to 10% of the Capital Sum Insured

— Miscarriage or Premature Childbirth Benefit to $2,500

— Kidnapping Benefit to 10% of Capital Sum Insured.

Note: The benefits outlined are a broad summary of cover. Refer to the policy wording for terms and conditions.

2. Public Liability Insurance ☐ YES ☐ NO

If YES, please complete the following:

Select Gold or Silver cover from below by ticking the relevant box.
If an optional $1,000 excess is required tick the relevant box.

(a) GOLD cover ☐

— Public liability – Limit of Indemnity any one event $20,000,000

— Product liability – Limit any one event and in the aggregate $20,000,000

(b) SILVER cover ☐

— Public liability – Limit of Indemnity any one event $10,000,000

— Products liability – Limit any one event and in the aggregate $10,000,000

The standard Gold and Silver public liability cover has no excess.

Tick the box if a $1,000 excess is required with a discount applying to the premium. ☐

3. Professional Indemnity Insurance for Coaches, Referees/Umpires and Match Officials ☐ YES ☐ No

If YES, please complete the following:

Note: Professional Indemnity cannot be taken in isolation.
It can only be taken in conjunction with Public Liability cover.

Select Gold or Silver cover from below by ticking the relevant box.
If an optional $1,000 excess is required tick the relevant box.

(a) GOLD cover ☐

Professional Indemnity – Limit any one event and in the aggregate $2,000,000

(b) SILVER cover ☐

Professional Indemnity liability – Limit any one event and in the aggreagate $1,000,000

The standard Gold and Silver professional indemnity cover have no excess.

Tick the box if a $1,000 excess is required with a discount applying to the premium. ☐

Retroactive Data (refer to note on page 7). _________ / _________ / _________

Claims/Insurance History

Current Policy Due Date ____________________

Current Broker ____________________

Please advise the name of previous and current Insurers

1. ____________________ Years on Risk From __________ to __________
2. ____________________ Years on Risk From __________ to __________
3. ____________________ Years on Risk From __________ to __________

Have you, or any director/partner/manager of the organisation ever:

Sustained any loss or damage or incurred liability during the last 5 years whether insured or not of a type against which insurance is now sought?	☐ YES	☐ NO
Are there any circumstances of which you are aware which could give rise to a claim under the proposed policy?	☐ YES	☐ NO
Had any insurance been declined or cancelled?	☐ YES	☐ NO
Had an insurer refused or not invited renewal?	☐ YES	☐ NO
Had any special conditions been imposed?	☐ YES	☐ NO
Had an excess been imposed, other than a standard excess?	☐ YES	☐ NO
Had a claim been rejected?	☐ YES	☐ NO
Been declared bankrupt, or put into receivership or voluntary liquidation?	☐ YES	☐ NO
Been charged/convicted of any criminal offence in the last 10 years?	☐ YES	☐ NO
Are there any other matters you should disclose (see "Your duty of disclosure")?	☐ YES	☐ NO

If you have answered YES to any of the above questions please supply full details. For incurred claims please advise data of loss, total amount paid, total amount outstanding, legal costs and describe occurrence and associated injury or damage. Confirmation of claims history on insurers letterhead may be requested. Details of the insurance cover in place at the time of these claims may also be required.

____

____

____

____

____

Sports Insurance Claim Form

1. Please complete Parts 2, 3, 4, 5, 6, 7 and 8 of this claim form (pages 2 and 3), plus the injury data collection questions on pages 5 and 6
2. Ask Your doctor to complete the 'Medical Statement' (pages 7 and 8)
3. If Your claim is for loss of earnings:
   (a) Ask Your employer to complete Part 9 (page 4). If You are self-employed please have Your accountant complete these details
   (b) Forward a medical certificate every two weeks if Your disability is continuing
4. An authorised official of Your club must complete Part 10 (page 4)
5. Please refer to 'Notes for claimants' on page 9

The Association

1

Sport played
Regional body
Association name
Club
Team
Age group
Grade [ ] Seniors [ ] Reserves [ ] (If applicable)

The Member

2

Name
Address
P/code
Phone Work Mobile
Email Address
Occupation
Date of Birth .... Sex: Male [ ] Female [ ]
Registration number

Details of the Member's Disability or Injury

3

What is the nature of Your injury?
What body part/s have been injured?
Is it a recurrence of a previous injury? Yes [ ] No [ ]
How did it happen?

Where were **You** when it happened?
Type of location Sportsground [ ] Gymnasium [ ] Swimming pool [ ]
Other [ ]
If 'Other' please describe
When did the injury occur? Date: ..../......../........ Time:
What were **You** doing? Playing match [ ] Warm up [ ] Training [ ]
Other sport [ ] Gradual onset [ ]
What was the event? Competition [ ] Regular training [ ] Training camp [ ]
Private training [ ] Other [ ]
If 'Other' please describe

Details of the Member's treatment

4 Name and address of each hospital **You** attended

Date of Admission: ....../....../...... Discharge: ....../....../....../

Name, address and phone numbers of all attending doctors

Name, address and phone number of **Your** usual doctor

Details of the Member's previous Disabilities, injuries or claims

5 Were You suffering any previous medical condition? Yes ☐ No ☐

If 'Yes', give details of the condition

Have You ever made a claim under a sports' injury or personal accident insurance policy? Yes ☐ No ☐

If 'Yes', what was the date of injury ....../....../......

Who was the insurer?

How much were **You** paid?

What was the injury?

Name and address of the doctor P/code

Details of the Member's insurance

6 Are **You** a member of a health fund Yes ☐ No ☐

If 'Yes', what type of membership do **You** have? Hospital cover only Ancillary cover only Hospital plus ancillary benefits

Name of health fund

Membership number

Any other details regarding private health cover

Do **You** have any other insurance to cover this disability or Injury? Yes ☐ No ☐

If 'Yes', please show name and address of insurer P/code

Drugs and intoxicating liquor

7 Were You under the influence of any drug or intoxicating liquor when the disability or injury took place? Yes ☐ No ☐

If "Yes", please give details

Have You taken any performance enhancing drugs? Yes ☐ No ☐

The Member's declaration

8 By signing this claim form I declare that

a. All the information that I have given in this form is correct
b. I authorise any doctor, hospital or other person who has treated me to provide OAMPS Insurance Brokers Ltd. or its representative with any medical records for any illness or injury I have suffered.
c. I authorise my employer to provide OAMPS Insurance Brokers Ltd. or its representative with details of my salary and working hours.
d. I agree that a photocopy of this authorisation will be accepted as valid.
e. I agree to allow the insurer to ask or tell other Insurers or Insurance reference bureaux about this or any other claim I have made.

Must be completed by the injured **Member** or their guardian if the member is under 18 years

Signature

Date

The Member's employment details (Must be completed by pay clerk/paymaster)

9

Employer's name	
Employer's address	
	P/code
Phone number	
What was your employee's gross weekly income at the date of injury for the 12 calendar months immediately preceding injury. (excluding bonuses, commissions, overtime or any other allowances)	$ p.w.
Date You expect Your employee to resume work	........./........./.........
Date **You** expect **Your** employee to resume normal duties (fully fit)	........./........./.........
What is Your employee's gross annual salary?	$
What date did he or she commence employment?	........./........./.........
If self-employed please attach proof of income over the Past 12 calendar months immediately preceding injury (net of business expenses, but before income tax and personal deduction e.g. Tax Return).	
What is the name of **Your** pay clerk?	
What is Your pay clerk's phone number?	
Signature of pay clerk / paymaster	
Date	........./........./.........

The Club's declaration

10 Must be completed by the club Secretary or Treasurer

If the Player was injured participating in a game please attach a copy of the team sheet to this claim form

I ....
Secretary or Treasurer

of ....
Name of club and association

Confirm that ....
Member's name

Sustained the injuries resulting in this claim on

.... at ....
Date time

While playing or training for ....
Team

against ....
Opposition Team

or while taking part in ....
Activity

against ....
Opposition Team

at ....
Place of game or activity

The first consultation with a doctor for this injury was on

....
Date

at ....
Address of doctor

Signature

Date ..../........./.........

Club mailing address	
	P/code
Phone number	

Injury data collection

OAMPS Insurance Brokers Ltd is committed to Safer Sport. Analysis of sporting injuries is critical to implementing injury prevention strategies OAMPS Insurance Brokers Ltd, in association with your sport and with your cooperation, is being proactive in collecting injury data with the aim of decreasing injuries. Thank you for assisting with this project.

What was Your role at the time of Your injury? Participant ☐ Coach ☐ Umpire/Referee ☐ Other Official ☐ Voluntary Worker ☐ Spectator ☐ Other ☐

If other, please provide details

How far into the activity were You at the time of the injury? (Note: Your answer relates to the time into the activity, rather than the period/stage of the game) Warm up ☐ 1st Quarter ☐ 2nd Quarter ☐ 3rd Quarter ☐ 4th Quarter ☐ Cool Down ☐

On what surface were You participating? Grass ☐ Synthetic Surface ☐ Wooden Floor ☐ Gravel ☐ Concrete/Bitumen ☐ Other ☐

If 'Other', please provide details

What was the condition of the surface? Normal ☐ Hard ☐ Wet ☐ Muddy ☐ Other ☐

If 'Other', please provide details

What were the weather conditions at the time of injury? Fine ☐ Light Rain ☐ Heavy Humid ☐ Other ☐

If 'Other', please provide details

What were the temperature conditions at the time of injury? Very Hot ☐ Hot ☐ Hot & Humid ☐ Mild ☐ Cold ☐ Very Cold ☐ Other ☐

If 'Other', please provide details

How was the onset of injury? Sudden ☐ Gradual ☐ Started Play With Pre-Existing Injury ☐

If a collision injury, what did You collide with? Ground ☐ Equipment ☐ Player ☐ Other Structure ☐

If 'Other', please provide details

What was Your activity leading to the injury? Landing ☐ Jumping ☐ Twist/Turn ☐ Side Stepping ☐ Starting ☐ Stopping ☐ Running ☐ Applying Tackle ☐ Being Tackled ☐ Receiving Ball ☐ Passing/Throwing ☐ Hitting ☐ Kicking ☐ Scrum ☐ Ruck ☐ Maul ☐ Other ☐

If 'Other', please provide details

Was protective equipment, tape or support being own on the injury site? Yes ☐ No ☐

If yes, please provide details Taping ☐ Protective Equip. ☐ Other Support ☐

If protective equipment, please provide details

If other support, please provide details

How did the injury severity affect Your playing? Unable to Continue Playing ☐ Continued to Play After Treatment ☐ Continued to Play Without Treatment ☐

What was the immediate treatment? (more than one box may be ticked) Rest ☐ Ice ☐ Compression ☐ Elevation ☐ Stretching ☐ Mobilisation ☐ Taping ☐ Bandaging ☐ Sling ☐ Splint ☐ Other ☐ Unknown ☐

If 'Other' please provide details

If 'Other' please provide details Yes ☐ No ☐ Unknown ☐

If Your injury required referral, to whom were **You** referred? Hospital ☐ Doctor ☐ Physiotherapist ☐ Dentist ☐ Other ☐

If 'Other', please provide details ____________________

If immediate off sitetreatment was necessary, What mode of transport was used? Ambulance ☐ Private Vehicle ☐ Other ☐

If 'Other', please provide details ____________________

Please indicate the site of your injury on The appropriate diagram below

Back

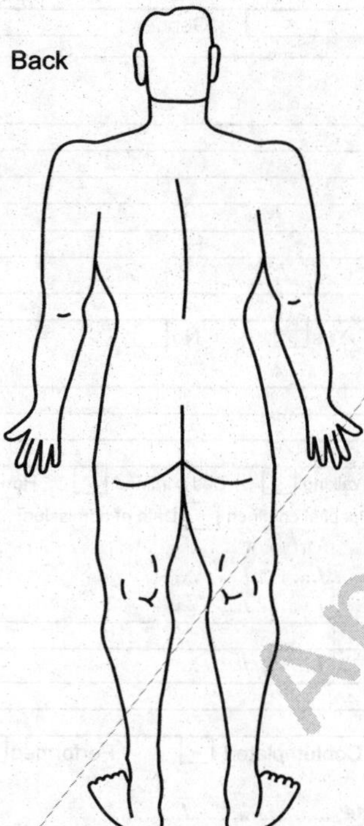

Front

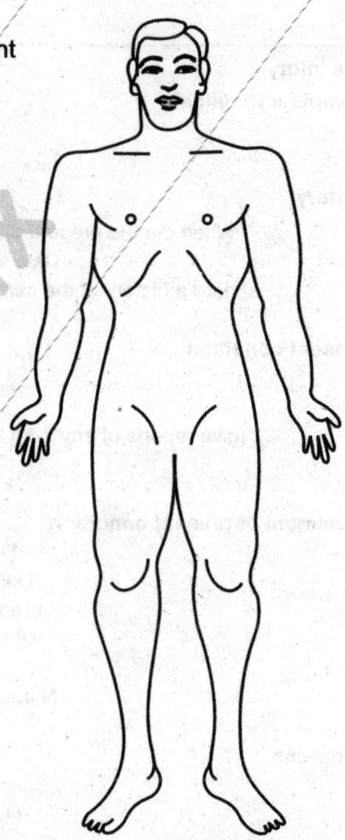

Head

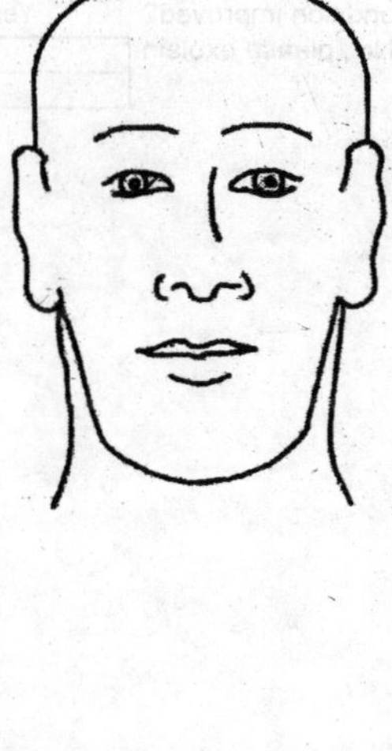

Medical statement

This form must be completed by the registered medical doctor treating the injury

The Association and Club

Association name

Club name

Type of sport

The Member

Name

Address

P/code

Age

Gender

The injury

Complete Diagnosis

History

When did the present disability or injury occur?

Date the player ceased work ..../.... . ..../.... . ....

Is there a history of the same or similar condition?

Is this a recurrence? Yes ☐ No ☐

Present condition

Subjective symptoms

Objective finding

(give reports of any x-rays, ECGs or other tests)

Is the player Walking ☐ Bed confined ☐ House confined ☐

Hospital confined ☐ Date of admission: ... ./... . .../... . ...

Treatment of present condition

Date of first consultation ..../.... . ..../.... . ....

Date of latest consultation ..../.... . ..../.... . ....

Frequency of consultations

Date of last hospitalisation ..../.... . ..../.... . ....

Name of hospital

Nature of surgical procedure

Contemplated ☐ Performed ☐

Progress

If performed Date: ..../.... . ..../.... . ....

Has condition improved? Yes ☐ No ☐

If 'No', please explain

Degree of disability

Has the patient been able to do any work?

If 'No', from what date Regular work: ... ./... . .../... . ... Light duties: ... ./... . .../... . ...

When will the patient be able to resume for Regular work: ... ./... . .../... . ... Light duties: ... ./... . .../... . ...

Other treatment

If the patient was seen in consultation by another doctor, .../... . .../... . ...

please give the date, name and address of that doctor.

P/code

If the patient is no longer under your care,

What date were your services terminated? ... ./... . .../... . ...

Other conditions

Describe any other disease or infirmity

Affecting the patient's present condition

Cardiac-circulatory

Please complete the appropriate section if disability or injury is due to:

Blood pressure

Circulatory disorder – please describe

Visual

Is the patient totally or industrially blind? Yes No

If 'No', what was the vision at last observation With glasses: Distant Near Date: ...../...../...../

Without glasses: Distant Near Date: ...../...../...../

What is the extent of any gross visual field defect?

Could vision be improved by treatment, surgery or lenses? Yes No

What are the rehabilitation prospects?

Orthopedic

Please report findings of specialist if referred?

Neurological

Please report findings of specialist if referred?

Prognosis

Remarks

Please apply doctors name stamp below

Signature

Date ..../..... . ...../..... . .....

Degree

Name of Doctor (please print)

Address

P/code

Notes for claimants

To ensure your claim is processed quickly and efficiently please follow steps below. Please read thoroughly and keep for your own reference.

Non Medicare medical expenses claim

1. Please note that due to Federal Government Legislation (Section 126, Health Insurance Act 1973) General Insurers are unable to provide benefits on any Medicare related expenses, including gap payments.
2. Refer to instructions on page 2 of claim form.
3. Claims for treatment given by a chiropractor, masseur, naturopath, osteopath or physiotherapist must be accompanied by a referral from a registered medical doctor.
4. If you hold private health insurance you are required to claim all expenses from your private health fund first. Once you have claimed from your health fund please forward your 'Statement of Benefits Paid', the account and receipt to us.
5. If you have already incurred non-Medicare medical expenses, please attach the original tax invoices along with a reciept confirming the account has been paid.

Loss of income claim

1. Refer to instructions on page 2 of claim form.
2. If you are self-employed have your accountant complete 'The Member's Employment Details' and supply us with a copy of your last tax assessment.
3. If you are an employee please forward payslips for the four weeks preceding your injury, or a letter from your employer on company letterhead confirming the gross amount earned per week for the four weeks preceding your injury.
4. Loss of income payments will not be made until the Medical Statement, medical certificates and proof of earnings are received.

Important

1. **Your claim cannot be processed if the claim forms are incomplete or illegible. To ensure your claim is processed without delay please make certain all sections on the *Sports Injury Claim Form, Medical Statement, Injury Data Collection* questionnaire and any applicable *Addendums to Injury Data Collection* questionnaires are fully complete.**
2. **Please forward your completed Sports Injury Claim Form to our office within 30 days of your injury. Do no wait for all your medical accounts. Forward them to us as you receive them.**
3. **Your Personal Accident Sports insurance policy covers medical expenses incurred within 365 days of the date of the event that caused the injury.**

If you have any questions or problems please contact us, we are always ready to help.

Complaints and disputes

If you are dissatisfied with a product or service provided by your Adviser, please contact the Manager of the Branch in your State.

If the Branch Manager is unable to resolve the complaint to your satisfaction, you may ask that the matter be referred to the National Complaints Manager for OAMPS Insurance Brokers Ltd. The National Complaints Manager will acknowledge your complaint in writing and endeavour to resolve your problem within 20 working days.

If you remain dissatisfied, you have the right to refer to your complaint to the Insurance Brokers Disputes Ltd. (IBD). Each of the licensed entities subscribes to the external facility for the handling of complaints. You can refer your complaint to an IBD Case Manager who will conciliate with a view to seeking a solution that is acceptable to both parties.

If either you or OAMPS reject the IBD Case Manager's finding and the dispute remains unresolved, it will be referred to the IBD's Referee whose decision is binding on us (but not on you). Further information about the IBD is available for all OAMPS Insurance Brokers Lid offices.

Contacts

Claim forms should be sent to the OAMPS Insurance Brokers office servicing your association. Details can be found via www.oamps.com.au, by calling our national sports insurance number 1800 SPORT 1 (800 776 781) or at our State and Territory capital city offices listed below:

Adelaide	**Brisbane**	**Canberra**	**Darwin**
168 Greenhill Road	Lvl 2, 8 Gardner Close	Ground Floor, 10 Geils Court	Lvl 2, 71 Smith Street
Parkside, Adelaide, SA 5063	Milton, Brisbane, QLD 4064	Deakin ACT 2600	Darwin, NT 0801
T: (08) 8172 8000	T: (07) 3367 5000	T: (02) 6283 6555	T: (08) 8942 5000
F: (08) 8172 8100	F: (07) 3367 5100	F: (02) 6283 6556	F: (08) 8942 5050
Hobart	Melbourne	Perth	Sydney
Lvl. 4, 85 Macquarie Street	176 Wellington Parade	Lvl 1, 21 Teddington Street	Lvl 1, 25 Grose Steet
Hobart, TAS 7000	East Melbourne, VIC 3002	Burswood, WA 6100	Nth Parramatta, NSW 2151
T: (03) 6235 1222	T: (03) 9412 1555	T: (08) 6250 8300	T: (02) 8838 5700
F: (03) 6235 1221	F: (03) 9412 1666	F: (08) 6250 8400	F: (02) 8838 5701

E. Shopkeeper's Insurance

Middlesea Insurance p.l.c.

Middle Sea House, Floriana GPO 01, Malta, Tel: 246262 - Fax: 248195

PROPOSAL FOR TRADERS COMBINED INSURANCE

IMPORTANT NOTE

Insurers, their Agents and Insurance Associations share information with each other to prevent fraudulent claims and for underwriting purposes. In the event of a claim, some or all of the information you supply in this form and in the claim form together with other information relating to the claim may be provided to other Insurers, their Agents and Insurance Associations.

All questions must be answered fully. Ticks and dashes are not sufficient.

PROSPECTUS

The following summary of the Policy is necessarily condensed but a Specimen Policy setting out the full terms and condition is available on request.

The Policy has been specially designed to cover in one document the insurance requirements of retail shopkeepers and for Traders.

The Middle Sea Shopkeepers/Traders Combined Policy contains the following different forms of protection:

SECTION 1 - TRADE CONTENTS	SECTION 7 - EMPLOYER'S LIABILITY
SECTION 2 - LOSS OF INCOME	SECTION 8 - GLASS
SECTION 3 - MONEY	SECTION 9 - BUILDINGS
SECTION 4 PERSONAL ACCIDENT ASSAULT	SECTION 10 - DETERIORATION OF STOCK
SECTION 5 - PUBLIC LIABILITY	SECTION 11 - ALL RISKS
SECTION 6 - TENANTS LIABILITY	SECTION 12 - GOODS IN TRANSIT

An important feature of this Policy is the 'New for Old' Basis of settlement under SECTION 1 - TRADE CONTENTS and SECTION 9 - BUILDINGS.

The Sums Insured under these Sections must therefore reflect the total value as new of such property.

PROPOSAL FOR SHOPKEEPERS/TRADERS COMBINED POLICY

Name of Proposer (in full) ____________________

Address of Proposer ____________________

Tel. No.: ______ I.D. Card Nr. ______ Insurance Required from ______ to ______

Business or Occupation: ____________________

Address of property to be insured:

____

____

____

____

State nature of the Business carried on in the premises containing the property to be insured:

____

____

____

SECTION 1 - TRADE CONTENTS **SUM INSURED**

1. Tobacco in any form including cigarettes and cigars.............................. ☐
2. Wines and Spirits.. ☐
3. All other stock and goods in trust.. ☐
4. Shop front and facia.. ☐
5. All other contents including interior decoration and additions to landlords' property and landlord's fixtures and fittings for which you are responsible (Sum insured must reflect value as new)........................ ☐

TOTAL

SECTION 2 - LOSS OF INCOME **SUM INSURED**

1. Estimated annual net takings.. ☐
2. Allowance for additional expenditure and trading trends.......................... ☐

TOTAL

SECTION 3 - MONEY

1. Limits as specified under relative Section of Policy
2. Estimated Annual Carryings ☐

SECTION 4 - PERSONAL ACCIDENT ASSAULT

1. Benefits as specified under relative Section of Policy

SECTION 5 - PUBLIC LIABILITY

1. Limits of Indemnity..Lm 100,000
2. If Hairdressers Liability Extension is required please state

   number of Ladies Operators.. ☐

   number of Gentlemen Operators... ☐
3. Are treatment risks undertaken?.. ☐
4. If yes, are all dyes, bleaches and tints of proprietary brands only?........ ☐
5. Do you work away from your premises?... ☐

SECTION 6 - TENANTS LIABILITY

1. Automatically included if applicable

SECTION 7 - EMPLOYER'S LIABILITY

1. Number of Employees... ☐
2. Estimated Annual Wages, Salaries and other earnings

   (a) Clerical Staff...Lm ☐

   (b) All others..Lm ☐
3. By virtue of a collective agreement of provisions made under the condition of Employment (Regulation) Act 1952, employers are liable in certain circumstances for payment of wages during injury leave to employees in respect of injuries occurring during the discharge of their duty. The indemnity under the Company's usual form of policy does not extend to include this liability but may do so on payment of additional premium.

   Please therefore indicate whether you will require this cover. ● YES ● NO

SECTION 8 - GLASS **SUM INSURED**

1. Total replacement value of Glass to be insured.. [ ]

SECTION 9 - BUILDINGS **SUM INSURED**

1. Buildings (Sum Insured must reflect value as new).............................. [ ]
2. Rent.. [ ]

SECTION 10 - DETERIORATION OF STOCK

1. Number of refrigerators and/or frozen foods cabinets............................ [ ]
2. Indicate requirements for each item in Table below:

Description of Unit	Age	Sums Insured of contents
(a)		
(b)		
(c)		
(d)		
	TOTAL	L m

SECTION 11 - "ALL RISKS"

1. Specify each item to be insured in Table below:

Description of Unit	Age	Sums Insured
(a)		
(b)		
(c)		
(d)		
(e)		
(f)		
(g)		
(h)		
	TOTAL	L m

SECTION 12 - GOODS IN TRANSIT

1. What is the nature of the Property to be insured?............................... [ ]
2. State number of vehicles used.. [ ]
3. Sum to be insured per vehicle..Lm [ ]

INFORMATION TO BE PROVIDED BY PROPOSER

1. Are the premises built of brick, stone and concrete and roofed with incombustible materials? If no, give particulars:

2. Are the premises in a good state of repair? • YES • NO
3. Are there any other occupants on the premises? • YES • NO
   (a) If yes, state trade or business carried on
4. Are the premises occupied at night by you or your staff? • YES • NO
5. Please state hours of Business
6. How are the following secured and protected?
   (a) Outer doors on ground floor and basement
   (b) Front windows on ground floor and basement
   (c) Back or side windows on ground floor and basement
   (d) Trap doors and skylights
7. Is any alarm system fitted? If so give details and state which parts of the premises are protected:

   (a) Is there any maintenance agreement? • YES • NO
8. Do you carry out work elsewhere than at your premises? If so give particulars:

9. Have you ever had a proposal for similar insurance, or renewal of policy, declined or policy cancelled? If so give particulars:

10. Have you ever had any accidents or losses in respect of any other Sections to be selected? If so give particulars

11. Do you keep any mineral oils for sale? If so, please advise quantities and where stored

12. Will a complete record of stock received and sold be kept?

Declaration

I/We hereby declare that the above information and statements are, to the best of my/our knowledge and belief, correct and complete.

I/We agree that his proposal shall be the basis of the contract between me/us and the MIDDLESEA INSURANCE PLC. and I/we agree to accept the Company's standard form of Policy for the class of Insurance.

If the answers to all or any of the above questions have been written by others at my/our dictation or instruction I/We confirm that I/We have read those answers and that they are correct.

Signature .... Date ....

Name in block letters ....

The Insurance will not be in force until the proposal has been accepted by the Company and the premium paid.

Important Note

Any other facts known to you which are likely to affect acceptance or assessment of the risks proposed for insurance must be disclosed. Should you have any doubt about what you should disclose, do not hesitater to tell us or your insurance adviser. This is for your own protection, as failure to disclose may mean that your policy will not provide you with the cover you require or may perhaps invalidate the policy altogether.

F. LPG INSURANCE

THE NEW INDIA ASSURANCE COMPANY LIMITED

Head Office: 87, MG Road, Fort, Mumbai-400001

PROPOSAL FORM FOR LIQUIFIED PETROLEUM GAS DEALERS POLICY

1. Name of proposer in full :

   (IN BLOCK LETTERS)

2. Address of the Business premises :
3. Period for which insurance is Required : From ______ To ______
4. Have you previously held any insurance in respect of any of the risks proposed for insurance. If yes, give details. :
5. Has any insurance company ever
   (*a*) declined your proposal? :

   (*b*) refused to renew or cancelled the policy? :

   (*c*) imposed any special conditions?

SECTION I

FIRE AND ALLIED RISK (BUILDING AND CONTENTS) INSURANCE

1. Nature of trade or business: ______________

2. Property to be insured

	Sum to be Insured	**Showroom Items 2 to 7**	**Godown Items 2 to 7**
(*i*) Building – Godown/showroom	(*i*) ₹		
(*ii*) Stock in trade including cylinders in Godown/Showroom	(*ii*) ₹		
(*iii*) Furniture, fixture and fittings in Godown/Showroom	(*iii*) ₹		

3. Construction: State materials used e.g. concrete or bricks, iron sheets or timber etc.
   (*a*) Walls

   (*b*) Roof

4. State whether premises solely occupied by the proposer.
   If not, give details of other Occupants and trade carried on

5. State whether the building is completely detached on all four sides. If not, give particulars of how attached.

6. Have you insured your Building and contents/stock-in-trade elsewhere, if so, state (*i*) name and place of issuing office (*ii*) Policy No. (*iii*) period (*iv*) sum insured.

7. Addresses of Showroom and Godown

SECTION II
BURGLARY AND HOUSEBREAKING

1. Property to be insured: ____________________

	Value	Showroom Items 1 to 4	Godown Items 1 to 4
		Sun Insured 25% of value	
(*i*) Stock-in-trade including cylinders In attached godown	(*i*) ₹		
(*ii*) Furniture, fixture and fittings	(*ii*) ₹		

N.B. : The Sun Insured is on First Loss Basis for an amount equivalent to 25% value to the Property at risk.

2. Are all doors protected by lock/locks?

3. Are all windows protected by bars?

4. Do you keep daily sales and purchases invoices and other books of accounts?

SECTION III
GAS CYLINDERS IN TRANSIT

1. Maximum No. of cylinders carried at any one time.
2. Mode of carriage
3. Value of cylinders.
   (*i*) Gas-filled cylinders.
   (*ii*) Empty cylinders
4. Maximum distance between the Proposer's premises and the Customer's premises/house.
5. Are the cylinders carried during normal office hours or beyond office hours also. If they are carried beyond office hours also, please state up to what hours they are carried?
6. Who authorizes issue of cylinders to customers?

SECTION IV
CASH IN TRANSIT

1. How is money carried and between what hours? :
2. How many employees will carry money at a time? :
3. State per transit limit other than delivery boys. :
4. State per transit limit of delivery boys. :
5. Whether money collected are retained in the proposer's premises? :
   If so, where and what arrangements are made for their safety?
6. Insurance required for cash in safe/fixed cash bos : ₹
7. Particulars of the safe
   (*i*) Measurement of safe/s
      (*a*) Height, Width
      (*b*) Depth, Weight, Makers Name

SECTION V

FIDELITY GUARANTEE

Name of Employee	Designation and nature of duties	Total Monthly remuneration	Amt. of guarantee per employee ₹

1. How often and by whom are your cash and Bank balances agreed, entries in cash books verified with vouchers and stocks checked?
2. Are the books audited by an independent auditor and if so, how often?
3. Has/have the proposed employee/s been suspected of dishonesty in the past?

SECTION VI

PEDAL CYCLE TRICYCLE

Maker and Name of Manufacturer	Year of Mfg. Frame No.	Accessories attached, if any	Estimated present value

SECTION VII

PUBLIC LIABILITY INSURANCE

1. State the existing number of customers the proposer has and the number estimated during the year.
2. Are the gas-filled cylinders tested for leakage before delivery to customers?
3. Whether the employees carrying cylinders are trained on safety methods for installing gas cylinders.
4. Amount of indemnity desired | ANY ONE ACCIDENT ₹ ________
   ANY ONE YEAR ₹ ________
   ANNUAL SALES TURNOVER ₹ ________

SECTION VIII
WORKMEN'S COMPENSATION

Name of Employee (s)	Nature of work	Monthly wages

SECTION IX
PERSONAL ACCIDENT FOR PROPRIETORS/PARTNERS/EMPLOYEES

Name	Age	Details of existing infirmity/ disability	Occupation	Table of Benefits	Name of Assignee and Relationship

SECTION X
P.A. BENEFIT TO CUSTOMERS

1. Are you interested in covering your customers for personal accident Risk?
2. Please state how many customers you are servicing?
3. Please also state Number of cylinders sold domestic/industrial.

SECTION XI
ACCIDENTAL BREAKAGE OF PLATE GLASS

1. Please give the details of glasses :

Sr.No.	Type (i.e. Plate/Sheet/ Plain etc.)	No. of Squares	Size each square	Position where fixed	Estimated Replacement value

2. Is any of the glasses proposed for Insurance scratched, damaged or Insecurely fixed? If yes, give full details,

SECTION XII

LOSS OF OR DAMAGE TO NEON SIGNS/GLOW SIGNS

1. Please give the particulars of Signs:

Sr. no.	Description of Signs	Situation	Date when created	Date when last inspected and by whom	Estimated replacement

2. Are the signs in good state of repair and will be so maintained?

DECLARATION

I do hereby declare that all the information given and statements made above are true and complete and that I have withheld no information whatever regarding the insurance applied for therein. Further, I declare that the premises are in sound condition and in a good state of repair and they are not specifically exposed to the risk of fire, or theft. Further I also declare that the premises will not be left uninhabited for more than a continuous period of SEVEN days. I also declare that aggregate value of the Building and contents/stock-in-trade relevant to Section of the cover does not exceed Rs. whether insured under one or more policies or whether issued by one or more officers of the subsidiaries.

I further agree that this Declaration and the information given, and statements made above by me, shall form the basis of the contract between me and the company and I further agree to accept Indemnity subject to the conditions in and endorsed on the Company's Policy.

Place ......

Date ...... **Proposer's Signature ....**

Note 1. The liability of the company does not commence until the proposal has been accepted.
2. If space is found insufficient, please attach separate sheets for details.
3. Insurance is the subject matter of solicitation.
4. Premium will be quoted on application.

PROHIBITION OF REBATE -- Section 41 of the Insurance Act 1938

No person shall allow or offer to allow, either directly or indirectly, as an inducement to any person to take out or renew or continue an insurance in respect of any kind of risk relating to lives or property in India, any rebate of the whole part of the commission payable or any rebate of the premium shown on the policy nor shall any person taking out or renewing or continuing a policy accept any rebate, except such rebates as may be allowed in accordance with the published prospectuses or tables of the Insurer.

Any person making default in complying with the provisions of this section be punishable with fine which may extend to Five Hundred Rupees.

For Office Use -

MARKETING/DEVELOPMENT OFFICER'S REPORT

The Proposer is known to me/my agent/Broker for_____years and I recommend acceptance of this proposal.

Name and Code No. Signature of Dev. Officer / A/AO-D

ACCEPTED BY DATE & TIME RATE REMARKS

CODES - OFFICE/DEV. OFFICER/AGENT/BROKER-

COLLECTION/SCROLL NO POLICY NO.

TATA AIG INSURANCE

MULTI LINE PACKAGE CLAIM FORM
ISSUANCE OF THIS FORM DOES NOT CONSTITUTE ADMISSION OF LIABILITY

As soon as Loss or damage has become known the Company must be notified without any delay. If any detail or information is not readily available please do not delay dispatch of this form and such particulars may be sent later. In any case, duly completed form together with relevant vouchers, etc., must be returned within fourteen days of the loss.

Claim No. Policy No/Coupon Nos.

A. INSURED

1. Name	:	
2. Address	:	
City	:	
3. Telephone Number	:	
4. Period of Insurance	:	From To
5. Occupation	:	

B. DETAILS OF THE PREMISES WHERE LOSS HAS OCCURRED

1. Address	:	
City	:	Pin Code:
2. What was the premises used for?	:	
3. How was the entry to/exit from the premises effected?	:	
4. Which portion of the premises was affected by the entry or exit?	:	
5. Whether the premises was occupied at the time of loss. If not, at what date and time was it last occupied?	:	
6. Are you the sole owner of	:	
(a) The property lost or damaged?	:	
(b) The premises?	:	
7. Are you responsible for repair of the premises?	:	
8. State the total value of property upon the premises at the time of loss.	:	

Tata AIG General Insurance Company Ltd.

Corporate Office: Ahura Centre, 4th Floor, 82, Mahakali Caves Road, Andheri (E), Mumbai-400093.

(Regd. Office: Bombay House, 24 Homi Mody Stree, Mumbai 400001.)

Offices also at: Bangalore, Chennai, Delhi, Hyderabad, Kolkata.

For more information, call the Tata AIG Toll-free-24-hour Helpline at 1-600-119966

C. DETAILS OF THE LOSS:

1. Data and Time of Loss.	
2. When discovered and by whom?	
3. Give brief details of how exactly the loss occurred. (Specify overleaf the property damaged/articles stolen).	
4. Is anybody suspected in this incident? If yes, state full details.	● YES ● NO
5. Was information given to the Fire Brigade? If so, when and by whom? (Attach Copy of the Fire Report)	● YES ● NO
6. Has a complaint been lodged with the Police Station?	● YES ● NO
If Yes, by whom, when and at which Police Station? (Attach a copy of the police report).	
If not, this may be done immediately.	
7. Has the police apprehended any person?	● YES ● NO
If yes, give details.	

D. DETAILS OF OTHER INSURANCES

Give details of other Insurances, if any, covering the present loss.	

E. DETAILS OF PREVIOUS LOSSES

Give details of Previous losses, if any, on the affected property.	

I/We heregby declare that the foregoing particulars are true and correct in every respect and that the articles or properties described herein belong to the person/s named, with no other person having any interest therein, whether as Owner, Mortgage, Trustee or otherwise.

Place ......

Date ......

Signature of the Insured

J. EXPORT RISK INSURANCE

Sample Insurance Certificate

ORIGINAL

OPEN POLICY NO.	CERTIFICATE NO.
A2310	2952305

FOREMAN'S FUND INSURANCE COMPANY
SAN FRANCISCO, CALIFORNIA
ATLANTIC DIVISION, 110 WILLIAM STREET
NEW YORK, NEW YORK 10038

$ 125000.00

The company named above in consideration of premium in the amount of and at rates as arranged and subject to the Conditions and Warranties specified and/or attached hereto, does by this policy insure

ASSURED **Metalworking Machines, Inc.**

as well in their own name as in that of those to whomsoever the subject matter of this Policy does, may or shall appertain.

IN THE SUM OF **One hundred twenty-five thousand and 00/100 - - - - - - - - - -**

UPON **steel grinders with accessories**

CONTAINER-HOUSE/HOUSE [X]
CONTAINER-PORT/PORT [ ]
CONTAINER-OTHER [ ]
NON-CONTAINER [ ]

VALUED AT SUM OR SUMS INSURED

LADEN (UNDER DECK) ON BOARD THE VESSEL/AIRLINE: S/L Adventurer B/L OR SAILING DATE: 9-30-97

(LOST OR NOT LOST) AT AND FROM (INITIAL POINT/PORT) interior USA via Baltimore TO: (FINAL POINT/PORT) Taipei Taiwan via Keelung

LOSS IF ANY PAYABLE TO THE ORDER OF THE ASSURED AT destination

Insured against all risks of physical loss or damage from any external cause irrespective of percentage, but excluding the risks excluded by the "F.C.&S." and/or "S.R. & C.C." warranties on the reverse side of this policy except to the extent that such risks may be specifically covered by endorsement; also warranted free from any claim arising out of the inherent price of the goods insured or consequent upon loss of time or market.

This insurance attaches from the time the goods leave the warehouse at the place named in the policy for the commencement of the transit and continues during the ordinary course of transit until the goods are delivered to the final warehouse at the destination named in the policy.

It is a condition of this insurance that there shall be no interruption or suspension of transit unless due to circumstances beyond the control of the Assured.

The risks covered by this policy include loss, damage or expense resulting from explosion howsoever or whensoever occurring, irrespective of percentage, but it is especially understood and agreed that this wording is not intended to cover any of the risks excluded by the F.C.&S. and/or S.R.&C.C. Warranties set forth elsewhere in the policy.

In the event of the vessel, craft, [illegible] or other cargo being [illegible] by order of properly constituted authority and damage arising therefrom to the goods insured hereunder, this Company agrees to indemnify the Assured for such damage irrespective of percentage.

General Average and Salvage Charges payable according to United States laws and usage and/or as per Foreign Statement and/or as per York-Antwerp Rules (as prescribed in whole or in part) in accordance with the Contract of Affreightment.

In case of any loss or misfortune, it shall be lawful and necessary for the Assured, his or their factors, servants and assigns, to sue, labor, and travel for, in and about the defense, safeguard, and recovery of the interest insured, or any part thereof, without prejudice to this insurance; to the charges whereof this Company shall contribute according to the rate and quantity of the sum hereby insured; nor shall the acts of the Assured or the Company in recovering, saving, or preserving the property insured, in case of disaster, be considered as a waiver or acceptance of abandonment.

In case of any agreement, act or omission of the Assured, prior or subsequent to loss, whereby any right of recovery of the Assured for loss or damage to any property insured hereunder against any Carrier or Bailee, is released, impaired or lost, which would on acceptance of abandonment or payment of loss by this Company have inured to its benefit, but for such agreement, act or omission, this Company shall pay for the loss only to the extent its right of recovery was not released, impaired or lost.

This insurance is subject to the American Institute Marine Extension Clauses (1943) and the following American Institute Clauses as if the current form of each were endorsed hereon.
South America 60-Day Clause S.R.&C.C. Endorsement War Risk Insurance

It is hereby understood and agreed that in case of loss or damage to the property insured under this policy, same shall be immediately reported as soon as the goods are landed, or the loss is known or expected, to the nearest agent of this Company as designated on the reverse side hereof.

(See reverse side for further terms and conditions which are hereby made a part of this Policy.)

NOTE—It is necessary for the assured to give prompt notice to underwriters when he becomes aware of an event for which he is "held covered" under this policy and the right to such cover is dependent on compliance with this obligation.

In witness whereof the company named above has caused this policy to be signed by its duly authorized officers, but this policy shall not be valid unless countersigned by an authorized representative of this Company or the Assured.

SECRETARY PRESIDENT

Endorsement — Countersigned at Baltimore MD 9-30-97
DATE

35

RURAL INSURANCE AND PROSPECTS OF AGRICULTURE INSURANCE IN INDIA

SCOPE OF RURAL INSURANCE

The scope of rural insurance is very high although it is poorly realised. Rural areas having 70 per cent of total population, livelihood to two-third of the total population, supply of raw materials to industrial production and other economic activities have compelled the insurance educators to make the insurance companies enter in the rural population. The agriculture is full of vagaries and natural calamities. which impede the sustainable growth of the country by sustaining agricultural development. The natural risks and disasters have pulled back the rural development. Therefore, there is dire needs of insurance of rural risks. Crop insurance, cattle insurance, life and property insurance, general insurance etc. have abundant scope of development.

CROP INSURANCE

Crop insurance is the main rural insurance wherein the product, price and income risks are insured. If the farmers do not get a standard amount of product, required price and income from the farms; they are compensated by insurance companies under crop insurance. In past insurance companies did not approach for the crop insurance because of non availability of records of land-ownership yield per acre, inputs used and expected outputs. The scattered and fragmented land holdings posed another problems. Large varieties of crops, simultaneous harvesting, small premiums and non-availability of records of labour, cost and input costs have discourged the insurer to insure the crop risk.

The General Insurance Corporation of India had prepared are approach of crop insurance in 1979. The area yield for each to tehsil and block have be standardised and was compared with the actual yield to find out the indemnity amount. It has paved the way for Comprehensive Crop Insurance Scheme (CCIS) in 1985 which was later on modified as National Agricultural Insurance Scheme (NAIS). At present NAIS has covered 30 million hectares of cropped area for 18 million farmers throughout the country.

Area Based Insurance

The natural hazards differ from state to state and district to district in one state. Weather indices have been prepared to decide the indemnity amount. The catastrophic income losses have been estimated for each year. Area based crop insurance covers the risks of drought, flood etc. in the respective districts and tehsils. The crop insurance covers these, the value of protection desired for meeting the cost of cultivation and value of production etc. Farmers in the same region will receive the same rate of payment of claims in the area. The area based rainfall data is used for deciding the premium amount and claims to be paid in the area.

Rainfall Index

The rainfall index of the last 30 years are used to demonstrate the rainfall index. It is decided weekly for 30 years to know the capped rainfall. The average of the week of the month in each year is taken for 30 years. Thus the average arrived at is modified with 2 standard deviation to find out the copped rainfall of the week of the month. If the rainfall in less than capped rainfall, the payment is made proportionately.

Similarly multiple weather parameter such as rainfall, temperature, frost, humidity, wind speed etc., are decided for fruits and vegetable insurance.

Revenue Insurance Products

Besides products, price is another factor of loss to farmers. For example, despite normal production, farmers often fail to maintain their level of income due to price fluctuations. Government has introduced Farm Income Insurance Scheme (FIIS) during Rabi 2003-2004 season. It encourages crop diversification for cash and ready income.

Individual farmers are also assessed for payment. Plant risks have been the significant example of such insurance. The resource poor farmers can get the insurance protection at the behest of the governments premium. The banking institutions and other financial institutions can ask for crop insurance so that their dues can be paid in time.

REGULATIONS OF IRDA

The IRDA has imposed social obligations on life and non life insurance companies. The rural obligation is one important social obligations for the insurers. It applied to all insurers separately covering five thousand lives in the first financial year, seven thousand lives in the second year, ten thousand lives in the third year, fifteen thousand lives in the fourth year and 20 thousand lives in each year. The Rural sector obligations in respect of a life insurer is defined as terms of total policies underwritten – 7% in first year, 9% in the second year, 12% in the third year, 14% in the fourth year 16% in the subsequent each year. Such obligations in respect of general insurers are in terms of total gross premium income underwritten each year: 2% in the first year, 3% in second year and 5% thereafter. Non fulfillment of these obligations invites penalties from the regulator.

Imposing such obligations would help the companies discover the appropriate paradigm. The rural obligations are meant to tap commercial as well as semi-commercial segments of rural areas. Social obligations are meant to extend insurance to the subsistence sector which are not pragcitable. Now every insurer has a separate cell/unit for rural and social obligations. The insurance products are sold with the help of NGOs and development agencies. Some insurance companies have taken rural and social obligations in a positive spirit and they have done more than the prescribed limits in rural areas and social sector.

MICRO INSURANCE

IRDA has come out with microinsurance and has paved the principles of role defining of agents with small and segmented insurance products. It is interested to develop insurance awareness in the remote corner of the country. It has adopted traditional techniques of motivations and joining hands with State governments. Postal Life Insurance (PLI) is very effective form of microinsurance. IRDA has approached postal authority to extend its insurance facilities to general public also. Cooperative societies should come forward to start insurance business for the benefits of the masses. Gujarat, Maharashtra and Karnataka have started such micro insurance. IFFCO has started insurance with the joint venture of Tok. Thus IFFO—Tokio has started micro insurance. Self Help Groups, Mahila Mandals, Panchayats etc. are motivated to extend insurance in rural areas.

The GIC and the four subsidiaries viz., National Insurance Co. Ltd., The New Assurance Co. Ltd., The Oriental Insurance Co. Ltd., and United India Insurance Co. Ltd., hereby known as National, New India, Oriental and United India have taken the responsibilities of insuring the rural masses against the growing risks in the areas of personal, property, livestock and packages. Their brief descriptions will highlight how far the General insurance industry has been successful to harness the existing opportunities in rural areas. Now private non-life insurance have taken the responsibility of rural insurance.

1. Personal Insurance

The personal insurance to rural people is granted in the form of Janata Personal Accident—Individual and Group and Gramin Personal Accident—Individual and Group.

(i) Janata Personal Accident (Individual). Persons between age group of 10 to 65 years are covered under Janata Personal Accident (Individual) policy whereby ₹ 15,000 is paid at the death or permanent total disablement due to accident. ₹ 7,500 is paid at the loss of one eye or one limb due to accident.

Sterilisation risks and claims arising out of racing on wheels, big game hunting, mountaineering whilst engaged in winter sports skiing or ice hockey are also covered. The premium is ₹ 12 per annum. The nominee should submit death certificate, original policy and claim form at the death of the assured due to accident.

(ii) Janta Personal Accident (Group). Persons between the age group of 10 to 65 years are entitled for Janata Personal Accident (Group). The benefits are ₹ 15,000 at the time of death or permanent disablement due to accident. At the loss of one eye or one limb in an accident is paid ₹ 7,500. The premium is ₹ 12 per annum:

The Janata Personal Accident Insurance has increased from ₹ 129.00 lakhs in 1982 to ₹ 440.24 lakhs in the form of direct insurance premium. During the period of five years, it became just double. In the form of number of persons covered; it has increased from 20.16 lakhs in 1982 to 42.26 lakhs in 1987. It shows that this non-traditional policies can be more popular if efforts are made systematically to increase the business. The growth rate has been not satisfactory as the premium income increased at faster rate in the beginning. The growth rate was 44.8 per cent in 1983 but there was also decline by 9.5 per cent in 1986. The persons covered has declined in 1986 by 6.8 per cent.

Table 35.1 Janata Personal Accident Insurance

(₹ in lakhs)

	Premium Income		*Number of persons covered*	
	₹	*% increase over previous year*	*Lakhs*	*% increase over previous year*
1980				
1981				
1982	219.00	—	20.16	—
1983	317.00	44.8	30.75	52.5
1984	361.00	13.9	35.10	14.2
1985	458.00	27.1	43.44	23.8
1986	414.97	–9.5	40.50	–6.8
1987	440.24	6.1	42.26	+4.4

(iii) Gramin Personal Accident (Individual). This policy is applicable to persons between the age group of 10 to 65 years living in rural areas. The benefits are ₹ 6,000 at death or permanent disablement due to accident or ₹ 3,000 at the loss of two eyes or two limbs or one eye and one limb due to accident. Sterilisation risks and claims arising out of racing on wheels, big game hunting, mountaineering whilst engaged in winter sports, skiing or ice hockey. The premium amount is ₹ 6 per annum. The nominee is required to submit death certificate, original policy and claim form at the death claims and medical certificate and bills in other cases.

(iv) Gamin Personal Accident (Group). This policy is issued to a large number of persons insured under one policy. The benefits are the same as discussed earlier in the case of Gramin Personal Accident (Individual). Basic premium for one year is ₹ 500 for 100 persons in two instalments. The discount is available if the number of persons have been higher.

Table 35.2 Gramin Personal Accident Policy

	Premium Income		Persons covered	
	₹ in Lakhs	*% increase over previous year*	*Lakhs*	*% increase over previous year*
1982	6.47	—	1.30	—
1983	9.05	39.9	1.74	33.8
1984	18.27	101.9	3.04	74.7
1985	37.75	106.6	7.52	144.1
1986	39.67	9.1	7.06	6.1
1987	40.96	3.3	7.62	7.9

The premium income under Gramin Personal Accident Policy increased from ₹ 6.47 lakhs in 1982 to ₹ 40.96 lakhs in 1987. The persons covered has also increased from 1.30 lakhs to 7.62 lakhs in the respected years. The number of persons covered increased by more than 4 times. The premium income has increased by the same fold. The traditional policies during this period has increased by not more than twofold. It reveals that the non-traditional policies are becoming more popular in India.

2. Property Insurance

(i) Agricultural Pumpset. Agricultural pumpsets insurance policy indemnifies the insured against unforeseen and sudden physical damage to the pumpsets caused by/or solely due to mechanical/electrical breakdown, fire and lightning, theft and burglary. The minimum premium is ₹ 50 for electric pumpset and ₹70 for diesel pumpset. No claim discount is applicable on renewable premium at the rate of 10 per cent if no claim arises for one year. 15 per cent if no claim arises for two consecutive years and 20 per cent if no claim arises for three consecutive years. Long Term Discount is also available at the rate of 15 per cent if taken for 2 years and 25 per cent if taken for three years. Group discount is also applicable if a number of pumpsets are insured together. Annual premium depends on horse power types of pumpset and deductible franchise. The deductible franchise will be first borne by the Insured, out of each and every machinery breakdown claim where more than one item is lost or damaged in one and the same occurrence. The insured shall not be called upon to bear more than the highest deductible franchise applicable to any one such item.

Table 35.3 Agricultural Pumpset Insurance

	Premium Income		Number of Pumpsets	
	In Lakhs of ₹	*% Increase over previous year*	*In Lakhs*	*% increase over previous year*
1982	105.30	—	1.35	—
1983	125.50	19.2	1.68	24.4
1984	170.00	35.8	2.36	40.5
1985	258.00	51.4	2.96	25.4
1986	373.82	44.9	3.66	23.7
1987	481.38	28.8	4.44	21.3

The number of pumpsets insured increased from 1.35 lakhs in 1982 to 4.44 lakhs in 1987. The premium income has also increased from ₹ 105.30 lakhs in 1982 to ₹ 481.38 lakhs in 1987. The premium became more than fourfold during the period 1982 to 1987. The growth rate has been maximum in 1985. The traditional business had risen only to twofold during this period. Considering the growning demand of pumpsets for the economic development of rural areas; the insurance opportunities are expanding every year. The subsidiary companies have to effort maximum to exploit the growing opportunities in rural insurance.

(ii) Animal Driven Carts Insurance. The Animal Driven Cart Insurance cover risks against death or permanent total disablement of the animals driving the cart. Gramin accident cover for driver while driving the cart at no extra premium. Damage to the cart/tonga and its accessories by accident, external means like fire, lightning, flood, cyclone and other allied perils while in transit by road, rail and inland waterways. Third party liability upto ₹ 5,000 per accident and maximum ₹ 10,000 for all accidents in a policy year. Insured will bear first ₹ 100 of each cart and ₹ 200 of each tonga claim. The age group of animals covered is 3 to 12 years for bullocks, male buffaloes, 2 to 6 years for horses and mules, 1 to 5 years for donkey and 5 to 15 years for camels. The sums assured will be the market value of cart tonga and animal. Premium rate is 2.00 per cent of the insured value. The insured value is decided on the basis of market value after deducting reasonable amount of depreciation for the number of years for which the cart has been in use. If diseases cover required, the premium applicable in respect of the animal covered will be charged. The scope of cover is loss or damage to the animal driven cart, death or permanent disablement of animal, liability to third parties and passengers and personal accident cover to person driving the cart.

Loss or damage due to any accident is subject to an excess of ₹ 100 per policy excluding wear and tear. In case of vehicles fitted with preumatic or hard rubber tyres only 50 per cent of value of the tyre is payable. Death or permanent disability of the animal used for pulling the cart provided that death/disablement arises out of and during the course of accident to insured cart and provided the animals are insured under the policy. Liability arising out of the accident to the insured cart resulting into injury, fatal or non-fatal and damage to the properties of the third party upto ₹ 5,000 in any accident and ₹ 10,000 for all the accidents in a year. Personal injury or death of passengers is also covered within this limit. The liability is covered even when the vehicle is being loaded or unloaded. It is not extended to cover damage to the goods carried. The policy will not make any distinction between the use of the cart for private and professional purposes and for hire or reward. Personal accident cover to person driving the cart is upto ₹ 5,000 which becomes payable to the cart driver who whilst driving the cart meets with death following accident to the cart and or for loss of two entire feet, or two arms or complete loss of sight of two eyes and or loss of one entire foot and or arm and loss of sight of one eye. No information about the progress of insurance for animal driven cart is available.

(iii) Hut Insurance. Hut insurance policy indemnifies the insured against all accidental losses or damages due to fire, earthquake, inundation, storm, tempest, impact damage, riot, strike, malicious damage and aircraft damage subject to the exclusions of war, invasion, act of foreign enemy, hostilities, civil war, rebellion, revolution, insurrection, mutiny, military or usurped power. The maximum sum insured is ₹ 6,000. The maximum 200 huts situated in on contiguous area. In case the number of huts is more than 50 in contiguous area the insurer will accept the risk after inspection. The premium rate is ₹ 3 per mille per annum. 50 per cent of the premium is shared by Government. In practice, Government pay the premium in full in advance and recover 50 per cent of the premium from hut owner. Insurer shall pay compensation on the basis of a certificate issued by the Tehsildar regarding occurrence of the fire loss where compensation is less than ₹ 10,000. However, where the amount of loss involved is more than ₹ 10,000 or number of huts is more than 5, the Tehsildar shall report the occurrence to the company immediately who will depute their officer for inspection and assessment of the loss. The payment of compensation is made within a month of the occurrence.

A scheme to provide fire insurance cover for huts and belongings of landless labourers, small farmers, artisans and other poor families in rural areas which was introduced from May 1, 1988 was in operation in 406 districts of the country as on 31.3.1989. The scheme provides compensation not exceeding ₹ 1,000 for a hut and ₹ 500 for belongings therein the entire premium cost is being borne by the Central Government. Continuous efforts are on to propagate the benefits of the scheme among the poor families in rural areas. About 11,000 claims amounting to ₹ 1.24 crores have been settled upto the end of March 1989. National Insurance settled 18455 Hut Insurance claims, New India settled 457 claims, amounting ₹ 6.85 lakhs; 52.01 lakhs settled by Oriental and ₹ 242.56 lakhs by United India during 1994-95.

(iv) Gobar Gas Insurance. The Gobar Gas Insurance is applicable to all Khadi and Village Industries workers/artisans, IRDP beneficiaries, schedule castes, schedule tribes and such other identifiable groups. The risks covered are fire, lightning, explosion, riot, strike malicious damage, impact by rail/road vehicles or animals, aircraft and other aerial/devices, storm, cyclone, typhoon, tempest, hurricane, tornado, flood, landslide, earthquake and shock. The sum assured is inclusive of digester, gas holder and cost of construction depending on type and cubic capacity. Master policy agreement is preferable in respect of this insurance in view of the concessional rate of premium and to reduce overall administrative expenses. The rate of premium is Re. 1 per mille for widest cover subject to minimum premium of ₹ 15.

(v) New Well Insurance. The new well insurance is applicable to dugwells or borewells which are being newly installed. It does not apply to existing well. The cover is given to financing banks or individuals. The sum insured shall be limited to a maximum of ₹ 12,000 per well. The 75 per cent of sum insured is settled for complete failure and 50 per cent is paid for partial, failure. 500 imperial gallons of water per hour pumped intermittently for six hours by 2 to 3 horse power submersible pump and yield measured in contained of known capacity of at least 200 litres. If yield is between 300 to 500 gallons, the well shall be derived partially failed and compensation will be paid at 50 per cent of sum insured. Natural calamities like flood, earthquake, riot and strike are excluded from this insurance.

3. Cattle and Livestock

The cattle and livestock insurance was demanded since independence. No worth mentioning progress was made till 1972 when the general insurance was nationalised. Recently some progress has been made and figure of the progress is available since 1982. Cattle and livestock insurance have included cattle, sheep and goat, horse/pony/mule, pig, camel, duck, rabbit, elephant and dog.

(i) Cattle Insurance Schemes. The cattle insurance policy under market agreement covers milch cows, and buffaloes, calves/heifers, stud bulls, bullocks and castrated male buffaloes whether idigeneous or exotic or cross-bred. Exotic animal means an animal whose both parents are of foreign breed. This policy provides indemnity in event of death of insured cattle due to accident inclusive of fire, lightning, flood, cyclone, famine, surgical operation, strike, riot, civil commotion, diseases inclusive of anthrax, blackquarter foot and mouth disease haemorrhagic septicaemia, rinderpest and theileriasis; contracted or occurring during the period of policy and shall be subject to exclusions of theft and clandestine sale of the insured animal, partial disability of any type, whether permanent or temporary; permanent total disability, which, in case of milch cattle result in permanent and total incapacity to conceive or yield milk in the case of stud bulls, war, invasion, hosilities, civil war and military.

The age group of animals to be covered are 2 years to 10 years for milch cows, 3 years to 12 years for milch buffaloes, 3 years to 8 years for stud bulls, 3 years to 12 years for bullocks. The market value of cattle will be the amount of sum insured which varies from breed to breed, from area to area and from time to time. In the case of permanent total disablement, insurers, liability is limited to 75 per cent of sum insured. The premium rates are governed by market agreement varying from 2.75 per cent to 4.00 per cent. The premium rate is 3 per cent for milch cattle. The premium for cattle

Rural Insurance

No. of Policy Issued Lacs

	GIC	National	New India	Oriental	United India
1999-2000		36.83		75.53	—
2000-2001		36.97		79.34	—
2001-2002		34.04		44.39	—
				Number crossed in lacs	
1999-2000		73.65		226.6	—
2000-2001		73.94		238.02	—
2001-2002		68.07		133.17	—
				Premium Received Rs. in crores	
1999-2000		76.92		45.32	50.78
2000-2001		86.25		47.60	78.41
2001-2002		75.50		26.63	58.04
				Incurred Claim in Rs. crores	
1999-2000		66.25		4.40	3.00
2000-2001		67.82		14.69	9.09
2001-2002		58.03		20.03	30.84
				Incurred Claim Ratio % (Claim to Premium)	
1999-2000		86.13		9.72	5.91
2000-2001		78.63		30.87	11.60
2001-2002		77.00		75.20	53.13

owned by individuals/institutions and bank financed oattle which do not provide regular and efficient veterinary attention is per cent. Cattle owned by well organised government, cooperative/private dairies/apex bodies providing regular and efficient veterinary attention are charged premium at the rate of 4.00 per cent if there are less than 50 animals, 3.95 per cent of number of animals insured is 50 to 250 and 3.90 per cent if number of animals insured is over 250. The market agreement helps decide the premium rates in other cases. The bullocks and male buffaloes are charged premium at the rate of 2.75 per cent. There are extra premium of 2 per cent for exotic milch cattle and stud bulls and 1 per cent for covering permanent total disablement. The minimum premium rate is ₹25/- per annum per animal and ₹20/- per annum per bullock. All the insured animals are suitably identified by one or more of the following methods: (*i*) ear tag made of aluminium or any other metal (*ii*) branding with hot iron and tattooing. The natural identification marks are clearly noted in the proposal form and veterinarian's report.

Cattle insurance schemes are also available under IRDP Project for cattle subsidised under SPDA/MFAL/DPAP/IRDP/TADP, Antyodaya projects. Milch cows, milch buffaloes and stud bulls of indigeneous or cross-bred variety between age group of 2 to 12 years are insurable for the sum assured agreed upon provided it does not exceed market value. The permanent total disability shall be covered at extra premium of 0.85 per cent. The premium rate is 2.25 per cent of sum insured per annum to be subsidised by the Project Authorities and financing bank. The risks covered are as mentioned in market agreement plan. The common exclusions are malicious or wilful injury or neglect overloading, unskilfully treatment or use of animal for purpose other than stated in the policy without the consent of the insurer, accident occurring and/or diseases contracted prior to commencement of risk, intentional slaughter of the animal except in cases where destruction is necessary to terminate incurable suffering on humane consideration on the basis of certificates insured by qualified veterinarian or in cases where destruction is resorted to by the order of lawfully constituted authority; theft and clandestine sale of the insured animal; war invasion, act of foreign enemy, hostilities, civil war, rebellion, revolution, insurrection, mutiny tumult military or usurped power, any accident, loss, destruction, damage or legal liability directly or indireclty caused by or contributed to by or arising from nuclear weapon and consequential losses.

(*ii*) *Sheep and Goat Insurance.* The sheep and goat insurance provides indemnity in the event of death of insured animals due to disease or accident contracted during the period of risk in the age group 4 months to, 7 years of the sheeps. Ramsused for breeding and aged more than 75 per cent of its market value. Goats are covered between age group of 6 months to 5 years. The sum assured will be restricted to 80 per cent of market value as certified by veterinary surgeon or 100 per cent bank advance whichever is higher. The premium rates are 8 per cent of sum assured in case of sheep and 10 per cent in case of goat of indigeneous breed for private insureds. This premium is 10 per cent for exotic breed. The premium rate for bank financed and IRDP project is 2.75 per cent in both the cases of sheep and goat. The foot rot is excluded for sheep under this category. The policy shall provide indemnity against death of sheep and goats due to accident including fire, lightning, flood, cyclone, famine, strike, riot and civil commotion or diseases contracted or occurring during the period of insurance.

(*iii*) *Horse/Pony/Mule Insurance.* The policy for horse/pony/mule insurance includes draught horses, half draught horses, ponies, mules against death due to accidents and/or specified diseases contacted during the period of insurance and subject to usual terms, conditions and exclusions of the policy. The age group for such animals to be insured are 2 years to 8 years. Indigeneous, cross-bred and exotic are insured. The sum assured is 100 per cent market value or bank loan which is higher. The non-scheme animals are charged premium at the rate of 4 per cent of sum assured whereas the scheme animals are charged at 2.75 per cent per annum.

(*iv*) *Pig insurance.* Pig insurance policy covers death risk due to accident or disease. The minimum number of animals covered is 10. Swire fever disease is excluded. The age group insurable is one month to 5 years. All indigeneous cross-bred and exotic pigs are insured. The maximum sum insured per pig is ₹ 500. The premium rate is 6 per cent per annum but pigs under SFDA/IRDP scheme are charged at 3.5 per cent per annum. The sum assured will be linked to 100 per cent of market value for organised breeding farms whereas in other cases it is 80 per cent of market value.

(*v*) *Camel Insurance.* The camel insurance policy is applicable to all male and female camels in India including camel subsidised by SFDA/DPAP/MFAL between age group of 3 years to 10 years. The sum assumed will be 80 per cent of market value or bank finance. The maximum sum insured is ₹ 3000 in case of bank finance SFDA/DPAP/MFAL. In case of PTD claim, 75 per cent of sum assured is payable. The premium rate is 4 per cent per annum for non-IRDP scheme camels and 2.25 per cent (net) for IRDP scheme camels. 'Surra' disease is excluded. The minimum premium is ₹ 25 per annum per animal. The policy provides indemnity only for death due to accident at inclusive of flood, cyclone, famine or disease inclusive of Rinderpest, Blackquarter, Haemorrhagic Septicaemia/ Anthrax contracted or occurring during the period of policy or strike, riot and civil common risks. The exclusions are common exclusions and specific exclusions.

Common exclusions are applicable to all types of cattle insurance. They are malicious or wilful injury or neglect over-loading, unskilful treatment or use of animal for purpose other than stated in the policy without the consent of the insurer in writing. Accident occurring and/or diseases contracted period to commencement of risk. Intentional slaughter of the animals except in cases where destruction is necessary to terminate incurable suffering on humane consideration on the basis of certificates issued by qualified veterinarian or in cases where destruction is resorted to by the order of lawfully constituted authority. Theft and clandestine sale of the insured animal, war, invasion, act of foreign enemy, hostilities whether war be declared or not, civil war rebellion, revolution, insurrection, mutiny, tumult, military or usurped power or any consequences thereof or attempt threat. Any accident, loss, destruction, damage or legal liability directly or indirectly caused by or contributed to by or arising from nuclear weapons. Consequential loss of whatsoever nature. Specific exclusion are transport by air and sea, partial disability of any type. Death of camel due to disease Surra. Diseases contracted prior to and within 15 days of commencement of risk.

(*vi*) *Rabbit Insurance.* The rabbit insurance policy is applicable to all breeds of Rabbits in India, in the age group of 1 day to 4 years, but death of rabbits due to disease till they complete the age of 30 days is not covered. The risks covered, death of rabbits due to accident and/or disease contracted during the period of insurance. The exclusions have common exclusions as described in camel insurance and specific exclusions of transport by air and sea, permanent and partial disablement of any nature pasteurellosis, culling, cannibalism and intentional slaughter, undergrowth, myxomatosis and coocidissis. The insured is compensed only 70 per cent of the sum assured, the rate of premium is 7 per cent of sum assured.

(*vii*) *Elephant Insurance.* The elephant insurance policy indemnifies the owner for death due to accident or disease contracted or occurring during the period of insurance subject to certain exclusions stipulated. The insurable age group is one year to 60 years. The policy is applicable to the elephants including those owned by temple, circus companies and individuals. The sum assured is 80 per cent of market value. The value of sum assured does not exceed ₹ 50,000. The premium rate is 5 per cent per annum. The common exclusions clause as mentioned under Cattle Market Agreement is also applicable in this case. Specific exclusions are surgical operations, disability, breeding and calving and certain specific diseases such as tuberculosis, foot, and mouth diseases etc.

(*viii*) *Dog Insurance.* The dog insurance policy insures the risks against death due to accident and/or disease contracted during the period of insurance subject to usual theory and conditions. The insurable age group is 8 weeks to 8 years. Dogs of indigeneous cross-bred and exotic breeds are insured under this policy. The minimum value of any breed should not be less than ₹ 200 and maximum value of any dog should not exceed ₹ 2,000 each dog. The premium rate is 5 per cent per annum. In the event of death of the insured dog, any amount received or receivable by the insured from third parties and the value of the salvage recovered if any would be deducted from the claim amount.

(*ix*) *Livestock Insurance Master Policy.* An open policy is issued without specifying the sum insured. This will be stamped document stating the type of cover grantee, perils covered, conditions exclusions etc. When loans are granted by the branch of the bank, the animals purchased will be covered under the insurance scheme. The insurance cover will commence from the time the animals are purchased by the beneficiaries and will be valid for one year. The declaration forms are supplied to bank's branches by the insurance company. As and when animals are financed, the branch will send to the insurance company the declaration giving details of the borrowers financed alongwith the certificate of veterinary doctor. Under the livestock insurance scheme livestock as milch cows, buffaloes, calves/heifers, stud bulls and bullocks castrated bulls and male buffaloes whether indigeneous cross-bred or exotic, sheep, goats and pigs are insured. This policy covers death of livestock due to any accident inclusive of fire, lightning, flood, inundation, storm, hurricane, earthquake, cyclone, tornado, tempest, famine snakebite etc., diseases inclusive of rinderpest, blackquarter, haemorrhagic septicaemia anthrax, foot and mouth diseases, surgical operation strike, riot and civil commotion.

The cattle and livestock insurance has shown an increase of ₹ 75.58 crores during 1982 to 1988-89 from ₹ 26.3 crores to ₹ 101.88 crores. It is about four-fold increase which far more above those of traditional increase. The percentage increase over previous year was maximum at 35.6 per cent in 1984 whereas it was the lowest in 1986. So for cattle number is concerned, it has in creased from 82.4 lakhs in 1982 to 256.22 lakhs in 1988-89 giving about three-fold increase. The growth rate as compared to previous year was maximum at 34.9 per cent in 1984 and the decline at 2.3 per cent in 1987. It shows that the year 1984 and 1985 have been very promising for non-traditional business. The subsidiaries of GIC have to expand their business through pragmatic strategies.

Table 35.4

	Premium Income		Number Insured	
	In Crores of ₹	*% Increase over previous year*	*In Lakhs*	*% increase over previous year*
1982	26.3	37.9	82.4	45.1
1983	33.9	28.7	105.8	28.4
1984	45.96	35.6	143.0	34.9
1985	51.36	11.8	161.0	12.7
1986	59.35	15.6	189.69	18.0
1987	69.45	17.0	185.36	–2.3
1988-89	101.88	17.0	256.22	10.6
1989-90	86.04	—	199.21	—

4. Poultry Insurance

The general insurance companies have taken another big to insurance poultry, duck and other birds.

(*i*) *Poultry Insurance.* The poultry insurance policy cover poultry farms consisting of 100 or more pure and hybrid chicks, hens and cocks. All birds in a farm should be covered. The policy covers death of birds due to accident or disease contracted or occurring during the period of insurance subject to certain exclusions. Birds are covered from 0 to 72 weeks. The cover is for epidemics *i.e.* Ranikhet disease, Fowl Pox and Gamhoro. The sum assured is as per poultry market agreement. The sum insured is as per valuation table. The premium rate is ₹ 1.20 per bird where SFDA and other subsides are applied, the premium is Re. 0.90 per bird. Extra premium will be charged in case of addition of fresh birds. Each proposal is rated according to flock strength mortality and management of farm. The compulsory inspection of the risk by Company's Veterinary surgeon before assumption of risk, besides periodical routine inspection at intervals.

(*ii*) *Poultry Insurance Master Policy (IRDP).* Poultry Insurance Master Policy as Cattle Master Policy is issued to benefits the benefactors of IRDP.

(*iii*) *Duck Insurance.* The duck insurance policy provides indemnity against death of ducks due to accident including fire, lightning, flood, cyclone, famine, strike, riot, civil commotion or diseases contracted or occurring during the period of insurance subject to specific exclusions. This policy is applicable to all types of migratory and non-migratory birds in India, ducks farms consisting of minimum 100 ducks for non-IRDP and 50 ducks for IRDP and other subsidised schemes. The insurable age is first week to 52 weeks. The premium is Re. 1.00 per bird and Re. 0.90 per bird for IRDP and other scheme birds. Common exclusions are as mentioned under Cattle Market Agreement. Specific exclusions are improper management cannibalism, sun stroke virus, transit diseases such as Coli Aspirgillosis etc.

Table 35.5 Poultry Insurance

	Premium Income		Number of Birds	
	In Lakhs of ₹	*% Increase previous year*	*In Lakhs*	*% increase over previous year*
1984	42.68	—	40.48	—
1985	68.63	60.8	63.49	56.8
1986	84.51	23.1	65.07	2.5
1987	111.74	32.2	85.71	31.7

The premium income under poultry insurance has, increased from ₹ 42 68 lakhs in 1984 to ₹ 111.74 lakhs in 1987 giving about two-fold increase. The growth rate has been declining from 60.8 per cent to 32.2 per cent. The number of birds insured increased from 40.48 lakhs in 1984 to 85.71 lakhs giving two-fold rise during 1987.

5. Insurance of Species

The general insurance industry has started insuring other species such as brackish water prawn, inland fish, silkworms and honey bees.

(*i*) *Brackish Water Prawn Insurance.* The brackish water prawn insurance policy cover risks against total loss of prawn, nursed seeds in hatcheries owned by State Government; FFDAS, State Fisheries Corporations, MPEDA or such other organisations. It is issued to provide insurance cover to the engaged in brackish water prawn farming against total loss of seedlings/Juveniles/prawns of all species raised in brackish waters after being transferred to the farm. It also provides cover to financial institutions to protect their interests and recover loans advanced for such brackish water prawn farming in the event of loss. The policy covers either the input cost or fixed value of the produce. The period of cover is from the stage prawn seeds being sown in hatcheries for rearing till the post larvae/ removed from the hatcheries. The period of cover for farms is from the stage of transferring of post larvae to the brackish-water till actual harvesting. The premium rate is 4 per cent of mean value declared for insurance for each crop period. The insurance covers total loss or destruction of prawns due to accident and disease such as summer kill, pollution, posioning riot and strikes, malicious acts of third parties, earthquakes, explosion, storms, tempest, cyclone, typhoon, hurricane, tornado, flood, inundation, volcanic eruption and other comulsions of nature, aircraft and other aerial devices or articles dropped therefrom, impact with any road vehicle, horses and cattle, shell disease, vibriosis aeromanas celiades and other viral form of opidemics and parasitical attacks. Wilful destruction losses due to natural mortality, overcrowding, loss due to negligence and error, theft, dacoity, war invasion, hostilities etc. arc excluded from this policy.

(*ii*) *Fish Insurance Policy.* The fish insurance policy indemnifies the insured against total loss due to accident or disease of Fry/Fingerlings/Fish in ponds, lakes and other still fresh water. This policy covers death or loss of fish due to disease of any kind, epidemic, parasitic infestation, poisoning, malicious act by third parties, pollution, summer kill, riot and strike, explosion, fire, aircraft damage and aerial devices, impact by any vehicle, storm, tempest, flood, innudation. The exclusions are loss due to improper management and bad handling, loss due to neglect and carelessness, loss due to malicious act, wilful injury, error or omission, partial loss of any kind, losses sue to dangerous insects, predators, competitions etc. losses due to variation in pH factor, physical, chemical status of the water and soils, asphyxia, losses due to natural mortality, burglary, house breaking, theft infidelity of any person, land and air accident loss, destruction damage or legal liability directly or indirectly caused by contributed to by or arising from nuclear weapons material. 80 per cent of fish as per valuation is indemnified. The premium rate is 2.5 per cent per annum on average value of fish.

(*iii*) *Silk Worms Insurance.* The silk worms insurance policy is applicable to mulberry silkworms only of Univoltine, Bivoltine or Multivoltine Breed. The disease free layings purchased from licensed seed preparers/Graineurs or Government Grainages are covered. Silkworms from egg stage to cocoon stage are insured. This policy covers death of silkworm due to accident or disease contracted during the period of insurance subject to the usual terms and conditions. The cover is in respect or total loss only. The malicious wilful act of insured his family member/person/worker; theft, clandestine sale, missing of the worms and non supply of adequate quality suitable quality of mulberry leaves. The valuation is done by Sericulture officer. The insured will send monthly declaration statement to the insurer based upon which premium is collected or adjusted. The premium is 5 per cent per annum of the sum assured on the market value of cocoon at the 5th stage.

(*iv*) *Honey Bee Insurance.* The honey bee insurance policy indeminfies the insured against all accidental losses or damages to the Hive and/or Bee Colony subject to the exclusion of loss of production, malicious or wilful act or neglect or improper management; theft, clandestine sale or missing of worms, war invasion, act of foreign enemy, hoslilities, civil war, rebellion, revolution, insurrection, mutiny, military or usurped power or any consequences thereof or attempt thereat; accident loss, destruction, damage or legal liability directly or indirectly, caused by or contributed to by or arising from nuclear weaks material. The rate or premium is 3 per cent of total insured value. Risk of theft can be covered on payment, of additional premium of 2 per cent.

The form subsidiary companies have underwritten small volume of business under pondfish insurance, silkworm insurance, agriculture insurance and animal driven cart insurance.

6. Package Insurance

The General Insurance Corporation and its four subsidiaries have evolved insurance policy known as package insurance with a view to offer complete, all round protection to the weaker sections of societies in respect of their dwelling premises and belongings from various hazards. They are composite package and farmers' package.

(*i*) *Composite Package Insurance.* The composite package insurance has been evolved to protect the weaker sections and tribes. The properties covered under this scheme are huts, dwelling, cottage industry sheds, contents including belongings personal accident and hospitalisation. The risks covered under this policy are fire, lightning, riots and strikes, malicious damage, aircraft damage, flood, inundations, cyclone, storm, tempest, typhoon, tornado, hurricane. The sum assured under Hut coverage is ₹ 2,000 and premium rate is 3 per cent annum. The contents are for ₹ 1,000 at 3 per cent premium. Personal accident covers ₹ 10,000 at the premium of ₹ 10. Hospitabsation for accidents and major diseases are for ₹ 4,000 at the premium of ₹ 40.00. Thus, the total premium ₹ 59 for covering all the above risks under one policy.

(*ii*) *Farmers' Package Insurance.* The farmers' package insurance policy has been issued to provide insurance coverage to the farmers for dwelling hut/houses, agricultural implements, seeds, fertilisers, pesticides against the risks of fire, lightning, cyclone, earthquake, flood upto ₹ 5000; cattle insurance against death due to accident and discase, permanent total disablement and breeding and calving risks upto ₹ 4000; agricultural pumpsets against fire, theft/burglary and machinery breakdown upto their market price, bullock cart against death/permanent disabilities to animal due to accident upto ₹ 2000, loss/damage to cart due to accident upto ₹ 1000, third party liability personal accident to cart driver and Gramin Personal Accident against death/permanent total disablement upto ₹ 6000 under single policy known as farmers' package insurance.

The premium is decided as per separate insurance policy.

7. Crop Insurance

The countrywide comprehensive crop insurance scheme introduced by the Government of India commenced from kharif 1985-86. The GIC has been entrusted with the task of administering the scheme on behalf of the Government. The insurance charges and claims in respect of crops insured in any state is shared between the Central Crop Insurance Fund and Crop Insurance Fund set up by the State Government concerned in the ratio of 2 : 1. GIC maintains close and constant liaison with State Governments, RBI, NABARD, State Cooperative Banks, Commercial Banks, Regional Rural Banks, and other agencies involved for smooth implementations of the scheme.

The number of farmers covered under crop insurance has increased from 26.30 lakhs in 1985 (Kharif) to 29.64 lakhs in 1988. The premium income has declined from ₹ 9.42 lakhs to ₹ 8.82 lakhs under Kharif. The number of farmers covered has declined from 12.13 lakhs in 1985-86 to 8.71 lakhs in 1988-89. The premium has also declind from ₹ 4.48 crores to ₹ 3.12 crores. This shows that the crop insurance is not being properly managed by the GIC and its four subsidiaries.

Table 35.6
Crop Insurance

		Kharif							*Rabi*						
		1985	*1986*	*1987*	*1988*	*1989*	*1997-98*	*2001*	*1985-86*	*1986-87*	*1987-88*	*1988-89*	*1989-90*	*1997-98*	*2001-02*
1. No of farmers covered (in Lakhs)		26.31	40.66	46.31	29.64	42.26	51.35	85.69	12.13	11.28	21.28	8.79	6.61	6.82	20
2. Sum Insured	Rs.	542.73	856.20	1140.15	547.89	873.86	2230.74	7300.9	238.41	242.37	475.44	163.87	148.76	322.37	1600
3. Premium	Rs.	9.42	14.99	19.09	8.82	14.44	34.32	256.96	4.48	4.57	8.55	3.12	2.72	5.72	
4. Incurred claims	Rs.	83.00	159.54	277.38	27.84	28.05	—	508.10	2.96	7.80	12.07	3.10	—	—	—

Table 35.7

Statement of New Business Under Janashree Bima Yojana & Krishi Shramik Samajik Suraksha Yojana-2001 as at 31-03-2003 by the LIC

Zone	*Janashree Bima Yojana*						*Krishi Shramik Samajik Suraksha Yojana 2001*			*Total for The Year 2002-03*		
Growth Rate (March 2003)				*For the Year 2002-03*			*For the Year 2002-03*					
	SCH	*Lives*	*Premium*	*SCH*	*Lives*	*Premium*	*SCH*	*Lives*	*Premium*	*SCH*	*Lives*	*Premium*
Northern	–56	82	82	292	36914	3691400	164	7909	1735600	456	44823	5427000
Central	–66	88	88	372	71523	7152300	43	8333	1001595	415	79856	8153895
North Central	19	–1	–1	398	78525	7852500	137	2674	240660	535	81199	8093160
Eastern	115	48	48	370	33290	3329000	435	26283	4590839	805	59573	7919839
Southern	337	848	848	387	62376	6237600	688	22372	4212165	1075	84748	10449765
South Central	–35	1055	1055	516	122597	12259700	429	8694	3010575	945	131291	15270275
Western	43	109	109	950	230891	23089100	890	33748	5364610	1840	264639	28453710
Corporation	–7	199	199	3285	636116	63611600	2786	110013	20156044	6071	746129	83767544

*Budget 2002-03 include targets of Krishi Shramik Suraksha Yojana.

Since Government finding is involved, the scheme lacks smooth management. The triangular decisions and processes *i.e.*, GIC, Central Government and states have caused less efficiencies in crop insurance. The GIC may be given certain regular premium by the Central government who may get reimbursed from respective states for its proper management. The crop insurance in India needs thorough revision and systematic management.

The Government of India introduced National Agricultural Insurance Scheme (NAIS) replacing the Comphrehensive Crop Insurance Scheme (CCIS) with effect from Rabi 1999-2000 season. The scheme cover all farmers-loance and non-loance. Sugarcane, Potato and cotton. Onion Ginger, Gonlic and termeric are also covered. Similarly Jute, Tapioca Banana and Pineapple are introduced and covered.

Oriental Insurance has introduced Rice Insurance Policy. Khalihan Bima Policy, Jan Arogya Bima and Agricultural tractor Policies got much appreciation by villagers.

8. Rural Insurance Business

The overall performance, under Rural Insurance Business for 1994-95 has shown good progress. The premium income received was ₹ 31.26 crores by National Insurance. The Solatium Final Schemes were operative in all the insurance companies. United India paid death claim amounting to ₹ 23.95 lakhs and ₹ 1.45 lakhs injury to victims in "Hit and Run" accident cases during 1994-95. Under Personal Accident Social Security Insurance Scheme out of Claims amounting 2063 claims of ₹ 61.88 were settled by New India, ₹ 24.69 lakhs by Oriental Insurance and ₹ 218.86 lakhs by United India during 1994-95. All the companies have procured ₹ 336 crores during 1997-98.

PROSPECTS OF AGRICULTURE INSURANCE IN INDIA

Agriculture is the oldest occupation and is primary sector of the economy. Industrialisation and technological upgrading has increased the degree of risks in agriculture. The risks to be scaled up continuously to bring the much needed prosperity in the rural economy. The risks in agriculture are classified under production risk, pest risks, market risk, investment and credit risk, institutional risk, technology risks and personal risks. Production risks include rainfall, temperature variation, frost, solar radiation, wind and vapour pressure pest risks include soil, its fertility, PH texture, physiology, phenology and morphology, farmyard manners, pest management and irrigation.

MANAGING AGRICULTURAL RISKS

Agriculture insurance has to manage a number of agricultural risks which are production risk, operational risk, market risk, financial risk, technological risk, institutional and regulation risks and infrastructural risk. All these risks are interrelated.

Production risks refer to a shortfalls in output or sub-standard quality due to various operations weather and social factors. Its impacts range from revenue loss for the individual farmer to chronic food shortages at the national level. Predicting output and quality with certainity is challenging especially due to adverse weathers such as droughts, floods, windstroms, hailstorm, nons-availability of water and irrigation facilities; pests and crop diseases and social risks such as war, terrorism, riots or social instability.

Operational risks relates to liability, currency and business interruption, non-availability of labour, input shortages, equipment failure; theft, fire or accidents. The contaminations of food processing, growingc use of genetically modified seeds and complex fertilisers.

Market risks relates to uncertain input and output prices triggered by demand and supply conditions in the local or global market place. Price volatility affects farmers and others through operating costs and revenues. They may face rising inputs as compared by market price and suffer loss. This discourages investment in farm production.

Financial risk relates to uncertainty about the availability and cost of farm credit. The risk arises because of non availability of funds or non availability of the resources at tolerant price and current foreign exchange. Agriculture production usually incurs a funding gap due to long production cycle. Short term as well as long-term financing is required for purchases inputs and investing in farming equipment farmers many times are forced to borrow from moneylenders who exploit them severally.

Technological risk involves advances in technology such as the launch of an advanced fertiliser or new genetically modified reds, equipment. In absence or use of modern technology farm products are bound to be less compared to those who use them.

Intitutional risk arises from policy changes at local or national government level. Many times this policy framework supports and protects the farmers. In absence of such supports they may suffer losses. Price support, agricultural subsidies and other facililatting measures help farmers. These may be detrimental policies also such as export restrictions to meet domestic demand. Farmers, thus, cannot get full benefits of higher international price.

Infrastructure risk originates from inadequate infrastructure for agricultural productions and distributions. infrastructurd challenges may stem from warehouses to financial institutions. An unsufficient distribution network or poor warehousing setup can result loss of perishable products.

The agricultural risks require a holistic risk management. Insurers have to educate and support the farmers although government and others institutions have been supporting farmers from time to time. Insurers may train the farmers for cropsharing, individual savings, production diversification. They should adopt through farmer risk, prevention, risk control and financing. Government and insurance sector should come together to manage the agricultural risk to maintain constant flow of qualitative agricultural products. Agricultural insurance can help fill the void in risk financing and risk management.

ROLE OF INSURANCE IN MANAGINGRS AGRICULTURAL RISK

Insurance provides cover for weather relate losses, enables farm investment, promots the development of support infrastructure and enables income stability. Weather related losses are reduced through effective risk transfer, expediate recovery of losses and reducing governments contingent liability generation risk awareness and encouraging structural reformers. Investment is facilitated through bank government nexus, improving credit available insurance and bank help investment equipment and better technology for agricultural sector Agricultural insurance is sometime required for collateral financing and credit. Agriculture crop insurance is compulsory in India for requiring agricultural credit from financial institutions.

Insurance provides protection against various non-weather relates risks such as import shortfalls, food processing, infrastructure and transport risk. It helps ensure the farmer's earnings and other requirements.

Microinsurance in agriculture facilitates saving insurance products, family health protection and other assistançes.

Agriculture Insurance Company of India Limited (AIC)

The Government and the Agriculture Insurance Company of India Limited (AIC) have passed through the leaning curve in all areas of crop insurance and are looking to make crop insurance reachable and affordable to a majority of cultivators. Based on the data supplied by Indian Agriculture Research Institute (IARI), AIC is able to offer products on climate variation and locational differences in around 250 locations spread over around 50 districts of the country. AIC has been experimenting with unique insurance models in the management of crop insurance. AIC has kept management costs below a level of 2% and intermediary costs of low level. It has used the large banking network numbering 1.5 lakhs branches of commercial banks. Cooperative Banks and Rural Banks and Primary Agricultural Cooperative societies AIC has collaborator with the various Boards and Authories in the agriculture sector such as the Coffee, Rubber, Coconut, Spices Boards, Floriculture and all types of plantations.

Index based weather insurance is rapidly gaining interest in India. More than 5,00,000 Indian farmers have taken weather insurance policies through schemes provided by AIC and private sector insurance companies including ICICI Lombard and IFFCO Tokio, Swiss Reinsuring the schemes of micro-finance. AIC is actively promoting crop insurance, strengthening marketing, education and awareness of the benefits of insurance.

CROP INSURANCE

Crop insurance is a part of agriculture insurance. It has included the risks of weather, yield and so on.

Weather Insurance : Weather insurance is part of crop insurance which started since Kharif 2003 season through BASIX, a micro-finance institution. Agriculture Insurance Company of India Limited (AIC), a government entity is created to ensure agriculture risks. ICICI Lombard General Insurance Company and IFFCO. Tokio General Insurance Company have been piloting weather based crop insurance. Farmers have not responded positively because of unaffordable premium rates and lack of subsidies from the Government, technical challenges, unrealistic expectations, poor communication and lack of clarity AIC has been running a pilot weather insurance scheme since Kharif 2004. It has started weather based crop insurance scheme during Kharif 2007 in Karnataka. AIC designed the weather indices using weather parameters us unseasonal rains, frost heat relative humidity and technical inputs from the apex scientific institutions in designing the customised insurance product for Rabi 2007-08 season. Weather insurance seems to score better when it causes to data accuracy. transparency and quick settlement of payouts. Weather based crop insurance program and the challenges are designing a proxy weather index with predictive capability to realistically measure crop losses and is closer to the indemnity principle and the basis risk. A good insurance product should be able ensure either no claim if the crop is good or high claim of the crop is poor.

Role of Weather Insurance

Weather insurance has a role to play, particularly, as complimentary to the existing area yield crop insurance weather insurance is the solution for the areas where yield data are not available. Weather index is used to make early payments under area yield crop insurance. It is also used to design double trigger insurance products. Triggers are weather index and area yield estimate. Weather insurance is designed for micro level insurance products. It is an ideal tool for protecting a large port- folio at District/Regional/State level against droughts or floods. Weather, insurance produce design is to taken to minimise to basis risk creating realistic and appropriate communication, adopting reliable and sustainable pricing and product servicing.

Yield Insurance : Yield insurance covers the loss of Hurricane, Tornado, Flood, Inundation and Landslide, Drought, Dry Spells, Pests and diseases. Yield based crop insurance covers Food Crops, Cereals, Millets and Pulses, Oilseeds and Animal Crops, Commercial Crops and Horticultural Crops. It operates on 'Area Approach'. Individual assessment of losses is also being implemented on experimental basis. The size of area is Block/Mandal/ Nyaya Panchayat/Gram Panchayat. Village may be area for selected crops.

Sum Assured : The amount of crop loan is the minimum sum assured which is on compulsory basis. Additional coverage upto 150% value of average yield by paying premium at acturial rate. For the non-loanee farmers, the coverage is available at normal flat rates of premium for the value of normal coverage of yield. The value of sum assured is arrived at by multiplying the thresh hold yield/

average yield with the latest available Minimum Support Price (MSP) announced by the Government or the market price is MSP is not announced.

Premium : The premium at acturial rate as (AIC) communicated by Agriculture Insurance Company of India Ltd. (AIC) is generally 3.5% of Sum Insured for bagra and oilseeds, 2.5% for other food crops, 1.5% for wheat and 2% for other food crops. The premium for small and marginal farmers is subsidised to the extent of 10% which is shared by the State Government and Government of India.

Settlement of claims : Claim is a Notified Area, automatically payable if these is a shortfall in (NFA) become yield, i.e., current season's yield is less than the guaranteed yield. The shortfall is converter into claims by multiplying the percentage shortfall with sum insured. The guaranted yield or Threshold Yield (TY) for a crop in an insurance unit based on moving average of the preceding 3/5 years multiplied by the idemenity level, i.e., 90% or 80% or 60% depending upon the variability in the yield of the crop.

Coverage : The summary of coverage under National Agricultural Insurance Scheme (Rabi 1999-2000 to 2006-07 season) is given in the tables.

Table 35.8

National Agriculatural Insurance Scheme

Kharif Season

Season Kharif	*Loanee farmers*		*Non Loanee farmers*		*Loanee Loss of*	*Non-Loanee*	*Loanee Benefited*	*Non-Loanee benefited*
	In lakhs	*%*	*In lakhs*	*%*	*cost %*	*cost %*	*% of covered*	*%covered*
2000	82.17	97.71%	1.92	2.29	17.42	38.3	38.3	64.37
2001	79.75	91.70	7.22	8.30	5.67	26.94	16.97	53.86
2002	84.20	86.19	13.49	13.81	17.59	31.19	39.54	71.14
2003	70.12	87.97	9.59	12.03	5.19	37.99	12.14	89.83
2004	110.58	87.16	16.29	12.84	7.08	17.15	18.40	39.32
2005	105.64	83.35	21.10	16.65	7.59	9.86	19.08	30.44
2006	98.38	76.06	30.97	23.94	11.82	13.74	22.25	26.04
Total	630.83	85.25	100.58	13.75				
Rabi Kharif								
1999-2000	5.60	96.64	0.19	3.36	2.04	7.18	8.14	49.56
2000-2001	19.22	91.91	1.69	8.09	2.90	21.32	22.89	51.14
2001-2002	18.79	96.10	0.76	3.90	3.24	41.83	20.34	93.34
2002-2003	19.66	84.48	3.61	15.52	8.85	25.41	36.65	57.05
2003-2004	22.55	51.01	21.66	48.99	3.41	20.33	14.04	81.08
2004-2005	32.74	92.72	2.57	7.28	4.07	9.33	21.90	21.75
2005-2006	37.18	91.84	3.31	8.16	6.54	11.57	24.65	19.47
2006-2007	42.00	84.38	7.78	15.62	–	–	–	–
Total	197.75	82.63	41.58	17.37				

Insurance Coverage Under National Agriculture Insurance Scheme

Season Kharif	*Farmers Covered*		*Area Covered*		*Sum Insured*		*Premium*		*Claims ₹ in crore*	*Farmers Benefitted in Lakhs*
	Lakhs	*% Increase*	*Lakhs Hectare*	*%*	*Crores*	*% Increase*	*Crore*	*% Increase*		
2000	84	–	132		69.3		207		1222	36
2001	87	3.4	129	–2.5	7502	8.7	262	26.5	494	17
2002	98	12.3	155	20.1	9432	25.6	325	24.4	1824	43
2003	80	18.4	124	–20.0	8114	–13.9	283	12.9	653	17
2004	127	59.2	243	95.9	13171	62.3	459	62.0	1038	27
2005	127	0	205	–15.4	13519	2.6	450	–1.9	1060	27
2006	199	2.1	197	–4.2	14759	9.2	467	3.8	1774	31
2007	134	3.6	208	5.7	17008	15.2	524	12.1	913	16
2008	130	–2.9	178	–14.4	15656	–7.9	514	–1.9	1476	30
2009										
Total	996	–	1571		94210		3491		10454	244
Rabi										
1999 -2000	6	–	8	–	356	–	5		8	1
2000 -2001	21	260.6	31	298.3	1603	349.6	28	412.7	59	5
2001 -2002	20	– 6.5	31	1.1	1498	– 6.6	30	8.5	65	5
2002 -2003	23	19.0	40	28.3	1838	22.7	39	27.7	189	9
2003 -2004	44	89.9	65	60.2	3049	65.9	64	66.4	497	21
2004 -2005	35	–20.1	53	–17.4	3774	23.7	76	18.4	161	8
2005 -2006	40	14.6	72	35.1	5072	34.4	105	38.2	338	10
2006 -2007	50	22.9	76	5.7	6543	28.9	143	36.2	515	14
2007 -2008	50	0	74	–2.6	7466	14.1	159	11.1	798	16
2008 -2009										
Total	289	–	450	–	31199	–	649	–	2630	89

Cropwise Coverage Under
National Agriculature Insurance Scheme (2000 to 2006)

Crops	*Farmers covered*	*Sum Insured (Crore)*	*Premium crore*	*Claims crore*	*Loss cost %*	*Claim Ratio (%)*
Paddy	332	30447	752	2412	7.92	3.21
Maize	18	1508	38	166	11.00	4.32
Bajra	39	2517	88	332	13.19	3.75
Redgram	27	1943	50	258	13.29	5.21
Ground nut	111	17105	591	3200	18.71	5.41
Soyabean	70	6779	234	494	7.28	2.11
Wheat	70	5670	86	334	5.90	3.89
Jawar	40	1458	36	298	20.42	8.19
Horsegram	15	924	20	187	20.24	9.26
Sunflower	11	813	23	95	11.64	4.03
Sugarcane	37	6477	91	130	2.01	1.43
Cotton	57	6277	496	528	8.42	1.06
Onion	4	519	39	97	18.69	2.49
Potato	17	2207	95	209	9.47	2.20
Food Crop and oil seeds (FCOS)	802	73869	2039	8381	11.35	4.11
Annual Commercial Horticulture (ACH)	119	16721	763	996	5.95	1.30
Total	921	90590	2802	9377	10.35	3.35

Percentage Coverage of
Natural Agriculture Insurance Scheme.

Crop	*Farmers covered*	*Sum Insured*	*Premium*	*Claims*	*Loss*	*Class Ratio*
Paddy	36.07	33.61	26.85	25.72	7.92	3.21
Maize	1.97	1.66	1.37	1.77	11.00	4.32
Bajra	4.20	2.78	3.16	3.54	13.19	3.75
Redgram	2.59	2.14	1.77	2.75	13.29	5.21
Groundnut	12.00	18.88	21.10	34.13	18.71	5.41
Soyabean	7.57	7.48	8.35	5.27	7.28	2.11
Wheat	7.59	6.26	3.07	3.56	5.90	3.89
Jowar	4.39	1.61	1.30	3.17	20.42	8.19
Horsegram	1.63	1.02	0.72	1.99	20.24	9.26
Sunflower	1.17	0.90	0.84	1.01	11.64	4.03
Sugarcane	4.04	7.15	3.26	1.39	2.01	1.43
Cotton	6.19	6.93	17.71	5.63	8.42	1.06
Onion	0.44	0.57	1.38	0.92	18.69	2.49
Potato	1.82	2.44	3.38	2.24	9.47	2.20
FCOS	87.07	81.54	72.77	89.38	11.35	4.11
ACH	12.93	18.46	27.23	10.62	5.95	1.30
Total %	100.00	100.0	100.0	100.0	100.0	100.0
Figure Lacs/ in crore	921	90590	2802	9377	10.35	3.35

Table 35.9A

Per Famer/hectare coverage under

National Agriculture Insurance Scheme (NAIS)

In ₹

Kharif Season	*Per Farmer Sum Assured*	*Per hecatre Sum Assured*	*Per Farmer Premium*	*Per Farmer Claims*
2000	8209	5222	246	3362
2001	8627	5821	301	2833
2003	9655	6072	333	4245
2004	10180	6567	355	3811
2005	10381	5426	362	3811
2006	11411	7502	361	5659
2007	12692	8193	391	5786
2008				
2009				
Total				
1999–2000	7662	5150	133	1129
2000–2001	7658	4760	154	1426
2001–2002	7897	4550	165	2035
2002–2003	6897	4714	144	2369
2003–2004	10688	7063	214	2078
2004–2005	12527	7026	258	3450
2005–2006	13142	8571	287	3663
2006–2007	14776	9911	314	
2007-2008				
2008-2009				

Total Source : Agriculture = Insurance company of India Ltd.

Table 35.9B

Level of Penetration and Coverage

State	*Level of Penetration*	*Farmers covered*	*Lakhs % to Total*	*Service Insurance*	
Andhra Pradesh	22.02	165	14.9	24497	
Gujarat	22.20	83	7.5	16066	
Karnataka	10.24	77	7.0	8804	
Madhya Pradesh	30.51	136	12.5	12618	11.0
Maharashtra	18.63	189	18.6	10782	9.4
Orissa	24.54	82	7.4	7946	6.9
Rajasthan	52.85	91	8.4	8769	7.7
Uttar Pradesh	11.29	97	8.8	9946	8.7
West Bengal	16.08	56	5.0	4031	3.5
All India	15.96	11.04	100.8	114186	100.0

Table 35.9 C

Coverage of Crop Insurance	
Total number of farmers covered	9,70,73,736
Total Area covered (Hectares)	15,62,10,772
Total Sum Insured (₹ crore)	97,180
Total Insurance changes (₹ crore)	2943
Total claim (₹ crore)	9763
Claim Ratio	1:3

International Agriculture Insurance

Agriculture Insurance in world in gaining ground. The Private Insurance are taking interest in agricultural insurance

Table 35.10

	Premium	*USD (Million)*	*Private Insurer*
Asia of which	428		
India		141	Low
South Korea		69	Medium
China		94	Medium
Latin America of which	309		
Argentina		92	High
Brazil		111	Low
Clule		3	Moderate
Mexico		30	Moderate
Eastern Europe of which	230		
Russia		15	Moderate
Poland		20	Moderate
Czech Republic		30	Moderate
Turkies		36	Moderate
Africa of which	103		
South Africa		60	High
Nigeria		1	Low
Mauritius		19	Low
Total	**1070**		

Agricultural Insurance in BRICS Countries in 2011

	Agricultural Land as % of total Land Area	*Employment in Agricultural as % of total Employment*	*Agriculture Value % of Total GDP*	*Agriculture Insurance in USD (million dollars)*	*Agriculture Insurance in Penetration*
Brazil	31.9	17.0	5.8	430	0.35%
Russia	13.2	9.7	4.0	552	0.35%
India	60.5	51.1	19.0	673	0.98%
China	56.2	39.6	10.1	2543	0.197%
South Africa	81.7	5.1	2.5	153	0.36%
Emerging marketing				5176	1.77%
Aggregate				11400	1.23%
United States				23511	7.15%
World					0.83%

QUESTIONS

1. How far rural masses have been benefited by the rural insurance schemes?
2. What is cattle insurance? How many livestock are insured under cattle insurance?
3. 'Crop insurance in India is not very popular'. Discuss it.

36

URBAN TRADITIONAL AND NON-TRADITIONAL INSURANCE

TRADITIONAL INSURANCE

The Traditional Insurance includes burglary and personal accidental insurance

BURGLARY INSURANCE

Burglary Insurance is one of the major classes of business underwritten in the miscellaneous department and accounts for a sizeable portion of the department's premium income. For the business house Burglary insurance is as essential as Fire insurance, as it enables them to recoup the losses suffered by them consequent on burglary or house breaking. In addition to the burglary policy, other types of policies giving wider covers have also been devised by the burglary department.

The main types of policies are as follows:

(*i*) Business Premises Policy,
(*ii*) Private Dwelling Policy,
(*iii*) Jewellary and Valuable Policy,
(*iv*) All Risk Policy, and
(*v*) Money in Transit Policy

Definitions

Burglary

The criminal law of the country does not speak of an offence called burglary. Hence it becomes necessary for the insurers to lay down in the policy the definition of the term. As normally understood burglary is:

(*a*) Theft of property from the premises following upon felonious entry of the said premises by violent and forcible means, or

(*b*) Theft by a person in the premises who subsequently breaks out by violent and forcible means provided there shall be visible marks made upon the premises at the place of such entry or exit by tools, explosives, electricity or chemicals. Use of force may be against property and person.

Theft

Indian Penal Code in Section 378 defines theft as follows: "whoever intending to take dishonestly any movable property out of the possession of any person without the consent of that person or of any person having for that purpose authority, moves that property in order to such taking is said to commit theft."

House-breaking

The word in practice is equal to 'Burglary'. Section 445 of the Indian Penal Code has laid down a definition of the term. A person is said to commit housebreaking who commits house trespass if he effects his entrance into the house (or any part of it), or if being in the house (or any part of it) for the purpose of committing an offence, or having committed an offence therein he quits the house, such entrance or exit being made by use of force in one of the six ways as described in the Indian Penal Code.

Robbery

Section 390 of the Indian Penal Code laid down, "If in order to the commission of or in committing of the theft or in carrying away property obtained by theft, the offender, for that end, voluntarily causes (or attempts to cause) to any person death or hurt or wrongful restraint or fear of instant death or hurt or wrongful restraint or fear of instant death or hurt or wrongful restraint".

Dacoity

Section 391 of the Indian Penal Code states dacoity as "where five or more persons conjointly commit or attempt to commit a robbery or are present and aid such commission or attempt, everyone of them is said to commit dacoity".

Coverage

Business premises are generally covered against burglary and house breaking only. Mere theft without the use of force and violence is not covered, robbery and dacoity being aggravated forms of theft. It also covers risk of holdup. Burglary and house breaking fall within the scope of this cover. Under policies issued for private dwellings, the contents are covered against burglary, house-breaking and theft risks. Similarly Jewellery and valuables are also insured in the same manner.

Money in Transit

Policies, as a matter of rule, cover robbery, hold-up and dacoity in addition to burglary, house-breaking and theft.

Business Premises Insurance Policies

Policics issucd to business premises cover stock-in-trade, goods in trust or on commission, fixtures and fittings, tools of trade such as typewriters, calculators and other similar property and cash and currency notes in locked safe against the risk of burglary and house-breaking. Loss or damage to contents or to any part of the building caused by burglary or any attempt therefore is also covered. In regard to stock-in-trade and other goods the policy may be issued on full value basis or on "first loss" basis.

A "*First Loss*" 'Policy insures the property up to a specified amount only which is calculated to be the maximum likely loss on any one occasion. This type of policy is taken where a total loss is a physical impossibility. First loss policies are usually taken for bulk commodities. The amount insured is always specified as a certain percentage of the full value, say, 10% or 12.5% of the full value.

The amount of premium-loss reinsurance was ₹ 16.60 crore by New India in 1994-95. It has got profit of ₹ 12.12 crore in that year.

Cash-in-Safe Insurance

The cover includes only when the cash is secured in a safe and is granted only if the safe is burglar proof and is of an approved make and design. Safe which is permanently installed in the premises is a better risk than a safe which can be shifted. The cover is granted subject to the following two clauses.

(*a*) The loss of cash obstructed from the safe following the use of the key to the said safe or any duplicate these of belonging to the insured is not covered unless such key has been obtained by violence or through means of force. The use of force need not necessarily be against the person or an individual. It can be against property as well. Thus cupboard is removed after forcing open the cupboard, the loss is covered by the policy.

(*b*) A complete list of the amount of cash in safe should be kept secure in some places other than the safe and the liability of the insurer is limited to the amount actually shown by such records.

All Risks (Jewellery and Valuables) Insurance

Policies under this form of insurance cover risks in respect of jewellery, plate, watches, personal ornaments and other valuables. Loss or damage by any accident or misfortune including fire, theft, robbery from the person, defective settings or fastening and accidental damage are thus covered. The policies do not, however, cover loss or damage:

(*i*) occasioned by or in consequence of war, invasion, act of foreign enemy, hostilities, civil war, nuting, rebellion, revolution, insurrection, military or usurped power, riot, civil commotion, earthquake or other convulsions of nature;

(*ii*) caused by or arising from any process of repairing, restoring or renovating any property insured;

(*iii*) due to moth, wildew, wear or other deterioration or inherent defect in any property insured. The insurance is applicable in all places within the geographical limits provided for in the policy.

Exclusions

The exceptions peculiar to a burglary (business premises) policy are:

(*i*) loss or damage where any member of the insured's household or his business staff is concerned as principal or accessory or resulting from any act committed by any other person lawfully on the premises wherein the property may happen to be;

(*ii*) loss or damage which can be insured against by a fire or a plat glass or a motor insurance policy;

(*iii*) loss of or damage to deeds, bonds, bills of exchange, promissory notes, cash, treasury, bank notes, cheques, securities for money, stamps, stamp collections, books of accounts, manuscripts, documents of any kind and medals and coins, unless specially mentioned and agreed to be covered.

Extension Under the Policy

An extension of the policy frequently sought is in respect of riot and strike damage which is a common exclusion in all policies. Riot as included in the policy is deemed to mean riot as defined in the Indian Penal Code.

Insurance of Money in Transit

This is a modified version of Burglary Insurance covering money or securities in transit between the insured's premises and bank or post office or other specified place or between the insured's (main) premises and branch premises. The cover is granted only to commercial and industrial establishments.

The coverage of money in transit policy is as below:

(*a*) Wages in transit from bank to insured's premises.

(*b*) Cash in transit from insured's premises to post office for purchase of postal orders, money orders and postage or Revenue Stamps.

(*c*) Postal orders, money orders and postage or revenue stamps in transit from Post Office to insured premises.

(*d*) Wages in transit from the insured's (main) premises to insured branch premises.

(*e*) Cash other than wages in transit from Bank to insured's premises from insured's to bank and between insured's premises and the insured's branch premises.

(*f*) Cheques, bills of exchange, money orders and postal orders in transit from the insured's premises to bank.

(*g*) Cash collected by employees from the time of collection during rounds and until delivered at the insured's premises or bank on the day of collection.

(*h*) Cash (other than wages) secured in locked safe when the insured's premises or closed.

(*i*) Cash (other than wages) contained in the insured's premises whilst occupied for business purposes.

In a money-in-transit policy, two sums are significant:

(*i*) Limit of the insurer's liability for anyone loss; and

(*ii*) Estimated amount in transit during the year.

Extension (Infidelity of Employees)

The normal policy does not cover loss to the insured arising through the acts of dishonesty by the employees entrusted with the carrying of the money. The policy is extended at additional premium to cover any loss to the insured of the property insured by any act of fraud or dishonesty committed by the employees or employees carrying the property. This is known as 'Infidelity Extension'.

UNDERWRITING

Underwriting of burglary insurance includes the following steps:

1. Nature of Insured property

The value of the property and the weight and/or volume of the property are two aspects of risk considerations. Small volume/weight having high value are attached more risks of burglary.

2. Premises in which the insured property is housed

The class of construction of the premises situation of the premises, etc. are considered for risk evaluation premises situated in densely populated areas are less risk prone than those situated in lonely areas.

3. Occupancies

It is noted how many hours the premises are occupied. The hours for which the premises are unoccupied are noted.

4. Safety Measures

Safety measures if adequately taken will give less risk.

5. History

History of post claim and insurance policies are considered for risk evaluation.

6. Moral Hazard

Underwriters take into consideration moral hazard of the proposer. Survey of heavy sum assured and special attributes thereof are taken into consideration.

7. Books of Accounts

Books of accounts enable underwriter to assets correctly amount of liability. Information relating to stock taking and airdib is useful for the purpose.

8. Identification

Correct description of goods are given for proper identification.

9. Conditions

Whether sum insured have been given separately against the insured's own stock, similar goods held in trust or on commission, furniture, etc., cash or valuables in safe.

Survey Report

Acceptance and the terms of cover of are based on the report given by the surveyors for the following particulars:

(i) Proposer's name, address and business
(ii) Exact description of the property proposed for insurance
(iii) Highest value of a single article
(iv) Whether the stock books are properly maintained and whether the exact amount of loss can be ascertained
(v) Maximum possible loss
(vi) Whether the proposer resides on the premises
(vii) Hours and time the premises are left unoccupied
(viii) History of burglary in the locality and steps taken to present them
(ix) Number of doors, windows, skylights and other openings
(x) Whether there is special precautions like alarms, collapsible gates, warning clock, etc.
(xi) Points of entry, exit, guards, etc.

Rating

Rating is done as per standard percent of the sum assured. The rate varies according to type of goods location and construction of premises, security measures such as close circuit T.V., armed guard, locked Bars, electronic alarms.

Claim Procedures

Immediate notice is given to the insurer about the circumstance of loss, happening or event giving rise or likely to give rise to a claim under the policy. Within 7 days of the notice, the insured has to lodge with the insurer a detail statement in writing of the loss or damage with an estimate of the intrinsic value of each article lost and the amount of damage sustained.

Prevention and Minimisation of Loss

The insured is required to exercise reasonable steps to safeguard the property insured and to secure all doors windows and upper openings.

The insured has to give immediate notice to the police. He will take all reasonable steps to apprehend the guilty and to recover property lost. If insurer requires the insured has to take steps for the prosecution and conviction of the guilty persons to recover the property. The expenses will be borne by the insurer.

Indemnification of Loss

The insurer may reinstate replace, repair the property or premises, as the case may be instead of paying the amount of the loss or damage. The doctrine of subrogation applies after payment is made.

The insurer will pay only prorata of the loss or damage. Where the property insured at the time of loss or damage shall be greater value than the sum insured thereon.

BURGLARLY (PRIVATE DWELLINGS) INSURANCE

Similar to Burglarly (Business Premises) Insurance Burglarly insurance is also applicable to property of private dwellings. The policy does not pay more than the value of any particular article. The private dwellings insurance may be All Risk Insurances and Baggage Insurance.

All Risks Insurance Policy

The policy seeks to cover loss or damage by fire or burglary or theft or any other accidental or fortuituous circumstances.

The policy is suitable for Jeweller, valuables, antiques, paintings, watches, clocks, works of art cameras, trumpets, and other similar articles. The insured values in respect of these items are decided on an agreed value basis. For Jewellery, gold and silver plates, the values are fixed in consultation with a professional Jewellery appraiser.

Full description of jewellery, number of precious stones, amount of gold, type of ornament and valuation made by reliable recognised jeweller.

Baggage Insurance Policy

This policy provides indemnity to the insured to the extent of the insurisic value of the accompanied personal baggage of the insured or member of his family while the insured is travelling on tour and/or holiday.

Exclusions:

The specific exclusions are loss or damage

(*i*) Occurring during routine travel

(*ii*) Articles which do not form part of the baggage when the journey commenced, unless declared and accepted by the insurer.

(*iii*) Articles of consumable and perishable nature.

(*iv*) Loss of articles like sticks, umbrellas etc. properly in use on the voyage or journey, articles or clothes whilst being worn or carried out.

(*v*) Loss arising from leakage, spilling of liquids, oils, etc.

(*vi*) Damage caused by repairing or renovating.

(*vii*) Loss or damage arising through delay detention or confiscation by customs or by other authorities.

Conditions

1. Baggage must be insured for its full value condition of average will apply.
2. The cover inscripts from the time travel begins and cover continues during the stay also at intermediate places and destination and ends at the original place, expires the policy-period.
3. The value is specifically declared when the article is fragile and high value in nature. Premium increases if the value is very high.
4. Notice has to be sent to the nearest office of the company during the journey. Secondly, a written notice on Railway Authorities, Shipping Co. Airline or Hotel may be necessary where the loss has taken place.
5. Notice to police in the case of theft is required to investigate into the matter.

Underwriting

The baggage insurance policy covers accompanied baggage (not dealer's stock or traveller's samples) during specified journey. Which includes air, sea, rail or road travel undertaken by the insured.

Proposal form fully describes the content and value of each package. All descriptions and individual values should be given for jewellery.

It is necessary to have a full inventory and individual valuation of each item. It is essential to have adequate valuation at the time when the policy is effected. Separate valuations are insisted for each item such as cameras, watches, jewellery, etc.

Claims

The following steps are involved for claims settlement

(*i*) an immediate written notice of the occurrence must be given for claim.

(*ii*) It is necessary to take all possible steps to discover the guilty person and to recover the stolen property.

(*iii*) It is necessary to furnish such evidence of the loss as the insurers may require.

(*iv*) It is to furnish to the insurers the claims form duly completed by him.

(*v*) It is to cooperate fully with the insurers and with the claims survey/inspection who many be appointed by insurer.

(*vi*) It is to abstain form fraud or intentional exaggeration in the particulars of the claims.

(*vii*) Claim form includes.

(*a*) The description and value of the property stolen.

(*b*) Allowance has to be made for depreciation and wear and tear to arrive at the amount of the claim.

(*c*) Details are required in respect of date and time of loss.

(*viii*) The claim is processed on the basis of the claim form, survey report, the policies report and the various vouchers, proof of ownership and other evidence submitted by the insured to substantiate the loss.

(*ix*) There must be evidence of a broken lock, broken window, broken roof, etc. to substantiate the claim. These would be violent and forcible entry.

PERSONAL ACCIDENT INSURANCE

Introduction

Personal accident insurance is one of the popular classes of accident insurance and as a supplement to life insurance, it provides an ideal protection against death or disability. Though the majority of the policies still issued are to individuals, it has found favour with employers who offer personal accident insurance benefits as a part of the service benefits to their employees.

Due to rapid industrialisation, and more and more use of complex machinery, industrial accidents are more frequent. To cater to the varying and increasing needs, different forms of cover are available. Individuals are granted this cover under an individual personal accident insurance' policy. For a group of individuals, the insures have devised a group personal accident insurance policy.

Coverage

Personal accident policy provides for specific benefits of insured person suffering injury, resulting in death or disablement arising solely and directly from an accident caused by violent external and visible means. The bodily injury within twelve calendar months (period varies) from occurrence thereof shall solely and directly cause or result in—

1. Death,

2. Loss by Physical Separation at or above the wrist or ankle of:

(*i*) both hands or feet or one hand and one foot (known as loss of limbs).

(*ii*) complete and irrecoverable loss of sight in both eyes.

(*iii*) loss of one limb and complete and irrecoverable loss of sight in one eye.

In these above cases capital sum insured is given.

(*iv*) loss of one limb or complete and recoverable loss of sight of one eye—in this regard 50% of capital sum insured.

3. Temporary total disablement—in this respect 33% of capital sum insured, maximum ₹ 500 per week.

Features of the Policy

1. The maximum liability of the insurer is the capital sum insured.
2. The amount of the claim is payable to the insured person or his legal representative in case of death. Appointment of nominee is desirable.

3. No weekly compensation shall become payable, until total amount shall have been ascertained and agreed.
4. Personal accidents cover (other than coupon insurance) with another insurer must be within the knowledge and written permission of the insurer or else policy becomes void.
5. Age limits between 16 and 25 years. The upper age limit may be relaxed in certain cases on merit.

Rating

The rate of premium to be charged depends mainly on the type of cover desired and the insured person's occupation. This is a non-tariff business. The rates or premium charged by the various insurers for the same risk may, therefore, vary. The proposal and the policy forms used by the various insurers also differ widely. The rates are usually charged per mile of the capital sum insured by the policy.

Extensions of Policy (Motorcycling)

In most parts of India, motor cycling and scooter riding have become so common that if accidents arising out using them are not covered, the policy is hardly of any practical significance. Most of the insurers are, therefore, willing to grant cover against these risks with or without additional premium.

Exceptions

1. War and kindered risk, riot, strike and civil commotion or intentional self-injury whether criminal or not.
2. Injury sustained whilst the insured person is under influence of intoxicants or is suffering from insanity.
3. Injury occasioned by or contributed to by venereal disease or pregnancy.
4. Flying for the purpose of any trade of technical operation or as a member or an aircrew or any other aerial activities.
5. Hunting, stable-chasing, racing of any kind (other than one foot), rugby, football, polo, motor cycling or winter sports, underwater pastime or pot-holding except insofar as the company have by endorsement agreed to extend the insurance.

Classification of Occupations

Profession or occupation is an important factor to guide the underwriter as regards assessment of risk in each case and consequently it stands to serve as the basis of rating. A representative classification is given as under:

Class I—Accountants, Bankers, Member of Legal and Medical Profession, teachers, consulting engineers, mercantile assistants and those engaged in executive, administrative, etc., duties.

Class II —Architects, engineers (Superintendents) only, Planters, Salesmen and master tradesmen who supervise but do not do manual work.

Class III—Engineer (superintending and working), engineering contractors engaged in manual work not involving unusual hazards.

Class IV—Any occupation involving unusual hazards.

It is not possible to give an exhaustive list and the classification given above is only indicative of the considerations involved.

Personal Accident and Specified Diseases Insurance

In addition to the death and disablement arising out of accidental bodily injury, insurance may also provide for benefits for disablement arising out of specified diseases. This is provided by issuing personal accident and specified diseases insurance policies. These policies contain the usual personal accident.

Extensions

Certain diseases like malaria, influenza, etc., which are not included in the list of diseases specified in the policy, can be included within the scope of the cover afforded by the policy, on payment of additional premium. The additional premium is usually charged @ 0.1 % of the capitalism insured for each additional disease included.

Underwriting Consideration

Underwriting involves the selection of risks for insurance. Based on the information collected, the underwriter has to decide to accept, particular risk and if he decides to accept, at what premium and on what terms. In fulfilling this task in respect of personal accident insurance the underwriter is guided broadly by the following considerations:

(*i*) age of the insured person;

(*ii*) health and physical build of the insured person;

(*iii*) occupation of the insured person;

(*iv*) other pursuits of the insured person; and

(*v*) medical history and family history in case cover is extended to diseases.

Medical Benefits and Hospitalisation Schemes

As part of their service benefits, many employers reimburse to their employees the expenses incurred by their employees for medical treatment. Insurers have, therefore, devised medical benefits and hospitalization schemes which they offer to the employers. There is a tendency on the part of many employers to buy such insurance schemes rather than electing to reimburse the employees from their funds, because such scheme reduce the cost of providing medical facilities for the employees and cut out clerical work for them.

NON-TRADITIONAL INSURANCE

The non-traditional insurance applicable in urban areas may be personal insurance, property insurance, liability insurance and package insurance. These insurances are also used by the rural population but urban populations are more familiar with these insurances.

1. Personal Insurance

Personal insurance covers personal accident insurance, medi-claim hospitalisation, overseas medi-claim policy, students, safety insurance, urban child welfare insurance and cancer medical expenses policy.

(*i*) *Personal Accident Insurance.* Personal accident insurance covers death, total or partial disablement due to accident. The insurable age is 12 to 70 years. The capital sum-insured is generally ₹ 10,000 wherein the sum assured is payable at death or at loss of two limbs, two eyes or one limb and one eye. ₹ 5,000 is paid at loss of one limb or one eye, ₹ 10,000 is paid at the permanent total disablement from injuries other than those named above. Medical expenses arising out of an accident upto 10 per cent of the capital sum insured or 25 per cent of the admissible claim whichever is lower at additional premium at the rate of 10 per cent of basic premium. The normal premium is ₹ 6.00 for ₹ 10,000 sum assured to be paid at death. ₹ 12.50 is charged for the benefits of death loss of two limbs, two eyes or one limb and one eye or loss of one limb or one eye permanent total disablement and permanent partial disablement. The normal risks and heavy risks are required to pay ₹ 6.00 and ₹ 9.00 respectively for death and ₹ 12.50 and ₹ 19.00 respectively for death and other benefits as given above. Heavy risks include persons working in underground mines, explosives, magazines, jockeys circus personnel, big game hunting mountaineering, winter sports, skiing or ice hockey, ballooning or polo and persons engaged in occupation of similar nature, due to the very nature of their profession. The cover is worldwide. Normal risks are others than those given in heavy risks.

(*ii*) *Personal Accident Insurance* (*family*). The family package cover is granted on the following pattern. The personal accident insurance family package incorporates all the conditions as mentioned in the personal accident insurance (individual). The cover for earning member (person insured) and spouse if earning will be 100 per cent of the capital sum insured for each *i.e.,* ₹ 10,000 (base figure). The cover is 50 per cent of the capital sum insured or ₹ 1 lakh whichever is lower if spouse is not earning member. 25 per cent of the capital sum insured or ₹ 50,000 whichever is lower per child, will be insured for children between age of 5 years and 19 years. For children the cover shall be limited to Death and Permanent Disablement (total and partial) only and premium payable will be at table II benefits and corresponding rates. Premium payable for husband and wife will be on the total Sum Insured at table III benefits and corresponding rates. A discount of 5 per cent may be granted on the gross premium under the Family Package Cover. It is applicable for the proposal exceeding ₹ 1,00,000 also.

(*iii*) *Medi-claim Hospitalisation and Domiciliary Hospitalisation Insurance.* The policy insures payment of 80 per cent of medical expenses actually and necessarily incurred in India by or on behalf of insured person. The age of insurable person is 12 to 70 years. Hospitalisation cover starts after 30 days for diseases from the commencement of the policy. It is not applicable to renewal policy. The categories of expenses to be reimbursed are mentioned in the table of benefits which are generally room, board and nursing expenses, surgeon and anaesthetist fees, oxygen and blood expenses, X-ray, medicines end drugs. The annual premium rates vary with the benefits required and categories of insurance. Personal accident insurance can also be sought alongwith this policy wherein the insured amount is paid at death or at loss of two limbs, loss of sight of two eyes or loss of one limb and loss of sight of one eye or loss of one limb or loss of sight of one eye or permanent total disablement from injuries other than the insured diseases. Mediclaim policy to persons above the age of 70 years subject to reduced limits of liability is being introduced. For the benefits of Mediclaim policyholder, tie up arrangements have been finalised with two hospitals in Bombay, and one each in Calcutta, Madras, Hyderabad and Pune. The subsidiary companies are negotiating such tie up arrangements in other centres also.

(*iv*) *Overseas Medi-claim, Policy*. Overseas medi-claim policy insures reimbursement of medical expenses incurred in connection with sickness/accident/disease/death outside India subject to applicable deductible. The persons eligible for this policy are persons undertaking bonagide trips abroad for business, official, professional purposes including training assignment officially sponsored; for holiday either in groups or as an individual and accompanying spouse and children of persons eligible as above. The maximum cover is 180 days for business tour, 60 days for plan A and 30 days under plan B for holiday travel. The proposals in excess of this are to be referred to GIC with medical reports. Plan A is worldwide excluding USA and Canada and plan B is worldwide including USA and Canada. The sum assured is $ 50,000 under Plan A and $ 1,00,000 under Plan B. The adults are insurable upto 70 years and children are insurable above 5 years. Claims are settled in foreign currency through authorised agents of G.I.C.

(*v*) *Student's Safety Insurance*. The student's safety insurance is intended to be issued to the schools/colleges or any other educational institution for the benefit of the student studying therein. The students are covered against death, total loss of two limbs, two eyes or one limb and one eye, total loss of one limb or one eye and permanent total or partial disablement. The benefits per student are ₹ 10,000 at death, ₹ 10,000 at loss of two limbs, two eyes or one limb and one eye or at permanent total disablement from injuries other than those mentioned above and ₹ 5,000 at the loss of one limb or one eye. There are other compensations verify from one per cent at the loss of more than one toe to 50 per cent at the loss of two ears. In addition to the above, the policy will provide for reimbursement of medical expenses subject to limb of ₹ 500. Claims are payable to parent or guardian of the student as mentioned in the school register. The premium is ₹ 6.00 per thousand of sum assured if students are

500 and ₹ 1.50 per thousand if students are 5000. The premium rates vary from ₹ 1.50 per thousand to ₹ 6.00 per thousand as per number of students included under this policies.

(vi) Unborn Child Welfare Insurance. The unborn child welfare insurance policy is applicable for expectant mothers in the age group of 18 to 40 years with pregnancy up to 3 months. The scheme provides for reimbursement of medical expenses for treating a child born with congenital anomalies and for its maintenance if the anomalies are certified as permanent total disablement. For permanent partial disablement, a proportion of the sum insured is payable as the percentage of disability certified by the doctor. Medical expenses are reimbursed upto 50 per cent of the capital sum insured as per table of benefits in case of congenital anomalies which are curable. Medical expenses are reimbursed as per Table of Benefits besides a certain percentage of the balance (unspent) amount will be paid as deposit in a bank or Unit Trust in case of congenital anomalies which are certified by a qualified doctor as 'Permanent Partial Disability'. Medical expenses are reimbursed and the balance unspent amount is put in a Bank or Unit Trust in case of congenital anomalies which are certified as 'Permanent Total Disability'. On the death of the insured, the monthly benefits will be paid to the legally appointed guardian or failing that to the legally appointed guardian under whose care the child is placed. The premium rate is 2 per cent for capital sum insured and so on upto ₹ 75,000 sum assured. Claims under this policy is payable in Indian currency. All medical treatment for the purpose of this insurance will have to be taken in India only. The limit of liability in respect of hospitalisation is as for table of Hospitalisation and Domiciliary Hospitalisation Benefits.

(vii) Cancer Medical Expenses Policy. The cancer medical expenses policy covers medical expenses due to cancer for insured person or spouse. The sum assured is ₹ 50,000 at the premium of ₹ 100. The period covers treatment expenses started during the policy period till the sum assured is exhausted. Cover starts after 30 days of the issue of the policy. It is not applicable for renewals. Cumulative bonus at the rate of 5 per cent on continuous claim free medical renewal subject to maximum sum insured of ₹ 75,000. This cumulative bonus is not applicable to group policy. The group discounting applicable at the rate of 15 per cent if persons insured are below 100 and above 25. This discount is 66.7 per cent if persons covered increased 25,000. The Indian Cancer Society allows the above group discount on the membership fees for the number of persons covered by the Group. The group policy is issued to the member of the Indian Cancer Society. The members of Indian Cancer Society, Ratan Tata Medical and Research Centre, Bombay are benefited one free check up at Cancer Society, Detection Centre. The members are required to pay ₹ 200 per annum. The premium is paid by the Indian Cancer Society for its members under group insurance.

2. Property Insurance

The general insurance industry insures property of people, under boiler and pressure plant insurance, cold storage insurance domestic pumpset insurance, machinery insurance policy, pedal cycle insurance and baggage insurance.

(i) Boiler and Pressure Plant Insurance: The boiler and pressure plant insurance policy is taken for Boiler or Pressure Vessel against the risks of due explosion due to steam pressure. The explosion is causing damage to the boiler or pressure vessel and also the machines surrounding the boilers as well as personnel working in the boiler house. It will also damage the property of neigh bouring industry involving third party liability. Collapse of pressure vessels due to vacuum conditions to created due to lack of steam pressure or condensation of steam is also covered. Explosion shall mean the sudden and violent rending or tearing apart of the permanent structure of a boiler plant or any part or parts thereof by force or internal steam pressure causing bodily displacement of the said structure and accompanied by the forcible ejectment of its contents. Collapse shall mean the sudden and dangerous distortion of any part of a boiler plant by bending or crushing caused by steam pressure whether attended by rupture or not. It shall not mean any slowly developing deformation due to any cause. The premium rate is decided as per Tariff rate.

(ii) Cold Storage Insurance: The cold storage insurance covers potatoes and frozen food. It cover deterioration of stocks stores due to rise in temperature in the storage chamber on account of mechanical or electrical breakdown of machinery insured under concurrent machinery breakdown policy. The cause of machinery breakdown should be sudden and unforeseen damage to machinery insured by the concurrent machinery breakdown policy from any accidental cause, escape of refrigerant in the refrigerated chamber as a result of breakdown of the machines insured under concurrent machinery breakdown policy. The average price of stocks will be sum insured. The premium rate, terms and conditions are decided as per Tariff rate.

(iii) Domestic Pumpset Insurance. The domestic pumpset insurance policy covers domestic pumpset against the risks of loss due to short circuit, single phasing, faulty design, lack of skill, fluctuations in power supply, theft, burglary, fire and lightning. The premium is based on horse power. For example upto 3 H.P. premium is ₹ 50 and upto 10 H.P., the premium is ₹ 100 per annum.

(iv) Machinery Insurance. The machinery insurance policy covers machinery like compressors, pumps, turbines etc. as also electrical machines such as transformers, electrical motors etc. The cover may be accident caused by faulty materials, action of centrifugal forces contributing to disruption of the rotating parts, malfunctioning or failure of safety devices, failure of lubrication due to malfunctioning of the lubricating oil pump or its own breakdown, electrical short-circuit including electrical fire originating from failure of insulation and/or over-voltage or under- voltage conditions, about and sudden stoppage of other connected machinery, entry of foreign bodies into a running machine and inexperienced operators causing damage due to error of judgement. The replacement value is considered for deciding the sum assured. The premium is decided as per Tariff-rate and inspection by the engineer of the insurer.

(v) Pedal Cycle Insurance: The pedal cycle insurance policy covers pedal cycle against the risks of loss or damage of pedal cycle by accident, fire, external explosion, malicious damage, theft and liability to third parties. Death of or bodily injury to any person damage to the property. Maximum limit is ₹ 10,000. The premium rate is 5 per cent of the sum insured.

(vi) Baggage Insurance. The baggage insurance policy covers baggage of travelling person except costly item like jewellery. It covers risks of loss, destroyed or damage at any time while travelling by accident, fire or theft. The premium rate per thousand is ₹ 4 upto 15 days, ₹ 6 upto 3 weeks, ₹ 8 for 1 month and ₹ 30 upto 12 months. The minimum premium is ₹ 30.

3. Liability Insurance

Liability insurance includes doctors, composite package insurance, lift insurance, public and product liability.

(i) Doctors' Composite Package Insurance. The doctors' composite package insurance policy is devised to meet the insurance requirements of the doctors through a single composite package policy. There are seven coverage under this policy viz., fire and allied perils including burglary, house breaking, theft; fidelity guarantee insurance for cashier/compounder/any other authorised employee; money-in-transit by self/cashier/compounder/any other authorised employee; loss or damage to doctor's kit by fire, theft accident during visits within municipal city limits; all risks for ECG and other electronic machines and such other equipment pertaining to doctor's profession; signboard and doctor's professional indemnity, The coverage of fire and burglary is compulsory. More than two covers will entitle the proposer to a special discount of 15 per cent maximum.

(ii) Lift Insurance. The lift insurance is liability insurance against for compensation of any accidental death or bodily injury sustained by any person whilst in the lift. The premium is ₹ 200 for ₹ 1,00,000 and ₹ 700 for ₹ 5,00,000.

(iii) Product and Public Liability. A market agreement on product and public liability with standardised terms and conditions and scientific premium rating structure has been brought into force from January 1, 1988.

4. Package Insurance

Package insurance include a number of risks under one policy. There are certain insurances which are included under package in the beginning of the policy or during the currency of policy. The householders' insurance, shopkeepers' insurance all risks cover and social security scheme.

(*i*) *Householders' Insurance*. The householders' insurance policy is designed to cater to the requirements of the householder by combining under a single policy a number of contingencies which are otherwise covered separately. The policy covers are building of class 'A' construction; burglary, housebreaking, larcency or theft; all risks; plate glass; breakdown of domestic appliances; T.V. set; pedal cycles; baggage insurance, personal accident and public liability. The policy does not cover inter-alia loss or damage by war, civil war and the like, depreciation, wear and tear, consequential loss etc. The damage to building against fire, lightning explosion of gas in domestic appliances, bursting and overflowing of water tanks, apparatus or pipes, aircraft or articles dropped therefrom, riot and strike, earthquake, malicious act, flood, inundation, storm, cyclone, subsidence and landslide damage and impact damage are covered by this policy. Jewellery and valuables against loss or damage by accident or misfortune. Legal liability upto ₹ 25,000 and damage to insured's own property due to collapse of antenna upto ₹ 3000 under T.V. set insurance. Public liability is pertaining to insured's legal liability for bodily injury or loss of or damage to property of third party limited to amount specified in the schedule and workmen's compensation liability to domestic servants.

(*ii*) *Shopkeeper's Insurance*. The shopkeeper's insurance policy includes fire and allied perils, burglary and housebreaking, money, insurance, pedal cycle, plate glass neon and glow sign, baggage insurance, personal accident, fidelity guarantee, public, liability and workmen's compensation liability. The premium rate per thousand varies from the minimum of ₹ 0.50 for public liability to ₹ 20.00 per thousand for pedal cycle. The Premium rate varies contentwise.

(*iii*) *All Risks Cover Insurance*. Personal jewellery and valuable articles are insured against loss, damage or destruction by accident or misfortune. The premium rate varies from 1.00 per cent to 1.5 per cent of sum assured.

(*iv*) *Social Security Scheme*. A composite policy specifically designed for tribals had been introduced in 1985 to provide insurance cover in respect of huts, cottage industry, dwellings sheds, contents including belongings personal accident and hospitalisation. Composite package insurance policy was also introduced for beneficiaries under District Rural Development Agency Scheme. This policy is designed to provide all round protection to weaker sections of the society covering their residences and personal belongings from various hazards. Among the items covered by the policy are pedal cycles, electrical mechanical appliances, carts, milch cows and working animals, fishing boats, agricultural implements etc. Comprehensive insurance for artisans, village and cottage industries, tiny industries etc., against the fire and other perils for the plants and equipment not exceeding ₹ 10 lakhs. From 15th August 1985, the Government of India introduced a scheme for providing social security through an insurance cover in the event of accidental death of earning members of poor families. The scheme covers all earning members at the age group of 18 to 60 years and provides compensation of ₹ 3,000 to the dependents in the event of accidental death of any of the earning members.

Table 36.1 Social Security Scheme

	Districts Covered	*Claims Settled*
1985	91	—
1986	192	53
1987	214	155
1988-89	415	341
1989-90	417	482

The social security scheme under personal accident insurance increased from 192 districts in 1986 to 415 districts in 1988-89, settling the claims from ₹ 53 lakhs to ₹ 341 lakhs in the respective years.

India International Insurance

The general insurance industry has extended its activities in foreign countries besides the traditional and non-traditional insurance in rural and urban areas. The international insurance is considered under this scheme. India International Insurtence PTE Ltd. has been established as on 3rd Dec., 1987, The principal activities of the company are to undertake the business of insurance and reinsurance of all classes of the general insurance and to perform investment functions incidental thereto. There have been no significant changes in the nature of these activities. The total gross premium earned by this company for 1988 and 1989 respectively were $ 6.641 and 6.0051 million for fire, $16 .628 million and $ 18.466 million for marine, $ 21.675 million and $ 23.853 million for miscellaneous and $ 44.944 million and $ 48.370 million for the total general insurance. It has earned profit of $ 796 thousand and $ 58 thousand for fire, $ 1600 thousand and $ 425 thousand for marine and loss $ 3065 thousand and $ 2285 thousand for miscellaneous. It is expected that this company will earn profit in coming years. The profit before tax was $ 9.68 million and profit retained was $ 5.68 million in 1994-95.

QUESTIONS

1. Why is there non-traditional insurance in urban India?
2. What are the salient features of boiler and pressure plant insurance ?
3. Discuss the future of India International Insurance PTE Ltd.

37

PROGRESS OF MISCELLANEOUS GENERAL INSURANCE

The General Insurance Corporation of India was formed on 22nd Nov. 1972 under the General Insurance Business (Nationalisation) Act, 1972 and by virtue of the same Act, 55 Indian general insurance companies became subsidiaries of the General Insurance Corporation of India and the undertaking of other erstwhile insurance were merged in undertakings of one or other four selected ultimate companies which were to operate in the nationalised set-up, viz., National Insurance Co. Ltd., New India Assurance Co. Ltd., Oriental Fire and General Insurance Co. Ltd., and United India Fire and General Insurance Co. Ltd.

The progress of miscellaneous insurances before nationalisation has been analysed in the following paragraphs:

The gross premium of Indian Insurers has increased from ₹39.78 crores in 1969 to ₹ 45.90 crores in 1970 and ₹50.65 crores in 1971 and further to ₹57.28 crores in 1972. The gross premium received by the Indian insurers has increased from 85.5 per cent of total gross premium in 1969 to 87.4 per cent in 1971 and further to 88.5 per cent in 1972. This shows that the Indian insurers are getting increasing business. Consequently, the shares of non-Indian insurers were also declining from 14.5 per cent in 1969 to 11.5 per cent in 1972. Thus, the total gross premium of miscellaneous insurance a had increased from ₹ 46.55 crores in 1969 to ₹ 57.93 crores in 1971 and further to ₹ 64.70 crores in 1972.

As compared to total insurances, the share of Indian insurers to miscellaneous insurance had been higher. It was 82.6 per cent in case of total insurances and 88.5 per cent in ease of miscellaneous insurances. Thus the miscellaneous insurances of Indian insurers have been at higher level. Consequently the share of non-Indian insurer has been decreasing. The total gross premium has increased from ₹ 116.88 crores in 1969 to ₹ 131.62 crores in 1970 and further to ₹ 147.53 crores in 1971 and again to ₹ 195.83 of ores in 1972. In both the cases, the share of Indian insurers to gross premium has increased from ₹ 116.88 crores in 1969 to ₹ 131.62 crores in 1970 and further to ₹ 147.53 crores in 1971 and again to ₹ 195.83 crores in 1972. In both the cases, the share of Indian insurers to gross premium was rising.

The share of net claims payable to net premium hall increased from 56.8 per cent in 1970 to 57.20 per cent in 1972. It means the amount of claim has been Increasing m case of miscellaneous Insurances. The net commission has also increased from 11.4 per cent of net premium in 1970 to 11.8 per cent in 1971 and further to 12.5 per cent in 1972. However, the percentage of management expenses has also been declining. The reserve has decreased but the balance of Income has increased from 8.5 per cent of net premium in 1970 to 11.2 per cent in 1971 and declined to 10.3 per cent in 1972.

Table 37.1 Gross Premium

Year	*Miscellaneous Insurances*					*Total Insurances*				
	Indian Insurers		*Non-Indian Insurers*		*Total*	*Indian Insurers*		*Non-Indian Insurers*		*Total*
	₹	*%to total*	₹	*% to total*		₹	*%to total*	₹	*% to total*	
1969 ..	39.78	85.5	6.76	14.5	46.55	91.96	78.7	24.91	21.3	116.88
1970 ..	45.90	86.9	6.94	13.1	62.83	105.38	80.1	26.24	19.9	131.62
1971 ..	50.65	87.4	7.28	12.6	67.93	118.80	80.5	28.73	19.5	147.53
1972 ..	57.25	88.5	7.42	11.5	64.10	132.00	82.6	27.83	17.4	159.83
1975					84.34					247.07
1977					103.88					299.23
1978					123.09					339.05
1977					133					338
1978					155					378
1979					176					415
1980					218					503
1981					275					623

Table 37.2 Percentage Ratio to Net Premium

Year	*Indian Insurances*						*Non-Indian insurers*					
	Net claim payable	*Net comm-ission*	*Exp. of manag ement*	*Increase in Reserve*	*Misc. Income*	*Balance of Income*	*Net claim pay-able*	*Net comm-ission*	*Exp. of maney*	*Increase in Reserve*	*Misc. income*	*Balance of Income*
1970 ..	56.8	11.4	21.3	4.6	3.0	8.5	50.1	6.3	32.7	1.9	1.1	8.5
1971 ..	57.2	11.8	19.4	3.7	3.5	11.2	43.5	5.7	33.3	1.5	0.6	15.5
1972 ..	57.0	12.5	19.2	4.4	3.7	10.3	46.9	6.2	34.3	2.8	0.6	9.8
1975 ..	58.5	26.6	0.8	9.7	—	42						
1977 ..	54.3	26.3	1.2	4.3	—	14.0						
1978 ..	60.9	25.7	1.3	7.1	—	5.3						
1980 ..	72.2	28.3	1.1	8.5	—	−10.2						
1981 ..	70.1	28.2	0.9	11.6	—	−10.6						

The non-Indian Insurers have paid lesser amount in the shape of claims whereas the Indian insurers have paid more amount as compared to net premium. Expenses of management in case of non Indian insurers are also increasing. It had increased from 32.7 per cent of net premium to 34.3 per cent in 1972. The balance of income bass increased from 8.5 per cent in 1970 to 15.5 per cent in 1971, but declined to 9.8 per cent in 1972. Thus. The non-Indian insurers were increasing their balances at higher speed.

The gross claims payable has been 40.7 per cent of gross premium in 1958. 64.9 per cent of gross premium in 1970 and again 51.8 per cent in 1972. Thus, the share of gross claims payable has been decreased in 1971. The percentage of direct commission has been constantly decreasing. The percentage of management expenses has been declining from 32.6 per cent in 1958 to. 20.7 per cent in 1970 and further to 19.2 per cent in 1971 but increased to 20.1 per cent in 1972. The miscellaneous income has been increasing in both the cases. Similarly the balance of income in case of Indian insurers has increased from 13.5 per cent of gross premium in 1958 to 22.0 per cent of gross premium in 1971 and declined to 21.2 per cent in 1972. The Non-Indian insurers have lesser balance of income than the Indian insurers had.

Table 37.3 Gross Direct business written outside India by Indian Insurers

Ratio to Gross Direct Premium income	*1958*	*1970*	*1971*	*1972*
1. Gross claims Payable		68.2	70.8	53.8
2. Direct Commission		27.5	27.6	27.8
3. Expenses of Management		15.2	15.0	14.0
4. Increase in Reserve		–1.2	0.8	6.6
5. Miscellaneous Income		2.2	4.3	5.5
6. Balance of Income		–8.7	–11.7	2.1

The Indian insurers have experienced increasing loss in case of miscellaneous insurance. The loss has gone up from 8.7 per cent in 1970 to 11.7 per cent in 1971. It was most probably due to increasing amount of claims payable and direct commission.

From the analysis of progress of different types of insurance it has been revealed that the Indian insurers were doing well more in marine insurance than in other types of general insurances.

Table 37.4

Net Premium Income
Miscellaneous Insurance

	1975	**1977**				
In India	63.33	77.70				
Outside India	25.92	25.46				
Total	89.25	103.16				
	Total Insurance					
	1975	1977	1978	1979	1980	1981
In India	166.12	196.97	287	323	385	486
Outside India	63.75	71.46	83	75	96	113
Total	229.87	268.43	370	398	481	599

The net premium income of Miscellaneous insurance outside India has declined from ₹ 25.92 crores in 1975 to ₹ 25.46 crores in 1977. Thus, the miscellaneous insurance has lesser scope outside India.

Table 37.5 Percentage to Gross Premium

	Indian insurers						*Non-Indian Insurers*					
Year	*Gross claims payable*	*Direct commission*	*Expenses of Management*	*Increase in Reserve*	*Misc. Income*	*Balances of Income*	*Gross claims payable*	*Direct commission*	*Expenses of Management*	*Increase in Reserve*	*Misc. Income*	*Balance of Income*
1985 ..	40.7	13.1	32.6	..	..	13.6	48.9	12.6	27.9	–	..	10.6
1970 ..	64.9	7.7	20.7	4.5	2.1	4.2	49.6	8.9	28.0	1.0	0.5	12.0
1971 ..	50.4	6.9	19.2	3.8	2.4	22.0	40.8	8.6	28.3	1.9	0.5	20.0
1972 ..	51.8	7.7	20.1	1.3	2.3	2.12	46.2	8.9	30.7	0.8	0.5	13.4

Table 37.6 General Insurance: Income and, Outgo in respect of General Insurance excluding L.I.C

(₹ *in crore)*

	1958	*1970*	*1971*	*1972*
1. Premium less reinsurance: In India	12.96	75.84	86.45	10.3.13
Out India	12.02	35.26	41.24	44.74
2. Net Interest Div. and Rents	0.37	3.21	4.18	5.16
3. Other Incomes	0.21	0.13	0.27	1.34
Total Incomes	25.56	132.14	132.14	154.37
1. Claims loss reinsurance	12.56	57.04	62.80	73.58
2. Net Commission	3.33	12.51	14.89	18.72
3. Expenses of Management	6.77	23.38	24.45	28.78
4. Misc. Outgo	0.24	0.60	0.37	0.41
Outgo	22.90	93.53	102.51	121.49
Excess of Income over Outgo	2.66	20.91	29.63	32.88
Increase in Reserve	1.57	7.31	12.61	9.40

The execess of income over outgo has been increasing from ₹ 2.66 crores in 1958 to ₹ 20.91 crores in 1970 and further to ₹ 32.88 crores in 1972. Thus, the reserve has also been increasing from ₹ 1.57 crores in 1958 to ₹ 7.31 crores in 1970 and further to ₹ 9.40 crores in 1972. The premium income in India has been constantly increasing from ₹ 12.96 crores in 1958 to ₹ 75.84 crores in 1970 and further to ₹ 86.45 crores in 1971 and again to ₹ 103.13 crores in 1972. The total income has increased from ₹ 25.56 crores in 1958 to ₹ 132.14 crores in 1971, and further to 154.37 crores in 1973, but the increase in total outgo was lesser than this, so the excess of income over outgo and increase in reserve has been rapidly rising.

The general insurance could not increase rapidly as industrial production did up to 1967. The general insurance would have risen at least parallel to the development of industries. If the general insurance is rising at a faster speed than the industria production does, it is a clear indication of satisfactory development or general insurance. The Index of general insurance reveals that it had gone up to 137.5 in 1967 and 158.9 in 1968 whereas the index of industrial production has gone up 143.2 in 1967 and 152.9 in 1968. Thus the general insurance started rising more rapidly after 1967 and touched the maximum of 22.5 in 1971 while the index of industrial production has gone only up to 173.6 in 1971 making a gap of 27.4 in 1971 which was maximum up to 1970. The index number of general insurance was 202.8 whereas the index number of industrial production was 182.6 in 1972. It reveals that the general insurance business was satisfactorily progressing.

Table 37.7 Profit & Loss of All General Insurance Business

			In lakhs of ₹	
	1975	*1978*	*1980*	*1981*
1. Interest Dividends & Rents	869.02	1484.36	2286.23	2658.20
2. Profit of				
Fire Insurance	560.97	548.60		

Contd...

Murine	210.32	2341.21	622.20	642.01
Miscellanoolls	74.15	131.08	—	27.55
3. Profits on sale of Investments	4.69	5.77	3.05	2.82
4. Capital gains	0.13	0.07	0.18	0.26
5. Miscellaneous	0.05	4.03	5.35	6.25
Total	1719.33	2515.12	2917.01	3337.02
1. Interest Payable	0·93	0·54	0.53	5.72
2. Preliminary Expenses	1.14	1.13	1.14	1.14
3. Other Amounts written off		0.23	610.10	514.89
4. Transferred to share Capitate Redemption	190.00	360.00	350.00	–
5. Provision for relation	937.00	1030.00	603.00	805.00
6. Balance	590.26	1133.20	1339.74	2002.45
Total	1719.33	2515.12	2917.01	3337.08

Progress of Miscellaneous Insurance After Nationalisation

The progress of miscellaneous insurance after nationalisation has been analysed under (*i*) gross premium, (*ii*) net premium and (*iii*) underwriting experiences.

1. Gross Premium in Miscellaneous Insurance

The gross direct premium has increased from ₹ 114.00 crores in 1980 to ₹ 218.00 crores in 1980 and again to ₹ 610.18 crores in 1985 and ₹ 1302.16 crores in 1988-89. The miscellaneous insurance increased by 590.32 per cent during 1980 to 1988-89. The maximum amount of miscellaneous insurance has been ₹ 75.00 crores in 1980 and ₹ 424.86 crores in 1988-89 in New India. It has increase by 744.06 per cent. The United India has increased its business from ₹ 47.60 crores in 1980 to ₹ 318.82 crores by 669.79 per cent. Oriental has increased its business by 701.56 per cent from ₹ 39.13 crores in 1980 to ₹ 274.52 crores in 1988-89. National has increased its business from ₹ 39.92 crores in 1982 to ₹ 234.41 crores in

Table 37.8 Gross Direct Premium in Miscellaneous Insurance

	GIC	*National*	*New India*	*Oriental*	*United India*	*Total*
1975						114.00
1980	34.25	39.92	57.10	39.13	47.60	218.00
1982	17.84	66.78	120.62	74.44	89.52	362.20
1983	22.73	80.40	141.23	91.07	108.94	444.37
1984	24.32	93.71	162.69	104.15	125.16	510.03
1985	33.31	115.65	195.07	121.67	144.48	610.18
1986	41.51	139.32	232.12	150.15	178.29	741.39
1987	49.80	162.13	279.32	181.21	215.32	887.78
1988-89	40.55	243.41	424.86	274.52	318.82	1302.16
1989-90	21.11	236.28	406.55	275.15	316.16	1234.16
1994-95	119.51	536.72	878.89	641.58	707.70	1367.69

1988-89 by 609.74 per cent. It shows that New India having maximum amount of gross direct premium has increased its business at the highest rate followed by Oriental, United India and National. The higher amount of miscellaneous Insurance in New India and United India has been attributed to several non-traditional policies issued by them. They have tried to attain the socio-economic objectives of the nationalisation. Oriental and National have been lagging behind. The GIC has no fixed trend. It deals only in aviation insurance which depends on the flights frequencies. It has to compete with foreign companies. The gross direct premium amounted to ₹ 1367.69 crore in 1994-95; out of which the contribution of all companies was ₹ 119.51 crores by GIC, ₹ 536.72 crore by National, ₹ 878.89 crore by New India by India, ₹ 641.58 crores by Oriental and ₹ 707.70 crore by United India.

2. Net Premium

The net premium of miscellaneous insurance has increases from ₹ 89.00 in 1973 to ₹ 207.90 crores in 1980 and again to ₹ 576.12 crore in 1980 and ₹ 1221.74 crores in 1988-89. It shows the rising trend of insurance business. The net premium increased by 344.31 per cent from ₹ 354.84 crore in 1982 to ₹ 1221.74 crore in 1988-89. The net premium of GIC increased from ₹ 66.55 crore in 1982 to ₹ 239.77 crore in 1988-89 by 360.29 per cent. National Insurance has increased its net premium from ₹ 52.26 crore in 1982 to ₹ 188.26 crores in 1988-89 by 360.24 per cent. New India increased from ₹ 103.60 crores to ₹ 337.99 crore by 326.25 per cent during 1982 to 1988-89. Oriental increased its net premium by 368.11 per cent from ₹ 57.55 crore in the corresponding period. United India has increased from ₹ 74.88 crore to ₹ 243.87 crore by 325.68 per cent during the period. Oriental increased its business at faster rate followed by National, New India and United India. The net amount has been the highest in New India followed by United India, Oriental and National. The net premium was ₹ 2811.89 crore in 1994 95. The highest net premium was ₹ 804.27 crore by New India and the lowest was ₹ 428.04 crores by National.

Table 37.9 Net Premium in Miscellaneous Insurance

In crores of Rupees

	GIC	*National*	*New India*	*Oriental*	*United India*	*Total*
1973						89.00
1975						107.00
1980	66.55	52.26	103.60	57.55	74.88	354.84
1983	82.07	61.66	116.21	69.67	89.35	418.96
1984	96.60	75.54	137.09	81.76	102.92	493.91
1985	112.12	89.56	160.79	94.40	119.25	576.12
1986	136.63	108.06	183.92	114.70	144.92	688.23
1987	155.56	125.14	221.98	139.26	168.36	810.32
1988-89	239.77	188.26	337.99	211.85	243.87	1221.74
1989-90	233.42	181.33	317.51	212.35	243.55	1188.16
1994-95	553.62	428.04	804.27	492.74	533.22	2811.89
1997-98	910.40	806.07	1251.67	788.09	859.24	4615.47

3. Underwriting Progress Experiences

The underwriting experiences has shown negative result. The underwriting loss has increased from ₹ 4.33 crores, in 1982 to ₹ 40.77 Crores in 1985 and ₹ 296.12 crores in 1988-89. The underwriting loss to net premium has gone up from 1.2 per cent in 1982 to 7.1 per cent in 1985 and again to 24.4 per cent. The maximum loss ratio has been in the case of United India *i.e.,* 26.4 per cent in 1988-89, 11.6 per cent in 1985 and 2.2 per cent in 1982. The reason has been the highest claims ratio ranging from 69.4 per cent to 96.7 per cent. However, the expense-ratio has been the lowest of all the companies in 1988-89. Oriental has the second largest loss followed by New India and National. The underwriting experience has shown that National and New India have experienced less loss-ratio because of less claims ratio. Underwriting experience in 1994-95 has revealed loss of ₹ 209.91 crores. All companies have incurred loss in 1994-95.

Table 37.10 Financial Highlights of Miscellaneous Insurance

	GIC	*National*	*New India*	*Oriental*	*United India*	*Total*
			In India			
1998-1999	55.7	1199.1	1750.0	1287.1	1381.2	5617.4
1999-2000	76.6	1334.5	1908.8	1429.3	1465.7	6138.3
2000-2001	280.1	1506.0	2073.1	1540.5	1635.4	6755.0
2001-2002		1666.7	2313.15	1719.16	1763.86	
			Out of India			
1998-1999	00	25.7	186.6	26.0	38.5	276.8
1999-2000	00	42.3	221.8	28.0	41.0	333.1
2000-2001	00	101.9	307.5	31.3	81.8	522.5
2001-2002		65.58	415.50	33.84	125.43	
			Total of India			
1998-1999	55.7	1224.8	1936.6	1313.1	1419.7	5949.9
1999-2000	76.6	1376.8	2130.6	1457.3	1506.7	6548.0
2000-2001	280.1	1607.9	2380.6	1571.8	1717.2	7557.6
2001-2002	311.57	1732.05	2728.65	1753.00	1889.29	—

Table 37.11 Miscellaneous Insurance

Year	*Net Premium*		*Net Claims*		*Commission*		*Expenses of Management*		*Other outgo*		*Increase in Reserve*		*Investment Income*		*Under writing*	
	₹	%	₹	%	₹	%	₹	%	₹	%	₹	%	₹	%	₹	%
							General Insurance Corporation									
1998-1999	1079.0		987.0	91	271.7	25					84.3	8			–264.0	–24
1999-2000	1201.94		1216.02	101.2	290.56	24.2	12.34	1.0	–0.12	0.0	61.49	5.1			–378.35	31.5
2000-2001	1580.63		1531.20	96.9	330.72	20.9	14.33	0.9	2.40	0.1	189.34	12.0	381.1	27.39	–487.36	30.8
2001-2002	1828.65		1807.83	106.05	381.24	22.36	15.77	0.93	1.17	0.07	–		446.92	26.22	–501.37	–29.41
							Nationaı									
1998-1999	968.0	79	861.0	89	282.3	29					81.0	8			–256.3	–26
1999-2000	1079.84		1029.43	95.32	1.49	–0.47	325.27	30.12	–0.72	0.07	55.98	5.18			–.324.98	–30.09
2000-2001	1289.92		1225.66	95.01	19.28	–1.49	336.22	26.06	–2.52	–0.19	104.99	8.13			393.71	30.52
2001-2002	1312.71		1454.66	110.81	14.03	1.06	399.58	30.43	–2.63	–2.0	11.39	0.86	245.00	18.66	–319.32	–24.32
							New India									
1998-1999	1469.9		1253.8	85	3368	23					109.1	7			.229.8	–15
1999-2000	1629.61		1486.54	91.22	–5.06	–0.31	415.23	25.48			79.86	4.9			–346.96	–21.29
2000-2001	1883.72		1745.20	92.65	23.27	1.24	484.43	25.72			127.06	6.75	312.96		496.33	26.35
2001-2002	2099.30		2052.04	97.75	81.66	3.89	490.40	23.36			107.79	5.13	336.51		–632.59	–30.13

(Contd.)

Year	Net Premium		Net Claims		Commission		Expenses of Management		Other outgo		Increase in Reserve		Investment Income		Under writing	
	₹	%	₹	%	₹	%	₹	%	₹	%	₹	%	₹	%	Rs.	%
Oriental																
1998-1999	956.3	73	998.2	104	235.4	25					84.1	9			−361.4	−38
1999-2000	1087.23	74.6	1061.99	97.7	26.98	−2.5	341.52	31.4			65.44	6.0			−354.74	−32.6
2000-2001	1210.21	77.0	1144.43	94.6	−19.07	−1.6	336.01	27.8			61.49	5.1			−312.66	−25.8
2001-2002	1287.17	73.43	1560.90	121.3	23	0.0	422.44	32.81			−38.48	3.0	−16.71	1.3	−476.32	−37.0
United India																
1998-1999	1043.8	74	1000.9	96	245.7	23					92.3	9			−295.1	−28
1999-2000	1115.84		1269.79	113.79	−20.99	−1.88	310.51	27.83			36.02	3.23			−479.49	−42.97
2000-2001	1329.27		1369.89	103.06	1.14	0.09	340.22	25.59			106.71	8.03			−488.69	−36.76
2001-2002	1438.18		1523.58		35.21		387.78		−58.60		54.46	106.71	373.35		−248.10	
Indian Market Total																
1998-1999	5517.0	93	5100.9	92	1371.9	25					45.08	8.0			−1406.6	−25
1999-2000	6114.4	93	6063.7	99	163.65	27					298.8	5.0			−1884.6	3.1
2000-2001	7293.27	97	7016.4	96	1866.5	26					589.5	8.0			−2178.7	−30
2001-2002																

Table 37.12 Underwriting Experience in Miscellaneous Insurance

	Net Premium In ₹ Crores	*Net Claims Payable*	*Net Commission*	*Expenses Management*	*Miscellaneous Outgo*	*Undereriting Risks Reserve*	*Underwriting Profi/Loss(–)*	*Underwriting Profit/Loss(–) ₹ Crores*
1985	112.12	69.5	27.8	1.2	–0.9	6.9	–4.5	–5.04
National	89.56	70.4	–2.3	28.8	–	7.8	–4.7	–4.26
New India	160.79	76.4	1.6	21.8	0.4	7.4	–6.8	–10.91
Oriental	94.40	76.2	–2.0	26.6	–0.3	6.7	–7.2	–6.77
United India	119.25	82.9	–0.5	22.3	0.1	6.8	–11.6	–13.79
Total	576.12	75.4	5.1	19.8	–0.3	7.1	–7.1	–40.77
1989-90								
GIC	233.42	79.4	21.0	1.7	–0.6	8.9	16.4	–38.31
National	181.33	89.4	–	29.3	–	8.5	–27.2	–49.36
New India	317.51	89.9	–	25.4	–	7.4	–22.7	–72.87
Oriental	212.35	86.9	–	25.9	–	10.1	–22.9	–48.62
United India	243.55	88.9	–	24.8	–	10.0	–23.7	51.61
Total	1188.16	86.9	–	25.5	–	8.98	22.58	266.77
1994-95								
GIC	553.62	105.8	23.3	1.0	–0.9	6.8	–36.0	–198.94
National	428.04	105.6	–2.5	27.5	0.1	5.6	–36.3	155.56
New India	804.27	101.9	–0.8	20.8	–	6.6	–28.5	–299.04
Oriental	492.74	110.9	–3.3	24.9	–	6.2	–38.7	–190.44
United India	533.22	114.4	–3.2	22.2	–	5.2	–38.6	–205.58
Total	2811.89	107.7	–2.7	9.28	–	6.1	35.62	–209.91
1997-98								
GIC	910.40	94.1	24.0	0.9	–0.1	5.3	–24.3	–220.78
National	806.07	92.93	–0.86	–26.09	0.13	5.05	–23.09	–186.09
New India	1251.67	86.25	–1.95	–24.74	–	4.04	–13.48	168.74
Orintal	788.09	94.1	24.0	–0.1	–	5.9	–28.5	224.99
United India	859.24	104.0	–31.2	28.6	20.9	5.2	–34.2	293.76

38

PROGRESS OF TOTAL GENERAL INSURANCE

The progress of total general insurance has been analysed under gross direct premium, net premium, underwriting experiences, return on total assets, number of employees and number of offices.

1. Gross Direct Premium

The gross direct premium of all general insurance has increased from ₹ 208 crore in 1973 to ₹ 284 crore in 1975 and again to ₹ 503 crore in 1980, ₹ 1204.31 crore in 1985 and ₹ 2348.92 crore in 1988-89. Thus, the total insurance has been increasing at a faster rate after nationalisation. It has increased by 466.98 per cent during 1982 to 1988-89. United India increased its business by 504.67 percent from ₹ 121.08 crore in 1980 to ₹ 611.05 crore in 1988-89. The gross direct premium of New India has increased from ₹ 128.03 crore in 1980 to ₹ 733.54 crore in 1988-89 by 572.94 per cent. The insurance business of Oriental has from ₹ 111.26 crore in 1980 to ₹ 511.01 crore in 1988-89, by 459.29 per cent. National has increased its business from ₹ 98.59 crore in 1980 to ₹ 452.82 crore 1988-89 be 459.30 per cent. The maximum growth rate in business has been. New India followed by United India, National and Oriental. The maximum amount of business has been done by New India followed by United India, Oriented and National. GIC has only aviation insurance which fluctuating as per flights frequency. New India and United India took lead in this field. They have maximum number of employees and offices. They did commendable task in expansion of insurance business although they did at the cost of lower underwriting profit. Their investment income has been comparati-vely higher. The lower business of Oriental and National has not affected underwriting profit. Their profits have been comparatively higher because they manag, risks and selected only few business working with profits. The total amount of gross premium was ₹ 4959.43 crore in 1994-95.

Table 38.1 Gross Direct Premium in All Types of Insurance

	GIC	*National*	*New India*	*Oriental*	*United India*	*Total*
1973						208
1980	44.04	98.59	128.03	111.26	121.08	503.00
1981	17.84	142.56	232.32	171.29	197.38	761.39
1983	22.73	168.21	274.37	202.53	227.25	895.09
1984	24.32	199.26	315.80	227.12	267.98	1034.48
1985	33.31	239.25	370.11	258.27	303.27	1204.31
1987	41.51	277.96	433.82	306.24	363.60	1423.13
1988	49.80	317.08	502.63	354.23	428.44	1652.18
1988-89	40.50	452.82	733.54	511.01	611.05	2348.92
1994-90	21.11	443.02	717.40	500.49	596.64	2278.66
1994-95	119.51	945.36	1524.49	1074.35	1295.72	4959.43
1997-98	88.38	1604.82	2433.73	1677.95	1930.64	7735.52

2. Net Premium

The net premium has increased from ₹ 222.0 crore in 1973 to ₹ 281.0 crore in 1975 and again to ₹ 481.0 crore in 1980, ₹ 1190.50 crore in 1985 and again to ₹ 2255.24 crore during 1982 to 1988-89. New India in 1988-89. The rate of increased has been 311.03 per cent has increased its business from ₹ 187.66 crore in 1982 to ₹ 576.76 crore in 1988-89 by 307.34 per cent. The business of United India has increased from ₹ 158.20 crore in 1982 to ₹ 466.38 crore by 294.80 per cent. The net premium of Oriental has increased from ₹ 125.86 crore in 1982 to ₹ 384.71 crore in 1988-89 by 305.67 per cent. National increased its business from ₹ 110.43 crore in 1982 to ₹ 366.42 crore in 1988-89 by 331.81 per cent. GIC has increased its business from ₹ 142.93 crore in 1982 to ₹ 460.98 crore in 1988-89 by 322.52 per cent. The net premium of New India has been maximum whereas of National has been the lowest. Although growth rate of business in National has been the maximum followed by GIC has been higher than the direct premium because it deals with reinsurance business also. The total amount of net premium was ₹ 4879.43 crore in 1994-95. National Insurance has given the lowest amount of premium.

Table 38.2 Net Premium in All Types of Insurance

	GIC	*National*	*New India*	*Oriental*	*United India*	*Total*
1973						222.00
1975						281.00
1980						481.00
1982	142.93	110.43	187.66	125.86	158.20	725.08
1983	176.69	132.74	225.60	152.52	193.72	881.27
1984	224.15	159.73	253.48	174.33	218.88	1030.57
1985	262.23	186.47	296.98	191.39	253.43	1190.50
1986	287.32	220.00	341.67	227.99	289.36	1366.34
1987	321.79	255.07	398.63	265.89	338.43	1579.81
1988-89	460.98	366.42	576.75	384.71	466.38	2255.24
1989-90	434.23	348.46	569.66	380.66	452.75	2085.76
1994-95	1018.31	768.93	1333.44	821.89	936.86	4879.43
1997-98	1510.16	1263.24	1945.00	1235.84	1402.73	5846.8

3. Underwriting Experiences

The total underwriting experiences has been very unfavorable. The profit of ₹ 66.04 crore in 1982 declined to ₹ 12.42 crore in 1985 and became loss of ₹ 145.72 crore in 1988-89. All the companies have faced loss in 1988-89 because of higher claim ratio which was between 70.7 per cent to 79.4 per cent. The expense ratio has varied from 25.6 per cent in New India to 29.00 per cent in National. The unexpired risks reserve could not increased as per their previous years figure. The maximum loss suffered was by United India which experienced loss-ratio of 7.7 per cent. GIC has different pattern of aviation insurance. Its loss is not comparable with those of other companies. The lowest loss-ratio was 5.2 per cent in New India because of comparatively lower expense-ratio. New India and United India has higher claims-ratio and National and Oriental have higher expense ratio. The underwriting experience has shown loss of ₹ 141.18 crore in 1994-95 by the companies and gone down to 35 crore in 2001.

4. Investment Income

The investment income of general insurance industry has increased industry has increased from ₹ 130.99 in 1982 to ₹ 244.09 crore in 1982 to ₹ 244.99 crore in 1985, ₹ 487.39 crore In 1988-89 and ₹ 1206.83 crore in 1994-95. As percentage to total assets, it has increased from 7.57 per cent to 8.27 per cent and again to 10.33 per cent in the respective years; but it declined to 8.58 per cent in 1994-95. It shows that the investment income has an increasing trend. On the other hand, the underwriting profit has declined from ₹ 66.04 crore to ₹ 39.60 crore, ₹ –145.72 crore and ₹ –110.92 crore in the respective years. They have also gone down as percentage to total asset from 3.82 per cent to 1.34 per cent, –3.09 per cent and –5.02 per cent in the corresponding years. The loss experience is mainly on account of losses faced under miscellaneous insurance, particularly nontraditional insurance. The other income has given loss for 1982 to 1988-89 and in 1994-95. Consequently the profitability before taxes has declined from 11.00 per cent in 1982 to 8.35 per cent is 1985,7.17 per cent in 1988-89 and 3.67 per cent in 1994-95, although the profit amount has increased from ₹ 190.40 crore in 1982 to ₹ 247.43 crore in 1985 and again to ₹ 338.43 crore in 1988-89 ₹ 502.51 crore in 1994-95 and ₹ 2057.75 crore in 2000-2001. The amount of profit increased mainly due to increase in investment income. The profitability of investment income has also increased. Had there not been this trend, the insurance industry would have faced loss. The investment income is shock absorber of the underwriting loss. They should try to increase investment income at faster rate to serve the society better by providing more insurance coverages because coverage of higher insurance will essentially have loss-bearing subject-matter.

Table 38.3 Total General Insurance Business
Gross Direct Premium

	GIC	*National*	*New India*	*Oriental*	*United India*	*Total*
			In India			
1998-1999		1821.4	2729.5	1930.8	2221.3	8703.0
1999-2000		1993.32	2979.53	2124.17	2348.57	9445.4
2000-2001		2117.88	3041.17	2199.67	2441.09	9799.8
2001-2002		2365.47	3512.33	2446.48	2654.96	9042.04
			Out of India			
1998-1999		32.10	288.1	39.1	39.5	398.8
1999-2000		48.79	327.00	42.38	42.01	460.2
2000-2001		109.85	451.88	47.43	82.91	692.0
2001-2002		73.94	685.73	52.15	126.52	938.34
			Total of India			
1998-1999	55.7	1853.5	3017.6	1969.9	2260.8	9157.5
1999-2000	76.60	2042.11	3306.53	2166.55	2390.58	9982.2
2000-2001	280.08	222.73	3493.05	2247.10	2524.00	10771.9
2001-2002	311.57	2439.41	4198.06	2498.63	2781.48	9980.38

Table 38.4 Underwriting Experience in Total Insurance

			% to Net Premium					
Underwriting Profi/Loss(–)	*Net Premium* *Profit/Loss(–)*	*Net Claims In Rs. Crores* ₹ *Crores*	*Net Payable*	*Expenses Commission*	*Other Management*	*Undereriting Outgo*	*Underwriting Risks Reserve*	
1985								
GIC	262.23	60.6	26.9	1.2	–0.4	9.3	2.4	6.21
National	186.47	65.1	–3.6	28.5	–0.2	8.4	1.8	3.32
New India	296.98	67.3	–0.7	23.5	–0.6	8.7	1.8	5.31
Oriental	191.39	68.8	–5.0	29.1	–0.5	5.1	2.4	4.51
United India	253.43	72.1	–1.1	23.4	0.1	8.2	–2.7	–6.93
Total	1190.50	66.8	4.1	20.3	–0.3	8.1	1.0	12.42
1989-90								
GIC	434.23	61.7	27.1	1.9	–0.3	9.1	0.5	2.27
National	348.46	73.3	–	29.0	–	9.2	–11.5	–40.06
New India	569,66	68.9	–	21.1	–	11.1	–5.1	–29.29
Oriental	380.66	70.0	–	27.0	–	10.7	–7.7	–29.51
United India	452.75	70.7	–	24.3	–	10.0	–5.0	–22.63
Total	2185.76	68.9	–	26.02	–	10.02	5.7	24.75
1994-95								
GIC	1018.31	80.2	25.4	1.3	–0.7	6.7	–12.9	131.42
National	768.93	91.6	2.44	28.6	0.3	2.6	–20.1	155.56
New India	1333.45	89.6	–4.6	23.3	–	5.0	–13.3	177.43
Oriental	821.80	88.8	–4.9	27.1	–	4.9	–15.9	130.79
United India	936.86	90.0	–5.0	24.5	–	3.2	–11.8	110.92
Total	4879.43	88.0	–1.5	21.0	–	4.5	15.0	141.18
1997-98								
GIC	1510.16	72.7	25.8	1.1	–0.1	4.7	–4.2	63.53
National	1263.24	78.42	–2.84	27.4	–0.3	4.39	–7.35	–92.81
New India	1945.00	71.43	–4.47	26.99	–	3.11	2.94	57.13
Orintal	1235.84	80.2	–	29.5	–5.4	4.8	–9.1	–112.09
United India	1402.7	82.3	5.9	30.8	22.0	5.1	–12.3	–172.33

Table 38.5 Underwriting Experience in Total Insurance

Year	Net Premium		Net Claims		Commission		Expenses of Management		Other outgo		Increase in unexpired Risks Reserve		Investment Income		Under writing profit	
	₹	%	₹	%	₹	%	₹	%	₹	%	₹	%	₹	%	₹	%
General Insurance Corporation																
1998-1999	1710.3		1252.3	73	455.9	27					103.8	6	592.1		–101.7	–6
1999-2000	1886.31		1515.63	80.4	486.42	25.8	23.32	1.2	0.45	0.0	90.02	4.8	635.2		–229.53	–12.2
2000-2001	2186.54		1851.83	84.7	496.10	22.7	23.51	1.1	3.14	0.1	146.85	6.7	652 6	25.24	–334.89	–15.3
2001-2002	2617.23		2295.08	94.12	636.34	26.10	24.45						569.33	233.5	–517.40	–21.22
National																
1998-1999	1466.0	79	1150.9	79	423.1	29					104.9		296.3		–212.9	–15
1999-2000	1614.72	79	1302.74	80.7	–31.91	–1.98	503.86	3120	–0.45	0.03	72.39	4.48	332.3		–231.91	–14.36
2000-2001	1804.55	81	1461.63	81.0	–1.82	–0.10	492.30	27.28	–2.04	0.11	99.84	5.53	17.64		–245.37	–13.60
2001-2002	1813.12		1725.11	95.14	–10.14	–0.55	564.34	31.12	–2.33	0.21	–3.88	0.21	319.96		–140.02	–7.72
New India																
1998-1999	2186.9	72	1561.5	71	490.3	22					121.8	6	551.4		133	
1999-2000	2477.45	75	1906.25	76.94	–71.65	2.89	674.67	27.23			146.16	5.90			–177.98	7.18
2000-2001	2671.48	76	2279.74	85.34	4.80	0.18	737.96	27.62			95.02	3.56	423.37		–446.04	–16.70
2001-2002	3068.23		2555.14	83.28	790.82	2.60	753.51	24.56			209.36	6.82	445.22		–529.60	–17.26

Contd...

Year	Net Premium		Net Claims		Commission		Expenses of Management		Other outgo		Increase in unexpired Risks Reserve		Investment Income		Under writing profit	
	₹	%	₹	%	₹	%	₹	%	₹	%	₹	%	₹	%	₹	%
Oriental																
1998-1999	1423.7	72	1233.0	87	350.0	25					98.0	7	324.4		–257.3	–19
1999-2000	1632.0	375.33	1332.17	81.6	–40.36	2.5	534.60	32.8			104.12	6.4	359.3		–298.50	–18.3
2000-2001	1725.35	76.78	1502.06	87.1	–45.57	–2.6	502.98	29.2			41.48	2.4	–314.68	–17.3	–275.60	–16.0
2001-2002	1818.50	72.78	1827.92	100.5	–23.07	–1.3	609.03	33.5			–223.0	0.1	21.74	1.2	–256.73	–.14.1
United Indian																
1998-19991	1615.6	71	1262.6	78	377.3	23					103.7	6	389.4		–128.0	–7
1999-2000	1753.00	73	1528.9	87.21	–85.26	–4.80	515.41	29.40			70.57	4.03	427.0	–276.63	–15.78	
2000-2001	1884.37	75	1776.93	94.30	–56.19	2.98	521.64	27.68			62.32	3.31	428.5		–420.33	–22.31
2001-2002	12045.06		1780.82		–17.53		577.88		–76.64		72.26		476.61		31.60	
Indian Market Total																
1998-1999	8402.5	92	6460.3	77	2096.6	25					532.21	6	21536		–686.6	–8
1999-2000	9363.4	94	7585.6	81	2509.1	27					483.2	5	2367.1		4214.5	–13
2000-2001	10272.1	45	8872.1	80	2670.0	25					445.4	2	2454.1		1722.2	–7

The profitability has been the lowest in United India as the percentage of profit-before tax to total assets has been 9.26 per cent in 1982, 9.52 per cent in 1985 and 4.91 per cent in 1988-89 and 3.86 per cent in 1994-95. The investment income-ratio has been the second lowest and the underwriting profits has given the highest loss-ratio. The company should increase its investment income ratio, to set off the losses of underwriting. The highest profitability has been 7.51 per cent in 1988-89 in New India, wherein the investment income-ratio has been the maximum and the underwriting loss ratio has been the lowest consequently the profitability has been the highest. Oriental have experienced maximum profitability in 1982 wherein the percentage of profit before tax to total assets has been 13.56 per cent. The highest investment income ratio and underwriting profit have given more profitability. The maximum underwriting profitability has been 6.40 per cent in 1982 in Oriental whereas the maximum investment income ratio has been 14.27 per cent in 1988-89 in GIC. It shows that the insurance companies should try to increase investment income as well as the underwriting profit. The profitability in case of insurance business is not very certain in insurance because of high uncertainty of risks. The general insurance can not predict correctly the claims because the accidents and other eventual factors are mostly unpredictable. However, the profitability of insurance companies in India is higher than those of USA, Japan, West Germany, France and Switzerland wherein the profitability in 1985 has been respectively 0.6 per cent, 1.3 per cent, 2.1 per cent 1.0 per cent and 1.2 per cent.

5. Number of Employees

The total number of employees in general insurance industry has been increasing from 41582 in 1982 to 50.559 in 1985 and again to 70940 in 1988-89 and 84561 in 1994-95. The number of employees has been maximum in New India followed by United India, Oriental and National. In the beginning National has the second lowest number of employees which be came the lowest in 1988-89. Thus, National did not attempt to increase number of employees tried to increase their business and the productivity per employee in National and Oriental.

6. Number of Offices

The number of offices of insurance industry has increased from 1550 in 1982 to 2731 in 1985, ₹ 3739 in 1988-89 and ₹ 4202 in 1994-95. It has also increased its branch offices from 1075, 2003, 2706 and 2997 in the respective years. The branch offices have been the main factors to procure business from the field. The productivity per branch office has been increasing constantly. The lowest number offices has been in National whereas United India has been the maximum. The productivity per office has been the highest in New India followed by United India, Oriental and National.

7. Overall Performances

The general insurance industry is progressive in India. At the companies particularly New India and United India have increased general insurance business rapidly. They have increased their productivity, claims per employee and investment income. They have tried to achieve the social subjectively of the nationalisation. The progress of non-traditional business given an impetus to general insurance industry to serve the society fully well.

Table 38.6 Investment Income and Underwriting profits in Companies

	Major Heads of Income						*Profit Before Tax*		
	Investment Income		*Underwriting Profit*		*Other Income*				
	₹	*% to Total Asset*	₹	*% to Total Assets*	₹	*% to Total Assets*	₹	*Total Assets*	*Total Assets*
1985									
GIC	72.26	11.79	–39.01	–6.37	0.50	–0.08	23.35	3.81	612.80
National	33.08	10.32	10.18	3.17	–0.41	–0.13	36.82	11.48	320.63
New India	60.36	7.29	26.10	3.15	–0.42	–0.05	76.87	9.28	828.51
Oriental	40.50	7.93	23.89	4.68	–0.96	–0.19	57.80	11.32	510.75
United India	38.79	7.03	18.44	3.34	–0.69	–0.12	52.59	9.52	552.14
Total	244.99	8.27	39.60	1.34	–1.60	–0.05	247.43	8.35	2961.69
1989-90									
GIC	137.24	14.27	–38.88	–4.04	–1.15	–0.12	97.21	10.10	962.06
National	66.58	9.37	–20.27	–2.86	0.33	0.05	46.60	6.57	709.81
New India	129.51	9.77	–30.05	–2.27	0.02	0.02	99.98	7.51	1325.34
Oriental	74.04	8.78	–20.78	–2.47	–1.28	–0.15	51.48	6.17	842.76
United India	80.06	9.11	–35.74	–4.07	–1.16	–0.13	43.16	4.91	878.69
Total	487.39	10.33	–145.72	–3.09	–3.24	–0.07	338.43	7.17	4718.86
1994-95									
GIC	304.95	9.88	–131.42	–4.26	0.23	0.01	173.53	5.62	3085.85
National	169.17	8.94	–154.84	–8.18	2.47	0.13	16.80	0.89	1892.14
New India	342.19	8.05	–177.43	–4.18	3.51	0.08	168.27	3.96	4248.14
Oriental	178.51	7.95	–130.79	–5.82	–4.01	0.18	43.71	1.95	2245.51
United India	212.01	8.16	–110.92	–4.27	–0.89	0.03	100.26	3.86	2598.35
Total	1206.83	8.58	–705.49	5.02	1.31	0.01	502.51	3.67	14059.98
1997-98									
GIC	522.06	10.81	–63.53	–1.31	–4.28	–0.09	440.31	9.12	4829.38
National	284.69	8.76	–92.81	–2.86	–6.03	–0.19	185.85	5.72	3249.60
New India	573.90	9.45	57.13	0.94	–10.37	–0.17	67.66	11.05	6071.67
Oriental	312.23	9.24	–112.69	–3.34	–15.86	–0.47	183.68	5.44	3378.03
United India	364.69	9.04	–172.33	–4.27	+0.52	+0.01	192.88	4.78	4033.34
Total	2057.57	9.54	–348.55	–1.61	–36.02	–0.16	1673.38	7.76	21562.02

Table 38.7 Number of Employees

	Employees in Each Category				
	Officer	*Development Officers*	*Supervisory & Clerical Staff*	*Subordinate Staff*	*Total*
1982					
GIC	90	—	157	33	280
National	1219	2440	5135	1202	9996
New India	1467	2817	6102	670	11056
Oriental	1599	2476	4762	926	9727
United India	1474	2628	5361	1040	10523
Total	5849	10381	21418	3871	41582
1985					
GIC	145	—	209	16	400
National	1726	2042	5782	1299	11894
New India	1820	3393	7048	1269	13536
Oriental	2030	2972	5586	1190	1175
United India	2117	2958	6720	1200	12995
Total	7845	12365	25345	5004	50559
1988-89					
GIC	266	—	379	107	752
National	2684	3342	7616	2043	15685
New India	3425	3974	10272	2447	20118
Oriental	3065	3614	7861	2148	16695
United India	3297	3586	8838	1969	17690
Total	12737	14516	34973	8714	70940
1990-90					
GIC	282	—	380	105	767
National	3062	2328	8265	2514	7169
New India	3647	3923	10976	2790	21336
Oriental	3098	3488	8307	2622	17516
United India	3605	3463	9503	2063	18634
Total	13694	14202	37431	10095	75422
1994-95					
GIC	224	—	365	135	724
National	3470	3070	9987	2542	19069
New India	4072	3533	12681	3358	23644
Oriental	3643	3291	10325	2475	19734
United India	3918	3274	11487	2711	21390

Contd...

Total	15327	13168	44845	11221	84561
2000-2001					
GIC	224	—	346	113	683
National	3588	3004	10156	2419	19167
New India	4219	3579	13305	2942	24045
Oriental	3600	3185	10449	2499	11793
United India	3974	3210	11622	2699	21505
Total	15665	12978	45878	10672	85193
GIC	327	—	254	116	697
National	4055	2662	9800	2366	18883
New India	5229	3720	11700	2635	23284
Oriental	4397	2821	9271	2380	18869
United India	4684	2844	10907	2481	20916
Total	18692	12047	41932	20916	82649

Table 38.8 Non-Life Insurers Investment Statistics for The period Ended March 2005 and March 2006

Name of the Insurer	*Central Govt Securities*		*State govt Securities and Other approved Securities including Central Govt securities*		*Loans to Housing and Fire Fighting Equipments*	
	31-Mar-05	*31-Mar-06*	*31-Mar-05*	*31-Mar-06*	*31-Mar-05*	*31-Mar-06*
GIC of India	2,744	2,789	3,849	3,973	927	1,012
New India	2,398	2,826	3,658	4,166	495	617
National	1,083	1,346	1,596	1,942	385	486
United India	1,585	1,654	2,645	2,856	321	392
Oriental Insurance Co	1,395	1,692	1,977	2,214	308	280
Public Sector (A)	9,205	10,307	13,725	15,151	2,435	2,787
Reliance	97	75	97	75	13	15
Royal Sundaram	89	132	99	147	36	45
Iffco Tokio	128	245	128	245	21	41
Tata Aig General	207	198	207	238	26	41
Bajaj Allianz	257	294	257	294	55	79
ICICI Lombardy	160	210	227	382	30	64
Cholamandalam	140	133	140	133	16	26
HDFC Chubb	80	75	80	75	15	15
Private Sector (B)	1,158	1,364	1,235	1,590	212	320
Total (A+B)	10,362	11,670	14,960	16,740	2,647	3,107

Note: 1. Investments of Agricultural Insurance Corporation of India have not been included

2. The above figures are based on provisional returns filed with IRDA.

Table 38.9

Infrastructure and Social Sector		Investment Subject to Exposure Norms (Incl.Otal)		Other Than Approved Investments (OTAL)		Total Investments	
31-Mar-05	*31-Mar-06*	*31-Mar-05*	*31-Mar-06*	*31-Mar-05*	*31-Mar-06*	*31-Mar-05*	*31-Mar-06*
1,199	1,275	4,905	6,269	1,456	1,584	10,880	12,530
1,050	1,206	3,201	3,415	771	611	8,404	9,404
600	720	1,725	1,537	460	410	4,306	4685
691	685	2,556	2,720	706	734	6,211	65,52
460	527	2,312	2,228	540	592	5,056	5,249
4,001	4,413	14,695	16,169	3,932	3930	34,857	38,520
26	30	56	99	12	35	193	219
67	110	70	79	17	14	217	381
45	77	117	245	0	0	310	607
41	60	38	94	1	3	312	433
78	87	223	342	35	26	613	797
79	136	133	377	11	49	469	959
27	41	16	16	10	5	198	216
26	26	55	70	6	16	177	187
387	567	709	1,323	92	148	2,542	3,799
4,388	4,980	15,404	17,492	4,024	4,079	37,399	42,319

Table 38.10 Gross Direct Premium in India (₹ in crores)

Insurer	*2003-04*	*Market shares*	*2004-05*	*Market shares*	*2006-07*	*Market shares %*	*Previous Growth over year in 2005*	*2007*
Royal sundram	211.33	1.61	270.00	1.83	600.03	2.40	27.76	30.63
Tata A/G	300.49	2.20	386.38	2.59	741.56	2.97	28.58	21.09
Reliance General	145.22	1.00	146.64	0.89	912.23	3.65	0.98	461.96
IFFCO Tokio	265.32	1.84	403.78	2.80	1150.32	4.60	52.18	28.37
ICICI Lombard	403.63	3.16	752.14	4.89	3003.45	12.0	86.35	88.66
Bajaj Allianz	385.02	2.97	701.62	4.71	1804.60	7.22	82.23	40.48
HDFC	83.93	0.70	142.98	0.98	190.16	0.76	70.34	– 7.59
Chclamandalam	76.45	0.60	145.05	0.94	314.59	1.26	89.74	41.57
New India	3229.49	25.23	–	23.25	5024.15	20.01	–	4.86
National	2839.11	21.31	–	21.14	3810.88	15.24	–	8.15
United India	2564.20	18.94	2473.62	16.31	3509.95	14.04	–3.53	11.26
Oriental	2368.64	17.66	2565.03	16.79	3940.53	15.76	8.29	11.26
ECGL	355.01	2.78	414.15	2.86	618.05	2.47	16.66	6.84
Total	13227.86	–	8401.38	–	25002.45	2.45	–	22.37

Table 38.11 Office of Subsidiary Companies

Offioce	Nationa						New India						Oriental						United India						Total					
	1982	1985	1989 -90	1994 -95	1997 -98	2001 -01	1982	1985	1989 -90	1994 -95	1997 -98	2001 -02	1982	1985	1989 -90	1994 -95	1997 -98	2001 -02	1982	1985	1989 -90	1994 -95	1997 -98	2001 -02	1982	1985	1989 -90	1994 -95	1997 -98	2001 -02
Regional	6	11	16	17	19	20	10	13	18	21	21	26	8	11	16	18	18	21	7	12	20	21	22	25	31	47	70	77	80	92
Divisional	94	149	223	248	254	286	115	185	285	315	352	397	113	157	229	251	274	309	222	190	293	311	322	368	444	681	1030	1128	1202	1360
Branch	222	462	642	677	681	662	327	555	793	827	788	688	243	474	686	701	680	626	283	512	804	792	777	723	1075	2003	2925	2997	2926	269
Total	322	622	881	942	954		425	753	1096	1163		1161	364	642	931	973	972	412	714	117	1124		1124	1	1550	2731	4025	4202	4208	

GROSS PREMIUM UNDERWRITTEN BY NON-LIFE INSURERS WITHIN INDIA (SEGMENT WISE) : FOR THE PERIOD APRIL-MARCH, 2010 (PROVISIONAL & UNAUDITED)

(Rs. in Crores)

Sl. No.	Insurer	Fire	Marine	Marine Cargo	Marine Hull	Engineering	Motor	Motor OD	Motor TP	Health	Aviation	Liability	Personal Accident	All Others	Grand Total
1.	**Royal Sundaram**	**42.49**	**23.02**	**22.54**	**0.47**	**36.81**	**617.19**	**478.50**	**138.70**	**116.11**	**0.00**	**16.21**	**26.62**	**28.63**	**907.08**
	Previous Year	50.84	19.97	19.50	0.47	37.84	529.91	419.10	110.81	114.39	0.00	9.33	28.05	15.46	805.79
2.	**TATA-AIG $**	**156.75**	**113.84**	**113.84**	**0.00**	**38.86**	**236.36**	**203.66**	**32.70**	**83.39**	**0.00**	**141.21**	**104.10**	**17.34**	**891.84**
	Previous year	163.78	111.82	111.82	0.00	35.62	249.77	217.37	32.40	78.95	0.00	116.05	118.02	13.48	887.49
3.	**Reliance**	**129.78**	**44.42**	**27.35**	**17.07**	**103.86**	**1,318.71**	**905.71**	**413.00**	**238.75**	**40.61**	**18.64**	**43.63**	**41.26**	**1,979.65**
	Previous year	126.42	61.65	32.23	29.42	119.23	1,164.87	828.87	336.00	310.83	11.01	25.74	53.44	41.68	1,914..87
4.	**IFFCO Tokio**	**202.38**	**135.12**	**70.54**	**64.58**	**93.57**	**849.01**	**501.67**	**347.34**	**164.22**	**41.91**	**43.98**	**20.60**	**88.75**	**1,639.56**
	Previous year	209.01	116.13	80.71	35.42	81.54	797.53	473.39	324.14	140.99	16.15	34.18	24.87	95.12	1,515.52
5.	**ICICI Lombard**	**270.06**	**146.57**	**81.59**	**64.98**	**152.83**	**1,379.16**	**957.22**	**421.94**	**911.81**	**57.32**	**104.91**	**79.69**	**192.72**	**3,295.06**
	Previous year	289.50	223.85	87.76	136.08	185.37	1,321.30	874.66	446.64	1,031.70	52.20	80.23	112.52	123.18	3,419.84
6.	**Bajaj Allianz**	**261.40**	**74.76**	**68.41**	**6.35**	**100.47**	**1,445.77**	**1,052.08**	**393.69**	**295.36**	**28.62**	**73.81**	**52.73**	**182.75**	**2,515.70**
	Previous year	267.43	88.44	73.87	14.56	126.48	1,500.97	1,061.14	439.83	332.02	25.13	70.11	65.76	164.17	2,640.49
7.	**HDFC ERGO**	**142.78**	**25.01**	**15.49**	**9.52**	**29.31**	**289.92**	**201.00**	**88.93**	**268.74**	**18.28**	**69.18**	**72.90**	**12.29**	**928.42**
	Previous year	64.73	8.42	5.89	2.53	14.51	185.33	124.17	61.16	56.01	1.83	33.38	7.66	2.16	374.03
8.	**Cholamandalam**	**47.77**	**42.39**	**41.44**	**0.95**	**22.41**	**450.10**	**312.82**	**137.28**	**149.51**	**0.00**	**12.11**	**29.42**	**31.15**	**784.85**
	Previous year	53.84	36.56	35.27	1.28	27.33	319.53	246.32	73.20	165.89	0.00	12.94	29.49	39.86	685.44
9.	**Future Generali**	**42.38**	**15.50**	**15.50**	**0.00**	**15.20**	**210.40**	**150.86**	**59.55**	**69.32**	**0.00**	**8.93**	**13.15**	**11.82**	**386.72**
	Previous year	17.17	6.79	6.79	0.00	14.01	95.67	71.07	24.60	41.25	0.00	4.83	9.56	5.56	194.85
10.	**Universal Sompo**	**42.15**	**3.84**	**3.84**	**0.00**	**3.22**	**79.10**	**61.66**	**17.44**	**17.40**	**0.00**	**0.77**	**9.83**	**33.04**	**189.36**
	Previous year	10.65	0.51	0.51	0.00	1.30	3.92	3.92	0.00	3.24	0.00	0.08	0.72	9.60	30.03
11.	**Shriram**	**1.74**	**0.01**	**0.01**	**0.00**	**1.47**	**410.51**	**202.13**	**208.38**	**0.00**	**0.00**	**0.16**	**1.63**	**0.39**	**415.91**
	Previous year	0.22	0.00	0.00	0.00	0.63	112.72	58.01	54.70	0.00	0.00	0.10	0.03	0.06	113.76
12.	**Bharti Axa**	**27.29**	**5.44**	**5.44**	**0.00**	**13.18**	**179.97**	**137.33**	**42.64**	**35.20**	**0.00**	**3.19**	**23.64**	**2.74**	**290.65**
	Previous year	2.25	0.61	0.61	0.00	5.57	17.39	14.00	3.38	1.51	0.00	0.53	0.43	0.21	28.50
13.	**Raheja QBE***	**0.16**	**0.02**	**0.02**	**0.00**	**0.40**	**0.17**	**0.15**	**0.02**	**0.00**	**0.00**	**1.00**	**0.18**	**0.02**	**1.94**
	Previous year	0.00	0.00	0.00	0.00	0.00	0.00	0.00	0.00	0.00	0.00	0.00	0.00	0.00	0.00

14.	**New India**	**914.80**	**477.79**	**192.76**	**285.04**	**297.75**	**2,067.42**	**1,171.19**	**896.23**	**1,541.90**	**55.32**	**119.51**	**101.03**	**437.92**	**6,013.44**
	Previous year	773.33	446.10	175.17	270.92	247.74	2,000.29	1,088.43	911.86	1,355.67	78.20	104.68	97.12	405.70	5,508.83
15.	**National**	**429.16**	**239.91**	**141.98**	**97.93**	**185.59**	**2,168.76**	**1,361.54**	**807.22**	**1,021.71**	**36.92**	**57.05**	**95.36**	**386.46**	**4,620.92**
	Previous year	397.08	201.16	136.70	64.46	164.03	2,137.10	1,341.13	795.97	854.02	57.79	50.91	71.86	345.94	4,279.90
16.	**United India @**	**647.93**	**451.97**	**275.68**	**176.29**	**306.43**	**1,817.13**	**963.74**	**853.39**	**1,256.14**	**30.02**	**91.43**	**109.17**	**527.11**	**5,237.32**
	Previous year	572.79	336.93	221.60	115.33	249.86	1,563.48	758.77	804.72	900.72	32.22	88.68	137.05	396.04	4,277.77
17.	**Oriental**	**575.03**	**390.45**	**183.42**	**207.03**	**281.80**	**1,610.19**	**868.39**	**741.80**	**1,063.51**	**92.08**	**99.85**	**101.12**	**504.73**	**4,718.75**
	Previous year	436.51	332.53	167.24	165.29	262.99	1,490.53	803.34	687.19	713.45	90.07	82.86	147.30	404.33	3,960.57
	Grand Total	**3,934.07**	**2,190.06**	**1,259.85**	**930.22**	**1,683.14**	**15,129.88**	**9,529.64**	**5,600.23**	**7,233.10**	**401.08**	**861.94**	**884.78**	**2,499.12**	**34,817.17**
	Previous year	3,435.55	1,991.46	1,155.69	835.77	1,574.05	13,490.31	8,383.71	5,106.60	6,100.65	364.60	714.65	903.86	2,062.54	30,637.68
	SPECIALISED INSTITUTIONS														
18.	**ECGC**													**813.71**	**813.71**
	Previous year													744.67	744.67
19.	**Star Health & Allied Insurance**									**965.53**			**10.50**	**4.01**	**980.04**
	Previous year									488.84			16.47	4.56	509.86
20.	**Apollo MUNICH**									**106.43**			**4.26**	**3.97**	**1.4.66**
	Previous year									44.35			2.46	2.14	48.95
21.	**Max BUPA#**									**0.13**			**0.00**	**0.00**	**0.13**
	Previous year									0 00			0.00	0.00	0.00

Source = IRDA = Journal June 2010

 # Commenced operations in March, 2010 Source: IRDA-Journal June 2010

$ Figures revised by Insurer for March, 2009

@ There is variation between Segment-wise figures and Monthly Business figures for March, 2010

Complied on the basis of data submitted by the Insurance companies

Report Card: General

GROSS PREMIUM UNDERWRITTEN AND UP TO THE MONTH OF MARCH, 201

(₹ in Crores)

INSURER	MARCH		APRIL-MARCH		GROWTH OVER THE CORRESPONDENCE PREVIOUS YEAR
	2013-14	2012-13*	2013-14	2012-13*	
Royal Sundaram	120.21	153.80	1,437.00	1,561.09	-7.95
Tata-AIG	222.95	231.78	2,362.71	2,135.08	10.66
Reliance General	165.00	156.74	2,388.82	2,010.01	18.85
IFFCO-Tokio	339.11	240.74	2,930.92	2,570.18	14.04
ICICI-lombard	557.57	478.72	6,856.16	6,133.98	11.77
Bajaj Allianz	486.91	473.17	4,516.45	4,001.40	12.87
HDFC ERGO General	336.10	251.43	2,906.99	2,453.20	18.50
Cholamandalam	248.75	161.71	1,854.45	1,620.89	14.41
Future Generali	111.96	101.67	1,264.42	1,105.27	14.40
Universal Sompo	71.59	70.55	540.45	534.35	1.14
Shriram General	150.61	171.42	1,510.59	1,541.38	-2.00
Bharti AXA General	120.90	119.71	1,407.43	1,218.43	15.51
Raheja QBE	1.61	1.75	23.28	21.26	9.51
SBI General	146.76	117.68	1,187.57	770.85	54.06
L&T General	31.82	36.38	252.82	182.07	38.86
Magma HDI	47.81	28.39	424.93	95.14	346.64
Liberty	22.17	1.33	129.82	2.19	NA
Star Health & Allied Insurance	152.65	119.82	1,097.21	860.22	27.55
Apollo MUNICH	93.88	72.34	692.48	619.99	11.69
Max BUPA	42.29	32.01	308.85	207.22	49.05
Religare	11.55	5.80	152.31	38.80	292.59
Cigna TTK	0.29	NA	0.34	NA	NA
New India	1,222.95	1,081.47	11,523.04	10,037.95	14.79
National	1,155.74	1,026.32	10,244.43	9,165.73	11.77
United India	954.83	954.60	9,705.69	9,266.04	4.74
Oriental	670.05	700.43	7,131.28	6,543.51	8.98
ECGC	160.64	132.43	1,303.85	1,157.22	12.67
AIC	258.11	226.57	3,383.95	3,235.25	4.60
PRIVATE TOTAL	**3,482.50**	**3,026.65**	**34,246.01**	**29,682.99**	**15.37**
PUBLIC TOTAL	**4,422.32**	**4,121.83**	**43,292.24**	**39,405.70**	**9.86**
GRAND TOTAL	**7,904.83**	**7,148.78**	**77,538.25**	**69,088.69**	**12.23**

Note: Compiled on the basis of data submitted by the insurance companies IRDA

THE ORIENTAL FIRE AND GENERAL INSURANCE COMPANY LIMITED

INCORPORATED IN INDIA

Regd. Office : Jeevan Udyog,
Asaf Ali Road, New Delhi

Issuing Office

PROHIBITION OF REBATE

Section 41 of the Insurance Act 1938 as amended provides as follows:

1. No person shall allow or offer to allow, either directly or indirectly, as an inducement to any person to take out or renew or continue an insurance in respect of any kind of risk relating to lives or property in India, any rebate of the whole or part of the commission payable or any rebate of the premium shown on the Policy nor shall any person taking out or renewing or continuing Policy accept any rebate except such rebate as may be allowed in accordance with the published prospectuses or tables of the insurer.
2. Any person making default in complying with the provisions of this section shall be punishable with fine which may extend to five hundred rupees.

Specimen

COMBINED HOUSEHOLD INSURANCE

For your Jewellery and other valuables particularly those worn or taken out of your residence, the best Insurance is an "ALL Risk" Policy from The Oriental Fire & General Insurance Company Ltd.

The Oriental
Fire & General Insurance
Company Limited

THE ORIENTAL FIRE AND GENERAL INSURANCE COMPANY LIMITED

Incorporated in India

Subsldiary to General Insurance Corporation of India

Registered Office:

Jeevan Udyog, Asaf Ali Road, NEW DELHI-1

For the Contents of

Privaate Dwelling houses and Flats

(*as detailed on the Proposal Form*)

The Sum Insured must represent the full value of property covered)

COVER

A. Loss or Damage caused by any of the undermentional perils:

(*i*) FIRE

(*ii*) LIGHTING

(*iii*) EXPLOSION

(*iv*) AIRCRAFT OR ARTICLES DROPPED THEREFROM (excluding enemy aircraft)

(*v*) BURSTING OR OVERFLOW OF WATER TANKS, APPARATUS OR PIPES (excluding damage caused thereto)

(*vi*) BURGLARY OR HOUSEBREAKING or any attempt thereat.

(*vii*) LARCENY OR THEFT excluding (*a*) Larceny or Theft of Cash, Currency Notes, Bank Notes or Stamps and (*b*) Larceny or Theft whilst the dwelling house or any part thereof is lent, let or sublet in whole or in part.

Extensions

If and so far as said Contents are not otherwise insured the Policy extends except as regards property removed for sale or exhibition or to Furniture Depositories and subject in every case to the exclusion and limitations specified to cover the same whilst temporarily removed and contained in any private dwelling house, club, hotal, boarding or lodging house but remaining in India, against all the said perils except Laceny and Theft.

The amount recoverable under these extensions shall be limited to 15% (fifteen per cent) of the declared full value of the contents.

B. Damage to the Buildings and/or Landlord's Fixtures and Fittings

Damages (other than by fire) but only for which the Insured is liable as Tenant and not as Owner directly caused by

(*i*) Bursting or Overflow of Water Tanks, Apparatus or Pipes:

(*ii*) Burglary, House breaking or any attempt thereat, except while the Dwelling is left unfurnished, Excluding in the case of (*i*) the first ₹ 100 of each and every loss and not exceeding in aggregate 10% of the declared full value of the contents.

C. Liability to the Public or Householders:

As occupier of the Premises only, not arising under any contract, in respect of accidents happening in or about the Insured's Private Dwelling house. Domestic Offices, Garages or Out Buildings covering:

(*i*) Bodily Injury (excluding the Insured's family household or servant).

(*ii*) Damage to property (excluding Property of the insured a family household or servants).

Limited to ₹ 2,00,000 in respect of any one one occurrence and in additions costs and expenses incurred with the Company's consent, Excluding liability for injury or damage arising out of or incidental to the Insured's Profession or Business or the use of lifts of Vehilcles.

D. Compensation for Death of the Insured or the wife or the husband the Insured:

By violence in his private dwelling house, caused by Byrglan or House-breakers or Fire, if death occurs within three months or injury (limited to 50% of the declared full value of the contents or ₹ 10,000/- whichever is the less).

Special Note

Policies do not cover any contingency occasionaed by or happening through:

(*a*) Earthquake, volcanic eruption or other convlusions of nature.

(*b*) Typhoon, hurricane, tornado, cyclone or other atmospheric disturbance.

(*c*) War, invasion, act of foreign enemy, hostilities or warlike operations (whether war be declared or not), civil war.

(*d*) Mutiny, riot, strike, military or popular rising, insurrection, reballion, revolution, military or usurped power, material law or state of siege or any of the events or causes which determine the proclamation or maintenance of material law or state of stage.

(*e*) Redioactive contamination.

EXTRA RISKS

The following additional covers are obtainable or request:

PERSONAL PUBLIC LIABILITY

The liabilities of the Insured and of members of his family reding with him in respect of claims by Third Parties for bodily injury or damage to property arising from accidents happening in the insure of private personal activities, but EXCLUDING accidents arising from the ownership or use of any mechanically propelled vehicle, aircraft vessel or craft (other than hand-propelled craft); the ownership or occupation of land or buildings, the carrying on of any trade, business or profession.

Proposer and un-named members of his family residing with him — Annual Premium ₹ 7.50

Limit of Indemnity ₹ 2,00,000

ACCIDENTS TO SERVANTS

The Liability of the Insured under the Workmen's Compensation Acts and at Common Law for accidents to Servants, Rate:

Indoor Servants	—₹ 4 per capita	Syces	—₹ 12 per capita
Mails	—₹ 6 ,, ,,	Drivers	—₹ 23 per capita

N.B.: A separate Proposal Form must be completed for this cover.

PROPOSAL FORM **AGENCY** ....

1. **Proposer's Name (in full)** ....

Address .. ..

.. ..

Occupation .. ..

2. **Property to be Insured**

Situation ....

Household Goods and Personal Effects (except as specifically excluded below*) belonging to the Insured (or for which he is responsible) or permanently resident member of his family and fixtures and fittings the Insurerd's own (or for which he is responsible).

Sum to be Insured .... ₹. .... If the value of Jewellery, Good and Silver articles exceeds one-third of the Sum to be Insured please state their total value Rs. ....

The sum proposed must represent the full value of the property * Exclusions

(*i*) This Proposal does not apply to property more specifically insured, nor, unless specifically mentioned, to Deeds, Bonds, Bills of Exchange, Promissory Notes, Cheques, Securities for money, Documents of any kind, Manuscripts, Medals and Coins, Motor Vehicles and Accessories whilst thereon or Livestock, and,

(*ii*) No one Article, Curio, Picture or other work of art, stmap Collection or article of Gold, Silver or other Precious metal, Jewellery or Fur shall be deemed to be of greater value than 5% of the sum to be Insured, unless specifically insured under a separate item.

(*iii*) Cash, Currency Notes, Bank Notes and Stamps not forming part of or Stamp Collection are included up to 5% of the Sum to be Insured not exceeding Rs. 300/-. Loss by Larceny or Theft in respect of such property is not covered.

3. **Dwelling**

(*a*) Is it built of brick, stone or concrete, with state tiles, metal or concrete, with state tiles, metal or concrete root? ....

If not, please give full particulars ....

(*b*) Is it a private house? ....

If not, is it a self-contained flat with separate entrance? ....

(*c*) Is it exclusively occupied by yourself and family? ....

(*d*) State type of lockl securing door .... (*i*) Front ....

(*ii*) Stack ....

(*e*) Does it communicate with or is it over any trade risk or is any trade or business carried or is any trade or business carried on in the building? ....

(*f*) Except for shopping and the life, for what periods is it left without an occupant? ....

4. (*a*) Is the building in a good state of repair and will it be so maintained? ... .

(*b*) State approximate age of the building ....

5. In respect of any of the contingencies specified in the proposal have you ever

(*a*) been proviously insured? ... .

If so, with which Company? ... .

(*b*) sustained a loos? ... .

If so, please give particulars. ... .

6. Have you ever had:

(*a*) a proposal for insurance or renewal of a Policy declined? ....

(*b*) a Policy canclled? ... .

(*c*) special conditions or rates imposed? ... .

If so, please give full particulars. ... .

7. Do you wish to effect these insurances?

(*a*) Personal Public Liability ....

(*b*) Accidents to Serants ... .

(see previous pages for details.)

DECLARATION TO BE SIGNED BY THE PROPOSER

I hereby declared that the above statements are true and that I have withheld no information that might influence the acceptance of this Proposal and I further declare that the sum proposed for insurance represents and will be maintained at no loss than the full value of the property and I agree that this Proposal shall be the Contract between me and The Oriental fire & General Insurance Company Limited and shall be deemed to be incorporated therein.

Dated .... Signature of Proposer ....

No insurance is in force until the Premium has been paid and the Proposal has been accepted by the Company.

Agency ....   Policy No. ....

THE ORIENTAL FIRE AND GENERAL INSURANCE COMPANY LIMITED

(INCORPORATED IN INDIA)

Registered Office:

Telegrams: Oriential Buildings, Mahatma Gandhi Road,

"ORIENTFIRE" BOMBAY   **BOMBAY-400001**   Telephone No. : 253911

PROPOSAL FOR MACHINERY BREAKDOWN INSURANCE

Name : ....

Postal Address : ....

Nature of Business : ....

Works Address : ....

1. Give list of Machinery to be insured on the reverse bearing in rained the guiding notes.	
2. Do the items listed represene the whole of the machinery? If not, state items not included and reasons why they are not proposed for insurance.	
3. Is all or any of the machinery subject to periodical inspection? Is so, which by whom and at what intervals?	
4. Are you at present insured? Or have you ever made a proposal for machinery breakdown insurance? If so, has any such proposal (or renewal) been:	

(*a*) declined by any Insurance Co.? If so, give details. (*b*) subject to increased premium or special conditions?	
5. Have you ever suffered loss due to machinery breakdown? If so, give particulars of each breakdown (apart from small damages) during the past three years, giving the cause of the damage and the total cost of repairs in each case.	
6. State the time and date when the insurance is to commence:	

Date : .... Month : .... 19 Period of Insurance will be till noon of the same date and month the following year.

I/We hereby warrant that the answers stated above are true, that I/we have withheld no information which might influence the acceptance of this proposal, and that the warrantly hereby given shall be the basis of the Contract between me/us and the Company. I/we undertake to exercise all reasonable and ordinary precautions for the safety of the said machinery, and I/we agree to accept the conditions of Company's Policy, which I/we have read and understood.

Date : ....

Signature : ....

Section 41 of the Indian Insurance Act, 1938, which is in force from the 1st July, 1939 reads as follows:

(1) No person shall allow or offer to allow, either directly or indirectly as an inducement to any person to take out or renew or conditions an Insurance in respect of any kind of risk relating to lives or property in India, any rebate of the whole or part of the commission payable or any rebate of the premium shown on the policy, nor shall any person taking out or renewing or continuing a policy accept any rebate, except such rebate, as may be allowed in accordance with the published prospectuses or tables of the insurer.

(2) Any person making default in complying with the provisions of this section shall be punishable with fine which may extend to five hundred rupees.

THE OTHER, PAYMENT OR ACCEPTANCE OF A REBATE OF THE PREMIUM HEREUNDER IS THEREFORE A BREACH OF THE LAW

SCHEDULE OF MACHINERY TO BE INSURED

Guiding notes for the completion of the Schedule of Machinery

1. Each machine should be entered separately with necessary identification particulars from the name plate stating the market's name, number, size, power, capacity, speed. Additional particulars for electrical equipments such as voltage, amperage, cycles & for steam equipments, pressure and temperature should be given.
2. If (*a*) foundation and/or masonry and brickwork: (*b*) oil in transformers and/or switchgear, are to be included separate entry and valuatin should be given.
3. All protable machines must be so designated. All outside items must be so described separately.
4. To avoid under insurance the sum insured on each machine must be on the basis of its present-day new replacement value including provision for Packing, Freight, Erection and customers and other duties.
5. If any of machines are "standby" or only intermittently inuse, this fact should be mentioned and the extent of use should be specified.

Situation of Machinery: ....

Serial No. (1)	Number of (2)	Description (3)	Year of make (4)	Sum Insured (5)	Excess (6)

Signature of Propeser' --------..........................

THE ORIENTAL FIRE AND GENERAL INSURANCE COMPANY LIMITED

(INCORPORATED IN INDIA)

Subsidiary to General Insurance
Corporation of India
Registered Office :
Jeevan Udyog, Asaf Ali Road, New Delhi

Issuing Office

PROHIBITION OF REBATE

Section 41 of the Insurance Act 1938 as amended provides as follows:

1. No person shall allow or offer to allow, either directly or indirectly, as an inducement to any person to take out or renew or continue an insurance in respect of any kind of risk relating to lives or property in India, any rebate of the whole or part of the commission payable or any rebate of the premium shown on the Policy, nor shall any person taking out or renewing or continuing Policy accept any rebate except such rebate as may be allowed in accordance with the published prospectuses or tables of the insurer.
2. Any person making default in complying with the provisions of this section shall be punishable with fine which may extend to five hundred rupees.

FIDELITY
Gurantee
(Individual or Collective)

The Oriental
Fire & General Insurance
Company Limited

The Oriental Fire and General Insurance Company Limited

FIDELITY

GURANTEE

Present -day loss experience in Fidelity Gurantee emphasies the importance of this type of insurance, and various types of Fidelity Policies issued provide Insurance against loss of cash and stock occasioned by the fraud or dishonesty of employees.

All monies or funds standing to the credit of a defaulting Employee are deducted from the loss and not from the amount of the Guarantee.

Policies are issued to meet every need whether a single Employees, or an entire Staff and workpeople, in the latter case without the name of Employees being submitted.

Quotations are available to meet all requirement.

THE ORIENTAL FIRE & GENERAL INSURANCE CO. LTD.

(Incorporated in India)

Subsidiary of General Insurance Corporation of India

Registered Office: Jeevan Udyog, Asaf Ali Road, New Delhi

FORM OF PROPOSAL FOR INDIVIDUAL OR COLLECTIVE FIDELITY GUARANTEE

Agency : .... Policy No.

1. Full name of Employer .... Business

....

Address ....

2. Has any application for Fidelity Insurance been made to any other Company or Underwriters? If so, state date, name of Company or Underwriters, and the result? .. .. ..

3. Give particulars of any Losses suffered during the last five years through the dishonesty of your Employees and the steps taken to prevent a recurrance. .. ..

4. (*a*) Has any Employee power to operate on your Banking Account? .. .. (*a*)

   (*b*) State maximum amount of any one cheque:

   (*i*) on his signature alone. .. .. .. (*b*) (*i*)

   (*ii*) jointly with another Employee. .. .. (*ii*)

5. What system do you use to prevent inclusion of fictitious names in the Pay Roll? .. ..

6. How soon after receipt of money are Employees required to amount for same? .. ..

7. Are they required to bank collections in full to your credit at once or remit to you forthwith?

8. How often and by whom are:

(*a*) Employees Receipt Book Counterfoils checked against collections their reported collections?	(*a*)		by
(*b*) Accounts prepared and rendered direct to customers, and also the subsequent procedure to clear outstanding accounts?	(*b*)		by
(*c*) Cash Book entire checked with Pass Book Recepit Counter-foils and Vouchers?	(*c*)		by
(*d*) Petty Cash payments similary checked and the capability of the Employees to produce the balance tested?	(*d*)		by
(*e*) Your books balanced?	(*e*)		by
(*f*) Your professional audit arrangement carried out? ..	(*f*)		by
(*g*) Traveller's Stocks physically checked?	(*g*)		by
(*h*) Other Stocks Physically checked?	(*h*)		by
(*i*) Physical surprise and spot checks operated?	(*i*)		by

FULL NAMES AND PARTICULARS OF EMPLOYEES FOR WHOM GURANTEES ARE REQUIRED

Note: Porposal Forms are required to be completed by each Employees named unless he has been in your service for three years or more when he may be included without completing an Application Form

Surame	Christian Name(s)	Capacity	Amount of	Address	No. of Years in Employ-yer's Service	Salary and Commission (if any)

I/We hereby Declare that the particulars and statements in this Proposal Form are true and that this and any other written statement made by me/us or on my/our behalf for the purpose of the proposed Guarantee shall be the basis of and incorporated in the Contract between me/us and The Oriental Fire & General Insurance Co. Ltd., not only in respect of the persons named herein but also in respect of any other person or persons who may hereafter be included in the said Guarantee and I/we also declare that the conduct and accounts of the said persons have always been satisfactory.

Date .... Signature of Employer ....

This insurance will not be in force until the Proposal has been accepted by the Company and the Premium paid.

FULL NAMES AND PARTICULARS OF EMPLOYEES FOR WHOM GURANTEES ARE REQUIRED

Surame	Christian Name(s)	Capacity	Amount of	Address	No. of Years in Employ-yer's Service	Salary and Commission (if any)

THE ORIENTAL FIRE AND GENERAL INSURANCE COMPANY LIMITED

(INCORPORATED IN INDIA)

Subsidiary to General Insurance Corporation of India
Registered Office :
Jeevan Udyog, Asaf Ali Road, New Delhi

Issuing Office

PROHIBITION OF REBATE

Section 41 of the Insurance Act 1938 as amended provides as follows:

1. No person shall allow or offer to allow, either directly or indirectly, as an inducement to any person to take out or renew or continue an insurance in respect of any kind of risk relating to lives or property in India, any rebate of the whole or part of the commission payable or any rebate of the premium shown on the Policy, nor shall any person taking out or renewing or continuing Policy accept any rebate except such rebate as may be allowed in accordance with the published prospectuses or tables of the insurer.
2. Any person making default in complying with the provisions of this section shall be punishable with fine which may extend to five hundred rupees.

CASH INSURANCE

The Oriential Fire & General Insurance Company Limited

CO. LTD

(INCORPORATION IN INDIA)

Subsidiary to General Insurance Corporation of India
Registered Office :
Jeevan Udyog, Asaf Ali Road, New Delhi

INSURANCE AGAINST LOSS OF CASH

The Company issues policies providing indemnity in respect of loss of Cash in the circumstances or situation as described in the Schedule overleaf subject to the followig exceptions:

(*a*) Shortage due to error or omission.
(*b*) Loss of cash entrusted to any person other than the Insured or an employee of the Insured.
(*c*) Loss due to the fraud or dishonesty of any employee of the Insured unless such loss is discovered within 48 hours of its occurance.
(*d*) Loss for which at the time of its occurrence indemnity is provided by or would but for the existence of this Policy by provided by any other existing Poliy or Policies except in respect of any excess beyond the amount which would have been payable under such other Policy or Policieis had this insurance not been effected.
(*e*) Less occasioned by riot or civil commotion.
(*f*) Any consequence of war invasion act, of foreign enemy hostilities (whether war be declared or not) civil war rebellion revolution insurrection or military or usured power.

Rates will be quoted on receipt of completed Proposal. An annual premium based on the sum insured is charged for Cash on the premises vide Item 4 of the Schedule overleaf, but in respect of Cash insured under Items 1, 2 and 3 is adjustable according to the total amount actually in transit per annum.

LOCAL REPRESENTATIVE

THE ORIENTAL FIRE & GENERAL INSURANCE CO. LTD.

(Incorporated in India)

Subsidiary of General Insurance Corporation of India

Registered Office: Jeevan Udyog, Asaf Ali Road, New Delhi

Branch : .... Policy No. ....

Agency : ....

PROPOSAL FOR CASH INSURANCE

Definition:— For the purpose of this Insurance the terms "Cash" means current coin, bank and currency notes, cheques, postal ordersm, money orders and current postage stamps.

1. Name in Full .... Business

....

2. Address ....

3. Trade or Business ....

4. (*a*) Description of premises e.g., Shop, Office, Warehouse, Factory, etc ....

   (*b*) Are the whole of the premises occupied by you? If not, give particulars of other tenent. ....

   (*c*) Are the premises occupied at night? ....

   (*d*) ....

5. Are the employees engaged in the Handing of Wages and/or Cash guaratned under a Fidelity Policy? ....

6. Description of Cash to be insured: (If no insurance required for any items inser 'Nil")

Item No.	CIRCUMSTANCE OR SITUATION	Limit any one loss	Estimated total amount of cash (other than crosed cheques) in transit during onsuring twelve months
1.	Cash for the payment of wages, salaries and other earnings or for petty cash in the direct transit from the bank to the Insured's premises from the time the cash is received at the bank by the Insured or authoried employees of the Insured until delivered at the premises or other place of disbursement an whilst there until paid out provided that out of business hours Cash shall be secured in locked safe or locked strong room on the premises. Cheques drawn by the Insurance to provide for such Cash are covered in transit from the premises to the bank.		
2.	Cash (other than described in Item 1) in the personal custory of the Insured or the authorised employees of the Insured whilst in transit between the premises and the bank or post office or in night safe at the bank.		
3.	Cash (other than described in Item 1 and 2) collected by and in the personal custody of the Insured or the authorised employees of the Insured whilst in transit to the premises or bank within a period not exceeding forty-eight hours from the time of collection.		
4.	Cash (other than described in Item 1) whilst on the premises during business hours or whilst secured in locked safe or locked strong room on the Insured's premises out of business hours.		

ESTIMATED TOTAL AMOUNT OF CASH IN TRANSIT per annum

7. Approximate distance between Bank and Proposer's premises. ....

8. (*a*) Is there any transit to or form branches, outlying contract or elsewhere? ....

(*b*) Is so, give particulars, includind addresses. ....

(*c*) How is the Cash conveyed and how many employees have change of it? ....

9. State estimated maximum amount of wages salaries and petty cash retaied

in sate or strong room overnight ....

10. (*a*) State following particulars of safe and/or strong room in which cash will be kept out of business hours : ....

Maker's Name	Weight	Dimensions	Identification Number

(*b*) Where and on which floor is the safe situated? ....

(*c*) Is it fixed to the walls or floor, If so, how? ....

(*d*) By whom are the keys of the safe and/or strong room held? ....

(*e*) Are all such keys removed from the premises after business hours? ....

11. (*a*) Are you now, or have you been insured in respect of loss of Cash? If so, state name of Insurer ....

(*b*) Has any Insurer in respect of an insurance against loss of Cash

(*i*) Declined your proposal or renewal? ....

(*ii*) Terminated your Insurance? ....

(*iii*) Required an increased premium? ....

or imposed special conditions? ....

12. Have you ever sustained any loss of Cash? If so, give particulars. ....

I/We desire to effect an insurance with THE ORIENTAL FIRE & GENERAL INSURANCE COMPANY LIMITED, as set forth above. I/We warrant that the above statements are true and complete and that nothing materially afterting the risk has been conceled by me/us. I/We undertake to keep the records necessary for the due adjustment of the premium and to rendeer at the end of each period of insurance a statement in the form required by the Company of the total amount of Cash in transit which is the subject of this proposal and I/we agree that this Proposal and Declaration shall be held to be promissory and shall form the basis of the contract between me/us and The oriential fire & general insurance company limited.

Date .... 19 ....   Signature of Proposer ....

No insurance is in force until a premium or Deposit has been paid and no acknowledgement of any premium or depoist is valid unless upon the Official Printed Form of the Company.

PART SIX

PROSPECTS OF INSURANCE COMPANIES

39

PROSPECTS OF INSURANCE

Prospects of insurance during second millennium have been forecasted as very bright because people accept it as essential cover of life. Privatisation of insurance brings additional technique of business. It has been assessed in the present chapter and succeeding chapter, 'Privatisation of Insurance'. The prospects of life insurance and general insurance have been analyzed based on their performances during last decade, *i.e.,* 1991-2000.

LIFE INSURANCE

Life insurance business is analyzed under new business individual insurance, rural new business, development of new products, new business projects under group insurance, new business projects under group superannuation schemes, business in force, individual and group schemes, lapsation of policies, valuation, working results, investment operations, number of active agents and their business, and social responsibilities.

New Business Individual Insurance

New business of the Life Insurance Corporation of India has increased rapidly after decentralisation of its functions in 1985-86. The impact has been clearly observed in 1990-91 when the total number of life policies has crossed 80 lakh of policies assuring more than ₹ 25,000 crores. During five years (1990-91 to 1994-95) The new business has additional increment of about 20 lakh policies of ₹ 25,000 crores. It reveals that the end of the century will witness total new business of ₹ 80,000 crores under 150 lakh of policies. LIC should reach to the level of ₹ 1,01,000 crore new business under 176 lakh of policies in 2004-2005. With the presence of foreign insurance business in India, it has to compete hard. The existing normal servicing has to be improved to get its outstanding place in insurance business. Business outside India has increased slowly. It is not very satisfactory as the number of policies per year has not increased more than 9 thousand. Sum assured increased by about ₹ 30 crores only per annum.

It is to be seen how much insurance business outside India would increase after entry of foreign insurers. LIC has to strike outside India as foreign insurers plan to achieve maximum business which was untapped by LIC. Challenges before LIC would be greater in the coming years. It is expected that life insurance business would take new turn during the years as people would be fully aware of insurance as a result of massive advertising practices of foreign insurers who believe in offensive advertising and sophisticated services. Many consumer goods have increased their market share as foreign companies have resorted to massive advertising. Coming years would be more materialistic and full of uncertainties. Science and technology would reach to common man. They would not spare any opportunities untapped. If income and uncertainties have increased, insurance desire would convert into insurance-craze.

Rural New Business

Rural LIC business has increased from ₹ 10,294.55 crores under 36.15 lakh policies in 1990-91 which increased to ₹ 21,263.59 crore under 52.47 lakh policies. The percentage share of policies to total new policies increased from 42.5 lakh to 49.2 lakh during the period. It is expected that the sum assured would increase upto ₹ 30,000 crore under 72 lakh policies in 1999-2000, and ₹ 45,000 crore under 85 lakh policies in 2004-2005. The percentage share of rural business in the total business would not change. The LIC would not devote much time and energy for procuring new business in rural areas, as it has to compete with foreign insurers who would devote only in urban areas. Profit motive is the basic object of foreign insurers. They would devote for enhancing business. Rural business would be ignored by the LIC and foreign insurers.

Table 39.1A New Business Individual Insurance (Excluding Annuities)

Mo. of Policies in Lakhs
Sum Assured in crores of ₹

Year	New Business in India		Out of India		Total New Business	
	No. of Policies	Sum Assured	No. of Policies	Sum Assured	No. of Policies	Sum Assured
1990-91	86.45	28,139.07	.086	100.03	86.54	.28,239.10
1991-92	92.38	32,064.44	.096	131.86	92.48	32,196.30
1992-93	99.58	35,956.82	0.102	158.98	99.68	36,115.80
1993-94	107.26	41,913.83	0.124	199.07	107.38	42,012.90
1994-95	108.75	55,228.50	0.133	240.32	108.88	55,468.82
1995-96	110.21	51,815,54	0.133	255.99	110.34	52,071.53
1996-97	122.68	56,740.50	0.123	253.44	122.81	56,993.94
1998-99	148.43	75,316.28	0.170	283.72	148.60	75,600.00*
1999-2001*	150.00	80,000.00	0.250	300.00	150.25	80,300.00*
2004-2005*	175.00	100,000.00	1.00	1000.00	176.00	101,000.00*

*Expected as per crude estimate.

Table 39.1B New Business Individual Insurance of LIC

No. of Policies in Lakhs
Sum Assured in Crores of ₹

Year	New Business in India		Out of India		Total New Business	
	No. of Policies	Sum Assured	No. of Policies	Sum Assured	No. of Policies	Sum Assured
1998-99	148.43	75316.28	0.14	289.98	14857	75606.26
1999-2000	169.77	91214.25	0.12	276.69	169.89	91490.94
2000-2001	196.56	124771.62	0.08	179.01	196.64	124950.63
2001-2002	224.91	192572.27	0.09	212.69	225.00	192784.96
2002-2003	242.67	179504.34	0.10	298.95	242.78	179803.27
2003-2004	264.56	198707.12	0.11	341.40	264.68	199048.52
2004-2005	218.18	179481.39	0.14	405.27	218.32	179886.66

The new business of LIC has increased to the level of ₹ 179886.66 Crore under 218.32 Lakh policies in 2004-2005 after touching the highest figure of ₹ 199048.52 Crore under 264.68 Lakh policies in 2003-2004. It is expected to enhance further in 2005-2006. It reveals that the life insurance new business has increased more than the forecasted at straight line fitting methods *i.e.,* ₹ 101000.00 crore under 176.00 Lakh policies in 2004-2005. Thus the prospects of life insurance is very light in India.

Table 39.2A Rural New Business

Year	Rural New Business		Percentage share of Rural New Business in total new business	
	No. of Policies (in Lakhs)	Sum Assured (₹ in crore)	Policies	Sum Assured
1990-91	36.75	10,294.55	42.50	36.60
1991-92	41.27	12,439.93	44.70	38.80
1992-93	44.39	14,085.03	44.30	39.20
1993-94	48.56	16,680.03	45.30	39.90
1994-95	49.02	21,571.00	45.10	39.10
1995-96	52.57	21,263.59	47.70	41.00
1996-97	60.33	24,278.73	49.20	42.80
*1998-99	70.00	28,000,00	47.16	37.18
*1999-2000	72.00	30,000.00	48.00	37.50
*2004-2005	85.00	45,000.00	48.57	45.00

* Expected

Table 39.2B Rural New Business

Year	Rural New Business		Percentage share of Rural New Business in total new business	
	No. of Policies (in Lakhs)	Sum Assured (₹ in crore)	Policies	Sum Assured
1997-98	68.40	27550.69	51.4	43.3
1998-99	81.23	3537294	54.7	47.0
1999-2000	97.04	44168.19	57.5	48.7
2000-2001	35.33	17955.88	55.53	47.78
2001-2002	37.01	25461.94	16.94	13.65
2002-2003	45.23	23547.69	18.90	13.37
2003-2004	62.19	35651.99	22.97	17.85
2004-2005	55.03	46037.01	22.97	25.18
2005-2006				

The figures since 2000-2001 are as per the definitions of rural/social set as approved by IRDA.

The rural new business of LIC has increased to the level of 25.18 per cent under 22.97 per cent policies in 2004-2005. It is more than expected in 2000-2001 the traditional definition has revealed 47.78 per cent of sum assured and 55.53% of policies as compared to 14.59 per cent and 18.18 per cent respectively based on latest definition of IRDA.

The role of LIC in enhancing rural business would socially be essential but commercially, it would be loss-making endure because LIC's urban share would be snatched by foreign and domestic insurers. The inertia of large-number applies in insurance. The mortality is comparatively lower in urban people than that of rural-people. Cream-people would be insured by private insurers, whereas the inferior stuff would be left to the LIC. It would cause deterioration in rural business. The spirit would not enhance for social-upliftment because profit is the index of achievement for which every insurer would aspire their functions and policies.

Development of New Product

People are not attracted with the traditional insurance products (policies) like whole-life, endowment and pure endowment. During 1996-1997, Jeevan Suraksha, Jeevan Sneha, and Jeevan Sanchaya were introduced. Under Jeevan Suraksha plan, retirement income is provided from a chosen date. The policy is with life cover but can be taken without life cover under certain conditions. The policyholder taking policy with life cover provides minimum of 50 per cent of the target pension to spouse on death during the deferment period. On vesting date, the policyholder has the option to receive 25% of the notional cash options in lumps urn and balance in annuity.

Jeevan Sneha: This plan is a without profits money back type plan with the added features of guaranteed addition. Loyalty addition, encashment of survival benefit as and when required. Flexibility to pay premium in advance, in-built accident cover, free insurance cover: for a period of 3 years from the date of first unpaid premium provided at least 2 full years premium have been paid and option to receive pension in lieu of maturity benefits.

Jeeven Sanchaya: This is a without profits money back type plan with provision of loyalty addition and guaranteed addition. Accident benefit will also be granted under the plan with an upper limit of ₹ 5,00,000 in addition to existing limit of ₹ 5,00,000 under other plans.

New Business under Group Insurance

Group insurance provides insurance cover to those persons who are unable to purchase their own policies. It is purchased mainly by different institutions for the benefit of its employees. Many new organisations are approached by the LIC to insure their employees' life under group insurance and superannuation schemes.

New Group Insurance: The number of new members insured under new group insurance has been highest *i.e.,* 34.83 lakhs in 1991-92 when a large number of institutions was attached to this scheme. Since 1993-94, the number of new members under new schemes has been constantly increasing. The annuity amount (sum assured) was ₹ 3837.23 crore in 1991-92. There was no definite trend in the business of group insurance, but it is expected to increase to ₹ 4000.0 crore under 20 lakh policies in 1999-2000 and ₹ 4200.0 crore under 21 lakh policies in 2004-2005.

New Group Superannuation Scheme: The popularity of pension schemes are increasing rapidly. LIC has take some of its efforts in this direction, but it is negligible. The new members covered under group superannuation scheme has been less than a lakh during 1990-91-1995-96. It has increased slightly to 1.25 lakhs in 1996-97 and is expected go upto 2.00 lakh by 2005. It is not encouraging sign. LIC has to effort hard in this direction. The minimum expected annuity of ₹ 200.00 crore has to be crossed by 2005. However, considering the late entry of LIC in this field, the progress is comparable with other private insurers.

Table 39.3A New Business Under Group Scheme

Year	*New Group Insurance*		*Group Superannuation Scheme*	
	No.of Members (in Lakhs)	*Sum Assured (₹ in Crore)*	*No. of Members (in Lakh)*	*Sum Assured (₹ in Crore)*
1990-91	17.08	3392.05	0.12	5.49
1991-92	34.83	3837.23	0.15	6.78
1992-93	26.4	2923.43	0.28	9.10
1993-94	9.94	2382.77	0.32	11.65
1994-95	10.49	2773.06	0.31	14.85
1995-96	11.77	2657.22	0.75	49.34
1996-97	18.89	3237.59	1.25	78.42
*1999-2000	20.00	4000.00	1.70	150.00
2004-2005	21.00	4200.00	2.00	200.00

*Expected

Table 39.3B New Business Under Group Scheme

Year	*New Group Insurance*		*Group Superannuation Scheme*	
	No.of Members (in Lakhs)	*Sum Assured (₹ in Crore)*	*No. of Members (in Lakh)*	*Sum Assured (₹ in Crore)*
1996-97	18.89	3237.59	1.25	78.42
1997-98	15.80	3692.24	0.33	122.45
1998-99	15.84	3793.93	0.51	80.92
1999-2000	17.59	3571.12	0.64	82.62
2000-2001	14.91	4563.20	0.94	84.35
2001-2002	21.57	6703.08	0.62	92.45
2002-2003	24.91	16707.57	1.09	110.94
2003-2004	44.48	128047.85	1.72	214.90
2004-2005	81.00	117662.56	0.43	82.50
2005-2006				

The new group insurance has increased to ₹ 117662.56 crore covering 81.00 lakh members in 2004-2005. It is more than the expected of ₹ 4200.00 crore covering 21.00 lakh. Similarly Group Insurance has reached to the level of ₹ 214.90 crore as compared to expected of ₹ 50.00 crore although it has declined to ₹ 82.50 crore in 2004-2005.

The group business of LIC has increased faster than the expected. It reveals that the prospects of insurance is very high in India.

Table 39.4A Business in Force (Individual Assurance)

Year	*In India*		*Out of India*		*Total*	
	No. of Policies (in lakhs)	*Sum Assured & Bonus (₹ in crore)*	*No. of Policies (in lakhs)*	*Sum Assured & Bonus (₹ in crore)*	*No. of Policies (in lakhs)*	*Sum Assured & Bonus (₹ in crore)*
1990-91	455.08	1,18,651	0.60	528	455.68	1,19,179
1991-92	508.63	1,45,929	0.63	748	509.26	1,46,677
1992-93	566.12	1,77,268	0.67	852	566.79	1,78,120
1993-94	608.00	2,07,601	0.73	1,018	608.73	2,08,619
1994-95	654.52	2,53,333	0.77	1,239	655.29	2,54,572
1995-96	708.78	2,94,336	0.82	1,422	709.60	2,95,758
1996-97	776.60	3,43,018	0.84	1,601	777.50	3,44,619
1999-2000	950.00	4,50,000	1.10	2,200	951.10	4,52,200
2004-2005	1200.00	700,000	4.00	6,000	1204.00	7,06,000

*Expected

Table 39.4B Business in force (Individual Assurance)

Year	In India		Out of India		Total	
	No. of Policies (in lakhs)	Sum Assured & Bonus (₹ in crore)	No. of Policies (in lakhs)	Sum Assured & Bonus (₹ in crore)	No. of Policies (in lakhs)	Sum Assured & Bonus (₹ in crore)
1996-97	776.60	3,43,018	0.84	1,601	777.50	3,44,619
1997-98	849.15	398959	0.88	1889	850.03	400748
1998-99	916.37	457435	0.89	1766	917.26	459201
1999-2000	1012.99	534589	0.90	1862	1013.89	536451
2000-2001	2230.24	643241	0.87	1801	1131.11	645042
2001-2002	1257.89	809170	0.87	1847	1258.76	811017
2002-2003	1387.88	954501	0.90	2174	1388.77	956675
2003-2004	1539.21	925033	0.93	2039	1540.15	927072
2004-2005	1629.51	1029839	1.00	2213	1630.51	1032053
2005-2006						

The individual business in force has increased to ₹ 1032053 crore under 1630.51 policies in 2004-2005 whereas the expected business was ₹ 706000 under 1204.00 policies in the same year. It is realised that the real business have always been higher than the expected business the prospects of insurance business is very high.

Table 39.5A Business in Force (Group Insurance)

Year	New Group Insurance		Group Superannuation Scheme	
	No.of Members (in Lakhs)	Sum Assured (₹ in crore)	No. of Members (in lakh)	Amount of Annuities per Annum (₹ in crore)
1990-91	169.57	30,501.57	2.43	253.12
1991-92	189.53	32,973.46	2.54	301.77
1992-93	212.54	43,086.83	2.69	358.93
1993-94	227.31	46,742.95	3.14	403.51
1994-95	241.88	51,034.1	3.54	427.66
1995-96	246.49	64,651.54	4.19	483.05
1996-97	238.97	64,606.60	5.54	545.59
*1999-2000	270.00	81,000.00	7.00	700.00
*2004-2005	250.00	1,18,000.00	14.70	1,470.00

* Expected

Table 39.5B Business in Force (Group Insurance)

Year	New Group Insurance		Group Superannuation Scheme	
	No.of Members (in Lakhs)	Sum Assured (₹ in crore)	No. of Members (in lakh)	Amount of Annuities per Annum (₹ in crore)
1996-97	238.97	64606.60	5.54	545.59
1997-98	245.22	74798.75	6.71	682.84
1998-99	234.85	77918.65	7.54	815.96

(Contd.)

1999-2000	234.93	76384.53	8.09	971.15
2000-2001	236.68	89326.19	8.84	1137.72
2001-2002	247.19	100597.64	9.80	1271.94
2002-2003	240.99	124312.26	10.86	1488.98
2003-2004	252.46	143398.20	12.34	1705.05
2004-2005	306.50	136286.92	12.73	1916.64
2005-2006				

The group insurance business in force was ₹ 136286.92 crore for 306.50 Lakhs members in 2004-2005, and superannuation was ₹ 1916.64 crore covering 12.73 lakh members on the other hand the expected business was ₹ 118.000.00 crore for 250.00 lakhs members of group insurance and ₹ 1470.0 crore for 14.70 lakhs members of group superannuation scheme. It is very clear that the real business has been enhaving faster than the expected. It was also correct in 1999-2000.

Business-in-Force

Business-in-force has been constantly increasing alongwith bonus amount. It has been analysed under individual assurance and group insurance during last decade of 20th century.

Individual Assurance: Business-in-force (individual assurances) has increased from ₹ 1,19,179 crore in 1990-91 to ₹ 3,44,619 crore in 1996-97. It is expected that the sum assured and bonus would be ₹ 4,50,000 crore in 1999-2000 and ₹ 7,00,000 in 2004-2005 under 950 lakh policies and 1200 lakh policies respectively in India. Business outside India is not very encouraging. Number of policies would be expected to go up to 4.00 lakh for ₹ 6000 crore sum assured in 2004-2005. Thus, the total business in force has increased to ₹ 706000 crore. It is the minimum amount expected to be achieved in the beginning of 21st century. If LIC is unable to achieve the expected amount of business in business, its effectiveness is not praiseworthy.

Group Insurance: Business-in-force (group insurance) has increased from ₹ 30,501.57 crore in 1990-91 to ₹ 64,66.60 crore in 1996-97. Number of members increased from 169.51 lakh to 238.97 lakh during the period, which is expected to be 350.00 lakh in 2005. It is the minimum expected business that ₹ 1,18,000 crore would be in 2005. If LIC is unable to achieve that much, it would be a failure in this field. Group insurance is the cheapest form of insurance available to people. It is based on term insurance.

Group Superannuation Scheme: The amount of annuities has increased from ₹ 253.12 in 1990-91 to ₹ 545,59 in 199.6-97 and is expected to go upto ₹ 1470 crore in 2005. Similarly the number of members is expected to upto 14.70 lakh in 2005 although it was 2.43 lakh in 1990-91. LIC must increase its business at faster rate as there is enough scope of superannuation business in India.

Table 39.6A Lapsation of Policies

Year of New Business	*Percentage of Net Lapses to Mean Life Insurance Business in Force*	*New Lapse Ratio at Mean Duration of New Business*				
		0	1	2	3	Total
1990-91	6.0	0.5	13.5	8.0	3.4	25.4
1991-92	6.1	0.9	14.5	8.9	3.5	27.8
1992-93	5.9	1.0	15.6	8.9	3.8	29.3
1993-94	6.3	0.6	17.0	8.5	2.6	28.7
1994-95	6.1	0.6	17.0	8.0		
1995-96	6.4	0.9	15.6			
1996-97	5.1	1.1				
1999-2004	5.5					25.0
2004-2005	4.0					20.00

Note: Mean duration is year of lapse minus year of New business.

Table 39.6B Lapsation of Policies

Year of New Business	Percentage of Net Lapses to Mean Life Insurance Business in Force	New Lapse Ratio at Mean Duration of New Business				
		0	1	2	3	Total
1996-97	5.1	1.1	16.3	9.4	2.4	29.2
1997-98	5.0	0.8	16.4	9.8	2.3	29.3
1998-99	4.9	0.1	17.9	11.2	2.0	31.2
1999-2000	5.1	0.7	16.2	7.2	2.4	26.5
2000-2001	4.9	0.8	16.0	8.7		
2001-2002	5.5	0.7	16.0	8.7		
2002-2003	5.5	0.7	15.3			
2003-2004						
2004-2005						
2005-2006						

The reposition of policies has shown dismall results as the total lapses for three years in 1998-99 had louched the English figure of 31.2 per cent of new business. It was 26.5 per cent of new business in 1999-2000 although the expected was 25.5 per cent. The per cent of Net lapses to mean life insurance in force has not been declining. It remain constantal 5.5 per cen.

Table 39.7A Valuation Results

(In crores of ₹)

Year	Valuation Surplus	Shares of Central Govt.	Taxes Paid to Govt.	Reversionary Bonus on Sum Assured	
				Whole-life	Endowment
1990-91	1800	90.00	254.90	80	64
1991-92	2108	105.41	326.60	96	75
1992-93	2368	118.42	407.15	96	75
1993-94	2803	140.15	431.92	96	75
1994-95	3219	160.94	508.98	96	75
1995-96	3434	171.69	582.28	95	78
1996-97	3967	198.35	585.06	95	78
1999-2000	5000	250.00	750.00	100	90
2004-2005	7000	350.00	1050.00	125	100

* Expected

Table 39.7B Valuation Results

Year	Valuation surplus ₹	Shares of central Govt. ₹	Taxes Paid to Govt. ₹
1996-97	3967	198.35	585.06
1997-98	4673	233.64	563.06
1998-99	5300	265.00	726.96
1999-2000	6333	316.55	758.62
2000-2001	7613	380.66	709.65
2001-2002	8667	433.25	868.17
2002-2003	9767	488.10	1258.62

Contd...

2003-2004	10987	548.13	1506.28
2004-2005	13952	696.60	5365.16
2005-2006			

The total surplus has increased to ₹ 13952 crore in 2004-2005 as ₹ 7000 expected. It is much more than the expected figure. Similarly the share of central government and taxes paid to government have been much higher than expected. It shows that LIC has worked hard for the development of insurance business.

Lapsation of Policies

The new business increased fastly but some of them did not continue for the stipulated period. They are known as lapsed policies. It should be analysed systematically. It reveals that the percentage of net lapses to mean Life Insurance Business in force has gone down from 6.0 in 1990-91 to 5.1 in 1996-97 and is expected to go down to 5.5. in 1999-2000 and 4.0 in 2004-2005. The net lapse ratio at mean duration has gone to 17.0 percent of new business during one year of new business. The total amount of percentage of percentage to new business has been 25.4. percent in 1990-91 which has gone upto 29.3 percent in 1992-93. It reveals that more than one fourth of new business did not continue for its term. It is failure of LIC and increase discredit and loss of expenses of business. If it is not very serious of its business loss the private insurers would procure higher amount of business. However, it is not correct to believe that private insurers would not face lapsation problems. In any case, it is great drawback of LIC's business.

Valuation of Results

The valuation surplus of LIC has increased from ₹ 1800 crore in 1990-91 to ₹ 3967 crore in 1996-97 and is expected to go upto ₹ 3000 crore in 2004-2005. The share of government is 5 percent of surplus. Thus, it should be ₹ 350 crore in 2005 and tax amount would be ₹ 1050 crores in that year. Reversionary bonus is expected to increase to 125 per thousand sum assured on whole life policies, and 100 per thousand sum assured on endowment policies. The LIC must meet the expectation of people at higher rate because the sum assured is highly hit with inflation. A person insured for 10 lakh will not get ₹ 10 lakh in real term after 20 years. Although long term activities/ investment/ agreement is bound to be hit of inflation, LIC has to be very careful and the bonus rate is to be increased for the benefit of policy and compete with banking deposits:

Working Results

Working results is calculated by finding the life insurance fund which is equal to total income minus total outgo. Total income includes premium income, income from investments and miscellaneous. Premium income is denoted by first year premium and renewal premium as well as single premium. Total outgo includes commission etc., to agents, salary and other benefits to employees and other expenses. The transfer to reserve and surplus share paid to Government are also included under outgo. The comparison of real work-up results with the expected in 1999-2000 and 2004-2005 has revealed the outstanding performance of LIC.

Table 39.8 Working Results

(In crores of ₹)

Year	*Total Income over*	*Total Outgo*	*Excess of Income over outgo*	*Fund at the end*	*Fund % increase over Previous year*
1990-91	8,517.98	3,588.85	4,929.13	28,400.91	21.00
1991-92	10,690.69	4,400.27	6,290.42	34,691.39	22.15
1992-93	12,244.23	5,937.33	6,306.90	40,998.29	18.18
1993-94	15,212.31	6,544.78	8,667.53	49,665.82	21.14
1994-95	18,102.32	7,789.24	10,313.08	59,978.90	20.76
1995-96	22,046.76	9,24,5.60	12,801.16	72,780.06	21.34

Contd...

1996-97	25,933.09	10,841.54	14,979.90	87,759.96	20.58
1999-2000	44729.6	18101.93	26,627.67	1,54,043.73	20.92%
2004-2005	48460.70	63885.54	3,85,639.07	1,12,346.24	19.86%

Table 39.9 Expense Ratio, Interest and Claims Ratio

Year	*Expense Ratio Overall Expense Ratio*	*Renewal Ratio*	*Interest Earned Rate of interest Realised on Mean Life insurance Fund*	*Ratio of outstanding claims to claims Payable*
	%	%	%	%
1990-91	23.24	3.52	11.44	5.51
1991-92	22.27	3.49	11.95	5.50
1992-93	22.89	5.37	11.56	5.27
1993-94	21.83	4.95	12.43	4.86
1994-95	21.39	6.32	12.21	5.26
1995-96	20.79	7.00	12.29	5.99
1996-97	21.43	7.09	12.39	5.32
1999-2000	21.16	5.63	12.08	4.10
2004-2005	16.57		9.93	0.80

The excess of income over outgo has been ₹ 4,929.13 crores in 1990-91 and ₹ 14,979.90 crore in 1996-97 which re expected to go upto ₹ 30,000 crore in 2004-2005. From the total funds every year, claims amount are also deducted. The total fund at the end of 1996-97 was ₹ 87,759.96 crore which is expected to go upto ₹ 1,75,000 crore in 2004-2005. The corporation has to accumulate that amount by 2005 for investment. The LIC investment is made in social and economic projects.

Expense Ratio: Overall expense ratio has gone down from 23.24% of total premium income in 1990-91 to 21.43% in 1996-97 and expected to go down to 20.00% in 2000. Renewal ratio is increasing from 3.52% in 1990-91 to 7.00% in 1996-97 and expected to go upto 10.0% in 2005. It reveals that LIC is unable to restrain renewal rates, while some improvements are expected in overall expense ratio. But real experience showed at LIC has curtailed its expanses.

Rate of Interest Realised: The rate of interest increased from 11.44% in 1990-91 to 12.39% in 1996-97 and expected to go upto 13.5% in 2004-2005. It reveals that LIC is able to earn more interest. The rate in 2004-2005 is outcome or market positive.

Ratio of Outstanding Claims: The percentage of outstanding claims to claims payable has been rounding from the lowest 4.86% to 5.99%. It is expected to be at 5.00% in 2000 and 4.50% in 2005. Thus the outstanding claims have not been improved and could not go down to 4.00 per cent. It has improved to the label of 6.80 per cent on 2004-2005.

Investment Operations: The total Investment has increased from ₹ 24,899.65 crore in 1990-91 to ₹ 77,935.19 crore in 1996-97 and is expected to go upto ₹ 1,25,000.00 crore in 2005. It shows that LIC has taken serious step for socio-economic development of the country. The investment has gone to 84.58 percent in 1996-97 in Public Sector, whereas investment in private sector has declined from 14.00% to 12.93% in 1990-91 and 1996-97 respectively. It reveals that investment in public sector is given more importance. Public Sector enterprises are engaged in socio-economic development of India. Many infrastructure development projects have been taken up by public sector. The investment in private sector is expected to increase as a result of private insurers. The trend of investment would reverse in next century *i.e.,* private investment would increase as compared to investment in public sector. The real investment has increased to ₹ 4,13,800.00 crores in 2004-2005 as against the expected investment of ₹ 115.00. It reveals that the LIC profound excellently.

Table 39.10 Investment Operations

Year	Public ₹ in Crore	Sector % to Total	Cooperative ₹ in Crore	Sector % to Total	Private ₹ in Crore	Sector % to Total	Total ₹ in Crore
1990-91	19,979.76	80.2	1,444.47	5.80	3,475.12	14.0	24,899.65
1991-92	24,457.27	80.4	1,562.63	5.10	4,382.51	14.5	34,402.41
1992-93	28,983.24	79.8	1,657	56 4.60	5,681.31	15.6	36,322.11
1993-94	36,246.48	82.10	17,106.06	3.90	6,199.01	14.00	44,161.55
1994-95	44,318.93	82.87	1,793.05	3.35	7,367.49	13.78	53,479.47
1995-96	54,245.63	84.63	1,857.63	2.90	7,996.52	12.47	64,099.78
1996-97	65,917.41	84.58	1,938.98	2.49	10,078.80	12.93	77,935.19
1999-2000	1,17,058.95	84.20	2,129.31	1.53	19,843.89	14.27	1,39,032.15
2004-2005							4,13,200.45

Table 39.11 Productivity

Year As on 31st March	Number of Active Agents	Average Business (₹) per Agent
1991	4,14,820	6,78,344
1992	4,64,505	6,90,293
1993	4,95,745	7,25,309
1994	5,24,427	7,97,324
1995	5,19,504	10,63,101
1996	5,13,897	10,08,286
1997	5,33,133	10,64,284
2000	6,83,190	13,28,292
2005	10,41,737	16,97,997

Productivity of Agents

Productivity of agents is calculated dividing total new business (individuals) by number of active agents. The average business per agent has increased from ₹ 6,78,344 in 1990-91 to ₹ 10,84,284 in 1996-97 and is expected to touch ₹ 15,00,000 in 2005 as the number of active agents is expected to go up to 7,00,000. The technological improvements will enhance their productivity. It is, therefore, more than the expected new businesses.

Computerisation has facilitated many branch offices of LIC to upgrade the services. Many agents have modernised their activities through application of computer. The agents have modernised their activities through application of computer. The agents' productivity is expected to increase in coming years. The productively of insurance agent has been ₹ 16,97,997 as compared to expected ₹ 15,00,000 in 2004-2005. It discloses the increased producing by of LIC. Business is expected to increase in future.

Table 39.12 Social Responsibilities

(In crores of ₹)

Year	*Socially Oriented Investment* (₹)	*New Lives Insured under Social Security Group Schemes*	*Loans to Housing Schemes* (₹)
1990-91	2,705.78	4,21,113	323.13
1991-92	3,189.58	19,42,913	456.52
1992-93	3,196.82	15,17,466	636.14
1993-94	8,19,9.00	7,01,207	548.30
1994-95	7,927.40	2,94,090	536.90
1995-96	9,535.59	3,96,326	733.00
1996-97	11,794.95	9,91,327	940.50
*1999-2000	26,026.56	49,49,987	1,651.10
*2004-2005	67,209.00	81,43,000	7,424.00

Social Responsibilities

The social responsibilities have been analysed under investment in social schemes, new lives insured under social security group schemes and loans to housing schemes.

Socially Oriented Investment: The socially oriented investment has increased from ₹ 2,705.78 crore in 1990-91 to ₹ 11,794.95 crore in 1996-97 and is expected to increase to ₹ 30,000 crore by 2005. These investments help to improve the quality of life of the people at large through improvement of basic amenities like potable water, drainage, housing, electrification and transport. In 2004-2005, it has been more than expected.

New Lives Insured under Social Security Group Schemes: New lives insured under social security group schemes has increased from 4,21,113 in 1990-91 to 9,91,327 in 1996-97 and expected to go up 28,00,000 by 2005. LIC made considerable efforts for creating greater awareness and benefits provided under Landless Agricultural Labourers (LALG- 1) and IRDP Group Insurance Scheme. The accidental death cover has been increased and Disability benefits have been included under Social Security Group Insurance with effect from 16th-October, 1995. In case of death or total permanent disability due to accident (including loss of two limbs of use) an amount of ₹ 25.00 is payable and in case of loss of limb of use, due to an accident, a sum of ₹ 12,500 is payable under these schemes irrespective of basic sum assured. These additional benefits have been provided from Social Security Fund without charging any additional premium. The performance of LIC in 2004-2005 have been for table than expected.

GENERAL INSURANCE

General insurance business in India came into hands of public sector under the caption of General Insurance Corporation of India and its four subsidiaries viz., National Insurance Company Ltd., New India Assurance Company Ltd., Oriental Insurance Company Ltd. and United India Insurance Company Ltd. in 1972. The prospects of General Insurance business is analysed under Gross Direct Premium Income, Investment Income, Profit After Tax, underwriting experience, Crop Insurance, Rural Insurance and foreign business.

Gross Direct Premium Income

The gross direct premium income has been analysed under fire insurance, marine insurance, miscellaneous insurance and total.

Fire Insurance: The amount of gross direct premium income in fire insurance has increased from ₹ 683 crore in 1990-91 to ₹ 1,997 crore in 1997-98 and is expected to go upto ₹ 3,500 crore in 2005. The business of fire insurance is comparatively better than marine insurance but better than miscellaneous insurance.

Marine Insurance: The gross direct premium income of marine insurance has increased from ₹ 524 crore in 1990-91 to ₹ 1,055 crore in 1997-98 and is expected to increase upto ₹ 1,550 crore in 2004-2005. It is very slow progress of marine insurance.

Miscellaneous Insurance: The gross direct premium income of miscellaneous insurance has increased from ₹ 1,706 crore in 1990-91 to ₹ 5,034 crore in. 1997-98 and is expected to rise up to ₹ 9,000 crore in 2004-2005. The insurance of motor vehicles and other accident insurance have become compulsory. So the miscellaneous insurance has increased faster than those of fire insurance and marine insurance. The general insurance in India is not progressing as expected.

Total Insurance: The gross direct premium income of all the insurance has increased form ₹ 2,913 crore in 1990-91 to ₹ 8,086 crore in 1997-98 and is expected to increase to ₹ 14,050 crore in 2004-2005. The increase of gross direct premium has increased by more than three times which would increase by more than five times during 1990-2005. The gross direct premium of General Insurance has been significantly higher than the expected ones.

Table 39.13 Gross Direct Premium Income.

(In crores of Rupees)

Year	*Fire Insurance*	*Marine Insurance*	*Miscellaneous Insurance*	*Total*
1990-91	683	524	1,706	2,913
1991-92	839	659	2,005	3,503
1992-93	988	803	2,279	4,070
1993-94	1.164	875	2,727	4,766
1994-95	1,323	852	3,096	5,271
1995-96	1,578	999	3,800	6,377
1996-97	1,800	1,021	4,527	7,348
1997-98	1,997	1,055	5,034	8,086
*1999-2000	2,300	1,250	6,000	9,550
*2004-2005	3,500	1,550	9,000	14,050
2004-2005				51,554.50
2005-2006				57,846.49

*Expected

Table 39.14 Investment Income and Profit After Tax

(Rupees in crores)

	Investment Income (Gross)	*Profit After Tax*
1990-91	566	334
1991-92	752	428
1992-93	859	503
1993-94	957	670
1994-95	1,150	377
1995-96	1,475	551
1996-97	1,687	719
1997-98	1,978	1,255
1999-2000	2,400	1,500
2004-2005	3,500	2,300

The gross direct premium is indication of the insurance business, but it does not increase so fastly as expected by public.

Investment Income

Investment income of General Insurance Business has increased from ₹ 566 crore in 1990-91 to ₹ 1978 crore in 1979-98 and is expected to go upto ₹ 3500 crore in 2004-2005. It shows that general insurance business has increased its investment income by more than two times during 1990-91 to 1997-98 and by about six times during 1990-91 to 2004-2006. It reveals that the investment income has increased faster than the gross direct premium income.

Table 39.15 Underwriting Experience

(Income of ₹)

	Net Premium	*Net incurred claims*	*Expenses commission and other outgo*	*Increased in unexpired risk reserves*	*Underwriting Profit (+) Loss (–)*
1990-91	2,742	1,898 (69.2%)	652 (23.8%)	310 (11.3%)	–118 (4.3%)
1991-92	3,450	2,303 (66.8%)	802 (23.2%)	422 (6.2%)	– 77 (2.2%)
1992-93	3,868	2,839 (73.4%)	908 (23.5%)	240 (12.2%)	–119 (3.1%)
1993-94	4,427	3,050 (68.9%)	983 (22.2%)	312 (70%)	+ 82 (1.9%)
1994-95	4,879	4,289 (87.9%)	1,070 (21.9%)	225 (4.6 %)	–705 (14.4%)
1995-96	5,956	4,427 (74.3%)	1,567 (26.3%)	608 (10.2%)	– 646 (10.8%)
1996-97	6,731	5,105 (75.8%)	1,900 (28.2%)	357 (5.3%)	– 628 (7.3%)
1997-98	7,357	5,625 (76.5%)	1,799 (24.4%)	317 (4.3%)	–384 (5.2)
1998-99					–200 (4.0%)
1999-2000					–100 (2.0%)
2004-2005					

Profit After Tax

The profit after tax increased from ₹ 334 crore in 1990-91 to ₹ 1,255 crore in 1997-98 and is expected to increase to ₹ 2,300 crore by 2004-2005. Thus, the profit has increased faster than the investment income and gross direct premium income. The profit is expected to increase by more than six times to 2004-2005.

Underwriting Experience

Net premium of general insurance business has increased from ₹ 2,742 crore in 199-91 to ₹ 7,357 crore in 1997-98. Expenses of management have also increased from ₹ 652 crore in 1990-91 to ₹ 1,799 crore in 1997-98. Although unexpired risk reserves have also increased but in a slow rate. The underwriting loss has gone upto ₹ 705 crore in 1994-95 after getting profit of ₹ 82 crore in 1993-94.

All the performances of general insurance business have been discouraging. With the entry of private insurers, the performances of GIC and its subsidiaries are expected to go up because of competition and availability of measurement parameter. If private insurers enter for profit, why not GIC and its subsidiaries should earn profit. The causes of profit and the diagnose of losses reveal the points of modifications.

Crop Insurance

Crop insurance scheme was implemented in India since 1985. State Government is required to share the premium and claim in the ratio of 2 : 1. At present, the scheme is implemented in 15 states and 2 union territories. It is available for crop loans in selected areas for selected crops. During 1997-98 51.35 lakh farmers and 6.82 lakh farmers were covered for a sum insured of ₹ 2,230.74 crore and ₹ 322.37 crore in kharif 1997 season and Rabi 1997-98 season, respectively. The premium income for the period was ₹ 34.32 crore and, ₹ 5.72 crore for Kharif and Rabi season, respectively.

During 1997-98 season, Experimental Crop Insurance Scheme for non-loa nee small and marginal farmers was implemented in selected 24 districts of 8 states. The premium is totally subsidised for small and marginal, farmers and premium and claims are shared between Centre and State Government in the ratio of 4 : 1. Under this scheme, 4.78 lakh farmers are covered for a sum insured of ₹ 172 crore in 14 district of 5 states.

Rural Insurance

During 1997-98, new schemes have been devised such as Foetus Insurance Scheme and the Calf Heifer Rearing Insurance Scheme as recommended by the Task Force Committee on Cattle Insurance constituted by the Government of India. Farmers Package Policy was introduced to cover all the assets of the farmers under one policy. Aquaculture Insurance Scheme is also introduced for the benefit of rural population.

Foreign Business

GIC and its subsidiaries operate foreign business. During 1997-98, direct overseas operations of the four subsidiary companies produced a gross premium income of ₹ 382.95 crore as against ₹ 367.05 crore in 1996-97. Net claims amounted ₹ 245.41 crore during 1997-98. Foreign business of GIC and its subsidiaries is expected to increase as a result of foreign insurers.

GROWING ECONOMY AND INSURANCE

With the introduction of globalisation and privatisation, insurance industry in India is grooving more than 15% per annum. It is second highest after IT industry. The GDP in expected to grow by 10.00 per cent agriculture by 4 per cent and industry by 12.00. The insurance industry is developing in number, quality and class fication. The population and per capita income have been instrument for the growth of the industry. The quality life of people demands distills free lining. Insurance has increased several quality products to meet their requirement the different classes of prospects have started demanding deferent types of products. The company which is expert in diversification of its products and CRM can develop leap and found. The insurance intermediation has become a full time qualified profession. Professionally qualified agents of insurance can earn more than a doctor, engineer, CA and other professional expects.

Now, people are approaching insurance agents for their financial advises rater than business. Insurance in started to be bought by the people rater than previous thinking of bold. People are seeking now best publication for their lives, health, property, business and economic activities. IT and IRDA have asked agents to serve people better. The policyholders are getting more satisfaction today as compared to past year-experiences. Telecommunication has helped people to develop themselves through insurance. The business of insurance is expected to grow more than 18 per cent annum in future.

40

PRIVATISATION OF INSURANCE INDUSTRY

Public Enterprises in any country cannot perform all the economic and business activities efficiently. Even in a socialist country, public enterprises in all the fields cannot discharge their full responsibilities. Complete governmentalisation or nationalisation will lead towards serfdom or anarchism. In absence of free will personal interests; the economic activities will not provide adequate and qualitative production. This is the reason that some troubles have started in some parts of the USSR and China. In Indian conditions where we have adopted mixed economy, expecting too much from public enterprises will distort the economy and ultimately will lead towards wastage of precious resources. Supporting and subsidising by the Government indirectly punish the tax-payers and the country-men. Therefore, it is the high time to recast our Industrial Policy and should consider the productivity and efficiency as criteria to continue a particular unit whether public enterprises or private enterprises. The public enterprises cannot be sustained as sacred cow without milk. Similarly, the unscrupulous private enterprises declaring themselves sick cannot be put on ambulance for a longer time. It is a matter of satisfaction that the Government has started taking pragmatic approaches to revive the productivity and efficiency base criteria for the development of an enterprise. The restrictions on utilisation of full capacity by private enterprises are being removed gradually to increase production and productivity of the economy. The public enterprises will have to come at the compative of the private enterprises. If the formers are loosing in the efficiency and productivity criteria, they should be closed down and the private enterprises having more efficiency and productivity should be encouraged to increase production of the economy. The industrial policy that public enterprises provide more employment opportunities although production is nominal should be changed to bring them under productivity criterion. Providing employment for the sake of employment is adding fuel to the fire of inflation any trend in the economy because the productivity is very low. The Government decision to denationalise certain production undertaking is welcome step because they remain idle without production or very small production. Other political parties should realise the gravity of productivity and discard the public enterprises for the sake of political system.

The Government cannot perform all the functions with equal efficiency. The regulatory role, promotional role, entrepreneurial role and planing role have not been fully discharged by Government. Barring few enterprises as envisaged in the Industrial Policy 1956, rest of the public enterprises should be returned back to the private institutions if their productivities are not improved to the level of a private enterprise. The government should concentrate more on regulatory, and planning roles. The entrepreneurial role should be confined only to those areas where the private entrepreneurs are hesitant and cannot discharge their functions satisfactorily at national level. Non-profitable business activities, defence, transport, education, communication and such types of public activities should be undertaken by the Government. W.A. Levis observed: "The nationalisation of industry is not essential to planning, a government can do nearly anything it wants to do by way of controlling industry without resorting to nationalisation". Neither state monopoly nor private monopoly is desirable in the economy. The competition, being the backbone of the productivity should be encouraged to promote the economy. The competition may be between and amongst the public and private enterprises. The productivity and efficiency are the important criteria to permit the continuation of an enterprise. The public enterprises in some areas performed better than the private enterprises and, therefore, should be permitted to continue to accelerate the growth of the economy. On the other hand, many public enterprises are wasting public money because of continuous loss and less production. Such enterprises should be handed over to the competent private companies. On the reverse, some private enterprises are at loss and declaring themselves sick. They should be taken over by the Government companies of the area or by the private houses as the circumstances and nature of the business may be prevailing at that time. The privatisation may be done after analysing the efficiency of the organisation and their role in the economy. The problem of public enterprises, inefficiency of public enterprises and efficiency of private enterprises, are considered under privatisation and efficiency.

Problems of Public Enterprises

A large number of public enterprises and their size and variety have given complex problem. Some of them are on account of procedural defects and too much rigidity in their operation, but many problems are inherent due to the basic tenets of the public enterprises. They lack flexibility, effectiveness and efficiency of private enterprises. Over the last decades, the experiences of public enterprises particularly of departmental undertakings have been very discouraging. The control over performance and routine operations have been too rigid or too timid to yield higher productivity. The functioning of government companies have been better than those of other forms of public enterprises but they could not excel the private enterprises. It was considered that the public corporations could perform better than, other public enterprises but many corporations did not comply the expectations. The political parties and government hindered routine functioning of many public enterprises. Frequent changes of top management and alterations of policies and procedures have adversely affected their operations. The sense of belongingness which is the soul and spirit of success of any business is absent at top, middle and lower level of management in public enterprises. The workers of public enterprises are more reckless than those of private enterprises. The sense of belongingness is not common in many of the socialist countries, whereas the Japanese organisations have excelled on this pattern as the result of ringi (family) system of employment. The work-culture of Japan is being imitated by the U.S.A. The public enterprises are least suitable in the political upheavals. Many organisations are facing interferences by the Government. Overlapping and absence of power and authority are served at several levels.

The Government has modified the appointment policy recently. Instead of appointing politically supported bureaucrats, business experts are appointed at the top. The productivity improved consequently. Many committees have recommended that the Board of Directors should consist technical skill, representatives of labour and personnel management, financial talent and management experts. But, the Government has not paid full attention towards such suggestions. The appointment of Members of Parliament and civil servants are considered unhealthy and full of political backing which creates groupism in the organisation. It is also suggested that full time managing director should be appointed to manage that concern effectively and efficiently.

Decentralisation of power should be implemented to avoid the problems of overlapping and fraud. Recently, postal saving accounts have experienced a large number of fraud, corruption and red tapism because of too much centralisation and dual functioning of the operation. The branch as well as head post offices are maintaining account-books without entrusting responsibility to any one. On the other hand, banking operation because of decentralisation of power, authority and responsibility are functioning properly. The postal saving accounts should be transferred to banking systems to avoid the problems of public and retain the goodwill of post offices. The suggestions of

Administrative Reform Commissions have not been fully complied to regulate and manage the public enterprises. During the last three decades many public enterprises are running at loss and wasting public money in several forms. These organisations should be handed over to the private houses. The Government can exercise control on them. The regulatory and administrative functions of the Government should be strengthened to control the business activities. The Government should not take up entrepreneurial operations where it cannot function profitably and economically. Giving the picture of inefficiency and inactiveness, it cannot control the business to improve efficiency and effectiveness. The inefficiency and failure at business-front reflects the efficiency of the Government at large. It is in the interest of the nation and the public individually to denationalise sick government organisations.

The appointment policy of many public enterprises are defective. Redundant staff and scarcity are observed in many cases. Proper planning and recruitment is absent in these organisations. Labour relations in several public enterprises are not congenial inspite of maximum amenities and facilities to the labour. The productivity of labour in public enterprises is lower than their counterpart in private enterprise, whereas the salaries and amenities are higher in the former case than that in the latter case. The public enterprises in the name of socialistic approach adopting no profit no loss have resorted the practices of concealing low productivity. Many organisations fix their prices arbitrarily and at the instructions of the Government. It is observed that their pricing policies are no cheaper than those of private enterprises. The depending on competition and pricing systems help promote rational allocation of scarce resources, optimal utilisation of resources and accelerate the growth of economy. The retained earnings should be encouraged to strengthen the enterprisi but in absence of adequate profit, these organisations are depending on Government for financial strain and expansion. In any case the productivity cannot be at the altar of the socialistic pattern of the society. If any concern has not reached even the level of break even after 10 years of establishment, it should be handed over to competent business houses. The cost of production in several public enterprises is very high because of improper use of resources and absence of competition. The enterprises are left free at the cost-front. They are not personally liable for the higher cost of production. The Parliamentarians can be satisfied on this or that pretext if the performances of the public enterprises are below the standard. Comparing the performances of public enterprises with those of private enterprises is considered traditional approach as well as pre-capitalism. But this is the only criteria whereby the public enterprises performance can be judged to reveal their efficiencies and inefficiencies. Monopolistic protection either to public enterprises or private enterprises will lead only towards wastage of public money and exploitation of their dire needs. Therefore, the private enterprises should be left free to utilise their full capacity and public enterprises should be accountable if they do not come up to the standard. The techniques of financial control should be exercised by the public enterprises. The financial manager should be given the power of using the funds on business-exigencies rather than on the bureaucratic system. The problems of too much unnecessary reporting and auditing have obstructed the proper functioning of public enterprises. The government should realise that public enterprises should not be allowed to function for the sake of political motto. The national funds should be used economically and effectively. These enterprises should be given the autonomy of using the business principles to prove themselves worthy of continuation in the society. If a public enterprise after 5-10 years has not achieved the break-even-level, it should be handed over to some private organisation with the condition that they will bring them at profitable stage within specified time.

Insurance industry along with other financial institutions has been constantly under pressure of privatisation without going into the grass-root of the problems and its potential consequences. Many committees and government agencies have been arguing for privatisation, denationalisation and permitting foreign institutions to conduct insurance business in India. Insurance industry was nationalised at the behest and considerate thoughts of devoted and honest leaders. They have observed the increasing ills of private insurers and scope of socio-economic development with the help of insurance institutions.

In 1956, the then Finance Minister, Mr. Deshmukh had stated, "the misuse of power, position and privilege that we have reason to believe occurs under existing conditions in one of the most compelling reasons that have influenced us in deciding to nationalise life insurance". Thus, they have foreseen the misuse of power by the private insurers. The motives of private insurers have not changed today and will not change in future too because they work for self interest and maximisation of wealth. While putting arguments for privatisation at present, one should see whether the objectives of nationalisation have been fulfilled. If it is not fulfilled, arguments for privatisation may be accepted with the assumption that the privatisation would remedy all the problems and help succeed the nation to achieve its socio-economic development. One should not forget that insurance is not purely commercial industry, it is socialinstitution, too. Government should provide social security, safety and welfare to people of India. It is not possible for a government to achieve all these objectives at a time while carrying the responsibility of governance; it should entrust these responsibilities to an institution of national character. Basic duty of a Government is to protect its people from any sort of disturbances and invasion. If the social security and welfare is left to a national institution which can survive and grow on its own while providing social security and welfare to people; it would be an appropriate proposition for the government rather than leaving it to private hands who care for profits and appropriation of funds.

The government while having a nationalised insurance institution serves both the purposes at a time, *i.e.,* governance and social welfare an security to people. The arguments for privatisation can be judged on the basis of achievements of nationalised insurance institutions, critical analysis of the reports given for liberalisation and privatisation of insurance industry and past practices of private insurers.

Whether Objectives are Fulfilled?

The objectives of nationalisation have been incorporated in the form of corporate objectives of LIC. If the objectives of nationalisation are not fulfilled, whether the private insurers can fulfil those objectives, what can be the next step if both institutions, *i.e.,* the nationalised and private insurers have not achieved the objectives of insurance? These questions are dispassionately analysed.

1. *Rural Insurance*: The nationalisation of life insurance business in 1956 had aimed to spread the gospel of life insurance business in the remote corners of the country. In the word of the then Finance Minister: "The purpose of nationalisation was to see that the gospel of insurance is stored as far and wide as possible so that we reach out beyond the more advanced urban areas well into the hitherto neglected rural areas. Millions of lives in rural areas were left uninsured because the private insurers did not like to carry their business there. Now question arises whether private insurers including foreign companies would like to conduct their business in rural areas. The answer is certainly not because they would not be getting profit there. No private insurer would like to do business on loss. If the government is not agreeing to this logic, then why private airlines are not operating their business in non-remunerative areas. The nationalised institutions are doing satisfactory business in rural areas. They have national mission and performing the business in urban as well as rural areas. The insurance principles, inertia of large number is being followed by LIC and GIC. No private insurer can work longer on national mission to help peoples 'progress and security because they have the main motives of profit-making.' The Life Insurance Corporation has developed corporate objectives. "Spread life insurance much more widely and in particular to the rural areas reaching all insurable persons in the country and providing them adequate financial cover against death at a reasonable cost".

Table 40.1 New Business of LIP

(in crores of Rupees)

Year	*Individual New Business*	*Group Insurance*	*Rural Business*
1955	260.84	—	—
1962-63	745.96	18.33 (1966–67)	233.45 (31.8%)
1984-85	7,088.45	8,409.90	1,569.62 (29.7%)
1994-95	55,468.82	50,651.85	21,571.00 (39.0%)
1997-98	63,617.69(P)	76,619.21	

(P) = Provisional

The rural business was unheard before 1955. After nationalisation, it has increased to ₹ 21,570 crore which was 39.0 percent of individual new business. Rural business of LIC in 1995-96 was 49 lakh policies out of the total 110 lakh policies issued in that year giving rural business to the extent of 45% of total new policies issued. Can anyone think of such achievement by private insurer? Logics are hurled that nonbanking institutions are fetching maximum business from rural areas. It should be analysed from safety and security point of view. The business procured by them are not safe and secure because many non-banking institutions are getting business pressurising the rural people. It should be known that many non-banking institutions are eloping with the money of people. They open an office for some months and then close the office forever after extracting money from the people.

One finds it difficult to understand whether the government is unaware or unable to prevent such nefarious activities. If the government is unable to govern, it should not talk of privatisation or denationalisation of insurance industry. LIC and GIC are national institutions which are working for the nation and people. The LIC has covered a large number of people by insuring them under group insurance otherwise they would have been uninsured on account of low premium paying capacity. The new business under group insurance increased from ₹ 18.33 crore in 1966-67 to ₹ 50,651.43 crore in 1994-95.

Table 40.2 Business of General Insurance

(In crores of Rupees)

Year	*Gross Direct Premium*	*Net Premium*
1971	147.53	127.69
1980	503.00	481.00
1985	1,204.31	1,190.50
1994-95	4,959.43	4,879.43
1997-98	8,086.00	7,357.00

All the four subsidiaries of General Insurance Corporation have tried to procure maximum business for the benefit of people at large. General insurance in rural areas have increased considerably under Personal Accident Social Security amounting more than ₹ 300 crores and Hut Insurance Scheme amounting about ₹ 300 crore. Hit and Run schemes have benefited a large number of beneficiaries.

Life Insurance Corporation of India has formulated corporate objective "Meet the various life insurance needs of the community that would arise in the changing social and economic environment.

The total payment under social security group/schemes amounted more than ₹ 240 crore in 1991-92 and ₹ 550 crore in 1995-96. The LIC and GIC have been working hard to benefit rural people through its branches which have been respectively 2024 and 2997 as, on March 1996.

The second objective of nationalisation of life insurance business was to conduct business with utmost economy as the Finance Minister said, "The business must be conducted with utmost economy and with the full realisation that money belongs to the policyholders. The premium must be no higher than is warranted by strict actuarial consideration". The LIC has accepted the corporate objectives. "Act as trustees of the insured public in their individual and collective capacities. Conduct business with utmost economy and with the fuu realisation that money belongs to the policyholders". The trusteeship principle has been carried by the LIC as it has tried to reduce the expense-ratio.

Table 40.3 Expense Ratios of LIC

Year	*Total Premium Income (in crores of ₹)*	*Overall Expense Ratio*	*Renewal Expense Ratio*
1957	88.65	27.20%	15.89%
1984-85	1,559.33	24.68%	13.92%
1994-95	11,527.80	21.39%	6.32%
1997-98	19,252.07	20.54%	6.00%

The expense ratio which were very high before nationalisation were brought to a lower level in 1995. The overall expense ratio declined from 27.20% In 1957 to 21.35% in 1995 and the renewal expense ratio have come down from 15.89% to 6.32% in the respective years. The corporation would have reduced the expense ratio further had there been complete computerisation. General Insurance Corporation along with its subsidiaries has attempted to reduce the expenses considerably. The benefits of reduced expenses have been given to the policyholders in the form of enhanced bonus and reduced premium. The bonus of life policy per thousand sum assured has increased from ₹ 16 in 1956 to ₹ 86 varying to ₹ 95 in 1996 on whole life policies and ₹ 12.80 in 1952 to ₹ 69 varying to ₹ 78 on endowment policies. The lapse ratio to mean life insurance business in force has gone down from 7.6 per cent in 1955 to 3.1 per cent in 1991-92. With increase life fund from ₹ 410.40 crores in 1956 to ₹ 72,780.06 crore-in 1996; the LIC has achieved its corporate objective, *i.e.,* maximise mobilisation of people's savings by making insurance linked savings adequately attractive. The life insurance carrying capacity that is the ratio of business in force to national income has increased from 7.95% in 1951 to 30.30 per cent in 1995-96. The LIC has provided adequate financial cover to the people of India. It is also evident from the Table 41.4.

Table 40.4 Comparative Progress of LIC

Year	*% of business force to National Income*	*% of Premium Income to National Income*	*% of Annual Life Fund to National Income*
1951	7.95	0.38	0.2
1962-63	20.62	0.82	0.6
1984-85	25.42	0.90	0.7
1995-96	30.39	1.50	0.9

The rising rate of business in force has clearly shown that the, LIC has attempted to provide adequate financial cover to the people of India. The premium income as compared to national income has revealed the capacity of LIC for enhancement of business.

The third objective of nationalisation of life insurance business was to develop national economy as put in the words of the then Finance Minister, "Help development of National Economy in the right perspective for the benefits of the societies as a whole." Based on the objective, the corporate objective of LIC has been, "Bear in mind, in the investment of funds, the primary obligation to its policyholders whose money it holds in trust, without losing sight of the interest of the community as a whole". The LIC is performing this job through decentralised investment. The percentage of LIC investment, to national income has increased from 3.4 percent in 1956 to 6.26 percent in 1996. It had contributed to ₹ 184 crores during the Second Plan and ₹ 40303 crore during four years of Eighth Plan. No private sector enterprise can sacrifice so much for nation. It is illogical and anti-national to think to hand over the most contributing financial sector to private entrepreneurs including foreign companies. The money procured in the form of premium is helping reduced inflationary pressure because so much of money is withdrawn from circulation and is channelised for productive sector. The inflationary gap caused by the difference of money supply and production has been reduced at both the fronts, *i.e.*, reducing money supply through premium collection and increasing production through investment. The investment of LIC has increased from ₹ 372 crore in 1956 to ₹ 65057 crore in 1996, whereas the premium has increased from ₹ 88.65 crore to ₹ 14182 crore which were 0.2 percent and 2.4 percent respectively of the money in circulation, in the respective years.

The diversified investment policy of LIC has served almost all the industries, all the states and infrastructure from the drinking water facilities to development of hardcore industries, LIC has invested for their growth. The corporate objectives of LIC says. "Meet the various life insurance needs of the Community that would arise in the changing social and economic environment".

Table 40.5 Infrastructure Development through LIC Investment

(In crores of ₹)

Year	*Housing*	*Transport*	*Water Supply*	*Electricity*
1967	121	30 (1980)	16	61
1995-96	8,731	477	1,881	7,580

The objectives of nationalisation was also to discourage greater concentration of economic power which have been achieved through diversified investment policy of LIC. The public sector has got a lion's share in the total investment of LIC.

Table 40.6 LIC Investment

	% of total investment in			
Year	*Public Sector*	*Other*	*Private Sector*	*Total (In crores of Rupees)*
1955	—	—	—	318.90
1962-63	76.8	3.8	19.4	623.64
1984-85	79.6	2.3	8.10	9,954.20
1995-96	82.87	3.35	13.78	53,479.47

The LIC investment in public sector has been approximately 80 percent of its total investment. Similarly, the general insurance companies have invested about 65 percent of its total investment in public sector. It has been varying from 6.3 percent to 73 percent in different subsidiary companies.

The Life Insurance Corporation of India has been contributing in the socio-economic development through its payment to government.

Table 40.7 Payment to Government

Year	*Surplus*	*Income Tax*	*Total*
1957	1.45	0.30	1.75
1961	1.28	0.09	1.37
1990-91	90.00	254.90	344.90
1995-96	160.94	582.28	743.22

Government has invested only ₹ 5 crore as capital of LIC but has received ₹ 160.94 crore as dividend in 1995-96. It is unthinkable ratio of dividend which is 32 times of capital employed. The tax money given to government is very high amount *i.e.,* more than ₹ 500 crore. Can any private insurer pay so much taxes to government and government may receive so much high of dividend rate? Certainly not. Therefore, the logic of government to denationalise the LIC is irrational and full of unwise step. Similarly, General Insurance Industry has given more than ₹ 100 crore as income tax and more than ₹ 800 crore as dividend. Taking the total funds received by life insurance and general insurance industry together, the government has received more tan ₹ 1,600 crore in 1995-96. If government is going to part with this revenue by throwing the insurance industry to private entrepreneurs doubts may arise on the rational functioning of the government. It may be on account of some concrete reasons *e.g.,* government is being run by irrational people, government does not care for the welfare of society, government is thinking to borrow money from international agencies rather than mobilising domestic savings. The scope of domestic saving is considerably high in India. There is need of honest and sincere attempt to mobilise people's saving for people's welfare. Government should not adhere on some of the reports on insurance because they have been prepared on government's liking and people's mood. The reports cannot be relied on considering the broader and wider interest of the country.

It has been anticipated that the funds required for Ninth Five-Year Plan can be met by insurance industry alone if the industry is given freehand for operation and investment. There will not be any need for inviting foreign investment and incurring socio-economic and political risks. Privatisation of insurance industry is totally out of context, irrational and antinational decision.

Life insurance business was nationalised with the objective of rendering prompt and efficient services to policyholders. Consequently, corporative objective, Involve all people working in the Corporation to the best of their capability in furthering the interests of the insured public by providing efficient service with courtesy.

Table 40.8 Business per Active Agent in LIC

Year	*No.*	*New Business per Agent (₹)*
1955	8,900	31,000
1985	1,47,783	3,63,772
1995	5,19,504	10,63,101

The business per active agent has increased to ₹ 10,63,101 in 1995 from the lowest level of ₹ 31,000 in 1955. The LIC has fulfilled the responsibility of claims payment of which amounted to ₹ 4,532.22 crore on 42 lakh policies in 1995-96 from the lowest figure of ₹ 28.7 crore in 1956.. Outstanding claim which was 50% in 1956 came down to the level of 5.99 % in 1995-96. This shows that LIC has attempted hard to render prompt and efficient services to take policyholders.

Table 40.9 Production of Employees in LIC

Year	No. of Employees	*Average Business per Employee (Productivity) In terms of*			
		New Business Policy No.	*Business in force Policy No.*	*Premium Income (₹)*	*Claims Payment (₹)*
1957	30,768	26	185	28,810	10.940
1962-63	48,080	37	198	31,420	10,270
1984-85	62.977	43	422	2,68,210	1,18,420
1994-95	1,21,410	89	569	9,49,000	1,85,100

The business of LIC has been constantly increasing. The productivity in terms of new business has increased from 26 policies in 1957 to 89 policies in 1994-95. An employee who was required to serve 185 policies in 1957 is serving 539 policies in force in 1994-95. No one can argue that employees productivity has declined as has been in other public sector enterprises. The case of LIC is totally different from other public sector units which are running on losses and have been under constant pressure of government. LIC and GIC having the benefits of corporate character under statutory act of 1956 and 1972 are demonstrating its efficiency. They improve further if political interference whatever is there is eliminated from the horizon of the business. Statutory corporations having their autonomy and management techniques can perform better than any private entrepreneurs or government organisation. Departmental undertakings are always on the mercy and methods of government. The Indian Government has vididly demonstrated its corrupt practices during the last five years and cannot be relied upon for better management of nation and industry. But statutory corporations being free from direct involvement of government and performing efficiency in India and helping the society at large which is not possible by individual entrepreneurs who are always profit minded and least bothered to public welfare and nation-building. Many sick units are the glaring examples of unscrupulous motives of private entrepreneurs.

SUCCESS OF MULTI-PRODUCT DISTRIBUTION OF LIC

Customer loyalty depends on satisfaction of his multiple needs. They know them only when they are told about those needs. The Life Insurance Corporation of India has devised several life policies to satisfy these diversified needs of the customers. The research cell has explored these policies which are put in circulation. The outcome of each new product is tested generally for two-three years. On the basis of their acceptability by public, they are launched permanently in the field. Multi-product distribution has become a success for LIC, but it has failed on multi-channel. Only life insurance offices are sellers of the product. If the distribution channel is increased; people may purchase more diversified products from Financial Institutions, educational houses, hospital, health centres, village community centres, commercial and regional rural banks, public enterprises and big business houses may be appointed as distribution channel of life insurance policies. The LIC has not thought on this front but the researches conducted by me under exploring insurance avenues have revealed glaring avenues of insurance. The paper analyses the success of multi-product distribution of Life Insurance Corporation of India.

Analysis of Multi-Product

The multi-product distribution of Life Insurance Corporation of India (LIC) has been analysed under four periods:

1. Period of early growth (1956–1970)
2. Period of Fluctuation Business (1970–71 to 1979–80)

3. Period of Reorganisation (1980–81 to 1989–90)
4. Period of Product Diversification (1990–91 to 1997–98).

The period division has been done on the basis of product introduction. Early growth has shown introduction of the traditional policies and product diversification has demonstrated multiple policies to meet the requirements of policyholders.

1. Period of Early Growth (1956–1970)

The life insurance business in India increased rapidly during 1956–70 after nationalisation of life insurance business in January 1956; the private insurers were not taking serious interest in insurance particularly in rural areas. The average growth rate of business was about 5.00 percent per annum during this period.

New Schemes

During the period of early growth salary saving scheme and non-medial schemes and anticipated endowment insurance were introduced.

Table 40.10 Salary Saving Scheme as Compared to New Business

(₹ in crores)

	Salary Saving Scheme		*Individual Insurance*		*% of Salary Saving Scheme to individual Insurance*	
Year	*Policy Number in Lakhs*	₹	*Policy Number In Lakhs*	₹	*% of Total Policies*	*% of Total sum assured*
1957	—	—	8.16	283.07	—	—
1970-71	4.86	252.06	16.16	1,224.14	30.07	20.58
1980-81	5.58	551.67	19.58	2,896.95	28.50	19.04
1985-86	9.25	1,535.62	32.94	7,088.45	28.08	21.66
1990-91	19.62	5,870.62	86.54	2,239.10	22.67	20.72
1991-92	21.29	7,071.16	92.48	32,196.30	23.83	21.96
1992-93	22.35	7,904.96	99.68	36,115.80	22.42	21.89
1993-94	22.58	8,468.11	107.38	42,012.90	21.03	20.16
1994-95	21.88	10,768.25	108.88	55,468.82	20.00	19.41
1995-96	38.06	16,750.22	110.34	52,071.53	34.49	32.16
1996-97	23.22	10,578.83	122.81	56,993.94	18.91	18.55

Salary Saving Scheme: The salary saving scheme was introduced to help salaried employees in paying their premium regularly. The employer is required to deduct premium from salaries and remit them to the Corporation (LIC). It waves the usual monthly extra and gives rebate on the tabular premium. It was introduced in 1958 booking only ₹ 13.93 crore during the year. The number of new policies under Salary Saving Scheme has been constantly increasing from 4.86 lakh in 1970-71 to 23.22 lakh in 1996-97. Similarly, the sum assured has also increased from ₹ 252.06 crore in 1970-71 to ₹ 10578.83 crore in 1996-97 under this scheme. The percentage share of salary saving scheme in the total individual insurance has not been less than 18 per cent in any year. It reveals that the LIC is relying on salary saving scheme for its business. If it is compared with the different segments of policyholders, it has major role in insuring a large number of people under salaried class. The different segments of potential policyholders are businessmen, labourers, advocates, farmers, people in small scale industries, traders and transporters.

Table 40.11 Contribution of Different Sectors to Net Domestic Product in India in 1997

Primary Sector	35.67%	Agriculture 31.55, Forestry 1.70, Fishing 0.91, Mining 1.51
Secondary Sector	24.19%	Manufacturing 17.07, Construction 6.17, Electricity, etc. 0.95
Transport, Communication Munication and Trade	19.87%	Transport, Storage and Communication 6.50, Trade, Hotel and Restaurant 13.17
Finance and Real Estate	7.98%	Banking and insurance 5.13, Real Estate, Ownership, Dwelling, Business services 2.85
Community and Personnel services	12.29%	Public Administration and Defence 5.75, Other Services 6.54
Total	100.00	

The salary saving scheme is mainly confined to community and personal services which account only 12.29 percent of total national income. There is enough scope of expansion of this scheme to other sectors, too, such as manufacturing, construction, electricity, transport, communication, trade, hotels, restaurants, etc.

Table 40.12 Number of People Employed in 1997 (in thousands)

	Public Sector	*Private Sector*	*Total*
1. Agricultural, etc.	551	876	1427
2. Mining and Quarrying	963	100	1063
3. Manufacturing	1856	4374	6230
4. Electricity, gas and water	862	41	903
5. Consumption	1188	63	1251
6. Wholesale and retail trade	144	285	429
7. Transport, storage, communication	3020	51	3071
8. Financing, insurance, real estate	1108	241	1349
9. Community, Social and Personnel service	8792	1426	10218
Total	18,484	2,457	25,941

The number of employees ranges from 14 lakh in agriculture to 102 lakh in community, social and personnel services, wnereas the total number of employees have been 259 lakh in all sectors. The number of policies issued under salary saving schemes have not been more than 38 lakh in any year. The self-employed are not included under this schemes. Thus, there is enough scope of expansion of salary saving scheme.

The salary saving scheme is very traditional in its procedure. There is need of its renovation, use of computers have started. If the LIC links its computer with those of employees associated with salary saving scheme, will be immediately credited in the account of LIC. Thus, crores of rupees lying unsettled with the employers will come in use with LIC. The return of premium saved would increase tremendously.

Non-Medical Scheme: Non-medical scheme was introduced in 1960 with a view to reduce premium rates in respect of lives, where medical examination is not likely to produce any tangible results. Many employees of government, armed forces and public sector enterprises have been insured under this scheme.

Table 40.13 Progress of Non-medical Scheme

(Policy in lakh/₹ in crore)

Year	*Non-Medical*	*Scheme*	*Total*	*New Business to total*	*% of Non-Medical*	
	Policy	*Rs Sum assured*	*Policy*	*₹ Sum assured*	*Policy (%)*	*Sum assured*
1970-71	18.25	3,240.50	16.16	1,224.14	51.05	26.47
1980-81	8.20	552.87	19.58	2,896.95	41.88	19.08
1985-86	16.02	2,006.61	32.94	7,088.45	48.63	28.31
1990-91	47.08	12,436.87	86.54	28,239.10	55.10	44.04
1991-92	55.96	15,987.01	92.48	32,196.30	60.51	49.65
1992-93	85.34	19,381.87	99.68	38,115.80	85.55	53.87
1993-94*	68.72	22,048.25	107.38	42,012.90	64.00	52.48

*No information is available thereafter.

Many employees of government sector, public enterprises, educational institutions, defence forces and so on are insured under non-medical schemes. More than 50 percent of total individual insurance is coming under medical examinations in certain categories of people. The conditions of non-medical examination have been laid down to safeguard any loss to the LIC.

Anticipated Endowment Policy: Anticipated endowment policy increased due to inherent merits of periodical payment. It was introduced in 1962-63. The importance of anticipated endowment policy increased upto 1975-76. It was popular because of three reasons *viz.*; (*i*) policy holders prefer endowment policy where a part of the sum assured is returned in instalment earlier than the normal maturity date while enjoying the benefits of insurance protection during the currency of policy. (*ii*) Income Tax relief continues to be available for the full term of the policy even though part of the sum assured is received earlier. (*iii*) Policyholders continue to receive bonus of the full sum assured although 40 per cent of the sum assured is returned to the policyholders before maturity. Anticipated endowment insurance declined from 9.93 per cent in 1962-63 to 0.92 per cent of the total individual insurance in 1980-81. It has been closed and now children's anticipated policy is in vogue which amount to ₹ 9.80 crore in 1996-97. Whole life and without profit schemes were declined as policyholders were not interested in them because of their long term agreement.

2. Period of Fluctuating Business (1970-71 to 1979-80)

Life insurance business during 1970-71 to 1979-80 experienced a wide ups and downs. Indian business declined in some years very drastically due to natural calamities and economic distress. The average rate of growth was below 4.00 per cent per annum. Industrial relations were not very much favourable during this period. Financial institutions posed problems of competition. People prefer bank deposits and postal saving certificates. In the later year of the period discipline and work culture improved. Consequently business increased in the later part of the period.

New Schemes

1. *Money Back Policy*: It was introduced in 1976-77 and got good response from public as the sum assured was 36.18 per cent and the policy was 28.15 percent of total individual business in 1980-81. People are interested in those policies which provide more benefits to policyholders during the currency of policy. From the detailed analysis of policy-planes, it has been revealed that people like such types of policies which provide money during policyholder's life for meeting different types of needs of life. They do not prefer those policies which provide money only at the end of certain period whether maturity or death. People prefer saving to protection. The percentage of sum assured under money back policy was 36.18 per cent to total individual insurance in 1980-81.

Table 40.14 Progress of Money Back Policy

Year	*Money Back Policy*		*Individual Insurance*		*% of Money Back to*	
	No. of Policy in Lakhs	*Sum Assured in ₹ crores*	*No. of Policy in lakhs*	*Sum Assured in crores*	*Total Individual Insurance Policy*	*Sum Assured in ₹ lakhs*
1980-81	—	—	—	—	28.15	36.18
1990-91	34.29	12,979.08	86.54	28239.10	39.62	45.96
1991-92	35.13	13,567.94	92.54	23196.30	37.99	42.14
1992-93	41.15	16,401.67	99.68	36115.80	41.28	45.41
1993-94	42.71	17,025.18	107.38	42012.90	39.77	40.52
1994-95	34.43	1,588.69	108.88	55468.82	31.62	28.10
1995-96	36.38	16,396.08	110.34	5271.53	32.97	31.49

The number of policies issued under Money Back Policy have been varying from the lowest number of 34.29 lakh in 1990-91 to the highest number of 42.41 lakh in 1996-97. Similarly sum assured has increased from ₹ 12,979.08 crore to ₹ 19,426.77 crore in the corresponding years. Their percentage to total individual insurance has been 31.61 percent in 1994-95 and 41.28 percent in 1992-93 in case of policy number and 31.49 percent in 1995-96 and 45.96 percent in 1990-91 in case of sum assured. It reveals that more than one third of individual business came from money back policy.

3. Period of Re-organisation (1980-81 to 1989-90)

The new business of LIC has increased by more than 7 percent per annum. The branch offices were given more authority. Decentralisation has yielded more business. New policies were introduced. Group insurance business increased during this period. The Group Insurance Scheme have several advantages over individual insurance. It has low cost and higher benefits. Many underprivileged persons also get the benefits of insurance. LIC laid considerable stress on development of Group and Superannuation Schemes because it is only through the group approach that rapid progress of insurance and protection of life insurance cover to society is possible. Employers can give the benefits of insurance through this scheme.

Group Insurance Schemes: Group Insurance Schemes were extended to various groups such as teachers of primary and junior high schools, employees of State Electricity Boards of several states, employees of central and state governments, employees of three defence services, employees of big business houses, employees of cooperative societies in Gujarat, Maharashtra, Tamil Nadu, Uttar Pradesh and Orissa. There are renewable term insurance issued to a particular group. If death does not take place within the contract period, the insured is refunded the amount of premium along with the prevailing rate of interest. Persons who cannot get the policy on medical ground can get insurance coverage under this scheme. Persons who cannot save adequate amount for payment of premium can also get the benefits of insurance if their employers agree to pay the premium amount.

Superannuation Scheme: The scheme provides pension (annual maturity) benefits to retired employees when they are old and not able to earn for their maintenance. The number of beneficiaries and schemes have increased fastly during this period. The superannuation is becoming more popular because of people's preference to investment.

Janashree Bima Yojana

On 10th August 2000, the Janashree Bima Yojana, a group insurance scheme was launched in order to extend the benefit of Social security and life insurance cover to poorer segments of the population. This scheme is being implemented with the help of non-governmental organisations and self-help groups who will help in identifying the groups of persons to be covered. In addition to persons below the poverty line, persons marginally above the poverty line also can be covered under the scheme, which provides cover and cover against accidental death and disability. During 2000-2001, 3,35, 052 new lives were covered under the 40 approved occupations pertaining to the Social Security Schemes and the Janashree Bima Yojana. The First Premium Income under these schemes during the year 2000-2001 registered a significant increase of 192% and grew to ₹ 2.33 crore. During the year 778 new group schemes were brought into the book. The number of new lives covered was 98,603 under various Group Superannuation and Annuity Schemes which were for a sum of assured of ₹ 70,614.80 crore during 2000-2001.

Table 40.15 Group Insurance Business and All Business in Force

	Individual (All)		*Group Insurance including Superannuation*		*Total Business Policy No.*	*% of Group Insurance to Total Business*	
Year	*Policy ₹ in Lakhs*	*₹*	*Member covered*	*₹*	*in Lakhs*	*Policy Member*	*Sum Assured*
1957	56.83	1473	—	—	56.83	—	—
1970-71	147.85	7067	—	123	147.85		1.71
1980-81	228.12	21,057	64.45	6,980	292.57	22.03	24.49
1985-86	280.47	40,617	92.65	11,799	373.12	24.83	22.51
1990-91	455.68	1,19,179	172.00	30,755	627.68	27.40	20.51
1995-96	709.90	2,95,758	250.68	64,135	960.28	26.10	17.82
1996-97	777.50	3,44,619	244.48	65,152	1021.98	23.92	15.90

The business under group insurance and superannuation schemes has been constantly increasing. The policy number and members covered under group insurance and superannuation have increased to the level of 244.48 lakh in 1996-97. The share of group insurance and superannuation scheme have been 21.40 percent of the total policy and members. The assessed sum under this scheme was 24.49 percent of the total insurance in 1980-81. It accounts about one fifth of the total business of Life Insurance Corporation of India. The people are made aware of this scheme.

4. Period of Product Diversification (1990-91 to 1997-98)

The Life Insurance Corporation of India realised the importance of product diversification. Business increased by selling different types of policies. Product diversification is essential to meet the varying needs, changing preferences and rising aspirations of the customers.

The importance of whole life policies and endowment assurances are reducing gradually, that total sum assured under these policies are increasing although in relation to total individual business, they are not increasing.

Money back policies have increased to the level of 20,000 crore. It is prominent assurance policy because of its advantages of investment. The amount of children's anticipated endowment is reducing year after year. It has come down to nearly 10 crore.

Jeevan Raksha Policy has yielded insurance to the tune of ₹ 1,600 crore in 1996-97. It is rapidly increasing. Similarly Jeevan Mitra has crossed the level of ₹ 1,900 crore. Jeevan Sathi is also becoming popular. The sum assured was ₹ 566.70 crore in 1996-97. The marriage Endowment and Educational amenities have increased considerably to meet the requirements of marriage and education of children. Convertible whole life has gone down to the level of ₹ 165.74 crore in 1996-97. Jeevan Balya/Jeeven Kishore have been popular as they crossed the level of ₹ 800 crore. Similarly, Jeevan Chhaya has been gradually increasing although Bima Sandesh declined to ₹ 51.78 crore in 1996-97.

Those policies are becoming popular, which have features of investment and periodical payment alongwith coverage of risk.

Table 40.16 Progress of Insurance Plans in India

Sum assured in crores

S.No.	*Name of Plans*	*1985-86*	*1990-91*	*1995-96*	*1996-97*	*2001-02*
1.	Whole Life Policies	41.22	130.03	113.33	281.14	643.78
2.	Endowment Assurance	2900.77	9538.92	10699.36	12314.79	34702.84
3.	Money Back	2628.83	12979.08	16396.08	19426.77	23202.67
4.	Children's Anticipated Endowment	87.33	82.08	9.96	9.80	—
5.	Jeevan Raksha Policy (All)	35.11	525.22	1375.39	1666.05	8781.73
6.	Jeevan Mitra	751.25	1885.55	1769.17	1927.46	3725.19
7.	Jeevan Sathi	59.47	544.36	554.64	566.74	1108.37
8.	Marriage/Educational Endowment/Annuity	—	271.90	637.12	647.70	3547.43
9.	Convertible Whole Life	273.92	473.62	198.16	165.74	291.20
10.	Jeevan Balya Kiran	—	1090.65	834.96	865.67	
11.	Jeevan Chhaya	—	84.40	363.54	357.90	1728.85
12.	Bima Sandesh	—	205.01	64.69	51.78	

Product Development

The Life Insurance Corporation of India has diversified insurance products. Under this scheme, Asha Deep with some novel features was introduced in 1993-94. This plan besides providing death and maturity payment, provides benefits in case the life assured suffering from any of four major ailments, *viz.*, cancer, paralytic stroke leading to permanent disability, renal failure of both kidneys and coronary artery diseases, where bypass surgery has been done.

1. *Asha Deep–I:* Asha Deep-I increased from 7th September 1993 to 30th November, 1993. The total business under Asha Deep-I was ₹ 4,573.70 crore under 6.42 lakh policies in 1993-94. Asha Deep-I did not continue later on.

Table 40.17 Progress of New Insurance Plans Policies

Sum assured in crores of ₹

	1990-91	*1991-92*	*1992-93*	*1993-94*	*1994-95*	*1995-1996*	*1996-97*	*2001-02*
Bhavisya Jeevan	1.58	1.46	1.33	1.13	0.84	0.39	45.60	3.55
Jeevan Swathi	—	—	1157.07	1003.83	2084.62	3360.78	4858.71	1108.37
Jeevan Sukanya	—	—	151.90	102.67	42.66	30.37	17.69	34.39
Asha Deep-I	—	—	—	4573.70	—	—	—	
Asha Deep-II	—	—	—	—	—	1362.341	886.11	
Jeevan Sarita	—	17.32	17.62	11.61	5.92	10.12	8.30	0.82
Jeevan Griha	—	55.66	132.54	169.85	141.07	129.89	136.58	299.07
Bima Kiran	—	—	—		19366.71	10944.84	9441.15	
Jeevan Shree	—	—	—		411.76	1320.34	1396.07	60212.66
Jeevan Adhar	—	—	—	—		21.12	19.52	15.15
Jeevan Sanjay	—	—	—	—	—		287.39	7267.5
Jeevan Sneha	—	—	—	—	—		251.07	3352.67
Children's Money	—	—	—	—	935.31	1583.50	1253.88	7040.89

2. *Asha Deep-II:* The Asha Deep Plan was first introduced in September 1993 on an experimental basis for a period of 3 months. In response to public demand the plan was reintroduced as Asha Deep-II in the month of November, 1995. This plan besides death and maturity payment, provides for benefits in case the life assured is affliated by any of four major ailments *viz.*, cancer, paralytic stroke leading to permanent disability, renal failure of both kidneys and coronary artery diseases where bypass surgery has been done. The amount of sum assured under this scheme was ₹ 1,362.34 crore in 1995-96 and ₹ 886.11 crore in 1996-97.

3. *Jeevan Aadhar:* Jeeven Aadhar introduced in January 1996 is specially designed for the benefit of handicapped dependents. Contributions under this Plan are eligible for income tax relief under Section 88 DDA of the Income Tax Act. This plan is basically a limited payment whole life assurance on the life of the proposer with provision for Guaranteed Additions and Terminal Addition to the basic sum assured. The claim amount will be payable partly in lumpsum and partly in the form of annuity to the handicapped dependents. The sum assured under Jeevan Aadhar was ₹ 21.12 crore in 1995-96 and ₹ 19.52 crore in 1996-97.

4. *Jeevan Suraksha:* Jeeven Suraksha was introduced on 15th August, 1996. It enables individuals to provide for retirement income from a selected date. The policy is with life cover but can be taken without life cover under certain conditions. The policyholder taking policy with life cover provides minimum of 50% of the target pension to spouse on death during the deferment period. Spouse's pension is not provided under without life cover plan. On vesting the policyholder has the option to receive 25 per cent of the notional case plan in lump sum and balance in annuity. The amount of Jeevan Suraksha was ₹ 102.65 crore in 1997-98.

5. *Jeevan Sneha:* Jeevan Sneha was introduced on 16th January, 1997 for women. It is a without profit money back type plan with the added features of guaranteed additions *viz.*, encasement of survival benefit as and when required. Flexibility to pay premium in advance, inbuilt accident cover, for insurance cover for a period of 3 years from the date of first unpaid premium provided atleast 2 full years premium have been paid and option to receive pension in lieu of maturity benefits. The sum assured under this scheme was ₹ 251.07 crore in 1996-97.

6. *Jeevan Sanchaya:* Similar to Jeevan Sneha, this plan was introduced on 16th January, 1997. It is without profits money back type of plan with provision of loyalty addition and guaranteed addition. Accident benefit is also granted under this plan with an upper limit of ₹ 5 lakhs in addition to existing limit of ₹ 5 lakhs under other plan.
7. *Children's Money Back:* Children's Money Back has assured ₹ 935.31 crore in 1994-95, ₹ 1,583.50 crore in 1995-96 and ₹ 1,253.88 crore in 1996-97. It is becoming popular because of inherent advantages to children. People want insurance for their children.

Impact of Product Diversification on Insurance Business

Product diversification of life insurance business yielded considerable results. People are attracted to purchase new policies of insurance which met their demands of children's education, marriage of daughter, their risk coverage, pension benefit to spouse and self, periodical monetary requirements and risk coverage. Different policies as discussed above have added more business as is clear from the foregoing tables. Had these policies not been issued, the insurance business would not have expanded so high. Being encouraged with the result of new schemes of life insurance, the LIC has introduced a very important scheme known as Jeevan Suraksha in 1998 and many other schemes are in pipe-lines. Jeevan Suraksha is available in three types to suit individual needs of person with life cover, pension without life cover and pension with endowment type.

Table 40.18 Impact of Product Diversification on Insurance Business

Policy Number in Lakh/
Sum Assured in Rupees Crore

	Individual Business		*Group Insurance*		*Superannuation*		*Total*	
Year	*Policy*	*Sum Assured*	*Members*	*Sum Assured*	*Members*	*Sum Assured*	*Policy Members*	*Sum Assured*
1957	45.18	1374	—	—	—	—	54.18	1374
1970-71	146.93	6952	3.10	119	—	4	150.00	7075
1980-81	227.58	20923	64.45	6960	—	20	292.03	27903
1985-86	279.89	40404	79.83	11764	—	35	359.72	52203
1990-91	455.08	118651	169.57	30502	2.43	253	627.08	149076
1991-92	508.63	145929	189.53	32973	2.54	302	700.70	179204
1992-93	566.12	177268	212.54	43087	2.69	359	781.35	220714
1993-94	608.00	207601	227.31	46743	3.14	404	838.45	254748
1994-95	654.52	253333	241.88	51035	3.54	428	899.94	304796
1995-96	708.78	294336	246.49	64652	4.19	483	961.48	359471
1996-97	776.66	343018	238.97	64607	5.54	546	1021.17	408171

The sum assured increased upto the level of ₹ 4,08,171 crore in 1996-97 under 1021.47 lakh policy/member. The business increased very fastly after 1985-86 on account of diversified business.

The percentage of population covered increased from 1.35 percent in 1957 to 8.30 percent in 1996-97 under individual business and from 1.35 percent to 10.91 percent under total insurance business. The percentage of policy number to total population was merely 4.79 percent in 1985–86 which rose to 7.47 per cent in 1990-91 due to product diversification scheme introduced in 1990. The role of group insurance and superannuation schemes was not very significant in expanding business per population as the percentage of the member number reanged between 2.68 to 1.06 during 1985-86 to 1996-97. Similarly, superannuation did not increase significantly. It is only individual business which contribute to insurance expansion. Only individual business has introduced new schemes of insurance. Group insurance and superannuation insurance continued on traditional scheme. Then the contribution to new insurance product is significant in business expansion.

Table 40.19 Percentage of Population Covered with Life insurance Schemes

Policy/Members in lakhs

Year	Individual Policy	Group Member	Supernal nuation Member	Total policy/ Members	Population	Percentage of Policy Member Number to the total population Individual	Group	Supern-nuation	Total
1957	54.18	—		54.18	40.00	1.35	—	—	135
1970-71	146.93	3.10	—	150.00	53.70	2.73	0.06	—	2.79
1980-81	227.58	6445	—	292.03	68.38	3.33	0.94	—	4.27
1985-86	279.89	79.83	—	359.72	75.00	3.73	1.04	—	4.79
1990-91	455.08	169.57	2.43	627.08	83.90	5.48	2.02	0.02	7.47
1991-92	508.83	189.53	2.54	700.70	85.61	5.94	2.21	0.03	8.18
1992-93	566.12	212.54	2.69	781.35	87.20	6.44	2.44	0.11	8.96
1993-94	608.00	227.31	3.14	838.45	88.80	6.84	2.58	0.04	9.44
1994-95	654.52	241.88	3.54	899.94	90.40	7.24	2.68	0.03	9.95
1995-96	708.78	256.49	4.19	961.46	92.00	7.70	2.68	0.07	10.45
1996-97	776.66	238.97	5.54	1021.17	93.60	8.30	2.56	0.06	10.91

*It is assumed that every policy-holder/member has one policy.

Table 40.20 Life Insurance Carrying Capacity in India

₹ in crores

Year	Total Insurance Business in Force in India	Net National Production in India (at current prices)	% of Total Insurance Business Force to NNP
1957	1374	11390	12.06
1970-71	7075	34476	20.52
1980-81	27903	104201	28.78
1985-86	52203	185333	18.25
1990-91	149078	416495	35.79
1991-92	179204	477868	37.50
1992-93	220714	684935	39.06
1993-94	254748	638979	39.87
1994-95	304796	759597	40.13
1995-96	359471	881216	40.79
1996-97	408171	996022	40.98

The Life Insurance carrying capacity is increased as the percentage share of insurance business in force to net national product increased. The life insurance carrying capacity in India increased from 12.06 in 1957 to 40.98 in 1996-97. The insurance carrying capacity was 18.25 in 1985-86 which rose to 35.79 in 1990-91 due to introduction of several new insurance schemes in 1990. Since then the life insurance carrying capacity is gradally increasing. It is on account of diversification of individual insurance business. Group insurance and Superannuation have not been diversified.

The per capita insurance increased rapidly in context to individual insurance from ₹ 33.68 in 1957 to ₹ 538.72 in 1985-86 and again to ₹ 3,664.72 in 1998-97. Thus population in India is insured on an average of ₹ 3,664.72 in 1996-97 although there are a large number of uninsured population still left out. Only 8.30 percent of the population is insured if policy number is taken only one by a policyholder. But policyholder has more than one policy. It is established fact that not more than 8.00 percent is insured in India. If group insurance and superannuation are taken together, it has not crossed 10 percent. The 10 percent of population who are insured have given average insurance of ₹ 4,360.80 under all schemes. The government of India has insured all the weaker sections of the society to the range of ₹ 5000 to ₹ 10,000 to provide social benefits. It is free of cost in the sense that the beneficiaries are not required to pay the premium. The government bears the premium amount. It is unique scheme in India which is not present probably in other countries.

Table 40.21 Per Capita Insurance in India

Year	*Individual Insurance*	*Total Insurance*	*Policy No. per ten thousand of population*	
	(₹)	(₹)	*Individual*	*Total*
1957	33.68	33.68	133	133
1970-71	129.46	131.75	274	279
1980-81	305.98	408.06	333	427
1985-86	538.72	696.04	373	497
1990-91	1,414.19	1,776.82	548	747
1991-92	1,704.58	2,093.26	594	818
1992-93	2,032.89	2,531.72	649	896
1993-94	2,337.84	2,868.78	684	944
1994-95	2,802.36	3,371.64	724	995
1995-96	3,199.30	3,907.29	770	1045
1996-97	3,664.72	4,360.80	830	1091
2000-01	6,432.41	15,489.32	1,130	1,131

The Role of Private Sector in Agriculture Insurance

With the opening up of insurance sector in 2000, the scenario of insurance industry has taken a dramatic turn. There exists a vast potential in rural and semi urban, particularly in agriculture where benefit of insurance is highly solicited but not reached. It is to be mentioned that despite regulatory requirements, companies are not taking much initiatives to spread their reach in rural sector. Most of their initiatives are just to fulfill the regulatory requirements of IRDA. One of the prominent features of rural sector is that of strong saving habits, and hence providing a huge potential to various industries including insurance. But lack of cost effective service delivery model and perception of huge investments in the sector deters them to exploit the opportunities.

Role of private sector in agriculture insurance had been limited to certain index based weather schemes. It started in year 2003 when ICICI Lombard, a private general insurance company, started its pilot program on rainfall insurance to protect the farmers of specified crop against deviation in rainfall. Since it was a pilot approach, the numbers were limited. Following the path, during Kharif 2004, IFFCO-Tokio General Insurance, another private general insurance company, launched its own variant of index based rainfall insurance program during karif season, initially in four states and as on date in ten states. Having learnt valuable lessons from such enterprises, pilots are now being done on protection from weather vagaries occurring during Rabi crops.

Private weather insurance products have been gaining momentum in agricultural market. Some of the prominent features of these products are :

- Point of sale policy insurance - receipt cum policy,
- Policy and promotion in vernacular language,
- Revision of policy every year based on past data / experiences,
- Local IMD weather station to be considered as reference stations.

Issues with private weather insurance schemes which curtail expansion in wider geographical areas are as :

- Service and claims issues,
- Price not affordable,
- Farmers perceiving insurance as investment with sure returns instead of risk mitigation tool,
- Absence of relevant weather data,
- Absence of government infrastructure in setting up weather stations to be used as reference weather stations,
- Misappropriate data correlation with risk occurrence,
- Small Holding size and wide variety of agricultural practices,
- Moral hazards.

Growth of life insurance in the post liberalization era:

With the advent of liberalization, privatization and globalization popularly known as IPG, productivity has enhanced. New products are marketed with greater innovation and utilization of technology has become a necessity not only to reduce the cost of production but also the cost of distribution as well. Liberalization creates a conducive climate for faster economic growth, allows up-gradation of technology, provides economy of scale and market expansion, domestically and internationally. The wave of LPG has influenced the insurance market globally. As of now, almost all the countries in the world have opened their insurance sector for the global players. The greatest advantage of allowing foreign partners is the inflow of direct foreign capital. Expertise of the foreign partner in the highly competitive insurance market in the other countries would definitely be leveraged by Indian partners. It leads to management efficiency and product innovation. Increased competition, technology-lead services, wide range of products and cost effective operations would finally benefit the customers. In the recent year there has been a slow growth of insurance market in the developed countries. The Insurance Market in the developed countries is almost saturated. During 2003 global life insurance witnessed a decline of 8% while the life insurance business in emerging markets grew by 6.6%. In the years to come the foreign insurance companies in the developed countries would therefore like to spread their wings to the emerging markets. Among emerging economies, India is one of the high growth countries with huge untapped potential, with the rise of middle class, increase in per capita income, rise in literacy rate and growth of service sector, there is certainly a huge scope of insurance penetration in India.

Role of IRDA :

The Insurance Regulatory and Development Authority has a very important role to play when more players join the market. Its primary function is to regulate the insurance sector allowing healthy growth but without compromising on consumer interest. This means ensuring proper disclosures, keeping affordable prices and making sure that the claims are paid by the insurers. Further ensuring the solvency of insurance companies is a very important function of the regulatory authority. It has to be ensured that not only regulatory authority. It has to be ensured that not only at the end of the financial year but also at all times an insurance company should be solvent. Consumer education is also one of the important functions that the regulator has to perform.

IRDA has issued guidelines on all aspects of insurance business like product pricing, itermediary, social responsibility, rural business, investment, solvency margin etc. As on 31/3/2008,

18 life insurance companies are operating in India and the composition of new business of these companies is below:-

Sr. No.	Insurer	Premium March, 2008 (₹ in Crs.)
1.	Bajaj Allianz	6491.72
2.	ING Vysya	704.67
3.	Reliance Life	2752.76
4.	SBI Life	4792.86
5.	Tata AIG	967.78
6.	HDFC Standard	2679.61
7.	ICICI Prudential	8305.84
8.	Birla Sunlife	1965.01
9.	Aviva	1059.08
10.	Kotak Mahindra Old Mutual	1106.62
11.	Max New York	1594.21
12.	Met Life	826.79
13.	Sahara Life	122.17
14.	Shriram Life	309.87
15.	Bharati AXA Life	113.11
16.	Future Generali Life	2.50
17.	IDBI Future Life	11.90
18.	LIC	59182.20
	Grand Total	**92988.70**

Challenges

With the financial services becoming market driven and with unforeseen fluctuations in the interest rates, Life Insurance Companies have to exercise utmost care in product pricing. When the interest rates started moving southward in 200001, without-profit policies which gave some sort of interest guarantee were withdrawn by LIC. In respect of insurance, what is important is not the return on capital but the return of capital. Hence if the rates of interest fall below the assumed rate of interest on investment when the product was designed, it is always advisable to withdraw the product and limit the liability. Even the Unit Linked Products need to be reviewed at appropriate intervals.

The greatest challenge before the new entrants in the insurance sector is to establish their presence in the minds of the public. The most popular three letter word is said to be 'LIC'. LIC's presence is seen even in small villages with a population of 1000 or 2000 where a policyholder of LIC or an agent of LIC is seen. Insurance is always sold and never bought. To convince prospects who are comparatively not well informed about the intangible benefits of the life insurance is indeed an onerous task. On the top of it, to establish brand equity of a new name in a new field is also a great challenge. The second most important challenge faced by the new entrants is going to be setting up an infrastructure and reaching out to the geographically well spread areas of the country. Life insurance is based on probability of numbers and wider the spread, greater is the probability of business sustainence.

Pension Administration

All over the world life insurance companies manage two types of risks: (*i*) the risk of dying too early and (*ii*) the risk off living too long. Although commonly insurance is attributed to the first risk *i.e.* the risk of dying too early, the insurance companies have an important and significant port folio of pensions. The annuity (pension) business is developing very fast with improvement in health conditions has led to increase in longevity. Annuity business is a more risky business than life insurance business. Designing products that attract the changing needs of the people and managing the funds in the volatile interest rate scenario are two important challenges that need to be faced by all players in insurance industry in the days to come.

Product Innovation

Since the sector opened up, all the insurance companies started promoting Unit Linked Insurance Plans (ULIP). During that period the stock market was also booming. Since the NAVs were going up, it was easy to convince clients of benefits of the Unit Linked Insurance Plans and handsome growth we reported by most of the insurance compaines by marketing Unit Linked Insurance Plans. It was said that these products were for the benefit of the customers, but they were basically designed to suit the insurers. Insurance Companies undertake three major risks viz.

The risk of death is passed on to the reinsurer to a great extent. In case of Unit Linked Plans, even the risk of return and the risk of investment is passed on to the customers. Thereby the insurance companies retain a very small portion of mortality risk with them. The lesser the risk retained, the lesser is the requirement for solvency margin. Since solvency margin is to be provided by the owners, they always feel happy to do business at lower capital requirements. As it is, capital is scarce and with every sale effected, insurance companies require additional capital to be pumped in. Although insurance sector has shown extraordinary growth in new business due to sale of Unit Linked Products, the stability of the company may get affected once the sensex starts moving southwards.

This is precisely what has happened since 18th Jan., 2008. The sensex which had crossed 21,000 mark was stated to cross 25,000 by 31/3/2008. However, the sensex started melting down and has reached a three year low of less than 8,000. The consumers who have invested in Ulip products have lost heavily. The insurance companies are having a tough time in convincing the existing customers to continue their policies despite reduction in NAV. It is even more difficult to promote new customers to induce them to put their money in Unit Linked Products.

Every company has now started promoting conventional products which are not linked to equity market. In this type of non-unit linked products, surplus is valued at the end of the year and distributed to customers as 'Bonus'. Private Insurance Companies may take a long period to declare bonus on par with LIC. The insurance companies are thus caught between the grave and the great sea. On one hand they find it difficult to market Unit Linked Products due to slump in equity market and on the other, they are finding it difficult to market conventional products as the return on these products will be pretty low as compared to LIC. With the global recession faced by financial sector all over the world, bringing more inflow of capital is going to be a big question mark. Since more capital will be required for every increases in sale, whether to reduce operations in order to obviate the capital requirements is going to be a great challenge for the new insurance companies.

Future scenario

In India only 10% of the market share has been tapped by LIC and the balance 90% remains to be tapped. This vast population can be tapped only by a large number of insurers to serve the population of more than 100 Crs. Indian Insurance Market offers tremendous opportunities to the new insurance companies. Every financial company would like to be a financial conglomerate marketing banking, Mutual Fund, Credit Card and Insurance as well, through their sister companies, Mergers and acquisition seem to be inevitable. AMP Sanmar, an Australian Insurance Company decided to close its operations in India due to lack off interest shown by the Indian partner. The company was taken over by Reliance Capital and is now Reliance Life. Hostile takeovers can also not be ruled out. The insurance regulator has a great challenge to ensure ethical practices. LIC will have to come out with new products and advancement of technology in insurance market will need to be tackled. LIC will have to ensure that the trust of the people is not jeopardized and that it continues to be the insurer of choice.

The Regulator has to play an important role and should be strong enough to check the wrong practices of the new insurance companies. If properly regulated, the future of insurance industry looks bright.

SUMMARY

The research study has revealed that the life insurance business in India increased mainly on account of product diversification. The LIC authorities realised that different types of products are needed to meet diverse requirements of the people. Many new insurance schemes were launched to meet the investment and protection needs of the public. People are more concerned with the Children's welfare. So many policies such as Jeevan Balya/Jeevan Kishore, Children's Anticipated Endowment and Children's Money Back were introduced which became very popular. Similarly people are much concerned with old age regular income. Superannuation plans under ground insurance became very popular. Individual pension plans be came more useful for them. They purchased Asha Deep, Bima Kiran, Jeevan Shree, Jeeven Sanchay and Jeevan Sneha. The Life Insurance Corporation of India has rightly realised different needs of people and procured adequate amount of business on account of new policies. Restructuring of plans has been a continued exercise as the market rates of interest and yields available on securities have been changing from time to time. Accordingly Jeevan Dhara, jeevan Akshay and Jeevan Suraksha have been revised and have been put in the market as New Jeevan Dhara, New Jeevan Akshay and Jeevan Suraksha (revised). One can well appreciate the business in force figure which has been increasing from ₹ 1,473 crore in 1957 to ₹ 7,190 crore in 1970-71 and again to ₹ 1,49,934 crore in 1990-91. The business increased very rapidly after 1990-91, when many new schemes were launched. The total figure of business in force as on 31st March, 1997 was ₹ 4,09,771 crore which is a big jump in the area of insurance business. Not only the absolute figure, but life insurance increased as compared to net national product and other economic indicators. The per capita insurance in India was more than ₹ 2000 as on 1997 which was merely ₹ 34 in 1957. The number of persons insured have been more than 10 crore. All these progressive results are on account of introduction of new insurance schemes. It is concluded that the multiproduct diversification has captured more market and more insurable people in India.

Table 40.22 Business of Life Insures Individual Non-Single Premium

Insures	In crores to Rs. Premium V/w			In Lakhs No.of Policies/Schemes			In Lakhs Group Schemes No.			Market Share % Premium			Market Share % Policies/Schemes			Market Share % Group Schemes		
	2003-04	2004-05	2005-06	2003-04	2004-05	2005-06	2003-04	2004-05	2005-06	2003-04	2004-05	2005-06	2003-04	2004-05	2005-06	2003-04	2004-05	2005-06
1. Bajaj Allianz	156.29	401.23	1184.84	1.82	2.46	6.53	1.01	3.62	3.95		3.39	7.29		1.10	2.17		3.31	
2. ING Vysya	70.84	266.26	243.41	0.79	1.03	1.24	0.14	0.47	0.54		1.11	0.75		0.42	0.40		0.49	
3. Relince Life	—	23.26	64.55	—	0.27	0.62	—	0.95	1.29		—	0.59		—	0.23			
4. SBI Life	53.09	98.30	309.37	0.78	1.18	2.63	7.00	7.03	8.57		1.91	1.85		0.49	0.75		8.84	
5. Tata Aig	123.87	250.21	380.50	1.62	2.29	2.96	0.94	2.34	4.18		1.18	1.60		0.87	1.12		2.89	
6. HDFC Standard	209.33	353.23	774.77	1.64	2.107	2.55	—	0.49	0.22		1.92	2.97		0.79	1.23		1.89	
7. ICICI Prudential	622.11	1344.39	2101.03	4.26	6.07	7.86	0.07	0.56	2.07		6.25	7.20		2.34	2.78		1.00	
8. Birla Sunlife	267.41	507.80	562.95	1.27	1.48	1.97	1.95	0.77	0.48		2.45	1.80		0.76	0.84		0.75	
9. Aviva	71.54	179.63	391.31	0.70	0.81	1.62	0.89	2.96	1.90		0.76	1.12		0.32	0.52		2.71	
10. Kotak Mahindra Old Mixture	92.73	174.50	348.84	0.50	0.61	0.90	0.53	0.94	1.32		1.48	0.76		0.24	0.30		0.86	
11. Max New York	125.60	216.02	439.36	1.45	2.16	4.23	1.18	0.70	0.67		0.89	1.38		0.83	1.57		0.63	
12. Met Life	22.36	48.55	127.47	0.24	0.46	0.94	0.41	1.59	3.32		0.22	0.43		0.18	0.35		1.45	
13. Schara Life	—	1.65	4.49	—	0.10	0.19	—	0.02	0.00		0.01	0.06		0.04	0.08		0.02	
14. Sri Ram Life	—		10.31			2.08		0	0									
15. LIC	11195.69	11380.70	12945.82	266.34	223.34	292.98	—	00	00		78.07	72.30		91.50	87.67		74.31	
Total	18669.40	15245.83	19889.04	286.27	244.35	327.44	62.53	22.45	28.51		100.00	100.00		100.00	100.00		100.00	

Table 40.23 First Year Premium of Life Insurers for the Period Ended January, 2009

	Insurer	Premium u/w (Rs. in Crores)			No. of Policies/Schemes			No. of lives covered under Group Schemes		
		January, 09	Up to January, 09	Up to January, 08	January, 09	Up to January, 09	Up to January, 08	January, 09	Up to January, 09	Up to January, 08
1	**Bajaj Allianz**									
	Individual Single Premium	55.75	324.82	509.08	11544	80807	70066			
	Individual Non. Single Premium	267.72	2920.36	3903.45	194141	1932899	2648502			
	Group Single Premium	0.92	3.93	8.30	3	5	0	2274	4542	6177
	Group Non-Single Premium	19.02	97.26	41.47	86	558	246	718946	5558528	870858
2	**ING Vysya**									
	Individual Single Premium	0.93	20.55	19.08	121	2524	1862			
	Individual Non-Single Premium	46.57	477.46	449.59	30780	270112	256120			
	Group Single Premium'	0.56	12.04	3.05	0	1	1	335	5008	627
	Group Non-Single Premium	0.32	17.82	251	5	95	18	3613	56564	91908
3	**Reliance Life**									
	Individual Single Premium	30.08	306.90	197.97	6132	73885	44431			
	Individual Non-Single Premium	288.73	2215.85	1283.32	266143	1553224	660922			
	Group Single Premium'	2.13	79.66	205.72	0	20	47	151	46586	69553
	Group Non-Single Premium	3.27	24.79	21.06	32	277	217	37080	585417	317412
4	**SBI Life**									
	Individual Single Premium	38.44	421.30	916.89	7421	74079	126514			
	Individual Non-Single Premium	203.70	2042.20	1532.75	70138	601345	465952			
	Group Single Premium'	22.43	219.20	177.12	0	5	0	35321	157575	89362
	Group Non-Single Premium	47.23	1319.46	247.70	6	95	48	685993	4828926	527163
5	**Tata AIG**									
	Individual Single Premium	1.86	32.68	32.04	428	6782	5448			
	Individual Non-Single Premium	75.22	666.37	555.34	64578	537318	354040			
	Group Single Premium'	1.87	27.96	51.69	0	7	4	2913	77704	307813
	Group Non-Single Premium	31.92	86.91	50.49	8	63	60	27111	282081	182428
6	**HDFC Standard**									
	Individual Single Premium	27.83	119.57	103.83	1982	38202	210775			
	Individual Non-Single Premium	137.16	1798.75	1591.61	83229	690246	529952			
	Group Single Premium'	21.12	86.14	75.61	15	121	108	22944	176900	141062
	Group Non-Single Premium	1.78	23.13	51.68	1	9	40	192	15810	33467

7	**ICICI Prdential**									
	Individual Single Premium	18.98	174.37	300.37	2605	30145	47359			
	Individual Non-Single Premium	472.19	4102.91	4800.95	274016	2128522	2087810			
	Group Single Premium'	2.44	181.91	216.93	4	188	136	44857	567361	409902
	Group Non-Single Premium	133.31	844.30	474.17	10	319	291	17185	537534	377126
8	**Birla Sunlife**									
	Individual Single Premium	3.12	28.86	20.02	14941	129952	72526			
	Individual Non-Single Premium	196.27	1799.78	1147.20	98764	795382	346737			
	Group Single Premium'	0.97	16.22	4.47	0	1	3	2265	41633	5131
	Group Non-Single Premium	14.23	158.44	87.53	8	154	102	12535	214617	131962
9	**Aviva**									
	Individual Single Premium	1.01	34.40	17.11	179	4106	2588			
	Individual Non-Single Premium	50.93	510.11	697.24	28390	281560	268683			
	Group Single Premium'	0.00	0.05	1.73	0	0	0	1	66	984
	Group Non-Single Premium	0.82	15.62	22.33	4	60	93	90995	901109	536146
10	**Kotak Mahindra Old Mutual**									
	Individual Single Premium	0.89	15.87	22.94	142	2017	3066			
	Individual Non-Single Premium	76.93	863.38	582.28	25892	417595	199657			
	Group Single Premium	2.15	29.02	20.09	2	10	2	9669	110784	149333
	Group Non-Single Premium	8.77	52.69	50.54	37	319	206	39354	441562	381628
11	**Max New York**									
	Individual Single Premium	10.00	195.80	208.95	647	13398	13683			
	Individual Non. Single Premium	88.30	1254.27	885.50	68284	955234	595231			
	Group Single Premium	0.14	7.61	0.00	0	10	0	–38	206659	0
	Group Non-Single Premium	0.91	15.77	36.01	7	296	263	8784	204846	457349
12	**Met Life**									
	Individual Single Premium	0.65	5.39	17.37	119	1786	2726			
	Individual Non. Single Premium	92.83	754.95	475.35	30860	220216	157974			
	Group Single Premium	6.59	31.86	9.75	28	129	53	29184	268187	152744
	Group Non-Single Premium	0.00	0.00	0.00	0	0	0	0	0	0

13	**Sahara Life**									
	Individual Single Premium	5.07	37.62	30.22	1647	10304	7819			
	Individual Non. Single Premium	7.52	57.87	48.44	9197	68109	67279			
	Group Single Premium	0.00	0.00	0.00	0	0	0	0	0	0
	Group Non-Single Premium	0.00	0.02	0.00	0	9	6	0	770	271
14	**Shriram Life**									
	Individual Single Premium	1.25	126.15	135.21	246	20015	24466			
	Individual Non. Single Premium	4.46	142.04	90.93	3478	75618	56495			
	Group Single Premium	0.00	0.00	0.04	0	0	2	0	0	4633
	Group Non-Single Premium	0.02	0.40	0.00	0	3	2	2196	25744	623
15	**Bharti Axa Life**									
	Individual Single Premium	0.31	4.53	2.36	41	985	367			
	Individual Non. Single Premium	25.83	207.67	63.88	17778	142718	50222			
	Group Single Premium	0.73	6.13	0.69	1	2	1	1076	27699	371
	Group Non-Single Premium	0.00	0.00	0.00	0	0	0	0	0	0
16	**Future Generali Life**									
	Individual Single Premium	0.74	2.90	0.00	165	606	0			
	Individual Non. Single Premium	18.01	43.93	0.12	14046	41396	6			
	Group Single Premium	0.02	0.07	0.00	0	1	0	64	420	0
	Group Non-Single Premium	3.17	11.61	1.79	13	54	6	19737	242460	66213
17	**IDBI Fortis Life**									
	Individual Single Premium	9.34	84.48		1673	13472				
	Individual Non. Single Premium	12.20	112.88		4319	39028				
	Group Single Premium	0.00	0.00		0	0		0	0	
	Group Non-Single Premium	0.00	0.02		0	1		2955	16308	
18	**Canara HSBC OBC Life**									
	Individual Single Premium	1.83	4.07		147	285				
	Individual Non. Single Premium	34.68	180.01		4216	19862				
	Group Single Premium	0.00	0.00		0	0		0	0	
	Group Non-Single Premium	0.00	0.00		0	0		0	0	

19	**Aegon Religare**									
	Individual Single Premium	**0.93**	1.63		109	**203**				
	Individual Non. Single Premium	**7.15**	15.67		3041	**14166**				
	Group Single Premium	**0.00**	0.00		0	**0**		**0**	0	
	Group Non-Single Premium	**0.00**	0.00		0	**0**		**0**	0	
20	**DLF Pramerica #**									
	Individual Single Premium	**0.00**	0.00		0	**0**				
	Individual Non. Single Premium	**0.31**	0.79		467	**1068**				
	Group Single Premium	**0.00**	0.00		0	**0**		**0**	0	
	Group Non-Single Premium	**0.00**	0.00		0	**0**		**0**	0	
	Private Total									
	Individual Single Premium	**209.03**	1941.89	**2533.46**	50289	**503553**	633696			
	Individual Non. Single Premium	**2106.70**	20167.25	**18107.95**	1291757	**10785618**	8745582			
	Group Single Premium	**62.08**	701.80	**775.18**	53	**500**	357	**151016**	1691124	**1337692**
	Group Non-Single Premium	**264.77**	2668.26	**1087.28**	217	**2312**	1598	**1666676**	13912276	**3974554**
21	**LIC**									
	Individual Single Premium	**8189.60**	18608.49	**15965.85**	1648611	**4538003**	4330794			
	Individual Non. Single Premium	**1607.29**	12631.80	**18076.25**	2713141	**20370473**	22061778			
	Group Single Premium	**604.24**	8617.97	**6581.94**	1669	**15564**	17675	**5033985**	26200359	**17548930**
	Group Non-Single Premium	**0.00**	0.00	**0.00**	0	**0**	0	**0**	0	**0**
	Grand Total									
	Individual Single Premium	**8398.63**	20550.38	**18499.31**	1698900	**5041556**	4964490			
	Individual Non. Single Premium	**3714.00**	32799.06	**36184.20**	4004898	**31156091**	30807360			
	Group Single Premium	**666.32**	9319.78	**7357.13**	1722	**16064**	18032	**5185001**	27891483	**18886622**
	Group Non-Single Premium	**264.77**	2668.26	**1087.28**	217	**2312**	1598	**1666676**	13912276	**3974554**

Note. *1. Cumulative premium / No. of policies upto the month is net of cancellations which may occur during the free look period.*

2. Compiled on the basis of data submitted by the Insurance companies

3. # Started operations in September, 2008

Source : *IRDA Journal.*

Table 40.24

GROSS PREMIUM UNDERWRITTEN BY NON-LIFE INSURERS WITHIN INDIA (SEGMENT WISE):

Sl. No.	Insurer	Fire	Marine	Marine Cargo	Marine Hull	Engineering	Motor
1	Royal Sundaram	45.51	15.05	15.05	0.00	28.54	375.36
	Previous year	55.19	12.35	12.35	0.00	29.73	285.77
2	TATA-AIG	132.01	90.47	90.47	0.00	28.49	171.75
	Previous year	105.73	72.48	72.48	0.00	22.68	182.37
3	Reliance	104.95	55.19	25.69	29.50	88.37	870.02
	Previous year	112.87	32.14	25.14	7.00	74.95	982.71
4	IFFCO Tokio	157.14	91.16	63.95	27.21	60.05	506.90
	Previous year	190.70	49.34	41.62	7.73	67.19	320.62
5	ICICI Lombard	257.22	193.99	72.04	121.96	160.05	982.99
	Previous year	401.54	178.02	48.16	129.86	144.58	955.49
6	Bajaj Allianz	184.53	69.22	56.95	12.28	95.13	1,162.77
	Previous year	221.33	62.47	56.34	6.13	107.12	954.66
7	HDFC ERGO	30.46	5.72	4.03	1.69	7.83	105.55
	Previous year	6.23	2.20	2.20	0.00	4.54	102.17
8	Cholamandalam	48.76	29.86	28.68	1.17	19.35	238.19
	Previous year	58.39	25.64	24.16	1.48	22.98	153.71
9	Future Generali $	11.69	4.22	4.22	0.00	8.97	57.63
	Previous year	0.23	0.52	0.52	0.00	0.18	0.11
10	Universal Sompo*	2.46	0.29	0.29	0.00	0.03	1.04
	Previous year	0.00	0.00	0.00	0.00	0.00	0.00
11	Shriram	0.14	0.00	0.00	0.00	0.22	56.88
	Previous year	0.00	0.00	0.00	0.00	0.00	0.00
11	Bharti Axa	1.02	1.18	0.18	0.00	1.43	4.93
	Previous year	0.00	0.00	0.00	0.00	0.00	0.00
11	New India	577.55	356.15	139.51	216.64	193.16	1,457.63
	Previous year	603.14	307.27	130.32	176.94	161.37	1,487.00
12	National	300.27	157.88	102.92	54.97	107.77	1,623.86
	Previous year sign	287.43	131.60	90.55	41.05	100.17	1,561.37
13	United India	429.11	251.92	146.14	105.78	177.18	1,138.01
	Previous year #	412.10	223.36	125.58	97.78	153.07	1,022.59
14	Oriental	361.27	253.01	127.45	125.56	188.57	1,107.09
	Previous year	402.92	262.49	121.70	140.80	162.90	1,196.26
	Grand Total	2,644.09	1,574.32	877.56	696.76	1,165.13	8,860.60
	Previous year	2,857.80	1,259.90	751.13	608.77	1,051.48	9,204.83
	SPECIALISED INSTITUTIONS						
15	ECGC						
	Previous year						
16	Star Health & Allied Insurance						
	Previous year						
17	Apollo DKV $						
	Previous years						

Note: In case of public sector insurance companies, the segment-wise data submitted may vary from the flash Nos filed with the Authority. As such, the industry totals may vary from the flash figures published for the month of September-2008.
$ Commenced operations in November, 2007.
* Commenced operations in February, 2008.
# There is variation between Segment-wise figures and Monthly Business figures for December, 2008.
Compiled on the basis of data submitted by the Insurance companies

Table 40.25 FOR THE PERIOD APRIL-DECEMBER-2008 (PROVISIONAL & UNAUDITED)

(Rs. Crores)

Motor OD	Motor TP	Health	Aviation	Liability	Personal Accident	All Others	Grand Total
299.45	75.91	88.95	0.00	6.49	21.39	11.23	592.51
231.48	54.30	80.10	0.00	4.08	22.62	6.05	495.90
146.95	24.80	60.16	0.00	89.44	90.88	7.68	670.87
152.01	30.35	52.07	0.00	73.90	78.20	2.04	589.48
622.51	247.51	259.75	9.67	21.86	48.25	37.13	1,495.20
713.26	269.45	221.10	5.99	11.86	36.56	46.27	1,524.47
351.91	154.99	94.05	9.48	27.54	20.60	74.53	1,041.46
219.86	100.77	66.99	4.03	20.14	15.17	65.96	800.13
657.01	325.98	819.54	46.21	67.98	97.82	96.08	2,721.87
679.74	275.75	674.41	30.07	67.71	94.33	78.52	2,624.67
813.70	349.07	214.58	17.91	52.90	40.96	159.35	1,997.34
695.48	259.17	181.57	9.81	35.92	29.02	111.00	1,712.89
87.17	18.38	38.76	0.59	27.72	4.77	12.97	234.36
90.53	11.65	25.69	0.00	17.41	4.46	5.81	168.51
181.50	56.69	127.89	0.00	11.00	19.15	31.73	525.93
123.68	30.03	82.59	– 0.15	11.63	9.09	23.64	387.52
43.59	14.04	27.01	0.00	3.45	7.71	3.15	123.83
0.10	0.02	0.00	0.00	0.00	0.00	0.00	1.04
1.04	0.00	0.41	0.00	0.01	0.87	1.94	7.06
0.00	0.00	0.00	0.00	0.00	0.00	1.94	1.94
29.13	27.75	0.00	0.00	0.07	0.00	0.00	57.31
0.00	0.00	0.00	0.00	0.00	0.00	0.00	0.00
4.08	0.85	0.00	0.00	0.18	0.04	0.06	7.83
0.00	0.00	0.00	0.00	0.00	0.00	0.00	0.00
798.29	659.34	1,042.37	45.53	79.85	64.93	296.30	4,113.48
811.44	675.56	856.74	51.26	66.03	62.78	315.31	3,910.90
1,027.23	596.63	628.63	45.56	36.60	53.71	244.21	3,198.40
981.45	579.92	466.74	38.24	29.93	47.41	259.22	2,922.10
648.26	489.75	631.01	13.05	57.52	53.49	392.11	3,143.40
613.79	408.79	448.33	20.59	50.34	64.33	370.24	2,764.96
645.67	461.42	525.79	66.16	60.57	68.02	335.22	2,965.71
737.55	458.71	402.52	58.94	51.58	67.47	289.81	2,894.90
6,357.49	3,503.11	4,558.90	254.06	543.18	592.60	1,703.68	22,896.56
6,050.36	3,154.47	3,558.84	218.79	440.53	531.42	1,575.81	20,799.41
						537.39	537.39
						473.96	473.96
		363.24			15.15	3.22	381.62
		136.00			14.87	2.63	153.50
		31.02					31.02
		0.00					0.00

Table 40.26 General Insurance

Insure	*Gross Crors Premune*	*Premium In ₹*	*Underwritten crores*	*Market*	*Shares in %*	
	2003-04	*2004-05*	*2005-06*	*2003-04*	*2004-05*	*2005-06*
1. Royal Sundaram	258.02	303.71	453.57	1.61	1.83	
2. Tata AIG	353.31	468.87	612.38	2.20	2.59	
3. Reliance General	161.05	161.68	162.33	1.00	0.89	
4. IFFOO-Tokio	295.64	501.28	896.11	1.84	2.80	
5. ICICI Landlord	506.72	885.16	1592.00	3.16	4.89	
6. Bajaj Allianz	476.31	856.07	1287.68	2.97	4.71	
7. HDFC CHUBB	3111.67	183.84	202.37	0.70	0.98	
8. Cholanandalam	96.68	170.10	220.42	0.60	0.94	
9. New India	4045.69	4210.81	4762.12	25.23	23.25	
10. Nitional	3417.00	3799.91	3524.00	21.3	21.14	
11. Until India	3038.05	2944.59	3146.98	18.94	16.37	
12. Oriental	2832.11	3017.78	3518.64	17.66	16.79	
Print Total		3557.72	5426.87			
Public Total		13973.10	14951.74			
Grand Total	1665.53	17530.81	20378.61	100.00	100.00	
Specialised Instance						
FCGC	445.12	515.54	578.46	2.78	2.86	

Table 40.27 Gross Premium Underwritten For and upto the Month of January 2009

Insurer	**January**		**April - January**		**Growth over the Corresponding period of previous year**
	2008-09	**2007-08**	**2008-09**	**2007-08**	
Royal Sundaram	70.52	70.30	663.03	566.20	17.10
Tata-AIG	76.19	82.81	749.72	672.28	11.52
Reliance General	140.70	149.17	1635.90	1673.64	–2.26
IFFCO-Tokio	120.07	127.34	1161.53	927.47	25.24
ICICI-lombard	317.80	278.43	3039.67	2903.10	4.70
Bajaj Allianz	217.09	212.57	2214.43	1925.46	15.01
HDFC ERGO General	33.62	17.46	267.97	185.98	44.09
Cholamandalam	62.04	48.00	587.97	435.52	35.01
Future Generali $	26.38	4.42	150.14	5.43	2662.80
Universal Sompo #	4.99	0.00	12.05	0.00	
Shriram General @	24.63	0.00	81.94	0.00	
Bharti AXA General @	6.47	0.00	14.30	0.00	
New India	456.58	451.30	4569.98	4359.75	4.82
National	360.55	373.96	3558.95	3296.06	7.98
United India	351.33	316.13	3491.07	3081.08	13.31
Oriental	338.93	328.68	3304.64	3223.58	2.51
Private Total	**1100.48**	**990.50**	**10578.65**	**9295.08**	**13.81**
Public Total	**1507.39**	**1470.07**	**14924.64**	**13960.47**	**6.91**
Grand Total	**2607.87**	**2460.57**	**25503.29**	**23255.55**	**9.67**
Specialised Institutions :					
1. Credit Insurance ECGC	62.15	56.99	599.53	530.95	12.92
2. Health Insurance					
Star Health & Allied Insurance	102.76	4.29	484.38	157.79	206.98
Apollo DKV	4.71	0.49	38.01	0.61	6167.24
Health Total	**107.47**	**4.78**	**522.39**	**158.39**	**229.80**
3. Agriculture Insurance AIC	71.54	126.57	653.12	700.16	–6.72

Note : Compiled on the basis of data submitted by the Insurance companies
$ Commenced operations in November, 2007 # Commenced operations in February 2008
@ Commenced operations in July, 2008 * Figures revised by insurance companies

Table 40.28: Average Productivity of the tied agents of the life insurers as on 31.03.2012

Insurers	*Average Productivity of Agents*	*Insurers*	*Average Productivity of Agents*
Aegon Religare	4	ING Vysya	6
Aviva	3	Kotak Mahindra	3
Bajaj Allianz	3	Max Life	6
Bharti Axa	4	Metlife	3
Birla Sunlife	3	Reliance	4
DLF Pramerica	5	Sahara	5
Edleweiss Toko	12	SBI Life	6
Future Generaili	2	Shriram Life	5
HDFC Standard	3	Star Union Dai-Ichi	12
ICICI Prudential	2	Tata AIA	2
IDBI Federal	3	LIC	27
India First	5	Industry Average	16

Source: IRDA Annual Report 2011-12

Table 40.29. Persistency Ratios (based on Number of Policies) of some leading life insurers during 2011-12

Insurers	*Persistency Ratios*				
	13 month	*25 month*	*37 month*	*49 month*	*61 month*
Aviva	58.00	47.00	25.00	24.00	19.00
Bajal Allianz	54.57	85.76	19.03	51.85	43.50
Bharti AXA	58.20	51.60	46.80	52.20	39.60
Birla Sulife	82.00	77.00	72.00	62.00	53.00
HDFC Standard	75.35	88.11	63.50	66.38	78.40
ICICI Prudential	77.00	86.70	31.80	50.60	65.30
ING Vysya	65.00	55.00	38.00	36.00	38.00
Kotak Mahindra	70.00	61.00	50.00	40.00	40.00
Max Life	75.00	62.00	42.00	39.00	31.00
Metlife	63.56	56.84	50.32	47.44	44.82
Reliance	55.90	78.10	29.10	70.30	76.70
Sahara	73.73	65.14	43.04	39.92	41.74
SBI Life	71.77	60.52	20.54	16.27	23.35
Shriram	51.40	82.30	39.10	80.30	84.70
Tata AIA	44.71	18.10	17.32	16.31	14.03
LIC	67.00	61.00	53.00	46.00	51.00

Source: IRDA Annual Report 2011-12

Table 40.24 Progress of General Insurance

Year Ended March, 2007 (Provisional & Unaudited)

(Rs. in Crores)

S. No.	Insurer	Fire	Marine	Marine Cargo	Marine Hull	Engineering	Motor	Motor OD	Motor TP	Health	Aviation	Liability	Personal Accident	All Others	Grand Total
1.	Royal Sundaram (March 2007)	102.47	18.32	17.73	0.59	37.73	303.39	261.46	41.93	97.45	0.00	8.45	25.08	7.14	600.03
	Previous year (March 2006)	92.39	18.30	17.72	0.58	28.07	233.09	209.78	23.31	50.59	0.00	6.73	24.47	5.71	459.35
2.	TATA-AIG	130.25	71.31	71.31	0.00	26.29	288.09	262.21	25.88	45.35	0.25	73.47	79.40	27.15	741.56
	Previous year	119.00	49.11	49.11	0.00	21.71	259.34	239.56	19.78	30.62	0.02	57.61	58.48	16.50	612.39
3.	Reliance	146.15	24.92	16.45	8.47	93.68	454.99	408.60	46.39	67.69	7.23	10.03	16.47	91.07	912.23
	Previous year	46.68	20.75	10.18	10.57	23.73	26.41	26.19	0.32	8.61	7.00	4.95	5.98	18.12	162.33
4.	IFFCO Tokio	294.76	129.96	52.24	77.73	90.91	448.90	348.63	100.27	71.89	4.74	12.70	17.44	79.03	1,150.32
	Previous year	226.43	46.24	36.11	10.13	65.82	379.69	318.73	60.96	51.97	0.73	10.09	16.65	98.51	896.11
5.	ICICI Lombard	403.05	155.25	56.23	99.02	177.54	1,143.34	956.73	186.60	735.85	32.07	84.02	113.74	158.59	3,003.45
	Previous year	311.87	85.71	42.14	43.57	85.98	458.80	404.05	54.75	274.46	16.60	60.90	76.25	221.43	1,592.00
6.	Bajaj Allianz	383.67	72.99	60.43	12.56	154.77	843.87	668.39	175.48	158.26	7.94	29.73	24.31	129.07	1,804.60
	Previous year	360.79	55.73	41.42	14.31	99.88	536.61	357.76	178.85	97.69	4.75	23.59	15.50	90.02	1,284.57
7.	HDFC Chubb	7.65	2.37	2.37	0.00	5.98	132.36	123.83	8.53	10.18	0.00	4.76	7.69	19.17	190.16
	Previous year	5.82	1.72	1.72	0.00	3.52	158.03	149.85	8.18	4.55	0.00	2.81	11.77	17.56	205.77
8.	Cholamandalam	80.54	26.56	25.66	0.90	23.72	97.16	80.53	16.63	38.60	0.40	14.70	7.63	25.27	314.59
	Previous year	73.07	17.00	16.67	0.33	20.71	52.35	47.86	4.49	21.11	0.94	13.08	12.57	11.37	222.21
9.	New India	909.98	321.03	158.72	162.31	210.31	2,034.73	1,233.71	801.02	765.29	115.27	60.65	79.39	518.07	5,014.71
	Previous year	839.63	299.78	149.34	150.45	144.70	2,174.50	1,394.35	780.16	669.28	116.85	64.34	95.78	386.63	4,791.50
10.	National	491.21	196.97	120.29	76.68	134.95	1,980.16	1,310.14	670.03	333.12	84.49	36.42	55.24	498.30	3,810.88
	Previous year	482.01	172.29	126.84	45.45	109.11	1,853.29	1,289.60	563.69	294.25	71.26	35.68	66.87	438.91	3,523.67
11.	United India	674.77	264.35	135.31	129.05	203.96	1,219.18	767.30	451.88	434.64	45.36	67.79	95.31	504.59	3,509.95
	Previous year	645.48	203.96	125.01	78.95	184.96	1,138.16	703.26	434.90	359.26	37.07	59.14	98.98	427.76	3,154.78
12.	Oriental	538.50	349.78	168.76	181.02	214.27	1,732.26	1,158.88	573.39	440.53	119.54	61.61	85.69	398.35	3,940.53
	Previous year	546.89	325.12	166.92	158.20	187.01	1,495.36	981.27	514.10	359.72	149.65	58.17	97.05	308.16	3,527.13
	Grand Total	4,163.00	1,633.81	885.49	748.32	1,374.09	10,678.43	7,580.41	3,098.02	3,198.83	417.29	464.32	607.42	2,455.81	24,993.01
	Previous year	3,750.06	1,295.71	783.17	512.54	975.22	8,765.75	6,122.26	2,643.49	2,222.09	404.86	397.06	580.35	2,040.68	20,431.80
	Specialised Institutions														
13.	ECGC*													618.05	618.05
	Previous year (March 2006)													578.46	578.46
14.	Star Health & Allied Insurance**									11.05			11.38		22.42
	Previous year (March 2006)									0.00			0.00		0.00

Note : In case of public sector insurance companies, the segment wise data submitted may very from the flash Nos filed with the Authority. As such a industry totals may vary from the flash figures published for the month of March, 2007.

Life Insurers

S.No	Name of the Company Principal Actuary	Name of Appointed Web Address	Name of Fax No./E-male	Telephone No. Officer
1.	Bajaj Allianz Life Insurance Company Limited GE Plaza, Airport Road, yerawada Pune 411 006	Mr. Sam Ghosh	Mr. Andrew Wakeling	Tel: 020-4026666 Fax: 020-4026789
2.	Birla Sun Life Insurance Co. Ltd 6th Floor, Vaman Centre, Makhwana Road, off Andheri-Kurla Road Andheri(E), Mumbai-400 059.	Nani B Javeri	Mr. Kedar Mulgund	Tel: 022 56783333 Fax: 022 56783232
3.	HDFC Standard Life Insurance Co. Ltd "Trade Star" 2nd floor, 'A' Wing, Kondivita Road Junction Andheri-Kurla Road Andheri (East) Mumbai 400 059.	Mr. D.M. Satwalekar	Mr. Nick Taket	Tel: 022-8222234/ 5551 6551 Fax: 022-2822-8844
4.	ICICI Prudential Life Insurance Co. Ltd ICICI Prulite Towers, 1089, Appasahcb Marathe Marg, Prabhadevi, Mumbai 400 025	Ms. Shikha Sharma	Mr.V. Rajagopalan	Tel: 022-56621996 Fax: 022-5622031
5.	ING Vysya Life Insurance Company Pvt. Ltd. ING Vysya Home, 5th Floor, # 22 Mahatma Gandhi Road Bangalore-560 001.	Mr. Kshitij Jain	Ms. Hemamalini Ramakrishnan	Tel: 080-2532800 Fax:080-25559764
6.	Life Insurance Corporation of India Yougakshema, Jeevan Bima Marg, Post Box No. 19953 Mumbai 400 021	Shri T.S. Vijayan	Mr. Gorakh Nath Agarwal	Tel: 56598701: 56598702 Fax: 22824386 E-mail: chairman@licindia.com
7.	Max New York LIfe Insurance Co. Ltd. 11th Floor, DLF square, Jacaranda Marg, DLF City, Phase-II, Gurgaon 122 002.	Mr. Gary R. Benett	MR. John Charles Poole	Tel: 0124-2561717 Fax:0124-2561764
8.	Met Life India Insurance company Pvt. Ltd. Brigade Seshamahal, No. 5, Vani Vilas Road Basavanagudi, Bangalore -560 004.	Mr. Venktesh Mysore	Mr. K. P. Sarma	Tel: 080-26438638 Fax:080-26521970 Toll Free No. 1-600-44-6969

Note: This table was prepared at the time of formation of the companies

Continue...

9.	Kotak Mahindra Old Mutual Life Insurance Limited 6th Floor Penisula Chambers, Penisula Corporate Park, Lower parel, Mumbai-400 013.	Mr. Gaurang Shah	Mr. A. Venkatasubramanian	Tel: 022-56635000 Fax: 022-56635111
10.	SBI Life Insurance Co. Ltd. Turner morrison Building 2nd Floor, 16 Bank Street, Fort Mumbai-400 023.	Mr. S. Krishna Murthy	Mr. I Sambasiva Rao	Tel: 022-56392000 Fax:022-56621471
11.	Tata AIG Life Insurance Co. Ltd. 5th 7 6th Floor, Peninsula Tower, Peninsula corporate Park Ganpatrao kadam Marg, Lower Parel, Mumbai 400 013.	Mr. Trevor Bull	Mr. Heerak Basu	Tel: 022-56516000 Fax:022-56550711
12.	Reliance Life Insurance Company Limited "The Trapezium" 39, First Floor, Nelson Manickam Road Chennai- 600 029	Mr. P Nandagopal	Ms. Pournima Gupte	Tel: 044-30588200 Fax:044-30588220
13.	Aviva Life Insurance Co. India Pvt. Ltd. 5th floor, JMD Regent Square, Mehrauli road, Gurgaon - 122001	Mr. Stuart Purdy	Mr. KK Wadhwa	Tel: 0124-2804141 Fax:0124-2804151
14.	Sahara India Life Insurance Co. Ltd. Sahara India Bhawan, Kopoorthala Complex, Lucknow 226024	Mr. N C. Sharma	Mr. K K Dharni	Tel: 0522-2337777 Fax:0522-2378200
15.	Shriram Life Insurance Co. Ltd. Regd. Office : 3-6-478, 3rd Floor, Anand Estate, Liberty Road, Himayat Nagar, Hyderabad - 500029	Mr R Duruvasan	Mr N S Sastry	Tel: 040-23434466-72 Fax: 040-23434488
16.	Bharti AXA Life Insurance Company Ltd. 61/62, Kalpataru Synergy, Vakola, Opp. Grand Hyatt Hotel, Santacruz (E) Mumbai-400 055	Mr. Nitin Chopra	Mr. K. S. Gopalakrishnan	Tel: 022-40306300/6301 Fax: 022-40306347

Continue...

Non-Life Insurance

	Name of the Company	Name of the Principal Officer	Name of the Appointed actuary	Telephone No. Fax. No./Email. & Web Address
1.	Bajaj allianz General Insurance Co. Ltd. GE Plaza, Airport Road, Yerawada, Pune 411 006.	Mr. Kamesh Goyal	Ms. Asha J. Joshi	Tel: 020-6602 666 Fax: 020-6602 666
2.	ICICI Lombard General Insurance Co. Ltd. Zenith House, Keshavrao Khade Marg, Mahalaxmi Mumbai-400 034	Mr. Sandeep Bakshi	Mr. Liyaquat Khan	Tel: 022-2490699 Fax: 022-2492762
3.	IFFCO Toko General Insurance Co. Ltd 4 and 5th Floors, IFFCO Tower, Plot No. 3, Sector 29, Gurgaon-122001 (Haryana)	Mr. Ajit Narain	Mr. A. Peetambaram	Tel: 0124-285010 Fax: 0124-257792
4.	National Insurance Co. Ltd. 3, Middleton Street, P.B. No. 9229, Kolkata 700 071.	Mr. V. Ramasaamy	Mr. Bhudeb Chatterjee	Tel: 033-2283170 Fax: 033-2283171
5.	The New India Assurance Co. Ltd. New India Assurance Bldg. 87, M. G. Road, Fort, Mumbai 400 011.	Mr. B Chakrabarthi	Mr. A. R. Prabhu	Tel: 022-2267461 Fax: 022-2265281
6.	The Oriental Insurance Co. Ltd. A-25/27, Asaf Ali Road New Delhi 110 002.	Mr. M. Ramadoss	Mr. P. C. Gupta	Tel: 011-23279221 Direct: 23265024 Fax: 23287192,232 23283971
7.	Reliance General Insurance Co. Ltd. 19 Reliance Centre Walchand Hirachand Marg, Ballard Estate, Mumbai-400 038	Mr. K.A. Somasekaran	Mr. Gopalakrishna Pai	Tel: 022-3023750 Fax: 022-3027123
8.	Royal Sundaram Alliance Insurance Co. Ltd. "Sundaram Towars" 45-46, Whites Road, Royapetah Chennai-600 014.	Mr. Antony Jacob	Mr. O. Lakshminarayana	Tel: 044-4222737 Fax: 044-28517370 Email: customer.services@
9.	Tata AIG General Insurance Co. Ltd.	Mr. Dalip Verma	Mr. K. Hanumanth Rao	Tel: 022-6669969

	Peninsula corporate Park, Nicholas Piramal Tower, 9th Floor Ganpatrao Kadam Marg Lower parel Mumbai 400 013			Fax: 044:2851737
10.	United India Insurance Co. Ltd. 24, Whites Road Chennai - 600 014.	Mr. M. K. Garg	Mr. S. Krishnan	Tel: 044-2852016 Fax: 044-2852382
11.	Cholamandalam MS General Insurance Co. Ltd. "Dare House" 2nd Floor New No. 2 (Old No. 234) N. S. C. Bose Road, Chennai-600 001	Mr. M. Anandan	Mr. Venkatesan	Tel: 044-4216600 Fax: 044-4216600
12.	HDFC-Chubb General Insurance Co. Ltd. 5th Floor, Express Towers, Nariman Point, Mumbai 400021	Mr. Shrirang V Samant	Mr. Narayannan Laksmanan	Tel: 022-6638 36 Fax: 022-6638 36
13.	Export Credit Guarantee Corporation Ltd. 10th Floor, Express Towers, Nariman Point, Mumbai-400021	Shri Christy Fernandez, IAS		Tel: 022-56590512-515 Fax: 022-5659051 022-5659053
14.	Agriculture Insurance Co. of India Ltd. 13th Floor, 14 K. G. Marg Connaught Place, New Delhi -110001	Mr. M. Parshad	Mr. Nalin Kapadia	Tel : 011-4108199 Fax: 011-4108199 Email: aicho@aicofi
15.	Star Health and Allied Insurance Company Limited No.1, New Tank Street, Vlluvarkottam High Road, Nungambakkam, Chennai-600 034	Mr. V. Jagannathan	Mr. R. Soundararajan	Tel: 044-2826005 Fax: 044-2826006

मरीन कार्गो विभाग/ MARINE CARGO DEPARTMENT

एम ए/MA3

प्रति/ To,

युनाइटेड इंडिया इन्श्योरेन्स कम्पनी लिमिटेड
पंजीकृत व प्रधान कार्यालय :
24, व्हाइट्स रोड चेन्नै - 6000 01

United India Insurance Co. Ltd.
Redg. & Head Office:
24, Whites Road Chennai - 600 014

कृपया आप द्वारा जारी ओपेन पॉलिसी क्रमांक .... के अन्तर्गत निम्नलिखित माल की किश्त भुगतान के आधार पर बीमित करें :-

Please Insure the following goods under Open Policy No. .... Issued by you on account of

रेल/लारी द्वारा रे.र./प्र.स. .... के अन्तर्गत दिनांक .... को प्रेषित

Despatch by Rail/Lorry, under R.R./c. No. .... dated ....

पोत एस.एस. ".. ल.बि.सं. .... दिनांकित ....

Vesel S.S. ".." B/L No. .... dated ....

डेक के अन्तगंत या पर .... से .... तक .... प्रेषित

Shipped on or under deck .... from .... to ....

आवरित किया जाने वाले जोखिम ....

Risk to be cover ....

मार्क और सं. **Marks or Nos.**	माल का विवरण **Description of Goods**	बीमित की जाने वाली राशि/मात्रा **Amount to be Insured**

केवल कार्यालय के प्रयोगार्थ/For Office Use Only

घोषणा सं. .... के अन्तर्गत बीमित/Insured under Declaration No.

ओपन पॉलिसी सं............. / Open Policy No.

दिनांक .... को अभिलेखित / Record on Date

प्रीमियम रु./ Premium Rs.................................

हस्ताक्षर/ Signature

आद्याक्षर / Initials

स्थान / Place

दिनांक / Date

Tata AIG General Insurance Company Limited
Marine Insurance Application Form

TATA AIG INSURANCE
WITH YOU ALWAYS

1. Name and Address of the applicant/Bank, if any* [ ]
2. Phone & Fax nos. & e-mail address [ ]
3. Merchandise/Goods to be insured* [ ]
4. Nature of Packing* [ ]
5. Marks & Nos. [ ]
6. Conveyance* ☐ Sea ☐ Air ☐ Closed Rail wagons Covered Trucks
   ☐ Courier ☐ Post ☐ Others
7. Name of the Vessel [ ]
8. B/L, AWB, RR/CN no. and date [ ]
9. Voyage/Transit* From [ ] To [ ]
10. Transshipment &/or storage if any (specify place and period) [ ]
11. Basis of Valuation* [ ]
12. Value declared for insurance*
    In foreign currency [ ]
    In Indian Rupees [ ]
13. Terms of cover required* ☐ All Risks ☐ Basic
14. Specify LC wordings, if any, to be incorporated: [ ]
15. Any other details about the risk: [ ]
16. Producer Name & Code, if applicable: * [ ]

Corporate Office: Ahura Centre, 4th Floor, 82 Mahakali Caves Road, Andheri (E), Mumbai-4000093.
(Regd. Office: Bombay House, 24 Homi Mody Street, Mumbai - 400001)
For more information, call the Tata AIG Toll-free-24 hours Helpline at - 1-600-119966

1 of 2

Declaration by Applicant

I/We here by declare that the statement made by me/us herein and in attachments here to are true to the best of my/our knowledge and belief and I/We hereby agree that this Proposal shall form the basis of the insurance contract between me/us and Tata AIG General Insurance Company Ltd. (referred to as the Company). I/We further confirm that if any additions or alterations are carried out in the risk proposed for insurance herein after the submission of this Proposal then particulars of such shall be forthwith conveyed to the Company. I/We further agree that the submission of this Proposal to the Company and its receipt thereof shall not constitute an acceptance of the risk by the Company.

Place		Signature of Applicant	
Date		Name & Designation	
Time		Cheque no. and Date	
Amount of Cheque			

ATTACHMENTS

Invoice/Packing List/LC wordings/BL or contract of affreightment/if other, specify.

(IMPORTANT) Prohibition of Rebates (Section 41 of the Insurance Act 1938)

1. No person shall allow or offer to allow either directly or indirectly as inducement to any Person to take out renew or continue an Insurance in respect of any kind of risk relating to lives or property in India any rebate of the whole or part of the commission payable or any rebate of the premium shown on the Policy, nor shall any person taking out or renewing or continuing a Policy accept such rebate except such rebate as may be allowed in accordance with the published prospectuses or tables of the insurer.
2. Any person making default in complying with the provision of this section shall be punishable with fine which may extend to five hundred rupees only.

NOTE.

1. Premium cheque to be drawn in favour of Tata AIG General Insurance Company Limited.
2. Policies proposed and taken after commencement of transit shall be deemed to be null and void.
3. Non-disclosure or misrepresentation in application form will render the contract null and void.
4. For Sea shipments-Institute Classification Clause (extended for Vessels upto 20 years).
   Vessels < 20 years > 25 years additional premium @ 0.125%. VESSELS NOT TO EXCEED 25 YEARS
5. Insurance policy taken should run concurrent to your sale terms and not exceeding the same.
6. This application shall form part of the policy and in case of a dispute referred to as base document.
7. Fields marked in* are Mandatory fields.
8. Please ask for copy of the Clauses in case you require it alongwith the Policy document
9. Shipment details to be furnished within 7 days of sailing

FOR OFFICE USE

Corporate Office: Ahura Centre, 4th Floor, 82 Mahakali Caves Road, Andheri (E), Mumbai-4000093.
(Regd. Office: Bombay House, 24 Homi Mody Street, Mumbai - 400001)
For more information, call the Tata AIG Toll-free-24 hours Helpline at - 1-600-119966

- Ordinary leakage, ordinary loss in weight or volume, ordinary wear and tear and inherent flaws in the cargo insured;
- Delay
- Insolvency and financial distress of the carriers;
- Un-seaworthiness of vessel
- Strike, riot, civil commotion, war and nuclear risks

In appropriate cases, however, loss or damage to cargo insured due to strike, riot, civil commotion and/or war can be covered upon payment of additional premium.

Premium Payable

Sum insured for cargo for insurance purposes would be on the following basis:

Cost of cargo + Insurance + Freight (CIF) + 10% of CIF towards incidental charges.

Sum insured for Customs Duty shall be the actual duty payable.

The Company will determine the premium payable for the Policy from time to time depending on:

(*i*) Nature cargo
(*ii*) Mode of conveyance
(*iii*) Nature of packing
(*iv*) Risks to be covered
(*v*) Destination
(*vi*) Past experience with respect to claims, if any, under any Policy/Policies
(*vii*) Any other matters connected with or incidental to the risks to be covered

About us

Reliance General Insurance is one of the fastest growing general insurance companies in India with innovative product offerings and customer service standards that are benchmarked to the best in the world. The company aims to increase its presence in the retail and corportate sectors with a focus on customer centric products, multiple distribution channels and technology.

Reliance General Insurance is a 100% subsidiary of Reliance Capital Limited. Relaince Capital is a part of the Reliance Anil Dhirubhai Ambani group.

Some of our other product:

▪ Reliance HealthWise Policy ▪ Reliance Shopkeeper's Package Policy ▪ Reliance HomeProtect Policy ▪ Reliance Office Package Policy ▪ Reliance Industry Care Policy ▪ Reliance SME care Policy ▪ Reliance Standard Fire & Special Perils Insurance Policy ▪ Reliance Burglary & Housebreaking Insurance Policy

This product brochure gives the salient features of the plan only. For further details on all the conditions and exclusions related to Reliance Marine Cargo Policy, please contact us.

1800 3002 8282 (toll free)
3989 8282 (local charges apply)

sms **'protect'** to **55454**
www.reliancegeneral.co.in

RELIANCE General Insurance
Anil Dhirubhai Ambani Group
A Reliance Company

Reliance General Insurance Company Limited
Registered office Reliance Centre, 19, Walchand Hirachand Marg, Ballard Estate, Mumbai 400 001.

Insurance is the subject matter of solicitation. MC-01

Reliance Marine Cargo Policy

RELIANCE General Insurance
Anil Dhirubhai Ambani Group
A Reliance Company

Welcome to Reliance General Insurance

The term safety is strongly associated with transport and cargo business. However, sometimes even despite the best effort, an uncontrollable factor can cause an untoward event. This always leads to a considerable loss of valued goods, money and time. At such times, what you need is a Policy that offers you financial protection and saves you mental agony. Reliance General Insurance is pleased to offer you such a Policy, which ensures seamless coverage whether you cargo is on land, at sea, in the air or in the hands of any postal service.

Key Advantages

- Comprehensive coverage for your cargo during transit from ne place to another
- Provides cover for cargo sent by all modes of transport-be it Rail/Road/or Air
- World class service standards to facilitate prompt and quick claims settlement

Types of Policies

Specific Policy:

Covers specific transit of a cargo between specified locations.

Open Policy:

Covers a series of transits of cargo during a specific period of insurance.

Open Cover:

Similar to Open Policy but limited to covering imports.

Scope of Cover

Provides cover against loss or damage to cargo during transit from one place to another by any one or more modes of transport on 'strict liability basis', that is to say, whether or not fault or negligence on the part of the carrier is proved.

Coverage provided under Marine Cargo policies ranges from a restricted form of cover to the widest available form of cover, namely, All Risks as opted by the client.

Transit	Clauses available
Inland Transit	Inland Transit (Rail/Road) Clauses C (Basic cover) Inland Transit (Rail/Road) Clauses B (Restricted cover) Inland Transit (Rail/Road) Clauses A (All Risk cover)
Overseas Transit (by Sea)	Institute Cargo Clauses C Institute Cargo Clauses B Institute Cargo Clauses A Institute Commodity/Trade Clauses
Transit by Air	Institute Cargo Clauses (Air)

Institute Cargo Clauses

Coverage available under the Institute Cargo Clauses are given here.

Inland Transit Clauses

Insurance of goods carried by Rail, Road, Inland waterways are covered as per coverage granted under Inland Transit (Rail/Road) Clauses A, B, C, Inland Transit (Inland Vessels Clauses).

Inland Transit (Rail/Road) B and C Clauses and Inland Transit (Inland vessels) Clauses are restrictive in nature. Where as Inland Transit (Rail/Road) A Clause provides all risk cover subject to certain specific exclusions.

Exclusions

At Reliance General Insurance, we would like things to be as transparent as possible. To ensure that you do not face any misunderstandings when you make a claim, we would like you to know some of the major exclusions under the Policy:

- Willful misconduct of the Insured
- Insufficiency or unsuitability of packing or preparation of the cargo insured;

Institute Cargo Clauses A	Institute Cargo Clauses B	Institute Cargo Clauses C
All Risk Cover	**Restricted Cover**	**Basic Cover**
■ Fire of Explosion ■ Standing, Grounding, Sinking or Capsizing ■ Overturning or Derailment ■ Collision or contact of vessel craft or conveyance with any external object other than water ■ Discharge of cargo at point of distress ■ Earthquake, volcanic eruption or lightining and water damage by entry of sea/river water (excluding rainwater) ■ Total loss of package lost overboard ■ Total loss of package dropped during loading and unloading ■ Breakage ■ Scratching, Chipping, Denting & Bruising ■ Theft ■ Malicious Damage ■ Non Delivery ■ All water damage including rain damage	■ Fire or Explosion ■ Standing, Grounding, Sinking or Capsizing ■ Overturning or Deraliment ■ Collision or contact of vessel craft or conveyance with any external objects other than water ■ Discharge of cargo at point of distress ■ Earthquake, volcanic eruption or lightning and water damage by entry of sea/river water (excluding rainwater) ■ Total loss of package lost overboard ■ Total loss of package dropped during loading and unloading	■ Fire or Explosion ■ Standing, Grounding, Sinking or Capsizing ■ Overturning or Derailment ■ Collision or contact of vessel craft or conveyance with any external objects other than water. ■ Discharge of cargo at point of distress.

SURVEY REQUEST FORM

To: Ian Short BEng CEng MRINA, 8 Queens Park Gardens, Seaford, East Sussex BN 25 2QE
Fax: +44 (0) 1323 896861 Tel: + 44 (0) 1323 873267 email : info@marine-surveys. org

I/we having obtained permission from the owners (if applicable) hereby request that you carry out a pre-purchase condition/insurance condition & valuation/partial survey (please delete as applicable), subject to your normal terms of survey as set out below, which I have received, read and understood, and to any special instructions listed below, on the vessel named:

Name of vessel							
Type or class of vessel							
Length		Beam		Draft		Year built	
Builder				Construction material			
Vessel located at							
Arrangement for keys							
Owner/Brokers name				Telephone			
Please advise of any special instructions							

I/we hereby agree to pay any fees and expenses reasonably incurred and charged by the Surveyor and understand that I am/we are responsible for all charges for botat movements, slipping, docking, removals, replacement and reinstatement work arising in preparation for and process of the survey.

It is understood and agreed that the surveyor's report will be a factual statement of the examination carried out within stated limitations and with opinions given in good faith as far as seen and accessible at the time of survey. It carries with it no guarantee against faulty design or latent defects or suitability of the vessel for any particular purpose, nor any guarantee of compliance with any particular national or international rule, requirement, regulation, law, standard or code unless specifically requested on this form and confirmed in the text of the report. Liability for the report is solely to the instructing client and to no other third party unless otherwise specified and agreed. It is further agreed that no liability will arise for any consequential or economic loss, loss of profits, business interruption or loss of use.

I/we acknowledge that this survey contract shall be governed by and construed in accordance with English law and that any dispute arising hereunder shall be submitted to the exclusive jurisdiction of the courts of England and Wales.

Survey reports are normally released within 5 working days of the date of survey, subject to all outstanding accounts being settled.

Fee quoted	£	Date				
Name		Signed				
Address						
Tel day		Tel mobile				
Fax		email				
Where did you hear about Marine Surveys (tick box)		Internet		Magazine ad		other

Cover Note Request Form

Thank you for selecting National Transport Insurance.

To ensure that your client's interests are fully protected we require the following information.

You acknowledge that completion and submission of this document represents that you act on behalf of your client.

You acknowledge that you have provided your client with advice in relation to the DUTY OF DISCLOSURE, AVERAGE/UNDER INSURANCE, THIRD PARTY INTERESTS AND SUBROGATION clauses.

You acknowledge that if requested by National Transport Insurance, your client agrees to obtain from the appropriate Commissioner of Motor Transport within 14 days of receiving notice thereof, a complete and up to date record of offences in respect of which your client has been reported and/or convicted.

You acknowledge that all particulars and statements contained in the original quote request are those of your client, and are true and correct, and that together with this declaration they shall form the basis of the contract between your client and National Transport Insurance and be incorporated therein.

You acknowledge that neither your client nor yourself have with held any information to our questions that is likely to affect our cover, in that we may reduce or refuse to pay a claim on this Cover Note.

You acknowledge that if your client answered our question fraudulently, we may refuse to pay a claim and treat the cover as not have been effected.

Please indicate your acceptance by ticking ☐ **I accept the terms of this declaration**

Cover Note Details

* Quotation Number :

* Cover Required From:

Note: Cover will commence at 4pm local time on the above date unless specified by NTI Express.

Proposer Details

* Name of the Proposer:

ABN Number:

*Trading Name:

*Phone Number: Mobile Phone Number :

*Street No & Name:

*Suburb:

*Postcode:

Email Address:

Trailers in Control

* If you have been quoted for Trailer in Control, do you require cover to be placed on the quoted Trailer in Control items: Select

No Claim Bonus

* Are you entitled to a No Claim Bonus? Select

*Name of Previous Insurer:

*Name of Policy Owner:

*Policy Number: * Expiry Date: dd mm yy

*Vehicle Insured:

(or "As Above" if applicable)

Liability Cover

* If NTI Express has quoted you for Liability Cover, do you require Liability Cover? Select

Marine Cargo Cover

* If NTI Express has quoted you for Marine Cargo Cover, do you require Marine Cargo Cover? Select

Business Interruption Cover

* If NTI Express has quoted you for Business Interruption Cover, do you require Business Interruption Cover? Select

Submit Cover

* Intermediary Email Address:

Print Form Send

RELIANCE General Insurance
Anil Dhirubhai Ambani Group

A Reliance Capital Company
1800 3002 8282 (toll free)
3989 8282 (local charges apply)
www.reliancegeneral.co.in

Proposal Form for Reliance Marine Cargo Policy

The policy does not commence until the proposal is accepted and premium paid

Intermediary Details (To be filled in BLOCK LETTERS)

Intermediary Name ______ Code ______

Branch Name ______ Code ______

Sales Manager Name ______ Code ______

Personal Details

1. Name of the Proposer M/s ______
2. Address
   Flat Building ______
   Road/Street/Sector ______
   Area ______
   Taluka/Village/District City ______ Pin Code ______
   State ______ Country ______
3. Customer ID, if any ______
   Contact Person, if any ______ Phone ______
   Email ______

Cargo Details

In addition to questions i to ix, you are also required to answer questions x and xi only in case of specific policy and questions xii, xiii and xiv only in case of policies other than specific policy.

4. Goods proposed for insurance ______
5. Specify whether New or Secondhand ______
6. Packing used ______
7. Conveyance(s) ______
8. Containerization details ______
9. Terms of Sale ______
10. RR/GR/BL/AWB No. and date, if any ______
11. Details of the carrying vessel/vehicle such as name/no. and name of the transporter ______
12. Basis of valuation ______
13. Value of Cargo ______
14. Sum proposed for Insurance ______
15. Annual turnover ______
16. Limit per sending ______
17. Limit per location ______

Cover Details

18. Type of Policy required (Please tick whichever is applicable)
    1. Specific Policy/Open Policy ______
    2. Others (Please specify): ______

Reliance General Insurance Co. Ltd. Registere Office 19, Reliance Centre, Watchand Hirachand Marg, Ballard Estate, Mumbai 400 001

19. Voyage details [d|d|m|m|y|y|y|y] To [d|d|m|m|y|y|y|y]
20. Distance less than 100 kms ☐ Yes ☐ No
21. Policy period [| | | | | | |] To [| | | | | | |]
22. Multi transit involved ☐ Yes ☐ No
23. Is storage extension required? ____________________
24. Periodicity of Declaration (other than specific policy) ☐ Monthly ☐ Quarterly ☐ Others
25. Type of Cover (Please specify) ____________________
26. Do you wish to bear a protion of each and every loss (voluntary excess): ☐ Yes ☐ No
If YES, please specify the % of loss: ____________________

Claims Experience: (For last three years excluding current year)

Department	Year	Cover	Premium (Rs.)	Claims (Rs.) Paid	Outstanding
Marine					
Total					
Other than Marine					
Total					

Others

27. Has any other insurer refused to accept this insurance or imposed conditions to accept the same. If YES, give details, ____________________
28. Rate of premium charged by previous Insurer, if any. ____________________

Payment Details

☐ Cheque ☐ DD

Cheque or DD Amount [| | | | |] /- Amount in words (____________________)

Bank Name [| | | | | | | | | | | | | | | | | | | | | | | |]

Cheque/DD No. [| | | | | | | | | | | | |] Cheque/DD Date [d|d|m|m|y|y|y|y]

Declaration

Duty of disclosure: The policy shall be void and all premium paid shall be forfeited to the Company in the event of misrepresentation, mis-description or non disclosure of any material fact.

I/We declare that the answers given by me/us are true and correct and that I/We have not with held any information, which might influence acceptance of this proposal. I/We agree that this declaration and the answers given by me/us shall be the basis of the insurance contract between me/us and Reliance General Insurance Company Limited and shall deemed to be incorporated in the policy.

I/We agree and undertake to covey to Reliance General Insurance Company Limited any additions/alterations carried out in the risk proposed for insurance after submission of this proposal form.

Place : ____________________

Date : ____________________

Signature of the Proposer

Prohibition of rebates-Section 41 of The Insurance Act 1938

1. No person shall allow or offer to allow, either directly or indirectly, as an inducement to any person to take out or renew or continue an insurance in respect of any kind or risk relating to lives or property in India, any rebate of the whole or part of the commission payable or any rebate of the premium shown on the policy, nor shall any person taking out or renewing or continuing a policy accept any rebate, except such rebate as may be allowed in accordance with the published prospectuses or tables of the insurer.

2. Any person making default in complying with the provisions of this section shall be punishable with fine which may extend to Rs. 500/-

Allianz
Marine
Commercial

Marine Hull/Liability Claim Form

The supply and acceptance of this form is not to be implied as as admission of liability on the part of Allianz.

Claim Number

Name of Insured

Contact Person

Home Phone No. Work Phone No. Mobile No.

Email

Postal Address

Post code

Broker/Agent Phone No.

Policy No. Excess $

Inception Date Expiry Date

Interested Parties : Is the vessel being claimed for under a Financial Agreement? Yes ☐ No ☐

Name of Financier

G.S.T. : Are you registered for GST purposes Yes ☐ No ☐ A.B.N.

To what extent are you entitled to claim an Input Tax Credit on the GST for this policy?

To what extent are you entitled to claim an Input Tax Credit on the GST for this vessel?

Details of Insured Vessel:

Vessel Name Registration No. Sail No.

Type of Vessel Motor Make Serial No.

Motor Type Inboard ☐ Outboard ☐ Petrol ☐ Diesel ☐

Is there any other Insurance Policy that would indemnify you in respect of this accident? Yes ☐ No ☐

If Yes, give details

Details of Damage to Insured Vessel:

Where can Vessel be inspected?

Name of Repairer

Address

Postcode

Telephone No. Estimate of Repair Costs $

Prior to this incident, was the Vessel in a fit condition to be used and seaworthy? Yes ☐ No ☐

Give Details

Details of Person in Charge of Vessel:

Name Age Years

Relationship to you

Address

Postcode

Phone No. (Home) Phone No. (work) Mobile No.

Boat Licence No. Expiry Date Place of Issue

Allianz Australia Insurance Limited AFS Licence No. 234708 ABN 15 000 122 850 Registered Office: 2 Market Street Sydney NSW 2000

Does the Person have any physical defect or infirmity in limbs, eyesight, or hearing, or have they ever suffered from a fit of any kind? Yes ☐ No ☐

If Yes, give details ______________________

Was the Person injured? ______________________

If Yes, give details ______________________

Particulars of Incident Date __________ Time __________ am/pm

Place of Incident ______________________

Estimated Speed at Time of Accident __________ Km/Hour

Estimated Speed of other Craft at time of Accident __________ Km/Hour

Speed Limit in area of the Accident __________ Km/Hour

Give a general description of the Accident with all the Circumstances and particulars

Diagram of Location of Accident/Loss (show direction of Vessels, Wind, Tide, etc.)

Personal Injury: Name of Injured Person __________ Occupation __________

Age __________ Years Sex Male ☐ Female ☐

Address ______________________

______________________ Postcode __________

Phone No. (Home) __________ Phone No. (work) __________ Mobile No. __________

Vessel Name __________ Registration No. __________ Sail No. __________

Describe where they were and how they were injured ______________________

Was treatment given at the scene of the incident? Yes ☐ No ☐

If Yes, by whom (if ambulance or doctor, give details) ______________________

Was transport provided to hospital Yes ☐ No ☐

Details of Other Vessel

Vessel Name __________ Registration No. __________ Sail No. __________

Type of Vessel __________ Motor Make __________ Serial No. __________

Motor Type Inboard ☐ Outboard ☐ Petrol ☐ Diesel ☐

Owner's Name ______________________

Address ______________________

______________________ Postcode __________

Name of the Insurer (if known) ______________________

Were there any passengers in the Other Vessel? Yes ☐ No ☐ How many? __________

Damage to Other Vessel or Property (Do Not Approach the Other Party to obtain this information)

Details of Damage ______________________________

Has a Claim been made to you by a Third Party? Yes ☐ No ☐

If Yes, give details ______________________________

Person(s) injured in other Vessel

Name ______________________________

Injury Details ______________________________

Name ______________________________

Injury Details ______________________________

If you have received any written communication, do not answer. Please attach it to this Form.

Witness: Were there any witnesses to the even? Yes ☐ No ☐ (if yes, please complete the following)

Name ______________________________

Address ______________________________

______________________________ Postcode __________

Phone No. (Home) __________ Phone No. (work) __________ Mobile No. __________

Where was the witness? ______________________________

Notifying Authority: Has the Accident or loss been reported to a Police or Maritime Services Officer? Yes ☐ No ☐

Name of Officer __________ Time reported __________ am/pm Date __________

Police Station __________ Police Report/MSB No. __________

In your opinion, who was at fault? ______________________________

Why? (Give details) ______________________________

Has the person responsible ever had their licence endorsed, suspended or cancelled?

Yes ☐ No ☐ If Yes, give details.

____

Was any liquor consumed by the person during the 12 hours before the accident?

Yes ☐ No ☐ If Yes, give details.

____

History:

Have you or the person in charge of the vessel had any insurance or renewal of insurance declined or cancelled or special conditions imposed in the last 5 years? Yes ☐ No ☐

Have you or the person in charge had an accident or made a claim on a marine insurance policy in the last 5 years? Yes ☐ No ☐

Have you or the person in charge been charged or convicted of any boating or marine offence in the last 5 years? Yes ☐ No ☐

Have you or the person in charge been charged or convicted of any criminal offence? Yes ☐ No ☐

If Yes to any history questions, please give details

____

Privacy: The Privacy Act 1988 requires us to tell you that as an insurer we collect your personal and sensitive information in order to calculate your loss and entitlements, determine our liability, compile data and handle claims.

When handling claims, we may have to disclose your personal and other information to third parties such as other insurers, reinsurers, loss adjusters, external claims data collectors, investigators and agents or other parties as required by law.

You have the right to seek access to your personal information and to correct it at any time. Please contact us on 1300 360 529 EST 9am-5pm, Monday-Friday and advise us of the changes.

IDR Statement: Disputes are not an everyday occurrence at Allianz. However we do provide an internal dispute resolution process should any dispute arise. Please feel free to ask for details.

If You are not satisfied with the outcome of this process, we will advise you how to contact the insurance industry's external independent complaints scheme (subject to eligibility).

Declaration: I/We certify that the information given in this form is truthful, accurate and complete. No information likely to affect trhis claim has been with held. I/We understand that this claim may be refused if information is untrue, inaccurate or concealed.

I/We acknowledge that I/we have read and understood the Privacy Act 1988 information referred to above and consent to the collection, storage, use and disclosure of personal and sensitive information of all persons affected by this claim, with their approval. I/we acknowledge that if I/we do not agree to the collection of this personal and sensitive information then Allianz will be unable to process my/our claim.

Signature of Insured ______________________ Date __________

Signature of Vessel Operator ______________________ Date __________

41

INSURANCE INNOVATION AND LONG TERM CARE INSURANCE

Innovation involves the development of ideas into marketable products and processes in order to add economic value. The value added is judged by the commercial success of renewed or changed product or service in terms of increased sales and ultimately profits for the innovating firm.

The main forms of innovation

According to the Oslo manual, there are four broad types of innovation:

1. *Product innovation*–the introduction of a good or service that is new or significantly improved with respect to its characteristics or intended uses. Product improvements could include significant changes to technical specification, components and materials, user friendliness or other functional characteristics.
2. Process Innovation–the implementation of a new or significantly improved production of delivery method. This includes significant changes in techniques. equipment and/or software. Process innovations can also occur to reduce the number of steps in an existing process so as to cut the overall cost of running a process and consequently lower the cost of the end product.
3. Market innovation–the implementation of a new marketing method involving important changes in product design or packaging, product placement product promotion of pricing.
4. Organisational innovation–the implementation of a new organisational method in a firm's business practices, workplace organisation or external relations. This term may also include business model innovation: the creation of reinvention of how companies or industries structure themselves to deliver value to customers.

Alongside the overall type of innovation, it is also helpful to differentiate developments according to the degree to which they represent a departure from existing arrangements. Specifically, innovation can be through of as forming a spectrum, at the most conservative end of which is incremental innovation, focusing on making small but significant improvements to existing products and services. Examples from the high street might be producing detergent with bleach, detergent with scent etc. Such incremental innovation is sometimes called "continuous improvement" and relates to the ongoingpursuit of enhancements to a company's products and processes from design through assembly, sales, and service. At the other end of the spectrum are transformational innovations that fundamentally shift the way things are doen or the set of available products. And in between are evolutionary innovations. There introduce an existing technology into a new market, a new technology into an existing market, or change the way the offering is delivered.

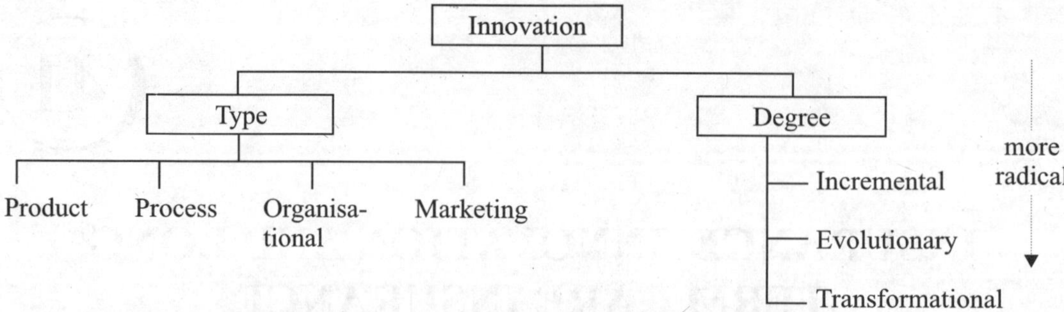

Source: Swiss Re Economic Research & Consulting

Above figure summarises the technical and market impact dimensions of innovation. The lower left quadrant represents innovations that levarage existing technologie and service existing customers. This is everyday innovation, with firms looking to respond to the changing needs of their clients with modest technical changes in the product offering. In the upper left quadrant, existing knowledge and resources are leveraged to create new revenue streams by exploring new markets. When such innovations seek out new clients they can offer significant organic growth at relatively low risk, especially when the firms is familiar with the product/service.

The upper right-hand quadrant embodies the archetypal notion of innovation; new technology in a new market. But while the rewards from capturing market share and potentially significant the corresponding risk are also high. According to some researchers, up to 90% of product innovations fail in the market place.

The risks associated with new technology are also present in the bottom right hand quadrant. But the motivation fo the technical innovation is different. Firms don't seek to find new market opportunities, but rather try to address changes in customer behviour in order to retain their loyalty.

Financial and physical product innovations

Physical product innovations refer to the development of new technologies, techniques or solutions that directly impact the productive potential of an economy, through improvements or the development of physical products or services. A classic modern-day example would be the development of computers, which have vastly improved the ability of individuals and firms to carry out complex, time-constrained in their ability to exploit their ideas and inventions—for example, they may have limited initial funds to finance the building of prototypes or stock or the cost of failure may be too great for one person or firm to take on financial product innovation can help to overcome these problems by allowing redistribution of risks and facilitating the intermediation of savings to firms for investment in new productive capital.

In practical, the boundaries between incremental and progressively more radical innovations are subject to considerable interpretation. In fact, there are at least two dimensions that separate an incremental from a radical innovation. First, there is the technical aspect of how far the innovation expands existing knowledge and its applications. An incremental innovation will typically build upon existing knowledge and resources within a company or industry. A transformational innovation, on other hand, will require completely new knowledge and/or resources and will be, therefore, technically more challenging.

The second dimension relates to the market impact of the innovation. Specifically, some innovations can completely change the competitive landscape in an industry to market place in the sense that they create their own market, and generally displace existing ones. As a result, incumbent firms might rapidly lose market share at the expense of innovators. There so-called 'disruptive' innovations might be associated with a major technical breakthrough, although this need not be the case. Equally, significant technical advances may or may bot be disruptive, And by the same token, minor, or incremental innovations can be disruptive–for example, LCD and LED televisions.

New market

	Incremental innovation	*Transformational innovation*	
			Disruptive innovation
	Low risk; potential significant source or organic growth	Prototypical innovation offering potentially high reward but at high risk	
Modest technical change			**Significant technical change**
	Focus on existing customers; process/product improvements	High risk, defensive innovation aimed at retaining customers with new product/services	*Sustaining innovation*

Existing market

Source: Swiss Re Economic Research and Consulting

The opposite of disruptive is 'sustaining' innovation. This is where a product or process is developed to meet the needs of current customers but serves to sustain leading firms in their market position. Sustaining innovation could simply involve a firm adopting existing product ideas and applying them in new regions or local markets. for example, an established product line developed by the same firm or indeed other firms might be rolled out to emerging markets where demand is still nascent. In this way, while product innovations may not always be completely novel, the diffusion of existing ideas is nonetheless an integral part of companies' innovative activities. Indeed, the economic impact of such innovation can be very significant in terms of growing firms overall business. A number of commentators suggest that exploiting nearby market opportunities that are adjacent to a strong core business offer one of the surest paths to new growth, whether industries are stable or changing rapidly.

Innovation of Insurance business has taken accelerated development in India since 2000. It has been observed by international agencies, too. All the insurers in India are busy with New Product Development, Underwriting Simplification and Distribution strategies. The Government is cautious about fraud and misappropriation by insurers as well as insureds. Regulations are being framed by IRDA in India to safeguard the policyholders' interest and facilitate insurance development.

IRDA has its role cut out as stated in the insurance Act and the IRDA Act. Its primary function is to protect the interests of the policyholders and secondary role is to regulate, promote and ensure orderly growth of the industry. How does 'product innovation' fit into the twin objectives? Currently, the 'File and Use' guidelines are circumscribed by the circulars issued by the IRDA on 28th September 2006 that has over 31 paragraphs of guidance information.Too many?

Most of the guidelines of IRDA deal with underwriting aspect, pricing and internal control systems of the insurers, which, in my view, should be left to the insurers themselves. To the extent that there is no mis-selling of the product and that enough market research has gone into designing the new product, the current guidelines need revamping. Again there should be 'life' tenure to the product approved, say for three years, so that the performance of the product gets reviewed for extension of its tenture.

The IRDA should also make it clear that the new product approved has no patent or copyrights to it. Any other insurer can also market it on identical terms and conditions except on price, which is a subject of competitive forces. Many insurers believe (wrongly) that these new products approved have patent protection from the IRDA. This implied assumption needs clarity. The product and its approval are more important than who sells it.

'Riders' should be distinguished from radical products. All 'rider' approvals should be based on as 'endorsements' to the main policy structure and are not to be regarded as a new product except for its wording. The basic policy structure that has survived several decades should be inviolate unless it is a radical product. Customers have gotten used to them.

Rampant mis-selling has taken place in the life insurance sector; and the industry is fully aware of it. Intentional or unintentional mis-selling, it is true that many customers have suffered financially and have complained to the IRDA. The sale of ULIPS, though these products were approved by the IRDA, was twisted by insurers to carry credibility in the market.

When the growth rates are down, as has happened in the life insurance sector, in FY 2011/12, extraneous excuses have been invented and publicized. This kind of lobbying is a global phenomenon by several disheartened Insurers must need to look within.

FACT FINDING

There are a few issues that need broad agreement between the insurance industry and IRDA of what constitutes a 'product innovation' and who should bear the underwriting and marketing accountability for it? The other issue to be agreed is: does the promoter of the new product get patent and copy right rights, according to the IRDA; and if so, for how many years, as exclusive peddler of this product? If another insurer wants to sell the identical product, without any changes, is mere advice of it to the IRDA sufficient or has he to go through the process, all over? There has to be clarity on it. In the absence of patents and copyrights, any insurer should be allowed to sell an approved product on identical terms and by mere intimation to the IRDA.

Is there a 'product life' to an approved product? From the circular issued on 28th September 2006, it would appear that it is a life time approval and the product cannot be withdrawn for a period of at least five years. Is it not advisable, from a marketing and statistical review point of view to get data and review the product performance every three years? A product must be allowed to expire, if it cannot be sold in sufficient numbers. Products are filled for approval by insurers without any market research of its selling potential. The format of IRDA applications prescribed are more related to underwriting and pricing of risks, more to do with protecting the insurer filling the product than the customer, who needs real protection. There is very little on claims in the formats to show that the forms are customer-friendly. There has to be absolute clarity of who needs IRDA protection, from the point of view of misselling and fair claim settlement process. There is currently no review process how the so-called new products have performed from the point of view of the provider and the customer.

PRODUCT DEVELOPMENT

Different customers have different types of insurance needs for life, property and general interest. The product development has helped development of life insurance spectacularly as was never expected. There are abundant opportunities of development of property and general insurance, too. The Product Development has been analysed under Life Insurance and Non-Life Insurance.

LIFE INSURANCE

The premium income of life insurance has touched the highest ever level of ₹ 49,474 crore in 2005-2006 as compared to ₹ 25,316 crore in 2004-2005 and ₹ 17,716 crore in 2003–2004. The growth rate was 95.4 per cent in 2005-2006 and 34.4 per cent in 2004-2005. The main contribution for this phenomenal growth is because of individual insurance which was ₹ 23,528 crore in 2005-2006 and ₹ 6,332 crore in 2004-2005. Out of these, the non-single premium was ₹ 33,468 crore in 2005-2006 and ₹ 15,034 crore in 2004-2005. The linked policy explained ₹ 29,164 crore premium in 2005-2006 and ₹ 7981 crore in 2004-2005. It reveals the popularity of linked policies.

Link policy concept is expected to be more popular in future as it has the benefits of life-cum-investment cover. People are interested in investment mainly. On the other hand the potential market is waiting for cheap policies to cover risk only. Insurers are trying to develop life policies to cover the risk only.

Price: The potential buyers are looking for cheaper product. The risk cover policies are the cheapest. The premium is decided on the basis of mortality, interest and expenses. The mortality is natural factor wherein, the insurers can do nothing in this regard. The interest should be increased and expenses should be curtailed to minimise the premium rate. With the success of unit-linked insurance, the efficiency of the insurers count a lot in managing premium rate in the era of competition.

Process: Product development is outcome of opportunities available in the market. New products are introduced and developed to meet the competitive challenges and changes. Product development process involves analysis of environment, idea generation, market research, production concepts, process design, testing, product modification and launch. Insurers go through the process and adopt the product development promotion strategies for enhancing the business. In India, product development increased dramatically from various product line of whole life, endowment and term insurance. The market research and environment analysis explore the product mixed to be launched by the insurer. The legal framework, consumer demand and behaviour, competitive stage, economic and political conditions and social needs are the important factors to be considered under product innovation.

The product development is broadly divided into non-linked policies and linked policies which are further sold under individual business single premium, individual business non-single premium, group new business single premium and group new business non-single premium.

Table 41.1 Individual New Business Single Premium

(₹ in Crores)

Non-Linked	Premium (₹) 2004-05	Premium (₹) 2005-06	Policies in Lakhs 2004-05	Policies in Lakhs 2005-06	Sum Assured (₹) 2004-05	Sum Assured (₹) 2005-06
	1	2	3	4	5	6
1. Life						
(a) With Profit	396.99	242.34	0.44	0.32	534.24	367.53
(b) Without Profit	380.52	1,259.47	1.68	4.71	1,810.62	4,489.36
2. General Annuity						
(a) With Profit	0.27	0.40	—	—	0.44	0.78
(b) Without Profit	0.26	1.44	—	—	—	—
3. Pension						
(a) With Profit	129.32	62.13	0.75	0.12	4.49	1.46
(b) Without Profit	56.56	125.90	0.03	.03	0.39	1.81
4. Health						
(a) With Profit	—	—	—	—	—	—
(b) Without Profit	—	—	—	—	—	—
A. Sub Total	963.92	1,691.68	2.90	5.18	2,350.39	4,860.94
Linked						
1. Life						
(a) With Profit	0.71	0.05	—	—	0.72	0.04
(b) Without Profit	2,861.43	2,950.91	5.72	3.39	3,587.87	3,625.06
2. General Annuity						
(a) With Proifit	—	—	—	—	—	—
(b) Without Profit	—	0.63	—	—	—	—
3. Pension						
(a) With Profit	—	—	—	—	—	—
(b) Without Profit	2,078.06	6,355.33	9.45	18.39	10.73	5.17
4. Health						
(a) With Profit	—	—	—	—	—	—
(b) Without Profit	—	—	—	—	—	—
B. Sub Total	4,940.20	9,306.93	15.16	21.79	3,599.33	3,630.27
C. Total (A + B)	5,904.12	10,998.61	18.55	26.96	5,949.72	8,491.22

Source: IRDA Journal, Aug. 2006 / June 2007

First Year Premium of the Insurers for the Year Ended March 2007 (Provisional & Unaudited)
Individual Single Premium (Including Rural & Social)

(₹ *in Crore*)

S. No.	Particulars	Premium Mar 2006	Premium Mar 2007	Policies Mar 2006	Policies Mar 2007	Sum Assured Mar 2006	Sum Assured Mar 2007
1.	**Non linked**						
	Life						
	with profit	242.34	291.20	31601	26200	367.53	386.87
	without profit	1259.47	784.28	470784	485730	4489.36	3987.38
2.	**General Annuity**						
	with profit	0.40	0.00	10	0	0.78	0.00
	without profit	1.44	12.55	145	642	0.00	0.68
3.	**Pension**						
	with profit	62.13	159.57	11567	10178	1.46	2.52
	without profit	125.90	2.26	3532	100	1.82	1.95
4.	**Health**						
	with profit	0.00	0.00	0	0	0.00	0.00
	without profit	0.00	0.00	0	0	0.00	0.00
A.	**Sub total**	1691.68	1249.85	517639	522850	4860.95	4379.40
	Linked						
1.	**Life**						
	with profit	0.05	0.00	5	1	0.05	0.00
	without profit	2950.91	4342.15	339740	764066	3625.06	7062.59
2.	**General Annuity**						
	with profit	0.00	0.00	0	0	0.00	0.00
	without profit	0.63	1.20	0	0	0.00	0.00
3.	**Pension**						
	with profit	0.00	0.00	0	0	0.00	0.00
	without profit	6355.33	17952.47	1839374	5430530	5.17	3.63
4.	**Health**						
	with profit	0.00	0.00	0	0	0.00	0.00
	without profit	0.00	0.00	0	0	0.00	0.00
B.	**Sub total**	9306.93	22295.83	2179119	6194597	3630.28	7066.22
C.	**Total (A + B)**	10998.61	23545.68	2696758	6717447	8491.23	11445.61
	Riders:						
	Non linked						
1.	Health	0.03	0.04	21	32	0.33	0.57
2.	Accident	0.18	0.06	1755	1050	12.47	7.07
3.	Term	0.03	0.01	135	33	0.82	0.25
4.	Others	0.00	0.00	0	0	0.00	0.00
D.	**Sub total**	0.24	0.10	1911	1115	13.63	7.90
	Linked						
1.	Health	0.04	0.04	59	89	0.78	1.04
2.	Accident	0.09	0.16	357	13043	8.10	84.56
3.	Term	0.00	0.00	4	8	0.05	0.12
4.	Others	0.00	0.00	0	0	0.00	0.00
E.	**Sub total**	0.14	0.20	420	13140	8.92	85.72
F.	**Total (D + E)**	0.38	0.31	2331	14255	22.55	93.62
G.	**Grand Total (C + F)**	**10998.99**	**23545.99**	**2696758**	**6717447**	**8513.77**	**11539.23**

Individual Non-Single Premium (Including rural & Social)

(*₹ in Crore*)

S. No.	Particulars	Premium		Policies		Sum Assured	
		Mar 2006	Mar 2007	Mar 2006	Mar 2007	Mar 2006	Mar 2007
	Non linked						
1.	**Life**						
	with profit	12819.57	16484.03	28409713	21169366	266239.86	201760.82
	without profit	702.42	1930.10	2087776	1048344	41343.05	24442.02
2.	**General Annuity**						
	with profit	0.86	0.23	845	242	15.54	4.13
	without profit	0.00	0.00	0	0	0.00	0.00
3.	**Pension**						
	with profit	70.87	48.61	52458	25323	294.28	187.93
	without profit	8.84	21.23	3649	6337	0.00	0.00
4.	**Health**						
	with profit	0.00	0.00	0	0	0.00	0.00
	without profit	7.37	27.88	34020	169703	1166.45	7604.73
A.	**Sub total**	13609.93	18512.07	30588461	22419315	309059.18	233999.62
	Linked						
1.	**Life**						
	with profit	0.97	0.18	330	87	6.71	1.96
	without profit	5676.56	16627.45	1950273	15704231	48030.97	215674.25
2.	**General Annuity**						
	with profit	0.00	0.00	0	0	0.00	0.00
	without profit	117.74	0.00	72527	0	224.42	0.00
3.	**Pension**						
	with profit	0.22	0.09	49	8	0.00	0.00
	without profit	452.80	2737.74	132032	1287337	51.32	1694.83
4.	**Health**						
	with profit	0.00	0.00	0	0	0.00	0.00
	without profit	0.00	0.00	0	0	0.00	0.00
B.	**Sub total**	6248.28	19365.45	2155211	16991663	48313.43	217371.03
C.	**Total (A + B)**	19858.22	37877.53	32743672	39410978	357372.60	451370.66
	Riders:						
	Non linked						
1.	Health	5.28	3.77	31807	20553	406.32	287.96
2.	Accident	9.31	6.79	417513	419127	8631.99	6969.34
3.	Term	1.37	0.53	24272	8884	221.00	95.09
4.	Others	5.53	17.65	10185	4814	434.84	2466.35
D.	**Sub total**	21.49	28.73	483777	453378	9694.15	9818.74
	Linked						
1.	Health	3.53	5.33	15119	18806	945.28	601.54
2.	Accident	3.78	7.96	87687	192737	1530.88	10907.00
3.	Term	0.87	1.70	8999	20881	189.19	585.88
4.	Others	1.16	1.27	22886	22573	25.09	1095.28
E.	**Sub total**	9.34	16.25	134691	254997	2690.43	13189.70
F.	**Total (D + E)**	30.83	44.99	618468	708375	12384.58	23008.44
G.	**Grand Total (C + F)**	**19889.04**	**37922.51**	**32743672**	**39410978**	**369757.18**	**474379.10**

Table 41.2 Individual New Business-Non Single Premium

(₹ in Crores)

	Premium (₹)		*Policies in Lakhs*		*Sum Assured (₹)*	
	2004-05	*2005-06*	*2004-05*	*2005-06*	*2004-05*	*2005-06*
1	*2*	*3*	*4*	*5*	*6*	*7*
None-Linked						
(*a*) With profit	10,680.77	12,819.51	211.54	284.10	1,69,480.55	2,66,239.86
(*b*) Without Profit	740.55	702.42	14.05	20.88	27,122.63	41,343.05
General Annuity						
(*a*) With Profit	4.39	0.86	0.05	—	96.54	15.54
(*b*) Without Profit	—	—	—	—	—	—
Pension						
(*a*) With Profit	448.22	70.87	4.11	0.52	852.46	294.28
(*b*) Without Profit	—	8.84	—	0.03	—	—
Health						
(a) With Profit	115.79	—	2.32	—	2,739.00	—
(*b*) Without Profit	3.19	7.36	0.16	0.34	246.06	1166.45
A. Sub Total	11,992.92	13,609.93	232.23	305.88	2,00,537.26	3,09,059.18
Linked						
1. Life						
(*a*) With Profit	7.70	0.96	0.03	—	69.51	6.71
(*b*) Without Profit	2,599.84	5,676.56	8.02	19.50	21,454.06	48,030.96
2. General Annuity						
(*a*) With Profit	—	—	—	—	—	—
(*b*) Without Profit	220.96	117.74	2.10	0.73	445.86	224.42
3. Pension						
(*a*) With Profit	2.35	0.22	—	—		—
(*b*) Without Profit	210.31	452.80	1.43	1.32	171.95	51.32
4. Health						
(*a*) With Profit	—	—	—	—	—	—
(*b*) Without Profit	—	—	—	—	—	—
Sub Total	3,041.16	6,248.28	11.58	21.55	22,141.38	48,313.42
Total (A + B)	15,034.08	19,858.22	243.81	327.44	2,22,678.64	3,57,372.60

Table 41.3 Group New Business-Single Premium

(₹ in Crores)

Non-Linked	Premium (₹)		No. of Schemes		Lives Covered		Sum Assured (₹)	
	2004-05	2005-06	2004-05	2005-06	2004-05	2005-06	2004-05	2005-06
1	2	3	4	5	6	7	8	9
1. Life								
(*a*) **Group Gratuity Schemes**								
(*i*) With Profit	—	—	—	—	—	—	—	—
(*ii*) Without Profit	1042.83	1581.90	2203	2167	570718	766005	2848.61	3364.70
(*b*) **Group Savings Linked Schemes**								
(*i*) With Profit	—	—	—	—	—	—	—	—
(*ii*) Without Profit	18.75	58.25	675	1835	135101	502607	1266.79	4664.91
(*c*) **EDLI**								
(*i*) With Profit	—	—	—	—	—	—	—	—
(*ii*) Without Profit	2.73	5.47	990	1213	543330	718411	1595.44	3122.57
(*d*) **Others**								
(*i*) With Profit	—	—	—	—	—	—	—	—
(*ii*) Without Profit	529.78	574.51	14522	13051	7412858	10220727	36941.14	47257.92
2. General Annuity								
(*i*) With Profit	850.53	672.02	7	5	57.80	38.26	—	—
(*ii*) Without Profit	591.46	735.13	10	22	11284	7974	—	—
3. Pension								
(*i*) With Profit	—	—	—	—	—	—	—	—
(*ii*) Without Profit	964.93	678.70	214	113	25889	59599	—	—
4. Health (No pension)								
A. Sub Total	4001.02	4305.99	18621	18406	8704960	12279149	42651.99	58390.10
Linked								
1. Life								
(*a*) **Group Gratuity Schemes**								
(*i*) With Profit	—	—	—	—	—	—	—	—
(*ii*) Without Profit	4.91	86.85	12	24	1021	45962	0.08	4.60
(*b*) **Group Savings Linked Schemes**								
(*i*) With Profit	—	—	—	—	—	—	—	—
(*ii*) Without Profit	—	—	—	—	—	—	—	—
(*c*) **EDLI (No Business)**	—	—	—	—	—	—	—	—
(*d*) **Others**								
(*i*) With Profit	—	—	—	—	—	—	—	—
(*ii*) Without Profit	3.98	3.63	2	1	1623	352	0.17	0.03
2. General Annuity								
(*i*) With Profit	—	—	—	—	—	—	—	—
(*ii*) Without Profit	3.14	—	—	—	14	—	3.03	—
3. Pension								
(*i*) With Profit	—	—	—	—	—	—	—	—
(*ii*) Without Profit	1.82	8.66	1	3	10	3936	—	—
4. Health (No Business)	—	—	—	—	—	—	—	—
B. Sub Total	13.86	99.14	15	28	2668	50250	3.28	4.63
C. Total	4014.88	4405.13	18636	18434	8707628	12329399	42655.27	58394.73

Source: indicates no business.

First Year Premium of Life Insurance for the Year Ended March 2007 (Provisional & Unaudited)
Group Single Premium (Including Rural & Social)

S. No.	Particulars	Premium		No. of Schemes		Lives Covered		Sum Assured	
		Mar 2006	Mar 2007	Mar 2006	Mar 2007	Mar 2006	Mar 2007	Mar 2006	Mar 2007
	Non linked*								
1.	Life								
a)	Group Gratuity Schemes								
	with profit	0.00	0.00	0	0	0	0	0.00	0.00
	without profit	1581.190	2473.23	2167	2287	766005	926223	3364.70	4086.88
b)	Group Savings Linked Schemes								
	with profit	0.00	0.00	0	0	0	0	0.00	0.00
	without profit	58.25	30.89	1835	1022	502607	281244	4644.91	2163.39
c)	EDLI								
	with profit	0.00	0.00	0	0	0	0	0.00	0.00
	without profit	5.47	5.69	1213	1047	718411	923126	3122.57	2585.38
d)	Others								
	with profit	0.00	0.00	0	0	0	0	0.00	0.00
	without profit	574.51	6477.96	13051	16296	10220727	12708409	47257.92	25847093
2.	General Annuity								
	with profit	672.02	1039.19	5	9	3826	3525	0.00	0.00
	without profit	735.13	883.32	22	61	7974	11275	0.00	0.00
3.	Pension								
	with profit	0.00	0.00	0	0	0	0	0.00	0.00
	without profit	678.70	1173 17	113	239	59599	101111	0.00	0.00
4.	Health								
	with profit	0.00	0.00	0	0	0	0	0.00	0.00
	without profit	0.00	0.00	0	0	0	0	0.00	0.00
A.	Sub total	4305.99	12083.45	18406	20961	12279149	14954913	58390.11	267306.58
	Linked*								
1.	Life								
a)	Group Gratuity Schemes								
	with profit	0.00	0.00	0	0	0	0	0.00	0.00
	without profit	86.85	233.14	24	88	45962	200027	4.60	629.76
b)	Group Savings Linked								
	Schemes with profit	0.00	0.00	0	0	0	0	0.00	0.00
	without profit	0.00	0.00	0	0	0	0	0.00	0.00
c)	EDLI								
	with profit	0.00	0.00	0	0	0	0	0.00	0.00
	without profit	0.00	0.00	0	0	0	0	0.00	0.00
d)	Others								
	with profit	0.00	0.00	0	0	0	0	0.00	0.00
	without profit	3.63	15.62	1	4	352	13225	0.04	1.32
2.	General Annuity								
	with profit	0.00	0.00	0	0	0	0	0.00	0.00
	without profit	0.00	0.00	0	0	0	0	0.00	0.00
3.	Pension								
	with profit	0.00	0.00	0	0	0	0	0.00	0.00
	without profit	8.66	89.15	3	18	3936	12448	0.00	0.00
4.	Health with profit	0.00	0.00	0	0	0	0	0.00	0.00
	without profit	0.00	0.00	0	0	0	0	0.00	0.00
B.	Sub total	99.14	337.90	28	110	50250	225700	4.63	631.09
C.	Total (A + B)	4405.13	12421.35	18434	21071	12329399	15180613	58394.74	267937.67
	Riders:								
	Non linked								
1.	Health#	0.37	0.40	25	19	18228	9237	344.21	0.00
2.	Accident ##	0.75	0.28	21	39	37362	23415	1994.04	0.00
3.	Term	0.00	0.00	0	0	0	0	0.00	0.00
4.	Others	0.00	0.00	0	0	0	0	0.00	0.00
D.	Sub total	1.11	0.68	46	58	55590	32652	2338.25	0.00
	Linked								
1.	Health#	0.00	0.00	0	0	0	0	0.00	0.00
2.	Accident # #	0.00	0.00	0	0	0	0	0.00	0.00
3.	Term	0.00	0.00	0	0	0	0	0.00	0.00
4.	Others	0.00	0.00	0	0	0	0	0.00	0.00
E.	Sub total	0.00	0.00	0	0	0	0	0.00	0.00
F.	Total (D + E)	1.11	0.68	46	58	55590	32652	2338.25	0.00
G.	**Grand Total (C + F)	4406.24	12422.04	18434	21071	12329399	15180613	60732.99	267937.67

* Excluding rider figures : ** for no. of schemes & lives covered Ground Total is C. # All riders related to critical illness benefit, hospitalisation benefit and medical treatment. # # Disability related riders. The Premium is actual amount received and not annualised premium. Complied on the basis of data submitted by the Insurance companies.

Group New Business – Non - Single Premium (Including Rural & Social)

(₹ *in Crore*)

S. No.	Particulars	Premium		No. of Scheme		Lives Covered		Sum Assured	
		Mar 2006	Mar 2007	Mar 2006	Mar 2007	Mar 2006	Mar 2007	Mar 2006	Mar 2007
	Non linked*								
1.	Life								
a)	Group Gratuity Schemes								
	with profit	0.00	0.00	0	0	0	0	0.00	0.00
	without profit	126.60	247.96	56	59	58456	95517	370.57	346.49
b)	Group Savings Linked Schemes								
	with profit	0.00	0.00	0	0	0	0	0.00	0.00
	without profit	0.14	44.34	6	0	7543	446142	153.10	7221.68
c)	EDLI								
	with profit	0.00	0.00	0	0	0	0	0.00	0.00
	without profit	5.22	5.79	272	282	402135	420048	3330.62	3599.31
d)	Others								
	with profit	0.66	0.00	29	0	35994	0	408.24	0.00
	without profit	63.36	314.68	2539	1195	2075517	3348604	32364.88	61621.13
2.	General Annuity								
	with profit	0.00	0.00	0	0	0	0	0.00	0.00
	without profit	0.00	0.00	0	0	0	0	0.00	0.00
3.	Pension								
	with profit	0.00	0.00	0	0	0	0	0.00	0.00
	without profit	0.75	5.97	1	4	885	79	2.18	0.00
4.	Health								
	with profit	0.00	0.00	0	0	0	0	0.00	0.00
	without profit	0.00	0.00	0	0	0	0	0.00	0.00
A.	Sub total	196.73	618.74	2903	1540	2580530	4310390	36629.60	72788.61
	Linked*								
1.	Life								
a)	Group Gratuity Schemes								
	with profit	0.00	0.00	0	0	0	0	0.00	0.00
	without profit	222.17	473.52	253	369	257452	361554	705.32	2122.81
b)	Group Savings Linked								
	Schemes with profit	0.00	0.00	0	0	0	0	0.00	0.00
	without profit	0.00	0.00	0	0	0	0	0.00	0.00
c)	EDLI								
	with profit	0.00	0.00	0	0	0	0	0.00	0.00
	without profit	0.00	0.00	0	0	0	0	0.00	0.00
d)	Others								
	with profit	0.00	0.00	0	0	0	0	0.00	0.00
	without profit	4.24	11.39	13	14	249	167	1.79	1.97
2.	General Annuity								
	with profit	0.00	0.00	0	0	0	0	0.00	0.00
	without profit	15.59	38.26	11	12	906	2547	15.59	38.26
3.	Pension								
	with profit	0.00	0.00	0	0	0	0	0.00	0.00
	without profit	164.32	372.35	73	135	12549	62451	0.00	0.00
4.	Health								
	with profit	0.00	0.00	0	0	0	0	0.00	0.00
	without profit	0.00	0.00	0	0	0	0	0.00	0.00
B.	Sub total	406.32	895.52	350	530	271156	426719	722.69	2163.04
C.	Total (A + B)	603.05	1514.26	3253	2070	2851686	4737109	37352.29	74951.65
	Riders:								
	Non linked								
1.	Health #	0.15	0.34	7	21	1496	14141	124.08	601.01
2.	Accident # #	0.46	0.67	52	34	60348	46185	1807.32	1936.96
3.	Term	0.00	0.00	1	1	153	114	5.03	8.03
4.	Others	0.01	0.01	1	5	32	3987	20.67	216.56
D.	Sub total	0.63	1.02	61	61	62029	64427	1957.10	2762.55
	Linked								
1.	Health #	0.00	0.00	0	0	0	0	0.00	0.00
2.	Accident # #	0.00	0.70	0	47	0	48838	0.00	1635.54
3.	Term	0.00	0.00	0	0	0	0	0.00	0.00
4.	Others	0.00	0.00	0	0	0	0	0.00	0.00
E.	Sub total	0.00	0.70	0	47	0	48838	0.00	1635.54
F.	Total (D + E)	0.63	1.72	61	108	62029	113265	1957.10	4398.10
G.	** Grand total (C + F)	603.68	1515.98	3253	2070	2851686	4737109	39309.39	79349.75

Table 41.4 Group New Business — Non-Single Premium

(₹ in Crores)

	Premium (₹)		*No. of Schemes*		*Lives Covered*		*Sum Assured (₹)*	
	2004-05	*2005-06*	*2004-05*	*2005-06*	*2004-05*	*2005-06*	*2004-05*	*2005-06*
1	*2*	*3*	*4*	*5*	*6*	*7*	*8*	*9*
Non-Linked								
1. Life								
(a) **Group Gratuity Schemes**								
(i) With Profit	—	—	—	—	—	—	—	—
(ii) Without Profit	25.78	126.60	26	56	13975	58456	40.76	370.57
(b) **Group Savings Linked Schemes**								
(i) With Profit	—	—	—	—	—	—	—	—
(ii) Without Profit	17.59	0.14	1	6	24240	7543	913.78	153.10
(c) **EDLI**								
(i) With Profit	0.74	—	57	—	29293	—	297.26	—
(ii) Without Profit	5.39	5.22	205	272	278770	402135	2256.31	3330.62
(d) **Others**								
(i) With Profit	0.41	0.66	25	29	29361	35994	302.52	408.24
(ii) Without Profit	58.66	63.36	4197	2539	1724647	2075517	18639.65	32364.88
2. General Annuity								
(i) With Profit	—	—	—	—	—	—	—	—
(ii) Without Profit	—	—	3	—	1766	—	8.54	—
3. Pension								
(i) With Profit	—	—	—	—	—	—	—	—
(ii) Without Profit	2.94	0.75	7	1	226	885	—	2.18
4. Health (No Business)—								—
A. Sub Total	111.52	196.73	4521	2903	2102278	2580530	22458.83	36629.60
Linked								
1. Life								
(a) **Group Gratuity Schemes**								
(i) With Profit								
(ii) Without Profit	179.23	222.17	171	253	135115	257452	217.94	705.32
(b) **Group Savings Linked Schemes (No Business)**								
(c) **EDLI (No Business)**								
(d) **Others**								
(i) With Profit	—	—	—	—	—	—	—	—
(ii) Without Profit	3.55	4.24	10	13	179	249	12.75	1.79
2. General Annuity								
(i) With Profit (No Business)								
(ii) Without Profit	25.78	15.59	7	11	1994	906	25.78	15.59
3. Pension								
(i) With Profit	—	—	—	—	—	—	—	—
(ii) Without Profit	43.95	164.32	64	73	9964	12549	17.50	—
4. Health (No Business)—		—	—	—	—	—	—	—
B. Sub Total	252.52	406.32	252	350	147252	271156	263.97	722.69
C. Total (A + B)	364.04	603.05	4773	3253	2249530	2851686	22722.80	37352.29

(–) Indicate No Business.

These four tables have revealed that life insurance is being diversified to meet different requirement of society. Health insurance is not becoming popular. The LIC has issued a large number of policies which are different degree mix of endowment and term insurance. On its anniversary, LIC issues some new policies in September of each year. Many of the policies are brand name starting with Jeevan *e.g.*, Jeevan Suraksha, Jeevan Kishore, Jeevan Sukanya, Jeevan Sneha, Jeevan Nidhi etc. Private sector insurers have been dependent on term insurance as it is the cheapest form of insurance.

NON-LIFE INSURANCE

Non-life insurance has invented new products to meet the different requirements of customers. The new products are Mediclaim Insurance, Terrorism cover, Janata Personal Accident, Insurance for plantations, cattle, pump sets, Hut Insurance, Social Security Scheme. Many insurers feel that it is prevalence of tariff coverage that prevented the growth of product innovation. The lack of market research, consumer behaviour, inability to identify customer needs and their buying habits and the lack of acturial talent in non-life insurance have inhibited promoting new products.

The future of market innovation lies mainly with the new players. The cost of operation will be reduced considerably. Bringing down transactional and distribution costs and adding value to current and future products are expected to popularise new products. Product innovation is bound to take off in a big way. It is another new game in the competitive arena, which would be more vigorously fought in the post-detariffication era. Insurers have to create need-based and differentiated products to suit various segments and within those segments, offer necessary choices and options to suit target customers. Design and pricing of products are based on certain basic requirements in the context of consumer choice, safety and competitions.

Role of NGO's and Self Help Groups

Insurance is expected to increase with the help of NGOs and Self Help Groups (SHGs). It is for the insurance to come forward to find out the SHGs who can undertake insurance business.

Risk Evaluation and Product Formation

The premium is fixed after proper evaluation of risk. Clear and transparent cover is valuable to the insured who get cover insurable risk. Standard clauses across policies should be used to help customer understanding. Products should be developed with the compliances of IRDA (Production of policyholders' Interests) Regulations 2002. Terms and conditions should be fair between the insurer and the insured. The product is innovated bases on the market needs and competitive position, The evaluation of risk bases on costs as stipulated by the acturial assessment. The product is sub-classified and segmented as per market requirements. Each product has operative clause, the schedule, exclusions, general conditions and warrantees. There are several other clauses such as cancellation, renewal, claim, settlement processes, dispute resolution and grievance redressal mechanisms.

Risk is insured on the basis of experience of rating or exposure rating based on circumstances, internal tariff rate, packaged products and insurance of large risks. In non-tariffed, rating is done on the basis of available data of industry, pricing decisions and policy terms, The acturial experience and rate components are evaluated to frame rate of the product. The pricing covers all costs and return on investment. The loss-calculation essential for determination of premium. The price cutting is resorted only in the hope of image-building which helps repositioning, repackaging of the product, used of temporary discounts, increased publicity and advertising.

Future of Product Development

The future of product development is very bright in the detariff era. Before pre-nationalisation period in 1972, the product development was not done as the insurers followed the practices of American and British insurers. After 1972, the entire conduct of insurance was vesting into the holding companies of the General Insurance Corporation of India. The GIC with the help of the Tariff Advisory Committee (TAC) regrouped the existing products in more than 130 products. It has introduced a lot of products.

A Mediclaim Policy was introduced in 1980 with great success. During the post-liberalisation private companies brought new idea to the insurance industry and a lot of product has taken place.

The insurers have ample scope of designing new product and redesigning the old product to meet the individual requirements of the buyers. The future of non-life insurance exists in:

1. Combination of health and accident as well as life cover.
2. A first loss policy of households.
3. A multi-year policy for motor-vehicles.
4. Consequential loss policies.
5. Insurance of various products, property and business machines as well as industrial inputs and outputs.
6. Agricultural inputs, machine and outputs.
7. Work-in-progress of industrial and agro-bases industries.

UNDERWRITING

Underwriting is a process of accepting a risk, analysing the risks, framing terms and conditions and deciding the chargeable premium rate. It needs to know the risk features and factors of every risk offered for acceptance. Risk analysis determines the physical hazards and inherent moral hazards attacked to the cover of the products. Steps of risk management are adopted for underwriting purposes. Safety audit, staff drills, investigations and remedial steps are taken to prevent recurrence of risk. Moral hazard is minimised by staff-relations, compliance with legal enactments and affectiveness of corporate governance.

The acceptance of risks and pricing them has been the basic statutory function of the Tariff Advisory Committee (TAC) till detariffed market is governed by IRDA since January 1, 2007. The TAC has prescribed cover wordings and the minimum prices to be charged by insurers who breach them. The disciplinary standards are imposed by the TAC to safeguard the consumers' interest. The TAC has been working in India for more than 50 years. With liberalisation of market and entry of foreign players, the detariffication has started.

It has observed by the experience of 2005-2006 that only 6% claim has been reported in India as against 20 per cent losses in international markets. Only 1.2 lacks out of 32 lakhs insured persons reported for mediclaim. The claims paid as said by insurers are 120 per cent. Thus, the underwriting redesigning is needed for the purpose. The underwriting process is studied under life insurance, non-life insurance and detariffed era underwriting.

Life Insurance Underwriting

Life insurance underwriting is not merely selling of life insurance products. It is sold to those who qualify to be suitable person to buy insurance. It assesses proposers' needs, paying capacity and determining the price rate. Life insurance is embedded with an element of social responsibility with cooperative spirit. The risk qualifications and determination of price (premium-rate) for each class is essential function of underwriting. The insurer underwrites a policy to an insured by assessing his own experience of claims payment, expenses incurred and return on investment besides his ability to retain the risk and products.

In life insurance, underwriting is done by insurance agents or advisors. Based on the disclosures of the proposal forms, medical reports; the insurer may exercise his own investigation to insure the insurable risk. The underwriting takes two phases *i.e.,* financial underwriting and medical underwriting. The former deals with determining the eligible total amount of life assurance coverage. The latter deals with medical and diagnostic reports. There is need of close monitoring early death and should check the reasons of early death. The life insurance underwriting is based on mortality, expenses and interest.

Mortality: The cost of insurance depends on mortality insurers have to monitor whether the present tables of mortality and morbidity are in tune with the present rate of premium. Life Insurance

Council and Acturial Society of India are working in this area. They will decide the extra premiums to be charged from the sub-standard lives and ensure fair premium rate to standard lives. Certified Life Underwriter is preparing professionals of underwriting life insurance.

Expenses: The life insurers incur certain expenses which are loaded on the net premium based on mortality and interest. Since there are different insurers having different expense rate, The premium rate may differ but under Tariff Advisors committee, the rates cannot vary significantly.

Interest: The interest or return on investment made of life fund. The post liberalisation has facilitated several insurers to earn varied rate of interest depending on the investment methodology.

The life insurance agents known as intermediates are playing significant role in underwriting of life insurance business. Medical development has reduced mortality and premium rate is expected to decline accordingly. On the other hand, pollution and crowd have created unexpected deaths. Occupation is considered as one of the key elements affecting the longevity of the insured. Stress and occupational hazards have added more risk.

INNOVATION IN NON-LIFE INSURANCE

Insurance innovation in the areas in the areas of non-life insurance are policy ammendements, bundling and unbundling and deal by deal innovation.

Policy amendments

Often product innovation look to flex traditional insurance methods by expanding the scope of coverage and making amendments to terms and conditions of prevailing insurance policies.The sample in Table 1 indicates that around a quarter of all product announcements could be described as policy refinements which look to improve the current level of insurance cover.

The typical policy modifications revolve around changes to market wordings or sublimits, which can have important implications for the overall level of cover. this is what is often labelled "deal-by-deal" innovation and happens quite frequently (especially in reinsurance). Through the use of underwriting tools like deductibles, co-insurance profit commissions, flexible payment programs and policy limits, insurers can not only maintain the scope of cover but in addition can incentivise policy holders to adopt rish reduction measures (see Box on "Deal-by-deal innovation").

"Deal-by-deal" innovation usually happens in a piecemeal fashion as part of an on-going relationship with a particular client. This enables the insurer to estimate projected earnings across the suit of products sold to that customer. A dowside to ths approach is that over time, products can become complex, at least from a pricing perspective. So, from time to time, policy amendments are geared towards simiplification.

Budling and unbundling

Product bundling involves combining different (sometimes new) risk cover within the same product. Again the overall aim is typically to provide a more holistic service to customers, For example, policies might look to combine engineering with liability cover or mortgages and earthquake insurance. Payment protection insurance also covers a borrower against an accident, sickness, unemployment or death.

The attraction for policyholders may be that a common aggregate deductible or "excess" on a portfolio of risks may allow a reduction in teh total insurance cover and hence lower costs. Bundling may also enable policy limits to be minimised. More generally, the packaging of different risks can be popular option for small industrial companies who don't necessarily have deep risk management expertise. Larger companies tend to seek tailor-made solutions for particular risk, not least because the nature of their operations often gives rise to multiple types of risk. The exception is umbrella liability insurance which offers risk protection against claims above and beyond the amount covered by primary policies or for claims not currently covered.

Deal-by-deal innovation

Deductibles/co-payments – These refer to the amount of loss that an insurance policy-holder has to absorb before reimbursement is triggered–sometimes called an "excess" or an attachment point. This sharing of losses provides incentives to the insured to take preventative actions to minimise risk and/or not make claims for losses that, in the absence of insurance, they would not incur.

Profit-commissions–These are a type of contingent commission whereby the commission paid from the risk carrier or underwriter to the producer/distributor depends on the defined "profitability" of a specific book of business over a fixed period of time.

Cover limits–These policy clauses limit the maximum loss that the insurance company may face. Such limits may transform unquantifiable, underlying risks into known maximum exposures. They are very common in reinsurance agreements and often take the form of excess-of-loss agreements where the reinsured is only compensated if the loss suffered exceeds a predetermined level and then usually up to a maximum.

Duration of cover–Insurance policies normally provide cover for one year with an annual renewal. But depending on the nature of the risk, some policyholders might prefer to lock in insuracne cover a agreed terms for multiple years. In this way, there may be diversification benefits over time-because the risk might be serially uncorrelated-that can be exploited and shared between insurer and the insured. Moreover, such long-term insurance may help in reducing insurers' administrative costs and lower search costs, providing stability to consumers and incentivizing property owners to invest in risk-reducing measures.

Scope of cover–A "named perils" insurance policy covers losses or perils that occur that are specifically listed on the insurance policy. In contrast, an "all risk" insurance policy covers all perils unless they are specifically exculded on the insurance policy. An exclusion is a provision within an insurance policy that eliminates coverage for certain acts, property, types of damage or locations.

Multiple triggers–Traditional insurance contracts have one trigger: a physical event or occurrence that activates a payout on the policy. Multiple trigger contracts are designed to respond to both physical hazards-type events and resultant financial movements. For example, a multiple trigger (also known as a dual trigger) program might cover not only property loss due to a fire or windstorm but also the resulting quarterly earning loss caused by the physical event.

Underwriting requires a kind of discipline which can exist on pure risk. Commercial considerations are adjusted for the purpose. The premium rate varies in non-tariff products like health, accident and so on. The clear examples of commercial consideration is Group Health policy which is renewed at 50-60% of average claims paid during last 3 years. It is below the underwriting principle. The insurer can adjust the loss experience in future premium calculation.

The premium calculation is based on individual risk and industry's experience, maximum potential loss attached to the proposed risk, estimate the customers capabilities for prevention and minimisation of losses, terms and conditions and expected moral hazard.

There is no one single indicator within the surveys that adequately captures innovation activities. But the responses to three types of questions provide a useful read-out on innovation developments. Specifically.

- the number of firms that report having undertaken innovative activities. Often labelled the "innovation rate", this indicator provides a guide as to the **importance** of innovation in that country or sector.
- expenditure on research and development (R&D). While this will likely under-estimate innovation efforts in services relative to manufacturing, such spending may potentially inform about the priority companies attach to the search for new products. It may therefore provide a measure of innovation **intensity**.
- firms product innovation that are "new to the firm" compared with "new to market". This suggests whether new products are genuinely novel and inventive *-ie* it may indicate the degree of **ingenuity**.

UNDERWRITING IN DETARIFFED ERA

The non-life insurers would go for detariffed era since January 1, 2007. Detariffing refers to freedom to the underwriters to conduct the business with their own individual experience. Underwriting had been understood as routine work of accepting the proposals to be operated under restricted and regulated market. Now underwriting is total management of product to be sold considering all factors influencing sale-decision *i.e.,* loss or profit related to underwriting, income generated through premium and investment and expenses of the company. The underwriting is designing the product to cover the risks price to be charged and claims management. In tariff regime, designing the product and pricing was done by Tariff Advisory Committee (TAC) and claim management was left to the insurance companies.

Detariff era is expected to make the insurer free to design the products and pricing them as per their insurance experience. The tariff will be deregulated with effect from January 1, 2007. Thus, the current product *i.e.,* perils covered, exclusions, add-one terms and conditions etc. Will continue to be regulated by TAC till 31-3-2008. Now the insurers will be free to design their products as per their exposure to risk, expense management, premium rate and underwriting losses. The insurers assess the risk and fix the premium as per their experiences. But they will fix the price judiciously in the competitive market. The insured will be benefited with the lower price in the competitive situations. Detariffing refers to differential rates depending on the rate factors but unfair discrimination *i.e.,* differentiation not based on scientific and credible structure should not be practiced. It emphasises a higher regulatory role of IRDA.

Tele Underwriting

Underwriting is estimated to be more than USD 1500 billion world-wide. The IT industry is helping insurance business to grow. The process of modernisation and IT services has started gaining ground. In near future, the insurance will depend on tele-communication. The old system of underwriting was slow and expensive. The present system of computerisation, internetting, websites and satellite communication have accelerated growth of insurance business. The risk evaluation was slow process, issue of policy took long time and price fixation was manually done. Not only underwriting but serving the policyholders and payment of claims was time consuming. The IT facilitates faster, cheaper and better service. The processing and evaluating of risk will be done mechanically. Application of electronics gadgets make underwriting, price determination serving policyholders and claim-payment easy and faster.

Teleunderwriting starts with telephone interview with insurance applicants. It saves times and money. Similarly the policyholders ask for the services on telephone. Gradually it will extend to mail, fax, internetting and so on.

DISTRIBUTION CHANNEL

Distribution Channel have become a useful components of insurance innovation. The banks have taken the responsibility of insurance-distribution. The *Bancassurances* have started in India. Its best example is Aviva which has developed link with more than 20 banks. It is spread in 378 town and cities in India. The two way flow is *easened* with Bancassurances *i.e.* Payment of premium of insured too insurers and payment of claims, health, pension, etc. by insurers to the insureds. Potentials of market have increased with the number deposits, consumer loans and housing finances, agricultural and industrial loans. The wide network of RRBs can be utilised for underwriting. Distribution and servicing the masses. Bancassurances have become cheaper than the agents for underwriting and servicing of insurance. Since banks' branches are available in rural areas, the rural insurance will extent with the help of banks.

Inspite of the growing needs of bancassurances, the personal approaches of agents are helpful to extend insurance business and serve the policyholders in a better manner. The distribution channel is analysed under life insurance, insurance intermediation and non-life insurance agents.

Insurance Intermediation

With the opening up of the insurance sector, one channel *i.e.,* broker is added as an effective intermediary. They are acting as consultant to the customer and agents of insurance company. Agents are very important for expansion of business, who provide personal services to the clients *i.e.,* the policyholders and the prospects of insurance. In the competitive atmosphere, the company will survive and grow, who can provide high level of services, back office and front office staff, consumer awareness and prompt and sensitive response to the clients' grievances.

Corporate agent may be allowed to tie up with more than one life or non-life insurer. This facilitates corporate agents to develop professionalism and competitiveness.

Life Insurance

Life insurance Agents are full of knowledge, compassion and sound people management. Life insurance agent of LIC have been gaining their role as club-members of Branch manager, Club Divisional Manager Club, Zonal Manager Club and Chairman's Club. The motivation of LIC has gone further to guide the agents become member of Million Dollar Round Table. Life Underwriters' Guild of India (LUGI) is also guiding the insurance agents to be professional. Life insurance agents quickly engage in their duties and contribute silently although discipline culture is not present there. There is competition amongst the agents to grow themselves higher and higher.

Technology in LIC

Innovation and technology have to go hand in hand so that some real and palpable results could be achieved. Innovation without technology is shapeless and technology without innovation is of no use. The relevance of technology in the insurance sector is of paramount importance today, because to-day's customer is more demanding than ever before, he has plenty of choices to shift his loyalty and finally the volume of work that can only be done through computers. Be it processing of proposals, the need for a standard practice of underwriting, the management of the records, valuation of surplus, preparation of Balance Sheets, keeping track of customers, reaching them in no time, you name the area — It is unthinkable and incomplete without a sound system of technology. Technology again is a vast subject. You need to make research for Productive Development. It is to be followed by product-Mix and Marketing, Obtaining feedback and finally Dissemination of Information. At every stage, the role of most advanced and modern technology comes to the fore. Consider the Case of LIC. It has established connectivity among all its officers, has opened Satellite officers, launched Websites (internet/intranet), Portals, Touch Screen Kiosks, IVRs, Corporate Messaging Service, Call Centres and the like. Its FEAP system has got several user-friendly modules. Its Touch Screen system works on a visual BASIC or C ++ front end and the like. Its internet site 'Jeevan Sanchar' is hosted on the most powerful operating system LINUX and designed by adapting the latest technologies of C, C++, Java, Perl, Oracle and COBOL. LIC has also embraced Online Data Sore and manages a Data Warehouse envied by many. It is pertinent to note that LIC has won the prestigious IT Excellence Award from NASSCOM for excellence in IT. Just imagine the plight of the corporation and the consumers under its 23 Crore policies without the advancement of these technologies. The entire purpose of the usage of these technologies, apart from managing its gigantic size of business, is ensuring consumer delight in an age what is called - digital. Can we say in a lighter vein, a person who does not know 'Windows' in this era of computers will be shown the door? But satisfaction of customers needs by launching new products and services through innovation and technology.

This life insurance agents have developed themselves as full-fledged persons maintaining work records, meeting clients and help them in calamity and serve them in a better way. They have great hopes and aspirations for a better standard of life, social acceptability and readiness to work hard although they are not highly educated, have less financial strength and inadequate skill, knowledge and experience. They have become financial advisors to the clients. Customer Relationship Management is present there. Many insurance agents have started selling shares and debentures of companies. They advise their clients in totality.

Non-Life Insurance

Non-Life insurance agents are less professional as the public sector organisations do not treat as business associates. They get scant training. Even the Agents Manuals and other knowledge tools such as product literature are not available to them as is available to life insurance agents.

MARKETING MANAGEMENT

Insurance innovation passes through transitional stages where at many problems are faced by the insurer. The marketing management is required for the purpose. The marketing management includes marketing audit and segmented approach.

Marketing Audit

In India, majority of the population have been unaware of the benefits of insurance although they need insurance. The psychological and emotional forces alongwith economic needs of the prospect should be completed, audited and forecasted by the management. The feelings of people are against insurance. It has to be averted. The insurer should develop marketing audit of the potentials and opportunities available for business and should be very clear of the weaknesses and threats of market. The saving and risk management has to be designed to meet the requirements of potential buyers of insurance. The role of marketing agents is generally doubted. They have to develop themselves in such a way as to make them helping agents of people.

The technique of recruiting, selecting, training and motivation of insurance agents should be modernised to train the insurance agents as social servers, economic adviser, friend and philosopher. The competition strategies are to be analysed and developed by them. Life Insurance is a need but not felt by people. Marketing manager should develop its force in such a way as to make people realise the need of insurance.

Segmented Approach

Insurance marketing needs segmented approach. The different needs of people are met differently by the insurer through its agents. Training and motivation of insurance agents are essential in this direction. They have to evaluate the present, guide the future and inspire people to come willingly for insurance products. Product development is a function of insurer and its distribution is the responsibility insurance agents.

REGULATORY MEASURES

Development of stable and strong insurance system is essential for economic development of the Country. Regulatory measures are required for instilling public confidence in insurance companies, deliver reliable and quality services. It has to secure the long-term stability of financial services through monitoring of their financial soundness and fair treatment of their customer. With the experience of failure of non-banking financial institutes and loss of depositors' money, regulatory measures have to very effective, considering the interests of insurers, government has changed its traditional regulatory role to control with facilitating investment and trade. Insurance Act 1938 is being modified as per the suggestions of IRDA. Globalisation of financial activity, innovations is financial instruments and practices have to be strictly controlled.

There is oftenly a conflict between strict regulation and development. Regulation is based on past experience whereas development is future oriented. Developing new products, processing and servicing is no easy matter. It is expected that regulations will work as driver for change to force players to do things in a better way. Regulations by IRDA in India is praireworthy as it is pro-development. It has emerged as prudential supervisor and developer of capacity in terms of risk pooling, reinsurance and skills. It has guide for insurance penetration and insurance density. It makes insurance available to poor in rural areas. Insurance companies have to provide risk cover as well as contribute to long term investment.

USE OF ELECTRONIC PAYMENT SYSTEM

Reserve Bank of India has been impressing upon banks the need to migrate to electronic modes for initiating and receiving payments, so that the dependence on paper-based clearing products is brought down and the payment systems universe becomes safe, secure, sound and efficient. Electronic payment systems also speed up the clearing process, apart from reducing incidence of fraud inherent in cheques, draft and other paper modes of payment. Individuals, corporates and government departments are using electronic payment products like ECS, NEFT and RTGS extensively as per guidelines of IRDA.

The following paragraphs detail some of the various retail electronic payment products presently available –

1. Electronic Clearing Service (ECS) – Credit Clearing : ECS (Credit) is designed for repetitive and bulk payment such as salary, pension, ITRO refunds, etc. The system works on the basis of T+1 settlement which means that payment instructions submitted up to the cut-off time on day 'zero' will be settled with credits given to all the account holders on the next working day. The system is available in two different mods (*i*) ECS Local and (*ii*) National ECS. Local ECS is presently available at 75 locations and covers all bank branches in the jurisdiction of the clearing house. National ECS (NECS), has the coverage of over 26,000 bank branches across the country and is operated by RBI at Mumbai . This system leverages on the Core Banking System installed at banks to provide credit to beneficiary accounts from a central location, with settlement on T + 1 basis.

2. Electronic Clearing Service (ECS) – Debit Clearing: ECS (Debit) is designed for the collection of repetitive and bulk receipts such as electricity bills, telephone bills, EMI payments, Insurance Premia, etc. This system also works on the basis of T + 1 settlement whereby payment instructions submitted up to the cut off time on day 'zero' will be settled on the next working day and debits raised from all the account holders will be credited to the beneficiary company's account. The system is presently available at 75 location and covers all bank branches in the jurisdiction of the clearing house.

3. National Electronic Funds Transfer (NEFT) System : This is designed to cater to the need of ad-hoc and individual fund transfer requirement of bank customers. The system replaces the requirement of DDs, TTs and usage of cheques for effecting such payments. NEFT has been operational since November 2005 and covers around 56,000 bank branches across the country. The system works on net settlement basis and provides same-day settlement across 6 settlement batches every day. NEFT is robust, reliable and a secure mechanism to transfer funds from one bank account to another, and can also cater to the demands of walk in customers who do have any bank account. Many banks have also provided facilities to their net banking customers for originating NEFT transfer instructions online.

Self Regulatory Organisationn (SRO)

The key to effective market depends on public disclosure and consumer education. The role of self regulation is realised in the developing market. So Self Regulatory Organisation (SRO) is empowered to give greater rights and responsibilities to market participants. It anticipates and assists the industry to meet the needs of consumers, improves industry's image, promotes insurance awareness, encourages improvement of services and effectively manages the insurance resources.

SRO will develop link with Government, industry, public, consumer forum and technical researches. All the insurance companies will be the member of SRO. It will supply information to member companies, develop codes of conduct for member companies, develop compliance programmes, The SRO will have a separate secretariat headed by a secretary general and chairperson elected from the member. The international standards and practices will be adopted for the purpose.

Fraud

The possibilities of fraud exist in insurance business. The possibilities of fraud to agents are there if premium rates are not published. They may charge higher amount from the policyholder. The insured may inflate the value of the assets and get more amount than the assets in case of damage. The company can deduct some amount from the claim. Fraud may occur during underwriting by agents and brokers, surveyors and clients. The fraud is prevented by designing product step by step providing sufficient information to customers, customer identification and claim determination and direct contact with company by customers to prevent fraud created by agents. There have been a number of fraud cases which occur with connivance of claimant, lawyers and authorities. The insurer should develop fraud risk management.

Money Laundering

Money Laundering is the process through which criminals attempt to disguise the origin of the proceeds. International agencies are very much concerned with Money Laundering. RBI and SEBI have come out for anti money laundering guidelines for banking and capital market sectors. IDRA is planning to formulate such laws for insurance companies. If money laundering is not prevented, the company's reputation is at stake. The company may fail to comply the insurance contract due to risks involved in money-laundering. The IDRA has emphasised that insurer should know the customer. Agents if conscious of such movements can easily explore the money-laundering and anti-money laundering (AML) process may be adopted by them. IRDA has provided Anti money laundering in Aug. 2006.

1. Every insurer has to put in place an AML policy which should include following:
   (*i*) Internal policies, control and procedures for protection and detection of instances of money laundering.
   (*ii*) Appointment of a Principal Compliance Officer.
   (*iii*) Recruitment and Training.
   (*iv*) Internal control and audit of the AML framework.
2. Establish processes for carrying out 'Know Your Customer' (KYC) :
   (*i*) Identity the customers.
   (*ii*) Conduct detailed due diligence.
   (*iii*) Careful look at cash transactions.
   (*iv*) Conduct KYC also at payment stage.
3. Create a risk matrix for various classes of customers.
4. Defining suspicious transaction.
5. Internal Audit to deploy modules to list the efficacy of AML framework.

LONG TERM CARE (LTC) INSURANCE

Most rapid ageing population need long term care of instrumental activities of daily living (IADL), activities of daily living (ADL) and medical conditions (comorbid. Long term care (LTC) insurance is considered a modern solutions of IADL, ADL and comorbid. IADL includes bathing, dressing, walking, feeding, mobility and continence. ADL includes housework money management medications adherence, shopping and getting around outside the house chronic diseases, disability, cognitive impairments and functional impairments are important comorbid.

"You'll never walk alone" – a multi-stakeholder approach

The challenge of providing care for the ageing population requires a comprehensive solution, including all stakeholders: insurers, governments, healthcare institutions current and potential care providers, and current and future potential consumers of care. Starting from different points, most countries will have to reform their systems to find sustainable solutions for growing care demands. This chapter looks at possible policy and other responses.

As a starting point, governments could help raise consumer awareness of the risks and costs of care solutions by clearly communicating what care is provided by the state. This would help individuals make more informed decisions about how best to provide for their old-age care needs. It would also give insurers a better-defined backdrop from which to develop care products.

Governments could partner with insurance companies as potential investors in care facilities. At present, governments often house patients inappropriately and very expensively in hospitals, and do not have the financial capacity to invest in care infrastructure. By partnering with insurers, governments would benefit from lower costs and funding needs. For insurers care infrastructure could be an interesting asset class because their returns are positively related to the development of care needs. Therefore, care infrastructure would be a good asset match for care risk on insurers liability side.

Policymakers also need to be mindful of regulations which may hinder the development of a private market. For example, excessive capital requirements on very long-term products, can create impediments to insurers' willingness to participate in the market, and also make products more expensive.

Another approach would be to work with employers to institute programs similar to voluntary pensions, such as the 401 (k) in the US. Employer involvement can also help raise awareness of LTC risks. Group LTC insurance does exist in certain markets such as the US and France, but employers typically do not contribute towards the cost of premiums. With the right design (for example opt out instead of opt in) and tax or other financial incentives, it may be possibie to make some people start paying for policies early when it is still affordable, as in Singapore. It is along these lines that the Taiwanese government is expected to launch a LTC insurance system in 2016, financed collectively by the state, private employers and the insured. Similarly, in the UK there is discussion about a ring-fenced pension system dedicated to care solutions and with additional tax incentives. The idea is that this "Care Pension Fund" is to be used only to fund care expenses. Further, if the fund is not used, it can be passed on to family descendants without inheritance tax.

The care solutions challenge is also about social behaviour. Many people have the mind-set that retirement begins at a certain age, say 60 or 65 with no flexibility. They also expect that any available government programs in retirement will also begin at this age and cover their care needs. These attitudes could be encouraged to shift towards the possibility of working longer through incentives and labour market flexibility and by removing and structural and legal barriers or other disincentives to working longer. The work could be on a full-or part-time basis and would give individuals more time to save for future care needs.

An ounce of prevention

Health prevention initiatives can generate significant cost savings. Lifestyle-related chronic diseases such as coronary artery disease, stroke, diabetes and some cancers are a growing burden on individuals and national health systems. Yet many of the major risk factors for non-communicable diseases like these and thus the resultant ADL limitations are preventable.

Obesity and smoking, for example are key contributors to chronic disease trends. In the US estimates attributes 12% of type 2 diabetes and 22% of coronary heart disease as well as other conditions to lack of physical activity. Meanwhile, several studies have concluded that improved diets and increased levels of physical activity reduce the risk of chronic conditions and associated disability and that appropriate management of the conditions can limit or reverse ADL limitations. A study in France found that intellectual and physical activity could even help hold back mental deterioration. Specifically, the report cities a 15% reduction in Alzheimer's detection in workers who retired at age 65 over those who retired at age 60.

Service innovation through technology

Just as health insurers have realized the value of subsidising gym memberships, care solutions insurers and public payers for care services may benefits from subsidies that encourage the application of technologies and devices that help older people live alone longer. Or, insurers could provide the distribution channels for these types of technologies.

Technological innovation can enable better health monitoring, care coordination and a longer period of living unassisted/alone. For example remote monitoring devices can track glucose levels in diabetics, detect falls and in more advanced cases, even be linked to analytical systems that predict impending heart failure. Similarly, medication adherence can be tracked by smart pill bottles that notify a caregiver via text message of cases of non-compliance. Locator devices can assist with the management of dementia patients. And various tele-health initiatives can reduce admissions to hospitals, number of home visits and visits to general practitioners. These and other remote interventions can be less expensive than constant monitoring in a nursing facility, and increase quality of life by helping people stay at home.

To prolong a pension's independence, home modifications may be necessary. This includes non-medical equipment such as special chairs, hoists, rails, ramps into the house, adapted toilets, showers and baths, lifting equipment and more. Paying for such equipment and modifications rather than for nursing home care may be more cost-efficient and also improve quality of life.

A step up from basic modifications is the concept of smart homes with an array of wireless sensors that address "intelligent health services, home automation, security and safety, communication and entertainment". Insurers are unlikely to find efficiencies in paying for such customs-built houses as part of LTC solutions, but the sensors could help those who may well be living in smart homes in the not-so-distant future retain their independence for longer than is possible today. Robots capable of simple tasks like lifting could also be part of care services in the coming years, both in the home and in support facilities. Overall, the elder care tech industry is projected to be a USD 20 billion market by 2020."

Purpose-built "retirement cities" consisting of independent and assisted-living apartments a nursing home-type facility and a hospitals are gaining popularity. Sometimes, this concept is referred to as a Continuing Care Retirement Community. In Florida, a retirement village in this vein with golf courses and social amenities for retirees alongside healthcare facilities is the fastest growing metropolitan areas in the US. In similar residential developments in China financed by China Life and Ping An Life apartments are "fitted with remote sensing equipment to monitor the vital sings of high-risk residents." Other countries have retirement developments of this nature also.

INNOVATIVE PRIVATE INSURANCE CARE SOLUTIONS FOR OLDER LIVES

Insurance alone cannot solve all care service and solution issues, but it can help diversify the risks and make care more efficient. However, to meet the growing demand and the same needs as classic LTC products, but in a more tangible and easily sold way a fundamental re-think of the design and purpose of current care insurance products in required.

Annuity products

Immediate-needs annuities (INAIS) have been introduced in some markets. This single-premium product is bought at the point when a dependant has to move to a nursing home so the benefit is very tangible compared to a traditional deferred LTC policy. The issuer of the policy agrees to pay the costs of the stay, no matter how long the dependant will require institutional care.

Hybrid products

Hybrid products combine LTC insurance with life, retirement/pension or critical illness products. They pay out the death benefits early, or increase the monthly payment from the annuity at the onset of the LTC need. Their advantage over traditional LTC products for the consumers is that if care is not needed, the underlying life or retirement product still gives the insured a payout. This can help overcome the loss aversion and the mental accounting challenges traditional LTC insurance faces.

From the insurers' perspective hybrid products have a lower risk profile than stand-along LTC insurance, as some risks diversify. In particular, the sensitivity to changes in assumptions, (about investment income, lapses mortality and incidence rates) is materially lower for hybrid products. This reduces the costs and hence the price of these products. The LIC feature can also be a rider on a traditional life/annuity product, rather than a full combination product. For example, in Hong Kong a global life insurer offers a rider to a term annuity that pays an extended income for life if the policyholder becomes unable to perform certain specified activities of daily life.

Services and financing

Assisted living insurance (also known as short-term care insurance) is intended to help support a policyholder and his/her family in the initial stages of dependency. It provides financial support for a set period and advice in cases of unexpected care costs, allowing the individual and family some time to organize financing for future care costs. The insurance also provides access to a suite of services from care, assistance, financial advice, to offering solutions and taking over arrangement as needed.

Other insurance approaches

In some cases, it may be better to address specific aspects of the care need rather than the entire range of care solutions in one product. This would make the insurance products more affordable and less complex for consumers. For example in South Korea, targeted products in senior health and cancer acre have met with some success. Dementia and arthritis have been some of the other targeted conditions with success largely due to appropriate distribution, low price and simple and understandable lump-sum benefits. This could be replicated in other markets by finding niche needs and addressing them from the ground up as opposed to analysing and trying to address the total need at once. However, this is very country-specific because of cultural reasons and the different public schemes in place.

Re-labelling existing LTC insurance products in more positive terms could also help. The current LTC insurance products focus on compensation for loss of independence and in particular ADL failures, which for many consumers seems like a horrendous personal state to experience. This is an additional psychological reason not to buy. Products which extend independence may have a much more positive marketing message and be purchased more readily than current LTC products. Marketing with wording reference to lifestyle maintenance or independence assistance for example, may lead to higher sales of LTC insurance.

SELECT COUNTRIES AND LTC INSURANCE

The US – private LTC insurance is the main mechanism for risk sharing

The largest private LTC insurance market is the US. LTC insurance policies were very popular in the 1990s and premium volume grew from about USD 2 billion in 1995 to USD 11.5 billion in 2012. Around 80% of these premiums were for individual business, and the rest sold as group business. In recent years, however, business growth has been weak and often driven by rate increases rather than new sales.

A key driver of demand for private LTC insurance in the US in the lack of a universal LTC scheme. Medicaid does finance LTC but only on a means-tested basis, and private funds virtually have to be exhausted before one becomes eligible.

The typical insurance solution offers reimbursement of LTC costs to a daily cap. The vast majority of policies provide comprehensive coverage, which pays for both home care and care in nursing facilities. Often there is a limited benefit period, but lifetime contracts are (were) also available.

Most contracts have a waiting period of around three months before the insurer starts to pay care costs that acts as deductible.

Despite its size, the US is not the showcase for private LTC insurance. Life insurers have suffered heavy losses and were forced to increase rates on large blocks of policies, which upset many policyholders and resulted in a loss of reputation of the industry. Moreover, many insurers have exited the market.

The main issues confronting the US LTC insurance market were lower-than-expected lapse rates, low investment returns, high capital requirements, underwriting challenges, and problems with distribution networks (high commissions).

However, the Pension Protection Act of 2006 improved the tax treatment of LTC insurance and allowed for the dvelopment of hybrid products. These new prodcuts, mainly life insurance with acceleration riders, where the death benefit from the life insurance can be withdrawn for LTC or chronic illiness needs, have been introduced and sold successfully in the past five years. Specificially, premiums for hybrid products grew strongly between 2009 and 2013 (CAGR 34%) and new business for 2013 reached USD 2.6 billion.

Germany – mandatory LTC and supplementary private LTC insurance

In Germany compulsory universal LTC insurance was introduced in 1995. There are two parallel mandatory schemes: social LTC insurance for those with social health insurance and private LTC insurance for those with private health insurance. The social LTC insurance is pay-as-you-go-financed through payroll contributions. Private LTC insurance is pre-funded through premium payments.

Benefit eligibility criteria and payments are equivalent for both systems. Benefits comprise daily allowances for informal care formal care, at home and in nursing homes. The amount paid for each of the three benefit types is explicitly defined and graded depending on the level of dependency.

France – social health insurance, government and private LTC solutions

In France, financial support for LTC at home or in an institution is mainly provided for by the universal public health insurance system and personalized allowances for autonomy (APA). APA is intended for people aged 60 and above to help pay for expenses linked with loss of independence. The level of benefit is a function of an individual's degree of independence. However, APA is also means tested and depending on one's income, benefits can be reduced by up to 90%.

For formal home-care, APA provides support towards any expenses incurred in line with a personalized care plan identified by a social-medical term. In 2010, benefits varied from EUR 1235 per month for the most severe cases to EUR 530 for low dependency levels. Neither level of benefits is sufficient to cover the full estimated costs of home-care of EUR 1500 to 4000 per month.

The costs of staying in a nursing home were estimated at EUR 34 705 in 2012, with three components; (1) the health cost of EUR 11844, which is borne by social health insurance (2) the accommodation cost of EUR 11616, which is paid fully by the dependent; and (3) the care cost (i.e., non-medical care needs such as feeding, help with dressing etc.) of EUR 11844, for which APA makes means-tested contributions, with any remaining portion borne by the dependent and his/her family. It is estimated that families spent at least EUR 6 billion in 2007 for accommodation and dependency fees (total LTC expenditures were estimated to be EUR 34 billion in 2007, for 1.8% GDP).

Life insurers provide supplementary LTC insurance to reduce the remaining gap. Premium income was EUR 466 million in 2012 with 1.8 million insured (or which 75% were individual contracts). So called *Mutuals* 45 and *Institutions de Prévoyance* also offer LTC insurance and generated premium income of EUR 138 million and EUR 25 million, respectively, in 2011 from 3.6 million and 0.3 million insured. The vast majority of the contracts are written on a group basis. In France, more than

16% of the population over 40 years of age has private LTC insurance (2012) compared with about 5% in th US.

The contracts provided by French life insurers are defined benefit. In other words, once the policyholder is eligible a regular fixed amount of money is paid for life (although there are also lump-sum policies and contracts with limited payment period). For contracts covering light and severe dependency benefits averaging EUR 371 per month were paid in 2012. For contracts only covering severe dependency, benefits were EUR 574 on average.

Japan - social LTC insurance crowds out private solutions

In 2000, Japan created a public LTC insurance system funded by a combination of premiums and taxes that finances approved in-kind services. The scheme covers the population aged 65 and above as well as age-related illnesses for those aged 40-64. Benefits are only provided in the form of services (in kind), with no possibility of receiving a cash benefit. The fact that cash benefits are not offered was a specific design feature to avoid the burden of care falling on (unpaid) female family members (sometimes referred to in Japan as "daughter-in-law syndrome").

Israel - high risk awareness helped develop a LTC market

In Israel, the Long-term Care insurance Program (LTCIP, a publicly-1, funded LTC scheme) provides services and benefits designed to supplement informal care provided by family and friends, and encourages elderly people to remain in their communities as long as possible. Individuals must be citizens or permanent residents of Israel and be above the retirement age of 67 (for men) or 62 (for women).

Eligibility for services from the program is means-tested. However, the means test is sufficiently high so that only the very wealthy are excluded. The LTCIP services cover about 80% of the elderly population at a cost of approximately USD 1 billion in 2011 or 0.5% of Israel's GDP.

Awareness of LTC risk is widespread and Israel is one of the biggest private LTC iusurance markets. Claimants receive compensation for the cost of care in a nursing home or care provided at home up to a specified amount. Benefits are ADL-triggered and tiered. Premium income grew from USD 118 million in 2003 to USD 710 million in 2012. making LTC insurance the fastest growing L&H line of business. Two thirds is written on a group basis, typically sold through affinity groups and employers.

Singapore - a public-private partnership

Singapore has a mandatory national medical savings scheme called Medisave, which helps individuals put aside part of their monthly income into individuals Medisave accounts to meet their own or their family's healthcare expenses. LTC costs are financed through a mix of government subsidies and disability insurance (ElderShield), the premiums of which can be paid for from individual's Medisave accounts. In addition, families unable to afford remaining LTC costs even with subsides and insurance can receive further assistance from Medifund, a safety net for needy Singaporeans.

The ElderShield program was launched in 2002. It is a public-private partnership designed by the government but priced, sold and managed by private insurers. ElderShield provides automatic enrolment for individuals at the age of 40. However, individuals can opt out of the plan within the first three months. By 2013, premium income amounted to about USD 160 million/SGD 199 million. The number of ElderShield policies increased from 0.75 million in 2008 to 1.1 million in 2013, an increase of 5.2% annum.

The UK - almost no public LTC funding

In the UK, the National Health Service (NHS) provides universal healthcare. LTC, however, is not included and the bulk of the old-aged care costs must be borne by the dependant and their families.

For LTC benefits, there is a means-tested safety net requring individuals to significantly spend down their assets (including property if not occupied by the dependent or spouse). Only once assets are below a certain threshold is the person eligible for state support. As a consequence. the dependent is often forced to sell their home or liquidate any available assets to fund nurshing or residential home care.

The LTC protection gap in the UK is significant. Private LTC insurance has been sold since the early 1990s, but the market has grown slowly and there are only a few players, mainly offering immediate-needs annuities (INAs). The traditional products pre-funded LTC insurance with ADL and cognitive impairment triggers — has not been popular and the last provider to offer pre-funded LTC insurance exited the market in 2010. LTC bonds are similar to pre-funded care plans but allow inheritance or unused capital. Even so, UK consumers have likewise not been big buyers of LTC bonds.

The most promising products in the UK insurance market are INAs. These are purchased with a single premium when an individuals is already in need of care. INAs have been relatively successful, aided by certain tax efficiencies, although premium income was only about GBP 130 million in 2012.

Given the tough eligibility requirements for state support, it is surprising that LTC insurance penetration in the UK is so low. Either the products on offer do not meet consumer's needs, or many people are simply not aware of the LTC risks they face.

QUESTIONS

1. Discuss the present positions of insurance innovation.
2. What is product development ? How is it done in insurance industry? Explain.
3. Evaluate the various types of life insurance in India. Give the details of their progress.
4. Examine the product management of non-life insurance.
5. Forecast the future of product development in India.
6. What is underwriting ? Explain its role in insurance management.
7. What is detariffed Era ? What are its advantages ? Illustrate them.
8. Give the benefits and processes of telemarketing of insurance.
9. What is marketing audit of insurance ?
10. Explain the benefits of SRO.
11. Examine the role of Anti Money Laundering Act for developing insurance business in India.
12. Discuss long term care Insurance Program in developing countries.

42

RISK-MANAGEMENT

Risk Management is emerging an important area of insurance. The insurer succeeds if he is able to manage the risk properly. The risk may be insurance or uninsurable. Insurer transfers the risks to reinsurance companies. Risk is uncertainty or loss or profit. It may arise because of hazards routine business and dynamic functions. The risk may be financial and non-financial. Business risks and individual risks are also insured. Business risks include profit, price, credit and other risks. Personal risks include property risk and liability risk.

The risk management involves loss control, loss financing and risk reduction. Loss control is loss prevention method which reduces frequency of loss. Control devices to prevent loss are installed in property to prevent fire. Loss financing is done through retention, insurance hedging and risk transfers. Risk reduction is possible through better forecasts and diversification.

Risk is uncertainly of loss or profit. If business enterprises is not managing the potential risk, it may suffer incredible loss. The insurance industry ensuring risk has to be very particular about the risk management. The need and objectives of risk management, risk identification, principles of risk management, strategies of risk management and functions of important association of risk management will illustrate how to manage a risk effectively.

NEED AND OBJECTIVES

Risk management is essential to prevent financial disasters and achieve the objectives of capital management. The success must be sustainable, for which risk has to be prevented and managed. The aspirations of insurance customers can be easily met if the risk is properly managed. It helps right things performances and assists carrying out the duties of care, loyalty and good faith. The competition is beaten over by proper planning of risks. The shareholders' stake will remain intact if the risks are systematically managed. Many time policyholders and shareholders have competing interests. The insurer has to balance them. The development and solvency requirements are contradictory, sometimes. The disclosures, transparency and performance have become routine functions of insurance. The investor, suppliers of inputs and marketing management have credibility. Their interests should not be deluded in the organisation.

RISK IDENTIFICATION

Risk identification is a prime functions of underwriting and marketing management. The employees and agents of insurance companies are trained to identify the risk and also quantify the amount of risk. The risk is identified on the basis of economic and financial factors, accounting system, reputation, regulation and property and liability risk. The risks are managed by providing minimum interest rates, accounting guidance, premium calculation and knowing the unknown sources of risks.

Insurer uses rigorously technique to identify, monitor and manage the risks. Some of the techniques are stockastic modelling, value at risk, tail risk, economic capital calculations, stress tests and more and identify negative impa-ct. The U.S. Enterprise, Risk Management (ERM) uses culture, currency, regulation, economic factors, geographical differences, Time Zone Language, distance from home office, credentials, loss of control etc. are used for identification of a risk.

Risk management involves identification, measurement and control of risk.

Identification of Risk

Identification of risk is determination of risk where does it lie. The risk may be relating to property, Life, Liability and Nature. Fire, theft, damage, natural calamities are the various hazards.

Property Loss: The factors responsible for loss are identified and evaluated for the purpose. The insured and uninsured perils are identified. Replacement possibilities and operational expenses of business, revenue loss, normal levels of production, pre-loss situation and post-loss situation are studied to identify the risk.

The book value is the minimum loss value of the property because it denotes the purchase price and depreciation of the property. But it is not economic value which is the real loss of the property. Market value is very near to economic value.If the firm does not get value of the property *i.e.,* no benefits of use of value, it will be equal to market value. Replacement cost is considered for insurance as it is the cost of replacemet of damaged property but it exceeds the market value as the new property value increases due to inflation, Fire insurance, marine insurance, motor insurance,machine insurance, profit insurance etc. are the methodologies of loss deduction due to risk.

Life Risk: Human life is exposed of several risks *e.g.,* old. age, death, health, accident and so on. Some responsibilities such as education and marriage of children, starting of their career, business responsibilities, key men employees, etc. are also attached with human life. Life insurance policies, health insurance, keyman insurance etc. are prevailing to minimise the loss of human life.

Liability: Liability mainly legal liabilities arise because of contractual relationship. Third party insurance of motor insurance, product liability and professional liability and many new liabilities are added in recent years.

Other Risks: There are several other risks which influence the cost and production. Profit insurance is taken for the purpose. Machine breakdown and crop insurance etc. are the recent examples of other risks which are separately insured to reduce the loss can used by such risks.

Risks are measured using probability methods. Last experiences and variance analysis with standard deviation are used for measuring risks. The probability is modified with the present situation and future expectation.

Control of Risk

The risks are controlled through insurance with the principle of pooling, cooperation and transfer of risks, Insurance of risks are becoming a gradual and continuous process. The Indian experience is very positive wherein insurance is expanding with more than 15 percent per annum.

PRINCIPLES OF RISK MANAGEMENT

The principles of risk management includes top level involvement, culture of accountability, risk prevention, appropriate control, discipline and forecasting negative events. Investment and accountability are important factors of risk management.

Investment

Risk management is embedded in insurance industry from the date of proposal to the final payment of claims. After sale services reveal the techniques of risk management. It reveals the investment process in Industry itself discovers the principles of risk management . The senior managers have knowledge of risk and risk management technique. There are a set procedure *e.g.,* LIC has agents manuals to guide them how to identify the risk and manage it properly. The L.I.C. provides oversight integration, coordination and consolidation of corporate functions, Many company has a separate department of risk management.

Accountability

The responsibility vested on the executive reduces the risk and forces them to manage risk. There are rating agencies (Tariff Advisory Committee) analysts, surveyors etc. who evaluate the risk. Management is responsible for identifying the risk setting the risk limits implementing process to back and identify new risks. Applying constant testing and monitoring. The agents, development officers and branch managers are responsible for risk evaluation and rate fixation. They sell right policy to right person.

STRATEGIES OF RISK MANAGEMENT

The risk management strategy is fully aligned with the company's overall strategy while ensuring a separation of duties between risk policy setting, monitoring and controls and business management. The strategies of minimise risk are formulated keeping into account the risk profile, reporting risk issues, implementation of risk management and so on. Corporate Risk Unit (CRU) is developed to assess and formulate risk management strategies. Risk model is developed with the help of actuaries, technical analysts, expertised consultancy pricing, financial management and capital management are analysed for the purposes. The strategies are formulated by imagination and identifying weaknesses.

Imagination

The insurer imagines control-devices. Regular dynamic reviews and current risk factors are adjusted. Liquidity, derivatives, rescuing credit exposure, counter-party exposure and reinsurer exposure are estipulated for the purpose. The depth study of previous losses due to epidemic mumps, meningitis etc. are conducted by the management.

Identifying Weaknesses

The risk management weaknesses are identified and remedied. The risk profiles, measure and metrics are thoroughly analysed for the purpose.

ASSOCIATIONS OF RISK MANAGEMENT

The risk management assoiations are formed for meeting the challenges of risk. There are two associations viz., International Federation of Risk and Insurance Management Association (IFRIMA) and Federation of European Risk Management Association in Europe (FERMA) which are guiding insurers to manage the potential risks.

INTERNATIONAL FEDERATION OF RISK AND INSURANCE MANAGEMENT ASSOCIATION (IFRIMA)

Risk management involves loss prevention and safety programmes. Insurers manage the risk in very effective manner so that policyholders may not suffer on account of higher premium. Reinsurance is practiced to avoid the loss. There is great pressure on the reinsurance companies as natural disasters are increasing. Catastrophe management is resorted to which insurance companies are financially helping for effective management of risks.

Risk management depends on good corporate governance. The insurance company increases its image through corporate governance. IFRIMA is motivating education of risk management. Insurers will have to manage hazards, operational risk, financial risk and so on.

Federation of European Risk Management Association in Europe (FERMA)

Every day people are coping with new types of risk. They have to manage them through insurance and insurers manage them through reinsurance. Insurance is needed for all those risks which could not actuarially be calculated by the insurers who have put them under exclusions. For example, storms were excluded previously, but now they need to be insured. Many insurers have started insuring those risks which were uninsurable. The resort risk management through risk transfer and risk financing.

FERMA having 14 members are looking into risk management issues. Many new companies are looking FERMA to help them. They have to comply the regulations of solvency, directives of intermediation and environmental issues. FERMA is providing education and training of risk management as well as global insurance learning.

RISK MANAGEMENT IN LIFE INSURANCE

Solvency Margin

The insurer makes assumptions into future for parameters such as mortality, morbidity, expenses, interest etc. Sub regulation (b) of Regulation 5 of IRDA Regulations (Assets, Liabilities and Solvency

Margin of Insurers) 2000; specifies that the best estimate assumption shall be adjusted by an appropriate Margin for Adverse Deviation (MAD) which is dependent upon the degree confidence. The purpose of MAD is to build a buffer for mis-estimations of the best estimate or adverse fluctuations. But it does not cover for volatility and catastrophe risks for which a separate excess assets known as Solvency Margin should be provided by the insurer.

Risk Based Capital

Risks based capital includes asset default risk, mortality morbidity risk, volatility risk, catastrophe risk, margin risk and fund risk. Each company needs to develop implement and maintain appropriate and effective procedures to manage its capital position, *i.e.*, on going minimum capital requirements, and future capital requirements. The capital management planning identifies the quantity, quality and sources of additional capital required, availability of any external sources, estimating the financial impact of raising additional capital, taking into account the plans and requirements of various business units of the company. Risk Based Capital is an amount of capital based on an assessment of risk that a company should hold to protect policy holders against adverse developments. Risk based capital involves identifying the key risks and quantifying them.

1. Insurance Risk
2. Market Risk
3. Credit Risk
4. Liquidity Risk
5. Operational Risk

These risks are analysed with special references.

Insurance Risk : It is underwriting risk associated with the uncertainty of business written in the furture.

Market Risk : It is the risk associated with movements in interest rates, foreing exchange rates or asset prices lead to an adverse movement in asset values.

Credit Risk : If another party fails to perform them in time *i.e.* If the party fails to pay the credit. So, allowance should be made for the financial effect of non-payment of reinsurance and of the non payment of premium debtors.

Liquidity Risk : It is the risk that a firm has insufficient financial resources to meet its obligation as they fall due or can only secure the resources at excessive cost.

Operational Risk : It in the risk of direct or indirect loss resulting from inadequate or failed internal proceses, people and system or from external events.

RISK MANAGEMENT IN GENERAL INSURANCE

Solvency Margin Formula

IRDA's relevant regulations prescribe required solvency margin (RSM) at 20% of the net premiums or 30% of net increased claims whichever in higher.

Risk Based Capital

Risk Based Capital (RBC) formula comprises asset risk, credit risk, underwriting loss, underwriting premium risk and off balance sheet risk.

Reserving

The importance of proper reserving cannot be over-emphasised. The failure to provide adequately for future claims is attributed to 'under reserving' or 'under provisioning'. Reserves can be classified as unearned premium reserves (UPR), Unexpired Risk Reserve (URR) outstanding Claims Reserve (OCR), Chain Ladder Method (CL), Average Cost Per Claim Method (ACPC) and Incurred but not reported Reserve (IBNR).

Alternate Risk Management

These are several alternate risk management strategies such as risk transfer (reinsurance), ris' hedging through interest ratio etc. longevity bonds and managing financial market risks.

Solvency I

Solvency I is based on minimum solvency standards. The solvency I directive adopted in 2002 left the solvency calculation unchanged but only adjusted some other components. Solvency requirements should be fulfilled at all times rather than only at the time the financial statements are drawn up. All life insurers are required to Gold capital of at least the Solvency I minimum guarantee fund, or the Solvency I required solvency margin plus the resilience capital requirement. Solvency capital requirement will be calculation by applying either the standard approach or the insurer's won internal risk model.

Solvency I requires insurers to hold capital funds equal to the required solvency margin or the minimum guarantee fund, whichever is the higher. Solvency I for non-life insurance is defined as the higher of the premium and the claim index.

Premium Index = 18% of gross premium × retention rate

Claims Index = 26% of gross claim × retention rate

Retention = Net claims ÷ Gross claims (3 year average but not less than 50%)

Solvency I for Life Insurance is Required Solvency Margin

= 4% × gross mathematical provision × retention rate mathematical provision + 3% × capital at risk × retention rate capital at risk.

Solvency II

Solvency II requires adequate capital backing for the volatility of claims. The assess which lives of business may exhibit above-average volatility the loss rations of five non-life lives of business. European union (EU) adopted solvency I 2002 which was converted to solvency II in early 2003. EU commission is expected to adopt the solvency II directive in mid 2007. After its adoption by EU Parliament and the council of Ministers, the implementation is scheduled to be complete by 2010.

One of the objectives of Solvency II is to establish a solvency capital requirement which is better matched to the risks of an insurance company. The characteristic of solvency II are based on principles and not rules. These are two levels of capital requirements under solvency II, *i.e.*, The Minimum Capital Requirement (MCR) and Solvency Capital Requirement. MCR is the minimum level below which ultimate supervisory action will be triggered. SCR should deliver a level of capital that enables an insurance undertaking to absolute significant unforeseen losses and gives reasonable assurance to policy holders that payment will be made as they fall due. Solvency II deals with quantitative requirements, supervisory review powers and for insurer's internal control and risk management and disclosure and transparency to reinforce market mechanism and risk based supervisors. It reinforces on risk/return fundamentals.

IRDA Role

The reporting framework for published accounts for insurance companies in prescribed by the IRDA and is mainly armed at demonstrating solvency and protecting the interest of policy holders. The IRDA reviews the functioning of the insurance company, from time to time, through inspections meetings with the CEO, CFO, the Appointed Actuary and other senior officials to form a view of compliance and how risk issuer are addressed by the company. The solvency requirements are related to mathematical reserves and sum at risk reflecting solvency I. The insurers are required to maintain, at all times, solvency margin at not less than 150% of the required level as per the regulators. As of now, the regulations allow only equity as the accepted form of capital.

Solvency framework in India is similar to some of the Asian countries which follow Solvency I. Although there is a move towards a risk based capital which is principles based and focuses on the specific risks to which the business is exposed. The IRDA is a number of International Association of Insurance Supervisors (IAIS) which is working towards a common structure and common standards for assessing insurer solvency as a new framework for insurance supervision. The risks faced by an insurer have been categorised under five heads viz., underwriting risk, credit risk, market risk. operational risk and liquidity risk.

De-tariffing

De-tariffing has provided significant opportunities in tapping more markets and will provide even more opportunities after product liberalisation. It has placed the onus of correct pricing on the players themselves. While this has resulted in players preparing to identify risk parameters and pricing products based on risks, the immediate response has been to drop the rates in hitherto non-profitable business. The price war will erose capital. The general insurances players are exposed to memerous such risks as financial and non-financial.

Financial risks include capital risks asset liability management risks insurance risks and credit risks. Capital risks relates to capital structure risks and capital adequacy risks. Asset Liability Management Risks takes into consideration of exchange rate risks, interest rate risks and investment management risks. Insurance risks are underwriting risks, catastrophic risks, reserves risks, pricing risks and claim and management risks. Credit risks include re-insurer's risks, policy holder premium, brokers, claim recoveries and other debtors.

Non Financial Risks are enterprise risks and operational risks. Enterprise risks include reputation risks parents risks and competitor behavior risks. Operational risks are regulators risks, business continuity risk, IT obgolescence risks, people and process risks, risks of frouds process-related risks regulatory compliance risks and outsourcing related risks.

Trained and devoted personnel as well as agents can manage these risks effectively. The impact of detariffing was realised by discounting the rates endlessly. It creates problems to them. So, they were given freedom in Policy wording. 1RDA issued guidelines for relaxion in terms and Relaxations in Detariffing condition.

Insurers are permitted to file Add.-on. covers over and above the erstwhile tariff covers in Fire, Engineering, Industrial All Risks and Motor insurance. Insurers are permitted to file variations in deductible from those prescribed.

They are permitted to extend engineering insurance to movable and portable equipments.

As a result of detariffing, friendly policies are issued. The insured are paid claims without deducting depreciation The Add-on cover provides for payment of loan installment to the finances during the period of accident repairs. This cover provides for payment of incidental expenses, providing alternative vehicle, reimburse loss of personal items kept in the car.

Housebreaking risk can be covered as an extension to fire insurance of residential property, thereby avoiding the necessity of taking separate burglary cover. Loss of or damage to the property insured caused by its own fermentation, natural heating or spontaneous combustion can be covered as an extension. Fire policy can be extended to cover jetties. Hotel, holiday resorts and private properties erected on sea shore can be caused in fire policy itself. Insurers have extended coverage to cover the loss or damage to boiler. ecouonnser, other vessel, apparatus or their contents resulting from their own explosion/implosion. Accidental damage coverage is included under property insurance. Marine risk can be combined with storage risk.

Current Impact

The abolition of the tariffs has lead to price war in Fire and Engineering insurance. This caused negative impact on commission because the cost is not sustainable. Many insurers are facing pressure on profitability the customers are in advantageous position as they can bargain better they can increase their insurance levels.

The tariff abolitions in international markets suggests that the market reacts with a sharp drop in the premium rates the followers may also reduce the rates and price-war may cause problems to industry. It has a major concern on the continued solvency of the insurance companies.

INSURANCE AS PART OF RISK MANAGEMENT

Risk management is the process of managing an organisation's exposure to loss. It consists of identifying and measuring potential exposure, developing and executing a plan to manage those potentials exposures. Companies are many times prepared to manage their own risks.

Risk Feeling and Preparedness of Risk Management

Rank	Discription	2007 Prepara-tions in %	Rank	Description	2009 Prepara-tions in %	Rank	Description	2011 Prepara-tions in %
1.	Damage to do Reputation	48	1	Economic slowdown	60	1	Economic slowdown	64
2.	Business Industry	70	2	Regulatory	65	2	Regulations	65
3.	Third Party Liablity	75	3	Business Interrupt	79	3	Increasing competitions	71
4.	Distribution	63	4	Increasing competition	71	4	Damage to Reputation	61
5.	Market Environment	35	5	Commodities price Risk	77	5	Business interruptions	69
6.	Regulatory Changes	41	6	Damage to reputation	58	6	Failure to innovate	68
7.	Failure to attract or retain staff	55	7	liquidity Risk	75	7	Failure to attract or retain staff	60
8.	Market Risk (financial)	56	8	Distributions	70	8	Commodities Price Risk	76
9.	Physical Damage	77	9	Third parties Liability	81	9	Technologies system failure	76
10.	Merger/Acquisition Pesticulturing	69	10	Failure to attract or retains retaurns	68	10	Liquidity Risk	77

Source: Swiss Re Economic Research & Consulting.

Among the above risks, Business Interruption, Third Party liability and Physical Damage are insurable. The financial and economic crisis began clouding the scene although economic slowdown and regulations changed have topped the list. Many of the above risks such as market environment increasing competitions; failure to attract or retain staff and damage to reputation are related to the core risk of running a business. Risk which are not insurable are managed by commercial insurer or via self insurance. Most of the company's riks are entrepreneurial by nature and not insured. The insurable risks as mentioned earlier are managed through risk preventions and loss reduction. Risk prevention can be achieved via safety education programme. Loss reduction measures save lives and property from death and damages to a greater event.

COMMERCIAL INSURANCE

Commercial insurance is to stabilise revenue and profit. The catastrophic risk is transferred to the insuring companies. Insurance contributes to the financial stability of a company by providing funds when companies need it most, reducing cash flow volatility, normalising tax burdens and stabilising earnings. Insurence can relieve financial stress from unfavourable borrowing terms, strained relationship with suppliers and clients, departure of key personnel, the need to pay high retention wages or drop in a company's stock price and can minimise the disruption of investment plans. Commercial insurance provides goodwill to the purchasing company that it has mechanism to reduce loss and financial distress.

Substitutes for Commercial Insurance

Instead of purchasing commercial insurance, the companies generally use self insurance, captives, pools and capital markets.

Self Insurance: Company takes control of low-level risks by becoming its own insurer. It is an in-house insurance used to cover company's assets and risks. Self insurance is also useful when risks are difficult to insure and for which commercial insurance industry cannot provide adequate cover in every circumstances. They are third party liability for pharmaceutical risk, errors and omissions insurance, terrorism risk insurance, environment impavement liability insurance.

Captives insurance have become a standard tool for large corporations to perform integrated risk management. Multinational companies can through captives, better bundle and diversify their risks. They develop better loss prevention, incentives and claims settlements. It does not bear insurer's overhead and broker commission. The captives insurance companies are formed by the larger companies to manage their own risks and sometime other business too. Captives insurance companies may obtain license to perform insurance functions.

More than 2000 captive insurers were domiciled in USA. It has 35 per captives of world's; total captive insurers. Europe has merely 17 per cent capatives of total world's captives. Carribbean has maximum number of captives *i.e.* 45 per cent of the total world's captive insurers.

Pools are risk sharing arrangement between member companies or insurers to mobilise sufficient capacity for very large risks. It is organised generally on national basis. It may operate reinsurance business wastes the individual member ceding the risk and their premiums to the pool to cover a specific risk class. Aviation and nuclear power plants are covered by pools.

Capital markets can be a source of capacity for insurance risks and could play a significant role in the future.

Progress of Commercial Insurance

In spite of the alternatives, commercial insurance has become very popular in the world insurance market.

Direct Premium in Billion USD

Rank	*Country*	*Commercial insurance USD*	*Total non-Life insurance USD*	*Commercial share of market*	*Premium as a % of GDP (Insurance Penetration)*
1	United States	236.8	479.4	49%	1.6%
2	Japan	35.4	82.8	43%	0.6%
3	China	30.7	59.4	52%	0.5%
4	U.K.	28.3	69.7	41%	1.2%
5	Germany	26.5	76.7	35%	0.8%
6	France	24.4	81.1	30%	1.0%
7	Canada	13.9	45.0	31%	0.9%
8	Italy	12.7	47.5	27%	0.6%
9	Australia	11.7	26.6	44%	0.9%
10	Russia	9.3	17.6	53%	0.6%
	World	**600.0**	**1450.0**	**41%**	**1.0%**

Prospects of Commercial Insurance

The prospects of commercial insurance is very bright as it started with diversified risks coverage. The risks which are to be covered or which have already been covered under commercial insurance are property and business risks, liability risks workers compensation risks, motor risks of commercial vehicle and speciality risks, property risks which are generally not insured under fire insurance are covered under commercial insurance such as flood, earthquake, tsunami and terrorism, wind and water damage and vandalism risks. Business interruption risks are cover under commercial insurance as Business Owner's Policy Liability risks include product liability, professional liability, directors and officer's liability and environmental liability. Worker's compensation covers the consequences of occupational accidents and occupational diseases. Specially Risk Insurance includes marine insurance, offshore energy insurance, aviation and space insurance, credit and surety insurance, engineering insurance. Environmental risks include the cost of clean up, bodily injury and property damage liability and legal defence costs.

Progress of Commercial Insurance Markets

As a % of total commercial premium

Country	*Property*	*Liability*	*Worker Compensation*	*Commercial Automobile*	*Other*	*Total*
US	30	30	17 /-	10	13	100
Canada	37	28	-	19	16	100
UK	31	24	10	20	15	100
Germany	31	27	-	12	30	100
France	38	24	-	10	28	100
Japan	21	17	2	41	19	100
Australia	29	28	10	14	19	100
China	13	6	N.A	65	16	100
Russia	33	5	-	16	46	100
Brazil	50	7	-	N.A	43	100
India	24	10	-	21	46	100
Subtotal	**29**	**25**	**11**	**19**	**17**	**100**

Source : Swiss Re Economic Research & Consulting.

QUESTIONS

1. What is risk ? Discuss the methods of its identification.
2. Explain the methods of evaluation of risk.
3. Illustrate the techniques of controlling various types of risk.
4. Discuss the risk management techniques in India.
5. Explain the International Risk Management Association.

43

HEALTH INSURANCE

Health Insurance has been realised as an instrument for the health of the economy. If the people of the country are healthy, they can contribute significantly in the economic development of the country. The health insurance industry would provide protection to social development. The insurance industry should come forward to provide health to the masses like life insurance and property insurance. The Government provisions for health have not succeeded for want of initiative on the part of government officers and beneficiaries. It is hoped that commercial bases of health insurance will be more suitable for health development of people. There is need of products, designs, structural facilities and sustainability of insurance products. Adequate environment is to be developed for the introduction and development of health insurance.

Environment

Health insurance requires sufficient information and data for development of a good product, proper pricing and health management. Many insurers are interested to provide health insurance provided consumers are properly educated in this area. Recently with the break of joint family system, the need of health insurance is more thrusting. Maintaining health responsibilities on commercial basis to insurance companies, economic growth, human resource development and prosperity will enhance in future.

Product Design

There is need of well designed health insurance product that may protect family savings in case of unexpected medical charges. People are interested in higher achievement than paid by them in the form of premium. Insurer, therefore is expected to invest the premium money in such a way as to earn sufficient money for meeting the expenses of insurance and insurance claims. Insurer has to meet the challenges of expenses and health services. The insurance cover should be reasonably comprehensive without counter productive gaps.

Mediclaim policies provide coverage of medical services rendered during hospitalisation. But, there is need of broader set of services. There is need of outpatient costs because a large number of persons are treated satisfactorily without being admitted in the hospital. Health insurance should cover all such types of expenses. The third need of health insurance is preventive measures by providing health education and quality life. Premium may be reduced on such types of proposals.

Additional incentives should be provided for purchasing health insurance. The tax exemption on health premium and medical saving accounts are few of the examples of financial incentives for health insurance. The alternative choices should be there for selecting a suitable hospitals nearby the insured persons. There is need of new products of non-patient services. The premium should be competitive and fair to the policy holders.

Educating to consumers about health consciousness is very essential in health insurance. It increases people's awareness of diseases, cost of treatments, alternative treatment options. People should know quality of health and health care services. Employers should be motivated to provide health cover to their employees. Like group insurance and group superannuation; employers should purchase policies for their employees and pay the premium. It enhances the images of the organisation.

Cost Effective Health Insurance: The product of Health Insurance should be designed in such a way as to reduce cost of premium. The insurer should design the product to attract more customers. People should get incentives to purchase health policies. Low premium rate attracts a larger number of persons to purchase health policies. The developed nations have popularised the health insurance as the insurers meet the most expensive treatments. People are ready to pay higher premium to meet the high cost of medical bill.

Investment cum Health Service Product: In India, people are interested mainly in investment. They went that health protection should be part of savings. While saving schemes are spreading Health Insurance should be linked with that. If people get health cover with a slight deduction of money from their saving rate, they would not mind as it becomes a regular feature after some time. They will fell that health cover is given free of cost.

Product of Causal and Usual Risks: Health product should cover the casual risks such as epidemics risk and claims uncertainty risks and usual risks *e.g.,* overhead expenses, interest and other business risks. With the past experience of claim payment, insurer should design a number of suitable policies to meet different requirements of the customers. Product design and pricing are key factors for enhancing insurance. High price reduces business and less price increases loss of insurer. Therefore, proper balance is established with the help of data analysis.

Trust and Confidence: The insured should have trust and confidence in the insurance company that premium rates are at the lowest possible and they will get the claim amount at the time of need. The insurer should influx the confidence of solvency, proper risk selection, reasonable cost of operation and timely payment of claims. Solvency plus financial and operational performance monitoring will be essential.

Structural Facilities

The structural facilities are provided by the government. Regulatory authority properly guide the insurer to design insurance for health care. The insurer should feel free to approach hospitals, doctors physicians and others for getting adequate information. International Classification of Diseases-10th Revision (ICD-10) and Procedure Classification System (PCS) are good guide for health care and developing structural facilities of health insurance.

The health insurance reduces the charges for health care. The structural facilities of health care are told to the insured on websites and electronic format. The insurer should assure that reimbursement for their services are fair and sufficient. It will cover all the costs of medical treatment. The possibilities of litigation are minimised to provide confidence to the insureds.

Sustainability of the Products

The insurance products should be sustained for developing the trust and confidence amongst the policyholder. The insurer has to adopt proper management of funds, pricing, product-designs and follow the regulatory features. Facilities of electronic data is crucial for long-term success of the insurance industry. It will improve efficiency of the employees who will provide quality services to the insureds. The insurers maintain risk capital for meeting the contingency of unexpected losses. The scope of insurance cover is expanded to include impatient, out patient facilities, physicians and pharmacy charges.

Health insurance as a class, is very young in the Indian insurance. But, it occupies the third place among the different non-life insurance classes. It has registered more than 50% rise in 2006-2007. While non-life insurance business increased only by 10%. However, health insurances has not received more attention because the customers awareness is very low. The insurers should make the classes very explicit and explain the exclusions in detail. The role of Third Party Administrators should be effectively ensured by them. They should take care of the customers' interests.

Retailing Health Insurance

Retailing health insurance requires products innovation channel innovation, risk based pricing and prevention.

Causes of Low Level of Health Insurance

Inspite of health insurance provided by public sector insurance companies as well as private sector insurance. Only 2 per cent of the population is covered under health insurance schemes. The causes of low level of health insurance are :

1. Low level of awareness of the common public.
2. Limited insurance products to cover health problems.
3. Low level of medical facilities.
4. Moral hazard.
5. Adverse selection of underwriting process.
6. Insufficient data and information.
7. Variation in costs of insurance.

The unorganised sector workers below poverty line (BPL) and their families are proposed to be covered under Rashtriya Swasthya Bima Yojana (RSBY) during the next five years (2008-09 to 2012-2013). The coverage of health services is on a daycare basis, cashless coverage of all health services, provision for pre and post-hospitalisation expenses for one day prior and 5 days after hospitalisation and provision for transport allowance.

Product Innovation

Individuals face a number of exposures driven by health and health-related events and costs, the risks of which they can bear to differing degrees. These risks range from low ticket-size expenses (*e.g.*, for routine care) to higher ticket-size discretionary expenses (*e.g.*, for elective surgery), catastrophic expenses (*e.g.*, due to major illness, accident), end-of-life care expenses (*e.g.*, due to life threatening illness), expenses related to chronic diseases and income risk (*e.g.*, disability).

Channel Innovation

Health insurance products are likely to require additional distribution channels beyond the dominant agency force. Based of the U.S. experience, several innovations hold promise:

- **Direct-response channels.** These include a captive sales force, call centres, the Internet, direct mail, and television commercials. A leading U.S. player primarily uses the Internet, for example, to sell a product aimed at consumers aged 18 to 29 ("young invincibles") who think they do not need health insurance.
- **Retail stores.** Health insurers in the U.S. are now offering health benefit products through leading retail and pharmacy chains. One of the biggest success stories for payers has been selling Medicare-related products to the elderly through bricks-and-mortar retailers.
- **Affinity-marketing relationships.** Health insurance have entered successful affinity partnerships with diverse players.

Risk-based Pricing

Product and channel innovations alone are not enough, Health insurers need to understand the risk profile of individuals and their ability and willingness to pay, which often varies by sement and channel.

Actuaries could determine now consumer behaviour would change *a priori* and build that into product pricing rather than wait for years to study observed behaviour, they could benefit from substantive gains. Insurers in the U.S. have leveraged detailed data to build sophisticated actuarial models, that are more powerful by a factor of over 1,000 relative to competitors.

Insurance Coverage Beyond Hospitalization Benefits

Private sector group and individual health insurance coverage in India today focuses on hospitalisation benefits with a limited sum assured. While this provides valuable coverage, preventive care techniques are important to improve medical outcomes and to provide cost-effective health insurance. In India, there remains a huge need for simple primary prevention that largely falls into the public domain. However, the private health insurance can make important contributions at the secondary and tertiary prevention levels.

Primary vs Advanced Prevention

In assessing the cost-benefit equation of a number of techniques and determining who is best positioned to provide these services it is helpful to distinguish between three levels of preventive care:

- **Primary prevention** entails reduction in the level of one or more identified macro risk factors to reduce the probability of the initial occurrence of a disease. Examples include road safety, clean water, food fortification and vaccinations, which are typically Government-led.
- **Secondary prevention** aims at detecting a disease at a very early stage to prevent or delay its progression. Examples include screening programme for cancer and diabetes, which could be provided for and funded by the private sector.
- **Tertiary prevention** consists of ongoing interventions aimed at decreasing or delaying the severity and frequency of recurrent events of chronic or episodic diseases. Example include family-oriented disease management therapies for cardio-vascular diseases, or disease management programs for diabetes patients, where again the private sector can play an important role.

  WHO statistics indicate that 8 million people die prematurely every year in India from diseases that are relatively easily preventable, if certain primary preventive measures were adopted by the public authorities.

HEALTH INSURANCE IN INDIA

The government has asked the public sector non-life insurance companies to devise an affordable health insurance scheme. Universal Health Insurance Policy is issued by them. It has failed to attract policy holders and people to get its benefits. The role of NGOs have been realised to benefit the poor by health insurance. There is urgent need of health insurance to product the masses against health hazards.

Government has subsidised the health insurance for the poor.

Health insurance in India is not gaining ground because people are skeptical about the payment of claims and services provided by insurance companies. Lack of health care services and infrastructure, illiteracy and lack of trust in health schemes and insurance companies have impeded the health insurance in India.

PROSPECTS OF HEALTH INSURANCE

The prospects of health insurance are very bright in future as the cost of medical treatment is escalating although it is not gaining at present. The underwriting practices have to be tightened. The health care utilisation increases with affluence of society. The socio-economic development in India is increasing fastly and need of insurance is realised gradually. Low premium is not always good because the coverage may be small. The medical inflation index provides the guidance for designing the product and pricing reasonably. In absence of medical inflation index, consumer price index is used for the purpose.

In India, medical claims and losses occur but they are not reported to any organisation. People suffer and get totally secret medicine inherent getting any receipts of purchases. Such types of activities are not useful for managing health insurance. Insurers have to anticipate such claims and manage in their total claims. It is observed that unhealthy lives would remain with insurer causes like in claims losses. They donot go to other insurers because they have to pay higher premium for new health policy. The insurer has to classify the healthy and unhealthy lives for proper insurance management and portfolio management. Information and data should be updated for future planning and product designing.

Health insurance is personal insurance that provides coverage for the cost of hospital and medical expenses arising from illness or injury. Benefits are paid as a fixed lump sum or as a proportion of actual treatment costs. It includes individually hospital cash, critical illness and disability benefits.

Indemnity mediclaim has covered only inpatient facility and professional claims along with some of the pre-admission and post admission expenses. Covering all outpatient expenses in additon to inpatient expenses would be a huge broadening of the scope of policy benefits and would represent a major shift in the philosophy of health insurance in India. Those companies in India that have experimented with such policy broadening have experienced huge increased in claim volumes and the associated administrative expenses. To this point, the focus has been on offering policies which protect the policyholder from costly care that might threaten a person's financial security. This has been done with an indemnity policy that has a sum insured cop on the insurer's ability.

Hospital Cash

In the case of hospital cash benefits, the actuary will need to tailor the pricing assumptions to the target popoulations being insured. Variables such as age, gender, geographic location, occupation and income level are known to correlate with hospital utilization and hence will be important considerations in pricing this benefit. The cash benefit usually makes a payment to a person that is hospitalized at some scheduled amount, typically on a per day basis and usually is limited to 60-90 days of cover per hospitalization. Certain types of hospitalization stays are excluded for specific surgeries and hospitalizations that commerce within 30 days of policy issuance.

As with all medical insurance policies, careful benefit design is crucial. Moral hazard is a concern. For example, an insurer will not want to offer a hospital cash benefit that covered more than the expected patient out-of-pocket expenses during a hospital stay; otherwise the patient would stay to gain financially by being in the hospital! The key here is not to create in incentive to such a degree that it encourages hospital admissions.

Critical Illness

Critical illness benefits are most commonly sold by life insurers as riders to life policies. They are usually structured in a way which pays a defined percentage of the policy amount in the event a policyholder is diagnosed with one of several designated critical illnesses. Some insurers are offering these policies on a stand alone basis.

A variation on the critical illness rider offers coverage for the treatment of the disease conditions as opposed to a cash payout if the diagnosis is present. Payment is made under the terms of these policies only to indemnify the insured for the cost of treatments. As with the Critical Illness benefit, adverse selection is always of great concern under these policies, and so offering these benefits requires skillful and expert underwriting.

Just as in the Critical Illness benefit, it is important to have some sense of the prevalence and incidence of the covered diseases. The Indian incidence rates, for these diseases, are not well known, particularly in an insured population. Public health officials have made estimates for the overall population of the prevalence of critical illness (see Table 1). Incidence of disease and the related treatment are of utmost interest to insurers. The mere existence of a disease in a population does not necessarily translate into incidence of treatment at any given point in time, given some people are asymptomatic and go from day to day without using the healthcare system.

Disability Benefits

Health Insurance products in India narrowly cover hospitalization benefits with a sum-assured limit. India's private health insurance sector could cover a number of secondary and tertiary preventive measures such as screening for cancer or diabetes, and preventive health check ups as well as disease management programs for specific conditions, which would be beneficial for insured and insurers alike.

Innovative Health Insurance

Insurers are working innovative health insurance over in the market and as both as service and products and as part of package for production. The inclusion of pre-existing diseases after a waiting period not exceeding 48 months is a similar, innovative and industry-wide initiative. Rom coverage point of view, the insurers are now offering a wide variety of comprehensive products including expansion of the standard hospitalization policy. E.g. listing of day care procedures which do not require 24-hour hospitalization whch has not only enhanced the coverage, but also facilitate to minimize the costs towards unnecessary overnight stay in the hospitals. Similarly, the expenses towards organ transplantation as well as the treatment for the donor, external medical aids, are also being offered under coverage, which were otherwise considered exclusions. Even the maternity cover, which was earlier not available in the case of individual health insurance policies, is now being offered after a certain waiting period.

Increasingly, health insurance policies now offer fixed benefit product like daily hospital cash benefit–which is a fixed allowance to cover incidental costs at a nominal premium and is unliked to expenditure actualy incurred. Policyholder can opt for the allowance based on his needs. which policies available already offering a wide range from ₹ 100 to ₹ 5000 per day. Initiatives such as linking of sub-limits against sum insured, co-payments and compulsory and voluntary deductibles are not only means of cost effectiveness, but also minimize the moral hazard elements, thereby containing claim costs and help keep premium costs in check. Comprehensive coverage for disease management such as products for Diabetes are already into the market. Recent clarification of insurance beneficiaries also mean that they can get benefited if they have additional health insurance in addition to their entitlements in CGHS, subject to the total not exceeding the total expenditure incurred.

Critical illness benefit is another regular element appearing in most of the comprehensive health policies, and with the recent attempts at standardization of nomenclature and definitions of critical illness products, this area may see greater activity too. Treatment of major diseases like cancer, Heart problems etc. is very costly; and many expenses may not be covered by hospital indemnity policies. Critical illness policies pay a lump sum amount of the diagnosis of any of specified critical illness, and both life and non-life insurers offer critical illness benefit either as standalone products or as rider to policies or as a components of packaged health insurance product.

Gradually, health insureres are also offering OPD coverage in limited way. Features like e-opinion or second opinion, telemedicine treatment are also increasingly becoming regular feature of comprehensive policies.

Product and Pricing: There are a number of health insurance policies available in the market which have been more publicized after the advent of the private insurance players. The products of additional prominence introduced into the market include Critical Illness or Dreaded Disease Cover; Hospital Daily Cash cover to take care of incidental costs and non-admissible expenses; and Specific Disease Cover for Cancer, HIV, and Diabetes in addition to standard consequents Health insurance premium in patient grew from ₹ 380 crores in 1999-2000 to ₹ 6625 crores in 2008-2009 from predominates single product *i.e.*, Mediclaim by the four non-life insurers, to more than 300 health insurance products that are offered by over 30 insurance companies, both general and life; in less than a decade.

Universal Health Coverage

Defined in simple terms, UHC means ensuring access, availability and affordability of healthcare to all citizens at all times. The broader definition of health also includes preventive and promotive part such as clean drinking water, nutrition, immunization, awareness compaign against use of tobacco etc. However for the purpose of this paper, we shall focus on consumption of healthcare at the time of need *i.e.* sickness-whether the same pertains to out-patient consultation, drugs, diagnostics or in-patient services including tetiary care. And how Health insurance could step in to support goverment's efforts to extend the same to maximum chunk of population in short to medium term, create a win-win situation of all stakeholders in a feasible, sustainable manner.

With WHO's report 'Health Systems Financing - The Path to Universal Coverage' in 2010. UHC has caught the attention of governments all over the world; especially in those low/middle income countries where out of pocket spend has been high, causing further financial impoverishment to already distressed and vulnerable population. For the past many decades, high income and developed nations have evolved models – tax funded (like NHS in UK) or social health insurance (like Germany), further organised around single payer, multiple payers, managed competition model, care provisioning by mix of public and private providers, with parying payment mechanisms – case based payment, Fee for service, capitation global budgets etc. The models seem to have worked reasonably well for these economies with high level or organised sector, high per capita income and overall educated and developed comunities, through some adjustments continue to be made with evolution of health care and modern diseases.

UHC Pakage and its Dellivery

It is expected that a person covered under UHC should be able to access all types of care as per need and occassion. Thus a comprehensive 'package' under UHC would consist of combination of preventive, promotive and curative services. The sheer magnitude of financing, providing and managing all services under one umbrella is challenging. Add to that some of the inefficiency and indifference of public health system, it is not difficult to imagine that the result would not be any different from what exists today. Thus it seems more feasible to split different types of services and the ownership/responsibility shared between entities that can help deliver the relevant services.

Amongst the gamut of health services required under UHC, insurance mechanism is most suited for curative services-outpatient, inpatient ICU etc. forming part of secondary and teriary case while public health system should be utilised for the rest such as primary care, immunization etc, refer Table 2 in the Annexure. The nature of services under public system is such that it need not have any upper limit or capping from beneficiary perspective though from budgetary perspective the outgo can be estimated. The insurance cover can be a combination of a basic package of secondary care (on the lines of RSBY), say up to a limit of ₹50,000, topped up by a tertiary care/critical care package of ₹1.5 lac.

HIV/AIDS Coverage

HIV/AIDS Coverage Insurance companies across the globe normally do not exclude HIV in their life policies. It means a death, even due to or related to HIV, merits to be paid under the policy.

This sounds good. But the fate of coverage is filered at the beginning of the acceptance of proposal at underwriting level. It is seen that comes from a person with HIV, the underwriters well decline acceptance. It means, pre-existing HIV is out of scope of acceptance under life policies. But once the proposal is accepted, the insurer has no ground to decline the claim irrespective of whether the illness is pre-existing or post infected.

Life insurance companies, like all other Non-life insurance companies or stand alone Health insurance companies offering Health insurance, also provide Health insurance cover either in indemnity or benefit based policies. Under this all Life/Non-life/Standalone Health insurers adopt almost similar underwriting principles, while dealing with acceptance of proposals and settlement of claims. (*i*) it is found that the proposals with HIV are not accepted for underwriting, because HIV patient is vulnerable to many other illnesses. (*ii*) All policies carry exclusion clauses which categorically treate HIV as a permanent exclusion. It means none of the Health insurance policies normally cover HIV- either pre- or post-infected. Miserably, declining a proposal is more dangerous than accepting a proposal with HIV exclusion, because the later merits for illness not related to HIV/AIDS. The exclusion wordings in most of the policies more or less read similar to "expenses arising out of any condition directly or indirectly caused by or associated with Human T-Cell, Lymphotropic virus type III (HTLB-III) or Lymphadinopathy associates virus (LAV) or mutants derivates, or knows deficiency syndrome or similar syndes are called AIDS.

Recently, it is found that some insurance companies both in life and Non-life segments have gradually and slowly started granting cover for HIV patients also. The reasons can be attributed to the legislations, product innovations and mass coverage. But it is also seen that these are too little for a patient, which either come under too many restrictions (adherence to ART) and/or with too little compensation amounts.

Indian National Accreditation Structure

The attempts to evolve a voluntary accreditation system began in late 1980s with the Bureau of Indian Standards putting down standards for 30, 100 and 250 bed hospitals. The National Institute of Health and Family Welfare had also specified rules for more than 50 bed hospitals. Since health is a state subject, there have been attempts in some states to incorporate standards for hospitals. Compartmentalized initiatives have led to a fragmentation of an already segmented industry.

To overcome this lack of single system to monitor the functioning of hospitals in India and the stringency of compliance to established standards that was suitable to the Indian conditions and credible in the eyes of international markets; an inter-ministerial task force was set-up up in 1991. The report of the task force was brought out in January 1993 and Quality Council of India (QCI) was established in 1997 as an autonomous body as a result of the recommendations of the task force. The mandate given to QCI was to establish and operate the national accreditation structure and obtain international recognition for its accreditation schemes. Accordingly National Accreditation Board for Hospitals and Healthcare Provides (NABH) was established.

Objective of NABH

The broad objectives of the accrediting system is to develop and update standards to cover various areas of hospitals functioning. It also aims to monitor hospitals compliance with the standards prescribed, assist hospitals that need to upgrade their levels and awards accreditation to those insutitutions demonstrating them. specific objective of NABH is to enhance health system and promote continuous quality improvement and patient safety.

Organization and affiliations of NABH

The board is supported by many stakeholders including industry, consumers, government and has a full functional autonomy in its operational activities. NABH provides accreditation to various Healthcare Organizations and entities independent of their ownership status in a non discriminatory way.

The categories of health entities for which currently the standards have been laid out and for which the accreditation process is available are:

- Allopathic Clinics
- AYUSH Hospitals
- Blood Banks
- Blood Storage Centre
- Dental Facilities
- Hospitals
- Medical Imaging Services
- Medical Laboratory Programme
- OST Centre
- PHC/CHC Accreditation
- Small Healthcare Organizations
- Wellness Centre

Outline of NABH Standards

Patient Centered Standards
• Access, Assessment and Continuity of Care (AAC
• Care of Patient (COP)
• Management of Medication (MOM)
• Patient Right and Education (PRE)
• Hospital Infection Control (HIC)

Organisation Centered Standards
• Continuous Quality Improvement (CQI)
• Responsibility of Management (ROM)
• Facility Management and Safety (FMS)
• Human Resource Management (HRM)
• Information Management System (IMS)

NABH Standards

NABH Standards for hospitals prepared by technical committee contains complete set of standards for evaluation of hospitals for grant of accreditation. The standards provide the broad framework for quality of care for patients and quality improvement for hospitals. Thee standards help to build a quality culture at all level and across all the function of hospital. NABH Standards include ten chapters that incorporate 102 standards and 636 objective elements.

II. National Accreditation Board for Testing and Calibration Laboratories (NABL)

NABL is an autonomous body under the aegis of Department of Science & Technology, government of India. NABL has been established with the objective to provide government, regulators and industry with a scheme of laboratory accreditation through third-party assessment for formally recognizing the technical competence of laboratories. The accreditation services are provided for testing, calibration and medical laboratories in accordance with International Organization for Standardization (ISO) standards.

III. Indian Public Health Standard (IPSH)

The Primary Health Centres (PHCs) and Community Health Centers (CHCs) which constitute the primary and secondary level of health care were designed to provide referral as well as specialist health care to the rural population.

In order to provide quality care in these CHCs India Public Health Standards (IPHs) are being prescribed to provide optimal expert care to the community and achieve and maintain an acceptable standard of quality of care. These standards would help monitor and improve the functioning of the CHCs.

IV. Joint Commission International

JCI provides a premier set of international standards. An international committee develops the standards that JCI implements, while regional advisory councils— Guided by experts—ensure local and cultural relevance. JCI's standards are accreditation programs are accredited by the international Society for Quality in Health Care, demonstrating that JCI meets the highest international benchmarks for accreditation entities.

Hospitals, laboratories, medical transport organizations, care continuum (non-acutesettings from assisted living to private homes), ambulatory care, and primary care providers undergo setting-specific evaluations to achieve The Gold Seal of Approval. Organizations can also pursue Clinical Care Program

Certification to demonstrate excellence in the integration and coordination of care for specific diseases. World Health Organization (WHO) partnered with JCI and The Joint Commission to establish the first WHO Collaborating Centre for Patient Safety Solutions.

Current Status of Accreditation in India:

In India, accreditation is a voluntary act. As of August 2013, the status of NABH accredited HCO's is as follows:

- Allopathic Clinics : 6
- Blood Banks : 56
- Hospitals : 188
- Primary Health Centres : 10
- Community Health Centres : 1
- Wellness Centre : 05
- AYUSH Hospitals : 8
- Dental Health Care Service Providers (DHSP) : 04
- Medical Imaging Services : 07
- Oral Substitution Theory (OST) Centre : 51
- Small Healthcare Organisations : 22

There are 22 hospitals in India with JCI accreditation. Of these, 9 have obtained re-accreditation.

The demand for accreditation is spurred by emerging new markets, like medical tourism, and the insistence by Health insurance companies and third-party administrators for the purpose of reimbursement.

Government Initiatives:

The government too is taking keen interest in providing services to the population by entering into various kinds of Public Private Partnerships were service delivery is through accredited centers.

A. The Janani Suraksha Yojana (JSY) of the Government of India, Under the National Rural Health Mission (NRHM), has also made accreditation mandatory for private health organizations wishing to participate in order to promote quality and encourage institutional deliveries (MoHFW, 2005; 12, 39).

B. In 2006, the Government of India constituted a 'Working Group on Clinical Establishments, Professional Services Regulation and Accreditation of Health Care Infrastructure' for the 11th Five Year Plan. The report of the group (Planning Commission, 2007; 11-12) raised the following concerns relating to enforcement, effectiveness and implementation:

1. Out-of-date legislation, which are cumbersome and irrelevant in the current scenario.
2. Ineffective implementation of relevant laws due to weak regulatory controls.
3. Absence of rules for the implementation of the Clinical Establishment Act, 2010.
4. Ineffective content of rules, which refer only to registration without spelling out standards.
5. Non-coverage of other private institutional providers, such as laboratories and diagnostic centres.
6. No uniformity in the standards specified in the acts enacted by different states.

C. The fifth India Health Summit on "Optimising Healthcare Delivery in India: A Patient Centric Approach", jointly organised by CII (Confederation of Indian Industry), MOHFW (Ministry of Health and Family Welfare) and IHCF (Indian Health Care Federation) on December 15-16 2008, has come out with useful recommendations that will have a far-reaching impact on the health industry, one of the important recommendations being:

"**Insurance companies driving accreditation:** Globally, medical insurance is linked to accredited delivery centres. Once there are a sizable number of accredited hospitals, a directive mandating medical reimbursement to be allowed only from accredited hospitals will be a welcome move, which is likely to induce hospitals to embrace accreditation."

D. Kerala takes 'Quality' leap in public health:

Today with its many initiatives, Arogya Keralam has started making its impact on the health sector. To ensure holistic development of healthcare in the state, the government had to

Hospitals selected for accreditation

District	Hospital	Bed Strength
Thiruvanthapuram	W and C Hospital, Thiruvanthapuram	428
Kollam	District Hospital, Kollam	471
Pathanamthitta	General Hospital, Pathanamthitta	414
Alappuzha	Taluk Head Quarters Hospital, Cherthala	251
Kottayam	District Hospital, Kottayam	374
Idukki	Taluk Head Quarters Hospital, Thodupuzha	304
Ernakulam	General Hospital, Ernakulam	779
Thrissur	Taluk Head Quarters Hospital, Chavakkad	140
Palakkad	District Hospital, Palakkad	562
Malappuram	District Hospital, Manjeri	501
Kozhikode	W and C Hospital, Kozhikode	295
Wayanad	Taluk Head Quarters Hospital, Sulthan Bathery	57
Kannur	District Hospital, Kannur	616
Kasaragod	District Hospital, Kanhangad	400

counter the shortage of qualified healthcare workers. Before embarking on a process of recruitment of medical and paramedical personnel in the state through NRHM, the critical requirement of the hour was a need assessment survey in the state, through which the critical gaps in human resources could be identified. At the same time, upgradation of the CHCs to IPHS was essential, since facilities available in these institution hardly satisfied the prescribed norms.

E. Vibrant Gujarat

In an effort to improve the quality of healthcare in the state, the Government of Gujarat has introduced Total Quality Management (TQM) system in its key medical institutions. The system covers the state's Medical College, Hospitals and District Hospitals, as per the NABH and NABL standards. Simultaneously, its strived to develop a pool of healthcare professionals in the public health sector, trained in the implementation of healthcare quality standards and information technology, to bring productivity and effectiveness in the healthcare delivery system of the state. Under the system, a policy framework for NABH and NABL accreditation of public hospitals and laboratories, as approved by the state government, was launched, and empanelment of NABH and NABL consultants was undertaken in coordination with QCI.

Hospitals for NABH & NABL accreditation

1st Phase (2007-2008	2nd Phase (2008-2009)	3rd Phase (2009-2010)
District Hospital Rajpipla	District Hospital Surendranagar	District Hospital Dahod
District Hospital Godhara	District Hospital Porbander	District Hospital Kheda
District Hospital Valsad	District Hospital Petlad	District Hospital Patan
District Hospital Junagadh	District Hospital Nadiad	District Hospital Morvi
District Hospital Kutchch	District Hospital Navsari	District Hospital Limdi
District Hospital Sola	District Hospital Amreli	District Hospital Ahwa Dang
District Hospital Gandhinagar	District Hospital Himatnagar	District Hospital Bharuch
District Hospital Mehsana Medical	Jamana Bai Hospital Baroda	District Hospital Khambhaliya
	Medical College Hospital Baroda	Old Civil Hospital Surat
	Medical College Hospital Surat	
	Medical College Hos. Jamnagar	
	Medical College Hos. Bhavnagar	
	Medical College Hos. Ahmadabad	

Some examples of how accreditation ensure quality of care and lead to improved outcomes:

1. Wockhardt Hospital in Bangalore, under JCI accreditation implementation, achieved noteworthy decreases in the monthly rate of ventilator-associated pneumonia (from 17 to 7); surgical site infections (from 3.25 to 0.9); hospital associated urinary tract infections (from 15 to 4) and blood stream infections ((from 19 to 3) during the period May 2007 to May 2008 (Cooper, Helfrick and de Silva, 2009).
2. Indraprastha Apollo Hospitals in Delhi reduced medication errors by 78 per cent, and its revenue grew by 20 per cent in the six months after it received international accreditation from JCI (http://johnpunnoose.com/yahoo_site_admin/assets/docs/Indraprastha_Apollo_Hospital_Delhi_-India. 30354104.pdf). The Apollo Hospitals Group, with 8,000 beds across 47 hospitals (7 accredited by JCI, 2 by NABH) performed over 7,600 cardiac surgeries during 2009-10 with a 99.2 per cent success rate (Apollo Hospitals, 2010: 18).

The future of accreditation:

Medical Tourism: Cost-effectiveness and quality cares are the mainstay of Indian hospitals, which have created a new market of medical tourism. There are several corporate hospitals and some private medical college hospitals with accreditation from Joint Commission International that enjoy a good reputation among the citizens to the US, the UK and other developed countries. These hospitals offer timely and cost-effective treatment, coupled with wellness management, a value addition to medical care, helping the patient to recuperate faster.

India's National Health Policy declares that the treatment of foreign patients is legally an "export" and deemed "eligible for all the fiscal incentives extended to export earnings (MoHFW, 2002:)" Government and private sector studies in India estimate that medical tourism, which is growing by 30 per cent a year, could bring anywhere between US$ 1 billion and US$ 2 billion into the country by 2012 (Gupta, 2004).

Health Insurance and TPAs: By insisting on acceptable standards for doctors as well as hospitals, Health insurance companies can improve the quality of care provided by the private sector hospitals. Public-private partnerships (PPP) are proving to be successful in Health insurance in India. Many state Government has implemented mass insurance schemes in PPP mode via a trust to improve access to quality care for the below poverty line (BPL).

COVERAGE IN SOME COUNTRIES (FOR EXAMPLE)

UK: Life insurers do not normally exclude AIDS in life policies. But HIV exclusion is more common in all health insurance policies. Claims unrelated to HIV are paid. Now, past infected HIV is covered under critical illness policies where one time lump sum compensation is paid as full and final payment. Unlike many other countries, UK has the biggest advantage of having its government owned National Health Scheme (NHS) where all citizens are covered for all illness including HIV.

USA: The American Disability Act prohibits discrimination on the basis of disability. It considers contagious disease as impairment and entitles PLHA the same Health insurance covers that are offfered to those not having HIV. That apart, the state has a number of government supported health schemes, where the citizens can be members to benefit for illness. The American healthcare system is principally financed by medical insurance schemes. These fall into three primary categories: (*i*) Private work-based schemes, run either directly by the employer, or through a union, (*ii*) Government funded programmes (such as Medicaid and Medicare) available to over-65s, those on limited incomes and people with limited disabilities.

Status of Universal Health Coverage in India

As on 2010, approximately 200 million lives were covered in India under formal Health insurance mechanism, *i.e.* organised through licenced commercial insurers (both public and private) Extrapolating the same based on growth in various segements the insured number would be approximately 319 million in March 2013 (official data for all not yet available). Since most Health insurance products in India cover in-patient treatment costs, this means that close to 26% of Indian population has been covered by the insurance industry against financial risk, to varying extent, associated with hospitalization. These include people covered under group health covers organised by employers, individual and family covers bought by households and mass segments (comprising of Below Poverty Line and vulnerable sections) covered under government insurance schemes of both Centre and State governments. Here we are not discussing beneficiaries who are covered under non-insurance/self-funded schemes *e.g.* CGHS, ESIS, Yeshasvini or uninsured part of Aarogyasri.

There has been substantial increase, rather a quantum jump in number of lives insured with the introduction of government insurance schemes, starting with Aarogyasri in Andhra Pradesh in 2007. A major boost to the insured population was received with the introduction up of RSBY– Rashtriya Swasthya Bima Yojna, a central government scheme covering all Below Poverty Line (BPL) population across India. Experts further project that the number of insured lives would touch 470 million by 2015. On benefit utilisation side, the total claims reported/paid in 2010 stood at 38.43 lacs under group and individual covers and approximately 7.43 lacs under government health insurnace schemes as on 2009-2010. Thus it can be said that these many hospitalisations have been paid for by the insurance mechanism wherein people did not have pay from pocket for episode of hospitalisation

LIC's New Health Insurance plan '**Jeevan Arogya**' (T-903) has won the most prestigious "**Golden Peacock**" for innovative Product/Service **Award 2011**" at a glittering ceremony in Bangalore on January 2012 Latest health insruance plan has been selected out of a gamut of such plans introduced by 22 Life insurers and another 22 Non-life insurers (including 3 Stand-Alone Health Insurers).

This honour has been possible due to the team effort of the Product Development Department and then Health Insurance Division designing the product, Actuarial department developing the premium rates making it affordable to all, IT/SD Department providing the necessary modules for the new plan, F & A Department giving back-end support and the Visibility created by the Corporate Communications Department through multiple Publicity Channels and all other Departments working in unison to bring out the winning product.

Thereby LIC's market share increased four-fold to 60% from 15% last year. They completed health insurance cover to 1 million lives and ₹ 400 Crore First Premium cumulative since HI Division was formed 4 years ago in February, 2008 on the same day.

Meeting the sudden health care expenses is a major concern for many families. Due to increase in health costs, sudden ill-health of any family member erodes all the hard earned savings of the family. If there are no savings, the family is pushed into poverty. 30% of people fall below poverty line (BPL) due to health related expenses like sudden hospitalization or surgery alone. There is increased realization to seek cover for this medical risk leading to enhanced public awareness and more demand for health insurance cover. Also, only a healthy society can drive growth. Hence, a lot of initiatives are being taken by the Government as well as the Regulator (IRDA) to spread the concept of health insurance.

It's the sheer comprehensiveness and popularity of the plan that's given it an edge, garnering good coverage in the print media. Undoubtedly, LIC's 'Jeevan Arogya' is tailor-made for the customers' health insurance needs at an affordable cost. The product has many innovative features and benefits as recognized by the award. Health insurance is LIC's our fastest growing sector with 42% CAGR. There is a good demand for health insurance and LIC has the best product. However, They have just touched the tip of the iceberg. There is mammoth potential.

For out agents to take the policy to the masses, besides sales strategies, LIC sha some of the servicing strategies. During this year. LIC took up a project of reviewing the 1000 Claims (10% of total) 10000 helath claims last year) closed due to non-submission of claim requirements by the policyholders. LIC re-opened these claims to give another opportunity our health customers to resubmit their medical documents for their reconsideration by the TPA &/or our end. We settled 300 such claims, *i.e.*, 30%.

This was part of the Health insurance action plan to improve perception of claims and servicing amongst the general and our field force. Vigorous follow up was done by our Branch Health Insurance

Nodal Officers with the claimants.

The most enriching learning is experiential. To share some of the successful innovative marketing strategies adopted by our field force and marketing officials in various regions across the country resulting in good new business for the benefit of the readers:-

Holding 'Health Days': Often, getting started is the most difficult part of a task. Dedicating one full day to a single cause definitely creates more awareness as it results in publicity buzz. Many initiatives like 'Pulse Polio' etc. used this strategy sucessfully. Divisions like Bangalore-I & II have earmarked one day for each branch this week for Health Insurance to give fillip to its new business. Bhavnagar Division in Western Zone & Lucknow Division in North Central Zone have given a call to observe January 28 & 30 respectively as 'Health Day' in each of their Branches.

Status of Health Insurance Business in India Players

Currently the major participants in Health Insurance business are General Insurance companies, Standalone Health insurers and Life insurance companies. Besides that there are State and Central government schemes similar in nature to Health Insurance for target groups like employees, BPL (below poverty line) Population. NGO's (Non Government Organisations) and SHG(Self Help Groups) also have some schemes mainly for BPL population.

Dominance of General Insurers

In India for the first time a well defined private Health Insurance product called "Mediclaim" was introduced in 1986 by the public sector General insurance companies.

Life insurers were late entrants in Health insurance business in India. Ashadeep product sold by LIC of India circa 1994 was having some elements of Health insurance. The real begining in selling Health insurance. The real begining in selling Health insurance products from Life insurer happened only after liberalisation of the sector in the year 2000.

Due to these historic reasons the General Insurance Industry in India is the dominant player in Health insurance business.

Phenomenal Growth over last decade

Before the liberalization of the Insurance Sector in the year 2000, Health insurance sector hardly had any growth. In the year 1990-91 total Health Insurance premium collected by all Players was Just ₹27.64 crore. This was only a small fraction of total General Insurance business in India at that time. The business was so low that General Insurers classified Health insurance premium under miscellaneous insurance. This rose to ₹380.40 crores by 1999-2000 mainly due to group Health insurance for large corporate and PSU's (Public sector undertakings).

Health insurance premium grew phenomenally after the year 2000 to reach about ₹13350 crores in 2011-12. This was due to growth in, group as well as Individual Health insurance.

The graph below clearly shows this phenomenal growth of Health Insurance since liberalisation of the insurance sector.

Why Life Insurers are keen on Health Insurance Business

The total first premium collected by Life insurers in the year 2011-12 was ₹114232.73 crores.

Thus total Health insurance business in the same period was almost 12% of total Life insurance business. But Health Insurance business grew by oveer 20%. In fact Health Insurance is currently the fastest growing segment of the insurance industry in India.

Health insurance is expected to grow rapidly for quite some time due to several reasons like

- Increased awareness
- Higher treatement costs
- Rising expectations of customers about quality of healthcare
- Demographic changes towards more ageing population
- Nuclar families
- Higher incidence of "Lifestyle" related conditions like diabetes.

This current high rate of growth and the future potential of Health insurance business make it very attractive for the Life insurers. Also there are some synergies between these two businesses.

How Life insurer currently stands in Health Insurance Business:-

Globally Life insurance companies are big Players in Health insurance business in many countries. But in India the picture is exactly opposite.

Thus Health Insurance is an attractive area but Life insurers have not made much headway in it. Despite entering the sector several years back even today Life insurers have a negligible market share of Health Insurance premiums. As per latest IRDA data the total Health Insurance premium collected in a year by all General Insurers was about ₹12000 crores. While Life insurers collected only about ₹400 crores.

One of the reason could be the difference in nature of these two businesses. Let us take a look at some of these with an aim to create a better understand of the Health insurance business.

Fundamental differences

We cover the risk of untimely death in Life insurance. Health insurance covers the expenses associated with treatment of "bad health".

Thus Life Insurer is concerned with Mortality while Health Insurer is concerned with Morbidity. Mortality is a well defined event legally and otherwise which is CERTAIN to happen one day and ONLY ONCE.

We need to define what "good health" is before we go to define "Bad Health".

WHO (World Health Organisation) has defined health as physical, social and mental wellbeing. This definition is extremely difficult to implement practically from an insurers viewpoint. Physical health may be evaluated based on some parameters but mental health is extremely difficult to define and it may not be possible to give a definition of social health. Even in case of physical health the factors responsible for bad health are so many that listing them is not feasible and possible. Also what kind of "bad health" and at what level of severity will be insured by the insurer varies.

There is no universally accepted definition of morbidity. The probability of its occurence is UNCERTAIN and varies from ZERO to MANY.

Product complexity

Morbidity definition is far more complicated than mortaility definition. Often a restrictive definition of morbidity is used in practice. Each Health Insurance product thus will have a product specific restrictive definition of "bad health" for the purpose of risk coverage. This leads to number of exclusions and restrictive clauses which are mentioned in the product. Premiums are linked to this definition of "bad health". More liberal is the definition, higher is the premium and vice a versa.

The possible repetitive nature of risk and all this clauses and restrictions make Health insurance product inherently more complex than Life insurance products.

Underwriting

Physical parameters vary greatly from person to person depending on their build. Life insurers have a build chart for few critical parameters like pulse rate, blood pressure etc... which is concerned mainly with mortaility risks.

But it's extremely difficult to sepcify a chart giving the normal healthy condition for every single human body functions.

When and how a person shifts from good to bad health is difficult to determine other than few critical body functions.

The lack of reliable past morbidity data in India makes the underwriting of Health Insurance even more difficult.

All this make Underwriting Health Insurance more complicated. Thus greater underwriting expertise is necessary than that required for Life Insurance underwriting.

To make matters simple most General Insurance companies in India rely heavily on past claim data to underwrite Health Insurance. Life Insurer cannot do this as they don't have such past data.

Relationships

In Life Insurance the relationship is direct between the insurer and the beneficiaries of the product.

Relationships: Life Insurance

In case of Health Insurance the relationship is more indirect and involves multiple stakeholders. Customers purchases Health Insurance for covering health care costs. Thus he needs to approach care providers for health treatment. Health care providers are independent entitites over whom insurance companies have no control whatsoever. Customer will approach Insurer only for cost of treatment and that is often managed through TPAs (Third Party Administrators).

Relationships: Health Insurance

Due to this multiple relationship there are several issues in Health Insurance servicing. One factor that will affect Life Insurer is their lack of understanding of healthcare business. Often they tend to rely on TPAs. Any issues with TPA will affect the image of the insurer. Health Insurance servicing involves multiple agencies and needs to be handled in a different manner than Life insurance servicing.

Claims

Frequency of claim payment is rather simple straight forward process in Life insurance based on death certificate and other papers like discharge form. Amount paid is generally the sum assured.

In Health insurance claim payment frequency can be multiple times and more unpredictable. The amount of claim payment is determined by health care costs. These are not uniform across different providers. Even same provider may charge different rates for two patients undergoing similar treatment.

The terms and conditions for health claims are more in number and more complicated. Health Claim needs careful evaluation and considerable medical expertise which is not commonly available with most Life Insurers.

Summing Up

Health Insurance is a tempting area of insurance due to its growth rate and potential. But Life Insurance companies need to understand that it's a more demanding business in terms of expertise and customer servicing. They need to build expertise at underwriting level. The servicing aspects will need to be carefully looked at specially at TPA level which could make a difference. The product complexity necessitates better training and a difference approach at the marketing level.

If they do so then only they can increase their market share in future. Being a future growth area this will positively impact their overall profitability and growth in the long run.

Progress of RSBY in Premium

Insurance Company	*RSBY (2010-11) Premium in Billion ₹*	*RSBY % to Total Premium*
ICICI Lombard	1.84	26.5%
Cholamandalam	1.10	15.8%
United India Insurance Ltd.	1.09	15.7%
Oriental Insurance Company	1.04	15.0%
National Insurance Company	0.99	14.2%
Royal Sundaram Alliance Insurance Ltd.	0.59	8.5%
New India Assurance Co. Ltd.	0.17	2.5%
Appollo Munich Health Ins. Co. Ltd.	0.04	0.6%
Star Health and Allied Ins. Co. Ltd.	0.04	0.6%
Tata AIG General Insurance Co Ltd.	0.04	0.5%
IFFO-TOKIO General Ins. Co. Ltd.	0.01	0.1%
Grand Total	6.95	100.0%

LIC'S HEALTH PLUS UNIT LINKED HEALTH INSURANCE PLAN

"In this policy, the Investment Risk in Investment Portfolio is Borne by the Policy-Holder"

Heal this a major concern on everybody's mind these days. With sky rocketing medical expenses, the possibility of any illness leading to hospitalization of surgery is a constant source of anxiety unless the family has actively provided for funds to meet such an eventuality. Most families rarely provide for healthcare, and even if they do, it is grossly inadequate. Given this scenario, LIC has launched LIC's Health Plus plan, a unique long term health insurance plan that combines health insurance covers for the entire family (husband, wife and the children) - Hospital Cash Benefit (HCB) and Major Surgical Benefit (MSB) along with a ULIP component (investment in the form of Units) that is specifically designed to meet domiciliary treatment related (DTB) expenses for the insured members.

1. Vital Information

1. Age	**Principal Insured**	**Spouse Insured**	**Child Insured**
Min Policy Entry Age -Age Last Birthday	18	18	3 months
Min Age -HCB Cover -Age Last Birthday	18	18	3 months
Min Age - MSB Cover -Age Last Birthday	18	18	18
Maximum Entry Age Age Nearest Birthday	55	55	17

2. Premium Payment

Mode of Payment

Yearly, Half-Yearly, & Monthly (ECS Mode only)

Minimum Annual Premium Conditions

Number of Lives covered	Higher of the two conditions in each category listed below:
Single Life	6 times the HCB of the Principal Insured OR ₹ 5000 p.a.
Two Lives	The qarithmetic sum of 6 times the HBC of PI and 3 times the HCB of the second insured OR ₹ 7500 p.a.
More than two Lives	The arithmetic sum of 6 times the HCB of PI and 3 times the HCB of each of the others insured OR ₹ 10,000 p.a.

Annualized Premiums are payable in multiplies of ₹ 500.

3. Sum Assured. The Principal Insured must first choose the respective levels of HCB for each member to be covered under the policy. The Sum assured for major surgical benefits will be 200 times of the HCB you choose.

Major Surgical Sum Assured	**Principal Insured**	**Spouse Insured**	**Child Insured**
	200 times the HCB applicable to each insured life under the policy		

4. Term of the Policy. The term of the policy is upto the policy anniversary on which the age nearer birthday of the principal insured in 65 years.

Age Nearest Birthday	Pincipal Insured	Spouse Insured	Child Insured
Max. Cover creasing age	65	65	25
Premium Ceasing Age	65 Years Nearest Birthday of the Principal Insured		

5. Addition of New Members. It is important for the principal Insured (the person taking the policy) to decide which of the existing family members are to be covered and include them at the beginning (proposal state) itself. Eligible existing family members cannot be added at a later stage. New members can however be added under the following three situations.

Situation	When to include?	The cover starts from
Marriage/remarriage of the Principal insured after taking the policy	Within one year from the date of marriage	The following policy anniversary
A Child born or Legally adopted child less than 3 months after taking the policy	Health Cover Starts from the policy anniversary falling immediately after the child completes 3 months	
Legally adopted child is more than 3 months old	From the policy anniversary falling after date of adoption	

- The new members will be eligible for the cover only if they satisfy the conditions of minimum premium and benefits.
- New members must be included by the Principal Insured only. No new members will be allowed after the death of the principal insured.

6. Increase/Decrease of Premiums. Increase or decrease of premiums is allowed during the term of the policy. Increase in premium must be in multiples of ₹ 500. In case of decrease, the minimum premium conditions must be satisfied. However, increase/decrease in premiums does not affect the level of health cover and HCB and MSB benefits.

Your Health is your most important Asset;
Take care of your Health

II. Benefits

1. Hospital Cash Benefit (HCB). A daily benefit is payable in case the insured is hospitalized due to either accidental body injury or sickness. The quantum of benefit depends upon the level of cover opted.

Insured	Initial Daily Benefit (IDB)* #	
	Minimum	Maximum
Principal Insured	₹ 250	₹ 2500
Spouse/Child	₹ 250	₹ 1500

* The Applicable Daily Benefit IDB is applicable during the first year of risk cover. The daily benefit will increase @5% p.a. simple of the IDB on each policy anniversary until it hits a cap of 1.5 times the initial benefit.

IDB of the spouse cannot exceed the Principal Insured's IDB; IDB of the children cannot exceed the spouse's IDB.

The initial HCB must be in multiples of ₹ 50. # Initial daily benefit that is payable in respect of stay in a non-ICU room or ward. In case the insured is required to stay in the ICU of a hospital, an enhanced rate of daily benefit is payable, which is twice the eligible daily cash benefit.

2. Major Surgical Benefit (MSB). In the event of the insured undergoing one of the major surgeries defined in the table in page 4, a lump sum benefit (regardless of the actual costs incurred) equivalent to the percentage of the sum assured mentioned against that surgery will be payable on providing proper proof of surgery to the satisfaction of the corporation.

3. Domiciliary Treatment Benefit (DTB). The Principal Insured can withdraw an amount equivalent to the actual expense he or she has incurred in respect of any domiciliary treatment or to meet the medical expenses incurred over and above the hospital cash/major surgical benefits in respect of either oneself or the others insured under the policy.

Minimum domiciliary claimable	**₹ 2500**
Maximum amount that can be claimed/payable*	Up to 50% of the policy fund at the date of payment

* Subject to a minimum balance of one annualized premium being left in the policy fund after making the payment.

Note: 1. A maximum of **two payments** will be allowed in a policy year subject to the above conditions - on production of supporting proof of treatment and bills of expenses **DTB is available only after at least 3 years premiums are paid.**

2. DTB is payable for the children covered until the health cover ceasing age.

4. Death Benefit. No death insurance cover is available under the plan. Following benefits/ changes will take place on the happening of unfortunate death of Principal Insured (PI) and/or other insured member.

1. Where only a single life (Principal Insured) is insured under the policy:

Fund value of units held in the policy fund is payable to the nominee or legal heir(s) of the principal insured.

2. Where two or more are covered under the policy: Where the death of PI has occurred within 3 years from the commencement: The policy will terminate and the policy Fund Value will be payable to the nominee/legal heir.

Where death of PI has occurred after 3 years from the commencement. The premiums payment will cease but the health cover for the other insured, if any, will continue until the fund is sufficient to recover the charges or until the cover ceasing age, which ever is earlier.

3. On the death of insured members, other than the PI. Premium payment as well as the Risk cover will continue for the other members insured under the policy.

4. On the death of all the insured members. Fund value of units held in the policy fund is payable to the nominee or legal heir(s) of the principal insured.

5. On the death of the PI and the spouse (whether insured or not under the policy) after 3 years from the commencement. The benefits in respect of the insured children, if any, shall continue and can be claimed by the eldest major child covered under the policy it all children covered are minors, the legal guardian can claim the health cover benefits.

PROHIBITION OF REBATES SECTION 41 OF INSURANCE AT 1938

(1) No person shall allow or offer to allow, either directly or indirectly, as an inducement to any person to take out or renew or continue an insurance in respect of any kind of risk relating to lives or property in India, any rebate of the whole part of the commission payable or any rebate of the premium shown on the policy, nor shall any person taking out or renewing or continuing a policy accept any rebate, except such rebate as may be allowed in accordance with the published prospectus or tables of the insurer provided that acceptance by an insurance agent of commission in connection with a policy of life insurance taken out by himself on his own life shall not be deemded to be acceptance of a rebate of premium within the meaning of this sub-section if at the time of such

acceptance the insurance agent satisfies the prescribed conditions establishing that he is a bona fide insurance agent employed by the insurer.

(2) Any person making default in complying with the provisions of this section shall be punishable with fine which may extend to five hundred rupees.

List of Surgical Procedures Covered **CARDIOVASCULAR SYSTEM**	**Sum** **Assured%**
Major Surgery of Aorta	100%
CABG (two or more coronary arteries must be bypassed) via open chest surgery	100%
Valve Replacement using mechanical prosthesis via open chest surgery	100%
Pericardiotomy/Pericardectomy done in chronic constrictive pericarditis	100%
Open chest surgery for repair of any of the heart valves	100%
Initial implantation of permanent pacemaker in the heart	60%
Coronary Angioplasty with stent implantation (two or more corronary arteries must be stented)	40%
HAEMIC AND LYMPHATIC SYSTEM	
Bone Marrow transplant (as recipient)	60%
Splenectomy for hematological conditions	60%
NERVOUS SYSTEM	
Surgery to remove cerebral tumors (benign or malignant) and space occupying lesions requiring "craniotomy"	100%
Repair of Cerebral or, Spinal Arterio-Venous Malformations and, Cerebral Aneurysms	100%
Other intra-cranial operations requiring craniotomy	100%
Excision of pineal gland	100%
Excision of the pituitary gland	100%
Operations of Surbaracahnoid space of brain	60%
Intracranial ransaction of Cranial nerve	60%
Drainge of Extradural space	40%
Drainge of Subdural space	40%
RESPIRATORY SYSTEM	
Lung Transplant or combined Heart-Lung Transplant	100%
Isolated Heart Transplant	100%
Pneumonectomy or Pleuro-pneumonecnomy -total lung of one side	100%
Pleurectomy or Pleural decortication	60%
Thoractoplasty	60%
Open Lobectomy of Lung	60%

Excision of begin medistinal, mediastinal lesions (evidence of thoracotomy needs to be ascertained	60%
Partial Extirpation of Bronchus	60%
Partial of Total Pharyngectomy	60%
Total Laryngectomy	60%
DIGESTIVE SYSTEM	
Resection and Anastomosis of any part of digestive tract	60%
Open Surgery for treatment of Peptic Ulcer	60%
Total excision of oesophagus	60%
Total excision of stomach	60%
Excision of oesophagus and stomach	100%
Artificial opening into stomach	40%
ENDOCRINE SYSTEM	
Complete excision of adrenal glands	60%
Partial excision of adrenal glands	40%
Complete excision of Thyroid gland	60%
Partial excision of Thyroid gland	40%
Complete excision of Parathyroid gland	60%
Partial excision of Parathyroid gland	40%
Thymectomy	60%
EYE	
Any eye surgery requiring corneal or retinal repair due to accident	40%
LIVER, GALL BLADDER & PANCREAS	
Partial Resection of Liver	60%
Partial Pancreatectomy	60%
MUSCULOSKELETAL SYSTEM	
Total Replacement of Hip or knee joint following accident	60%
Amputation of Arm or hand or Foot or Leg due to trauma or accident	60%
ORO-MAXILLOFACIAL SURGERY	
Major reconstructive oro-maxillafacial surgery due to trauma or burns and not for cosmetic purpose	60%
KIDNEY AND URINARY TRACT	
Renal transplant (recipient)	100%
Nephrectomy due to medical advice (not as a transplant donor)	60%

III. Conditions & Restrictions

1. Waiting Period. Both HCB and MSB covers are available subject to a waiting period from the commencement of the risk cover specified hereunder - in respect of each insured member:

Waiting Period from	Principal Insured	Spouse Insured	Child Insured
Dater of the cover	180 days	180 days	180 days
Date of revival/ reinstatement	90 days	90 days	90 days

No waiting period in respect of Accidental Bodily Injury. Also incase of children for MSB

2. Benefit Period Limits - Hospital Cash Benefit

HCB	Maximum Annual Benefit Period		Maximum Lifetime Benefit Period
	1st year	2n year & after	
Principal Insured Spouse Insured Child Insured*	18 days incl. 9 days for ICU	60 days incl. 30 days for ICU	365 days

*Maximum period of HCB for an insured child until he or she completes 5 years age is limited to 90 days.

Important Note : HCB is available only in respect of hospitalization in a ward or ICU for continuous period of 24 hours of part there of over and above 48 hours, provided such part stay exceeds 4 hours.

3. Conditions for Availing Major Surgery Benefit

MSB	Principal Insured	Spouse Insured	Child Insured
Max. Annual benefit	100% of the Sum Assured applicable in respect of the each insured member		
Max. Lifetime Benefit	3 times the Sum Assured applicable in respect of the each insured member		

MSB is payable only if the surgery is performed in India

NOTE : Various HCB and MSB Benefit limits and restrictions applicable under this policy in respect of each insured shall solely and exclusively apply to that insured only and are not transferable to any other insured.

4. Limits on Availing Domiciliary Treatment Benefit

DTB Conditions	
Minimum domiciliary claimable	₹ 2500
Maximum amount that can be payable during the policy term -for each payment	50% of the policy fund the date of payment
Maximum amount that can be claimed/ payable during the last policy anniversary by the Principal insured.	100% of the policy fund at the date of payment

*Equal to actual amount spent subject to a minimum balance of one annualized premium being left in the policy fund after making the payment.

5. Termination of HCB and MSB Benefits.

On attainment of the insured's maximum cover ceasing age 65 years n.b.d. for Pl/spouse insured and 25 years n.b.d. for the children insured

One reaching the maximum lifetime benefit limits under HCB (365 days) and MSB (3 times the sum assured).

On the death of the insured; End of policy term or on the date of termination of the policy for any other reason.

Insured spouse's cover terminates on the date of divorce/legal separation.

On the date of lapsation: See 7 below.

6. Premium Discontinuance and Revival. The policy will lapse if the premiums are not paid within the days of grace. The Pl shall have the option to revive the policy any time within a period of two years from the due date of first unpaid premium.

If the Policy lapses before payment of 3 years premiums. THE HEALTH COVER WILL STOP FOR ALL THE INSURED. THE POLICY CAN BE REVIVED ANYTIME DURING A PERIOD OF two years from the due date of first unpaid premium by payment of all the arrears of premium without interest but subject to proof of continued insurability.

If the policy is lapsed after payment of at least 3 years premiums. The policy can be revived with 2 years from due date of first unpaid premium by payment of arrears of premiums or by availing Premium Holidays. During the period of discontinuity, the charges for HCB and MSB covers will continue to be deducted from the policy fund till whichever of the following happens earlier.

i. the policy fund falls below one annualized premium, or
ii. the lives covered reach the benefit ceasing age, or
iii. the maximum lifetime benefits are exhausted, or
iv. the policy has reached the end of revival period/end of policy term.
v. the policy is terminated due to death or any other reason.

7. Premium Holidays. If the policy lapses after at least 3 years premiums have been paid the Principal Insured has the option of either paying all the due premiums in full or avail of premium holiday by just paying the latest instalment premium without any interest. The premium holidays can be availed only as long as the policy fund has a balance of at least one annualized premium at the time of revival.

8. Surrender. The surrender value, it any, is payable only on completion of the third policy anniversary. The policy can be surrendered by the Principal Insured. If the request for surrender is received with 3 years from the Date of Commencement (DOC), the monetary value of the fund as on the date of application is payable after 3 years from commencement date.

The Monetary Value of the fund is the NAV as on the date of application for surrender or the date when the revival period is over (in respect of compuslory surrender) as the case may be, multiplied by the number of units in the policyholder's fund as on that date. There will be no surrender charge.

9. Compulsory Surrender

a. Where the premiums are paid for less than 3 years. In case the policy is not renewed and the fund value is not sufficient to cover relevant charges, the policy shall compulsorily be terminated and the balance amount, if any, will be refunded to the Pl immediately.

b. Where the premiums are paid for at least 3 years. The balance in the policy fund value is at all times, subject to a minimum balance of one annualized premium. In case the fund value falls below this limit, the policy shall compulsorily be terminated with a notice to the Pl and the balance amount in the policy fund, if any shall be refunded to the Pl.

10. Benefit Payable at the end of the term. At the end of the policy term, the balance in the policy fund, if any, will be payable to the principal insured.

11. Policy Loans. No policy loan will be available under this policy.

12. Assignment. No assignment will be allowed under this policy.

INCOME TAX BENEFIT AVAILABLE

"COOLING OFF" PERIOD

If you are not satisfied with the "Terms and Conditions" of the policy, you may return the policy to us within 15 days.

Important : If a person is covered under various policies of the corporation under this plan, then the maximum benefit available to such insured life shall not exceed the cap on benefits under this plan.

IV. Exclusions

1. Common Exclusions in respect of HCB & MSB Benefits:

No benefits are available hereunder and no payment will be made by the Corporation for any claim for Hospital Cash Benefit and Major Surgical Benefit under this Policy on account of Hospitalization directly or indirectly caused by, based on, arising out of or howsoever attributable to any of the following.

a. **"Pre-existing condition"**- any medical condition or any related condition (*e.g.* illnesses, symptoms, treatments, pains and surgery) that have arisen at some point prior to the commencement of this coverage, irrespective of whether any medical treatment or advice was sought. Any such condition or related condition about which the Pl or insured dependant know, knew or could reasonably have been assumed to have known, will be deemed to be pre-existing. The following conditions will also be deemed to be "pre-existing".

i. Conditions arising between signing the application form and confirmation of acceptance by the Corporation.

ii. Any **Sickness,** illness, complication or ailment arising out of or connected to the pre-existing illness.

b. Any **Sickness** that has been classified as an Epidemic by the Central or State Government.

c. Self afflicted injuries or conditions (attempted suicide), and/or the use of misuse of any drugs or alcohol.

d. Any sexually transmitted diseases or any condition directly or indirectly caused to or associated with Human immuno Deficiency (HV) Virus or any Syndrome or condition of a similar kind ommonly referred to as AIDS.

e. War, invasion, act of foreign enemy, hostilities (whether war be declared or not), civit war rebellion revolution, insurrection military or usurped power of civil commotion or loot or pillage in connection herewith.

f. Naval or military operations (including duties of peace time) of the armed forces or air forces or air force and participation in operations requiring the use of arms or which are ordered by military authorities for combating terrorists, rebels and the like.

g. Any natural peril (including but not limited to avalanche, earthquake, volcanic eruptions or any kind of natural hazard).

h. Participation in any hazardous activity or sports including but not limited to racing scuba diving, aerial sports, bungee jumping and mountaineering or in any criminal or illegal activities.

i. Radioactive contamination.

j. Non-allopathic methods of surgery and treatment.

2. Additional Exclusions in respect of Hospital Cash Benefit:

No benefits are available hereunder and no payment will be made by the Corporation for any claim for Hospital Cash Benefit under this Policy on account of Hospitalization directly or indirectly caused by, based on, arising out of or howsoever attributable to any of the following:

a. Hospitalization due to illness within the first 180 days from the Date of Cover commencement and 90 days from the date of revival/reinstatement after discontinuance of the cover.

b. Removal of any material that was implanted in a former surgery before Date of Cover commencement.

c. Any diagnosis or treatment arising from or traceable to pregnancy (whether uterine or extra uterine), childbirth including caesarean section, medical termination of pregnancy and/or any treatment related to pre and post natal care of the mother or the new born.

d. Hospitalization for the sole purpose of physiotherapy or any ailment for which hospitalization is not warranted due to advancement in medical technology.
e. Any treatment not performed by a Physician or any treatment of a purely experimental nature.
f. Any routine or prescribed medical check up or examination.
g. Medical expenses relating to any hospitalization primarily for diagnostic, X-ray or laboratory examinations.
h. Circumcision, cosmetic or aesthetic treatments of any description, change of gender surgery, plastic surgery (unless such plastic surgery is necessary for the treatment of illness or Accidental Bodily Injury as a direct result of the insured event and performed with in 6 months of the same).
i. Hospitalization for donation of an organ.
j. Hospitalization for correction of birth defects or congenital aromalies.
k. Dental treatment of surgery of any kind unless necessitated by Accidental Bodily Injury.
l. Convalescence, general debility, nervous or other breakdown, rest cure, congenital diseases or defect or anomaly, sterilization or infertility (diagnosis and treatment), any sanatoriums, spa or rest cures or long term care or hospitalization undertaken as a preventive or recuperative measure.

3. Additional Exclusions in respect of Major Surgical Benefit:

No benefits are available hereunder and no payment will be made by the Corporation for any claim for Major Surgical Benefit under this Policy directly or indirectly caused by, based on, arising out of or howsoever attributable to any of the following:

a. Surgeries not listed in the "List of surgical procedures covered" under item II.
b. Surgery triggered by health related causes (and not by Accident) within the first 180 days from the commencement date and 90 days from the date of revival/reinstatement after discontinuance of the cover.
c. Any Surgery for which claim has already been made and paid by the Corporation.
d. Any treatment not performed by a Physician/Surgeon.
e. Any treatment including Surgery that is performed unconventionally under experimental conditions and purely experimental in nature.
f. Circumcision, cosmetic or aesthetic treatments of any description, change of life surgery or treatment, treatment (including surgery) for obesity, plastic surgery (unless necessary for the treatment of illnes or accidental Bodily Injury as a direct result of the insured event and performed within 6 months of the same).
g. Surgery for donation of an organ.
h. Removal or correction or replacement of any material that was implanted in a former surgery before date of cover commencement.
i. Surgery for correction of birth defects or congenital anomalies.
j. Any diagnosis or treatment or surgery arising from or traceable to pregnancy (whether uterine or extra uterine).

V. Investment of Funds

The premiums allocated to purchase units will be strictly invested in a Health Plus Fund (Income and Growth – Low Risk) as follows:

A. Government/Government guaranteed/ Corporate securities/debt	**Not Less Than 50%**
B. Short term investments: Money Market instruments including A above	Not more than 90%
C. Investment in listed equity shares	Not less than

10% & Not more than 50%

1. Method of Calculation of Unit Price: Unit will be allotted based on the Net Asset Value (NAV) on the date of allotment. There is no Bid-Offer spread. The NAV will be computed on daily basis and will be based on investment performance, Fund Management Charge and whether the fund is expanding or contracting.

a. Applicability of Net Asset Value (NAV) : The premiums received upto 3 p.m. (as per IRDA guidelines) by the servicing branch of the corporation by a local cheque or by a demand draft payable at par at the place where the premium is received, the closing NAV of the day on which premium is received shall be applicable. The premiums received after such time by the servicing branch of the corporation by a local cheque or by a demand draft payable at par at the place where the premium is received, the closing NAV of the next business day shall be applicable.

b. Redeeming of Units : In respect of valid applications received for reimbursement of medical expenses, death claim, etc up to such time by the servicing branch of the Corporation closing NAV of that day shall be applicable. For the valid applications received in respect of Domiciliary Treatment Benefit, death claim etc after 3 p.m. as per IRDA guidelines by the servicing branch of the Corporation the closing NAV of the next business day shall be applicable.

2. Charges Under the Plan :

a. Premium Allocation Charge: This is the percentage of the premium appropriated towards charges from the premium received. The balance known as allocation rate constitutes that part of the premium which is utilized to purchase (investment) units for the policy. The allocation charges are as below:

First year	thereather
30%	6%

The above allocation charges shall be applicable for all premiums including any additional premium paid in that particular policy year.

b. Health Insurance Charge: There will be two separate charges for the following benefits:

Hospital Cash Benefit **Major Surgical Benefit**

These charges will be taken every month in respect of all the members covered by canceling appropriate number of units out of the Policy Fund.

These charges, during a policy year, will be based on the age nearer birthday, of the each of the members covered, as at the Policy anniversary coinciding with or immediately preceding the due date of cancellation of units and hence may increase every year on each policy anniversary. The charges will also depend on whether the person covered is male or female and standard or sub-standard as per the underswriting decision.

If more than one member is covered under the policy then the total charges shall be based on the individual ages of all the members and the amount of cover for each such member.

In case of Hospital Cash Benefit, the charges will be applied on the Initial Daily Benefit as mentioned in the policy Schedule.

The charges for Hospital Cash Benefit and/or Major Surgical Benefit will not be deducted once the benefit terminates.

Specimen charges for ₹ 100/- per day for HCB & ₹ 1000/- SA for MSB for standard lives are given as under:

Age	HCB		MCB	
	M	F	M	F
5	24.43	24.43	0	0
15	20.71	20.71	0	0
25	31.39	24.34	1.02	1.38
35	33.59	29.96	1.58	1.75
45	49.29	53.20	3.54	2.64
55	76.08	72.53	7.28	5.16

Note: M & F stand for male & female lives.

Other Charges:

Policy Administration Charge	₹ 75/- per month during the first policy year and ₹ 25/- per month during the subsequent year.
Fund Management Charge	Levived @ 1.25% per annum of the unit fund at the time of computation of NAV which will be done on daily basis.
Bid/Offer Spread	Nil
Surrender charges	Nil.

Service Tax Charge service tax charged at applicable rates. Currently the effective service rate is 12.36% which includes education cess @ 3%

Right to revise charges

The Corporation reserves the right to revise all or any of the above charges (subject to a maximum limit) except the Premium Allocation charge. The modification in charges will be done with prospective effect with the prior approval of IRDA.

SECTION 45 – INDISPUTABILITY CLAUSE

No policy of Life Insurance shall, after the expiry of two years from the date on which it was effected, be called in question by an insurer on the ground that a statement made in the proposal for insurance or in any report of a medical officer or referee or friend of the Insured or in any other document leading to the issue of the Policy, was inaccurate or false, unless the insurer shows such statement was on a material matter or suppressed facts which is it was material to disclose and that it was fraudulently made by the policy holder and that the policy holder knew at the time of making it that the statement was false or that it suppressed facts which it was material to disclose.

Note : "Material" shall mean and include all important, essential and relevant information in the context of underwriting the risk to be covered by the corporation.

BENEFIT ILLUSTRATION

Frequency of Premium Payment. Annual	Annual Premium ₹ 12,000
Number of Lives Covered. Single Male	Per Day Hospital Cash Benefit (HCB) ₹ 2000 Per Day Hospital Cash Benefit in ICU. ₹ 4000 Major Surgical Benefit (MSB). ₹ 4,00,000
Age at Entry: 35 years	

End of Policy Year	Cumulative Premium Paid Till the Year	Maximum Guaranteed Benefit		Fund Value Available for Domiciliary Treatment Benefit	
		HCB	MSB	Variable SCENARIO 1	Variable SCENARIO 2
1	12000	54000	400000	6367	6649
2	24000	189000	400000	16600	17565
3	36000	198000	400000	27258	29369
4	48000	207000	400000	38350	42125
5	60000	216000	400000	49865	55883
6	72000	225000	400000	61787	70694
7	84000	234000	400000	74043	86555
8	96000	243000	400000	86739	103650
9	108000	252000	400000	99882	122068
10	120000	261000	400000	113464	141898
11	132000	270000	400000	127512	163265
12	144000	270000	400000	142005	186260
13	156000	270000	400000	156965	211024
14	168000	270000	400000	172410	237706
15	180000	270000	400000	188338	266447
16	192000	270000	400000	204790	297441
17	204000	270000	400000	221842	330938
18	216000	270000	400000	239442	367071
19	228000	270000	400000	257613	406066
20	240000	270000	400000	276346	448131
21	252000	270000	400000	295678	493544
22	264000	270000	400000	315609	542565
23	276000	270000	400000	336179	595518
24	288000	270000	400000	357406	652729
25	300000	270000	400000	379294	714541
26	312000	270000	400000	401870	781343
27	324000	270000	400000	425063	853464
28	336000	270000	400000	448692	931148
29	348000	270000	400000	472562	1014654
30	360000	270000	400000	496383	1104180

i. This illustration is applicable to a non-smoker male/female standard (from medical, life style and occupation point of view) life.

ii. The non-guaranteed benefits (1) and (2) in above illustration are calculated so that they are consistent with the Projected Investment Rate of Return assumption of 6% p.a. (Scenario I) and 10% p.a. (Scenario 2) respectively. In other words, in preparing this benefit illustration, it is assumed that the Projected Investment Rate of Return that LICI will be able to earn throughout the term of the policy will be 6% p.a. or 10% p.a., as the case may be. The Projected Investment Rate of Return is not guaranteed.

iii. The main objective of the illustration is that the clinet is able to appreciate the features of the product and the flow of benefits in different circumstances with some level of quantification.

iv. LIC does not authorise its agents/intermediaries, staff and officials to express their opinion on the future performance of the "ULIP" fund, excepting the above illustrative rate of 6% and 10% growth.

v. Domiciliary Treatment Benefit can be claimed from the 3rd year onwards after at least 3 years premiums have been paid.

1. For variable amounts in the benefit illustration, it is assumed that premiums have been paid as and when due and no domiciliary treatment benefit has been availed earlier.
2. Maximum HCB shown above is inclusive of 9 days stay in ICU in the first year and 30 days in subsequent years.

STATUTORY WARN : "Some benefits are guaranteed and some benefits are variable with returns based on the future performance of your life insurance company. If your policy offers guaranteed returns then these will be clearly marked "guaranteed" in the illustration table on this page. If your policy offers variable returns then the illustrations on this page will show two different rates of assumed investment returns. These assumed rates of return are not guaranteed and they are not upper or lower limits of what you might get back as the value of your policy is dependant on a number of factors including future investment performance."

RISKS BORNE BY THE POLICYHOLDER

i. LIC's Health Plus is a Unit Linked Health Insurance product which is different from the traditional insurance products and is subject to risk factors.

ii. The premium paid in Unit Linked Insurance policies are subject to investment risks associated with capital markets and the NAVs of the units may go up or down based on the performance of fund and factors influencing the capital market and the insured is responsible for his/her decisions.

iii. Life Insurance Corporation of India is only the name of the Insurance Company and LIC's Health Plus is only the name of the unit linked health insurance contract and does not in any way indicate the quality of the contract, its future prospects of returns.

iv. Please know the associated risks and the applicable charges, from your Insurance agent or the Intermediary or policy document of the insurer.

v. The fund offered under this contract is the name of the fund and do not in any way indicate the quality of these plans, their future prospects and returns.

vi. All benefits under the policy are also subject to the Tax Laws and other financial enactments as they exist from time to time.

Appendix

Private health insurance schemes in select emerging markets

Asia

Market	Overview	Type of system	Coverage and benefits	Financing
China	As of 2013 the three pillars of the national health insurance scheme covered 95% of the total population. The target is to increase that to 98% by 2015 according to the Report of the 18th National Congress.	1. Urban Employee Basic Medical Insurance (UEBMI): 265 million people enrolled in 2013.	Mandatory basic health insurance for urban citizens working in state owned or private enterprises.	Funded employers and employees
		2. Urban Resident Basic Medical Insurance: 271 million people enrolled 2013.	Voluntary basic health insurance for urban residents not eligible for UEBMI (eg. senior citizens. unemployed, children, students, disabled).	Funded by government (general taxes) and by individuals.
		3. New Rural Cooperative Medical System: 805 million people enrolled in 2013.	Voluntary basic medical insurance for rural residents.	Funded by government (general taxes) and by individuals
		4. PHI: The private sector is still small, but growing rapidly. Total premiums were CNY 86.3 billion in 2012, up 25% from 2011.	Basic Medical Insurance (BMI) as a supplement to national health schemes. Also high-end VIP medical insurance and critical illness insurance.	Funded by individuals and employers
India	Public sector healthcare schemes dominate. The term "health insurance" includes "Medical insurance" (mediclaim) and "health insurance". Mediclaim is reimbursement-type policies generally sold by non-life insurers; health insurance is mainly critical illness and long-term care (LTC) type- plans, sold mostly by life insurers. The PHI sector has grown rapidly since 2000, with premiums up by an annual average of	1. Government/social health insurance.	Targeted mainly at rural and poorer segments of society and is characterized by low sum insured and premiums. This includes the launch of central and state government-funded SHI schemes such as Rashtriya Swasthya Bima Yojana (RSBY) which provides coverage up to INR 30000.	Largely funded by general taxes to government. For RSBY, insureds must pay an annual nominal fee of INR 30.
		2. State and Central government employee health insurance schemes.	As of 1950, health insurance for state and central government employees. Two branches: the Employee State Insurance Scheme (ESIS) and the Central	ESIS and CGHS are funded by contributions from government tax collections and employees.

	28.4% in 2001-2012. However, the growth is from a very low starting point. Out-of-pocket payments still make up a large chunk of total healthcare expenditure.		Government Health Scheme (CGHS).	
		3. Private health insurance	According to latest data from the IRDA, just 1.9% of the population (23.6 million people) bought private health insurance voluntarily. Basic and intermediate to comprehensive covers are available.	
		4. Public private partnership (PPP) health insurance	India has championed the use of PPP to increase health insurance penetration. Funded by indivisuals and employers PPP is usually with lower sums insured and lower premiums. Goverment subsidies have helped increase penetration.	Government/non-profit organisations team up with commercial insurers to provide health insurance at a subsidised rate. Only a minimal contribution from the end consumer is required.
The Philippines	About 84% of the population is enrolled in the National Health Insurance Program (NHIP), including those under the Social Security System and their dependents, the Government Service Insurance System and their dependents and workers in the informal sector. PHI is available on an individual and group basis from life and non-life insurers. Health Maintenance Organizations (HMOs) and other self administered plans. PHI cover is relatively low given the high enrolment in NHIP.	1. Social health insurance is represented by the NHIP administered by the Philippine Health Insurance Corporation	The NHIP provides extensive cover and benefits including in and out-patient treatment and personal preventive, emergency and transfer services.	Contributions from employers and employees and government subsidies.
		2. Private health insurance	(1) PHI on offer includes traditional reimbursement products for in-patient costs, together with hospital cash benefits and optional covers for out-patient expenses, including dental and optical treatment costs. (2) HMO plans are used to supplement the state heath plan and provide cover for in-and out-patient costs. HMO cover levels are generally lower than PHI from insurers.	Contribution from individuals employers and employees.
Indonesia	In January 2014, Indonesia launched its universal healthcare programme known locally as Jaminan Kesehatan Nasional (JKN). The goal is to provide health insurance to the entire	1. National health insurance	JKN provides comprehensive benefits, from the treatment of infectious diseases such as influenza to expensive medical intervention like open-heart surgery, dialysis and cancer therapies.	Government subsidies and contribution from employers and employees. Those earning wages from either formal state-or private-sector

	population by January 2019. After stage 1 implementation in 2014, the JKN covers almost half of the population. The PHI sector is still in early stage of development.			employment pay a premium equivalent to 5% of their salary (4% payable by employers, 1% by employees) All other members, including informal workers the self-employed and investors pay monthly premiums of between IDR 25500-59500 each.
		2. Private health insurance	Private insurance companies are allowed to sell health insurance products including traditional indemnity, managed care, personal accident and other forms of health insurance.	Individuals, employers / employees.
Malaysis	The Malaysian healthcare system consists of tax-funded and government-run universal services and a fast-growing private sector. Public sector health services are organised under a civil service structure and are centrally administered by the Ministry of Health.	1. National health insurance	Comprehensive coverage ranging from preventive and primary healthcare to tertiary hospital care.	General taxes (direct and indirect) and non-tax revenues collected by the federal government. The allocation of funds by the Treasury to the Ministry of Health is based on past spending plus any additional increment in inflation (CPI). The Treasury provides additional funds in times of need such as during disease outbreaks.
		2. Private health insurance	The private sector offers clinics and hospitals, mainly in urban areas.	Mostly funded by out-of-pocket payments.
Thailand	The Universal Health Care policy of 2002 has resulted in 99% universal coverage. The system based on primary healthcare. The network of health institutions provides good coverage, with strong "pro-poor" bias.	1. National health insurance	A comprehensive package of care, including both curative and preventing care.	The schemes in financed by general tax revenues.
		2. Private health insurance	There are many private medical facilities across. Thailand, including hospitals, clinics and medical centres. There is no general practitioner system. People go directly to a hospital for	Individuals, employers and employees.

			treatment, which is available on a same-day basis to private-paying patients.	Individuals, employers and
Vietnam	Vietnam is working to develop a universal healthcare system to provide all citizens with basic care. it has signed a memorandum of understanding on health cooperation with Thailand and will get help from the latter to develop its scheme.	State-owned enterprises, public offices, foreign and foreign-invested enterprises, export processing zones, and private firms with 10 or more workers are required to provide compulsory medical insurance to employees. Demand for PHI is growing.	The compulsory medical insurance does not cover occupational illness or disease. HIV/AIDS, some mental illnesses and sexually-transmitted diseases.	employees.
Brazil	In 2013 the publicly-provided healthcare system covered about 150 million or 75% of the population. There were 50.3 million PHI/health plan policyholders, mostly middle and high-income families and through group insurance programs.	1. Single public healthcare system (SUS)	Constitutionally guaranteed free medical assistance for all from public hospitals or private providers reimbursed by the state.	Primarily financed by central government via general taxes the remainder by state and municipal governments via taxes development bank and multi-lateral borrowing and PHI
		2. Male Saude a comprehensive primary care programme	The programme includes various initiatives to improve Brazil's healthcare provision. family planning, family health old age care vaccinations, dental care improving public awareness, organ donor registrations. sexual health and medical training.	General taxes
		3. Private health insurance	PHI supplements state provisions in Brazil. Voluntary PHI is available from medical co-operatives, HMOs, specialised health insurers and self-administered plans. LTC insurance is generally not available. Critical illness is available as an add-on to PHI plans.	Contribution from individuals, employers and employees.
Mexico	Healthcare provision is decentralised. Services are provided by three branches of public-sector schemes and through private health cover.	1. Social Security Institute (IMSS): in 2013, covered about 35% of the population (40 million people).	Private-sector workers and their families. Provisions include consultations, basic out-and in-patient care and medical benefits.	Funded by employer and employee contributions.

		2.	Public sector institutions: Government Workers Security and Social Services Institute (ISSSTE): state oil company employee scheme (PEMEX): separate schemes for army. Ministry of Defence. National Defence Secretariat, and the navy.	These schemes cover employees of public sector institutions. Benefits include consultations, basic outpatient and hospital care.	Funded by employer and employee contributions, and transfers from the federal government revenues to avoid insolvency.
		3.	Social health protection system (Seguro Popular, SISSP): covered around 35% of the population (41 million people) in 2013. Ten million people had affiliation to both SISSP and IMSS. The government's conditional cash-transfer scheme Prospera also provides cash incentives to the poor to visit clinics and receive health education.	SISSP is aimed at informally-employed "independent workers" and their families.	Users pay a meanstested subscription. Federal and state governments supplement each local area as necessary from general tax funds, depending on the number of people affiliated.
		4.	Private health insurance covered 7% of the population (8 million people) in 2013. PHI is provided by private medical establishments. Insurance companies and specialist health institutions (ISES) which own healthcare establishments directly.	PHI uptake is mainly by the affluent. Covers range from basic, intermediate to comprehensive, and tend to be purchased by those looking for a more complete health service.	Funded by individuals, and employers.
Argentina	The public sector accounted for 69% of total healthcare spending in 2012 and private expenditure the rest. Traditionally PHI has provided cover for about 10% of the population.	1.	The Ministry of Health runs a network of hospitals and health centres.	Uninsured and underinsured have access to public hospitals providing free healthcare for most in-and out-patient treatments.	General tax revenues.
		2.	Social insurance trusts (Obras sociales) run by trade unions and professional	SHI schemes for employees and dependents, providing cover for all types of medical attention. Certain exclusions	Pay-as-you-go system funded) by employers and employees via compulsory payroll

			associations under the supervision of the National Social Security Administration and Superintendent of Health Services.	such as dentistry and psychiatric treatment.	deductions (3% of wages) and employer contributions (6%)
		3.	Special Schemes : Plan Remediar and Programa de Atención Médica Integral (PAMI)	Free medicine for those below the poverty line (Plan Remediar); LTC for retirees (PAMI).	General tax funds and support from the inter-American Development Bank (IADB).
		4.	Private health insurance is provided by conventional insurance firms. pre-paid plans, and insurance schemes run by private hospitals.	Cover can be comprehensive and can also act as a top-up to public-sector provisions.	Privately funded, 28% from prepaid plans.
Chile	Dual healthcare system: both public and private systems provide mandatory healthcare. The Ministry of Health oversees the entire system and also public healthcare system comprising 29 decentralized regional health services (SNSS), the National Health Fund (FONASA), the Public Health institute, and a network of locally-based primary care facilities. Guaranteed universal access was introduced under the plan AUGE in 2005.	1.	Social health insurance: National Health Fund (FONASA), which covers 80% of the population.	FONASA covers all employed persons in Chile but also the unemployed and most low-income households. There are a few exceptions: the police, armed services and universities. All citizens are guaranteed medical care under FONASA. There are no exclusions for age, gender earnings level or pre-existing conditions.	All employed persons make a mandatory contributions of 7% of monthly gross earnings. Dependents included free of charge. The self-employed will make full contributions as of 2018. The unemployed are not charged. Employee contributions account for 40% of funding, central government (taxes) 40% and co-payments the rest.
		2.	Private health providers (ISAPRE): open or closed pre-paid medical plans, covering 17% of the population.	ISAPRE plans must at a minimum provide cover equivalent to FONASA ISAPRE tends to attract higher-income individuals. Those who do not choose ISAPRE are automatically enrolled in FONASA.	Affiliates payroll deductions vary according to the specific coverage plan and co-payments at the time of service (10-30 % of service's cost). It is common for members to make additional payments for wider cover.
		3.	Other private health insurance schemes.	Provide cover over and above that provided by FONASA and ISAPRE	Privately funded

Colombia	Universal healthcare insurance scheme the Plan Obligatorio de Salud (POS). The scheme covers formal-sector workers and employers, the unemployed and very poor. The government plans to extend universal cover to the 3% of Colombians who remain uninsured and who tend to live in remote regions. Private pre-paid medicine companies and conventional insurance make up the rest.	1.	Social health insurance delivered by public health system (Nueva EPS) and private healthcare providers (EPS)	All employed or self-employed persons. Basic POS benefits cover common disease of accident and maternity.	All employed persons make compulsory contributions equal to 12.5% of salary (employers pay 8.5%) employees 4%): the self-employed pay the full 12.5%. One percentage goes to a solidarity fund used for treatment of subsidised members. Government subsidies cover the unemployed and very poor.
		2.	Pre-paid medicine companies (EMPs) and conventional life and non-life insurance companies.	Complementary to POS, therefore only cover gaps. For most consumers POS is the principal cover. It is common for companies wishing to attract and retain talent to offer additional healthcare covers for their workers.	Privately funded
		3.	Special schemes	magistrates, armed forces the police. Ecopetrol, universities.	Publicly funded from general taxes.
Venezuela	Around 75% of the population (20 million) used the public health system (IVSS) in 2011, through that number is likely to have declined significantly due to chronic under-funding and mismanagement. Private health insurance covers around 10% of the population. The remainder are covered under the Barrio Adentro scheme.	1.	Social Security Institute (IVSS).	State healthcare is available to those who contribute to the social security system. Also to the old aged and pensioners.	Central government funded general taxes. Specific projects receive additional funds from the World Bank and and IADB. As part of a Sino-Venezuela agreement in 2011. China supplied 13500 health centres with medical equipment.
		2.	Mision Barrio Adentro Program	Mostly low income and rural households which access healthcare via "People Health Centers" and "People's Clinics". Services are provided in parallel with the public health system.	Oil-for-health arrangement with Cuba, including around 30000 Cuban health-sector professionals.
		3.	Private health insurance: pre-paid providers (prepagas)	Generally covers middle and high-income households. The deterioration of	Direct payments, only rarely matched by contributions from

		and conventional healthcare insurers.	facilities and service and public hospitals in recent years has led to increasing demand. The government mandates uniform policy wording and tariffs apply.	public-sector and private employers.
Russia	In 1993, a mandatory health insurance (MHI) scheme was adopted. MHI is financed through payroll taxes with supplementary funding from general taxes. MHI funds are administered by insurance companies, which bear no risk. Everyone can access public sector healthcare but even so, voluntary health insurance has grown strongly, and is often offered as an employee benefit.	1. Government-funded healthcare.	Emergency, specialized and tertiary care and medication for certain vulnerable groups and conditions.	General tax revenues.
		2. Mandatory Health Insurance (MHI)	Covers almost all outpatient and inpatient services.	Payroll taxes administered by insurance companies.
		3. Voluntary Health Insurance (VHI).	VHI offers supplementary cover to state system benefits.	Employers and individuals.
Poland	Post communism Poland moved from a free and universal state-provided healthcare system to a compulsory social insurance health system. Initially several sickness funds, these were later merged into one national health fund (NFZ). Today the NFZ covers about 98% of the population. Private sector and employer-provided PHI schemes are available.	1. Compulsory social health insurance	Comprehensive cover for in-and out-patient care at state hospital and institutions. Income replacement (loss of income in case of sickness) is no longer covered.	Mainly through payroll taxes. Informal payments are common as a means to get faster access to healthcare from state institutions.
		2. Private health insurance.	Not very popular as supplementary cover is not effectively possible under current legislation. There are a wide range of group and individual covers, offered as riders to life policies or as stand alone non-life cover.	Employers and individuals.
Crech Republic	Compulsory SHI system administered through seven quasi-public health insurance funds covering the whole population with high-quality healthcare. All permanent residents are covered.	1. Social health insurance	Encompasses cover for all healthcare services provided by private and public institutions. A recent proposal to limit the state system to basic services has not materialised.	Payroll tax split between employers (9% of gross income) and employees (4.5%); self-employed contribute a fixed percentage of their pfofits (13.5% of 50% of their profits): general taxes public-sector employees and the unemployed.
		2. Private health insurance	Medical assistance services, cash plans due to illness and critical illness (Cancer) cover	Employers and individuals.

South Africa	There is no national health insurance scheme is South Africa, although the government remains committed to the development of one as a means to reduce inequities in access to health-care. Medical schemes (not-for-profit mutual funds) reimburse scheme members for medical expenses. Both individuals and companies can join the schemes. PHI is available but is typically restricted to fixed-benefit cover.	Medical schemes are regulated by the Medical Schemes Act of 1998, under the Council of Medical Schemes (CMS). At the end of 2013, there were 87 registered medical schemes. Despite consolidation among schemes the number of beneficiaries increased to 8.78 million (6.2% of total population) in 2013 from 6.66 million (4.6%) in 2004. This represents an increase of 31.7 over the course of a decade although it still means that a large proportion of the South African population is not covered.	Medical schemes must provide prescribed minimum benefits (PMBs). The PMBs are diagnosis driven meaning that it is irrelevant how a beneficiary acquires a condition. The PMBs cover the diagnosis and treatment of roughly 300 of the most serious and most expensive health conditions, including emergency conditions 25 chronic conditions and diseases such as cancer and tuberculosis. The medical schemes must pay for PMB conditions in full. They cannot use members personal medical savings accounts.	Members contribute to the schemes fund. Each year the CMS analysis key economic indicators that have a bearing on private healthcare costs in order to determine reasonable assumptions the schemes can use to calculate annual increases in member contributions. Scheme contributions increased by 10.4% in 2013.
		Private health insurance polices are regulated by the Financial Services Board (FSB).	Fixed-benefit cover according to policy features.	Private policy premiums are paid by individuals.
Nigeria	The National Health Insurance Scheme was established in 2005. It was launched as a pilot initially targeting federal employees, the army and police force. By law, firms with more than 10 employees must enrol but overall uptake had been limited so far. The target is to cover 30% of the population by 2015. There are additional schemes for rural and self-employed individuals. Most private healthcare is from administered funds schemes, not insurers.	1. National Health Insurance Scheme.	Employees in the formal sector (both public and private sector employees).	Funded by employer (10% of payroll) and employee (5% contribution).
		2. Private health insurance.	Not common, mostly administrated funds.	Mostly employers, but some plans are open to individuals.
Kenya	There are state-run hospital and healthcare providers, and private ones. Most are in Nairobi. Access to state hospitals in not free, but the cost has been lowered recently. About 35% of the population have access to healthcare though the National	1. National Hospital Insurance (Fund (NHIF).	Compulsory insurance for all formal sector employees; available on a voluntary basis for the self-employed, informal sector workers, retirees and the unemployed. Comprehensive medex fover for inpatient care with annual limits for non-state hospitals.	Funded by general taxes and employer contributions.

	Hospital Insurance Fund. Many people benefit from group medical schemes offered by their employers and the self-employed can take out voluntary cover. Micro health insurance schemes are becoming increasingly popular in rural areas.	2. Private health insurance.	Wide cover of inpatient medical expenses, typically with different limits on the annual cover.	Companies that run their own-self-funded and self-administered medical schemes: companies that provide a management service for self-funded schemes; and schemes run by the insurance sector.
Saudi Arabia	Healthcare services mostly public-sector provided through the Ministry of Health. Other public agencies such as the national oil company ARAMCO, armed forces, securities forces, national guard etc provide healthcare to employees and their dependants. In 1999 the Council of Health Insurance was established to introduced and supervise PHI to the country.	1. Ministry of Health: free service for all Saudi nationals.	Employees in the formal sector (both public and private sector employees)	Funded by employer (10% of payroll) and employee (5% contribution).
		2. Public agencies provide free healthcare to employees and their families.	Healthcare treatment at all levels.	Public-sector organisations.
		3. Cooperative Health Insurance Compulsory for expects and Saudi nationals working in the private sector.	Majority of the out patient and in patient services.	Employers and individuals.
Turkey	The Universal Health Insurance System was established in 2008, providing healthcare services for all. Total healthcare spending is between 6% and 7% of GDP. There is a small PHI sector in Turkey.	1. Universal Health Insurance System	In principle, all Turkish citizens are covered. Expatriates employed under a contract of service are covered by the system, provided that they make contributions.	Mostly funded by general taxes to the federal budget. Co-funding from employers, employees.
		2. Private health insurance	3.8% of the population is covered by PHI. Of those, 64% are insured on an individual and 36% on a group basis.	Individuals and employers.

Source: Swiss Re Sigma

QUESTIONS

1. What is health insurance?
2. Discuss the products of health insurance.
3. Explain the structural facilities needed for health insurance.
4. Examine the sustainability of the health products.
5. Project the future prospects of health insurance in India

44

CATASTROPHE INSURANCE

The tragic and unforeseen evenly of catastrophe causes multiple losses to society such as loss of life, destruction of property, loss of revenue, and additional expenses. Due to dislocation of such things, consequential losses occur such loss of business, non-availability of social facilities. The society expects that insurers should provide quick and effective indemnity of such losses. Insurance industry practively support the economic recovery process.

The insurers should manage the crises through insurance schemes by coordinating with the Insurance Councils, by quick survey and assessment of losses, develop response system and educate the policy-holders and general public against the catastrophe losses. The insurers should coordinate the loss compensation process through the General Council by taking the help of police, hospital and government machineries. The insurers after occurring of catastrophe should try to contract the beneficiaries at the earliest possible. They should through surveyors try to compensate the losses as quickly as possible on humanitarian grounds. The insurers and not the insured should take the responsibilities of verification and assessment of loss through photographs, newspaper, ratio and televisions. Insurers should waive documents other than essential ones in settlement of claims, work with other insurers and all other authorities in quick settlement of claims, allows disposal of salvage and settlements of other dues.

The catastrophe is unforeseen and unpredictable but it brings fury and ferocity to human life and property. The destruction is unimaginable. The resultant losses of life, property and other will take long time to recompensate. There is need of insuring and losses. The insurers have to be very careful in designing suitable product at a reasonable price. The insurers and government should educate people of the serious consequences of catastrophe *e.g.*, floods, earth-quake and tsunamies. India is prone to serious socio-economic consequences and natural calamities. In India, Tariff Advisory Committee (TAC) is guiding fire insurance to protect catastrophe losses. Riot, strike and terrorism perils are the high profile social risks. The risks of flood, earthquake and convulsions are caused by nature. Therefore they are natural catastrophe. The catastrophe insurance covers social risks (such as, riots strikes, terrorism, perils) and natural risks (such as flood, earthquake and Tsunami etc.).

Riot

Generally property and generally insurance do not cover riot risks, but the increasing incidents of riots have compelled the insurer to consider its insurance. People in India, can get fire insurance policy plus coverage of riot at an additional premium payment. Since people have not purchased riot risk policies, they are denied of claims arising out riots. The Causa proxima is used to decide the riot risks and its payment. Government has been very particular about the purchase of riot policies. It motivates people to purchase fire policy wherein riots etc. are insured with payment of extra premium.

Riots have posed various problems in various parts of country. Even in U.S.A., riots killed 200 people and billions of dollars were destroyed in 1960. Insurers were unwilling to ensure riots risks because of his potential losses, inadequate premiums and moral hazard. Government provided reinsurance to insurance of riot-risks. Thus the riot insurance started since then.

Strikes

Strikes are also unforeseen and causing damage to property and life and also loss of revenue. Previously it was uninsured. But now it is insured under fire policy with payment of extra premium. The public sector companies have started insuring strike risks. The insurance act is amended accordingly.

Terrorism Risks

Terrorism is increasing fastly. Loss of life, property and revenue become unthinkable events. The extra-premium is paid under fire policy to cover terrorist risks. The devasting attack on the World Trade Centre and Pentagon on 11 September, 2001 forced insurers to confront the international terrorism. Companies have come forward for the protection against terrorism. They have started terrorism insurance policy covering terrorism risks.

Problems of terrorism insurance are non-availability of data for proper measurement of risks, absence of information of total loss exposure and high loss potential of terrorist actions. Insurance and reinsurance can contain terrorism risk. Insurers can insist on how to deal with terrorism and maintain minimum security standards and educate clients on best practices for protecting individuals and properties from attack. Government also help overcome the terrorist risk. Government can declare terrorism insurance mandatory. Terrorism premium surcharde is levied on all property policies. Spreading the risk throughout society expand the risk pool.

Besides terrorism insurance, fixed investment in risk securities is being practised. Multi-event securities may become a partial long-term solution for privately insuring terrorism risk.

Terrorism Risk Insurance Act was passed on 26th November, 2002. Now, all licensed/admitted primary insurers, surplus lives insurers, state workers' compensation funds and residual market will offer coverage for certified acts of terrorism. The federal government will pay upto 90 per cent of any insured losses arising from such acts but does not grant any backstop for "non-certified" terrorism.

Austria developed terrorism pool from January 1, 2003. The pool gives automatic protection against property damage and business interruption for industrial, commercial and private properties.

Floods

The cover of floods was excluded till March 2001 when it was offered on extra premium to fire policy. The fire policy covers the flood-risks today. If any one does not like to get cover of floods certain discounts will be made in the usual premium rate. Insurance cover for natural disasters have become socially oriented concept in India. The fire policy in this context reads as "Loss destruction or damage directly caused by storm, cyclone, typhoon, tempest, hurricane, tornado, flood or inundation excluding those resulting from earthquake, volcanic, eruption or other convulsion of nature" would be idemnified.

Heavy mansoon rains trigged landslides and floods in Mumbai of India in July 2005 and August 2006. All the losses were not insured although insured property was USD 0.8 billion. Insurers have received 20,000 incidents of claims ranging more than ₹ 2,000 crore.

In USA, National Flood Insurance Program (NFIP) has started to insure flood risks. The maximum limit was USD 2.50 lacs for buildings and USD 1.00 has for contents of buildings private insurers provide flood cover for large industrial risks as a part of comprehensive policies.

Building insurance in Switzerland covers fire and flood damage. It is compulsory to insure buildings.

Earthquake

Fire policy as social obligation has started providing cover for earthquake on an additional premium. It does not cover loss due to volcanic eruption or convulsions of nature. Fire policy, now, cover flood as well as losses due to an earthquake.

Pakistan, Afghanistan and India were hit by earthquake on 8th October, 2005 causing fatalities to 73,300 people. They were uninsured. Similarly the earthquake looses in China and Iran have also been uninsured. The life and property losses have been very high. Insurance has paid US USD 2068 million in 2004 out of total damage of USD 13442 in 2004. It reveals that there is need of insurance of earthquake losses.

Table 44.1 (a): Catastrophes in 2011

Region	Number	Victims	Insured loss in%	Insured loss in USD m	Total loss in%	Total loss in USD m
North America	50	768	2.2%	39756	34.3%	63460
Latin America & Caribbean	36	1880	5.4%	631	0.5%	5558
Europe	34	1158	3.3%	4340	3.7%	8712
Africa	51	2894	8.3%	323	0.3%	1560
Asia	104	26189	75.4%	49249	42.5%	260149
Oceania	10	233	0.7%	19106	16.5%	27814
Seas/Space	40	1607	4.6%	2409	2.1%	3633
World total	**325**	**34729**	**100.0%**	**115814**	**100.0%**	**370887**

Source: Swiss Re Economic Research & Consulting

Table 44.1 (b): 2011 Economic Losses by Region and as a % of GDP

Region	*Economic loss in USE m*	*as a % of GDP*
North America	63460	0.38%
Latin America & Caribbean	5558	0.10%
Europe	8712	0.04%
Africa	1560	0.08%
Asia	260149	2.09%
Oceania	27814	1.80%
Seas/Space	3633	–
World Total	**370887**	**0.31%**

Source: Swiss Re Economic Research & Consulting

Total economic losses estimated at about USD 186 billion in 2012

Natural catastrophes and man-made disasters cost society about USD 186 billion in 2012. Most of the losses were due to Hurricane Sandy, which devastated the north-eastern coast of the US. The storm also affected the Caribbean and Canada, making it the largest North Atlantic hurricane on record in terms of wind span. The impact of the winds and ensuing flooding from the storm surge caused about USD 70 billion in economic losses. Last year, Italy suffered the most damaging earthquake in its history in terms of total economic losses. The earthquake caused significant property damage and disrupted local manufacturing activity, estimated to be over USD 16 billion.

Man-made disasters are estimated to have caused roughly USD 8 billion in damages. The cruise liner Costa Concordia running aground off the Tuscan coast in Italy and damaging fires and explosions on drilling platforms and in other oil and gas facilities were among the costliest man-made disasters of 2012.

Region	*USD bn*	*% of GDP*
North America	119	0.68%
Latin America & Caribbean	4	0.08%
Europe	27	0.13%
Africa	1	0.08%
Asia	30	0.13%
Oceania/Australia	1	0.07%
Seas/Space	3	–
Total	**186**	**0.13%**

Source: Swiss Re Economic Research & Consulting

Insured losses of USD 77 billion make 2012 the third most expensive year ever

Of the USD 186 billion in total damage caused by catastrophic events in 2012, more than USD 77 billion (see Figure 3), were covered by insurance. According to the sigma records, this makes 2012 the third-most expensive year for the insurance industry, after 2011, the year in which record earthquakes and floods contributed to losses of over USD 126 billion, and 2005, when Hurricanes Katrina, Wilma, and Rita alone caused claims of over USD 100 billion. Most of the losses in 2012 resulted from weather-related events in the US, such as Hurricane Sandy, the drought in the Corn Belt.

Of the USD 71 billion insured losses from natural catastrophes, USD 69 billion were due to weather-related events, while roughly USD 2 billion were triggered by earthquakes.

Regional overview

As a consequence of the extreme weather in the US, both the insured and the economic losses were highest in North America (84% of the insured losses), while Europe came a distant second with only 7%.

Region	*Number*	*Victims*	*in %*	*Insured loss in USD bn*	*in %*	*Total loss in USD bn*
North America	43	560	4.0%	64.6	83.6%	118.5
Latin America & Caribbean	30	1167	8.4%	0.9	1.2%	4.2
Europe	33	1480	10.7%	5.5	7.1%	26.8
Africa	53	2300	16.5%	0.2	0.3%	1.5
Asia	115	7177	51.5%	3.4	4.4%	30.5
Oceania/Australia	7	97	0.7%	0.3	0.4%	1.1
Seas/Space	37	1148	8.2%	2.4	3.1%	3.1
Total	**318**	**13929**	**100.0%**	**77.2**	**100.0%**	**185.7**

Source: Swiss Re Economic Research & Consulting

North America

North America was the most affected region in 2012. in terms of both insured losses (roughly USD 65 billion) and economic losses (over USD 118 billion). Losses were primarily caused by Hurricane Sandy and the severe drought in the Corn Belt.

An early-season tornado outbreak hit the Ohio Valley and south-eastern regions of the US on 2-3 March 2012. According to the US Storm Prediction Centre. 75 tornadoes were reported over the two-day period. making it one of the largest March tornado outbreaks on record (since 1950) and causing the highest tornado-related number of victims (42) for one single outbreak. Insured claims totalled about USD 2.5 billion. Later on, more severe weather in the Midwest and Ohio Valley (on 28 and 29 April) again spawned tornadoes and large hail storms causing a similar amount of insured claims. At the end of June, a fast-moving, violent line of storms known as derecho developed in lowa and travelled through the Ohio Valley into the Mid-Atlantic within ten hours, causing insured damage across the various states of about USD 2 billion and also 28 fatalities. The storm highlighted severe failures in the emergency communication infrastructure of the affected states.

In terms of the number of both recorded tornadoes and victims the 2012 tornado season ranked 25th since 1950 and was below the average for the past 30 years. Nevertheless. tornadoes and related storms led to insured losses of around USD 14 billion. the second highest on *sigma* records. although significantly lower than historic losses recorded in 2011. when the top two tornado outbreaks triggered a combined USD 15 billion in insured claim&. Loss potential from tornadoes and related thunderstorms has consistently shown an upward trend in recent decades. One reason is the advancing urbanisation. which has exposed more insured assets.

Table 44.1 (c): Insured Fresh Water Flood Losses

Date	*Country*	*Insured loss, USD M, at 2011 Prices*	*Insured loss as a % of country's property premiums*	*Insured loss as a % of country's non-life premiums*	*Insured loss as % of GDP*	*Total loss as % of GDP*
July-Nov 2011	Thailand	12000	1846%	203.5%	3.4%	8.6%
Aug-2002	Germany & Czech Republic	2886	20%	3.0%	0.1%	0.5%
Jun-2007	United Kingdom	2697	12%	2.2%	0.1%	0.1%
Aug-2005	Switzerland	2444	76%	11.7%	0.6%	0.9%
Jan-2011	Australia	2255	24%	5.9%	0.2%	0.4%
Jul-Aug-1997	Poland & Czech Republic	2241	213%	42.3%	0.7%	2.3%
Jul-2007	United Kingdom	2158	9%	1.7%	0.1%	0.1%
Dec-2010	Australia	2114	27%	5.9%	0.2%	0.4%
Apr-1973	United States	1873	5%	0.6%	0.03%	0.1%
Jun-Aug-1993	United States	1600	3%	0.3%	0.02%	0.2%

Table 44.1 (d) Earthquake Losses

Date	*Country*	*Dead or missing*	*Injurd*	*Total Loss in USD in million*	*Insured Loss in USD in million*
07.01.2000	China	2,55,000	NA	19,222	0
26.01.2001	India, Pakistan Nepal	15,000	1,66,835	4,964	110
26.12.2003	Iran	26,271	30,000	2,018	0
26.12.2004	Indonesia, Thailand	2,20,000	1,25,000	13,442	2068
08.10.2005	Pakistan, India Afghanistan	73,300	74,000	5,000	0
27.05.2006	Indonesia, Sumatra	5778	37883 (1173742 homeless)	3,000	40
27.02.2010	Chile	562	...	...	8000
04.09.2010	New Zea Land	...	...	...	4453
12.01.2010	Haiti	222570	...	...	100
14.04.2010	China	2968	...	...	1

Hurricanes and Windstorms

The insured property damaged amounts to USD 48 billions due to hurricanes in Charley, Frances, Iran in 2005. The windstorm insured losses were to the extent of USD 69 billion in 2005. Katrina, Rita and Wilma have caused damage to property and life.

Winter storm in Europe caused damage totalling $ 1.9 billion in 2006. Insurance companies helped Denmark, Sweden, UK and Germany.

Japan was hit by 10 typhoons in 2004. The catastrophe losses particularly wind losses would increase in future as a result of global warming. It is for the insurance companies to come forward to insure wind losses exclusively over 26°C temperature of sea causes sea-storm which lashes the land. Property and life are endagered. Insurance is needed for the purpose. Since 2004, sea warming is common phenomena. So, the coastal areas of all the countries are facing the problems of wind losses, when wind speed is 150 km per hour, the sea surges with 1.7 metre and if the wind speed is more than 250 km per hour, the sea-tide taken more than 5 metre.

Tsunami

Tsunami has posed a great threat to the public for its survival and rehabilitation. It provides huge opportunity for insurance to enhance risk awareness of natural calamities. Insurance is most suitable financial protection to public in natural calamities. Underwriting natural catastrophe risk posses serious challenges to insurers. The immeasurability low frequency and high severity of catastrophe risks have made insurers to decide whether to sell or not catastrophe insurance decides the underwriting process and premium rate involving geology, engineering and economics Insurers refine their risk estimates by collecting and assessing additional data. Nanotechnology is an example of a new technology which is used by the insurers.

The Tsunami on 26th December 2004 hit 12 coastal states on the Indian Ocean and has been highest number of fatalities which ranged to more than 2,80,000. The scale of the catastrophe triggered worldwide sympathy. Wind storms and flood claimed 6,700 people in Haitti in 2004. Out of the total losses caused by catastrophes in 2004, USD 49 billion was covered by property insurance.

Insurance cover could be an effective way of minimising the tsunami damage, but it is very low in India.

Table 44.2 (i) Insurance and Catastrophe Loss (Number)

	North America	*Caribean and Latin America*	*Oceania Australia*	*Europe*	*Asia*	*Africa*	*Seas/ Space*	*World Total*
2004								
No.	46	16	5	46	169	36	14	332
%	13.9%	4.8%	1.5%	13.9%	50.9%	10.8%	4.2%	100.0%
2005								
No.	54	21	6	59	208	41	8	397
%	13.6%	5.3%	1.5%	14.9%	52.4%	10.3%	2.0%	100.0%
2006								
No.	43	11	2	45	169	50	29	349
%	12.3%	3.2%	0.6%	12.9%	48.4%	14.3%	8.3%	100.0%
2007								
No.	47	19	7	35	146	32	49	335
%	14.0%	8.7%	2.1%	10.4%	43.6%	9.6%	14.6%	100.0%
2008								
No.	54	13	7	45	129	29	34	311
%	17.3%	4.2%	2.3%	14.5%	41.5%	9.3%	10.9%	100.0%
2009								
No.	54	13	7	32	125	26	31	288
%	18.8%	4.5%	2.4%	11.1%	43.4%	9.0%	10.8%	100.0%
2010								
No.	36	39	7	37	139	32	14	304
%								

Table 44.2 (ii) Insurance and Catastrophe Loss (Victims)

	North America	*Caribean and Latin America*	*Oceania Australia*	*Europe*	*Asia*	*Africa*	*Seas/ Space*	*World Total*
2004								
No.	7.342	718	39	1042	290412	2666	216	302435
%	2.4%	0.2%	0.0%	0.3%	96.27	0.9%	0.1%	100.0%
2005								
No.	3781	943	26	659	86633	1851	125	97018
%	3.9%	1.0%	0.0%	0.7%	92.4%	1.9%	0.1%	100.0%
2006								
No.	517	485	14	4166	19789	3569	2531	31071
%	1.7%	1.6%	0.0%	13.4%	63.7%	11.5%	8.1%	100.0%
2007								
No.	983	1216	303	1088	13748	2215	2000	21553
%	4.6%	5.6%	1.4%	5.0%	63.8%	10.3%	9.3%	100.0%
2008								
No.	1230	534	4	506	235276	1543	1367	240460
%	0.5%	0.2%	0.0%	0.2%	97.9%	0.6%	0.6%	100.0%
2009								
No.	543	547	706	874	9386	932	1928	14916
%	3.7%	3.7%	4.7%	5.9%	62.9%	6.2%	12.9%	100.0%
2010								
No.	139	225784	50	56490	17955	2640	515	303573
%								

Table 44.2 (iii) Insurance and Catastrophe Loss (Insured loss in USDM)

	North America	*Caribean and Latin America*	*Oceania Australia*	*Europe*	*Asia*	*Africa*	*Sea/ Space*	*World Total*
2004								
No.	32911	2	1261	1203	12094	577	578	48626
%	67.7%	0.0%	2.6%	2.5%	24.9%	1.2%	1.2%	100.0%
2005								
No.	72633	47	359	7039	2660	49	609	83396
%	87.1%	0.1%	0.4%	8.4%	3.2%	0.1%	0.7%	100.0%
2006								
No.	9658	587	335	2569	1814	68	850	15881
%	60.8%	3.7%	2.1%	16.2%	11.4%	0.4%	5.4%	100.0%
2007								
No.	8767	228	1283	12431	3533	46	1276	27564
%	31.8%	0.8%	4.7%	45.1%	12.8%	0.2%	4.6%	100.0%
2008								
No.	39881	360	2272	5806	3014	426	745	52504
%	76.0%	0.7%	4.3%	11.1%	5.7%	0.8%	1.4%	100.0%
2009								
No.	12655	50	1297	7697	2436	180	1955	26270
%	48.2%	0.2%	4.9%	29.3%	9.3%	0.7%	7.4%	100.0%
2010								
No.	15348	8977	8860	6303	2240	124	1623	43475
%								

Table 44.2 (iv) Insurance and Catastrophe Loss (Economic Loss)

(No. in USDM and % as a % of GDP)

	North America	*Caribean and Latin America*	*Oceania Australia*	*Europe*	*Asia*	*Africa*	*Seas/ Space*	*World Total*
2009								
No.	20086	559	2048	20107	16744	483	1990	62017
%	0.12%	0.02%	0.19%	0.11%	0.07%	0.03%	...	0.10%
2010								
No.	20551	53378	13131	35204	74840	337	20623	218064
%	0.13%	1.10%	0.95%	0.19%	0.28%	0.02%	...	0.31%

Table 44.3
Major Catastrophe in world

	2007			*2008*			*2010*		
Events	*Number*	*victims*	*Insured loss in USDM*	*Number*	*Victims*	*Insured loss in USDM*	*Number*	*Victims*	*Insure loss in USDM*
Natural catastrophes	142	14630	23269	137	234842	44692	167	297127	39869
In%	(42.4%)	(67.9%	(84.4%)	44.1%	97.7%	85.1%	54.9%	97.9%	91.7%
Flood	53	5798	6022	44	3184	2059	69	11027	6393
Storms	57	6729	14318	62	14191.3	39288	63	1702	20126
Earthquakes	9	636	437	12	87820	422	13	227050	12943
Major Fire Explosive	34	611	2145	45	454	5255	27	783	1060
In %	(10.1%)	(2.8%)	(7.8%)	(14.5%)	(0.2%)	(10.0%)	8.9%	0.3%	2.4%

	2007			*2008*			*2010*		
Events	*Number*	*victims*	*Insured loss in USDM*	*Number*	*Victims*	*Insured loss in USDM*	*Number*	*Victims*	*Insure loss in USDM*
Aviation Disasters	19	732	1239	17	496	758	16	820	1070
	(5.7%)	(3.4%)	(4.5%)	(5.5%)	(0.2%)	(1.4%)	5.3%	0.3%	2.5%
Shipping Disasters	52	2180	582	41	1598	548	27	1192	1262
	(5.5%)	(10.1%)	(2.1%)	(13.2%)	(0.7%)	(1.0%)	8.99%	0.4%	2.9%
Rail Disasters	14	220	–	6	166	...	7	337	117
	(4.2%)	(1.0%)	–	(1.9%)	(0.1%)		2.3%	0.1%	0.3%
Mining Accident	19	909	62	15	686	476	18	903	78
	(5.7)	(4.7%)	(0.2)	(4.8%)	(0.2%)	(1.0%)	5.9%	0.3%	0.2%
Collision of Building	11	393	–	6	204	...	6	283	...
	(3.3%)	(1.8%)	–	(1.9%)	(0.1%)	...	2.0%	0.1%	...
Miscellaneous	44	1878	267	44	20.4	775	36	2128	18
	(3.1%)	(8.8%)	(1.0%)	(14.1%)	(0.8%)	(1.5%)	11.8%	0.7%	0.0%
Total	–	–	–	–	–	–	304	303.573	43475

Insured loss of total catastrophe has increased from USD 48626 mn in 2004 to USD 83396 mn in 2005. The maximum loss paid by insurance has been in North America followed by Asia and Europe. The catastrophe loss was 5 billion in 1987 which increased to 40 billion in 2005. It reveals rising trend of catastrophe loss which should be insured to the possible extent.

Table 44.4. List of Major Losses in 2011 According to Loss Category.

					insured loss[10]	
	Number	*in%*	*Victims (11)*	*in%*	*(in USD m)*	*in%*
Natural catastrophes	**175**	**53.8%**	**29026**	**83.6%**	**110021**	**95.0%**
Floods	65		5093		16262	
Storms	76		3301		41152	
Earthquakes	15		20264		49194	
Droughts, bush fires, heat waves	9		8		2432	
Cold, frost	8		360		350	
Hail	2				630	
Man-made diasasters	**150**	**46.2%**	**5703**	**16.4%**	**5794**	**5.0%**
Major fires, explosions	**25**	**7.7%**	**390**	**1.1%**	**2463**	**2.1%**
Industry, warehouses	9		30		933	
Oil, gas	8		96		1490	
Department stores	1				40	
Other buildings	3		163			
Other fires, explosions	4		101			
Aviation disasters	**21**	**6.5%**	**463**	**1.3%**	**710**	**0.6%**
Crashes	11		463		26	
Explosions, fires	1		1			
Damage on ground	2				108	
Space	8				576	
Maritime disasters	**39**	**12.0%**	**1986**	**5.7%**	**1833**	**1.6%**
Freighters	2		22		67	
Passenger ships	29		1873			
Tankers	1				125	
Drilling platforms	6		53		1641	
Other maritime accidents	1		38			
Rail disasters (incl. cableways)	**9**	**2.8%**	**272**	**0.8%**		**0.0%**
Mining accidents	**8**	**2.5%**	**185**	**0.5%**	**377**	**0.3%**
Collapse of buildings/bridges	**3**	**0.9%**	**103**	**0.3%**		**0.0%**
Miscellaneous	**45**	**13.8%**	**2304**	**6.6%**	**411**	**0.4%**
Social unrest	14		1495		411	
Terrorism	16		492			
Other miscellaneous losses	15		317			
Total	**325**	**100.0%**	**34729**	**100.0%**	**115814**	**100.0%**

Source: Swirs Re Economic Research & Consulting

Tables for reporting year 2012

Table 44.5 The 20 most costly insurance losses in 2012

Insured loss[(19)] *(in USD m)*	*Victims* [(20)]	*Date start*	*Event*	*Country*
35000[21]	237	24.10.2012	Hurricane Sandy	US, et al
11000[22]	123	15.07.2012	Drought in the Corn Belt	US
2500	42	02.03.2012	Severe storms, tornadoes	US
2500	1	28.04.2012	Thunderstorms, large hail. tornadoes	US
2000	28	28.06.2012	Derecho storm with winds up to 146 km/h. tornadoes. hail	US
1700	—	25.05.2012	Thunderstorms, hail, tornadoes	US
1622	26	May 2012	Earthquakes (Mw 5.9 and Mw 5.7), aftershocks	Italy
1600[23]	40	26.08.2012	Hurricane Isaac	US, et al
1000	—	06.06.2012	Thunderstorms, large hail, tornadoes	US
950	—	11.06.2012	Thunderstorms, large hail, tornadoes	US
910	6	13.04.2012	Thunderstorms, >100 tornadoes, hail, flooding (Wichita)	US
841	4	03.04.2012	Storms with winds up to 150 km/h	Japan
813	1	June 2012	Floods caused by heavy rains (two events)	UK
813	4	23.11.2012	Floods caused by heavy rains	UK
775	—	02.04.2012	Thunderstorms, tornadoes, hail, heavy rains	US
532	—	12.08.2012	Hailstorm	Canada
515	32	13.01.2012	Cruise liner Costa Concordia capsizes after hitting rocks	Italy
450	2	24.06.2012	Waldo Canyon Fire; 346 houses destroyed	US
443	5	04.01.2012	Windstorm Andrea	Germany, et al
npa[24]	2	31.03.2012	Explosion at chemical plant	Germany

Source: Swiss Re Economic Research & Consulting

Table 5. The 20 worst catastrophes in terms of victims 2012

Victims [(20)]	*Insured loss*[(19)] *(in USD m)*	*Date start*	*Event*	*Country*
1901	—	04.12.12	Typhoon Bopha	Philippines
824	250	21.01.2012	Cold wave, severe frost	Europe
455	—	03.09.2012	Floods caused by heavy monsoon rains	Pakistan
361	—	15.02.2012	Fire in a prison started by an inmate	Honduras
317	—	07.12.2012	Cold wave	Eastern Europe
306	—	11.08.2012	Earthquakes (Mw 6.2 and Mw 6.0)	Iran
286	—	04.03.2012	Explosion at arms depot caused by a short circuit	Congo, Republic
252	—	01.06.2012	Cold wave	Peru
246	—	02.02.2012	Overcrowded ferry capsizes	Papua New Guine
244	10	22.07.2012	Floods caused by heavy rains	Nigeria. et al
240	—	12.09.2012	Fire at garment factory	Pakistan
237	5000[17]	24.10.2012	Hurricane Sandy	US. etal
205	—	30.04.2012	Ferry capsizes on Brahmaputra River	India
185	—	20.01.2012	Armed attacks on police buildings	Nigeria
172	30	07.07.2012	Flash floods; 7200 houses destroyed	Russia
169	—	18.07.2012	Floods caused by heavy rains	North Korea
153	npa[24]	03.06.2012	Dana Air McDonnell Douglas MD-83 crashes	Nigeria
149	140	21.07.2012	Floods caused by heavy torrential rains	China
144	—	18.07.2012	Ferry capsizes in rough weather	Tanzania
135	—	07.04.2012	Avalanche from,Himalaya glacier hits military base	Pakistan

Source: Swiss Re Economic Research & Consulting

Table 44.7 List of major losses in 2012 according to loss category

	Number	*in%*	*Victims (25)*	*in%*	*insured less*[26] *(in USD m)*	*in%*
Natural catastrophes	**168**	**52.8%**	**8948**	**64.2%**	**71278**	**92.3%**
Floods	63		2979		2712	
Storms	61		3129		54065	
Earthquakes	15		717		1787	
Droughts, bush fires, heat waves	8		139		11524	
Cold, frost	13		1806		250	
Hail	5				900	
Other natural catastrophes	3		178			
Man-made disasters	**150**	**47.2%**	**4981**	**35.8%**	**5960**	**7.7%**
Major fires, explosions	**40**	**12.7%**	**1367**	**9.8%**	**2933**	**3.8%**
Industry, warehouses	19		497		1 137	
Oil, gas	12		94		1696	
Department stores						
Other buildings	5		454			
Other fires, explosions	4		322		100	
Aviation disasters	**11**	**3.5%**	**449**	**3.2%**	**557**	**0.7%**
Crashes	8		449		142	
Explosions, fires						
Damage on ground						
Space	3				415	
Maritime disasters	**43**	**13.5%**	**1701**	**12.2%**	**2208**	**2.9%**
Freighters	4		14		224	
Passenger ships	26		1679		719	
Tankers	3		6		130	
Drilling platforms	6		2		929	
Other maritime accidents	4				206	
Rail disasters (incl. cableways)	**5**	**1.6%**	**141**	**1.0%**		**0.0%**
Mining accidents	**2**	**0.6%**	**66**	**0.5%**		**0.0%**
Collapse of buildings/bridges						
Miscellaneous	**49**	**15.4%**	**1257**	**9.0%**	**262**	**0.3%**
Social unrest	15		152		116	
Terrorism	25		785			
Other miscellaneous losses	9		320		147	
Total	**318**	**100.0%**	**13929**	**100.0%**	**77238**	**100.0%**

Source: Swiss Re Economic Research & Consulting

Atomic Risk Insurance

The Atomic Energy Commission in USA appointed insurance industry as a leader to study nuclear facilities and current state of the field. The commission concluded that the only solution was to creater risk pools. Share and Stock companies formed the Nuclear Energy Liability Insurance Association to write third party liability coverage and the Nuclear Energy property Insurance Association to write physical damage cover. Mutual insurers formed a combined reinsurance pool to write back types of coverage. The Price-Anderson Act in 1957 was passed to fix the maximum liability for any licensed nuclear facility at the amount of private liability insurance available. The Government was ready to pay to the extent of USD 500 million.

PROSPECTS OF CATASTROPHE INSURANCE

Catastrophe are unexpected occurrences and therefore, best protected through insurance pools. Catastrophes can be extremely large and destructive and hence uninsurable in the absence of the ability to create capacities. Its insurability requires coordinated action on the part of governments and insurers. There could be tie-up and coordination at regional and international levels for diversifying pools and lowering costs. The insurance facilitates risk taking and asset building across the economy and enables a virtuous cycle of wealth creation. Risk betterment is best possible in open underwriting one innovative approaches to rating or risks.

Insurance industry has been traditionally innovative inensuring insurability in all areas of the economy and has the capability to tailor insurance requirements. The sharing of the risk can be advantageously shared from the level of the policy holder to that of the insurer in catastrophe coverage.

The insurer, global reinsurer, capital markets and government should pool the funds for meeting catastrophic risks in such a way as occurrence of large magnitude do not prove a setback for the economy. There is need to make all economic losses as insured losses. Appropriate pricing and offering of terms require that the insured is motivated to reduce both physical and moral hazards. The insurer can use mathematical and technological tools and create maps and models to analyse and understand various risk profile across reforms and risk clusters. Mandatory insurance coverage may be experienced to couple people to join the pool High quality data is required by insurers to control exposures and determine risk premium as well as probable maximum losses.

Once the insurers and government come to take change of risk management in catastrophic area, many risk control measures will fall in place acrose the economy. Insurers have definite role in giving a dynamic impetus to an insured economy in hazard identification, risk assessment, risk, preventions and mitigation in the area of catastrophic risks.

Mumbai flood has taken insurance companies by surprise. In 2006, all insurance companies had purchased more catastrophic reinsurance cover. With the increased reinsurance cover purchased.

Table 44.8

Major Catastrophe in India *(₹ in crore)*

Event	*Year*	*Market Loss*	*Equicted to 2006*	*Gross Premium*	*% to GDP*
Gujarat Cyclone	1998	1096	1591	8703	0.71
Orissa Cyclone	1999	170	215	9454	0.54
Gujarat Earth quabe	2001	431	500	9799	0.56
Mumbai Floods	2005	2500	2500	21337	0.61

Setting up of National Disaster Management Authority is a holistic approach to disaster prevention, mitigation and relief by Government Authority the role of Disaster and catastrophe insurance is very much realised in present age.

QUESTIONS

1. What is Catastrophe Insurance? Discuss its scope and feature.
2. "Catastrophe is natural or man made or both" Examine.
3. Explain the loss caused by strikes and riots.
4. Discuss how terrorism risks are insured. Explain its coverage.
5. Examine the progress of earthquake insurance.
6. Examine how hurricane and wind storms are insured.
7. Evaluate the total catastrophe insurance.
8. Illustrate the Atomic Risk Insurance.

45

LIABILITY INSURANCE

Liability insurance does not have direct impact on policy-holder. Insurer does not deal with policy-holder but deals with third parties. Each liability policy has different nuances in its wording. The claim handling is largely dependent on policy wording. The right to defend exists on the insurer. Claims procedures are worded in the policy. The insured risks and excluded risks are properly given in the policy. Liability claims deserve more attention.

Doctors are liable for ill-treatment of their patients. Employers are liable for accident or death of employees during performance. There are several other examples which can cause liability to a party. Liability claims to be more complicated because of the sheer number of parties. The insurer is liable to pay the claims as per the contract of liability insurance and policy clause. The insured has to prove his liability to third party for which insurance is taken.

Liability policies may be assured either on claims. Made or an occurrence Based Wording Claims. Made Wording indicates that claim should have occurred during the period of insurance. The claim should be made during the policy period of 12 months during which the policy is in force. In an occurrence Based Wording, the event giving risk to the claims must occur during the policy period. The insurer would respond whenever the claim is made.

In a recent business risk survey by Travelers, liability issues appeared to be the fastest growing worry for businesses, with medical cost inflation, legal liability and computer technology ranking as the three risks that increased most over the past five to 10 years. While 67% of businesses thought medical cost inflation was a leading risk for their business, 58% cited legal liability issues, such as errors and omissions, and 52% reported concerns in understanding and complying with US government laws, rules, and regulations. Meanwhile, 53% were concerned about technology, including data risks such as hacking and viruses.

Third-party liability is one of the most important insurable risks that firms need to manage. Faulty products, wrongdoings and negligence can cause harm to third parties, who are compensated under the rules of tort law. Tort events are relatively rare but when they do occur, the awards can be high, which is why insurance is purchased. Even if the firm is found not liable, legal defence costs can be significant.

Liability coverage is generally broader than property coverage. Liability insurance may cover unknown and unexpected risks, including significant losses that may arise from changing interactions between technological innovation, society and the legal environment. In contrast, property insurance is mostly designed on the basis of "named perils". It provides cover for losses arising from explicitly defined causes, and claims cannot exceed the value of the insured goods. See the Appendix for an explanation of the various types of liability products.

Commercial liability insurance	Commercial property insurance
Usually all events which are not excluded from the policy terms.	Confined to named perils.
Legal liability claims of insured, often including defence costs.	Mostly refers to an observable insured object.
Payout restricted by policy limit defence costs are sometimes within the limit sometimes not.	Payout restricted by policy limit and the value of the insured object.
Claims recognition may come with a lag and settlement can require longer time.	Short recognition lag and relatively quick settlement.

Source: Swiss Re Economic Research&Consulting

The size of insured liability claims is primarily restricted by policy limits, which are calculated to allow for unexpected events. Liability claims are not tied to the value of assets of the insured, but to the bodily injury or physical damage claims of third parties. Liability risks are therefore more dependent on changes in the risk landscape than property coverage.

Liability claims are subject to changes in social costs

Liability claims are highly exposed to economic, social and legal dynamics. This can lead to unexpected additional costs for insurers. There are two reasons for this:

- In a liability claim it can often take years to reach final settlement. In the time between the underwriting of a policy and settlement of claims the variables determining the final claims payable often change. For instance, inflation can pick up, healthcare standards can improve and the general trend on size of legal awards may move upwards, all of which increase the claims burden. This problem becomes more acute the longer the tail. Thus for example asbestos and pollution claims have been even more vulnerable to unexpected spikes in cost burdens.
- Liability risks can accumulate since a single loss event may result in many claims being filed under different policies and across policy types by many injured parties. Accumulation risk can occur especially in lines such as product and environmental liability (including asbestos). It can also affect employment practices liability, directors' & officers' liability and professional indemnity, where significant changes in judicial rulings may have implications for a large number of similar claims. Because of the risk of very large claims. the insureds demand larger limits, which are often provided by layering umbrella or excess liability policies (see Appendix for a description of these and other products).

The insurability of liability risks

Some liability risks are uninsurable, and it can be challenging to distinguish between what is and what is not insurable. Insurable risks have several key attributes: they are measurable, loss occurrences are independent, actuarial premium rates are acceptable to both insurer and insured, and there are enough insurers who believe in the insurability to offer sufficient aggregate protection for maximum losses.

A key factor limiting the insurability of liability risk is the difficulty of projecting claim costs, which is essential for the pricing of risk. This is usually referred to as ambiguity or parameter uncertainty, and includes the problem of estimating the probability distribution used for pricing. The uncertainties may be more acute due to a lack of historical claims or related data, or to imperfect scientific knowledge about the risk.

Another key problem is that liability risk evolves with economic and social conditions. More so than natural catastrophe or mortality risks, liability risks involve human behaviour and complex societal relationships, which are difficult to predict with quantitative models. Also, the law is constantly changing, making past experience a poor predictor of the future. Trials gain relevance quickly through the evolution of case law and the adaptive behaviour of plaintiffs and their trial lawyers. In addition, frequency and severity are difficult to estimate for new technologies whose adoption is uncertain and whose impacts will not be known for many years. Insurers respond to parameter uncertainty by charging higher risk premiums which in turn reduces the demand for insurance protection.

What is insurable in the market can change over time. For example, the application of advanced data analytics may help overcome some of these underwriting restrictions by closing the information gap increasing insurability. On the other hand, if an insured risk has sharp increases in frequency or severity in ways not envisioned by the insurer, the additional substantial losses may even bankrupt the insurer. In such cases, a risk once deemed insurable can become challenging to insure or uninsurable, as has happened with asbestos liability, pharmaceutical product liability, and professional liability for financial institutions.

Property and Casualty Risks

Liability insurance in USA deals with property and casualty insurance. Controlled Master Programs (CMP) are widely used by insurers. It aims to provide global risk managers with the ability to manage and control worldwide exposure. CMP is a group of linked insurance policies. The set of local policies is issued in conjunction with the master policy in any territories. Underwriters and intermediaries must asses, the local laws and regulations. Certain laws require admitted liability policies. Non-admitted coverage is allowed.

CMP provides uniform coverage and uniform liability limits. Given the difference in the content of liability policies in different countries which is achieved through master policy. Difference in conditions allows the coverage provided by the master policy. CMP specifies worldwide jurisdiction and territory, so that the insurance company can respond to third party claims regardless of where they arise.

Local Insurance Requirements

The laws and regulations of local country govern the issue and operation of liability insurance. The business practices of the country also decide the procedure of insurance business. Warehousing, manufacturing, after sale services, maintenance or specific contract would call for an admitted policy of liability insurance. The local country's requirement of standard policy and compulsory provisions should be followed by the multinational insurance companies. For example, General liability policies are prevalent in Germany.

Local policies limit the clause of operation. For example, mandatory risk retention is imposed in Brazil. Insurers should issue all policies on economical and efficient bases.

Contracts' Liability Insurance

The contracts are given by the principal business house when the contractors give the proof of insurance for workmen's compensation, employers liability and general liability insurance.

American International Group Inc. (AIG) through its member companies around the world provides effective services to the contractors and business companies with its global experience and network. Multinational Companies admit to their membership only which have experienced claim professionals familiar with the legal requirements of the country to provide effective services and handling worldwide liability claims. CNP provides its services to member countries with a true worldwide risk management tool.

Progress of Liability Insurance

The liability claims totalled $ 84 billion in 2002 worldwide. It is one-sixth of all non-life claims. The costs of general liability claims grew faster than overall economic activity in developed nations. The most problematic lives of liability insurance are product liability, medical malpractices, directors and officers, errors, omissions and employment practices liability.

Insurers face the problems of premium calculation as the traditional methods of actuarial calculations are not suitable for it. So, they adopt risk prevention measures, limit accumulated risk. Insurers have to be vigilant in pricing and offering cover for liability risks. They pay more attention to wording and policy language. Insurers should cease underwriting if the limit may cross insurability and beyond imagination.

The growth of liability insurance depends upon economic factors, medical expenses, property value and wages, life spans, legal expenses and others. The severity of claims is affected by rising medical costs, property value and wages. Trust and compensation are also influencing liability claims.

The growth rate of liability insurance during 1998-2004 was 8.8% twice than the growth rate in non-life insurance. Brazil, Chile and Colombia recorded the highest growth rates ranging from 13% to 15%.

Table 45.1 Liability Insurance Claims (2002)

Country	*$ Billion*	*General Liability*			*Motor Liability $ billion 2002*	*Total Non-Life $ billion 2002*
		Average Loss Ratio 1997-2002	*% of total Non-life*	*% of TDP*		
US	66.7	99.7	2.1	0.64	86.4	318.0
Canada	1.3	73.5	7.0	0.18	3.4	18.8
Germany	4.2	65.1	10.0	0.21	11.1	40.8
UK	3.1	99.0	12.0	0.20	15.2	25.9
France	2.8	113.2	9.0	0.19	6.5	30.6
Italy	2.3	102.0	10.0	0.19	13.0	22.3
Spain	0.5	N.A.	4.0	0.08	3.9	12.7
Netherlands	0.4	N.A.	3.0	0.10	3.1	14.1
Japan	1.5	53.37	5.0	0.04	7.2	32.4
Australia	0.9	124.2	15.0	0.25	2.1	6.1
10 Countries	83.8	98.2	16.0	0.37	151.9	521.8

EMERGING MARKETS

Liability Insurance is growing in emerging markets. It has taken diversified forms of development *viz.*, commercial general liability, product liability, professional indemnity, directors and officers D & O liability, product recall, personal liability, motor liability, social security systems. The liability insurance has taken the form of third party risks, export financial protection. Liability insurance covers the financial consequences arising out of the insured's obligation to pay compensation for harm caused to third parties. There may be commercial as well as personal risks.

Liability insurance is called, "Long-tail" business where the claim picture will be fully developed long after the policy has expired. Globalisation and burgeoning international trade stimulate demand for liability insurance. Ethical, moral, cultural, religious and social norms and standards play an important role for development of liability insurance.

Liability insurance penetration varies significantly even among industrialised economies. Technological and industrial development also contribute liability insurance. In many emerging markets, traditional principle of fault applies to liability insurance but recent changes have shifted the burden of proof onto defendant. The introduction of punitive damages and liability extension have destorted the economic functioning of liability insurance.

PROSPECTS OF LIABILITY INSURANCE

Indian mindset pertaining to happening, *i.e.*, what is allotted cannot be blotted has hindered liability insurance in India. 'Liability and accidents are sure to happen and cannot be obviated, have been the main drawback of insurance. Liability insurance has taken a good start with the education and realization of one's responsibilities and duties. It keeps pace with global business where ventures have crossed the domestic boundaries. It contemplates exporting of products and services to tough and unknown jurisdiction.

Liability insurance has become only source of financial recourse in the event of litigation compared with the normal course or business, if unfortunate entrepreneur is faced with litigation finds no help for expensing legal fees and compensation duty to defend claims handling also makes a compulsive case for buying liability insurance. Liability insurance makes it possible for the insured to outsource adverse litigation management. It provides definite value addition through the intervention in risk management and insurance buying. The coverage depends on interpretation and negotiation skills of product knowledge. Specialised brokers are required for liability programmes and insurance buyers.

The liability insurance claim is very low in India. It makes insurers to decide premium rate. Many of the enterprepreneurs and professionals are encouraged to seek liability insurances. Liability insurance permits the insurer to heave a higher risk so that a large number of persons are willing to take this insurance. It keeps overall claim ratios within controllable limits. The insurers should keep adequate reserves to meet an unexpectedly large claim if ever it arises.

The Future

With the current growth of the Indian economy, there is much hope of liability insurance. It requires Training, Expanding, Self-reliance and Targeting (TEST) strategies for growth. Training is need to make the insurer-people expert in the line of liability procedures. The insurance players need intensive training 90 most classes of liability insurance demand intensive and sophisticated underwriting. The insurers have to find new avenues of insurance, long term growth is possible through analysing the market, seeing the need for liability insurance. There is need of developing underwriting capability and expertise. In is a must to set up a liability department within the company to gain experience of foreign underwriter, local adaptability and quick decision making. The industrial sectors and economic trends are helpful for developing liability insurance. Liability insurance has grown with IT sector. India has leap-frogged to the top of the heap in the provision of these services to the rest of the world.

With the explosion in internet usage and services together with hardware and software advances, it is surprising that insurance mechanisms to transfer risk have not been able to match these studies in equal measures. Legal liability led a rather blithe and low level existence in insurers' minds and consciousness in the form of compulsory third party motor insurance and workmen's compensation mandated by law. Public Liability Insurance ACT, 1991 has offered Indian insurer marketplace for premises, products and environmental pollution coverage, as a consequence of development tort and judicial reform. The technology insurance areas have physical assets, human assets liabilities, employee dishonesty and crime. The liabilities include premises, professional and management liabilities including directors and officers liability, employment practices liability, fiduciary liability, professional errors and omissions, intellectual property, internet liability and cyber crime. Physical assets included automobiles, equipment, property, catastrophes, terrorism and machinery Human assets include sickness and long term disability, workmen's compensation and employer's liability key man liability, kidnap and ransom.

Cross-border characteristics include the country's Political Risk arising out of confiscation, expropriations, currency inconvertibility, mergers and acquisious risk, tax liability risk, investor management and professional liability risk, outside directorship liability and need for admitted insurance placements in different countries. Intellectual property, multi-jurisdictional disputes, individual's identity, difficulty in assessing damages, technical exposures including mechanical faults, software errors, performance efficacy, programming errors. Exposures arising from errors, omissions, libel and trademark violations arising from the use of internet for a huge volume of transactions which could be laid waste by therefore, virus attacks.

Companies began to contractually require their vendors to obtain some form of insurance to protect them from accident or criminal losses. Litigation against the clinical trials industries has increased manifold. Clinical trials insurance can offer protection against some of the liabilities companies with inadequate risk management practices require insurance. The clinical trials insurance includes, liabilities arising from death or injury, property damage, lack of care, improper disclosures, conflicts of interests.

The clinical trial insurance covers the trials carried out by the insured causing death, physical injury and harm to health. The damage involves claimants' fees, cost, expenses etc. The maximum liability under this policy is limits to the indemnity chosen by the insured and stated in the policy. The deterioration of health occurred without participation in clinical trial is excluded. The clinical trial insurance does not cover claims arising out of war ionizory radiation, hepatitis AIDS deliberate disregard of the need to be taken reasonably to prevent claims and so on. If any event occurs that may affect this insurance, the insured must report it to the insurer without delay. Any death occurrence must be notified to the insurer early enough so that it can arrange for a post mortem. The insured must help insurance company to ascertain the facts and reduce the damages.

The liability on the part of Directors and officers of the company has been increasing in recent times. The majority of these proceeding relate to white collar crime like insider trading, fraud, tax liabilities, tax evasion or corporate manslaughter issues like the breach of health and safety offences statutes.

LIABILITY INSURANCE IN FOREIGN COUNTRIES

Need for Commercial Liability Insurance

Third party liability is one of the most important risks that corporations face. Faulty products, wrongdoings, negligence and the conduct of risky activities can cause harm to third parties who are compensated under the rules of tort law. Tort events are relatively rare; however, the severity can be high, which is why insurance is purchased. Even if there is ultimately no liability, legal defence costs can be significant.

In a recent survey among risk managers, third party liability ranked third after damage to reputation and business interruption. Because third party liability is insurable and is normally insured, corporations felt significantly better prepared to cope with these kinds of risks versus non-insurable risks.

Of insurable risks, third party liability carries the highest cost.

Based on data provided by the Risk and Insurance Management Society (RIMS), liability risks accounted for 48% of the total insurance premiums of larger US corporations in 2008, followed by property with 30%, workers' compensation with 13% and other risks with 9%. According to data from Market Stance, US companies spend an average of 2% of revenues on liability insurance premiums.

Data from Marsh on the excess liability market provide some further details.

- The health care, transportation services, construction, utilities, manufacturing and chemicals and pharmaceuticals sectors have the highest cost of excess liability insurance in relation to their revenues. The financial services and trade sectors have the lowest cost of excess liability insurance in relation to revenues due to their high-volume, low-margin business models.
- The mining, energy, chemicals and pharmaceuticals, utilities, food, agriculture and financial services sectors purchase the largest limits. This may be due to their higher risk profile as well as their larger average size. The government, healthcare, metal products, construction, education and non-profit sectors purchase the lowest average limits.
- Larger companies profit from economies of scale and spend less on risk transfer in relation to exposure or revenues. Larger companies also tend to retain a higher share of the losses. Due to both effects, larger companies spend considerably less on insurance premiums than smaller companies, despite the fact that they purchase significantly higher limits.
- Corporations are particularly concerned about US liability risks. European companies with significant North American operations purchased nearly twice as much coverage as companies with no North American operations and paid about 60% more for insurance premiums.
- The demand for liability cover is also higher for companies that previously incurred a large loss. In the US, companies that have experienced large losses (> USD 5m) tend to purchase limits that are about 3.5 times higher than those that have not incurred such losses. In Europe, limits are roughly twice as high for companies that have incurred large losses.

Types of liability cover

A commercial general liability policy basically provides coverage against legal liability exposures of a business unless specifically excluded. Legal defence costs, which can be severe and often need to be borne by the defending party even if a case is won or settled, are typically also covered. The policy may cover "...bodily injury and/or property damage on the premises of a business, when someone is injured as the result of using the product manufactured or distributed by a business, or when someone is injured in the general operation of a business." Such covers within one policy are usually only provided to small and medium-sized enterprises. For small businesses that are not exposed to specific risks, multi-line contracts including property risks are also provided.

Historically, general liability has been classified into different sub-categories of liability insurance. The broadest scope of specified liability covers exists in the US market. Some of the covers listed below are integrated in the general liability policies in other markets.

Commercial umbrella/excess liability insurance supplements the limits of a corporation's underlying policies, such as general liability, automobile liability and employers' liability. The coverage is triggered when the limits of the underlying insurance have been exhausted. Terms and conditions usually follow the provisions of the underlying primary policies. Less commonly, the cover of the umbrella may be broader than the underlying policies, although it typically does require some self-retention of risks. Higher limits are achieved by adding layers of excess liability on top of the lead umbrella cover.

Environmental impairment liability insurance covers liability and sometimes cleanup costs due to pollution of the environment.

Product liability insurance, typically purchased by manufacturing firms, covers losses which originate from defects in conception, design, manufacture or storage of the product; or from improper use by the consumer. Liability is triggered by the defective nature of products, not by their hazardous characteristics.

Product liability is increasingly complemented by special statutory regulations aimed at ensuring product safety, obliging entrepreneurs to take certain measures to guarantee the safety of the products brought into circulation throughout their entire life cycle. Insurance for **product recall and product integrity;** reimburses the expenses that are incurred by the recall of faulty products, thus reducing the risk of accidents and related product liability claims.

Professional liability or errors and omissions insurance is the corresponding protection for companies rendering professional services. This cover is typically purchased by accounting, auditing and consulting firms, as well as lawyers, architects, engineers and travel agents. Policies are intended to cover claims for damages based on violations of the duty to exercise care and prudence, or failure to follow state-of-the-art or other generally applicable professional standards and practices. A wide range of customised products exists, for example, for banks and other financial services firms. A special form of professional indemnity is **medical malpractice** insurance, which is particularly important in the US.

Directors and officers liability insurance covers the consequences of violations of the duty to exercise care on the part of the members of the board of directors, supervisory boards or management of legal entities (such as stock corporations or companies with limited liability). For public companies, this type of policy protects them against certain types of claims from shareholders who suffer investment losses.

Workers' compensation and **employers' liability** insurance cover the consequences of occupational accidents that occur due to a lack of adequate safeguards on machines, tanks and vessels, and facilities. Occupational diseases, such as those due to inadequate ergonomic conditions at the workplace, are also covered. The compensation of occupational accidents and diseases is usually not dependent on fault and therefore strongly regulated by governments. Systems vary by country or by state in the US. Workers' compensation is often compulsory and is, to some extent, considered part of the social security system. Depending on the regulation, cover is provided by social security schemes, specialised mutual insurers or the private insurance industry.

Beyond bodily injury, employers are also liable under specific laws (*e.g.* anti-discrimination and sexual harassment) for general conduct towards employees, which can be insured through **employment practices liability** insurance.

In 2008, corporations spent USD 142bn worldwide on commercial liability insurance. Their total spending on insurance was approximately USD 600bn. The developed economies alone generate USD 135bn of the world's commercial liability premiums. The top ten markets - which include China - accounted for 91 % of commercial liability premiums in 2008 (see Table 2). Premiums in the emerging markets are still comparatively low (USD 7bn).

Premiums & GDP (USD billions) in 2008 and 2013 Percentage Shares%

Rank		Liability 2008	Liability 2013	Total Non-Life 2008-2013		GDP 2008	GDP 2013	Liability/ Total Non-Life 2008	Liability/ Total Non-Life 2013	Liability/ GDP 2008	Liability/ GDP 2013
1	US	77.2	84.0	492.9	531.2	**14301**	**16802**	15.7%	15.8%	0.54%	0.50%
2	UK	11.7	9.9	107.0	99.2	**2673**	**2521**	11.0%	9.2%	0.44%	0.36%
3	Germany	11.5	7.8	132.1	90.4	**3684**	**3713**	8.7%	8.7%	0.31%	0.21%
4	France	6.9	6.8	83.9	83.1	**2864**	**2750**	8.3%	8.2%	0.24%	0.25%
5	Canada	4.9	5.2	40.9	50.5	**1517**	**1823**	11.9%	10.3%	0.32%	0.29%
6	Italy	4.9	5.0	55.1	47.6	**2312**	**2073**	8.9%	10.6%	0.21%	0.24%
7	Japan	4.7	6.0	71.3	81.0	**4932**	**4964**	6.6%	7.3%	0.10%	0.12%
8	Australia	3.8	4.8	21.8	32.7	**966**	**150.6**	17.5%	14.8%	0.40%	0.32%
9	Spain	2.7	2.2	46.6	31.0	**1614**	**1361**	5.8%	7.0%	0.17%	0.16%
10	China	1.2	3.5	35.9	105.5	**4405**	**9345**	3.3%	3.3%	0.03%	0.04%
	Top 10	**129**	**135**	**1052**	**1152**	**34865**	**46857**	**12.3%**	**11.7%**	**0.37%**	**0.2%**
	World	**142**	**160**	**1585**	**1550**	**60775**	**61709**	**9.0%**	**10.3%**	**0.23%**	**.26%**

Sources: National Supervisory Authorities. Oxford Economic Forecasts,
Swiss Re Economic Research & Consulting

The United States is by far the largest market for liability insurance, accounting for 54% of gross liability premiums worldwide in 2008. This is due to the size of the economy and the high penetration of liability insurance (0.54% of the country's GDP). Most other developed countries spend significantly less; liability premiums in the emerging markets were, on average, just 0.04% of GDP. In 2008, businesses spent USD 77.2bn on commercial liability covers in the US. Of this amount USD 50bn was spent on general liability, including USD 9bn for Errors and Omissions (E&O) and USD 8bn for Directors and Officers (D&O). Businesses spent another USD 13bn on commercial multi-peril policies, USD 11 bn for medical malpractice and USD 3bn for product liability covers.

The US is by far the largest market, with 51% of the global liability premiums written in 2013. This is due to the size of the US economy and high penetration of liability insurance (0.5% of GDP). In 2013. US businesses spent USD 84 billion on commercial liability covers, of which USD 50 billion was on general liability, including USD 12 billion for Errors and Omissions (E&O and USD 5.4 billion for Directors and Officers (D&O). US businesses spent another USD 13 billion on the liability portion of commercial multi-peril policies. USD 9.5 billion for medical malpractice and USD 3 billion for product liability covers.

General liability	33%
Product liability	4%
Directors and officers	7%
Professional liability, E&O	17%
Medical malpractice	12%
Umbrella/excess liability	8%
Commercial multiple peril (liability)	16%
Warranty	3%

The US legal system produces most liability awards of USD 1 billion or more

One of the highest damages award ever made was in April 2014, when a US jury in Louisiana ordered a Japanese drug maker and its American partner to pay a combined USD 9 billion in punitive damages to the plaintiffs over a diabetes drug that was linked to cancer. The US legal system produces most of the world's awards of USD 1 billion or greater. US juries awarded three such verdicts between 2011 and 2013 and also three between 2006 and 2010. The rise of billion-dollar verdicts reflects a pipeline of class action cases related to corporate misconduct during the financial crisis. Many of the cases combine the elements of large public corporations as defendants, class actions and punitive damages.

The UK is the world's second largest market for liability insurance, with USD 9.9 billion of liability premiums in 2013. The largest sub-line of business is public and product liability. This is followed by professional indemnity and employers' liability (cover for employment-related accidents and illnesses). There has been a significant shift in the sub-segments of UK liability insurance. In the last decade, the share of professional indemnity has increased from about 14% to 32%, highlighting the shift towards a more services-driven economy. Manufacturing, meanwhile, comprises a lower share of liability claims as accidents related to injuries and property damages have declined.

Most UK liability business originates in London. As the principal marketplace for international commercial insurance and reinsurance, the London market deals with risks both inside and outside the UK. The outside-UK business (called "home-foreign") contains a significant portion of risks located in the US and other parts of the world and is transacted by Lloyd's and other internationally active insurers. It generated overall premium income of approximately USD 9 billion in 2013.

- Public and product liability 39%
- Professional indemnity 32%
- Employers' liability 26%
- Directors' and officers' liability 3%

The continental Europe, the largest liability insurance markets are Germany, France, Italy and Spain. Together they made up almost USD 22 billion of global liability premiums in 20'13. Typically governed by civil law systems, these markets rely on local conditions and historical experience to determine which liability policies and covers are available. Penetration ranges from 0.16% to 0.25%, which is low compared to the common law countries such as the US, the UK and Australia.

The German commercial liability market, with USD 7.8 billion in total premiums in 2013, is dominated by general and product liability covers. This is partly due to the country having a still-significant manufacturing sector relative to other European countries. However, the share of professional indemnity is increasing because of medical malpractice insurance which, contrary to the other liability segments, has experienced a rapidly worsening of loss ratios (claims/premiums) since 2004. The weakening loss ratios led to reserve strengthening and market exits of major insurance providers. Hospitals and doctors were subject to significant rate increases due to malpractice risks. The rates became unaffordable for many, particularly midwives and obstetricians because these are high-risk specialists.

In France, third-party liability premiums totalled USD 6.8 billion in 2013. These were mostly professional indemnity covers because in France more than 100 professions require compulsory covers. Décennale (or decennial) construction liability insurance (10-year building warranty cover) alone counts for a third of the premiums. Medical malpractice accounts for about USD 800 million.

In Italy, with USD 5 billion in premiums, professional indemnity is also becoming increasingly important. Medical malpractice became mandatory in 2012, addressing some of the structural issues that had affected this line. Although work-related injuries are covered by the social security system, employers often buy employers' liability cover as an extension to general third-party insurance. This bridges the gap between the reimbursements provided by the INAIL (social security system) and the damage payments ordered by Italian courts.

The Spanish liability market generated premiums of USD 2.2 billion in 2013. The market has shrunk significantly during the recent recession years, with penetration falling to 0.16% of GDP last year from 0.18% in 2010. The main lines of business are liability and professional indemnity, followed by construction.

Canada is one of the few countries outside of the US where securities class action litigation has become well-established, even though frequency remains low. With extensive cross-border trade, Canadian companies are highly exposed to US litigation, and this has increased demand for D&O cover. The Canadian liability market is currently the sixth-largest in the world with USD 5.2 billion in premiums (2013). It has been growing at a rapid average annual rate of 9% since 2000. Recent regulatory rulings finding companies liable for environmental clean-up costs are also expected to increase demand for environmental coverage in Canada.

Japan and Australia are the largest markets in the Asia Pacific region, with commercial liability premiums of USD 6.0 billion and USD 4.8 billion, respectively, in 2013. At 0.12% of GDP, the penetration of liability insurance in Japan is much lower than in other advanced economies. In Australia, penetration is much higher at 0.32% of GDP. This is due to the country's Anglo-American legal framework, which has increased demand for employers liability insurance. Australia has mandatory covers for aviation, maritime oil pollution and residential construction and, in certain states, for medical practitioners, property brokers and stock brokers. Liability insurance premiums have grown at an average annual rate of 11 % since 2000.

The Canadian liability market is the second largest in the Americas with premiums of USD 4.9bn. Since 2000, premiums have been growing at an average annual rate of 15%. Latin American markets account for roughly USD 1 bn in commercial liability, premiums. Penetration is low, but the average growth has been at 14% per year since the beginning of the decade.

The market for large liability risks is dominated by a few players

The commercial liability insurance market is dominated by a few global insurers and large predominantly national insurers. The market concentration is higher in the lines that cover complex risks or require larger amounts of cover. The key global players competing for business in North America and Europe are ACE, Chartis, Allianz, AXA, Chubb, QBE, The Travelers, XL Insurance, Zurich Financial Services and Lloyd's.

	Equity (USD m)	US	UK	Germany	France	Italy	Canada
AXA	55 000		6	3	1	6	8
Chartis	52 700	1	3		8		2
Allianz	49 500	12	9	1	4	3	29
The Travelers	25 300	2	10				13

Zurich	22 100	3	2	5		5	6
Lloyd's	18 300		1				1
ACE	14 400	7	7				14
Chubb	13 400	4	11				7
QBE	9 500		8				
XL Capital	6 600	10					23

Sources: National insurance associations, AM Best

In the US, Chartis was the market leader with 12% of liability lines in 2008, followed by the Travelers and Zurich Financial Services with 6% each. The top ten firms in the US accounted for 48% of total liability lines premiums. In the United Kingdom, however, the top five liability insurers- Zurich Financial Services, Royal & Sun Alliance, Chartis, Aviva and AXA - generated almost half of the premiums. Lloyd's share was 15%. The leading liability insurers in other selected markets were Allianz (Germany), AXA (France), General (Italy), Lloyd's (Canada) and Tokio Marine (Japan).

The market share of Lloyd's is difficult to measure in various markets because it is not a single carrier, but rather a marketplace. It often does not operate through licensed carriers, and it assumes cross-border risks. Distribution is exclusively through brokers. The market share of the global players in Continental Europe is also difficult to measure because national data do not fully capture the business written by companies domiciled in other European Union (EU) member states. All the above-mentioned non-European global players write considerable amounts of liability business in various countries through their UK subsidiaries.

Apart from the global players, there are many "domestic" insurers that dominate the regional liability markets. Typically, the specialised liability insurers focus on the primary layer, for which they may provide integrated programmes. They mostly offer traditional lines of business and a few specialty lines. However, they are highly committed to their local clients, maintaining capacity through swings in the underwriting cycle. Examples of such companies are SMABTP in France, and HDI-Gerling in Germany.

The following are some of the important characteristics of the market leaders:

Large balance sheets: are necessary in order to provide sufficient capacity for the substantial exposures of large corporations, although large programmes are often co-insured. Currently, the market leaders are providing individual capacity of USD 100m or more.

Solvency: strong capitalisation is necessary to provide the full benefit of risk transfer. Extreme risk scenarios are often correlated and equity capital provides the buffer for these unforeseen loss events. The financial strength of many clients and insurers is influenced by the same developments in financial markets. The value of risk transfer is highest in times of financial or economic crisis.

Reinsurance cover: Risk transfer via reinsurance - in lieu of balance sheet capital - is an option for dealing with extreme risk events. The leading players are protected by large reinsurance treaties providing cover on a fully automatic basis.

International experience: most large corporations are operating globally and are exposed to different liability regimes via export or foreign operations. Insurers must be able to service and support their clients relative to their international exposure. Globally operating insurance companies maintain respective networks, whether through their own operation or through partnership with other carriers, at least in major countries or around the world.

QUESTIONS

1. What is liability insurance?
2. Explain the property and casualty risks.
3. Discuss the local insurance requirements for liability insurance.
4. Examine the contractor's, liability insurance.
5. Illustrate the progress of liability insurance.
6. Describe the emerging markets of liability insurance.

46

MICRO INSURANCE TOTAL AND CREDIT INSURANCE

MICRO INSURANCE TOTAL

Microinsurance typically refers to insurance products designed for low-income individuals. The wordd 'micro' represents the relatively small transaction size of lower premiums, a concept similar to microfinance with small ticket loans. Microinsurance differs from traditional insurance in many ways. Such as the size of premiums, coverage limits, product features, distribution, policy administration and target customers. The objectives of microinsurance also vary amongst different stakeholders. For governments and policymakers, for instance, microinsurance is a way to ensure inclusive growth and support the livelihoods of the vulnerable segment of the society. For social and developmental organizations, microinsurance can be an effective tool to help alleviate poverty. For insurers and other market participants. It is an opportunity to tap into new market segments and support economic and insurance growth of emerging markets.

Characteristics of microinsurance

Though the concept of microinsurance is gaining in popularity across the globe, there is no commonly accepted definition. The *sigma* study defines microinsurance by the following characteristics:

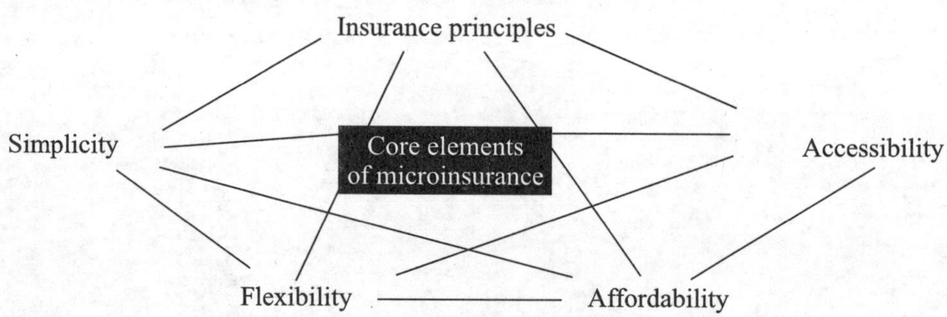

Source: Swiss Re Economic Research and Consulting

- ***Insurance Principles:*** It based on insurance principles and involves payment of premiums by the policyholders (or on the policyholder's behalf by government developmental agencies and donors) in exchange for the promise of indemnification by the insurer in the event of a covered loss.
- ***Accessibility:*** Microinsuance targets the segment of society with low and unstable incomes who would not otherwise be able to afford conventional insurance. It extends the reach of insurance to the remote sections of the society, thus ensuring the availability of risk protection for a wider segment of the society.

- ***Affordability:*** Premiums and coverage are kept at a low level in order to make products affordable for the target population. Premium subsidies provided by governments or developmental agencies also help to ensure products are affordable.
- ***Flexibility:*** Since the low-income segment of the society is not a homogeneous cluster, microinsurance products require customization to meet the community requirements in an effective way. For instance, premium collections can be tailored to suit the irregular income stream of policyholders.
- ***Simplycity:*** Microinsurance should be structured simply in terms of product design, underwriting conditions, premiums collection, policy language and claims handling. This takes into consideration the lack of actuarial data in many cases and helps to make the products easy to understand and more acceptable.

Distinguishing Features of Microinsurance and Conventional Insurance

	Microinsurance	Conventional Insurance
Target market	• Low-income individuals • Extremely limited insurance awareness/knowledge	• High and medium income individuals • Market is largely aware of insurance benefits
Product design	• Simple product design with easy-to-understand features • Community or group pricing: limited actuarial data	• Multiple coverage and features • Risk-based pricing driven by multiple parameters: good data quality
Marketing and distribution	• Innovative distribution with multiple tie-ups • Usually sold as combined products through micro-finance institutions	• Employs conventional channels including agents, blanks, internet • Insurance sold by licensed intermediaries
Underwriting	• Simple underwriting practices (often no screening); small sum assured • Simple policy language with minimal or no exclusions	• Comprehensive underwriting; large sum assured • Complex language with multiple exclusions and terms and conditions
Administration	• Irregular premium payments by cash or bundled with other products	• Regular payments paid by cheque direct bank debit, credit card
Claims handling	• Simple and quick claims turnaround process; limited documentation	• Comprehensive process: detailed documentation
Asset management	• As per regulatory norms or investment rules of the risk-carrier	• As per regulatory norms or investment rules of the risk-carrier

Source: Swiss Re Economic Research and Consulting

Benefits of Microinsurance

Benefits of microinsurance are discussed as to individuals, social and economic development and growth opportunities.

Individual Benefits

- *Health risks:* Such as illness, accidents and disability can results in high expenditure on medical treatment and also indirect costs including loss of income.
- *Lifecycle risks:* The death of the breadwinner can lead to acute poverty conditions for family members with no or limited alternative sources of income. Many low-income households are also not prepared to face major life cycle events such as old-age and retirement.
- *Financial risks:* Such as crop spoilage, lower market prices for the produce, death of livestock or loss of business properties can significantly impact the earnings of low-income families.
- *Disaster risk:* Events such as windstorm, flood, tsunami and earthquake will not only result in casualties, but also widespread economic damages that impact the livelihood of low-income individuals.

Source: Swiss Re Economic Research and Consulting.

DIFFERENT FORMS OF MICRO INSURANCE

Life microinsurance

Simple life insurance is the most popular and successful microinsurance offering across the world. Its success has been due to the following:

- a strong push from MFIs to bundle life protection with microcredit
- the relative ease in creating awareness and understanding of the product
- the profitability of risk carriers and distributors (as life products are comparitively easy to price)

Though credit life and funeral insurance remain the most popular life products, risks carriers are increasingly designing products that offer more comprehensive life protection, mobilise savings and enable wealth accumulation. Interestingly, as per the landscape study, pensions was the largest category of life products, though skewed by large scale institutions providing such offerings in China and India. Aon Bolivia recently was reported to have launched a new retirement product targeting the working class population, which requires regular payments for 100 months and thereafter entities policy-holders to receive double the monthly payment for the next 70 months. In India, ICICI Prudential Life has partnered with a tea producer to offer unit-linked endowment products to company workers at tea plantations. The product comes with premium gurantee and flexible liquidity options. There are also instances where providers are exploring links between remittances and insurance offerings. Seguros Futuro, a cooperative insurance company in EI Salvador, is developing remittance-linked microinsurance products to cover the death and repatriation of migrant workers. PICC of China, meanwhile, initiated in 2009 a pilot microinsurance programme insuring internal migrants against accidents and diseases.

There are numerous programmes which make extensive use of both formal and informal distribution channels. The objective is to improve accessibility to remote customers and help ease the process of premium collection/claims payment. Max New York Life Insurance Company in India developed 'Max Vijay', a simple life insurance product with a built-in savings component ensuring protection as well as wealth creation. It focuses on the retailer network for its distribution – eg telecom, grocery and retail stores – in addition to tie-ups with NGOs and MFIs. The company uses handheld terminals, mobile phones and portals to manage flexible payments that are small and irregular. Hollard in South Africa teamed up with PEP stores to distribute funeral insurance products. The product is a prepaid 'starter pack' available off the shelf, containing a policy card and document. Monthly premiums can be paid in the store. Distribution is also being explored through the utility corporations, religious institutions, postal offices etc. Codenso, the largest power distribution compnay in Columbia leverages its client base to target microinsurance products in partnership with Seguros Mapfre. increasingly, mobile technology is also being lever leveraged by providers to ease premium payment.

Heath microinsurance

Health microinsurance offer a high value proposition to the low-income population. Since health shocks are more frequent, impact household earnings capacity and result in recurring expenditure. On the other hand, the product is complex, since it is dependent on the availability of healthcare providers and infrastructure. Health products are also difficult to price due to limited actuarial data, susceptibility to adverse selection and abuse. Nevertheless, health microinsurance is emerging as an effective solut on to manage health/financial shocks as it reduces out-of-pocket expenditure on health for low-income families, and provides a steady flow of revenues for providers, which ensures the feasibility of operations and drives investment in quality healthcare infrastructures. Health microinsurance is provided by private insurers, mutuals/cooperatives and other informal solidarity groups. In the case of solidarity groups, the contributions are collected from group members to set up a 'pot', which is then used for members requiring major medical expenses.

Health microinsurance can help in achieving social protection objectives since social security systems are either non-exsitent or lacking in many emerging economies. A recent study suggested that health microinsurance has had a major impact on improving the poverty status of rural households in Bangladesh. RSBY in India (see earlier Box) is a case where government subsidies along with private sector expertise contribute towards improving access to healthcare services for the poor. There are numerous health initiatives which have been launched across emerging countries, especially in South Asia and Africa. Grameen Kalyan, a sister NGO of Grameen Bank in Bangladesh is both the insurer as well as provider of primary health services. It offers coverage for preventive and curative health services and requires co-payment which helps to reduce over-usage of services. In Namibia, the Okambilimbili pilot project, which concluded in 2009, provided a low cost micro-health insurance scheme offering full coverage of HIV/AIDS treatment. The insurance was sold through employers who contribute at least 50% of premiums, thereby subsidsing the premiums for the employees.

Agriculture microinsurance

Agricultural production a is mainstay for millions of low-income families across the world and contributes significantly to the national output of many emerging economies. Therefore protecting agricultural output from risks and uncertainties related to weather events (e.g. hail, drought or flood), pests and diseases, and adverse economic developments (e.g. price fluctuations, interest rates and change in demand) is critical. Agricultural microinsurance aimed at low-income farmers involves the transfer of agricultural risks through conventional and index-based parametric solutions. It provides a safety net to small-scale farmers by insuring them against loss of income. At the national level, it allows governments to shift from ex-post to ex-ante risk-coping mechanisms by transferring agricultural risks to the insurance sector and capital markets. Conventional agricultural insurance programmes face various challenges in supporting small-scale farmers, such as high administrative and loss assessments costs, risks of adverse selection, moral hazard and fraudulent claims. These challenges can be overcome through the use of index-based solutions with payouts defined as a function of a weather parameters of an index that is highly correlated with agricultural production. Examples of indices include rainfall (e.g. flood or drought), temperature (minimum or maximum), relative humidity, sunshine hours etc. To structure an index requires product design expertise, historical weather data from a dense network of weather stations and agriculture production statistics.

The microinsurance supply chain consists of reinsurers, risk carriers, distributors and policyholders (including beneficiaries). The risk carriers are mainly comprised of insurance providers, including private and public insurers, non-governmental organisations (NGOs). mutuals and community organisations/cooperatives. A study showed that 48% of lives wre covered by commercial microinsuress, while a similar portion was covered by NGOs. Reinsurers support underwriting capacity by assuming part of insurance risks. In disaster-prone business lines or regions, reinsurers play an important role in absorbing some of the peak risks and stabilising underwriting results. They also offer technical advice to help risk carriers design viable products.

Efficiency in distribution is perhaps one of the key success factors in microinsurance. A major challenge for microinsurance operators is to secure the best and most cost-efficient channel to reach customers. Existing microinsurance channels include micro-finance institutions (MFIs). NGOs, community organisations and cooperatives, retail/departmental stores, trade unions, utility companies, religious faith groups, post offices and commercial banks.

The role and significance of different channels varies across regions and product segments. In India and the Philippines, for instance. MFIs play an important role in distributing microinsurance (more specifically credit life) insurance products, while utility and telecom companies are increasingly being used in Brazil. Retail distribution has gained significance in Latin American markets as well as in South Africa. Funeral insurance, on the other hand, continues to be dominated by informal burial socicties, funeral parlours and cooperative societies. One of the noteworthly achievements in the microfinance sector has been the continuous innovation by risk carriers in designing channels and selecting intermediaries. New technology-based solutions (eg mobile banking) are increasingly being used in the operations and distribution process and are likely to drive also the mass market distribution of micro-insurance products in the future.

Other key participants include governments, which are instrumental in setting up the appropriate regulatory framework as well as being sponsors of some microinsurance programmes. There are also supporting institutions and organisations such as services providers (eg claims administration, IT, market research), International Developmental Organisations (IDOs), donors and investors. Collectively, they play a key role in operations, market development, knowledge transfer and mobilising capital. IDOs and donors in particular have been instrumental in providing funding support in the launch and development of microinsurance schemes and supporting risk carriers and distributors.

A range of institutional and delivery models have been tested in the microinsurance space; however, the effectiveness has varried considerably across the schemes (see Table 1). The common models for microinsurance are partner agent and self-help arrangements, such as mutuals/cooperatives/ community organisations launching their own microinsurance programmes. For insurers following a focused approach towards microinsurance, direct distribution, has been successfully deployed while keeping costs under control.

The microinsurance sector is also seeing innovative models that leverage brokers. Service providers are also entering the market. In this space, some organisations offer front and back-end services such as product and distribution design, claims handling and database management to risk carriers as well as support the search for suitable (re) insurance arrangements for microinsurance programmes. The international brokers are now showing increasing interest in the microinsurance sector and are offering placement and advisory services. While it is too early to tell which model is the best, success is largely dependent on understanding the needs and characteristics of the target population, ensuring a lean and efficient operational structure and selecting the best available channel.

Different Business Models for Microinsurance

Models	*Details*
Direct	Insurers develop products for the low-income segment and use own distribution channels (including alternative channels)
Partner Agent	Co-development of products by insurers and MFIs/NGOs/cooperatives. Insurers bear risk while other organisations distribute products.
Mutuals/ Communities/ Cooperatives	Local communities, member-based organisations, NGOs, co-operative organisations develop and distribute own products.

Provider	Banks/microfinance institutions, for example, offer insurance to protect against default risk. Healthcare providers offer insurance with health services.
Takaful	Takaful operators or other institutions offer takaful products compliant with the islamic principles of shariah
Public Private Partnership (PPP)	Government in partnership with private sector. NGOs/MFIs to offer subsidised products or directly buy catastrophe covers from re/insurers or capital markets.

Source: Swiss Re Economic Research & Consulting

Microinsurance is not a new concept; its history can be tracked back to the numerous informal mechanisms that have been prevalent in developing markets, specifically for the benefit of the low-income population. Microinsurance in the institutional setup started off as a form of charity in the 1990s, when scaled down insurance policies were offered. However, it has been only in the past decade that there have been commercial interest and activities in microinsurance. In Africa, for instance, many of microinsurance scheme grew by over 80% between 2006 and 2008. Growth has also been strong in India and certain Latin American countries, while large scale pilots have been initiated in China. So what has changed in the past decade that is driving strong growth in microinsurance and facilitating increased market participation? It has been a confluence of factors, such as increasing microfinance penetration, the focused approach by market practitioners, the active involvement of governments in certain cases as well as innovative channel/product offerings corresponding to the needs of the target markets.

Key issures and challenges

Though recent developments in the microinsurance sector have been encouraging in most regions and product segments, the actual reach is not yet broad-based and covers only a fraction of the potential market. Numerous challenges remain that need to be overcome before microinsurance growth accelerates. Fundamentally, market practiners have to realise that providing insurance products to the low-income population is much more complex than providing credit.

On the demand side, the microinsurance sector faces the biggest challenge in creating insurance and product awareness at the bottom of the income pyramid. Socio-cultural factors, such as dependence on informal or traditional arrangements, religious practices, and negative perceptions of insurance also affect demand. Sometimes customers are not fully informed about the benefits of the insurance products, which results in lower utilisation. Insurance may even be seen as having limited value.

Micrinsurance providers also need to provide need-based and relevant products rather than delivering standardised or scaled-down insurance products. For example, microinsurance providers tend to push credit and simple life insurance products. These products usually fail to provide adequate protection and are often issued to protect microfinance lenders. Providing additional value to low-income clients is also vital; this is often missing in many microinsurance offerings. This could involve for instance the provision of preventive healthcare services or consultation with doctors. It could also involve providing weather forecasts/data, advice on crops or farming technology. By addressing these issues, microinsurance providers can improve the product take-up and policy renewal rates.

Building a cost-effective infrastructure is a major challenge for microinsurance providers, given the high operating and administrative costs involved in reaching remote areas. In the current market environment, a number of insurers resort to traditional business models to offer microinsurance. Exclusive microinsurance business models that provide microinsurance products at the lowest cost are required to ensure long-term success and sustainability. The costs need to be continuously reviewed and minimised across the entire value chain through use of technology and innovation. Limited knowledge of the low-income market segment is another barrier to entry for insurers and other practitioners. There are issues in the claims handling process which need to be simplified, such as faster settlement and less documentation to file claims. A short-sighted focus on results or attempts to exclude certain segments of the population to cap downside risk could restrict the expansion of microinsurance programmes.

On the underwriting side, the lack of quality data makes it challenging for risk carriers to effectively assess and price the risk. The issue becomes more complicated since the products need to be affordable, yet profitable. Also, certain risks are hard to insure at lower primiums, which results in products that provide narrow coverage and limited benefits to customers. The providers should aim to simplify the policy language with few or no restrictive clauses such as co-payments, exclusions and deductions. For products such as health and agriculture, a high level of operational expertise and scale are key success factors.

Distributions models, infrastructure availability and instituional support are other challenges faced by microinsurence practitioners. Identification, availability and support of appropriate intermediaries remain major concerns for risk carriers as existing distribution channels tend to be weak. The staff of informal channels as well as local community/cooperative networks quite often are not trained or motivated to sell microinsurance products. MFIs, on the other hand, tend to focus their efforts on credit products. The feasibility of certain products is also dependent on the availability of infrastructure. Which is often lacking or low in quality.

Conventional insurance regulations could hinder the development of microinsurance Barriers such as high capital requirements or extensive compliance often limit the development of the sector. There is a need for focused approach from policymakers to encourage participation by offering a regulatory framework that is conductive to the development of microinsurance. Table 4 below summarises the key issues and challenges facing microinsurance in emerging markets.

Issues and Challenges Related to Microinsurance

Demand	*Lack of insurance awareness; socio-cultural factors; limited perceived value*
Operational	Maintaining low-cost operational framework; providers' limited knowledge of low-income segment and lack of skilled staff and resources; non-diversified risk portfolios; claims settlement issues.
Underwriting	Lack of quality data; coverage for herd-to-insure risks; policy language.
Distribution	Selection of channel partners; training; motivation level
Market	Skepticism about profitability; short-sighted focus of providers; low renewal rate
Infrastructure	Lack of quality healthcare infrastructure/providers and weather stations
Regulatory	No specific provisions for microinsurance: lack of or limited government support
Insurance	Over-usage, fraud, adverse selection, moral hazard and covariant risk

Source: Swiss Re Economic Research & Consulting

Role of government in creating an enabling environment for microinsurance

The role of government is important in facilitating the development of microinsurance, especially since microinsurance contributes towards meeting socio-economic developmental goals. Given the fact that serving the low-income population may not be the first priority for many of the private sector participants due to concerns about profitability and operational hurdles, governments can play a critical role in shaping the development of the microinsurance sector in emerging economies. The key objectives for governments and policymakers in this regard should be to ensure:

- *Financial inclusion:* Governments can improve access to financial services for the low-income population and empowering them with risk management solutions to cope with uncertainities.
- *Development of sound regulatory framework:* Regulators, through market enabling policies and reforms, play a critical role in further developing the microinsurance market. At the same time,

balance needs to be maintained since over-regulation tends to increase costs and operational obstacles.

- *Ease barriers and develop efficient markets that encourage innovation and competition:* Governments can lower barriers such as high capital requirements, licensing norms for intermediaries, stringent regulatory requirements, and restrictions on product offerings and reinsurance placement in order to facilitate further growth of the microinsurance market. A level playing field will result in increased participation/focus from private sector players and innovative practices which ultimately benefit consumers.
- *Increase awareness and ensure consumer protection:* By increasing insurance awareness amongst the low-income population, government can help to create a market for demand-driven microinsurance products. Also, since this section of the society has very limited resources at their disposal, governments should formulate mechanisms to ensure that policyholders interests are adequately protected.

The increased focus on financial inclusion and the role of policymakers in this regard has grabbed the attention at the highest level world forums such as the G-20, which has now developed a set of nine pricinciples for innovative financial inclusion, derived from experiences of developing countries. It forms the basis of a paragmatic action plan for improving the access to financial services amongst the low-income population.[35] This is a major step towards establishing international best practices and principles.

- So how can policymakers help develop the microinsurance sector? The following are multiple approaches that can create a favourable environment:
- Adopting microinsurance regulations (eg lower capital requirements) that lead to more focused approaches by market players to address the needs of the low-income population.
- Requiring insurers to serve the low-income population in order to obtain a license.
- Offering financial assistance aimed at building up necessary infrastructure and insurance awareness; educating low-income individuals about the benefits of insurance through large scale initiatives.
- Sponsoring insurance schemes to better address the issues of effectiveness and penetration. Since commercially viable operations may not be feasible for the extremely poor segment of the population, sponsoring insurance schemes may be an effective way to give specific population groups access to insurance products. However, such support needs to be provided over the long-term and become part of a clear transition strategy in order to ensure sustainability.

Government Initiatives and Proposals in the Microinsurance Sector

Country	*Regulatory initiatives/proposals in microinsurance*
India	Separate regulations for microinsurance; mandate on rural and social obligations as part of licensing conditions.
Brazil	Proposed regulation with provisions including specific license for microinsurance providers and consumer protection regulations.
South Africa	National treasury framework being proposed with measures such as dedicated microinsurance licenses, simplified distribution etc.
Phillippines	Recent launch of National Strategy and Regulatory Framework for Microinsurance allows second tier mutual benefit associations which are subjected to separate rules and favorable treatment
West Africa	Microinsurance regulation in 8 countries for mutual social health organisations.

Peru	Separate regulations for microinsurance
Taiwan	Proposed draft microinsurance regulations for a programme covering traditional life and personal injury insurance

Sources: Swiss Re Economic Research & Consulting; Presentation by Arup chatterjee. IAIS on "The case for a regulatory framework to protect policyholders and develop an inclusive microinsurance market". June 2010.

Public private partnership (PPP) and microinsurance

PPP in the context of microinsurance involves a multi-stakeholder response from the private and public sectors in order to address the risk management and risk transfer needs of the low-income population (see Table 6). The rationale behind such partnerships is to create synergies by leveraging the capabilities of multiple stakeholders. The public sector has the power to set conditions that facilitate adaptive responses by individuals and private market participants. In contrast, the private sector often has the expertise, operational and financial capabilities, but generally lacks the power to set appropriate conditions. Hence such partnerships, if designed properly, can help to create market-based and commercially sustaiable solutions for the low-income population. A PPP approach is of particular importance in the start-up and early expansion phase of microinsurance schemes, when offering products to the extremely poor population of market segments which are commercially unviable for private and economically driven operators. PPP is also important for the design and implementation of disaster risk transfer solutions.

Affective Risk Management

Contribution	*Governments*	*NGOs, IDOs, multilaterals*	*Re/insurer*
Education to raise awareness for risks and solutions	✓	✓	✓
Build/improve infrastructure and regulatory framework	✓	(✓)	✓
Distribution channels	✓	✓	(✓)
Improve product design and efficiencies	×	✓	✓
Financial support. particularly in start-up pahse and pilots	✓	✓	(✓)
Manage risks	×	×	✓

(✓) donotes part contribution

Source: Swiss Re

Social and Economic Development

Governments and developmental agencies have been heavily involved in launching and suplementing social security schemes to improve the livelihood of low-income individuals. However, it is believed that many low-income households have yet to benefit from such schemes and available benefits could be insufficient. At the same time, the use of conventional insurance to manage risks, after having improved significantly in emerging markets in the past, still remains less prevalent among low-income households who either do not have access to or cannot afford insurance.

Microinsurance has thus emerged as a viable alternative for low-income households to manage their risks. Risks related to health, lifecycle events, natural disasters and loss of property can be covered at affordable premiums with microinsurance. The development of microinsurance was largely driven through microfinance as life insurance has been increasingly bundled with credit products to limit uncertainties related to the death of loan-holders. This not only resulted in increased awareness of insurance, but also created a platform to develop other microinsurance products. The development of microfinance over the last two decades has shown that the low-income population is a commercially viable segment as well as a huge potential market for financial services.

A key objective of microinsurance is to offer insurance and risk management products to the low-income population. By reducing the vulnerability of low-income households, microinsurance supports the macroeconomic development of emerging markets and limits the impact of shocks. It also helps protect the income streams of low-income families, thus reducing their vulnerability of falling back into extreme poverty. These families can therefore begin to focus on the education of their children, health, improving their quality of life, upgrading skill sets and launching entrepreneurial ventures that result in the social uplift of the rural areas.

Providing access to financial service across all segments of the society is vital to ensure broad level economic development. Through credit, savings and insurance products, low-income households are able to mitigate their risks, gain access to credit that can be used to establish new business ventures, and expand their income-generating options. Financial services thus create economic opportunity, which enables people to manage their assets in a way that generates income and options.

For the extremely poor segment of the society, where commercial microinsurance may not be viable, governments through public private partnerships (PPP) can engage insurers to administer microinsurance products by fully funding or subsidizing premiums. Such mechanisms are high relevant, especially in markets where social security schemes are inadequate. In fact, government-sponsored microinsurance programmes can be an effective alternative to social security schemes, especially in helping to cope with life and health risks. Such programmes extend the reach of social protection measures to a wider population. They also allow governments to leverage private sector involvement to improve effectiveness and efficiency. Government-sponsored programmes significantly reduce government expenditure and administrative expenses required to establish and sustain comprehensive social security schemes. Lastly, these programmes encourage infrastructural investments by the private sector, such as the setting up of healthcare facilities and enhancing service quality.

Growth Opportunity for the Insurers

Offering insurance to the low-income segment of the society is no longer simply a part of corporate social responsibility. But is becoming a focused growth strategy of insurers. Insurance markets in industrialized countries fast becoming saturated, insurers must identify new markets which can drive future business growth. Emerging markets offer enormous opportunities for the insurance sector. It is estimated that low-income individuals constitute a USD 5 trillion global consumer markets. This is potentially a substantial market opportunity for the financial service sector, including insurance.

Microinsurance supports the insurance sector's long-term development. With favourable trends, such as rising personal and household income, improving economic fundamentals and increased efforts on poverty reduction, it is expected that a high percentage of present low-income households will move into the middle income segment in the near future. This socio-economic transformation will offer huge business opportunities to the financial services industry. In particular, insurers can look forward to a growing client base seeking higher premium/coverage conventional insurance products. Insurers targeting microinsurance are not only serving current unmet risk protection needs, but also creating for their long-term growth a strong brand value, a large client base, and credibility and recognition for future development.

A key contribution of microinsurance is the strong drive to raise insurance awareness by insurers, market practitioners and governments. Lack of insurance awareness has often been regarded as one of the major reasons for low insurance penetration in emerging economies, especially in the lower-income segment. Efforts to raise insurance awareness will not only result in immediate benefits, such as higher uptake of microinsurance products, but will also help in developing an insurance-buying culture amongst low-income individuals, supporting long-term demand for insurance products, but will also help in developing an insurance-buying culture amongst low-income individuals, supporting long-term demand for insurance products and thereby increasing the insurance penetration levels in emerging economies.

Microfinance in India-a sector in transition

The to much thriving microfinance industry in India is now under increasing pressure from regulators, government and local political parties/organisations to adapt its business model to strike a better balance between profitability and social responsibility. The sector came into the spotlight when SKS Microfinance Ltd, the country's largest microfinance institution, went public in August 2010. The company's market capitalisation quickly soared to USD 2.4 billion, sparkling the interest of other microfinance institutions (MFIs) and institutional investors. However, the sector's image was soon marred by reports that some firms charged exceptionally high interest rates and intimidated borrowers who fell behind in their payments.

The Andhra Pradesh state government tightened regulations by issuing an ordinance that restricted the operations of MFIs in a move to protect the interests of the low-income population (The state accounts for a large proportion of MFIs loan portfolios). The provisions of the ordinance include for example the compulsory registration of MFIs, a change in how often payments are collected (from weekly to monthly), the prohibition of multiple loans to borrowers and the possible arrest of employees who use coercion to collect debts. This was accompanied by political pressure and moves to encourage public banks not to give loans to MFIs unless they lowered the interst rates they charged their borrowers. As a result, many of hte MFIs reduced their interest rates from over 30% to around 24%. The financial results to the MFIs are likely to be adversely affected in the short-term as net interest rate margins narrow, loan growth slows and credit risks increase.

Although the microfinance sector has garnered negative publicity, the sector has played a significant role in increasing financial inclusion. The major MFIs have extended credit to the poor, built a strong distribution network and improved operational efficiency. The microfinance sector has also been successful in reaching out to an estimated 27 million low-income individuals-a feat which major commercial banks could not achieve on their own due to the lower penetration rate in rural areas and the high distribution and transaction costs.

The microfinance sector will benefit from sound regulations that protect the interst of borrowers and foster the development of the sector. The policies should promote the establishment of well-managed MFIs with sound corporate governance and ethical practices. Regulations that are too stringent could discourage market entry and increase costs, which may be passed on to millions of low-income individuals who rely on MFIs for funding. The microfinance sector is currently in transition despite its tremendous growth potential. Once sound regulations are in place, the scope of microfinance is likely to expand to include savings, remittances and microinsurance.

Rashtriya Swasthya Bima Yojana (RSBY): heath microinsurance for the poorest in India

Sigma Swiss Re Economic Research and Consulting has properly assessed RBSY in India. With the objective of providing health insurance to the "below poverty line" (BPL) households, the Government of India in 2008 launched the RSBY initiative, which is a healthcare financing model making use of public private partnership (PPP). the model leverages government financing, legislation and private sector expertise to improve BPL households' access to healthcare services.

The scheme provides cashless health insurance covers to BPL families who gain access to more than 700 in-patient medican procedures for a nominal registration fee. The health insurance providers are selected after a competitive bidding process. With their smart card, individuals can use the health service facilities in any of the empanelled hospitals (both public and private) across India. The insurance is also portable, benefiting migrant workers across India.

The initiative has now become one of the major government health insurance schemes in India with over 19 million families enrolled. It has successfully leveraged the PPP model and made use of information technologies to improve accessibility and efficiency. Initial findings suggest that the programme has led to improved access to healthcare, higher quality care, lower out-of-pocket medical expenditure and more investment in healthcare infrastructures. It has also resulted in the development of a better tracking mechanism of health services.

Furthermore, economic growth in emerging markets will also benefit from improving savings and investment flows. Uninsured low-income families usually keep small cash reserves to manage daily requirements and unforeseen risks; most do not save for the long-term. The availability of microinsurance helps to ensure that most major risk are covered and encourages long-term savings. Life products such as those with a savings component or pensions can also help to achieve this objective. At the macroeconomic level, funds collected by microinsurance operators are usually invested in government bonds and other corporate securities, to the benefit of the overall economy, particularly in infrastructure and capital market development.

Insurance and banking partnership

There cohesive partnership between banking industry and life insurance industry, the same synergy could further percolate down to the rural India population as a perfect combination model of providing "one stop financial solution" to the rural population, which needs the most.

Possible route of distribution of Microinsurance product through bancassurance: Today, many of the PSU banks have promoted their own insurance company (Life and Non Life) or have tied up with some insurance company as a corporate agent.

In addition to their own branch network these PSU Banks also have another approx 15,723 branches of Regional Rural Banks (RRB) jointly sponsored by various State Government, NABARD and these public sector banks. These RRBs operate in specific geographical areas and cater to the speciffic rural population with a large number of PSU bank branches are schemselves hugely involved in the formation Self Help Group (SHGs) which is a huge community that could be carered through Micro Insurance products. In such cases banks become an aggregator of such SHGs, who in many cases are also involved in lending towards the activity of these SHG

These rural bank branches of PSU banks and RRBs are a wonderful vehicle for distribution of Microinsurance products to its customers giving tremendous benefits and wing-to-wing customer service, which is of prime importance in Micro Insurance.

In a typical Micro insurance product (where the sum assured (SA) is betweeen 5000 and 50000), the premiums are relatively very low as most of these products are pure tem or term with return of premium. Some insurers also offer products which are on Endowment and Money Back platform in the market, which also fall under the categorization of Microinsurance. There is need of specially designed products of microinsurance and microfinance in rural areas.

Microinsurance in the next decade – trends to watch out for ! Due to the rapid growth of microfinance in recent decades, there is now little doubt that demand for financial services among the low-income population exists and has huge potential. Given the strong growth of microinsurance in recent years and its role in meeting socio-developmental objectives. 2010-2020 can become a 'decade of further financial inclusions', where microinsurance, along with microcredit and other microfinance products will change the way the world sees the low-income market segment.

Key microinsurance trends that may develop between 2010 and 2020 include the following.

- Insurers will continue to target low-income families. The hiehtened interest and more focused approach of insurers will result in more choices for policyholders. New players will enter the market, resulting in evolution and innovation in business models and product offerings. Rising incomes and reduction in poverty will result in higher demand for conventional insurance and risk management products.
- Demand will rise for health microinsurance (a priority for many governments in the emerging market countries), for savings/accumulation life products (including pension and education products) and for parametric solutions (index-based agriculture products for farmers as well

as catastrophe covers). Also, there is likely to be a stronger focus on developing bundled microinsurance products that can offer comprehensive protection at low costs.

- Demand for microfinance will increase from the low-income group's particularly as their needs expand from emergency credit to housing and educational loans.
- Governments will play an increasingly important role in fulfilling the needs and requirements of the extremely poor segment of society. They will increasingly engage private sector (re)insurers to design and implement innovative mechanisms to serve the risks management needs of low-income households. Products such as health and agriculture insurance will continue to be subsidised by governments in order to keep premiums at a low level.
- The need for more sophisticated approaches to disaster risk management will be come vital and lead to comprehensive national policies. Innovative risks transfer mechanisms will be adopted. As the need to deal with the financial consequences of large scale natural disasters on the low-income population increases, the use of PPP will become more important for governments and developmental agencies.
- Technological innovation will have a significant impact on the operational and distribution models, resulting in reduced transactional costs and increased efficiency across the microinsurance value chain. Mobile phones and related technologies will enable fast-paced growth and penetration of microinsurance products. Better technology and management information systems are also likely to result in improved data quality as required for effective pricing and risk assessment of microinsurance products.
- Formal mechanisms of risk management will gain in popularity and eventually take over the market for informal schemes. Institutions, which are currently not regulated for the purpose of providing microinsurance, will increasingly be controlled or montored by the relevant supervisory authorities.
- Microtakaful is expected to become more popular in the Middle East North Africa (MENA) region and in certain Asian economies with huge islamic populations such as Indonesia and Malaysia.

The role of insurance and reinsurers

Global and local (re)insurers are catering to the needs of low-income household with number of small to large scale microinsurance projects initiated in the past few years across various product lines and major markets.

Private insurers currently provide the largest number microinsurance products and have the largest outreach. However, their product offering is often skewed towards credit life, although there are increased efforts to provide a more diverse product range. In fact, the largest the number of microinsurance products in the last decade were introduced by commercial insurers. The commercial issurers are not engaged in the product design and delivery, but they also support NGOs, communities, cooperatives, governments and other providers of microinsurance.

For insurers, the low-income market segment is expected to become the driver of growth. As the sector expands, local insurers and other microinsurance providers will need capital support, catastrophic protection, holistic risk management solutions, technical expertise, and innovative solutions, all of which are provided by reinsurers. Reinsurance solutions offer loss stabilisation for microinsurance programmes, thereby limiting the loss impact and reducing underwriting costs. This greatly enhances the institutions capability to build sustainable operations, increases their solvency and supports the expansion of microinsurance programmes. Reinsurance offers the following benefits:

- *Innovative risk transfer mechanisms*: Insurers can manage the risk of insuring the low-income population through innovative reinsurance arrangement, including those making use of parametric indices and capital market solutions. For large MFIs,which already absorb a variety of risks such as credit, investments and liquidity insurance-related risks can be effectively transferred to reinsurers.

- *Hedging the corporate portfolio*: Insurers and other risk carriers such as mutuals and community-based microinsurance providers-at both the national and local level-face covariate risk in that their assets and operations can be severely impacted by a catastrophic event or large scale loss. They need protection at the institutional level to cope with such extreme events.
- *Capacity expansion:* To develop large scale microinsurance programmes or to scale up existing programmes, risk carriers require support from reinsurers to expand underwriting capacity. Reinsurers also provide capacity for peak risks or portfolios which are difficult to insure.
- *Disaster risk management:* With support from reinsurers, natural catastrophe protection can be provided through traditional as well as capital market solutions. Such mechanisms ensure guaranteed access to required funds for recovery up to agreed cover limits, and are an efficient way to cope with the financial consequences of disasters.
- *Provision of technical and risk management expertise:* To make microinsurance profitable, insurers have to deal with major issues including lack of data, control of antiselection, moral hazard and fraud. Reinsurers have the expertise and know-how to support insurance companies in adequately assessing and pricing risks and to design innovative and attractive products for both the providers and the policyholders.

Increasingly, insurers and other risk carriers are teaming up with reinsurers to co-develop microinsurance programmes or transfer the insurance risk. Reinsurance arrangements have not just been limited to private programmes, but also extended to public sector initiatives. Recently, micro reinsurance was used to protect a government-sponsored critical microinsurance was used to protect a government-sponsored critical microinsurance scheme that covers 10 million low-income families in Tamil Nadu, India. The programme uses several reinsurance structures and has the support of major international reinsurers. The deal, believed to be the largest contractual transfer of microinsurance risk, highlights how reinsurers aid the development of the microinsurance market.

CREDIT INSURANCE

Credit insurance and surety is closely tied to the economic development. Credit insurance is a risk management tool the compensates policyholder when their clients fails to pay for goods and services. Credit insurance enables sellers to extend credit more liberally. Surety compensates the beneficiary if a contractual, legal or regularly obligation is not met. The legal need for surety is more important for the economic well-being of the country. Companies undertaking projects for government or semi-public institutions guarantee their work with surety bonds.

Credit insurance and surety are differently used in different countries according to their specific rules and regulations. The need for credit insurance is observed because of rising of international trade faster than GDP and growing specialisation. Export and domestic trade have opined emerging markets for credit insurance. The global surety insurance is expected to grow with rising GDP. It is oftenly demanded in Asian and European markets. The general insurers are the underwriters of credit insurance and surety. The credit insurance depends upon financial markets particularly banking products. The factoring companies in USA by company's receivable for immediate and discounted payment. Therefore, the factors often by credit insurance to cover the risk of not collecting then trade receivables.

Credit insurance companies control their exposures through limit management as they provide cover for 60 to 120 days. They gain better with the use of information technology for credit quality of policy-holder and risks accumulations. Reinsurance Companies cover 50% of the credit insurance. Similarly surety guarantees also increase. Credit insurance and surety bonds are guarantees insurance that the commitments will be fulfilled. Credit insurance assures payment and surety assures performances.

Suretyship is a bond and contract in which the insurer provides a guarantee to the policyholder or beneficiary that a third party *i.e.*, the principal will meet its contractual, legal or regulatory obligations. 'For example, a contractor is engaged to construct a building as per specification but the office room should be constructed first within 3 months. If the contractor fails to finish the work on some valid ground, the surety company undertakes the construction work. The contractor is known as principal and the building owner is beneficiary. The contract may be of any commercial nature. Suretyship includes performance bond, advance payment bond, labour and material payment bond and maintenance bond. Similarly commercial bonds includes customs bond, tax bonds, license and permit board and court bonds.

An surety bond increases the likelihood of a project being completed as initially agreed. It enhances the principal's credit worthiness. The surety company's expertise in pre-qualifying the principal. Surety involves disciplined underwriting, exposure management and use of reinsurance.

Background of Credit Insurance and Surety

The first credit insurance yook place in 1820 principally offer fire and life insurance by British Commercial Insurance Company. The surety market started in 1894 in USA which required the purchase of surety bonds on construction projects. The credit insurance and surety could not develop much. Credit insurance policies have covered commercial risks with the experience of last years. It has developed gradually since last 15 years. The political risks are covered only in combination of commercial risks coverage.

Short term credit covered provide for consumer goods, spare parts and raw materials. Medium term credit covers capital goods. Credit insurance is being helped.

The premium volume of credit insurance has increased from \$ 4340 million in 1998 to \$ 6591 million in 2004. Western Europe constitutes more than 70 per cent of share premium. 0.016 per cent of GDP is collected as premium credit insurance worldwide. The Suretyship premium has increased from \$ 5391 million in 1998 to \$ 7644 million in 2004. 0.019 per cent of GDP is collected as premiums for surety ship.

Functions of Credit Insurance

Credit insurance protects a seller from the risk of buyer nonpayment, which may occur due to commercial or political risks. The commercial risks cover buyer insolvency and extended late payment and, failure to pay within a fixed days of the due date. Extended late payment is protracted default. Political risks involves nonpayment on an export contract or project due to government's actions. It includes intervention to prevent the transfer of payment, cancellation of a license, acts of war or civil conflict or the government's enactment of laws or other measures.

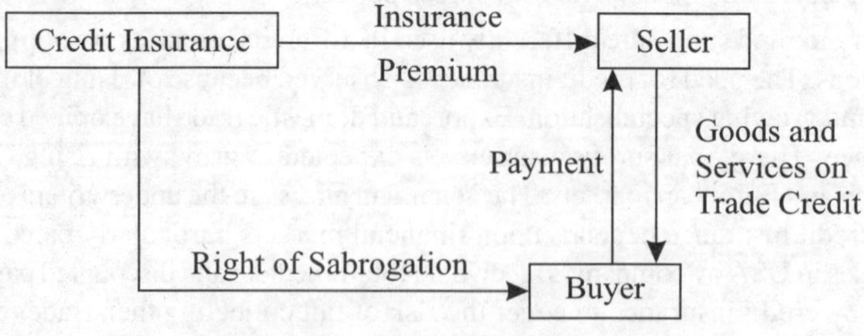

Fig. 46.1 Functions of credit Insurance.

The credit insurance gets the right of collection directly from buyer who failed to pay to seller. The credit insurer pays the amount of trade credit to seller if buyer fails to pay to the seller.

TYPES OF CREDIT INSURANCE

Credit insurance covers all the commercial trade receivable under 'Comprehensive Policy'. When the insurer finds that the individual buyer is not creditworthy, it does select the risk. Credit insurance policies are annually renewable. Premium rate is set at the inception of the policy. The insurer declares its turnover either monthly, quarterly or annually depending upon the policy. The renewal policy is issued at a discount of 10 to 20 percent, in non-claim. The insurer manages its trade credit relationship efficiently. There are specific account policies which cover only certain named accounts. Single Account Policies cover a single named account. The catastrophe credit policies insure risk from catastrophic trade credit default. It carries larger premium.

Credit insurers have started selling credit information to the sellers who will be cauthous in selling their creditworthy customers that is decided on the basis of capital character and capacity. Capital refers to the financial strength which is evaluated on the basis of 3–5 years of financial statements including balance sheet, income statement, statement of cash flows and statement of owners' equity. Cost records are used for contractors' jobs. Character refers to reputation for fair and business like dealings. Capacity refers to the ability to perform which is assessed by the buyers' capacity of operation and marketability.

Proper policy design is essential for credit insurance management. Self retention, coinsurance, limit setting, short term cover etc. are adopted for risk management. Reinsurance and risk scrutinisation are also done proper management of credit risks.

REINSURANCE

When credit insurers are confronted with default, reinsurance helps to smooth the loss impact. The loss ratio of an individual credit insurer tends to vary even more than that of overall market. It require transfer of risk through reinsurance. Reinsurance lowers the cost of capital of credit insures by reducing their earnings volatility.

Types of Reinsurance

There are two types of reinsurance *i.e.*, proportional and non-proportional. The insurer and the reinsurance share premiums and losses at a contractual defined ratio under proportional reinsurance. A treaty is set for an amount up to which the direct insurer will pay all losses and reinsurer pays all or predetermined percentage of losses above this amount upto a cover limit. The reinsurance is feasible through equity, debt and hybrid securities. Non-proportional reinsurance protects against exceptionally large losses. The advantage of reinsurance is that it is indemnity base and have no basis risk. Hedging tools leave the insurer exposed to the risk that the losses it incurs will not be covered.

CREDIT INSURANCE IN INDIA

In India, Export Credit and Guarantee Corporation of India (ECGC) is providing cover for credit insurance. It has been termed specialised institution for conducting non-life (general) insurance.

Table 46.1 Gross Direct premium of ECGC

Gross Direct Premium	*2003-04*	*2004-05*	*2005-06*
In Crore ₹	445.12	515.54	578.46
Market share in % of total	2.78	2.86	—
Growth %	7.0	16.36	12.20

Source: Sigma various Issues

ECGC has done ₹ 445.12 crore in 2003-2004 as compare ₹ 374 crore in 2002-2003. It has increased to ₹ 578.46 crore in 2005-2006.

Appendix

सर्व शक्ति सुरक्षा बीमा (Traditional)

1. सिर्फ 5 प्रीमियम प्लान

₹ 600	₹ 1,200	₹ 2,400	₹ 4,800	₹ 9,600

2. बीमा धन

₹ 25,000	₹ 50,000	₹ 1,00,000	₹ 2,00,000	₹ 4,00,000

3. बीमा धन दुर्घटना मृत्यु दर

₹ 50,000	₹ 1,00,000	₹ 2,00,000	₹ 4,00,000	₹ 8,00,000

4. प्रवेश आयु सीमा - 18 से 65 वर्ष।
5. 5 साल तक प्रीमियम अवधि।
6. हाथों हाथ बीमा
7. टैक्स में बचत, टैक्स फ्री लाभ स्कीम
8. पिछले दो सालों से 8.50% से ज्यादा का प्रतिफल / लाभांश घोषित किया गया।

QUESTIONS

1. Discuss the main proviso of Industrial Life Insurance.
2. 'Group Life Insurance is becoming more popular', discuss its appealing feature.
3. 'Disability and Pension Plans are useful to under-privileged,'—comment it.
4. What is Credit Insurance and Surety? Discuss their salient features.
5. Examine the background of credit insurance and surety.
6. Explain the functions of Credit Insurance.
7. What are the types of Credit Insurance? Explain.
8. Illustrate the role of reinsurance in Credit Insurance and Surety.
9. Examine the progress of credit insurance in India.

47

REINSURANCE

Reinsurance is an arrangement whereby an original insurer who has insured a risk insures a part of that risk again with another insurer, that is to say, reinsures a part of the risk in order to diminish his own liability. The difference between the retention and the total amount of acceptance is reinsured. The limiting or retention and effecting of reinsurance brings about a wider distribution of the risks and secures to the insurer the full advantages of the law of average. It creates an automatic capacities to accept a large amount of risks.

Insurance is a contract between the insurer and the original insured. Reinsurance is a contract between the reinsured (the insurer) and the reinsurer.

Therefore, the original insured is not a party to the contract of reinsurance. Now, if insurer goes into liquidation can the original insured sue the reinsurer for recovery of loss under the policy?

This question involves the protection of the rights of the reinsured's policyholders. In America, a special provision is made in the reinsurance contracts to safeguard the interests of the reinsured's policyholder, that is the original insured. A specific clause called 'loss assumption clause' is incorporated in the body of the reinsurance contract whereby the original insured can recover his loss on the policy from the reinsurers, if the reinsured goes into liquidation.

Limits

It is usual to fix a limit up to which the insurer is prepared to lose on risks in a specified class. The limit depends upon the following circumstances:

1. The financial status and premium income of the insurer. A new insurer with small premium income cannot afford to sustain a loss which might be borne with ease by established insurer with ample reserve.
2. The experienced in a particular class of risk:
   (*i*) The degree of the fire hazard present.
   (*ii*) The extent of the damage likely to be sustained.
   (*iii*) The fire extinguishing facilities available.
3. The limit will vary according to the nature and size of the concerns proposing for insurance.
4. Location and other factors affecting the risk are also taken into account while calculating the amount of limit.

Retention

After deciding the limit, retention can be easily fixed. Retention is the amount of maximum liability which the insurer can assume on a particular risk. The retention is determined according to the class to which it belongs and to its merit and demerits. The retention is also decided upon the total amount of insurance in force, the average size of its policies and the amount of surplus fund available with it. It also depends upon the size of company, age of issue, the type of policy and the class of risk. Retention is also known as 'limit' or 'Net holding' of the insurer. The 'Limit' is based on physical nature of the risk, construction and occupancy, probability to fire, exposure, fire protection, situation of risk, conflagration (adjoining) hazards, special peril Maximum Probable Loss (PML) is also influencing factor of deciding Maximum Amount of Loss (MAL) for the insurer. The different between these two is for reinsurance.

Reinsurance

Reinsurance is the transfer of insurance business from one insurer to another. The insurer transferring the business is called the 'principal' or ceding or original office and the office to which the business is transferred is called for 'reinsurer or guaranteeing office'. It is also a contract of indemnity. The original company must disclose all the material facts to the reinsurer. At the time of loss the reinsurer indemnifies the loss up to the amount of reinsurance. The reinsurance amount is obtained by deducting retention amount from the original policy amount.

Advantages of Reinsurance

1. The original insurer can accept the risk to the extent of his limit. In absence of reinsurance, a person desiring a large amount of insurance will have to take a number of policies from several insurers. This reinsurance contract makes it possible to purchase only one policy from an insurer.
2. Reinsurance makes it possible to accept each risk for the very amount desired by the proposer and to transfer the excess above the 'retention limit' to another insurer.
3. The reinsurance gives the benefit of the greater stability resulting from a widespread of business. By accepting many risks and scaling down, by reinsurance, all those that are larger than the normal carrying capacity of the insurer justifies, certainty in business is substituted for uncertainty through the better application of the law of average.
4. The reinsurance makes stability in underwriting and consistency in underwriting results over a period.
5. It provides a safeguard against serious effects of conflagration.
6. The reinsurance has the effect of stabilizing income and losses over a period of years.

METHODS OF REINSURANCE

1. Shopping or 'Street' Reinsurance

Under this method, there is no standing agreement regarding reinsuring of risk of one company by the other. Each policy is treated on an individual basis. The reinsurer is sought only when the need of reinsurance on a policy arises. The reinsurer serutinises each case on its merits and may accept the risk on any terms and conditions or may decline it. Since the ceding company is not certain about the availability of reinsurance and a term, it will exercise a greater care in selecing the risk.

2. Facultative Reinsurance

The essential feature of this method is that each individual risk is submitted by the ceding office to the reinsurer who can accept or decline whatever sum they consider appropriate subject to the amount of their acceptance being approved by the ceding office. The reinsurer is offered the particulars of original contract. The reinsurer will see the plan and report on the risk offered for reinsurance. The reinsurer may qualify the acceptance subject to plan and report. The ceding office may retain certain amount on the insurance. The agreement does not make it binding upon the reinsuring company to provide reinsurance on a particular risk. The ceding office is under no obligation to submit all its business to the insurer. When reinsurance facultatively, the insurer may obtain reinsurance coverage before accepting to insurer a client to ensure that the reinsurance term do not exceed those applying to direct insurance and to back up the judgment of the original underwrite at the insurer's office who will after benefit from the reinsurer.

This method differs from the 'Shopping' in the sense that the two companies are agreed in advance as to the form in which risks, premium, terms and other details are to be submitted. Thus, many expenses connected with 'shopping' are reduced. Under this method also, the ceding office may have to wait before accepting the original risk till it is accepted for insurance. When the underwriting rules of the two companies are similar and the plan of insurance seems to be fairly satisfactory, it can be assumed with reasonable safety that the required reinsurance will be available.

The ceding office knowing that the risk may also be declined for reinsurance will be more careful in accepting the original risk and may avoid the higher risk. It may receive valuable advice from the reinsurer.

Facultative reinsurance policies

As mentioned earlier, a reinsurance policy is essentially different from a reinsurance contract. A reinsurance policy is in respect of risk which is already written and the reinsurance is required for limits in excess of net retention limits and other reinsurance capacities. It is not obligatory for the reinsured to effect facultative reinsurances and the reinsurers have option open to accept or reject a risk. Facultative reinsurances are of two types, *viz*., poro rata or Contributing Facultative Reinsurance and Facultative Excess of Loss Reinsurance. Reinsurance policies are contracts for risks already written and not for future risks to be written.

A reinsurance policy is issued under Facultative reinsurance and such a policy contains detailed description of the risk, its location, its period of coverage, perils covered, exclusions if any, territorial scope, premium rate, limits of liability, reinsurance commission, etc. Such policy is for each individual risk reinsured. Generally, there is a convention of not providing profit commission on such reinsurances. Premium and losses are accounted separately as provided therein.

Reinsurance Treaties and Reinsurance policies are not synonymous; reinsurance treaties are contracts for insurance and reinsurance policies or cessions are contracts of insurance.

Facultative reinsurance is not for creation of capacity but it is for risks already underwritten, where limits are beyond the capacity of the insurer. It is a contract of insurance by way of a reinsurance policy for current single risk.

Under Reinsurance Treaty method, the reinsurance contract is for creation of capacity for future portfolio of risk to be underwritten and declared therein.

Again, under Quota Share treaty and Excess of Loss treaty the risk accepted by the ceding office of insurer are automatically reinsured according to the terms of the treaty. But under Surplus treaties, a risk is reinsured once it crosses the retained limit of liability. Thus under Surplus treaties the reinsured has to declare a risk by an entry on bordereau.

Open covers or Automatic Facultative covers or Facultative obligatory covers are agreements to make future reinsurance where the reinsured has got an option to declare a risk but, once declared, the reinsurer has to accept it as on obligation under the contract. Thus such reinsurance is 'Facultative' for reinsured but 'Obligatory' for the reinsurer.

3. Automatic or Treaty Reinsurance

Under this method, there is an agreement between the ceding office and reinsurer office that the amount of insurance on a policy above the retention of the ceding office shall be submitted by it for reinsurance and the same shall be accepted by the reinsuring company. As soon as the original contract is completed the excess above retention amount becomes automatically reinsured under the agreement. The ceding office need not even inform the reinsuring office immediately that a risk has been accepted by it. The terms and conditions of the reinsurance contract are the same as of the original insurance contract. The maximum reinsurance amount acceptable to the reinsurer bears a definite relationship with the retention limit of a ceding company.

TREATIES ARE OF THREE TYPES

(*i*) Quota Share Treaty

Under this method, the ceding insurer is bound to cede and the reinsurer is bound to accept a fixed share of every risk coming within the scope of the treaty. This treaty is used where the direct insurer is new in the field with little or no past experience or has had adverse experience in the past. This method is favourable to the reinsurers. The liability of the reinsurer attaches as soon as the ceding office assumes the risk. Then the ceding office furnishes the accepting office with full particulars of each cession, copies of proposal papers. It does not give the reinsurer an option of acceptance or rejection. It enables the reinsurer to consider any marked divergence of underwriting standards and if persistent to its disadvantage, it may indicate the need for revision or cancellation of the treaty in respect of new business.

(*ii*) The Surplus Treaty

The purpose of this treaty is to reinsure the surplus of a risk beyond the amount of the ceding insurer's retention. Up to what extent the surplus can be reinsured is determined by the size of the treaty measured in terms of lines—not retention. There may be second surplus treaty to absorb the amounts which are beyond the capacity of the first surplus treaty.

The scope of treaty is defined with the scope of geographical area, class of business, etc. The liability of the insurer commences obligatorily and simultaneously with that of the ceding insurer as soon as retention of the ceding insurer is exceeded. The ceding insurer has the right to demand immediate payment from the reinsurer of the latter's share of any loss exceeding an agreed value.

There may be two problems under this method

(*a*) There may be selection against the reinsurer as the ceding insurer will retain more of the better type of business with type result that the bulk of the business under a treaty will be of an inferior nature.

(*b*) There may be problem of accumulation of acceptances.

(*iii*) Excess of Loss Treaty

This method provides against catastrophic loss. The excess of loss reinsurance comes into operation when the total net loss suffered by the insured due to one event exceeds the figure agreed in the treaty. Such excess of the amount or a proportion of it, being paid by the reinsurer subject to a maximum limit. The net loss means the loss computed after taking into account recoveries from facultative and treaty reinsurers. If the total net loss exceeds the maximum limit provided in the treaty the excess amount is paid by the reinsurer. The premium depends upon the nature and extent of reinsurance.

ADVANTAGES OF TREATY METHOD OVER FACULTATIVE

1. The Treaty-method provides obligatory and automatic nature of reinsurance acceptances. The reinsurer cannot decline to accept any cession coming within its scope.
2. The risk commences simultaneously with that of the ceding insurer. Under the facultative method, the reinsurance cover operates only from the time the reinsurer accepts the risk.
3. The treaty method involves much less clerical work and costs as compared to the costs involves in the facultative reinsurance.
4. The rights and obligations of each party are clearly defined in the treaty agreement, whereas in facultative, it has not been so easy.
5. The treaty-method ensure a constant and regular flow of business.

4. "Pool or Syndicate Method"

Under this method, a number of insurer agrees to pool together all their business to a leading office and the payment is made by this leading office. The profit of this association is distributed amongst the insurers according to their shares to the business.

Reinsurance Treaty Contracts

A reinsurance treaty is a contract for reinsurances. A set of terms and conditions for a given class of business is provided and the reinsurance capacity is created for the reinsured to underwrite any risk which will be written in future. As opposed to facultative reinsurance it is meant to create capacity and it gives a reinsurance facility to cede risks after retentions. All future writing of risks has got an automatic, simultaneous and continuous reinsurance cover.

A reinsurance treaty is an agreement for twelve months between the reinsured on one part and the reinsurer on the other whereby the reinsured agrees to cede and the reinsurer agrees to accept the reinsurance business, pursuant to the provisions.

Treaty reinsurance is a contract for future reinsurance. It is offered before its inception and main terms of the treaty are specified on a SLIP. The prospective reinsurer goes through the slip and decides his acceptance. After its acceptance, the reinsurer signs one copy of the slip and returns it to the reinsured. Such signed slip is called a Binder, when a broker is given an order for placement of a treaty. When he completes his order he issues a Cover Note to the reinsured giving list of participating reinsurers along with slip terms of the treaty. The reinsured then issues full contract wording called Treaty Document or Treaty Wording to each reinsurer. There should not be any discrepancy between the slip terms and the terms in the contract. Any such discrepancy is to be cleared off before executing the Treaty Document.

In the event of any discrepancy between the slip and the treaty document discovered subsequent to signing, in strict legal sense, document supercedes the slip.

Reinsurance treaties are placed before the inception of the treaty year on the basis of a slip which summarises 'main' terms and conditions of the treaty arrangement, Generally, it contains name of the company, type of treaty, class of business, perils covered, territorial scope, retention, limits of reinsurance cession, commission percentage, profit comission formula and percentage, portfolio provision or reserve provision, if any with interest (less tax) on reserves, cash loss limits, frequency of accounts rendering and underwriting information with mention of specific exclusions essential for the reinsurer's acceptance. Once the treaty is placed on the basis of the slip, the broker prepares a cover note with names and shares of reinsurers. Such cover note serves the basis of reinsurance agreement and later on treaty wording is preparted. The treaty wording is to be corrected if there is any error in the main terms as compared to the slip.

If the slip is wrong and wording is correct, the ceding company must give satisfactory explanation and obtain agreement of the leader to be followed by other reinsurers.

Treaty wordings have a number of variations in form and structure but standardised London market clauses are common in use. American market treatise contain American market standard clauses. Every market has its own peculiar provisions of law and the wordings may vary. Again, wordings will vary according to type of treaties as shown in the following chart:

TREATIES

- Proportional
  - Quota Share / Surplus
    - Direct Business
    - Retro Business
  - Facob. Open Covers
- Non-Proportional
  - Working XL
  - Cata XL
  - Stop Loss XL
  - XL Pools

Again, from class to class there will be variation of clauses in treaty wordings. Therefore, the best way, according to me, is to generalise common pattern of treaty wording and then add special clauses peculiar to the type of treaty or particular class of business.

The Reinsurance Officers Association has made valuable contribution to standardise Treaty Wording in late seventies and eighties. With computerisation and standardization, Treaty Clauses are drafted and are available in a CD.

After WTC attack losses, leading global reinsurers like Munich Re/ Swiss Re have drafted Terrorism Exclusion Clauses, Political Risks Exclusion Clauses and introduced Treaty Slip formats with attached main clauses to avoid any misgiving. Such Treaty Slips are standardised by them and run into 100 pages instead of earlier slips of 3 or 4 pages.

Some Legal Conventions

Follow the Fortune Clause means Reinsurers follow Legal and Technical Fortune of the Reinsured in respect of claims settlements.

Reinsurers do not follow Exgratia payment of claims.

Claims Co-Operation Clauses provide that Reinsured must seek Reinsurer's advices before entering into litigation in respect of a disputed claim.

Claims payable by Reinsurers **can be more than TSI** to the extent of legal expenses, court awards, punitive damages, etc.

Proportional Treaty Contract Clauses

- Time Clause
- Territorial Scope Clause
- Covered Perils Clause
- Exclusion Clause
- Operative Clause
- Premium Clause
- Commission Clause
- Claims Settlement Clause
- Borderaux Clause
- Accounts Clause
- Profit Commission Clause
- Inspection of Records Clause
- Error, Omissions and Alternation Clause
- Portfolio Adjustment Clause
- Reserves Clause
- Cash Loss Clause
- Arbitration Clause
- Intermediary Clause
- Insolvency Clause
- Currency Conversion Clause
- Cut-Through Clause
- Special Termination Clause like Sun-Set Clause

Changes by Way of Addendum

XL Treaties : Some clauses in addition to common clauses between proportional Treaties and XL Treaties.

- Definition of Loss Occurrence
- Ultimate Net Loss Clause
- Net Retained Lines Clause

- Definition of GNPI Clause
- Reinstatement Clause
- Extended Expiration Clause
- Notification of Claims and Loss Settlement Clause

PRACTICAL EXAMPLE

Premium

The reinsurance premium paid by the ceding insurer to the reinsurer is a percentage of original premium paid by the insured. The percentage paid to the reinsurer is the same as the percentage of the sum insured ceded by the ceding company.

Example 1

Ceding company reinsurer

sum assured	₹ 20,000	₹ 5000	₹15,000
premium	₹ 40	₹10	₹ 30

Quota share

The quota share treaty is an automatic reinsurance whereby the ceding insurer is bound to part with a fixed percentage of every risk written by it. The same percentage is applied to every risk to determine cession in the class of insurance as reinsured no matter how large or small the sum insured and irrespective of whether the risk is 'good' or 'bad'. But in the case of surplus method, the percentage reinsured varies with each risk. If there is 90% quota share treaty:

Example 2

	case 1	*case 2*	*case 3*
	Rs	₹	₹
Sum Assured	5,000	20,000	80,000
Ceding Company	500	2,000	8,000
Reinsurer	4,500	18,000	72,000

The premium and claim will be shared according to the ceding company will received 10% and reinsurer will receive 90%.

Claims

The claim falling within the scope of a treaty will be shared between the ceding insurer and the reinsurer in the same proportions as the original sum insured was reinsured.

Example 3

	Sum Assured	*Loss*
Ceding Company retained	₹ 40,000	₹ 2000
Ceded to Surplus Treaty	5000	250
	35,000	1750

If there are more than one reinsurer. They will share the loss in proportion to their share to sum assured

Example 4

	Sum Assured	*Loss*
	₹ 50,000	₹ 5,000
Ceding company	5000	500
Reinsurer A	20,000	2,000
Reinsurer B	25,000	2,500

The premium is also shared in proportion to the Sum Assured.

Evolution of Excess of Loss Reinsurance

In the history of the business, up to the middle of the nineteenth century, reinsurance was effected between one direct insurer and another, at first on facultative basis, subsequently by treaty and for a good many years by both methods concurrently. But, though the methods of reinsurance continued for many years on these lines, the march of events brought certain inevitable developments which had a marked effect on the mechnism of risk transfer. Sharing of risk began changing the forms due to increased nature and complexity of risk requiring reduction of the magnitude of exposure, initially on micro basis, risk by risk, later on macro form on portfolio basis. While facultative reinsurance reduces peak exposure, surplus and quota share treaty reduce individual exposure. Yet there is another side to the picture of risk accumulation. Increased loss ratio arising from attrition of losses together with increased magnitude of loss caused by several risks exposed to a single catastrophic event arising from conflagration or natural disaster, gave rise to the emergence of excess of loss reinsurance. This is formed on non-proportional basis to provide protection of balance sheet of the ceding company. Therefore, while the proportional treaty which is a contributory type is more of a "Risk Reinsurance", the excesss of loss insurance which is non-contributory is a form of "Loss reinsurance". The non-proportional covers are thus based, not on the Sum Assured, but on the claims cost or loss portfolio of the reassured. This cost could be measured in various ways and the covers are:

- Individual risk exposure on First Loss basis,
- Cost of single claim on any one risk on a given portfolio,
- Cost of claim or series of claims caused by a single event,
- Cost of claim caused by a "second event",
- Unknown accumulation of the entire portfolio comprising all classes,
- Aggregate cost of all claims in any one year,
- Cost of claims exceeding available Indemnity and
- Reinstatement premium protection.

Compulsory Tarrff and IRDA

The IRDA is yet to roll-out and approve the phased dismantling of the prevalent tariff system and usher in market-based pricing. The challenge in this endeavour will be to develop a database of reliable premium and claims information to which insurance pricing can be pegged. While India's insurance market has historically lacked such as a database, the Tariff Advisory Committee has painstakingly compiled this information which will help insurers and reinsurers with their rate-making decisions in the long run.

Mandatory Reinsurance Cessions

The purpose of compulsory cessions has been to maximize retentions within the country while the market was in the process of restructing. Nevertheless, this is a restrictive practice and permits limited flexibility in the reinsurance portfolio of domestic entities. IRDA's reinsurance advisory committee proposed a gradual reduction of 5 percent on a year on year basis; however, the IRDA is yet undertake concrete steps to enforce the comittee's recommendations.

Nuclear Insurance Pool in Indfia:

The nuclear suppliers groups agreements have led to opening up the industry for foreign players but the agreements cannot be implemented unless we have the defined limits of liability in case of accidents. This was brought in with the passing of The Civil Liability for Nuclear Damage Act.

The liability upto the specified limit can be arranged by creating a fund of 1500 cr. by the nuclear industry in India with the central government addressing anything over this level. A better alternative would be to make arrangements in the form of insurance up to the limits as provided by the law as is the global practice. The insurance industry along with the nuclear industry can come together to develop the Nuclear Insurance Pool with adequate capacity garnered locally as well as from the international market.

The pool can provide cover to the operators to the extent required by the legislation that is 1500 cr. per incident per operator. Beyond the pool limit the state normally accepts responsibility as insurer of last resort upto a limit of SDRs 300 mn. Balance if any will be passed on to "Convention for Supplementary Compensation".

Inernational insurers and reinsurers who provide capacity for the insurance of these nuclear facilities insist on inspection of the plants by global nuclear pool agencies. In India apparently there is a restriction on inspection of facilities by international pools. Periodic inspections are carried out by specialist teams for the purpose of identifying insurance with the aspects of nuclear safety.

Global Reinsurance Market:

Global RI market would iclude (1) Re insurance treaties, (2) Internal pools (terrorism), (3) Industry pools (nuclear risks), (4) Non-voluntary pools (Motor TP Pool) and (5) Reciprocal insurance exchanges (Rotterdam and Chicago). For the Indian market, the European reinsurers are the major sources for placing reinsurance, followed by the London market. While reinsurance capacities are abundant in Europe, the infrastructure and man-power required for palcement and servicing reinsurance business is dominated by the professional UK broking community. Rating of reinsurers by recognized international rating agencies is relied upon for the financial strength of a reinsurer.

Professional reinsurance brokers are big in reinsurance to offer advisory services about the nature of the RI Kontract and the quality of hte reinsurer, and they assist in negotiating the most favorable price and conditions. But they would charge for their services. London brokers command a lot of rcspcct for their integrity, professional conduct and expertise and are much sought after in reinsurance.

There are too many business incentives for 'no entry', without any apparent disincentives to access the Indian reinsurance market! Reinsurance placements are an annual feature, and do not involve soil-presence to nurture relationships. Indian business is growing in Motor and Health, which do not need reinsurance in a big way. Risks of huge values will have to ncessarily come to Europe, as local capacity is limited. Hence opening liaison offices to making and influencing insurer-friends is considered as good enough for their interests.

Lacking the active presence of professional risk-sharing foreign reinsurers, on the Indian soil, there is only the GIC, which can really change the market dynamics, and correct the operating market deficiencies. The GIC now has a free run of Indian reinsurance business, with obligatory cessions of 10% automatically flowing in. But even the GIC considers the obligatory cessions, as burdensome and is pursuing global business (44%) to grow its premiums. If the GIC is shunning the local market, what signals are we sending?

IRDA Regulations

All insurers in India can write inward reinsurance business from other domestic insurers and from overseas. They must have a well defined underwriting policy for underwriting inward reinsurance business. The insurer needs to ensure that decisions on acceptance for reinsurance business are made by person with necessary knowledge and experience. The insurer is required to file with the IRDA a note his underwriting policy.

QUESTIONS

1. Discuss the methods of reinsurance.
2. What are the principles of reinsurance ?

48

CORPORATE GOVERNANCE

The insurance and consumer community is well protected by good corporate governance. There is need to involve consumers to express their responses through an effective method. The dominant shareholders should work for the interests of the consumers and not purely in their self interest. There is need to develop an effective mechanism to cheek corporate behaviour. Only market mechanism and regulatory frameworks cannot control their behaviour. Till market mechanism, the company has accumulated sufficient funds of policyholders and declare himself insolvent. Thus, the financial conditions of consumers are made unfavourable.

The management is made responsible for some failures towards consumers' interest whereas the shareholders are enjoying their supremacy. The healthy relationship between policyholders and shareholders should be developed for the economic and social development of country. The Board of shareholders and Management must see that the policyholders' interests are fully served by the company. The corporate Governance in Indian Insurance Companies have got momentum but its progress is very slow as the management is not very efficient. There are lack of experienced directors, inadequate information systems, inadequate system of control, individual and accountability is not developed. Ownership structure and lack of enforcement capabilities have caused poor governance.

COMPONENTS OF CORPORATE GOVERNANCE

The corporate governance is mainly concern with how ownership influence, promoting corporate fairness, transparency ana accountability Briefly, Corporate Governance means doing everything, to improve relationship between companies and their shareholders to improve the quality. If directors, to encourage people to think long-term, to ensure that information needs of all stakeholders. Corporate Governance becomes an organise system when companies are directed and controlled by the management in the best interest of the stakeholders and insuring greater transparency and financial reporting. The investors' confidence should be instilled and not shaken by the management practices. Corporate Governance in insurance companies makes corporate entities, institutional investment and business opportunity.

Insurance Companies are important constituent of Corporate Governance. Keeping an open mind, listening and learning from others, ready to share ideas and thoughts recognising and rewarding cooperation and franchise, development skill of employees. Concerned for delivering on promises inducing teamwork and inspiring management to their best are the various examples of corporate Governance.

TRANSPARENCY

The insurers should develop transparency of financial resources. The examples of transparency present in public sector *i.e.* LIC and GIC have been a guide line for the private insurers. The Board of Directors consists one Chairman (CMD). Two Executive Directors, three Nominee Directors and four independent Directors. The Board of Directors has set up *Audit Committees, Investment Committees, IT Committees and, Personnel and Administration Committees* apart from *policy-holders' Council* at divisional level and *Zonal Advisory Board* at Zonal Office.

The corporate performance is subject to public scrutiny. Insurance companies are directly and indirectly link with banking industry, financial markets and the industrial and agricultural development alongwith the protection of policyholders' interest. They are accountable to policy-holders and shareholders. The competitive atmosphere of insurance industry forces them to cut down their costs of operation.

Efficient and Independent—Directors

Directors are link between policyholders and shareholders. Their primary duty is to monitor management on behalf of the shareholders as well as for the interest of policyholders. There should be systems and mechanism to make management accountable to them. The directors must exercise due deligence in making decisions by collecting adequate information. They should supervise and approve financial objectives, major strategies and plans. They have to review the internal control system to mitigate risk exposures. The Board is responsible for the overall picture and not the daily business decisions. It has to create momentum, movement, improvement and direction. The Board should have information of financial statements, market intelligence, competitors role, regulations, measures, management, performance.

Management is dominant in day to day functionary. It has to enhance creativity and productivity. Management is accountable to Board of Directors which oversees whether management is effective and satisfying the consumers', policyholders and employees' interests. In this context Chief Executive Officer (CEO) is the main functioning body. His ability, expertise, resources, motivation and authority are sufficient for making the company grow alongwith servicing the interests of policyholders and shareholder. His decision should not invite conflicts. His accountable for within be should watch himself to make the appropriate decisions according to changing times and needs.

The most important aspects of Corporate Governance are Supervision of Management through proper discharge of its statutory responsibility, enforcement of effective internal control systems ensuring operation and monitoring of adequate and proper risk management and handling consumers grievances. The management should see that quality of the corporate Governance is very high. The insurance companies should follow the stricter norms of Corporate Governance formulate by SEBI.

The marketing systems have been self regulatory to monitor the activities of insurance companies apart from the IRDA regulations, SEBI guidelines and Insurance Acts. Insurers are an important class of institutional investors. It is needed to control the activities of management for investment system. They are required to observe the investment principles of safety, solvency and liquidity etc. RBI has Forex control. They have to develop public trust and confidence apart from strictly following the provisions of various rules and regulations for governing insurance companies.

The insurers should fairly deal with employees insured people and others avoiding manipulation, comcealment, abuse of priviledged information, misrepresentation of material facts and unfair dealings. There should be willing compliance with the law, refusal to take unfair advantages, concern and respect for others, prevention of harm, trustworthiness, benevolence and fairness.

NEED OF CORPORATE GOVERNANCE IN INSURANCE INDUSTRY

Insurance industry bears a fiduciary relationship with policyholders and has long term performances. The honesty and integrity of insurers are paramount important as the industry has financial functions. Officers and employees can break the regulatory measures and enjoy the money of policyholder. No insurer will be successful unless his integrity is tested as sound and useful for the effective performances of the functions. The need of Corporate Governance is realised for confidence building change-management, investment and viability.

Confidence

Insurance is based on confidence. New insurance companies can develop only if the old insurance companies have demonstrated honestly and integrity. For example, LIC has proved the insurance has sorereign guarantee. Long-term contract is built only on confidence. Insurance particularly life insurance is long-term contract. There should be benchmark standards against which insurers should demonstrate public image.

Change Management

Insurance companies are facing several changes in the society. They have to cope with the changes and come forward to challenge the changes. It has been observed that insurance industry is growing faster than GDP. Specialised insurance companies are entering in the market. Many foreign companies have entered in India to conduct insurance business. Health insurance is becoming a need of the hour. The insurance companies have to manage themselves for maintaining safety and solvency. Non-insurers are growing in detarrified era challenging their fair play, policyholders servicing and transparency.

Investment

Insurance companies manage their funds through investment which involves safety solvency risk management and protection of policyholders' interest. The acturial experiences also help decide insurance expansion. It graples greater challenges such as increasing number of claims. There is need of good governance standard against which the companies conduct and performance would get measured against these backdrops. They have to live up with securities market and governing rules. SEBI has formulated several rules and regulation which have to be followed by the insurer.

Viability

The insurers have to prove their viability. Many new and existing companies now enter in the insurance business. Foreign, insurance companies have to prove their viability. Public Sector insurers have proved their viability and private sector insurers have to follow them. They have to operate in a safe and sound manner and in accordance with the applicable rules and regulations.

Social Responsibility

Approaches to Corporate Social Accounting & Reporting

Descriptive	Programme Management
	Corporate Rating
Quantitative	C.B. Analysis
	Se Statement
	Input Cost
	Index Cost
Others	Social Audit by Group
	Goal oriented
	Pictorial

Measurement of Social Benefits

Steps		*Particulars*	*Effect*
1. Input		Socially significant Action and cost	Installation of Equipment
2. Process	(*a*)	psychological changes in peoples effected	Clear Air, better Health, positive felling for the area
	(*b*)	Physical changes	More people try to move to the area.
3. Output		Behavioural change	
4. Economic		(Measured by Accounting)	

ANALYSIS OF BALANCE SHEET

Both the "Financial Balance Sheet" and "Social Balance Sheet" are analysed mainly to evaluate the following:

Four Major Aspects

Aspects	*Financial Balance Sheet*	*Social Balance Sheet*
1. Scale and Work of resources	Net-worth *i.e.*, Amount invested in business	Resources required and resources available for different projects.
2. Productivity	Earnings on capital employed	Degree of social impact per unit of resource invested.
3. Liquidity or flexibility of resources	Current nation (Current assets) (Current liabilities)	Capacity to adopt to social changes and disinvest.
4. Efficiency	Return on Assets	Benefits to be measured by alternatives.

Associates, Inc. of Social and Financial Balance Sheet

	Amount	*Amount*
1. Staff Assets		
Staff Available with one year	...	...
Staff Available after one year	...	...
Training Investment	...	...
Less: Accumulated Training Obsolescence	...	...
Total Staff Assets	...	...
Total Organisational assets	...	...
2. Use of public Goods		
Public Services paid for through taxes (Net of Consumption)	...	...
3. Financial Assets		
Cash	...	...
Accounts Receivable Net	...	...
Untill add contract costs and fees	...	...
Other current financial assets	...	...
Other Long-Term Financial assets	...	...
Total Financial Assets	...	...
4. Physical Assets	...	...
Land	...	...
Buildings	...	...
Improvements	...	...
Equipment, Furniture & Fixtures	...	...
Loss: Accumulated Appreciation	...	...
Total physical Assets	...	...
Total Assets	...	...

* Social Asset sand liabilities are identified in black types, and physical and financial assets and liabilities are indicated in lighter types.

I. Liabilities and Equity		
1. Staff Liabilities		
Staff wages payable	...	...
2. Organisational Liabilities		
Organisations Financing Requirements	...	...
3. Public Liabilities		
Environmental Resources Used through pollution	...	...
Electricity	...	...
Commuting	...	...
Other	...	...
Total Public Liabilities		
4. Financial Liabilities		
Notes Payable (Short-term)	...	...
Accounts Expenses	...	...
Federal Income Taxes	...	...
Reformed Federal Income Taxes	...	...
Household Interest in Property	...	...
Total Financial Liabilities	...	...
5. Stockholder's Equity		
Common Stock	...	...
Additional paid-in Capital	...	...
Retained Earnings	...	...
Total Stockholder's Equity	...	...
6. Society's Equity		
Society's Equity generated by increases ( ) in net social assets	...	...

Abt Associate, Inc. Social and Financial Income Statement

	Amount	*Amount*
(Income)		
1. to company / Stockholders		
Contract Revenue and other Income	...	...
Federal Services Consumed	...	...
State Service Consumed	...	...
Local Services Consumed	...	...
Developmental Resources Need through pollution	...	...
Electricity	...	...
Commuting	...	...
Other	...	...
Total	...	...

*Net Social Income and expenditure are indicate in black type.

2. To Staff		
Salaries for time period	...	...
Current Advancement and Holidays	...	...
Health and Life Insurance	...	...

Sick Leave	...	...
Services	...	...
Facility of Space	...	...
Child care	...	...
Credit Union	...	...
Total	...	...
3. To Clients/General Public		
Value of Contract work at cost	...	...
Staff Overtime Worked but not paid	...	...
Federal taxes paid by company	...	...
State and Federal tax with of net jobs created	...	...
State Taxes paid by Company	...	...
Contribution to knowledge (publications)	...	...
Total	...	...
4. To Community	...	...
Local taxes paid by company	...	...
Local Tax worth of net jobs created	...	...
Environment Improvements	...	...
Total	...	...
Costs (Expenditures)		
1. No Company Stockholders		
Salaries Paid (Exclusive of Training on Fringe Benefits)	...	...
Training Investment in Staff	...	...
Direct Contract Costs	...	...
Overhead/General and Administrative	...	...
Expenditure not Item	...	...
Vocation and Holidays	...	...
Improvements, Space and Environment	...	...
Federal Taxes paid	...	...
Health and Life Insurance	...	...
Sick Leave	...	...
State Taxes paid	...	...
Local Taxes paid	...	...
Services	...	...
Child Care	...	...
Company School and Tuition Reimbursement	...	...
Fiscal and Public offerings of Stock	...	...
Interest Payments	...	...
Income Foregone an paid-in Capital	...	...
Total		
2. To Staff		
Opportunity Costs of Total Time Worked	...	...
Absence of Retirement Income plan	...	...
Day-offs and involuntary termination	...	...
Inequality of Opportunity	...	...

Uncompensated losses through theft	...	...
Total	...	...
3. To Clients/General public	...	...
Cost of contracted work	...	...
Federal services consumed	...	...
State Services consumed	...	...
Environmentai Resources used through pollution	...	...
Electricity	...	...
Commuting	...	...
Other	...	...
Total	...	...
4. To Community		
Local Services consumed	...	...
Total	...	...
NET INCOME	...	...
5. To Community/Shareholders		
Financial	...	...
Social	...	...
2. To Staff		
3. To Clients		
4. To Community	...	...
Total Net Social Income	...	...
Total Net Social and Financial Income Generated by Company Operations	...	...

II. SOCIO-ECONOMIC OPERATING MODEL—BY DAVID D.F. LINOWES

Statement Model – By David Lionwes Operating

Statement model presents the positive and negative aspects of its social activities. The positive aspects are broadly termed as, 'Social Benefits' and negative aspects as 'Social Costs'. The net social contribution of a firm is represented by the difference between social benefits and social costs. Under this model, social income statement and social balance sheet are not prepared. Instead, the firm presents, focusses the negative and positive aspects of social activities.

David Linowes concept of 'Social-economic Operating Statement' aims at focussing on 'what the corporation has done for the society on the one hand' and 'what it has failed to do on the other'. He suggested that a firm should prepares social statement periodically showing expenditure made for improvement in social areas, offset against the cost of programmes which were not undertaken but which would have resulted in improvement.

Linowes 'Socio-Economic Statement' contains the following sections:

— Section related with people;

— Section related with environment;

— Section product related with

and the net figure are reported within each section and a net total is also reported before the entity for the period.

The operating statement model has some advantages. These are: (*i*) it includes detriments in the statement (*ii*) it can be used for comparative analysis of firms within an industry and also for inter-industry comparability. But the main weakness of this model is the assumption that total cost measures the total benefits of the programme which is not true.

Socio-Economic Operating Statement for the year ended December 31, 19 ....

I. Relations with people:

A. Improvements:

1. Training programme for handicapped worked.
2. Contribution to black college.
3. Extra turnover costs because of minority hiring programme.
4. Cost of Nursery School for children of employees, voluntarily set up.

B. Less: Detriments

1. Postponed installing new safety devices on cutting machines (cost of the devices).

C. Net Improvement Deficit people actions for the year :

II. Relation with Environment:

A. Improvements:

1. Cost of reclaiming and landscaping old dump on company property.
2. Cost of installing pollution control devices on plant and smoketacks.
3. Cost of detoxifying waste from finishing process this year.

Total Improvements:

Less: Detriments:

1. Cost that would have been incurred to relendscape strip mining site used this year.
2. Estimated cost to have installed purification process to neutralise poisonous liquid being dupmed into stream.

Net Deficit/Improvement in Environment one for the year: Relations with Product:

Improvements:

1. Salary of V.P. while serving on Government Product Safety Commission.
2. Cost of substituting leave free pait for previously used poisonous lend paint.

Total Improvement:

Less: Detriments

1. Safety device recommended by safety Council but not added to product.

Net Improvements/Deficit in product actions for the year:

Total : Socio-Economic Deficit for the year.

Add : Net cumulative socio-economic Improvements as on January 1, 19....

Grand Total Net Socio-Economic Action to December 31, 19...

Source: David F. Linowes, Strategies for Survival (New York), The presidents Association, American Management Association, Inc.

III. COST BENEFIT STATEMENT MODEL—BY RALPH W. FASTES

Ralph W. Fastes has proposed an accounting model that systematically reflects the worth of all resources consumed, including those resources are values which are free to the consuming entity (non-internalised costs of external diseconomies), and then of all benefits produced, including those that provide no compensation to the producing entity (external economies). Estates defines the two terms, social benefits and social costs in the following way:

Social Benefits—any benefit to society (or to any element of society) whether economic or non-economic, internal or external. These social benefits include those benefits provided by an entity for which it is compensated as well as those external economies and bargains for which no compensated as well as those external economies and bargains for which no compensation (or inadequate compensation) is received.

Social Cost: Any cost, sacrifice or detriment to society (or to any element of society), whether economic or non-economic, internal or external. Social costs include sacrifices for which compensation is made (such as human services used and paid for an well detriments not paid for (such as air pollution); any payments are treated separately as benefit to society.

Allocation of resources at prewent depend heavily on information provided through the financial accounting model, which excludes certain benefits (external economies) and detriments (external diseconomies). Pastes notices that the financial accounting model generally reflects the view of entity looking out, towards society; benefits (products and services) provided to society are thus indicated by the surrogate of revenue received, whereas costs are measured only by the entity's expenditure. He proposed that improved resource allocations could result from a different view-point, that of society looking towards the entity. Benefits to society, in his proposal, would then be measured by the values or utilities actually received by society (which may differ from the amount paid to the entity); while costs would reflect the full detriments to society, and not only those for which the entity pays.[21] These opposing view-points are illustrated in Table given below:

Reporting View-Points

	Utility Produced	***(Social Benefits)***	
Entity			Society
	Utility Consumed	(Social Costs)	
	Financial Reporting view point	Social Reporting view point	

Source: Ralph W. Enstes, Corporate Social Accounting, New York, John Woley & Sons, 1976, p. 93.

Estates has argued that care must be taken in defining the reporting entity or system. The term reporting entity, according to Estates, includes the organisation or corporation itself, all activities of employees carried on behalf of the entity and while 'on duty', activities of a Board of Directors and of shareholders acting, collectively for the entity. The term 'reporting entity' for reporting purposes excludes personal activities of employees, including commenting: activity of customers, including use or misuse of the product; and all other secondary or indirect effects. Estates[22], in this regard, argues:

"The proposed model is a comprehensive report of the direct effects of a single entity or society. It is not designed to show that happens (how society would be better or worse off) if the entity has not existed during the reporting period; this would require the reporting of such indirect effects as a prorate share of pollution caused by suppliers and detriments produced by users of the entity's products. A model including such information would certainly be useful but would involve substantial double counting among entities."

The present model could, in fact, reflect indirect effect, but only if they were internalised (*i.e.*, built into entity's cost and reward structure.) This would occur if (*a*) each element of society accurately measured and reported all social benefits and costs created, (*b*) each element were periodically assessed or rewarded an amount equal to its net social surplus or deficit, and (*c*) each element then adjusted the prises of its goods and service upward in response to assessments or down-ward for rewards ofcourse, these condition do not presently obtain; consequently, the proposed model reflects significant indirect effects only in footnotes.

If all significant costs and benefits are reported 'gross' netting is avoided. For example, the cost to society of human services used by the reporting entity and the benefits to society in compensation paid might logically be netted against each other, but in the proposed report each would be separately disclosed. This approach permits the disclosure of total benefits and total-costs-useful information for evaluating the total impact of the organisation on society. It also focusses attention on value separate from exchange price; the latter may disguise bargain purchase, fraud, lack of information, and various market aberrations.

However, according to ebstes, this model is somewhat idealistic and may not be presently practical for all firms the objective is to suggest a standard, a goal, for social reporting. Nevertheless, much of the information is already available in every company, and a serious effort should produce adequate estimates for completion of the report in most companies.

Social Impact Statement for the year ending December 31st

	(₹)	(₹)	(₹)
Social benefits			
Products and services provided		×××	
Payments to other elements of society:			
Employment provided (salaries and wages)	×××		
Payment for goods and other services	×××		
Taxes paid	×××		
Contributios	×××		
Dividends and interest paid	×××		
Loans and other payments	×××	×××	
Additional direct employee benefits		×××	
Staff, equipment and facility services donated		×××	
Environmental improvement		×××	
Other benefits		×××	×××
Total social benefits			×××
Social costs:			
Goods and metals required		×××	
Buildings and equipments purchases		×××	
Labour and services used		×××	
Discrimination			
In hiring (External)		×××	
In placement and promotion (internal)		×××	×××
Work-related injuries and illness			×××
Public services and facilities			×××
Other resources used			×××
Environmental damage:			
Terrain damage		×××	
Air pollution		×××	
Water pollution		×××	
Noise pollution		×××	
Solid waste		×××	
Visual and aesthetic pollution		×××	
Other environmental damage		×××	×××
Payment from other elements of society:			
Payment for good and services provided		×××	

Additional capital investment loans	×××	
Other payment received	×××	×××
Other costs		×××
Total Social Costs		×××
Social surplus (Deficit) for the year		×××
Accumulate surplus (Deficit) current year		×××
Accumulated surplus (Deficit) precious year		×××

Standard Footnotes

1. Significant indirect effects associated with inputs.
2. Significant indirect effects associated with outputs.
3. Bases for measurement and estimates.
4. Progress in areas of current social concern (such as environmental protection outlays and activities, employment and promotion of minorities and women, and energy conservation efforts).

A. Environmental Concern:

I. Contributions

1. Installation of pollution abatement equipment required by Environmental Agencies.
2. Installation of pollution equipment on a voluntary basis.
3. Reclamation of land (Mandatory of Voluntary) .
5. Aesthetics.

II. Consumption:

1. Estimate of investment required for pollution abatement equipment.
2. The following environment pollution is unavoidable to the nature of the production process.
   — Amount of Air pollution
   — (*e.g.*, tons of surphur participants per unit time)
   — Noise
   — Scenic disturbance
   — Amount of water Pollution
3. Utilisation of other physical and social environment (If quantification is not possible, a narrative description).

B. Product Concern:

I. Contributions

(*a*) Improvement in design.

(*b*) Improvement in packaging.

(*c*) Improvement in use of new material.

2. Reduction of pollution resulting from the product:

(*a*) Change in product to make it recyclable.

(*b*) Reduction in pollutive effects of using product.

II. Improvement Needed:

1. Estimated cost to fully meet the safety standards.
2. Complaints or legal cases pending resulting from the lack of product safety.

C. Human Resources:

Social Accounting and Reporting.

I. Contributions:

1. Hiring of employees from minority groups (Number of employees from each group).
2. Training programme for advancement of minorities
   (*a*) Training programme for all employees
   (*b*) Special programme for advancement of minorities.
3. Working Conditions:
   (*a*) Improvement in safety Conditions.
   (*b*) Other improvement in Working Environment.
4. Medical Plan for employees.
5. Leisure and recreation facilities for employees.

D. Community Investment:

I. Contribution.

1. Cash contributions to Educational Institutions.
2. Cash contributions to Social Institutions.
3. Cash contributions to Religious Institutions.
4. Other than cash contributions (man hours etc.).

PROSPECT OF CORPORATE GOVERNANCE IN LIC

Corporate management has become an essential feature of any organisation. It involves corporation strategies particularly marketing strategy, financial strategy and human resources strategy. The Life Insurance Corporation has failed in corporate management although it has theoretically considered its importance.

Corporate Strategies

The LIC has formulated corporate objectives in 1974 to spread life insurance business much more widely particularly in rural areas, maximize insurance linked savings, investing insurance funds for the best advantage of investors, conduct business with utmost economy, act a business of the insured public, meet the various life insurance needs, involve people of the Corporation to the best of their capability, promote sense of participation and job satisfaction. The LIC has failed to achieve the objectives, as it has not formulated proper strategies to achieve them. It has not properly analysed the impacts of environmental factors. The economic, political, cultural, social and geographical factors have been accepted as constraints. The SWOT analysis has not been applied. The threats have been accepted as blocked barriers. No attempt has been made to convert the threats into opportunities. Similarly, the weakness of LIC has not been identified for its conversion into strength. It is smoothly sailing in the ocean of abundant market opportunities. Many untapped resources are lying idle. The poverty, need of insurance, political unawareness, demographic segments natural vagaries and competition have been taken as accepted parameters of non-development. Strategic audit is naive idea in the corporation although it is essential for success of a Corporation.

Marketing Strategy

The LIC has several attractive schemes of insurance but they are least utilized. Many field force personnel are unaware of the schemes. They do not have adequate knowledge of the insurance plans. The agent and development officers are working with routine knowledge. They have become merely sellers of insurance product from door to door; "Insurance is sold and not brought" has been accepted by them. The LIC only pushing them to increase their sale from time to time through organizing seminars of Chairman's club, Zonal Manager's club, Divisional Manager's club and Branch Manager's club. The practice of organising such seminars has its utilities but many officers discourage such seminars and do not take deep interest for their success. This is the only strategy of pushing up business without caring the upgrading of their knowledge of the product, pricing, promotion and placement. There is only pushing strategy after patting their shoulders. There is no clear guidance to accomplish the objection, no positioning strategy, no customer research and no Lest marketing. After 15 years of establishment, the L.I.C. has been unknown of market penetration strategies, market development strategies, reformulation strategies and market extension strategies; product line strategies, concentric diversification strategies and so on.

Product Strategy

The LIC depends on market stretching by increasing usage of product among current users and not creating new users for the new product. The field force is more traditional and is unaware of the new insurance policies. New products are not adequately known to them. The agents who are the only business-procurers are not adopting psycho-graphic techniques of product-expansion, product modification change marketing strategy and product elimination and adoption strategy. The Central Office of LIC has done some jobs of market research but its findings have not been used by the field force.

Pricing Strategy

Pricing strategy' is rigid in the LIC. It has recently given some concessions in non-payment of regular premium. Pricing is not used for enhancing business. It believes that people have to purchase policies on the highest rate of premium because insurance is their needs. But the LIC has forgotten that insurance business has not reached to the level of being brought by purchasers. Only few policies and their rates of premium are known to the agents. The agent-manuals are not available to many agents who can understand the premium rates on their own. They totally depend on the development officer. The time lag between initiation of proposal talk and meeting with D.O. reduces the business prospects. Interest rate has been increasing till the end of the twentieth Century. Morality has declined and expenses have to be curtailed to reduce the premium rates for attracting potential prospects of insurance.

Promotion Strategy

The mass communication has been absent till 2000 in LIC Recently. It has started to educate people about its products, but it is merely half promoted. The terms and conditions of the policies are not advertised. They are left to be told by field force who do not oftenly know them. Market targets and position strategy, effective advertising, creative strategy and successful personal selling are absent in LIC. Publicity and public relations are inadequate and less appealing. Message, media and methods of promotion are not properly selected to make people aware, create desire, increase interest and behave for adopting insurance policies. Advertising effectiveness has not been measured.

Place Strategy

The objective of the LIC has been to increase insurance business to rural areas but the LIC has not adopted any dynamic place strategy. Unlike Regional Rural Bank, the LIC officers are present only in district headquarters or tehsil places. RRBs have benefited the masses at the maximum through their branches almost in every village of the country. The LIC has only theoretically decided to enhance business in rural and hitherto neglected areas. The link of people with LIC is only agents who are not properly trained. Many agents are totally unaware of LIC products and marketing techniques, channel strategy is inadequate and tardy.

Financial strategy

The cast benefits analysis is used in the LIC for launching new products but the income and outgo strategic management in inadequate. Premium income has increased significantly but its collection is incurring float cost and opportunity-cost. Premium collected by the agents are not received by the LIC the same day because of inadequate collection staff. It is a matter of pure mathematics that if crores of rupees are lined up in float persday, the interest thereon will be not less than the rate of bank deposit. The problems of salary saving scheme are more acute. It has been observed that the premium so collected by the employers is lying with them usually for six months. The LIC argues that the employer must submit its premium in time. If LIC is not very serious about collection of its own money, how the employer would be serious for remittances. It is the greatest fault of LIC corporate management. Similarly, premium are put in only in transit. More than a crore is lost per day in float and opportunity return; similarly, interest income is not promptly collected. The problem of float lies here too.

The expenses per policy in force continue to rise without any control and restrain. My study on LIC for 1957-1986 has revealed it. It has increased recently, too. No cost control is exercised similarly advances to agents have been rising rapidly. The financial management is very poor in LIC.

Human Resource Development

The specific strategy of HRD has been adopted by the LIC. The agents and the office staff are never trained on the corporate management. They are routinely motivated on money which is obsolete strategy. The recognition, learning and personality, perception and attitude development are totally absent in the LIC. The only traditional HRD is conferences of ZMs, DMs, BNs at some costly hotel. It is purely bureaucratic strategy of development. Unless the shop floor level employees are developed, HRD is impossible. Management must involve employees participation in development process. When employees are laggard and management is leader, the gap creates conflicts. The product and people oriented leadership cannot function effectively unless people are learnt about organisational belongingness. Employees are afraid of function and management is suppressed off under top management pressure. Job involvement is satisfaction that must be known by the employees. Agents do selling without developing their marketing attitudes, perception, learning and personality. Opening of only sales Training Centres and participation in insurance. Academy by few employees do not serve the purpose. Passing of examination by agents have become a difficult task for getting agency license. They are compelled to opt the classroom teaching, which is not efficient at functional level in office. Many officers who are unable to perform better in office are sent to train the agents in STC even if STC is telling about selling but is purely absence of actuating and motivating. The office staff and agents should be actuated to function on job satisfaction after proper attitude change, perception, formation, learning practices, personality development and self-motivation. The Life Insurance Corporation of India has to adopt dynamic strategies of marketing, finance and HRD to become successful Corporate Model in Insurance industry.

IV IRDA GUIDELINES, 2009 FOR CORPORATE GOVERNANCE

1. General

1.1 Corporate Governance is understood as a system of financial and other controls in a corporate entity and broadly defines the relationship between the Board of Directors, senior management and shareholders. In case of the financial sector, where the entities accept public liabilities for fulfillment of certain contracts, the relationship in fiduciary with enhanced responsibility to protect the interests of all stakeholders. The Corporate Governance framework should clearly define the roles and responsibilities and accountability within an organization with build-in checks and balances. The importances of Corporate Governance has received emphasis in recent times since poor governance and weak internal controls have been associated with major corporate failures.

It has also been appreciated that the financial sector needs to have a more intensive governance structure in view of its role in the economic development and since the safety and financial strength of the institutions are critical for the overall strength of the financial sector on which the economic growth is built upon. As regards the insurance sector, the regulatory responsibility to protect the interest of the policy holders demands that the insurers have in place, good governance practices for maintenance of solvency, sound long term investment policy and assumption of underwriting risks on a prudential basis. The emergence of insurance companies as a part of financial conglomerates has added a further dimension to sound Corporate Governance in the insurance sector with emphasis on overall risk management across the structure and to prevent any contagion.

1.2 The Insurance Regulatory and Development Authority (IRDA) has outlined in general terms, governance responsibilities of the Board in the management of the insurance functions under various regulations notified by it covering different operational areas. It has now been decided to put them together and to issue the following comprehensive guidelines for adoption by Indian Insurance Companies. These guidelines are in addition to provisions of the Companies Act, 1956, insurance Act, 1938 and requirement of any other laws or regulations framed thereunder. Where any provisions of these guidelines appear to be in conflict with the provisions contained in any law or regulations, the legal provisions will prevail. However, where the requirements of these guidelines are more rigorous than the provisions of any law, these guidelines shall be followed. Recently IRDS has opened toll free no. 155255 to make insurance business more transparent.

2 Objectives

2.1 The objective of the guidelines is to ensure that the structure, responsibilities and functions of Board of Directors and the senior management of the company fully recognize the expectations of all stakeholders as well as well those of the regulator. The structure should take steps required to adopt sound and prudent principles and practices for the governance of the company and should have the ability to quickly address issues of non-compliance or weak oversight and controls. These guidelines therefore amplify on certain issues which are covered in the Insurance Act, 1938 and the regulations framed thereunder and include measures which are additionally considered essential by IRDA for adoption by insurance companies.

2.2 The guidelines accordingly address the various requirements broadly covering the following major structural elements of Corporate Governance in insurance companies —

- Governance structure
- Board of Directors
- Control functions
- Senior management :
  - CEO & other senior functionaries
  - Role of Appointed Actuaries
  - External Audit—Appointment of Statutory Auditors
- Disclosures
- Outsourcing
- Relationship with stakeholders
- Interaction with the Supervisor
- Whistle blowing policy

2.3 In these guidelines, the reference to the "Board" would apply to the "Board of Directors" and "Senior Management" to the team of personnel of the company with core management functions. Normally, this would include officials at one level below the Executive Director (including Functional Heads.) In regards to insurers, the Appointed Actuary has a special executive and statutory role.

3. Significant Owners, Controlling Shareholders and Conflict of Interest—Role of Board

3.1 IRDA prescribes a minimum lock-in period of 5 years from the date of certificate of commencement of business of an insurer (R_3) for the promoters of the insurance company and no transfer of shares of the promoters would be permitted within this period.

3.2 Section 2 (7-A) of the Insurance Act, 1938 has prescribed the ceiling of FDI in Indian Insurance Companies at 26%. It could be capped at such percentage as may be notified by the Government of India[1] in future.

The manner of computation of FDI to satisfy this requirement is detailed at Regulation 11 of the IRDA (Registration of Insurance Companies) Regulations, 2000.

3.3 The Insurance Act stipulates prior approval of the IRDA for registration/transfer of shares, exceeding one per cent and / or which involve holding of share capital, after such transfer, in excess of 5 per cent of the paid-up capital of the company (2.5 per cent for banking or Investment Company). The Board of Directors of the company shall ensure that the registration of shares is in compliance with the above provisions of the Act and Circular No. 022/IRDA/F&A/Aug-05 dated 25th August, 2005 on regulatory framework on (i) issue of shares in any form other than equity and (ii) transfer of shares.

3.4 Sections 297 & 299, of the Companies Act, 1956, *inter-alia*, deal with the potential areas of conflicts of interest and the obligation of the Directors and the disclosures thereof. Primarily, the conflicts of interest in insurance companies aries whenever there are conflicting intersects of shareholders, policyholders and management, and there is therefore a duty on the Board to act in the interest of policyholders or prospective policyholders. The Authority may in due course also define significant ownership that could attract potential conflicts of interest. AS 18 of ICAI also casts obligations for the disclosures of transactions involving related parties. There should be adequate systems, policies and procedures to address potential conflicts of interest, compliance with AS 18. These include Board level review of key transactions, disclosures of any conflicts of interest to manage and control such issues.

3.5 Auditors, Actuaries, Directors and Senior Managers shall not simultaneously hold two positions in the insurance company that could lead to conflict or potential conflicts of interest.

3.6 The Board should ensure ongoing compliance with the statutory requirements on capital structure while planning or examining options for capital augmentation of the Company.

4. Governance Structure

4.1 **General.** — Currently, the private insurers in India are yet to go public and get their shares listed on the stock exchanges. The composition of the Boards of the Public Sector Undertakings in the insurance sector is also laid down by the Government of India. It is relevant to observe here that the Corporate Governance requirements of companies listed in the Stock Exchanges have evolved over time and are outlined in Clause 49 of the Listing Agreement of the Stock Exchanges. As the listing requirements are available in public domain they are not being repeated. However, since the Indian Insurance Companies are as yet unlisted the Authority advises all insurer to familiarize themselves with Corporate Governance structures and requirements appropriate to listed entities. The companies are also well advised to initiate necessary steps to address the extant "gaps" that are so identified to facilitate smooth transition at the time of their eventual listing in course of time.

4.2 Varying structure of the board. — Subject to the above, the insurance companies presently could have different structures with the Board of Directors headed by a Full-Time or Part-Time Chairman with distinct executive and oversight responsibilities among the other Directors and Senior Management. It is expected that whatever form is taken, the broader elements of good Corporate Governance are present.

4.3 Group and Conglomerates. — The governance structure of the insurer could also be influenced by its association with an insurance group or a larger financial/non-financial conglomerate. Insurers who are a part of a financial group could also be subject to the regulatory requirements on governance policies and practices established for the group level and implemented uniformly across the group. However, these practices should be re-oriented at the level of the insurer taking into account its specific business and risk profile. Such insurers should nevertheless strive to maintain consistency in policies and practices in order to reinforce controls across the group.

V BOARD OF DIRECTORS

5.1 Composition

- The insurance Act stipulates that the insurance companies in India would be public companies and hence, would require a properly constitute Board.
- Insurers should ensure that the Board comprises of competent and qualified Directors to drive the strategies in a manner that would sustain growth and protect the interest of the stakeholders in general and policyholders in particular.
- The size of the board in addition to being complaint with legal requirements (where applicable), should be consistent with scale, nature and complexity of business. The size and composition should ensure that they collectively provide knowledge, skills experience and commitment along with independence. Further, the Board Members should be in a position to dedicate sufficient time and commitment to fulfilling their reponsiblities.
- It is expected that the shareholders of the companies elect or nominate Directors from various areas of financial and management expertise such as accountancy, banking, insurance, finance, economics etc., with qualifications and experience that is appropriate to the company.
- It is essential that the Directors possess the knowledge of group structure, organizational structure, process and product of the insurer and the Board generally complies with the following requirements :–
    - The Board of Directors and Senior Management understand the operational structure of the insurer and have a general understanding of the lines of business and products of the insurer, more particularly as the insurer grows in size and complexity.
    - The Board of Directors of an insurer belonging to a larger group structure/conglomerate should understand the material risks and issues that could affect the group entities, with attendent implication on the insurer.
- The Board of Directors is required to have a significant number of "Independent Directors:" (as laid down in the Listing Agreement). The optimum contribution of Independent and Non-Executive Directors enhances the quality of business judgement and benefits the shareholders and policyholders. This is especially important in respect of insurance companies under conglomerate structure and where there is potential scope for transfer of risks and conflicts of interests that affect the group entities. At a minimum, where the company has a non-executive Chairman, at least one third of the directors should be independent and in other cases at least fifty percent of the directors should be independent. While the above intention is desirable and would facilitate smooth transition on the listing of the companies, the companies should have a minimum of two independent directors so long as they are unlisted.
- Similarly, where the Chairman of the Board is non-executive, the Chief Executive Officer should be a whole time director of the Board.
- As a matter of prudence, not more than one member of a family or a close relative as defined in the Companies Act or an associate (partner director etc.) should be on the Board of an insurer.

5.2 The Role and responsibility of the Board and their Discharge. – The specific areas of responsibilities of the Board of the Insurance Companies are detailed in the Annexure 1. The Board would primarily concentrate on the direction, control and governance of the insurer and in particular should articulate and commit to a corporate philosophy and governance that will shape the level of risk adoption, standards of business conduct and ethical behaviour of the company at the macro levels. The Board should also set clear and transparent policy framework for translation of the corporate objectives. The Board can delegate its authority to the Board Committees in the discharge of this responsibility but such delegation does not absolve the Board from its primary responsibilities. In this regard, the management through well documented agenda notes and also devise appropriate systems to serve as effective monitoring arrangements. As the Boards generally do not meet at frequent intervals, it is imperative that the senior management is clearly made accountable for the two ways information flow.

The structure of the Board of Directors should be oriented to setting-up of objectives to meet the expectations of various stakeholders, strategies for their fulfillments and for monitoring the achievements. The insurers need to consider interests of all stakeholders, and especially their policyholders as a specific group. Further, since there could arise a conflict of interest amongst the various stakeholders, a key board function is to establish strategies and policies that define ethical individual and corporate behaviour and ongoing effective processes that ensure adherence to these strategies and policies.

Thus, with a view to being effective, the board in active consultation with the Management should set strategies and policies to address, at the minimum, a broad range of areas, as indicated below. There should concurrently be arrangements to review the policies from time to time to ensure that they are dynamic.

- overall direction of the business of the insurer, including projections on the capital requirements, revenue streams, expenses and the profitability. While laying down the projections, the Board must address the expectations of the shareholders and the policy holders.
- obligation to fully comply with the Insurance Act and the regulations framed thereunder, and other statutory requirements applicable to it;
- addressing conflicts of interest;
- ensuring fair treatment of policyholders and employees;
- ensuring information sharing with an disclosures to stakeholders, including investors, policyholders, employees, the regulators, consumers, financial analyst and / or rating agencies.
- establishing channels for encouraging and facilitating employees raising concerns or reporting a possible breach of law or regulations, with appropriate measures to protect against retaliation against reporting employees;
- developing a corporate culture that recognizes and rewards adherence to ethical standards.

5.3 Fit and Proper Criteria. — In line with the international and domestic norms, the Directors of insurance companies have to meet the "fit and proper" criteria. The criteria to be satisfied, at a minimum, would relate to integrity demonstrated in personal behaviour and business conduct, soundness of judgement and financial soundness. The Insurance Act prohibits (i) a life insurance agent to be the Director of the life insurance company; and (ii) the common directorship among life insurance companies. Currently, the fit and proper requirements seek to ensure that the Director should not have been convicted or come under adverse notice of the laws and regulations involving moral turpitude or of any professional body. With a view to ensuring that the Directors comply with the above requirement, a due diligence enquiry should be undertaken on the person to be appointed as Director or for the continuance of the existing Directors only after obtaining a declaration from the proposed/existing Directors in the format given in *Annexure 2*, at the time of their appointment/re-appointments.

It is desirable that the Boards constitute a Nomination Committe to scrutinize the declarations of intending applicants before the appointment/re-appointment/election of Directors by the shareholders at the General meetings. The Nomination Committee could also make independent/ discreet references, where necessary, well in time to verify the accuracy of the information furnished by the applicant. The insurance companies are further advised that they should obtain an annual declaration from the Directors that the information provided in the declaration at the time of appointment/re-appointment has not undergone any change subsequently and the changes, if any, are apprised by the concerned Director to the Board.

The Directors are also required to enter into a Deed of Covenant as per the format placed at *Annexure 3*, with the insurance company, duly approved by the Board, pursuant to their terms of appointment to ensure that there is a clear understanding of the mutual role of the company, the Directors and the Board in Corporate Governance.

5.4 Conduct of Meetings. — The Board should also lay down systems that would make the Company Secretary responsible for proper conduct of the Board meetings and with adequate time to deliberate on the major issues in detail. The Minutes should be recorded as soon as possible after the meeting and get circulated. There should be a system of familiarizing new Directors with the background of the company's governance philosophy, duties and responsibilities of the Directors, etc. Well structured arrangements should be in place for ongoing briefing of Directors on dynamic changes in the financial sector in general and in the insurance in particular for updating the Directors through formal and informal programmes covering regulatory systems, market growth trends, future strategic plans/operations etc.

6. Control, Functions. —Given the risks that an insurer takes in carrying out its operations, and the potential impact it has on its business, it is important that the Board lays down the policy framework to put in place :

- robust and efficient mechanisms for the identification, assessment, quantification, control, mitigation and monitoring of the risks;
- appropriate processes for ensuring compliance with the Board approved policy, and applicable laws and regulations;
- appropriate internal controls to ensure that the risk management and compliance policies are observed;
- an internal audit function capable of reviewing and assessing the adequacy and effectiveness of, and the insurer's adherence to its internal controls as well as reporting on its strategies, policies and procedures; and
- Independence of the control functions, including the risk management function, from business operations demonstrated by a credible reporting arrangement.

6.1 The responsibility for the oversight of control functions of an insurer should be entrusted to Directors possessing the appropriate integrity, competence, experience and qualifications.

6.2 For insurers within a group, appropriate and effective group-wide risk control systems should be in place in addition to the control systems at the level of the insurer. it is essential to manage risks appropriately on a group-wide basis as well as at the level of the insurer. The Boards of the respective insurers are required to lay down requisite policy framework to ensure that such risks are adequately addressed.

7. Delegation of Functions.—With a view to providing adequate Board time for discharge of the significant corporate responsibilities, the Board can consider setting up of various Committees of Directors by delegating the overall monitoring responsibilities after laying down the roles and responsibilities of these Committees to the Board. In particular, the following aspects need to be defined in respect of the role and functions of the Committees:

- Constitution
- Objectives
- Responsibilities
- Frequency of meeting/quorum requirements
- Appointment and removal of members
- Reporting to the Board

The company can establish several committees to undertake specific functions depending on the size and level of the complexity of the operations. Typically, the Committees that assist the Board are Audit Committee, Risk Management Committee, Nominations Committee, Remuneration Committee, Investment Committee and Asset-Liability Management Committee. However, the Authority advises insurers that it is mandatory to establish Audit; Investment; Risk Management; Policyholder Protection; and Asset Liability Management (in case of life insurers) Committees that have a critical role in strengthening the control environment in the company. Establishment of the other Committees is left to the option of the insurer. The role and responsibilities of the Committees would generally be as detailed below :—

7.1 Audit Committee (mandatory)

- The Audit Committee shall oversee the financial statements, financial reporting, statement of case flow and disclosure processes both on an annual and quarterly basis. It shall et-up procedures and processes to address all concerns relating to adequacy of checks and control mechanisms.
- The Chairman of the Audit Committee should be an independent Director of the Board and should ideally be a professional Chartered Accountant or a person with strong financial analysis background. The association of the CEO in the Audit Committee should be limited to eliciting any specific information concerning audit findings.
- The Audit Committee will oversee the efficient functioning of the internal audit department and review its reports. The Committee will additionally monitor the progress made in rectification of irregularities and changes in processes wherever deficiencies have come to notice.
- The Audit Committee shall be directly responsible for the recommendation of the appointment, remuneration, performance and oversight of the work of the auditors (internal/statutory/concurrent). In case of statutory audit, the independence of the external auditors shall be ensured (although the approval of appointment, remuneration and removal of the statutory auditors shall be done by the shareholders at the general body meeting).
- The Audit Committee shall have the oversight on the procedures and processes established to attend to issues relating to maintenance of books of account, administration procedures, transactions and other matters having a bearing on the financial position of the insurer, whether raised by the auditors or by any other person.
- The Audit Committee shall discuss with the statutory auditors before the audit commences, about the nature and scope of audit as well have post-audit discussions to address areas of concern.
- Any additional work other than statutory/internal audit that is entrusted to the auditor or any of its associated persons or companies shall be specifically approved by the Board keeping in mind the necessity to maintain the independence and integrity of the audit relationship. All such other work entrusted to the auditor or its associates shall be specifically disclosed in the notes to Accounts forming part of the annual accounts of the insurer.

7.2 Investment Committee (mandatory)

- The board of every Insurer shall set up an Investment committee comprising of at least two non-Executive Directors, the Chief Executive Officer, Chief of finance, Chief of Investment Division and wherever an appointed actuary is employed, the Appointed Actuary.
- The Committee's role in managing the investments out of the policyholders' funds in crucial and hence the constitution of the Investment Committee should be approved by the Board of Directors and any new appointment or removal of any member of the Investment Committee shall also be approved by the Board and be communicated to the Authority within 30 days.
- The Committee shall be responsible for laying down an overall investment policy and operational framework for the investment operations of the insurer. The policy should focus on a prudential Asset Liability Management (ALM) supported by robust internal control systems. The investment policy and operational framework should, *inter alia*, encompass aspects concerning liquidity for smooth operations, compliance with prudential regulatory norms on investments, risk management/mitigation strategies to ensure commensurate yield on investments and above all protection of policyholders' fund. It is also responsible for a periodic review of the Investment Policy based on the performance of investments and the evaluation of dynamic market condition.
- Members of the Committee should be fully conversant with the various responsibilities cast on them by the IRDA (Investment) Regulations 2000 as amended from time to time as well as the guidelines issued on the system of risk management.
- The members of the Committee should not be solely influenced by the credit rating agencies. The committee should independently review their investment decisions duly supported by the due diligence process required to be carried out by the Investment Team.
- It shall also put in place an effective reporting system to ensure compliance with the policy set out by its apart from Internal/Concurrent Audit mechanisms for a sustained and on-going monitoring of Investment Operations.
- The IC shall atleast meet once in a quarter and look into various aspects of investment operations and monitor them.
- The IC shall furnish a report to the Board on the performance of Investments atleast on a quarterly basis and provide analysis of its Investment portfolio and on the future outlook to enable the board to look at possible policy changes and strategies.

7.3 Risk management Committee (mandatory).– It is now well recognized that the sound management of an insurer as in the case of other financial sector entities, is dependent on how well the various risks are managed across the organization. In pursuit of development of a strong risk management system and mitigation strategies, insurers shall set up a separate Risk Management Committee to lay down the company's Risk management Strategy. The risk management function shall be organized in such a way that it is able to monitor all the risks across the various lines of business of the company and the operating head has direct access to the Board. Conventionally this function is under the overall guidance and supervision of the Chief Risk Officer (CRO) with a clearly defined role. The insurers can, however, presently organize the function appropriately to the size, nature and complexity of their business keeping in view the need for operative independence of the Head of the risk management function.

Broadly, the Risk Management Committee shall :

- assist the Board in effective operation of the risk management system by performing specialised analyses and quality reviews;

- maintaining a group—wide and aggregated view on the risk profile of the insurer in addition to the solo and individual risk profile;
- report to the Board details on the risk exposures and the actions taken to manage the exposures;
- advise the Board with regard to risk management decisions in relation to strategic and operational matter such as corporate strategy, mergers and acquisitions and related matters.

7.4 Asset Liability management Committee (mandatory for life insurers).—ALM is an ongoing process of formulating, implementing, monitoring and revising strategies related to assets and liabilities to achieve an organization's financial objectives, given the organization's risk appetite, risk tolerances and business profile. The need for ALM cannot be over-emphasized as it lays down the framework to ensure that the insurer invests in a manner which would enable it to meet its cash flow needs and capital requirements at a future date.

The responsibilities of the ALM Committee shall include:

- Setting the insurer's risk/reward objectives and assess policyholder expectations.
- Quantifying the level of risk exposure and assessing the expected rewards and cost associated with the risk exposure.
- Formulating and implementing optimal ALM strategies and meeting risk/reward objectives. The strategies must be laid down both at product level and enterprise level.
- Laying down the risk tolerance limits.
- Monitoring risk exposures at periodic intervals and revising ALM strategies where required.
- Placing the ALM information before the board at periodic intervals.

7.5 Policyholder Protection Committee (mandatory). — The Authority places significant emphasis on the protection of policyholder's interests and on the adoption of sound and healthy markct conduct practices by insurers. Towards meeting these objectives, IRDA has notified the (i) Protection of Policyholders' Interests Regulations, 2002 and (ii) Insurance Advertisements and Disclosure Regulations, 2002. The Authority has also put in place the Guidelines on Advertisements, Promotion & Publicity of Insurance Companies and Insurance Intermediaries in January, 2006. Insurers are also required to report on the number and nature of complaints to the IRDA at monthly intervals to enable IRDA to assess the governance and market conduct issues with respect to each insurer. With a view to addressing the various compliance issues relating to protection of the interest of policyholders, as also relating to keeping the policyholders well informed of and educated about insurance products and complaint-handling procedures, each insurer shall set up a Policyholder Protection Committee which shall directly report to the Board. The committee should but in peace systems to ensure that policyholders have access to redressal mechanisms and shall establish policies and procedures, for the creation of a dedicated unit to deal with customer complaints and resolve disputes expeditiously.

Thus, the responsibilities of the Policyholder Protection Committee shall include :

- Putting in place proper procedures and effective mechanism to address complaints and grievances of policyholders including misselling by intermediaries.
- Ensure compliance with the statutory requirements as laid down in the regulatory framework.
- Review of the mechanism at periodic intervals.
- Ensure adequacy of disclosure of "material information" to the policyholders. These disclosures shall, for the present, comply with the requirements laid down by the Authority both at the point of sale and at periodic intervals.
- Review the status of complaints at periodic intervals to the policyholders.
- Provide the details of grievances at periodic intervals in such formats as may be prescribed by the Authority.
- Provide details of insurance ombudsmen to the policyholders.

7.6 Other Committees.—The other Committees which are optional, which can be set up by the Board, include the Remuneration Committee, Nomination Committee and the Ethics Committee. In cases where Board decides not to constitute, their functions responsibilities can be addressed in such manner as the Board may deem fit.

7.6.1 Remuneration Committee (not mandatory). — It is pertinent to draw attention to the provisions of Section 34(A)(1) of the Insurance Act, 1938 which stipulates that the remuneration of CEOs/Whole-time Directors of Indian insurance companies is subject to statutory approval of the IRDA. Further, the overall management costs of the insurer are also additionally governed by the limits prescribed statutorily in the Insurance Act and Rules framed there under in order to protect the interests of the policyholders.

The setting up of a Remuneration Committee should keep the above requirements in view. Further, the envisaged role of the Committee includes the following aspects :

- The Remuneration Committee is required to determine on behalf of the Board and on behalf of the shareholders with agreed terms of reference, the insurer's policy on specific remuneration packages and any compensation payment, for the CEO and the Executive Directors of the company.
- The remuneration package shall be closely connected with the performance objectives laid down for the senior management.
- To avoid conflicts of interest, the Remuneration Committee, which would determine the remuneration packages of the Executive Directors may comprise of at least three directors, all of whom should be non-executive directors, with the Chairman of the Committee being an independent Director.
- The Chairman of the Remuneration Committee could be present at the Annual General Meeting, to answer the shareholders' queries. However, it would be up to the Chairman to decide who should answer the queries.

7.6.2 Nomination Committee (not mandatory).— The role of the Nomination Committee has been discussed in para 5.3.

7.6.3 Ethics Committee (not mandatory).—Responsibilities of the Ethics Committee typically include :

- monitoring the compliance function and the insurer's risk profile in respect of compliance with external laws and regulations and internal policies, including the insurer's code of ethics or conduct.
- receiving reports on the above and on proactive compliance activities aimed at increasing the insurer's's ability to meet its legal and ethical obligations, on identified weaknesses, lapses, breaches or violations and the controls and other measures in place to help detect and address the same.
- supervising and monitoring matters reported using the insurer's whistle blowing or other confidential mechanisms for employees and other to report ethical and compliance concerns or potential breaches or violations.
- advising the board on the effect of the above on the insurer's conduct of business and helping the board set the correct "tone at the top" by communicating, or supporting the communication, throughout the insurer of the importance of ethics and compliance.
- approving compliance programmes, reviewing their effectiveness on a regular basis and signing off on any material compliance issues or matters.

8. Senior Management

8.1 CEO & Other Senior Functionaries.—The Chief Executive Officer of the company and other key functionaries are responsible for the operations and day to day management of the company in line with the directions of the Board and the Committees set up by the Board. Section 34-A of the Insurance Act, 1938 requires prior approval of the Authority for appointments, re-appointment or termination of the Chief Executive Officer and the Whole Time Directors. The Authority expects the CEO to be responsible for the conduct of the company's affair in a manner which is not detrimental to the interests of the policyholders and is consistent with the policies and directions of the board. The Board should, therefore, carry out effective due diligence to establish that the new incumbent is 'fit and proper' before recommending the name for Authority's approval. In case the CEO resigns, the Authority should be kept informed of such resignation and the reasons therefore. The Insurance Act also prohibits the CEO of a **Life insurance company** from being a Director on the Board of any other Indian insurance company/bank/investment company.

As the appointment of the CEO is made with the prior approval of the IRDA the Board should take proactive steps to decide on the continuance of CEO well in time before the expiry of his tenure or to identify the new incumbent. The Authority requires the proposal to be submitted with the approval of the Board at least a month before the completion of the tenure of the incumbent. as a corollary, the board should also have practices in place for succession planning for the key senior functionaries through a process of proper identification and nurturing of individuals for taking over senior management positions.

8.2 Role of Appointed Actuaries. —IRDA has brought out detailed Regulations on Appointed Actuary *vide* IRDA (Appointed Actuary) Regulations, 2000, detailing the procedure for his appointment, qualifications, powers along with his duties and obligations. The Regulations also stipulate that prior approval of the Authority shall be taken for the appointment of the Appointed Actuary. The Board should ensure that the requirements are scrupulously complied with. In brief, it is re-iterated that :

- A procedure for appointment of Appointed Actuary should be put in place.
- The Appointed Actuary should qualify and satisfy the 'Fit & Proper' criteria.
- The insurer shall clearly set forth the Actuary's responsibilities and any advisory role *vis-a-vis* the board or the management as well as his/her rights and obligations. These shall be in addition to the duties of the Appointed Actuaries as specified in the IRDA Regulations and any other directions of IRDA in the matter.
- As soon as the Appointed Actuary realizes that the entity does not comply or is likely to fail in complying with the requirements of solvency and other parameters of sound operations, he/she shall inform the board of the management. If no viable/acceptable solution is taken, then he/she has to inform IRDA.
- The board shall interact directly with the Appointed Actuary wherever it considers it expedient to secure his advice, it may do so in such manner as it may deem fit.

The Appointed Actuary shall provide professional advice or certification to the Board with regard to :

- estimation of technical provisions in accordance with the valuation framework set up by the insurer
- identification and estimation of material risks and appropriate management of the risks
- financial condition testing
- solvency margin requirements
- appropriateness of premiums (and surrender value)
- allocation of bonuses to with-profit insurance contracts

- management of participating funds (including analysis of material effects caused by strategies and policies)
- product design, risk mitigation (including re-insurance) and other related risk management roles.

While the areas of advice/certification listed above are with specific reference to life companies, the Appointed Actuaries in case of non-life insurance companies shall provide such advice/ certification to the extent applicable.

In order to facilitate the Appointed Actuary in discharge his responsibilities he shall at all times be provided access to the information as required.

8.3. External Audit—Appointment of Statutory Auditors.—The IRDA (Preparation of Financial Statements and Auditors Report of Insurance Companies) Regulations, 2002 empower the Authority to issue directions/ guidelines on appointment, continuance or removal of auditors of an insurance company. These guidelines/directions may include prescriptions on qualifications and experience of auditors, their rotations, period of appointment, etc., as may be deemed necessary by the Authority.

8.3.1. Appointment.—The statutory auditors recommended by the Audit Committee are required to be appointed at a general body meeting of the shareholder of the insurer. For the present, the statutory auditors of insurers are required to certify the insurer's accounts on an annual basis. The Board should therefore ensure that the statutory auditors are compliant with the regulatory requirements and there are no conflicts of interest in their appointment.

The auditors should possess the competence and integrity to alert the appropriate authorities promptly of any event that could seriously affect the insurer's financial position or the organization of its administration or its accounting and of any criminal violations or material irregularities that come to his notice.

8.3.2 Guidelines on eligibility Conditions/Qualifications.— The Authority, *vide* Circular No. 368/7/F&A/EMPL/74/July/05 dated 25th July, 2005, while discontinuing maintenance of the panel of auditors, has laid down the requirements to be complied with for a firm to be eligible to be appointed as statutory auditor of an insurance company. The guidelines provide for joint audit of each insurance company by two statutory Auditors. In order for an audit firm to be eligible to be appointed as statutory auditors the following conditions must be complied with :

- Be in continuous practice for a period of fifteen years;
- Minimum number of partners, their qualification and experience in the audit firm as employee/partner;
- At least one partner/employee should have CISA/ISA or equivalent qualification.
- One of the joint auditors may have a term of 5 years and the other 4 years in the first instance. Thereafter, the maximum duration for which an auditor can be retained is a period of five years.
- In appointment of the statutory auditors, the insurer must ensure compliance with the requirements on 'cooling off' period of two years on completion of the tenure of 4/5 years as the case may be.
- No Audit Firm shall carry out more than two statutory audits of Insurance Companies (Life/Non-Life/R-insurance).

8.3.3 Access to board and Audit Committee. —The Audit Committee should have discussions with the statutory auditors periodically about internal control systems, the scope of audit including the observations of the auditors (where applicable) and review the quarterly/half yearly and annual financial statements as the case may be before submission to the board of Directors and also ensure compliance with the internal control systems.

The statutory auditors should have access to the Board of Directors through the Audit Committee.

9. Disclosure Requirements.—The IRDA (Preparation of Financial Statements) Regulations, 2002, have prescribed certain disclosures in the financial statements and the Authority is in the process of finalizing additional disclosures to be made by insurers at periodical intervals. In the meantime it may be ensured by the board that the information on the following, including the basis, methods and assumptions on which the information is prepared and the impact of any changes therein are also disclosed in the annual accounts : —

- Quantitative and qualitative information on the insurer's financial and operating ratios, namely, incurred claim, commission and expenses ratios.
- Actual solvency margin details *vis-a-vis* the required margin.
- Life insurers shall disclose policy lapse ratio.
- Financial performance including growth rate and current financial position of the insurer.
- A description of the risk management architecture.
- Details of number of claims intimated, disposed of an pending with details of duration.
- All pecuniary relationships or transactions of the Non-Executive Directors *vis-a-vis* the insurer shall be disclosed in the Annual Report.
- Any other matters, which have material impact on the insurer's financial position.

10. Outsourcing

10.1 The IRDA (Registration of Insurance Companies) Regulations. 2000 requires that he insurer should be able to carry on all functions in respect of insurance business including management of investments within its own organizations. An insurer shall not, therefore, outsource any of the company's substantive functions other than those that have been explicitly permitted. Each proposal to outsource any function of the insurer as permitted by the Authority (*e.g.,* as in the case of calculation of NAV of investments) shall be reported to IRDA before entering into the arrangement. Where the IRDA issues any guidance in the matter, it shall be complied with. All outsourcing arrangements of the company shall have the approval of the Board. Every outsourcing contract shall contain explicit safeguards regarding confidentiality of data and all outputs from the data, continuing ownership of the data with the insurer and orderly handing over of the data and all related software programmes on termination of the outsourcing arrangement. The arrangement shall be for a defined duration of not more than 3 years and should have provision for premature cancellation without attracting penalties. The Authority would issue in due course guidelines on functions that cannot be outsourced.

10.2 The Company shall monitor and review the performance of agencies to whom operations have been outsourced at least annually and report findings to the Board.

10.3 The Authority reserves the right to access the operations of the outsourced entity to the extent these are relevant to the insurance company and for the protection of policyholder.

11. Relationship with Stakeholders.— A stakeholder is any person, group or organization that has a direct or indirect stake in an insurer. The stakeholder can affect or be affected by the insurer's actions, objectives and policies.

11.1 The key stakeholders in case of an insurer include shareholders, employees, policyholders and supervisors. Other stakeholders could include creditors, service providers, unions, rating agencies, equity analysts and the community at large.

11.2 The stakeholders are interested in the operations of the insurers in terms of:

- Its profitability and thus its capacity to provide a return on capital to shareholders, hire employees, expand its operations and contribute to economic and social activity.
- Its ability to meet its obligations to the various stakeholders as they come due, thereby also promoting trust and confidence in the financial system.

11.3 Towards protecting the interests of the various stakeholders the insurer must ensure complete transparency in operations and make periodic disclosures.

The disclosures stipulations must at the minimum address the following :

- financial statements accurately and fairly represent the financial condition of the insurer; and
- The insurer is running its business soundly and will be viable over the long term.

In particular, the disclosure requirement of the participating policyholders and the unit linked policyholders must be duly addressed.

12. Interaction with the Supervisor

12.1 Effective corporate governance practices in the office of the insurer will enable IRDA to have greater confidence in the work and judgement of an insurer's board, senior management and control functions.

12.2 in assessing the governance practices in place, the IRDA would :

- Seek confirmation that the insurer has adopted and effectively implemented sound corporate governance policies and practices;
- assess the fitness and propriety of Board members;
- monitor the performance of Boards;
- assess the quality of insurers' internal reporting, risk management, audit and control functions;
- evaluate the effects of the insurer's group structure on the governance strategies;
- assess the adequacy of governance processes in the area of crisis management and business continuity.

12.3 The IRDA would at periodic intervals bring to the attention of the Board and senior management, concerns which have been detected through supervisory activities.

12.4 Reporting to IRDA

12.4.1. Insurers should examine to what extent they are currently complying with these guidelines and initiate immediate action to achieve compliance (where not already in compliance) within a period of six months from the date of these guidelines. It is expected that all the arrangements would be in place to ensure full compliance with the guidelines from the financial year 2010-2011. Where such compliance is not possible for any specific reason, the insurer should write to the IRDA for further guidance.

12.4.2 Each insurer should designate an officer as the Compliance Officer whose duty will be to monitor continuing compliance with these guidelines.

13. Whistle Blowing Policy

13.1 The insurers are well advised to put in place a "whistle blowing" policy, where by mechanisms exist for employees to raise concerns internally about possible irregularities, governance weaknesses, financial reporting issues or other such matters. These could include employee reporting in confidence directly to the Chairman of the Board or of a Committee of the Board or to the external auditor.

The policy illustratively covers the following aspects :

- awareness of the employees that such channels are available, how to use them and how their report will be handled.
- handling of the reports received confidentially, for independent assessment, investigation and where necessary for taking appropriate follow-up actions.
- a robust anti-retaliation policy to protect employees who make reports in good faith
- Briefing of the Board of Directors.

13.2 The appointed Actuary and the statutory internal auditors have the duty to 'whistle blow', *i.e.*, to report in a timely manner to the IRDA if they are aware that the insurer has failed to take appropriate steps to rectify a matter which has a material adverse effect on its financial condition. This would enable the IRDA to take prompt action before policyholders' interests are undermined.

ANNEXURE 1
Responsibilities of the Board of Directors

(1) The Board should ensure that the Governance principles set for the insurer comply with all relevant laws, regulations and other applicable codes of conduct.

(2) The Board should set the following policies in consultation with the Management of the Company as indicated.

(a) Define and periodically review the corporate business policy.

(b) Define the underwriting policy of the insurer.

(c) Determine the retention and re-insurance policy and in particular, the levels of retentions of risk by the insurer and the nature and extent of re-insurance protection to be maintained by the insurer.

(d) Define the policy of the insurer in investment of its assets consistent with an appropriate asset liability management structure.

(e) Define the insurer's policy on appointments and qualification requirements for staff at all levels and for fixing their remuneration and benefits; the remuneration policy should not include incentives that encourage imprudent behaviour.

(3) The Board should define and set the following standards :—

(a) Define the standards of business conduct and ethical behaviour for Directors and senior management.

(b) Define the standards to be maintained in policyholder servicing and in redressal of grievances of policyholders.

(4) The Board would be responsible to provide strategic guidance for implementation of business policy and structure a management information system for review and course correction.

(5) As an integral part of the proper implementation of the guidelines of the business and other policies, the Board should take action as under : —

(a) Establish appropriate systems to regulate the risk appetite and risk profile of the Company. It will also enable identification and measurement of significant risks to which the company is exposed in order to develop an effective risk management system.

(b) Ensurer that all supervisory/regulatory directions are submitted to the Board and the supervisor's recommendations are utilized in the assessment of the performance of the senior management in the implementation of board philosophy.

(c) Define the role of the Appointed Actuary and the degree of his involvement in the designing and pricing of products and in determination of labilities.

(d) Ensure that the Appointed Actuary has directed access to the Board and reports on important matters to the board in a timely manner.

(e) Ensure that the IT systems in the company are appropriate and have built-in checks and balances to produce data with integrity.

(f) Ensure that the company has in place a robust compliance system for all applicable laws and regulations.

(g) Prescribe the forms and frequency of reporting to the board in respect of each of the above areas of responsibility.

(6) In the discharge of the above and other Governance functions, the Board should delegate the responsibilities to mandated/other recommended Empowered Committees of Directors while retaining its primary accountability.

(7) The Board should ensure that the insurer is compliant with its directions and all statutory provisions and regulations framed thereunder through :

(a) A sound system of internal controls and audit in respect of all aspects of the insurer's activities and accounts, including financial, operational and compliance controls and such systems should be annually reviewed by the board for their effectiveness.

(b) The Internal Audit function should perform in an objective, independent and risk oriented manner, with timely feedback to the Board.

(c) Prescribing and reviewing all delegations of authority to various levels of management, especially in underwriting, claims, re-insurance, investments and financial transactions. Ensure that critical decisions are taken under the 'four eyes' principle.

ANNEXURE 2

Name of the Insurance Company :

Declaration and Undertaking by Directors

(With enclosures as appropriate as on ....)

I. Personal details of Director

a. Full Name

b. Date of Birth

c. Educational qualifications

d. Relevant Background, knowledge and Experience

e. Permanent Address

f. Present Address

g. E-mail Address/Telephone Number

h. Permanent Account Number under under the Income-tax Act and name and address of Income-tax circle

i. Any other information relevant to Directorship or the Insurance Company.

II. Relevant relationships of Director

a. List of relatives, if any who are connected with the insurer (Refer Section 6 and Schedule 1-A of the Companies Act, 1956)

b. List of entities, if any, in which he/she is considered as being interested (Refer Section 299 (3) (a) and Section 300 of the Companies Act, 1956)

III. Records of professional achievements

a. Relevant professional achievements

IV. Proceedings, if any, against the Director

a. If the Director is a member of a professional association/body, details of disciplinary action, if any pending or commenced or resulting in conviction in the past against him/her or whether he/she has been banned from entry of at any profession/occupation at any time.

b. Details of prosecution, if any, pending or commenced or resulting in conviction in the past against the Director and/or against any of the entries listed II (b) and (c) above for violation of economic laws and regulations.

c. Details of criminal prosecution, if any, pending or commenced or resulting in conviction in last five years against the Director.

d. Whether the Director attracts any of the disqualifications envisaged under Section 274 of the Company's Act, 1956 ?

e. Has the Director or any of the entities at II (b) and (c) above been subject to any investigation at the instance of Government department or agency ?

f. Has the Director at any time been found guilty of violation of rules/regulations/legislative requirements by customs/ excise/ income-tax/foreign exchange/other revenue authorities, if so give particulars.

g. Whether the Director at any time came to the adverse notice of a regulator such as SEBI, RBI, MCA,

h. Whether the Director was associated as Director or officer with any entity that was wound up or that was penalized for violation of any law.

i. Any other explanation/information in regard to items I to III an other information considered relevant for judging his/her fit and proper compliance.

V Other directorships or senior executive positions held by the Director.

Undertaking/— I confirm that the above information is, to the best of my knowledge and belief, true and complete. I undertake to keep the insurer fully informed, as soon as possible, of all events which take place subsequent to my appointment which are relevant to the information provided above.

I also undertake to execute the deed of covenant required to be executed by all Directors of the insurance company.

Place: Signature of the Director

Date :

VII. Remarks of Board of Directors of Insurer

Place:

Date:

Signature

ANNEXURE 3
Form of deed of Covenants with a Director

THIS DEED OF COVENANTS is made this ....day of ....Two thousand ....BETWEEN................having its registered office at ....(hereinafter called the 'Insurance Company') of the one part and Mr/Ms ....of ....(hereinafter called the Director') of the other part.

WHEREAS

A. The Director has been appointed as a Director one the Board of the Insurance Company (hereinafter called 'the Board') and is required as a term of his/he appointment to enter into a Deed of Covenants with the Insurance Company.

B. The Director has agreed to enter into this Deed of Covenants, which has been approved by the Board, pursuant to his said terms of appointment.

NOW IT IS HEREBY AGREED AND THIS DEED OF COVENANTS WITNESSETH AS FOLLOWS:

(1) The Director acknowledges that his/her appointment as Director on the Board of the Insurance Company is subject to applicable laws and regulations including the Memorandum and Articles of Association of the Insurance Company and the provisions of the Deed of Covenants.

(2) The Director covenants with the Insurance Company that :

(i) The Directors shall disclose to the Board the nature of his/her interest, direct or indirect, he/she has any interest in or is concerned with a contract or arrangement or any proposed contract or arrangement entered into or to be entered into between the Insurance Company and any other person, immediately upon becoming aware of the same or at meeting of the Board at which the question of entering into such contract or arrangement is taken into consideration or if the Director was not at the date of that meeting concerned or interested in such proposed contract or arrangement, then at the first meeting of the Board held after he/she becomes so concerned or interested and in case of any other contract or arrangement, the required disclosure shall be made at the first meeting of the Board held after the Director becomes concerned or interested in the contract or arrangement.

(ii) The Director shall disclose by general notice to the Board his/her other Directorships, his/her memberships of bodies corporate, his/her interest in other entities and his/her interest as a partner or proprietor of firms and shall keep the Board apprised of all changes therein.

(iii) The Director shall provide to the Insurance Company a list of his/her relatives as defined in the Companies Act, 1956 and to the extent the Director is aware of Directorships and interests of such relatives in other bodies corporate, firms and other entities.

(iv) The Director shall in carrying on his/her duties as Director of the Insurance Company :

(a) use such degree of skill as may be reasonable to expect from a persons with his/her knowledge or experience;

(b) in the performance of his/her duites take such care as he/she might be reasonably expected to take on his/her own behalf and exercise and power vested in him/her in good faith and in the interests of the Insurance Company:

(c) shall keep himself/herself informed about the business, activities and financial status of the Insurance Company to the extent disclosed to him/her;

(d) attend meetings of the Board and Committees there of (collectively for the sake of brevity hereinafter referred to as Board') with fair regularity and conscientiously fulfil his/her obligations as Director of the Insurance Company;

(e) shall not seek to influence any decision of the Board for any consideration other than in the interests of the Insurance Company;

(f) shall bring independent judgment to bear on all matters affecting the Insurance Company brought before the Board including but not limited to statutory compliances, performance reviews, compliances with internal control systems and procedures key executive appointments and standards of conduct;

(g) shall in exercise of his/her judgment in matters brought before the Board for entrusted to him/her by the Board be free from any business or other relationship which could materially interfere with the exercises of hsi/her independent judgement; and

(h) shall express his/her views and opinions at Board meetings without any fear or favour and without any influence on exercise of his/her independent judgement;

(v) The Director shall have:

(a) fiduciary duty to act in good faith and in the interests of the Insurance Company and not for any collateral purpose;

(b) duty to act only within the powers as laid down by the Insurance Company's Memorandum and Articles of Association and by applicable laws and regulations; and

(c) duty to acquire proper understanding of the business of the Insurance Company.

(vi) The Director shall :

(a) not evade responsibility in regard to matters entrusted to him/her by the Board;

(b) not interfere in the performance of their duties by the wholetime Directors and other officers of the Insurance Company and wherever the Director has reasons to believe otherwise, he/her shall forthwith discloses his/her concerns to the Boards; and

(c) not make improper use of information disclosed to him/her as a member of the Board for his/her or someone else's advantage or benefit and shall use the information disclosed to him/her by the Insurance Company in his/her capacity as Director of the Insurance Company only for the purpose of performance of his/her duties as a Director and not for any other purpose.

(3) The Insurance Company covenants with the Director that :

(i) the Insurance Company shall apprise the Director about :

(a) Board procedures including identification of legal and other duties of Director and required compliances with statutory obligations;

(b) Control systems and procedures;

(c) voting rights at Board meetings including matters in which Director should not participate because of his/her interest, direct or indirect therein;

(d) qualification requirements and provide copies of Memorandum and Articles of Association;

(e) corporate policies and procedures;

(f) insider dealing restrictions;

(g) constitution of delegation of authority to and terms of reference of various committees constituted by the Board;

(h) appointments of Senior Executives and their authority;

(i) remuneration policy;

(j) deliberations of committees of the Board, and

(k) communicate any changes in policies, procedures, control systems, applicable regulations including Memorandum and Articles of Association of the Insurance Company, delegation of authority, Senior Executives etc. and appoint the Compliance Officer who shall be responsible for all statutory and legal compliance.

(ii) the Insurance Company shall disclose and provide to the Board including the Director all information which is reasonably required for them to carry out their functions and duties as Directors of the Insurance Company and to take informed decisions in respect of matters brought before the Board for its consideration or entrusted to the Director by the Board or any committee thereof;

The insurance company shall provide training on an on-going basis to enable the directors to discharge their role effectively.

(iii) the disclosures to be made by the Insurance Company to the Directors shall include but not be limited to the following :

(a) all relevant information for taking informed decisions in respect of matters brought before the Board;

(b) Insurance Company's strategic and business plans and forecasts;

(c) organisational structure of the Insurance Company and delegation of authority;

(d) corporate and management controls and systems including procedures;

(e) economic features and marketing environment,

(f) information and updates as appropriate on Insurance Company's products;

(g) information and updates on major expenditure;

(h) periodic reviews of performance of the Insurance Company; and

(i) report periodically about implementation of strategic initiatives and plants;

(iv) the Insurance Company shall communicate outcome to Board deliberations to Directors and concerned personnel and prepare and circulate minutes of the meeting of Board to Directors in a timely manner and to the extent possible within two business days of the date conclusion of the Board meeting; and

(v) advise the Director about the levels of authority delegated in matters placed before the Board.

(4) The Insurance Company shall provide to the Director periodic reports on the functioning of internal control system including effectiveness thereof.

(5) The Insurance Company shall appoint a Compliance Officer who shall be a Senior Executive for reporting to Board/respective Committees of the Board and be responsible for setting forth a framework no compliance responsibility and for implementation thereof. He/she shall also monitor adherence to the applicable laws and regulations and policies and procedures including but not limited to directions of Insurance Regulatory and Development Authority and other concerned statutory and governmental authorities.

(6) The Director shall not assign, transfer, sublet or encumber his/her office and his/her rights and obligations as Director of the Insurance Company to any third party provided that nothing herein contained shall be construed to prohibit delegation of any authority, power, function or delegation by the Board or any committee thereof subject to applicable laws and regulations including Memorandum and Articles of Association of the Insurance Company.

(7) The failure on the part of either part of either party hereto to perform, discharge, observe or comply with any obligation or duty shall not be deemed to be a waiver thereof nor shall it operate as a bar to the performance, observance, discharge or compliance thereof at any time or times thereafter.

(8) Any and all amendments and/or supplements and/or alterations to this Deed of Covenants shall be valid and effectual only if in writing and signed by the Director and the duly authorized representative of the Insurance Company.

(9) This Deed of Covenants has been executed in duplicate and both the copies shall be deemed to be originals.

IN WITNESS WHEREOF THE PARTIES HAVE DULY EXECUTED THIS AGREEMENT ON THE DAY MONTH AND YEAR FIRST ABOVE WRITTEN.

For the Insurance Company **Direction**

By.......................... ....

Name: Name:

Title:

In the presence of :

1. .... 2. ....

Companies Act, 2013

The corporate governance requirements under the Companies Act, 2013 are as under :

Regulatory Framework for Insurance Companies

In addition to the requirements under the Companies Act 2013 and Rules there under, or the Insurance Act 1938, IRDA has vide guidelines on Corporate. Governance prescribed following requirements.

Requirement(s)	General description
Duties of Directors (166)	For the first time the duties of the Directors are defined under Section 166 of the Act and the most important shifts from the current regime is duties of the Directors towards company, employees, shareholders, community and environment. Besides above, directors are expected to promote the objectives of the Company, act in good faith, without any conflict of interest, no undue gains. In case of contravention, a director may be penalized with fine which shall be not less than ₹ 1 lakh and can go up to ₹ 5 lakh. It is noteworthy to mention that all the above behaviors were expected from the directors and were covered under the fiduciary duties. However, since the same has now been clearly provided under the Act, there will be less ambiguity in interpretation.
Independent Directors	Every listed company is required to have 1/3 of its Board comprising of Independent Directors. Other Public Companies having paid up share capital of ten crore rupees or more; or having turnover of one hundred crore rupees or more; which have, in aggregate, outstanding loans, debentures and deposits, exceeding fifty crore rupees need to have at least two Independent Directors. 'Independent Director' has been defined under Section 149(6) of the Companies Act. Additionally, an Independent Director is required to submit a declaration to the board about his meeting the criteria of independence as provided under Section 149 on annual basis. Ordinarily, an Independent Director can hold office for five consecutive years and can be reappointed by passing special resolution and subject to specific disclosure of such appointment in the Board's report.

Loan to Directors	The provisions related to loan to directors have been made stricter. Under Section 29 of the Insurance Act, 1938 Loans to director is anyway prohibited.
Resident Director	The Act mandates Companies to have at least one resident Director and this has significant impact on wholly owned foreign subsidiaries, which are being managed by persons outside India.
Women Directors	To bring women representation in the Boardrooms, the Act mandates Companies I having paid up capital of ₹ 100 crore or more or turnover of ₹ 300 crore to have women Directors. In view of the capital requirement for the Insurance Companies, every Company shall have a woman Director on their Board.
Audit Committee	Audit Committee shall comprise of at least three Directors, majority of the same shall be the Independent Directors. Chairperson of the Audit Committee should be person of ability to read and understand the financial statement.
Corporate Social Responsibility (CSR)	Under Section 135 of the Companies Act, 2013, a new requirement has been triggered for the companies haying paid up capital of ₹ 500 crore or more or turnover of ₹ 1000 crore or more or profit of ₹ 5 crore or more to constitute a CSR Committee and spend 2% of the net profit on the CSR activities. An indicative list of CSR activities is provided in the Act. To undertake the CSR activities, the Companies are required to frame a CSR Policy and in the event of failure to spend required money towards CSR, a statement in the Board's report is required to be made explaining the reasons thereto.
Managerial Remuneration	There are two dimensions to the Managerial Remuneration under the Act, (1) the overall remuneration payable to the Directors under Section 198 of the Companies Act and (2) the constitution of the Remuneration and Nomination Committee under Section 178. The said Committee is expected to formulate a policy to attract good quality directors; define the relationship with the performance Vs. remuneration; provide for the short term and long term performance objectives striking the balance between the fixed and variable pays. Additionally, Companies are required to disclose in the Board's report median salary paid to the employees Vs. Manage rial remuneration.
KMP- Role of Company Secretary	New set of management professionals has been created including CEO, CFO and Company Secretary as Key Managerial Personal (KMP). Under Section 205, the functions of Company Secretary has been clearly defined viz., reporting to the Board about the compliance with the provisions of the Act and Rules (2) compliance with the Secretarial standards (c) discharge other duties as may be prescribed. IRDA vide its Circular dated 09th October, 2013 defined the Key persons of the insurance Companies to include CEO, CMO,

	Appointed Actuary, CIO, Chief Internal Audit, CFO, CRO and Chief Compliance Officer.
Secretarial Audit	Section 204 the Act has prescribed the secretarial audit for 'such companies having paid up capital of ₹ 50 crore or more or having turnover of ₹ 250· crore or more.
Disclosures and Reporting	The Act has revised the formats of various registers and returns to be prepared by the Companies and have asked for exhaustive information. Additionally, Section 117 of the Act requires companies to submit certain resolutions/ agreement with ROC. The Section has wide coverage and the same will have greater transparency from the shareholders point of view.

CORPORATE SOCIAL RESPONSIBILITY

Background

Corporate Social Responsibility ("CSR" for short) is a form of corporate self-regulation integrated into a business model. CSR policy functions as a built-in, self-regulating mechanism whreby business monitors and ensures its active compliance with the spirit of the law, ethical, standards, and international norms. It is also called by different names such as 'corporate conscience' or 'sustainable and responsible business'. The goal of CSR is to embrace responsibility for the company's actions and encourage a positive impact through its activities on the environment, consumers, employees, communities, stakeholders and all other members of the public sphere. Furthermore, CSR-focused business would proactively promote the public interest by encouraging community growth and development, and voluntarily eliminating practices that harm the public sphere, regardless of legality. CSR is the deliberate inclusion of public interest into corporate decision-making, and the honouring of a triple bottom line: "people, planet, profit".

Corporate Social Responsibility in foreign Countries :

Viewing globally, the United States has had a strong tradition of corporate philanthropy. Corporate social programs have always been very popular there. The government is a quiet but key player especially in the regulation of Corporate Social Responsibility (CSR). The USA Community Reinvestment Act (CRA) regulates CSR in financial services sector. The CRA sets minimum requirements, monitors compliance; and incentivizes through tax credits. It can be said CSR is fairly developed in US. Waren Buffett, the chairman of Berkshire Hathway Inc., and Bill Gates, the chairman of Microsoft Corp., are expanding the philanthropic effort by meeting billionaires and they've been asking their peers to sign the "Giving Pledge," which promises they'll give the majority of their fortunes to charity. With their efforts the number of participants has risen to 57 in the U.S. since the project was announced in June. There has also been a Minister appointed for CSR (in Department of Trade and Industry) since 2000 in the United Kingdom. CSR Asia, the Asia Pacific CSR Group shows the status of CSR in Asia and Asia Pacific countries. Insurers also occupied a position among the top 20 donors in international scene. Their effects are leading to address issues on the environment, education and human rights.

Government Initiatives

The Ministry of Corporate Affairs had brought out a set of voluntary guidelines in December, 2009. Following are the core elements of those guidelines :

- Care for all stake holders: It includes shareholders, employees, customers, suppliers, project-affected people, society at large.

- Ethical functioning: The governance systems should not engage in business practices that are abusive, unfair, corrupt or anti-competitive.
- Respect for worker' Rights and Welfare: Providing safe and hygienic workplace environment, access to training and development of necessary skills for career advancement, on an equal and non-discriminatory basis. They should not employ child or forced labour. They should give freedom of association and right to collective bargaining of labor and they should have an effective grievance redressal system.
- Respect for human rights
- Respect for Environment: It suggests that companies should take measures to check and prevent pollution: recycle, manage and reduce waste, should manage natural resource in a sustainable manner and ensure optimal use of resources like land and water, should proactively respond to the challenges of climate change by adopting cleaner production methods, promoting efficient use of energy and environment friendly technologies.
- Activities for social and inclusive development: These could include: education, skill building for livelihood of people, health, cultural and social welfare etc., particularly targeting at disadvantaged sections of society.

To implement CSR strategies, companies are advised to partner with local authorities, associations and are advised to allocate specific amount in their budgets related to profits after tax for CSR activiies. They are also asked to disseminate information on CSR policy, activities and progress to all their stakeholders and the public through website, annual reports and media.

1. Role in awareness generation :

The following action plan serves both as CSR and promotes long-term business interests.

- Getting involved in
- Improving educational and training institutions, relevant to the company.
- Sponsoring awareness generation/Spreading information on various hazards and the step to be taken for mitigating
- Making people aware of their vulnerabilities and the need for prevention, mitigation and preparedness measures
- Research and development of products for suiting the needs of the customers.
- Focusing on need based selling instead of target based selling.
- Providing climate-friendly and climate-proof products and services.
- Partnering with government, suppliers and other stakeholders in disaster risk management.
- Building on existing dialogue with consumers
- Offering contracts acorss many states, for many crops, covering a range of risks, from excessive rainfall to extreme temperatures through public and private programs
- Formation of a group of insurance companies and organizations, committing them to take action to reduce climate change risk, support climate change awareness and lead the way in analyzing and reducing risks.

Role beyond commercial interests :

Insurers can design products and extend insurance covers to supplement the Government social security schemes for the vulnerable and weaker sections like women, old aged, unemployed, rural poor of the BPL families. Further, though it is not directly related to their core business, they can establish their brand image with the following activities via fulfilling their social responsibility. Some of them are

- Maintaining traffic roundabouts
- Maintaining parks for children and elderly
- Advertising for socially important causes
- Promoting road safety
- Taking village development projects
- Deforestation
- Building effective bridges amongst all important stakeholders for the successful implementation of CSR initiatives.
- Floating foundations to conduct CSR projects
- The involvement of small and medium enterprises (SMEs),
- Synergy of corporate houses and NGOs,
- Public Private Partnerships,
- Government's Encouragement in rewarding and recognizing corporate house CSR activities.
- Introduction of CSR as a subject at business schools and in colleges and universities.
- Insurers should spend atleast 2 per cent of their profits for social benefits of the society.

Insurance companies and CSR

Insurance companies can contribute to the CSR initiative in a number of ways. Given the sheer size of the industry – with nearly three million agents alone apart from the employees, this industry is one of the highest people-intensive industries in the country.

Insurance companies by virtue of being engaged in the business of providing life insurance coverage to the society, have their core business intertwined with the social objectives. By providing the claim cheque to the nominee, the life insurance companies provide the succour needed to the bereaved family at a time when they most need - upon death of the bread winner - in financial form. No other business can give the moral satisfaction which an insurance person gets when he hands over the claim cheque to the nominee and wipes off a tear or two from her eyes.

Private insurance companies have also gone beyond their boundaries when it comes to servicing of customers. Dedicated calls centers and touch points to serve customers is one example. Even in places where they do not have branches, customer touch points have been created through the business partners. With the advent of email and mobiles, the extent of automation by private insurance companies has resulted in faster customer service at a touch of the button.

On the employees front, insurance companies, especially the private sector, have done exceedingly well. Apart from monetary compensation, the employee engagement initiatives are worth noting. Sensing the employee satisfaction levels by conducting assessment surveys, conducting offsites to unwind and relearn, focus more on training and skill sets, nurcuring and retention of talents, to quote a few.

One of the other areas, eventhough due to regulatory requirements, where insurance companies have contributed to the CSR initiatives, are the coverages the weaker sections and persons residing in rural areas in the wake of discharge of their rural and sector obligations. Micro insurance products which provide coverage to the down trodden at affordable prices have gone a long way in delivering their obligations to the society. In fact many life insurance companies have gone beyond the regulatory mandate and have extended coverage to more persons in these sectors voluntarily.

Sector externalities

An externally or transaction spillover is a cost or benefit, not transferred through prices, incurred by a party who did not agree to the action causing the cost or benefit. In these cases in a competitive market, prices do not reflect the full costs or benefits of producing or consuming a product or service, producers and consumers may either not been all of the costs or not reap all of the benefits of the economic activity and too much or too little of the good will be produced or consumed in terms of overall costs and benefits to society. A manufacturing unit releasing untreated effluents causes damage to environment and society as a whole; as did excessive risk taking by large financial institutions leading to global credit crisis and subsequent recession and job losses.

Insurers by the nature of their business identify pool and transfer risk, hence are therefore in a strong position to identify the risk associated with an underdeveloped society and the impact it can have on their business. Sustaining a healthy and vibrant community is much more critical for insurers to ensure a sustained demand for their products and services.

Sectrol relevance

The insurance and financial service sector is very important in a capitalist economy which is measured in terms of economic growth, aggregate consumption and production capacity with the support of capital and labour. The sector is a channel of captial directing the flow from surplus to deficit sectors and the impact of importance and interconnection can be felt in the backdrop of the global financial crisis which affected not just these businesses and economy but the society at large. The negative externality for the society is seeing a backlash from authorities trying to curb and control many operational aspects of financial firms.

Management of risks

Insurance companies transform individual insecurity into transferable risk and by doing so they create a higher level of assurance. As it is desirable to prevent damage than ractify it, insurers need to send clear market signals to accurately price risks and reward socially and environmentally well managed companies- as will no doubt happen as the industry matures and develops sophisticated methodologies to accurately measure and price risk. The premium for bad behavior will be high as in the case of smokers buying protection.

Aligning CSR to business operations

An analytical Framework proposed by porter and Kramer "Inside-out" and "Outside-in" linkage can help identify the points of interconnection for insurers. Inside-out linkages refer to the impact a company has on seciety through the normal course of business. Bu working through each step of the value chain, the company can work but positive and negative consequences of its actions eg. hiring practices, waste disposal etc. Outside-in linkages refer to external social conditions that may affect an organisation – availability of talant, intellectual property protection, rule of law etc. The company needs to work out what it can and can't influence; and accordingly align their CSR strategy to overall business stategy. Insurance being a long term business globally insurers have embraced causes with long term impact likeclimate renewable energy green energy and reduction of green house gases.

A company's impact on society also changes over time, as social standards evolve and science progresses. India has had strong economic growth in the last decade however the country still faces many social development challenges. Some of the points of intersections for insurers with society are:

- Education
- Skills and Leadership Development
- Health and Welfare
- Environmental Protection

Indian insurance industry though young is actively involved in CSR acitivities. There are insurance companies that support primary education of underprivileged children, yet another supports poverty relief, education and health. One life insurer is focussing on providing a safe and secure future to the children in the age group 0-12 years through improved healthcare; another focuses on eyecare for the elderly through 'Gift Dristhi' campaign and primary education. Another life insurer goes into several socially responsible areas and focuses its efforts in two areas: financial inclusion (child education, women empowerment, skill development, capacity building for youth, women etc) and environment (biodiversity/wildlife, natural resources and livelihoods). Many more examples abound of insurers as well as other corporporates undertaking meaningful CSR initiatives.

CSR-global perspective

Insureres globally have embraced causes that benefit society as well as have business linkages like climate, green energy and leadership, diversity and equality, health and welfare, environmental protection and animal health are also supported.

Insurers in Europe and US have laid out a well-defined CSR policy, which is aligned to their operations.

Insurance agents and CSR

Insurance agents have exhibited their CSR in many ways. Many senior agents in life insurance sector stand as the role model, when it comes to customer service – walking that extra mile in various ways. For example, opening of policyholders' service centre which provide free service to any customer who walks in. These senior agents maintain a parallel office of their own, where the records of customers are maintained up to date. Premium reminders go well ahead of the insurance company's notice. They collect the premium and deposit with insurance companies on time to ensure continued coverage to their customers. They maintain a cordial relationship with their customers throughout the year – they do not forget to wish them on birthday or any other anniversaries in the family with a simple greeting card. Agents of private life insurance companies who have taken up agency as a full time profession also follow this practice.

When it comes to settlement of claims, these agents extend full support to the family, right from the time of filling claim intimation till handing over the claim cheque to the nominee.

Value Oriented Corporate Social Responsiblility:

Some of the key areas where insurance companies should display corporate social responsibility are:

- Towards customers : The insurance company should aim to be the most trusted financial services company by developing customer centric, cost-effective products to meet the needs of financial security of a diverse range of clients and providing peace of mind and high service standards including fast TATs (turnaround time), timely claim payments, response and resolutions etc.
- Sound risk management principles for all stakeholders, including shareholders, employees, customers, suppliers, society at large etc and create value for all of them. Insurers should develop mechanism to actively engage with all stakeholders, raise awareness, inform them of inherent risks and mitigate them where they occur and continue to gain knowledge about sustainable economic, social and environmental development.
- Corporate governance to be the responsibility of each department and governance systems to be underpinned by ethics, transparency and accountability; while striving to maintain high ethical standards at all times, insurance companies to pursue strict compliance in all aspects of business activities. The insurance company should not engage in business practices that are abusive, unfair and corrupt.

- Transparency and communication to disclose information timely and appropriately; and to promote dialogue with all stakeholders to ensure effective corporate management.
- Towards employees: Spell out KPls (Key performance indicators) and focus on diversity, employee engagement, transparency, trust, feedback, motivation, development and health, with the aim of the employer of choice; a strong code of conduct to be in place that focuses on integrity and fairness; a workplace environment that is safe, hygienic and humane and which upholds the dignity of employees.
- Protecting the environment: Insurance companies, as risk managers should take proactive measures to check and prevent pollution, focus on recycling, manage and reduce waste, manage natural resources in a sustainable manner and ensure optimal use. Further, the insurance companies should proactively respond to the challenges of climate change by adopting cleaner production methods, promoting efficient use of energy and environment friendly technologies. Acknowledging that protection and security is the aim of insurance, insurance companies should be at the forefront in improving the global environment.
- Promote employee volunteering: While marching ahead on the path of progress, we cannot think and plan only for a few sections of the population. Any scheme of development will not be complete unless we ensure that the benefits percolate to the grassroots and therefore, the Indian insurance regulator too promoted the concept of Corporate Social Responsibility through mandated business for Rural and Social Sectors - a commitment to deliver innovative solutions addressing the needs of the rural population and economically weaker sections of the society.

Thus by exhibiting ethically, socially and environmentally responsible behaviour in day-to-day governance of operations, business can generate value and long term sustainability for itself, while making positive contribution in the betterment of the society.

QUESTIONS

1. What is corporate Governance? Discuss its main features.
2. Explain the components of Corporate Governance.
3. What is transparency? Describe how is it maintained in insurance industry.
4. Explain the role of accountability in insurance industry.
5. Examine the investment and viability of Corporate Governance.
6. Explain Social Responsibility and Social Accounting with reference to Corporate Governance.
7. Project the future of corporate Governance in General Insurance and Life Insurance.

49

BANCASSURANCE

Insurance and Banking are coexisting financial institution while complementing and supplementing each other. The Insurance Regulatory and Development Authority Act, 1999 have created more opportunities to them for expansion of their markets. They can serve the society in a very effective manner. Banking Institutions have got the opportunities to enter in insurance business while insurance institutions have already under the autonomy of starting their banking business. Many non-banking institutions have been opened, acquired funds and dissolved with public money at their stakes. Since they were totally in the hands of private persons, the Government control became ineffective. Banking institutions in India are mainly under the control of Reserve Bank of India. People need insurance but they prefer investment over risk coverage although latter is more important. Indian mentally for insurance is very bleak people do not feel need of insurance although they have dire-necessity for that. Insurance institutions in India have not considered forced insurance. The voluntary-purchasing of insurance policies is rare phenomena. They prefer to go to bank-offices rather than going to insurance offices for getting risk coverage. The insurance institutions procure the business through their agents who are the main link between people and the company. Agents attitude and environment may work against the free will environment of insurance. The IRDA, Act is expected to mobiles insurance coverage and resources for investment in the economy. The Government has assured that there would not be any disinvestment in the LIC, GIC and their subsidiaries. Insurance Act, 1938, has not been sufficient to regulate the insurance business in India. Foreign companies would not be allowed to hike their equity in the country through their Indian subsidiaries. It has opened a great opportunities for the banking and insurance institutions. They can perform both the functions.

INSURANCE AS BANKING INSTITUTE

The life insurance and general insurance corporations are performing their respective functions with the help of banks. LIC and GIC have opened their accounts with banks. Policyholders have to approach the banks for realisation of cheques. Indirectly banks have to intervene in their business. If the insurance companies perform the business of banking institutions, they get benefits of business in financial transactions. Policyholders are also benefited as they have not to run from pillar to post. The claim amounts will be deposited in insurance banks. The account holders get all the benefits and facilities of banks. It can be analysed under premium Collection, claims, payment, pension plans, funds, investment consultant and employment opportunities.

Bancassurance is a strategy adopted by banks or insurance companies arming to operate in the financial market in a more or less integrated manner. It is inter-linkage of different financial services as well as the distribution of these products.

Premium Collection

Insurance as bank will facilitate deposits of premium. The burden on cash-counter is lessened or the cash transaction is shifted to insurance bank. The premium amount is regularly collected without any pressure on other activities of insurance. Insurance business is expanded with extra zeal and effort as people working in the marketing areas develop specialisation. They devote with additional knowledge and equipment for the expansion of insurance business on the other hand. Management of premium collection becomes easy as the insurance banks has diversified its activities. New bank customer get information about insurance. They collect, analyses and reinforce the available information at insurance-bank counter from the fellow depositor of premiums and receivers of claims-amount. Insurance policy is accepted by its realisation of actual benefits towards which Indian population is apathetic. The premium account is regularly collected as the customers visit often the insurance-bank for their daily transaction. They are reminded of premium-deposits. The premium collected are deposited in a commercial bank who use the money for their transactions and investment. If so much money is retained by insurance-bank, it would be utilised by them for getting some profit on the money.

Table 49.1 Premium Collected by (₹ in Crores)

Years	*Life Insurance corporation of India*	*General Insurance*	*Total*
1990-91	5600	2742	8342
1991-92	6960	3450	10410
1992-93	7987	3868	11855
1993-94	9735	4427	14162
1994-95	11527	4879	16406
1995-96	14182	5956	20138
1996-97	16240	6734	22974
1997-98	19252	7357	26609
2000-01	34207.78		
2004-05	75083.37		

Table 49.1 reveals that the total premium collected by insurance industryes has gone from ₹8,342 crores in 1990-91 to ₹26,609 crores in 1997-98 by 3.18 times during the period of 7 years. If this much of money is retained by insurance industry they would earn enough profit margins. But, at present insurance industry operates its financial functions through a commercial banks. The functions of commercial banks should be performed by the insurance industry itself. There are many other income than the premium income which are also deposited in banks.

Table 49.2 Total Income

(₹ in Crores)

Years	*Life Insurance*	*General Insurance*	*Total*
1990-91	8518	3308	11,826
1991-92	10691	4202	14,893
1992-93	12244	4727	16,971
1993-94	15212	5384	20,596
1994-95	18102	6029	24,131
1995-96	22047	7431	29,478
1996-97	25821	8431	34,252
1997-98	30732	8335	40,067
2000-01	53968.46		
2004-05	112346.24		

The public is accustomed to get insurance and banking services at a place. Insurance industry will work like a multiple shop store werein all the financial functions would be performed by them. The investor would also come to the insurance offices for getting all the information and services fulfilled. However the insurance-bank should not have to confine only on insurance-investment but should have widen its horizon to help all types of people seeking financial suggestions.

Payment of premium would be easy and prompt if the policyholder has opened account with the insurance-bank. It would be like salary saving scheme wherein no policyholder would bother for monthly remittance of premium. Merely accounting transaction in the insurance-bank facilitate the payments. The account holder would be reminded of the minimum balance in the account for payment of premiurn. The insurance bank becomes total bank of people as it takes cares of all financial transactions. Payment of electricity bill income tax and business-invoices would be easy by insurance-bank.

Total income received by insurance industries comes through banks. In other-words, banks maintain its total income which increased from ₹ 11,826 crore in 1990-91 to ₹ 40,067 crores in 1997-98 by 3.39 times during the period of seven years. If this amount is not deposited or transacted through commercial banks all these money is used by insurance industries as bank too. Therefore, it is advisable for the insurance industry to start its own bank wherein public is also invited to transact as bank-customer. Thus the deposit of insurance industry in a year would exceed ₹ 50 thousand crore at the minimum. Bank certainly gets some benefit on the amount deposited by insurance. They maintain their liquidity level and invest rest of the money received from insurance. This earning would be earned by insurance companies as commercial banks if they transact business of a commercial bank.

Claims Payment

The claims-amount paid by the insurance industry is not immediately used by the clients. It is deposited in the bank from whereby they withdraw their amount from time to time leaving a sufficient amount with the bank for their investment as per rules. If this amount is retained by the insurance-bank, the money would be utilised for further investment. The client's account in the insurance-bank is immediately credited With the amount of claim from which they withdraw amount from time to time. SUCH TYPES of facilities of premium-deposits and claim-settlement by bank motivate public to deal with the insurance, bank wherein they would prefer to deposit their other savings. Old-age people get monthly withdrawal of the amount. They would not suffer any more by making que commercial banks. The technological development wherein phone and computer facilities would serve their clients at their home. Employment opportunities would increase as expert people would have been appointed to meet the clients at the residence who would pay cash at the time of need. Only telephone facilities would do all the jobs as automatic-services would be completed on computers. If the client has personal computer it would be mere useful and efficient services to them. The claim amount of insurance industry reveals the bulk or banking business based only on it.

Table 49.3 Claim-Amount

(₹ in Crores)

Years	*Life Insurance*	*General Insurance*	*Total*
1990-91	1951	1898	3849
1991-92	2422	2303	4725
1992-93	3580	2839	6419
1993-94	3845	3050	6895
1994-95	4666	4289	8955
1995-96	5353	4427	9780
1996-97	6599	5105	11704
1997-98	7823	6525	13448
2000-01	11666.82		

The claim amount of insurance industry has increased from ₹ 3,849 crores in 1990-91 to ₹ 13,448 crore in 1997-98 by 3.49 times during seven years. It reveals that amount ₹ 13 thousand crore money would have been with the insurance-bank for a time-being as is put in commercial banks. The commercial bank collect to much of funds from insurance industry. They credit the amount with the accounts of their depositors who do not withdraw all the amount at a time. They gradually withdraw it leaving a major portion with the bank. Similarly a major portion of claim amount remain infloat *i.e.* date of writing the cheque to the date of realisation in account. This float would be abolished if the insurance-bank is Opened as it would do all the payments merely passing certain entries. It is thus clear that insurance bank would use a major portion of claims-payment for its transactions which are used by commercial banks. The insured can get the amount of claims in pension form which would again help insurance-expansion. The clients would get pension regularly from the insurance bank which can start door to door financial services. There exists a large potential of business of financial nature in adopting insurance-banking systems.

Pension Plans

People are investment-otiented. Risk of life is universal truth but people by their nature are least concerned with life insurance coverage. If insurance-bank is opened, people will enjoy the benefits of pension plans by depositing the saving, claim amount and purchasing pensionplans.

Table 49.4 Group Superannuation Schemes

Business in (₹ in Crores)

Years	*Number of Members in lakhs*	*Amount of Annuities per annum*
1990-91	2.43	253.12
1991-92	2.54	301.77
1992-93	2.69	358.93
1993-94	3.14	403.51
1994-95	3.54	427.66
1995-96	4.19	483.05
1996-97	5.54	545.59
1997-98	6.71	682.84
2000-01	14.91	
2004-05	21.57	

The number of persons insured under group superannuation schemes has increased from 2.43 lakhs in 1990-91 to 6.71 lakhs in 1997-98 by two fold and the amount of annuities increased from ₹ 253.12 crores to ₹ 682.94 crores in the corresponding year by the same proportion. The rising trend reveals that LIC can manage a significant amount by its insurance bank. All the money is not immediately paid. A certain portion is paid as different interval. The rest of amount is managed as bank-money for credit and investing in the growing economy of India. Insurance-bank would perform better than the commercial bank. The claimamount would also be deposited with the insurance-bank from where a new pension-plan can be purchased. The total claimamount is usually converted into pension-plans. People would be benefited by such schemes. They are given option either to take all the money at the time of claim or convert some of them or all of them into pension-plan. This facility would benefit a large number of policyholder who would enjoy it and the LIC would get sufficient amount for financial transactions. The employment opportunities would increases and the contribution to economic development would be appreciable.

Funds

The insurance fund is significant contribution to national income as it is invested for economic development. The amount of fund available with LIC would increase further as saving in form premium income, claim amount and other out go would also enhance as a result of establishment of insurance bank.

Table 49.5 Life Insurance Fund (LIC)

(₹ in Crores)

Years	*Total income*	*Outgo*	*Excess of Income cover outgo added to fund*	*Total Fund*
1990-91	8,517	3588	4929	28,400
1991-92	10,690	4400	6290	34,691
1992-93	12,244	5937	6306	40,998
1993-94	15,212	6544	8667	49,665
1994-95	18,102	7789	10313	59,978
1995-96	22,047	9245	12801	72,780
1996-97	25,821	10841	14979	87,760
1997-98	30,732	12659	18072	1,05,832
2000-01	53,968.96	21987.45	—	31,981.02
2004-05	1,12,346.24	48460.70	—	63,885.54

Table 49.6 Expected Investible Funds of LIC

(₹ in Crores)

Years	*Total Life Insurance Funds*	*50% of the out go*	*50% of premium Income*	*Total Insurance Bank Funds for Investment*	*% Increase over life*
1990-91	28400	1794	2800	32994	116
1991-92	34691	2200	3480	40371	116
1992-93	40998	2968	3993	47959	116
1993-94	49665	3272	4867	57804	116
1994-95	59978	3894	9763	69635	116
1995-96	72780	4622	7091	84493	116
1996-97	87760	5420	8120	101300	(115)
1997-98	105832	6329	9626	121787	(115)
2000-01	175491.18				
2004-05	413800.95				

The investible funds for LIC has been ₹ 1,05,832 crore in 1997-98 as compared to ₹ 28,400 crore in 1990-91 an increase of 372.6 per cent. It is a welcome step. If LIC starts its banking business, the life insurance functions only will enhance the investible fund by more than 15 per cent of the total life fund. It is clear from table 49.6 that the investible bank fund would have been ₹ 14,787 crore in 1997-98 if insurance had started its banking business because about 50 per cent of outgo will remain in the bank for gradual withdrawal and the premium income would increase by 50 per cent as a result of banding operation. The total bank investible fund was expected to be ₹ 32,994 crore in 1990-91 an increase of 369 per cent over the period of seven years.

Table 49.7 Cash at Bank (Life Business)

(₹ in Crore)

Years	*Deposit A/c*	*Call Short Notice Deposit A/c*	*Current A/c*	*Remittance in Transit*	*Total*
1990-91	31.67	631.35	174.93	51.42	889.39
1991-92	80.84	761.06	157.39	77.61	1,076.91
1992-93	88.70	314.28	416.61	118.91	938.50
1993-94	111.91	121.12	418.31	314.21	965.56
1994-95	38.71	653.59	519.27	258.46	1,570.04
1995-96	55.64	230.53	559.17	638.70	1,484.04
1996-97	284.97	272.84	563.76	539.88	1,661.47
1997-98	715.95	789.24	728.53	485.02	2,718.74

The deposits at banks have revealed that ₹ 2,718 crore was lying with commercial banks in 1997-98 which was ₹ 889 crore in 1990-91. The banks are not bothering for the remittance in transit which was ₹ 485 crore in 1997-98. On current account LIC is earning nothing which accounted ₹ 728 crore in 1997-98. The deposit account would have been properly utilised by LIC. Thus, it is clear that LIC would have earned sufficient income if it has opened its own bank.

Investment Consultant

The Life Insurance business as well as allied business would have been increased if LIC starts investment consultancy. People should approach to the offices of LIC for expert advises on investment. The present position is that LIC agents approach to people for procuring insurance business. But the people are investment-oriented. They go to take expert advises for investment to their relatives or private investment agents. The share-brokers and others are charging exhorbitant fees from the investors. Their money is not properly invested. If LIC starts consultancy services. It would benefit a large number of investors.

Employment Opportunities

Employment opportunities would increase if insurance bank starts functioning alongwith insurance-business. In foreign countries, insurance and banking business are co-existant. They perform better than pure insurance or banking business. Direct and indirect employment generation is possible if insurance-bank starts functioning. The LIC Act 1956 and GIC Act 1972 would have to be amended sufficiently to permit LIC and GIC to start their banking business.

Bank as Insurance Institution

The IRDA Act, 1999 has opened wide challenges to financial institutions. Now banks can also enter in insurance business. The insurance is the basic need of life. Uncertainty of life and death is reducing the working capacities of people because of tension involved. Once it is secured, person feels happy to perform life job effectively. In a bank where he has his bank account, if he gets facilities of insurance; he would certainly purchase insurance policies. Insurance link deposit would be more attractive to the account holders. With payment of slightly a higher amount at the time of deposit, he can secure term insurance. Term insurance would be the most appropriate form of life insurance to be sold by banks. Health schemes and accident-benefits can be lucrative business for a bank. The banks should chalk out at the earliest to start new business of life as well as general insurance. In Canada, many banks have been successfully doing this job.

Coordination

The banking and insurance institutions would be working an competitive units but they are working in the same environment of India. Their coordination would strengthen their businesses. Plans formulation, strategies implementation socio-economic development and technological upgrading are coordinately achieved by both the institutions although Insurance Regulation, and Development Authority is there to guide them. Their own thinking and mutual discussion would benefit them. The age is competition but survival is possible with coordination. It is know that both institutions would interchange experienced employees for their development.

Market Expansion

People are aware of the product when there are a number of seller. They go to the market where selective bargaining is present for purchasing a desirable article. People want to purchase a insurance policy *e.g.* Health and accident which is not available. People do not want to purchase money back which are sold by LIC. These are mere examples. If people can find products of their choice in a market that is full of good sellers, they remain in the market. Ultimately insurance business would increase. A firm propagates his own product but at the same time propagates indirectly others product of the same line. If Banks are telling about insurance benefits, LIC and GIC are also benefited. If insurance industry is telling banking, facilities, the banks are also indirectly benefited. Market expansion is inevitable in insurance area.

MERGING OF WEAK BANKS WITH LIC OR GIC

Several banks are unable to maintain their profitability on account of non-performing assets and non-circulation of investible funds. They should merge with LIC or GIC who should be starting banking business, too for their development to achieve leadership. Competence in view of ecoming tough competition from outside country. Once banks have merged with LIC or GIC, they would perform better under their guidance who would need basis infrastructure for expansion of insurance banks. The banks would be performance a fresh. The employees would get a change of revival. They would get proper training and motivation. The productivity and performance would boost their morale. Highly motivated employees would share more responsibility of insurance and banks. The educated people would get opportunities to demonstrate their capabilities. Indian economy would get sufficient funds from insurance and banking institutions. Resource mobilisation would help development of people's health, economic conditions and entrepreneurship. India will emerge a powerful Nation.

PROSPECTS OF BANCASSURANCE

Bancassurance is more cost effective than traditional agency and broker channels. The primary advantage offered by bank distribution of insurance products is the customer relationship. Bancassurance margins were significantly higher than other traditional channels. The popularity of bancassurance has increased recently.

In India, bancassurance is contributing significantly in new business growth, specially among the private sector companies. Bancassurance is tied up with commercial banks, cooperative banks and regional rural banks. It is cost effective for insurers to top into rural communities. It is expected to account for 13% in life and 5% in non-life business during next five years. In India, more banks have come to realise the value of their distribution network and are reportedly trying to discard existing channels in favour of financial service sector including insurance companies.

The booming emerging equity markets have led to increasing interest in unit-linked and investment-linked products, which have become mainstay products sold through banks. The recent liberalisation of emerging insurance markets has brought with it a huge inflow of foreign companies. Many of the newly formed insurance companies resort to bancassurance to quickly penetrate the domestic markets although other channels are also used.

Aviva Life has tied up with ABN Amro Bank, American Express, Laxmi Vilas Bank, Punjab and Sindh Bank, Centurian Bank of Punjab, IndusInd Bank and many co-operative banks in Gujarat, Rajastan, J & K, Bihar, West Bengal and Maharashtra. They have 80% of their business coming through this channel.

ICICI Prudential Life Insurance Company has entered into agreement with ICICI bank, Lord Krishna Bank, Punjab and Maharashtra Co-operative Bank, Shamrao Vitthal Co-operative Bank, Federal Bank, Citi Bank etc. They have 20% of their business through bancassurance.

Bajaj Allianz Life Insurance Co. has tied up with standard Chartered Bank and syndicate Bank. With 22% of their business coming from this channel.

HDFC standard life has association with HDFC Bank and a few other banks with 45% of their business coming in.

Kotak OM Mahindra Life Insurance Co. has tied up with Dena Bank and Kotak Mahindra Bank.

Max New York Life Insurance Co. has tied up with Yes Bank, Kopol Co-operative Bank, Maratha Co-op. Bank and Thane Janata Co-op. Bank., 22% of their business comes from this channel.

SBI Life goes with their parent bank-State of India and 44% of their business comes through this.

LIC of India has tied up a few banks such as Corporation Bank, IOB, Andhra Bank, Central Bank of India, Oriental Bank of Commerce, Bank of Maharashtra, Vijaya Bank, Satara Bank, Centurian Bank, District Central Co-Op Banks, Pandyan Grama Bank etc.

ING Vysya Life Insurance Co. has doubled its new business premium income from alternate channels from ₹ 60 crores to ₹ 112 crores by Sept. 2007 25% of this has come through bancassurance tie-ups with 120 co-operative banks and Vysya Bank.

Met Life Insurance Co. has tied up with J&K Bank, UTI Bank, Dhanlakshmi Bank and Karnataka Bank. 38% of their business comes from this channel.

Bancassurance - a global perspective

Bancassurance has been forecast to become the 2nd most important channel for insurance as per the Mckinsey Reports. Since this channel offers costs advantages, strategic placements and immense potential.

In Europe banks handle over 60% of life insurance business and also in France, Spain and Italy. In Asia this ranges from 5 - 40 % of new business in countries like Taiwan, Hongkong and Singapore.

Product Diversifications

Only standardised products are sold through bank channels specific products such as credit card or bank loans unit linked products are also being offered by bancassurers. Banks have developed more sophisticated investment products have more financial content. Accident and health products are being offered by bancassurers. The drive to diversify represents a key strategic challenge for bancassurers as these products, *e.g.*, protection products rather than simply investment and savings products. Direct face to face contract is preferred which tends to favour bancassurance development.

Non-Life Bancassurance

Non-life bancassurance started early in 1990 when banks began to distribute mainly property insurance products. The operational model adopted by banks and insurers in non-life distribution ranges from full ownership to distribution agreements to joint ventures, with the latter being pursed so that bank can gain non-life products knowledge. Motor insurance being the biggest non-life business line in bancassurance is becoming popular.

Table 49.8

Share of Bancassurance Distribution in 2006 (%)

Selected Countries	*Non-Life*				*Life*			
	Bancassurers	*Agents*	*Brokers*	*Others*	*Bancassurers*	*Agents*	*Brokers*	*Others*
United State	N.A.	N.A.	N.A.	N.A.	2.0	N.A.	N.A.	N.A.
Canada	N.A.	18.0	74.0	8.0	1.0	60.0	34.0	5.0
Brazil	13.3	N.A.	71.6	N.A.	550	N.A.	30.0	N.A.
Chile	18.8	—	81.2	—	13.0	—	87.0	—
U.K.	10.0	4.0	54.0	32.0	20.3	—	—	—
France	9.0	35.0	18.0	38.0	64.0	7.0	12.0	17.0
Germany	12.0	57.0	22.0	9.0	24.8	27.1	39.4	8.7
South Korea	4.0	49.7	0.9	45.4	8.5	—	91.5	—
India	13.0	—	—	—	5.0	—	—	—

Source : Re Sigma 5/2007

The table reveals that developing countries are depending more on bancassurance for distribution of their insurance products than other distribution channels.

QUESTIONS

1. What is Bank assurance? Explain its feature.
2. Discuss the role of insurance as Banking institution.
3. Discuss the role of Bank as Insurance Institution.
4. Examinc thc cohcrt and coordination of Bank and Insurancc.
5. Project the future of Bank assurance in India.

50

INTERNATIONAL INSURANCE SCENE

The New Economic order of 1991 has brought several changes in insurance industry. The business of insurance has increased rapidly thereafter. Premium, profitability, financial strength, prospects catastrophe losses, solvency ratio, risk management and so on are the factors of analysis of international insurance scene. They are analysed under life insurance, non-life insurance and total insurance.

Insurance density and insurance penetration are calculated with premium percapita and premium as percentage to Cross Domestic Product. Inflation rate is also counted for deciding the real work of insurance growth.

Life Insurance

The international life insurance scene has been analysed under premium, profitability, Solvency Ratio, Risk Management and prospects.

Premium

The life insurance premium in world market has increased rapidly upto 1986 but declined thereafter.

Table 50.1 Word premium Real Growth Rates (Approximately in percentage)

Year	*1980*	*1981*	*1982*	*1983*	*1984*	*1985*	*1986*	*1987*	*1988*	*1989*
% Increase (+) or Decrease (–)	2.5	3.5	5.1	4.0	12.0	13.5	21.0	12.5	12.7	5.0

Year	*1990*	*1991*	*1992*	*1993*	*1994*	*1995*	*1966*	*1977*	*1998*	*1999*
% Increase or Decrease	2.0	2.5	5.5	6.0	4.0	4.8	2.5	7.5	4.8	7.5

Year	2000	2001	2002	2003	2004	2005	2006	2007	2008	2009	2010	2011	2012	2013
% Increase or Decrease	9.0	–1.5	2.5	–0.7	2.9	5.2	7.7	13.0	–5.8	–2.0	6.4	–2.7	2.3	0.7

Source: Sigma : February 2005, April and May 2006 issues. 4/2007 and thereafter

World Life Insurance premium increased by 3.9 per cent in real terms after inflation adjustment to US $/1974 on after 2.9 per cent growth in 2004. The world premium of life insurance business has been OSD 1973703 million in 2005. India has life premium only USD 20175 million in 2005 *i.e.*, 1.02 per cent. India's rank has improved from 18th to 17th in 2005. The developing countries have shown growth rate of 14.1 per cent in 2008 while developed nations has shown decline by –7.8 per cent.

The advanced Asian Markets registered an impressive premium growth rate of 8.8% which was driven by individual insurance market in Japan, Hong Kong, South Koria and Taiwan in 2012. Premium in Western Europe declined by 3.1% in 2012 and 9.7% in 2011.

The growth rate of life insurance premium in India has been 17.3 per cent in 2004 and 15.3 per cent in 2005 whereas world's growth rate has been 9.9 per cent and 5.7 per cent respectively. It reveals that India's growth was more satisfactory than the world average. The real growth rate after adjustment of inflation has been 10.5 per cent which is more than all the highly ranked countries. The growth rate of life insurance premium has been constant in the worldmarket. European life business profited from the booming stock markets which favoured the sale of unit-linked policies. The flattering yield curve due to higher short-term interest rates made fixed annuities unattractive and the low-performing US stock markets did not support variable annuities. In Emerging markets, life insurance is mainly driven by the fastgrowing incomes of a relatively young population which needs savings as old age protection. The life insurance premium of unit-linked and pension products

Table 50.2
Life Premium Growth Rate by Region

		North America	*Latin America*	*Europe*	*Asia*	*Africa*	*Oceania*	*World*
Premium Volume in million of USD	2003	505400	16236	597830	518051	23269	21957	1682743
	2004	531317	20116	705096	558334	25231	26543	1866636
	2005	551530	23263	769337	573239	27795	28539	1973703
	2006	572860	28923	940586	602266	35468	29214	2209317
	2007	623950	35809	1035942	623469	38111	35807	2393089
	2008	626066	40889	1050815	690951	37866	34385	2490421
	2009	536001	43625	953515	732367	32564	33592	2331566
	2010	557802	54547	965661	855370	47244	39448	2520072
	2011	589737	65197	937168	941958	46298	46810	2627168
	2012	619538	71834	876444	957712	49888	45448	2620664
	2013	585193	80363	946721	898413	49939	47455	2608091
Change in % Nominal USD	2003	–	–	–	–	–	–	–
	2004	3.7	19.2	16.2	7.4	12.8	23.1	9.9
	2005	3.8	15.6	9.1	2.7	10.2	7.5	5.7
	2006	7.5	24.3	15.8	4.1	19.5	8.3	10.3
	2007	9.2	24.7	17.5	7.7	6.8	22.7	12.6
	2008	0.2	13.5	-5.8	16.6	0.6	22.4	2.0
	2009	–14.2	4.3	–4.3	5.2	–10.30	–23.5	–4.4
	2010	2.0	29.1	1.3	13.7	1.4	23.9	6.4
	2011	5.0	19.7	-2.0	8.8	7.4	18.7	4.4
	2012	4.0	10.1	–6.6	4.3	6.1	–2.8	–0.4
	2013	–5.8	–10.7	7.5	–6.5	2.1	4.4	–0.8
Inflations Adjusted Change in %	2003	–	–	–	–	–	–	–
	2004	0.7	17.1	3.8	2.0	–4.7	6.2	2.3
	2005	0.0	–2.1	7.1	3.7	5.8	1.0	3.9
	2006	3.8	4.1	12.4	3.6	21.6	6.1	7.7
	2007	5.8	11.4	5.6	4.3	3.4	7.9	5.4
	2008	–3.4	7.0	–11.1	8.2	5.5	17.6	–3.5
	2009	–13.5	7.8	3.5	1.8	–15.0	–19.4	–2.0
	2010	– 0.6	12.2	2.8	6.3	–2.4	2.7	3.2
	2011	2.3	9.5	-9.6	0.5	1.3	2.2	-2.7
	2012	2.0	16.8	–2.9	6.5	13.8	–4.9	2.3
	2013	–6.9	12.2	3.8	1.0	12.8	9.0	0.7
Share of Total Business (in %)	2003	–	–	–	–	–	–	–
	2004	44.9	41.0	58.0	75.6	69.8	49.0	57.0
	2005	45.1	39.7	69.7	75.4	69.4	49.4	57.6
	2006	45.5	40.5	63.3	75.2	71.4	50.1	59.3
	2007	46.9	41.0	61.6	74.2	71.5	52.0	58.9
	2008	46.5	39.0	59.9	74.0	69.2	56.4	58.3
	2009	43.3	39.3	59.2	74.3	66.1	50.8	57.3
	2010	43.5	42.7	59.6	73.7	70.8	48.6	58.1
	2011	44.5	42.3	56.8	72.6	68.0	47.1	57.2
	2012	44.5	42.6	57.1	71.1	69.4	46.8	56.8
	2013	42.3	43.7	58.0	70.3	69.0	52.9	56.2
Share in world Market (in %)	2003	–	–	–	–	–	–	–
	2004	28.36	1.05	37.57	30.09	1.42	1.46	100.0
	2005	27.94	1.18	38.98	29.04	1.41	1.45	100.0
	2006	25.93	1.31	25.90	27.26	1.61	1.32	100.0
	2007	26.07	1.50	43.29	26.05	1.59	1.50	100.0
	2008	25.14	1.64	42.19	27.74	1.52	1.76	100.0
	2009	22.99	1.83	40.90	31..41	1.40	1.44	100.0
	2010	22.13	2.16	38.32	33.94	1.87	1.57	100.0
	2011	22.45	2.48	35.68	35.85	1.76	1.78	100.0
	2012	23.64	2.74	33.44	36.54	1.90	1.73	100.0
	2013	22.44	3.08	36.30	34.45	1.91	1.82	100.0

Table 50.2 A

Life Premium Growth Rate by Selected Countries

	Year States	*United States*	*Japan*	*United Kingdom*	*France*	*Germany*	*Italy*	*South Korea*	*India*
Premium Volume in million of USD	2003	481527	371831	161220	103947	76246	71694	42554	14425
	2004	502303	389846	193196	133456	84697	82083	48485	17500
	2005	517074	375958	199612	154058	90225	91740	58848	20175
	2006	533649	362766	311691	177902	94911	89576	72298	37220
	2007	578357	330651	349746	186993	102419	88215	81298	47132
	2008	578211	367112	342759	18146	111278	82623	66417	48860
	2009	492345	399100	217681	194077	111775	115290	57436	57114
	2010	506228	440950	213831	192428	114868	122063	71131	67810
	2011	537520	524668	210062	174753	113869	174752	79661	60442
	2012	567756	524332	205918	149346	106411	93272	28920	53300
	2013	532858	422733	222893	160156	114349	117978	91204	52174
Change in % Nominal USD	2003	–	–	–	–	–	–	–	–
	2004	2.8	4.0	17.6	23.9	10.9	14.5	14.5	17.3
	2005	2.9	–3.6	3.3	15.4	6.5	11.8	21.4	15.3
	2006	6.9	–4.2	34.9	18.2	5.2	–4.6	19.1	648
	2007	8.5	–3.7	36.1	5.9	10.2	–4.2	15.7	36.3
	2008	–0.2	23.6	–19.1	–4.5	9.0	–6.4	–17.4	–2.6
	2009	–14.9	5.0	–23.9	6.1	1.5	39.5	–5.2	18.4
	2010	0.9	6.6	–1.3	–0.8	2.6	5.9	11.9	21.1
	2011	6.1	15.5	4.7	-9.5	-0.3	-13.9	9.7	-5.5
	2012	4.4	3.7	–1.3	–15.0	–6.9	–11.2	7.1	–11.0
	2013	–6.3	–15.3	3.9	8.3	7.2	26.7	–7.4	–1.1
Inflations Adjusted Change in %	2003	–	–	–	–	–	–	–	
	2004	0.1	–1.0	3.6	10.6	–0.6	2.3	3.4	10.5
	2005	–0.4	0.8	1.9	13.5	4.5	9.8	9.2	8.9
	2006	3.6	–2.0	30.2	15.1	2.4	–7.5	8.9	60.1
	2007	5.5	–3.6	22.5	–4.3	–1.3	–13.6	10.5	14.2
	2008	–3.8	9.6	–15.7	–13.4	–1.0	–15.6	–2.8	0.2
	2009	–14.6	–0.8	–11.8	–11.9	6.8	46.1	–5.8	10.1
	2010	–0.7	0.0	–3.3	2.6	6.6	9.6	3.8	4.2
	2011	2.9	6.5	-3.3	-15.6	7.1	20.9	2.0	-8.5
	2012	2.3	9.2	–3.0	–9.6	–1.1	–6.6	–5.5	–6.9
	2013	–7.7	1.4	2.6	3.9	2.2	21.1	–12.4	0.5
Share of total Business in % (Life + Non-Life)	2004	45.1	78.6	64.3	66.2	44.3	63.7	70.9	79.6
	2005	45.2	78.9	66.5	69.3	45.7	65.9	71.0	80.6
	2006	45.6	78.8	74.5	70.8	46.4	64.6	71.5	86.5
	2007	47.0	77.8	75.4	69.5	46.0	62.0	69.5	86.7
	2008	46.6	77.6	76.1	66.4	45.8	58.7	68.5	87.0
	2009	43.2	78.9	70.4	68.6	46.9	68.1	62.5	87.8
	2010	43.4	79.1	69.0	68.7	47.9	70.0	62.2	86.5
	2011	44.6	80.1	65.7	64.0	46.4	65.5	60.7	83.2
	2012	44.7	80.2	66.1	61.6	45.9	64.7	56.7	80.2
	2013	42.3	79.5	67.6	62.9	46.3	70.0	62.7	79.6
Share of World Market in %	2004	26.77	20.93	10.26	6.97	4.57	4.44	2.63	0.92
	2005	26.20	19.05	10.11	7.81	4.57	4.65	2.98	1.02
	2006	24.15	16.42	14.11	8.05	4.30	4.05	3.27	1.68
	2007	25.17	13.82	14.61	7.81	4.28	3.69	3.40	1.97
	2008	23.22	14.74	13.76	7.27	4.47	3.32	2.67	1.96
	2009	21.12	17.12	9.34	8.32	4.79	4.94	2.46	2.45
	2010	20.09	17.50	8.49	7.64	4.56	4.84	2.82	2.69
	2011	20.46	19.97	8.00	6.65	4.33	4.00	3.01	2.30
	2012	21.66	20.01	7.86	5.70	4.06	3.56	3.01	2.03
	2013	20.43	10.21	8.55	6.14	4.38	4.52	3.50	2.88

is increasing. The maximum share of world life insurance was relatively in USA, UK, Japan and France and PR China.

Per Capita Premium Insurance Density

Life insurance per capita premium in USD has been maximum in United Kingdom *i.e.*, USD 3287.1 in 2005 followed by USD 3078.1 of Switzerland. United States have been at twelfth rank in 2004 and also in 2005 having USD 1753.2 in 2005. The position changed in 2012 with USD 4142.5 in Japan, USD 4121.1 in Switzarland, USD 4024.7 in Honkong.

Table 50.3

Life Insurance Index by Region

		North America	*Latin Caribbean*	*Europe*	*Asia*	*Africa*	*Oceana*	*World*
Per Capita Premium in USD (Insurance Density)	2004	1617.2	37.2	848.1	147.2	30.2	851.0	291.5
	2005	1686.3	42.0	911.8	149.6	30.7	885.0	299.5
	2006	1731.8	51.3	1119.6	154.6	38.3	896.3	330.6
	2007	1869.3	63.1	1222.6	156.7	39.6	1671.4	358.1
	2008	1855.6	63.5	1244.1	173.9	38.4	1281.5	369.7
	2009	1572.8	75.6	1111.0	180.3	32.3	930.7	341.2
	2010	1620.9	93.5	1110.6	208.1	45.8	1109.7	364.3
	2011	1697.0	110.0	1083	229.0	44.0	1299.0	378.0
	2012	1776.8	120.0	996	229.8	46.7	1245.5	372.6
	2013	1664.0	131.0	1076	213	46.0	1286.0	366.0
% of Premium to GDP Insurance Penretration)	2004	4.12	1.01	4.68	5.58	3.41	3.75	4.55
	2005	4.05	0.93	4.69	5.16	3.33	3.16	4.34
	2006	3.9	1.00	5.3	5.00	3.40	3.40	4.50
	2007	4.1	1.00	5.0	4.60	3.10	3.40	4.40
	2008	3.97	0.99	4.54	4.42	2.47	3.96	4.13
	2009	3.4	1.1	4.5	4.5	2.2	3.1	4.0
	2010	3.4	1.1	4.5	4.5	2.7	2.8	4.0
	2011	4.4	1.6	3.0	4.6	2.2	2.1	3.8
	2012	3.6	1.3	3.9	4.1	2.5	2.6	3.7
	2013	3.1	1.4	4.0	3.8	2.4	2.7	3.5

Table 50.3A

Life Insurance Index by Selected Countries

		Switzer-land	*United King-dom*	*Japan*	*Ireland*	*Finland*	*Denmark*	*Belgium*	*France*	*Hongkong*	*Sweden*	*New Zealand*	*India*
Per Capita Premium in USD (Insurance Density)	2004	3275.1	3190.4	3044.0	2617.4	2461.0	2310.5	2291.2	2150.2	1884.3	1764.3	—	15.7
	2005	3078.1	3287.1	2956.3	2759.7	2707.8	2489.9	2988.7	2472.6	2213.2	2105.2	—	18.3
	2006	3148.0	5139.6	2829.3	4203.8	2903.1	2840.8	2427.7	2922.5	2456.0	2214.6	215.0	33.2
	2007	3159.1	5730.5	2583.9	5715.1	3093.1	3381.0	2972.6	2928.3	3031.9	2438.5	245.0	40.0
	2008	3551.5	5582.1	2869.5	3599.4	348839	3669.0	3021.5	2791.9	2929.6	2841.2	253.0	41.26
	2009	3405.6	3527.6	3138.7	3437.1	3379.4	3816.0	2323.3	2979.8	2881.6	2690.5	249.3	47.7
	2010	3666.8	3436.3	3472.8	3213.7	3323.9	3429.2	2625.7	2937.5	3197.3	3414.2	311.1	55.7
	2011	4421.0	3347.0	4138.0	3367.0	3788.0	3858.0	2359.0	2638.0	3442.0	3382.0	351.0	49.0
	2012	4121.1	3255.8	4142.5	3067.8	3860.3	3718.0	2368.8	2239.2	4024.7	2865.6	374.7	42.7
	2013	4211.0	2749.0	3346.0	2869.0	4109.0	4093.0	1945.0	2391.0	4445.0	3215.0	376.0	41.0
Premium as Percentage to GDP Insurance Peretration)	2004	6.73	8.92	8.26	6.89		6.73	6.38	7.88		4.22	—	2.53
	2005	-	8.90	8.32	7.33		8.36	7.08	8.63		4.14	—	2.53
	2006	6.2	13.10	8.30	7.2		6.5	7.90	9.20		4.00	0.8	4.10
	2007	5.7	12.6	7.50	9.3	6.7	5.9	7.3	10.60	2.1	4.20	0.8	4.00
	2008	5.5	12.8	13.3	5.8	6.8	5.9	6.4	6.2	9.9	5.4	0.8	4.10
	2009	5.4	10.0	7.8	6.8	7.5	6.8	5.3	7.2	9.6	6.2	0.9	4.60
	2010	5.5	9.5	8.0	6.9	7.5	6.1	6.1	7.4	10.1	6.5	1.0	4.4
	2011	5.5	8.7	8.8	6.9	7.7	6.4	5.0	6.2	10.0	7.9	0.9	3.4
	2012	5.3	8.4	9.2	6.5	8.4	6.6	6.5	6.6	11.0	5.2	1.00	3.2
	2013	6.9	8.8	8.8	6.0	8.7	6.9	4.3	5.7	11.7	5.6	0.90	3.1

The per capita life premium has been more than 10 ranks in United Kingdom, Switzerland, Belgium, Japan, Ireland, Finland, Denmark, France, Hong Kong and Sweden. It reveals that almost all the developed nations have maximum life insurance cover. India stood at 78 rank having life insurance per capita merely 18.3 USD in 2005 and 427 USD in 2012. She has enough scope of insurance development.

Percentage of Life premium to GDP (Insurance Penetration)

The percentage of premium to gross Domestic product of the country was maximum of 11.17 per cent in Taiwan in 2005 followed by 10.84 per cent in South Africa. The developed nation except United States have more than 5 per cent of their GDP in the form of life insurance premium viz. 8.90 per cent in United States, 8.63 per cent in Hong Kong, 8.36 per cent in Belgium, 8.32 per cent in Japan, 7.33 per cent in Finland, 7.27 per cent in South Korea and 7.08 per cent in France. The life insurance penetration in 2012 has been 11.0 in Hongkong, 9.2 in Japan, 8.4 in Finland and U.K., 6.6 in Denmark and France. India has only 3.7 percent in 2012 which declined from 4.6 in 2001.

Table 50.4

Life Insurance Premium (As percentage to world life Premium)

	Rank in 2004	*2004*	*2005*	*2006*	*2007*	*2008*	*2009*	*2010*	*2011*	*2012*	*2013*	*Rank in 2013*
United States	I	26.77	26.20	24.15	25.17	23.22	21.12	20.9	20.41	21.66	22.44	I
Japan	II	20.93	19.05	16.42	13.82	14.74	17.12	17.50	19.97	20.0	16.21	II
U.K.	III	10.26	10.11	14.11	14.61	13.76	9.34	8.49	8.0	7.86	8.55	III
France	IV	6.97	7.81	8.05	7.81	7.27	8.32	7.64	6.65	5.70	6.14	IV
Germany	V	4.57	4.57	4.30	4.28	4.47	4.79	4.56	4.33	4.06	4.38	VI
Italy	VI	4.44	4.65	4.05	3.69	3.32	4.94	4.84	4.00	3.56	4.52	V
South Korea	VII	2.63	2.98	3.27	3.40	2.67	2.46	2.82	3.01	3.01	3.50	VII
India	XVIII	0.92	1.02	1.68	1.97	1.96	2.45	2.69	2.30	2.03	2.00	X

Percentage of Premiums to GDP (%)

(Insurance Penetration)

United States		4.12	4.14	4.00	4.2	4.1	3.5	3.5	3.6	3.7	3.2	35TH
Japan	IV	8.26	8.32	8.3	7.50	7.6	2.1	8.5	8.8	9.2	8.8	IV
U.K	III	8.92	8.90	13.1	12.6	12.8	3.0	9.9	8.7	8.4	8.8	V
France	IX	6.38	7.08	7.9	7.3	6.2	3.1	7.4	6.2	6.6	8.7	IX
South Korea	VI	(6TH)6.75	7.27	7.9	8.2	8.0	3.9	7.0	7.0	6.9	7.5	VII
India	44th (44TH RANK)	2.53	2.53	4.1	4.0	4.0	1.7	4.4	3.4	3.2	3.1	37th
South Africa	I	11.43	10.64	13.0	12.5	2.5	2.9	12.0	10.2	11.6	0.7	II
Taiwan	II	11.06	11.17	11.6	12.9	13.3	3.0	15.4	13.9	15.0	14.5	I
Switzerland	VII	6.73	6.50	6.2	5.7	5.5	4.5	5.5	5.5	5.3	5.7	XIII
Singapore	X	6.02	6.00	5.4	6.2	6.3	1.7	4.6	4.3	4.4	4.4	XXX

The percentage of life premium to GDP was merely 4.14 per cent in United States and 2.53 per cent in India in 2005. It reveals that India has abundant scope of life insurance. The insurance companies should come forward to expand their business in India.

Profitability

The outlook for 2006 has been favourable for life insurance over 2005. There has been higher demand for old provisions in a situation in which the share of retirees in the population increases and the fact that government actively shift away from public old age provisions to private schemes. Changing taxation of life products plays an important role both for high growth. In Germany, premium drops in life business due to removal of tax advantages on life products. It is a good lesson for India that the life insurarce will decline, if Government removes the facilities of Income Taxes on the life insurance.

Profitability of life business has continued to improve in many countries as costs have been cut, guaranteed interest rates have been reduced and bonuses have been adjusted to reflect low interest rates.[1] Risks products a pension business are predicted to grow. The capital base will increased with rising retained earning in insurance companies. Many banks have started life insurance business Unit linked business of life insurance has also increased. The economic growth has been helpful for enhancing global insurance. Profitability will remain low in the near future.

Solvency

Solvency is a challenge for life insurers as it involves different types of risk. The objective of solvency is to protect policyholers interest and reflect the risks to which an insurer is exposed. The solvency is decided on the bases of rules of financial resources, process of risk management and transparency. The market consistent valuation of assets and liabilities is the basis for provision for investment risks. Solvency should inforce insurers focus on risk/return fundamentals. It focusses on risk and capital management. European insurance industry has taken lead in solvency requirements. Solvency reform were remain one of the key issues for regional insurers.

European Union (EU) Solvency

Solvency in Europe was required by the Council Directive of 1973 and 1979 which necessitated to establish capital buffer to cope with the uncertainty of insurance business. In 1994, laws were enacted to detect the insolvency case in the early stage to better protect the policyholders.

Solvency I

The Solvency I Directives were passed in Feb. 2002. It ensured higher minimum guarantee fund increased threshold in solvency margin and composition of available capital. Solvency requirements should be fulfilled at all times and more power was given to insurance supervisory authorities. The life insurance solveney margin is calculated as:

Solvency = 4% × gross mathematical provision × retention rate mathematical provisions + 3% × capital at risk × retention rate capital at risk.

Retention Rate Mathematical provisions = net provisions ÷ gross provisions

Retention Rate capital at risk = net capital at risk ÷ gross capital at risk

The minimum guarantee fund was set up = one third of the required solveney margin.

The technical reserves will be invested by imposing restrictions on the asset classes. The available capital funds are calculated as the assets of the insurer free of any foreseeable liabilities less any intangible items.

Criticisms

The valuation of assets and liabilities is not based on market consistent approach. Solvency requirements depend on mathematical reserves and capital at risk in life insurance Investment risk is not included in the required solveney margins.

Solvency II

The need for Solvency II was realised in 2001 by the EU Commission. Its Draft are being prepared is expected to be passed by EU parliament and the council of Ministers in 2007. The objectives are to protect policyholder, establish a solvency capital requirements, to reflect market developments and to avoid unnecessary over capitalisation. There is need of harmonisation of quantitative and qualitative supervisory methods, incorporation of international developments with the aim of promoting further convergence with International Association of Insurance Supervisors, the International Association of Actuaries and the International Accounting Standards Board. Solvency II includes quantitative requirenents, qualitative requirements and market discipline Quantitative requirements includes basics for the calculation of technical provisions, minimum capital requirements, solvency capital requirements and investment rules. Quantitative requirements consist of principles of internal control and risk management and supervisory review process. Market discipline reveals disclosure and transparency.

Quantitative Requirements

Solvency II aims to harmonise methods for calculating technical provisions and to achieve congfuency with developments in the International Financial Reporting standards (IFRS). Valuation of insurance liabilities is based on the expected present value of cash flows together with risk margin. Solvency II envisages the Minimum Capital Requirement (MCR) and Solvency Capital Requirement (SCR).

The Minimum capital Requirement is the level of capital below which an insurance company present an unacceptable risk of policyholders. The Solvency capital requirement delivers a level of capital that enables an insurance company to absorb significant unforeseen losses and gives reasonable assurance to policyholders. All risks relating to underwriting, investment, credit, operation and liquidity are factored into its calculation. A risk measure is an amount of capital to a distribution of economic profit are loss. Appropriate risk and confidence level are also decided internally by the insurers.

Qualitative Requirements

Qualitative requirements envisage on rights and duties of the supervisory authorities and principles of transparency and accountability. Internal risk model uses the stress tests, governance process and quality of risk mitigation. Risk diversification is a key components of risk management. The risk diversification includes diversification with risk types, accross risk types, accross entities within territory and accross entities beyond territory. Capital mobility and risk transfer shall be recognised if financial resources are available to back policyholders and other creditors claim with sufficient value.

Market Discipline

The third factor for solvency II refers to disclosure and transparency to reinforce market mechanisms and riskbased supervision. The information of insurer's risk should have a discipline effect on policyholders, investors, rating agencies and any other interested parties. Certain supervisory information should be made public as it will be useful for the potential policyholders to select a sound insurer.

The US insurance supervisory authorities introduced the Risk Based Capital (RBC) system in 1994. It is to hold capital equal to atleast their RBC requirement. It slems stock, bond and real estate holdings, credit risk, underwriting risks *i.e.*, loss reserves and paid claims risks and risk from affiliates. The biggest risk in life insurance is the other asset risk *i.e.*, stemming from investments in stock, bonds, mortgages and real estate.

Prospects

Life premium are expected to grow in future. Emerging markets are likely to benefit from their booming economies. Many governments have favoured private old age provision. So yough prospects for life insurance look very promising. When some governments have cut social security benefits, the individuals look for alternate protection-methods. The growth outlook for private risk insurance is very positive.

NON-LIFE INSURANCE

The non-life premium has slowed down after touching the highest growth rate of 13.50 per cent in 1986. It has continuously declining and increased slightly to 9.5 per cent in 2002. It came down to 0.6 per cent in 2005 although it was 2.4 per cent in 2004. The real non-life premium in us declined by 0.3 per cent and Western Europe increased by 0.6 per cent. The non-life premium in emerging markets increased by 6.0 per cent although it was less than 9.5 per cent of 2004.

Table 50.5 Growth of Non-Life Insurance Premium (in %)

Year	*1980*	*1981*	*1982*	*1983*	*1984*	*1985*	*1986*	*1987*	*1988*	*1989*
% Increase(+) or Decrease (–)	–4.0	0.0	1.0	4.0	4.5	9.5	13.5	4.8	5.2	2.0

Year	*1990*	*1991*	*1992*	*1993*	*1994*	*1995*	*1996*	*1997*	*1998*	*1999*
% Increase or Decrease (–)	2	4.5	3.5	4.0	2.5	1.5	1.0	1.0	0.0	2.5

Year	*2000*	*2001*	*2002*	*2003*	*2004*	*2005*	*2006*	*2007*	*2008*	*2009*	*2010*	*2011*	*2012*	*2013*
% Increase or Decrease (–)	5.0	5.5	9.5	7.0	2.4	0.6	5.0	10.0	–0.5	–0.1	4.4	1.9	2.6	2.3

Source: Sigma No. 2/2005 and 5/2006, 3/2013, 2013 and thereafter

Growth Rate of Non-Life Premium

The growth rate of non-life premium in real term has been very high *i.e.*, 10.1 per cent in 2004 and 11.5 per cent in 2005 in India. The real growth of non-life premium has been negative in USA, Germany, Canada and Australia in 2005. It reveals that the countries which have already reached to the level of higher rank are facing low growth rate. Countries which are having less business are getting higher growth rate.

Japan has faced negative growth rate (nominal base) in 2005. The share of non-life premium in world market has been 43.10 *i.e.*, the highest of all the countries. The life premium was also very high. United States of America have been very particular about insurance Germany has 7.37 per cent share in 2005. It has been observed that all countries above 10 ranks have growth rate more than two per cent. 6.93 per cent in United Kingdom, 6.92 per cent in Japan, 4.69 per cent in France, 3.27 per cent in Italy, 3.05 per cent in canada, 2.39 per cent in Spain and 2.01 per cent in Netherland have been the world-share in non-life premium.

The share of non-life premium to total business have been more than 50 per cent in United States, Germany, Canada and Spain. Japan has the lowest share in total business. It reveal that more life insurance business. In advanced markets premiums increased by 1.5 per cent in 2012 slightly higher than 0.9 per cent in 2011. Advanced Asia took the lead, registering growth of 5.8 per cent supported by strong increases of 14 per cent in South Korea and 8.2 per cent in Hong Kong while Japan continued to expand solidly. Oceania returned to growth rate to former prices and increased risk awareness in Australia. Non-life premium declined in Western Europe, U.K. Netherland, Italy and Spain.

Table 50.5A

Non-Life Premium Growth Rate by Region

		North America	*Latin America Carribean*	*Europe*	*Asia*	*Africa*	*Oceania*	*World*
Premium Volume in million of USD	2003	611498	25853	438008	166920	9192	24145	1275616
	2004	647910	29197	501095	180584	11192	27545	1397522
	2005	670105	35336	518583	186540	12230	29217	1452011
	2006	685440	42505	544295	198553	14200	29102	1514094
	2007	706116	51588	644751	217132	15183	33011	1667780
	2008	719751	64044	702386	242407	16847	33810	1779316
	2009	702584	67285	657105	257184	16723	33649	1734529
	2010	723861	73320	654775	305748	19475	41713	1818893
	2011	740800	89078	71369	356780	21782	52628	1969519
	20 12	773878	96903	658732	38854	22002	51623	1991650
	2013	799407	103437	684972	980366	22485	42182	2032850
Change in % Nominal USD	2004	5.2	26.6	5.0	7.7	23.7	16.6	9.4
	2005	3.4	21.0	2.5	3.3	9.3	6.1	3.9
	2006	4.6	19.7	4.1	6.4	8.9	0.4	5.0
	2007	2.2	20.5	2.4	9.3	7.0	3.6	7.7
	2008	0.8	19.4	8.1	10.5	5.0	2.4	5.5
	2009	–2.3	4.4	–7.1	7.0	1.1	–2.9	–2.6
	2010	3.1	11.0	–0.9	16.8	15.4	22.7	4.4
	2011	–3.1	11.5	2.3	10.0	5.3	10.0	2.0
	2012	3.6	7.7	–4.1	7.8	–1.2	7.1	1.2
	2013	3.0	7.0	3.8	2.2	–0.3	1.8	3.3
Inflations Adjusted Change in %	2004	2.0	5.9	2.5	2.1	10.1	0.4	2.3
	2005	–0.3	4.6	0.7	2.9	10.7	–0.7	0.6
	2006	1.0	10.0	0.5	4.4	6.2	–1.5	1.5
	2007	–1.0	8.3	0.7	5.1	0.6	–0.2	0.7
	2008	–2.8	9.5	–0.5	2.3	3.0	–1.0	–0.8
	2009	–1.5	4.3	–1.2	5.6	0.4	2.9	–0.1
	2010	0.5	5.5	0.3	9.8	4.1	2.0	2.1
	2011	–1.1	10.7	1.3	7.8	3.3	8.1	1.9
	2012	1.7	7.8	0.0	8.1	–1.0	4.6	2.6
	2013	1.9	7.2	0.0	6.0	2.1	5.1	2.3
Share of total Business in % (Life + Non-Life)	2004	55.1	59.0	42.0	24.4	30.2	51.0	43.0
	2005	54.9	60.3	40.3	24.6	30.6	50.6	42.4
	2006	54.5	59.5	36.7	24.8	28.6	49.9	46.7
	2007	53.1	59.0	3834	25.8	28.5	48.0	41.1
	2008	53.5	61.0	40.1	26.0	30.8	43.6	41.7
	2009	56.7	60.7	40.8	26.0	33.9	50.0	42.7
	2010	56.5	57.3	40.4	26.3	29.2	51.4	41.9
	2011	56.0	57.3	41.0	27.0	29.7	52.4	42.1
	2012	55.5	57.4	42.9	28.9	30.6	53.4	43.1
	2013	57.7	56.3	42.0	29.7	31.0	47.1	43.8
Share of World Market in %	2004	46.10	2.09	36.10	12.88	0.81	2.02	100.0
	2005	46.15	2.43	35.71	12.85	0.84	2.01	100.0
	2006	45.27	2.81	35.95	13.11	0.94	1.92	100.0
	2007	42.34	3.09	38.66	13.02	0.91	1.98	100.0
	2008	40.45	3.60	39.48	13.62	0.95	1.90	100.0
	2009	40.51	3.88	37.88	14.83	0.96	1.94	100.0
	2010	39.80	4.03	36.00	16.81	1.07	2.29	100.0
	2011	37.40	4.53	36.26	18.08	1.11	2.67	100.0
	2012	38.86	4.87	33.07	14.51	1.10	2.59	100.0
	2013	39.32	5.09	33.70	18.71	1.11	2.08	100.0

Table 50.5 B
Non Life Insurance Index by Region

		North America	*Latin America Caribbean*	*Europe*	*Asia*	*Africa*	*Oceania*	*World*
Per Capita Premium in USD (Insurance Density)	2004	1984.0	53.7	579.8	47.1	13.1	885.9	220.0
	2005	2048.8	63.8	601.9	48.3	18.5	904.3	219.0
	2006	2072.2	75.4	626.0	50.4	15.3	891.0	224.2
	2007	2115.5	91.0	739.8	54%	15.8	988.1	249.6
	2008	2133.2	107.3	799.8	60.4	17.1	990.5	264.2
	2009	2061.7	116.6	750.6	62.8	16.6	932.2	253.9
	2010	2103.5	125.6	739.6	73.5	18.9	1173.4	263.0
	2011	–2117.9	150.5	802.5	85.4	20.9	1460.3	283.2
	2012	2219.5	161.9	728.3	91.9	20.9	1414.7	283.1
	2013	2273.0	169.0	758.0	91.0	21.0	1143.0	285.0
% of Premium to GDP (Insurance Penetration)	2004	5.05	1.46	3.20	1.79	1.48	3.90	3.43
	2005	4.92	1.42	3.10	1.67	1.47	3.22	3.18
	2006	4.70	1.40	3.00	1.60	1.40	3.30	3.0
	2007	4.60	1.50	3.00	1.60	1.20	3.20	3.10
	2008	4.57	1.55	2.92	1.53	1.10	3.06	2.95
	2009	4.00	1.50	3.10	1.60	1.10	3.10	3.00
	2010	4.00	1.50	3.00	1.60	1.10	3.00	2.90
	2011	4.41	1.59	3.01	1.59	1.16	3.15	2.83
	2012	4.46	1.72	2.84	1.64	1.12	2.98	2.81
	2013	4.30	1.80	2.80	1.60	1.10	2.40	2.80

Table 50.5C
Non Life Insurance by Selected Region

		Switzerland	*United States*	*Nether-land*	*Luxem-berg*	*Ireland*	*United Kingdom*	*Denmark*	*Germany*	*Canada*	*Australia*	*New Zealand*	*India*
Per Capita Premium in USD (Insurance Density)	2004	2441.2	2062.6	1663.1	1555.8	1473.8	1318.0	1309.9	1262.3	1262.6	1204.4	—	4.0
	2005	2480.3	2122.9	1785.5	1643.8	1417.4	1311.9	1386.3	1268.4	1377.1	1247.7	—	4.4
	2006	2450.1	2134.2	1152.9	1817.4	1360.9	1327.1	1430.6	1306.7	1504.3	1292.1	1155.9	5.2
	2007	2581.7	2164.6	4070.5	2000.0	1456.4	1383.2	1722.1	1427.9	1667.0	1430.9	1299.0	6.2
	2008	2827.9	2177.4	4483.5	2191.7	1315.0	1275.7	1750.0	1572.7	1728.0	1568.5	1316.0	6.2
	2009	2852.1	2107.3	4508.5	1997.6	1078.6	1051.2	1712.9	1518.7	1643.7	1307.9	1317.8	6.7
	2010	2966.9	2127.2	4333.3	1954.9	1082.9	1060.2	1655.1	1501.6	1886.9	1603.0	1626.3	8.7
	2011	3591.0	2130.0	4777.0	2226.0	1075.0	1188.0	1760.0	1578.0	2010.0	2017.0	1926.0	10.0
	2012	3401.1	2239.2	4235.1	2012.0	943.6	1094.4	1586.2	1505.3	2040.4	1934.7	1975.1	10.5
	2013	3490.0	2296.0	4466.0	2254.0	914.0	1087.0	1687.0	1585.0	225.0	1472.0	2047.0	11.0
% of Premium to GDP (Insurance Penetration)	2004	5.02	5.14	4.67	—	—	3.68	—	3.86	4.05	—	—	0.65
	2005	4.99	5.01	4.67	—	—	3.55	—	3.73	3.92	—	—	0.61
	2006	4.90	4.8	2.50	—	—	3.40	—	3.60	4.70	3.2	4.5	0.60
	2007	4.60	4.7	8.70	1.9	2.4	3.00	3.0	3.60	3.80	3.2	4.3	0.60
	2008	4.40	4.6	8.5	1.8	2.1	2.9	2.8	3.50	3.8	2.40	4.4	0.60
	2009	4.5	4.5	9.3	2.0	2.1	3.0	3.1	3.70	4.1	3.0	4.8	0.60
	2010	4.4	4.5	9.2	2.9	2.4	2.9	2.7	1.9	4.1	3.0	5.0	2.9
	2011	4.5	4.5	9.5	1.9	2.2	3.1	2.9	3.6	4.0	3.0	5.2	0.7
	2012	4.3	4.5	9.2	1.9	2.0	2.8	2.8	3.6	3.9	2.8	5.3	0.8
	2013	4.4	4.3	9.4	2.0	1.9	2.8	2.0	3.6	4.0	2.1	5.1	0.8

Table 50.6 A (Total Insurance)
Total Premium Growth Rate by Selected Countries

		United States	*Japan*	*United kingdom*	*France*	*Germany*	*Italy*	*South korea*	*Canada*	*Netherland*	*Spain*	*India*
Premium Volume in million of USD	2003	1057162	472820	254363	161483	170137	112410	60138	59735	52037	47282	18132
	2004	110929	494735	292199	199863	190811	128405	68806	69935	59919	56002	21608
	2005	1142912	476481	300241	222220	197251	139194	82933	78723	61073	60275	25024
	2006	11701011	4460261	418366	251164	204544	138079	101179	88200	62669	65813	43.32
	2007	1229648	424832	463686	268900	222825	142328	116990	100398	10283	74696	54375
	2008	1240643	473197	450152	273007	243085	140689	97023	105174	112611	87038	56190
	2009	1139746	505956	312165	283070	238366	169360	91963	98840	108144	82775	65085
	2010	1166142	557439	310022	280082	239817	174347	114422	115521	97057	76082	78373
	2011	1204477	655408	319553	273112	245162	160514	130363	121213	110931	79987	75628
	2012	1270884	654112	311418	242459	231908	144218	139296	122532	100.342	71991	66441
	2013	1259255	531506	329643	254254	247162	168554	145427	125344	101140	71510	65526
Change in % Nominal USD	2004	3.8	4.1	15.9	0.5	12.1	14.6	14.1	16.8	12.6	18.2	17.2
	2005	3.0	–3.7	2.8	11.2	3.4	8.4	20.5	3.6	1.9	7.6	15.8
	2006	543	–3.75	24.46	13.65	3.32	–1.89	18.90	12.99	5.19	8.92	56.99
	2007	4.69	–3.31	28.16	10.09	7.47	1.27	16.28	14.74	11.98	13.50	34.8
	2008	0.22	20.37	–16.56	0.06	8.75	–1.20	–15.97	4.38	9.74	16.22	–2.76
	2009	–8.07	4.73	–21.84	2..61	–1.48	20.38	1.48	–5.29	–5.57	–4.63	17.21
	2010	1.42	6.76	–0.69	–1.39	–0.05	2.94	16.25	16.11	–6.14	–7.86	21.95
	2011	3.66	14.71	6.43	–3.57	4.34	7.93	13.92	6.61	8.46	9.66	2.35
	2012	4.0	2.5	–0.5	–11.1	–5.6	–10.3	10.7	1.2	–7.8	–12.6	–8.2
	2013	–10.6	–15.19	2.37	7.22	6.34	17.06	–4.94	0.57	5.51	0.46	–0.39
Inflations Adjusted Change in %	2004	1.1	–0.9	2.1	7.6	0.6	2.3	3.1	6.5	–	4.6	10.4
	2005	–0.3	6.7	1.3	9.3	1.4	6.5	8.5	–0.2	0.3	4.2	9.4
	2006	2.17	–1.49	20.9	10.61	0.55	–4.90	8.73	3.72	2.92	4.11	52.56
	2007	1.78	–3.17	15.31	–2.90	–1.33	–8.82	11.06	6.35	1.05	1.25	13.00
	2008	–3.44	6.75	–12.99	–9.33	–1.26	–10.93	–15.97	4.38	–0.24	4.04	0.13
	2009	–7.77	–1.06	–9.43	8.20	3.64	26.07	0.81	1.02	–1.51	0.95	9.02
	2010	–0.22	–0.09	–2.66	2.07	3.86	–2.59	7.85	2.94	–2.59	–4.88	4.91
	2011	0.50	5.76	–1.77	–10.05	–2.84	–14.68	5.34	–0.49	0.95	1.04	5.46
	2012	1.9	7.9	–2.4	–5.5	–5.3	–0.7	9.0	0.7	–2.5	–7.6	–3.9
	2013	2.49	1.49	1.16	2.84	1.32	11.89	–8.04	2.68	0.42	–4.16	1.22

Non-Life Insurance Index

Per Capita Premium

The per capita non-life premium in USD was maximum in switzerland *i.e.*, USD 2441.2 in 2004 and USD 2480.3 in 2005 followed by United States, Netherland, Luxumburg and Ireland. Their ranks have not changed. The other countries under ten ranks have been United Kingdom, Denmark, Germany, Canada and Austria. All the developed nations have maximum non-life per capita insurance. India is at 78th rank having per capita non-life premium USD 4.0 in 2004 and USD 4.4 in 2005. The non-life premium per capita is USD 1204.4 in 2004 and USD 1247.7 in 2005. India has to develop the non-life insurance, which was USD 10.5 in 2012. Maximum business was down by Netherland (USD 4235.1) followed by (USD 3401.1) Switzerland, USA (USD 2239.2) Luxumberg (2012) and Canada (2040.4) in 2012.

Percentage of premium to Gross Domestic Premium

North America has 5.05 per cent premium to GDP in 2004 and 4.92 per cent of GDP in 2005. The lowest percentage was in Latin America *i.e.*, 1.46 per cent and 1.42 per cent in the respective years. United States has maximum share of non-life insurance to GDP *i.e.*, 5.14 per cent in 2004 and 5.01 per cent in 2005. Switzerland stood second, Netherland was third and Newzealand was fourth in this comparison in all the two years. Other countries within 10 ranks are Canada, Slovenia, Germany, Australia, United Kingdom and France. India stood at 44th rank in 2004 and 43th rank in 2005. Maximum penetration percentage in 2012 was 9.2 percent in Netherland followed by 5.3 percent in Newzealand and 4.5 percent in USA, 4.3 per cent in Switzerland, 3.9 per cent in Canada and 3.6 per cent in Germany. India had only 0.8 per cent.

Table 50.6 (Total Insurance)
Total Premium Growth Rate by Region

		North America	*Latin America & Carbean*	*Europe*	*Asia*	*Africa*	*Oceana*	*World*
Premium Volume in million of USD	2003	1116897	42089	1035838	684970	32461	46103	2958359
	2004	1179226	49313	1206191	738918	36422	54088	3264158
	2005	221635	58599	1287920	754779	40025	57756	3425714
	2006	1258301	71428	1484881	800819	49667	58316	3723412
	2007	1330066	87397	1680693	84060	53294	68818	4060870
	2008	1345816	104933	1753200	933358	54713	77716	4269737
	2009	1238586	110910	1610620	989451	49287	67241	4066095
	2010	1281664	127867	1620437	1161118	66719	81160	4338964
	2011	1275854	127930	1615190	1172176	63072	81466	4335687
	2012	1393416	168737	1535176	1346223	71891	97071	4012514
	2013	1384599	183800	1631699	1278780	72825	89698	4640941
Change in % Nominal USD	2004	4.5	17.2	15.7	7.5	15.9	19.7	9.7
	2005	3.6	18.8	6.8	2.8	9.9	6.8	4.9
	2006	5.93	21.50	11.22	4.65	16.27	3.78	8.0
	2007	5.39	22.18	15.47	8.09	6.86	18.17	10.50
	2008	0.54	17.06	–0.66	14.94	1.92	12.82	3.44
	2009	–7.85	4.33	–5.46	5.87	–6.70	–14.39	–3.65
	2010	2.59	18.06	0.37	14.46	16.13	23.31	5.58
	2011	3.92	20.59	2.21	10.75	7.94	22.06	5.98
	2012	3.8	8.7	5.6	5.3	3.8	2.2	1.00
	2013	0.91	8.59	5.91	–4.09	1.33	3.18	0.91
Inflations Adjusted Change in %	2004	1.4	10.5	3.2	2.1	–1.3	3.2	2.3
	2005	–02	1.9	4.4	3.5	7.1	0.1	2.5
	2006	2.24	11.61	7.47	..83	17.55	2.17	4.97
	2007	2.10	9.61	3.43	4.52	2.80	3.89	3.22
	2008	–3.09	8.41	–6.20	6.60	4.88	8.63	–1.96
	2009	–7.08	5.79	1.83	2.78	–11.13	–9.57	–1.07
	2010	0.03	8.19	1.81	7.16	–1.11	2.32	2.73
	2011	0.41	10.13	–5.15	2.17	1.77	5.23	–0.81
	2012	1.8	11.7	–1.7	6.9	10.5	–0.1	2.4
	2013	–2.03	9.39	2.16	2.38	10.23	7.15	1.44

TOTAL INSURANCE

The total insurance has increased considerably. The growth rate of total insurance premium had –1.0 per cent in 1980 which increased to 17.0 per cent in 1986. The growth rate has declined to 2.0 per cent in 1990 and became 7.0 per cent in 2000. It remained constant at 2.5 per cent in 2005 and declined in 2011 as the real permium growth was –0.8% in 2011.

Growth Rate

The total premium growth rate has been highest *i.e.*, 20.5 per cent in 2004 in France and 20.5 per cent in 2005 in South Korea. The lowest growth rate has been 3.8 per cent in 2004 in United States and –3.7 per cent in 2005 in Japan although the total premium volume in USD has been second highest in Japan. The total premium volume has been the highest in United States and the growth in 2005 was modest there. United Kingdom having third rank in total premium volume has been satisfactory in growth rate *i.e.*, 15.9 per cent in 2004 and 2.8 per cent in 2005. France has significantly high growth rate in premium volume and also has fourth rank in total premium volume. Germany and Italy have also maintained their ranks in total premium volume. After interchanging the growth rates with South Korea and Canada. Netherlands and Spain have maintained their ranks. India is 19th in total premium volume. It is good sign for India. The growth rate is moderately high *i.e.*, more than 15 per cent although its share in world's total insurance premium is merely 0.66 per cent in 2004 and 0.73 per cent in 2005. Inflation-adjusted growth rate is the highest in India *i.e.*, 10.4 per cent in 2004 and 9.4 per cent in 2005. United States have maximum share of world market *i.e.*, 33.84 per cent in 2004 and 33.36 per cent in 2005.

Table 50.6. C
Total Insurance Index
By Region

		North America	*Latin America Caribbean*	*Europe*	*Asia*	*Africa*	*Oceania*	*World*
Per Capita Premium in USD (Insurance Density)	2004	3601.1	90.9	1427.9	194.3	43.4	1736.9	511.5
	2005	3735.1	105.7	1513.8	197.9	44.2	1789.3	518.5
	2006	3804.0	126.7	1745.7	205.0	53.6	1787.3	554.8
	2007	3984.8	154.1	1962.4	210.7	55.3	2059.5	607.7
	2008	3988.8	175.8	2043.9	234.3	55.6	2271.9	633.9
	2009	3634.5	192.2	1861.5	243.1	48.8	1862.9	595.1
	2010	3724.4	219.1	1850.2	281.5	64.7	2283.1	627.3
	2011	38150	261.0	18860	314.0	65.0	2259.0	641.0
	2012	3996.0	281.9	1724.4	321.7	67.3	2660.2	655.7
	2013	3938.0	300.0	1833.0	303.0	66.0	2429.0	652.0
% of Premium to GDP (Insurance Penetration)	2004	9.17	2.47	7.89	7.37	4.89	7.65	7.99
	2005	8.97	2.35	7.78	6.83	4.80	6.38	7.52
	2006	8.7	2.40	8.30	6.60	4.80	6.70	7.50
	2007	8.7	2.50	8.00	6.20	4.30	6.60	7.50
	2008	8.5	2.50	7.5	6.00	3.6	7.0	7.10
	2009	7.9	2.8	7.6	6.1	3.3	6.2	7.0
	2010	7.9	2.7	7.5	6.2	3.9	5.8	6.9
	2011	7.3	2.8	7.1	5.8	3.6	5.9	6.6
	2012	8.3	3.0	6.7	5.7	3.7	5.6	6.5
	2013	7.4	3.2	6.8	5.4	3.5	5.2	6.3

Total Insurance Index

The premium of total insurance has been analysed on the basis of per capita in USD and percentage share of Gross Domestic products (GDP).

Table 50.7 A
Total Insurance Index by Selected Countries
Insurance Penetration (% of Premium to G.D.P)

	South Africa	*Taiwan*	*U.K.*	*Switzerland*	*Japan*	*Netherland*	*Belgium*	*South Korea*	*France*	*U.S.A*	*Hong Kong*	*New-zealand*	*India*
2004	14.36	14.13	12.60	11.75	10.51	10.10	9.62	9.52	9.52	9.36	9.27	–	3.17
2005	13.87	14.11	12.45	11.19	10.54	9.79	11.15	10.25	10.21	9.15	9.93	–	3.14
2006	16.0	14.5	16.50	11.0	10.50	10.40	9.2	11.10	11.0	8.8	10.50	5.3	4.8
2007	15.3	15.7	15.70	10.3	9.6	13.40	9.6	11.18	10.3	8.9	11.80	5.2	4.7
2008	15.3	16.2	15.7	9.9	9.8	12.9	9.1	11.80	9.2	8.7	11.20	5.4	4.6
2009	12.9	16.8	12.9	9.8	9.9	13.6	8.0	10.4	10.3	8.0	11.0	5.8	5.2
2010	14.8	18.4	12.4	9.9	10.1	12.4	8.8	11.2	10.5	8.0	11.4	6.0	5.1
2011	12.9	17.0	11.8	10.0	11.4	13.2	7.9	12.9	9.5	8.1	11.4	6.1	4.1
2012	14.1	18.29	11.3	9.6	11.4	13.0	8.1	12.1	8.9	8.2	12.4	6.3	4.0
2013	15.4	17.6	11.5	9.6	11.1	12.6	7.1	11.9	9.0	7.5	13.2	6.1	3.9

Table 50.7
Total Insurance Index by Selected Countries
Insurance Density (Per capita Premium in USD)

		Switzerland	*United Kingdom*	*Ireland*	*Belgium*	*Dnmark*	*United States*	*Japan*	*Netherland*	*France*	*Finland*	*New Zealand*	*India*
Per Capita Premium in USD	2004	5716.4	4508.4	4091.2	3275.6	3620.4	3755.1	3874.8	3599.6	3207.9	3134.41	–	19.7
	2005	5558.4	4599.0	4177.0	3985.6	3876.2	3875.2	3746.7	3739.7	3568.5	3389.3	–	22.7
	2006	5561.9	6466.7	5564.7	3681.2	4271.4	3923.7	3589.6	4075.4	4271.4	3828.8	1370.9	38.4
	2007	5740.7	7113.7	771.4	4131.5	5103.1	4086.5	3319.9	6262.9	5103.1	3905.8	1569.0	46.6
	2008	6379.4	6857.8	4914.5	4298.8	5418.9	4078.0	3698.6	6849.5	4298.8	4393.2	1569.0	47.4
	2009	6257.6	4578.8	4515.7	3494.0	5528.9	3710.0	3979.0	6554.6	4269.0	4253.0	1567.1	54.3
	2010	6633.7	4496.6	4296.6	3736.0	5084.2	3758.9	4390.2	5845.3	4186.6	4181.5	1937.3	64.4
	2011	8012.0	4716.0	4449.0	3622.0	5619.0	3846.0	5169.0	6647.0	4041.0	4716.0	2277.0	59.0
	2012	7522.1	43502	4011.3	3574.7	5304.1	4042.3	5167.5	5984.9	3543.5	4770.7	2349.8	53.2
	2013	7701.0	4561.0	3783.0	3235.0	5780.0	3979.0	4207.0	6012.0	3736.0	5073.0	2423.0	52.0

Per Capita Premium

The per capita premium has been the highest in Switzerland *i.e.*, USD 5716.4 in 2004 and USD 5558.4 in 2005 followed by United Kingiom having per capita premium of USD 4508.4 in 2004 and USD 4599.0 in 2005 and Ireland USD 4091.2 in 2004 and USD 4177.0 in 2005. Belgium, Denmark, United States, Japan, Netherlands, France and Finland have been within 10 ranks. India has 78th rank so far per capita premium is concerned although it has 19th rank in total premium volume.

Table 50.8
Total Insurance Index (Share of World Market in %) by
Region and selected countries

	North America	*Latin America & caribbean*	*Europe*	*Asia*	*Africa*	*Oceania*	*World*
	–	–	–	–	–	–	–
2004	35.99	1.52	36.94	22.69	1.16	1.70	100.0
2005	35.66	1.71	37.60	22.18	1.17	1.69	100.0
2006	33.79	1.92	39.88	21.51	1.33	1.57	100.0
2007	32.75	2.15	41.39	20.70	1.30	1.69	100.0
2008	31.52	2.46	41.06	21.86	1.28	1.82	100.0
2009	30.46	2.73	39.61	24.33	1.21	1.65	100.0
2010	29.54	2.95	37.35	26.76	1.54	1.87	100.0
2012	30.21	3.66	33.28	29.19	1.56	2.10	100.0
2011	28.85	3.36	35.93	28.24	1.48	2.16	100.0
2012	30.21	3.66	33.28	29.19	1.56	2.10	100.0
2013	29.83	3.96	35.16	27.55	1.56	1.93	100.0

Selected Countries

	United States	*Japan*	*United kingdom*	*France*	*Germany*	*Italy*	*South korea*	*Canada*	*Netherland*	*Spain*	*New Zealand*	*India*
2004	33.84	15.18	9.09	6.00	5.88	3.97	2.12	2.15	1.81	1.72	–	0.66
2005	33.36	13.91	8.76	6.49	5.76	4.06	2.42	2.30	1.78	1.76	–	0.73
2006	31.43	12.36	11.24	6.75	5.49	3.72	2.72	2.73	1.69	1.77	0.15	1.16
2007	30.28	10.41	11.42	6.62	5.49	3.50	2.88	2.47	2.53	1.84	0.16	1.34
2008	29.06	11.08	10.54	6.39	5.69	3.30	2.27	2.46	2.64	2.04	.15	1.32
2009	28.03	12.44	7.61	6.96	5.86	4.17	2.26	2.43	2.66	2.04	0.16	1.60
2010	26.88	12.86	7.15	6.46	5.53	4.02	2.64	2.66	2.24	1.75	0.19	1.81
2011	26.22	14.26	6.95	5.94	5.34	3.49	4.83	2.64	2.41	2.16	0.22	1.58
2012	27.55	14.18	6.75	5.26	5.03	3.13	3.02	2.66	2.18	1.56	0.23	1.44
2013	27.13	11.45	7.10	5.49	5.33	3.63	3.13	2.70	2.18	1.35	0.24	1.41

Total Insurance Penetration. (% of Premium to GDP)

The highest percentage of premium to GDP has been in South Africa *i.e.*, 14.38 per cent of GDP in 2004 and 13.87 per cent in 2005 followed by Taiwan, United Kingdom and Switzerland. Japan stood at 5th and 6th position in 2004 and 2005 respectively. Netherlands, Belgium, South Korea and France have been with 10 ranks. India has 44th rank covering 3.17 per cent of GDP in 2004 and 43th rank having 3.14 per cent of GDP. The Total Insurance Penetration in 2012 was 18.19 per cent in Taiwan, 14.16 per cent in South Africa 12.44 per cent in Hon Kong, 12.12 per cent in South Korea, 12.99 per cent in Netherland, 11.44 in Japan, 11.27 per cent in U.K.

Total Insurance Density (Per Capita Insurance in USD)

The total insurance density in 2004 was USD 5716.4 in Switzerland, USD 4508.4 in U.K, USD 4091.2 in Ireland, USD 3874.8 in Japan, USD 3755 in USA, USD 3620.4 in Denmark, USD 3599.6 in Netherland, USD 3275.6 in Belgium, USD 3207.9 in France and USD 3134.4 in Finland. India had 19.7 USD in 2004. The total insurance density has increased in 2012 in some of the new markets. The USD 7522.1 in Switzerland, USD 5984.9 in Netherlands, USD 5304.1 in Denmark, USD 5167.5 in Japan, USD 5079.4 in Haemberg, USD 4770.7 in Finland , USD 4543.9 in Honkong, USD 4487.8 in Norway, USD 4350.2 in U.K, USD 4047.3 in USA, USD 4011.3 in Ireland. India increased its total insurance density to USD 53.2 in 2012. Thus, new insurance market emerged in the world.

Outlook for 2015 and 2016

Swiss Re Economic Research and consulting has prepared a thorough report for insurance Development. Some of the points of the report are given herewith for the insurance minded people.

The macroeconomic and financial market environment along with interest rates will be critical for the future of the life insurance industry. The short to mid-term outlook remains challenging. Global real premium income will increase in the next two years, by an estimated 4.3% and 4.2% in 2015 and 2016, respectively. Premiums in the advanced markets are expected to grow by 3.0% in 2015 and by 2.8% in 2016. In emerging markets, they are forecast to grow by 10.4% in 2015 and 10.7% in 2016.

The bulk of life insurers' premium income (about 85%) stems from saving-type insurance business, in which policyholders are refunded when an insurance contract matures. The share of savings (as a percentage of total premiums paid) in advanced countries has declined slightly since 2000. In emerging markets, the share has been moving up to levels similar to that in advanced markets as insurance markets develop and household incomes increase.

Savings-type solutions are often more appealing for consumers than pure risk protection products as consumers receive part of the premium and a share of the investment return at maturity. This is in contrast to pure risk products like term-life insurance, which provide no return unless the insured event occurs. Another reason for the success of savings-type insurance is that it often comes along with tax advantages.

A drawback of savings-type insurance versus other savings vehicles such as mutual funds and bank products is that the costs of insurance and administration can absorb some of the accumulated returns. In times when interest rates were "normal", these costs were less visible to policyholders and at maturity, savings-type insurance still offered an attractive return on investment. In recent years, however, record low interest rates have made it more challenging for insurers to earn enough investment income and in many countries, guarantees and profit sharing arrangements have been reduced.

This has made savings-type insurance less attractive for policyholders. For example, in China many consumers have moved their investments to so-called "wealth management products", including trust loans, which offer higher yields. In the UK, pension reforms are expected to impact demand for annuities also (see Box: *UK pension reform and implications for life insurers*). In addition to weak demand, the supply of savings-type insurance has become more expensive for regulatory reasons (eg. higher capital requirements for long-term guarantees or asset liability mismatches), reducing insurers' willingness to make these kinds or product available.

UK pension reform and implications for life insurers

In a surprise move, in its March 2014 Budget the UK government announced significant changes to the annuity market which could have far reaching implications for UK life insurers. From April 2015, individuals will be able to take as much or as little as they want from their defined contribution pension pot when they reach the minimum pensionable age (normally 55). Under the existing arrangements, most pensioners are effectively mandated to buy an annuity upon retirement. The market for annuities only generates around one-fifth of UK life insurance sales, but it represents around two-thirds of major UK insurers' new business profits. Those insurers which rely heavily on annuity business will therefore need to adapt to the new market environment.

Insurance in emerging markets in 2015-2016: Outlook still favourable

The near-term outlook for insurance in emerging markets remains favourable. However, the balance of risks is tilted to the downside, with some markets still vulnerable to external shocks and rising geopolitical risks. The coming normalisation of US interest rates could result in higher financial market volatility and threaten the economic growth outlook of some emerging countries.

The non-life business in emerging markets is expected to recover in 2015-2016. Emerging Asia is expected to maintain strong growth, in part driven by the Chinese government's recent pledge of stronger support for the insurance business (see special topic below on *China's new Insurance Directives*). Sales of non-life insurance in Malaysia could be hit by the introduction of sales tax in April 2015, while Thailand could see stronger growth assuming a stabilisation of the political environment. Premium growth will likely be more sanguine in other regions, including a return to modest 1.9% growth in CEE in 2015 after this year's 5.2% contraction. This reflects an improving economic environment and consumer sentiment, and also anticipated firmer rates on the expectation that after years of underwriting losses, larger players will finally be persuaded to consolidate loss-making portfolios. The outlook, however, hinges on how the Russia-Ukraine conflict plays out (see special topic on *Impact of Russian Ukraine conflict on Europe*).

Life premium growth is expected to remain strong in Emerging Asia, while other regions will likely see a steady return to trend growth levels. The improvement will begin early in Latin America, the Middle East and North Africa, but come more slowly in CEE and Sub-Saharan Africa. In particular, tough economic conditions in Russia and Ukraine will continue to constrain demand for life lump-sum products. The implementation of Solvency II, due 1 January 2016, will also drive a shift in insurers' focus to protection products and riders, which will come in with lower premium volume compared to traditional saving-type products. In India, an extension in the limit of tax benefit on premiums will support insurance demand. Overall, life business is expected to expand robustly in emerging Asian markets over the next two years.

Insurance regulations in the emerging markets continue to converge towards international best practices. China has unveiled details of its next-generation solvency regime called the "China-Risk Oriented Solvency System (C-ROSS)", which brings insurance supervision standards in China closer to those in the advanced markets. In Latin America, Brazil, Maxico and Chile are in advance stage of implementing risk-based capital regimes (see special topic below on *Development on insurance solvency regimes in Latin America*). The upcoming formation of the ASEAN Economic Community in December 2015 should encourage national of the regulators to strengthen and align their solvency and capital standards. The changes could result in more capital volatility and heightened risk awareness. Many insurers will also consider revising product design and pricing and also revamp their data systems to cope with these regulatory changes (see special topic below on *Recent regulatory changes in India and Indonesia*).

Non-life insurance: economic headwinds hold back premium growth

Non-life premium growth in the emerging markets has been supported mainly by the strong performance of emerging Asia in 2014. There has been solid growth in China. India and Southeast Asia, with the exception of Thailand where business was adversely affected by economic recession in the first half of the year. In China, non-life premiums rose strongly by 15%, underpinned by an expanding motor sector and faster increases in other sectors including agriculture and liability insurance. Tackling the challenge of natural catastrophes remains a key theme in the region. In the Philippines, for instance, the government is considering the introduction of a compulsory earthquake insurance pool for private residential properties.

Non-life premium growth in Latin America has slowed to 2.4% this year from 7.5% in 2013. Premiums were stagnant in Mexico and grew notably slower in Brazil and Argentina. In Brazil, motor premium growth has remained relatively firm despite a sharp drop-off in vehicle sales. An extension in tax incentives for new car purchases may have buoyed demand in the first half of the year, but the trend is not expected to have sustained into the second half. Other regional markets also fared poorly against the backdrop of a more challenging economic environment.

Life insurance in emerging markets: robust growth in Asia, weaker elsewhere

Life Insurance premiums in emerging markets have grown by 9.1% in 2014, up from a 4.6% gain last year. The improvement has also been due to stronger growth in emerging Asia and a gradual stabilisation in CEE. Growth in other emerging regions has weakened, particularly in the Middle East and Africa.

Emerging Asia accounts for 67% of total emerging market life premiums in 2014, up from 64% in 2013. A sustained recovery in China, where premiums are rising by 15.7% in 2014 compared with 5.1% in 2013 and 1.4% in 2012, is the main reason for the strong momentum in Asia. Chinese insurers have been tapping into new distribution channels and cross-selling opportunities to offset the drag from tougher bancassurance rules introduced earlier this year. At the same time, India and Southeast Asia continue to report solid performance. Premium growth in the Philippines remains very strong at close to 30%, having expanded by more than 30% per annum in 2013 and 2012. The growth has been based on a surge in sales of variable insurance policies.

Special topics — emerging markets

This section reviews four issues that are topical for the insurance sector in emerging market: (1) new insurance directives in China; (2) recent regulatory changes in India and Indonesia; (3) the development of insurance solvency regimes in Latin America; and (4) the impact of the Russian-Ukraine conflict in Europe.

1. *New insurance directives issued in China*

The State Council of China issued a new set of Directives on the Development of Insurance ("The Directives") on 13 August this year, detailing the government's view on the role of insurance in China's social and economic development. The Directives are comprehensive and cover all major aspects of the insurance value chain.

- The Directives acknowledge the role of insurance as an important economic sector and as a risk management tool for modern societies. This significantly raises the status of insurance in contributing to China's growth and development.
- Insurance is now seen as a means to help resolve and manage many of the social issues high on the government's policy agenda, including environmental protection, food safety, rural-urban inequality and ageing population.
- The Directives will likely bring better policy coordination among different government agencies. Government bureaus and agencies are urged to initiate measures (e.g., in the areas of tax, fiscal budget, land use and supervisions) to support the further development of insurance.
- The Directives commit to further market liberalisation and deregulation, including the expected removal of interest rate caps in the L&H sector and de-tariffication in the motor business in non-life.
- The Directives call for the internationalisation of China's insurance sector, including overseas expansion of Chinese insurance companies, the provision of insurance services to Chinese overseas direct investment raising funds and capital in international capital markets and promoting the export of insurance services.

The Directives pinpoint numerous insurance lines of business that could qualify for government support, such as tax-deferred annuities and subsidised natural catastrophe insurance. However, a key feature is the quantitative targets: the government says it expects insurance penetration to grow to 5% of GDP in 2020 and insurance density (per capita premiums) to CNY 3500 (USD 570). That compares with penetration of 3% in 2003 (life: 1.6%; non-life: 1.4%) and density USD 201 (life USD 110; non-life: USD 91). This implies total insurance premiums will need to grow by around 17% per year between 2014 and 2020.

The aggressive target is likely to drive insurers to explore new growth areas. In non-life, it is expected that agricultural insurance, liability insurance and disaster insurance will benefit most. In L&H, old-age related insurance products and health insurance will received the biggest push from these new directives. The government is expected to support higher insurance penetration with different initiatives. For instance, there could be tax concessions to support the development of health and annuities products, regulations will be so formulated as to encourage enterprises to cover themselves adequately against liabilities, and governments will be more willing to subsidise insurance premiums.

The new Directives will support premium growth, but also competition (e.g., due to motor de-tariffication). At the same time, the Directives send a strong message to domestic insurers to consider overseas expansion, in particular to support Chinese overseas direct investment. China's insurers have limited experience operating overseas but some larger companies might start to look for M&A opportunities in foreign markets.

2. *Recent regulatory changes in India and Indonesia*

In its budget 2014, the newly-elected Indian government announced that it proposes to raise the ceiling on foreign direct investment (FDI) in the insurance sector to 49% from 26% currently, subject to certain proposed safeguards and restrictions including "full Indian management and control".[25] The proposal is included in the Insurance Laws (Amendment) Bill. 2008 (the Bill), which has been approved by the Indian Cabinet and is now awaiting parliamentary approval.

The increase in the FDI ceiling would allow domestic insurers to raise more capital from foreign partners, boost operating efficiency and competition, and contribute to higher penetration. However, before the Bill is signed into law, foreign insurers or investors may want clarification from the Indian authorities on, for example, the proposed conditions in regard to "full Indian management and control". Joint ventures with current de facto foreign management or effective control could run into difficulties under the proposed changes if the foreign partners choose to increase their stake to 49%.

There are currently 19 joint ventures in the non-life sector in India, and 21 in life.

Many foreign insurers have already established a foothold in the Indian market and the relaxation of the FDI ceiling is unlikely to spur another influx. The higher ceiling could, however, alleviate some of the capital pressures on Indian insurers, particularly in cases where the domestic partner has been unable or unwilling to inject additional capital.

In Indonesia, the re/insurance industry has seen a number of important developments over the past two years, including:

- In late 2013, the insurance regulator Otoritas Jasa Keuangan (OJK) established a premium rating agency to determine benchmark rates in order to reduce "unhealthy competition". Floor and ceiling tariffs for property, flood and motor insurance were introduced in March 2014, with different rates depending on the type of property and motor, as well as zones (whether flood-prone or not).
- In December 2013, the OJK issued letters to the industry on the "responsibility to optimise domestic reinsurance capacity". For all life businesses as well as motor, medical, personal accident and credit & surety in non-life, insurers are asked to place reinsurance of these businesses domestically, and are required to submit their reinsurance plans to the OJK.
- A new Insurance Law was passed in September 2014 covering issues such as "Single Presence" and "Controller". Under the "Single Presence" rule, a party can only be a controlling shareholder in one company in each of the following categories: life, non-life, reinsurance, Sharia life, Sharia non-life and Sharia reinsurance. At least one 'Controller' has to be specified by the re-insurer which will be held responsible the policyholders and other participants. If the insurance company fails, the OJK may ask the Controller to take responsibility. The new Insurance Law retained the maximum foreign shareholding at 80%, despite earlier reports that the government is planning to reduce this to 49%.

3. *Development on insurance solvency regimes in Latin America*

Latin America has joined the global trend towards risk-based insurance supervision. Regulatory modernisation is progressing across most of the region, with Brazil, Chile, d Mexico expected to adopt frameworks similar in design to Solvency II over the next one to three years. Colombia and Peru are laying the groundwork for more comprehensive regulatory reforms while simultaneously instituting certain risk capital (RBC) provisions, such as those covering investment and operational risks, in a piecemeal fashion. Argentina and Venezuela are the notable outliers of this trend. Neither has committed to modernise nor submitted timetables for insurance and solvency reform.

Three main changes are expected to impact the insurance regulatory landsçape in Latin America in 2015. First Mexico is due to implement its landmark Law of Insurance and Bonding Institutions (LISF) in April next year. The law, which will be phased in over the course of the year, ushers in a three-pillar solvency framework encompassing capital adequacy and valuation (Pillar I), enterprise risk management (ERM. Pillar II) and market disclosure (Pillar III). Capital requirements will target major risk exposures (including underwriting, market credit and operational risks) while an Institutional Risk and Solvency Self-Assessment (ARSI which falls under Pillar II) will cover qualitative risks not captured by Pillar I.

Second, Brazil is due to introduce market risk capital requirements and proposals for an Own Risk Solvency Assessment (ORSA) by the end of 2014. The capital requirements add to existing charges for underwriting, credit and operational risks, while the ORSA is intended to improve risk sensitivity of insurers' ERM and corporate governance practices. Together the new rules will give Brazil a three-pillar framework equivalent — both practically and legally — to Solvency II. Finally, in 2015 Chile is expected to pass enabling legislations for RBC supervision that, once implemented will complete a Solvency II-styled reform process, that began in 2004.

The repercussions of the reforms will vary from country to country depending on the final model design. The region's three incoming RBC models all incorporate diversification benefits and reinsurance capital relief which will help mitigate the impact of additional risk capital charges and in some instances, may lead to a reduction in capital requirements. In general, however, the tighter operating requirements are likely to squeeze insurers' margins. Smaller and-less-diversified carriers will be at a particular disadvantage, marking some as candidates for takeovers and others for exit. A shift in product mix may be another consequence as insurers will be incentivised to focus on products and lines of business that are less capital intensive.

4. *Impact of Russian-Ukraine conflict on Europe*

The Russia-Ukraine conflict has exacerbated the economic downturn in Russia and prompted a sharp recession in Ukraine. The weaker economic environment in the conflict countries and the sanctions imposed by the EU and the US will also negatively affect other countries. CEE countries in particular will be affected due to their trade links with the conflict countries, but the negative repercussions remain small for most countries in Europe unless the conflict escalates rapidly. A scenario of prolonged interruption to gas supplies would have a severe negative impact, but this currently looks unlikely.

At the end of September-2014, the EU upheld its sanctions on Russia noting that while there were positive political developments, more needs to be done to resolve the conflict. Travel bans and the freezing of assets of more than 100 individuals in Russia remain in place, as well as bans on borrowing by large Russian banks and companies. There are also restrictions on the export of military and dual-use goods and oil extraction technologies to Russia. In retaliation, Russia has banned agri-food imports from the EU and is restricting the freedom of its own citizens to travel to the west.

QUESTIONS

1. Examine the International Insurance Scene.
2. Explain the progress of life Insurance in India and World.
3. Discuss the progress of non-life insurance in world.
4. What is solveney? How is it judged? Explain.
5. Examine the progress of total insurance in world.

PART SEVEN

INSURANCE LEGISLATION

51

INSURANCE LEGISLATION IN INDIA

History

From the writings of Manu, Yajnavalkya that the carrier in India was also an insurer in a restricted sense; yet is "not certain if the ancient Hindus also had a system of life insurance and practised it, though it seems highly problematical as legal codes do not reveal traces of any such system. Insurance against death was regarded till very recently, as want of belief in God which was not a very fertile soil for the growth of the insurance.

Up to the end of nineteenth century, the insurance was in its inceptional stage. Therefore, no legislation was required till that time. Usually the Indian Companies Act 1883 was applicable in business concerns, banking and insurance companies. New Indian Insurance companies and Provident Societies started at the time of national movement; but most of them were financial unsound. It was asserted that the Indian Companies Act, 1883 was inadequate for the purpose. *Therefore, two Acts were passed in 1912, namely, Provident Insurance Societies Act V of 1912 and Indian Life Insurance Companies Act VI of 1912.* These two Acts were in pursuit of the English Insurance Companies Act of 1909 with the difference that the Indian Life Insurance Companies related to Life insurance only and excluded the non-life business from its fold. The Act put the life insurance business in India on sounder footing and resulted in creating a healthier atmosphere than before. It was also instrumental in the dissolution of some unsound Indian as well as non-Indian life offices or in the merging of some of them with the others. The legislation in India was confining of some of them with the others. The legislation in India was confining to life business because there were very few general insurance companies and did not call for any legislation. To prevent financial weakness the insurers were required to keep certain stated deposits. The Indian insurers were required to submit returns giving particulars of their business. The foreign insurers were exempted from submitting separate particulars regarding the business done in India. Some English companies ceased to underwrite further business with a view to avoid submission of reports to the Government of India Insurance Legislation in India. Some Indian Companies which conducted business on assessments or on actuarially unsound basis, either dropped or mortgaged them to conform to actuarial requirements. The policies issued by these companies were not less than ₹ 1,000. The aim of the Provident Insurance Societies Act 1912 was to govern Provident Insurance Societies which were engaged in issuing life policies worth ₹ 1,000 or less and marriage and disease policies, of very nominal amount. This act was purely based on the Friendly Societies Act.

These two enactments were governing only life insurance. There were no control on general insurance since such businesses were not so developed. Besides, there were the following defects of these Acts:

Defects

1. There were no regulation pertaining to investment. The need for restriction on investments was felt in India because unenlightened public was not able to judge the position of a company. But simply because there was no restriction on investment in England, no restriction was placed in India.

2. The control and enquiry was slight. Non-compliance of rules and regulations was not strictly penalised.
3. The foreign companies were to submit report of their total business both in India and outside India. But separate particulars regarding business done in India were not demanded and the absence of these made it impossible to get any idea of the cost of procuring business in India for foreign companies and comparing them with similar data of the Indian companies.
4. The Government Actuary was not vested with the power to order investigation into the conduct of a company even when it appeared that the company was insolvent under the power of exemption, several new underwriters were granted exemption even from submitting reports to the Governments although the business transacted continued to be in force.
5. Any one can start life insurance business only with the sum of ₹ 25,000. It was too low to prevent the mushroom growth of companies. Foreign insurarer was not bound to deposit a certain sum of life policy issued in India. Thus, it was not sufficient to check the floatation of unhealthy concerns and provided discrimination in India.

These defects were compelling the above Acts to be replaced. Public was aware of the fact that the Indian companies in foreign countries or in England were directed to have a certain sum in the shape of reserve as contrary to above regulation. The law in India was not in line with the law in force in other countries. Persistent demands were made by various important public bodies in the country for statutory provisions which would provide for disclosure and publication of the business carried on in India by foreign companies. After a few years it was realised that there should be another efficient and adequate act.

Reasons of Replacement Act of 1912

(*i*) The above defects compel the replacement.

(*ii*) Persistent demands were made by various important public bodies and Swadeshi Movements.

(*iii*) The general insurance business should also be controlled.

(*iv*) The insurance companies particularly Fire, Marine and Accident insurance companies developed very fast during 1914-18 due to First World War. Therefore, it was essential to control such new companies and to provide them with some proper guidance.

(*v*) The important underwriters and business units demanded that there should be a full-fledged insurance Act.

(*vi*) The Foreign-underwriters should also be governed by the Indian Legislation.

(*vii*) Some guiding principles for starting new business or for completing the jobs were required.

So, the Government placed a bill for essential amendment of the Act, in 1924. The bill was containing a wide scope of insurance business. The bill came to the legislative assembly after a thorough comments by different bodies.

During the time, an important thing happened miraculously about the enactments of insurance business in England. The Government of India thought it fit to watch the course of new legislation on Insurance Law in England. Great Britain appointed Clauson (under the chairmanship of Mr. A. C. Clauson) Committee to report the possible and required changes in the Legislation. Therefore, the Government of India thought it wise to postpone the bill to include the reports of Clauson Committee. The Clauson Committee submitted its report in February, 1927, but no action was taken on its recommendations by the Government of England. The Government of India in 1928 passed a stop-gap legislation with the main object of collecting statistics regarding insurance matters so that the information collected would be of value when the time would come to pass a comprehensive Act. This act was not very comprehensive. The Government of India wanted to wait the English Legislation which was expected to be passed in 1929 or so and base the law for India on the British model but the legislation was not passed in Britain. The slow progress of events in Britain again revived the agitation for amendment of the law of Insurance in India.

Demand for another Act

Since the Act of 1928 was not very comprehensive, demand for another act was made. There were forceful and constant demand of such legislation which can control Indian as well as non-Indian insurance companies and can reduce the competition between these companies. The Government accepted the genuine demand and appointed one special officer for investigations the special and required reform of legislation in 1935. He was a well-known Calcutta Solicitor and was placed on special duty to report on the amendments necessary to modernise insurance legislation in India. His report was considered by the Advisory Committee appointed by the Government of India from representatives of all branches of insurance. The committee made several changes and the Government of India introduced the bill in the Legislative Assembly in 1937 and after much debate and several changes, it emerged as the Insurance Act of 1938.

Act of 1938

The Act does not follow the principle of minimum interference with maximum publicity and direct control. It was well balanced and was the first comprehensive piece of insurance legislation in this country governing both life and non-life branches of insurance. This Act provided to prevent the growth of mushroom companies, to enforce working on sound principles, to prevent misappropriation of funds and to protect the assets.

This Act of 1938 was wide and more comprehensive. There was strict control over the insurance business. This Act was amended from time to time. Since 1938, there were six amendments up to 1945. In 1945, it was deemed necessary to protect the interest of Insured Companies. Therefore in the Chairmanship of Sri Kavas Ji Jahangir, a meeting was appointed which was to investigate all the misconduct of the insurance business. The committee gave its reports after a thorough inquiry on which recommendation was made for amending many important sections and to introduce new sections. On this basis one amendment bill was made and was sent to different select committees and at last it was enacted on 18th April, 1950 by the Parliament. According to this amended Act, there are provisions pertaining to administration. The total right of control is with the Central Government. The Central Government controls the insurance business by appointing Controller of Insurance. The rules and regulations must be followed by the insurance companies, otherwise they will be penalised under this Act. The life insurance business was nationalised in 1956 and certain provisions of this Act apply to the Life Insurance Corporation of India. General Insurance Corporation of India Act was passed in 1972 to govern the business of general insurance which were nationalised in 1972.

THE INSURANCE ACT 1938

The Salient Features of Insurance Act 1938 have been discussed under the following headings:

1. Wide Scope
2. Requirements as to Capital
3. Deposits
4. Registration
5. Submission of Returns
6. Prohibition of Rebates, Restriction of Commission.
7. Licensing of Insurance Agents
8. Investment
9. Prohibition of loan
10. Investigation
11. Duties and Power of Controller of Insurance.

THE INSURANCE ACT 1938

The Salient Features of the Act

1. Wide Scope

(*a*) Application

The Act applies to all types of insurance business—life, fire, marine etc.—done by companies incorporated in India or elsewhere. It also governs the provident companies, mutual offices and cooperative-societies. Assessments in or dividing insurance business is Prohibited.

(*b*) Prohibition

According to Section 2-c of the .Act, there is prohibition of transaction of insurance business by certain persons.

"Save as hereinafter provided, no person shall, after the commencement of the Insurance Act, begin to carry on any class of insurance business in India and no insurer carrying on any class of insurance business in India shall after the expiry of one year, from such commencement, continue to carry on any such business unless he is

(*i*) a public company or,

(*ii*) a society registered under the Cooperative Societies. Act, 1912 or under any other law for any country outside India not being of the nature of a private company;

(*iii*) a body corporate incorporated under the law of any country outside India not being of the nature of a private company;

(*iv*) every notification issued under the Sub-section shall be laid before Parliament as soon as may be after it is issued.

2. Requirement as to Capital

(*a*) Section 6

No insurer incorporated after or who contained carrying on the business of life insurance in the States whether solely or in connection with any other business after the 26th day of January, 1937, shall be registered unless he has a working capital of a net sum of not less than fifty thousand rupees excluding of the deposit to be made before registration under sub-section (5) of Section 7 of this Act, and exclusive in the case of a company of any sums payable as preliminary expenses in the form of the company.

(*b*) Voting Powers

Notwithstanding anything to the contrary contained in any law for the time being in force or in the memorandum or articles of association but subject of the other provisions contained in this section, the voter's right of every shareholder of any public company as aforesaid in all cases be strictly proportionate to the paid up amount of the shares held by him.

(*d*) Maintenance of Registers of Members

A public company shall maintain in addition to the register of members to be maintained under the Indian Companies Act, a register of shares in which shall be inserted the name, occupation and address of the beneficial owner of each share and shall incorporate there any change of beneficial owner declared to it within 14 days from the receipt of such declaration.

3. Deposits

To prevent the growth of insurers of small financial resources or speculative concerns, the Act provided for registration of all insurers and a substantial deposit with the Reserve Bank.

Section 7

"Every insurer not being an insurer specified in sub-clause (*iii*) of clause (*i*) of Section 2 shall in respect of the insurance business carried on by him in India, deposit and keep deposited with the Reserve Bank of India in one of the offices in India of the bank for and on behalf of the Central Government. The amount hereafter specified, either in cash or in approved securities, estimated at the market value of the Securities on the day of deposit or partly in cash and partly in approved securities so estimated.

(*i*) Where the business done or to be done is life insurance only, two hundred thousand rupees.

(*ii*) Where the business done or to be done is fire insurance only, one hundred and fifty thousand rupees.

(*iii*) Where the business done or to be done is marine insurance only, one hundred and fifty thousand rupees.

(*iv*) Where the business done or to be done is miscellaneous insurance only, one hundred and fifty thousand rupees.

(*v*) Where the business done or to be done is life insurance and any one of the three classes specified in clauses (*ii*), (*iii*) and (*iv*), three hundred thousand rupees of which two hundred thousand rupees shall be the deposit for life insurance business.

(*vi*) Where the business done or to be done is life insurance and any two of the three classes specified in clauses (*ii*), (*iii*) and (*iv*), four hundred thousand rupees of which two hundred thousand shall be the deposit for life insurance business.

(*vii*) Where the business done or to be done is life insurance and all three classes specified in clauses (*ii*), (*iii*) and (*iv*) four hundred and fifty thousand rupees of which two hundred thousand rupees shall be the deposit for life insurance business:

(*viii*) Where the business done or to be done, does not include life insurance but is any two of the classes specified in clauses (*ii*), (*iii*) and (*iv*), two hundred and fifty thousand.

(*ix*) Where the business done or to be done does not include life insurance but is all three classes specified in clauses (*ii*) and (*iii*), Three hundred and fifty thousand rupees.

4. Registration

Section 3

1. No person shall, after the commencement of this Act, begin to carry on any class of insurance business in India and no insurer carrying on any class of insurance business in India shall after the expiry of three months from the commencement of this Act, continue of any or carry on any, such business, unless he has obtained from the controller a certificate of registration for the particular class of insurance business.

Provided that in the case of an insurer who was carrying on any class of insurance business in India at the commencement of this Act, failure to obtain a certificate of registration in accordance with the requirements of this Sub-clause shall not operate to invalidate any contract of insurance entered into by him if before such date as may be fixed in this behalf by the Central Government by notification in the Official Gazette, he has obtained that certificate.

Every application for registration shall be accompanied by:

(*i*) a certified copy of the memorandum and articles of association.

(*ii*) Name, address and occupation of directors.

(*iii*) a statement of the class or classes of insurance business done or to be done.

(*iv*) principal place of business or domicile outside India.

(*v*) a certified copy of the published prospectus.

(*vi*) the receipt showing payment in the prescribed manner of the prescribed fee which shall not be more than five hundred rupees.

2—A

On receipt of an application for registration and after making such inquiry as he deems fit the controller is satisfied that:

(*a*) The financial condition and the general character of management of the applicant are sound.

(*b*) The volume of business likely to be available to, and the capital structure and earning prospects of the applicant will be adequate.

(*c*) The interests of the general public will be served.

The controller may register the applicant as an insurer and grant him a certificate of registration.

The controller shall withhold registration or shall cancel a registration already made if any requirement is not satisfied.

2—4

The controller shall cancel the registration of an insurer either wholly or in so far as it related to a particular class of insurance business as the case may be:

(*a*) Insurer fails to apply Section 7 or 8 of deposits.

(*b*) Insurer is in liquidation or adjudged an insolvent.

(*c*) The business has been transferred to any other insured.

(*d*) Deposits have been returned to insurer.

(*e*) When clause 9 of Section 2 related to insurer's definition ceased or cancelled or suspended.

(*f*) Defaults in complying with any rules.

(*g*) Insurer has reason to cancel.

(*h*) Carry any business other than insurance business or any prescribed business.

Controller will give notice of his decision not more than two months before termination.

5. Submission of Returns

The Act provided for the creation of a past of Superintendent of Insurance and it was made obligatory on all companies–including the foreigner returns to submit all the quinquennial in the prescribed form within a stated period. The Superintendent had been given wide powers to reject all incomplete and inaccurate returns, etc.

Section 14

1. The audited accounts and balance sheet and actuarial report and abstract and four copies thereof shall be furnished as returns to the controller in the case of the accounts and balance sheet and the acturil report and abstract within nine months from the end of the period to which they refer. If the principal place is outside India, the period of submission may be extended by three months.
2. Of the four copies so furnished one shall be signed in the case of company by the Chairman and two directors and by the principal officer of the Company and if the Company has a managing director or managing agent, by that director or managing agent, in the case of a firm, by two partners of the firm, and in the case of an insurer being an individual by the insurer himself and one shall be signed by the auditor who made the audit or the actuary who made the valuation, as the case may be.
3. Where the insurer's principal place of business or domicile is outside India, he shall forward to the controller, along with the documents, a certified statement showing the total assets and liabilities of the insurer at the close of the period covered by the said documents.

16—2

The insurer, established outside India, shall, within the time specified in sub-section (1) of Section 15, furnish to the controller four certified copies in the English language of every balance-sheet, account abstract, report and statement supplied to the public authority and in addition thereto four certified copies in the English language of each of the following statement:

(*a*) a statement audited by an auditor or by a person duly qualified under the law of the insurer's country showing the assets held by the insurer in India at the date if any balance sheet so furnished;

(*b*) a separate account of receipts and payments and a revenue account for the period covered by any account so furnished;

(*c*) a separate abstract of the valuation report in respect of all business transacted in India in each class or sub-class of insurance business; and

(*d*) a declaration in the prescribed form stating that all amounts received by the insurer directly or indirectly whether from his head office or from any other source outside and have been shown in the revenue account.

6. Prohibition of Rebating, Restriction of Commission and Licensing of Agents

Section 40

"Prohibition of payment by was of commission of otherwise for procuring business."

1. No person shall, after the expiry of six months from the commencement of this Act, pay or contract to pay any remuneration or reward whether by way of commission or otherwise for soliciting or procuring insurance business in India to any person except an insurance agent or a principal, chief or special agent.
2. No Insurance agent shall be paid or contract to be paid by way of commission or as remuneration in any form an amount exceeding, in the case of life insurance business, 40% of the first year's premium payable on any policy or policies effected through him and 5% of a renewal premium, payable on such a policy, or, in the case of business of any other class 15%.

Provided that insurers, in respect of life insurance business only, may pay, during the first ten years of their business, to their insurance agents 55% of the first year's premium payable on any policy or policies effected through them and 6% of the renewal premium payable on such policies.

(40—A) Limitations of Expenditure on Commission

No person shall pay or contract to pay to an insurance agent, and no insurance agent shall receive or contract to receive by way of commission or remuneration in any form in respect of any policy of life insurance issued in India by an insurer after the 31st day of December 1950, and effected through an insurance agent, an amount exceeding.

(a) where the policy grants an immediate annuity or a deferred annuity in consideration of a single premium, or where only one premium is payable on the policy, 2% of that premium,

(*b*) where the policy grants a differed annuity in consideration of more than one premium, $7\frac{1}{2}$% of the first year's premium, and 2% of the each renewal premium payable on the policy, and

(*c*) in any other case, 35% of the first year's premium, $7\frac{1}{2}$ % of the second and third year's renewal premium and there after 5% of each renewal premium payable on the policy.

Provided that in a case referred to in clause (*c*), an insurer during the first 10 years of his business, may pay to an insurance agent, and an insurance agent may receive from such an insurer, 40% of the first year's premium payable on the policy.

2. No person shall pay or contract to pay to a special agent, and no special agent shall receive or contract to receive, by way of commission or as remuneration in any form, in respect of any policy of life insurance issued in India by an insurer of the 31st day of December, 1950 and effected through a special agent, an amount exceeding:

(*a*) in a case referred to in clause (*a*) of Sub-section (1) one half per cent of the premium;

(*b*) in a case referred to in clause (*b*) of Sub-section (1) two per cent of the first year's premium payable on the policies.

(*c*) in a case referred to in clause (*c*) of Sub-section (1) fifteen per cent of the first-year's premium payable on the policies.

Section 41

Prohibition at rebates

1. No person shall allow or offer to allow either directly or in· directly as an inducement to any person to take out or renew or continue an insurance in respect of any kind of risk, relating to lives or property in India, any rebate of the whole or part of the commission payable or any rebate of the premium shown on the policy, nor shall any person taking out or renewing or continuing a policy accept any rebate, except such rebate as may be allowed in accordance with the published prospectuses or tables of the insurer.

   Provided that acceptance by an insurance agent of commission in connection with a policy of life insurance taken out by himself on his own life shall not be deemed to be acceptance of a rebate of premium within the meaning of this sub-section if at the time of such acceptance the insurance agent satisfies the prescribed conditions establishing that he is bona fide insurance agent employed by the insurer,

2. Any person making default in complying with the provisions of this section shall be punishable with fine which may extend to ₹ 500.

7. Licensing of Insurance Agents

Section 42

The controller or an officer authorised by him in this behalf shall, in the prescribed manner and on payment of the prescribed form which shall not be more than ten rupees, issue to any person making an application in the prescribed manner and a licence to act as an insurance agent for the purpose of soliciting or procuring insurance business:

Provided that:

(*a*) in the case of an individual, he does not suffer from any of the disqualification:

(*i*) that the person is a minor;

(*ii*) that he is found to be of unsound mind by a court of competent jurisdiction;

(*iii*) that he has been found guilty of criminal misappropriation or criminal breach of trust or cheating or forgery or an abetment of or attempt to commit any such offence by a court of competent jurisdiction:

Provided that, where at least five years have elapsed since the completion of sentence imposed on any person in respect of such person that his conviction shall cease to operate as a disqualification under this clause;

(*b*) in the case of a company or firm, any of its directors or partners does not suffer from any of the said disqualifications, and the company or firm was immediately before the 1st day or August 1957, holding a certificate issued under Section 42-A entitling, it to act as a principal agent for the purpose of procuring insurance business.

(42—2)

A licence issued under this section shall entitle the holder to act as an insurance agent for any insurer.

(42—3)

A licence issued under this section, after the commencement of the Insurance (Amendment) Act 1950, shall remain in force for a period of three years only from the date of issue, but shall, if the applicant does not suffer from any of the disqualification mentioned above and the application for renewal of the licence reaches the issuing authority at least thirty days before the date on which the licence ceases to remain in force, be renewed for a period of three years at any one time on payment of the prescribed fee which shall not be more than ten rupees, and an additional fee of a prescribed amount, not exceeding three rupees by way of penalty if the application for renewal of the licence does not reach the issuing authority at least thirty days before the date on which the licence ceases to remain in force.

8. Investments

It was laid down that 55% of net life liabilities of an Indian or a British insurer should be invested in India Government and Approved Securities with at least 25% in Indian Government Rupee Securities. All other companies had to invest 100% of their Indian liabilities in Indian Government and Approved Securities with at least one-third in Indian Government Rupee Securities. This provision had been made for the prevention of the misapplication of assets and for their preservation so that the funds of every insurer could not only be safely invested but they could also be so invested as to make them readily available and, if necessary, to be readily convertible into liquid funds.

5.27—A

1. No insurer shall invest or keep invested any part of his controlled fund otherwise than in any of the following approved investment, namely,
   (*a*) Approved securities.
   (*b*) Securities guaranteed by Government of U.K.
   (*c*) Debentures of Municipality in a State.
   (*d*) Debentures issued by a body constituted by any Central Act or Act of State Legislature.
   (*e*) First Mortgage on immovable property under any housing or building scheme.
   (*f*) Debentures secured on first charge on immovable property.
   (*g*) First debentures secured by a floating charge on all its assets.
   (*h*) Preference share of any company.
   (*i*) Shares of any company which is guaranteed by any company.
   (*j*) First Mortgage on immovable property.

Every insurer shall also submit to the controller a return in the prescribed form showing all the changes that occurred in the investments aforesaid during each of the quarters ending on the last day of March.

9. Prohibition of Loan

Section 29—1

No insurer shall grant loans or temporary advances either on hypothecation of property or on personal security or otherwise except loans on life Policies issued by him within their surrender value to any director, manager, managing agent, actuary auditor, or officer of the insurer if the company or where the insurer is a firm to any partner therein, or to any other company or firm in which any such director, manager, managing agent, actuary officer or partner holds such position.

10. Investigation

Section 33

The Central Government may, at any time, by order in writing direct the controller or any other person specified in the order to investigate the affairs of any insurer and to report to the Central Government on any investigation made by him.

11. Duties and Power of Controller of Insurance

The duties and power of controller are discussed under general duties. special duties and rights about investigation.

General Duties and Power

The controller is authorised to grant the certificate of registration, to inquire about deposit, and to receive reports and accounts from the insurers. He is empowered to issue licences to agents and to accept the amalgamations and reorganisation. He is also authorised to compose the dispute regarding claim of smaller amount, and may ask any report in this connection. He can delegate his Powers and duties to his subordinate.

Special Duties and Power

According to Section 21 (1), he is authorised to get completed the incomplete reports. He may require from the insurer such further information, certificate and documents as he may consider necessary. He may call upon the insurer to submit for his examination at the principal place of business of the insurer in the states any book of account, register, etc. He may examine any officer of the insurer on oath in relation to the return. He may decline to accept any such return unless the inaccuracy has been corrected or the deficiency has been supplied. He may examine the accounts and reports of past years. He is empowered to rectify the mistakes.

Rights about Investigation

The controller is authorised to investigate the organisational set-up and administration of the insurer. He may get special audit or actuarial or any reports by the auditors, actuaries or investigators appointed by him. He is authorised, after giving a short notice, to cancel the registration of an insurer and may order for liquidation or may take action for breach of law.

THE LIFE INSURANCE CORPORATION ACT, 1956

The essential features of the Act of 1956 have been discussed in the following headings:

(A) Termination of Personal Management.

(B) Termination of Private Ownership.

(C) Establishment of the Life Insurance Corporation of India:

1. Constitution.
2. Capital.
3. Functions of the Corporation.
4. Transfer of Services.
5. Set-up of the Corporation.
6. Committee of the Corporation.
7. Authorities.
8. Zonal Bodies.
9. Finance, Accounts and Audit.
10. Investment provisions.
11. Provisions pertaining to commission.
12. Provisions to Policy-holder's rights.

THE LIFE INSURANCE CORPORATION ACT, 1956

The process of nationalisation of Life Insurance is divided into two parts:

(A) Termination of Personal or Private Management; and

(B) Abolition of Private Ownership.

(A) Termination of Personal Management

The private management was eliminated on March 21, 1956 and was replaced by the Corporation management governed by the Life Insurance Corporation Act, 1956.

1. According to Section 3 of Life Insurance (Emergency Provisions) Act 1956, the management of controlled business were vested in Government on commencement of this Act (Emergency). On and from the 19th January, 1956 the appointed date, the management of the controlled business of all insurers shall vest in the Central Government, and pending the appointment of a custody for the controlled business immediately before the appointed day shall, on and from the appointed day, be in charge of the management of the business for and on behalf of the Central Government; and the controlled business of the insurer shall be carried on by them subject to the provisions contained in Sub-sections (3) and (5) and to such further directions, if any, as the Central Government may give to them by notice addressed and sent to the principal officer of the insurer.
2. Any contract, whether express or implied, providing for the management of the controlled business of an insurer made before the appointed day between the insurer and any person in charge of the management of the business immediately before the appointed date shall be deemed to have terminated on the appointed day.
3. No insurer shall, without the previous approval of the person specified by the Central Government in this behalf in respect of that insurer (hereinafter referred to as the authorised person):
   (*a*) make any payment or grant any loan in respect of a policy of life insurance otherwise than in accordance with the normal practice observed by him in respect of such matters immediately before the appointed day;
   (*b*) incur any expenditure from the assets appertaining to the controlled business otherwise than for the purpose of making routine payments of salaries or commission to employees, insurance, agents, special agents or chief agents or for the purpose of meeting the routine day-to-day expenditure;
   (*c*) transfer or otherwise dispose of any such assets or create any charges hypothecation in or other encumbrance thereon;
   (*d*) invest in any manner any money forming part of such assets;
   (*e*) acquire any immovable property out of any moneys forming part of such assets;
   (*f*) enter into any contract of service or agency, whether expressly or by implication, for purposes connected wholly or partly with the controlled business or vary the terms and conditions of any such contract subsisting on the appointed day; and
   (*g*) enter into any other transaction relating to controlled business other than a contract relating to the issue of a new policy of life insurance or vary the terms and conditions of any agreement relating to any such transaction subsisting at the commencement of this Act.

Appointment of Custodian

Section 4

The Central Government may, as soon as it is convenient administratively so to do, appoint any person as custodian for the purpose of taking over the management of the controlled business of an insurer.

On the appointment of a custodian all persons in charge of the management of the controlled business of the insurer for and on behalf of the Central Government immediately before such appointment shall cease to be in charge of such management and shall be bound to deliver to the custodian all books of account, registers or other documents in their custody relating to the controlled business of the insurer.

The custodian shall receive such remuneration as the Central Government may, by order, direct that the whole or any part of the deposit fix and the Central Government may at any time cancel the appointment of any person as custodian and appoint some other person in his stead.

Refund of Deposits Made under Insurance Act

The Central Government may, by order, direct that the whole or any part of the deposit appertaining to his controlled business made by an insurer under Section 7, 73 or 98 of the Insurance Act, as the case may be, shall be returned to the custodian who has been appointed to take over the management of the controlled business of the Insurer, and every such order shall have effect notwithstanding anything contained in the Insurance Act.

5.3 (6) Every insurer shall deliver forthwith at the place and to the person specified in this behalf by the Central Government in respect of that insurer the following documents:

(*i*) The minute book or any other book in India containing all resolution up to the appointed day of the persons in charge of the management of the controlled business before the appointed day.

(*ii*) The current cheque books relating to the controlled business which are at the head office of the principal office of the insurer;

(*iii*) All registers or other books containing particulars relating to the investments of any money appertaining to the controlled business including investment on mortgaged properties and all loans granted and advances made otherwise than on policies.

(*iv*) All brokers' notes, or certificates in the possession of the insurer in respect of any orders for the investment of any money appertaining to the controlled business.

Compensation for Acquiring Management

(*i*) Where the controlled business of an insurer has been transferred to and vested in the corporation under this Act, compensation shall be given by the corporation to that insurer in accordance with the principles contained in the first Schedule.

There the amount of compensation is determined as: One-twelfth of annual average of the Surplus determined according to the last two valuations of such surplus.

If the surplus cannot be determined, the basis of Income on premium is taken into account. Re. 1 on the income of ₹ 2,000/ or part there of is the basis of amount of compensation.

(B) Abolition of Private Ownership

The official management of Life Insurance continued for 6 months from January 19, 1956 to June 30, 1956. During this period the Act was passed. The Act commenced from July 1, 1956 and from this date the Act was implemented.

(C) Organisation, and Functions of Life Insurance Corporation

1. Constitution

Section 3

"Establishment and Incorporation of Life Insurance Corporation of India".

1. With effect from such date as the Central Government may, by notification in the official gazette, appoint there shall be established a corporation called the Life Insurance Corporation of India.

2. The corporation shall be a body corporate having perpetual succession and a common seal with power, subject to the provisions of this Act to acquire, hold and dispose of property and may by its name sue and be sued.

Section 4: "Constitution of the Corporation".

1. The corporation shall consist of such number of persons not exceeding fifteen as the Central Government may think fit to appoint thereto and one of them shall be appointed by the Central Government to be the Chairman thereof.
2. Before appointing a person to be a member the Central Government shall satisfy itself that the person has no such financial or other interest as is likely to affect prejudicially the exercise or performance by him of his functioning as a member, and the Central Government shall also satisfy itself from time to time with respect to every member that he has no such interest; and any person who is, or whom the Central Government proposes to appoint and who has consented to be a member shall, whenever required by the Central Government so to do, furnish to it such information as the Central Government considers necessary for the performance of its duties under this sub-section.
3. A member who is in any way directly or indirectly interested in a contract made or proposed to be made by the corporation shall as soon as possible report to the Corporation.

2. Capital

Section 5.

Capital of the Corporation:

1. The original capital of the corporation shall be five crores of rupees provided by the Central Government after due appropriation made by Parliament by law for the purpose and the terms and conditions relating to the provisions of such capital shall be such as may be determined by the Central Government.

3. Function of the Corporation

1. Subject to the rules, if any, made by the Central Government in this behalf it shall be the general duty of the Corporation to Carry on life insurance business, whether in or outside India, and the Corporation to carry on life insurance business, whether in or outside India, shall so exercise its powers under this Act as to secure that life insurance business is developed to the best advantage of the community.
2. Without prejudice to the generality of the provisions contained in Sub-section (1) but subject to the other provisions contained in this Act, the Corporation shall have power.
   (*a*) to carry on capital redemption business, annually certain business, or reinsurance business in so far as such reinsurance business appertains to life insurance business;
   (*b*) subject to the rules, if any, made by the Central Government in this behalf, to invest the funds of the Corporation in such manner as the Corporation may think fit and to take all such steps as may be necessary or expedient for the protection or realise of any investment, including the taking over of and administering any property offered as security for the investment until a suitable opportunity arises for its disposal;
   (*c*) to acquire, hold and dispose of any property for the purpose of its business;
   (*d*) to transfer the whole or any part of the life insurance business carried on outside India to any other person or persons, if in the interests of the Corporation it is expedient so to do;
   (*e*) to advance or lend money upon the security of any movable or immovable property or otherwise;

(*f*) to borrow or raise any money in such manner and upon such security as the Corporation may think fit;

(*g*) to carry on either by itself or through any subsidiary any other business in any case where such other business was being carried on by a subsidiary of an insurer whose controlled business has been transferred to and vested in the Corporation under this Act.

(*h*) to carry on any other business which may seem to the Corporation to be capable of being conveniently carried on in connection with its business and calculated directly or indirectly to render profitable the business of the Corporation; and

(*i*) to do also such thing as may be incidental or conducive to the proper exercise of any of the powers of the Corporation.

4. Transfer of Services

All the employees except chief agent will be vested into new life-business. The salary and terms of employment will remain the same unless insurance business think fit to change the terms of employment for the benefit of the policyholder.

If any term is not acceptable to an employee, he can be terminated by paying three months' salary as compensation.

Section 12

Subject to such rules as the Central Government may make in this behalf, every whole-time salaried employee of a Chief Agent of an insurer whose controlled business has been transferred to and vested in the Corporation and

(*a*) who was employed by the Chief Agent wholly or mainly in connection with the controlled business of the insurer;

(*b*) whose salary on the appointed day did not exceed five hundred rupees per mensem; and

(*c*) who was in the employment of the Chief Agent for a continues period of not less than one year immediately before the appointed day.

Shall, on and from the appointed day, become an employee of the Corporation and the provisions of Section 11 shall, so far as may be, apply in relation to such employee as they apply in relation to a whole-time employee of the insurer.

Provided that this section shall not apply except in cases where the Chief Agent of the insurer was required under the terms of his contract with the insurer to render the prescribed service top policy holders of the insurers.

Section 14

Power of Corporation to modify contracts of life insurance is given in certain cases.

Section 15

Right of Corporation to seek relief in respect of certain transaction of the insurer:

1. Where an insurer whose controlled business has been transferred to and vested in the corporation under this Act, has at any time within five years before the 19th day of January, 1956,

(*a*) made any payment to any person without consideration,

(*b*) sold or disposed of any property of the insurer without consideration or for an inadequate consideration,

(*c*) acquired any property or rights for an excessive consideration,

(*d*) entered into or varied any agreement so as to require an excess consideration and

(*e*) entered into any other transaction.

Section 18

(*i*) The Central Office of the Corporation shall be at such a place as the Central Government may, by notification in the Official Gazette, specify.

(*ii*) The Corporation shall establish a Zonal Office at each of the following places *i.e.* Bombay, Calcutta, Delhi, Kanpur and Madras and subject to the previous approval of the Central Government, may establish such other zonal offices as it thinks fit.

(*iii*) The territorial limits of each zone shall be such as may be specified by the corporations.

(*iv*) There may be established as many divisional offices and branches in each zone as the Zonal Manager thinks fit.

6. Committee of the Corporation

Section 19

1. The corporation may entrust the general superintendence and direction of its affairs and business to an executive committee consisting not more than five of its members and the executive committee may exercise all powers and do all such acts and things as may be delegated to it by the Corporation.
2. The Corporation may also constitute an Investment Committee for the purpose of advising it in matters relating to the investment of its funds, and the Investment amount shall consist of not more than seven members of whom not less than three shall be members of Corporations and the remaining members shall be person (whether members of the corporation or not) who have special knowledge and experience in financial matters, particularly matters relating to investment of funds.
3. The corporation may constitute such other committees as it may think fit for the purpose to discharge such of its functions as may be delegated to them.

7. Authorities

(*a*) Managing Director

The corporation may appoint, one or more persons to be the Managing Director or Directors of the Corporation and every Managing Director shall be a whole-time officer of the Corporation, and shall exercise such power and perform such duties as may be entrusted or delegated to him by the Executive Committee or the Corporation.

Corporation to be Guided by the Directions of Central Govt.

In the discharge of its function under this Act, the Corporation shall be guided by such directions in matters of policy involving public-interest as the Central Government may give to it in writing.

(*b*) Zonal Managers

1. The Corporation may entrust the superintendence and direction of the affairs and business of a zonal office to a person, whether a member or not, who shall be known as a Zonal Manager and the Zonal Manager shall perform all such functions of the Corporation as may be delegated to him with respect to the area within the jurisdiction of the Zonal Office.
2. The Corporation may constitute for each zone a Board consisting of such number, of persons as it thinks fit to appoint thereto for the-purpose of advising the zonal manager in respect of such matters as are referred to it under the regulations made by the Corporation.
3. The Corporation shall constitute in the prescribed manner for each zonal office an Employee and Agents Relations Committee consisting of such number of person as it thinks fit and every such committee shall consist of representatives of the Corporation.

8. Zonal Bodies

(*a*) Zonal Board

The Corporation will establish one board at every zone. The appointment of members and the numbers are determined according to corporation. These board suggests on the zonal management, on the rules and regulations of the Corporation.

(*b*) Employees of Agents Relations Committee

The Corporation shall constitute in the prescribed manner for each zonal office an Employees and Agents Relations Committee consisting of such number of the persons at it thinks fit and every such committee shall consist of representation of the Corporation and of its employees and agents, so that the number of representatives of the employees and agent on the Committee shall not be less than the number of representatives of the Corporation and it shall be the duty of the Committee to advise the Zonal Manager on matters which relate to the welfare of the employees and agents of the Corporation or which are likely to promote and secure amity and good relations between them and the Corporation.

9. Finance, Accounts and Audit

(*a*) Audit

The accounts of the Corporation shall be audited by auditors duly qualified to act as auditors of companies under the law for the time being in force relating to companies, and the auditors shall be appointed by the Corporation with the previous approval of the Central Government and shall receive such remuneration from the Corporation as the Central Government may fix.

1. Every auditor in the performance of his duties shall have at all reasonable time access to the books of accounts and other document of the Corporation.
2. The auditors shall submit their report to the Corporation and shall also forward a copy of their report to the Central Government.

(*b*) Actuarial Valuation

The Corporation shall, once at least in every two years, cause an investigation to be made of actuaries into the financial condition of the business of the Corporation, including a valuation of the liabilities of the Corporation and submit the report of the actuaries to the Central Government.

(*c*) Annual Report of activities of Corporation

The Corporation shall, as soon as may be, after the end of each financial year, prepare and submit to the Central Government in such form as may be prescribed a report giving an account of its activities during the previous financial year, and the report shall also give an account of the activities, if any, which are likely to be undertaken by the Corporation in the next financial year.

(*d*) Surplus how to be utilised

If as a regular of any investigation undertaken by the Corporation under Section 26 and surplus re-merges, not less than 95% of such surplus shall be allocated to or reserved for the policyholders, of the Corporation and the remainder may be utilised for such purposes and in such manners as the Central Government may determine.

(*e*) Reports to be laid before Parliament

The Central Government shall cause the report of the auditors under Section 25, the report of the actuaries under Section 26 and the report giving an account of the actuaries of the Corporation under Section 27 to be laid before both Houses of Parliament as soon as may be after each such report is received by the Central Government.

Section 30. Corporation to have the exclusive privilege of carrying on Life Insurance Business

Except to the extent otherwise expressly provided in this Act, on and from the appointed day the Corporation shall have the exclusive privilege of carrying on life insurance business in India; and on and from the said day any certificate of registration under the Insurance Act held by any insurer immediately before the said day shall cease to have effect in so far as it authorises him to carry on life insurance business in India.

Section 31. Exception in the case of Insurance business in respect of persons residing outside India

1. Notwithstanding anything contained in Section 30 or in the Insurance Act, the Central Government may, by order, permit any person who has made an application in that behalf, to carry on life insurance business in India in respect of the lives of persons ordinarily resident outside India, subject to such restrictions and conditions as may be specified in the order and any such order shall be deemed to have effect as if it were a certificate of registration issued by the Controller to such person under Section 3 of the Insurance Act in respect of that class of business.
2. Nothing in sub-section 1 shall authorise any person permitted to carry on life insurance business of the nature referred to in that sub-section, to insure the life of any person ordinarily resident outside India, during any period of his temporary residence in India.

Section 32. Power of Corporation to have official seal in certain cases

The Corporation may have for use in any zonal office, divisional office or in any office outside India an official seal which shall be a fascimile of the common seal of the Corporation, with the addition on its facc of thc name of the zonal office, divisional office other office where it is to be used and any such official seal may be affixed to any deed or document to which the Corporation is a party.

Section 33. Requirement of foreign laws to be complied with in certain cases

Where any property or rights appertaining to the controlled business of an insurer are transferred to and vested in the Corporation under this Act on would be so transferred and vested but for the fact that such transfer and vesting are governed otherwise than by the law of India, the insurer shall comply with such directions as may be given to him by the Corporation for the purpose of securing that the ownership of the property or, as the case may be, that the right is effectively transferred to the Corporation.

Section 34. Revesting of certain shares vested in the Administrator-General

Notwithstanding anything contained in the Insurance Act, all shares which have vested in the Administrator-General of any State under sub-section (8) of Section 6A of that Act and which have not been disposed of in accordance with the provision of that sub-section before the appointed day, shall, on payment of the amount of expenditure, if any, incurred by the Administrator-General in relation to such shares by the persons who would have been entitled to those shares if the said sub-section had not been enacted revest in such persons.

Section 35. Repatuation of assests and liabilities in the case of foreign insurers in certain cases

1. Any insurer incorporated outside India may, before the appointed day, make an application to the Central Government stating that among the assets appertaining to the controlled business of the insurer there are assets brought into India by the insurer for the purpose of building up his

life insurance business in India which, notwithstanding anything contained in Section 7, should not be transferred to and vested in the Corporation.

2. On receipt of an 'application under sub-section 1, the Central Government shall determine the value of the assets of the insurer appertaining to his controlled business in existence on the 31st day of December, 1955, computed as at that date in accordance with the provisions contained in paragraph 3 of part B of the First Schedule, and deduct therefrom the total amount of the liabilities of the insurer appertaining to this controlled business in existence on the 31st day of December, 1955, computed as at that date in accordance with the provisions contained in the Second Schedule and if there is any excess, the Central Government may, by order, direct that such assets equivalent in value to tiie excess as may be specified in the order shall not be transferred to or vested in the Corporation, or where the order is made after the appointed day, that the Corporation shall be divested of the said assets.
3. In the case of any insurer incorporated outside India, the Central Government may also, by order, direct that any such liabilities in respect of life insurance policies expressed in any foreign currency issued on the lives of persons who are not citizens of India as are specified in the order together with any such assets necessary to meet the liabilities, as may be so specified, shall not be transferred to or vested in the Corporation or, if the order is made after the appointed day, that the Corporation shall be divested of such liabilities and assets as aforesaid.
4. The amount of liabilities in respect of the policies referred to in an order made under sub-section 3. shall be computed as at the 31st day of December. 1955:
   (*a*) in any case where in respect of the insurer concerned an order has been made under sub-section 2. in accordance with the provisions contained in clause of the Second Schedule; and
   (*b*) in any other case, in accordance with method A specified in the Second Schedule.

   Explanation—In computing the amount of labilities in respect of the policies referred to in this sub-section, allowance shall be made for receipts and payments in respect of such policies from the 31st day, of December, 1955, up to the date of the order.
5. Every order made by the Central Government under this section shall be carried out by the Corporation in such manner as the Central Government may direct.

Section 36. Contracts of chief agents and special agents to terminate

Notwithstanding anything contained in the Insurance Act or in any other law for the time being in force, every contract appertaining to controlled business subsisting immediately before the appointed day—

(*a*) between an insurer and his chief agent or between an insurer and special agent; or

(*b*) between the chief agent of an insurer and a special agent; shall as from the appointed day, cease to have effect and all rights accruing to the chief agent or the special agent under any such contract shall terminate on that day.

Provided that in every such case compensation shall be given by the Corporation to the chief agent or the special agent, as the case may be, in accordance with the principles contained in the Third Scheduled, and the provisions of sub-Section 2 of Section 16 shall, so far as may be, apply in every such case.

Section 37. Policies to be Guaranteed by Central Government

The sums assured by all policies issued by the Corporation including any bonuses declared in respect thereof and, subject to the provisions contained in Section 14 the amounts assured by all policies issued-by any insurer the labilities under which have vested in the Corporation under this Act, and all bonuses declared in respect thereof, whether before or after the appointed day, shall be guaranteed as to payment in cash by the Central Government.

Section 38. Liquidation of Corporation

No provision of law relating to the winding up of companies for corporations shall apply to the Corporation established under this Act, and the Corporation shall not be placed in liquidation save by order of the Central Government and in such manner as that Government may direct.

Section 39. Special provisions for winding up of certain insurers

Where any insurer being a company (other than a composite insurer) whose controlled business has been transferred to and vested in the Corporation under this Act has in accordance with the provisions of this Act collected and distributed any moneys paid to him by the Corporation by way of compensation or otherwise and has also complied with any direction given to him by the Corporation for the purpose of securing that the ownership, of any property or any right is effectively transferred to the Corporation, the Central Government may on application being made to it in this behalf by such insurer grant a certificate to the insurer that there is no reason for the continued existence of the insurer and where such a certificate has been granted shall cause the certificate to be published in the Official Gazette and upon the publication thereof the insurer shall be dissolved.

Section 40. Penalty for

If any person wilfully withholds or fails to deliver to the Corporation as required by Section 13, any property or any books, documents or other papers which may be in his possession or unlawfully retains Possession of any property of an insurer which has been transferred to and vested in the Corporation under this Act or wilfully applies any such property to purposes other than those expressed in or, authorised by this Act, he shall, on the Complaint of the Corporation, be punishable with imprisonment which may extend to one, year, or with fine which may extend to one thousand rupees, or with both.

Section 41. Tribunal to have exclusive jurisdiction in certain matters

No civil court shall have jurisdiction to entertain or adjudicate upon any matter which a Tribunal is empowered to decide or determine under this Act.

Section 42. Enforcement of Decisions of Tribunals

Any decision of a Tribunal may be enforced in any civil court within the local limits of whose jurisdiction the person against whome the decision is to be enforced actually and voluntarily resides or carries on business or personally works for gain or owns any property, as if it were a decree passed by that court.

Section 43. Application of the Insurance Act.

1. The following sections of the Insurance Act shall, so far as may be, apply to the Corporation as they apply to any other insurer, namely:

   Sections 2, 2B, 3, 18, 26, 33, 41, 46, 47 A, 50, 51, 52, 110A, 110B, 110C, 119, 121, 122 and 123.

2. The Central Government shall, as soon as may be after the commencement of this Act, by notification in the Official Gazette, direct that the following sections of the Insurance Act shall apply to the Corporation subject to such conditions and modifications as may be specified in the notification, namely:

   Sections 2D, 10, 11, 13, 14, 15, 20, 21, 22, 23, 25; 27A; 28 A; 35, 36, 37, 40, 40A, 40B, 43, 44, 102 to 106, 107 to 110, 111, 113, 114 and 116A.

(2A) Section 42 of the Insurance Act shall have effect in relation to the issue to any individual of a licence to act as an agent for the purpose of soliciting or procuring life insurance business for the

Corporation as if the reference to an officer authorised by the Controller in this behalf in sub-section 1. thereof included a reference to an officer of the Corporation authorised by the Controller in this behalf.

3. The Central Government may, by notification in the official Gazette, direct that all or any of the provisions of the Insurance Act other than those specified in sub-section 1. or sub-section 2, shall apply to the Corporation subject to such conditions and modifications as may be specified in the notification.
4. Every notification issued under sub-section 2 or subsection 3 shall be laid for not less than 30 days before both Houses of Parliament as soon as possible after it is issued, and shall be subject to such modifications as Parliament may make during the session in which it is so laid or the session immediately following.
5. Save as provided in this section, nothing contained in the Insurance Act shall apply to the Corporation.

Section 44. Act not to apply in certain cases

Nothing contained in this Act shall apply in relation to:

(*a*) any, insurer whose business is being voluntarily wound up or is being wound up under the orders of the court;

(*b*) any insurer to whom the Insurance Act does not apply by reason of the provisions contained in Section 2E thereof;

(*c*) any composite insurer in respect of the management of whose affairs an Administrator has been appointed under Section 52A of the Insurance Act;

(*d*) the scheme run by the Central Government known as the Post Office Life Insurance Fund;

(*e*) any approved superannuation fund as defined in clause (*a*) of Section 58N of the Indian Income-tex Act 1922 which is in existence on the appointed day;

(*f*) any scheme in existence on the appointed day or any scheme framed after the appointed day with the approval of the Central Government whereby, in consideration of certain compulsory deductions made by Government from the salaries of its employees as part of the conditions of service, the payment of money is assured by Government on the death of the employee concerned or on the happening of any contingency dependent on his life.

Section 45. Special provisions regarding transfer of controlled business of certain composite insurers

Notwithstanding anything contained in clause (*c*) of section 44, the Central Government may, by notification in the Official Gazette, direct that on and with effect from such date as may be specified in the notification the assets and liabilities appertaining to the controlled business of a composite insurer in respect of the management of whose affairs an Administrator has been appointed under section 52A of the Insurance Act shall be transferred to and vested in the Corporation, and on the issue of such a notification the provisions of this Act shall so far as may be, apply in relation to such insurer and to the transfer and vesting of the assets and liabilities of his controlled business in the Corporation as they apply in relation to all other insurers and to the transfer and vesting of the assets and liabilities of their controlled business in the Corporation, subject to the modification that references in this Act to the appointed day shall be construed as references to the day specified in the notification.

Section 46. Defects in constitution of corporation or committees not to invalidate acts or proceedings

No act or proceeding of the Corporation or of any Committees of the Corporation shall be called in question on the ground merely of the existence on any vacancy or defect in the constitution of the Corporation or Committee, as the case may be.

Section 47. Protection of action taken under act

No suit, prosecution or other legal proceeding shall lie against any member or employee of the Corporation for anything which is in good faith done or intended to be done under this Act.

Section 48. Power to make rules

1. The Central Government may, by notification in the Official Gazette make rules to carry out the purposes of this Act.
2. In particular, and without prejudice to the, generality of the foregoing power, such rules may provide for all or any of the following matters, namely:
   (*a*) the term of office and the conditions of service of members.
   (*b*) the manner in which the moneys and other assets belonging to any such fund as is referred to in Section 8 shall be apportioned between the trustees of the fund and the Corporation;
   (*c*) the services which the chief agent should have rendered for the purpose of the proviso to Section 12;
   (*d*) the jurisdiction of the Tribuals constituted under Section 17;
   (*e*) the manner in which, and the persons to whom, any compensation under this Act may be paid;
   (*f*) the time within which any matter which may be referred to a Tribunal for decision under this Act may be so referred;
   (*g*) the manner in which and the conditions subject to which investments may be made by the Corporation;
   (*h*) the manner in which an Employees and Agents Relations Committee may be constituted for each zonal office;
   (*i*) the form in which the report giving an account of the activities of the Corporation shall be prepared.
   (*j*) the conditions subject to which the Corporation may appoint employees;
   (*k*) the fees payable under this Act and the manner in which they are to be collected;
   (*l*) any other matter which has to be or may be prescribed.
3. All rules made under this section shall be laid for not less than thirty days before both Houses of Parliament as soon as possible after they are made, and shall be subject to such modifications as Parliament may make during the session in which they are so laid or the session immediately following.

Section 49. Power to Make Regulations.

1. The Corporation may, with the previous approval of the Central Government, by notification in the Gazette of India, make regulations not Inconsistent with this Act and the rules made thereunder to provide for all matters for which provision is expendient for the purpose of giving effect to the provisions of this Act.
2. In particular, and without prejudice to the generality of the foregoing power, such regulations may provide for—

(*a*) the powers and functions of the Corporation which may be delegated to the Zonal Managers;

(*b*) the method of recruitment of employees and agents of the Corporation and the terms and conditions of service of such employees or agents;

(*bb*) the terms and conditions of service of persons who have become employees of the Corporation under sub-section (1) of Section 11;

(*c*) the number, term of office and conditions of service of members of Boards constituted under Section 22;

(*d*) the territorial limits of each zone established under this. Act and the business to be transacted in each zone;

(*e*) the manner in which the Fund of the Corporation shall be maintained;

(*f*) the maintenance of separate funds and accounts at each of the zonal office;

(*g*) the jurisdiction of each divisional office and the establishment of Councils representative of policy-holders in each area served by a divisional office for the purpose of advising the divisional office in respect or any matter which may be referred to it;

(*h*) the conduct of business at meetings of the Corporation;

(*i*) the formation of Committees of the Corporation and the delegation of powers and functions of the Corporation to such Committees, and the conduct of business to meetings of such Committees;

(*j*) the form and manner in which policies may be issued and contracts binding on the Corporation may be executed;

(*k*) the classification or by any insurer whose controlled business has been transferred to and vested in the Corporation for the purpose of declaring differential bonuses wherever necessary.

(*l*) the manner in which and the interval within which the accounts of the various zonal offices, divisional offices and branch offices may be inspected are their accounts audited;

(*m*) the conditions subject to which any payment may be made by the Corporation.

10. Investment Provisions

The Section 27-A of the Insurance Act, 1938 was made applicable to the Corporation with slight modifications. The investments of the Corporation were divided into three broad categories: (*i*) the government and approved securities which generally mean gilt-edged securities; (*ii*) investments approved under Section 27 A of the insurance Act; and (*iii*) other investments. The Corporation has to hold at least 50 per cent of the total funds in government and approved securities and the rest in approved investments. Not more than 15 per cent of the total funds may, however, be held in the form of other investments, provided that such investments is unanimously approved by the Investment Committee of the Corporation or by a resolution of the Corporation with a two-thirds majority.

11. Provisions Pertaining to Commission

The maximum amount of commission or remuneration in any form payable in respect of life insurance is 35 per cent of the first year's premium, 7½ per cent of the second and third years' renewal premium and 5 per cent of the renewal commission thereafter. In case of an immediate annually or a deferred annuity in consideration of a single premium or a single premium life policy, the maximum allowable rate is 2 per cent of the premium. In case of a defferred annuity, where consideration is payable in more than one Premium, the limit is $7\frac{1}{2}$ per cent for the first year and 2 per cent for other years.

The limit to the expenses of management can be prescribed by the controller. The controller may fix a further limit within which the actual expenses of an insurer may exceed the prescribed limit.

12. Provisions to Policyholders Rights

Section 37

The Central Government guarantees the payment in cash of the sums assured by all policies issued by the Corporation including any bonuses declared in respect thereof .

Section 38

A life insurance policy can be freely assigned to anybody.

Section 39

Similarly, the holder of a policy of life insurance may without any restriction nominate any person or persons to whom the money secured by the policy may be paid in the event of his death.

Section 45

After the expiry of two years from the date of the issue of a policy, the validity of it cannot be contested on grounds of breach of utmost good faith if the breach is unintentional.

Sections 51 and 52 made the payment of claims easier and smoother. Section 113 of the Insurance Act 1938 deals with the acquisition of surrender value.

THE MARINE INSURANCE ACT, 1963
(NO. 11 OF 1963)

An Act to codify the law relating to marine insurance.

[18th April, 1963.]

Be it enacted by Parliament in the Fourteenth Year of the Republic of India as follows:

1. Short title and commencement:

(*i*) This Act may be called the Marine Insurance Act, 1963.

(*ii*) It shall come into force on such date as the Central Government may, by notification in the Official Gazette, appoint.

2. Definitions. In this Act, unless the context otherwise requires

(*a*) "contract of marine insurance" means a contract of marine insurance as defined by Section 3;

(*b*) "freight" includes the profit derivable by a ship-owner from the employment of his ship to carry his own goods or other movables, as well as freight payable by a third party, but does not include passage money;

(*c*) "marine adventure" includes any adventure where:

(*i*) any insurable property is exposed to maritime perils;

(*ii*) the earnings or acquisition of any freight, passage money, commission, profit or other pecuniary benefit, or the security for any advances loans, or disbursements is endangered by the exposure of insurable property to maritime perils;

(*iii*) any liability to a third party may be incurred by the owner of, or other person interested in or responsible for, insurable property by reason of maritime perils;

(*e*) "maritime perils" means the perils consequent on, or in cidental to, the navigation of the sea, that is to say, perils of the seas, fire, war perils, pirates, rovers, thieves, captures, seizures restrains and detainments of princes and peoples, jettisons, barratry and any other perils which are either of the like kind or may be designated by the policy;

(*f*) "movables" means any movable tangible property, other than the ship, and includes money, valuable securities and other documents;

(*g*) "policy" means a marine policy;

(*h*) "ship" includes every description of vessel used in navigation;

(*i*) "suit" includes counter claim and set-off.

MARINE INSURANCE

3. Marine insurance defined. A contract of marine insurance is an agreement whereby the insurer undertakes to indemnify the assured, in the manner and to the extent thereby agreed, against marine losses, that is to say, the losses incidental to marine adventure.

4. Mixed sea and land risks;

(*i*) A contract of marine insurance may, by its express terms, or by usage of trade, be extended so as to protect the assured against losses on inland waters or on any land risk which may be incidental to any sea voyage.

(*ii*) Where a ship in course of building, or the launch of a ship, or any adventure analogous to a marine adventure, is covered by a policy in the form of a marine policy, the provisions of the Act, in so far as applicable, shall apply thereto, but, except as by this section provided, nothing in, this Act shall alter or affect any rule of law applicable to any contract of insurance other than a contract of marine insurance as by this Act defined.

Explanation—'An adventure analogous to a marine adventure' includes an adventure where any ship, goods or other movables are exposed to perils incidental to local or inland transit.

5. Lawful Marine Adventure. Subject to the provisions of this Act, every lawful marine adventure may be the subject of a contract of marine insurance.

INSURABLE INTEREST

6. Avoidance of wagering contracts.

(*i*) Every contract of marine insurance by way of wagering is void.

(*ii*) A contract of marine insurance is deemed to be a wagering contract—

(*a*) where the assured has not an insurable interest as defined by this Act, and the contract is entered into with no expectation of acquiring such an interest; or

(*b*) where the policy is made 'interest or no interest', or "without further proof of interest than the policy itself" or "without benefit of salvage to the insurer, or subject to any other like term.

Provided that, where there is no possibility of salvage, a policy may be effected without benefit of salvage to the insurer.

7. Insurable interest defined.

(*i*) Subject to the provisions or this, Act every person has an insurable interest who is interested in a marine adventure.

(*ii*) In particular a person is interested in a marine adventure where he stands in any legal or equitable relation to the adventure or to any insurable property at risk therein, in consequence of which he may benefit by the safety or due arrival of insurable property, or may be prejudiced by its loss, or by damage thereto or by the detention thereof, or may incur liability in respect thereof.

8. When interest must attach.

(*i*) The assured must be interested in the subject-matter insured at the time of the loss, though he need not be interested when the insurance is effected;

Provided that, where the subject-matter is insured "lost or not lost", the assured may recover although he may not have acquired his interest until after the loss, unless at the time of effecting the contract of insurance the assured was aware of the loss, and the insurer was not.

2. Where the assured has no interest at the time of the loss, he cannot acquire interest by any act or election after he is aware of the loss.

9. Defeasible or contingent interest

(*i*) A defeasible interest is insurable, as also is a contingent interest.

(*ii*) In particular, where the buyer of goods has insured them, he has an insurable interest, notwithstanding that he might, at his election, have rejected the goods, or have treated them as at the seller's risk, by reason of the latter's delay in making delivery or otherwise.

10. Partial interest—A partial interest of any nature is insurable.

11. Reinsurance.

(*i*) The insurer under a contract of maring insurance has an insurable interest in his risk, and may reinsure in respect of it.

(*ii*) Unless the policy otherwise provides, the original assured has no right or interest in respect of such reinsurance.

12. Bottomry. The lender of money on bottomry or respondentia has an insurable interest in respect of the loan.

13. Master's and Seamen's Wages. The master or any member of the crew of a ship has an insurable interest in respect of his wages.

14. Advance freight. In the case of advance freight, the person advancing the freight has an insurable interest, in so far as such freight is not repayable in case of loss.

15. Charges of insurance. The assured has an insurable interest in the charges of any insurance which he may effect.

16. Quantum of interest. Where the subject-matter insured is mortgaged the mortgagor has an insurable interest in the full value thereof, and the mortgagee has an insurable interest in respect of any sum due or to become due under the mortgage.

(*i*) A mortgagee, consignee, other person having an interest in the subject-matter insured may insure on behalf and for the benefit of other persons interested as well as for his own benefit.

(*ii*) The owner of insurable property has an insurable interest in respect of the full value thereof, notwithstanding that some third person may have agreed, or be liable to indemnify him in case of loss.

17. Assignment of interest. Where the assured assigns of otherwise parts with his interest in the subject-matter insured, he does not thereby transfer to the, assignee his rights under the contract of insurance, unless there be an express or implied agreement with the assignee to that effect. But the provisions of this section do not affect transmission of interest by operation of law.

INSURABLE VALUE

18. Measure of insurable value. Subject to any express provision or valuation in the policy, the insurable value of the subject-matter insured must be ascertained as follows:

(*i*) In insurance on ship, the insurable value is the value, at the commencement of the risk, of the ship, including her outfit provisions, and stores for the officers and crew, money advanced for seamen's wages, and other disbursements (if any) incurred to make the ship fit for the voyage or adventure contemplated by the policy, plus the charges of insurance upon the whole:

The insurable value, in the case of a steamship, includes also the machinery, boilers and coals and engine stores if owned by the assured; in the case of a ship driven by power other than steam includes machinery and fuels and engine stores if owned by the assured; and in the case of a ship engaged in a special trade, includes also the ordinary fittings requisite for that trade;

(*ii*) In insurance on freight, whether paid in advance or otherwise, the insurable value is the gross amount of the freight, at the risk of the assured, plus the charges of insurance;

(*iii*) In insurance on goods or merchandise, the insurable value is the prime cost of the property insured, plus the expenses of and incidental to shipping and the charges of insurance upon the whole;

(*iv*) In insurance on any other subject-matter, the insurance value is the amount at the risk of the assured when the policy attaches, plus the charges of insurance.

DISCLOSURE AND REPRESENTATIONS

19. Insurance is uberrimae fidei. A contract of marine Insurance is a contract based upon the utmost good faith, and if the utmost good faith be not observed by either party, the contract can be avoided by the other party.

20. Disclosure by assured.

(*i*) Subject to the provisions of this section, the assured must disclose to the insurer, before the contract is concluded, every material circumstance which is known to the assured, and the assured is deemed to know every circumstance which, in the ordinary course of business, ought to be known to him. If the assured fails to make such disclosure, the insurer may avoid the contract.

(*ii*) Every circumstance is material which would influence the judgment of a prudent insurer in fixing the premium, or determining whether he will take the risk.

(*iii*) In the absence of inquiry the following circumstances need not be disclosed, namely:

(*a*) Any circumstance which diminishes the risk;

(*b*) any circumstance which is known or presumed to be known to the insurer. The insurer is presumed to know matters of common notoriety or knowledge and matters which an insurer in the ordinary course of his business as such, ought to know;

(*c*) any circumstance as to which information is waived by the insurer;

(*d*) any circumstance which it is superfluous to disclose by reason of any express or implied warranty.

(*iv*) Whether any particular circumstance, which is not disclosed, be material or not is, in each case, a question of fact.

(*v*). The term "circumstance" includes any communication made to, or information received by, the assured.

21. Disclosure by agent effecting insurance. Subject to the provisions of the preceding section as to circumstances which need not be disclosed, where an insurance is effected for the assured by an agent, the agent must disclose to the insurer:

(*a*) every material circumstance which is known to himself, and an agent to insure is deemed to know every circumstance which in the ordinary course of business ought to be known by, or to have been communicated to him; and

(*b*) every material circumstance which the assured is bound to disclose, unless it comes to his knowledge too late to communicate it to the agent.

22. Representations pending negotiation of contract.

1. Every material representation made by the assured or his agent to the insurer during the negotiations for the contract, and before the contract is concluded, must be true. If it be unture the insurer may avoid the contract.
2. A representation is material which would influence the judgment of a prudent insurer in fixing the premium, or determining whether he will take the risk.
3. A representation may be either as to a matter of fact, or as to a matter of expectation or belief.
4. A representation as to a matter of fact is true, if it be substantially correct, that is to say, if the difference between what is represented and what is actually correct would not be considered material by a prudent insurer.
5. A representation as to a matter of expectation or belief is true if it be made in good faith.
6. A representation may be withdrawn or corrected before the contract is concluded.
7. Whether a particular representation be material or not, is, in each case, a question of fact.

23. When contract is deemed to be concluded. A contract of marine insurance is deemed to be concluded when the proposal of the assured is accepted by the insurer, whether the policy be then issued or not; and for the purpose of showing when the proposal was accepted, reference may be made to the slip, covering note or other customary memorandum of the contract, although it be unstamped.

THE POLICY

24. Contract must be embodied in policy. A contract of marine insurance shall not be admitted in evidence unless it is embodied in a marine policy in accordance with this Act. The policy may be executed and issued either at the time when the contract is concluded, or afterwards.

25. What policy must specify. A marine policy must specify—

1. the name of the assured, or of some person who effects the insurance on his behalf;
2. the subject-matter insured and the risk insured against;
3. the voyage, or period of time, or both, as the case may be, covered by the insurance;
4. the sum or sums insured ;
5. the name or names of the insurer or insurers.

26. Signature of insurer.

1. A marine policy must be signed by or on behalf of the insurer.
2. Where a policy is subscribed by or on behalf of two or more insurers, each subscription, unless the contrary be expressed, constitutes a distinct contract with the assured.

27. Voyage and time policies.

1. Where the contract is to insure the subject-matter at and from, or from one place to another or others, the policy is called a 'voyage policy', and where the contract is to insure the subject-matter for a definite period of time, the policy is called a "time policy". A contract for both voyage and time may be included in the same policy.
2. A time policy which is made for any time exceeding twelve months is invalid.

28. Designation and subject-matter.

1. The subject-matter insured must be designated in a marine policy with reasonable certainty.
2. The nature and extent of the interest of the assured in the subject-matter insured need not be specified in the policy.
3. Where the policy designates the subject-matter insured in general terms, it shall be construed to apply to the interest intended by the assured to be covered.

4. In the application of this section regard shall be had to any usage regulating the designation of the subject-matter insured.

29. Valued policy.

1. A policy may be either valued or unvalued.
2. A valued policy is a policy which specifies the agreed value of the subject-matter insured.
3. Subject to the provisions of this Act, and in the absence of fraud, the value fixed by the policy is, as between the insurer and assured, conclusive of the insurable value of the subject intended to be insured, whether the loss be total or partial.
4. Unless the policy otherwise provides, the value fixed by the policy is not conclusive for the purpose of determining whether there has been a constructive total loss.

30. Unvalued policy. An unvalued policy is a policy which does not specify the value of the subject-matter insured, but subject to the limit of the sum insured, leaves the insurable value to be subsequently ascertained, in the manner herein-before explained.

31. Floating policy by ship or ships.

1. A floating policy is a policy which describes the insurance in general terms, and leaves the name or names of the ship or ships and other particulars to be defined by subsequent declaration.
2. The subsequent declaration or declarations may be made by endorsement on the policy, or in other customary manner.
3. Unless the policy otherwise provides, the declarations must be made in the order of dispatch or shipment. They must, in the case of goods, comprise all consignments within the terms of the policy, and the value of the goods or other property must be honestly stated, but an omission or erroneous declaration may be rectified even after loss or arrival, provided the omission or declaration was made in good faith.
4. Unless the policy otherwise provides, where a declaration of value is not made until after notice of loss or arrival, the policy must be treated as an unvalued policy as regards the subject-matter of that declaration.

32. Construction of terms in policy.

1. A policy may be in the form in the Schedule.
2. Subject to the provisions of this Act, and unless the context of the policy otherwise requires, the terms and expressions mentioned in the Schedule shall be construed as having the scope and meaning assigned to them in the Schedule.

33. Premium to be arranged.

1. Where an insurance is effected at a premium to be arranged, and no arrangement is made, a reasonable premium is payable.
2. Where an insurance is effected on the terms that an additional premium is to be arranged in a given event, and that event happens but no arrangement is made, then a reasonable additional premium is payable.

DOUBLE INSURANCE

34. Double insurance

1. Where two or more policies are effected by or on behalf of the assured on the same adventure and interest or any part thereof, and the sums insured exceed the indemnity allowed by this Act, the assured is said to be over-insured by double insurance.
2. Where the assured is over-insured by double insurance:

(*a*) the assured, unless the policy otherwise provides, may claim payment from the insurers in such order as he may think fit, provided that he is not entitled to receive any sum in excess of the indemnity allowed by this Act;

(*b*) where the policy under which the assured claims is a valued policy, the assured must give credit as against the valuation for any sum received by him under any other policy, without regard to the actual value of the subject-matter insured;

(*c*) where the policy under which the assured claims is an unvalued policy he must give credit, as against the full insurable value, for any sum received by him under any other policy;

(*d*) where the assured receives any sum in excess of the indemnity allowed by this Act, he is deemed to hold such sum in trust for the insurers, according to their right of contribution among themselves.

WARRANTIES, ETC.

35. Nature of warranty.

1. A warranty, in the following sections relating to warranties, means a promissory warranty, that is to say, a warranty by which the assured undertakes that some particular thing shall or shall not be done, or that some condition shall be fulfilled, or whereby he affirms or negatives the existence of a particular state of facts.
2. A warranty may be express or implied.
3. A warranty, as above defined, is a condition which must be exactly complied with, whether it be material to the risk or not. If it be not so complied with, then, subject to any express provision in the policy, the insurer is discharged from liability as from the date of the breach of warranty, but without prejudice to any liability incurred by him before that date.

36. When breach of warranty excused.

1. Non-compliance with a warranty is excused when, by reason of a change of circumstances, the warranty ceases to be applicable to the circumstances of the contract, or when compliance with the warranty is rendered unlawful by any subsequent law.
2. Where a warranty is broken, the assured cannot avail himself of the defence that the breach has been remedied, and the warranty complied with, before loss.
3. A breach of warranty may be waived by the insurer.

37. Express warranties.

1. An express warranty may be in any form of words from which the intention to warrant is to be inferred.
2. An express warranty must be included in, or written upon, the policy, or must be contained in some document incorporated by reference into the policy.
3. An express warranty does not exclude implied warranty unless it be inconsistent therewith.

38. Warranty of neutrality.

1. Where insurable property, whether ship or goods, is expressly warranted neutral, there is an implied condition that the property shall have a neutral character at the commencement of the risk, and that, so far as the assured can control the matter, its neutral character shall be preserved during the risk.
2. Where a ship is expressly warranted "neutral", there is also an implied condition that, so far as the assured can control the matter, she shall be properly documented, that is to say, that she shall carry the necessary papers to establish her neutrality, and that she shall not falsify or suppress her papers, or use simulated papers. If any loss occurs through breach of this condition, the **insurer may avoid the contract.**

39. No implied warranty of nationality. There is no implied warranty as to the nationality of a ship, or that her nationality shall not be changed during the risk.

40. Warranty of good safety. Where the Subject-matter insured is warranted "well" or "in good safety" on a particular day, it is sufficient if it be safe at any time during that day.

41. Warranty of sea-worthiness of ship.

1. In a voyage policy there is an implied warranty that at the commencement of the voyage the ship shall be seaworthy for the purpose of the particular adventure insured.
2. Where the policy attaches while the ship is in port, there is also an implied warranty that she shall, at the commencement of the risk, be reasonably fit to encounter the ordinary perils of the port.
3. Where the policy relates to a voyage which is performed in different stages, during which the ship requires different kinds of or further preparation or equipment, there is an implied warranty that at the commencement of each stage the ship is seaworthy in respect of such preparation or equipment for the purposes of that stage.
4. A ship is deemed to be seaworthy when she is reasonably fit in all respects to encounter the ordinary perils of the seas of the adventure insured.
5. In a time policy there is no implied warranty that the ship shall be seaworthy at any stage of the adventure, but where, with the privity of the assured, the ship is sent to sea in an unseaworthy state, the insurer is not liable for any loss attributable to unseaworthiness.

42. No implied warranty that goods are seaworthy.

1. In a policy on goods or other movables there is no implied warranty that the goods or movables are seaworthy.
2. In a voyage policy on goods or other movables there is an implied warranty that at the commencement of the voyage the ship is not only seaworthy as a ship but also that she is reasonably fit to carry the goods or other movables to the destination contemplated by the policy.

43. Warranty of legality. There is an implied warranty that the adventure insured is a lawful one, and that so far as the assured can control the matter, the adventure shall be carried out in a lawful manner.

44. Implied condition as to commencement of risk.

1. There the subject-matter is insured by a voyage policy "at and from" or "from" a particular place, it is not necessary that the ship should be at that place when the contract is concluded, but there is an implied condition that the adventure shall be commenced within a reasonable time, and that if the adventure be not so commenced the insurer may avoid the contract.
2. The implied condition may be negatived by showing that the delay was caused by circumstances known to the insurer before the contract was concluded, or by showing that he waived the condition.

45. Alteration of port of departure. Where the place of departure is specified by the policy, and the ship instead of sailing from that place sails from any other place, the risk does not attach.

46. Sailing for different destination. Where the destination is specified in the policy, and the ship, instead of sailing for that destination, sails for any other destination, the risk does not attach.

47. Change of voyage.

1. Where, after the commencement of the risk, the destination of the ship is voluntarily changed from the destination contemplated by the policy, there is said to be a change of voyage.
2. Unless the policy otherwise provides, where there is a change of voyage, the insurer is discharged from liability as from the time of change, that is to say, as from the time when the determination

to change is manifested; and it is immaterial that the ship may not in fact have left course of voyage contemplated by the policy when the loss occurs.

48. Deviation.

1. Where a ship, without lawful excuse deviates from the voyage contemplated by the policy, the insured is discharged from liability as from the time of deviation, and it is immaterial that the ship may have regained her route before any loss occurs.
2. There is a deviation from the voyage contemplated by the policy—
   (*a*) where the course of the voyage is specifically designated by the policy, and that course is departed from; or
   (*b*) where the course of the voyage is not specifically designated by the policy, but the usual and customary course is departed from.
3. The intention to deviate is immaterial; there must be a deviation in fact to discharge the insurer from his liability under the contract.

49. Several ports of discharge.

1. Where several ports of discharge are specified by the policy, the ship may proceed to all or any of them, but, in the absence of any usage or sufficient cause to the contrary, she must proceed to them, or such of them as she goes to, in the order designated by the policy. If she does not there is a deviation.
2. Where the policy is to "ports of discharge" within a given area, which are not named, the ship must, in the absence of any usage or sufficient cause to the contrary, proceed to them, or such of them as she goes to, in their geographical order. If she does not there is a deviation.

50. Delay in voyage. In the case of a voyage policy, the adventure insured must be prosecuted throughout its course with reasonable despatch, and if without lawful excuse it is not so prosecuted, the insurer is discharged from liability as from the time when the delay became unreasonable.

51. Excuse for deviation or delay.

1. Deviation or delay in prosecuting the voyage contemplated by the policy is excussed—
   (*a*) where authorised by any special term in the policy; or
   (*b*) where caused by circumstances beyond the control of the master and his employer; or
   (*c*) where reasonably necessary in order to comply with an express or implied warranty; or
   (*d*) where reasonably necessary for the safety of the ship or subject-matter insured; or
   (*e*) for the purpose of saying human life or aiding a ship in distress where human life may be in danger; or
   (*f*) where reasonably necessary for the purpose of obtaining medical or surgical aid for any person on board the ship; or
   (*g*) where caused by the barratrous conduct of the master or crew, if barratry be one of the perils insured against.
2. When the cause excusing the deviation or delay ceases to operate the ship must resume her course, and prosecute her voyage with reasonable despatch.

ASSIGNMENT OF POLICY

52. When and how policy, is assignable.

1. A marine policy may be transferred by assignment unless it contains terms expressly prohibiting assignment. It may be assigned either before or after loss.
2. Where a marine policy has been assigned so as to pass the beneficial interest in such policy, the assignee of the policy is entitled to sue thereon in his own name; and the defendant is entitled to

make any defence arising out of the contract which he would have been entitled to make if the suit had been brought in the name of the person by or on behalf of whom the policy was effected.

3. A marine policy may be assigned by endorsement thereon or in other customary manner.

53. Assured who has no interest cannot assign. Where the assured has parted with or lost his interest in the subject-matter insured, and has not, before or at the time of so doing expressly or impliedly agreed to assign the policy, any subsequent assignment of the policy is inoperative:

Provided that nothing in this section affects the assignment of a policy after loss.

THE PREMIUM

54. When premium payable. Unless otherwise agreed, the duty of the assured or his agent to pay the premium, and the duty of the insurer to issue the policy to the assured or his agent, are concurrent conditions, and the insurer is not bound to issue the policy until payment or tender of the premium.

LOSS AND ABANDONMENT

55. Included and excluded losses.

1. Subject to the provisions of this Act, and unless the policy otherwise provides, the insurer is liable for any loss proximately caused by a peril insured against, but, subject as aforesaid, he is not liable for any loss which is not proximately caused by a peril insured against.
2. In particular
   (*a*) the insurer is not liable for any loss attributable to the wilful misconduct of the assured, but, unless the policy otherwise provides, he is liable for any loss proximately caused by a peril insured against, even though the loss would not have happened but for the misconduct or negligence of the master or crew;
   (*b*) unless the policy otherwise provides, the insurer on ship or goods is not liable for any loss proximately caused by delay, although the delay be caused by a peril insured against;
   (*c*) unless the policy otherwise provides, the insurer is not liable for ordinary wear and tear, ordinary leakage and breakage, inherent vice or nature of the subject-matter insured, or for any loss proximately caused by rats or vermin, or for any injury to machinery not proximately caused by maritime perils.

56. Partial and total loss.

1. A loss be either total or partial. Any loss other than a total loss, as hereinafter defined, is a partial loss.
2. A total loss may be either an actual total loss, or a constructive total loss.
3. Unless a different intention appears from the terms of the policy, an insurance against total loss includes a constructive, as well as an actual, total loss.
4. Where the assured brings a suit for a total loss and the evidence proves only a partial loss, he may, unless the policy otherwise provides, recover for a partial loss.
5. Where goods reach their destination in specie, but by reason of obliteration of marks, or otherwise, they are incapable of identification, the loss, if any is partial and not total.

57. Actual total loss.

1. Where the subject-matter insured is destroyed, or so damaged as to cease to be a thing of the kind insured, or where the assured is irretrievably deprived thereof, there is an actual total loss.
2. In the case of an actual total loss no notice of abandonment need be given.

58. Missing ship. Where the ship concerned in the adventure is missing, and after the lapse of a reasonable time no news of her has been received, an actual total loss may be presumed.

59. Effect of transhipment, etc. Where, by a peril insured against, the voyage is interrupted at intermediate port or place, under such circumstances as apart from any special stipulation in the contract of affreightment; to justify the master in landing and reshipping the goods or other movables, or in transhipping them, and sending them on to their destination, the liability of the insurer continues, notwithstanding the landing or transhipment.

60. Constructive total loss defined.

1. Subject to any express provision in the policy, there is a constructive total loss where the subject matter insured is reasonably abandoned on account of its actual total loss appearing to be unavoidable, or because it could not be preserved from actual total loss without an expenditure which would exceed its value when the expenditure had been incurred.
2. In particular, there is a constructive total loss—

   (*i*) where the assured is deprived of the possession of his ship or goods by a peril insured against, and

   (*a*) it is unlikely that he can recover the ship or goods, as the case may be, or

   (*b*) the cost of recovering the ship or goods, as the case may be

   would exceed their value when recovered; or

   (*ii*) in the case of damage to a ship; where she is damaged by a peril insured against that the cost of repairing the damage would exceed the value of the ship when repaired.

   In estimating the cost of repairs, no deduction is to be made in respect of general average contributions to those repairs payable by other interest, but account is to be taken of the expense of future salvage operations and of any future general average contributions to which the ship would be liable if repaired; or

   (*iii*) in the case of damage to goods, where the cost of repairing the damage and forwarding the goods to their destination would exceed their value on arrival.

61. Effect of constructive total loss. Where there is a constructive total loss the assured may either treat the loss as a partial loss, or abandon the subject-matter insured to the insurer and treat the loss as if it were an actual total loss.

62. Notice of abandonment.

1. Subject to the provisions of this section, where the assured elects to abandon the subject–matter insured to the insurer, he must give notice of abandonment. If he fails to do so the loss can only be treated as a partial loss.
2. Notice of abandonment may be given in writing, or by word of mouth, or partly in writing and partly by word of mouth, and may be given in any terms which indicate the intention of the assured to abandon his insured interest in the subject-matter insured unconditionally to the insurer.
3. Notice of abandonment must be given with reasonable diligence after the receipt of reliable information of the loss, but where the information is of a doubtful character the assured is entitled to a reasonable time to make enquiry.
4. Where notice of abandonment is properly given, the rights of the assured are not prejudiced by the fact that the insurer refuses to accept the abandonment.
5. The acceptance of an abandonment may be either express or implied from the conduct of the insurer. The mere silence of the insurer after notice is not an acceptance.
6. Where notice of abandonment is accepted the abandonment is irrevocable. The acceptance of the notice conclusively admits liability for the loss and the sufficiency of the notice.
7. Notice of abandonment is unnecessary where at the time when the assured receives information of the loss, there would be no possibility of benefit of the insurer if notice were given to him.

8. Notice of abandonment may be waived by the insurer.
9. Where an insurer has reinsured his risk, no notice of abandonment need be given by him.

63. Effect of abandonment.

1. Where there is a valid abandonment the insurer is entitled to take over the interest of the assured in whatever may remain of the subject-matter insured and all proprietary rights incidental thereto.
2. Upon the abandonment of a ship, the insurer thereof is entitled to any freight in course of being earned, and which is earned by her subsequent to the casualty causing the loss, less the expenses of earning it incurred after the casualty; and, where the ship is carrying the owner's goods, the insurer is entitled to a reasonable remuneration for the carriage of them subsequent to the casualty causing the loss.

PARTIAL LOSSES (INCLUDING SALVAGE AND GENERAL AVERAGE AND PARTICULAR CHARGES)

64. Particular average loss.

1. A particular average loss is a partial loss of the subject-matter insured, caused by a peril insured against, and which is not a general average loss.
2. Expenses incurred by or on behalf of the assured for the safety or preservation of the subject matter insured, other than general average and salvage charges are called particular charges. Particular charges are not included in particular average.

65. Salvage charges.

1. Subject to any express provision in the policy, salvage charges incurred preventing a loss by perils insured against may be covered as a loss by those perils.
2. "Salvage charges" means the charges recoverable under maritime law by a salver independently of contract. They do not include the expenses of services in the nature of salvage rendered by the assured or his agents, or any person employed for hire by them, for the purpose of averting a peril insured against. Such expenses, where properly incurred, may be recovered as particular charges or as a general average loss, according to the circumstances under which they were incurred.

66. General average loss.

1. A general average loss is a loss caused by or directly consequential on a general average act. It includes a general average expenditure as well as a general average sacrifice.
2. There is a general average act where any extraordinary sacrifice or expenditure is voluntarily and reasonably made or incurred in time of peril for the purpose of preserving the property imperilled in the common adventure.
3. Where there is a general average loss, the party on whom it falls is entitled, subject to the conditions imposed by maritime law, to a rateable contribution from the other parties interested, and such contribution is called a general average contribution.
4. Subject to any express provision in the policy, where the assured has incurred a general average of expenditure, he may recover from the insurer in respect of the proportion of the loss which falls upon him; and in the case of a general average sacrifice, he may recover from the insurer in respect of the whole loss without having enforced his right of contribution from the other parties liable to contribute.
5. Subject to any express provision in the policy, where the assured has paid, or is liable to pay, a general average contribution in respect of the interest insured, he may recover therefor from the insurer.
6. In the absence of express stipulation, the insurer is not liable for any general average loss or contribution where the loss was not incurred for the purpose of avoiding, or in connection with the avoidance of a peril insured against.

7. Where ship, freight, and cargo, or any two of those interests, are owned by the same assured, the liability of the insurer in respect of general average losses or contributions is to be determined as if those interests were owned by different persons.

67. Extent of liability of insurer for loss.

1. The sum which the assured can recover in respect of a loss on a policy by which he is insured, in the case of an unvalued policy to the full extent of the insurable value, or, in the case of a valued policy to the full extent of the value fixed by the policy, is called the measure of indemnity.
2. Where there is a loss recoverable under the policy, the insurer, or each insurer if there be more than one, is liable for such proportion of the measure of indemnity as the amount of his subscription bears to the value fixed by the policy in the case of a valued policy, or to the insurable value in the case of an unvalued policy.

68. Total loss. Subject to the provisions of this Act, and to any express provision in the policy, where there is a total loss of the subject-matter insured—

1. if the policy be a valued policy, the measure of indemnity is the sum fixed by the policy;
2. if the policy be an unvalued policy, the measure of indemnity is the insurable value of the subject-matter insured.

69. Partial loss of ship. Where a ship is damaged, but is not totally lost, the measure of indemnity subject to any express provision in the policy, is as follows—

1. where the ship has been repaired, the assured is entitled to the reasonable cost of the repairs, less the customary deductions, but more exceeding the sum insured in respect of any one casualty;
2. where the ship has been only partially repaired, the assured is entitled to the reasonable cost of such repairs, computed as above, and also to be indemnified for the reasonable depreciation, if any, arising from the unrepaired damage, provided that the aggregate amount shall not exceed the cost of repairing the whole damage, computed, as above;
3. where the ship has not been repaired, and has not been sold in her damaged state during the risk, the assured is entitled to be indemnified for the reasonable depreciation arising from the unrepaired damage, but not exceeding the reasonable cost of repairing such damage, computed as above;
4. where the ship has not been repaired and has been sold in her damaged state during the risk, the assured is entitled to be indemnified for the reasonable cost of repairing the damage, computed as above, but not exceeding the depreciation in value as ascertained by the sale.

70. Partial loss of freight. Subject to any express provision in the policy, where there is a partial loss of freight, the measure of indemnity is such proportion of the sum fixed by the policy in the case of a valued policy or of the insurable value in the case of an unvalued policy, as the proportion of freight lost by the assured bears to the whole freight at the risk of the assured under the policy.

71. Partial loss of goods, merchandise, etc. Where there is a partial loss of goods, merchandise, or other movables, the measure of indemnity, subject to any express provision in the policy, is as follows:—

1. where part of the goods, merchandise or other movables insured by a valued policy is totally lost, the measure of indemnity is such proportion of the sum fixed by the policy as the insurable value of the part lost bears to the insurable value of the whole, ascertained as in the case of an unvalued policy;

2. where part of the goods, merchandise or other movables insured by an unvalued policy is totally lost, the measure of indemnity is the insurable value of the part lost, ascertained as in case of total loss;
3. where the whole or any part of the goods or merchandise insured has been delivered at its destination, the measure of indemnity is such proportion of the sum fixed by the policy in the case of a valued policy, or of the insurable value in the case of an unvalued policy, as the difference between the gross sound and damaged values at the place of arrival bears to the gross sound value;
4. "Gross value" means the wholesale price, or, if there be no such price, the estimated value, with, in either case, freight, lending charges, and duty paid beforehand; provided that, in the case of goods or merchandise customarily sold in bond, the bonded price is deemed to be the gross value. "Gross proceeds" means the actual price obtained at a sale where all charges on sale paid by the sellers.

72. Apportionment of valuation.

1. Where different species of property are insured under a single valuation, the valuation must be apportioned over the different species in proportion to their respective insurable values, as in the case of an unvalued policy. The insured value of any part of a species is such proportion of the total insured value of the same as the insurable value of the part bears to the insurable value of the whole ascertained in both cases as provided by this Act.
2. Where a valuation has to be apportioned, and particulars of the prime cost of each separate species, quality, or description of goods cannot be ascertained, the division of the valuation may be made over the net arrived sound values of the different species, quality or descriptions of goods.

73. General average contributions and salvage charges.

1. Subject to any express provision in the policy, where the assured has paid, or is liable for, any general average contribution, the measure of indemnity is the full amount of such contribution if the subject-matter liable to contribution is insured for its full contributory value; but, if such subject-matter be not insured for its full contributory value, of if only part of it be insured, the indemnity payable by the insurer must be reduced in proportion to the under-insurance, and where there has been a particular average loss which constitutes a deduction from the contributory value, and for which the insurer is liable, that amount must be deducted from the insured value in order to acsertain what the insurer is liable to contribute.
2. Where the insurer is liable for salvage charges the extent of his liabilities must be determined on the like principle.

74. Liabilities to third parties. Where the assured has effected an insurance in express terms against any liability to a third party, the measure of indemnity subject to any express provision in the policy, is the amount paid or payable by him to such third party in respect of such liability.

75. General provisions as to measure of indemnity.

1. Where there has been a loss in respect of any subject-matter not expressly provided for in the foregoing, provisions of this Act, the measure of indemnity shall be ascertained as nearly as may be, in accordance with those provisions, in so far as applicable to the particular case.
2. Nothing in the provisions of this Act relating to the measure of indemnity shall affect the rules relating to double insurance, or prohibit the insurer from disproving interest wholly or in part, or from showing that at the time of the loss the whole or any part of the subject-matter insured was not at risk under the policy.

76. Particular average warranties.

1. Where the subject-matter insured is warranted free from particular average, the assured cannot recover for a loss of part, other than loss incurred by a general average sacrifice, unless the contract contained in the policy be apportionable; but, if the contract be apportionable, the assured may recover for a total loss of any apportionable part.
2. Where the subject-matter insured is warranted free from particular average, either whôlly or under a certain percentage, the insurer is nevertheless liable for salvage charges, and for particular charges and other expenses properly incurred pursuant to the provisions of the suing and labouring clause in order to avert a loss insured against.
3. Unless the policy otherwise provides, where the subject matter insured is warranted free from particular average under a specified percentage, a general average loss cannot be added to a particular average loss to make up the specified percentage.
4. For the purpose of ascertaining whether the specified percentage has been reached, regard shall be had only to the actual loss suffered by the subject-matter insured. Particular charges and the expenses of and incidental to ascertaining and proving the loss must be excluded.

77. Successive losses.

1. Unless the policy otherwise provides, and subject to the provisions of this Act, the insurer is liable for successive losses, even though the total amount of such losses may exceed the sum insured.
2. Where, under the same policy, a partial loss, which has not been repaired or otherwise made good, is followed by a total loss the assured can only recover in respect of the total loss;

Provided that nothing in this section shall affect the liability of the insurer under the suing and labouring clause.

78. Suing and labouring clause.

1. Where the policy contains a suing and labouring clause, the engagement thereby entered into is deemed to be supplementary to the contract of insurance, and the assured may recover from the insurer any expenses properly incurred pursuant to the clause, notwithstanding that the insurer may have paid for a total loss, or that the subject-matter may have been warranted free from particular average, either wholly or wider a certain percentage.
2. General average losses and contributions and salvage charges, as defined by this Act, are not recoverable under the suing and labouring clause.
3. Expenses incurred for the purpose of averting or diminishing any loss not covered by the policy are not recoverable under the suing and labouring clause.
4. It is the duty of the assured and his agents, in all cases, to take such measures as may be reasonable for the purpose of averting or minimising a loss.

RIGHTS OF INSURER ON PAYMENTS

79. Right of subrogation.

1. Where the insurer pays for a total loss, either of the whole, or in the case of goods of any apportionable part, of the subject-matter insured, he there upon becomes entitled to take over the interest of the assured in what-ever may remain of the subject-matter so paid for, and he is thereby subrogated to all the rights and remedies of the assured in and in respect of that subject-matter as from the time of the casualty causing the loss.
2. Subject to the foregoing provisions, where the insurer pays for a partial loss, he acquires no title to the subject-matter insured, or such part of it as may remain, but he is thereupon subrogated to all rights and remedies of the assured in and in respect of the subject-matter insured as from, the time of the casualty causing the loss, in so far as the assured has been indemnified, according to this Act, by such payment for the loss.

80. Right of Contribution.

1. Where the assured is over-insured by double insurance, each insurer is bound, as between himself and the other insurers, to contribute rateably to the loss in proportion to the amount for which he is liable under his contract.
2. If any insurer pays more than his proportion of the loss, he is entitled to maintain a suit contribution against the other insurers, and is entitled to the like remedies as a surety who has paid more than his proportion of the debt.

81. Effect of under-insurance. Where the assured is insured for an amount less than the insurable value, or, in the case of a valued policy, for an amount less than the policy valuation, he is deemed to be his own insurer in respect of the uninsured balance.

RETURN OF PREMIUM

82. Enforcement of return. Where the premium, or a proportionate part thereof, is, by this Act, declared to be returnable—

(*a*) if already paid, it may be recovered by the assured from the insurer, and,

(*b*) if unpaid, it may be retained by the assured or his agent.

83. Return by agreement. Where the policy contains a stipulation for the return of the premium or a proportionate part thereof, on the happening of a certain event, and that event happens, the premium, or, as the case may be, the proportionate part thereof, is thereupon returnable to the assured.

84. Return for failure of consideration.

1. Where the consideration for the payment of the premium totally fails, and there has been no fraud or illegality on the part of the assured or his agents, the premium is thereupon returnable to the assured.
2. Where the consideration for the payment of the premium is apportionable and there is a total failure of any apportionable part of the consideration, a proportionate part of the premium is, under the like conditions, thereupon returnable to the assured.
3. In particular—

(*a*) where the policy is void, or is avoided by the insurer as from the commencement of the risk, the premium is returnable, provided there has been no fraud or illegality on the part of the assured, but if the risk is not apportionable, and has once attached, the premium is not returnable.

(*b*) where the subject-matter insured, or part thereof, has never been imperilled the premium, or, as the case may be, a proportionate part thereof, is returnable:
Provided that where the subject-matter has been;

(*c*) where the assured has no insured interest throughout insured "lost or not lost," and has arrived in safety at not returnable, unless, at such time, the insurer knew of the safe arrival;

the time when the contract is concluded, the premium is by way of wagering vided that this rule does not apply to a policy effected the currency of the risk the premium is returnable, pro-

(*d*) where the assured has a defeasible interest which is terminated during the currency of the risk, the premium is not returnable.

(*e*) where the assured has over-insured under an unvalued policy a proportionate part of the premium is returnable.

(*f*) subject to the foregoing provisions, where the assured has over-insured by double insurance, a proportionate part of the several premiums is returnable:

Provided that, if the policies are effected at different times, and any earlier policy has at any time borne the entire risk, or if a claim has been paid on the policy in respect of the full sum insured thereby, no premium is returnable in respect of that policy, and when the double insurance is effected knowingly by the assured no premium is returnable.

SUPPLEMENTAL

85. Ratification by assured. Where a contract of marine insurance is in good faith effected by one person on behalf of another, the person on whose behalf it is effected may ratify the contract even after he is aware of a loss.

86. Implied obligation varied by agreement or usage.

1. Where any right, duty, or liability would arise under a contract of marine insurance by implication of law, it may be negatived or varied by express agreement, or by usage, if the usage be such as to bind both parties to the contract.
2. The provisions of this section extend to any right, duty, or liability declared by this Act which may be lawfully modified by agreement.

87. Reasonable time, etc., a question of fact. Where by this Act any reference is made to reasonable time, reasonable premium, or reasonable diligence, the question what is reasonable is a question of fact.

88. Covering note as evidence. Where there is duly stamped policy, reference may be made, as heretofore, to the slip or covering note, in any legal proceeding.

89. Power to apply Act with modifications, etc., in certain cases. The Central Government may, by notification in the Official Gazette, direct that the provisions of this Act shall, in their application to contracts of marine insurance relating to any class of ships exclusively used in inland navigation, be subject to such conditions, exceptions and modifications as it may specify in the notification.

90. Centain provisions to override Transfer of Property Act 1882. Nothing in clause (*e*) of Section 6 of the Transfer of Property Act, 1882, shall affect the provisions of Sections 17, 52, 53 and 79.

91. Savings. The rules of law, including the law merchant, which applied to contracts of marine insurance immediately before the commencement of this Act, save in so far as they are inconsistent with the express provisions of this Act, shall continue to apply to contracts of marine insurance.

92. Repeals. Sub-sections (1), (2) and (3) of Section 7 of the Indian Stamp Act., 1899 and Sections 130A and 135A of the Transfer of Property Act, 1882 are hereby repealed.

SCHEDULE

FORM OF POLICY

(SEE SECTION 24)

BE IT KNOWN THAT .... as well in .... own name as for and in the name and names of all and every other person or persons to whom the same doth, may, or shall appertain, in part or in all doth make assurance and cause .... and them, and every of them, to be insured lost or not lost, at and from upon any kind of goods and merchandises, and also upon the body, tackle, apparel, ordnance, munition, artillery, boat and other furniture, of and in the good ship or vessel called the .... whereof is master for this present voyage .... or whosoever else go for master in the said ship or by whatsoever other name or names the said ship, or the master thereof, or shall be named or called; beginning the adventure upon the said goods and merchandises from the loading thereof aboard the said ship .... upon the said ship, etc .... and so shall continue and endure, during her abode there, upon the said ship, etc .... And further, until the said ship, with all her ordnance, tackle, apparel, etc., and goods and merchandises whatsoever shall be arrived at .... upon the said ship, etc., until she hath moored at anchor twenty-four hours in good safety; and upon the goods and merchandises, until the same be there discharged and safely landed. And it shall be lawful for the said ship, etc., in this voyage to proceed and sail to and touch and stay at any ports or places whatsoever without prejudice to this insurance. The said ship, etc., goods and merchandises, etc., for so much as concerned the assured by agreement between the assured and assurers in this policy, are and shall be .... valued at ....

Touching the adventures and perils which we the assurers are contented to bear and do take upon us in this voyage; they are of the seas, men of war, fire, enemies, pirates, roverbs, thieves, jettisons, letters of mart and countermart, surprisals, takings at sea, arrests, restraints, and detainments of all kings, princes, and people, of what nation, condition or quality so ever, barratry of the master and mariners, and of all other perils, losses, and misfortunes that have or shall come to the hurt, detriment, or damage of the said goods and merchandises, and ship, etc., or any part thereof.

And in case of any loss or misfortune it shall be lawful to the assured, their factors, servants and assigns, to sue, labour, and travel for, in and about the defence, safeguards and recovery of the said goods and merchandises and ship, etc., or any part thereof, without prejudice to this insurance; to the charges whereof we, the assurers, will contribute each one according to the rate and quantity of his sum herein assured.

And it is especially declared and agreed that no acts of the insurer or insured in recovering, saving, or preserving the property insured shall be considered as a waiver, or acceptance of abandonment. And so we, the assurers, are contented, and do hereby promise and bind ourselves, each one for his own part, our heirs, executors, and goods to the assured, their executors, administrators, and assigns, for the true performance of the premises, confessing ourselves paid the consideration due unto us for this assurance by the assured, at and after the rate of...

In witness whereof we, the assurers, have subscribed our names and sums assured in ....

MEMORANDUM N.B. Corn, fish, salt, fruit, flour, and seed are warranted free from average, unless general or the ship be stranded—sugar, tobacco, hemp, flax, hides and skins are warranted free from average, under five per cent, and all other goods, also the ship and freight, are warranted free from average, under three per cent, unless general, or the ship be stranded.

RULES FOR CONSTRUCTION OF POLICY

The following are the rules referred to by this Act for the construction of a policy in the above or other like form, where the context does not otherwise require:—

1. Lost or not lost. Where the subject-matter is insured "lost or not lost" and the loss has occurred before the contract is concluded, the risk attaches unless, at such time the assured was aware of the loss, and the insurer was not.

2. From. Where the subject-matter is insured "from" a particular place, the risk does not attach until the ship starts on the voyage insured.

3. At and from.

(*a*) Where a ship is insured "at and from" a particular place, and she is at that place in good safety when the contract is concluded, the risk attaches immediately.

(*b*) If she be not at that place when the contract is concluded, the risk attaches as soon as she arrives there in good safety, and, unless the policy otherwise provides, it is immaterial that she is covered by another policy for a specified time after arrival.

(*c*) Where chartered freight is inured "at and from" a particular place, and the ship is at that place in good safety when the contract is concluded, the risk attaches immediately. If she be not there when the contract is concluded, the risk attaches as soon as she arrives there in good safety.

(*d*) Where freight, other than chartered freight, is payable without special conditions and is insured "at and from" a particular place, the risk attaches pro rata as the goods or merchandise are shipped; provided that if there be cargo in readiness which belongs to the ship-owner, or which some other person has contracted with him to ship, the risk attaches as soon as the ship is ready to receive such cargo.

4. From the loading thereof. Where goods or other movables are insured "from the loading thereof", the risk does not attach until such goods or movables are actually on board, and the insurer is not liable for them while in transit from the shore to the ship.

5. Safety landed. Where the risk on goods or other movables continues until they are "safely landed", they must be landed in the customary manner and within a reasonable time after arrival at the port of discharge, and if they are not so landed the rise ceases.

6. Touch and stay. In the absence of any further licence or usage, the liberty to touch and stay "at any port or place whatsoever" does not authorise the ship to depart from the course of her voyage from the port of departure to the port of destination.

7. Perils of the Seas. The term "perils of the seas" refers only to fortuitous accidents or casualties of the seas. It does not include the ordinary action of the winds and waves.

8. Pirates. The term "pirates" includes passengers who mutiny and rioters who attack the ship from the shore.

9. Thieves. The term "thieves" does not cover clandestine theft or a theft committed by any one of the ship's company, whether crew or passengers.

10. Restraint of princes. The term "arrests, etc., of kings, princes, and people" refers to political or executive acts, and does not include a loss caused by riot or by ordinary judicial process.

11. Barratry. The term "barratry" includes every wrongful act wilfully committed by the master or crew to the prejudice of the owner, or, as the case may be, the charterer.

12. All other perils. The term "all other perils', includes only perils similar in kind to the perils specifically mentioned in the policy.

13. Average unless General. The term "average unless general" means a partial loss of the subject-matter insured other than a general average loss, and does not include "particular charges".

14. Stranded. Where the ship has stranded, the insurer is liable for the excepted losses although the loss is not attributable to the stranding, provided that when the stranding takes place the risk has attached and, if the policy be on goods, that the damaged goods are on board.

15. Ship. The term "ship" includes the hull, material and outfit, stores and provisions for the officers and crew, and in the case of vessels engaged in a special trade, the ordinary fittings requisite for the trade, and also, in the case of a steamship, the machinery, boilers, and coals and engine stores, if owned by the assured and also in the case of a ship driven by power other than steam, the machinery and fuels and engine stores, if owned by the assured.

16. Freight. The term "freight" includes the profit derivable by a ship-owner from the employment of his ship to carry his own goods or movables as well as freight payable by a third party, but does not include passage money.

17. Goods. The term "goods" means goods in the nature of merchandise, and does not include personal effects or provisions and stores for use on board.

In the absence of any usage to the contrary, deck cargo and living animals must be insured specifically, and not under the general denomination of goods.

THE GENERAL INSURANCE BUSINESS (NATIONALISATION) ACT, 1972

(57 OF 1972)

An Act provide for the acquisition and transfer of shares of Indian insurance companies and undertaking of other existing insurers in order to serve better the needs of the economy by securing the development of general insurance business in the best interests of the community and to ensure that the operation of the economic system does not result in the concentration of wealth to the common detriment, for the regulation and control of such business and for matters connected therewith or incidental thereto.

(20th September, 1972.)

Be it enacted by Parliament in the Twenty-third Year of the Republic of India as follows:—

CHAPTER 1

PRELIMINARY

1. Short title. This Act may be called the General Insurance Business (Nationalisation) Act, 1972.

2. Declaration as to the policy of the State. It is hereby declared that this Act is for giving effect to the policy of the State towards securing the principles specified in clause (c) of Article 39 of the Constitution.

Explanation. In this section, "State" has the same meaning as in article 12 of the Constitution.

3. Definitions. In this Act, unless the context otherwise requires,

(*a*) "Acquiring company" means any Indian insurance company and, where a scheme has been framed involving the merger of one Indian insurance company in another or the amalgamation of two or more such companies, means the Indian insurance company in which any other company has been merged or the company which has been formed as a result of the amalgamation;

(*b*) "Appointed day" means such day, not being a day later than the 2nd day of January, 1973, as the Central Government may, by notification, appoint;

(*c*) "Companies Act" means the Companies Act, 1956;

(*d*) "Corporation" means the General Insurance Corporation of India formed under Section 9;

(*e*) "Existing insurer" means every insurer the management of whose undertaking has vested in the Central Government under Section 3 of the General Insurance (Emergency Provisions) Act, 1971, and includes the undertaking of the Life Insurance Corporation in so far as it relates to the general insurance business carried on by it;

(*f*) "Foreign insurer" means an existing insurer incorporated under the law of any country outside India;

(*g*) "General insurance business" means fire, marine or miscellaneous insurance business, whether carried on singly or in combination with one or more of them, but does not include capital redemption business and annuity certain business;

(*h*) "Government company" means a Government company as defined in Section 617 of the Companies Act;

(*i*) "Indian insurance company" means an existing insurer having a share capital who is a company within the meaning of the Companies Act;

(*j*) "Insurance Act" means the Insurance Act, 1938;

(*k*) "Life Insurance Corporation" means the Life Insurance Corporation of India established under the Life Insurance Corporation Act, 1956;

(*l*) "Notification" means a notification published in the Official Gazette;

(*m*) "Prescribed" means prescribed by rules made under this Act;

(*n*) "Schedule" means the Schedule to this Act;

(*o*) "Scheme" means the scheme framed under Section 16;

(*p*) "Words and expressions used in this Act but not defined herein or in the Insurance Act and defined in the companies Act, shall have the meanings respectively assigned to them in the Companies Act.

CHAPTER II
TRANSFER TO PUBLIC OWNERSHIP OF GENERAL INSURANCE BUSINESS

4. Transfer of shares of Indian insurance companies.

1. On the appointed day all the shares in the capital of every Indian insurance company shall, by virtue of this Act, stand transferred to and vested in the Central Government free of all trusts, liabilities and encumbrances affecting them.
2. Out of the shares of transferred and vested, the Central Government shall, immediately thereafter, by notification, provide for the transfer of not less than ten shares of every such company to such persons as may be specified in the notification to enable the Indian insurance company to function as a Government company.
3. Every notification made under sub-section (2) shall specify the names and description of the persons to whom the shares are transferred and the particulars of the shares which are transferred to each such person.
4. A copy of every notification made under sub-section (2) shall, as soon as may be after it is made, be sent by the Central Government to the concerned Indian insurance company, who shall, on receipt of such copy, and notwithstanding anything contained in the Companies Act or in its articles of association, forthwith rectify its register of members by including therein the persons mentioned in the notification as the holders of the shares specified therein.
5. For the removal of doubts it is hereby declared that the transfer and vesting of shares effected under sub-section (1) shall not be deemed to affect any right of the Indian insurance company subsisting immediately before the appointed day against any shareholder to recover from him any sum of money on the ground that shareholder has not paid or credited to the insurer the whole or any part of the value of the shares held by him or on any other ground whatsoever.

5. Transfer of undertakings of other existing insurers.

1. On the appointed day, the undertaking of every existing insurer who is not an Indian insurance company shall stand transferred to and vested in the Central Government and the Central Government shall immediately thereafter provide, by notification, for the transfer to and vesting in such Indian insurance company, as it may specify in the notification, of that undertaking.
2. Any notification made under sub-section (1) may provide that any of the undertakings aforesaid may be transferred to and vested in more than one Indian insurance company in such manner and subject to such conditions as may be specified in the notification.

6. Effect of transfer of undertakings.

1. The undertaking of every such existing insurer as is referred to in Section 5 shall be deemed to include all assets, rights, powers, authorities and privileges and all property, movable and immovable, cash balances, reserve funds, investments and all other rights and interests in, or arising out of, such property as were immediately before the appointed day in the ownership, possession, power or control of such existing insurer in relation to the undertaking whether within or without India, and all books of accounts, records and all other documents of whatever nature relating thereto, and shall also be deemed to include all borrowings, liabilities and obligations of whatever kind then subsisting of the existing insurer in relation to the undertaking.

2. Unless otherwise expressly provided by this Act, all deeds, bonds, agreements, powers of attorney, grants of legal representation and other instruments of whatever nature subsisting or having effect immediately before the appointed day and to which any such insurer as is referred to in Section 5 is a party or which are in favour of such existing insurer shall be of as full force and effect against or in favour of the Indian insurance company in which the undertaking or the part to which the instrument relates, has vested and may be enforced or acted upon as fully and effectually as if, in the place of the existing insurer referred to in Section 5, the Indian insurance company in which the undertaking or any part thereof has vested had been a party thereto, or as if they had been issued in its favour.
3. If, on the appointed day any suit appeal or other proceeding of whatever nature in relation to any business of the undertaking which has been transferred under Section 5 is pending by or against any such existing insurer as is referred to in that section, the same shall not abate, be discontinued or be in any way prejudicially affected by reason of the transfer of the undertaking or of anything contained in this Act but the suit appeal or other proceeding may be continued, prosecuted and enforced by or against the Indian insurance company in which the undertaking or the part to which the proceeding relates has vested.
4. For the removal of doubts it is hereby declared that in the case of foreign insurer or as the cas may be, the Life Insurance Corporation the provisions of Section 5 and the preceding subsections shall only apply to the extent to which any property appertains in the former case to the general insurance business carried on in India and in the latter case to the general insurance business carried on whether within or without India and to rights and powers acquired and to debts, liabilities and obligations incurred and to contracts agreements and other instruments made by the foreign insurer of the Life Insurance Corporation as the case may be for the purpose of such general insurance business and to legal proceeding relating to those purposes and the said provisions shall be construed accordingly.
5. If any question arise as to whether any property appertains to any such general insurance business as is referred to in this section or whether any rights, powers, liabilities or obligations were acquired or incurred or any contract, agreement or other instrument was made by the foreign insurer or the Life Insurance Corporation, as the case may be, for the purposes of any such business or whether any documents relate to those purposes, the question shall be referred to the Central Government which shall, after giving an opportunity of being heard to the persons interested in the matter, decide it in such manner as it thinks fit.

7. Transfer of service employees in certain cases.

1. Every whole-time officer or other employee of an existing insurer other than an Indian insurance company who was employed by that insurer wholly or mainly in connection with his general insurance business immediately before the appointed day shall, on the appointed day, become an officer or other employee as the case may be, of the Indian insurance company in which the undertaking of that insurer or that part of the undertaking to which the service of the officer or other employee relates has vested, and shall hold his office or service under the Indian insurance company on the terms and same conditions and with the same rights to pension, gratuity and other matter as would have been admissible to him if there had been no such vesting and shall continue to do so unless and until his employment in the Indian insurance company in which the undertaking or part has vested is terminated or until his remuneration, terms and conditions are duly altered by that Indian Insurance company:

   Provided that nothing in this sub-section shall apply to any such officer or other employee who has given, in writing, notice to the Central Government or to any person nominated in this behalf by that Government before the appointed day intimating his intention of not becoming an officer or employee of the Indian insurance company in whom the undertaking or part thereof to which his service relates has vested.

2. If any question arises as to whether any person was a wholetime officer or employee, or as to whether any officer or employee was employed wholly or mainly in connection with the general insurance business of the existing insurer referred to in sub-section (1), immediately before the appointed day, the question shall be referred within a period of two years from the appointed day and not thereafter, the Central Government which shall, after giving an opportunity of being heard to the person concerned in the matter, decide it in such manner as it thinks fit and such decision shall be final.
3. Notwithstanding anything contained in the Industrial Disputes Act, 1947 or in any other law for the time being in force the transfer of the services of any officer or other employee under subsection (1) shall not entitle any such officer or other employee to any compensation under that Act or such other law and no such claim shall be entertained by any court, tribunal or other authority.

8. Provident, Superannuation, welfare and other funds.

1. Where an existing insurer has established a provident, superannuation, welfare or any other fund for the benefit of his employees and constituted a trust in respect thereof (hereafter in this section referred to as an existing trust), the moneys standing to the credit of such fund on the appointed day, together with any other assets belonging to such fund, shall stand transferred to and vested in the Indian insurance company on the appointed day free from any such trust.
2. Where all the employees of the Life Insurance Corporation or any other existing insurer do not become employees of an Indian insurance company, the moneys and other assets belonging to any such fund as is referred to in sub-section (1), shall be apportioned between the trustees of the fund and the Indian insurance company in the prescribed manner; and in case of any dispute about such apportionment the decision of the Central Government thereon shall be final.
3. Where the undertaking of an existing insurer has vested in more than one Indian insurance company, the Central Government may, by order, provide for the apportionment among such Indian insurance companies of moneys and other assets belonging to any existing trust relating to that undertaking in such manner as in its opinion may be appropriate.
4. The Indian insurance company shall as soon as may be after the appointed day constitute in response of the moneys and other assets which are transferred to and vested in it under this section one or more trusts having objects as similar to the objects of the existing trusts as in the circumstances may be practicable.
5. Where all the moneys and other assets belonging to an existing trust are transferred to and vested in an Indian insurance company under this section, the trustees of such trust shall, as from the appointed day, stand discharged from the trust, except as respects things done or omitted to be done before the appointed day.

CHAPTER III

GENERAL INSURANCE CORPORATION OF INDIA

9. Formation of General Insurance Corporation of India.

1. As soon as may be after the commencement of this Act, the Central Government shall form a Government company in accordance with the provisions of the Companies Act, to be known as the General Insurance Corporation of India for the purpose of superintending, controlling and carrying on the business of general insurance.

2. The authorised capital of the Corporation shall be rupees seventy-five crores, divided into seventy-five lakhs fully paid-up shares of one hundred rupees each, out of which rupees five crores shall be the initial subscribed capital of the Corporation.
3. Notwithstanding anything contained in the Companies Act, 1956, it shall not be necessary to add the word "Limited" as the last word of the name of the Corporation.

10. Transfer to Corporation of shares vested in Central Government. All the shares in the capital of every Indian insurance company which stand transferred to and vested in the Central Government by virtue of Section 4 [with the exception of the shares transferred to any person under sub-section (2) of that section] shall, immediately after such vesting, stand transferred to and vested in the Corporation and every Indian insurance company shall forthwith give effect to such transfer of shares and rectify its register of members by including therein the Corporation as the holder of such shares.

CHAPTER IV

AMOUNTS TO BE PAID ACQUISITIONS

11. Amounts to be paid for transfer and vesting of share or undertakings.

1. For the transfer of the shares of each Indian insurance company to, and vesting in, the Central Government, under Section 4, there shall be paid by the Central Government to the Corporation, for distribution to the shareholders of each such company, the amount specified against such company in the corresponding entry under column (3) of Part A of the Schedule.
2. For the transfer to, and vesting in, the Central Government, under Section 5, of the undertaking of each existing insurer who is not an Indian insurance company, there shall be paid by the Central Government to the Corporation, for payment to each such existing insurer, the amount specified against such insurer in the corresponding entry under column (3) of Part B of the Schedule.

12. Disbursement of amounts by Corporation.

1. The total amount Paid by the Central Government under Section 11 shall be treated as additional contribution to the subscribed capital of the Corporation and such additional subscribed capital shall stand allotted to, and vested in, the Central Government.
2. The Corporation shall distribute the amount paid to it under Section 11, to the shareholders of each Indian insurance company and to each existing insurer, who is not an Indian insurance company, in accordance with their rights and interests, and, if there is any doubt or dispute as to the right, or extent of the right, of any person to receive the whole or any part of such amount, refer such doubt or dispute to the Central Government for determination and thereafter act in accordance with the determination made by that Government.
3. Save as otherwise provided in sub-section (2), the amount referred to in Section 11 shall be given in accordance with the provisions of Section 13, Section 14 or Section 15, as the case may be.

13. Mode of Payment.

1. Where the amount referred to in Section 11 is to be given—

(*a*) to the members of an Indian insurance company, the amount due to each such member shall be paid in full, where it does not exceed twenty-five thousand rupees, and where it execeeds twenty-five thousand rupees, each such member shall be paid twenty-five thousand rupees and the balance of the amount due to such members shall be paid to him in three equal installments, the first of which shall fall due on the appointed day;

(*b*) to a foreign insurer, it shall be given to him in cash within three months from the appointed day;

(*c*) to the Life Insurance Corporation, it shall be given to it in three equal annual instalments, the first of which within three months from the appointed day;

(*d*) to an existing insurer who is a co-operative society, it shall be distributed as soon as may be after the appointed day in accordance with the rules of the society which will apply in case of dissolution of the society;

(*e*) to an existing insurer not falling within any of the foregoing provisions, it shall be apportioned by the acquiring company among the individual policy-holders of the insurer whose policies with that insurer were in force on the appointed day and were comprised in the undertaking of such insurer in proportion to the premiums paid by the policy-holder such policies and every such payment shall be made either—

(*i*) in cash, to be sent by postal money order, or

(*ii*) at the option of the policy-holder, as a deduction in the premium due at the time of the renewal of the policy and such option shall be exercised by the policy holder before the expiry of three months from the appointed day (or within such further time not exceeding three months as the Central Government may, on the application of the policy-holder, allow) and the option so exercised shall be final and shall not be altered or rescinded after it has been exercised;

Provided that if any policy-holder fails to exercise his option within the time allowed, he shall be deemed to have exercised his option in favour of payment in cash by postal money orders;

2. Where any amount is payable whether in instalments or otherwise under the provision of this section, the unpaid amount, where its payment has become due, shall carry interest at the rate of four per cent, per annum from the appointed day.

14. Amount payable to share-holders may be paid to named persons instead in certain cases.

1. Notwithstanding anything contained elsewhere in this Act, if a majority in number of the persons, who, immediately before the appointed day, were registered in the books of an Indian insurance company as the members thereof, and representing two-thirds in value of the amount payable to the Indian insurance-company, agree either in person or by proxy at a meeting specially convened for the purpose that the amount so payable instead of being distributed among the members shall be given to any such person or body of persons as the members may nominate either at that meeting or subsequently for the purpose of carrying on any business, and the Central Government is satisfied that due provision has been or will be made for the payment of the value of their respective shares to persons who have dissented from the resolution, the amount may be given to the person or body of persons so nominated in such manner and subject to such conditions as the Central Government may think fit.
2. No resolution passed at any such meeting as is referred to in sub-section (1) held after the appointed day shall have any effect unless the meeting has been convened after obtaining the approval of the Central Government.

15. Payment into court in case of rival claims. Where a claim to the amount payable under Section 11 is made by two or more persons adversely to one another, the Corporation may cause the amount to be deposited in any civil court having jurisdiction in that behalf and the court shall decide as to whom the payment shall be made.

CHAPTER V

SCHEME FOR REORGANISATION OF GENERAL INSURANCE BUSINESS

16. Schemes for mergers of companies, etc.

1. If the Central Government is of opinion that for the more efficient carrying on of general insurance business it is necessary so to do, it may, by notification, from one or more schemes

providing for all or any of the following matters:—

(*a*) the merger in one Indian insurance company of any other Indian insurance company, or the formation of a new company by the amalganation of two or more Indian insurance companies;

(*b*) the transfer to and vesting in the acquiring company of the undertaking (including all its business, properties assets and liabilities) of any Indian insurance company which ceases to exist by reason of the scheme;

(*c*) the constitution name and registered office and the capital structure of the acquiring company and the issue and allotment of shares;

(*d*) the constitution of a board of management by whatever namecalled for the management of the acquiring company;

(*e*) the alteration of the memorandum and articles of association of the acquiring company for such purposes as may be necessary to give effect to the scheme;

(*f*) the continuance in the acquiring company of the services of all officers and other employees of the Indian insurance company which has ceased to exist by reason of the scheme, on the same terms and conditions which they were getting or, as the case may be, which they were governed immediately before the commencement of the scheme;

(*g*) the rationalisation or revision of pay scales and other terms and conditions of service of officers and other employees wherever necessary;

(*h*) the transfer to the acquiring company of the provident superannuation, welfare and other funds relating to the officers and other employees of the Indian insurance company which has ceased to exist by reason of the scheme;

(*i*) the continuance by or against the acquiring company of legal proceedings pending by or against any Indian insurance company which has ceased to exist by reason of the scheme, and the initiation of such legal proceedings, civil or criminal, as the Indian insurance company might have initiated if it had not ceased to exist;

(*j*) such incidental, consequential and supplemental matters as are necessary to give full effect to the scheme;

2. In framing schemes under sub-section (1); the object of Central Government shall he to ensure that ultimately there are only four companies (excluding the Corporation) in existence and that they are so situate as to render their combined services effective in all parts of India.
3. Where a scheme under sub-section (1) provides for the transfer of any property or liabilities, then, by virtue of the scheme, the property shall stand transferred to and vested in, and those liabilities shall be transferred to and become the liabilities of, the acquiring company.
4. If the rationalisaton or revision of any pay scale or other terms and conditions of service under any scheme is not acceptable to any officer or other employee, the acquiring company may terminate his employment by giving him compensation equivalent to three months' remuneration, unless the contract of service with such employee provides for a shorter notice of termination.

   Explanation—The compensation payable to an officer or other employee under this sub-section shall be in addition to, and shall not affect, any pension, gratuity, provident fund or other benefit to which employee may be entitled under his contract of service.
5. Notwithstanding anything contained in the Industrial Disputes Act, 1947 or in any other law for the time being in force, the transfer of the services of any officer or other employee of an Indian insurance company to the acquiring company shall not entitle any such officer or other employee to any compensation under that Act or other law, and no such claim shall be entertained by any court, tribunal or other authority.

6. The Central Government may, by notification, add to, amend or vary any scheme framed under this section.
7. The provisions of this section and of any scheme framed under it shall have effect notwithstanding anything to the contrary contained in any other law or any agreement, award or other instrument for the time being in force.

17. Schemes to be laid before Parliament. A copy of every scheme and every amendment thereto framed under Section 16 shall be laid, as soon as may be after it is made, before each House of Parliament.

CHAPTER VI

FUNCTIONS OF CORPORATION, AND ACQUIRING COMPANIES AND THEIR MANAGEMENT

18. Functions of Corporation.

1. The functions of the Corporation shall include—
   (*a*) the carrying on of any part of the general insurance business, if it thinks it desirable to do so;
   (*b*) aiding, assisting and advising the acquiring companies in the matter of setting up of standards of conduct and sound practice in general insurance business and in the matter of rendering efficient service to holders of policies of general insurance;
   (*c*) advising the acquiring companies in the matter of controlling their expenses including the payment of commission and other expenses;
   (*d*) advising the acquiring companies in the matter of the investment of their funds;
   (*e*) issuing directions to acquiring companies in relation to the conduct of general insurance business.
2. In issuing any directions under sub-section (1) the Corporation shall keep in mind the desirability of encourageing competition amongst the acquiring companies as far as possible in order to render their services more efficiently.

19. Functions of acquiring companies.

1. Subject to the rules, if any, made by the Central Government in this behalf and to as memorandum and articles of association, it shall be the duty of every aquiring company to carry on generate insurance business.
2. Each acquiring company shall so function under this Act as to secure that general-insurance business is developed to the best advantage of the community.
3. In the discharge of any of its functions each acquiring company shall act so far as may be on business principles and where any directions have been issued by the Corporation, shall be guided by such directions.
4. For the removal of doubts it is hereby declared that the corporation and any acquiring company may, subject to the rules, if any; made by the Central Government in this behalf, enter into such contracts of reinsurance or reinsurance treaties as it—may think fit for the protection of its' interests.

20. Balance of profit how to be utilised.

1. After making provision for bad and doubtful debts, depreciation in assets, provident, superannuation, welfare and other funds; debts due to Government and all other matters for which provision is necessary under any law or which are usually provided for by insurance companies, every acquiring company shall distribute the balance of profit as dividends.

2. Any profit made by the Corporation and any sums received by the Corporation by way of dividends or otherwise shall be dealt, with by it in such manner as may be prescribed.

21. Interim provisions for management of Indian insurance companies.

1. Notwithstanding anything contained in the Companies Act, or in the memorandum and articles of association of any Indian insurance company, on and from the appointed day and until a new board of directors of the Indian insurance company is duly constituted the management of the company shall continue to vest in the Custodian in charge of the management of the undertaking of that company immediately before the appointed day by virtue of the provisions contained in the General Insurance (Emergency Provisions) Act, 1911, and the Custodian shall be entitled, subject to such directions as the Central Government may in this behalf, to exercise all the powers and do all acts and things as may be exercised or done by the company or by its board of directors:
2. Nothing contained in sub-section. (1) shall be deemed to prevent the Central Government from appointing any other person to take charge of the management of the undertaking of any Indian insurance company during period referred to in that sub-section if for any reason it becomes necessary so to do, and any person so appointed may exercise all the powers and do all acts and things which a Custodian may exercise or do under sub-section (1).
3. The Custodian referred to in sub-section (1) and the persons appointed under sub-section (2) shall be entitled to such salaries and other allowances as the Central Government may specify in this behalf and shall hold office during the pleasure of the Central Government.

22. Power of Central Government to transfer employees. The Corporation may at any time transfer any officer or employee from an acquiring company or the Corporation to any other acquiring company or the Corporation, as the case may be, and the officer or employee so transferred, shall continue to have the same terms and conditions of service as were applicable to him immediately before such transfer.

23. Power of Central Government to issue directions. The Corporation and every acquiring company shall, in the discharge of its functions, be guided by such directions in regard to matters of policy involving public interest as the Central Government may give.

CHAPTER VII

MISCELLANEOUS

24. Acquiring companies to have the exclusive privilege of carrying on general insurance business.

1. Except to the extent expressly provided in this Act, on and from the appointed day the Corporation and the acquiring companies shall have exclusive privilege of carrying on general insurance business in India.
2. Subject to the provisions of Section 36, any certificate of registration granted under the Insurance Act to any insurer other than an insurer referred to in sub-section (1) shall, on and from the appointed day, cease to have effect:

Provided that nothing in this sub-section shall apply to the carrying on by the Life Insurance Corporation of life insurance business and capital redemption and annuity certain business.

25. Properties in India not to be with foreign insurers except with permission of Central Government.

1. No person shall take out or renew any policy of insurance in respect of any property in India or any ship or other vessel or aircraft registered in India with an insurer whose principal place of business is outside India save with the prior permission of the Central Government.

2. If any person contravenes any provision of sub-section (I), he shall be punishable with imprisonment for a term which may extend to one year, or with fine which may extend to one thousand rupees or with both.

26. Acquiring companies and income-tax. For the purposes of the Income-tax Act, 1961, every acquiring company shall be deemed to be an Indian company and a company in which the public are substantially interested.

27. Power to reduce amounts of insurance in certain cases. An acquiring company may, having regard to its financial condition on the 13th day of May, 1971, or the financial condition on the said date of any existing insurer whose undertaking have been transferred to and vested in it under this Act reduce the liabilities which have arisen under contracts of general insurance entered in to before the said date in such manner and subject io such conditions as it thinks fit:

Provided that no such reduction shall be made except in accordance with specific proposals made by the acquiring company in this behalf and approved by the Central Government.

28. Right of acquiring company to seek relief in respect of certain transactions.

1. Where an existing insurer has at any time within five years before the 13th day of May, 1971—
   (*a*) made any payment to any person without consideration,
   (*b*) sold or disposed of any property of the insurer without consideration or for an inadequate consideration,
   (*c*) acquired any property or rights for an excessive consideration,
   (*d*) entered into or varied any agreement so as to require an excessive consideration to be paid or given by the insurer,
   (*e*) entered into any other transaction of such an onerous nature as to cause a loss to, or impose a liability, on the insurer exceeding any benefit accruing to the insurer and the payment, sale, disposal, acquisition, agreement or variation thereof or there transaction was not reasonably necessary for the purpose of the general insurance business of the insurer or was made with an unreasonable lack of prudence on the part of the insurer, regard being had in either case to the circumstances at the time, the acquiring company may apply for relief to the circumstances at the time, the acquiring company may apply for relief to the court in respect of such transaction, and all parties to the transaction shall, unless the court otherwise directs, be made parties to the application.
2. The court may make such order against any of the parties to the application as it thinks just having regard to the extent to which those parties were respectively responsible for the transaction or benefited from it and all the circumstances of the case.
3. Where an application is made to the court under this section in respect of any transaction and the application is determined in favour of the acquiring company, the court shall have exclusive jurisdiction to determine any claim outstanding in respect of the transaction.

29. Duty to deliver possession of property and documents relating thereto.

1. Where any property appertaining to an existing insurer has been transferred to and vested in an Indian insurance company under Section 5—
   (*a*) every person in whose possession, custody or control any such property may be, shall deliver the property to the Indian insurance company forthwith,
   (*b*) any person who immediately before such vesting has in his possession, custody or control any books, documents or other papers relating to an existing insurer shall be liable to account for the said books, documents and papers to the Indian insurance company, and shall deliver them to that company or to such person as that company may direct.

2. In particular, all the assets of an existing insurer appertaining to the undertaking held in deposit, by the Reserve Bank of India under the Insurance Act or by trustees in trust shall be delivered to the Indian insurance company.
3. Without prejudice to the other provisions contained in this section, it shall be lawful for each Indian insurance company to take all necessary steps for taking possession of all properties which have been transferred to and vested in it under this Act.

30. Penalty for withholding property, etc. If any person wilfully withholds or fails to deliver to an Indian insurance company as required by Section 29 any property or any books, documents or other papers which may be in his possession or unlawfully retains possession of any property of an existing insurer which has been transferred to and vested in an Indian insurance company under Section 5 or wilfully applies any such property to purposes other than those expressed in or authorised by this Act, he shall, on the complaint of the Indian insurance company, be punishable with imprisonment for a term which may extend to one year, or with fine may extend to one thousand rupees, or with both.

31. Officers and employees of Corporation or of acquiring companies to be public servants. Every officer or other employee of the Corporation or of an acquiring company shall be deemed to be a public servant for the purposes of Chapter IX of the Indian Penal Code.

32. Indemnity. Every officer of the Central Government and every officer or other employee of the Corporation and of any acquiring company shall be indemnified by the Central Government or the Corporation of the acquiring company, as the case may be, against all losses and expenses incurred by him in, or in relation to, the discharge of his duties under this Act except such as have been caused by his own wilful act or default.

33. Dissolution of Corporation and acquiring companies. No provision of law relating to the winding up of companies shall apply to the Corporation or to an acquiring company, and neither the Corporation nor any such company shall be placed in liquidation save by order of the Central Government and in such manner as it may direct.

34. Reference to existing insurer in other laws. Any reference to an existing insurer in any law other than this Act or any contract or other instrument shall, in so far as it relates to an acquiring company, be construed as a reference to that company.

35. Application of Insurance Act. Subject to such exceptions, restrictions and limitations, if any, as the Central Government may, by notification, specify in this behalf, the Insurance Act shall apply to or in relation to the Corporation and every acquiring company as if the Corporation or the acquiring company, as the case may be, were a insurer carrying on general insurance business within the meaning of that Act.

36. Exemptions.

1. Nothing contained in this Act shall apply in relation to—
   (*a*) any general insurance business carried on by a State Government, to the extent to which such insurance relates to properties belonging to it or undertakings owned wholly or mainly by the State Government; or to properties belonging to semi-government bodies, or any Board or body corporate established by the State Government under any statute or any industrial or commercial undertaking in which the State Government has substantial financial interest, whether as shareholder, lender or guarantor;
   (*b*) any general insurance business not falling within clause (*a*) which has been carried on by a state Government before the commencement of this Act, to the extent to which it is necessary to allow such business to run off :
   Provided that nothing contained in this clause shall be deemed to authorise the State Government to issue any new policies or renew any existing policies;

(*c*) any insurer whose business is being voluntarily wound up or is being wound up by a court;

(*d*) the insurance business carried on by the Calcutta Hospital and Nursing Home Benefits Association. Limited;

(*e*) the insurance business carried on by the Export Credit and Guarantee Corporation Limited and the Deposit Insurance Corporation established under Section 3 of the Deposit Insurance Corporation Act, 1961;

(*f*) any scheme in existence immediately before the 14th day of May, 1971, or an scheme framed after the said day with the approval of the Central Government for the insurance of crops or of cattle or of flood risks or of war or emergency risks.

2. If the Central Government is satisfied that an insurer, whether established before or after the appointed day, carries on only such general insurance business as is not carried on ordinarily by insurers, it may, by notification, direct that nothing contained in this Act shall apply to such insurer.

37. Vacancies, etc., not to invalidate proceedings. No act or proceeding of the Corporation or of an acquiring company shall be called in question merely on the ground of the existence of any vacancy in or defect in the constitution of the Corporation or the company.

38. Protection of action taken in good faith. No suit, prosecution or other legal proceeding shall lie against any officer of the Central Government or officer or other employee of the Corporation or of the acquiring company for anything which is in good faith done or intended to be done under this Act.

39. Power to make rules.

1. The Central Government may, by notification, make rules to carry out the provisions of this Act.
2. In particular, and without prejudice to the generality of the foregoing power, rules made under this section may provide for—

(*a*) the manner in which the profits, if any, and other moneys received by the Corporation may be dealt with;

(*b*) the conditions, if any, subject to which the Corporation and the acquiring companies shall Carry on general insurance business;

(*c*) the terms and conditions subject to which any reinsurance contracts or treaties may be entered into;

(*d*) the form and manner in which any notice or application may he given or made to the Central Government;

(*e*) the reports which may be called for by the Central Government from the Corporation and the acquiring companies;

(*f*) any other matter which is required to be, or may be, prescribed.

3. Every rule made under this section and every notification issued under Section 35 shall be laid, as soon as may be after it is made, before each House of Parliament, while it is in session, for a total period of thirty days which may be comprised in one session or in two or more successive sessions, and if, before the expiry of the session immediately following the session or the successive sessions aforesaid, both houses agree in making any modification in the rule or notification or both Houses agree that the rule or notification should not be made, the rule or notification shall thereafter have effect only in such modified form or be of no effect, as the case may be; so, however, that any such modification or annulment shall be without prejudice to the validity of anything previously done under that rule or notification.

APPENDIX—B

Whereas the Insured named in the Schedule below, carrying on the business mentioned therein and no other for the purpose of this Insurance has, by a Proposal and Declaration dated as stated in the said Schedule, which Proposal and Declaration it is hereby agreed shall be the basis of this Contract and be considered as in corporated herein, applied to the ORIENTAL FIRE AND GENERAL INSURANCE COMPANY LIMITED (hereinafter called the "Company") for the Insurance hereinafter contained for the period stated in the Schedule hereto and in consideration of the Insured having paid or agreed to pay to the Company the sum shown as the first premium for or on account of such Insurance.

Now this policy Witnesseth that if during the period stated in the Schedule hereto or during any subsequent period in respect of which the Insured shall have paid and the Company accepted a renewal premium this property or any part thereof described in the Schedule below, whilst contained within the premises (which expression shall not include any garden, yard or outbuilding or other appartenances) mentioned in the said Schedule and whilst the premises are occupied by the Insured as stated in the proposal above referred to shall be lost or damaged by.

HOUSE BREAKING OR BURGLARY

or any attempt, thereat or if there shall arise any damage to the said premises by the risks insured against falling to be made good by the Insured then the company shall pay or make good to the Insured such loss or damage to the extent of the intrinsic value of the property so lost or to the amount of the damage so sustained, but not exceeding, in respect of each or any of the several items specified, the sum set opposite thereto respectively, nor in the whole of any one year of insurance the total sum insured by this Policy.

Provided always that this Policy shall not cover

(*a*) loss or damage where any member of the Insured's household or of his business staff is concerned as principal or accessory, or resulting from any act committed by any other person lawfully on the premises wherein the property insured may happen to be;

(*b*) loss or damage upon the occasion of or consequent upon, fire or explosion within such premises or any loss or damage which can be insured against by a Fire or Glass Insurance Policy.

(*c*) Unless specially mentioned, deeds, bonds, bills of exchange, promissory notes, cash, treasury notes and bank notes, cheques, securities for money stamps, stamp collections, books of account, documents of any kind, manuscripts, medals and coins, motor vehicles and accessories or livestock;

(*d*) (*i*) any accident or any loss or destruction of or damage to any property whatsoever or any loss or expense whatsover resulting or arising therefrom or any consequential loss.

(*ii*) any legal liability of whatsover nature,

directly or indirectly cause by or contributed to by or arising from ionising radiations or contaminations by radioactivity from any nuclear fuel or from any nuclear waste from the combustion of nuclear fuel. Solely for the purpose of this exclusion, combustion shall include any self-sustaining process of nuclear fission.

The indemnity or compensation provided by this Policy shall not apply to nor include any accident, loss, destruction, damage or legal liability directly or indirectly caused why or contributed to by or arising from nuclear weapons material.

(*e*) loss, destruction or damage directly or indirectly proximately or remotely occasioned by contributed to by or traceable to or arising out or in connection with Hurricane, Volcanic Eruption, Earthquake or other convulsions of nature, Invasion act or Foreign Enemies, Hostilities or Warlike Operations (whether before or after Declaration of War), Civil War, Strike, Riot, Civil

Commotion, Mutiny, Rebellion Military or Usurped Power or by any direct or indirect consequences of any of the said occurrences and in the event of any claim hereunder the Insured shall prove that the loss, destruction or damage arose independently of and was in no way connected with or occasioned by or contributed to by or traceable to any of the said occurrences or any consequence thereof and in default of such proof the Company shall not be liable to make any payment in respect of such a claim.

Provided always that the due observance and fulfilment of the conditions contained herein or endorsed hereon shall so far as the nature of them respectively will permit be deemed to be conditions precedent to the right of the Insured to recover hereunder.

The Agents of the Company shall in no case be made personally responsible on account of any legal or other investigation which they may find it necessary to institute for the satisfaction of the Company; nor can their personal property be attached on account of any Claim by the Insured. If the insured should commence such proceedings against the Agents it is hereby declared and stipulated that the Insured shall foreit thereby all Claims upon the Company under this Policy and shall moreover be responsible for all expenses which shall accrue in consequence of such proceedings.

1. For the purposes of this Policy the term "Housebreaking or Burglary" shall mean:—
   (*a*) Theft of property from the premises described in the Schedule, to this Policy following upon felonious entry of the said premises by violent and forcible means or
   (*b*) Theft by a person in the premises who subsequently breaks out by violent and forcible means, PROVIDED there shall be visible marks made upon the premises at the plate of such entry or exit by tools, explosives, electricity or chemicals.
2. Each and every item specified in the Schedule to this Policy is separately but similarly subject to Average, that is to say, if the property insured. Shall at the time of no loss or damage be collectively of greater value than the sum insured thereon then the insured shall be considered to be his own Insurer for the different and shall bear rateable share of the loss or damage accordingly.
3. Every notice or communication to be given or made under this Policy shall be delivered in writing at the Registered Office or any Branch Office or Agency of the Company with which the Insured has been in communication
4. This Policy shall be void if there be any misstatement in or if a material fact be omitted from the proposal.
5. If any claim under this Policy shall be in any respect fraudulent or if any fraudulent means or devices are used by the insured or anyone acting on his behalf to obtain any benefit under this Policy or if books showing an purchases of goods or stock, particulars of articles or goods manufactured, and of goods or stock sold or otherwise disposed of shall not have been duly and correctly kept during the time the insured has carried on the business, then this Policy shall be void and all benefit thereunder shall be forfeited.
6. The Insured shall exercise reasonable care in the selection and suppervision of employees and shall take all reasonable precautions to safeguard the property insured and to secure all doors, windows and other openings.
7. Upon the happening of any event giving rise or likely to give rise to a claim under this Policy coming to the knowledge of the Jnsured, or of the Insured's representative for the time being, the Insured or the representative shall:
   (*a*) Give immediate notice to the Police and take all practicable steps to discover the guilty person or persons and to recover the property lost and shall also give immediate notice to the Company siating the circumstances of the case.
   (*b*) Within seven days after such notice deliver to the Company a detailed statement in writing of the loss or damage, with an estimate of the intrinsic value of each article lost and the amount of the damage sustained.

(*c*) Furnish to the Company all such particulars and evidence, documentary or otherwise and execute and do all such assurances and things and give all such access as the Company may reasonably require to substantiate the claim, to discover and punish the guilty person or persons, to trace and recover the property lost, and to recoup the Company, so far as may be in respect of the amount they shall pay, or be liable to pay under this Policy. The Company shall bear the expense of all such particulars, evidence, assurances and things as they may require with the above objects or any of them other than those required to substantiate the claim.

Unless notice as required in paragraph (*a*) of this condition be receivel by the Company within six weeks after the happening of such event, the Company will be under no liability for any loss or damage in connection therewith.

8. The Company may reinstate, replace, or repair the property or premises as the case may be or any part thereof, instead of paying the amount of the loss or damage, and may join with other Insurers in so doing. If the Company elect to reinstate or replace, the Insured shall furnish to them when required all such specifications, and information as may be deemed necessary or expedient for the purpose. Upon payment of any claim for loss under this Policy, the property in respect of which the payment is made shall belong to the Company.
9. If at the time of the happening of any loss or damage covered by the Policy there shall be any other insurance covering the same risk, whether effected by the Insured or not, then the Company shall not be liable to contribute more than its rateable proportion of any payment in respect of such loss or damage.
10. This Policy ceases to be in force as to any property which shall pass from the Insured to any other person otherwise than by Will or Operation of Law, unless notice thereof be given to the Company, and the subsistence of the Insurance in favour of such other person be declared by a memorandum endorsed thereon by or on behalf of the Company.
11. The Company may by notice in writing to the Insured to his last known address cancel this Policy at any time paying on demand a proportion of the premium corresponding to the unexpired period of the Policy.
12. This Policy does not cover loss of cash and or other property abstracted from safe is following the use of the key to the said after or any duplicate thereof belonging to the Insured unless such key has been obtained by threats or violence.

    A complete list of the amount of cash and or other property in the safe shall be kept secure in some place other than the said safe, and the liability of the Company shall be limited to the amount actually shown by such record to be in the safe at the time of Burglary not exceeding in all the sum insured.
13. If any difference arises as to the amount of any loss or damage such difference shall independently of all other questions be referred to the decision of an Arbitrator, to be appointed in writing by the parties in difference, or if they cannot agree upon a single Arbitrator, to the decision of two disinterested persons as arbitrators, of whom one shall be appointed in writing by each of the parties within two calendar months after having been required so to do in writing by the other party. In case either party shall refuse or fail to appoint an arbitrator within two calendar months after receipt of notice in writing requiring an appointment, the other party shall be at liberty to appoint a sole arbitrator; and in case of disagreement between the arbitrators, the difference shall be referred to the decision of an umpire who shall have been appointed by them in writing before entering on the reference and who shall sit with the arbitrators and preside at their

meetings. The death of any party shall not revoke or affect the authority or powers of the arbitrator, arbitrators or umpire respectively; and in the event of the death of an arbitrator or umpire, another shall in each case be appointed in his stead by the party or arbitrators (as the case may be) by whom the arbitrator or umpire so dying was appointed. The costs of the reference and of the award shall be in the discretion of the arbitrator, arbitrators or umpire making the award. And it is hereby expressly stipulated and declared that it shall be a condition precedent to any right of action or suit upon this Policy that the award by such arbitrator, arbitrators or umpire of the amount of the loss or damage if disputed shall be first obtained.

QUESTIONS

1. Describe the main features of the Insurance Act, 1938.
2. What are the duties and liabilities of the Controller of Insurance?
3. Discuss the main functions of Life Insurance Corporation of India.
4. Detail the set-up and organisation of Life Insurance Corporation of India.
5. Discuss the main Proviso of the Marine Insurance Act.
6. Discuss the functions of the General Insurance Corporation of India.

THE INSURANCE REGULATORY AND DEVELOPMENT AUTHORITY ACT, 1999[1]

(NO. 41 OF 1999)

(*December* 29, 1999)

CONTENTS

CHAPTER 1

PRELIMINARY

CHAPTER II

INSURANCE REGULATORY AND DEVELOPMENT AUTHORITY

CHAPTER III

TRANSFER OF ASSETS, LIABILITIES, ETC. OF INTERIM INSURANCE REGULATORY AUTHORITY

CHAPTER IV

DUTIES, POWERS AND FUNCTIONS OF AUTHORITY

CHAPTER V

FINANCE, ACCOUNTS AND AUDIT

CHAPTER VI

MISCELLANEOUS

An Act to provide for the establishment of an Authority to protect the interests of holders of insurance policies, to regulate, promote and ensure orderly growth of the insurance industry and for matters connected therewith or incidental thereto and for there to amend the Insurance Act, 1938, the Life insurance Corporation Act, 1956 and the General Insurance Business (Nationalisation) Act, 1972.

Be it enacted by Parliament in the Fiftieth Year of the Republic of India as follows:

Prefatory Note—Statement of Objects and Reasons—The insurance industry requires a high degree of regulation. The Insurance Act, 1938 provides for the institution of the Controller of Insurance to act as strong and powerful supervisory and regulatory authority with powers to direct, advise, caution, prohibit, investigate, inspect, prosecute, search, seize, fine, amalgamate, authorise, register and liquidate insurance companies. However, after the nationalisation of the life insurance

1. Received the assent of the President on December 29, 1999 and published in the Gazette of India, Extra., Part II, Section I, dated December 29, 1999, pp. 1-29, No, 54.

industry in 1956 and the general insurance industry in 1972, the role of the Controller of Insurance diminished in significance over a period of time.

2. In April 1993, the Government set up a high-powered committee headed by Shri R.N. Malhotra, former Governor, Reserve Bank of India, to examine the structure of the insurance industry and recommend changes to make it more efficient and competitive keeping in view the structural changes in other part of the financial system of the economy. The Committee which submitted its report on the 7th January, 1994 felt that the insurance regulatory apparatus should be activated even in the present set up of nationalised insurance sector and recommended, inter alia, the establishment of a strong and effective Insurance Regulatory Authority in the form of a statutory autonomous board on the lines of the Securities and Exchange Board of India.
3. The recommendations of the Committee were discussed at different forums including the Consultative Committee of the Parliament attached to the Ministry of Finance, managements of the Life Insurance Corporation, the General Insurance Corporation and its subsidiary companies, trade unions, chambers of commerce and consumer interest groups. The recommendation to set up an autonomous Insurance Regulatory Authority found wide support. In view of the general support received, the then Government decided to bring in a legislation to establish an independent Regulatory Authority for the insurance industry. Since enacting legislation for creating the Insurance Regulatory Authority was to take time, the then Government constituted through a Government resolution an Interim Insurance Regulatory Authority pending the enactment of a comprehensive legislation. The Chairman, Insurance Regulatory Authority has been notified as Controller of Insurance under the Insurance Act, 1938. The said Interim Insurance Regulatory Authority at present is discharging certain functions and exercising powers of the Controller.
4. In pursuance of the Budget Speech in July 1996, the then Government introduced on the 20th December, 1996, the Insurance Regulatory Authority Bill, 1996 for establishment of an authority to protect the interest of holders of insurance policies and to regulate, promote and ensure orderly growth of the insurance industry and for matters connected therewith or incidental thereto. The Bill was referred to the Department related Standing Committee on the Ministry of Finance. The Committee submitted its report on 9th May, 1997. However, the said Bill incorporating therein the recommendations of the said Standing Committee was taken for consideration but could not be passed and the Bill was withdrawn by the then Government.
5. In order to provide better insurance coverage to our citizens and also to augment the flow of long-term resources for financing infrastructure, in the Budget Speech, 1998, the policy of the Government was announced to open up the insurance sector and also to establish a Statutory Regulatory Authority. Accordingly, the Insurance Regulatory Authority Bill, 1998 was introduced in the previous Lock Sabha on the 15th December, 1998 providing for setting a Statutory Insurance Regulatory Authority and containing three Schedules incorporating amendments to the Insurance act, 1938, the Life Insurance Corporation Act, 1956 and the General Insurance Business (Nationalisation) Act, 1972 to permit the entry of private Indian companies into the insurance sector and to make certain consequential amendments to the Insurance Act, 1938. The Bill was referred to the Standing Committee on Finance on the 4th January, 1999 for examination and report. The Standing Committee while recommending the Bill suggested some amendments. These were accepted by the Government and amendments to the Bill were circulated on the 18th March, 1999. However, the Bill could not be taken up for consideration consequent on the dissolution of the Lock Sabha.
6. It is now proposed to re-introduce a fresh Bill by incorporating the provisions of the Insurance Regulatory Authority Bill, 1998 and the amendments suggested by the Standing Committee on Finance. The Bill will be titled Insurance Regulatory and Development Authority Bill on the

basis of the recommendation of the Standing Committee. In the main text of the Bill, provisions are incorporated to give a Statutory character to the Interim Insurance Regulatory Authority and the Three Schedules contain amendments to the Insurance Act, 1938, amendment to the Life Insurance Corporation Act, 1956 and the General Insurance Business (Nationalisation) Act, 1972.

7. The proposed Authority shall be a body corporate having perpetual succession and a common seal with power to acquire, hold and dispose of property and to contract. It will consist of a Chairperson and other members not exceeding nine in number, of whom not more than five shall serve full time, to be appointed by the Central Government from amongst persons of ability, integrity and standing who have knowledge or experience of life insurance, general insurance, actuarial science, finance, economics, law, accountancy, administration or any other discipline which in the opinion of the Central Government shall be useful to the Authority. The Chairperson and other whole-time members, shall hold office for a term of 5 years or until the age of 65 years in the case of Chairperson and 62 years in the case of other whole-time members whichever is earlier and they shall be eligible for reappointment subject to age consideration. A part-time member shall hold office for a term not exceeding 5 years.

8. The duties, powers and functions of Authority, inter alia, shall include:
   (*a*) Issue to the applicant a certificate of registration, renew, modify, withdraw, suspend or cancel such registration;
   (*b*) Protection of the interests of the policyholders in matters concerning assigning of policy, nomination by policyholders, insurable interest, settlement of insurance claim, surrender value of policy, and other terms and conditions of contracts of insurance;
   (*c*) Specifying requisite qualifications, code of conduct and practical training for intermediary or insurance intermediaries and agents;
   (*d*) Specifying the code of conduct for surveyors and loss assessors;
   (*e*) Promoting efficiency in the conduct of insurance business;
   (*f*) Promoting and regulating professional organisations connected with the insurance and reinsurance business;
   (*g*) Levying fees and other charges for carrying out the purposes of this Act;
   (*h*) Calling for information from, undertaking inspection of, conducting enquiries and investigations including audit of insurers, intermediaries, insurance intermediaries and other organisations connected with the insurance business;
   (*i*) Control and regulation of the rates, advantages, term and conditions that may be offered by insurers in respect of general insurance business not so controlled and regulated by the Tariff Advisory Committee under Section 64-U of the Insurance Act, 1938;
   (*j*) Specifying the form and manner in which books of account shall be maintained and statement of accounts will be rendered by insurers and other insurance intermediaries;
   (*k*) Regulating investment of funds by insurance companies;
   (*l*) Regulating maintenance of margin of solvency;
   (*m*) Adjudication of disputes between insurers and intermediaries or insurance intermediaries;
   (*n*) Supervising the functioning of the Tariff Advisory Committee;
   (*O*) Specifying the percentage of premium income of the insurer to finance schemes for promoting and regulating professional organisations referred to in clause(f).
   (*p*) Specifying percentage of life insurance business and general insurance business to be undertaken by the insurer in the rural or social sector; and
   (*q*) Exercising such other powers as may be prescribed.

9. The powers and functions mentioned above would enable the Authority to perform the role of all effective watchdog and a regulator for the insurance sector in India. To enable the Authority to function in a truly independent manner and discharge its assigned responsibilities effectively, it is proposed to vest the Authority with statutory status.
10. The First Schedule contains consequential provisions relating to amendments to the Insurance Act, 1938 to update certain outdated provisions and for smooth and efficient regulation of the opened up sector. The Second and Third Schedules contain amendment to the Life Insurance Corporation Act, 1956 and the General Insurance Business (Nationalisation) Act, 1972 respectively to remove the exclusive privilege of the nationalised companies to transact insurance business.
11. The Bill seeks to achieve the above objects.

CHAPTER I
PRELIMINARY

1. **Short title, extent and commencement:** (1) This Act may be called the Insurance Regulatory and Development Authority Act, 1999.
2. It extends to the whole of India.
3. It shall come into force on such date as the Central Government may, by notification in the Official Gazette, appoint:

Provided that different dates may be appointed for different provisions of this Act and any reference in any such provision to the commencement of this Act shall be construed as a reference to the coming into force of that provision.

Notes

Commencement of Act. There are two ways of the laws coming into operation. One way that in the law itself it is laid down that it shall come into force on a particular day. If that is not provided in the Act, then the Act comes into operation on the date of assent. *Chandrasekhar Singh v. State of Orissa,* (1967) 33 Cut LT 263.

2. Definitions.

1. In this Act, unless the context otherwise requires:
   (*a*) "Appointed day" means the date on which the Authority is established under sub-section (1) of Section 3;
   (*b*) "Authority" means the Insurance Regulatory and Development Authority established under sub-section (1) of Section 3;
   (*c*) "Chairperson" means the Chairperson of the Authority;
   (*d*) "Fund" means the Insurance Regulatory and Development Authority Fund constituted under sub-section (1) of Section 16;
   (*e*) "Interim Insurance Regulatory Authority" means the Insurance Regulatory Authority set up by the Central Government through Resolution No. 17(2)/94-Ins.-V, dated the 23rd January, 1996;
   (*f*) "Intermediary or insurance intermediary" includes insurance brokers, reinsurance brokers, insurance consultants, surveyors and loss assessors;
   (*g*) "Member" means a whole-time or a part-time member of the Authority and includes the Chairperson;
   (*h*) "Notification" means a notification published in the Official Gazette;

(*i*) "Prescribed" means prescribed by rules made under this Act;

(*j*) "Regulations" means the regulations made by the Authority.

2. Words and expressions used and not defined in this Act but defined in the Insurance Act, 1938 (4 of 1938) or the Life Insurance Corporation Act, 1972 (57 of 1972) shall have the meanings respectively assigned to them in those Acts.

Chapter II
Insurance Regulatory and Development Authority

3. Establishment and incorporation of Authority.

1. With effect from such date as the Central Government may, by notification, appoint, there shall be established, for the purposes of this Act, an Authority to be called "the Insurance Regulatory and Development Authority".
2. The Authority shall be a body corporate by the name aforesaid having perpetual succession and a common seal with power, subject to the provisions of this Act, to acquire, hold and dispose of property, both movable and immovable, and to contract and shall, by the said name, sue or be sued.
3. The head office of the Authority shall be at such place as the Central Government may decide from time to time.
4. The Authority may establish offices at other places in India.

4. Composition of Authority. The Authority shall consist of the following members, namely:

(*a*) a Chairperson;

(*b*) not more than five whole-time members;

(*c*) not more than four part-time members;

to be appointed by the Central Government from amongst persons of ability, integrity and standing who have knowledge or experience in life insurance, general insurance, actuarial science, finance, economics, law, accountancy, administration or any other discipline which would, in the opinion of the Central Government, be useful to the Authority;

Provided that the Central Government shall, while appointing the Chairperson and the whole-time members, ensure that at least one person each is a person having knowledge or experience in life insurance, general insurance or actuarial science, respectively.

5. Tenure of office of Chairperson and other members.

1. The Chairperson and every other whole-time member shall hold office for a term of—five years from the date on which he enters upon his office and shall be eligible for reappointment:

   Provided that no person shall hold office as a Chairperson after he has attained the age of sixty-five years:

   Provided further that no person shall hold office as a whole-time member after he has attained the age of sixty-two years.
2. A part-time member shall hold office for a term not exceeding five years from the date on which he enters upon his office.

6. Removal from office

7. Salary and allowances of Chairperson and members

8. Bar on future employment of members

9. Administrative power's of Chairperson

10. Meetings of Authority

11. Vacancies, etc., not to invalidate proceedings of Authority

12. Officers and employees of Authority
13. Transfer of assets, liabilities etc. of Interim Insurance Regulatory Authority
14. Duties, powers and functions of Authority
15. Grants by Central Government
16. Constitution of Fund
17. Accounts and audit
18. Power of Central Government to issue directions
19. Power of Central Government to supersede Authority
20. Furnishing of returns, etc. to Central Government
21. Chairperson, members, officers and other employees of Authority to be public servants
22. Protection of action taken in good faith
23. Delegation of powers
24. Power to make rules
25. Establishment of Insurance Advisory Committee
26. Power to make regulations
27. Rules and regulations to be laid before Parliament. Every rule and every regulation made under this Act shall be laid, as soon as may be after it is made, before each House of Parliament, while it is in session, for a total period of thirty days which may be comprised in one session or in two or more successive sessions, and if, before the expiry of the session immediately following the session or the successive sessions aforesaid, both Houses agree in making any modification in the rule or regulation or both Houses agree that the rule or regulation should not be made, the rule or regulation shall thereafter have effect only in such modified form or be of no effect, as the case may be; so, however, that any such modification or annulment shall be without prejudice to the validity of anything previously done under that rule or regulation.
28. Application of other laws not barred. The provisions of this Act shall be in addition to, and not in derogation of, the provisions of any other law for the time being in force.
29. Power to remove difficulties.

1. If any difficulty arises in giving effect to the provisions of this Act, the Central Government may, by order published in the Official Gazette, make such provisions not inconsistent with the provisions of this Act as may appear to be necessary for removing the difficulty:
   Provided that no order shall be made under this section after the expiry of two years from the appointed day.
2. Every order made under this section shall be laid as soon as may be after it is made, before each House of Parliament.

30. Amendment of Act 4 or 1938. The Insurance Act, 1938 shall be amended in the manner specified in the First Schedule to this Act.
31. Amendment of Act 31 of 1956. The Life Insurance Corporation Act, 1956 shall be amended in the manner specified in the Second Schedule to this Act.
32. Amendment of Act 57 of 1972. The General Insurance Business (Nationalisation) Act, 1972 shall be amended in the manner specified in the Third Schedule to this Act.

The First Schedule

(See Section 30)

Amendments to the Insurance Act, 1938

(4 of 1938)

1. In the Act, except in clause (5-B) of Section 2 and Section 2-B, for "Controller" wherever it occurs, substitute "Authority" and such consequential changes as the rules of grammar may require shall also be made.

2. In Sections 27, 27-A, 27-B, 31, 32-A, 40-A, 48-B, 64-F, 64-G, 64-1, 64-J, 64-L, 64-R, 64-UC, 64-UM, 113 and 115, for "Central Government" wherever they occur, substitute "Authority".
3. **Section 2**

(*a*) after clause (1), *insert* the following:

'(1-A) "Authority" means the Insurance-Regulatory and Development authority established under sub-section (1) of Section 3 of the Insurance Regulatory and Development Authority Act, 1999;';

(*b*) for clause (5-B), *substitute* the following:

(5-B) "Controller of Insurance" means the officer appointed by the Central Government under Section 2-B to exercise all the powers, discharge the functions and perform the duties of the Authority under this Act or the Life Insurance Corporation Act, 1956 (31 of 1956), or the General Insurance Business (Nationalisation) Act, 1972 (57 of 1972), or the Insurance Regulatory and Development Authority Act, 1999;' ;

(*c*) after clause (7), *insert* the following:

'(7-A) "Indian Insurance Company" means any insurer being a company

(*a*) which is formed and registered under the Companies Act, 1956;

(*b*) in which the aggregate holdings of equity shares by a foreign company, either by itself or through its subsidiary companies or its nominees, do not exceed twenty-six per cent paid-up equity capital of such Indian insurance company;

(*c*) whose sole purpose is to carry on life insurance business or general insurance business or re-insurance business.

Explanation—For the purposes of this clause, the expression "foreign company" shall have the meaning assigned to it under clause (23-A) of Section 2 of the Income Tax Act, 1961 (43 of 1961).

(*d*) in clause (14), for "*Section 114*" *substitute* "this Act".

4. **After Section 2, insert the following:**

"2-A. *Interpretation of certain words and expressions.* Words and expressions used and not defined in this Act but defined in the Life Insurance Corporation Act, 1956 (31 of 1956), the General Insurance Business (Nationalisation) Act, 1972 (57 of 1972) and the Insurance Regulatory and Development Authority Act, 1999 shall have the meanings respectively assigned to them in those Acts".

5. **Section 2-B, for sub-section (1), *substitute* the following:**

"(1) If at any time, the Authority is superseded under sub-section (l) of Section 19 of the Insurance Regulatory and Development Authority Act, 1999, the Central Government may, by notification in the official Gazette, appoint a person to be the Controller of Insurance till such time the Authority is reconstituted under sub-section (3) of Section 19 of that Act."

6. **Section 2-C, in sub-section (1), after the second proviso, *insert* the following:**

"Provided also that no insurer other than an Indian insurance company shall begin to carry on any class of insurance business in India under this Act on or after the commencement of the Insurance Regulatory and Development Authority Act, 1999."

7. **Section 3**

(*a*) in sub-section (1), after the first proviso, *insert* the following:

"Provided further that a person or insurer, as the case may be, carrying on any class of insurance business in India, on or before the commencement of the Insurance Regulatory and Development Authority Act, 1999, for which no registration certificate was necessary prior to such commencement, may continue to do so for a period of three months from such commencement or, if he had made an application for such registration within the said period of three months, till the disposal of such application:

Provided also that any certificate of registration, obtained immediately before the commencement of the Insurance Regulatory and Development Authority Act, 1999, shall be deemed to have been obtained from the Authority in accordance with the provisions of this Act.";

(*b*) in sub-section (2),

(*i*) in the opening portion, for "Every application for registration shall be accompanied by—", *substitute* the following:

"Every application for registration shall be made in such manner as may be determined by the regulations made by the Authority and shall be accompanied by—";

(*ii*) in clause (*d*), for "working capital", *substitute* "paid-up equity capital or working capital or working capital";

(*iii*) in clause (*f*), in the proviso, *omit* "and" occurring at the end;

(*iv*) for clause (g), *substitute* the following:

"(g) the receipt showing payment of fee as may be determined by the regulations which shall not exceed fifty thousand rupees for each class of business as may be specified by the regulations made by the Authority;

(*h*) such other documents as may be specified by the regulations made by the Authority;";

(*c*) after sub-section (2-A), *insert*—

"(2-AA) The Authority shall give preference to register the applicant and grant him a certificate of registration if such applicant agrees, in the form and manner as may be specified by the regulations made by the Authority, to carry on the life insurance business or general insurance business for providing health cover to individuals or group of individuals." ;

(*d*) in sub-section (4),—

(*i*) in clause (*f*), for "of any rule or order made thereunder, or" *substitute* the following: of any rule or any regulation or order made or, any direction issued thereunder, or;

(*ii*) in clause (*h*), *insert* "or" at the end;

(*iii*) after clause (*h*), *insert* the following:

"(*i*) if the insurer makes a default in complying with any direction issued or order made, as the case may be, by the Authority under the Insurance Regulatory and Development Authority Act, 1999, or

(*j*) if the insurer makes a default in complying with, or acts in contravention of, any requirement of the Companies Act, 1956 (1 or 1956) or the Life Insurance Corporation Act, 1956 (31 of 1956) or the General Insurance Business (Nationalisation) Act, 1972 (57 of 1972) or the Foreign Exchange Regulation Act, 1973 (46 of 1973),

(*e*) in sub-section (5-C),

(*i*) for "clause (*h*)", *substitute* "clause (*h*) or clause (*i*) or clause (*j*)";

(*ii*) for "any requirement of this Act or of any rule or order made thereunder" substitute the following

(*iii*) "any requirement of this Act or the Insurance Regulatory and Development Authority Act, 1999, or of any rule or any regulation, or any order made thereunder or any direction issued under those Acts";

(*f*) after sub-section (5-D), *insert* the following:

'(5-E) The Authority may, by order, suspend or cancel any registration in .such manner as may be determined by the regulations made by it:

Provided that no order under this sub-section shall be made unless the person concerned has been given a reasonable opportunity of being heard."

(*g*) for sub-section (7), *substitute* the following:

"(7) The authority may, on payment of such fee, not exceeding five thousand rupees, as may be determined by the regulations, issue a duplicate certificate of registration to replace a certificate lost, destroyed or mutilated, or in any other case where the Authority is of the opinion that the issue of duplicate certificate is necessary.".

8. Section 3-A,—

(*a*) in sub-section (1), for "the 31st day of December, 1941.", *substitute* the following:

"the 31st day of March, after the commencement of the Insurance Regulatory and Development Authority Act, 1999.";

(*b*) in sub-section (2),

(*i*) for "prescribed fee", *substitute* "fee as determined by the regulations made by the Authority";

(*ii*) for clause (*i*), *substitute* the following:

(*i*) exceed one-fourth of one per cent of such premium income or rupees five crores, whichever is less,";

(*iii*) for clause (*ii*), *substitute* the following:

"(*ii*) be less, in any case, then fifty thousand rupees for each class of insurance business:";

(*c*) in sub-section (3), for "prescribed fee", substitute "fee as determined by the regulations made by the Authority";

(*d*) in sub-section (4), for "prescribed fee", substitute "fee as determined by the regulations made by the Authority, and".

9. For Section 6, *substitute* the following:

"6. *Requirement as to capital*. No insurer carrying on the business of life insurance, general insurance or re-insurance in India on or after the commencement of the Insurance Regulatory and Development Authority Act, 1999, shall be registered unless he has,—

(*i*) a paid-up equity capital of rupees one hundred crores, in case of a person carrying on the business of life insurance or general insurance; or

(*ii*) a paid-up equity capital of rupees two hundred crores, in case of a person carrying on exclusively the business as are insurer:

Provided that in determining the paid-up equity capital specified under clause (*i*) or clause (*ii*), the deposit to be made under Section 7 and any preliminary expenses incurred in the formation and registration of the company shall be excluded:

Provided further that an insurer carrying on business of life insurance, general insurance or re-insurance in India before the commencement of the Insurance Regulatory and Development Authority Act, 1999 and who is required to be registered under this Act, shall have a paid-up equity capital in accordance with clause (*i*) and clause (*ii*), as the case may be, within six months of the commencement of that Act.".

10. Section 6-A,

(*a*) in sub-section (4), in clause (b),—

(I) in sub-clause (*i*), *omit* "and" occurring at the end;

(II) in sub-clause (*ii*), for "sanction of the Central Government has been obtained to the transfer.", *substitute* "approval of the Authority has been obtained to the transfer;";

(III) after sub-clause (*ii*), *insert* the following:

'(*iii*) where, the nominal value of the shares intended to be transferred by any individual, firm, group, constituents of a group, or body corporate under the same management, jointly or severally exceeds one per cent of the paid up equity capital of the insurer, unless the previous approval of the Authority has been obtained for the transfer.

Explanation. For the purposes of this sub-clause, the expressions "group" and "same management" shall have the same meanings respectively assigned to them in the Monopolies and Restrictive Trade Practices Act, 1969 (54 of 1969).';

(*b*) in sub-section (II),—

(*i*) for "Explanation 1", substitute "Explanation";

(*ii*) omit Explanation 2.

11. After Section 6-A, *insert* the following:

"6-AA. *Manner of divesting excess shareholding by promoter in certain cases.* 1. No promoter shall at any time hold more than twenty-six per cent or such other percentage as may be prescribed, of the paid-up equity capital in an Indian insurance company:

Provided that in a case where an Indian insurance company beings the business of life insurance, general insurance or re-insurance in which the promoters hold more than twenty-six per cent of the paid-up equity capital or such other excess percentage as may be prescribed, the promoters shall divest in a phased manner the share capital in excess of the twenty-six per cent of the paid-up equity capital or such excess paid-up equity capital as may be prescribed, after a period of ten years from the date of the commencement of the said business by such Indian insurance company or within such period as may be prescribed by the Central Government.

Explanation. For the removal of doubts, it is hereby declared that nothing contained in the proviso shall apply to the promoters being foreign company, referred to in sub-clause (*b*) of clause (7-A) of Section 2.

2. The manner and procedure for divesting the excess share capital under sub-section (1) shall be specified by the regulations made by the Authority.".

12. Section 7,—

(*a*) in sub-section (1),

(*i*) *omit* "not being an insurer specified in sub-clause (*c*) of clause (9) of Section 2";

(*ii*) for clauses (*a*) and (*b*), substitute the following:

"(*a*) in the case of life insurance business, a sum equivalent to one per cent of his total gross premium written in India in any financial year commencing after the 31 st day of March, 2000, not exceeding rupees ten crores;

(*b*) in the case of general insurance business, a sum equivalent to three per cent of his total gross premium written in India, in any financial year commencing after the 31 st day of March, 2000, not exceeding rupees ten crores;

(*c*) in the case of re-insurance business, a sum of rupees twenty crores:";

(*b*) *omit* sub-section (1-A), (I-B), (1-C), (1-D) and (1-E).

13. Section 11

(*a*) in sub-section (1), for "calendar year", *substitute* "financial year";

(*b*) after sub-section (1), *insert* the following:

"(I-A) Notwithstanding anything contained in sub-section (1), every insurer, on or after the commencement of the Insurance Regulatory and Development Authority Act, 1999, in respect of insurance business transacted by him and in respect of his shareholders' funds, shall, at the expiration of each financial year, prepare with reference to that year, a balance sheet, a profit and loss account, a separate account of receipts and payments, a revenue account in accordance with the regulations made by the Authority.

(I-B) Every insurer shall keep separate accounts relating to funds of shareholders and policyholders.".

14. Section 13,

(*a*) in sub-section (1),

(*i*) for "once at least in every three years", substitute "every year";

(*ii*) in the first proviso, for "not later than four years", substitute "not later than two years";

(*iii*) after the second proviso, *insert* the following:

"Provided also that for an insurer carrying on life insurance business in India immediately before the commencement of the Insurance Regulatory and Development Authority Act, 1999, the last date as at which the first investigation after such commencement should be caused by an actuary, shall be the 31st day of March, 2001:";

(*iv*) after the third proviso, *insert* the following:

"Provided also that every insurer on or after the commencement of the Insurance Regulatory and Development Authority Act, 1999, shall cause an abstract of the report of the actuary to be made in the manner specified by the regulations made by the Authority.";

(*b*) in sub-section (4), after the proviso, insert the following:

"Provided further that the statement referred to in sub-section (4) shall be appended in the form and in the manner specified by the regulations made by the Authority .".

15. After Section 27-B, *insert* the following:

"27-C. *Prohibition for investment of funds outside India.* No insurer shall directly or indirectly invest outside India the funds of the policyholders.

27-D. *Manner and conditions of investment.*

1. Without prejudice to anything contained in Sections 27, 27-A and 27-B, the Authority may, in the interests of the policy-holders, specify by the regulations made by it, the time, manner and other conditions of investment of assets to be held by an insurer for the purposes of this Act.
2. The Authority may give specific directions for the time, manner and other conditions subject to which the funds of policyholders shall be invested in the infrastructure and social sector as may be specified by regulations made by the Authority and such regulations shall apply uniformly to all the insurers carrying on the business of life insurance, general insurance, or re-insurance in India on or after the commencement of the insurance Regulatory and Development Authority Act, 1999.
3. The Authority may, after taking into account the nature of business and to protect the interests of the policy-holders, issue to an insurer the directions relating to the time, manner and other conditions of investment of assets to be held by him:

   Provided that no direction under this sub-section shall be issued unless the insurer concerned has been given a reasonable opportunity of being heard .".

16. Section 28-A, in sub-section (1), for "31st day of December", *substitute* "31st day of March".

17. Section 28-B, in sub-section (1), for "31st day of December". *substitute* "31st day of March".

18. Section 31-B,

(*a*) in sub-section (1), for ''Central Government" at both the places where they occur, substitute "Authority";

(*b*) in sub-section (2), for "a statement in the prescribed form", *substitute* "a statement, in the form specified by the regulations made by the Authority,";

(*c*) after sub-section (3), *insert* the following:

"(4) Every direction under this section shall be issued by an order made by the Authority:

Provided that no order under this section shall be made unless the person concerned has been given an opportunity of being heard .".

19. After Section 32-A, *insert* the following:

"32-B. *Insurance business in rural or social sector.* Every insurer shall, after the commencement of the Insurance Regulatory and Development Authority Act, 1999, undertake such percentages of life insurance business and general insurance business in the rural or social sector, as may be specified, in the Official Gazette by the Authority, in this behalf.

32-C. *Obligations of insurer in respect of rural or unorganised sector and backward classes.* Every insurer shall, after the commencement of the Insurance Regulatory and Development Authority Act, 1999, discharge the obligations specified under Section 32-B to provide life insurance or general insurance policies to the persons residing in the rural sector, workers in the unorganised or informal sector or for economically vulnerable or backward classes of the society and other categories of persons as may specified by regulations made by the Authority and such insurance policies shall include insurance for crops.".

20. For Section 33, *substitute* the following:

INVESTIGATION

33. *Power of investigation and inspection by Authority.*

1. The Authority may, at any time, by order in writing, direct any person (thereafter in this section referred to as "Investigating Authority") specified in the order to investigate the affairs of any insurer and to report to the Authority on any investigation made by such Investigating Authority:

   Provided that the Investigating Authority may, wherever necessary, employ any auditor or actuary or both for the purpose of assisting him in any investigation under this section.
2. Notwithstanding anything to the contrary contained in Section 235 of the Companies Act, 1956 (1 of 1956), the Investigating Authority may, at any time, and shall, on being directed so to do by the Authority, cause an inspection to be made by one or more of his officers of any insurer and his books of account; and the Investigating Authority shall supply to the insurer a Copy of his report on such inspection.
3. It shall be the duty of every manager, managing director or other officer of the insurer to produce before the Investigating Authority directed to make the investigation under sub-section (I), or inspection under sub-section (2), all such books of account, registers and other documents in his custody or power and to furnish him with any statement and information relating to the affairs of the insurer as the said Investigating Authority may require of him within such time as the said Investigating Authority may specify.
4. Any Investigating Authority, directed to make an investigation under sub-section (1), or inspection under sub-section (2), may examine on oath, any manager, managing director or other officer of the insurer in relation to his business and may administer oaths accordingly.
5. The Investigating Authority shall, if he has been directed by the Authority to cause an inspection to be made, and may, in any other case, report to the Authority on any inspection made under this section.
6. On receipt of any report under sub-section (1), or sub-section (5), the Authority may, after giving such opportunity to the insurer to make a representation in connection with the report as, in the opinion of the Authority, seems reasonable, by order in writing,

(*a*) require the insurer, to take such action in respect of any matter arising out of the report as the Authority may think fit; or

(*b*) cancel the registration of the insurer; or

(*c*) direct any person to apply to the court for the winding up of the insurer, if a company, whether the registration of the insurer has been cancelled under clause (*b*) or not.

7. The Authority may, after giving reasonable notice to the insurer, publish the report submitted by the Investigating Authority under sub-section (5) or such portion thereof as may appear to it to be necessary.

8. The Authority may by the regulations made by it specify the minimum information to be maintained by insurers in their books, the manner in which such information shall be maintained, the checks and other verifications to be adopted by insurers in that connection and all other matters incidental thereto as are in its opinion, necessary to enable the Investigating Authority to discharge satisfactorily his functions under this section.

Explanation. For the purposes of this section, the expression "insurer" shall include in the case of an insurer incorporated in India

(*a*) all its subsidiaries formed for the purpose of carrying on the business of insurance exclusively outside India; and

(*b*) all its branches whether situated in India or outside India.

9. No order made under this section other than an order made under (*b*) of sub-section clause (6) shall be capable of being called in question in any court.

10. All expenses of 'and incidental to any investigation made under this shall be defrayed by the insurer, shall have priority over that debts due from the insurer and shall be recoverable as an arrear of land revenue.'

21. Section 33-A, *omit* "Central Government or the".

22. Section 34-H,

(*a*) in sub-section (1),

(*i*) for "Controller", *substitute* "Chairperson of the Authority";

(*ii*) for "an Assistant Controller of Insurance", substitute "an officer thorised by the Authority";

(*b*) in sub-section 5. and 7. for "Controller" wherever it occurs, *substitute* "Chairperson of the Authority".

23. Section 35,

(*a*) sub-section (1) for "sanctioned by the Controller", *substitute* "approved by the Authority";

(*b*) in sub-section (3),

(*i*) in the first paragraph for "to sanction any such scheme", substitute "to approve any such scheme";

(*ii*) in the second paragraph, for "the amalgamation or transfer if sanctioned", substitute "the amalgamation or transfer if approved".

24. Section 36,

(*a*) in sub-section (1) for "may sanction the arrangement", *substitute* "may approve the arrangement";

(*b*) in sub-section (2),

(*i*) for "the insurers concerned in the amalgamation, the Controller may sanction", *substitute* "the insurers concerned in the amalgamation, the Authority may approve";

(*ii*) for "contracts as sanctioned by the Controller", *substitute* "contracts as approved by the Authority".

25. Section 37, in clause (c), for "scheme sanctioned", *substitute* "scheme approved".

26. In Section 40-A, in sub-section (3), for the portion beginning with the words "an amount exceeding" and ending with the words "ten per cent of the premium payable on the policy", substitute "an amount not exceeding fifteen per cent of the premium payable on the policy where the policy relates to fire or marine insurance or miscellaneous insurance."

27. Section 42,

(*a*) for sub-section (1), *substitute* the following :-

"(1) The Authority or an officer authorised by it in this behalf shall, in the manner determined by the regulations made by it and on payment of the fee determined by the regulations, which shall not be more than two hundred and fifty rupees, issue to any person making an application in the manner determined by the regulations, a licence to act as an insurance agent for the purpose of soliciting or procuring insurance business:

Provided that,

(*i*) in the case of an individual, he does not suffer from any of the disqualifications mentioned in sub-section (4); and

(*ii*) in the case of a company or firm, any of its directors or partners does not suffer from any of the said disqualifications:

Provided further that any licence issued immediately before the commencement of the Insurance Regulatory and Development Authority Act, 1999 shall be deemed to have been issued in accordance with the regulations which provide for such licence.";

(*b*) for sub-section (3), *substitute* the following:

"(3) A licence issued under this section, after the date of the commencement of the Insurance Regulatory and Development Authority Act, 1999, shall remain in force for a period of three years only from the date of issue, but shall, if the applicant, being an individual does not, or being a company or firm any of its directors or partners does not, suffer from any of the disqualifications mentioned in clauses (*b*), (*c*), (*d*), (*e*) and (*f*) of sub-section (4) and the application of renewal of licence reaches the issuing authority at least thirty days before the date on which the licence ceases to remain in force be renewed for a period of three years at anyone time on payment of the fee determined by the regulations made by the Authority which shall not be more than rupees two hundred and fifty, and additional fee of an amount determined by the regulations not exceeding rupees one hundred by way of penalty, if the application for renewal to the licence does not reach the issuing authority at least thirty days before the date on which the licence ceases to remain in force.";

(*c*) in sub-section (3-A), for the proviso, *substitute* the following:

"Provided that the Authority may, if satisfied that undue hardship would be caused otherwise, accept any application in contravention of this sub-section on payment by the applicant of a penalty of seven hundred and fifty rupees.";

(*d*) in sub-section (4), after clause (*d*), insert the following:

"(*e*) that he does not possess the requisite qualifications and practical training for a period not exceeding twelve months, as may be specified by the regulations made by the Authority in this behalf;

(*f*) that he has not passed such examination as may be specified by the regulations made by the Authority in this behalf:

Provided that a person who had been issued a licence under sub-section (1) of this section or sub-section (1) of Section 64-UM shall not be required to possess the requisite qualifications, practical training and pass such examination as required by clauses (*e*) and (*f*);

(*g*) that he violates the code of conduct as may be specified by the regulations made by the Authority":

(*e*) for sub-section (6), *substitute* the following:

"(6) The Authority may issue a duplicate licence to replace a licence lost, destroyed or mutilated, on payment of such fee not exceeding fifty rupees as may be determined by regulations.";

(*f*) in sub-section (7),

(*i*) for "fifty rupees", *substitute* "five hundred rupees";

(*ii*) for "one hundred rupees", *substitute* "one thousand rupees";

(*g*) in sub-section (8), for "fifty rupees", substitute "five thousand rupees".

28. Section 42-A, in sub-section (1)

(*a*) for "Controller or an officer authorised by him", *substitute* "Authority or an officer authorised by it";

(*b*) for "an application to him", *substitute* "an application to it".

29. After Section 42-C, insert the following:

"42-D. *Issue of licence to intermediary or insurance intermediary.* (1) The Authority or an officer authorised by it in this behalf shall, in the manner determined by the regulations made by the Authority, and on payment of the fees determined by the regulations made by the Authority, issue to any person making an application in the manner determined by the regulations, and not suffering from any of the disqualifications herein mentioned, a licence to act as an intermediary or an insurance intermediary under this Act:

Provided that,

(*a*) in the case of an individual, he does not suffer from any of the disqualifications mentioned in sub-section (4) of Section 42, or

(*b*) in the case of a company or firm, any of its directors or partners does not suffer from any of the said disqualifications.

2. A licence issued under this section shall entitle the holder thereof to act as an intermediary or insurance intermediary.

3. A licence issued under this section shall remain of force for a period of three years only from the date of issue, but shall, if the applicant, being an individual does not, or being a company or firm any of its directors or partners does not suffer from any of the disqualifications mentioned in clauses (*b*), (*c*), (*d*), (*e*) and (*f*) of sub-section (4) of Section 42 and the application for renewal of licence reaches the issuing authority at least thirty days before the date on which the licence ceases to remain in force, be renewed for a period of three years at anyone time on payment of the fee, determined by the regulations made by the Authority and additional fee for an amount determined by the regulations, not exceeding one hundred rupees by way of penalty, if the application for renewal of the licence does not reach the issuing authority at least thirty days before the date on which the licence ceases to remain in force.

4. No application for the renewal of a licence under this section shall be entertained if the application does not reach the issuing authority before the licence ceases to remain in force:

Provided that the Authority may, if satisfied that undue hardship would be caused otherwise, accept any application in contravention of this sub-section on payment by the applicant of a penalty of seven hundred and fifty rupees.

5. The disqualifications above referred to shall be the following:

(*a*) that the person is a minor;

(*b*) that he is found to be of unsound mind by a court of competent jurisdiction;

(*c*) that he has been found guilty of criminaless appropriation or criminal breach of trust or cheating or forgery or an abetment of or attempt to commit any such offence by a court of competent jurisdiction:

Provided that, where at least five years have elapsed since the completion of the sentence imposed do any person in respect of any such offence, the Authority shall ordinarily declare in respect of such person that his conviction shall cease to operate as a disqualification under this clause;

(*d*) that in the course of any judicial proceeding relating to any policy of insurance of the winding up of an insurance company or in the course of an investigation of the affairs of an insurer it has been found that he has been guilty of or has knowingly participated in or connived at any fraud dishonestly or misrepresentation against an Insurer or an insured;

(*e*) that he does not possess the requisite qualifications and practical training for a period not exceeding twelve months, as may be specified by the regulations made by the Authority in this behalf;

(*f*) that he has not passed such examinations as may be specified by the regulations made by the Authority in this behalf;

(*g*) that he violates the code of conduct as may be specified by the regulations made by the Authority.

6. If it be found that an intermediary or an insurance intermediary suffers from any of the foregoing disqualifications, without prejudice to any other penalty to which be may be liable, the Authority shall, and if the intermediary or an insurance intermediary has knowingly contravened any provision of this Act may cancel the licence issued to the intermediary or insurance intermediary under this section.

7. The Authority may issue a duplicate licence to replace a licence lost, destroyed or mutilated, on payment of such fee, as may be determined by the regulations made by the Authority.

8. Any person who acts as an intermediary or an insurance intermediary without holding a licence issued under this section to act as such, shall be punishable with fine, and my insurer or any person not licensed to act as such or transacts any insurance business in India through any such person, shall be punishable with fine.

9. Where the person contravening sub-section 8 is a company or a firm, then without prejudice to any other proceedings which may be taken against the company or firm, every director, manager, secretary or other officer of the company, and every partner of the firm who is knowingly a party to such contravention shall be punishable with fine.".

30. Section 64-UA, in sub-section (1), in sub-clause (*a*), for "Controller of Insurance", *substitute* "Chairperson of the *Authority*".

31. Section 64-UB

(*a*) for sub-section (1) *substitute* the following:

"(1) The Authority may, by notification in the Official Gazette, make regulations to carry out the purposes of this part.";

(*b*) in sub-section (2), for "*rules*", *substitute* "regulations";

(*c*) in sub-section (3), for "Central Government" at both the places where it occur, *substitute* "Authority';

(*d*) in sub-section (5), for "Controller of Insurance", *substitute* "Chairperson of the Authority".

32. Section. 64-UC, in sub-section (1), in proviso, for "the Controller may, with the previous approval of the Central Government", *substitute* "the Authority may".

33. Section 64-UD, after sub-section (1), *insert* the following:

"Provided that the Chairperson of the Authority shall become the Chairman of the Advisory Committee with effect from the commencement of the Insurance Regulatory and Development Authority Act, 1999 and function as such, and any Chairman of the Tariff Committee holding office immediately before such commencement shall cease to be the Chairman."

34. Section 64-UJ, in sub-section (5), for "Central Government", wherever it occurs, *substitute* "Authority".

35. Section 64-UM

(*a*) in sub-section (1),

(*i*) in paragraph (B), after "the Insurance (Amendment) Act, 1968", *insert* "but before the commencement of the Insurance Regulatory and Development Authority Act, 1999";

(*ii*) after paragraph (B), insert the following:

"(B-A) Every person who intends to act as a surveyor or loss assessor after the expiry of a period of one year from the commencement of the Insurance Regulatory and Development Authority Act, 1999, shall make an application to the Authority within such time, in such manner and on payment of such fee as may be determined by the regulations made by the Authority:

Provided that any licence issued immediately before the commencement of the Insurance Regulatory and Development Authority Act, 1999 shall be deemed to have been issued in accordance with the regulations providing for such licence.";

(*iii*) in paragraph (C), for "as may be prescribed", *substitute* "as may be determined by the regulations";

(*iv*) in paragraph (D), in clause (*i*),

(A) for item (*a*), *substitute* the following:

"(*a*) has been in practice as a surveyor or loss assessor on the date of commencement of the Insurance Regulatory and Development Authority Act, 1999, or";

(B) in item (*f*), for "prescribed", *substitute* "specified by the regulations made by the Authority";

(*b*) after sub-section (l), *insert*

"(I-A) Every surveyor and loss assessor shall comply with the code of conduct in respect of their duties, responsibilities and other professional requirements as may be specified by the regulations made by the Authority:".

36. Section 64-V,

(*a*) in sub-section (1),

(*i*) in clause (*i*), after sub-clause (*g*), insert the following:

"(*h*) such other asset or assets as may be specified by the regulations made in this behalf;";

(*ii*) in clause (*ii*),

(A) in sub-clause (*b*), in items (*i*) and (*ii*), for "40 per cent", *substitute* "50 per cent";

(B) after sub-clause (*t*), insert the following:

"(*g*) such other liability which may be made in this behalf to be included for the purpose of clause (*ii*).";

(*b*) for sub-section (2), *substitute* the following:

2. Every insurer shall furnish to the Authority with his returns under Section 15 or Section 16, as the case may be, a statement certified by an auditor approved by the Authority in respect of general insurance business, or an actuary approved by the Authority in respect of life insurance business, as the case may be, of his assets and liabilities assessed in the manner required by this section as on the 31st day of March of the preceding year.

3. Every insurer shall value his assets and liabilities in the manner required by this section and in accordance with the regulations which may be made by the Authority in this behalf.".

37. Section 64-VA,

(*a*) in sub-section (1), for "at all times", *substitute* "at all times before the commencement of the Insurance Regulatory and Development Authority Act, 1999";

(*b*) after sub-section (1), *insert* the following:

'(I-A) Every insurer shall, at all times, on or after the commencement of the Insurance Regulatory and Development Authority Act, 1999, maintain an excess of the value of his assets over the amount of his liabilities of not less than the amount arrived at as follows (hereinafter referred to in this section referred to as the "required solvency margin"), namely:

(*i*) in the case of an insurer carrying on life insurance business, the required solvency margin shall be the higher of the following amounts

(*a*) fifty crores of rupees (one hundred crores of rupees in case of re-insurers); or

(*b*) the aggregate sums of the results arrived at in items (I) and (II) stated below:

(I) the aggregate of the results arrived at by applying the calculation described in item (A) below (Step I) and the calculation described in item (B) below (Step II):

(A) for Step 1

(A.1) there shall be taken, a sum equal to a percentage determined by the regulations not exceeding five per cent of the mathematical reserves for direct business and reinsurance acceptances without any deduction for re-insurance cessions;

(A.2) the amount of mathematical reserves at the end of the preceding financial year after the deduction of reinsurance cessions shall be expressed as a percentage of the amount of those mathematical reserves before any such deduction; and

(A.3) the sum mentioned in item (A.1) above shall be multiplied;

(A.3.l) where the percentage arrived at under item (A.2) above is greater then eighty-five per cent (or in the case of a reinsurer carrying on exclusive re-insurance business, fifty per cent), by that greater percentage; and

(A.3.2) in any other case, by eighty-five per cent (or in the case of a re-insurer carrying on exclusive reinsurance business, by fifty per cent);

(B) for Step II

(B. 1) there shall be taken, a sum equal to a percentage determined by the regulations made by the Authority not exceeding one per cent of the sum at risk for the policies on which the sum at risk is not a negative figure, and

(B.2) the amount of sum at risk at the end of the preceding financial year for policies on which the sum at risk is not a negative figure after the deduction of reinsurance cession shall be expressed as a percentage of the amount of that sum at risk before any such deduction, and

(B.3) the sum arrived at under item (B.I) above shall be multiplied

(B.3.1) where the percentage arrived at under item (B.2) above is greater than fifty Per cent, by that greater percentage; and

(B.3.2) in any other case, by fifty per cent.

(II) a percentage determined by the regulations made by the Authority of the value of assets determined in accordance with the provisions of Section 64- V;

(*ii*) in the case of an insurer carrying on general insurance business, the required solvency margin, shall be the highest of the following amounts:

(*a*) fifty crores of rupees (one hundred crores of rupees in case of reinsurer); or

(*b*) a sum equivalent to twenty per cent of net premium income; or

(*c*) a sum equivalent to thirty per cent of net incurred claims, subject to credit for re-insurance in computing net premiums and net incurred claims being actual but a percentage, determined by the regulation, not exceeding fifty per cent:

Provided that if in respect of any insurer, the Authority is satisfied that either by reason of an unfavourable claim experience or because of sharp increase in the volume of the business, or for any other reason, compliance with the provisions of this sub-section would cause undue hardship to the insurer, the Authority may direct, for such period and subject to such conditions, such solvency margin not being less than the lower of the amount mentioned in sub-clause (*i*) or sub-clause (*ii*) above, as the case may be.

Explanation. For the purposes of this sub-section, the expressions

(*i*) "mathematical reserves" means the provision made by an insurer to cover liabilities (excluding liabilities which have fallen due and liabilities arising from deposit back arrangement in relation to any policy whereby an amount is deposited by re-insurer with the cedant) arising under or in connection with the policies or contracts for life insurance business. Mathematical reserves also include specific provision for adverse deviations of the bases, such as mortality and morbidity rates, interest rates, and expense rates, and any explicit provisions made, in the valuation of liabilities, in accordance with the regulations made by the Authority for this purpose;

(*ii*) "net incurred claims" means the average of the net incurred claims during the specified period of not exceeding three preceding financial years;

(*iii*) "sum at risk", in relation to a life insurance policy, means a sum which is

(*a*) in any case in which an amount is payable in consequence of death other than a case falling within sub-clause (*b*) below, the amount payable on death, and

(*b*) in any case in which the benefit under the policy in question consists of the making, in consequence of death, of the payments of annuity, payment of a sum by installments or any other kind of periodic payments, the present value of that benefit, less in either case the mathematical reserve in respect of the relevant policies.";

(*c*) after sub-section (2), *insert* the following:

"(2-A) If, at any time an insurer does not maintain the required solvency margin in accordance with the provisions of this section, he shall, in accordance with the directions issued by the Authority, submit a financial plan, indicating a plan of action to correct the deficiency to the Authority within a specified period not exceeding three months.

(2-B) An insurer who has submitted a plan under sub-section (2-A) to the Authority shall propose modifications to the plan if the Authority considers it inadequate, and shall give effect to any plan accepted by the Authority as adequate.

(2-C) An insurer who does not comply with the provisions of sub-section (2-A) shall be deemed to be insolvent and may be wound up by the court.";

(*d*) after sub-section (6), *insert* the following:

7. Every insurer shall furnish to the Authority his returns under Section 15 or Section 16, as the case may be, in case of life insurance business a statement certified by an actuary approved by the Authority, and in case of general insurance business a statement certified by an auditor approved by the Authority, of the required solvency margin maintained by the insurer in the manner required by sub-section (I-A).".

38. Section 70, in sub-section (1), for "the Controller a certificate of registration", *substitute* "the Authority, before the date of commencement of the Insurance Regulatory and Development Authority Act, 1999, a certificate of registration" .

39. Section 95, in sub-section (1), for "In this Part-", *substitute*, "In this Part, before the date of commencement of the Insurance Regulatory and Development Authority Act, 1999."

40. Section 101-A,

(*a*) in sub-section (1), for "the Central Government", substitute "the Authority, with the previous approval of the Central Government,";

(*b*) in sub-section (2), for "the Central Government", substitute "the Authority".

41. Section 101-B,

(*a*) in sub-section (1), for "the Central Government", *substitute* "the Authority with the previous approval of the Central Government.';

(*b*) in sub-section (2), for "prescribed"; substitute "determined by the regulations made by the Authority".

42. For Sections 102 to 105, *substitute* the following:

102. *Penalty for default in complying with, or act in contravention of, this Act.* If any person, who is required under this Act, or rules or regulations made thereunder,

(*a*) to furnish any document, statement, account, return or report to the Authority, fails to furnish the same; or

(*b*) to comply with the directions, fails to comply with such directions;

(*c*) to maintain solvency margin, fails to maintain such solvency margin;

(*d*) to comply with the directions on the insurance treaties, fails to comply with such directions on the insurance treaties, he shall be liable to a penalty not exceeding five lakh rupees for each such failure and punishable with fine.

103. *Penalty for carrying on insurance business in contravention of Sections* 3, 7 and 98. If a person makes a statement, or furnishes any document, statement, account, return or report which is false and which he either knows or believes to be false or does not belief to be true,

(*a*) he shall be liable to a penalty not exceeding five lakh rupees for each such failure; and

(*b*) he shall be punishable with imprisonment which may extend to three years or with fine for each such failure.

104. *Penalty for false statement in document.* If a person falls to comply with the provisions of Section 27 or Section 27-A or Section 27-B or Section 27-C or Section 27-D, he shall be liable to a penalty not exceeding five lakh rupees for each such failure.

105. *Wrongfully obtaining or withholding property.* If any director, managing director, manager or other officer or employee of an insurer wrongfully obtains possession of any property or wrongfully applies to any purpose of the Act, he shall be liable to a penalty not exceeding two lakh rupees for each such failure.

105-A. *Offences by companies.* (l) Where any offence under this Act has been committed by a company, every person who, at the time the offence was committed, was in charge of, and was responsible to, the company for the conduct of the business of the company as well as the company shall be deemed to be guilty of the offence and shall liable to be proceeded against and punished accordingly:

Provided that nothing contained in this sub-section shall render any such person liable to any punishment, if he proves that the offence was committed without his knowledge or that he had exercised all due diligence to prevent the commission of such offence.

2. Notwithstanding anything contained in sub-section (1) where any offence under this Act has been committed by a company and it is proved that the offence has been committed with the consent or connivance of, or is attributable to any neglect on the part of, any director, manager, secretary or other officer of the company, such director, manager, secretary or other officer shall be deemed to be guilty of that offence and shall be liable to be proceeded against and punished accordingly.

Explanation. For the purposes of this Section,

(*a*) "company". means any body corporate, and includes

(*i*) a firm; and

(*ii*) association of persons or a body of individuals whether incorporated or not; and

(*b*) "director", in relation to

(*i*) a firm, means a partner in the firm;

(*ii*) an association of persons or a body of individuals, means any member controlling the affairs thereof.

105-B. *Penalty for failure to comply with Section-32-B.* If an insurer fails to comply with the provisions of Section 32-B, he shall be liable to a penalty not exceeding five lakh rupees for each such failure and shall be punishable with imprisonment which may extend to three years or with fine for each such failure.

105-C. *Penalty for failure to comply with Section 32-G.* If an insurer fails to comply with the provisions of Section 32-C, he shall be liable to a penalty not exceeding twenty-five lakh rupees for each such failure and in the case of subsequent and continuing failure, the registration granted to such insurer under Section 3 shall be cancelled by the Authority.".

43. In Sections 110-A, 110-B and 110-C, for "Controller" wherever it occurs, *substitute* "Chairperson of the Authority".

44. In Sections 110-G, for "Controller" at both the places where it occurs, *substitute* "Chairperson of the Authority".

45. Section 100-H, in sub-section (l), for "under sections", *substitute* "under sections 27-D.".

46. Section 114, in sub-section (2).

(*a*) after clause (*a*), *insert* the following:

"(aa) such other percentage of paid-up equity capital in excess of twenty-six per cent of the paid-up equity capital and the period within which such excess paid-up equity capital shall be divested under sub-section (1) of Section 6-AA.";

(*b*) omit clauses (*g*) and (II).

47. After Section 114, *insert* the following:

114-A. *Power of Authority to make regulations.* (l) Authority may, by notification in the Official Gazette, make regulations consistent with this Act and the rules made thereunder, to carry out the purposes of this Act.

2. In particular, and without prejudice to the generality of the foregoing power, such regulations may provide for all or any of the following matters, namely:—

(*a*) the matters including fee relating to the registration of insurers under Section 3;

(*b*) the manner of suspension or cancellation of registration under sub-section (5-E) of Section 3;

(*c*) such fee, not exceeding five thousand rupees, as may be determined by the regulations for issue of a duplicate certificate of registration under sub-section (7) of Section 3;

(*d*) the matters relating to the renewal of registration and fee therefor under Section 3-A;

(*e*) the manner and procedure for divesting excess share capital under sub-section (2) of Section 6-AA;

(*f*) the preparation of balance sheet, profit and loss account and a separate account of receipts and payments and revenue account under sub-section (1-A) of Section 11;

(*g*) the manner in which an abstract of the report of the actuary to be specified under the fourth proviso to sub-section (1) of Section 13;

(*h*) the form and manner in which the statement referred to in subsection (4) of Section 13 shall be appended;

(*i*) the time, manner and other conditions of investment of assets held by an insurer under sub-section (1), (2) and (3) of Section 27-D;

(*j*) the minimum information to be maintained by insurer in their books the manner in which such information should be maintained, the checks and other verifications to be adopted by insurers in that connection and all other matters incidental thereto under sub-section (8) of Section 33;

(*k*) the manner for making an application, the manner and the fee for issue of a licenec to, act as an insurance agent under sub-section (1) of Section 42;

(*l*) the fee and the additional fee to be determined for renewal of licence of insurance agent under sub-section (3) of Section 42;

(*m*) the requisite qualifications and practical training to act as an insurance agent under clause (*e*) of sub-section (4) of Section 42;

(*n*) the passing of examination to act as an insurance agent under clause (f) of sub-section (4) of Section 42;

(*o*) the code of conduct under Clause (*g*) of sub-section (4) of Section 42;

(*p*) the fee not exceeding rupees fifty for issue of duplicate licence under sub-section (6) of Section 42;

(*q*) the manner and the fees for issue of a licence to an intermediary or an insurance intermediary under sub-section (1) of Section 42-D;

(*r*) the fee and the additional fee to be determined for renewal of licence of intermediaries or insurance intermediaries under subsection (3) of Section 42-D;

(*s*) the requisite qualifications and practical training of intermediaries or insurance intermediaries under clause (*e*) of sub-section (5) of Section 42-D;

(*t*) the examination to be passed to act as an intermediary or insurance intermediary under clause (*f*) of sub-section (5) of Section 42-D;

(*u*) the code of conduct under clause(*g*) of sub-section (5) of Section 42-D;

(*v*) the fee for issue of duplicate licence under sub-section (7) of Section 42-D;

(*w*) such matters as specified under sub-section (2) of Section 64-UB relating to the Tariff Advisory Committee;

(*x*) the matters relating to licensing of surveyors and loss assessors, their duties, responsibilities and other professional requirements under Section 64-UM;

(*y*) such other asset or assets as may be specified under clause (*h*) of sub-section (1) of Section 64-V for the purposes of ascertaining sufficiency of assets under Section 64-V A;

(*z*) the valuation of assets and liabilities under sub-section (3) of Section 64-V;

(*za*) the matters specified under sub-section (1-A) of Section 64-VA relating to sufficiency of assets;

(*zb*) the matters relating to re-insurance under Sections 101-A and 101-B;

(*zc*) the matters relating to redressal of grievances of policy-holders to protect their interest and to regulate, promote and ensure orderly growth of insurance industry; and

(*zd*) any other matter which is to be, or may be, specified by the regulations made of the Authority or in respect of which provision is to be made or may be made by the regulations.

3. Every regulation made under this Act shall be laid, as soon as may be after it is made, before each House of Parliament, while it is in session, for a total period of thirty days which may be comprised in one session or in two or more successive sessions, and if, before the expiry of the session immediately following the session or the successive sessions aforesaid, both Houses agree in making any modification in the regulation or both Houses agree that the regulation should not be made, the regulation shall thereafter, have effect only in such modified form or be of no effect, as the case may be; so, however, that any such modification or annulment shall be without prejudice to the validity of anything previously done under that regulation."

48. Section I 16-A, for "Central Government", at both places where they occur, *substitute* "Central Government, before the date of commencement of the Insurance Regulatory and Development Authority Act, 1999".

The Second Schedule

(*See Section 31*)

Amendments to the Life Insurance Corporation Act, 1956 (31 of 1956)

1. In the Act, for "Controller" wherever it occurs, *substitute* "Authority".
2. After Section 30, insert the following:—

"30-A. *Exclusive privilege of Corporation to cease*—Notwithstanding anything contained in this Act, the exclusive privilege of carrying on life insurance business in India by the Corporation shall cease on and from the commencement of the Insurance Regulatory and Development Authority Act, 1999 and the Corporation shall, thereafter, carry on life insurance business in India in accordance with the provisions of the Insurance Act, 1938 (4 of 1938).".

The Third Schedule

(*See Section 32*)

Amendment to the General Insurance Business (Nationalisation) Act, 1972 (57 of 1972)

After Section 24, *insert* the following:—

"24-A. *Exclusive privilege of Corporation and acquiring companies to cease.*—Notwithstanding anything contained in this Act, the exclusive privilege of the Corporation and the acquiring companies of carrying on general insurance business in India shall cease on and from the commencement of the Insurance Regulatory and Development Authority Act, 1999 and the Corporation and the acquiring companies shall, thereafter, carry on general insurance business in India in accordance with the provisions of the Insurance Act, 1938 (4 of 1938)."

Insurance Regulatory and Development Authority (obligations of insurers to rural or social sectors) Regulations, 2000.

(In exercise of the powers conferred by section 32C read with section 32B of the Insurance Act, 1938 (4 of 1938), the Authority in consultation with the Insurance Advisory Committee, hereby, markes the following regulation, namely:—

Short title and Commencement

1. 1. These regulations may be called the Insurance Regulatory and Development Authority (obligation of Insurers to Rural or Social Sectors) Regulations, 2000.

   2. They shall come into force from the date of their publications in the official gazette.

Definitions:

2. In these regulations, unless the context otherwise requires:

   (*a*) "Act" means the Insurance Act, 1938 (4 of 1938);

   (*b*) "Authority" means the Insurance Regulatory and Development Authority Act, 1999 (41 of 1999),

   (*c*) Rural Sector shall mean any place as per the latest census which has—

   (*i*) a population of not more than five thousand

   (*ii*) a density of population of not more than four hundred per square kilometer, and

   (*iii*) at least seventy five per cent of the male working population is engaged in agriculture.

   (*d*) "Social Sector" includes unorganised sector, informal sector, economically vulnerable or backward classes and other categories of persons, both in rural and urban areas.

   (*e*) "unorganised sector" includes self employed workers such as agricultural labourers, bill wokers, brick kiln workers, carpenters, cobblers, construction workers, fisherman, hamals, handicraft, artisans, handloom and khadi workers, lady tailors, leather and tannery workers, papad makers, powerloom workers, physically handicapped self employed persons, primary milk producers rickshaw puller, safai karmacharis, salt growers, sericulture workers, sugarcane cutters, tendu leaf colectors, toddy tappers, vegetable vendors, washer women, workilg women in hills, or such other categories of persons.

   (*f*) "economically vulnerable or backward classes" means persons who live below the poverty line.

   (*g*) "other categories of persons" includes person with disability as defined in the persons with Disabilities (equal opportunities protection of Right and full Participation) Act, 1995 ,and who may not be gainfully employed and also includes guardians who need insurance to protect spastic persons or persons with disability.

   (*h*) All words and expressions used herein and not defined herein but defined in the Insurance Act, 1938 (4 of 1938) or in the Insurance Regulatory and Development Authority Act, 1999 (41 of 1999) shall have the meanings respectively assigned them in those Acts.

Obligations:

3. Every insurer who begins to carryon insurance business after the commencement of Insurance Regulatory and Development Authority Act, 1999 (41 of 1999), shall for the purposes of Section 32B and 32C of the Act, ensure that he undertakes the following obligations, during the first five financial years, pertaining to the persons in—

   (*a*) Rural Sector

   (*i*) in respect of a life insurer:

   (I) five per cent in the first financial year;

(II) seven per cent in the second financial year;

(III) ten per cent in the third financial year;

(IV) twelve per cent in the fourth financial year;

(V) fifteen per cent in the fifth year;

of total policies, written direct in that year;

(*ii*) in respect of a general insurer:

(I) two per cent in the first financial year;

(II) three per cent in the second financial year;

(III) five per cent thereafter;

of total gross premium income written direct in that year;

(*b*) Social sector, in respect of all insurers;

(I) five thousand lives in the first financial year;

(II) seven thousand five hundred lives in the second financial year;

(III) ten thousand lives in the third financial year;

(IV) fifteen thousand lives in the fourth financial year;

(V) twenty thousand lives in the fifth year.

Provided that in the first financial year where the period of operation is less than twelve months, proportionate percentage or number of lives as the case may be, shall be undertaken.

Provided further that in case of a general insurers, the obligations specified shall include insurance for crops.

Provided further that the Authority may normally, once in every five years, prescribe or revise the obligations as specified in Regulations 3.

Obligations of Existing Insurers

4. 1. The obligations of existing insurers as on the date of commencement of IRDA Act shall be decided by the Authority after consultation with them and the quantum of insurance business to be done shall not be less than what has been recorded by them for the accounting year ended 31st Marct 2000.

2. The Authority shall review such quantum of insurance business periodically and give directions to the insurers for achieving the specified targets.

INSURANCE REGULATORY AND DEVELOPMENT AUTHORITY (OBLIGATIONS OF INSURERS TO RURAL OR SOCIAL SECTORS) REGULATIONS, 2000

In exercise of the powers conferred by section 32C, read with section 32B of the Insurance Act, 1938 (4 of 1938) the Authority, in consultation with the Insurance Advisory Committee, hereby makes the following regulations, namely:—

Short title and commencement

1. 1. These regulations may be called the Insurance Regulatory and Development Authority (Obligations of Insurers to Rural or Social Sectors) Regulations, 2000.

2. They shall come into force from the date of their publication in the Official Gazette.

Definitions

2. In these regulations, unless the context otherwise requires.

Gazette No. 102, Extra ordinary dated 19-7-2000.

(*a*) "Act" means the Insurance Act, 1938 (4 of 1938);

(*b*) "Authority" means the Insurance Regulatory and Development Authority established under the provisions of section 3 of the Insurance Regulatory and Development Authority Act, 1999 (41 of 1999);

(*c*) "Rural sector" shall mean any place as per the latest census which has:—

(*i*) a population of not more than five thousand;

(*ii*) a density of populatin of not more than four hundred per square kilometer; and

(*iii*) at least seventy-five per cent of the male working population is engaged in agriculture.

(*d*) "Social sector" includes unorganised sector, informal sector, economically vulnerable or backward classes and other categories of persons, both in rural and urban areas;

(*e*) "Unorganised sector" includes self-employed workers such as agricultutral labourers, bidi workers, brick kiln workers, carpenters, cobblers, construction workers, fishermen, hamals, handicraft artisans, handloom and khadi workers, physically handicapped selfemployed persons, primary milk producers, rickshaw pullers, safaikarmacharis, salt growers, seri-culture workers, sugarcane cutters, tendu leaf collectors, toddy tappets, vegetable vendors, washerwomen, working women in hills, or such other categories of persons:

(*f*) "economically vulnerable or backward classes" means persons who live below the poverty line;

(*g*) "other categories of person" includes persons with disability as defined in the Persons with Disabilities (Equal Opportunities, Protection of Rights and Full Participation) Act, 1995 and who may not be gainfully employed; and also includes guardians who need insurance to protect spastic persons or person with disabifity;

(*h*) All words and expressions used herein and not defined herein but defined in the Insurance Act, 1938 (4 of 1938), or in the Insurance Regulatory and Development Authority Act, 1999 (41 of 1999), shall have the meanings respectively assigned to them in those Acts.

Obligations.

3. Every insurer, who begins to carry on insurance business after the commencement of the Insurance Regulatory and Development Authority Act, 1999 (41 of 1999), shall, for the purposes of section 32B and 32C of the Act, insure that he undertakes the following obligations, during the first five financial years, pertaining to the persons in.

(*a*) Rural sector,

(*i*) in respect of a life insurer,

(I) five per cent in the first financial year;

(II) seven per cent in the second financial year;

(III) ten percent in the third financial year;

(IV) twelve percent in the fourth financial year;

(V) fifteen percent in the fifth year;

of total policles written direct in that year;

(*ii*) in respect of a general insurer;

(I) two per cent in the first financial year;

(II) three per cent in the second financial year;

(III) five per cent thereafter,

of total gross premium income written direct in that year.

(*b*) social sector, in respect of all insurers,

(I) five thousand Fives in the first financial year;

(II) seven thousand five hundred lives in the second financial year;

(III) ten thousand lives in the third financial year;

(IV) fifteen thousand lives in the fourth financial year;

(V) twenty thousand lives in the fifth year;

Provided that in the first financial year, where the period of operation is less than twelve months, proportionate percentage or number of lives, as the case may be, shall be undertaken, Provided further that, in case of a general insurer, the obligations specified shall include insurance for crops.

Provided further that the Authority may normally, once in every five years, prescribe or revise the obligations as specified in Regulation 3.

Obligations of existing insurers

4. 1. The obligations of existing insurers as on the date of commencement of IRDA Act shall be decided by the Authority after consultation with them and the quantum of insurance business to be done shall not be less than what has been recorded by them for the accounting year ended 31st March, 2000.

2. The Authority shall review such quantum of insurance business periodically and give directions to the insurers for achieving the specified targets.

INSURANCE REGULATORY AND DEVELOPMENT AUTHORITY (INSURANCE ADVERTISEMENTS AND DISCLOSURE) REGULATIONS, 2000

In exercise of the powers conferred by section 26 of the Insurance Regulatory and Development Authority Act, 1999 (41 of 1999), the Authority in consultation with the Insurance Advisory Comittee. hereby makes the following regulations, namely:—

1. Short title and commencement.

1. These regulations may be called the Insurance Regulatory and Development Atithority (Insurance Advertisements and Disclosure) Regulations, 2000.

2. Definitions. Unless the context otherwise requires:

(*a*) "Authority" means the Insurance Regulatory and Development Authority established under sub-section (1) of section 3 of the Insurance Regulatory and Development Authority Act, 1999 (41 of 1999);

(*b*) "Insurance advertisement" means and includes any communication directly or indirectly related to a policy and intended to result in the eventual sale or solicitation of a policy from the members of the public, and shall include all forms of printed and published materials or any material using the print and or electronic medium for public communication such as:

(*i*) newspapers, magazines and sales talks;

(*ii*) billboards, hoardings, panels;

(*iii*) radio, television, website, e-mail, portals;

(*iv*) representations by intermediaries;

(*v*) leaflets;

(*vi*) descriptive literature/circulars;

(*vii*) sales aids flyers;

Gazette No. 102, Extra ordinary dated 19-7-2000.

(*viii*) illustration form letters;

(*ix*) telephone solicitations;

(*x*) business cards;

(*xi*) videos;

(*xii*) faxes; or

(*xiii*) any other communication with a prospect or a policyholder that urges him to purchase, renew, increase, retain or modify a policy of insurance.

Explanation. The following materials shall not be considered to be an advertisement provided they are not used to induce the purchase, increase, modification or retention of a policy of insurance:—

(*i*) materials used by an insurance company within its own organisation and not meant for distribution to the public;

(*ii*) communications with policyholders other than materials urging them to purchase, increase, modify,

(*iii*) materials used solely for the training, recruitment and education of an insurer's personnel, intermediaries, counselors and solicitors, provided they are not used to induce the public to prrchase, increase, modify or retain a policy of insurance;

(*iv*) any general announcement sent by a group policyholder to members of the eligible group that a policy has been written or arranged.

(c) "intermediary or insurance intermediary" includes insurance brokers, reinsurance brokers, insurance consultants, surveyors and loss assessors, or any other person representing or assisting an insurer in one or more of the following:

(*i*) soliciting, negotiating, procuring or effectuating an insurance contract or a renewal of an insurance contnct;

(*ii*) disseminating information relating to coverage or rates;

(*iii*) forwarding an insurance application;

(*iv*) servicing and delivering an insurance policy or contract;

(*v*) inspecting a risk;

(*vi*) setting a rate;

(*vii*) investigating or assessing a claim or loss;

(*viii*) transacting a matter after the effectuation of a contract; or

(*ix*) representing or assisting an insurance or other person in any other manner in the transaction of insurance with respect to a subject of insurance resident, located or to be performed in India;

(*x*) servicing a policy or contract;

(*d*) "unfair or misleading advertisement" will mean and include any advertisement:

(*i*) that fails to clearly identify the product as hsurance;

(*ii*) makes claims beyond the ability of the policy to deliver or beyond the reasonable expectation of performance;

(*iii*) describes benefits that do not match the poley provisions;

uses words or phrases in a way which hides or minimizes the costs of the hazard insured against or the risks inherent in the policy;

omits to disclose or discloses insufficiently, important exclusions, limitations and conditions of the contract;

gives information in a misleading way;

illustrates future benefits or assumptions which are not realistic nor realisable in the light of the insurer's current performance.

where the benefits are not guaranteed, does not explicitly say so as prominently as the benefits are stated or says so in a manner or form that it could remain unnoticed;

implies a group or other relationship like sponsorship, affiliation or approval, that does not exist;

makes unfair or incomplete comparisons with products which are not comparable or disparages competitors.

(*e*) "prospect" means any party that enters or proposes to enter into an insurance contract directly, or through an insurance intermediary.

Words and expressions used and not defined in these regulations but defined in the Insurance Act, 1938 (4 of 1938), or the Life Insurance Corporation Act, 1956 (31 of 1956) or the General Insurance Business Nationalisation Act, 1972 (57 of 1972), or Insurance Regulatory and Development Authority Act, 1999 (41 of 1999) shall have the meanings respectively assigned to them in those Acts or the rules as the case may be.

3. Compliance and control

1. Every insurer or intermediary or insurance agent shall—
   - (*i*) have a compliance officer, whose name and official position in the organisation shall be communicated to the Authority, and he shall be responsible to oversee the advertising programme;
   - (*ii*) establish and maintain a system of control over the content, form, and method of dissemination of all advertisements concerning its policies;
   - (*iii*) maintain an advertising register at its corporate office which much include;
     - (*a*) a specimen of every advertisement disseminated, or issued or a record of any broadcast or telecast, etc.;
     - (*b*) a notation attached to each advertisement indicating the manner, extent of distribution and form number of any policy advertised; and
   - (*iv*) maintain a specimen of all advertisements for a minimum period of three years;
   - (*v*) file a copy of each advertisement with the Authority as soon as it is first issued, together with information:
     - (*a*) an identifying number for the advertisement;
     - (*b*) the form number (s) of the policy(ies) advertised and when the product/s were approved by the Authority;
     - (*c*) a description of the advertisement and how it is used;
     - (*d*) the method or media used for dissemination of the advertisement;
   - (*vi*) file a certificate of compliance with their annual statement stating that, to the best of its knowledge, advertisement disseminated by the insurer or by its intermediaries during the preceding year have complied with the provisions of these regulations an the advertisement code as stated in regulation 12.
2. The advertisement register shall be subject to inspection and review by the Authority for content, context, prominance and position of required disclosure, omissions of required information, etc.

4. Changes in advertisement.

1. Any change in an advertisement would be considered a new advertisement.

2. All the provisions of regulation 3 shall apply mutatis mutandis to an advertisement referred to in sub-regulations (1).
3. The Authority shall be informed at the time of filing the advertisement the extent of change the original advertisement.

5. Insurance company advertisement.

1. Every insurance company shall be required to prominently disclose in the advertisement and that part of the advertisement that is required to be returned to the company or insurance intermediary or insurance agent by a prospect or an insured the full particulars of the insurance company, and not merely any trade name or monogram or logo.
2. Where benefits are more that briefly described, the form number of the policy and the type of coverage shall be disclosed fully.

6. Advertisement by insurance agents.

1. Every advertisement by an insurance agent that affects an insurer must be approved by the insurer in writing prior to its issue.
2. It shall be the responsibility of the insurer while granting such approval to ensure that all advertisements that pertain to the company or its products or performance comply with these regulations and are not deceptive or misleading.

Explanation: An agent shall not be required to obtain written approval of the company prior to issue for:

(*i*) those advertisements developed by the insurer and provided to the agents;

(*ii*) generic advertisements limited to information like the agent's name, logo, address and phone number; and

(*iii*) advertisements that consist only of simple and correct statements describing the availability of lines of insurance, references to experience, service and qualifications of agents; but making no reference to specific policies, benefits, costs of insurers.

7. Advertising by insurance intermediaries. Only properly licensed intermediaries may advertise or solicit insurance through advertisements .

8. Advertisement on the Internet.

1. Every insurer or intermediary's website or portal shall
   (*i*) include disclosure statements which outline the site's specific policies vis-a-vis the privacy of personal information for the protection of both their own businesses and the consumers they serve;
   (*ii*) display their registration/license numbers on their websites.
2. For the purposes of these regulations, except where otherwise specifically excluded or restricted, no form or policy otherwise permissible for use shall be deemed invalid or impermissible if such form or policy accurately reflects the intentions of the parties in such form or policy as published electronically or transmitted electronically between parties.

9. Identity of advertiser. Every advertisement for insurance shall

(*i*) State clearly and unequivocally that insurance is the subject matter of the solicitation; and

(*ii*) State the full registered name of the insurer/intermediary/insurance agent.

10. Endorsements and other third-party involvement.

1. A third party, group or association shall not:
   (*i*) distribute information about an insurance policy, intermediary or insurer on its letterhead;
   (*ii*) allow an insurance intermediary or insurer to distribute information about an insurance policy, insurance or insurance company on its letterhead;

(*iii*) distribute information about an individual insurance policy, or about an intermediary or insurer in its envelopes, unless

(*a*) the third party is providing only a distribution service for the insurance advertisement and is not itself soliciting the coverage, and

(*b*) the insurance information is a piece separate from any other information distributed by the third party and clearly indicates its origin;

(*iv*) recommend that its members purchase specific insurance products;

(*v*) imply that a person must become a member of its organization in order to purchase the policy;

(*vi*) imply that a purchaser of a policy by becoming a member of a limited group of persons shall receive special advantages from the insurer not provided for in the policy;

Provided that a third party, group or association may:

(*i*) endorse an insurance company or insurance intermediary's product and provide truthful statements, quotes and testimonials endorsing the insurance products to the insurance company for use in the company's advertisements, so long as the language does not convey directly or indirectly a recommendation that members of the organisation purchase the products;

(*ii*) provide an insurance company with information about its membership and collect compensation based upon sales for that information.

11. Procedure for action in case of complaint.

1. If an advertisement is not in accordance with these regulations the Authority may take action in one or more of the following ways:

(*i*) issue a letter to the advertiser seeking information within a specific time, not being more than ten days from the date of issue of the letter;

(*ii*) direct the advertiser to correct or modify the advertisement already issued in a manner suggested by the Authority with a stipulation that the corrected or modified advertisement shall receive the same type of publicity as the one sought to be corrected or modified;

(*iii*) direct the advertiser to discontinue the advertisement forthwith;

(*iv*) any other action deemed fit by the Authority, keeping in view the circumstances of the case, to ensure that the interests of the public are protected.

The advertiser may seek additional time from the Authority to comply with the directions justifying the reasons therefore. The Authority, may, however, refuse to grant extension of time if it feels that the advertiser is seeking time only to delay the matters.

Any failure on the part of the advertiser to comply with the directions of the Authority may entail the Authority to take such action as deemed necessary including levy of penalty.

12. Adherence to advertisement code. Every insurer or intermediary shall follow recognised standards of professional conduct as prescribed by the Advertisement Standards Council of India (ASCI) and discharge its functions in the interest of the policyholders.

13. Statutory warning.

1. Every proposal for an insurance product shall carry the following stipulation, as prescribed in section 41 of the Insurance Act, 1938 (4 of the 1938):

"No person shall allow or offer to allow, either directly or indirectly, as an inducement to any person to take out or renew or continue an insurance in respect of any kind of risk relating to lives or property in India, any rebate of the whole or part of the commission payable or any rebate of the premium shown on the policy, nor shall any person taking out or renewing or continuing a policy accept any rebate, except such rebate as may be allowed in accordance with the published prospectus or tables of the insurer."

2. If any person fails to comply with sub-regulation (1) above, he shall be liable to payment of a fine which may extend to rupees five hundred.

INSURANCE REGULATORY AND DEVELOPMENT AUTHORITY (LICENSING OF INSURANCE AGENTS) REGULATIONS, 2000

F.No. IRDA/Reg./7/2000.

In exercise of the powers conferred by sub-section (6) of section 42 and clauses (k), (1), (m), (n), (0) and (p) of sub-section (2) of section 114A of the Insurance Act, 1938 (4 of 1938), the Authority, in consultation with the Insurance Advisory Committee, hereby makes the following regulations, namely:

1. Short title and commencement.

1. These regulations may be called Insurance Regulatory and Development Authority (Licensing of Insurance Agents) Regulations, 2000.
2. They shall come into force on tlhe date of their publication in the Official Gazette.

2. Definitions. In these regulations, unless the context otherwise requires:

(*a*) "Act" means the insurance, Act,1938 (4 of 1938);

(*b*) "Approved Institution' means an Institution engaged in education and/or training particularly in the area of insurance sales, service and marketing, approved and notified by the Authority;

(*c*) "Authority" means the Insurance Regulatory and Development Authority established under the provisions of Section 3 of the Insurance Regulatory and Development Authority Act, 1999 (41 of 1999);

(*d*) "Composite insurance agent" means an insurance agent who holds a licence to act as an insurance agent for a life insurer and a general insurer;

(*e*) "Corporate Agent" means a person other than an individual as specified in clause (*i*);

(*f*) "Designated person" means an officer normally in charge of marketing operations, as specified by an insurer, and authorised by the Authority to issue or renew licences under these regulations;

(*g*) "Examination Body" means an Institution, which conducts pre-recruitment tests for insurance agents and which is duly recognised by the Authority;

(*h*) "Licence" means a certificate of licence to act as an insurance agent issued under these regulations;

(*i*) "Person" means:

(i) an individual;

(*ii*) a firm' or

(*iii*) a company formed under the Companies Act, 1956 (1 of 1956), and includes a banking company as defined in clause (4A) of section 2 of the Act;

(j) "Practical Training" includes orientation, particularly in the area of insurance sales, service and marketing, through training modules as approved by the Authority;

(*k*) "Proposal form" means an application for purchase of an insurance product which shall be the basis of insurance contract;

(*l*) "Prospect" means a potential purchaser of an insurance product;

(*m*) "Recognised Board or Institution" means such board or institution as may be recognised by any State Government or the Central Government.

2. All words and expressions used herein and not defined but defined in the Insurance Act, 1938 (4 of 1938), or in the Insurance Regulatory and Development Authority Act, 1999 (41 of 1999), shall have the meanings respectively assigned to them in those Acts.

3. Issue or renewal of licence.

1. A person desiring to obtain or renew a licence (hereinafter referred to as "the applicant") to act as an insurance agent or a composite insurance agent shall proceed as follows:
   (*a*) the applicant shall make an application to a designated person:
      (*i*) in Form IRDA-Agents-VA, if the applicant is an individual;
      (*ii*) in Form IRDA-Agents-VC, if the applicant is a firm or a company;
      Provided that the applicant, who desires to be a composite insurance agent, shall make two separate applications.
   (*b*) The fees payable by the applicant to the Authority shall be as specified in Regulation 7.
2. The designated person may, on receipt of the application along with the evidence of payment of fees to the Authority, and on being satisfied that the applicant—
   (*i*) possesses the qualifications as specified-under Regulation 4;
   (*ii*) possesses the practical training as specified under Regulation 5;
   (*iii*) has passed the examination as specified under Regulation 6;
   (*iv*) has furnished the application complete in all respects;
   (*v*) has the requisite knowledge to solicit and procure insurance business; and
   (*vi*) is capable of providing the necessary service to the policyholders;
   grant or renew, as the case may be, a licence in Form IRDA-Agents-VB, along with identity card in Form IRDA-Agents-VZ:

   Provided that in the case of a corporate agent, the identity card shall be in Form IRDA-Agent -VY.

   Provided further that such identity card from one life insurer and such identity card from one general insurer shall be provided to the applicant seeking licence to act as a composite insurance agent.

   Provided further that in the case of a firm or a company, all of its partners or directors, as the case may be, shall fulfil the requirements of sub-clauses (*i*) to (*iii*).

   Provided further a licence issued in accordance with this regulation shall entitle the applicant to act as insurance agent for one life insurer or one general insurer or both, as the case may be.
3. If the designated person refuses to grant or renew a licence under this regulation, he shall give the reasons therefor to the applicant.

4. **Qualifications of the applicant.** The applicant shall possess the minimum qualification of a pass in 12th Standard or equivalent examination conducted by any recognised Board/Institution, where the applicant resides in a place wtth a population of five thousand or more as per the last census, and a pass in 10th Standard or equivalent examination from a recognised Board/Institution if the applicant resides in any other place.

5. **Practical Training.**

1. The applicant shall have completed from an approved institution, at least, one hundred hours practical training in life or general insurance business, as the case may be, which may be spread over three to four weeks, where such applicant is seeking licence for the first time to act as insurance agent.

   Provided that the applicant shall have completed from an approved institution, at least, one hundred fifty hours' practical training in life and general insurance business, which may be spread over six to eight weeks, where such applicant is seeking licence for the first time to act as a composite insurance agent.

2. Where the applicant, referred to under sub-regulation (I), is
   (*a*) an Associate/Fellow of the Insurance Institute of India, Mumbai;
   (*b*) an Associate/Fellow of the Institute of Chartered Accountants of India, New Delhi;
   (*c*) an Associate/Fellow of the Institute of Costs and Works Accountants of India, Calcutta;
   (*d*) an Associate/Fellow of the Institute of Company Secretaries of India, New Delhi;
   (*e*) an Associate/Fellow of the Actuarial Society of India, Mumbai;
   (*f*) a Master of Business Administration of any Institution/University recognised by any State Government or the Central Government; or
   (*g*) possessing any professional qualification in marketing from any Institution/University recognised by any State Government or the Central Govemment

   he shall have completed, at least, fifty hours practical training from an approved institution.

   Provided that such applicant shall have completed from an approved institution, at least, seventy hours practical training in life and general insurance business, where such applicant is seeking licence for the first time to act as a composite insurance agent.
3. An applicant, who has been granted a licence after the commencement of these regulations, before seeking renewal of licence to act as an insurance agent, shall have completed, at least twenty-five hours' practical training in life or general insurance business, as the case may be, from an approved institution.

   Provided that such applicant before seeking renewal of licence to act as a composite insurance agent shall have completed from an approved institution, at least, fifty hours' practical training in life and general insurance business.

6. Examination. The Applicant shall have passed the pre-recruitment examination in life or general insurance business, or both, as the case may be, conducted by the Insurance Institute of India, Mumbai, or any other examination body.

7. Fees payable.

1. The fees payable to the Authority for issue or renewal of licence to act as insurance agent or a composite insurance agent shall be rupee two hundred and fifty.
2. The additional fees payable to the Authority, under the circumstances mentioned in sub-section (3) of section 42 of the Act, shall be rupees one hundred.

8. Code of Conduct.

1. Every person holding a licence, shall adhere to the code of conduct specified below:
   (*i*) **Every insurance agent shall:**
   (*a*) identify himself and the insurance company of whom he is an insurance agent;
   (*b*) disclose his licence to the prospect on demand;
   (*c*) disseminate the requisite information in respect of insurance products offered for sale by his insurer and take into account the needs of the prospect while recommending a specific insurance plan;
   (*d*) disclose the scales of commission in respect of the insurance product offered for sale, if asked by the prospect;
   (*e*) indicate the premium to be charged by the insurer for the insurance product offered for sale;
   (*f*) explain to the prospect the nature of information required in the proposal form by the insurer, and also the importance of disclosure of material information in the purchase of an insurance contract;

(*g*) bring to the notice of the insurer any adverse habits or income inconsistency of the prospect, in the form of a report (called "Insurance Agent's Confidential Report") along with every proposal submitted to the insurer, and any material fact that may adversely affect the underwriting decision of the insurer as regards acceptance of the proposal, by making all reasonable enquiries about the prospect;

(*h*) inform promptly the prospect about the acceptance or rejection of the proposal by the insurer;

(*i*) obtain the requisite documents at, the time of filing the proposal form with the insurer; and other documents subsequently asked for by the insurer for completion of the proposal;

(*j*) render necessary assistance to the policyholders or claimants or beneficiaries in complying with the requirements for settlement of claims by the insurer;

(*k*) advise every individual policyholder to effect nomination or assignment or change of address or exercise of options, as the case may be, and offer necessary assistance in this behalf, wherever necessary;

(*ii*) **No insurance agent shall:**

(*a*) solicit or procure insurance business without holding a valid licence;

(*b*) induce the prospect to omit any material information in the proposal form;

(*c*) induce the prospect to submit wrong information in the proposal form or documents submitted to the insurer for acceptance of the proposal;

(*d*) behave in a discourteous manner with the prospect;

(*e*) interfere with any proposal inttoduced by any other insurance agent;

(*f*) offer different rates, advantages, terms and conditions other than those offered by his insurer;

(*g*) demand or receive a share of proceeds from the beneficiary under an insurance contract;

(*h*) force a policyholder to terminate the existing policy and to effect a new proposal from him within three years from the date of such termination;

(*i*) have, in case of corporate agent, a portfolio of insurance business under which the premium is in excess of fifty percent of total premium procured, in any year, from one person (who is not an individual) or one organisation or one group of organisations;

(*j*) apply for fresh licence to act as an insurance agent, if his licence was earlier cancelled by the designated person, and a period of five years has not elapsed from the date of such cancellation;

(*k*) become or remain a director of any insurance company;

(*iii*) Every insurance agent shall, with a view to conserve the insurance business already procured through him, make every attempt to ensure remittance of the premiums by the policyholders within the stipulated time, by giving notice to the policyholder orally and in writing;

9. Cancellation of Licence. The designated person may cancel a licence of an insurance agent, if the insurance agent suffers, at any time during the currency of the licence, from any of the disqualifications mentioned in sub-section (4) of section 42 of the Act, and recover from him the licence and the identity card issued earlier.

10. Issue of duplicate Licence. The Authority may issue a duplicate licence replace a licence lost, destroyed, or mutilated on payment a fee of rupees fifty.

11. Non-application to existing insurance agents. Nothing contained in Regulations 4 to 6 of these Regulations shall apply to the existing agents before the commencement of these Regulations.

FORM IRDA-AGENTS-VA
(SEE REGULATION 3)

Insurance Regulatory and Development Authority (Licensing of Insurance Agents) Regulations, 2000

APPLICATION FOR A LICENCE /RENEWAL OF LICENCE TO ACT AS AN INSURANCE AGENT

TO
THE INSURANCE REGULATORY
AND DEVELOPMENT AUTHORITY
DEPARTMENT OF LICENSING,
NEW DELHI

DEAR SIRS,

I request that -------

(*a*) a licence to act as an insurance agent*/a composite insurance agent* may be granted to me.

(*b*) *my licence bearing number ____________ and expiry date ____________ may be renewed for a further period of three years.

2. I hereby declare that particulars given below are true and that the licence for which I apply will be used only by myself for soliciting or procuring insurance business for one life insurance's */one general insurer*/both*.

(1) Name: [ ][ ][ ][ ][ ][ ][ ][ ][ ][ ][ ][ ][ ][ ][ ][ ][ ][ ][ ]

(2) Father's, Husband's

Name: [ ][ ][ ][ ][ ][ ][ ][ ][ ][ ][ ][ ][ ][ ][ ][ ][ ][ ][ ]

(3) Full Address:

House No.: [ ][ ][ ][ ][ ][ ][ ][ ][ ][ ][ ][ ][ ][ ][ ][ ][ ][ ]

Street: [ ][ ][ ][ ][ ][ ][ ][ ][ ][ ][ ][ ][ ][ ][ ][ ][ ][ ][ ]

Town: [ ][ ][ ][ ][ ][ ][ ][ ][ ][ ][ ][ ][ ][ ][ ][ ][ ][ ][ ]

District: [ ][ ][ ][ ][ ][ ][ ][ ][ ][ ][ ][ ][ ][ ][ ][ ][ ][ ]

State: [ ][ ][ ][ ][ ][ ][ ][ ][ ][ ][ ][ ][ ][ ][ ][ ][ ][ ][ ]

Pin Code:[ ][ ][ ][ ][ ][ ]

Tel No. [ ][ ][ ][ ][ ][ ][ ][ ][ ][ ][ ][ ][ ][ ][ ][ ][ ][ ][ ]
(STD Code — Number)

(4) Date of Birth: [ ][ ]—[ ][ ]—[ ][ ]
Day Month Year

(5) Title: State 1 if are Mr., 2 Mrs., 3 Miss:

(6) If you ever held a Licence, state No. and date of expiry, otherwise say "Nil".

(*a*) Licence Number: [ ][ ][ ][ ][ ][ ][ ][ ][ ][ ][ ][ ][ ][ ][ ]

(*b*) Date of Expiry: [ ][ ][ ][ ][ ][ ][ ][ ]
Day Month Year

(7) If you apply for licence to work for a life insurer, state 1, for a general insurer, state 2, for both state 3 in the box. [ ]

(8) If your are an applicant from a rural place, State 1, in the box . [ ]

(9) Education Qualifications:

State 1, if you passed Class X; 2: Class XII; 3: Graduate; 4: Post-graduate; 5: if you hold a professional qualification such as ACA, FASI, AICWA.): [ ]

(10) Give particulars of pass in pre-recruitment test conducted by the Insurance Institute of India or any examination body:

(*a*) Name of Examination Body: [ ][ ][ ][ ][ ][ ][ ][ ][ ][ ][ ][ ][ ]
[ ][ ][ ][ ][ ][ ][ ][ ][ ][ ]

(*b*) Candidate's Number: [ ][ ][ ][ ][ ][ ][ ][ ][ ][ ][ ][ ][ ][ ]

(*c*) Centre of Examination: [ ][ ][ ][ ][ ][ ][ ][ ][ ][ ][ ][ ][ ]
[ ][ ][ ][ ][ ][ ][ ][ ][ ][ ]

(*d*) Date of Passing: [ ][ ]—[ ][ ]—[ ][ ][ ][ ]
Day Month Year

(11) Give particulars of Practical raining completed from an approved institution.

(*a*) Training Hours completed: [ ][ ]

(*b*) Name of Training Institute: [ ][ ][ ][ ][ ][ ][ ][ ][ ][ ][ ][ ][ ]
[ ][ ][ ][ ][ ][ ][ ][ ][ ][ ]

(*c*) Candidate's Number: [ ][ ][ ][ ][ ][ ][ ][ ][ ][ ][ ][ ][ ][ ]

(*d*) Centre (Place) of Training:[ ][ ][ ][ ][ ][ ][ ][ ][ ][ ][ ][ ][ ]
[ ][ ][ ][ ][ ][ ][ ][ ][ ][ ]

(*e*) Starting Date of Training : [ ][ ]—[ ][ ]—[ ][ ][ ][ ]
Day Month Year

3. I further declare that:

(*a*) I have not been found to be of unsound mind by a court of competent jurisdiction;

(*b*) I have not been found guilty of criminal misappropriation or criminal breach of trust or cheating or forgery or an abetment of or attempt to commit any such offence by a court of competent jurisdiction;

(*c*) I have not been found guilty of or to have knowingly participated in or connived at any fraud, dishonestly or mis-representation against an insurer or an insured in the course of any judicial proceeding relating to any policy of insurance or the winding up of an insurance company or in the course of an investigation of the affairs of an insurer; and

(*d*) # have not violated the code of conduct specified under Regulation 8 of Insurance Regulatory and Development Authority (Licensing of Insurance Agents) Regulations, 2000.

4. I have made the payment of licence fee of rupees two hundred and fifty and for which I enclose the documentary evidence.

5. I enclose the following documents in supports of the educational qualification, pre-recruitment test, and the practical training.

(a) ____________________

(b) ____________________

Place: Yours faithfully,

Date:

Signature of applicant

(*Strike out portion not required).

(# not applicable to the applicants seeking licence for the first time.)

Notes and Instructions

1. An individual can apply for only one licence which will entitle him to solicit or procure insurance business of any class and to act as an insurance agent for one life insurer, one general insurer, or both.
2. The application should be filled in, as far as possible, in Hindi language or English language.
3. Any correction or alteration made many answer to the questions in the application should be initialled by the applicant.
4. An applicant must be at, least 18 years of age on the date of the application. If required the applicant shall furnish proof of age.
5. An applicant shall furnish the proof of educational qualification, pass in the pre-recruitment test conducted by the Insurance Institute of India, Mumbai or an examination body approved by the Insurance Regulatory and Development Authority, and completion of practical training from a training institution approved by the Insurance Regulatory and Development Authority, along with the application. This is not applicable where the applicant is an absorbed agent.
6. The fees payable by an applicant is rupees two hundred and fifty.
7. The name and licence No. given in the application are identical with those shown in the last licence held. If there is any subsequent change in the name, the reasons for the same should be stated furnishing documentary evidence for the name.
8. The application should reach the designated person before the expiry of licence held by the applicant but not more than three months before such expiry. If the application does not reach the designated person at least 30 days before the date on which the last licence ceases to be in force, an additional fee of one hundred rupees should be payable. In this connection please also refer to the provisions of subsections (3) and (3A) of section 42 of the Insurance Act, 1938.
9. If the applicant desires to work for a life insurer or a general insurer or both, as the case may be, he should enclose the documentary evidence of the relevant pass in the pre-recruitment test and the completion of the relevant practical training.

FORM IRDA-AGENTS- VB

(SEE REGULATION 3)

INSURANCE REGULATORY AND DEVELOPMENT AUTHORITY (LICENSING OF INSURANCE AGENTS) REGULATIONS, 2000.

INSURANCE REGULATORY AND DEVELOPMENT AUTHORITY, NEW DELHI

LICENCE NO. [ ][ ][ ][ ][ ][ ][ ][ ][ ][ ]

LICENCE TO ACT AS AN INSURANCE AGENT UNDER PART II OF THE INSURANCE ACT, 1938

NAME OF INSURANCE AGENT*/

COMPOSITE INSURANCE

AGENT*: ______________________________

ADDRESS:

Having paid the prescribed fee and having made the necessary declaration is hereby authorised to act an insurance agent for three years from ______________________ for procuring or soliciting insurance business of one life insurer*/ one general insurer*/both*.

(*strike out portion not required)

Place:

Date:

For Insurance Regulatory and Development Authority

Designated Person:

Signature of Licence holder:

This licence is not valid unless it bears a fascimile of the signature of the chairperson of the insurance and Regulatory and Development Authority and the initials of a person authorised by him in this behalf, the signature of the licence holder and the identity card (s). The licence holder should put his signature as soon as licence is received.

(See Notes on the reverse)

Notes

1. If it is desired to renew this licence for a further period the procedure laid down in Regulation 3 of INSURANCE REGULATORY AND DEVELOPMENT AUTHORITY (LICENSING OF INSURANCE AGENTS) REGULATIONS, 2000, SHALL BE FOLLOWED, AND APPLICATION for renewal should reach the Designated Person before the licence expires. In this connection attention is also invited to the provisions of sub-sections (3) and 3(A) of section 42 of the Insurance Act, 1938.
2. This licence authorises the licence holder to act as an agent for the insurance business specified thereunder, and therefore no identifying mark or note of any description by which the identity of an insurer might be established should be placed on the licence.
3. No correction in this licence will be valid unless initialled by the Insurance Regulatory and Development Authority or a person authorised by in this behalf.
4. The attention of the licence holder is drawn to the code of conduct specified under Regulation 8 of INSURANCE REGULATORY AND DEVELOPMENT AUTHORITY (LICENSING OF INSURANCE AGENTS) REGULATIONS, 2000, and any violation of code of conduct may result is cancellation of licence.

FORM IRDA-AGENTS-VC
(SEE REGULATION 3)

Insurance Regulatory and Development Authority
(Licensing of Insurance Agents) Regulations, 2000.

APPLICATION FORM A FIRM OR COMPANY FOR A LICENCE/ RENEWAL OF LICENCE TO ACT AS AN INSURANCE AGENT

TO
THE INSURANCE REGULATORY
AND DEVELOPMENT AUTHORITY
DEPARTMENT OF LICENSING,
NEW DELHI.

DEAR SIRS,

I request that —

(*a*) *a licence to act as an insurance agent*/a composite insurance agent* may be granted to our Firm/Company;

(*b*) *our licence bearing number ________________ and expiry date ________________ may be renewed for a further period of three years.

2. It hereby declared that particulars given below are true and that the licence for which our Firm/ Company apply will be used only by our Firm/Company for soliciting or procuring insurance business.

(1) Name: [ ][ ][ ][ ][ ][ ][ ][ ][ ][ ][ ][ ][ ][ ][ ][ ][ ][ ]

(2) Full Address: [ ][ ][ ][ ][ ][ ][ ][ ][ ][ ][ ][ ][ ][ ][ ][ ]

House No: [ ][ ][ ][ ][ ][ ][ ][ ][ ][ ][ ][ ][ ][ ][ ][ ][ ]

Street: [ ][ ][ ][ ][ ][ ][ ][ ][ ][ ][ ][ ][ ][ ][ ][ ][ ][ ]

Town: [ ][ ][ ][ ][ ][ ][ ][ ][ ][ ][ ][ ][ ][ ][ ][ ][ ][ ]

District: [ ][ ][ ][ ][ ][ ][ ][ ][ ][ ][ ][ ][ ][ ][ ][ ][ ]

State: [ ][ ][ ][ ][ ][ ][ ][ ][ ][ ][ ][ ][ ][ ][ ][ ][ ][ ]

Pin Code:[ ][ ][ ][ ][ ][ ]

Telephone No.: [ ][ ][ ][ ][ ][ ][ ][ ]—[ ][ ][ ][ ][ ][ ][ ]

(STD Code — Number)

(3) (*i*) (In the case of a Firm) the names of all the partners therein:

(*ii*) (In the case of Company) the names of the Directors:

(4) Whether the Partnership Deed*/Memorandum of Association* contains as main objects the carrying on of soliciling or procuring insurance business as an insurance agent. (Please enclose a certified copy of the Partnership Deed*/Memorandum of Association*).

(5) The date from when the licence should be effective:

(6) If you apply for licence to work for a life insurer, state 1, a general insurer, state 2, for both, state 3 in the box. [ ]

3. It is further declared that —

(*a*) any partner of our Firm*/any Director of our Company* has not been found to be of unsound mind by a court of competent jurisdiction;

(*b*) any partner of our Firm*/any Director of our Company* has not been found guilty of criminal misappropriation or criminal breach of trust or cheating or forgery or an abetment of or attempt to commit any such offence by a court of competent jurisdiction;

(*c*) any partner of our Firm*/any Director of our Company* has not been found guilty of or to have knowingly participated in or connived at any fraud, dishonestly or mis-representation against an insurer or an insured in the course of any judicial proceeding relating to any policy of insurance or the winding up of an insurance company or in the course of an investigation of the affairs of an insurer;

(*d*) any partner of our Firm*/any Director of our Company* has not violated the code of conduct specified under Regulation 8 of Insurance Regulatory and Development Authority (Licensing of Insurance Agents) Regulations, 2000;

(*e*) the application in Form IRDA-Agents-V for each partner of our Firm*/each Director of our Company* has been enclosed along with this form;

(*f*) any partner of our Firm*/any Director of our Company* is not a minor.

4. The payment of licence fee of rupees two hundred and fifty has been made and for which the receipt is enclosed.
5. The documents in support of the educational qualification, pre-recruitment test, and the practical training, in respect of all partners of our Firm*/all Directors of our Company* have been enclosed along with this form.

(* Strike out portion not required.)

Place: Yours faithfully,

Date:

Signature of applicant

Notes

1. The application should be filled in, as far as possible, in Hindi language or English language.
2. Any correction or alteration made in any answer to the questions in the application should be initialled by the applicant.
3. The fees payable by an applicant is rupees two hundred and fifty.
4. The name and the licence No. given in the application are identical with those shown in the last licence held. If there is any subsequent change in the name, the reasons for the same should be stated furnishing documentary evidence for the same.
5. The application should reach the designated person before the expiry of licence held by the application but not more than three months before such expiry. If the application does not reach the designated person at least 30 days before the date on which the last licence ceases to be in force, an additional fee of one hundred rupees should be payable. In this connection please also refer to the provisions of sub-sections (3) and (3A) of section 42 of the Insurance Act, 1938.
6. If the, Firm or Company desires to act as an insurance agent or a composite insurance agent, as the case may be, the documentary evidence of the relevant pass in the pre-recruitment test and the completion of the relevant practical training of partners of the Firm or directors of the Company should be enclosed.
7. In case of a Firm, the signatory to the application (being a partner) should enclose a certified copy of the resolution of all the partners authorising him to make the application. In the case of a Company, the signatory to the application (being a director) should enclose a certified copy of the resolution of Board of Directors authorising him to make the application.

FORM IRDA-AGENTS-VZ
(SEE REGULATION 3)

INSURANCE REGULATORY AND DEVELOPMENT AUTHORITY (LICENSING OF INSURANCE AGENTS) REGULATIONS, 2000)

Individual Insurance Agent's identity card

Photo	Agent's Licence No.: Name of the Agent: Father's/Husband's Name: Office of the Insurer with whom the agent is attached:
Agent's signature Male/Female	The holder of this card is authorised to sell our insurance products, as per our terms and conditions.
Issued on: [ ][ ]–[ ][ ]–[ ][ ]	Signature of Designated Person
Valid upto: [ ][ ]–[ ][ ]–[ ][ ]	Name of Insurer (With Seal)
born on: [ ][ ]–[ ][ ]–[ ][ ]	(Please see on the reverse)

Address and telephone number of the Insurer: (If required to be contacted by any one in connection with the holder of this card):

Address and telephone Numbers of the Agent:

IRDA (Protection of Policyholders' Interests) Regulations 2002

The Insurance Regulatory and Development Authority in exercise of the powers conferred by Section 114A of the Insurance Act, 1938 read with Sections 14 & 26 of the IRDA Act, 1999 and in consultation with the Insurance Advisory Council has made the IRDA (Protection of Policyholder's Interests) Regulations, 2002. These regulations have been notified on 26th April, 2002 and here we reproduce these regulations in full. These regulations establish the benchmarks in the quality of sales as well as service in life insurance and it is necessary that every employee and agent in the organisation is fully aware of regulations as well as their implications.

1. Short title and commencement

1.(1) These regulations may be called the Insurance Regulatory and Development Authority (Protection of Policyholder's Interests) Regulations, 2002.

(2) They shall come into force on the date of their publication in the Official Gazette and shall apply to all contracts of insurance effected thereafter, except regulation 4(1) which shall come into force on 1st October, 2002.

(3) These Regulations are in addition to any other regulations made by Authority, which may, inter alia, provide for protection of the interest of policyholders.

(4) These Regulations apply to all insurers, insurance agents, insurance intermediaries and policyholders.

2. Definitions

2. (1) in these regulations, unless the context otherwise requires:

(*a*) "Act" means the Insurance Act, 1938 (4 of 1938);

(*b*) "Authority" means the Insurance Regulatory and Development Authority established under the provisions of section 3 of the Insurance Regulatory and Development Authority Act, 1999 (41 of 1999);

(*c*) "Cover" means an insurance contract whether in the form of a policy or a cover note or a Certificate of Insurance or any other form prevalent in the industry of evidence the existence of an insurance contract;

(*d*) "Proposal form" means a form to be filled in by the proposer for insurance, for furnishing all material information required by the insurer in respect of a risk, in order to enable the insurer to decide whether to accept or decline, to undertake the risk, and in the event of acceptance of the risk, to determine the rates, terms and conditions of a cover to be granted.

Explanation: "Material" for the purpose of these regulations shall mean and include all important, essential and relevant information in the context of underwriting the risk to be covered by the insurer.

(*e*) "Prospectus" means a document issued by the insurer or in its behalf to the prospective buyers of insurance, and should contain such particulars as are mentioned in Rule, 11 of Insurance Rules, 1939 and includes a brochure or leaflet serving the purpose. Such a document should also specify the type and character of riders on the main product indicating the nature of benefits flowing thereupon;

(*f*) Words and expressions used and not defined in these regulations, but defined in the Act, or the Life Insurance Corporation Act, 1956, (31 of 1956) or the General Insurance Business (Nationalisation) Act, 1972 (57 of 1972), or the Insurance Regulatory and Development Authority Act, 1999 (41 of 1999) or the Insurance Rules, 1939 shall have the meanings respectively assigned to them in those Acts of the Rules.

3. Point of Sale

1. Notwithstanding anything mentioned in regulations 2(e) above, a prospectus of any insurance product shall clearly state the scope of benefits, the extent of insurance cover and in an explicit manner explain the warranties, exceptions and conditions of the insurance cover and, in case of life insurance, whether the product is participating (with-profits) or non-participating (without-profits). The allowable rider or riders on the product shall be clearly spelt out with regard to their scope of benefits, and in no case, the premium relatable to all the riders put together shall exceed 30% of the premium of the main product.

   Explanation: The rider or riders attached to a life policy shall bear the nature and character of the main policy, *viz.* participating or non-participating and accordingly the life insurer shall make provisions, etc., in its books.

2. An insurer or its agent or other intermediary shall provide all material information in respect of a proposed cover to the prospect to enable the prospect to decide on the best cover that would be in his or her interest.

3. Where the prospect depends upon the advice of the insurer or his agent or an insurance intermediary. such a person must advise the prospect dispassionately.

4. Where, for any reason, the proposal and other connected papers are not filled by the prospect, a certificate may be incorporated at the end of proposal form from the prospect that the contents of the form and documents have been fully explained to him and that he has fully understood the significant of the proposed contract.
5. In the process of sale, the insurer or its agent or any intermediary shall act according to the code of conduct prescribed by:
   (*i*) the Authority
   (*ii*) the Councils that have been established under section 64C of the Act and
   (*iii*) the recognised professional body or association of which the agent or intermediary or insurance intermediary is a member.

4. Proposal for Insurance

1. Except in cases of a marine insurance cover, where current market practices do not insist on a written proposal form, in all cases, a proposal for grant of a cover, either for life business or for general business, must be evidenced by a written document. It is the duty of an insurer to furnish to the insured free of charge, within 30 days, of the acceptance of a proposal, a copy of the proposal form.
2. Forms and documents used in the grant of cover may, depending upon the circumstances of each case, be made available in languages recognised under the Constitution of India.
3. In filling the form of proposal, the prospect is to be guided by the provisions of Section 45 of the Act. Any proposal form seeking information for grant of life cover may prominently state therein the requirements of Section 45 of the Act.
4. Where a proposal form is not used, the insurer shall record the information obtained orally or in writing, and confirm it within a period of 15 days thereof with the proposer and incorporate the information in its cover note or policy. The onus of proof shall rest with the insurer in respect of any information not so recorded, where the insurer claims that the proposer suppressed any material information or provided misleading or false Information on any matter material to the grant of a cover.
5. Where the benefit of nomination is available to the proposer, in terms of the Act or the conditions of policy, the insurer shall draw the attention of the proposer to it an encourage the prospect to avail the facility.
6. Proposals shall be processed by the insurer with speed and efficiency and all decisions thereof shall be communicated by it in writing within a reasonable period not exceeding 15 days from receipt of proposals by the insurer.

5. Grievance Redressal Procedure

Every insurer shall have in place proper procedures and effective mechanism to address complaints and grievances of policyholders efficiently and with speed and the same along with the information in respect of Insurance Ombudsman shall be communicated to the policyholder along with the policy document and as may be found necessary.

6. Matters to be Stated in Life Insurance Policy

1. A life insurance policy shall clearly state:
   (*a*) the name of the plan governing the policy, its terms and conditions,
   (*b*) whether it is participating in profits or not;
   (*c*) the basis of participation in profits such as cash bonus, deferred bonus, simple or compound reversionary bonus;

(*d*) the benefits payable and the contingencies upon which these are payable and the other terms and conditions of the insurance contract;

(*e*) the details of the riders attaching to the main policy;

(*f*) the date of commencement of risk and the date of maturity or date(s) on which the benefits are payable;

(*g*) the premiums payable, periodicity of payment, grace period allowed for payment of the premium, the date of the last instalment of Premium, the implication of discontinuing the payment of an instalment(s) of premium and also the provisions of a guaranteed surrender value.

(*h*) the age at entry and whether the same has been admitted;

(*i*) the policy requirements for (*a*) conversion of the policy into paid up policy, (*b*) surrender (*c*) non-forfeiture, and (*d*) revival of lapsed policies;

(*j*) contingencies excluded from the scope of the cover, both in respect of the main policy and the riders;

(*k*) the provisions for nomination, assignment, and loans on security of the policy and a statement that the rate of interest payable on such loan amount shall be as prescribed by the insurer at the time of taking the loan;

(*l*) any special clauses or conditions, such as, first pregnancy clause, suicide clause etc.;

(*m*) the address of the insurer to which all communications in respect of the policy shall be sent.

(*n*) the documents that are normally required to be submitted by a claimant in support of a claim under the policy.

2. While acting under regulation 6(1) in forwarding the policy to the insured, the insurer shall inform by the letter forwarding the policy that he has a period of 15 days from the date of receipt of the policy document to review the terms and conditions of the policy and where the insured disagrees to any of those terms or conditions, he has the option to return the policy stating the reasons for his objection, when he shall be entitled to a refund of the premium paid, subject only to a deduction of a proportionate risk premium for the period on cover and the expenses incurred by the insurer on medical examination of the proposer and stamp duty charges.

3. In respect of a unit linked policy, in addition to the deductions under sub-regulation (2) of this regulation, the insurer shall also be entitled to repurchase the unit at the price of the units on the date of cancellation .

4. In respect of a cover, where premium charged is dependent on age, the insurer shall ensure that the age is admitted as far as possible before insurance of the policy document. In case where age has not been admitted by the time the policy is issued, the insurer shall make efforts to obtain proof of age and admit the same as soon as possible.

7. Matters to be stated in general insurance policy

1. A general insurance policy shall clearly state:

(*a*) the name(s) and address(es) of the insured and of any bank(s) or any other person having financial interest in the subject matter of insurance;

(*b*) full description of the property or interest insured;

(*c*) the location or locations of the property or interest insured under the policy and where appropriate, with respective insured values:

(*d*) period of Insurance;
(*e*) sums insured;
(*f*) perils covered and not covered;
(*h*) any franchise or deductible applicable;
(*i*) premium payable and where the premium is provisional subject to adjustment, the basis of adjustment of premium be stated;
(*j*) policy terms, conditions and warranties;
(*k*) action to be taken by the insured upon occurrence of a contingency likely to give rise to a claim under the policy;
(*l*) the obligations of the insured in relation to the subject matter of insurance upon occurrence of an event giving rising to a claim and the rights of the insurer in the circumstances;
(*m*) any special conditions attaching to the policy;
(*n*) provision for cancellation of the policy on grounds of misrepresentation, fraud, non-disclosure or material facts or noncooperation of the insured;
(*o*) the address of the insurer to which all communications in respect of the insurance contract should be sent;
(*p*) the details of the riders attaching to the main policy;
(*q*) proforma of any communication the insurer may seek from the policyholders to service the policy.

2. Every insurer shall inform and keep informed periodically the insured on the requirements to be fulfilled by the insured regarding lodging of a claim arising in terms of the policy and the procedures to be followed by him to enable the insurer to settle a claim early.

8. Claims procedure in respect of a life insurance policy

1. A life insurance policy shall state the primary documents which are normally required to be submitted by a claimant in support of a claim.
2. A life insurance company, upon receiving a claim, shall process the claim without delay. Any queries or requirement of additional documents, to the extent possible, shall be raised all at once and not in a piece-meal manner, within a period of 15 days of the receipt of the claim.
3. A claim under a life policy shall be paid or be disputed giving all the relevant reasons, within 30 days from the date of receipt of all relevant papers and clarifications required. However, where the circumstances of a claim warrant an investigation in the opinion of the insurance company, it shall initiate and complete such investigation at the earliest. Where in the opinion of the insurance company the circumstances of a claim warrant an investigation, it shall initiate and complete such investigation at the earliest, in any case not later than 6 months from the time of lodging the claim.
4. Subject to the provisions of section 47 of the Act, where a claim is ready for payment but the payment cannot be made due to any reasons of a proper identification of the payee, the life insurer shall hold the amount for the benefit of the payee and such an amount shall earn interest at the rate applicable to a savings bank account with a scheduled bank (effective from 30 days following the submission of all papers and information).
5. Where there is a delay on the part of the insurer in processing a claim for a reason other than one covered by sub-regulation (4), the life insurance company shall pay interest on the claim amount at a rate which is 2% above the bank rate prevalent at the beginning of the financial year in which the claim is reviewed by it.

9. Claim procedure in respect of a general insurance policy

1. An insured or the claimant shall give notice to the insurer of any loss arising under contract of insurance at the earliest or within such extended time as may be allowed by the insurer. On receipt of such a communication, a general insurer shall respond immediately and give clear indication to the insured on the procedures that he should follow. In cases where a surveyor has to be appointed for assessing a loss/claim, it shall be so done within 72 hours of the receipt of intimation from the insured.
2. Where the insured is unable to furnish all the particulars required by the surveyor or where the surveyor does not receive the full cooperation of the insured, the insurer or the surveyor as the case may be, shall inform in writing the insured about the delay that may result in the assessment of the claim. The surveyor shall be subjected to the code of conduct laid down by the Authority while assessing the loss, and shall communicate his findings to the insurer within 30 days of his appointment with a copy of the report being furnished to the insured, if he so desires. Where, in special circumstances of the case, either due to its special and complicated nature, the surveyor shall under intimation to the insured, seek an extension from the insurer for submission of his report. In no case shall a surveyor take more than six months from the date of his appointment of furnish his report.
3. If an insurer, on the receipt of a survey report, finds that it is incomplete in any respect, he shall require the surveyor under intimation to the insured, to furnish an additional report on certain specific issues as may be required by the insurer. Such a request may be made by the insurer within 15 days of the receipt of the original survey report.
Provided that the facility of calling for an additional report by the insurer shall not be resorted to more than once in the case of a claim.
4. The surveyor on receipt of this communication shall furnish an additional report within three weeks of the date of receipt of communication from the insurer.
5. On receipt of the survey report or the additional survey report, as the case may be, an insurer shall within a period of 30 days offers a settlement of the claim to the insured. If the insurer, for any reasons to be recorded in writing and communicated to the insured, decides to reject a claim under the policy, it shall do so within a period of 30 days from the receipt of the survey report or the additional survey report, as the case may be.
6. Upon acceptance of an offer of settlement as stated in sub-regulation (5) by the insured, the payment of the amount due shall be made within 7 days from the date of acceptance of the offer by the insured. In the cases of delay in the payment, the insurer shall be liable to pay interest at a rate which is 2% above the bank rate prevalent at the beginning of the financial year in which the claim is reviewed by it.

10. Policyholders' Servicing

1. An insurer carrying on life or general business, as the case may be, shall at all times, respond within 10 days of the receipt of any communication from its policyholders in all matters, such as:
   (*a*) recording change of address;
   (*b*) noting a new nomination or change of nomination under a policy;
   (*c*) nothing an assignment on the policy;
   (*d*) providing information on the current status of a policy indicating matters, such as, accrued, bonus, surrender value and entitlement to a loan;
   (*e*) processing papers and disbursal of a loan on security of policy;
   (*f*) issuance of duplicate policy;

(*g*) issuance of an endorsement under the policy, nothing a change of interest or sum assured or perils insured, financial interest of a bank and other interests; and

(*h*) guidance on the procedure for registering a claim and early settlement thereof.

11. General

1. The requirements of disclosure of "material information" regarding a proposal or policy apply, under these regulations, both to the insurer and the insured.
2. The policyholder shall assist the insurer, if the latter so requires, the prosecution of a proceeding or in the matter of recovery of claims which the insurer has against third parties.
3. The policyholder shall furnish all information that is sought from him by the insurer and also any other information which the insurer considers as having a bearing on other risk to enable the latter to assess properly the risk sought to be covered by a policy.
4. Any breaches of the obligations cast on an insurer or insurance agent or insurance intermediary in terms of these regulations may enable the Authority to initiate action against each or all of them, jointly or severally, under the Act and/or the Insurance Regulatory and Development Authority Act, 1999.

NOTES

NOTES

NOTES

NOTES

NOTES

NOTES